GS SCORE

CONCEPT MAPPING WORKBOOK

The Ultimate Guide to Cover Concepts through MCQs for Civil Services, State PCS & Other Competitive Examinations

HISTORY

VOL-1

ANCIENT & MEDIEVAL HISTORY AND ART & CULTURE

Series Editor

MANOJ K. JHA

Editorial Team

PANKAJ DWIVEDI

ANKITA SHARMA

PRABHAKAR MISHRA

VISHAL GUPTA

SHUBHAM KANOJIA

PIYUSH KUMAR SINGH

SHIPRA UPADHYAY

PRABHAT EXAMS

Publisher

PRABHAT EXAMS

Imprint of Prabhat Prakashan Pvt. Ltd.

4/19 Asaf Ali Road, New Delhi–110 002

Ph. 23289555 • 23289666 • 23289777 • Helpline/ 7827007777

e-mail: prabhatbooks@gmail.com • Website: www.prabhatexam.com

Price

Five Hundred Fifty Rupees

ISBN 978-93-5521-674-8

Printed at

Nakshatra Art, Delhi

GSSCORE
CONCEPT MAPPING WORKBOOK
HISTORY
VOL-1
ANCIENT & MEDIEVAL HISTORY
AND ART & CULTURE

Series Editor

Manoj K. Jha

ISBN 978-93-5521-674-8

₹ 550.00

PREFACE

Public Service Examinations across the Board in India offers immense opportunity for young talent to secure not only employment at prestigious positions but also gives them the chance to serve the nation in various capacities. These examinations are of a highly diverse nature as they test the candidates on diverse subjects, further spanning multiple dimensions largely the subjects related to Polity, Economy, History, Geography, Science and Technology, Environmental Sciences and miscellaneous topics like sports, awards and other events of national and international importance. All of these demand not only to study of these varied subjects but also practice in tackling the questions which are asked in the examination.

This workbook is an attempt to be a companion to candidates in their success. The book involves not only questions along with their solutions, but also a guide to self-study, self-correct and self-evaluate marks and also find the direction via the concept mapping to pinpoint the weak areas and to re-orient their preparation as they proceed. The book also gets enriched with a concept section, which serves as a tool for revision and reference. All in all one-stop solution for all the needs of the candidates.

This volume attempts to demystify the section of History, (Ancient & Medieval History and Art & Culture) for the candidates, making it a “strength” and not a “weakness” to fetch maximum marks. The MCQs have been set as per the changing demands of the public service examinations. Adequate stress has been laid on various topics both in terms of question styles and syllabus coverage. The MCQs have been further enriched with detailed explanations and supplementary notes to help the candidates with solutions and quick revision of the key concepts.

It is our firm belief that the research and brainstorming to come up with this volume at our end will be highly popular among the aspiring young candidates and will act as a small yet significant contributor to their impending success.

GSSCORE

CONTENTS

Preface iii

ANCIENT HISTORY

Syllabus (Micro Topics) 3-4

1. POLITICAL STRUCTURE OF ANCIENT INDIA 5-84

1.1 Pre-Historic Times 5
Questions 5
Solutions 6

1.2 Indus Valley Civilisation 10
Questions 10
Solutions 13

1.3 Rig Vedic and Later Vedic Period 21
Questions 21
Solutions 23

1.4 Mahajanapadas Period 31
Questions 31
Solutions 32

1.5 Mauryan Empire 41
Questions 41
Solutions 44

1.6 Post-Mauryan India 55
Questions 55
Solutions 57

1.7 Gupta Period 66
Questions 66
Solutions 68

1.8 Harshavardhan 77
Questions 77
Solutions 78

1.9 Sangam Period 82
Questions 82
Solutions 82

2. ECONOMIC CONDITIONS OF ANCIENT INDIA 85-108

2.1 Stone Age 85
Questions 85
Solutions 87

2.2 Copper-Bronze Age 92
Questions 92
Solutions 93

2.3 Iron Age 97
Questions 97
Solutions 99

2.5 Mauryan Empire 104
Question 104
Solution 104

2.7 Gupta's Era 104
Questions 104
Solutions 105

2.8 Post-Gupta Era 106
Questions 106
Solutions 106

3. SOCIO-CULTURAL DEVELOPMENT OF ANCIENT INDIA 109-124

3.1 Socio-Cultural Life in Stone Age 109
Questions 109
Solutions 109

3.2 Indus Valley Civilization 110
Question 110
Solution 110

3.3 From Varna System to Caste System 111
Questions 111
Solutions 112

3.4 Indian School of Philosophy 116
Questions 116
Solutions 117

3.5 Emergence of Bhagwatism, Expansion of Casteism during Gupta Era 122
Questions 122
Solutions 123

MEDIEVAL HISTORY

Syllabus (Micro Topics) 127-128

4. Political Structure of Medieval India 129-203

4.1 Cholas and Other South Indian Kingdoms 129

Questions.. 129

Solutions.. 131

4.2 Early Muslim Invasions 138

Questions.. 138

Solutions.. 139

4.3 Delhi Sultanate 142

Questions.. 142

Solutions.. 147

4.4 Mughal Empire 160

Questions.. 160

Solutions.. 165

4.5 Vijayanagara Empire 183

Questions.. 183

Solutions.. 185

4.6 Marathas and Other Indian States and Society 192

Questions.. 192

Solutions.. 194

5. Economic Conditions of Medieval India ..204-222

5.1 Economic Conditions and Reform in Sultanate Period 204

Questions.. 204

Solutions.. 205

5.2 Economic Life during Mughal Period 209

Questions.. 209

Solutions.. 212

5.3 Economic Life of Regional States in India 219

Questions.. 219

Solutions.. 220

6. Socio-Cultural Development of Medieval India 223-242

6.1 Caste System and Feudalism in Medieval India 223

Questions.. 223

Solutions.. 224

6.2 Emergence and Spread of Islam and Its Impact 227

Questions.. 227

Solutions.. 227

6.3 Bhakti and Sufi Movements 230

Questions.. 230

Solutions.. 233

ART & CULTURE

Syllabus (Micro Topics) 245-246

7. Visual Arts 247-318

7.1 Architecture & Sculptures 247

Questions.. 247

Solutions.. 259

7.2 Paintings, Pottery and Numismatic 301

Questions.. 301

Solutions.. 304

8. Performing Arts 319-357

8.1 Music in India 319

Questions.. 319

Solutions.. 321

8.2 Dances in India 329

Questions.. 329

Solutions.. 330

8.3 Indian Theatre and Puppetry 337

Questions.. 337

Solutions.. 338

8.4 Sports in India 342

Questions.. 342

Solutions.. 345

9. Religion, Language & Literature 358-454

9.1 Religions in India 358

Questions.. 358

Solutions.. 366

9.2 Languages and Literature in India 393

Questions.. 393

Solutions.. 402

9.3 Miscellaneous 431

Questions.. 431

Solutions.. 436

ANCIENT HISTORY

Syllabus (MICRO TOPICS)

1. Political Structure of Ancient India

- Pre-Historic Times
  - Sources of Pre History
  - Periodisation of Indian pre history
- Indus Valley Civilisation
  - Geographical spread
  - Important centres
  - Political Organisation
  - Town planning
- Aryans and Vedic Period
  - Political Organisation
  - Tribal assemblies
  - Evolution of Monarchy
  - Aryan invasion
- Mahajanapadas Period
  - Rise of Magadha and Nandas
  - Formation of states
  - The Sixteen Mahajanapadas
  - Republics
  - Haryanka dynasty
  - Shishunaga dynasty
- Mauryan Empire
  - Foundation of Mauryan Empire
  - Rulers and Political History of the Mauryas
  - Chandragupta and Bindusara
  - Asoka and His Successors
  - Polity and Administration
- Post-Mauryan India
  - Satavahanas
  - Contacts with Central Asia
    - Sungas and Kanvas
    - Sakas
    - Kushanas
  - Iranian and Macedonian invasions
- Gupta Period
  - Rise of Guptas
  - Political history of Gupta's
  - Gupta Administration
  - Expansion and Consolidation
  - Huna invasion
  - Disintegration of Gupta empire
- Post Gupta Period
  - The Regional powers
    - The Maitrakas of Valabhi
    - The Maukharis of Kanauj
    - Harshavardhana and his Reign
    - The Later Guptas of Magadha
    - Yasodharman of Kanauj
    - Kashmir
  - Disintegration in the post Gupta period
- Harshavardhana
  - Changing political scenario in North India
  - Political Activities of Harsha
  - The Extent of Harsha's Kingdom
  - End of Harsha's Reign
- Sangam Period (South Indian dynasties)
  - South Indian Dynasties
    - Cholas
    - Cheras
    - Pandyas
  - Sangam Polity
  - Foreign Dynasties

2. Economic Conditions of Ancient India

- Pre-Historic times
  - Hunting and gathering (Paleolithic and Mesolithic)
  - Beginning of agriculture (Neolithic and chalcolithic)
- Indus valley Civilisation
  - Harappan Trade with outside world
  - Agriculture
  - Weights and Measures
- Aryans and Vedic Period
  - Significance of Vedic age
  - Economical life
  - Pastoralist society
- Mahajanapadas
  - The second urbanisation
  - Rise of Urban centres
  - Economic growth
  - Trade and traders
  - Gahapati and Setthis
  - Coinage

- ➤ Mauryan Empire
  - Use of Iron
  - Agriculture and land revenue
  - Organisation of trade
  - Growth of Urban economy
  - The Arthashastra
  - External contacts
- ➤ Post-Mauryan Period
  - Internal and External Trade Routes
  - Trade with West and Central Asia
  - Crafts and Industries
  - Guilds
  - Growth of urban centres
  - Coinage
  - Impact of Iranian and Macedonian invasions
- ➤ Gupta Period
  - Importance of agriculture and irrigation
  - Crafts production
  - Trade
- ➤ Post Gupta period
  - Decline of trade
  - Paucity of coins
  - Decline of towns
  - Agrarian relations
  - Rise in land grants
- ➤ Harshavardhana
  - Agriculture
  - Commerce and Trade
  - Coinage
- ➤ Sangam Period (South Indian Dynasties)
  - Economy of Sangam Period
  - Flourishing trade with Roman empire
  - Sangama Administration

3. Socio-Cultural development of Ancient India

- ➤ Pre-Historic Times
  - Socio-cultural life of Stone Age
- ➤ Indus Valley Civilisation
  - Artefacts
  - Religion
  - Pottery
  - Script and Language
- ➤ Aryans and Vedic Period
  - Religious and philosophical literature
  - Sources for Reconstructing Vedic Society and Culture
  - Social Organisation and Varna System
  - Vedic religion
- ➤ Mahajanapadas
  - The second urbanisation
  - Spread of Buddhism and Jainism
  - Varna and Jati
- ➤ Mauryan Empire
  - Pacifist policy of Ashoka
  - Ashok dhamma
  - Megasthene's Indica
  - Art and Architecture
- ➤ Post-Mauryan India
  - Contact with outside world
  - Development of religions
  - Mahayana Buddhism
  - Art and Architecture, Rock cut architecture
  - Different schools of art
  - Contribution in field of literature and science
- ➤ Gupta Period
  - Proliferation of castes
  - Position of shudras
  - Position of women
  - Emergence of Bhagwatism
  - Education and Educational Institutions: Nalanda, Vikramshila etc
  - Art and Architecture
  - Scientific literature
- ➤ Post Gupta Period
  - Rise in popularity of Buddhism
  - Rise in Vaishnavism and Shaivism
  - Emergence of Bhakti
  - Spread of North Indian religions to the South
  - Bhakti movement in South India
  - Emergence of Tantrism
  - Contribution in field of Sanskrit literature
- ➤ Harshavardhana
  - Account of Huien Tsang
  - Prayag assembly
  - Harshacharita
  - Priyadarshika, Ratnavali and Nagananda
- ➤ Sangam Period (South Indian Dynasties)
  - Sangam Literature
  - Sangam Society and Culture
  - Interaction between North India and South India traditions

1. POLITICAL STRUCTURE OF ANCIENT INDIA

1.1 PRE-HISTORIC TIMES

QUESTIONS

1. **Which of the following is correct about the Stone Age sites in India?**
   1. Belan Valley in UP is an important Palaeolithic site that shows the evidence of cattle exploitation.
   2. Bogar in Rajasthan, a Neolithic site, was a distinctive microlith industry.
   3. Maski, Brahmagiri and Hallur are important Neolithic sites in Karnataka.

   Select the correct option using the codes given below:

   (a) 1 and 2 only (b) 2 and 3 only
   (c) 1 and 3 only (d) 1, 2 and 3

2. **Consider the following statements regarding Palaeolithic or Old Stone Age:**
   1. The Old Stone Age sites are generally located near water sources.
   2. Several Rock shelters and caves were not used by the Palaeolithic people. They mostly lived in huts made of leaves.
   3. They used stone tools called Microliths and flaked-off large pebbles for hunting animals. But hunting was an individual affair.
   4. Some of the famous sites of Old Stone Age in India are: Bhimbetka, Adamgarh hill and Kurnool.

   Which of the above statements is/are correct?

   (a) 1 only (b) 1 and 4 only
   (c) 2 and 4 only (d) 1, 2, 3 and 4

3. **Which of the following archaeological sites have Palaeolithic, Mesolithic and Neolithic remains?**

   (a) Belan valley (b) Bhimbetka
   (c) Nevasa (d) Pushkar

4. **Match the following:**

Places of Old Stone Age Tools	States
A. Bhimbetka	1. Rajasthan
B. Luni Valley	2. Madhya Pradesh
C. Attirampakkam	3. Andhra Pradesh
D. Renigunta	4. Tamil Nadu

Select the correct answer using the code given below:

	A	B	C	D
(a)	3	4	2	1
(b)	2	1	4	3
(c)	4	3	1	2
(d)	1	2	3	4

5. **In which age did the Man moved from food-gathering to food-producing stage?**

   (a) Neolithic Age
   (b) Mesolithic Age

(c) Chalcolithic Age
(d) Palaeolithic Age

6. With reference to the Stone Age culture in India, consider the following statements:

1. The lower Palaeolithic tool technology is characterized by flake tool industry.
2. Middle Palaeolithic tools have mostly been found in Northern India.
3. Microliths are the tools of Mesolithic age characterized by parallel-side blades.

Which of the above statements is/are correct?

(a) 1 and 2 only (b) 2 only
(c) 3 only (d) 1 and 3 only

7. Which of the following statements regarding the Neolithic Age is/are correct?

1. The earliest Neolithic settlements in the Indian subcontinent developed in the west of River Indus.
2. The Kashmiri Neolithic culture was characterized by the complete absence of microliths.
3. Pottery first appeared in this phase.
4. People in this phase found settlements away from the hilly areas.

Select the correct answer using the code given below:

(a) 1, 2 and 3 only (b) 2 and 4 only
(c) 3 only (d) 1, 3 and 4 only

8. With reference to the pre-historic phase of Indian History, consider the following statements:

1. The Palaeolithic Age was spread in the alluvial plains of the Indus and Ganga.
2. The last phase of Mesolithic age saw the beginning of plant cultivation.
3. The first metal to be used was copper, though they also occasionally used bronze during Chalcolithic Phase.

Which of the above statements is/are correct?

(a) 1 and 2 only (b) 2 and 3 only
(c) 1 and 3 only (d) 1, 2 and 3

9. With respect to 'Megaliths' in the Indian historical period, consider the following statements:

1. Megaliths were people living in the deltaic region of the deep southern peninsular India as early as 1000 BC.
2. They were predominantly agriculturists with less advanced types of agricultural tools.
3. The social arrangement developed within their primitive societal setup is known as Tamizhakam.

Which of the above statements is/are correct?

(a) 1 and 2 only (b) 2 and 3 only
(c) 1 and 3 only (d) None of the above

10. "It is situated in Indian state of Uttar Pradesh. It is famous for prehistoric sites, which is related with Palaeolithic, mesolithic and megalithic periods".

Which of the following archaeological sites is discussed in the above passage?

(a) Belan valley (b) Hungsi valley
(c) Nevasa (d) Didwana

SOLUTIONS

1. Correct Option: (c)

Explanation:

- **Statement 2 is incorrect:** Bogar in Rajasthan, a Mesolithic site, was a distinctive microlith industry.

Supplementary Notes:

The Stone Ages in India:

- **Palaeolithic:**
  - The Palaeolithic Age in India is divided into three phases in accordance with the type of stone tools used by the people and also according to the nature of climatic change. The first phase is called Early or Lower Palaeolithic, the second Middle Palaeolithic, and the third Upper Palaeolithic.
  - The Lower Palaeolithic or the Early Old Stone Age covers the greater part of the ice age. The Early Old Stone Age may have begun in Africa around two million years ago, but in India it is not older than 600,000 years. This date is given to Bori in Maharashtra, and this site is considered to be the earliest Lower Palaeolithic site.
  - Lower Palaeolithic tools have also been found in the Belan valley in UP and in the desert area of Didwana in Rajasthan.
  - The Middle Palaeolithic industries were largely based upon flakes or small pieces of stone which have been found in different parts of India with regional variations. The principal tools comprise blades, points, borers, and scrapers, all made of flakes.
  - The artefacts of this age are found at several places on the river Narmada, and also at several places, south of the Tungabhadra river. The Belan valley (UP), which lies at the foothills of the Vindhyas, is rich in stone tools and animal fossils including cattle and deer. These remains relate to both the Lower and Middle Stone ages.
  - In the Upper Palaeolithic phase, we find 566 sites in India. This may be due to the general presence of grassland dotted with few trees. The climate was less humid, coinciding with the last phase of the ice age when the climate became comparatively warm. In the world context, it

marks the appearance of new flint industries and men of the modern type (Homo sapiens).

- **Mesolithic:**
  - In 9000 BC began an intermediate stage in Stone Age culture, which is called the Mesolithic Age. It intervened as a transitional phase between the Palaeolithic and the Neolithic or New Stone ages.
  - The characteristic tools of the Mesolithic Age are microliths or tiny tools. Mesolithic sites abound in Rajasthan, southern UP, central and eastern India, and also south of the river Krishna. Bogar in Rajasthan was a distinctive microlith industry.
- **Neolithic:**
  - In the world context, the New Stone or the Neolithic Age began in 9000 BC. The only known Neolithic settlement in the Indian subcontinent, attributed to 7000 BC, is in Mehrgarh, which is situated in Baluchistan, a province of Pakistan.
  - Neolithic settlements in South India: An important group of Neolithic people lived in south India, south of the Godavari river. They usually settled on the tops of granite hills or on plateaus near the river banks. They used stone axes and also a kind of stone blades. Fire-baked earthen figurines suggest that they kept a large number of cattle, besides sheep and goats. They used stone querns for grinding corn, which shows that they were acquainted with the art of producing cereals.
  - South India has the largest number of Neolithic settlements because of the easy availability of stone, with over 850 settlements spread across AP, Karnataka, and Tamil Nadu.
  - Some of the important Neolithic sites or those with Neolithic layers that have been excavated include Maski, Brahmagiri, Hallur, Kodekal, Sanganakallu, Piklihal, and Takkalakota in Karnataka, and Paiyampalli in Tamil Nadu. Utnur is an important Neolithic site in AP.

2. Correct Option: (b)

Explanation:

- **Statement 2 is incorrect:** Several rock shelters and caves used by the Palaeolithic people are scattered across the subcontinent.
- **Statement 3 is incorrect:** They used stone tools, hand-sized and flaked off large pebbles for hunting animals.

Supplementary Notes:

- The Old Stone Age sites are widely found in various parts of the Indian subcontinent. These sites are generally located near water sources. Several rock shelters and caves used by the Palaeolithic people are scattered across the subcontinent. They also lived rarely in huts made of leaves.
- In the Old Stone Age, food was obtained by hunting animals and gathering edible plants and tubers. They used stone tools, hand-sized and flaked-off large pebbles for hunting animals. Stone implements are made of a hard rock known as quartzite. Large pebbles are often found in river terraces.
- Microliths are tiny stone artefacts found in the Mesolithic Stone Age. The hunting of large animals would have required the combined effort of a group of people with large stone axes. A few Old Stone Age paintings have also been found on rocks at Bhimbetka showing hunting as a group activity and other places.

3. Correct Option: (a)

Explanation:

- **Option (a) is correct**

Supplementary Notes:

Pre-Historic India

- Belan River is a river in Indian state of Uttar Pradesh. It is famous for prehistoric sites on its banks. It originates from western part of Sonbhadra district, and then flows in southern part of Mirzapur and Allahabad districts. It is famous for prehistoric sites, which are related with Palaeolithic, mesolithic and megalithic periods. Chopanimando in Allahabad district is one of these sites, which deals with evidences of ancient cultivation of wild cereals like rice. Koldihwa and Mahagara (both in Allahabad district) are two important excavated sites, located on the northern fringes of Vindhyas on the banks of the Belan River.

4. Correct Option: (b)

Places of Old Stone Age Tools	States
A. Bhimbetka	2. Madhya Pradesh
B. Luni Valley	1. Rajasthan
C. Attirampakkam	4. Tamil Nadu
D. Renigunta	3. Andhra Pradesh

Supplementary Notes:

Old Stone Age

- Places in India where the Old Stone Age tools were found:
  - Madhya Pradesh - Son River bank, Bhimbetka, and Mageshwa.
  - Rajasthan - Luni Valley.
  - Andhra Pradesh - Kurnool caves, Renigunta.
  - Tamil Nadu - Vadamadurai, Athirampakkam, Pallavaram, Kancheepuram, Vellur, and Thiruvallur.

5. Correct Option: (a)

Explanation:

- **Option (a) is correct:** The Neolithic Age saw the man turning into food producer from food gatherer.

Supplementary Notes:

Characteristics of Neolithic Age

- The Neolithic Age saw the man turning into food producer from food gatherer. It also witnessed the use of pottery for the first time. People used microlithic blades in addition to tools made of polished stone. The use of metal was unknown.
- **Agriculture:** The people of Neolithic Age cultivated ragi, horse gram, cotton, rice, wheat, and barley and hence were termed as food producers. They domesticated cattle, sheep, and goats. Agriculture and animal domestication were the main economic activity of early Neolithic cultures.
- **Tools:** The people used microlithic blades in addition to tools made of polished stones. They used stone hoes and digging sticks for digging the ground. The ring stones of 1-1/2 kg of weight were fixed at the ends of these digging sticks. They also used tools and weapons made of bone; found in Burzahom (Kashmir) and Chirand (Bihar).
- **Weapons:** The people primarily used axes as weapons. The North-western part of Neolithic settlement used rectangular axes having curved cutting edge. The southern part used axes with oval sides and pointed butt while polished stone axes with rectangular butt and shouldered hoes were use in the north-eastern part.
- **Housing:** The people of Neolithic Age lived in rectangular or circular houses which were made of mud and reed. The people of Mehrgarh lived in mud-brick houses while pit-dwelling is reported from Burzahom, the Neolithic site found in Kashmir.
- **Pottery:** With the advent of agriculture, people were required to store their food grains as well as to do cooking, arrange for drinking water, and eating the finished product. That is why pottery first appeared in the Neolithic Age. The pottery of the period was classified under grey ware, black-burnished ware, and mat-impressed ware.
- **Architecture:** The Neolithic age is significant for its megalithic architecture.
- **Technology:** In the initial stage of the Neolithic Age, hand-made pottery was made but later on, the foot-wheels were used to make pots.
- **Community Life:** Neolithic people had common right over property. They led a settled life.

6. **Correct Option: (c)**

Explanation:

- **Statement 1 is incorrect:** The Middle Palaeolithic tool technology is characterized by flake tool industry.
- **Statement 2 is incorrect:** Middle Palaeolithic tools have mostly been found in Central and Deccan India.

Supplementary Notes:

The Stone Age Cultures

- The Old Stone Age or the Palaeolithic Culture of India developed in the Pleistocene period of Ice Age. The Palaeolithic Age in India is divided into three phases in accordance with the type of stone tools used by the people and also according to the nature of climatic change.
  - The first phase is called Early or Lower Palaeolithic. The main tool types in this phase were hand axes and cleavers, along with chopper-chopping tools. Lower Palaeolithic tools have been found over a large area, virtually from all over India, except the plains of the Indus, Saraswati, Brahmaputra and Ganga where raw material in the form of stone is not available.
  - The second phase is called Middle Palaeolithic. The Middle Palaeolithic tool technology is characterized basically by the flake tool industry. The tools are made on flakes obtained by striking them out from pebbles or cobbles. The tools show regional variations both in shapes and sizes. Middle Palaeolithic tools have mostly been found in Central India, Deccan, Rajasthan, Maharashtra, Tamil Nadu, Karnataka and Orissa.
  - The third phase is called Upper Palaeolithic. The basic technological innovation of the Upper Palaeolithic period is the method of producing parallel sided blades from a carefully prepared core. The upper Palaeolithic tools have been found in Rajasthan, parts of the Ganga and Belan valleys, Central and Western India, Gujarat, Andhra Pradesh and Karnataka.
- In 9000 BC began an intermediate stage in Stone Age culture, which is called the Mesolithic age or Late Stone Age. It intervened as a transitional phase between the Palaeolithic and the Neolithic or New Stone ages. The Mesolithic people lived on hunting, fishing, and food gathering; at a later stage they also domesticated animals. The characteristic tools of the Mesolithic age are microliths or tiny tools characterized by parallel-sided blades taken out from prepared cores of such fine material as chert, chalcedony, crystal, jasper, carnelian, agate, etc. Mesolithic sites abound in Rajasthan, southern UP, central and eastern India, and also south of the river Krishna.

7. **Correct Option: (a)**

Explanation:

- **Statement 4 is incorrect:** As the people had to depend almost entirely on tools and weapons made of stone, they could not found settlements far away from the hilly areas in this phase.

Supplementary Notes:

Neolithic or the New Stone Age

- In the world context, the New Stone or the Neolithic age began in 9000 BC but in the Indian subcontinent, it began around the seventh millennium BC. Some important crops, including wheat and barley, came to be cultivated in the subcontinent, and villages were established in this part of the world.
- Perhaps the most fundamental advance that has affected the course of human life was the domestication of a large number of animals and plants. The domestication of various species of animals produced the specialized pastoralists and the domestication and successful exploitation of various species of wild plants produced a shift towards sedentary settlements.
- Some important crops, including wheat and barley, came to be cultivated in the subcontinent, and villages were established.
- The earliest Neolithic settlement in the Indian subcontinent first developed in the west of the Indus. Mehrgarh is one of the largest Neolithic settlements between the Indus and the Mediterranean and is attributed to 7000 BC.
- The people of the Neolithic age used tools and implements of polished stone. Based on the types of axes used by Neolithic settlers, we notice three important areas of Neolithic settlements—north-western, north-eastern, and southern. The north-western group of Neolithic tools is distinguished by rectangular axes with a curved cutting edge; the north-eastern group by polished stone axes with a rectangular butt and occasional shouldered hoes; and the southern group by axes with oval sides and pointed butt.
- In the north-west, Kashmiri Neolithic culture was distinguished by its dwelling pits, wide range of ceramics, the variety of stone and bone tools, and the complete absence of microliths.
- Another area from which Neolithic tools have been recovered is situated in the hills of Assam. Neolithic tools have also been found in the Garo hills in Meghalaya on the north-eastern frontier of India.
- An important group of Neolithic people lived in south India, south of the Godavari River. They usually settled on the tops of granite hills or on plateaus near the river banks. They used stone axes and also a kind of stone blades.
- During the Neolithic phase, several settlements became acquainted with the cultivation of cereals and the domestication of animals. So they needed pots in which they could store their food grains, and also pots for cooking, eating, and drinking. Pottery, therefore, first appears in this phase, with handmade pottery in the early stage.
- The people of the New Stone/Neolithic Age suffered from one great limitation. As they had to depend almost entirely on tools and weapons made of stone, they could not found settlements far away from the hilly areas. They could settle only on the slopes of the hills in rock shelters and the hilly river valleys.

8. Correct Option: (b)

Explanation:

- **Statement 1 is incorrect:** It was spread in practically all parts of India except the alluvial plains of the Indus and Ganga.

Supplementary Notes:

Pre-historic phase of Indian History:

- The Palaeolithic Age is the earliest period of the Stone Age, which developed in the Pleistocene period or the Ice Age. It was spread in practically all parts of India except the alluvial plains of the Indus and Ganga. The Palaeolithic man of India are said to have belonged to the Negrito race and lived in caves and rock shelters.
- **Mesolithic Age:**
  - Pottery is absent at most Mesolithic sites, but it is present at Langhnaj in Gujarat and in the Kaimur region of Mirzapur (UP).
  - The Mesolithic era initiated rock art in pre-history.
  - The last phase of Mesolithic age saw the beginning of plant cultivation.
- The Chalcolithic age marked the emergence of the use of metal along with stone tools. The first metal to be used was copper, though bronze was also occasionally used.

9. Correct Option (d)

Explanation:

- **Statement 1 is incorrect:** Megaliths were people living in the upland portions of the southern peninsular India as early as 1000 BC.
- **Statement 2 is incorrect:** These were predominantly hunters and did not practice an advanced type of agriculture.
- **Statement 3 is incorrect:** Tamizhakam was the cultural and economic contact between the north and the deep south regions of India provided by traders, conquerors, etc.

Supplementary Notes:

Megaliths

- The beginning of the Megalithic Culture can be traced to 1000 BC.
- Megaliths were people who claimed the upland portions of the peninsula up to the second century BC and their concentration seems to be in eastern Andhra and in the Tamil Nadu region of the peninsula.
- They are known not from their actual settlements which are rare, but from their funerary structures.

- These were predominantly hunters and did not practice an advanced type of agriculture which is evident from the fewer number of agricultural tools buried in their graves than those meant for fighting and hunting.
- The graves are called megaliths because they were encircled by large pieces of stone.
- By the second century BC, the megalithic people had moved from the uplands into fertile river basins and reclaimed marshy deltaic areas.
- The stimulus of contact to northern India was provided by traders, conquerors, and Jaina, Buddhist, and some brahmana missionaries who brought with them elements of material culture from the north.
- This cultural and economic contact between the north and the deep south is profoundly known as Tamizhakam.
- The route to the south, called Dakshinapatha, was valued by the northerners because the south supplied gold, pearls, and various precious stones.
- This north-south connect is evident from the writings of Megasthenes which mention the Pandya state in the south.
- The earlier Sangam texts are familiar with the rivers Ganges and Son, and also with Pataliputra, the capital of the Magadhan empire.
- The Ashokan inscriptions mention the Cholas, Pandyas, Keralaputras, and Satyaputras living on the borders of the empire and the Tamraparnis, or the people of Sri Lanka.
- The Brahmanical influence also percolated in a large measure to Tamizhakam, but this really happened after the fourth century AD. Eventually, many elements of Tamil culture spread to the north, and in the Brahmanical texts, the Kaveri came to be regarded as one of the holy rivers of India.

10. Correct Option: (a)

Supplementary Notes:

Pre-Historic India

- Belan River is a river in Indian state of Uttar Pradesh. It is famous for prehistoric sites on its banks. It originates from western part of Sonbhadra district, and then flows in southern part of Mirzapur and Allahbad districts. It is famous for prehistoric sites, which are related with Palaeolithic, mesolithic and megalithic periods. Chopanimando in Allahabad district is one of these sites, which deals with evidences of ancient cultivation of wild cereals like rice. Koldihwa and Mahagara (both in Allahabad district) are two important excavated sites, located on the northern fringes of Vindhyas on the banks of the Belan River.

CONCEPT REVISION

Here is the list of concepts that have been covered as part of the previous exercise. Revise and Self-reflect on your concepts you covered.

- Palaeolithic Sites in India ☐
- Mesolithic Sites in India ☐
- Neolithic Sites ☐
- Megaliths ☐

1.2 INDUS VALLEY CIVILISATION

QUESTIONS

1. Consider the following statements with respect to Indus Valley Civilisation:

1. This civilisation belongs to Bronze Age.
2. Inhabitants of the ancient Indus river valley developed new techniques of metallurgy with respect to copper, bronze, lead and tin.
3. Bead making was the most important industry.

Which of the above statements is/are correct?

(a) 2 only (b) 1 and 2 only
(c) 2 and 3 only (d) 1, 2 and 3

2. Consider the following statements with respect to Harappa Site of Indus Valley Civilisation:

1. Harappa is known as the 'city of granaries'.
2. Town planning consisted of Centre bounded by fortified wall called citadel.
3. It was situated on the bank of River Ravi.

Which of the above statements are correct?

(a) 1 and 2 only (b) 1 and 3 only
(c) 2 and 3 only (d) 1, 2 and 3

3. Which of the following statements is/are correct regarding major sites in Indus valley civilisation?

1. Chanhudaro is the only Indus city with citadel.

2. Surkotada is the only Indus site where remains of horses have been found.

Select the correct answer using the code given below:

(a) 1 only (b) 2 only
(c) Both 1 and 2 (d) Neither 1 nor 2

4. The government has proposed to develop five archaeological sites as "iconic sites" with onsite museums in the Union Budget 2020-21. Which of the following sites are mentioned in it?

1. Rakhigarhi
2. Lothal
3. Sivasagar
4. Dholavira
5. Adichanallur
6. Banawali

Select the correct option using the codes given below:

(a) 1, 2 , 5 and 6 only (b) 2, 3, 4 and 6 only
(c) 1, 3, 4 and 5 only (d) 3, 4 and 5 only

5. The Harappan Civilisation is referred as a:

(a) Bronze Age civilisation
(b) Silver Age civilisation
(c) Golden Age civilisation
(d) Stone Age civilisation

6. Consider the following statements regarding the port city of Harappa culture –'Lothal'?

(a) Lothal is a city in early-Harappan.
(b) Lothal was surrounded by a massive brick wall.
(c) Lothal remained the most important port for trade with the Mesopotamia civilisation.
(d) Both (b) and (c).

7. Which of the following Harappa site is relevantly matched with the stage of origin and evolution it represents in Harappan culture?

Sites		Stage
1. Kot Diji	-	Reveals the existence of pre-Harappan culture
2. Amri	-	Transition from rural to urban life
3: Kalibangan	-	Its elaborate town planning and urban features prove mature phase

Select the correct answer using the code given below:

(a) 1 only (b) 2 and 3 only
(c) 1 and 2 only (d) 1, 2 and 3

8. Mohenjo-daro, one of the sites of Harappan civilisation was discovered by which of the following archaeologists?

(a) R. D. Banerjee (b) D. R. Salini
(c) B. K. Thapar (d) D. R. Bhandarkar

9. Which of the following statements is incorrect about the Indus Valley Civilisation?

(a) People of Indus Valley Civilisation used to practice metallurgy.
(b) No site of this civilisation has been found in Haryana region.
(c) Animals known to people of Indus Valley Civilisation include humped bull, rhinoceros and elephant.
(d) All of the above.

10. Consider the following statements regarding the sites of the Harappan Civilisation:

1. Rakhigarhi is known as the Manchester of Harappan civilisation for its cotton trade.
2. Lothal is the only site of the civilisation with an artificial dockyard.
3. Kalibangan is located on the banks of river Ghaggar.

Which of the above statements are correct?

(a) 1 and 2 only (b) 1 and 3 only
(c) 2 and 3 only (d) 1, 2 and 3

11. Consider the following statements regarding Harappan culture:

1. Its mature phase lay between 2200 BC and 2000 BC.
2. A fierce war between the Aryans and the Harappans was considered to be the main reason for the fall of Harappa.

Which of the above statements is/are correct?

(a) 1 only (b) 2 only
(c) Both 1 and 2 (d) Neither 1 nor 2

12. At which of the following Indus Valley Civilisation sites, yarns of spun cotton have been found?

(a) Harappa (b) Mohenjo-daro
(c) Lothal (d) Kalibangan

13. Match the following pairs:

Site	Archaeological Evidence
A. Harappa	i. Copper elephant
B. Daimabad	ii. Bronze dancing girl
C. Mohenjo-daro	iii. Granary outside citadel
D. Kalibangan	iv. Fire altars

Select the correct answer using the code given below:

(a) A-ii, B-i, C-iii, D-iv
(b) A-i, B-ii, C-iii, D-iv
(c) A-iv, B-iii, C-ii, D-i
(d) A-iii, B-i, C-ii, D-iv

14. Consider the following statements :

1. The first man-made port was found in Harappa.
2. The main crops of the Indus Valley civilisation were wheat and barley.
3. The largest Harappan settlement in India is Rakhigarhi in Haryana.
4. The largest number of settlements are in the Ghaggar-Hakra valley.

Which of the above statements are correct?

(a) 1 and 2 only (b) 2 and 3 only
(c) 2, 3 and 4 only (d) 1, 2, 3 and 4

15. Match the following pairs:

River	Site
A. Ghaggar	i. Mohanjodaro
B. Ravi	ii. Kalibangan
C. Indus	iii. Lothal
D. Bhogava	iv. Harappa

Select the correct answer using the code given below:

(a) A-i, B-ii, C-iii, D-iv
(b) A-iii, B-iv, C-i, D-ii
(c) A-ii, B-iv, C-i, D-iii
(d) A-ii, B-iii, C-iv, D-i

16. Which one is the biggest site of the Harappan Civilisation?

(a) Rakhigarhi (b) Harappa
(c) Lothal (d) Dholavira

17. The Indus Valley people knew the use of:

(a) Gold, copper, bronze but not iron
(b) Silver, iron, gold but not bronze
(c) Silver, lead, iron but not copper
(d) Gold, tin, bronze but not silver

18. Consider the following statements regarding the Indus Valley Civilisation.

1. People of Indus Valley Civilisation used to make red and black pottery.
2. People of Indus Valley Civilisation used to trade with other countries

Which of the above statements is/are correct?

(a) 1 only (b) 2 only
(c) Both 1 and 2 (d) Neither 1 nor 2

19. Consider the following statements regarding Indus Valley Civilisation:

1. The area occupied by the Harappan civilisation was triangular in shape.
2. Painting on a jar resembling the story of the cunning fox from the Panchatantra has been found in Lothal.

Select the correct answer using the code given below:

(a) 1 only (b) 2 only
(c) Both 1 and 2 (d) Neither 1 nor 2

20. Consider the following statements with reference to the seals found at Indus Valley Civilisation sites:

1. The standard Harappan seal was square shaped and made of steatite.
2. Pashupati Seal was depicted with a human figure sitting in the centre and animals around it.
3. The seals show the dresses, ornaments, hair-styles of the people of that era.

Which of the above statements is/are correct?

(a) 1 only (b) 2 and 3 only
(c) 1 and 3 only (d) 1, 2 and 3

21. Consider the following statements regarding Chalcolithic age:

1. Chalcolithic people were primarily rural communities who used only copper objects.
2. Both black-and-red pottery and ochre-colored pottery are associated with this phase.
3. The settlement pattern and burial practices suggest the beginnings of social inequalities in Chalcolithic society.

Which of the above statements is/are incorrect?

(a) 1 only (b) 1 and 2 only
(c) 2 and 3 only (d) 1, 2 and 3

22. Match the following:

Chalcolithic Culture	Regions
A. Svalda Culture	1. Rajasthan
B. Kayatha Cultue	2. Maharashtra
C. Malwa Culture	3. Gujarat

Select the correct answer using the code given below:

	A	B	C
(a)	1	2	3
(b)	3	2	1
(c)	2	1	3
(d)	3	1	2

23. Match the following:

Important Harappan Sites	Archeological Findings
A. Harappa	1. Remains of horse bones
B. Banawali	2. Red sandstone male torso
C. Ropar	3. City with radial streets
D. Surkotada	4. Dog buried with human

Select the correct answer using the code given below:

	A	B	C	D
(a)	1	4	3	2
(b)	2	3	4	1
(c)	3	1	2	4
(d)	4	2	1	3

24. Nearly 1400 settlements of the Harappan Civilisation have been discovered so far and these are distributed over a wide geographical area. In this context, consider the following statements:

1. The Harappan Civilisation extended from Jammu & Kashmir in the north to Maharashtra in the south.
2. Majority of the settlements are located on the banks of river Indus and its tributaries.

Which of the above statements is/are incorrect?

(a) 1 only (b) 2 only
(c) Both 1 and 2 (d) Neither 1 nor 2

25. Match the following:

Harappan Sites	Discoveries
A. Kalibangan	1. Rice husk
B. Surkotada	2. Fire altar
C. Mohenjo-daro	3. Horse bones
D. Lothal	4. Bronze dancing girl

Select the correct answer using the code given below:

	A	B	C	D
(a)	1	2	3	4
(b)	4	3	2	1
(c)	3	2	4	1
(d)	2	3	4	1

26. With reference to the economic aspects of Indus Valley Civilisation, consider the following statements:

1. The trade was carried out by both barter system and use of metal money.
2. Foreign trade was conducted mainly with Mesopotamia or Sumeria and Iran.

Which of the above statements is/are incorrect?

(a) 1 only (b) 2 only
(c) Both 1 and 2 (d) Neither 1 nor 2

SOLUTIONS

1. Correct Option: (d)

Explanation:

- **All statements are correct**

Supplementary Notes:

Indus Valley Civilisation

- In terms of culture, it is the only surviving civilisation in the world. The Indus valley civilisation reached its pinnacle in the Bronze Age.
- It was first discovered in 1921. Its discovery pushed back the antiquities of Indian history by another 2000 years.
- Bead-making was the most important industry.
- Inhabitants developed new techniques in metallurgy.
- Charles Mason in 1829 came across mounds of terracotta arts while laying tracks for railways. Local people called it Mohenjo-daro, i.e., the mounds of dead. His findings were collected by Alexander Cunningham, who visited the site in 1878. Sir John Marshal carried out extensive findings on this site.

2. Correct Option: (d)

Explanation:

- **All statements are correct**

Supplementary Notes:

Indus Valley Civilisation

- Harappa was situated on the left bank of river Ravi in Montgomery district in west Punjab and excavated by Dayaram Sahni.
- It is the first Indus valley site that was discovered and thus the entire civilisation is also named as Harappan civilisation.
- It is also known as a city of granaries as 12 granaries were found in two rows.
- Town planning was constituted of horizontal and vertical roads and drains, and a Centre bounded by fortified wall called citadel, outside which H type cemetery was alien to Harappa.

3. Correct Option: (b)

Explanation:

- **Statement 1 is incorrect:** Chanhudaro is the only Indus city without citadel.

Supplementary Notes:

Major Sites & Significance of Indus Valley Civilisation

Harappa	40% total seals found here, Great granary
Mohenjo-daro	Largest of all Indus cities, Great Bath & Granary, Ship on seal
'Heap of dead'	Woven cloth discovered, 9 levels of occupation (300 ft above MSL), impressive drainage system
Kalibangan	Pre-Harappan phase shows land ploughed unlike Harappan, double cropping
Chanhudaro	Only Indus city without citadel, metal workers, bead makers found here.
Surkotada	Only Indus site where remains of horses have been found, coastal city with port town
Banawali	Clay bangles, animal & human figures
Dholavira	Latest and one of the largest civilisations found in India, signboard, 3 citadel with important inner closure
Lothal	Only Indus site with artificial dockyard & hence main sea-port (coastal city with port town) earliest rice cultivation here, twin burial
Rangpur	Rice husk
Kalibangan	Ploughed field, camel bones, circular & square graves, neither bricks nor drainage system (TP not developed here)

4. **Correct Option: (c)**

Explanation:

- The government has proposed to develop five archaeological sites as "iconic sites" with onsite museums in Rakhigarhi (Haryana), Hastinapur (Uttar Pradesh), Sivasagar (Assam), Dholavira (Gujarat) and Adichanallur (Tamil Nadu) in the Union Budget 2020-21.

Supplementary Notes:

Five Iconic sites

- The government has proposed to develop five archaeological sites as "iconic sites" with onsite museums in Rakhigarhi (Haryana), Hastinapur (Uttar Pradesh), Sivasagar (Assam), Dholavira (Gujarat) and Adichanallur (Tamil Nadu) in the Union Budget 2020-21.
- **Rakhigarhi (Haryana):**
  - Rakhigarhi in Haryana's Hisar district is one of the most prominent and largest sites of the Harappan civilisation. It is one among the five biggest townships of the Harappan civilisation in the Indian subcontinent.
  - In one of excavations, the skeletal remains of a couple were discovered. Interestingly, of the 62 graves discovered in Rakhigarhi, only this particular grave consisted of more than one skeletal remains and of individuals of the opposite sex together.
- **Hastinapur**
  - Hastinapur, situated in Meerut district of Uttar Pradesh, finds mention in the Mahabharata and the Puranas.
  - One of the most significant discoveries made at this site was of the "new ceramic industry" named as Painted Grey Ware, which as per the report, represented the relics of the early Indo-Aryans.
  - The Painted Grey Ware would be associated with the early settlers on these sites, viz., the Pauravas, Panchalas, etc., who formed a part of the early Aryan stock in India.
  - Such an association may also explain the synchronism between the appearance of the Painted Grey Ware in the Ghaggar-Sutlej valleys and the probable date of the arrival of the Aryans in that area.
- **Sivasagar**
  - In Sivasagar, excavations at the Karenghar (Talatal Ghar) complex between 2000 and 2003 led to the discovery of buried structures in the north-western and north-eastern side of the complex.
  - Among the structural remains found at the site were ceramic assemblages including vases, vessels, dishes, and bowls, etc.
  - Terracotta smoking pipes were also found.
  - Another excavation site in Sivasagar district is the Garhgaon Raja's palace.
  - A burnt-brick wall running in north-south orientation was found along with the remains of two huge circular wooden posts.
- **Dholavira**
  - Dholavira in Gujarat is located in the Khadir island of the Rann of Kutch, and like Rakhigarhi is one of the sites where the remains of the Harappan civilisation have been found.
  - Dholavira is unique because remains of a complete water system have been found here.
  - The people who lived there for an estimated 1,200 years during the Harappan civilisation are noted for their water conservation system using rainwater harvesting techniques in an otherwise parched landscape.
- **Adichanallur**
  - Adichnallur lies in the Thoothukudi district of Tamil Nadu.
  - The urn-burial site was first brought to light during a "haphazard excavation" by a German archaeologist in 1876.
  - Following this, an Englishman Alexander Rae excavated the site between 1889 and 1905.
  - Over the years, the site has gained attention because of three important findings: the discovery of an ancient Tamil-Brahmi script on the inside of an urn containing a full human skeleton, a fragment of broken earthenware, and the remains of living quarters.

5. **Correct Option: (a)**

Supplementary Notes:

- The Harappan civilisation is referred to as bronze age civilisation, mostly unalloyed copper was used for manufacturing artefacts, and only rarely, tin was alloyed in copper to make bronze.

6. **Correct Option: (d)**

Explanation:

- **Option (d) is correct**

Supplementary Notes:

- In the late-Harappan stage, the decline of the Indus culture started. The excavations at Lothal reveal the stages of evolution. Lothal was established in early Harappan phase. Lothal was surrounded by a massive brick wall for flood protection as the city experienced frequent floods like the city of Mohenjo-daro. It was observed that the city of Mohenjo-daro was often hit by floods created due to changing course of river Indus. Lothal remained an emporium of trade between the Harappan civilisation and the remaining part of India as well as Mesopotamia.

7. **Correct Option: (b)**

Explanation:

- **Statement 1 is incorrect:** It gives evidence of early Harappan stages.

Supplementary Notes:

It gives evidence of early Harappan stage.

- There are four important stages or phases of evolution and they are named as pre-Harappan, early-Harappan, mature-Harappan and late-Harappan.
- The pre-Harappan stage is located in eastern Baluchistan. The excavations at Mehrgarh, 150 miles to the northwest of Mohenjo-daro, reveal the existence of pre-Harappan culture. In this stage, the nomadic people began to lead a settled agricultural life. In the early-Harappan stage, the people lived in large villages in the plains. There was a gradual growth of towns in the Indus valley. Also, the transition from rural to urban life took place during this period. The sites of Amri and Kot Diji remain the evidence for early-Harappan stage. In the mature-Harappan stage, great cities emerged. The excavations at Kalibangan with its elaborate town planning and urban features prove this phase of evolution.

8. **Correct Option: (a)**

Supplementary Notes:

- Rakhaldas Bandyopadhyay, also known as R. D. Banerji, was an Indian historian and a native Indian pioneer in the fields of Indian archaeology, palaeography and epigraphy. He was the Manindra Chandra Nandy Professor of Ancient Indian History and Culture at the Banaras Hindu University from 1928–30. He is mostly known as the discoverer of Mohenjo-daro, the principal site of the Harappa culture.

9. **Correct Option: (b)**

Supplementary Notes:

- Although the Harappan civilisation is referred to as a bronze age civilisation, mostly unalloyed copper was used for manufacturing artefacts, and only rarely tin was alloyed in copper to make bronze. Tools and weapons were simple in form. They included flat axes, chisels, arrowhead, spearheads, knives, saws, razors and fish hooks. People also made copper and bronze vessels. They made small plates and weights of lead, and gold and silver jewellery of considerable sophistication.
- The range of animals domesticated by the Harappan people is quite large. Bones of several animals have been found in excavations. Skeletal remains include sheep, goat, bull, buffalo, elephant, camel, pig, dog and cat, which were all domesticated. A large number of animal have been depicted on the seals. These include sheep, goat, humped bull, buffalo, elephant, etc. Bones of wild animals like spotted deer, sambhar deer, hog deer, wild pig, etc. are also found, which evidently were hunted for food. Several types of birds as well as fishes were also hunted for food. The bones of camels have been found in large number from various sites but the animal is not depicted on seals.

10. **Correct Option: (c)**

Explanation:

- **Statement 1 is incorrect:** Lothal is known as 'Manchester of Harappan civilisation' for its cotton trade.

Supplementary Notes:

Harappan Civilisation

- **Lothal:** The first man-made port was found in Lothal.
  - Lothal is located on the banks of river Bhogavo in Gujarat.
  - It is the only Indus site with an artificial dockyard and has the world's first tidal port.
  - Evidence of double burials from Lothal.
  - Copper furnaces have been found.
  - A circular button-shaped seal called 'Persian Gulf' was seen.
  - Two terracotta models of Egyptian mummies found wrapped in a muslin cloth.
  - The game of chess seemed to have been played at Lothal.
- **Kalibangan:** Lower fortified town, Fire.
- Evidence of cultivation of rice in Lothal and Rangpur.
- Beadmakers shop seen in Lothal, Chanhudaro.
- A sacrificial fire altar found both in Lothal and Kalibangan, suggesting medical and surgical skills.
- Kalibangan is located on the banks of river Ghaggar.

11. **Correct Option: (a)**

Explanation:

- **Statement 2 is incorrect:** There is no evidence of any mass scale confrontation between the Harappans and the Aryans.

Supplementary Notes:

Decline of Harappan Culture

- The Harappan culture existed between 2500 BC and 1750 BC Its mature phase lay between 2200 BC and 2000 BC.
- Throughout the period of its existence, it seems to have retained the same kind of tools, weapons and houses.
- The whole style of life appears to be uniform. Archeologists noticed the same town planning, the

same seals, the same terracotta works, and the same long chert blades.

- But the view stressing changelessness cannot be pushed too far. We do notice changes in the pottery of Mohenjo-daro over a period of time.
- Around 1750 BC, the two important cities of the Harappan culture – Harappa and Mohenjo-daro, disappeared, but the Harappan culture at other sites faded out gradually and continued its degenerated phase in the outlying fringes in Gujarat, Rajasthan and western Uttar Pradesh.
- While the ancient cultures of Mesopotamia continued to exist even after 1750 BC, the Harappan culture disappeared at about that time for which various causes have been suggested:
    - Some ascribe it to the decreasing fertility on account of the increasing salinity of the soil caused by the expansion of the neighbouring desert.
    - Others attribute it to a sudden subsidence or uplift of the land which caused floods. And still others point out that the Harappan culture was destroyed by the Aryans.
- There is no evidence of any mass scale confrontation between the Harappans and the Aryans.

12. Correct Option: (b)

Supplementary Notes:

- Mohenjo-daro is an archaeological site in the province of Sindh, Pakistan.
- Built around 2600 BC, it was one of the largest settlements of the ancient Indus Valley Civilisation.
- Important archaeological findings of Mohenjo-daro include Great Bath, Dancing Girl, Yarns of spun cotton, etc.

13. Correct Option: (d)

Supplementary Notes:

Indus Valley Civilisation

Site	Archaeological Evidence
A. Harappa	iii. Granary outside citadel
B. Daimabad	i. Copper elephant
C. Mohenjo-daro	ii. Bronze dancing girl
D. Kalibangan	iv. Fire altars

- Important Indus Valley sites and archaeological discoveries
    - **Harappa:** Cemetery H & R37, Coffin burial, Granary outside the fort, Phallus worship, Graveyard, Mother goddess.
    - **Mohenjo-daro:** Prepared Garments, Temple-like Palace, Pashupati seal, Statue of a dancing girl, Ivory weight balance, The Great Bath, The Great Granary, Priest king statue.
    - **Kalibangan:** Lower fortified town, Fire Altar, Boustrophedon style, Wooden drainage, Copper ox, Evidence of earthquake, Wooden plough, Camel's bone.
    - **Lothal:** Port Town, Evidence of rice, Fire altar, Graveyard, Ivory weight balance, Copper dog.
    - **Rangpur:** Evidence of rice.
    - **Surkotada:** Horse bone, Stonecovered grave.
    - **Malavan:** Canals.
    - **Chanhudaro:** Bangle factory, Ink pot, only city without citadel, Carts with seated driver.
    - **Balakot:** Bangle factory.
    - **Daimabad:** Bronze Buffalo.
    - **Amri:** Actual remains of Rhinoceros.
    - **Alamgirpur:** Impression of cloth on a trough.
    - **Ropar:** Buildings made of stone and soil, Dog buried with humans, one inscribed steatite seal with typical Indus pictographs, Oval pit burials.
    - **Banawali:** Oval shaped settlement, only city with radial streets, Toy plough, largest number of barley grains.
    - **Dholavira:** Only site to be divided into three parts, Giant water reservoir, Unique water harnessing system, Dams, Embankments, a stadium, Rock-cut architecture.

14. Correct Option: (c)

Explanation:

- **Statement 1 is incorrect:** The first man-made port was found in Lothal.

Supplementary Notes:

Indus Valley Civilisation

- The first man-made port was found in Lothal.
- Lothal in Gujarat, was excavated by S.R. Rao.
- Lothal is located on the banks of river Bhagava in Gujarat.
- The only Indus site with an artificial dockyard. The world's first tidal port at Lothal.
- Evidence of double burials from Lothal.
- Evidence of cultivation of rice in Lothal and Rangpur.
- Beadmakers shop seen in Lothal, Chanhudaro.
- Lothal is known as 'Manchester of Harrappan civilisation' for its cotton trade.
- Copper furnaces have been found.
- A circular button shaped seal called 'Persian Gulf' was seen.
- Two terracotta models of Egyptian mummies found wrapped in muslin cloth.
- A sacrificial fire altar found both in Lothal and Kalibangan suggesting medical and surgical skills.
- The game of chess seemed to have been played at Lothal.
- There are evidences of cultivation of wheat, barley, rice, date, melon, lemon, etc. People were cattle

herders and used milk and milk products. There are evidences that people made sweets. Half burnt bones give evidence of non-veg life.

- The discovery of two more mounds at the Harappan site of Rakhigarhi in Hisar district, Haryana, has led to archaeologists establishing it as the biggest Harappan civilisation site. Until now, specialists in the Harappan civilisation had argued that Mohenjo-daro in Pakistan was the largest among the 2,000 Harappan sites known to exist in India, Pakistan and Afghanistan. The archaeological remains at Mohenjo-daro extend around 300 hectares. Mohenjo-daro, Harappa and Ganweriwala (all in Pakistan) and Rakhigarhi and Dholavira (both in India) are ranked as the first to the fifth biggest Harappan sites.
- The Ghaggar-Hakra river system has the most concentration of settlements.

15. Correct Option: (c)

Indus Valley Civilisation

Supplementary Notes:

River	Site
A. Ghaggar	ii. Kalibangan
B. Ravi	iv. Harappa
C. Indus	i. Mohenjo-daro
D. Bhogavo	iii. Lothal

16. Correct Option: (a)

Explanation:

- **Option (a) is correct**

Indus Valley Civilisation

- The discovery of two more mounds at the Harappan site of Rakhigarhi in Hisar district, Haryana, has led to archaeologists establishing it as the biggest Harappan civilisation site. Until now, specialists in the Harappan civilisation had argued that Mohenjo-daro in Pakistan was the largest among the 2,000 Harappan sites known to exist in India, Pakistan and Afghanistan. The archaeological remains at Mohenjo-daro extend around 300 hectares. Mohenjo-daro, Harappa and Ganweriwala (all in Pakistan) and Rakhigarhi and Dholavira (both in India) are ranked as the first to the fifth biggest Harappan sites.

17. Correct Option: (a)

Supplementary Notes:

Indus Valley Civilisation

- The people of Indus Valley Civilisation were aware of Gold, Silver, Copper, Brass, Bronze and Tin but did not know much about Iron. Copper was the most widely used metal. Ganeshwar in Sikar District of Rajasthan is supposed to be the supplier of Copper to the cities of Indus Valley; however, the largest hoard of Copper came from Gungeria.
- Tools, arms and weapons were made up of Copper and Bronze. They were unaware of the use of Iron. The Harappan people were generally peace loving and had not much arms and weapons in their kitty.
- Weights and Measurements: The weights and measurements were calibrated to a considerable extent. The measures were standardized and perhaps there was a binary system in use. A scale made up of elephant tusk has been found at Mohenjo-daro and Lothal.
- Finance, Business and Industry: There was use of many kinds of metals including Gold, Silver, Copper, Lapis Lazuli, Turquoise, Amethyst, Alabaster, Jade etc. It is thought that Jade came from Central Asia, Turquoise came from Iran, Amethyst came from current Maharashtra and Lapis lazuli came from Afghanistan. A Jewellery hoard has been found at Allahdino, an Indus valley Site near congregation of Indus River and Arabian sea. It has a necklace of 36 carnelian beads, Bronze spacer beads and a copper bead covered with Gold foil and 20 Gold lumps. The trade was multifaceted. It was operated on intraregional as well as interregional basis and had a guild system coupled with nomadic trade. There are no evidences of monetary exchange well developed stoneware industry. The manufacturing of the stone bangles was most prevalent in Harappa and Mohenjo-daro. Harappan civilisation had an Economic Zone. This economic zone was along the bank of the Sirhind River.

18. Correct Option: (c)

Explanation:

- Both statements are correct.

Indus Valley Civilisation

- People of Indus Valley Civilisation used to make pottery.
- Mainly two types – Plain pottery and Red and Black Pottery with decoration, the majority being the former.
- Widespread use of potter's wheel made up of wood, use of firing technique, use of kiln.
- Variety of Pleasing Design—Horizontal strips, Check, Chess-Board Pattern, Interesecting Circles (Pattern exclusively found), Leaves & Petals, Natural Motif—Birds, Fish, Animals, Plants, Human Figure—Rare (A Man & Child found from Harappa), Triangles.
- Pottery had plain bases. Few ring bases have also been found.
- Mainly, colour of pot was pink. General design was on the red base horizontally, black with line on pots.

- Evidences of Trade: Sumerian text makes a mention of Meluha which is identified with Indus Civilisation and two intermediate trading stations—Dilmun (Bahrain) and Makan (Makaran Coast).
- Appearance of Indus seals in the Mesopotamian cities of Ur, Kish, Susa, Tell Asmar and Lagash.
- Cylindrical seals of Mesopotamian type have been found in Indus Valley (Mohenjo-daro).
- "Persian Gulf seals" of intermediate trading stations have been discovered from Indus region (Lothal).
- Discovery of 'Reserved slip ware' of Mesopotamian type from Harappa & Lothal.
- Internal Trade: With Saurashtra, Maharastra, South India, Rajasthan, parts of western UP.
- Ports: Port was found in Lothal.
- External Trade: With Mesopotamia (Modern Iraq), Persian Gulf region and probably Egypt.

19. Correct Option: (c)

Explanation:

- **Both statements are correct.**

Indus Valley Civilisation

- As the three of the world's civilisations developed along the river banks (Egyptian on Nile, Mesopotamian on Tigris– Euphrates, Chinese on the Yangtse), the Indus valley civilisation developed on bank of Indus and several other nearby rivers such as Ghaggar–Hakra, the now dried up Saraswati and the Drasadvati. Centre of the civilisation was in Sind and Punjab and from there, it spread in all directions. Its westernmost point was Suktagendor in South Baluchistan while easternmost point was Alamgirpur in Meerut district of Uttar Pradesh. In North, it extended Afghanistan while in South, its extent was upto Maharashtra state. So far, around 1400 settlements have been discovered, most of which are located on river banks. This civilisation was largest of the four ancient urban civilisations of Egypt, Mesopotamia, South Asia and China and covered an area of around 1.3 million square kilometers. This area is triangular in shape and no other ancient civilisation was extended to such a large area.
- Lothal (Gujarat):
  - Excavated by S. R. Rao in 1954.
  - Situated on the bank of river Bhogavo.
  - City was divided into Citadel and the lower town and dockyard.
  - Evidence of rice has been found here.
  - Painting on a jar resembling the story of the cunning fox of panchtantra has been depicted.

20. Correct Option: (d)

Explanation:

- **All statements are correct.**

Seals of Indus Valley Civilisation

- Archaeologists have discovered thousands of seals, usually made of steatite, and occasionally of agate, chert, copper, faience and terracotta, with beautiful figures of animals, such as unicorn bull, rhinoceros, tiger, elephant, bison, goat, buffalo, etc.
- The purpose of producing seals was mainly commercial. It appears that the seals were also used as amulets, carried on the persons of their owners, perhaps as modern-day identity cards.
- The standard Harappan seal was a square plaque 2×2 square inches, usually made from the soft riverstone, steatite. Every seal is engraved in a pictographic script which is yet to be deciphered. They all bear a great variety of motifs, most often of animals including those of the bull, with or without the hump, the elephant, tiger, goat and also monsters. Sometimes trees or human figures were also depicted.
- The most remarkable seal is the Pashupati Seal depicted with a figure in the centre and animals around. This seal depicts a human figure seated cross-legged. An elephant and a tiger are depicted to the right side of the seated figure, while on the left a rhinoceros and a buffalo are seen. In addition to these animals, two antelopes are shown below the seat. Seals such as these date from between 2500 and 1500 BCE and were found in considerable numbers.
- The seals show the culture and civilisation of the Indus Valley people. In particular, they indicate:
  - Dresses, ornaments, hairstyles of people.
  - Skill of artists and sculptors.
  - Trade contacts and commercial relations.
  - Religious beliefs.
  - Script.

21. Correct Option: (a)

Explanation:

- **Statement 1 is incorrect:** The Chalcolithic people mostly used copper objects along with stone objects and occasionally used those of low-grade bronze.

Supplementary Notes:

Chalcolithic Age

- The end of the Neolithic period saw the use of metals. The metal first used was copper, and several cultures were based on the use of copper and stone implements. Such a culture is called Chalcolithic, which means the copper-stone phase use.
- Technologically, the Chalcolithic stage is applied to the pre-Harappan phase. However, in various parts of

India the Chalcolithic cultures followed the Bronze Age Harappan culture.

- The Chalcolithic people were primarily rural communities spread over a wide area with hilly land and rivers unlike the Harappans who were urbanized on the basis of the produce from the floodplains in the Indus Valley.
- The Chalcolithic cultures are all characterized by painted ceramic, usually black-on-red, a specialized blade and flake industry of the siliceous material like chalcedony and chert, and copper and bronze tools, though on a restricted scale. Their economy was based on subsistence agriculture, stock-raising, hunting and fishing.
- In India, settlements relating to the Chalcolithic phase are found in southeastern Rajasthan, the western part of MP, western Maharashtra, and in southern and eastern India.
- The people of the Chalcolithic phase use different types of pottery, one of which is called black-and-red and seems to have been widely prevalent from nearly 2000 BC onwards, and OCP (Ochre Colored Pottery), which is a red-slipped ware often painted in black and largely in vase forms.
- In Maharashtra, people buried their dead in urns beneath the floor of their house in the north-to-south position. They did not use separate cemeteries for this purpose, as was the case with the Harappans. Pots and some copper objects were deposited in the graves obviously for the use of the dead in the next world.
- Terracotta figures of women suggest that the Chalcolithic people venerated the mother goddess, and some unbaked nude clay figurines were also used for worship.
- A kind of settlement hierarchy is visible in several Jorwe settlements of Maharashtra. Some of them are as large as twenty hectares, but others encompass only five hectares and even less. This would imply two-tier habitations.
- Both the settlement pattern and burial practices suggest the beginnings of social inequalities in Chalcolithic society.
- The Chalcolithic people domesticated cattle, sheep/goats. In all probability, the domesticated animals were slaughtered for food and not used for milk and dairy products.

22. Correct Option: (c)

Chalcolithic Cultures	Regions
A. Svalda Culture	2. Maharashtra
B. Kayatha Cultue	1. Rajasthan
C. Malwa Culture	3. Gujarat

Supplementary Notes:

Chalcolithic Cultures

- **Ahar-Banas Culture**
  - The sites of Ahar-Banas Culture were Aahar, balathal, Gilund, etc in the vicinity of Banas River in Rajasthan. The distinctive feature is black and red ware.
- **Kayatha Culture**
  - Located in Rajasthan near Chambal and its tributaries, the sturdy red slipped ware with chocolate designs is main feature.
- **Malwa Culture**
  - Narmada & its tributaries in Gujarat. One of the largest Chalcolithic settlements. The largest site of the Chalcolithic period is Daimabad situated on the left bank of the Pravara River. Major sites of Malwa Culture include Daimabad, Inamgaon, Kayatha, Nagda, Vidisha, Eran, Mandsaur, and Navdatoli (near Maheshwar). A massive fortification wall and a moat have been discovered at Eran.
- **Svalda Culture**
  - The well-known sites are in Dhulia district of Maharashtra.
- **Prabhas & Rangpur Culture**
  - Both of them are derived from the Harappa culture. The polished red ware is the hallmark of this culture.
- **Jorwe Culture**
  - Jorwe is a village and an archaeological site located on the banks of the Godavari River in Ahmednagar district of Maharashtra. The key features of this culture include red pottery, generally with matt surface bearing paintings in black.

23. Correct Option: (b)

Important Harappan Sites	Archeological Findings
A. Harappa	2. Red sandstone male torso
B. Banawali	3. City with radial streets
C. Ropar	4. Dog buried with human
D. Surkotada	1. Remains of horse bones

Supplementary Notes:

Important sites of Indus Valley Civilisation

- Some of the important sites of the Indus Valley civilisation and their archaeological findings are:
  - **Harappa:** Two rows of six granaries with big platform, stone symbol of lingam and yoni, mother goddess figure, wheat and barley in wooden mortar, dice, copper scale and mirror, a sculpture of dog chasing a deer in bronze metal, and a red sandstone male torso have been excavated.

- **Mohenjo-daro:** The citadel, the Great Bath, the Great Granary, post-cremation burial, sculpture of bearded priest, the famous bronze statue of the Dancing Girl and Pashupati seal.
- **Dholavira (Gujarat):** Giant water reservoir, unique water harnessing system, stadium, dams and embankments, inscription comprising 10 large-sized signs like an advertisement board.
- **Lothal (Gujarat):** Important site for naval trade had a dockyard, practice of burial of cremated remains, rice husk, fire altars, painted jar, modern day chess, terracotta figure of horse and ship, instruments for measuring 45, 90 and 180 degree angles, practice of burial of cremated remains.
- **Rakhigarhi (Haryana)** is considered to be the largest site of Indus Valley civilisation. Granary, cemetery, drains, terracotta bricks have been found.
- **Ropar (Punjab):** Dog buried with human, oval pit burials, copper axe.
- **Surkotada (Gujarat):** First actual remains of the horse bones.
- **Banawali (Haryana):** Toy plough, barley grains, lapis lazuli, fire altars, oval shaped settlement, only city with radial streets.
- **Alamgirpur (Uttar Pradesh):** Easternmost site of IVC. Major findings are broken blade made of copper, ceramic items and impression of a cloth on a trough.
- **Balathal and Kalibangan (Rajasthan):** Bangle factory, toy carts, bones of camel, decorated bricks, citadel and lower town, fire altar.

24. Correct Option: (b)

Explanation:

- **Statement 2 is incorrect:** As many as 1,100 (80%) settlements are located on the vast plain between the Indus and the Ganga, comprising mainly the Saraswati river system which is dry today.

Supplementary Notes:

Harappan Civilisation: Geographical Distribution

- The Harappan civilisation was discovered in 1920-21 following the excavations by R.D. Banerjee at Mohenjo-daro and by D.R. Sahni at Harappa.
- The 1400 settlements discovered so far are distributed over a very wide geographical area. Its known extent in the west is upto Sutkagendor in Baluchistan; Alamgirpur in Meerut District (Uttar Pradesh) in the east; Daimabad (Ahmadnagar District, Maharashtra) in south; and Manda (Akhnoor District, Jammu and Kashmir) in the north, covering an area of almost 1600 km east-west and 1400 km north-south.
- These settlements are mostly located on river banks.
- When we look at the distribution pattern of these settlements in terms of rivers, we find that:
  - Only 40 settlements are located on the Indus and its tributaries.
  - As many as 1,100 (80%) settlements are located on the vast plain between the Indus and the Ganga, comprising mainly the Saraswati river system which is dry today.
  - About 250 settlements are found in India beyond the Saraswati river system with a number of them in Gujarat, and a few in Maharashtra.
- It is clear from the above distribution pattern of settlements that the focus of Harappan civilisation was not the Indus but the Saraswati River and its tributaries which flowed between the Indus and the Ganga.

25. Correct Option: (d)

Harappan Sites	**Discoveries**
A. Kalibangan	2. Fire Altar
B. Surkotada	3. Horse bones
C. Mohenjo-daro	4. Bronze dancing girl
D. Lothal	1. Rice husk

Supplementary Notes:

Indus Valley Civilisation

Site	Excavated by	Important Findings
Harappa	Daya Ram Sahni, 1921	Sandstone statues of human anatomy; Granaries; Bullock carts
Mohenjo-daro (Mound of the Dead)	R.D Banerjee, 1922	Great bath; Granary; Bronze dancing girl; Seal of Pasupati Mahadeva; Steatite statue of bearded man; A piece of woven cotton
Sutkagendor	Stein, 1929	A trade point between Harappa and Babylon
Chanhudaro	N.G. Majumdar, 1931	Bead makers shop; Footprint of a dog chasing a cat
Amri	N.G. Majumdar, 1935	Antelope evidence
Kalibangan	Ghose, 1953	Fire altar; camel bones; Wooden plough
Lothal	R. Rao, 1953	First manmade port; Dockyard; Rice husk; Fire altars; Chess playing
Surkotada	J.P. Joshi, 1964	Bones of horses; Beads
Banawali	R.S. Bisht, 1974	Beads; Barley; Evidence of both pre-Harappan and Harappan culture
Dholavira	R.S. Bisht, 1985	Water harnessing system; Water reservoir

26. **Correct Option: (a)**

Explanation:

- **Statement 1 is incorrect:** Metal money was not used and trade was carried on by barter system.

Supplementary Notes:

Indus Valley Civilisation – Economy Aspects

- They did not use metal money. Most probably, they carried on all exchanges through barter system.
- In return for finished goods and possibly food grains, they procured metals from the neighbouring areas by boats and bullock carts.
- Inter-regional trade was carried on with Rajasthan, Saurashtra, Maharashtra, parts of western Uttar Pradesh and Bihar.
- Foreign trade was conducted mainly with Mesopotamia or Sumeria (modern Iraq) and Iran.
- Their cities also carried commerce with those in the land of the Tigris and the Euphrates.
- The importance of trade in the life of the Indus people is witnessed by the presence of numerous seals, uniform script and regulated weights and measures in a wide area.

CONCEPT REVISION

Here is the list of concepts that have been covered as part of the previous exercise. Revise and Self-reflect on your concepts you covered.

- Major sites in Indus Valley Civilisation ☐
- "Iconic Sites" with onsite museums ☐
- Port city of Harappan Culture ☐
- Chalcolithic Age ☐

1.3 RIG VEDIC AND LATER VEDIC PERIOD

QUESTIONS

1. **Consider the following statements with respect to Vedic civilisation:**
   1. Sabha and Samiti were legislative assemblies at tribal or territorial level.
   2. The king was autocratic with main responsibility of being protector of the tribe and the cattle wealth.
   3. Samiti was not open for women in Early Vedic Period.
   4. The Aryans travelled from Afghanistan to India through Khyber and Bolan passes.

   Which of the above statements are correct?

   (a) 1 and 2 only (b) 1, 2 and 4 only
   (c) 1 and 4 only (d) 1, 2, 3 and 4

2. **Consider the following statements about the Later Vedic Culture:**
   1. Sacrifices became more important.
   2. People of the Later Vedic Period used painted grey ware pottery.
   3. There was no standing army with the king.

   Which of the above statement (s) is/are correct?

   (a) 1 only (b) 2 only
   (c) 1 and 3 only (d) 1, 2 and 3

3. **Consider the following about Rig Vedic Period:**
   1. People during this period personified natural forces and gave them human or animal attributes.
   2. Both male and female gods enjoyed equal status during this time.
   3. The prayers were accompanied by rituals and sacrifices.

   Which of the above statements are incorrect?

   (a) 1 and 2 only (b) 2 and 3 only
   (c) 1 and 3 only (d) All the above

4. **Consider the following statements regarding geographical expansion of Rig Vedic Period:**
   1. Aryans settled in Saptasandhav region for the first time.
   2. Ganges was the main river of Rig Vedic Aryans.
   3. Rig Vedic Aryans have made no mention of the territories across the Yamuna river.

   Which of the above statements is/are correct?

   (a) 1 only (b) 1 and 3 only
   (c) 2 and 3 only (d) 1, 2 and 3

5. **Consider the following statements regarding Later Vedic Period:**
   1. The main geographical spread of the Later Vedic Period was in the Gangetic plains.
   2. Painted grey pottery is found in abundance in the Later Vedic Period.

3. Later Vedic sites can be found in western Uttar Pradesh and Punjab, Haryana and Rajasthan.

Which of the above statements is/are correct?

(a) 1 only (b) 1 and 3 only
(c) 2 and 3 only (d) 1, 2 and 3

6. Who were the ex-communicated and prohibited people of the tribe during Later Vedic Period?

(a) Chandalas (b) Nishads
(c) Kiratas (d) Antyajas

7. Also known as Parasaram-ka-khera, this settlement along the Yamuna River existed from 3300 BC to 1300 BC. Among major discoveries made here were several ceramic items like roof tiles, cups, vases, beads and carts, among others. Also a humped bull and broken copper blade were unearthed at this site. The site is:

(a) Dholavira (b) Alamgirpur
(c) Rakhigarhi (d) Kalibangan

8. Consider the following statements regarding Later Vedic Age Economy:

1. It was mainly based on use of copper.
2. Agriculture could not be performed due to lack of plough.
3. Tax collection was done by Sangrihitri.

Which of the above statements is/are correct?

(a) 1 and 2 only (b) 2 and 3 only
(c) 3 only (d) 1, 2 and 3

9. Consider the following statements regarding the Rig Vedic economy:

1. Land and Cows were the two most important well-established types of private property.
2. Ayas was the common term for both Copper and Iron.
3. Trade played an important role in the growth of Rig Vedic cities.

Which of the above statements are incorrect?

(a) 1 and 2 only (b) 2 and 3 only
(c) 1 and 3 only (d) 1, 2 and 3

10. Large scale human settlements generally spread from west to east in the Indian sub-continent. What can be the possible reasons for this?

1. Presence of various passes in north-west mountain ranges
2. Easier clearance of forests in the Himalayan foothills
3. Narrower width of rivers in the Himalayan foothills
4. Gradual increase in rainfall from west to east

Select the correct answer using the code given below:

(a) 1 only (b) 1 and 4 only
(c) 2 and 3 only (d) 1, 2, 3 and 4

11. Consider the following statements regarding Rig Vedic Period:

1. According to the vedic rituals, 'Agni' was considered as the divine messenger who conveyed the prayers to the heavenly spheres.
2. The term 'Askini' in the Rig Veda refers to Beas River.

Which of the above statements is/are correct?

(a) 1 only (b) 2 only
(c) Both 1 and 2 (d) Neither 1 nor 2

12. Consider the following statements regarding the Later Vedic polity:

1. It was a monarchical system.
2. It gave greater stress on hereditary rulership.
3. Vidatha replaced Sabha and Samiti as the popular assembly to check the king's authority.

Which of the above statements is/are correct?

(a) 1 and 2 only (b) 2 only
(c) 3 only (d) 1 and 3 only

13. Consider the following statements regarding Early Rig Vedic Period:

1. The Rig Vedic people were mainly pastoral and thus fought wars for the sake of cows.
2. Dasas and Dasyus were slaves and Shudras who were conquered by Aryans.

Which of the above statements is/are correct?

(a) 1 only (b) 2 only
(c) Both 1 and 2 (d) Neither 1 nor 2

14. Consider the following statements:

1. Rig Vedic tribal chiefs had unlimited powers.
2. Vrajapati was the officer responsible for collection of taxes in the Rig Vedic Period.
3. Status of women in the early Vedic Period was better than that in Later Vedic Period.

Which of the above statements is/are incorrect?

(a) 1 only (b) 1 and 2 only
(c) 2 and 3 only (d) 3 only

15. Consider the following statements regarding religious practices during the Rig Vedic Period:

1. There was no idol worship during this period.
2. The dominant mode of worshipping was recitation of prayers and performance of sacrifices accompanied by rituals.
3. Female gods were less important than male gods.

Which of the above statements is/are correct?

(a) 1 and 2 only (b) 1 and 3 only
(c) 2 and 3 only (d) None of the above

16. Consider the following statements regarding the Rig Veda:

1. Indus River is called naditama or the best of the rivers in the Rig Veda.

2. Rig Veda contains only archaic Sanskrit words.

Which of the above statements is/are correct?

(a) 1 only (b) 2 only
(c) Both 1 and 2 (d) Neither 1 nor 2

17. Which of the following is the correct ascending order of the political structure of the Rig Vedic times in India?

(a) Grama-Kula-Jana-vis-Rashtra.
(b) Jana-Kula-vis-grama-Rashtra.
(c) Jana-kula-grama-vis-rashtra
(d) Kula-grama-vis-jana-rashtra.

18. Consider the following with respect to Later Vedic Age:

1. The main center of Aryan settlement shifted from the Saptha Sindhu to Ganga Yamuna doab.
2. Shudras belonged to the dwija system.
3. The head of the craftsmen guild was called Sresti.

Which of the above statements is/are incorrect?

(a) 2 only (b) 2 and 3 only
(c) 1 and 3 only (d) 1 and 2 only

19. With reference to the social structure of Later Vedic Period, consider the following statements:

1. Marriage could take place between persons belonging to the same gotra or having the same ancestor.
2. The women were encouraged and permitted to attend public assemblies.
3. The Varna system became less based on occupation but more hereditary.

Which of the above statements is/are incorrect?

(a) 1 and 2 only (b) 3 only
(c) 2 only (d) 1, 2 and 3

20. Consider the following statements regarding the effects of Alexander's invasion of India:

1. It opened up the land routes between the Greek world in the West and the Indian subcontinent.
2. It augmented political unification in northern India under the Mauryas.

Which of the above statements is/are correct?

(a) 1 only (b) 2 only
(c) Both 1 and 2 (d) Neither 1 nor 2

21. With reference to the administration during the Rig Vedic Period, consider the following statements:

1. The king maintained a large number of regular or standing army,
2. Vrajapati was the officer who enjoyed authority over a large land or pasture ground.

Which of the above statements is/are correct?

(a) 1 only (b) 2 only
(c) Both 1 and 2 (d) Neither 1 nor 2

SOLUTIONS

1. Correct Option: (c)

Explanation:

- **Statement 2 is incorrect:** The king was also not autocratic. He had to abide by the decision of assemblies called sabha, samiti and vidhata. Sabha and samiti were legislative assemblies at tribal and territorial level.
- **Statement 3 is incorrect:** The samiti was a general assembly which was open for all including women.

Vedic Civilisation

- The Aryans travelled from Afghanistan to India through Khyber and Bolan passes. By 1500 BC, they settled in Saptasindhu region.
- The king was also not autocratic. He had to abide by the decision of assemblies called sabha, samiti and vidhata.
- Sabha and samiti were legislative assemblies at tribal and territorial level. Any decisions by sabha and samiti were binding on king.
- Sabha was a general assembly of elders and heads of families.
- The samiti was a general assembly which was open for all including women.
- This samiti was ultimate authority and its decisions were final.
- The king was also not autocratic. He had to abide by the decision of assemblies called sabha, samiti and vidhata. Sabha and samiti were legislative assemblies at tribal and territorial level. The samiti was a general assembly which was open for all including women.

2. Correct Option: (d)

Explanation:

- **All statements are correct.**

Supplementary Notes:

- People worshipped gods for the same material reasons in this period as they did in earlier times. However, the mode of worship underwent substantial change. Prayers continued to be recited, but they ceased to be the dominant mode of placating the gods. Sacrifices became far more important, and they assumed both a public and domestic character. Public sacrifices involved the king and the entire community, which still in many cases coincided with the tribe. Private sacrifices were performed by individuals in their houses because during this period the Vedic people maintained regular households.
- During this period, collection of taxes and tributes seems to have become common. These were probably deposited with an officer called sangrihitri who worked as the king's companion.

- The epics tell us that at the time of a grand sacrifice, large-scale distributions were made by the princes, and all sections of the people were sumptuously fed. In the discharge of his duties, the king was assisted by the priest, the commander, the chief queen, and a few other high functionaries.
- **Statement 3 is correct:** At the lower level, the administration was possibly run by village assemblies, which may have been controlled by the chiefs of the dominant clans. These assemblies also tried local cases. However, even in Later Vedic times the king did not have a standing army. Tribal units were mustered in times of war and, according to one ritual, for success in war, the king had to eat along with his people (vis) from the same plate.
- The most distinctive pottery of the period is known as Painted Grey Ware. It consisted of bowls and dishes, that were used either for rituals or for eating or for both, probably by the emerging upper orders. Glass hoards and bangles found in the PGW layers may have been used as prestige objects by a few persons.

3. **Correct Option: (b)**

Explanation:

- **Statements 2 is incorrect:** Rig Vedic people worshipped female divinities such as Aditi and Usha who represented the appearance of dawn. But they were not prominent in the time of the Rig Veda. In the patriarchal set up of the period the male gods were far more important than the female gods.
- **Statement 3 is incorrect:** The dominant mode of working during Rig Vedic times were through collective and individual prayers. But the prayers were not accompanied by any rituals or sacrifice. Sacrifices and rituals were started during Later Vedic times.

Supplementary Notes:

Rig Vedic Period

- The political, social and cultural life of the Rig Vedic people can be traced from the hymns of the Rig Veda. The basic unit of political organisation was kula or family.
- Several families joined together on the basis of their kinship to form a village or grama. The leader of grama was known as gramani. A group of villages constituted a larger unit called visu. It was headed by vishayapati. The highest political unit was called jana or tribe.
- The Rig Vedic society was patriarchal. The basic unit of society was family or graham. The head of the family was known as grahapathi. Monogamy was generally practiced while polygamy was prevalent among the royal and noble families. The wife took care of the household and participated in all the major ceremonies. Women were given equal opportunities as men for their spiritual and intellectual development. There were women poets like Apala, Viswavara, Ghosa and Lopamudra during the Rig Vedic Period. Women could even attend the popular assemblies. There was no child marriage and the practice of sati was absent.
- Both men and women wore upper and lower garments made of cotton and wool. A variety of ornaments were used by both men and women. Wheat and barley, milk and its products like curd and ghee, vegetables and fruits were the chief articles of food. The eating of cow's meat was prohibited since it was a sacred animal. Chariot racing, horse racing, dicing, music and dance were the favourite pastimes. The social divisions were not rigid during the Rig Vedic Period as it was in the Later Vedic Period.
- The Rig Vedic Aryans worshiped the natural forces like earth, fire, wind, rain and thunder. They personified these natural forces into many gods and worshipped them. The important Rig Vedic gods were Prithvi (Earth), Agni (Fire), Vayu (Wind), Varuna (Rain) and Indra (Thunder). Indra was the most popular among them during the early Vedic Period. Next in importance to Indra was Agni who was regarded as an intermediary between the gods and people. Varuna was supposed to be the upholder of the natural order. There were also female gods like Aditi and Usha. There were no temples and no idol worship during the early Vedic Period. Prayers were offered to the gods in the expectation of rewards. Ghee, milk and grain were given as offerings. Elaborate rituals were followed during the worship.
- Aryans found it difficult to explain the advent of rains, the appearance of sun and the moon and the existence of rivers, mountains, etc. So they personified these natural forces and looked upon then as living beings to whom they gave human or animal attributes.

4. **Correct Option: (b)**

Explanation:

- **Statements 2 is incorrect:** The Indus River was the most important and most often mentioned river.

Supplementary Notes:

Geography of Rig Vedic Period

- The reference of seas in the early Rig Vedic text is doubtful. However, in the later-Vedic literature, Samudram actually means the sea.
- The Aryans used the term 'Sapta Saindhavas' as the region where they settled down. They used this term in the context of the country.
- There are references to eastern and western oceans in the Satapatha Brahmana, which indicate acquaintance with the Bay of Bengal and the Arabian Sea in the Later Vedic era.

- The Rig Vedic Aryans were not familiar with any kind of desert. However, an implied reference to Maru as the country of desert mounds near Kurukshetra has been traced in Taittiriya Aranyaka.
- Vedic culture was essentially a rural culture, and cities had not emerged; no important place name is hence recorded.
- In the Rig-Veda it was because of the migratory nature of the tribes and in the Later-Vedic Period the regions came to be known by the names of the tribes who controlled them.
- The country of the Aryan was also designated as Aryavarta in the latter scriptures. The Rig Vedic Aryans had not yet established settlements in southern India.
- The Sapta Saindhavas country of the Rig Vedic Period was bounded by the Himalayas and Tibet in the east, Turkistan in the north, Afghanistan in the west and the Aravallis in the south.
- Indus was the most important river of Aryans. Saraswati was called naditama; best in rivers.
- The Ganga and the mountains of the Vindhya were the barriers not easy to cross in those days.
- When the Early Rig Vedic hymns were written, the focus of Aryan culture was the region between the Yamuna and Sutudri (Sutlej), and along the upper course of the river Saraswati.
- The Saraswati river is now an insignificant stream, losing itself in the desert of Rajasthan, but then it flowed broad and strong.
- Out of thirty-one rivers mentioned in the Vedic texts, about twenty-five names occur in the hymns of the Rig Veda alone.
- In the Nadistuti, the Rig Veda enumerates several streams most of which belong to the Indus system.
- The Rig Vedic people knew about the Himalayas but did not mention about the land south of the Yamuna, and they did not mention the Vindhyas Mountains or Satpura even.
- The other hills referred to are Arjika, Mujavant, Silament (Sulaiman range), etc., which were all ridges of the Himalayas.

5. **Correct Option: (d)**

Explanation:

- **All statements are correct.**

Supplementary Notes:

Geography of the Later Vedic Phases

- The period of 1500 BC and 600 BC was divided into Early Vedic Age (Vedic Period) and Later Vedic Age.
- During the Later Vedic Age (1000-600 BC) the Aryans thoroughly subdued the fertile plains watered by Rivers like: Yamuna, Ganges and Sadanira.
- Excavation in the upper Gangetic basin has led to the discovery of earthen bowls and dishes made of painted grey pottery.
- These wares are part of the same area and the same period (circa 1000-600 BC) as the post-Vedic compilations.
- Thus, these sites are called Painted Grey Ware (PGW) sites.
- These sites can be found in western Uttar Pradesh and adjoining areas of Punjab, Haryana and Rajasthan.
- Iron gained prominence from around 1000 BC and was also found inside burials in Pakistan and Baluchistan.

6. **Correct Option: (b)**

Explanation:

- **Option (b) is correct.**

Supplementary Notes:

Later Vedic Period

- Untouchability was of two types during Later Vedic Period: untouchability by birth and untouchability by profession.
- Chandals were born under pratiloma marriage (pratiloma- marriage between upper cast women and lower cast men).
- Nishads were excommunicated and prohibited people of the tribe.
- Antyajas were those who lived outside the villages. They were untouchables as they cleansed the society and hence were not allowed to stay within but outside the society.
- Kiratas were uncivilised, forest tribe.
- Nishads, Kiratas and Antyajas - all three were untouchable by profession.

7. **Correct Option: (b)**

Supplementary Notes:

Alamgirpur

- It is another prominent archaeological site of the Indus Valley Civilisation in Uttar Pradesh's Meerut district. Also known as Parasaram-ka-khera, this settlement along the Yamuna River existed from 3300 BC to 1300 BC from the Harappan-Bara period. Among major discoveries made here during the excavation were several ceramic items like roof tiles, cups, vases, beads and carts, among others. Also, a humped bull and broken copper blade were unearthed at this site.

8. **Correct Option: (c)**

Explanation:

- **Statement 1 is incorrect:** Later Vedic Age economy was mainly based on iron.
- **Statement 2 is incorrect:** Agriculture was performed to full potential due to availability of plough.

Supplementary Notes:
Later Vedic Age Economy

- The main factor in the expansion of the Aryan culture during the Later Vedic Period was the beginning of the use of iron. It was introduced around 1000 BCE and is mentioned as Krishna Ayas/Shyama Ayas.
- Agriculture emerged as the chief means of livelihood of the Later Vedic people. The forests were cleared by burning the trees. The ruler Videha Madhava burned the forests between river Saraswati to river Sedanira or Gandak. Cultivation was done by plough.
- The land was communally owned over which the 'vish' (clan) had many participatory rights, but it was recognised as property and the head of the household who owned the land was termed as 'Grahpati'.
- With the beginning of food production, agricultural produce began to be offered in the rituals. The items of dana and dakshina included cooked rice. Tila, from which the first widely used vegetable food-oil was derived, increasingly came to be used in rituals.
- Diverse arts and crafts were practiced in the Later Vedic Period. Tin, lead, silver, iron, gold, bronze, and copper were known to Later Vedic people.
- There were smiths and smelters as a lot of copper objects have been found at PGW sites. People had obtained knowledge of glass manufacturing too.
- Exchange was still via barter, but Niskha was used as a convenient unit of value although not as a typical currency.
- Wagons drawn by oxen were probably the most used mode of transport.
- The Later Vedic people were acquainted with four types of pottery:
  - Painted Grey Ware
  - Black and Red Ware
  - Black-slipped Ware
  - Red Ware
- Unlike the Rig Vedic Age where only voluntary offerings were taken and per se no revenue collection was done, in the Later Vedic Age, collection of taxes and tributes was made mandatory and were done by Sangrihitri.

9. **Correct Option: (d)**

Explanation:

- **Statement 1 is incorrect:** Land did not form a well-established type of private property.
- **Statement 2 is incorrect:** During the Rig Vedic Period, only copper was used for which the general term - 'ayas' was used.
- **Statement 3 is incorrect:** The Aryans did not live in cities, and possibly lived in some kind of fortified mud settlements.

Supplementary Notes:
Rig Vedic Economy

- The economic life of the Rig vedic people centered around agriculture, cattle rearing and trade, and commerce. Oxen were used for ploughing and drawing carts and horses for drawing the chariots.
- The Rig Veda attached great importance to agriculture. The plough was drawn by the oxen at times in teams of six, eight or even twelve.
- The grains were harvested with sickles. The grains were collectively called yava and dhanya.
- Pottery-making, weaving, carpentry, metalworking, leather-working, etc. were other noteworthy occupations.
- During the Rig Vedic Period, only copper was used for which the general term - 'ayas' has been used. In a later period when iron came into use, copper and iron came to be known as lohit ayas and Syam ayas respectively.
- Cow was the most important form of wealth. Whenever we hear of gifts made to priests, they usually consist of cows and women slaves and never of land.
- The Rig Vedic people may have occasionally occupied pieces of land for grazing, cultivation, and settlement, but the land did not form a well-established type of private property.
- The Aryans did not live in cities, and possibly lived in some kind of fortified mud settlements. The term pur mentioned in that text means either a dwelling unit or a cluster of such units, not a city or a fort.
- The trade and traders (vanik) were known in the Rig vedic era. Barter was also in vogue.

10. **Correct Option: (d)**

Explanation:

- **All statements are correct.**

Supplementary Notes:
Geographical Setting

- Large-scale human settlements generally spread from west to east.
- Reasons for such migration pattern are:
  - The Himalayas are sufficiently high to shield India against invasions from the north. This was especially true in pre-industrial times when communications were very difficult. However, on the north-west, the Sulaiman mountain ranges, which are a southward continuation of the Himalayas, could be crossed through the Khyber, Bolan, and Gomal passes. The Sulaiman ranges are joined southward in Baluchistan by the Kirthar ranges which could be crossed through the Bolan Pass. Through these passes, two-way traffic between India and Central Asia has continued from prehistoric times onwards.

- The foothills of the Himalayas lent themselves to easier clearance than the jungles on the alluvial soil of the plains. It was easy to cross rivers in these areas because of their narrower width, and hence the earliest routes skirted along the foothills of the Himalayas from the west to the east. It was, therefore, natural that the earliest agricultural settlements were founded in the foothills and uplands, and trade routes followed the terai route.
- Proceeding from west to east, we find the annual rainfall gradually increasing from 25 cm to over 250 cm. The Indus vegetation based on 25 to 37 cm rainfall and possibly the western Gangetic vegetation based on 37 to 60 cm rainfall could be cleared with stone and copper implements and made fit for cultivation, but this was not possible in the case of the mid-Gangetic vegetation based on 60 to 125 cm rainfall, and certainly not in the case of the lower Gangetic and Brahmaputra vegetation based on 125 to 250 cm rainfall. The thickly forested areas, which also had hard soil, could be cleared only with the aid of iron implements which became available at a much later stage. Therefore, the natural resources of the less rainy western area were utilized first.

11. Correct Option: (a)

Explanation:

- **Statement 2 is incorrect:** The term Askini in the Rig Veda refers to Chenab River.

Supplementary Notes:

Rig Vedic Period

- Indra was the chief deity cited in the Rig Veda.
- The sky God Varuna, fire God Agni, and the Sun God Surya were some of the other chief deities who were important in the Rig Veda beside older Aryan deities.
- The God of storms and mountains Rudra, as cited in the Rig Veda is the origin for Lord Shiva, the Hindu God.
- According to the vedic rituals, Agni is the divine messenger who receives the prayers and conveys them to the heavenly spheres.

Rig Vedic Name	Modern Names of Indian Rivers
Sindhu	Indus
Vitasta	Jhelum
Askini	Chenab
Vipasa	Beas
Purushini	Ravi
Satudri	Sutlej
Gomal	Gomati
Drishvadati	Ghaggar

12. Correct Option: (b)

Explanation:

- **Statement 1 is incorrect:** Later Vedic polity did not experience a monarchical system.
- **Statement 3 is incorrect:** Vidatha disappeared from the Later Vedic texts.

Supplementary Notes:

Later Vedic polity

- It covers the time period around 1000-600 BC.
- There was a conspicuous urge in the Later Vedic texts for increasing the power of the raja through performances of elaborated sacrifices such as Vajpeya, Asvamedha, etc.
- The raja's position became more powerful than his Rig Vedic counterpart.
- The polity gave greater stress on hereditary rulership, paving the way for dynastic succession as an integral feature of a monarchical polity of subsequent times.
- Despite the growth of the ruler's power, the Later Vedic Period did not experience a monarchical system. It was a proto-state, on the threshold of a state system.
- The absence of a regular well-defined revenue as the rate of Bali was nowhere specified indicating the absence of its proper and adequate assessment resulted in the absence of enough resources which precluded the formation of military organisation.
- Tribal units were mustered in times of war and, according to one ritual, for success in war, the king had to eat along with his people (vis) from the same plate.
- In Later Vedic times, the Rig Vedic tribal assemblies lost importance, and royal power increased at their cost. The vidatha completely disappeared. Sabha and Samiti appeared more prominently in Later Vedic texts.
- The sabha was a smaller select body and also functioned as the lower court, while the Samiti was the larger General Assembly of the people. Accordingly, the latter is referred to as expressing the voice of vis (people).

13. Correct Option: (c)

Explanation:

- **Both statements are correct.**

Supplementary Notes:

Early Vedic Period

- **Cattle Rearing and Agriculture:**
  - Agriculture was well known to pre-Aryans & ploughshare is first mentioned in early part of Rig Veda, but agriculture was perhaps used to produce fodder only.

- However, there are so many references to the cow and the bull in the Rig Veda that the Rig Vedic people can be called a predominantly pastoral people.
- Most of the wars were fought for the sake of cows as the term for war in Rig Veda is Gavishthi i.e. search for cows (Hence, cows seems to have been most important wealth).
- The Rig Vedic people may have occasionally occupied pieces of land for grazing, cultivation, and settlement, but land did not form a well-established type of private property.

- **Social Differentiation:**
  - The factor that contributed most to the creation of social divisions was the conquest of the indigenous inhabitants by the Indo-Aryans.
  - The dasas and the dasyus, who were conquered by the Aryans, were treated as slaves and shudras. The Rig Veda mentions the arya Varna and dasa Varna (Varna was the term used for colour).
  - Unequal distribution of the spoils of war created social inequalities, and this aided the rise of princes and priests at the cost of the common tribal people.
  - However, as the economy was mainly pastoral and not food-producing, the scope for collecting regular tributes from the people was very limited.
  - The tribal elements in society were stronger and social divisions based on the collection of taxes or accumulation of landed property did not exist, and thus, the society was still tribal and egalitarian.

14. Correct Option: (b)

Explanation:

- **Statement 1 is incorrect:** Tribal chief did not exercise unlimited powers but had to reckon with the tribal organisations.
- **Statement 2 is incorrect:** Vrajapati was an officer who enjoyed authority over a large stretch of land or pasture ground.

Supplementary Notes:

Administration in Rig Vedic Period

- The administrative machinery of the Aryans in the Rig Vedic Period functioned with the tribal chief, for his successful leadership in war, at the centre. He was called Rajan. It seems that in the Rig Vedic Period, the king's post had become hereditary. However, the Rajan was a kind of chief and did not exercise unlimited power, having to reckon with the tribal organisations.
- Several tribal or kin-based assemblies such as the sabha, samiti, vidatha, and gana are mentioned in the Rig Veda. They exercised deliberative, military, and religious functions. Even women attended the sabha and vidatha in Rig Vedic times.
- In the day-to-day administration, the king was assisted by a few functionaries. The most important of these seems to have been the purohita.
- Next in rank to the king was the senani or the head of the army. He used spears, axes, swords, etc.
- We do not learn of any officer concerned with the collection of taxes. In all probability, the people made voluntary offerings called bali to the rajan.
- The officer who enjoyed authority over a large stretch of land or pasture ground was called vrajapati. He led to battle the heads of the families called kulapas, or heads of the fighting hordes called gramanis.

15. Correct Option: (b)

Explanation:

- **Statement 2 is incorrect:** The dominant mode of worshipping the gods was through the recitation of prayers and performance of sacrifices but these were not accompanied by any ritual or sacrificial formulae.

Supplementary Notes:

Rig Vedic Gods

- The Aryans found it difficult to explain the coming of the rains, the appearance of the sun and the moon, and the existence of the rivers, mountains, and the like. They, therefore, personified these natural forces and looked upon them as living beings to which they attributed human or animal attributes. Thus, there was no idol worship at this time.
- We have a large number of such divinities in the Rig Veda:

Indra	Rain god
Agni	Fire god
Varuna	Personified as water and supposed to keep natural order in line
Soma	God of plants, and an intoxicating drink somras named after it
Marut	Personified as storm
Aditi	Goddess of eternity
Usha	Appearance of dawn

- The women divinities like Aditi and Usha were not that prominent during Rig Vedic times. Given the patriarchal nature of society, the male gods were far more important than female gods.
- The dominant mode of worshipping the gods was through the recitation of prayers and performance of sacrifices.
- Offerings of vegetables, barley, etc., were made to gods, but in Rig Vedic times this was not accompanied by any ritual or sacrificial formulae.

16. Correct Option: (d)

Explanation:

- **Statement 1 is incorrect:** Sarasvati is called naditama or the best of the rivers in the Rig Veda.
- **Statement 2 is incorrect:** Rig Veda is written in Sanskrit, and it also includes many Munda and Dravidian words.

Supplementary Notes:

Rig Veda

- The Rig Veda represents the earliest sacred book of India. It is the oldest and biggest amongst all the four Vedas. In it, we find the seeds of India's religious and philosophical development.
- We know about the Aryans in India from the Rig Veda. The term arya generally denotes a cultural community that speaks the Indo-Aryan language.
- The Rig Veda is the earliest text of the Indo-European languages. It is written in Sanskrit but also includes many Munda and Dravidian words. Probably these words percolated to the Rig Veda through the language of the Harappans.
- It is a collection of prayers offered to Agni, Indra, Mitra, Varuna, and other gods by various families of poets or sages. It consists of mandalas or books, of which books II to VII forms the earliest parts. Books I and X seems to have been the latest additions to it.
- The earliest Aryans lived in the geographical area covered by eastern Afghanistan, the North-West Frontier Province, Punjab, and the fringes of western UP.
- The entire region in which the Aryans first settled in the Indian subcontinent is called the Land of the Seven Rivers.
- The Sindhu, coterminous with the Indus, is the river par excellence of the Aryans, and it is repeatedly mentioned. Another river, the Sarasvati, is called naditama or the best of rivers in the Rig Veda. It is identified with the Ghaggar–Hakra channel in Haryana and Rajasthan, but its Rig Vedic description shows it to be the Avestanriver Harakhwati or the present Helmand river in south Afghanistan from where the name Sarasvati was transferred to India.

17. Correct Option: (d)

Supplementary Notes:

Rig Vedic Polity

- The polity of the Rig Vedic India was basically a tribal polity with the tribal chief in the center.
- There was a continuous struggle for supremacy among different kings and republics chief such as the Battle of Ten Kings. Tribal struggle was a part of the evolutionary process towards the formation of a larger political entity.
- The political structure of Rig Vedic India may be traced in the following ascending order:
  - The Family (kula)
  - The Village (grama)
  - The Clan (vis)
  - The People (jana)
  - The Country (rashtra)
- Kula (family) was the smallest unit. It included all the people living under the same roof (griha).
- An aggregate of several families or kulas made up the grama and its headman was called gramini.
- The next larger formation was called the vis, under the head called vispati.
- Larger than vis was jana. The tribe was called jana for e.g. tribes like Yadus. (Yadva-janaha) and Bharatas and the tribal chief was called rajana. The king is also called the protector of the jana or people.
- Above the jana in the order was rashtra. The kingdoms (rashtra) were generally small states ruled by kings (rajana).

18. Correct Option: (b)

Explanation:

- **Statement 2 is incorrect:** Shudras did not belong to Dwija.
- **Statement 3 is incorrect:** The association or guilds of merchants and craftsmen were called Sreni. The head of the merchant guild was called sresti.

Supplementary Notes:

Later Vedic Age

- Drastic changes took place in the society during this period. It was time of socio-political upheaval.
- The main centre of Aryan settlement shifted from sapthasindhu to Ganga Yamuna doab.
- The first three varnas were considered "twice born". The system was provided to qualification for performing Vedic rituals and ceremonies. It's called as Dwija system. Shudras did not belong to Dwija.
- Guilds were formed during this period-the association or guilds of merchants and craftsmen was called Sreni. The head of the merchant guild was called Sresti. The head of the craftsmen guild was called Jesatka.

19. Correct Option: (a)

Explanation:

- **Statement 1 is incorrect:** No marriage could take place between persons belonging to the same gotra or having the same ancestor.

- **Statement 2 is incorrect:** Women were not permitted to attend public assemblies like Sabhas and Samitis.

Supplementary Notes:

Later Vedic Period – Social Structure

- The Varna system of social distinction became more distinct. This became less based on occupation but more hereditary.
- The Institution of gotra appeared in Later Vedic times. Literally, it means the cow-pen or the place where cattle belonging to the whole clan are kept, but in course of time, it signified descent from a common ancestor. People began to practise gotra exogamy. No marriage could take place between persons belonging to the same gotra or having the same ancestor.
- In the family we notice the increasing power of the father, who could even disinherit his son. In princely families, the right of primogeniture was getting stronger, male ancestors came to be worshipped.
- Women were generally given a lower position. Although some women theologians took part in philosophic discussions and some queens participated in coronation rituals, ordinarily women were thought to be inferior and subordinate to men. Women were not permitted to attend public assemblies like Sabhas and Samitis.

20. Correct Option: (c)

Explanation:

- **Both statements are correct.**

Supplementary Notes:

Effects of Alexander's Invasion of India

- The Indian invasion of Alexander covered only a brief period of about two years. But it had its direct and indirect effects, permanent or temporary. These effects were political, commercial and cultural.
- Alexander's invasion of India carried both a political lesson and a political result. The lesson was that divided into small kingdoms, republics and tribal units, the North-West India suffered badly from hands of the foreign invaders. Unity and not the disunity became the need of the time. The presence of small Macedonian garrisons in the Indus valley was like a reminder of India's lack of political unity for some time at least.
- Alexander's invasion opened up the land routes between the Greek world in the West and the Indian sub-continent.
- The Greek invasion of India provided scope for such an exchange. India was rich in religion and philosophy at the time of the Greek invasion.

21. Correct Option: (b)

Explanation:

- **Statement 1 is incorrect:** The king did not maintain any regular or standing army.

Supplementary Notes:

Administration during Rig Vedic Period

- The king did not maintain any regular or standing army, but during times of war he mustered militias.
- The military element was strong in the tribal system of the government.
- The army mainly consisted of Patti (infantry) and Rathins (chariot warriors).
- The soldiers were organised into units known as Sardha, Vrata and Gana.
- Bali was the voluntary offerings from the people, and was probably received by the chiefs.
- There was no special officer for justice. But spies were employed to keep an eye on theft or burglary.
- Vrajapati was the officer who enjoyed authority over a large land or pasture ground.

CONCEPT REVISION

Here is the list of concepts that have been covered as part of the previous exercise. Revise and Self-reflect on your concepts you covered.

- Aspects of Vedic Civilisation ☐
- Aspects of Later Vedic Culture ☐
- Later Vedic Age Economy ☐
- Rig Vedic Economy ☐
- Later Vedic Polity ☐
- Religious practices during Rig Vedic Period ☐
- Effects of Alexander's invasion of India ☐

1.4 MAHAJANAPADAS PERIOD

QUESTIONS

1. Kushinagar, the site of Buddha's parinirvana, was the capital of:

(a) Malla Mahajanapada
(b) Vajji Mahajanapada
(c) Kasi Mahajanapada
(d) Kosala Mahajanapada

2. What could be the possible reason/s for the rise of Magadha ?

1. Magadha occupied a strategic position of geographical importance.
2. Rajgir was situated near deposits of iron.
3. The land of Magadha was rainfed area.

Select the correct answer using the code given below

(a) 1 only (b) 2 and 3 only
(c) 2 only (d) 1, 2 and 3

3. Identify the kingdom having the following characteristic features:

1. It is located near the confluence of the Ganges and Yamuna rivers.
2. Its capital was Kausambi.
3. Swapna Vasavadatta mentions about its king.

Select the correct answer from the kingdoms given below:

(a) Avanti (b) Vatsa
(c) Vajjis (d) Anga

4. When Alexander invaded India, who were the rulers of Magadha?

(a) Haryankas (b) Shishunagas
(c) Nandas (d) Mauryas

5. Match the following pairs:

Kingdom	Capital
A. Magadha	i. Champa
B. Anga	ii. Benaras
C. Kosala	iii. Rajgriha
D. Kasi	iv. Shravasti

Select the correct answer using the code given below:

(a) A-i, B-ii, C-iii, D-iv
(b) A-iii, B-iv, C-i, D-ii
(c) A-iii, B-i, C-iv, D-ii
(d) A-ii, B-iii, C-iv, D-i

6. Match the following pairs:

Ruler	Policy
A. Bimbisara	i. Matrimonial alliances
B. Ajatashatru	ii. Aggressive policy
C. Udayin	iii. Built Fort at Pataliputra
D. Shishunaga	iv. Shifted Capital to Vaishali

Select the correct answer using the code given below:

(a) A-i, B-ii, C-iii, D-iv
(b) A-iii, B-i, C-ii, D-iv
(c) A-ii, B-iii, C-iv, D-i
(d) A-i, B-iv, C-iii, D-iii

7. Match the following pairs:

City	Characteristics
A. Pataliputra	i. Capital of Kosala
B. Rajgriha	ii. Water fort
C. Ujjain	iii. Impregnable, as surrounded by hills
D. Shravasti	iv. Capital of Avanti

Select the correct answer using the code given below:

(a) A-i, B-ii, C-iii, D-iv
(b) A-iii, B-i, C-ii, D-iv
(c) A-ii, B-iii, C-iv, D-i
(d) A-i, B-iv, C-iii, D-ii

8. Consider the following statements:

1. The founder of the Haryanka dynasty was Bindusara.
2. Ajatashatru annexed Vaishali to his kingdom.
3. Shishunaga's greatest achievement was the destruction of the power of Avanti.
4. Mahapadma Nanda took the title of Ekarat.

Which of the above statements is/are correct?

(a) 1 and 3 only (b) 1 and 2 only
(c) 3 only (d) 2, 3 and 4 only

9. Match the following pairs:

List I	List II
A. Chedi	i. Shishupala
B. Magadha	ii. Bindusara
C. Taxila	iii. Ambhi
D. Avanti	iv. Pradyota

Select the correct answer using the code given below:

(a) A-i, B-ii, C-iii, D-iv
(b) A-iii, B-i, C-ii, D-iv
(c) A-ii, B-iii, C-iv, D-i
(d) A-i, B-iv, C-iii, D-ii

10. Consider the following statements:

1. The Shishunagas were succeeded by the Haryankas.
2. Ajatashatru fought with Alexander
3. Mahapadma Nanda acquired Kalinga.

Which of the above statements is/are incorrect?

(a) 1 and 2 only (b) 2 only
(c) 2 and 3 only (d) None

11. Consider the following statements regarding the Mahajanapadas:

1. Assaka was the only Mahajanapada situated to the south of the Vindhya Range.
2. Kasi was located on the confluence of Ganga and Gomati Rivers.
3. The seat of eight smaller clans/kingdoms called "Athakula" belonged to Vajji.

Which of the above statements are correct?

(a) 1 and 2 only (b) 1 and 3 only
(c) 2 and 3 only (d) 1, 2 and 3

12. Which of the following statements is incorrect regarding the republics and monarchies in Mahajanapadas?

(a) Ayodhya, Saketa and Shravasti were three important cities in Kashi.
(b) Champa, capital city of Anga, was annexed to Magadha in the time of Bimbisara.
(c) The earliest dynasty of Magadha was founded by Brihadratha. However, it came into prominence under Bimbisasra and Ajatsatru.
(d) The Vatsa country had a monarchical form of government with its capital at Kausambi.

13. Magadha became the most important Mahajanapada in about two hundred years. Consider the following statements regarding this kingdom:

1. Both Ganga and Son flowed through Magadha.
2. There were copper mines in the region that could be tapped to make strong tools and weapons.

Which of the above statement/s is/are incorrect?

(a) 1 only (b) 2 only
(c) Both 1 and 2 (d) Neither 1 nor 2

14. Consider the following statements regarding the Rise of urban centres in the period of Mahajanapadas:

1. The doab and western Ganges plain saw the growth of Northern Black Polished Ware Culture.
2. Religion played an important role in the urbanisation in the Gangetic Plain.
3. The smallest unit were called Nagaras and the larger towns were called the Mahanagaras.

Which of the above statement/s is/are correct?

(a) 2 and 3 only (b) 2 only
(c) 1 only (d) 1 and 2 only

15. With respect to economic condition during the period of the sixteen Mahajanapadas, consider the following statements:

1. One-tenth of the produce of the soil had to be paid as land revenue.
2. Arts and industries like ivory work, mural painting, and stone-carving were highly developed at that time.

Which of the above statement/s is/are correct?

(a) 1 only (b) 2 only
(c) Both 1 and 2 (d) Neither 1 nor 2

16. Which of the following statements is incorrect regarding trade and craft in ancient India in the period around 200 BC to AD 250?

(a) The period saw the decline of arts and crafts as compared to the pre-Mauryan period.
(b) Ayatana was the guild of merchants.
(c) The term Vyavahari was used for the one who transacts the business.
(d) None of the statement is incorrect.

17. Arrange the following Mahajanapadas that came into existence in 6th century BC from North to South:

1. Avanti
2. Taxila
3. Magadha
4. Koshala

Select the correct answer using the code given below:

(a) 1-3-2-4 (b) 2-1-3-4
(c) 1-2-3-4 (d) 2-4-3-1

18. Consider the following statements regarding the ancient Indian Mahajanapadas that came into existence during the sixth century BC:

1. No Mahajanapada was located in Gangetic delta.
2. All Mahajanapadas were monarchical where power was exercised by a king.
3. The term Janapada is known from the days of the vedic literature.

Which of the above statements is/are correct?

(a) 1 only (b) 1 and 2 only
(c) 1 and 3 only (d) 3 only

19. "It was located to the west of Panchala and south of Kurus and to the west of river Yamuna. As per the Pali literature, this Mahajanapada was generally linked with the Surasena. The capital of this Mahajanapada was Viratanagara."

Which of the following Mahajanapada has been referred to in the above quote?

(a) Avanti (b) Chedi
(c) Assaka (d) Matsya

SOLUTIONS

1. Correct Option: (a)

Supplementary Notes:

- The district of Kushinagar, UP is named after the sacred death place of Lord Buddha.
- At Kushinagar, Lord Buddha, attained Mahaparinirvana (salvation) in 483 BC.
- The present Kushinagar was called Kushinara during Buddha Period.

- Kushinara was the capital of Mallas which was one of the sixteen Mahajanapads of the 6th century BC
- According to the Valmiki's Ramayana, the Mallas was earlier part of Kosala Janapada.

2. **Correct Option: (d)**

Explanation:

- **All statements are correct.**

Supplementary Notes:

Magadhan Empire

- Magadha occupied a strategic position of geographical importance.
- It was bound on the north and west by the river Ganges and Son, on the south by the spurs of the Vindhyas, and on the east by the river Champa. The rich iron deposits were situated not far away from Rajgir. It was from this that its rulers could make effective and strong weapons.
- The land of Magadha was also fertile which yielded rich harvests. Heavy rainfall made the land more productive even without irrigation. They produced different varieties of paddy. Land taxes could be kept high which proved to be regular and substantial source of income to the state without which the maintenance of a big army could not be possible and the empire could neither be built nor consolidated. Neighboring forests provided timber for buildings and elephants for the army.

3. **Correct Option: (b)**

Supplementary Notes:

Mahajanapadas - Vatsa

- Vatsa was one of the solasa (sixteen) Mahajanapadas (great kingdoms) of Uttarapatha of ancient India mentioned in the Anguttara Nikaya. It was situated in the Gangetic Plain with Kausambi as its capital, now known as Kosam, a small town in Uttar Pradesh. There is an archeological site known as Kosam Ruins in this town which is believed to be the Kausambi of Ancient India. Vatsa's geographical location was near the confluence of the Ganges and Yamuna rivers.

4. **Correct Option: (b)**

Supplementary Notes:

Explanation:

- The Indian campaign of Alexander, the Great began in 326 BC.
- The Nanda dynasty, an ancient Indian dynasty that originated in Magadha region during the 4th century BCE and lasted between 345–321 BCE, was around the time of Alexander's invasion.

5. **Correct Option: (c)**

Explanation:

- **Option (c) is correct.**

Supplementary Notes:

- According to Anguttara Nikaya, there were following Mahajanapadas:
  - Anga (including the modern districts of Monghyr and Bhagalpur in Bihar) with its capital of Champa,
  - Magadha (covering the districts of Patna, Gaya and parts of Shahabad) with its earlier capital at Rajgriha or Girivraj,
  - Vajji (a confederacy of eight republican clans, situated to the north of the river Ganga in Bihar) with its capital, Vaisal Ji,
  - Malla (also a republican confederacy covering the modern districts of Deoria, Basti, Gorakhpur and Siddharthnagar in eastern Uttar Pradesh) with two capitals at Kusinara and Pawa,
  - Kasi with its capital at Varanasi,
  - Kosala (covering the present districts of Faizabad, Gonda, Bahraich, etc.), with its capital at Sravasti,
  - Vatsa (covering the modern districts Allahabad, Mirzapur, etc.), with its capital at Kausambi.
  - Chedi, (covering the modern Bundelkhand area with its capital at Shuktimati),
  - Kuru (covering the modern Haryana and Delhi area to the west of river Yamuna), with its capital at Indraprastha (modern Delhi),
  - Panchala (covering the area of western Uttar Pradesh up to the east of river Yamuna up to the Kosala Janapada) with its capital at Ahichhatra,
  - Surasena, (covering Brij Mandal with its capital at Mathura),
  - Matsya (covering the area of Alwar, Bharatpur and Jaipur in Rajasthan)
  - Avanti (modern Malwa), with its capital at Ujjayini and Mahishmati,
  - Ashmaka (between the rivers Narmada and Godavari) with its capital at Potana,
  - Gandhara (area covering the western part of Pakistan and eastern Afghanistan) with its capitals at Taxila and Pushkalavati, and Kamboja (identified with modern district of Hazara in Pakistan).

6. **Correct Option: (a)**

Supplementary Notes:

- Magadha came into prominence under the leadership of Bimbisara of the Haryanka dynasty and a contemporary of the Buddha. He began the policy of conquest and aggression which ended with the Kalinga War of Ashoka. Bimbisara acquired Anga and placed it under the viceroyalty of his son Ajatashatru at Champa. He also strengthened his position by marriage alliances.

- Marriage relations with the different princely families lent enormous diplomatic prestige and paved the way for the expansion of Magadha westward and northward.
- He had three wives. Bimbisara's first wife was the daughter of the king of Koshala and the sister of Prasenajit, the son and successor of the Koshalan king.
- According to the Buddhist chronicles, Bimbisara ruled for fifty-two years, roughly from 544 to 492 BC. He was succeeded by his son Ajatashatru (492–60 BC). Ajatashatru killed his father and seized the throne for himself. His reign saw the high watermark of the Bimbisara dynasty. He fought two wars and made preparations for the third. Throughout his reign he pursued an aggressive policy of expansion. This provoked a combination of Kashi and Koshala against him.
- Ajatashatru was succeeded by Udayin (460–44 BC). His reign is important because he is said to have built a fort at the confluence of the Ganges and Son at Patna. This was done because Patna lay at the centre of the Magadhan kingdom, which now extended from the Himalayas in the north to the hills of Chhotanagpur in the south. Patna's position, as will be seen later, was crucially strategic.
- Udayin was succeeded by the dynasty of Shishunagas, who temporarily moved the capital to Vaishali. Their greatest achievement was the destruction of the power of Avanti with its capital at Ujjain. This brought to an end the 100-year old rivalry between Magadha and Avanti. From now onwards Avanti became a part of the Magadhan empire and continued to be so till the end of Maurya rule.

7. **Correct Option: (c)**

Supplementary Notes:

- Magadha enjoyed certain other advantages. The two capitals of Magadha, the first at Rajgir and the second at Pataliputra, were situated at very strategic points. Rajgir was surrounded by a group of five hills, and so it was impregnable in those days when there was no easy means of storming citadels such as cannons.
- In the fifth century BC, the Magadhan princes shifted their capital from Rajgir to Pataliputra, which occupied a pivotal position commanding communications on all sides. Pataliputra was situated at the confluence of the Ganges, the Gandak, and the Son, and a fourth river called the Ghaghra joined the Ganges not far from Pataliputra. In preindustrial days, when communications were difficult, the army could move north, west, south, and east by following the courses of the rivers.
- The position of Patna itself was rendered invulnerable because it was virtually surrounded by rivers. While the Ganges and the Son girdled it on the north and west, the Punpun girdled it on the south and east. Pataliputra was, therefore, a true water fort (jaladurga)
- The sixteen Mahajanapadas were as follows:
  - **Kasi:** Its capital was Banaras. Kasi was located on the confluence of Ganga and Gomti rivers and somewhere around today's Varanasi.
  - **Kosala:** Its capital was Shravasti. It was located in the Eastern Uttar Pradesh. It covers today's districts Faizabad, Gonda, Bhahraich, etc. and was bordered by River Gomti on the west, River Sadaniva in the east, Nepal hills in the north and River Syandika in the south.
  - **Anga:** Its capital was Champa. It covered the modern districts of Munger and Bhagalpur in Bihar It was later annexed to Magadha by Bimbisar. Magadha was on its west and Raja Mahal hills on the west.
  - **Magadha:** The initial capital of Magadha was Girivraja or Rajgriha. It covered the modern districts of Patna, Gaya, Shahabad of Bihar. It was bordered by River Son on north and Ganga on south.
  - **Vajji or Vriji:** Its capital was Vaishali. It was located on the north of River Ganga in Bihar. The seat of 8 smaller clans/kingdoms called "Athakula" out of which Lichhavais, Janatriks, Videhas were very important. It was separated from Kosala from river Gandak.
  - **Malla:** Its capital was Kushinagar, Pawa. It covered the modern districts of Deoria, Basti, Gorakhpur in Eastern Uttar Pradesh.
  - **Chedi or Cheti:** It was located in the Bundelkhand division of Madhya Pradesh regions, to the south of river Yamuna and along river Betwa or Vetravati. Its capital was Suktimati or Sotthivati, located somewhere near Banda in Uttar Pradesh.
  - **Vatsa:** Its capital was Kausambi. It covered the modern districts of Allahabad and Mirzapur in Uttar Pradesh.
  - **Kuru:** Its capital was Indraprastha / Hastinapur / Isukara. It covered the modern Haryana & Delhi-Meerut-Ghaziabad region. Its eastern border was River Yamuna.
  - **Panchala:** Its capitals were Ahichhtra (Western Panchal) and Kampilya (eastern Panchala). It covered modern day Rohilkhand division & Upper Gangetic Plains of today's Uttar Pradesh & Uttarakhand.
  - **Matsya:** Its capital was Viratnagar. It was located in the Alwar, Bharatpur, Jaipur districts of Rajasthan.
  - **Surasena:** Its capital was Mathura. It was located on the junction of Uttarpatha and Dakshinpatha around Mathura of today.

- **Assaka:** Located on the banks of the Godavari River, its capital was Potali, Potana or Podana, which now lies in the Nandura Tehsil, Buldana district in the Indian state of Maharashtra and it was the only Mahajanapada situated to the south of the Vindhya Range, and was in Dakshinapatha.
- **Avanti:** Its capital was Ujjain & Mahismati. Located on present day Malwa region. It was divided into two parts by the Vindhyas, the northern part had its capital at Ujjayini and the southern part had its centre at Mahishmati.
- **Gandhara:** Its capital was Taxila. The place covered the regions between Kabul and Rawalipindi in North Western Provinces, Peshawar, the Potohar Plateau and on the Kabul River.
- **Kamboja:** Its capital Rajpur. It was located around Hindukush mountains of Kashmir.

8. **Correct Option: (d)**

Explanation:

- **Statement 1 is incorrect:** Brihadratha founded the dynasty around 566 BCE.

Supplementary Notes:

- The Haryanka dynasty is believed to have been the second ruling dynasty of Magadha, an empire of ancient India, which succeeded the mythological Brihadratha dynasty. The reign of this dynasty probably began in the middle of 6th century BCE. Initially, the capital was Rajagriha. Later, it was shifted to Pataliputra, near the present day Patna in India. Brihadratha founded the dynasty around 566 BCE, although Bimbisara, his grandson, significantly expanded the dynasty's boundaries during his rule from 544 BCE to 492 BCE. Thus, Bimbisara is considered as the main founder of the dynasty.
- **Ajatshatru (492 BC–460 BC):** Son of Bimbisara killed his father & seized the throne. Annexed Vaishali and Kosala (annexed Vaishali with the help of a war engine, which was used to throw stones like catapults. Also possessed a chariot to which a mace was attached, thus facilitating mass killings). Kosala was ruled by Prasenajit at that time. Buddha died during his reign; arranged the first Buddhist Council.
- Shishunaga dynasty was the successor of the Haryanka dynasty. The founder of the dynasty was Shishunaga (founded it around 413 BCE), who was previously the minister at the last ruler Nāgadāsaka of Haryanka dynasty. He temporarily moved the capital to Vaishali. His greatest achievement was the destruction of the power of Avanti with its capital at Ujjain. This put to an end the 100-year old rivalry between Magadha and Avanti. From then onwards, Avanti became the part of the Magadha until the end of Mauryan rule.
- Mahapadma Nanda was a powerful ruler of the Nanda dynasty. He uprooted the kshatriya dynasties in north India and assumed the title 'Ekarat'. The Puranas speak of the extensive conquests made by Mahapadma.

9. **Correct Option: (a)**

Supplementary Notes:

Mahajanapadas

List I	List II
A. Chedi	i. Shishupala
B. Magadha	ii. Bindusara
C. Taxila	iii. Ambhi
D. Avanti	iv. Pradyota

10. **Correct Option: (a)**

Explanation

- **Statement 1 is incorrect:** The Haryanka dynasty founded the Magadha Empire in 684 BC, whose capital was Rajagriha, and later Pataliputra. This dynasty was succeeded by the Shishunaga dynasty.
- **Statement 2 is incorrect:** Alexander was attracted to India's wealth. In northwest India, just before Alexander's invasion, there were many small rulers like Ambhi of Taxila, and Porus of the region of Jhelum (Hydaspes). Ambhi accepted Alexander's sovereignty but Porus put up a valiant though unsuccessful fight. Alexander was so impressed with Porus's fight that he granted him his territory back. Porus might have accepted lordship. The battle between him and Porus is called the Battle of Hydaspes. In northwest India, Alexander left four of his generals in charge of four regions, one of them being Seleucus I Nicator, who would later trade his territories in the Indus Valley with Chandragupta Maurya. Eudamas was the last General of Alexander in India.

Supplementary Notes:

- Mahapadma Nanda uprooted the kshatriya dynasties such as Aikshavakus of Kosala, Panchalas of the Upper Ganges and Doab the Kasis, the Haihayas of Narmada Valley, the Kalingas of Orissa, the Asmakas of Godavari Valley in Hyderabad, the Kurus of Upper Ganges region on the confines of Punjab, the Maithilas of Mithila of Nepalese Terai, the Saurasenas of Mathura on the banks of the Jumna and Vitihotras of Western India adjacent to Avanti.
- He also conquered Kalinga and it is proved by two passages of Hatigumpha Inscription of Kharavela. It is known from Hathigumpha Inscription that Nandaraja (Mahapadmananda) constructed some irrigation dams in the province and carried away the statue of first Jina from Kalinga as a war trophy.

11. **Correct Option: (d)**

Explanation:

- **All statements are correct.**

Supplementary Notes:

Mahajanapadas

- **Kasi:** Its capital was Banaras. Kasi was located on the confluence of Ganga and Gomati rivers and somewhere around today's Varanasi.
- **Kosala:** Its capital was Shravasti. It was located in the Eastern Uttar Pradesh. It covers today's districts of Faizabad, Gonda, Bhahraich, etc. and was bordered by River Gomati on the west, River Sadaniva in the east, Nepal hills in the north, and River Syandika in the south.
- **Anga:** Its capital was Champa. It covered the modern districts of Munger and Bhagalpur in Bihar. It was later annexed to Magadha by Bimbisar. Magadha was on its west and Raja Mahal Hills on the west.
- **Magadha:** The initial capital of Magadha was Girivraja or Rajgriha. It covered the modern districts of Patna, Gaya, Shahabad of Bihar. It was bordered by River Son on north and Ganga on south.
- **Vajji or Vriji:** Its capital was Vaishali. It was located on the north of River Ganga in Bihar. The seat of 8 smaller clans/kingdoms called "Athakula" out of which Lichhavais, Janatriks, Videhas were very important. It was separated from Kosala from river Gandak.
- **Malla:** Its capital was Kushinagar, Pawa. It covered the modern districts of Deoria, Basti, and Gorakhpur in Eastern Uttar Pradesh.
- **Chedi or Cheti:** It was located in the Bundelkhand division of Madhya Pradesh regions to the south of river Yamuna and along the river Betwa or Vetravati. Its capital was Suktimati or Sotthivati located somewhere near Banda in Uttar Pradesh.
- **Vatsa:** Its capital was Kausambi. It covered the modern districts of Allahabad and Mirzapur in Uttar Pradesh.
- **Kuru:** Its capital was Indraprastha/Hastinapur/Isukara. It covered the modern-day Haryana & Delhi-Meerut-Ghaziabad region. Its eastern border was River Yamuna.
- **Panchala:** Its capitals were Ahichhtra (Western Panchal) and Kampilya (eastern Panchala). It covered modern-day Rohilkhand division & Upper Gangetic Plains of today's Uttar Pradesh & Uttarakhand.
- **Matsya:** Its capital was Viratnagar. It was located in the Alwar, Bharatpur, Jaipur districts of Rajasthan.
- **Surasena:** Its capital was Mathura. It was located on the junction of Uttarpatha and Dakshinpatha around Mathura of today.
- **Assaka:** Its capital was Potali, Potana, or Podana. Located on the banks of the Godavari River, which now lies in the Nandura Tehsil, Buldana district in the Indian state of Maharashtra and it was the only Mahajanapada situated to the south of the Vindhya Range and was in Dakshinapatha.
- **Avanti:** Its capital was Ujjain & Mahishmati. Located in the present day Malwa region. It was divided into two parts by the Vindhyas, the northern part had its capital at Ujjayini and the southern part had its centre at Mahishmati.
- **Gandhara:** Its capital was Taxila. Covered the regions between Kabul and Rawalpindi in North-Western Provinces, Peshawar, and the Potohar plateau and on the Kabul River.
- **Kamboja:** Its capital was Rajpur. It was located around the Hindukush mountains of Kashmir.

12. Correct Option: (a)

Explanation:

- **Statement (a) is incorrect:** Ayodhya, Saketa and Shravasti were three important Kosalan cities.

Supplementary Notes:

Republics and Monarchies in Mahajanapadas

- The Buddhist literature, particularly the Anguttara Nikaya lists the sixteen Mahajanapadas given as – Gandhara, Kamboja, Assaka, Vatsa, Avanti, Surasena, Chedi, Malla, Kuru, Panchala, Matsya, Vajji, Anga, Kosala and Magadha.
- **Kashi:** With its capital as Banaras, Kashi was at first the most powerful among the sixteen states and perhaps played an important part in the subversion of the Videhan monarchy. Eventually, it had to submit to the power of Kosala and was later annexed by Ajatasatru to Magadha.
- **Kosala:** It embraced the area occupied by eastern Uttar Pradesh and has its capital at Shravasti, which is identical with Sahet – Mahet in the borders of Gonda and Bahraich districts in Uttar Pradesh. Kosala was bounded on the west by the river Gomati, on the south by the Sarpika or Syandika (Sai), on the east by the Sadanira (Gandak) which separated it from Videha and on the north by the Nepal Hills.
- **Anga:** Anga in the east of Magadha roughly corresponds to the modern districts of Monghyr and Bagalpur. Its capital Champa, situated on the bank of the river of the same name, was noted for its wealth and commerce. It was annexed to Magadha in the time of Bimbisara.
- **Magadha:** Between Anga and Vatsa, there lay the kingdom of Magadha, corresponding to modern Patna and Gaya districts, bounded on the north and west by the rivers Ganga and Son, on the south by the Vindhya outcrop and on the east by the river Champa. Rajagriha or Girivraja, rendered impregnable by a perimeter of five hills, was the Magadhan capital. The earliest dynasty of Magadha was founded

by Brihadratha. However, Magadha came into prominence under Bimbisara and Ajatshatru.

- **Vatsa:** The Vatsa country had a monarchical form of government. Its capital was Kausambi (identified with the village of Kosam, 38 miles from Allahabad). Kausambi, a very prosperous city was the most important entrepôt of goods and passengers from the south and the west. Udayana, the ruler of this country in the sixth century BC, had to struggle against king Ajatasatru of Magadha and king Pradyota of Avanti.

13. **Correct Option: (b)**

Explanation:

- **Statement 2 is incorrect:** There were iron ore mines in the region that could be tapped to make strong tools and weapons.

Supplementary Notes:

Magadha

- Magadha became the most important Mahajanapada in about two hundred years. Many rivers such as the Ganga and Son flowed through Magadha. This was important for (a) transport, (b) water supplies, and (c) making the land fertile.
- Parts of Magadha were forested. Elephants, which lived in the forest, could be captured and trained for the army.
- Forests also provided wood for building houses, carts and chariots. Besides, there were iron ore mines in the region that could be tapped to make strong tools and weapons.
- Magadha had two very powerful rulers, Bimbisara and Ajatasattu, who used all possible means to conquer other janapadas.
- Mahapadma Nanda was another important ruler. He extended his control up to the north-west part of the subcontinent. Rajagriha (present-day Rajgir) in Bihar was the capital of Magadha for several years.
- Later the capital was shifted to Pataliputra (present-day Patna).

14. **Correct Option: (b)**

Explanation:

- **Statement 1 is incorrect:** The doab and western Ganges Plain saw the growth of Painted Gray Ware Culture (120BC- 400 BC).
- **Statement 3 is incorrect:** The smallest unit was grama.

Supplementary Notes:

Rise of Urban Centres

- In the 6th century BC, different kinds of towns grew out in the areas of earlier settlement in the Gangetic plain. There are various factors responsible for urbanisation.
- First, some areas, which were the centres of political and administrative activities, emerged as towns. Capitals of different kingdoms thus soon became urban areas.
- In this regard we may mention the names of Rajagriha of Magadha, Sravasti in Koshala, Kausambi in Vatsa, Champa in Anga and Ahicchatra in Panchala. New government offices are opened and officers and employees start residing in their quarters. Shops and markets are opened to meet their demand. In this way, the process of urbanisation begins and grows.
- Secondly, in the 6th century BC some other township grew out of economic activities, particularly market.
- In such cases, different villages, producing different agricultural surplus, selected a particular convenient place.
- They brought their own commodities and exchanged them with that of others. This system of marketing is called the barter system.
- Some of such selected market places were located on trade routes. To such places goods were brought from the far distant places.
- The process of urbanisation was faster and more intense in such places. Ujjain was the most important urban center to grow out of such a process.
- Thirdly, religion played an important role in the urbanisation in the Gangetic plain. In the 6th century BC, people built temples in only a few places.
- There used to be big gatherings with people coming from distant places. Gradually, these religious places saw the emergence of towns. Vaishali was one of such town to grow out of religious importance.
- Fourthly, there were some places which had all the above mentioned characteristics. These were important places for administration, economy and religion. Kausambi was such an urban centre.
- In these urban centers, there was a greater concentration of people than in the villages. There were more alternative sources of livelihood and more products were available for their use.
- The process of urbanisation was also based on concentration of population and size of a place. The smallest unit was grama.
- The exchange centers and the local markets were known as nigama and pulabhedana. They were greater than the gramas.
- The towns were called nagaras. Larger towns were called the mahanagaras. These were well settled, economically prosperous and politically important centers.
- Kausambi was an important mahanagara. Buddhist sources refer to villages of different grades. These were grama or village, nigama or market and nagara or town.

- There were two main areas in the Gangetic Plain where urbanisation occurred. These were western or doab area and eastern plains.
- There was a concentration of population in these two areas. People used metals like copper, bronze, and iron. Therefore, the society is called a chalcolithic society.
- Along with urbanisation, states were also formed in these two areas. But there was a difference in these two societies.
- The doab and western Ganges plain saw the growth of Painted Gray Ware Culture (120BC-400BC). This means that people produced commodities, particularly, pots with gray paint on this surface.
- On the other hand, the eastern societies used potteries with black and red surface. Later on, soft, bright and luxurious pots were used there. It is known as the Northern Black Polished Ware (BC 700-200).

15. Correct Option: (c)

Explanation:

- **Both statements are correct.**

Supplementary Notes:

Economic Condition during the Period of the Sixteen Mahajanapadas

- The basis of the economic life of the period was agriculture. One-tenth of the produce of the soil had to be paid as land revenue.
- The agricultural land was divided into small plots and for the purpose of irrigation, cultivation and conservation of water, cooperative system was followed. Famine was not altogether unknown but it was of very rare occurrence.
- Besides agriculture, animal husbandry was an important source of economic life.
- Arts and industries like ivory work, mural painting, stone-carving, etc. were highly developed at that time.
- Business was carried on both within and without the country. Bharuch, Tamralipti, Sopara, etc. were the important ports of the time through which water-borne trade with Burma, Ceylon, Malaya, Babylonia, etc. was carried on.
- Silk, gold, embroidered cloth were the principal merchandise. There are proofs of co-operative system in the trade and commerce of the period.
- The medium of exchange was copper and silver Karshapana. The silver Karshapana was also known as Dharan. A silver Karshapana was one-tenth in value of the Vedic Niska.

16. Correct Option (a)

Explanation:

- **Option (a) is incorrect:** Arts and crafts in particular witnessed remarkable growth during this period.

Supplementary Notes:

Trade and craft during 200 BC to 250 AD

- The age of the Shakas, Kushans, Satavahanas (200 BC-250 AD) and the first Tamil states was the most flourishing period in the history of crafts and commerce in ancient India.
- Arts and crafts, in particular, witnessed remarkable growth.
- The Digha Nikaya, which relates to pre-Maurya times, mentions nearly two dozen occupations, but the Mahavastu, which relates to this period, catalogs thirty-six kinds of workers living in the town of Rajgir, and the list is not exhaustive.
- The Milinda Panho or the Questions of Milinda enumerates as many as seventy-five occupations, sixty of which are connected with various crafts.
- A Tamil text known in English as 'The Garland of Madurai' supplements the information supplied by the two Buddhist texts on crafts and craftsmen.
- Many artisans and merchants were organized into guilds called sreni and ayatana.
- Both merchants and craftsmen were divided into high, low and middle ranks.
- The Buddhist texts mention the "Sresthi", who was the chief merchant of the Nigama, and the "Sarthavaha", the caravan leader who was the head of the Corporation of Merchants (Vanijgramo).
- It also speaks of nearly half a dozen petty merchants called "Vanija". They dealt with fruits, roots, cooked food, sugar, barkcloth, sheaves of corn or grass, and bamboo.
- The term "Vyavahari", that is one who transacts business.

17. Correct Option: (d)

Explanation:

- **Option (d) is correct:** The correct order of Mahajanapadas from north to south is: Taxila-Koshala-Magadha-Avanti.

Supplementary Notes:

The Age of Mahajanapadas

- The sixth century BC was a period of intense and new political development besides socio-political and religious upheavals that brought two religions to the fore—Buddhism and Jainism. In the Later Vedic age, agriculture and iron tools helped people to settle down at one particular place.
- The permanent settlement led to the foundation of the janapadas or small territorial states under the control of a king. The main area of political activity gradually

shifted from western UP to eastern UP and Bihar. This region was not only fertile due to the rainfall and river systems, but also closer to iron production centres. The use of better iron tools and weapons along with sound economic growth resulted in the transformation of some territorial states into bigger and more powerful states, which came to be known as Mahajanapadas.

- There were 16 Mahajanapadas in ancient India. They were:
  - Anga
  - Magadha
  - Kasi
  - Vatsa
  - Kosala
  - Saurasena
  - Kuru
  - Matsya
  - Chedi
  - Avanti
  - Gandhara
  - Kamboja
  - Ashmaka
  - Vajji
  - Malla

18. Correct Option: (a)

Explanation:

- **Statement 2 is incorrect:** There were also oligarchical Mahajanapadas where power was exercised by a group of people.
- **Statement 3 is incorrect:** The term jana and not Janapada is known from the days of the Vedic literature.

Supplementary Notes:

The age of Mahajanapadas

- The sixth century BC was a period of intense and new political developments besides socio-political and religious upheavals that brought two religions to the fore – Buddhism and Jainism. In the Later Vedic age, agriculture and iron tools helped people to settle down at one particular place.
- The permanent settlement led to the foundation of the janapadas or small territorial states under the control of a king. The main area of political activity gradually shifted from western UP to eastern UP and Bihar. This region was not only fertile due to the rainfall and river systems, but also closer to iron production centers. The use of better iron tools and weapons along with sound economic growth resulted in the transformation of some territorial states into bigger and more powerful states, which came to be known as Mahajanapadas.
- There were 16 Mahajanapadas in ancient India.
- The formation of the state polity was not uniformly seen in the subcontinent and it was not present in peninsular India nor in the Ganga delta and in the north-eastern part of the subcontinent.
- The majority of these states were monarchical but some were also republics, known as ganasangha. Ganasangha had an oligarchic system for governance where the administration was headed by an elected king who had a large council for his aid.
- The term 'janapada' literally denotes an area where a group of people or a tribe/clan (jana) first set its foot/feet (pada). The word Janapada, therefore, clearly implies a well-defined and populated territory. The term 'jana' is known from the days of the Vedic literature but the word 'janapada' in the sense of territorial entity seems to have gained currency only from the post-Vedic times.

19. Correct Option: (d)

Supplementary Notes:

Mahajanapadas

- **Matsya:** It was located to south of the Kurus and west of the Panchalas. Its capital was at Viratanagar, which lies around present day Jaipur. As per the Pali literature, the Matsyas are generally linked with the Surasena.
- **Anga:** This Mahajanapada finds mention in the Atharva Veda and the 'Mahabharata'. During the reign of Bimbisara, it was taken over by Magadha Empire. It is located in present day Bihar and west Bengal.
- **Magadha:** It was situated in present day Bihar close to Anga, separated by river Champa.
- **Kasi:** It was loacted around Varanasi which was the capital as well. It is believed that this city got its name from rivers Varuna and Asi, as mentioned in the Matsya Purana.
- **Vatsa:** This Mahajanapada followed the monarchical form of governance. Its capital was located at Kausambi. Vatsa was located around the present day Allahabad.
- **Kosala:** It was located in modern Awadh region of Uttar Pradesh. Its capital was Ayodhya.
- **Saurasena:** Its capital was Mathura.
- **Panchala:** Its capital was Ahichchatra and Kampilaya for its northern and southern regions, respectively. It was located in present day western Uttar Pradesh. And it shifted from monarchy to being a republic later.
- **Kuru:** Their capital was Indraprastha in present day Meerut and Haryana. The region around Kurukshetra was supposedly the site for Kuru Mahajanapada. It shifted to a republic form of governance later.

- **Chedi:** Its capital was Sothivati. It lay around the present day Bundelkhand region.
- **Avanti:** Its capital was located at Ujjaini or Mahishmati. It was located around present day Malwa and Madhya Pradesh.
- **Gandhara:** Their capital was at Taxila.
- **Kamboja:** Kamboja had its capital named as Pooncha. It is located in present day Kashmir and Hindukush. Various literary sources mention that Kamboja was a republic.
- **Ashmaka or Assaka:** The capital of this Mahajanapada was located at Pratisthan or Paithan. Ashmaka was located on the bank of Godavari.
- **Vajji:** Its capital was Vaishali. The major races residing here were Licchavis, Vedehans, Jnatrikas and Vajjis.
- **Malla:** They were a republic (Samgha). Their capital was Kusinara located around present day Deoria and Uttar Pradesh. **(Map: 1.4.1)**

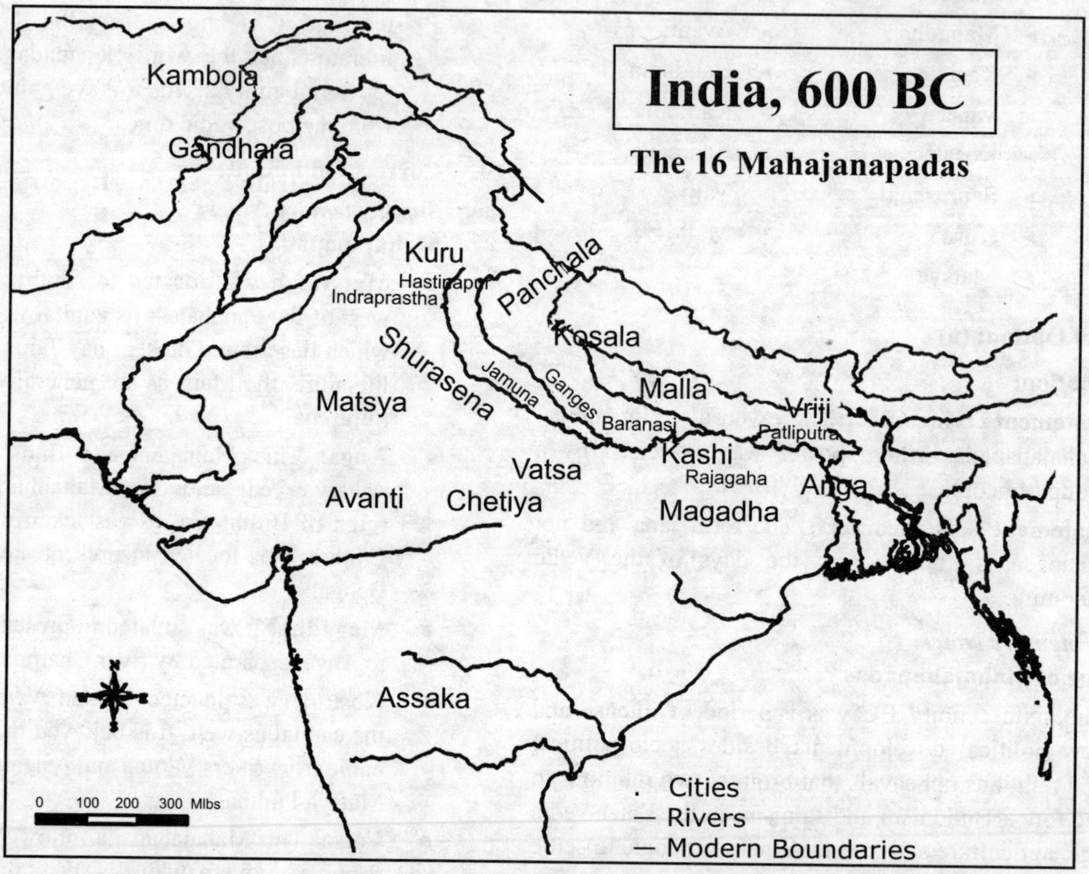

Map: 1.4.1

CONCEPT REVISION

Here is the list of concepts that have been covered as part of the previous exercise. Revise and Self-reflect on your concepts you covered.

- Aspects of Vedic Civilisation ☐
- Reasons for rise of Magadha ☐
- Characteristic features of Vatsa kingdom ☐
- All the 16 kingdoms along with their capitals ☐
- Different rulers and their administrative policies ☐
- Major cities and their characteristic features ☐
- Characteristic features of Magadha ☐
- Rise of urban centres in the period of Mahajanapadas ☐
- Trade and craft during the Mahajanapadas ☐
- Economy during the period of Mahajanapadas ☐

1.5 MAURYAN EMPIRE

QUESTIONS

1. **Which of the following scripts were respected during the Ashoka's reign?**
   1. Kharosthi 2. Aramaic
   3. Prakrit 4. Pali

   Which of the above statements are correct?
   (a) 1 and 2 only (b) 1, 2 and 3 only
   (c) 3 and 4 only (d) 1, 2, 3 and 4

2. **In 326 BC, Alexander invaded India. Consider the following statements regarding the effects of Alexander's invasion:**
   1. Alexander's campaign paved the way for Greek merchants and craftsmen and destroyed the existing facilities for trade.
   2. It provided the first occasion when ancient Europe came into close contact with ancient South Asia.
   3. It paved the way for the expansion of the Maurya Empire in north-west India.

   Which of the above statement/s is/are correct?
   (a) 1 and 3 only (b) 2 only
   (c) 2 and 3 only (d) 3 only

3. **Consider the following statements regarding Persian influence:**
   1. Bell-shaped capital of Asoka's rock edits.
   2. Kharosthi script written from right to left in one line and then from left to right in the next line.
   3. The influence on Mauryan Sculpture.

   Which of the above statements are correct?
   (a) 1 and 3 only (b) 1 and 2 only
   (c) 1, and 3 only (d) 1, 2 and 3

4. **With reference to the Persian invasions, consider the following statements:**
   1. Punjab and Sindh were annexed by Cyrus.
   2. Darius sent a naval expedition to explore the valley of the Sindhu River.

   Which of the above statements is/are correct?
   (a) 1 only (b) 2 only
   (c) Both 1 and 2 (d) Neither 1 nor 2

5. **Who were the 'Potwaadhyaksha' in Mauryan's admistration?**
   (a) Officers for the communication system
   (b) Quality controller of essential commodities
   (c) In charge of weights and measures
   (d) In charge of all mines except iron

6. **Which of the following statements regarding the foreign accounts of Ancient History is/are correct?**
   1. Indica of Megasthenese describes the social, religious and economic conditions of Mauryan administration.
   2. Hiuen Tsang describes the social, religious and economic conditions of India in the age of the Guptas.
   3. Fa-hien describes the social, religious and economic conditions of India in the age of the Harsha.

   Select the correct answer using the code given below:
   (a) 1 only (b) 1 and 2 only
   (c) 2 and 3 only (d) None

7. **Consider the following pairs with reference to Mughal administrative departments and their respective posts:**

Administrative		Department/ Post In charge of
1. Sadr-us-Sadr	-	In charge of Jagir land and control over Khalisa
2. Mir Bakshi		Head of military and intelligence department
3. Mir Saman	-	In charge of imperial household and karkhanas
4. Muhtasib	-	In charge of charitable and religious endowments

   Which of the above pairs are correctly matched?
   (a) 1 and 2 only (b) 2 and 3 only
   (c) 1 and 3 only (d) 1, 2, 3 and 4

8. **Consider the following statements with respect to Mauryans:**
   1. Mauryan state was the first welfare state in India.
   2. Ashoka received Deimachus as ambassador from Syrian king Antiochus I.
   3. Kautilya also wrote Kathasaritsagara.

   Which of the above statements is/are correct?
   (a) 1 and 2 only (b) 1 only
   (c) 2 and 3 only (d) 1, 2 and 3

9. **Consider the following statements about the consequences of Greek and Persian invasion:**
   1. Alexander's invasion led to political unification in northern India under the Mauryan Period.
   2. The impact of Persian invasion on Indian art can be seen through the Gandhara School of art.
   3. The Kharoshti script is derived from the Aramaic script and is written from right to left.

   Which of the above statements is/are correct?
   (a) 1 and 2 only (b) 1 and 3 only
   (c) 1, 2 and 3 (d) None of the above

10. Consider the following with reference to the disintegration and decline of the Mauryan Empire:

1. Brahmanical revolt
2. King Ashoka's pacifist policies
3. Invasions from outside
4. Weakness of Ashoka's successors

Which of the above reasons led to the disintegration and decline of the Mauryan Empire?

(a) 1, 2 and 4 only (b) 2 and 4 only
(c) 1 and 3 only (d) 1, 2, 3 and 4

11. Who among the following also had the name Devanamapiya Piyadasi?

(a) Mauryan King Ashoka
(b) Gautama Buddha
(c) Mauryan King Chandragupta
(d) Bhagwan Mahavira

12. Which of the following statements are correct about Ashoka?

1. He was viceroy of Taxila before he became king.
2. Kalinga War fought in 261 BCE changed his outlook towards violence.
3. In Rock Edict I, Asoka was referred as Devanamapiya Piyadassi
4. He sent his son Mahinda to China for propagating Buddhism.

Select the correct answer using the code given below:

(a) 1 and 2 only (b) 2 only
(c) 2, 3 and 4 only (d) 3 and 4 only

13. Consider the following statements:

1. There was no slavery during Mauryan times.
2. The Mauryas had an elaborate administrative structure.
3. Generally royal princes were appointed as viceroys.
4. Certain tests were conducted to check the suitability of the officers for different jobs.

Which of the above statements is/are correct?

(a) 2 and 3 only (b) 1 and 2 only
(c) 1, 2, and 3 only (d) 1, 2, 3 and 4

14. Match the following pairs:

List I	List II
A. Mahamattas	i. Village headmen
B. Adhyaksha	ii. Ministers/high officials
C. Anta	iii. Superintendent mahamattas
D. Gramika	iv. Frontier areas in charge

Select the correct answer using the code given below:

(a) A-i, B-ii, C-iii, D-iv
(b) A-iii, B-iv, C-ii, D-i
(c) A-ii, B-iii, C-iv, D-i
(d) A-iv, B-i, C-ii, D-iii

15. Consider the following statements regarding Mauryan Administration:

1. Chanakya wrote Arthashastra.
2. Taxes were paid in cash only.
3. Salaries were paid in kind.

Which of the above statements is/are correct?

(a) 1 only (b) 1 and 2 only
(c) 1 and 3 only (d) 2 and 3 only

16. Consider the following statements and mark the option which is correct.

1. Kautilya laid down a Saptanga theory of administration.
2. Ashoka believed in autocratic rule and not paternal despotism.
3. Bindusara is also known as the conqueror of the land between two seas.
4. Indica is survived in fragments and tells us about the Mauryan ways and life.

Which of the above statements is/are correct?

(a) 1 only (b) 1, 3 and 4 only
(c) 2 and 3 only (d) 1, 2, 3 and 4

17. Match the following pairs:

List I	List II
A. Bindusara	i. Amitraghat
B. Ashoka	ii. Devanampiya/ Piyadassi
C. Chandragupta Maurya	iii. Sandrocuttus
D. Chanakya	iv. Vishnugupta

Select the correct answer using the code given below:

(a) A-i, B-ii, C-iii, D-iv
(b) A-ii, B-i, C-iv, D-iii
(c) A-iv, B-ii, C-iii, D-i
(d) A-iii, B-ii, C-iv, D-i

18. Match the following pairs:

List I	List II
A. Bindusara	i. Propagated Buddhism to Ceylon
B. Ashoka	ii. Converted to Jainism
C. Chandragupta Maurya	iii. Great statesman
D. Chanakya	iv. Joined Ajivika Sect

Select the correct answer using the code given below:

(a) A-i, B-ii, C-iii, D-iv
(b) A-ii, B-i, C-iv, D-iii
(c) A-iv, B-i, C-ii, D-iii
(d) A-iv, B-ii, C-iii, D-i

19. Consider the following statements:

1. Dashratha was the last Maurya king who was killed by Pushyamitra Sunga.
2. Girnar inscription of Saurashtra relates to a provincial governor, Pushyagupta of Chandragupta's reign.

3. Chandragupta had defeated Seleucus Nikator.
4. Ashoka preached about non-violence and disbanded his army.

Which of the above statements is/are correct?

(a) 2 only (b) 2 and 3 only
(c) 3 and 4 only (d) 1, 2 and 3 only

20. Consider the following statements:

1. The last Mauryan ruler Brihadratha was assassinated by his commander-in-chief Pushyamitra Sunga.
2. Pushyamitra Sunga was succeeded by King Devabhuti.
3. The most famous ruler of the Satavahana dynasty was Gautamiputrasatkarni.

Which of the above statements is/are correct?

(a) 1 and 3 only (b) 2 only
(c) 3 only (d) 1, 2 and 3

21. Regarding the land revenue policy during the Mauryan age, which of the following pairs are correctly matched?

1. Sannidhata: Highest officer in charge of tax collection
2. Bhaga: Customary land tax
3. Pranaya: Gift of affection
4. Sitadhyaksa: Official in crown lands

Select the correct option using the codes given below:

(a) 1 and 2 only (b) 2 and 3 only
(c) 3 and 4 only (d) 1, 2, 3 and 4

22. Which of the following were the reasons for the disintegration of the Mauryan Empire?

1. Ashoka's preoccupation with missionary activities made him unable to pay attention to the north-western frontier.
2. His pacifist policies and extreme stand on this issue of non-violence.
3. The material advantages that were exclusive to the Magadha, reached to the peripheral provinces.

Select the correct option using the codes given below:

(a) 1 and 3 only (b) 1 and 2 only
(c) 2 only (d) 1, 2 and 3

23. Consider the following statements about the Persian invasion :

1. Absence of any strong political power in the western border of India led to invasion of Persians in India.
2. Sindh, north-western frontier and some part of Punjab constituted the 20th satrapy of Persian empire.
3. Indian subjects were also enrolled in the Persian Army.

Which of the above statements are correct?

(a) 1 and 2 only (b) 2 and 3 only
(c) 1 and 3 only (d) 1, 2 and 3

24. The Maurya period constitutes a landmark in the system of taxation in ancient India. In this context, consider the following statements:

1. The sannidhata was the highest officer in charge of assessment and collection.
2. The samaharta was the chief custodian of the state treasury and storehouse.
3. The assessor was far more important than the chief treasurer.

Which of the above statements is/are correct?

(a) 1 and 2 only (b) 2 and 3 only
(c) 3 only (d) 1, 2 and 3

25. Which of the following were the causes of the fall of Mauryan Empire?

1. Introduction of Vyavaharasamata and Dandasamata.
2. Financial crisis in the empire due to payment to bureaucracy.
3. Neglect of the north-west frontier and the creation of Great Wall of China.
4. Oppressive rule of bureaucrats.

Select the correct answer using the code given below:

(a) 1 and 4 only (b) 2 and 3 only
(c) 1, 2 and 4 only (d) 1, 2, 3 and 4

26. Consider the following statements regarding spread of material culture during Mauryan Age:

1. This period provides evidences for use of socketed axes, hoes, spades, sickles, and ploughshares.
2. Ringwells were first constructed under the Mauryas in the Gangetic plains.
3. Mauryan construction does not give any evidence of use of burnt bricks.

Which of the above statements are correct?

(a) 1 and 2 only (b) 1 and 3 only
(c) 2 and 3 only (d) 1, 2 and 3

27. Ashokan inscriptions, considered to be the earliest, were written in which of the following scripts?

1. Aramaic 2. Greek
3. Kharoshthi 4. Brahmi

Select the correct answer using the code given below:

(a) 1 and 4 only (b) 2 and 4 only
(c) 2, 3 and 4 only (d) 1, 2, 3 and 4

28. Which of the following achievements can be accredited to Ashoka's dynastic rule?

1. Political unification of the country through spreading Buddhist faith.
2. Adopted and preached tolerance.
3. Policy of military conquest.
4. Promotion of cultural contacts within and outside India.

Select the correct answer using the code given below:

(a) 2 and 4 only (b) 1, 2 and 3 only
(c) 1, 3 and 4 only (d) 1, 2 and 4 only

29. Consider the following statements regarding the Mauryan Empire:

1. Chandragupta Maurya was an autocrat who concentrated all power in his hands.
2. The largest expansion of the empire took place under King Ashoka.

Which of the statements given above is/are correct?

(a) 1 only (b) 2 only
(c) Both 1 and 2 (d) Neither 1 nor 2

30. Consider the following officials of Mauryan empire:

	Name		Occupation
1.	Panyadhyaksha	-	Director of trade
2.	Samsthadhyaksha	-	Director of market
3.	Lavanadhyaksha	-	Director of salt-making

Which of the above pairs are correctly matched?

(a) 1 and 2 only (b) 2 and 3 only
(c) 1 and 3 only (d) 1, 2 and 3

31. Consider the following statements regarding the administration of the Mauryan Empire:

1. There was a highly centralized administrative machinery.
2. The gramika was not a paid employee of the government but was elected by the village people.
3. The duty of the yukta was to tour the kingdom every five years and collect details of the administration.

Which of the above statements are correct?

(a) 1 and 2 only (b) 1 and 3 only
(c) 2 and 3 only (d) 1, 2 and 3

32. "He was the first king to have a standing army. He used the policy of marital alliances to expand his kingdom. He was contemporary to the Buddha. He send Jivaka, a Vaidya to the king of Avanti who was suffering from a disease, most probably jaundice."

The above quote refers to whom among the following rulers?

(a) Mahapadma Nanda
(b) Dhana Nanda
(c) Ajatashatru
(d) Bimbisara

SOLUTIONS

1. Correct Option: (a)

Explanation:

- **Option (a) is correct:** As Prakrit and Pali are the languages but not scripts, both 3 and 4 are eliminated.

Supplementary Notes:

Ashoka's Place in History

- Ashoka brought about the political unification of the country. He bound it further by one dharma, one language, and virtually one script called Brahmi which was used in most of his inscriptions. In unifying the country, he respected such non-Indian scripts as Kharosthi, Aramaic, and Greek. His inscriptions appear not only in different types of the Indian languages like Prakrit, but also in Greek and particularly in Aramaic which was a Semitic language of ancient Syria. His multi-script and multi-lingual inscriptions enabled him to contact literate people.
- Ashoka followed a tolerant religious policy, not attempting to foist his Buddhist faith on his subjects; on the contrary, he made gifts to non-Buddhist and even anti-Buddhist sects.
- Ashoka was fired with a zeal for missionary activity. He deputed officials in the far-flung parts of the empire. He helped administration and promoted cultural interaction between the developed Gangetic basin and distant backward provinces. The material culture, characteristic of the heart of the empire, spread to Kalinga, the lower Deccan, and northern Bengal.
- Above all, Ashoka is important in history for his policy of peace, nonaggression, and cultural conquest. He had no model in early Indian history for the pursuit of such a policy; nor was there any comparable example elsewhere except in Egypt where Akhnaton had pursued a pacific policy in the fourteenth century BC. But Ashoka was not aware of his Egyptian predecessor.
- Although Kautilya advised the king to be always intent on physical conquest, Ashoka followed quite the reverse policy. He asked his successors to give up the policy of conquest and aggression, followed by the Magadhan princes till the Kalinga War, and counselled them to adopt a policy of peace sorely needed after a period of aggressive wars lasting for two centuries. He consistently adhered to his policy, for though he possessed sufficient resources and maintained a huge army, he did not wage any war after the conquest of Kalinga. In this sense, Ashoka was certainly far ahead of his day and generation.

2. Correct Option: (c)

Explanation:

- **Statement 1 is incorrect:** Alexander's campaign opened up four distinct routes by land and sea, paving the way for Greek merchants and craftsmen, and increasing the existing facilities for trade.

Supplementary Notes:

Effects of Alexander's Invasion

- Alexander's invasion provided the first occasion when ancient Europe came into close contact with ancient South Asia.

- Alexander's Indian campaign was a triumphant success. He added to his empire an Indian province which was much larger than that conquered by Iran. However, the Greek possessions in India were soon lost to the Maurya rulers.
- The most important outcome of this invasion was the establishment of direct contact between India and Greece in various fields.
- Alexander's campaign opened up four distinct routes by land and sea, paving the way for Greek merchants and craftsmen, and increasing the existing facilities for trade.
- Although we hear of some Greeks living on the north-west even prior to Alexander's invasion, the invasion multiplied Greek settlements in this area.
- The most important of these were the city of Alexandria in the Kabul region, Boukephala on the Jhelum, and Alexandria in Sindh.
- Although the entire area was conquered by the Mauryas, the Greeks continued to live under both Chandragupta Maurya and Ashoka.
- Alexander was deeply interested in the geography of the mysterious ocean which he saw for the first time at the mouth of the Indus.
- He, therefore, dispatched his new fleet under his friend Nearchus to explore the coast and search for harbours from the mouth of the Indus to that of the Euphrates.
- As a result, Alexander's historians left valuable geographical accounts and also clearly dated records of Alexander's campaign, which enable us to definitively establish Indian chronology for subsequent events.
- Alexander's historians also provide us with important information about the social and economic conditions of the time.
- They tell us about the sad system, the sale of girls in marketplaces by poor parents, and the fine breed of oxen in north-west India. Alexander sent from there 200,000 oxen to Macedonia for use in Greece.
- The art of carpentry was the most flourishing craft in India, and carpenters built chariots, boats, and ships.
- By destroying the power of petty states in north-west India, Alexander's invasion paved the way for the expansion of the Maurya empire in that area.
- According to tradition, Chandragupta Maurya, who founded the Maurya empire, had seen something of the working of Alexander's military machine and had acquired some knowledge that helped him to destroy the power of the Nandas.

3. **Correct Option: (a)**

Explanation:

Statement 2 is incorrect: The Aramaic form of writing which the Persian introduced in the north-western India after their conquest, gradually developed into the Kharoshti script. It was written from right to left.

Supplementary Notes:

Persian Influence

- According to Megasthenes, the Greek Ambassador at the court of Chandragupta, the Mauryan ruler adopted certain Persian ceremonies and rituals. The Mauryan art was influenced by the Persian art to some extent.
- It was in Persia that the bell-shaped capital was evolved and it was that country which provided the technique for polishing the shafts of the Mauryan columns.
- Traces of the Persian influence can be seen in the Mauryan sculptures and in the Ashokan pillars. The polish of the Mauryan pillars manifests the Persian influence. The Persian masonry had this characteristic of high polish. Ashokan pillars were influenced by Persian pillars.
- Ashoka followed the Iranian custom of preaching ideals by inscribing them on the stone pillars. The architecture period of Ashoka was completely influenced by the Persian Architecture.
- The Aramaic form of writing which the Persians introduced in the north-western India after their conquest, gradually developed into the Kharoshti script. It was written from right to left.
- All the Ashokan rock inscriptions in the north-west India were engraved in the Kharoshti script. The idea of inscribing ethical exhortations on rocks in the form of royal proclamations might have been borrowed from Persia. Certain resemblances have been discovered between Achaemenid inscriptions and those of Ashoka. They both have the same style, especially in the construction of the opening sentence.

4. **Correct Option: (b)**

Explanation:

- **Statement 1 is incorrect:** Punjab and Sindh were annexed by Darius.

Supplementary Notes:

Persian Invasions

- The Indo-Iranian contact lasted for about 200 years. Iranian influence may also be traced in the preamble to Ashoka's edicts as well as in certain terms used in them. For instance, for the Iranian term 'dipi', the Ashokan scribe used the term 'lipi'. Also, it appears that through the Iranians, the Greeks learned about the great wealth of India, which whetted their greed and led to Alexander's invasion of India.
- The western borderland of India comprising the Punjab, Sindh, and Afghanistan did not have any strong political power during this period.

- Of the sixteen Mahajanapadas mentioned in the literature, only two, Kamboja and Gandhara, may be placed in this outlying region. It appears to have been divided into a large number of independent principalities which were frequently at war with one another, and were thus easy prey to foreign invaders.
- The powerful Achaemenian kings of Persia naturally cast their eyes towards this region, and perhaps Cyrus (558-530 BC) subjugated several principalities living to the south of the Hindukush mountains (parts of India). It was in the reign of Darius (522-486 I3C) that we have positive evidence of the extension of Achaemenian rule in the northwestern part of India. Two inscriptions of this monarch mention "Hindu" as a part of his dominion.
- The exact connotation of this term is not known, but it certainly comprised some territory to the east of the Sindhu, which Darius must have conquered about 518 BC. Herodotus, the Greek historian, tells us that in 517 BC Darius sent a naval expedition to explore the valley of the Sindhu river.
- The Iranian ruler Darius penetrated north-west India in 516 BC and annexed Punjab (earlier Gandhara), west of the Indus, and Sindh. This area was converted into the twentieth province or satrapy of Iran, which had a total number of twenty-eight satrapies.
- The Indian satrapy included Sindh, the north-west frontier, and the part of Punjab that lay to the west of the Indus. It was the most fertile and populous part of the empire. It paid a tribute of 360 talents of gold, which accounted for one-third of the total revenue Iran received from its Asian provinces. The Indian subjects were also enrolled in the Iranian army.

5. **Correct Option: (c)**

Supplementary Notes:

Potwaadhyaksha

- According to Megasthenese, royal officers called Agronomies were in charge officers for the communication systems.
- Panyaadhyaksha was quality controller of essential commodities.
- Potwaadhyaksha was in charge of weights and measures.
- Akaradhyakshya was in charge of all mines except iron.

6. **Correct Option: (a)**

Explanation:

- **Statements 2 and 3 are** incorrect: Hiuen Tsang describes the social, religious and economic conditions of India in the age of the Harsha.
- Fa-hien describes the social, religious and economic conditions of India in the age of the Guptas.

Supplementary Notes:

- The Indica of Megasthenes, who came to the court of Chandragupta Maurya, has been preserved only in fragments quoted by subsequent classical writers. These fragments, when read together, furnish valuable information not only about the system of Maurya administration but also about social classes and economic activities m the Maurya period.
- Hiuen Tsang describes the social, religious and economic conditions of India in the age of the Harsha.
- Fa-hien describes the social, religious and economic conditions of India in the age of the Guptas.

7. **Correct Option: (b)**

Explanation:

- **Statement 1 is incorrect:** Sadr-us-Sadr was an administrative position responsible for charitable and religious endowments.
- **Statement 4 is incorrect:** Muhtasib is a position responsible for censor of public morals.

Supplementary Notes:

Mughal Administration - Post & Departments

- Sadr-us-Sadr was an administrative position responsible for charitable and religious endowments.
- Muhtasib is a position responsible for censor of public morals.
- The Mughals drew heavily on the past, for the organisation of their government was on essentially the same lines as that of the sultanate. The principal officers of the central government were:
  - Diwan: The diwan, often called the wazir (the chief minister), was mainly concerned with revenue and finance.
  - Mir bakhshi: The mir bakhshi performed those duties which had been the responsibility of the ariz-i-mamalik during the earlier period. Owing to the organisation of the civil services on military lines, his power extended far beyond the war office, and some foreign travelers called him the lieutenant-general or the captain-general of the realm.
  - Mir saman: In charge of imperial household and karkhanas.

8. **Correct Option: (b)**

Explanation:

- **Statement 2 is incorrect:** Bindusara was called by Greeks as "Amitragatha" meaning slayer of enemies. And he received Deimachus as ambassador from Syrian king Antiochus. Bindusara wrote to Antiochus I asking for sweet wine, dried figs and sophist. Bindusara supported Ajivikas, a religious sect.

- **Statement 3 is incorrect:** Kautilaya wrote Arthashastra, and Kathasaritsagar was written by Soma Deva.

Supplementary Notes:
Mauryans

- The Maurya Empire was a geographically-extensive Iron Age historical power founded by Chandragupta Maurya which dominated ancient India between 322 BCE and 180 BCE. Comprising the majority of South Asia, the Maurya Empire was centralized by conquering the Indo-Gangetic Plain in the eastern extant of the empire and had its capital city at Pataliputra (modern Patna).
- Mauryan state was the first welfare state in India. It was the most centralized state in Indian history. It was also a state with well expanded and structured bureaucracy.
- Bindusara was called by Greeks "Amitragatha", meaning slayer of enemies. And, he received Deimachus as ambassador from Syrian king Antiochus. Bindusara wrote to Antiochus I asking for sweet wine, dried figs and sophist. Bindusara supported Ajivikas, a religious sect.
- Kautilaya wrote Arthashastra, and Kathasaritsagar was written by Soma Deva.

9. **Correct Option: (b)**

Explanation:

- **Statement (2) is incorrect:** Grecian impact on Indian art is often seen within the Gandhara school of art.

Supplementary Notes:
Greek Invasion:

- Alexander's invasion augmented political unification in northern India under the Mauryas. The destruction of the tiny states in north-west India by Alexander aided the Mauryan empire's easy expansion and also encouraged the Mauryas to capture the northwestern frontier of India.
- The most important results of this invasion was the establishment of direct contact between India and Greece in several fields.
- Post the invasion, there have been Indo-Greek rulers within the northwest part of India.
- Grecian impact on Indian art are often seen within the Gandhara school of art.

Persian Invasion:

- Iranian coins were also found within the northwestern frontier which points to the existence of trade with Iran.
- The Kharoshti script was introduced to north-west India by the Persians. It is derived from the Aramaic script.
- Kharoshti script is written from right to left.
- Probably, the rock inscriptions employed by Ashoka within the 3rd century BCE were inspired by the Persian king Darius.
- The monuments of Ashoka's time, especially the bell-shaped capitals and, therefore, the preamble of Ashoka's edicts have tons of Iranian influence.

10. **Correct Option: (d)**

Explanation:

- All statement are correct.

Supplementary Notes:

Causes of Mauryan decline were many. Some of them are listed below:

- **Weak successors:** It is a reason of decline of almost all the dynasties of world. The political power almost follows the same cycle of rise and fall.
- **External Invasions:** We can observe many Central Asian people and people from west invading India, for example, Indo-Greeks, Parthians etc.
- Emergence of regional kingdoms.
- Overcentralisation.
- Brahmanical anger due to the promotion of Buddhism.
- Financial crisis.

11. **Correct Option: (a)**

Supplementary Notes:

- King Ashoka held the name Devanampiya – Piyadasi (meaning 'Beloved of the gods') in his inscriptions.

12. **Correct Option: (a)**

Explanation:

Statement 3 is incorrect: In Babhru Inscription, he refers himself as 'Piyadassi laja Magadhe' (Piyadassi, King of Magadha). He assumes two titles Devanampiya and Piyadassi in his inscriptions.

Statement 4 is incorrect: He sent missions abroad to spread the word of the Buddha. Notably, he sent his son Mahinda and daughter Sanghamitra to Sri Lanka.

Asoka

- Ashokavardhana or Asoka was governor of Taxila and Ujjain during the reign of his father Bindusara. The Sri Lankan texts represent Asoka as "wading through a pool of Blood" quoting that he terminated all 99 of his brothers except his uterine brother, Tisya. This has been disputed by the scholars. For example, Rock Edict V of Asoka mentions about his brothers. It may be a falsified version of his bravery by the Buddhist monks who might have been interested in dark background of Asoka, who became the gentlest king after his conversion.
- The Kalinga War was a war fought between the Mauryan Empire and the state of Kalinga. Kalinga was an important kingdom because it controlled the trade routes with Southeast Asia. Because of this,

Ashoka, the Mauryan king, wanted to capture it. Therefore, he led his huge army to Kalinga in 261 BC.

- Only inscriptions in the Maski edicts refer his name as Asoka. Puranas refer his name as Ashokavardhana. Girnar Inscription of Rudradaman mentions him as Asoka Maurya. In Babhru Inscription, he refers himself as 'Piyadassi laja Magadhe' (Piyadassi, King of Magadha). He assumes two titles Devanampiya and Piyadassi in his inscriptions.
- Devanampriya Priyadarsi, Dhammarakhit, Dharmarajika, Dhammarajika, Dhammaradnya, Chakravartin, Samrat, Radnyashreshtha, Magadhrajshretha, Magadharajan, Bhupatin, Mauryaraja, Aryashok, Dharmashok, Dhammashok, Asokvadhhan, Ashokavardhan, Prajapita, Dhammanayak, Dharmanayak all are his titles.
- He sent missions abroad to spread the word of the Buddha. Notably, he sent his son Mahinda and daughter Sanghamitra to Sri Lanka.

13. Correct Option: (d)

Explanation:

- All statements are correct.

Supplementary Notes:

Mauryan Empire

- There was no slavery in the sense that people used to work as dasa, out of their own compulsions. No Arya, including a Shudra, could be made dasa forcibly. The 14th book of Arthashastra Secret Means (Aupanisadika) deals with a number of rites and practices.
- Indica was authored by Megasthenes who was the ambassador of Selecus Nikator in Chandragupta Maurya's court. It depicts administration in Mauryan Empire, 7-caste system and absence of slavery in India.
- After establishing the empire, the Mauryas organised a very elaborate system of administration. Megasthenes has left detailed accounts of the system of government under Chandragupta. His account can be supplemented by that of Kautilya.
- Provincial administration was under regional viceroys (Kumara or Aryaputra) with their own Mantriparishads and supervisory officials (Mahamattas) were present in Mauryan Empire.
- Kautilya's Arthasastra laid down certain specific tests to determine the suitability of appointment of persons as different Amatyas. In order that the Amatyas in charge of civil and criminal justice might be sufficiently religious-minded to adjudicate cases impartially, they had to be purified by religious tests.

14. Correct Option: (c)

Supplementary Notes:

List I	List II
A. Mahamattas	ii. Ministers/high officials
B. Adhyaksha	iii. Superintendent
C. Anta-mahamattas	iv. Frontier areas incharge
D. Gramika	i. Village headmen

15. Correct Option: (a)

Explanation:

- **Statement 2 is incorrect:** The taxes were levied both in cash and in kind.
- **Statement 3 is incorrect:** The salaries were paid in cash. It seems that the six wings of the armed forces, the army, the cavalry, the elephants, the chariots, the navy and the transport, were each assigned to the care of a separate committee.

Supplementary Notes:

- The Arthashastra is the title of a handbook for running an empire, written by Kautilya (also known as Chanakya, c. 350-275 BCE), an Indian statesman and philosopher, chief advisor and Prime Minister of the Indian Emperor Chandragupta, the first ruler of the Mauryan Empire.
- There was a well-developed "caste" system as per the accounts of Megasthenes. Megasthenes writes that there were 7 castes viz., philosophers (he indicated Brahmins), farmers, soldiers, herdsmen, craftsmen, magistrates and soldiers. So based upon this account, we can figure out that the caste system was based upon "occupation" rather than birth.
- The taxes were levied both in cash and in kind.
- The salaries were paid in cash. It seems that the six wings of the armed forces the army, the cavalry, the elephants, the chariots, the navy and the transport, were each assigned to the care of a separate committee.

16. Correct Option: (b)

Explanation:

- **Statement 2 is incorrect:** The Mauryan centralized monarchy became a paternal despotism under Ashoka. Ashoka in his Ist separate Edict (Dhauli and Jauguda) says "Savve Munisse Paja Mama" (All men are my children). The Mauryan king did not claim any divine origin yet they attempted to emphasize the connection between kinship and divine power.

Supplementary Notes:

The Mauryan Empire

- The Saptanga Theory: According to Kautilya, a state has seven elements or constituents, namely, Swamin—the King, Amatya—the Minister, Janapada—the Land, and the People, Durga—the Fortress, Kosha—the Treasury, Danda—the Army and Mitra—the Allies. This entire set-up of the kingdom was described as Saptanga theory in ancient India.

- The Mauryan centralized monarchy became a paternal despotism under Ashoka. Ashoka in his Ist separate Edict (Dhauli and Jauguda) says "Savve Munisse Paja Mama" (All men are my children). The Mauryan king did not claim any divine origin yet, they attempted to emphasize the connection between kinship and divine power.
- Bindusara brought sixteen states under the Mauryan Empire and thus conquered almost the entire Indian peninsula. That is why he is called the "conqueror of land between the two seas" – Arabian Sea and Bay of Bengal.
- Megasthenes was the Greek ambassador in the court of Chandragupta Maurya. Megasthenes' book 'Indica' has survived only in fragments. Yet, Indica gives details about the Mauryan administration, particularly, the administration of the capital city of Pataliputra and also the military organisation. His picture on contemporary social life is notable.

17. Correct Option: (a)

Supplementary Notes:

List I	List II
A. Bindusara	i. Amitraghat
B. Ashoka	ii. Devanampiya/Piyadassi
C. Chandragupta Maurya	iii. Sandrocuttus
D. Chanakya	iv. Vishnugupta

18. Correct Option: (c)

Supplementary Notes:

List I	List II
A. Bindusara	iv. Joined Ajivika Sect
B. Ashoka	i. Propagated Buddhism to Ceylon
C. Chandragupta	ii. Converted to Maurya Jainism
D. Chanakya	iii. Great statesman

19. Correct Option: (b)

Explanation:

- **Statement 1 is incorrect:** Sunga Dynasty was established by Pushyamitra Sunga in 185 BC. Pushyamitra Sunga was a Brahmin Commander-in-Chief of last Mauryan ruler called Brihadratha.

Supplementary Notes:

Asoka

- Sunga Dynasty was established by Pushyamitra Sunga, in 185 BC. Pushyamitra Sunga was a Brahmin Commander-in-Chief of last Mauryan ruler called Brihadratha.
- Brihadratha was a weak ruler and his Senapati, Pushyamitra Sunga, while parading the entire Mauryan army before Brihadratha to show him the strength of the army assassinated him and this was the end of the Mauryas. Pushyamitra Sunga founded the Sunga dynasty around 185-183 BC. Capital of Sunga Dynasty was Pataliputra and its major centres were Ujjain, Mathura, Saket, Sanchi, and Kapilvastu. Vidisha was capital of later Shunga rulers.
- The Junagarh Rock inscription of Rudradaman is considered as an early example of chaste Sanskrit, written in mid second century AD. It mentions that one of Chandragupta Maurya's governors, Pushyagupta, was responsible for building a dam on Sudarshana Lake near Girnar in Kathiawar. From another inscription of Skandgupta we came to know that this very dam was repaired during his reign, almost 800 years after it was built.
- Seleucus' wars took him as far as India, where, after two years of war (305–303 BC), he was defeated by the armies of the Mauryan Empire and made peace by marrying his daughter to King Chandragupta, whereupon he was rewarded a considerable force of 500 war elephants.
- Asoka admitted that war was sometimes necessary and never disbanded his army.

20. Correct Option: (a)

Explanation:

- **Statement 2 is incorrect:** Agnimitra, the second king of Shunga dynasty, succeeded his father Pushyamitra Shunga and reigned for a short period of 8 years.
- Sunga Dynasty was established by Pushyamitra Sunga, in 185 BC. Pushyamitra Sunga was a Brahmin Commander-in-Chief of last Mauryan ruler called Brihadratha.
- Brihadratha was a weak ruler and his Senapati Pushyamitra Shunga, while parading the entire Mauryan army before Brihadratha to show him the strength of the army assassinated him and this was the end of the Mauryas. Pushyamitra Shunga founded the Shunga dynasty in around 185-183 BC. Capital of Shunga Dynasty was Pataliputra and its major centers were Ujjain, Mathura, Saket, Sanchi, and Kapilvastu. Vidisha was capital of later Shunga rulers.
- Agnimitra, the second king of Shunga dynasty, succeeded his father Pushyamitra Shunga and reigned for a short period of 8 years. He is the hero of Malvikagnimitram of Kalidasa in which he has been referred to as Raja. By the times of Agnimitra, Vidarbha had become independent of the Maurays. Agnimitra was succeeded by Vasumitra around 131 BC. Who succeeded Vasumitra, not much details are available. Different accounts mention the name of

different kings such as Andhraka, Pulindaka, Ghosha or Vajramitra. The last rulers of Shunga dynasty were Bhagabhadra and Devabhuti, about whom we have some details.

- **Gautamiputra Satkarni (Reign 78-102 AD):** The lost power of Satavahana was revived by Gautamiputra Satkarni who is described as the 'Destroyer of the Shaka, Pahalava and Yavana Power'. Gautamiputra Satkarni is known to have made a total and sharp recovery of the Satavahanas. His achievements have been mentioned in the Nasik Inscription, by his mother Gautami. His empire extended from Eastern Malwa, Western Malwa, Narmada Valley, Vidarbha, Western Rajputana, Saurastra and even Kalinga. Nasik Prasasti describes Gautamiputra as the ruler of the Aparanta, Anupa, Saurashtra, Kukura, Akara, and Avanti. In south his reign was up to Kanchi. He assumed the title of 'Raja-Raja' and 'Maharaja'. After Gautamiputra Satkarni, the Puranic inscription name other Satavahanas such as Pulumayi, Sri Satkarni, Siva Sri, Sivaskanda Satkarni , Madhariptra Sakasena, Sri Yajna Satkarni. One more important king was Vasithiputra Pulumayi-II.

21. Correct Option: (c)

Supplementary Notes:

Economic Regulations: Land Revenue

- The essential resources needed for the Mauryan State could only be got from land revenue. Therefore, the land revenue collection had to be efficiently organised so as to expropriate the maximum possible surplus from the people. Maurya period constitutes a landmark in the system of taxation in ancient India. Kautilya names many taxes which were collected from peasants, artisans, and traders. This required a strong and efficient machinery for assessment, collection and storage. The Mauryas attached greater importance to assessment than to storage and deposit. The Samaharta was the highest officer in charge of assessment and collection, and the Sannidhata was the chief custodian of the state treasury and storehouse.
- Some lands were sita or crown lands. In these areas, the King's and the State's rights of possession, cultivation, mortgage and sale were naturally superior. In fact, in the Arthasastra, a Sitadhyaksa or superintendent of agriculture is mentioned, who supervised the cultivation works.
- The classical writers mention that 114th of the produce was paid in tax by the peasants. They also suggest that a tribute was paid by them.
- Land tax (bhaga) was the main item of revenue. According to the texts, it was levied at the rate of 1/6th of the produce.
- Sharecropping was another way by which the State collected agricultural resources. The sharecroppers were, in the first place, provided with seeds, oxen, etc., and received arable land for cultivation. In this kind of situation, the peasants probably gave half of the produce to the State.
- The Mauryas also introduced some new taxes and made already existing ones more effective. The peasants paid a tax called 'pindakara' paid by husbandsmen, which was assessed on groups of villages. This was also customary in nature.
- The exact nature of Hiranya is also not known, but it was probably a tax paid in cash because Hiranya literally means gold.
- Bali, the traditionally known levy from the Vedic times, continued under the Mauryas.
- The levy of Pranaya which literally meant a gift of affection. This is a tax first mentioned by Panini but elaborated upon for the first time in the Arthasastra. It is usually interpreted as a voluntary gift; but once put into practice, in reality, it must have become obligatory.
- Further, in times of emergency, the cultivators could be forced to raise two crops. The importance of these measures was constantly emphasized as the country did face famines, and during these bleak periods, the level of revenue collection must have naturally fallen.

22. Correct Option: (a)

Explanation:

- **Statement 2 is incorrect:** Trap: The policy of Ahimsa in no way weakened the army and administrative machinery of the Mauryan Empire. It is true that Asoka believed in non-violence as vital to Dhamma, however, there was no extreme stand on this issue.

Supplementary Notes:

Causes of the Fall of Mauryan Empire

- Several causes seem to have brought about the decline and fall of the Maurya empire:
  - The early three kings, Chandragupta, Bindusara and Asoka, had organised the administration in such a way that it needed strict supervision. The quick succession of kings made this difficult as none of the rulers could actually settle down and be in the control of things. Linked to this is the fact that dynastic empires depend much on the ability of its rulers. But the successors of Asoka failed in this respect. Each one of them ruled only for a short period of time and, therefore, could not formulate either new policies of governance or maintain the old ones.
  - **Brahmanical Reaction:** The brahmanical reaction began as a result of Ashoka's policy. There is no doubt that Ashoka adopted a tolerant policy and asked the people to respect even the brahmanas, but he issued his edicts in Prakrit

and not in Sanskrit. He prohibited the killing of birds and animals, and derided superfluous rituals performed by women. The anti-sacrifice attitude of Buddhism adopted by Ashoka adversely affected the incomes of brahmanas. Further, Ashoka appointed rajukas to govern the countryside and introduce vyavaharasamata and dandasamata. This meant the same civil and criminal law for all varnas. But the Dharmashastra compiled by the brahmanas prescribed varna discrimination. Naturally, this policy infuriated the brahmanas. Some new kingdoms that arose on the ruins of the Maurya empire were ruled by the brahmanas. The Shungas and the Kanvas, who ruled in MP and further east on the remnants of the Maurya empire, were brahmanas. Similarly, the Satavahanas, who founded kingdom in the western Deccan and Andhra, claimed to be brahmanas. These brahmana dynasties performed Vedic sacrifices that were discarded by Ashoka. However, there are no direct evidences to support the above arguments.

- **Financial Crisis:** The enormous expenditure on the army and payment to the bureaucracy created a financial crisis for the Maurya Empire. Mauryas maintained the largest army and the largest regiment of officers. Despite the range of taxes imposed on the people, it was difficult to maintain this huge superstructure. It seems that Ashoka made large donations to the Buddhist monks which left the royal treasury empty. Towards the end, in order to meet expenses, they were obliged to melt gold images.
- **Oppressive Rule:** Oppressive rule in the provinces was an important cause of the break-up of the empire. In the reign of Bindusara, the citizens of Taxila bitterly complained against the misrule of wicked bureaucrats (Dushtamatyas). Their grievance was redressed by the appointment of Ashoka, but when Ashoka became emperor, a similar complaint was made by the same city. The Kalinga edicts show that Ashoka was much concerned about oppression in the provinces, and, therefore, asked the mahamatras not to tyrannize the townsmen without due cause. For this purpose he introduced rotation of officers in Tosali (in Kalinga), Ujjain and Taxila. He himself spent 256 nights on a pilgrimage which may have helped administrative supervision. All this, however, failed to stop oppression in the outlying provinces, and after his retirement Taxila took the earliest opportunity to throw off the imperial yoke.
- **New Knowledge in the Outlying Areas:** Magadha owed its expansion to certain basic material advantages. Once the knowledge of the use of these elements of culture spread to central India, the Deccan, and Kalinga as a result of the expansion of the Magadhan empire, the Gangetic basin, which formed the heart of the empire, lost its special advantage. The regular use of iron tools and weapons in the peripheral provinces coincided with the decline and fall of the Maurya empire. On the basis of the material culture acquired from Magadha, new kingdoms could be founded and developed. This explains the rise of the Shungas and Kanvas in central India, of the Chetis in Kalinga, and of the Satavahanas in the Deccan.
- **Neglect of the North-West Frontier and the Great Wall of China:** Since Ashoka was primarily preoccupied with missionary activities at home and abroad, he was unable to pay attention to safeguarding the passes through the north-western frontier. This had become necessary in view of the movement of tribes in Central Asia in the third century BC. The Scythians were in a state of constant flux. A nomadic people principally reliant on the use of the horse, they posed a serious danger to the settled empires in China and India. The Chinese ruler Shih Huang Ti (247–210 BC) constructed the Great Wall of China in about 220 BC to shield his empire against the attacks of the Scythians, but Ashoka took no such measures. Naturally, when the Scythians made a push towards India, they forced the Parthians, the Shakas, and the Greeks to move towards this subcontinent. The Greeks had set up a kingdom in north Afghanistan which was known as Bactria, and they were the first to invade India in 206 BC. This was followed by a series of invasions that continued till the beginning of the Christian era.
- **Asoka's pacifist policies:** It is true that Asoka believed in non-violence as vital to Dhamma. There was, however, no extreme stand on this issue. A dislike for killing of animals for food and sacrifice did not, in fact, terminate the policy of the palace to continue killing animals for food, though on a reduced scale. Also, in governance and criminal justice, death penalty should have been done away with, but this was not so. Further, we have no evidence of the army having been demobilized, not even a hint in the inscriptions to such a policy is being intended. The evidence one has is that of only one campaign conducted against Kalinga which had ended in a ruthless defeat of the latter. Had Asoka been such a pacifist he should have reinstated Kalinga as an independent kingdom, but as a practical ruler, he maintained the supremacy of Magadha over it. There are innumerable other indications of Asoka's assertion of his control over the

different people of his empire, particularly his warning to the tribes. He had made it very clear that the misconduct of the tribes living within his empire would be to hated up to a point only and not beyond that. All these steps were taken by Asoka to see that the empire was kept secure. Thus, to conclude, the policy of ahimsa in no way weakened the army and administrative machinery of the Mauryan Empire.

23. Correct Option: (d)

Explanation:

- All statements are correct

Supplementary Notes:

Persian invasion

- The Indo-Iranian contact lasted for about 200 years. Iranian influence may also be traced in the preamble to Ashoka's edicts as well as in certain terms used in them. For instance, for the Iranian term 'dipi', the Ashokan scribe used the term 'lipi'. Also, it appears that through the Iranians, the Greeks learnt about the great wealth of India, which whetted their greed and led to Alexander's invasion of India.
- The western borderland of India comprising the Punjab, Sindh and Afghanistan did not have any strong political power during this period.
- Of the sixteen Mahajanapadas mentioned in the literature, only two, Kamboja and Gandhara, may be placed in this outlying region. It appears to have been divided into a large number of independent principalities which were frequently at war with one another, and thus, an easy prey to foreign invaders.
- The powerful Achaemenian kings of Persia naturally cast their eyes towards this region, and perhaps, Cyrus (558-530 BC) subjugated a number of principalities living to the south of the Hindukush mountains (parts of India). It was in the reign of Darius (522-486 BC) that we have positive evidence of the extension of Achaemenian rule in the northwestern part of India. Two inscriptions of this monarch mention "Hi(n)du" as a part of his dominion.
- The exact connotation of this term is not known, but it certainly comprised some territory to the east of the Sindhu, which Darius must have conquered about 518 BC. Herodotus, the Greek historian, tells us that in 517 BC Darius sent a naval expedition to explore the valley of the Sindhu river.
- The Iranian ruler Darius penetrated north-west India in 516 BC and annexed Punjab (earlier Gandhara), west of the Indus, and Sindh. This area was converted into the twentieth province or satrapy of Iran, which had a total number of twenty-eight satrapies.
- The Indian satrapy included Sindh, the north-west frontier, and the part of Punjab that lay to the west of the Indus. It was the most fertile and populous part of the empire. It paid a tribute of 360 talents of gold, which accounted for one-third of the total revenue Iran received from its Asian provinces. The Indian subjects were also enrolled in the Iranian army.

24. Correct Option: (c)

Explanation:

- **Statement 1 is incorrect:** The Samaharta was the highest officer in charge of assessment and collection.
- **Statement 2 is incorrect:** The Sannidhata was the chief custodian of the state treasury and storehouse.

Supplementary Notes:

Taxation System during Mauryan Age

- The Maurya period constitutes a landmark in the system of taxation in ancient India. Kautilya names many taxes which were collected from peasants, artisans, and traders.
- This required a strong and efficient machinery for assessment, collection, and storage. The Mauryas attached greater importance to assessment than to storage and deposit.
- The Samaharta was the highest officer in charge of assessment and collection, and the Sannidhata was the chief custodian of the state treasury and storehouse. The assessor-cum-collector was far more important than the chief treasurer.
- The damage inflicted on the state by the former was thought to be more serious than any inflicted by the latter.
- In fact, elaborate machinery for assessment was first set up during the Mauryan period. The list of taxes mentioned in the Arthashastra is impressive, and, if these were really collected, very little would have been left to the people to live on.

25. Correct Option: (d)

Explanation:

- All statements are correct

Supplementary Notes:

Causes of the fall of the Maurya Empire

- The Magadhan empire, which had been reared by successive wars culminating in the conquest of Kalinga, began to disintegrate after the exit of Ashoka in 232 BC. Several causes seem to have brought about the decline and fall of the Mauryan empire:

Brahmanical Reaction

- The brahmanical reaction began as a result of Ashoka's policy. He issued his edicts in Prakrit and not in Sanskrit. The anti-sacrifice attitude of Buddhism adopted by Ashoka adversely affected the incomes of brahmanas. Further, Ashoka appointed rajukas to govern the countryside and introduce vyavaharasamata and dandasamata. This meant the same civil and criminal law for all varnas. But the Dharmashastra compiled by the brahmanas prescribed varna discrimination. Naturally, this policy infuriated the brahmanas.

Financial Crisis

- The enormous expenditure on the army and payment to the bureaucracy created a financial crisis for the Maurya empire. It seems that Ashoka made large donations to the Buddhist monks which left the royal treasury empty. Towards the end, in order to meet expenses, they were obliged to melt gold images.

Oppressive Rule

- Oppressive rule in the provinces was an important cause of the break-up of the empire. In the reign of Bindusara, the citizens of Taxila bitterly complained against the misrule of wicked bureaucrats (dushtamatyas).

New Knowledge in the Outlying Areas

- The regular use of iron tools and weapons in the peripheral provinces coincided with the decline and fall of the Maurya empire. On the basis of the material culture acquired from Magadha, new kingdoms could be founded and developed.

Neglect of the North-West Frontier and the Great Wall of China

- Ashoka was unable to pay attention to safeguard the passes through the north-western frontier .The Scythians were in a state of constant flux. Due to the use of the horse, they posed a serious danger to the settled empires in China and India.
- The Chinese ruler Shih Huang Ti (247–210 BC) constructed the Great Wall of China in about 220 BC to shield his empire against the attacks of the Scythians, but Ashoka took no such measures.
- Naturally, when the Scythians made a push towards India, they forced the Parthians, the Shakas, and the Greeks to move towards this subcontinent.

26. Correct Option: (a)

Explanation:

- **Statement 3 is incorrect:** Mauryan constructions made of burnt bricks have been found in Bihar and UP.

Supplementary Notes:

Spread of Material Culture

- It appears that the contacts established by administrators, traders, and Jaina and Buddhist monks led to the spread of the material culture of the Gangetic basin to areas situated on the periphery of the empire.
- The new material culture in the Gangetic basin was based on an intensive use of iron, the prevalence of writing, punch-marked coins, an abundance of beautiful pottery called Northern Black Polished Ware, the introduction of burnt bricks and ringwells, and above all, on the existence of towns in north-eastern India.
- Thus, the Maurya period witnessed a rapid development of material culture in the Gangetic plains.
- Given the access to the rich iron ores of south Bihar, people used more and more of this metal. This period provides evidences of socketed axes, hoes, spades, sickles, and ploughshares.
- Besides these iron implements, the spoked wheel also began to be used.
- At the end of the Mauryan period, burnt bricks were used for the first time in north-eastern India. Maurya constructions made of burnt bricks have been found in Bihar and UP. Houses were made of bricks, and also timber, which was available in abundance because of the dense vegetation in ancient times.
- Excavations show that logs of wood were also used as an important line of defence against flood and invasion.
- Similarly, ring wells, which were first constructed under the Mauryas in the Gangetic plains, spread beyond the heart of the empire.

27. Correct Option: (d)

Supplementary Notes:

Inscriptions

- One of the most important reliable sources of history writing is inscription. An inscription, being a contemporary document, is free from later interpolations. It comes in the form it was composed in and engraved for the first time. It is almost impossible to add something to it at a later stage.
- The study of inscriptions is called epigraphy.
- Ashokan inscriptions are considered to be the earliest. These are found written in four scripts.
- In his empire in Afghanistan, he used Aramaic and Greek scripts for his edicts.
- In the Pakistan region Kharoshthi script was used.
- The Brahmi script was used for the rest of his empire from Kalsi in the north in Uttaranchal upto Mysore in the south.
- The inscriptions of Ashoka are a class in itself. These were recorded in different years of his reign and are called edicts because they are in the form of the king's order or desire. They also give a glimpse of Ashoka's image and personality as a benevolent king concerned with the welfare of not only his subjects but also of the whole humanity.

28. Correct Option: (a)

Explanation:

- **Statement 1 is incorrect:** Ashoka did not try to force his personal Buddhist faith on his subjects. He bound the whole country together by one dhamma (a social code of conduct).

- **Statement 3 is incorrect:** Ashoka abandoned the policy of physical occupation (bherighosha) in favour of cultural conquest (dhammaghosha).

Supplementary Notes:
Ashoka's legacy

- Ashoka was a great missionary ruler in the history of the ancient world. He has a number of achievements to his credit.
- Political unification of the country: He not only added Kalinga to Mauryan dynasty but also bound the whole country together by one dhamma, one language, and practically one script of Brahmi (which is used in most of his inscriptions).
- Spread of tolerance and respect: He adopted and preached tolerance in not only the religious sphere (did not try to force his Buddhist faith on his subjects and made gifts to non-Buddhist sects as well, such as, donating Barbara caves to Ajivika ascetics), but in the case of scripts (other than Brahmi, he respected other scripts like Kharosthi, Aramaic, and Greek), and languages (Greek, Prakrit, and Sanskrit) too.
- Promotion of cultural contacts: He not only brought innovative administrative changes, but also promoted cultural contacts between Indian states and between India and the outer world too. It would not be an exaggeration if Ashoka is considered the first global cultural ambassador of India.
- Policy of peace and non-aggression: Ashoka is famous in history for his policy of peace, non-conquest, and non-aggression. After his accession to the throne, Ashoka fought only one major war, called the Kalinga War. The war caused great suffering to the brahmana priests and Buddhist monks, and this in turn brought upon Ashoka much grief and remorse. He, therefore, abandoned the policy of physical occupation in favour of one of cultural conquests. In other words, bherighosha was replaced with dhammaghosha.

29. Correct Option: (a)

Explanation:

- **Statement 2 is incorrect:** The largest expansion of the empire took place under the rule of Chandragupta Maurya.

Supplementary Notes:
Mauryan Empire

- The Mauryan empire had an efficient administrative system which helped in its political integration. The region included within the empire was just too diverse so the administration seems to have recognized local and regional variations, which were accommodated and not wiped out.
- Chandragupta Maurya was an autocrat who concentrated all power in his hands.
- The largest expansion of the empire took place under Chandragupta Maurya.
- Chandragupta Maurya was the founder of the Maurya Empire in ancient India. He is credited with bringing together the small fragmented kingdoms of the country and combining them into a single large empire. During his reign, the Maurya Empire stretched from Bengal and Assam in the East to Afghanistan and Balochistan in the West, to Kashmir and Nepal in the North and to the Deccan Plateau in the South. Chandragupta Maurya, along with his mentor Chanakya, was responsible for bringing an end to the Nanda Empire.
- Bindusara and Asoka have contributed more to the consolidation of the empire whose expansion credits should go to Chandragupta.

30. Correct Option: (d)

Explanation:

- All pairs are correctly matched

Supplementary Notes:
Important Officials in the Mauryan Empire

Name	Occupation
A. Samnidhar	Director of Stores/Treasurer General
B. Panyadhyaksha	Director of trade
C. Pauthavadhyaksha	Director of weights and measures
D. Samsthadhyaksha	Director of market
E. Lavanadhyaksha	Director of salt-making
F. Sulkadhyaksha	Director of Customs and Octroi
G. Sitadhyaksha	Director of land
H. Suradhyaksha	Director of Alcoholic Beverages

31. Correct Option: (a)

Explanation:

- **Statement 3 is incorrect:** It was duty of the Pradesika to tour the kingdom every five years and collect details of the administration.

Supplementary Notes:
Mauryan Administration

- There was a highly centralized administrative machinery with a steel frame of bureaucratic institutions and machinery comparable to modern Indian administration.
- It is thought that the Maurya Empire was divided into 5 provinces.
- Each district was administered by three officers viz. Pradesika, Rajuka, & Yukta. Pradesika was senior and Rajuka was subordinate. Yukta was subordinate to both of them.
- It was duty of the Pradesika to tour the kingdom every five years and collect details of the administration.
- Village was the smallest unit of polity and it was called grama. The head of the grama was a Gramika. The Gramika was not a paid employee of the government but was elected by the village people.

32. Correct Option: (d)

Supplementary Notes:

Haryanka Dynasty - Bimbisara

- He was the first king to have standing army and was contemporary to the Buddha.
- He was the first who started matrimonial alliances to strengthen its position as a king after defeating Brahamadutta (Anga king).
- He married to the Mahakosaladevi (princes of Koshala and siter of Prasanjit), Licchhavi princes Chellana and Khema (Princes of Madra clan of Punjab).
- Pukkusati who was the ambassador of the Gandhara ruler of Taxila came to his court.
- He sent his personal physician Jivaka to his rival Chandapradyota Mahasena of Ujjain to cure him of jaundice.

CONCEPT REVISION

Here is the list of concepts that have been covered as part of the previous exercise. Revise and Self-reflect on your concepts you covered.

- Scripts used during Ashoka period ☐
- Influence of Persian Invasion ☐
- 'Potwaadhyaksha' in Mauryan Administration ☐
- Mughal Administrative Departments ☐
- Disintegration of the Mauryan Empire ☐
- Land Revenue Policy during Mauryan Age ☐
- Material Culture during Mauryan Age ☐
- Ashoka Inscriptions ☐
- Various Administrative Terminologies ☐

1.6 POST-MAURYAN INDIA

QUESTIONS

1. Consider the following statements:

1. Official language of the Satavahanas was Prakrit written in Brahmi script.
2. The Satavahanas mostly used lead coins.
3. The Satavahanas were the first to grant tax-free land to Brahmanas.

Which of the above statements is/are correct?

(a) 1 and 2 only (b) 2 only
(c) 3 only (d) 1, 2 and 3

2. Charaka was the famous court physician of:

(a) Harsha
(b) Chandragupta Maurya
(c) Ashoka
(d) Kanishka

3. Who among the following were contemporaries of Kanishka?

(a) Nagarjuna, Ashvaghosha, Vasumitra
(b) Kamban, Banabhatta, Ashvaghosha
(c) Ashvaghosha, Kalidasa, Banabhatta
(d) Kalidasa, Kamban, Vasumitra

4. Which of the following statements regarding the Indo-Greeks is/are incorrect?

1. The Indo-Greeks were also the first to issue gold coins in India.
2. The Indo-Greeks were the first rulers in India to issue coins that can be definitively attributed to particular kings.

Select the correct option using the codes given below:

(a) 1 only (b) 2 only
(c) Both 1 and 2 (d) Neither 1 nor 2

5. Consider the following statements with respect to post Mauryan kingdoms:

1. Sungas: They built the great Buddhist Stupa at Bharhut (in M.P.).
2. Kanvas: The Greek king Antialcidas-I sent his ambassador named Herodotus to the court of Kanvas.
3. Satavahanas: Both Buddhism and Brahmanism were practiced during their rule.

Which of the above statements is/are correct?

(a) 1 only (b) 2 only
(c) 2 and 3 only (d) 1 and 3 only

6. With reference to Satavahanas, consider the following statements:

1. They succeeded Mauryan rule in Deccan and Central India.
2. The society during their rule was patriarchal.
3. They claimed Brahmana decent but also promoted Buddhism.

Which of the statements is/are incorrect?

(a) 1 and 2 only (b) 2 and 3 only
(c) 3 only (d) None of the above

7. **Match the following pairs:**

List 1	List 2
A. Chola	i. Nedunjeliyan
B. Chera	ii. Karikala
C. Pandya	iii. Kharavela
D. Chedi	iv. Senguttuvan

Select the correct answer using the code given below:

(a) A-i, B-iii, C-iv, D-ii
(b) A-iii, B-i, C-iv, D-ii
(c) A-ii, B-iv, C-i, D-iii
(d) A-iv, B-iii, C-i, D-ii

8. **Consider the following statements regarding sources of revenue in Kushana period:**
1. Silk route
2. Trade with Roman Empire
3. Developed agriculture

Which of the above was the main source of tax revenue in the Kushana Empire?

(a) 1 only (b) 1 and 2 only
(c) 2 and 3 only (d) 1, 2 and 3

9. **Consider the following statements regarding Satavahanas:**
1. The earliest inscriptions of the Satavahanas belong to the first century BC
2. Rudradaman, the Shaka ruler of Saurashtra (Kathiawar), defeated the Satavahanas twice.
3. The empire of Gautamiputra Satakarni extended from Malwa in the north to Karnataka in the south.

Which of the above statements is/are correct?

(a) 1 only (b) 1 and 2 only
(c) 2 and 3 only (d) 1, 2 and 3

10. **Consider the following statements regarding the pattern of administration during the Satavahana phase:**
1. Gandhika was appointed as the provincial governor.
2. The ruler of each Ahara was Amatya.

Which of the above statements are correct?

(a) 1 only (b) 2 only
(c) 1 and 2 only (d) Neither 1 nor 2

11. **Consider the following statements about Satavahanas:**
1. The rulers were brahmanas and they represented triumphant Brahmanism.
2. The rulers promoted Buddhism by granting land to the monks.
3. Hinayana Buddhism commanded considerable following in their kingdom.

Which of the above statements are correct?

(a) 1 and 2 only (b) 1 and 3 only
(c) 2 and 3 only (d) All the above

12. **Which of the following statements regarding the Kushans is not correct?**

(a) Kushan rulers followed both Brahmanism and the Buddhism.
(b) Kanishka, the most famous Kushan ruler, started the Shaka era.
(c) Menander, a principal character of the Milinda Panho, was an earlier Kushan in India.
(d) The Kushans controlled the Silk Route which proved to be a source of substantial income for them.

13. **Consider the following statements regarding Satavahanas administration:**
1. Administrative units were influenced by the Mauryan Empire.
2. The gaulmika was the rural administrative head.
3. They started the practice of granting tax-free villages to Brahmanas and Buddhist monks.

Which of the above statements is/are correct?

(a) 1 only (b) 1 and 2 only
(c) 2 and 3 only (d) 1, 2 and 3

14. **Consider the following statements regarding the post Mauryan period:**
1. Mathura was famous for clothing products.
2. Yelleshwaram was the center of terracottas and their moulds.

Which of the above statements is/are correct?

(a) 1 only (b) 2 only
(c) Both 1 and 2 (d) Neither 1 nor 2

15. **Consider the following statements regarding the ruler of Rashtrakutas, Amoghavarsha – I:**
1. He set up a new capital of Manyakheta
2. He got converted to Buddhism.
3. Broach became the best port of the kingdom during his reign.

Which of the above statements are correct?

(a) 1 and 2 only (b) 1 and 3 only
(c) 2 and 3 only (d) 1, 2 and 3

16. **Which of the following statements with respect to Kushana is/are correct?**
1. Kanishka started an era in AD 78, which is known as the Saka era and officially used by Government of India.
2. Kanishka was also a great patron of art and Sanskrit literature.
3. Kushana inscriptions are distributed only in north-western India.

Select the correct answer using the code given below:

(a) 1 and 2 only (b) 1 and 3 only
(c) 1 only (d) 1, 2 and 3

17. Consider the following statements about Rashtrakutas:

1. Amoghavarsha is credited with writing the first Kannada book on poetics.
2. The Rashtrakuta rulers were not tolerant in their religious views and patronised only Vaishnavism.
3. Svayambhu, one of the great apabharamsha poet lived at the Rashtrakuta court.

Which of the above statements is/are correct?

(a) 1 and 2 only (b) 2 and 3 only
(c) 1 and 3 only (d) 1, 2 and 3

18. Consider the following statements regarding foreign trade carried out during ancient India.

1. The Romans first started trade with the southern-most portion of the country.
2. Wine amphorae and pottery were the main items of export by Romans to India.

Choose the correct statement/s by using the code given below

(a) 1 only (b) 2 only
(c) Both 1 and 2 (d) Neither 1 nor 2

19. They were nomadic people from the steppes of North-Central Asia living in the neighbourhood of China, first occupied Bactria or North Afghanistan and gradually moved to the Kabul valley and seized Gandhara by crossing the Hindu Kush. Their empire extended from the Oxus to the Ganges, from Khorasan in Central Asia to Pataliputra in Bihar.

Which of the following dynasties is described in above passage?

(a) Shakas (b) Kushans
(c) Parthians (d) Indo-Greeks

20. Which of the following were the consequences of Central Asian Invasion in India?

1. Better Cavalry
2. Promotion of Agriculture
3. Introduction of Gold coins on a wide scale.
4. Origin of Hinayana Buddhism

Select the correct answer using the code given below:

(a) 1, 2 and 3 only (b) 2 and 3 only
(c) 1 and 4 only (d) 1, 2, 3 and 4

21. Match the following:

List-I	List-II
A. Mahamatras	1. High Officials of administrative division
B. Gaulmika	2. Provincial Governor
C. Maharashtrikas	3. Head of Military Regiment
D. Senapati	4. District Officials

Select the correct answer using the code given below:

	A	B	C	D
(a)	3	4	1	2
(b)	3	4	2	1
(c)	4	3	1	2
(d)	4	3	2	1

22. He defeated the Shakas and destroyed many kshatriya rulers. His empire extended from Malwa in the north to Karnataka in the south. The fortunes of the Satavahanas were restored by him. He called himself the only brahmana.

Identify the ruler described in above passage?

(a) Rudradaman-I
(b) Gautamiputra Satakarni
(c) Vashishthiputra Pulumayi
(d) Yajna Sri Satakarni

23. Consider the following statements regarding family structure during Satavahanas phase:

1. The Satavahanas show traces of a matrilineal social structure.
2. Succession to the throne was passed to the male member.

Which of the above statements is/are correct?

(a) 1 only (b) 2 only
(c) Both 1 and 2 (d) Neither 1 nor 2

24. Consider the following statements:

1. Kalinga rose to power during the reign of King Kharvela of the Chedi dynasty.
2. The Sunga dynasty was followed by the Kanva dynasty.
3. The Junagadh inscription of Pushyamitra Sunga talks about the administration of Mauryan empire.

Which of the above statements is/are correct?

(a) 1 and 2 only (b) 2 only
(c) 3 only (d) 1, 2 and 3

25. Consider the following description:

'He was one of the greatest Rashtrakuta rulers who ruled for a long time. He preferred pursuit of religion and literature over war. He himself authored many books including the earliest Kannada book on Poetics'.

Which of the following rulers represent the above description?

(a) Dantidurga (b) Amoghvarsha I
(c) Govinda III (d) Krishna I

SOLUTIONS

1. Correct Option: (d)

Explanation:

- All statements are correct

Supplementary Notes:

Satavahana Dynasty

- The Satavahana rulers patronised Prakrit which was the official language used on documents. All the inscriptions were composed in Prakrit language and were written in the Brahmi script.

- The Satavahana coins give unique indications as to their chronology, language, and even facial features (curly hair, long ears and strong lips). They issued mainly lead and copper coins; their portrait-style silver coins were usually struck over coins of the Western Kshatrapa kings. The Satavahana coins also display various traditional symbols, such as elephants, lions, horses and chaityas (stupas), as well as the "Ujjain symbol", a cross with four circles at the end.
- The inscriptions of Gautamiputra Satakarni suggest the existence of a bureaucratic structure, although it is not certain how stable and effective this structure was. For example, two inscriptions from Nashik Cave 11 record donations of agricultural land to ascetic communities. They state that the ascetics would enjoy tax exemption and non-interference from the royal officials. The first inscription states that the grant was approved by Gautamiputra's minister Sivagupta on the king's verbal orders, and preserved by the "great lords". The second inscription records a grant by Gautamiputra and his mother, and mentions Syamaka as the minister of the Govardhana ahara. It states that the charter was approved by a woman named Lota, who according to archaeologist James Burgess' interpretation, was the chief lady-in-waiting of Gautamiputra's mother.

2. **Correct Option: (d)**

Supplementary Notes:

- Kanishka-I was the most power ruler of the Kushana Empire and is known for his military prowess. His main capital was Purushapura (Peshawar) and regional capitals were Taxila (Pakistan), Begram (Afghanistan) and Mathura (India).
- His date of accession is disputed. However, most sources agree that Kanishka was the founder of the Shaka Era of AD 78.
- This has been mentioned as Saka kala or Saka Nripa kala, probably because he was thought to be a Shaka.
- Under Kanishka, Kushana Empire reached its climax and it extended from Uzbekistan, Tajikistan to Mathura and Kashmir.
- Some of the scholars in the Court of Kanishka were Parsva, Vasumitra, Asvaghosa, Nagarjuna, Charaka and Mathara.
- Charaka has been called the Court Physician of Kanishka.
- Sushruta who wrote Sushruta Samhita has also been connected to Kanishka.
- Charaka (3rd century BC) was one of the principal contributors to Ayurveda, a system of medicine and lifestyle developed in Ancient India. He is known for authoring the medical treatise, the Charaka Samhita. Charaka was resident of Kapisthal (now known as Kapurthala), located between Iravati (Ravi River) and Chandrabagha (Chenab River) rivers in Panchanada (Punjab). Panchanada was name of Punjab in Mahabharata.
- He is well known as the "Indian father of medicine".
- Charaka is said to have studied at the University of Ancient Taxila and practiced there.

3. **Correct Option: (a)**

Explanation:

- **Option (a) is correct**
- The great scholars in the Court of Kanishka I were Asvaghosa (the Buddhist poet), Nagarjuna (the philosopher), Samgharaksha (the chaplain), Mathara (the politician), Vasumitra (the Buddhist scholar), Charaka (the physician) and Agisala (the engineer).
- Kanishka-I was the most power ruler of the Kushana Empire and known for his military powers. His main capital was Purushapura (Peshawar) and regional capitals were Taxila (Pakistan), Begram (Afghanistan) and Mathura (India).

4. **Correct Option: (d)**

Explanation:

- Both statements are correct

Supplementary Notes:

Indo-Greeks

- The most famous Indo-Greek ruler was Menander (165–45 BC), also known as Milinda. He had his capital at Sakala (modern Sialkot) in the Punjab; and invaded the Ganga–Yamuna doab. He had great many cities in his dominions including Sakala and Mathura. He is known for the variety and wide spread of coins in his dominions. He was converted to Buddhism by Nagasena, who is also known as Nagarjuna. Menander asked Nagasena many questions relating to Buddhism. These questions and Nagasena's answers were recorded in the form of a book known as Milinda Panho or the Questions of Milinda.
- Indo-Greek rule is important in the history of India because of the large number of coins that the Greeks issued.
- The Indo-Greeks were the first rulers in India to issue coins that can be definitively attributed to particular kings. This is not possible in the case of the early punch-marked coins, which cannot be assigned with certainty to any particular dynasty.
- The Indo-Greeks were also the first to issue gold coins in India, and these increased in number under the Kushans.
- Greek rule introduced features of Hellenistic art in the north-west frontier of India, but this was not

purely Greek but rather the outcome of Greek contact with non-Greek conquered peoples after Alexander's death. The best example of this was Gandhara art.

5. Correct Option: (d)

Explanation:

Statement 2 is incorrect: The Greek king Antialcidas-I sent his ambassador named Herodotus to the court of Sungas (not Kanvas).

Supplementary Notes:

Post-Mauryan Period

- Sunga Dynasty was established by Pushymitra Sunga, a Brahmin Commander-in-Chief of last Mauryan ruler named Brihadratha in 185 BC.
- The capital of Sungas was Vidisa in modern Madhya Pradesh. Pushyamitra didn't adopt any royal title and ruled with the name of Senani. He performed two horse sacrifices (Ashvamedha) and one of these was performed by Panini, the great grammarian. During the reign of Sungas, there was a revival of Brahmanical influence. The Bhagavata religion became important.
- The great Buddhist stupa at Bharhut (in M.P.) was built during the reign of Sungas. The fine gateway railing which surrounds the Sanchi stupa, built by Ashoka, was constructed during the Sunga period.
- Pushyamitra was succeeded by his son Agnimitra, the hero of Kalidasa's drama 'Malvikagnimitra'. The Greek king Antialcidas-I sent his ambassador named Herodotus to the court of Sungas.
- Herodotus constructed a pillar "Garuda-dhwaja" in the honor of God Vasudeva. After Agnimitra, a series of weak rulers such as Vasumitra, Vajramitra, Bhagabhadra, Devabhuti, followed, leading to the decline of the dynasty.
- Satavahana dynasty supported Brahmanism as well as Buddhism and patronized Prakrit literature.
- The Greek king Antialcidas-I sent his ambassador named Herodotus to the court of Sungas (not Kanvas).

6. Correct Option: (d)

Explanation:

- All statements are correct

Supplementary Notes:

Satavahanas

- Simuka was founder of the Satavahana Dynasty and was immediately active after Ashoka's death.
- The Satavahanas succeeded the Mauryas after a gap of almost 100 years in Deccan and in central India.
- There were numerous small political principalities that were ruling in different parts of the Deccan in this gap of 100 years. The Rathikas and Bhojikas mentioned in the Ashokan inscriptions gradually progressed into the maharathis and mahabhojas.
- The Satavahanas claimed Brahmana descent and performed Vedic rituals and worshipped gods like Krishna, Vasudeva, as evident in the Naneghat cave Inscription of Naganika (1st century BCE), which mentions the great sacrifices performed by Satkarni I.
- The kings pertaining to this dynasty used matronyms such as Gautamiputra and Vashishthiputra, although they were patriarchal.
- The Satavahanas assumed the title of Dakshinapathapati (Lord of the Dakshinapatha). The Satavahanas are also known in history for starting the practice of giving royal grants of land to Brahmanas and Buddhist monks, including those associated with tax exemptions.
- It is mentioned in one of the inscriptions of Gautamiputra Satkarni that the land gifted to the Brahmanas was not to be entered or disturbed by the royal troops, was not to be dug for salt, was free from the control of state officials, and was to enjoy all sorts of pariharas (immunities).
- They also promoted Buddhism by granting land to the monks.

7. Correct Option: (c)

Early historical period of South India

Supplementary Notes:

List I	List II
A. Chola	ii. Karikala
B. Chera	iv. Senguttuvan
C. Pandya	i. Nedunjeliyan
D. Chedi	iii. Kharavela

8. Correct Option: (d)

Explanation:

- All statements are correct

Supplementary Notes:

Impact of Central Asian Contact: Trade and Technology

- The Kushans controlled the Silk Route, which started from China and passed through their empire in Central Asia and Afghanistan to Iran, and Western Asia which formed part of the Roman empire in the eastern Mediterranean zone.
- This route was a source of great income to the Kushans, and they built a large prosperous empire because of the tolls levied from the traders.
- The coming of the foreigners established intimate contacts between Central Asia and India.
- As a result India received a good deal of gold from the Altai mountains in Central Asia.
- Gold also may have been received in India through trade with the Roman empire.
- It is significant that the Kushans were the first rulers in India to issue gold coins on a wide scale.

- The Kushans also promoted agriculture hence this was also a source of tax revenue.

9. **Correct Option: (d)**

Explanation:

- All statements are correct

Supplementary Notes:

Political History of Satavahanas

- The most important of the native successors of the Mauryas in the north were the Shungas, followed by the Kanvas. In Deccan and in Central India, the Satavahanas succeeded the Mauryas, although after a gap of about 100 years.
- 'The Satavahanas are considered to be identical with the Andhras who are mentioned in the Puranas.
- The Puranas speak only of the Andhra rule and not of the Satavahana rule. On the other hand, the name Andhra does not occur in Satavahana inscriptions.
- According to some Puranas, altogether the Andhras ruled for 300 years and this period is assigned to the rule of the Satavahana dynasty.
- The earliest inscriptions of the Satavahanas belong to the first century BC, when they defeated the Kanvas and established their power in parts of central India.
- The early Satavahana kings appeared not in Andhra, but in north Maharashtra where their earliest coins and inscriptions have been found.
- They set up their power in the upper Godavari valley.
- Gradually, the Satavahanas extended their power over Karnataka and Andhra.
- Gautamiputra Satakarni (AD 106-130) called himself the only Brahmana.
- The empire of Gautamiputra Satakarni extended from Malwa in the north to Karnataka in the south.
- He also enjoyed general authority over Andhra.
- He defeated the Shakas and destroyed many Kshatriya rulers. He claims to have destroyed the Kshaharata lineage to which his adversary Nahapana belonged.
- This claim is true because more than 8000 silver coins of Nahapana, found near Nasik, bear marks of being restock by the Satavahana king.
- The coins and inscriptions of Gautamiputra's immediate successor Vashishthiputra Pulumayi (AD 130-154) are found in Andhra.
- He set up his capital at Paithan on the Godavari in Aurangabad district.
- Rudradaman I (AD 130-150), the Shaka ruler of Saurashtra (Kathiawar), defeated the Satavahanas twice, but did not destroy them on account of matrimonial relations.
- Yajna Sri Satakarni recovered North Konkan and Malwa from the Shaka rulers.
- He was a lover of trade and navigation. His coins have been found not only in Andhra but also in Maharashtra, Madhya Pradesh and Gujarat. His love for navigation and overseas trade is shown by the representation of a ship on his coins.

10. **Correct Option: (b)**

Explanation:

- **Statement 1 is incorrect:** A Senapati was appointed as the provincial governor.

Supplementary Notes:

Pattern of Administration during Satavahana Phase

- The Satavahanas retained some administrative structures of Ashokan times.
- Their district was called ahara, as it was known in the time of Ashoka, and their officials were known as amatyas and mahamatras, as was the case in Maurya times.
- However, their administrative divisions were also called rashtra, and their high officials were styled maharashtrikas.
- We notice certain military and feudal traits in the administration of the Satavahanas. Significantly, the senapati was appointed provincial governor.
- As the tribal people in the Deccan were not thoroughly brahmanized and reconciled to the new rule, it was necessary to keep them under strong military control.
  - The administration in the rural areas was placed in the hands of a gaulmika, the head of a military regiment consisting of nine chariots, nine elephants, twenty-five horses, and forty-five foot-soldiers. The head of this regiment was posted in the countryside to maintain peace and order.

11. **Correct Option: (a)**

Explanation:

- **Statement 3 is incorrect:** In their kingdom, Mahayana form of Buddhism commanded considerable following, especially in the artisan class. Nagarjunakonda and Amaravati in Andhra Pradesh became important seats of Buddhist culture.

Supplementary Notes:

The Satavahanas

- The Satavahana rule is believed to have started around the third century BC, in 235 BC and lasted until the second century AD Some experts believe their rule started in the first century BC only.
- They are referred to as Andhras in the Puranas.
- The Satavahana kingdom chiefly comprised of modern-day Andhra Pradesh, Telangana and Maharashtra. At times, their rule also included parts of Karnataka, Gujarat and Madhya Pradesh.

- Their capital cities varied at different times. Pratishthana (Paithan) and Amaravati were its capitals.
- Simuka founded the dynasty.
- They were the first native Indian rulers to issue their own coins with the portraits of the rulers. This practice was started by Gautamiputra Satakarni who derived the practice from the Western Satraps after defeating them.
- The coin legends were in Prakrit language. Some reverse coin legends are in Telugu, Tamil and Kannada.
- They patronised Prakrit more than Sanskrit.
- They successfully defended their territories against foreign invaders and had many on-going battles with the Sakas (Western Satraps).
- The Satavahana rulers were brahmanas and they represented the march of triumphant brahmanism. From the very beginning, kings and queens performed the Vedic scarfices such as ashmedha, vajapeya, etc.
- However, the satavahana rulers promoted Buddhism by granting land to the monks.
- In their kingdom, Mahayana form of Buddhism commanded considerable following, especially in the artisan class. Nagarjunakonda and Amaravati in Andhra Pradesh became important seats of Buddhist culture. (Map: 1.6.1)

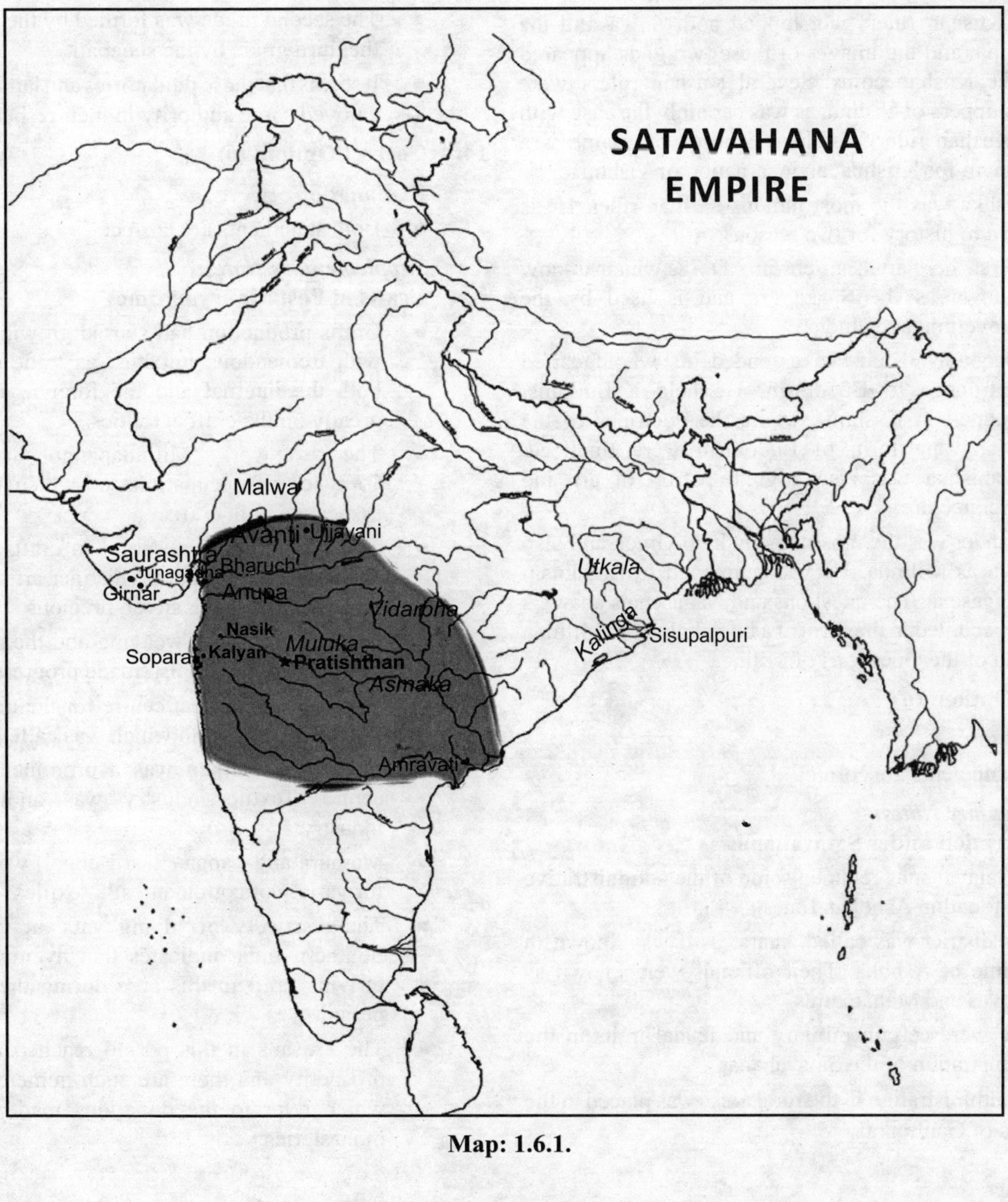

Map: 1.6.1.

12. **Correct Option: (c)**

Explanation:

- **Option (c) is correct:** Trap: Menander was an Indo-Greek.

Supplementary Notes:

Kushanas

- The Kushans controlled the Silk Route, Which started from China and passed through their empire in Central Asia and Afghanistan to Iran, and Western Asia which formed part of the Roman Empire in the eastern Mediterranean zone. This route was a source of substantial income for the Kushans, and they built a large prosperous empire on the strength of the tolls levied from traders.
- It is significant that the Kushans were the first rulers in India to issue gold coins on a wide scale.
- The Kushan rulers worshipped both Shiva and the Buddha, and the images of these two gods appeared on the Kushan coins. Several Kushan rulers were worshippers of Vishnu, as was certainly the case with the Kushan ruler Vasudeva, whose very name is a synonym for Krishna, an incarnation of Vishnu.
- Kanishka was the most famous Kushan ruler. He is known to history for two reasons.
  - First, he started an era in AD 78, which is now known as the Shaka era and is used by the Government of India.
  - Secondly, Kanishka extended his wholehearted patronage to Buddhism. He held a Buddhist council in Kashmir, where the doctrines of the Mahayana form of Buddhism were finalized. Kanishka was also a great patron of art and architecture.
- Menander was the most famous Indo-Greek and also known as Milinda. He was converted to Buddhism by Nagasena. The questions and Nagasena's answers were recorded in the form of a book known as Milinda Panho or the Questions of Milinda

13. **Correct Option: (d)**

Explanation:

- All statements are correct

Supplementary Notes:

Administration under Satavahanas

- The Satavahanas retained some of the administrative units found in Ashokan times.
- Their district was called Ahara, as it was known in the time of Ashoka. Their officials were known as Amatyas and Mahamatras.
- There were certain military and feudal traits in the administration of the Satavahanas.
- The administration in the rural areas was placed in the hands of Gaulmika.
- He was the head of a military regiment consisting of 9 chariots, 9 elephants, 25 horses and 45 foot-soldiers.
- The military character of the Satavahana rule is also evident from the common use of such terms as kataka and skandhavaras in their inscriptions.
- These were military camps and settlements which served as administrative centers so long as the king was there.
- The Satavahanas started the practice of granting tax-free villages to brahmanas and Buddhist monks. These areas therefore became small independent islands within the Satavahana kingdom.
- The Satavahana kingdom had three grades of feudatories. The highest grade was formed by the king who was called raja and who had the right to strike coins.
- The second grade was formed by the mahabhoja, and the third grade by the senapati.
- It seems that these feudatories and landed beneficiaries enjoyed some authority in their respective localities.

14. **Correct Option: (c)**

Explanation:

- Both statements are correct

Supplementary Notes:

Crafts in Post Mauryan times

- Crafts production had started growing in this period with tremendous impetus, as trade and commerce, both the internal and the foreign, were dependent greatly on the craft activities.
- The text work 'Milindapanho' has mentions of 75 types of occupations of which 60 were solely associated with crafts.
- The level of specialisation in crafts was very high and there were separate distinct artisans working in materials like gold, silver, precious stones, etc.
- Cloth-making, silk weaving and the making of arms and luxury articles also made progress.
- Mathura was a great centre for the manufacture of a special type of cloth which was called SATAKA.
- The city of Ujjain was a prominent bead making centre. Textile industry was another prominent industry.
- Mathura and Vanga (East Bengal) were very famous for variety of cotton and silk textiles.
- The discovery of 'dying vats' at various sites in Southern India indicates that dyeing clothes was a thriving craft in this area during the Post-Mauryan period.
- The artisans in this period reached new heights of prosperity and there are such numerous inscriptions which refer to the donations made by artisans to monasteries.

- The craftsmen also made fake Roman coins. Various coin-moulds belonging to the period have been found both in North India and in the Deccan.
- A coin-mould from the Satavahana level shows that through it, half a dozen coins could be turned out at a time.
- These urban handicrafts were supplemented by the manufacture of beautiful pieces of terracotta, which are found in profuse quantities.
- They have been found in almost all Kushan and Satavahana sites, but special mention may be made of Yelleshwaram in Nalgonda district, where we find the largest number of terracottas and the moulds in which they were manufactured.
- Like the merchants, roughly all craft vocations were also organised into the form of guilds, with each one under a headman called 'jyestha'.
- These included weavers, bamboo workers, corn dealers, oil manufacturers, potters and others, etc.

15. Correct Option: (b)

Explanation:

- **Statement 2 is incorrect:** Amoghavarsha I was converted into Jainism by Jinasena, a Jaina monk.

Supplementary Notes:
Amoghvarsha I—Rashtrakutas

- Amoghavarsha-I, also known as Amoghavarsha Nrupathunga-I, ruled between 800-878 CE was the greatest ruler of the Rashtrakuta dynasty, and one of the great emperors of India.
- His reign was of 64 years and is one of the longest dated monarchical reigns on record.
- He set up a new capital at Manyakheta (now Malkhed in Karnataka State) and Broach became the best port of the kingdom during his reign.
- He had lost control over Malwa and Gangavadi. Yet, his reign was popular for cultural development. He was a follower of Jainism. Jinasena was his chief preceptor. He was also a patron of letters and he wrote the famous Kannada work, Kavirajamarga. He had also built the Rashtrakuta capital, the city of Malkhed or Manyakheda, and Virupaksha temple at Pattadakkal.
- His writing Kavirajamarga is a landmark literary work in the Kannada language and became a guide book for future poets and scholars for centuries to come.

16. Correct Option: (a)

Explanation:

- **Statement 3 is incorrect:** Kushans inscriptions are distributed not only in north-western India and Sindh but also in Mathura, Sharavasti, Kaushambi and Varanasi.

Supplementary Notes:
Kushans

- The Kushan Empire was a syncretic empire, formed by Yuezhi, in the Bactrian territories in the early 1st century. It spread to encompass much of Afghanistan.
- The gold coins of the Kushans are found mainly west of the Indus. Their inscriptions are distributed not only in north-western India and Sindh but also in Mathura, Sharavasti, Kaushambi and Varanasi. Hence, they had set up their authority in the greater part of the middle Gangetic basin.
- Kanishka extended his wholehcarted patronage to Buddhism. He held a Buddhist council in Kashmir, where the doctrines of the Mahayana form of Buddhism were finalized. Kanishka was also patron of art and Sanskrit literature.
- Kanishka started an era in AD 78, which is known as the Saka era and officially used by Government of India.
- Kanishka was also a great patron of art and Sanskrit literature.
- Kushan inscriptions are distributed not only in north-western India and Sindh but also in Mathura, Sharavasti, Kaushambi and Varanasi.

17. Correct Option: (c)

Explanation:

- **Statement 2 is incorrect:** The Rashtrakuta rulers were tolerant in their religious views and patronised not only Saivism and Vaishnavism but Jainism as well.

Supplementary Notes:
Rashtrakutas

- While the Palas and the Pratiharas were ruling over north India, the Deccan was being ruled by the Rashtrakutas, a remarkable dynasty which produced a long line of warriors and able administrators.
- The kingdom was founded by Dantidurga who set up his capital at Manyakhet or Malkhed near modem Sholapur.
- The Rashtrakutas soon dominated the entire area of northern Maharashtra.
- Amoghavarsha ruled for 64 years but by temperament he preferred the pursuit of religion and literature to war.
- He was himself an author and is credited with writing the first Kannada book on poetics.
- He was a great builder, and is said to have built the capital city Manyakhet so as to excel the city of lndra.
- The Rastrakuta kings were great patrons of arts and letters. In their courts, we find not only Sanskrit scholars, but also poets and others who wrote in Prakrit and in apabhramsha, the-so called corrupt

languages which were the forerunners of the various modern Indian languages.

- The great apabharamsha poet, Svayambhu, and his son probably lived at the Rashtrakuta court.

18. Correct Option (c)

Explanation:

- Both statements are correct

Supplementary Notes:

- The Romans first started trade with the southern-most portion of the country, because their earliest coins have been found in Tamil Kingdoms which lay outside the Satavahanas dominions. The Romans mainly imported spices for which south India was famous. They also imported muslin, pearls, jewels and precious stones from central and south India.
- Wine amphorae and various pottery were the main items of export by Romans to India, which have been discovered in excavations at Tamluk, India.

19. Correct Option: (b)

Supplementary Notes:

The Kushans

- The Kushans are also called Yuechis or Tocharians. The Tocharians were considered to be the same as the Scythians. The Kushans were one of the five clans into which the Yuechi tribe was divided.
- A nomadic people from the steppes of north Central Asia living in the neighbourhood of China, the Kushans first occupied Bactria or North Afghanistan where they displaced the Shakas. Gradually they moved to the Kabul Valley and seized Gandhara by crossing the Hindu Kush, replacing the rule of the Greeks and Parthians in these areas. They eventually established their authority over the lower Indus basin and the greater part of the Gangetic basin.
- Their empire extended from the Oxus to the Ganges, from Khorasan in Central Asia to Pataliputra in Bihar.
- A substantial part of Central Asia now included in the Commonwealth of Independent States (in the former USSR), a portion of Iran, a portion of Afghanistan, almost the whole of Pakistan, and almost the whole of northern India were brought under one rule by the Kushans.
- Because of this, the Kushan empire in India is sometimes called a Central Asian empire. In any case, the empire created a unique opportunity for the interaction of peoples and cultures, and the process gave rise to a new type of culture which embraced nine modern countries.

20. Correct Option: (a)

Explanation:

- **Statement 4 is incorrect:** Mahayana Buddhism originated in India due to Central Asian invasion.

Supplementary Notes:

Cultural Consequences of Central Asia Invasion

Better Cavalry

- They introduced better cavalry and the use of the riding horse on a large scale. They popularized the use of reins and saddles, which appear in the Buddhist sculpture of the second and third centuries AD. The Shakas and the Kushans were excellent horsemen.

Trade and Agriculture

- The coming of the Central Asian people established intimate contacts between Central Asia and India. India received a great fund of gold from the Altai Mountains in Central Asia.
- The Kushans controlled the Silk Route, which started from China and passed through their empire in Central Asia and Afghanistan to Iran, and western Asia which formed part of the Roman empire in the eastern Mediterranean zone.
- It is significant that the Kushans were the first rulers in India to issue gold coins on a wide scale. The Kushans also promoted agriculture.

Religious Developments

- Some rulers and others from Central Asia adopted Vaishnavism, which means the worship of Vishnu, the god of protection and preservation. The Greek ambassador called Heliodorus set up a pillar in honour of Vasudeva at Besnagar near Vidisa (headquarters of Vidisa district) in MP around the middle of the second century BC. A few other rulers adopted Buddhism.

The Origin of Mahayana Buddhism

- Due to the large influx of people from Central Asia, Buddhism was especially affected. Discipline became so lax that some renunciated or even deserted the religious order or the samgha and restart the householder's life. This new form of Buddhism came to be called Mahayana or the Great Vehicle.

21. Correct Option: (c)

List-I	List-II
A. Mahamatras	4. District Officials
B. Gaulmika	3. Head of Military Regiment
C. Maharashtrikas	1. High Officials of Administrative Division
D. Senapati	2. Provincial Governor

Supplementary Notes:

Pattern of Administration during Satavahana Phase

- The Satavahanas retained some administrative structures of Ashokan times.
- Their district was called ahara, as it was known in the time of Ashoka, and their officials were known as amatyas and mahamatras, as was the case in Maurya times.

- However, their administrative divisions were also called rashtra, and their high officials were styled maharashtrikas.
- We notice certain military and feudal traits in the administration of the Satavahanas. It is significant that the senapati was appointed provincial governor.
- As the tribal people in the Deccan were not thoroughly brahmanized and reconciled to the new rule, it was necessary to keep them under strong military control. The administration in the rural areas was placed in the hands of a gaulmika, the head of a military regiment consisting of nine chariots, nine elephants, twenty-five horses, and forty-five foot-soldiers. The head of this regiment was posted in the countryside to maintain peace and order.

22. Correct Option: (b)

Supplementary Notes:

Satavahanas

- The founder of this dynasty is known as Simuka and he ruled from 235 BC to 213 BC. He was succeeded by his brother Krishna.
- The fortunes of the family were restored by Gautamiputra Satakarni (AD 106–30) who called himself 'the only Brahmana'. He defeated the Shakas and destroyed many kshatriya rulers.
- He claimed to have ended the Kshaharata lineage to which his adversary Nahapana belonged. This claim is true because over 8000 silver coins of Nahapana, found near Nasik, bear the marks of having been restruck by the Satavahana king.
- He also occupied Malwa and Kathiawar which were controlled by the Shakas. It seems that the empire of Gautamiputra Satakarni extended from Malwa in the north to Karnataka in the south, and he possibly also exercised general authority over Andhra.

23. Correct Option: (c)

Explanation:

- Both statements are correct

Supplementary Notes:

Family Structure during Satavahanas Phase

- The most interesting detail about the Satavahanas relates to their family structure. In the Aryan society of north India, the father enjoyed greater importance than the mother, and the north Indian princes generally belonged to a patriarchal society.
- The Satavahanas however show traces of a matrilineal social structure. It was customary for their king to be named after his mother. Such names as Gautamiputra and Vashishthiputra indicate that in their society the mother enjoyed a great deal of importance.
- Sometimes, an inscription is issued both under the authority of the king and his mother.
- At present in peninsular India, the son's name includes a part of the father's name, and there is no place in it for the mother's, indicative of patriarchal influence.
- Queens made important religious gifts in their own right, and some of them acted as regents.
- However, the Satavahana ruling family was basically patriarchal because succession to the throne passed to the male member.

24. Correct Option: (a)

Explanation:

- **Statement 3 is incorrect:** The Junagarh Rock Inscription of Rudradaman talks about Chandra Gupta Maurya's administartion.

Supplementary Notes:

Ancient Indian Dynasties

- After the decline of Mauryas, Kalinga rose to power around 1st century BC in the area of modern Odisha. We best know about the third ruler of this dynasty, named 'Kharavela'. Kharavela is known to have revived the past glory of Kalinga. King Kharavela belonged to the epic time of Chedi dynasty.
- Sunga Dynasty spanned from 185 BC to 73 BC and Kanva Dynasty spanned from 73 BC to 28 BC. The capital of Sunga Dynasty was Vidisha (MP) and the capital of Kanva Dynasty was Pataliputra.
- The Junagarh Rock Inscription of Rudradaman is considered as an early example of chaste Sanskrit, written in mid second century AD. It mentions that one of Chandragupta Maurya's governors, Pushyagupta, was responsible for building a dam on Sudarshana Lake near Girnar in Kathiawar. From another inscription of Skandgupta we come to know that this very dam was repaired during his reign, almost 800 years after it was built.
- Rudradaman I (AD 130–150) was a Saka ruler from the Western Kshatrapas dynasty. He was the grandson of the king Chastana. Rudradaman I was instrumental in the decline of the Satavahana Empire.

25. Correct Option: (b)

Supplementary Notes:

Amoghvarsha I – Rashtrakutas

- Amoghavarsha I, also known as Amoghavarsha Nrupathunga I, ruled between 800-878 CE was the greatest ruler of the Rashtrakuta dynasty, and one of the great emperors of India.
- His reign was of 64 years and is one of the longest dated monarchical reigns on record.
- He had lost control over Malwa and Gangavadi. Yet, his reign was popular for the cultural development. He was a follower of Jainism. Jinasena was his chief preceptor. He was also a patron of letters

and he himself wrote the famous Kannada work, Kavirajamarga. He had also built the Rashtrakuta capital, the city of Malkhed or Manyakhed a and Virupaksha Temple at Pattadakkal.

- His own writing Kavirajamarga is a landmark literary work in the Kannada language and became a guide book for future poets and scholars for centuries to come.

CONCEPT REVISION

Here is the list of concepts that have been covered as part of the previous exercise. Revise and Self-reflect on your concepts you covered.

- Satavahanas ☐
- Kushana Period ☐
- Rulers of Rashtrakutas ☐
- Central Asian Invasion ☐

1.7 GUPTA PERIOD

QUESTIONS

1. Fa-hien a Chinese Buddhist monk, visited India during the reign of ________ :

(a) Harshavardhana (b) Chandragupta II
(c) Deva Raya I (d) Rudramadevi

2. Consider the following statements with respect to Gupta administration:

1. The samantas were the bureaucrats which simultaneously discharged civil, military and judicial functions on behalf of the king.
2. Guptas were the first to grant lands to the civil servants.
3. The Gupta land grant system was responsible for the beginning of Indian feudalism.

Which of the above statements is/are correct?

(a) 1 only (b) 1 and 2 only
(c) 3 only (d) 1, 2 and 3

3. The Chinese traveller Fa-hien who visited India recorded the general conditions of the Gupta times. In this context, which of the following statements is/are correct?

1. There were no restrictions on people's movements and they enjoyed a large degree of personal freedom.
2. The administration was so efficient that the roads were kept safe for travelers, and there was no fear of thieves.
3. Administration was stricter than that of the Mauryas and restrictions on women were more.
4. Buddhism was flourishing in the north-western India but in the Gangetic valley it was in a state of neglect.

Select the correct answer using the code given below:

(a) 1, 2 and 4 only (b) 1, 2 and 3 only
(c) 2, 3 and 4 only (d) 1, 2, 3 and 4

4. Consider the following statements related to Satavahanas:

1. The Satavahanas started the practice of granting tax free villages to Brahmans and Buddhist monks.
2. Nagarjunakonda and Amravati in Andhra Pradesh became important seats of Buddhist culture under the Satavahanas.

Which of the above statements is/are correct?

(a) 1 only (b) 2 only
(c) Both 1 and 2 (d) Neither 1 nor 2

5. With respect to Gupta Dynasty, which of the following inscription is considered as the first written evidence on the custom of Sati?

(a) Allahabad Prashasti
(b) Eran Copper Plate Inscription
(c) Mehrauli Iron Pillar Inscription
(d) Halmidi Inscription

6. Consider the following statements with respect to Samudragupta:

1. He believed in a policy of peace and non-aggression.
2. Samudragupta was a patron of music & fine arts.
3. Samudragupta had built a Buddhist temple at Gaya to patronize Buddhism.

Which of the above statements is/are correct?

(a) 1 and 2 only (b) 2 and 3 only
(c) 2 only (d) 1, 2 and 3

7. Which of the following pairs is/are correctly matched?

	Kingdoms	**Famous king**
1.	Satavahana Dynasty	Gautamiputra Satakarni
2.	Saka Dynasty	Rudradaman
3.	Kushan Dynasty	Kanishka

Select the correct answer using the code given below:

(a) 3 only (b) 1 and 3 only
(c) 2 and 3 only (d) 1, 2 and 3

8. **With reference to administration in Gupta Empire, consider the following:**

Position		Responsibility
1. Sandhivigrahika	-	Foreign Minister
2. Dandapasika	-	Police Officers
3. Uparikas	-	Commander of the Cavalry
4. Nagara Sreshtis	-	Provincial Governors

Which of the above pairs are correctly matched?

(a) 1 and 2 only (b) 2 and 4 only
(c) 2 and 3 only (d) 1 and 4 only

9. **Aryabhatta and Varahmihira belong to which age:**

(a) Cholas (b) Guptas
(c) Mauryas (d) Mughals

10. **Arrange the following in increasing order of hierarchy of administrative unit during Gupta period:**

1. Bhuktis 2. Vithis
3. Vishaya 4. Village

Select the correct answer using the code given below:

(a) 1>3>2>4 (b) 3>2>1>4
(c) 1>2>3>4 (d) 3>1>2>4

11. **Consider the following pairs:**

Unit of Administration		Head
1. Bhukti	-	Rashtrapati
2. Mandala	-	Uparika
3. Pattala	-	Bhojapati
4. Grama	-	Mahattara

Which of above pairs are correctly matched?

(a) 1 and 2 only (b) 1, 3 and 4 only
(c) 3 and 4 only (d) 1, 2 and 4 only

12. **Which of the following statements represent the account of Fa-hien?**

1. The administration of the Guptas was liberal, the people enjoyed economic prosperity and the burden of taxes on them was not heavy.
2. Capital punishment was not given at all.
3. The public highways were secure and free from the menace of thieves and dacoits.

Select the correct option using the codes given below:

(a) 1 and 2 only (b) 2 and 3 only
(c) 1 and 3 only (d) 1, 2 and 3

13. **With reference to the Gupta administration, consider the following statements:**

1. Bhukti was the largest administrative zone in the empire.
2. Uparikas were entrusted only with military responsibilities.
3. Religious functionaries were empowered to punish criminals.

Which of the above statements are correct?

(a) 1 and 2 only (b) 1 and 3 only
(c) 2 and 3 only (d) 1, 2 and 3

14. **Consider the following statements:**

1. The inscription of the conquests of Samudragupta is engraved on the same pillar that carries the inscriptions of the Ashoka.
2. The prestige and influence of Samudragupta spread in South India and even outside India.
3. The republics, which flickered on the ruins of the Maurya empire, were finally crushed by Samudragupta.

Which of the above statements are correct?

(a) 1 and 3 only (b) 1 and 2 only
(c) 2 and 3 only (d) 1, 2 and 3

15. **Consider the following statements regarding a king:**

1. He wrote the Kavirajamarga, the earliest Kannada work on poetics and the Prashnottara Ratnamalika in Sanskrit.
2. For his religious temperament, his interest in the arts and literature and his peace-loving nature, he is called "Ashoka of the South".
3. He is also compared to Gupta king Vikramaditya in giving patronage to men of letters.

Which of the following kings is being described above?

(a) Govinda III (b) Amoghavarsha I
(c) Krishna I (d) Indra III

16. **The ending of Gupta era coincided with rise of various small and large states in north-eastern region. In this context, consider the following statements:**

1. Gauda was the region situated between the Ganga and Brahmaputra.
2. Dandabhakti was a fiscal and administrative unit formed is border areas between Bengal and Orissa.

Which of the above statements is/are correct?

(a) 1 only (b) 2 only
(c) Both 1 and 2 (d) Neither 1 nor 2

17. **Which one of the following statements is incorrect with respect to Gupta ruler, Chandragupta II?**

(a) The Gupta Empire was at its peak during the reign of Chandragupta II.
(b) Kalidasa and Amarasimha were scholars at the court of Chandragupta II at Ujjain.
(c) Chinese pilgrim Fa-hien visited India during his reign.
(d) Chandragupta II started the Vikrama samvat or era.

18. **With respect to the Gupta administration, consider the following statements:**

1. Absence of hereditary succession in high-ranking officials.
2. Grant of fiscal and administrative concessions to priests and administrators.

3. Both Visyapati and Uparika were appointed directly by the Gupta emperor.

Which of the above statements is/are correct?

(a) 1 and 2 only (b) 2 only
(c) 1 and 3 only (d) 2 and 3 only

19. Consider the following statements regarding Pala Empire:

1. This empire was founded by Dharmapala.
2. Dharmapala's reign was marked by a tripartite struggle between the Palas, the Pratiharas and the Rashtrakutas
3. The tripartite struggle was for the control of Kanauj and North India.

Which of the above statements is/are correct?

(a) 1 and 2 only (b) 3 only
(c) 2 and 3 only (d) 1, 2 and 3

20. Consider the following statements regarding Gupta period:

1. The Maitrakas as well as the Maukharies were subordinate rulers of the Guptas
2. The Maukharies used the title of samanta.

Which of the above statements is/are correct?

(a) 1 only (b) 2 only
(c) Both 1 and 2 (d) Neither 1 nor 2

21. Consider the following statements regarding the Gupta Empire:

1. Fa-hien, a Buddhist from China, visited India during the reign of Chandragupta I.
2. The Allahabad inscription describes the bravery of Chandragupta II.
3. Samudragupta gave permission to the king of Sri Lanka, Meghverman, to build a monastery in Bodh Gaya.

Which of the above statements is/are correct?

(a) 2 only (b) 1 and 3 only
(c) 3 only (d) None of the above

22. "He conducted the repair work of the Sudarshana Lake at Kathiawar. After becoming the king, he took up the title of Makakshatrapa. During his reign, the Greek writer Yavaneshwara lived in India and translated the Yavanajataka from Greek to Sanskrit."

The above quote describes which of the following ruler?

(a) Rudradaman I (b) Chashtana
(c) Rudrasimha III (d) Maues/Moga

23. Consider the following statements regarding Pala and Pratihara Empires:

1. The directly administered territories in the Pala and Pratihara empires were divided into Bhukti ,Mandala and Rashtra.
2. The Uparika collected land revenue and maintained law and order.

Which of the above statements is/are correct?

(a) 1 only (b) 2 only
(c) Both 1 and 2 (d) Neither 1 nor 2

SOLUTIONS

1. Correct Option: (b)

Supplementary Notes:

Fa-hien

- Fa-hien was a Chinese pilgrim who visited India during the reign of Chandragupta II (Vikramaditya).
- His primary aim was to visit the Buddhist religious places and to take with him the copies of the Buddhist religious texts.
- His voyage is described in his travelogue "Record of Buddhist Kingdoms".
- The account suggests that the administration of the Guptas was benevolent and successful and the rulers not only maintained peace and security within the empire but also looked after the welfare of their subjects.
- The people were prosperous and content with their lives. Public morality was high. Mostly the people were vegetarians and avoided meat and onions in their meals. They did not use alcohol and other intoxicants. Only Chandalas (Untouchables), who lived outside cities, engaged in hunting and fishing and were meat-eaters.
- He described the internal and foreign trade of India as well as its ports. According to him, both internal and external trade of India was in a progressive stage and the Indians carried on sea voyages. According to him, India had trade relations with China, countries of south-east Asia and western Asia as well as with Europe.

2. Correct Option: (d)

Explanation:

- All statements are correct

Supplementary Notes:

Gupta's administration

- The various inscriptions mention the following titles as usual for Guptas: Paraniadvaita, Pararnabhattaraka, Maharajadhiraja, Prithvipala, Paramesvara, Samrat, Ekadhiraja and Chakravartin.
- The king was assisted in his administration by a chief minister called mantri or sachiva.
- Pratiharas and Mahapratiharas were important officers in the royal court, though they did not participate in the administration.
- Among the important military officers are mentioned Senapati, Mahasenapati, Baladhyaksha; Mahabaladhyaksha, Baladhikrita and

Mahabaladhikrita who perhaps represented different grades.

- There were two other high military officers – the Bhatasvapati, commander of the infantry and cavalry and the Katuka, commander of the elephant corps.
- Another important official mentioned in the Basarh seals was Ranabhandagaradhikarana, chief of the treasury of the war office.
- One higher officer, mentioned for the first time in the Gupta records, was Sandhivigrahika or Mahasandhivigrahika, a sort of foreign minister.
- One of the inscriptions mentions Sarvadhyakshas, superintendents of all, but it is not clear whether they were central or provincial officers.
- The samanta system was the unique aspect of the Gupta administration. The Samantas were the civil servants simultaneously discharging civil, military and judicial functions on behalf of the king.
- Guptas were the first to grant land to the civil servants. They were given the lands called Bhuktis in lieu of salaries.
- The Gupta land grant system was responsible for the beginning of Indian Feudalism.
- The samantas who got lands from the Gupta king in course of time emerged as the Indian feudal class.

3. **Correct Option: (a)**

Explanation:

- **Statement 3 is incorrect:** Fa-hien's account on the Gupta administration provides useful information. He characterizes the Gupta administration as mild and benevolent. There were no restrictions on people's movements and they enjoyed a large degree of personal freedom. On the whole, the administration was more liberal than that of the Mauryas.

Supplementary Notes:

Gupta's administration

- The famous Chinese pilgrim, Fa-hien visited India during the reign of Chandragupta II. Out of his nine years stay in India, he spent six years in the Gupta Empire.
- Fa-hien provides valuable information on the religious, social and economic condition of the Gupta Empire.
- According to him, Buddhism was in a flourishing condition in the northwestern India but in the Gangetic valley it was in a state of neglect.
- He refers to the Gangetic valley as the 'land of Brahmanism'. Fa-hien mentions the unsatisfactory state of some of the Buddhist holy places like Kapilavastu and Kusinagara.
- According to him the economic condition of the empire was prosperous.
- Fa-hien's account on the Gupta administration provides useful information. He characterizes the Gupta administration as mild and benevolent.
- There were no restrictions on people's movements and they enjoyed a large degree of personal freedom.
- There was no state interference in the individual's life. Punishments were not severe. Imposing a fine was a common punishment. There was no spy system.
- The administration was so efficient that the roads were kept safe for travelers, and there was no fear of thieves.
- He mentioned that people were generally prosperous and the crimes were negligible.
- Fa-hien had also appreciated the efficiency of the Gupta administration as he was able to travel without any fear throughout the Gangetic valley. On the whole the administration was more liberal than that of the Mauryas.
- Fa-hien's account on the Gupta administration provides useful information. He characterizes the Gupta administration as mild and benevolent. There were no restrictions on people's movements and they enjoyed a large degree of personal freedom. On the whole, the administration was more liberal than that of the Mauryas.

4. **Correct Option: (c)**

Explanation:

- Both statements are correct

Supplementary Notes:

Satavahanas

- The Satavahanas rulers strove for royal ideal set forth in the Dharmashatras. The king was represented as the upholder of Dharma. To him were assigned a few divine attributes. The Satavahana king is represented as possessing the qualities of mythical heroes. The Satavahanas started the practice of granting tax free villages to Brahmanas and Buddhist monks.
- The Satavahana rulers promoted Buddhism by granting land to the monks. In their kingdom, the Mahayana form of Buddhism commanded considerable following, especially in the artisan class. Nagarjunakonda and Amravati in Andhra Pradesh became important seats of Buddhist culture under the Satavahanas and more so under their successors.

5. **Correct Option: (b)**

Explanation:

- **Option (b) is correct:** Eran copper plate inscription, founded in Sagar district of M.P., was issued by Bhanugupta.

Supplementary Notes:

Gupta Period

- It is the first written evidence on the custom of Sati. One of the earliest Sati Pillars of India was found in Eran. This was discovered by General Alexander Cunningham in 1874-1875 AD.
- This inscription shows that it was in the Gupta era 191. In addition to this, various Sati Pillars ranging from Early Medieval Period to the Modern Period have been noticed in Eran.
- The imprints taken from these 10 Sati Pillars, throw the new light about Eran and also on the position of women. The Saka Samvat is used in all Sati Pillars.
- The prayer to God occurs in the beginning of almost all the inscriptions.
- After mentioning the Samvat and date, the epigraph gives the name of the dead person and his wife who became Sati along with him.

6. **Correct Option: (c)**

Explanation:

- **Statements 1 is incorrect:** He was opposite of Ashoka. Ashoka believed in a policy of peace and non-aggression, but Samudragupta delighted in violence and conquest.
- **Statement 3 is incorrect:** According to Chinese source, Meghavarman, ruler of Sri Lanka, sent a missionary to Samudragupta for permission to build a Buddhist temple at Gaya. This was granted and the temple was developed into a huge monastic establishment.

Supplementary Notes:

Samudragupta

- Samudragupta was the fourth ruler of the Gupta Empire and the son and successor of Chandragupta I.
- He was opposite of Ashoka. Ashoka believed in a policy of peace and non-aggression, but Samudragupta delighted in violence and conquest.
- His rule was one of expansion marked first by the conquest of his immediate neighbors and then by campaigns to the east and the south where chiefdoms and kingdoms were subdued and forced to pay tribute to him.
- Much of the knowledge of Samudragupta's military exploits comes from the Allahabad Pillar of Ashoka which includes a prashasti extolling the deeds and virtues of the Gupta emperor.
- Samudragupta was a patron of music & fine arts.
- Going by the inscription, Samudragupta exerted direct or indirect control over much of the Indian subcontinent stretching from kingdoms in Nepal and the Punjab in the north all the way to the Pallava kingdom at Kanchipuram in the south-east.
- Samudragupta is the father of Gupta monetary system. He started minting different types of coins, known as the Standard Type, the Archer Type, the Battle Axe Type, the Ashvamedha Type, the Tiger Slayer Type, the King and Queen Type and the Lyre Player Type. They exhibit a fine quality of technical and sculptural finesse. At least three types of coins—Archer Type, Battle-Axe and Tiger type—represent Samudragupta in martial armour. According to Chinese source, Meghavarman, ruler of Sri Lanka, sent a missionary to Samudragupta for permission to build a Buddhist temple at Gaya. This was granted and the temple was developed into a huge monastic establishment.
- According to Chinese source, Meghavarman, ruler of Sri lanka, sent a missionary to Samudragupta for permission to build a Buddhist temple at Gaya. This was granted and the temple was developed into a huge monastic establishment.

7. **Correct Option: (b)**

Explanation:

- **Pair 2 is incorrectly matched:** Rudradaman I was a ruler from the Western Kshatrapas Dynasty. He was the grandson of the king Chastana. Rudradaman I was instrumental in the decline of the Satavahana Empire.

Supplementary Notes:

- Kanishka was a great Kushan king, great alike in war as in peace. His capability as a great conqueror had been proved by his conquests.
- Gautamiputra Satakarni is the most celebrated and successful king of the Satavahana Dynasty. He was the twenty third ruler of the Satavahana Dynasty and ruled for 24 years between 62 – 86 AD He was responsible for the rise of Satavahana Dynasty after its downfall in the first half of the 1st century in the Christian era. Born to Gautami Balashri and Sivasvati Satakarni, Gautamiputra Satakarni is described as the destroyer of Shakas, Pahlavas and Yavanas restoring the old prestige of Satavahana Dynasty.

8. **Correct Option: (a)**

Explanation:

- **Pair 3 is incorrectly matched:** Nagara Sreshtis were the officers looking after the city administration.
- **Pair 4 is incorrectly matched:** Provincial governors are known as Uparikas.

Supplementary Notes:

Administration under Gupta Dynasty

- The king was assisted in his administration by a chief minister called mantri or sachiva.
- There were two high military officers—the Bhatasvapati, commander of the infantry and cavalry and the Katuka, commander of the elephant corps.

- Another important official mentioned in the Basarh seals was Ranabhandagaradhikarana, chief of the treasury of the war office.
- One more high officer, mentioned for the first time in the Gupta records, was Sandhivigrahika or Mahasandhivigrahika, a sort of foreign minister.
- Numerous inscriptions mention Dutaka or Duty who communicated royal commands to officers and people concerned.
- Dandapasadhikarana represented the chief of the police.
- Ordinary police officials were known as Dandapasika, Chatas, Bhatas, Dandika (chastiser), and Chauroddharanika (officer apprehending thieves).
- The king maintained a close contact with the provincial administration through a class of officials called Kumaramatyas and Ayuktas.
- Provinces in the Gupta Empire were known as Bhuktis and provincial governors as Uparikas. They were mostly chosen from among the princes.
- Bhuktis were subdivided into Vishyas or districts. They were governed by Vishyapatis.
- Nagara Sreshtis were the officers looking after the city administration.
- The villages in the district were under the control of Gramikas.

9. Correct Option: (b)

Supplementary Notes:

- Aryabhata was an outstanding scholar of the Gupta age. His most original contribution was that the eclipses were not the work of Rahu (Saturn), as believed by some astrologers, but caused by the shadow of the earth falling on the moon, thus, asserting the movement of earth on its own axis around the sun, as was known in Vedic times. Aryabhata was the first to utilize sign functions in astronomy. He discovered an accurate formula to measure the decrease or increase in the duration of two consecutive days.
- In mathematics, Aryabhata wrote the book Aryabhattiya, in Kusumpura (Pataliputra) when he was 23 years old.
- Aryabhattiya is divided into four parts. As regards geometry, Aryabhata considers among other topics, an area of a triangle, the theorem on similarity of triangles, the area of circle and the theorem relating to rectangles contained by the segments. One of the most important features of Aryabhata's mathematical system is his unique system of notation. It is based on the decimal place-value system, unknown to other ancient people, but now in use throughout the civilized world. The other famous mathematician was Brahmagupta who wrote Brahmsiddhanta in c. AD 628 His other well known work was Khandakhadya, probably composed in AD 665. He developed rules for operating with negative qualities and with zero. He began to apply Algebra to astronomical problems.
- Varahamihira, who flourished in the court of Chandragupta II, has preserved in his Panchasiddhantika, written in AD 505, the accounts of five astronomical works which were evidently regarded as authority in his own time.
- These five works or siddhantas are known as Paitamaha, Romaka, Paulisa, Vasishtha and Surya.
- The Suryasiddhanta is the most important and complete work on the astronomy of the period. In the field of astrology, we are also much indebted to Varahamihira.
- He has, in his work Brihatsamhita, preserved a considerable amount of ancient knowledge on the subject.
- Varahamihira's son, Prithuyashas too was an ardent student of astronomy, and wrote, in about AD 600, a work called Harashatpanchashika.

10. Correct Option: (a)

Explanation:

- Option (a) is correct

Supplementary Notes:

- The kingdom (Rajya) was divided into a number of provinces and they were known as 'Bhukti' in the north and 'Mandala' or 'Mandalam' in the south.
- The provinces were sub-divided as 'Vishaya' or 'Bhoga' in the north (India) and 'Kottams' or 'Valanadu' in the south (India).
- The group of villages (i.e. modern tehsil) was known as 'Vithis' in the north (India) and 'Pattala' and 'Kurram' in the south (India).
- The villages were the lowest administrative units.

11. Correct Option: (c)

Explanation:

- **Pair 1 is incorrect:** Bhukti was governed by Uparika.
- **Pair 2 is incorrect:** Mandala was governed by Visyapati.
- **Elimination:** By eliminating 1, option (c) is correct.

Supplementary Notes:

Political Ideas and Organisation

- The king's position was hereditary, and normally, the eldest son succeeded the father, but the succession rules were not so rigid. The princes were mostly appointed as provincial governors and in some rare cases, princesses were also appointed to government posts.
- Kings were generally advised by a number of ministers. The ministers were chosen by the king, generally from leading families. Their position was often hereditary.

- The armed forces were very important for the maintenance and expansion of the empire. We have already cited evidence from Arab travellers that the Pala, Pratihara and Rashtrakuta kings had large and well-organised infantry and cavalry, and large number of war elephants. Elephants were supposed to be elements of strength and were greatly prized. The largest number of elephants was maintained by the Pala kings. Large numbers of horses were imported both by Rashtrakuta and Pratihara kings by sea from Arabia and West Asia, and over land from Khurasan (east Persia), and Central Asia. The Pratihara kings are believed to have had the finest cavalry in the country. There is no reference to war-chariots which had fallen out of use.
- The directly administered territories were divided into:
  - Rashtra, under the supervision of Rashtrapati or governor.
  - Bhukti (provinces), under the supervision of Uparika who was expected to collect land revenue and maintain law and order
  - Mandalas or Visaya (districts), whose head was called Visyapati and was expected to perform the functions of collection of revenue and maintaining law and order at district level.
  - Pattala (smaller unit of cluster of villages), which were headed by Bhojapati.
  - Village, headed by the village headman and village accountant whose posts were generally hereditary. He was often assisted by village elder called grama-mahajana or grama-mahattara.
- It is noteworthy to add that, almost all the officials were paid by giving them grants of rent- free land, and it also led to the rise of hereditary revenue officers called nad-gavundas or desa-gramakutas. Later, they were addressed as deshmukhas and deshpandes in Maharashtra. The revenue assignments called 'bhoga' or 'fief' granted by the rules to the officers were temporary in theory and were liable to be resumed whenever the ruler wanted but this was rarely practised except in case of outright rebellion or disloyalty.
- In terms of religion, most of the kings were tolerant in their views and behaviour and generously patronised the Hinduism (some were devout followers of Shiva or Vishnu), Buddhism or Jainism. Muslims were welcomed and allowed to propagate their faith by the Rashtrakuta kings. The kings like the earlier times were considered upholders of social hierarchy and generally the Chaturvarna system continued.
- However, the state was essentially secular as the politics and religion were in essence kept apart and kings were not dominated by the religious discourses.

12. Correct Option: (d)

Explanation:

- All statements are correct

Supplementary Notes:

Account of Fa-hien

- Fa-hien, a Chinese pilgrim, visited India during the reign of Chandragupta II. His primary aim was to visit the Buddhist religious places and to take with him the copies of the Buddhist religious texts. He, therefore, travelled through the Gupta empire and also wrote down his impressions about India. As his main interest was religion, we know nothing about the political condition of India from his account. However, his account helps us to know something about the social and religious condition of that period.
- It is inferred that the administration of the Guptas was liberal, the people enjoyed economic prosperity and the burden of taxes on them was not heavy.
- He wrote that corporal punishment was avoided and usually fines were exacted from the offenders according to the nature of their offence. Those who attempted repeated offences against the State were punished severely and in that case their right hands were cut off.
- Most importantly, capital punishment was not given at all.
- The primary source of income of the state was land-revenue. The people were free to move from one land to another. The government servants were paid in cash and they were barred from taking presents or bribery from the people. Monasteries, Sanghas, temples and their property and other religious endowments were free from government taxes. The public highways were secure and free from the menace of thieves and dacoits.
- The people were prosperous and content with their lives. Public morality was high. Mostly the people were vegetarians and avoided meat and onions in their meals. They did not use alcohol and other intoxicants. Only Chandalas (Untouchables), who lived outside cities, engaged in hunting and fishing and were meat eaters.
- Buddhism and Hinduism were the most popular religions at that time. Buddhism was more popular in Punjab, Bengal and the region around Mathura. In Mathura, there were many Buddhist monasteries and even government servants respected Buddhist monks. The Hindu religion was more popular in the 'middle kingdom' (Uttar Pradesh, Bihar and a part of Bengal) which formed the heart of Chandragupta II's dominions.
- The emperor worshipped Vishnu but he was tolerant to other faiths. Buddhism and Hinduism flourished

side by side which suggests that the people observed tolerance in religious matters.

- Fa-hien lived in Pataliputra for nearly three years and studied the Sanskrit language. He described that there were separate Sanghas both of the Hinayana and Mahayana sects, which provided education to students gathered from all parts of India.
- According to him, both internal and external trade of India was in a progressive stage and the Indians carried on sea-voyages. According to him India had trade relations with China, countries of south-east Asia and western Asia as well as with Europe. On its western sea-coast, India had ports like Cambay, Sopara and Baroach, while on its eastern coast Tamralipti was a famous port from where Fa-hien went to Sri Lanka on an Indian ship.

13. Correct Option: (b)

Explanation:

- **Statement 2 is incorrect:** Uparikas were entrusted with both civil and military responsibilities.

Supplementary Notes:

Gupta Administration

- There was an increase in the tendency to appoint high-ranking officers on a hereditary basis.
- Visyapati was appointed by the Uparika who was in turn appointed by the Emperor directly.
- Gupta Empire was divided into many regional units. It was a multi-layer administrative system.
- Bhukti was the largest administrative zone in the empire. The earliest known use of this administrative term is seen in the Allahabad pillar inscription of Samudragupta.
- Uparika were the highest regional authorities who were appointed directly by the emperor. They were entrusted with both civil and military responsibilities.
- The territorial-cum-administrative unit below the Bhukti was known as vishaya equivalent to a locality, close to the size of a district. The vishaya was entrusted to the district administrator (Vishyapati) who was appointed by the uparikas.
- The actual burden of administration and executive functions was borne by a large number of functionaries who were designated amatya, mantra, and sachiva. These were terms for high-ranking functionaries and ministers.
- A significant feature in the administrative system is the tendency to appoint high-ranking officers on a hereditary basis.
- There was also a growing tendency in the hierarchisation of offices, indicated by the use of the prefixes maha and sarva to the official designations. For e.g., dandanayaka, mahadandanayaka and mahasarvadandanayaka.
- Land donation to Brahmanas and other religious groups became far more prevalent and institutionalized during the Gupta period.
- The Gupta period saw the surfacing of feudal development in the form of the fiscal and administrative concessions to priests and administrators through various land grants. Although the practice was known since Satavahana times, it became far more institutionalized during the rule of Guptas. It became a regular and palpable institution.
- Religious functionaries were granted land, free of tax, for posterity, and they were authorized to collect from the peasants all the taxes that once went directly to the emperor. They were also empowered to punish criminals.

14. Correct Option: (d)

Explanation:

- All statements are correct

Supplementary Notes:

Conquests by Samudragupta

- Samudragupta was the opposite of Ashoka. Ashoka believed in a policy of peace and non-aggression, but Samudragupta delighted in violence and conquest. His court poet Harishena wrote a glowing account of the military exploits of his patron, and, in a long inscription, the poet enumerates the peoples and countries that were conquered by Samudragupta. The inscription is engraved at Allahabad on the same pillar that carries the inscriptions of the peace-loving Ashoka.
- The places and the countries conquered by Samudragupta can be divided into five groups.
- Group one includes the princes of the Ganga–Yamuna doab who were defeated and whose kingdoms were incorporated into the Gupta empire.
- Group two includes the rulers of the eastern Himalayan states and of some frontier states such as Nepal, Assam, and Bengal, which were made to feel the weight of Samudragupta's arms. It also covers some republics of Punjab. The republics, which flickered on the ruins of the Maurya empire, were finally crushed by Samudragupta.
- Group three includes the forest kingdoms situated in the Vindhya region and known as Atavika rajyas which Samudragupta brought under his control.
- Group four includes twelve rulers of the eastern Deccan and south India who were conquered and liberated. Samudragupta's arms reached as far as Kanchi in Tamil Nadu, where the Pallavas were compelled to recognize his suzerainty.
- Group five includes the names of the Shakas and Kushans, some of them ruling in Afghanistan. It is

said that Samudragupta swept them out of power and received the submission of the rulers of distant lands. The prestige and influence of Samudragupta spread even outside India.

- According to a Chinese source, Meghavarman, the ruler of Sri Lanka, sent a missionary to Samudragupta for permission to build a Buddhist temple at Gaya. This was granted, and the temple was developed into a huge monastic establishment.
- If we are to believe the eulogistic inscription at Allahabad, it would appear that Samudragupta never knew defeat, and because of his bravery and generalship he is called the Napoleon of India. There is no doubt that Samudragupta forcibly unified the greater part of India under him, and his power was felt in a much larger area than that of his predecessor.

15. Correct Option: (b)

Explanation:

- Option (b) is correct

Supplementary Notes:

The Rashtrakutas

- While the Palas and the Pratiharas were ruling over north India, the Deccan was being ruled by the Rashtrakutas, a remarkable dynasty which produced a long line of warriors and able administrators.
- The kingdom was founded by Dantidurga who set up his capital at Manyakhet or Malkhed near modern Sholapur.
- They achieved spectacular military successes in the north and south and in the tripartite struggle, they mostly defeated the Palas and the Pratiharas. It is significant to note that although their raids did not result in the extension of the Rashtrakuta empire to the Gangetic valley, they brought rich plunder, and added to the fame of the Rashtrakutas. They also constantly fought against the eastern Chalukyas of Vengi (Andhra Pradesh), the Pallavas of Kanchi and the Pandyas of Madurai.
- Probably the greatest Rashtrakuta rulers were Govinda III (793-814) and Amoghavarsha I (814-878).
- After a successful expedition against Nagabhatta of Kanauj and the annexation of Malwa, Govinda III turned to the south. In an inscription it is mentioned that Govinda 'terrified the Kerala, Pandya and the Chola kings and caused the Pallavas to wither. The king of Lanka and his minister who had been negligent of their own interests, were captured and brought over as prisoners to Halapur. Two statues of the lord of Lanka were carried to Manyakhet, and installed like pillars of victory in from of a Siva temple.
- Amoghavarsha I ruled for 64 years but by temperament he preferred the pursuit of religion and literature to war. He defeated the invading Eastern Chalukyas at Vingavalli and assumed the title 'Viranarayana'. It is interesting to note that unlike his father, he preferred to maintain friendly relations with his neighbours, the Gangas, the Eastern Chalukyas and the Pallavas with whom he also cultivated marital ties.
- He was a patron of literature and was an accomplished scholar in Kannada and Sanskrit himself. He wrote the Kavirajamarga – the earliest Kannada work on poetics and the Prashnottara Ratnamalika in Sanskrit, which is considered as a writing of high merit and was later translated into the Tibetan language.
- Because of his religious temperament, his interest in the arts and literature and his peace-loving nature, he is often compared to Emperor Ashoka and called "Ashoka of the South", and is also compared to Gupta king Vikramaditya in giving patronage to men of letters.
- The Rashtrakuta rule in the Deccan thus lasted for almost two hundred years, till the end of the tenth century. The Rashtrakuta rulers were tolerant in their religious views and patronised not only Saivism and Vaishnavism but Jainism as well. The famous rock-cut temple of Siva at Ellora was built by one of the Rashtrakuta kings, Krishna I, in the ninth century. Amoghavarsha is said to have been a Jain but he also patronised other faiths. The Rashtrakutas allowed Muslim traders to settle, and permitted Islam to be preached, in their dominions. This tolerant policy helped to promote foreign trade which enriched the Rashtrakutas.
- The Rashtrakuta kings were great patrons of arts and letters. In their courts, we find not only Sanskrit scholars, but also poets and others who wrote in Prakrit and the Apabhramsa. The great apabharamsha poet, Svayambhu, and his son probably lived at the Rashtrakuta's court.

16. Correct Option: (c)

Explanation:

- Both statements are correct

Supplementary Notes:

Rise of States in the Northeast Region

- The area situated between the Ganges and the Brahmaputra now covering Bangladesh, emerged as a settled and fairly Sanskrit-educated region in the fifth and sixth centuries.
- By AD 600, the area came to be known as Gauda and functioned as an independent state ruled by Shashanka, Harsha's adversary.
- The deltaic portion of Bengal formed by the Brahmaputra and called 'Samatata' was made to acknowledge the authority of Samudragupta in the fourth century.

- By the seventh century, there existed the state of the Khadgas in the Dhaka area, literally swordsmen.
- There was also the kingdom of a Brahmana feudatory called Lokanatha and that of the Ratas, both in the Comilla area.
- All these princes of south-east and central Bengal issued land grants in the sixth and seventh centuries.
- The practice of land charters attested to the expansion of cultivation and rural settlements.
- A fiscal and administrative unit called Dandabhukti was formed in the border areas between Bengal and Orissa.
- Danda means punishment and bhukti enjoyment. The unit was formed apparently to pacify and suppress the tribal inhabitants of that region and may have promoted Sanskrit and other elements of culture in the tribal areas.
- This was also true of Vardhamanabhukti (Burdwan) of which we hear in the sixth century.

17. Correct Option: (d)

Explanation:

- **Option (d) is incorrect:** Vikrama samvat or era in 58–57 BC was started by Ujjain ruler Shakari.

Supplementary Notes:

Chandragupta II

- The Gupta Empire saw its peak during the reign of Chandragupta II (AD 380–412).
- He extended the limits of the empire by marriage alliance and conquest.
- Chandragupta married his daughter Prabhavati to a Vakataka prince of the Brahmana caste and ruled in central India and exercised indirect control over the Vakataka kingdom in central India.
- He conquered Mathura from the Kushans and occupied western Malwa and Gujarat, which had for about four centuries been under the rule of the Shaka Kshatrapas.
- This gave him control over the western sea coast, famous for trade and commerce.
- The chief city Ujjain of Malwa region was made the second capital by Chandragupta II.
- He adopted the title of Vikramaditya, which had been first used by an Ujjain ruler in 58–57 BC as a mark of victory over the Shaka Kshatrapas of western India. This Ujjain ruler is traditionally called Shakari or the enemy of the Shakas. The Vikrama samvat or era was started in 58– 57 BC by Shakari.
- The court of Chandragupta II at Ujjain was adorned by numerous scholars including Kalidasa and Amarasimha.
- It was during Chandragupta's reign that the Chinese pilgrim Fa-hsien (AD 399–414) visited India and wrote an elaborate account of the life of its people.

18. Correct Option: (b)

Explanation:

- **Statement 1 is incorrect:** There was an increase in the tendency to appoint high-ranking officers on a hereditary basis.
- **Statement 3 is incorrect:** Visyapati was appointed by the Uparika who was in turn appointed by the Emperor directly.

Supplementary Notes:

Gupta Administration

- Gupta empire was divided into a number of regional units. It was a multi-layer administrative system.
- Bhukti was the largest administrative zone in the empire. The earliest known use of this administrative term is seen in the Allahabad pillar inscription of Samudragupta.
- Uparika was the highest regional authorties who were appointed directly by the emperor. They were entrusted with both civil and military responsibilities.
- The territorial-cum-administrative unit below the Bhukti was known as vishaya equivalent to a locality, close to the size of a district. The vishaya was entrusted to the district administrator (Vishyapati) who was appointed by the uparikas.
- The actual burden of administrations and executive functions was borne by a large number of functionaries who were designated amatya, mantri, and sachiva. These were terms for high-ranking functionaries and ministers.
- A significant feature in the administrative system is the tendency to appoint high-ranking officers on a hereditary basis.
- There was also a growing tendency in the hierarchisation of offices, indicated by the use of the prefixes maha and sarva to the official designations. For e.g., dandanayaka, mahadandanayaka and mahasarvadandanayaka.
- Land donation to Brahmanas and other religious groups became far more prevalent and institutionalised during Gupta period.
- The Gupta period saw the surfacing of feudal development in the form of the fiscal and administrative concessions to priests and administrators through various land grants. Although, the practice was known since Satavahana times, but it became far more institutionalised during the rule of Guptas. It became a regular and palpable institution.
- Religious functionaries were granted land, free of tax, for posterity, and they were authorized to collect from the peasants all the taxes that once went directly to the emperor. They were also empowered to punish criminals.

19. Correct Option: (c)

Explanation:

- **Statement 1 is incorrect:** This empire was founded by Gopala.

Supplementary Notes:

Pala Empire

- The Pala empire was founded by Gopala, probably in AD 750 when he was elected king by the notable men of the area to end the anarchy prevailing there.
- Gopala was not born in a high, much less a royal family, his father probably was a soldier. He unified Bengal under his control, and even brought Magadha (Bihar) under his control.
- Gopala was succeeded in AD 770 by his son, Dharamapala, who ruled till AD 810.
- His reign was marked by a tripartite struggle between the Palas, the Pratiharas and the Rashtrakutas for the control of Kanauj and north India.
- The Pratihara ruler advanced upon Gauda (Bengal), but before a decision could be taken, the Pratihara ruler was defeated by the Rashtrakuta ruler, Dhruva, and was forced to seek refuge in the deserts of Rajasthan. Dhruva then returned to the Deccan.
- This left the field free for Dharmapala who occupied Kanauj and held a grand darbar which was attended by vassal rulers from Punjab, eastern Rajasthan, etc.

20. Correct Option: (c)

Explanation:

- Both statements are correct

Supplementary Notes:

The Maitrakas

- The Maitrakas were tributary chiefs of the Guptas, who established an independent kingdom in western India ruling over Saurashtra in Gujarat.
- Dhruvasena II was the most important ruler of the Maitrakas, who was a contemporary of Harsha Vardhana and was married to his daughter.
- Hieun Tsang tells us that Dhruvasena II attended Harsha's assembly at Prayaga (Allahabad).
- The Maitrakas developed Vallabhi as their capital, which was also an important centre of learning.
- Being situated on the Arabian Sea, it was also a port town having flourishing trade and commerce.
- The Maitrakas continued to rule until the middle of the 8th century when Arab attacks weakened their power.

The Maukharies

- The Maukharies were also subordinate rulers of the Guptas and used the title of samanta.
- They ruled over Kannauj, a city in western Uttar Pradesh, which gradually replaced Pataliputra as the political centre of northern India.
- Harshavardhana's sister Rajyashri, was married to Grahavarmana.
- After the successful expedition of Harshavardhana, the kingdom of Kannauj, was then merged with that of the Pushyabhutis.
- Harsha shifted his capital from Thanesar (Kurukshetra) to Kannauj.
- The Maukharis are also mentioned in Patanjali's work.

21. Correct Option: (c)

Explanation:

- **Statement 1 is incorrect:** Fa-hien, a Buddhist from China visited India during the reign of Chandragupta II.
- **Statement 2 is incorrect:** The Allahabad inscription describes the bravery of Samudragupta as composed by his court poet, Harisena.

Supplementary Notes:

Samudragupta:

- The Allahabad inscription describes his bravery as composed by his court poet, Harisena.
- The Gupta emperor, Samudragupta, granted permission to Buddhist king of Ceylon Meghavarman to build a monastry at Bodh Gaya. Hence, he was also known as Anukampavan (full of compassion).

Chandragupta II:

- He used matrimonial alliances to expand his kingdom.
- He also annexed three Satrapa kingdoms and assumed the title Sakari (destroyer of the Sakas).
- His court had nine jewels or Navaratnas. It included the great Sanskrit poet Kalidasa, Harisena, Amarasimha (lexicographer) and Dhanvantari (physician).
- Fa-hien, a Buddhist from China visited India during his reign. He records the prosperity of the Gupta Empire.

22. Correct Option: (a)

Supplementary Notes:

Shakas—Rudradaman I (130 AD – 150 AD)

- He is from the Western Kshatrapa dynasty. He was the grandson of Chastana. He took up the title of Makakshatrapa after becoming king.
- His kingdom included Konkan, Narmada valley, Kathiawar, and other parts of Gujarat and Malwa.
- He conducted the repair work of the Sudarshana Lake at Kathiawar.
- He also issued the first long inscription in chaste Sanskrit.
- He maintained marital relationships with the Satavahanas.
- He regained through conquests most of the territories previously under Nahapana.

- It was during Rudradaman's reign that Yavaneshwara, the Greek writer lived in India and translated the Yavanajataka from Greek to Sanskrit.

23. Correct Option: (b)

Explanation:

- **Statement 1 is incorrect:** The directly administered territories in the Pala and Pratihara empires were divided into bhukti and mandala.

Supplementary Notes:

Pala and Pratiharas

- The directly administered territories in the Pala and Pratihara empires were divided into bhukti (provinces), and mandala or visaya (districts).
- The governor of a province was called uparika and the head of a district, visayapati. The uparika was expected to collect land revenue and maintain law and order with the help of the army. The visayapati was also expected to do the same within his jurisdiction. During the period, there, was an increase of smaller chieftains, called samantas or bhogapatis, who dominated over a number of villages.
- The visayapatis and these smaller chiefs tended to merge with each other, and later on the word samanta began to be used indiscriminately for both of them.
- In the Rashtrakuta kingdom, the directly administered areas were divided into rashtra (provinces), visaya and bhukti. The head of rashtra was called rashtrapati, and he performed the same functions as the Uparika did in the Pala and Pratihara empires.
- The visaya was like a modern district, and the bhukti was a smaller unit to it. In the Pala and Pratihara empires, the unit below the visaya was called pattala.
- The precise role of these smaller units is not known. It seems that their main purpose was the realisation of land revenue and some attention to law and order. Apparently all the officials were paid by giving them grants of rent-free land.
- This tended to blur the distinction between local officials and the hereditary chiefs and smaller vassals. Similarly, the rashtrapati or governor sometimes enjoyed the status and title of a vassal king.

CONCEPT REVISION

Here is the list of concepts that have been covered as part of the previous exercise. Revise and self-reflect on your concepts you covered.

- Foreign Travellers ☐
- Administration during Gupta Period ☐
- Inscriptions ☐
- Aryabhatta and Varahmihira ☐
- Important Gupta Rulers ☐
- Different units of administration and their heads ☐

1.8 HARSHAVARDHAN

QUESTIONS

1. Consider the following statements about Pushyabhutis Dynasty of Thanesar:

1. It rose after the downfall of the Gupta Empire in northern India.
2. The dynasty reached its zenith under Harshavardhana.

Which of the above statements is/are correct?

(a) 1 only (b) 2 only
(c) Both 1 and 2 (d) Neither 1 nor 2

2. Which of the following statements is/are correct about King Harsha?

1. Harsha belonged to Pushyabhuti Dynasty.
2. He was a Shaivite and so propagated Hinduism and did not patronized Buddhism.
3. He sent an envoy to the Chinese emperor and established the first diplomatic relations between India and China.

Select the correct answer using the code given below:

(a) 1 and 3 only (b) 2 only
(c) 1 and 2 only (d) 1, 2 and 3

3. Consider the following statements about the administration under Harsha:

1. Under his period taxation policy was very aggressive.
2. In his empire, the king's share was one-sixth of the agricultural produce.
3. One part of the revenue of the state was spent as reward to persons of high intellectual eminence.

Which of the above statements are correct?

(a) 1 and 2 only (b) 2 and 3 only
(c) 1 and 3 only (d) 1, 2 and 3

4. Consider the following statements pertaining to Hiuen Tsang's account of Harsha's Kingdom:

1. Pataliputra and Vaishali were in a state of decline while Prayag and Kanauj in the doab became an important center.
2. The Shudras were generally agriculturists and they could pursue agriculture independently.

Which of the above statement/s is/are incorrect?

(a) 1 only (b) 2 only
(c) Both 1 and 2 (d) Neither 1 nor 2

5. Consider the following statement regarding the Harsha's period:

1. The Buddhists were divided into eighteen sects during his period.
2. At Nalanda, the Monks were taught Buddhist philosophy of the Hinyana school.
3. As a devout Buddhist, Harsha convened a grand assembly at Thaneshwar to widely publicize the doctrines of Hinayana.

Which of the above statement/s is/are incorrect?

(a) 1 only (b) 1 and 3 only
(c) 1 and 2 only (d) 2 and 3 only

6. Which of the following statements is/are correct?

1. Harsha governed his empire on the same lines as did the Gupta did, but his administration became less feudal and more centralized.
2. Land grants to the officers and priestly class increased in the Harsha' reign which explains why there were much less coins issued by him.

Select the correct option using the codes given below:

(a) 1 only (b) 2 only
(c) Both 1 and 2 (d) Neither 1 nor 2

7. Consider the following statements regarding administration under Harsha:

1. It was a centralized system.
2. Gold coins were given as salary to officers.
3. Military camps were called skandhavaras.

Which of the above statements is/are correct?

(a) 1 and 2 only (b) 3 only
(c) 2 and 3 only (d) 1 and 3 only

8. Harsha is called the last great Hindu emperor of India. In this context, consider the following statements:

1. He was a staunch Hindu Ruler.
2. Kashmir, Rajasthan, Punjab, UP, Bihar, and Orissa were under his direct control.
3. His southward march was stopped by the Chalukya king Pulakeshin.

Which of the above statements is/are incorrect?

(a) 1 only (b) 1 and 2 only
(c) 3 only (d) None of the above

9. Which of the following travellers visited India during the reign of Harsha?

(a) Hiuen Tsang (b) Fa-hien
(c) Marco Polo (d) Francois Bernier

10. Which of the following statements about Pulakeshin II are correct?

1. He subjugated the Kadamba capital at Banavasi and compelled the Gangas of Mysore to acknowledge his suzerainty.
2. He defeated the Pallava king Narasimhavarman and assumed the title of Vatapikonda.
3. He also defeated Harsha's army on the Narmada and checked his advance towards the Deccan.

Select the correct answer using the code given below:

(a) 1 and 2 only (b) 1 and 3 only
(c) 2 and 3 only (d) 1, 2 and 3

SOLUTIONS

1. Correct Option: (c)

Explanation:

- Both statements are correct

Supplementary Notes:

Pushyabhutis Dynasty

- Also known as the Pushpabhuti dynasty or Vardhana dynasty, ruled parts of northern India during 6th and 7th centuries.
- The dynasty reached its zenith under its last ruler Harshavardhana, whose empire covered much of north and north-western India, and extended till Kamarupa in the east and Narmada River in the south.
- The dynasty initially ruled from Sthanvishvara (modern Thanesar, Haryana), but Harsha eventually made Kanyakubja (modern Kannauj, Uttar Pradesh) his capital, from where he ruled until 647 CE.
- It rose after the downfall of the Gupta Empire (3rd century CE - 6th century CE) in the 6th century CE in northern India.
- The fall of the Gupta Empire and the absence of any other empire instead led to the political disintegration of northern India.
- Along with the Pushyabhutis, there rose a number of similarly independent powers: the Maukharis of Kosala/Kanyakubja (present-day state of Uttar Pradesh), and the Later Guptas of Magadha and Malwa (present-day states of Bihar and Madhya Pradesh).
- The other kingdoms included those established in the present-day states of Odisha, Bengal, and Assam. In

the 7th century CE, the Gauda kingdom under King Shashanka (c. late 6th century CE - 637 CE) came into being, which comprised of the northern and most of the western parts of Bengal.

2. **Correct Option: (a)**

Explanation:

- **Statement 2 is incorrect:** Harsha was Shaivate but propogated Buddhism by constructing stupas.

Supplementary Notes:

Pushyabhuti Dynasty

- Harsha is considered the last great emperor in ancient Indian history.
- He also conducted Dharmayatras like Samrat Ashoka. Harsha belongs to Pushyabhuti Dynasty. Harsha was defeated by the south Indian Emperor Pulakeshin II.
- His biography Harshacharita ("Deeds of Harsha") written by Sanskrit poet Banabhatta.
- In 641 BC he sent an envoy to the Chinese emperor and established the first diplomatic relations between India and China.
- He established benevolent institutions for the benefit of travelers, the poor, and the sick throughout his empire. He was Shaivate but propogated Buddhism by constructing stupas.
- **Statement 2 is incorrect:** Harsha was Shaivate but propogated Buddhism by constructing stupas.

3. **Correct Option: (b)**

Explanation:

- **Statement 1 is incorrect:** In general, the taxation policy was liberal. The people were not subjected to oppressive economic measures.

Supplementary Notes:

Administration under Harsha

- Much light is thrown by the Chinese pilgrim on the revenue system of Harsha. As Hiuen Tsang says: "Official requirements are few ... families are not registered and individuals were not subject to forced labour contributions. Taxation being very light and forced service being sparingly used, everyone keeps to his hereditary occupation and attends to his patrimony".
- In Harsha's Empire, the king's share was one-sixth of the agricultural produce. It is known from the Madhuvana Copper Plate that the king's dues from a village were of two kinds.
  - One was the tulyameya or the tax depending on the weight and measures of the things sold. The other was the Bhagablioga kara-hiranyadi or the share of the produce, taxes, and payments in cash from other sources of income.
- Revenues were also earned from trade and commerce. But duties on goods were light.
- The revenue of the state, according to Hiuen Tsang, was spent for four main purposes as public expenditure.
- They were one part for the expenses of the Government, and state-worship; one part as the endowment of great public servants; one part as reward to persons of high intellectual eminence; and one part for gifts to various religious sects.
- The governments maintained records of good times and bad times like the times of natural or public calamities. The soldiers and smaller officers of the state were paid their salary in cash.

4. **Correct Option: (d)**

Explanation:

- Both statements are correct

Supplementary Notes:

Harshvardhan's Administration:

- The reign of Harsha is historically important because of the visit of the Chinese pilgrim Hiuen Tsang, who left China in AD 629 and travelled all the way to India. After a long stay in India, he returned to China in AD 645.
- He had come to study at the Buddhist university of Nalanda situated in the district of the same name in Bihar and to collect Buddhist texts from India.
- He spent many years in Harsha's court and travelled widely in India. Under his influence Harsha became a great supporter of Buddhism and made generous endowments to it.
- He vividly describes Harsha's court and life in those days, and this account is richer and more reliable than that of Fa-hien, shedding light on the social and economic life as well as the religious sects of the period.
- His account shows that Pataliputra was in a state of decline, as was Vaishali. On the other hand, Prayag and Kanauj in the doab had become important.
- The brahmanas and kshatriyas are reported to have led a simple life, but the nobles and priests led a luxurious life. This indicates differentiation in the ranks of each of the two higher varnas.
- Hiuen Tsang calls the shudras as agriculturists, which is significant. The earlier texts represent them as serving the three higher varnas BUT now they could do agriculture independently.
- He notes the living conditions of the untouchables such as scavengers, and executioners. They lived outside the villages and ate garlic and onion, and when they entered the town, they announced their

entry by shouting loudly so that people might keep away from them.

5. **Correct Option: (d)**

Explanation:

- **Statement 2 is incorrect:** At Nalanda, the Monks were taught Buddhist philosophy of the Mahayana school.
- **Statement 3 is incorrect:** As a devout Buddhist, Harsha convened a grand assembly at Kanauj to widely publicize the doctrines of Mahayana.

Supplementary Notes:

Buddhism and Nalanda during Harsha's Period:

- The Buddhists were divided into eighteen sects during the reign of Harsha. The old centers of Buddhism had fallen on bad days.
- The most famous center was Nalanda, which maintained a great Buddhist university meant for Buddhist monks.
- They were taught Buddhist philosophy of the Mahayana school.
- According to Hiuen Tsang, the monastery at Nalanda was supported from the revenues of 100 villages. I-Tsing raises this number to 200. Nalanda thus had a huge monastic establishment during the reign of Harshavardhana.
- Harsha followed a tolerant religious policy. A Shaiva in his early years, he gradually became a great patron of Buddhism.
- As a devout Buddhist he convened a grand assembly at Kanauj to widely publicize the doctrines of Mahayana. The assembly was attended not only by Hiuen Tsang and the Kamarupa ruler Bhaskaravarman, but also by the kings of twenty states and by several thousand priests belonging to different sects.
- After Kanauj, he held at Prayag a great assembly which was attended by all the tributary princes, ministers, nobles, etc.
- On this occasion, an image of the Buddha was worshipped, and discourses were given by Hiuen Tsang. At the end of it, Harsha made huge donations, and according to a tradition, he gave away everything except his personal clothing.
- Hiuen Tsang speaks of Harsha in glowing terms. The king was kind, courteous, and helpful to him, and the pilgrim was able to visit the various parts of the empire.

6. **Correct Option: (b)**

Explanation:

- **Statement 1 is incorrect:** His administration had become more feudal and decentralized.
- **Trap:** second part of the statement is incorrect.

Supplementary Notes:

Harsha: Administration

- Harsha governed his empire on the same lines as did the Guptas, but his administration had become more feudal and decentralized.
- It is stated that Harsha had 100,000 horses and 60,000 elephants. This appears astonishing because the Mauryas, who ruled over virtually the entire country except the deep south, maintained only 30,000 cavalry and 9,000 elephants.
- Harsha could have had a larger army only if he was in a position to mobilize the support of all his feudatories in the time of war. Evidently, every feudatory contributed his quota of foot soldiers and horses, and thus enormously added to the imperial army. The vast numbers of the imperial army suggests a great increase in population.
- Land grants continued to be made to priests for special services rendered to the state. More importantly, Harsha is credited with the grant of land to the officers by issuing charters. These grants allowed the same concessions to priests as were allowed by the earlier grants. The Chinese pilgrim Hiuen Tsang informs us that Harsha's revenues were divided into four parts. One part was earmarked for the expenditure of the king, a second for scholars, a third for the endowment of officials and public servants, and the fourth for religious purposes. He also tells us that ministers and high officers of the state were endowed with land. The feudal practice of rewarding and paying officers with grants of land seems to have begun under Harsha. This explains why we do not have very many coins issued by this king.

7. **Correct Option: (b)**

Explanation:

- **Statement 1 is incorrect:** The administration under Harsha was feudal and decentralised.
- **Statement 2 is incorrect:** Land grants, not coins, were given to officers as salary.

Supplementary Notes:

Administration under Harsha

- The administration under Harsha was feudal and decentralized.
- The leading feudatories of Harsha were Bhaskaravarmana of Kamarupa, Dhruvabhatta of Vallabhi, Purnavarman of Magadha, and Udita of Jalandhara.
- He had the support of a large army, which was also supplemented by contributory forces from feudatories in the times of need.
- The army consisted of infantry, cavalry, chariots, and elephants. The power shifted to military camps known as skandhavaras.

- Land grants to officers by charters in lieu of their salary were given. This is evident from the lesser number of coins issued by Harsha.
- People were taxed lightly and the revenues were divided into four parts:
  - One part earmarked for the king
  - Second part reserved for scholars
  - Third part for the endowments of officials and public servants
  - Fourth part for religious purposes
- The laws of the land were severe and generally robbery was considered as second only to treason, for which the right hand of robber was amputated.
- Later under the influence of Buddhism, the severity of punishment was mitigated and criminals were punished for life.
- The Brahmanas and Kshatriyas led a simple life, but the nobles and priests led a luxurious life.
- The Shudras were generally agriculturists and their status improved as compared to past. Earlier, they were meant to serve the other three varnas only, but they could now pursue agriculture independently.
- The state of untouchables such as the Chandalas continued to be pathetic and they suffered from all forms of disabilities.
- The forest guards were known as the Vanapalas and the chief of all the villages was an officer called sarva-palli-patti.

8. **Correct Option: (b)**

Explanation:

- **Statement 1 is incorrect:** He was not a staunch Hindu ruler.
- **Statement 2 is incorrect:** His authority was limited to north India excluding Kashmir.

Supplementary Notes:

Harsha's Kingdom

- Harsha is called the last great Hindu emperor of India, but he was neither a staunch Hindu nor the ruler of the whole country.
- His authority was limited to north India excluding Kashmir. Rajasthan, Punjab, UP, Bihar, and Orissa were under his direct control, but his sphere of influence spread over a much wider area.
- It appears that the peripheral states acknowledged his sovereignty. In eastern India he faced opposition from the Shaivite king Shashanka of Gauda, who felled the Bodhi tree at Bodh Gaya. However, Shashanka's death in AD 619 put an end to this hostility.
- Harsha's southward march was stopped at the Narmada River by the Chalukya king Pulakeshin, who ruled over a great part of modern Karnataka and Maharashtra with his capital at Badami in the modern Bijapur district of Karnataka.
- Apart from this, Harsha did not face any serious opposition and succeeded in giving a measure of political unity to a large part of India.

9. **Correct Option: (a)**

Explanation:

- Option (a) is correct

Supplementary Notes:

Harsha and His Times

- The early history of Harsha's reign is reconstructed from a study by Banabhatta, who was his court poet and who wrote a book called Harshacharita.
- This can be supplemented by the account of the Chinese pilgrim Hiuen Tsang, who visited India in the seventh century and stayed in the country for about fifteen years.
- Harsha's inscriptions speak of various types of taxes and officials.

10. **Correct Option: (b)**

Explanation:

- **Statement 2 is incorrect:** The Pallava king Narasimhavarman occupied the Chalukya capital at Vatapi in about AD 642, when Pulakesin II was probably killed in a battle against the Pallavas. Narasimhavarman assumed the title of Vatapikonda or the conqueror of Vatapi.

Supplementary Notes:

Pulakeshin II

- The first important event in long conflict between the Pallavas and the Chalukyas took place during the reign of Pulakeshin II (AD 609–42), the most famous Chalukya king.
- He subjugated the Kadamba capital at Banavasi and compelled the Gangas of Mysore to acknowledge his suzerainty. He also defeated Harsha's army on the Narmada and checked his advance towards the Deccan.
- In his conflict with the Pallavas, he almost reached the Pallava capital, but the Pallavas purchased peace by ceding their northern provinces to Pulakeshin II. Around AD 610 Pulakeshin II also conquered the entire area between the Krishna and the Godavari, which came to be known as the province of Vengi.
- Here, a branch of the main dynasty was set up and is known as the eastern Chalukyas of Vengi. However,

Pulakeshin's second invasion of Pallava territory ended in failure. The Pallava king Narasimhavarman (AD 630–68) occupied the Chalukya capital at Vatapi in about AD 642, when Pulakesin II was probably killed in a battle against the Pallavas.

- Narasimhavarman assumed the title of 'Vatapikonda' or the conqueror of Vatapi. He is also said to have defeated the Cholas, the Cheras, the Pandyas, and the Kalabhras.

CONCEPT REVISION

Here is the list of concepts that have been covered as part of the previous exercise. Revise and self-reflect on your concepts you covered.

- Pushyabhutis Dynasty ☐
- Administration under Harsha ☐
- Hiuen Tsang ☐
- Pulakeshin II ☐

1.9 SANGAM PERIOD

QUESTIONS

1. Which one of the following is considered as the Bible of Sangam literature?

(a) Tolkappiyam (b) Maduraikanji
(c) Thirukkural (d) Palamoli

2. Consider the following statement about the 'Sangam Economy':

1. The most important feature of the Sangam economy was flourishing trade with Romans.
2. Discovery of the monsoons and the use of a direct sea route between Indian coasts and the western world as well as south-east Asia was the main reason for the growth of trade.
3. The Chola king Karikala of the Sangam age is credited with constructing a dam on the river Kaveri.
4. Rice was the most important crop that formed the staple food as well as medium of barter exchange for inland trade

Which of the above statement/s is/are correct?

(a) 1 and 2 only (b) 1 and 3 only
(c) 3 and 4 only (d) 1, 2, 3 and 4

3. Consider the following statements regarding Kalabhra Revolt:

1. The revolt was directed against the existing social and political order in south India.
2. They captured power at the cost of the Cholas.
3. They were supressed through the joint efforts of the Pandyas, the Pallavas, and the Chalukyas.

Select the correct answer using the code given below:

(a) 1 and 2 only (b) 2 and 3 only
(c) 1 and 3 only (d) 1, 2 and 3

4. Match the following listed items with respect to Sangam Literature:

List I	List II
A. Arasar	1. Love story of Kovalan and a courtesan Madhavi of Kaveripattanam
B. Melkannakku	2. Ruling class
C. Tirukkural	3. Eighteen Major Works of Sangam Literature
D. Silappadikaram	4. Tamil text deals with philosophy and wise maxims

Select the correct answer using the code given below:

	A	B	C	D
(a)	2	3	4	1
(b)	3	4	1	2
(c)	4	3	2	1
(d)	3	2	1	4

5. Consider the following statements regarding Sangam Age of south India:

1. The Cholas are first mentioned by Megasthenes in his Indica
2. Chola king conquered Sri Lanka and ruled it over for nearly 50 years.
3. Cheras traded with the Romans.

Which of the above statements is/are correct?

(a) 1 and 2 only (b) 2 and 3 only
(c) 1 and 3 only (d) 1, 2 and 3

SOLUTIONS

1. Correct Option: (c)

Supplementary Notes:

Thirukkural

- The Tirukkural or Thirukkural, or shortly the Kural, is a Classic Tamil text consisting of 1330 couplets or kurals, dealing with the everyday virtues of an individual. Considered one of the greatest works ever written on ethics and morality, chiefly secular ethics, it is known for its universality and non-denominational nature. It was authored by Valluvar, also known in full as Thiruvalluvar. The text has been dated variously from 300 BCE to 7th century CE. The traditional accounts describe it as the last work of the third Sangam, but linguistic analysis suggests a later date of 450-500 CE. Its theme is ethics and moral values of the said period. It is also called Bible of Sangam Literature.

2. **Correct Option: (d)**

Explanation:

- All statements are correct

Supplementary Notes:

Economy of Sangam Period

- The people were engaged in various economic activities such as agriculture, crafts, and trade. Rice was the most important crop. It formed the main part of peoples' diet and also served as a medium of barter exchange for inland trade.
- The most important feature of the Sangam economy was flourishing trade with the Roman world. The best account of Indo-Roman trade is given in the book called the Periplus of the Erythrean Sea, which was written in the first century CE by an anonymous author.
- Major items of export to the Romans were the Indian products such as spices (included yavanapriya or pepper), perfumes, jewels, ivory and fine textiles (muslin especially), several precious and semi-precious stones like diamond, carnelian, turquoise, agate, sapphire, and so on, besides pearls, indigo, sandalwood, iron and steel cutlery. Against this import, Romans exported gold and silver to India.
- After the discovery of the monsoons by Hippatus, a Greek navigator, in 45 CE, more and more sea voyages were used for trading purposes. The discovery of the monsoons and the use of a direct sea route between Indian coasts and the western world as well as south-east Asia was the main reason for the growth of trade.
- The Chola king Karikala of the Sangam age is credited with constructing a dam on the river Kaveri. It is considered to be the earliest dam in the country.

3. **Correct Option: (d)**

Explanation:

- All statements are correct.

Supplementary Notes:

The Kalabhra Revolt

- It is one of the important revolt of the sixth century. The Kalabhras seem to have been a tribal people who captured power, particularly at the cost of the Cholas, and ruled for seventy five years.
- Their rule also affected the Pallavas as well as their neighbouring contemporaries.
- The Kalabhras are called evil rulers, who overthrew innumerable kings and established their hold on the Tamil land. The Kalabhra revolt was a powerful peasant protest directed against the landed Brahmanas.
- They put an end to the brahmadeya rights granted to the Brahmanas in numerous villages.
- It appears that the Kalabhras were of Buddhist persuasion as they patronized Buddhist monasteries.
- The Kalabhras' revolt was so widespread that it was be quelled only through the joint efforts of the Pandyas, the Pallavas, and the Chalukyas of Badami.
- By the last quarter of the sixth century, according to a tradition, the Kalabhras had imprisoned the Chola, the Pandya, and the Chera kings, which underlines how formidable their revolt was.
- The confederacy of the kings formed against the Kalabhras, who had revoked the land grants made to the brahmanas, shows that the revolt was directed against the existing social and political order in south India.

4. **Correct Option: (a)**

List I	List II
A. Arasar	2. Ruling class
B. Melkannakku	3. Eighteen Major Works of Sangam Literature
C. Tirukkural	4. Tamil text deals with philosophy and wise maxims
D. Silappadikaram	1. Love story of Kovalan and a courtesan Madhavi of Kaveripattanam

Supplementary Notes:

Tamil Societal Setup

- The Brahmanas first appear in the Tamil land in the Sangam age.
- The Tamil Brahmanas partook of meat and wine. The kshatriyas and vaishyas appear as regular varnas in the Sangam texts.
- The warrior class was an important element in the polity and society. The captains of the army were invested with the title of "Enadi" at a formal ceremony.
- Civil and military offices were held under both the Cholas and Pandyas by "Vellalas" or rich peasants.
- The ruling class was called "Arasar", and its members had marriage relations with the vellalas, who formed the fourth caste.
- Agricultural operations were generally the task of members of the lowest class or "Kadaisiyar".

Tamil Language and Sangam Literature

- Sangam was a college or assembly of Tamil poets held probably under the patronage of the chiefs or kings.
- The available Sangam literature, which was produced by these assemblies, was compiled in AD 300–600.
- The Sangam literature can roughly be divided into two groups, narrative and didactic.
  - The narrative texts are called "Melkannakku" or Eighteen Major Works. They comprise eighteen major works consisting of eight anthologies and ten idylls.
  - The didactic works are called "Kilkanakku" or Eighteen Minor Works.
- Besides the Sangam texts, we have a text called Tolkkappiyam, which deals with grammar and poetics.
- Another important Tamil text deals with philosophy and wise maxims and is called Tirukkural.
- The other important twin Tamil epics are Silappadikaram and Manimekalai. The two were composed around the sixth century.
  - The first is considered to be the brightest gem of early Tamil literature. It deals with a love story in which a dignitary called Kovalan prefers a courtesan called Madhavi of Kaveripattanam to his wedded wife Kannagi from a noble family.
  - The other epic, Manimekalai, was written by a grain merchant of Madurai. It deals with the adventures of the daughter born of the union of Kovalan and Madhavi. However, this epic is of greater religious than literary interest.

5. **Correct Option: (b)**

Explanation:

- **Statement 1 is incorrect:** The Pandyas are first mentioned by Megasthenes in his Indica.

Sangam Age of South India

- The Pandya territory occupied the southern-most and the south-eastern portion of the Indian peninsula. The Pandyas are first mentioned by Megasthenes in his Indica, wherein he refers to a Pandya Kingdom famous for pearls and ruled by a woman (which may suggest some matriarchal influence in the Pandya society).
- **Cholas:** The Chola kingdom (which in early medieval times was also known as Cholamandalam/ Coromandel) was situated to the north-east of the territory of the Pandyas and between the Pennar and the Velar rivers. Their chief centre of political power and capital Uraiyur was famous for cotton trade. They also maintained an efficient navy. It also appears that in the middle of 2nd century BCE, a Chola king named Elara conquered Sri Lanka and ruled it over for nearly 50 years. The Cholas were also rich and prosperous and the main source of their wealth was their trade in cotton cloth.
- The Cheras were situated to the west and north of the Pandyas. It was an important and prosperous kingdom owing to its trade with the Romans.

CONCEPT REVISION

Here is the list of concepts that have been covered as part of the previous exercise. Revise and self-reflect on your concepts you covered.

- Bible of Sangam Literature ☐
- Sangam Economy ☐
- Kalabhra Revolt ☐
- Sangam Literature ☐

☐☐☐

2. ECONOMIC CONDITIONS OF ANCIENT INDIA

2.1 STONE AGE

QUESTIONS

1. **Which of the following are the traits linked to Aryan culture?**
   1. Use of horse-drawn chariots
   2. Practice of pit dwelling
   3. Practice of cremating the dead
   4. Horse sacrifice

   Select the correct answer using the code given below:
   (a) 1 only (b) 2 and 3 only
   (c) 1, 2 and 3 only (d) 1, 2, 3 and 4

2. **Consider the following statements:**
   1. The Harappan Civilisation marked the beginning of the second urbanisation in India.
   2. Harappan people did not practice ploughing as iron was unknown to them.
   3. Animals depicted on the famous Pashupati seals excavated at Harappa are a rhino, a buffalo, an elephant and a tiger.

   Which of the above statements is/are incorrect?
   (a) 1 and 2 only (b) 2 only
   (c) 2 and 3 only (d) 1, 2 and 3

3. **Consider the following statements regarding Indus Valley Civilisation:**
   1. The people of this civilisation were the earliest people to produce cotton.
   2. The Indus Valley cities and towns had a rectangular grid pattern.

   Which of the above statements is/are correct?
   (a) 1 only (b) 2 only
   (c) Both 1 and 2 (d) Neither 1 nor 2

4. **Which of the following pairs related to period and occupation is/are correctly matched?**
   1. Old Stone Age - gathering food and hunting.
   2. New stone age - rearing of animals.
   3. Copper age - subsistence agriculture.

   Select the correct answer using the code given below:
   (a) 1 only (b) 1 and 3 only
   (c) 1 and 2 only (d) 1, 2 and 3

5. **Which of the following places in India where the Old Stone Age tools were found has been correctly matched?**
   1. Madhya Pradesh - Son River Bank
   2. Gujarat - Luni Valley
   3. Tamil Nadu –Kancheepuram

   Select the correct answer using the code given below:
   (a) 1 only (b) 1 and 2 only
   (c) 1 and 3 only (d) 1, 2 and 3

6. **Which of the following are sites of Mesolithic Period ?**
1. Langhnaj in Gujarat
2. Bhimbetka and Adamgarh in Madhya Pradesh
3. Bagor in Rajasthan

Select the correct answer using the code given below:
(a) 2 only (b) 1 and 3 only
(c) 1, 2 and 3 (d) 2 and 3 only

7. **Match the following pairs:**

Pre-Historic Age	Characteristics
A. Palaeolithic Age	i. Copper
B. Neolithic Age	ii. Discovery of Fire
C. Chalcolithic Age	iii. Microliths
D. Mesolithic Age	iv. Tools for harvesting crops

Select the correct answer using the code given below:
(a) A-i, B-iii, C-iv, D-ii
(b) A-iii, B-i, C-iv, D-ii
(c) A-ii, B-iv, C-i, D-iii
(d) A-iv, B-iii, C-i, D-ii

8. **Which was the first metal used by man?**
(a) Copper (b) Silver
(c) Bronze (d) Iron

9. **With which of the following periods do we associate the 'Microlith' implements?**
(a) Palaeolithic (b) Chalcolithic
(c) Neolithic (d) Mesolithic

10. **Match the following pairs:**

Sites	Age
A. Ahar and Gilund	i. Chalcolithic
B. Mohenjodaro	ii. Harappa
C. Burzahom	iii. Neolithic
D. Bagor	iv. Mesolithic

Select the correct answer using the code given below:
(a) A-i, B-iii, C-ii, D-iv
(b) A-iii, B-i, C-iv, D-ii
(c) A-i, B-ii, C-iii, D-iv
(d) A-iv, B-iii, C-i, D-ii

11. **Consider the following statements regarding Mesolithic age:**
1. During this period, stone tools called microliths are found in abundance.
2. Domestication of animals and plants was seen for the first time.
3. Climate became colder and dry due to major climate change

Which of the above statements is/are correct?
(a) 1 only (b) 1 and 2 only
(c) 2 and 3 only (d) 1, 2 and 3

12. **Which of the following statement is correct regarding the Neolithic Period?**
(a) The people during this period were predominantly hunters and gatherers.
(b) Domestication of animals was not known during this period.
(c) Pottery was not known to the people during this period.
(d) The period is significant for its megalithic architecture.

13. **Which of the following statements regarding the religious practices of Indus Valley Civilisation is/are correct?**
1. The people had faith in amulets and charms.
2. There was an absence of the worship of the mother goddess.

Select the correct answer using the code given below:
(a) 1 only (b) 2 only
(c) Both 1 and 2 (d) Neither 1 nor 2

14. **Consider the following statements about the religious practices of Indus Valley Civilisation:**
1. Indus people worshipped gods in the forms of trees and animals.
2. People believed in evil forces and used amulets as protection against them.
3. Pashupati was represented on seals as sitting in a yogic posture.

Which of the above statements are correct?
(a) 1 and 2 only (b) 2 and 3 only
(c) 1 and 3 only (d) 1, 2 and 3

15. **Consider the following statements regarding the food habits of Indus Valley Civilisation**
1. Indus Valley Civilisation (IVC) people were vegetarians only.
2. IVC people only consumed Dairy Products for protein needs.
3. There is no evidence of Rice consumption by IVC.

Which of the above statements is/are incorrect?
(a) 1 and 2 only (b) 1 and 3 only
(c) 1, 2 and 3 (d) None of the above

16. **Consider the following statement regarding the burial methods prominent among the Harappans:**

Sites		Stage
1. Mohenjodaro	-	Complete burial and post-cremation burial
2. Harappa	-	The practice of pot burial
3. Lothal	-	Wooden coffins were found here

Select the correct answer using the code given below:
(a) 1 only (b) 3 only
(c) 1 and 2 only (d) 1, 2 and 3

17. **Consider the following statements regarding religious beliefs of Harappan people:**
1. The chief male and female deities were Pasupati and mother goddess represented in figurines respectively.

2. Nature worship was prominent among Harappans.

Which of the above statements is/are correct?

(a) 1 only (b) 2 only
(c) Both 1 and 2 (d) Neither 1 nor 2

18. Which of the following is correct about Indus Valley Civilisation?

1. The cities were planned
2. Non-standardized weights were used
3. There was elaborate water drainage system

Select the correct answer using the code given below:

(a) 1 only (b) 2 only
(c) 1 and 3 only (d) 3 only

19. Which of the following deity was not worshipped in Indus Valley Civilisation?

(a) Vishnu (b) Peepal tree
(c) Pashupati (d) Mother goddess

SOLUTIONS

1. Correct Option: (d)

Explanation:

- All statements are correct

Supplementary Notes:

Aryan Culture

- **Texts for Traits of Aryan Culture:** The principal traits of Aryan culture are set out by Vedic, Iranian, and Greek literary texts and cognate terms found in the proto-Indo-European languages. The Rig Veda is assigned to roughly 1500 BC, although the later additions might be as late as 1000 BC. The earliest parts of the Zend-Avesta are roughly attributed to 1400 BC.
- **The Horse, its Domestication and Diffusion:** The horse is regarded as an indispensable trait of the Aryan culture, for it plays a crucial role in the life of the early Indo-Europeans. In its various forms, the term asva (horse) occurs 215 times in the Rig Veda; no other animal is mentioned so frequently. The Indo-Europeans widely used horse-drawn chariots. Aryans succeeded everywhere because they possessed chariot driven by horses & possibly with coats of mail & better armory. They also introduced these things for the 1st time in West Asia & India.
- Pit-dwelling can also be associated with the Aryan culture, and may have originated in cold conditions. The practice of pit-dwelling prevailed in Burzahom near Srinagar in Kashmir and also in Haryana. This may be due to the Central Asian influence on the borders of Kashmir.
- Cremation developed as an Aryan trait. Its practice is supported by the Vedic, Avestan, and Homeric texts.
- Animal sacrifice was an important Aryan ritual. However, given its almost universal practice among pastoral tribal people, it is difficult to make much of it. Animal sacrifice may have prevailed among many tribal peoples, but the horse sacrifice was typical of the Indo-Europeans, particularly of the Vedic people.
- Though two hymns are devoted to the horse sacrifice in the tenth book of the Rig Veda, the later Vedic texts transform the sacrifice into asvamedha. Animals may have been sacrificed in pre-Vedic times in the subcontinent, but despite cut marks found on the bones, it cannot be said that the horses were killed for religious purposes.

2. Correct Option: (a)

Explanation:

- **Statement 1 is incorrect:** The Harappan Civilisation marked the beginning of first urbanisation in India.
- **Statement 2 is incorrect:** Harappans probably used wooden ploughs drawn by oxen or camel.

Supplementary Notes:

Harappan Civilisation

- Agriculture
  - Agriculture was generally practiced along the river banks most of which were flooded during the summer and monsoons.
  - The granaries at some Harappan cities clearly suggest that cereals were produced in such large quantities that not only were all the immediate needs of people duly met with, but there was also enough reserve to face any future emergency.
  - The principal cereals seem to have been wheat and barley. Rice, though known, was a favored grain. Six varieties of millets including ragi, kodon, sanwa, and jowar were cultivated, as also peas and beans.
  - No hoe or ploughshare has been discovered, but the furrows discovered in the pre-Harappan phase at Kalibangan indicate that the fields were ploughed in Rajasthan during the Harappan period. The Harappans probably used the wooden plough drawn by oxen, and camels may also have been used for this purpose.
  - Gabarbands or nalas enclosed by dams for storing water were a feature in parts of Baluchistan and Afghanistan, but channel or canal irrigation was probably not practiced.
- Domestication of animals
  - Although the Harappans practiced agriculture, animals were raised on a large scale. Oxen, buffaloes, goats, sheep, and pigs were domesticated. Humped bulls were favored by the Harappans.
  - Evidence of the horse comes from a superficial level of Mohenjodaro and from a doubtful

terracotta figurine from Lothal. The remains of a horse are reported from Surkotada, situated in West Gujarat, and relate to around 2000 BC but the identity is doubtful. In any case, the Harappan culture was not horse-centered.

- Pashupati seal discovered at Mohenjo-daro, shows a seated figure of a Yogi, probably Shiva Pashupati, surrounded by four animals – a rhino, a buffalo, an elephant and a tiger. This seal may throw light on the religion of the Harappan age. Most of these seals have a knob at the back through which runs a hole and it is believed that they were used by different guilds or merchants and traders for stamping purposes. When not in use they could be worn round the neck or the arm like an amulet.

- Technology and Crafts
  - The rise of towns in the Indus zone was based on agricultural surplus, the making of bronze tools, various other crafts, and widespread trade and commerce. This is known as the first urbanisation in India, and the Harappan urban culture belongs to the Bronze Age.
  - The people of Harappa used many tools and implements of stone, but they were very well acquainted with the manufacture and use of bronze.
  - The bronze tools and weapons recovered from the Harappan sites contain a smaller percentage of tin.

3. Correct Option: (c)

Explanation:

- Both statements are correct

Supplementary Notes:

Indus Valley Civilisation

- The cities of the civilisation were planned in grid patterns with streets crossing at right angles.
- The use of burnt bricks in the Harappan cities is remarkable, because in the contemporary buildings of Egypt, mainly dried bricks were used.
- The drainage system of Mohenjodaro was very impressive.
- In almost all cities every big or small house had its own courtyard and bathroom.
- The earliest traces of cotton in the world were found here. The earliest evidence for the use of cotton was found in Mehrgarh dating back to the sixth millennium BC Most Harappan sites are located in semi-arid lands, where irrigation was probably required for agriculture.
- Traces of canals have been found at the Harappan site of Shortughai in Afghanistan, but not in Punjab or Sindh.
- Although the Harappans practised agriculture, animals were also reared on a large scale.

4. Correct Option: (d)

Explanation:

- All statements are correct

Supplementary Notes:

Pre-Historic India

- In the Old Stone Age, food was obtained by hunting animals and gathering edible plants and tubers. Therefore, these people are called as hunter-gatherers.
- The chief characteristic features of the Neolithic culture are the practice of agriculture, domestication of animals and animal rearing, polishing of stone tools and the manufacture of pottery.
- The Neolithic period is followed by Chalcolithic (copper-stone) period when copper and bronze came to be used. The new technology of smelting metal ore and crafting metal artifacts is an important development in human civilisation and they practised subsistence agriculture.

5. Correct Option: (c)

Explanation:

- **Statement 2 is incorrect:** Luni Valley is located in Rajasthan not Gujarat.

Supplementary Notes:

Old Stone Age

- Places in India where the Old Stone Age tools were found:
  - Madhya Pradesh-Son River bank, Bhimbetka, and Mageshwa.
  - Rajasthan-Luni Valley.
  - Karnataka-Pagalkhat.
  - Andhra Pradesh-Karnool caves, Renigunta.
  - Tamil Nadu-Vadamadurai, Athirambakkam, Pallavaram, Kancheepuram, Vellur, and Thiruvallur.
- Luni Valley is located in Rajasthan not Gujarat.

6. Correct Option: (c)

Explanation:

- All statements are correct

Supplementary Notes:

- Some of the important Mesolithic sites or the various sites of the Mesolithic period were located in:
- Langhnaj in Gujarat,
- Bagor in Rajasthan,
- Sarai Nahar Rai, Chopani Mando, Mahdaha, and Damdama in Uttar Pradesh,

- Bhimbetka and Adamgarh in Madhya Pradesh,
- Orissa,
- Kerala, and
- Andhra Pradesh

7. **Correct Option: (c)**

Supplementary Notes:

Pre-Historic Period

Pre Historic Age	Characteristics
A. Palaeolithic Age	ii. Discovery of Fire
B. Neolithic Age	iv. Tools for harvesting crops
C. Chalcolithic Age	i. Copper
D. Mesolithic Age	iii. Microliths

8. **Correct Option: (a)**

Explanation:

Chalcolithic Age

- **Option (a) is correct:** Chalcolithic period saw the use of the metals among which the Copper was first. It is called Chalcolithic which means use of stone and well as copper was prevalent in this period. The earliest settlements of the Chalcolithic period range from the Gangetic basin to Chhotanagpur Plateau.
- The economy of this period was based upon agriculture, stock raising, hunting and fishing.
- Limited number of Copper and bronze tools have also been recovered.
- The presence of painted pottery is a hallmark of the Chalcolithic period.
- The burial practice was another striking feature and the dead were buried in a particular direction all over a particular area.
- The largest site of the Chalcolithic period is Daima situated on the left bank of the Pravara River.
- The pottery ranges from red ware, deep red ware to deep brown and black, Pictographic red and black and polished red.

9. **Correct Option: (d)**

Supplementary Notes:

Mesolithic Age

- The Mesolithic tools smaller in size and better in finishing (more geometric) than the Palaeolithic age and are called Microliths. These microliths are tiny tools of one to five centimetres length, made by blunting one or more sides with steep retouch.
- The main tool types are backed blades, obliquely truncated blades, points, crescents, triangles and trapezes. Some of the microliths were used as components of spearheads, arrowheads, knives, sickles, harpoons and daggers. They were fitted into grooves in bone, wood and reed shafts and joined together by natural adhesives like gum and resin. Use of bow and arrows for hunting has been documented by Mesolithic man in rock art of that period. The bored stones, which had already appeared during the upper Palaeolithic, became common during this, and the Neolithic and Chalcolithic Periods. These are believed to have been used as weights in digging sticks and as net sinkers. Similarly, shallow querns and grinding stones also occur at several sites. These new technological elements led to enhanced efficiency in hunting, collecting and processing of wild plant foods.

10. **Correct Option: (c)**

Pre-Historic Sites

Supplementary Notes:

Sites	Age
A. Ahar and Gilund	i. Chalcolithic
B. Mohenjodaro	ii. Harappa
C. Burzahom	iii. Neolithic
D. Bagor	iv. Mesolithic

Important Mesolithic Sites

- In Rajasthan, Bagor is almost largest Mesolithic site in India.
- Other major Mesolithic sites in Rajasthan are Tilwara, Pachpadra basin and Sojat Area etc.
- In Guajarat, mesolithic sites include those on banks of river Sabarmati as such as Akhaj, Valsana, Hirpur and Langhanj.
- In Uttar Pradesh, Sarai Nahar Rai, Morhana Pahar and Lekkahia are important Mesolithic sites.
- In Madhya Pradesh, Bhimbetka along with Adamgarh, Chaturbhujnath Nala are major Mesolithic sites.
- In Jharkhand Chhotanagpur Plateau is a major Mesolithic site in India.
- In Odisha, Mayurbhanj, Keonjhar, Sundergarh are major mesolithic sites.
- In South India, Mesolithic sites are abundant in Karnataka, Tamil Nadu and Andhra Pradesh.

Important Neolithic Sites

- Mehrgarh, Baluchistan, Pakistan
- Burzahom (the place of birch), Kashmir
- Gufkral, Kashmir
- Chirand, Bihar
- Pikilihal, Brahmagiri, Maski, Hallur, Takkalakota, T. Narsipur, Kodekal, Sanganakallu, Karnataka
- Paiyampalli, Tamil Nadu
- Utnur, Andhra Pradesh
- **Indus Valley Civilisation Sites**
- So far nearly 1000 sites of nearly, mature and late phases of the Indus Civilisation are known in the sub-continent. But the number of the sites belonging

to the mature phase is limited, and of them only half a dozen like Mohenjo-daro, Harappa, Kalibangan, Lothal, Chanhu-daro and Banwali can be regarded as cities. Other sites include Kot-Diji, Amri, Surkotada, Sutkagendor, Ropar, Rangpur, Alamgirpur, Ali Murad, Dholavira.

Some Chalcolithic Cultures

- **Ahara Culture:** The sites of Ahara Culture were Aahar (Rajasthan), Balathal, Gilund etc. The distinctive feature is black and red ware.
- **Kayatha Culture:** Located in Chambal and its tributaries, the sturdy red slipped ware with chocolate designs is main feature.
- **Malwa Culture:** Narmada & its tributaries in Gujarat. One of the largest Chalcolithic settlements.
- **Svalda Culture:** The well-known sites are in Dhulia district of Maharashtra.
- **Prabhas & Rangpur Culture:** Both of them are derived from the Harappa Culture. The polished red ware is the hallmark of this culture.

11. Correct Option: (b)

Explanation:

- Statement 3 is incorrect: Climate became warmer not colder

Supplementary Notes:

Mesolithic Period (Late Stone Age)

- The Upper Palaeolithic Age came to an end with the end of the Ice Age around 8000 BC, and the climate became warm and dry.
- Climate change bought about changes in fauna and flora and made it possible for human beings to move to new areas. Since then there have not been any major changes in climatic conditions.
- From 8000 BC began an intermediate stage in stone age culture, which is called the Mesolithic Age.
- It intervened as a transitional phase between the Palaeolithic Age and the Neolithic or New Stone Age, and is also called the Late Stone Age.
- In the case of India it started about 8000 BC and continued up to about 4090 BC.
- Rainfall increased and so more availability of flora and fauna.
- Domestication of animals and plants was seen for the first time.
- First animal to be domesticated was the wild ancestor of the dog.
- Sheep and goats were the most common domesticated animals.
- Hunting and food gathering continued.
- First human colonisation of the Ganga plains.
- Microliths have been excavated.They are small stone tools that were probably stuck to stones to be used as saws and sickles.
- Tools used were blades, crescents, triangles, trapezes, spearheads, knives, arrowheads, sickles, harpoons and daggers.

Major sites:

- Brahmagiri (Mysore)
- Narmada
- Vindhya
- Gujarat
- UP
- Sojat,Pali (Rajasthan)
- Bhimbetka
- Godavari Basin

12. Correct Option: (d)

Supplementary Notes:

Neolithic Period

- The Neolithic Age saw the man turning into food producer from food gatherer. It also witnessed the use of pottery for the first time. People used microlithic blades in addition to tools made of polished stone. The use of metal was unknown.
- **Agriculture:** The people of Neolithic Age cultivated ragi, horse gram, cotton, rice, wheat, and barley and hence were termed as food producers. They domesticated cattle, sheep, and goats. Agriculture and animal domestication were the main economic activity of early Neolithic cultures.
- **Tools:** The people used microlithic blades in addition to tools made of polished stones. They used stone hoes and digging sticks for digging the ground. They also used tools and weapons made of bone; found in Burzahom (Kashmir) and Chirand (Bihar).
- **Weapons:** The people primarily used axes as weapons. The north-western part of Neolithic settlement used rectangular axes having curved cutting edge. The Southern part used axes with oval sides and pointed butt while polished stone axes with rectangular butt and shouldered hoes used in the north-eastern part.
- **Housing:** The people of the Neolithic Age lived in rectangular or circular houses were which were made of mud and reed. The people of Mehrgarh lived in mud-brick houses, while pit-dwelling is reported from Burzahom, the Neolithic site found in Kashmir.
- **Pottery:** Pottery first appeared in the Neolithic Age. The pottery of the period was classified under grey ware, black-burnished ware, and mat-impressed ware.
- **Architecture:** The Neolithic Age is significant for its Megalithic Architecture.

- **Technology:** In the initial stage of the Neolithic Age, hand-made pottery was made but later on the foot-wheels were used to make pots.
- **Community Life:** Neolithic people had common rights over the property. They led a settled life.

13. Correct Option: (a)

Explanation:

- **Statement 2 is incorrect:** The people in this civilisation worshipped mother goddess.

Supplementary Notes:

Indus Valley Civilisation

- The religion of the Indus people comprised:
  - The worship of the Mother Goddess
  - The worship of a male deity, probably of Siva
  - Worship of animals, natural, semi-human, or fabulous.
- The most common depiction of the seal is a unicorn, which is perhaps mythical. Thirdly, there are the natural animals, such as the water buffalo, the gaur or Indian bison, the Indian humped bull or zebu, the rhinoceros, a short-horned humpless bull the tiger, and the Indian elephant.
- Worship of trees in their natural state or their indwelling spirits; worship of inanimate stones or other objects, of linga and yoni symbol chrematheism as illustrated in the worship of the sacred "incense-burners".
- Faith in amulets and charms indicative of demonophobia: and practice of yoga: A large number of terracotta figurines depict the individuals in various yogic postures (asanas) indicating thereby that the Harappans practiced yoga.
- A striking oblong sealing found at Harappa represents the Earth or Mother Goddess, with a plant growing from her womb. Also depicted are a man with a knife in hand and a woman with raised hands. A male deity, "the prototype of the historic Siva," is portrayed on a seal with three faces, seated on a low throne in the typical posture of a Yogi. The depiction shows Siva as Pasupati. There is also the last characteristic of the historic Siva in this figure, a pair of horns crowning his head with a central bump that appears like the trisula or trident of the Saivas.
- Evidence of animal worship is also found in the animals represented on seals and sealings, or in terracotta, faience, and stone figurines.

14. Correct Option: (d)

Explanation:

- All statements are correct

Supplementary Notes:

- There are generally two aspects of religion: one conceptual or philosophical, and the other, practical or ritualistic. The former is enshrined in metaphysical texts while the latter is reflected in the material remains.
- Religion of the Indus people comprised:
  - The worship of the Mother Goddess;
  - The worship of a male deity, probably of Siva;
  - Worship of animals, natural, semi human, or fabulous;
  - The most common depiction on seal is unicorn, which is perhaps mythical. Thirdly, there are the natural animals, such as (i) the water buffalo, (ii) the gaur or Indian bison, (iii) the Indian humped bull or zebu, (iv) the rhinoceros, (v) a short-horned humpless bull (vi) the tiger, and (vii) the Indian elephant;
  - Worship of trees in their natural state or of their indwelling spirits;
  - Worship of inanimate stones or other objects, of linga and yoni symbol;
  - Chrematheism as illustrated in the worship of the sacred "incense-burners";
  - Faith in amulets and charms indicative of demonophobia; and
  - Practice of yoga: A large number of terracotta figurines depict the individuals in various yogic postures (asanas) indicating thereby that the Harappans practised yoga.
- A striking oblong sealing found at Harappa represents the Earth or Mother Goddess, with a plant growing from her womb. Also depicted are a man with a knife in hand, and a woman with raised hands. A male deity, "the prototype of the historic Siva," is portrayed on a seal with three faces, seated on a low throne in the typical posture of a Yogi. The depiction shows Siva as Pasupati. There is also the last characteristic of the historic Siva in this figure, a pair of horns crowning his head with a central bump which appears like the trisula or trident of the Saivas.
- Evidence of animal worship is also found in the animals represented on seals and sealings, or in terracotta, faience, and stone figurines.

15. Correct Option: (c)

Explanation:

- **Statement (1) is incorrect:** A new findings about the Harappan Civilisation states that IVC people are dependent on a variety of meat.
- **Statement (2) is** incorrect: IVC people only consumed Dairy Products and meat both for protein needs.
- **Statement (3) is** incorrect: IVC People ate variety of food from pulses, wheat, rice, millet.

Supplementary Notes:

- Recently new findings about Harappan Civilisation states that IVC people were dependent on a variety of meat for their consumption.

- IVC People ate variety of food from pulses, wheat, rice, millet, meat (variety of meats like buffalo, goat, pig).
- They were pastoral people dependent on dairy products.

16. Correct Option: (a)

Supplementary Notes:

- The cemeteries discovered around the cities like Mohenjodaro, Harappa, Kalibangan, Lothal and Ropar throw light on the burial practices of the Harappans. Complete burial and post-cremation burial were popular at Mohenjodaro. At Lothal the burial pit was lined with burnt bricks indicating the use of coffins. Wooden coffins are found at Harappa. The practice of pot burials is found at Lothal sometimes with pairs of skeletons.

17. Correct Option: (c)

Explanation:

- Both statements are correct

Supplementary Notes:

- The seals, terracotta figurines and copper tablets give an idea on the religious life of the Harappans. The chief male deity was Pasupati (proto-Siva) represented in seals as sitting in a yogic posture with three faces and two horns. He is surrounded by four animals (elephant, tiger, rhino, and buffalo each facing a different direction). Two deers appear on his feet. The chief female deity was the Mother Goddess represented in terracotta figurines. In latter times, Linga worship was prevalent. Trees and animals (Nature) were also worshipped by the Harappans. They believed in ghosts and evil forces and used amulets as protection against them.

18. Correct Option: (c)

Explanation:

- **Statements 2 is incorrect:** Indus Valley Civilisation is known for its city planning, extensive drainage system, grid pattern of settlements, sophisticated system of waste disposal, etc. Besides, standard weights are seen to have been used throughout the region. The weights that have been recovered have shown a remarkable accuracy.

Supplementary Notes:

- Indus Valley Civilisation is known for its city planning, extensive drainage system, grid pattern of settlements, sophisticated system of waste disposal, etc. Besides, standard weights are seen to have been used throughout the region. The weights that have been recovered have shown a remarkable accuracy.

19. Correct Option: (a)

Explanation:

- Option (a) is correct

Supplementary Notes:

- Archaeological evidences from Indus Valley Civilisation such as seals and figurines suggest that people worshipped Peepal tree, Neem tree, Pashupati, Mother Goddess, animals like bull and buffalo. Evidence of worshipping of Vishnu has not been found.

CONCEPT REVISION

Here is the list of concepts that have been covered as part of the previous exercise. Revise and self-reflect on your concepts you covered.

- Traits of Aryan Culture ☐
- Occupations prevalent during after Ages ☐
- Location of old age stones ☐
- First metal used by man ☐

2.2 COPPER-BRONZE AGE

QUESTIONS

1. Which one of the following statements is incorrect with respect to social developments in the Gupta period?

(a) The position of Shudras improved during this period.

(b) Gupta period is marked with the subordination of women of upper varnas.

(c) Brahmans became direct tillers of the soil due to the various land grants.

(d) Daughters were not allowed to inherit landed property due to patriarchal setup.

2. Consider the following statement regarding the Rigvedic society:

(a) Social mobility was affected due to the Varna system.

(b) The wife was the husband's partner in all religious and social ceremonies.
(c) Slaves were primarily used in agricultural activities.

Which of the above statements is/are incorrect?

(d) 1 only (e) 2 only
(f) 1 and 3 only (g) 1, 2 and 3

3. Which of the following statements regarding social institutions in Ancient India is/are correct?

1. Institution of Gotra appeared in later Vedic Period for widening the socio-political ties.
2. All the four institutions of Ashramas were established in early Vedic Period.

Select the correct answer using the code given below:

(a) 1 only (b) 2 only
(c) Both 1 and 2 (d) Neither 1 nor 2

4. Which of the following statement(s) correctly defines the difference between Harappan and Mesopotamian civilisation art and culture?

1. In Harappa, the houses were built to the East of citadel while in Mesopotamia, the houses were built around distinct palaces and temples.
2. The Harappans traded in cotton, beads, other art and jewellery, while the Mesopotamians traded in precious stones.

Select the correct answer using the code given below:

(a) 1 only (b) 2 only
(c) Both 1 and 2 (d) Neither 1 nor 2

5. Which of the following Indus Valley settlements is located in Rann of Kuchch?

(a) Kalibangan (b) Rakhigarhi
(c) Mohenjodaro (d) Ganawariwala

6. Consider the following statements about the Indus Valley Civilisation:

1. Barley has been found from one of the Indus Valley Civilisation sites.
2. People of Indus Valley Civilisation used to make pottery.
3. People of Indus Valley Civilisation used to trade with other countries.

Which of the above statements is/are correct?

(a) 1 only (b) 2 only
(c) 1, 2 and 3 (d) 2 and 3 only

7. Consider the following statements with respect to status of economy during Indus Valley Civilisation:

1. They were the first people in Indian history to go for international trade.
2. They were first to cultivate cotton in the entire pre-historic period.
3. The economy of Indus Valley Civilisation was based upon agriculture and trade.

Which of the above statements is/are correct?

(a) 1 and 2 only (b) 3 only
(c) 2 and 3 only (d) 1, 2 and 3

8. Which of the following statements related to the chalcolithic stage is/are incorrect?

1. Largest town of Jorwe culture was Inamagaon, situated along the right bank of the Ghod River.
2. The houses were mainly made up of burnt bricks plastered with cow dung and lime.
3. They produced wheat, rice, bajra and pulses.

Select the correct answer using the code given below:

(a) 1 and 3 only (b) 2 and 3 only
(c) 1 and 2 only (d) 3 only

9. Consider the following statements regarding the trade and commerce of chalcolithic culture:

1. Chalcolithic communities traded and exchanged materials with other contemporary communities.
2. It appears that Ahar people, settled close to the copper source, supplied copper tools and objects to other contemporary communities in Malwa and Gujarat.

Which of the above statement(s) is/are correct?

(a) 1 only (b) 2 only
(c) Both 1 and 2 (d) Neither 1 nor 2

10. Which of the following statements regarding the Chalcolithic period is/are correct?

1. The economy was based on subsistence agriculture, stock-raising, hunting, and fishing.
2. Painted pottery was the distinguishing feature among all the Chalcolithic cultures.

Select the correct answer using the code given below:

(a) 1 only (b) 2 only
(c) Both 1 and 2 (d) Neither 1 nor 2

SOLUTIONS

1. Correct Option: (c)

Supplementary Notes:

Social Developments in the Gupta Period

- Guptas, who were originally Vaishyas, became the great supporters of the Brahmanical order who in turn legitimized their position by looking upon Guptas as Kshatriyas.
- Shudras
  - Castes were proliferated into numerous sub-castes during this period and the position of Shudras improved during this period.
  - They were now permitted to listen to recitations of the Ramayana, the Mahabharata, and the Puranas.
  - They could also worship a new god called Krishna and were also permitted to perform certain domestic rites which naturally meant fees for the priests. This can all be linked to some improvement in the economic status of the Shudras.

- Untouchables
  - During this period, the number of untouchables increased, especially the chandalas.
  - Fa-hien mentions chandalas living outside the village and dealing in meat and flesh.
- Women
  - Like the shudras, women were also allowed to listen to the Ramayana, the Mahabharata, and the Puranas, and were advised to worship Krishna.
  - Women of Upper Varna
    - The Gupta period is marked with the subordination of women of upper varnas.
    - The principal reason for the subordination of women of the upper varnas was their complete dependence on men for their livelihood, and lack of proprietary rights.
    - The only property they could hold on was the "stridhana" which included presents received by the bride not only from her parents' side but also from her parents-in-law at marriage.
    - A daughter was not allowed to inherit landed property in the patriarchal communities of India.
  - Women of Lower Varna
    - Women of the two lower varnas were free to earn their livelihood, which gave them considerable freedom, but this was denied to women of the upper varnas.
  - In a patriarchal setup, higher order began to treat women as items of property, to such a degree that a woman was expected to follow her husband to the next world.
  - The first example of the immolation of a widow after the death of her husband occurred during the Gupta period in AD 510.
- Brahmana's material conditions improved immensely as the recipient of agraharas. They were now associated with agrarian life as an owner of the land or a landed intermediary, though not as a direct tiller of the soil.

2. **Correct Option: (c)**

Explanation:

- **Statement 1 is incorrect:** There were freedom and mobility for the adoption of a profession and the occupation-based differentiation was sharp.
- **Statement 3 is incorrect:** In Rig Vedic times, slaves mostly women, were not used directly in agriculture or other productive activities.

Supplementary Notes:

Rigvedic Society

- The social divisions were created by the conquest of the indigenous inhabitants by the Indo-Aryans. The Rig Veda mentions the arya varna and dasa varna.
- The tribal chiefs and the priests acquired a larger share of the booty and naturally became wealthy at the cost of their kinsmen, thereby creating social inequalities in the tribe.
- Gradually, the tribal society was divided into three occupational groups, warriors, priests, and the common people. The fourth division, called the Shudras appeared towards the end of the Rig Vedic Period. The term shudra is mentioned for the first time in the Rig Veda in its tenth book, which is the latest addition.
- These vocations of various groups were followed by persons according to their ability and liking, and the occupations had not become hereditary. Members of the same family took to different professions and belonged to different varnas.
- There were freedom and mobility for the adoption of a profession and the idea of hereditary trades and occupations was not envisaged in the society.
- Slaves were given as gifts to the priests. These were primarily women employed for domestic purposes. It is clear that in Rigvedic times, slaves were not used directly in agriculture or other productive activities.
- The tribal elements in society were stronger and social divisions was not highly iniquitous as the economy was mainly pastoral and not food producing. So the scope for collecting regular tributes from the people was very limited.
- The unit of society was family, primarily monogamous and patriachical. Child marriage was not in vogue. There are a few references to the freedom of choice in marriage. A widow could marry the younger brother of her deceased husband. The wife was the husband's partner in all religious and social ceremonies. The father's property was inherited by the son. The daughter could inherit it provided if she was the only child of her parents.

3. **Correct Option: (a)**

Explanation:

Statement 2 is incorrect: There are four ashramas in all: Brahmacharya (student life), Garhasthya (family life), Vanaprastha (retired life), and Sannyasa (life of renunciation). But only three are mentioned in the later Vedic texts. The last or the fourth stage had not been well-established in Later Vedic times. The 4th Ashrama is only mentioned in Jabala Upanishad.

Supplementary Notes:

The Gotra System:

- It is part of a system of classification or identification of various Brahmin families in ancient times. The gotra classification took form probably sometime during the Yajur Veda period, after the Rig Veda period.

- It is believed that the gotras (now account to a total of 49) started to consolidate some around 10-8 Century BC
- There are 49 established Hindu gotras today. All members of a particular gotra are believed to possess certain common characteristics by way of nature or profession.
- The institution of gotra (literally meaning-cow pen) appeared during later Vedic Period. As against tribal endogamy (marriage within tribe) people practised gotra exogamy (marrying outside the gotra).

Ashrams:

- These are an outstanding feature of the social organisation in ancient India. This system particularly developed during the later Vedic Period.
- Ashramas are the stages of life which provide training and environment for realising the ideal of our life.
- There are four ashramas in all: Brahmacharya (student life), Garhasthya (family life), Vanaprastha (retired life), and Sannyasa (life of renunciation). But only three are mentioned in the later Vedic texts. The last or the fourth stage had not been well-established in later Vedic times. The 4th Ashrama is only mentioned in Jabala Upanishad.

4. **Correct Option: (c)**

Explanation:

- Both statements are correct

Supplementary Notes:

Harappan and Mesopotamian Civilisation:

- In Harappan civilisation, the houses were built to the East of citadel while in Mesopotamian Civilisation, the houses were built around distinct palaces and temples & dedicated to the patron Gods or Goddesses.
- Most of the Harappan people lived in small villages while most of the Mesopotamians lived in cities and towns.
- The Harappans had walls built to protect their houses while the Mesopotamians had walls built to protect their cities and town.
- The Harppan people were peaceful in comparison to the Mesopotamians.
- The Harappans traded in cotton, beads, other art and jewellery while the Mesopotamians traded in precious stones.
- The Hrappans grew melons, lettuce, and general fruits and vegetables that they ate while the Mesopotamians grew flex and used it for oil, net, cloth & food.
- Harappans established exact measurement and weighing system and the Mesopotamians first created the wheel.

5. **Correct Option: (a)**

Supplementary Notes:

- Most of the 1400 settlements belonging to this civilisation can be classified as small villages (which are up to 10 hectares), a few larger towns and small cities (10 to 50 hectares). Some of the settlements like Mohenjōdaro (+250 hectares), Harappa (+150 hectares), Ganawariwala (+80 hectares) and Rakhigarhi (+80 hectares), Kalibangan (+100 hectares), and Dholavira (+100 hectares) can easily be classed as large cities. The first five are inland centres located approximately at equidistance in a zigzag pattern that covers Indus and Saraswati river plain. The last two are located in Rann of Kachchha.

6. **Correct Option: (c)**

Explanation:

- All statements are correct

Supplementary Notes:

- Harappan pottery represents a blend of the ceramic tradition of the pre-Harappan culture of both west of the Indus region as well as of the Saraswati area.
- The pottery technology was quite advanced. Most of the pots were wheel-made. Big storage jars were also produced. Pots were beautifully painted in black on the bright red surface with geometric designs, plants, animals, and a few paintings seem to depict scenes from stories.
- The occurrence of mature Harappan seals and other artefacts in contemporary Mesopotamian civilisation, and some of the MesopotaIman and Egyptian objects in Harappan civilisation, and the evidence of Mesopotamian documents, establish that the Harappans had trading relationship with that land.
- The granaries at some Harappan cities clearly suggest that cereals were produced in such large quantities that not only were all the immediate needs of people duly met with, but there was also enough reserve to face any future emergency. The principal cereals seem to have been wheat and barley. Rice, though known, was a favoured grain. Six varieties of millets including ragi, kodon, sanwa, and jowar were cultivated, as also peas and beans. Remains of rice have been found mainly from Gujarat and Haryana areas.

7. **Correct Option: (d)**

Explanation:

- All statements are correct

Supplementary Notes:

Indus Valley Civilisation

- Indus valley people were the pioneer in agriculture. They had knowledge of seasonal cultivation.
- They were also aware of all types of irrigation systems like tanks, canals, tank irrigation.

- They were first to cultivate cotton in the entire prehistoric period.
- They were first people in Indian history to go for international trade.
- The economy of Indus Valley Civilisation was based upon agriculture and trade. They traded with Mesopotamia, Sumeria, Greece, Egypt, and Mongolia. They also imported several items from different places.

8. Correct Option: (c)

Explanation:

- **Statements 1 and 2 are incorrect:** The Chalcolithic people were generally not acquainted with burnt bricks and their houses were made of mud bricks. The largest Jorwe site is Daimabad in the Godavari valley which contained about 4,000 people.

Supplementary Notes:

Chalcolithic Age

- People belonging to the Chalcolithic Age domesticated animals and practised agriculture. They produced not only wheat and rice, but also cultivated bajra and pulses. All these cereals have been found at Navdatoli, situated on the bank of the Narmada, in Maharashtra. People in the eastern regions lived on fish and rice as fish hooks have been found in Bihar and West Bengal.
- The Chalcolithic people were generally not acquainted with burnt bricks and their houses were made of mud bricks. However, stone-built houses were found in Ahar. The largest Jorwe site is Daimabad in the Godavari valley which contained about 4,000 people. The place was fortified with a mud wall having stone bastions.
- A large number of bronze goods is also found in Daimabad. At Inamgaon in western Maharashtra, large mud houses with ovens and circular pit houses have been discovered. In the latter phase of the Chalcolithic culture, a house with five rooms and a granary in its neighbourhood, have been found. Inamgaon was a large settlement which contained more than one hundred houses and numerous burials. The arts and crafts of the Chalcolithic age showed weapons and bangles of copper. Coppersmiths manufactured beads of semiprecious stones such as carnelian, steatite and quartz crystal.
- The Chalcolithic people were generally not acquainted with burnt bricks and their houses were made of mud bricks. The largest Jorwe site is Daimabad in the Godavari valley which contained about 4,000 people.

9. Correct Option: (c)

Explanation:

- Both statements are correct

Supplementary Notes:

- There is evidence to show that the Chalcolithic communities traded and exchanged materials with other contemporary communities. Large settlements like Ahar, Gilund, Nagada, Navdatoli, Eran, Prabhas, Rangpur, Prakash, Daimabad and Inamgaon would have served as major centres of trade and exchange. It appears that Ahar people, settled close to the copper source, supplied copper tools and objects to other contemporary communities in Malwa and Gujarat. It has been suggested that most of the copper axes found in Malwa, Jorwe and Prabhas cultures bear some identification marks, which are almost identical, suggesting that they may be the trademarks of the smiths who made them.

10. Correct Option: (c)

Explanation:

- Both statements are correct

Supplementary Notes:

Chalcolithic Age

- The end of the Neolithic period saw the use of metals. The metal first used was copper, and several cultures were based on the use of copper and stone implements. Such a culture is called Chalcolithic, which means the copper– stone phase.
- Technologically, the Chalcolithic stage is applied to the pre-Harappan phase. However, in various parts of India, the Chalcolithic cultures followed the Bronze Age Harappa culture.
- The Chalcolithic people were primarily rural communities spread over a wide area with hilly land and rivers, unlike the Harappans who were urbanized based on the produce from the flood plains in the Indus Valley.
- The Chalcolithic cultures are all characterized by painted ceramic, usually black-on-red, a specialized blade and flake industry of the siliceous material like chalcedony and chert, and copper and bronze tools, though on a restricted scale. Their economy was based on subsistence agriculture, stock-raising, and hunting and fishing.
- In India, settlements relating to the Chalcolithic phase are found in southeastern Rajasthan, the western part of MP, western Maharashtra, and in southern and eastern India.
- The people of the Chalcolithic phase used different types of pottery, one of which is called black-and-red, and seems to have been widely prevalent from nearly 2000 BC onwards and OCP (Ochre-Colored Pottery) which is a red-slipped ware often painted in black and largely in vase forms.
- In Maharashtra, people buried their dead in urns beneath the floor of their house in the north-to-south

position. They did not use separate cemeteries for this purpose, as was the case with the Harappans. Pots and some copper objects were deposited in the graves obviously for the use of the dead in the next world.

- Terracotta figures of women suggest that the Chalcolithic people venerated the Mother Goddess, and some unbaked nude clay figurines were also used for worship.
- A kind of settlement hierarchy is visible in several Jorwe settlements of Maharashtra. Some of them are as large as twenty hectares, but others encompass only five hectares and even less. This would imply two-tier habitations.
- Both the settlement pattern and burial practices suggest the beginnings of social inequalities in Chalcolithic society.
- The Chalcolithic people domesticated cattle, sheep/goats. In all probability, the domesticated animals were slaughtered for food and not used for milk and dairy products.

CONCEPT REVISION

Here is the list of concepts that have been covered as part of the previous exercise. Revise and self-reflect on your concepts you covered.

- Social and Economic institutions in Ancient India ☐
- Difference between Harappan and Mesopotamian Civilisation ☐
- Indus Valley Settlements ☐
- Status of economy during Indus Valley Civilisation ☐
- Trade and Commerce during Chalcolithic Culture ☐

2.3 IRON AGE

QUESTIONS

1. **This school believes in the physicality of the universe and is considered to be the realistic and objective philosophy that governs the universe. This school has a scientific approach and explains the phenomenon of this universe. It was also responsible for the beginning of physics in the Indian subcontinent.**
   Which of the following Schools of Philosophy is explained in the above passage?
   (a) Samkhya (b) Vedanta
   (c) Mimamsa (d) Vaisheshika

2. **Consider the following statements regarding six schools of Hindu Philosophy:**
   1. They believed in the infallibility of God.
   2. The first school to originate in Hindu Philosophy was Samkhya.

   Which of the above statements is/are correct?
   (a) 1 only (b) 2 only
   (c) Both 1 and 2 (d) Neither 1 nor 2

3. **With reference to Jain Councils, consider the following statements:**
   1. The first Jain council was held in Pataliputra in 310 BC
   2. The second Jain council was held in Vallabhi and it led to the final compilation of 12 angas of Jainism.

   Which of the above statements is/are incorrect?
   (a) 1 only (b) 2 only
   (c) Both 1 and 2 (d) Neither 1 nor 2

4. **Match the following philosophers of Bhakti movement with the theories they propounded:**

Philosophers	Theories
A. Sankaracharya	1. Dvaita
B. Ramanuja	2. Dvaita advaita
C. Madhavacharya	3. Advaita
D. Nimbraka	4. Shudhadvaita
E. Vallabhacharya	5. Vishista Advaitavada

Select the correct answer using the code given below:

	A	B	C	D	E
(a)	3	5	2	4	1
(b)	5	3	2	4	1
(c)	3	5	1	2	4
(d)	5	3	1	2	4

5. **Consider the following statements:**
   1. The Vedanta of Shankara, absolute monism, considers Brahman to be without any attributes and considers knowledge to be the chief means of salvation.
   2. The Visistadvaita Advaita of Ramanuja considers Brahman with attributes.

3. The Dvaita of Madhva considers God to be completely different from the individual soul and the world.

Which of the above statements is/are correct?

(a) 1 only (b) 1 and 3 only
(c) 2 and 3 only (d) 1, 2 and 3

6. **Consider the following statements:**
1. Kshatriya reaction against Brahmanical domination
2. Spread of new agricultural economy
3. Rise of new cities in northeastern India
4. Practicing the doctrine of non-violence

Which of the above is/are the reasons for the origin of Buddhism and Jainism?

(a) 1 only (b) 2 and 3 only
(c) 1, 3 and 4 only (d) 1, 2, 3 and 4

7. **Select the correct statement regarding Tantric worship:**
(a) Tantric practices were open to both men and women.
(b) Tantric practitioners recognized caste and class differences within ritual context.
(c) Tantric worship was confined to Eastern India.
(d) Tantric worshippers recognized the authority of vedas.

8. **Match the following:**

Philosophy	**Features**
A. Samkhya	1. Practice of control over pleasure and senses
B. Yoga	2. Atom Theory
C. Mimamsa	3. Rational and Scientific Theory
D. Vaisheshika	4. Considers Brahma as the only reality
E. Vedanta	5. Performance of vedic sacrifices to attain salvation

Select the correct answer using the code given below:

	A	B	C	D	E
(a)	1	5	4	2	3
(b)	5	2	3	1	4
(c)	3	1	5	2	4
(d)	4	3	1	5	2

9. **With reference to Buddhism, consider the following statements:**
1. It does not recognize the existence of soul.
2. In comparison with Brahmanism, Buddhism was more liberal and democratic.
3. The use of Prakrit language helped in the spread of Buddhism.

Which of the above statements is/are correct?

(a) 1 only (b) 1 and 2 only
(c) 2 and 3 only (d) 1, 2 and 3

10. **Consider the following statements**
1. Ramanuja considers brahma to be without any attributes.
2. Shankara considers Brahma to possess attributes.
3. Ramanuja's road to salvation lies in devotion.
4. Shankara's road to salvation lies in knowledge.

Which of the above statements is/are correct?

(a) 1 and 2 only (b) 3 and 4 only
(c) 1, 2 and 4 only (d) All of the above

11. **In Ancient India, large scale human settlements spread from west to east. What are the possible reasons quoted for this trend?**
1. Gradual increase in rainfall from west to east
2. Narrower width of rivers in the Himalayan foothills
3. Presence of various passes in north-west mountain ranges
4. Easier clearance of forests in the Himalayan foothills

Select the correct answer using the code given below:

(a) 1 only (b) 1 and 4 only
(c) 2 and 3 only (d) 1, 2, 3 and 4

12. **Consider the following statements:**
1. The craft of making steel was first developed in India.
2. Indian steel was called as Wootz and it was exported to many countries.
3. India had to import swords as quality of domestically produced Indian swords was not good.

Which of the above statements is/are correct?

(a) 1 only (b) 2 only
(c) 1 and 2 only (d) 1 and 3 only

13. **Consider the following statements regarding various sea ports in ancient India:**
1. Broach and Sopara were situated on the Western Coast.
2. Both Arikamedu and Tamralipti were situated on Eastern Coast.

Choose the correct statements using the codes given below:

(a) 1 only (b) 2 only
(c) Both 1 and 2 (d) Neither 1 nor 2

14. **Consider the following statements regarding Rig Vedic Period:**
1. Metal trade was in advanced stage during Rig Vedic Period.
2. The rural economy was mainly based on pastoralism.
3. Settlements were open and free for movement.

Which of the above statements is/are incorrect?

(a) 1 only (b) 1 and 3 only
(c) 2 and 3 only (d) 1, 2 and 3

SOLUTIONS

1. **Correct Option: (d)**

Explanation:

- **Option (d) is correct:** The above passage describes the Vaisheshika School of Philosophy.

Supplementary Notes:

Vaisheshika School

- The Vaisheshika school believes in the physicality of the Universe and is considered to be the realistic and objective philosophy that governs the universe.
- The Kanada who also wrote the basic text governing the Vaisheshika philosophy is often considered the founder of this school.
- They argue that everything in the universe was created by the five main elements: fire, air, water, earth and ether (sky). These material elements are also called Dravya.
- They also argue that reality has many categories, for example, action, attribute, genus, inherence, substance, and distinct quality
- As this school has a very scientific approach, they also developed the atomic theory, i.e. all material objects are made of atoms.
- They explain the phenomenon of this universe by arguing that the atoms and molecules combined to make matter, which is the basis for everything that can be physically touched or seen.
- This school was also responsible for the beginning of physics in the Indian subcontinent. They are considered to be the propounders of the mechanical process of the formation of this Universe.

2. **Correct Option: (b)**

Explanation:

- **Statement 1 is incorrect:** They did not believe in infallibility of God.

Supplementary Notes:

Six Schools of Hindu Philosophy

- There are six sub-schools that were called the Shada Darshana.
- These were known as Samkhya, Yoga, Nyaya, Vaisheshika, Mimamsa, and Vedanta.

Samkhya

- Samkhya, literally 'count', seems to have originated first. According to the early Samkhya philosophy, the presence of divine agency is not essential to the creation of the world. The world owes its creation and evolution more to Nature or prakriti than to God. This was a rational and scientific view. Around the fourth century AD, in addition to prakriti, purusha or spirit was introduced as an element in the Samkhya system, and the creation of the world was attributed to both.

3. **Correct Option: (d)**

Explanation:

- Both statements are correct

Supplementary Notes:

Jain Councils

- Towards the close of Chandragupta Maurya's rule a terrible famine broke out in South Bihar. It lasted for about 12 years.
- Bhadrabahu and his disciples migrated to Sravanabelgola in Karnataka.
- Other Jains remained in Magadha with Sthulabhadra as their leader.
- They summoned the first council at Pataliputra in about 310 BC.
- In that council, the sacred teaching of Mahavira was divided into twelve angas to replace Purvas. It was presided over by Sthulabhadra.
- The second Jain Council was held at Vallabhi (Gujarat) in 512 AD and was presided over by Derridhiganj.
- The purpose of this Council was to collect the sacred texts and write them down systematically.
- It led to a final compilation of 12 angas and 12 upangas.
- All the angas were written in Ardhamagadhi.

4. **Correct Option: (c)**

Philosophers	Theories
A. Sankaracharya	3. Advaita
B. Ramanuja	5. Vishista Advaitavada
C. Madhavacharya	1. Dvaita
D. Nimbraka	2. Dvaita advaita
E. Vallabhacharya	4. Shudhadvaita

Supplementary Notes:

Prominent Leaders of the Bhakti Movement

Sankaracharya

- 9th century philosopher
- He was born in Kaladi (Kerala) and propounded the Advaita (Monism) philosophy and NirgunaBrahman (god without attributes).
- In Advaita, the reality of the world is denied and Brahman is considered as the only reality.
- According to him, gyaan (knowledge) alone can lead to salvation.

Ramanuja

- Born at Sriperumbudur near modern Chennai in the 12th century.
- He opposed the mayavada of Shankara and advocated the philosophy of Vishista Advaitavada (qualified monism), and founded the Shrivaishnava sect. According to him, God is Saguna Brahman.

- In Vishista Advaita, the world and Brahman are also considered two equally real entities, as in dualism, but here the world is not separate from Brahman but is formed out of Brahman.

Madhavacharya

- In the 13th century, Madhava from Kannada region propagated Dvaita or the dualism of the Jivatma and Paramatma.
- According to this philosophy, the world is not an illusion but a reality, full of real distinction.
- According to Madhava, Brahman and the world are considered to be two equally real entities and not related in any way.

Nimbraka

- Younger contemporary of Ramanujam who propounded the Dvaita advaita philosophy and the philosophy of Bheda Abheda (difference/ non–difference).
- According to him, Brahman or the supreme soul transforms itself into the souls of the world, which are therefore real, distinct, and different from Brahman.
- Like Vishista Advaita, the Bheda Abheda school also believes that the world and Brahman are both equally real, and that the world is a part of Brahman.

Vallabhacharya

- Born in Benaras in the 15th century and lived at the court of Krishnadeva Raya.
- He propounded the Shudhadvaita (pure monism). In Shudhadvaita, as in Vishista Advaita, the world is taken to have a real existence, as also Brahman. But it is said that there is no change of Brahman into the world, and the world exists as it were as an aspect of Brahman without undergoing any change, being a part of Brahman.

5. **Correct Option: (d)**

Explanation:

- All statements are correct

Supplementary Notes:

Vedanta of Shankara

- Shankara was a major proponent of Vedanta in the 9th century.
- He considers Brahman to be without any attributes and considers knowledge or jnana to be the chief means of salvation.
- Shankara argues that the atman is completely identical with Brahman. He believed in only one reality.
- According to Shankara, the atman experiences a false sense of plurality and individuality under the influence of the delusive power of maya.
- While maya has the ambiguous ontological status of being neither real nor unreal, the only true reality is Brahman which is pure consciousness, eternal and unchanging.

Visistadvaita Advaita

- Visistadvaita Advaita or qualified monism/non-dualism of Ramanuja: Ramanuja wrote a commentary on Vedanta in 12th century and combined Vaishnava bhakti with Upanishadic monism.
- He identifies the Brahman with Vishnu, holding that Brahman is saguna (possesses attributes), in contrast to Sankara's attributeless or nirguna Brahman. The road to salvation lies in practising devotion or loving faith.
- Ramanuja asserts that the relationship between Brahman and the atman is similar to relationship of a red rose and redness.
- According to Ramanuja, atman and Brahman are distinct but inseparable.

Dvaita of Madhva

- The Dvaita or dualist school of Hindu Vedanta philosophy originated in 13th century South India with Sri Madhvacharya (Madhva).
- Madhva wrote commentaries on the Brahmasutra and Upanishads, and a work called the Bharatatatparyanirnaya, based on the Puranas and the epics.
- He considers God to be completely different from the individual soul and the world.

6. **Correct Option: (d)**

Explanation:

- All statements are correct

Supplementary Notes:

Causes of Origin of Buddhism and Jainism

- Post-Vedic society was clearly divided into four varnas: Brahmanas, Kshatriyas, Vaishyas and Shudras. Each Varna was assigned well-defined functions which generated tensions. The Kshatriya reaction against the domination of the Brahmanas, who claimed various privileges, was one of the causes of the origin of new religions. Vardhamana Mahavira, who founded Jainism, and Gautama Buddha, who founded Buddhism, belonged to the Kshatriya clan, and both disputed the authority of the Brahmanas.
- Spread of a new agricultural economy in north-eastern India including eastern U.P. and Bihar also led to rise of new religions. The agricultural economy based on the iron ploughshare required the use of bullocks, and could not flourish without animal husbandry. However, the Vedic practice of killing cattle indiscriminately in sacrifices hampered the progress of the new agriculture.
- Rise of a large number of cities in northeastern India like Kaushambi, Kusinagar, Vaishali, etc. facilitated

trade and commerce which added to the importance of Vaishyas. Naturally, they sought a religion that would improve their position.

- Jainism and Buddhism at the initial stage did not attach any importance to the existing Varna system.
- They preached the gospel of non-violence, which would put an end to wars between different kingdoms and consequently promote trade and commerce.
- The Brahmanical law-books, called the Dharmasutras, decried lending money at an interest, and condemned those who lived on interest. Therefore, the Vaishyas, who lent money because of the growing trade and commerce, were held in low esteem and looked for better social status.
- Both Jainism and Buddhism propounded simple, puritan, ascetic living which appealed to the old-fashioned people who did not like the use and accumulation of coins, new dwellings and clothes, new luxurious systems of transport, war and violence, etc.

7. **Correct Option: (a)**

Supplementary Notes:
Tantric Worship

- Tantric practices were open to women and men, and practitioners often ignored differences of caste and class within the ritual context.
- Many of these ideas influenced Shaivism as well as Buddhism, especially in the eastern, northern and southern parts of the subcontinent.
- Those engaged in tantric practices frequently ignored the authority of Vedas.
- The devotees of Tantricism often projected their chosen deity, either Vishnu or Shiva as supreme.
- Relations with other traditions, such as Buddhism or Jainism, were also often fraught with tension if not open conflict.

8. **Correct Option: (c)**

Explanation:

- Option (c) is correctly matched

Philosophy	Features
A. Samkhya	3. Rational and Scientific Theory
B. Yoga	1. Practice of control over pleasure and senses
C. Mimamsa	5. Performance of vedic sacrifices to attain salvation
D. Vaisheshika	2. Atom Theory
E. Vedanta	4. Considers Brahma as the only reality

Supplementary Notes:
6 schools of Philosophy

- By the beginning of the Christian era, six schools of philosophy developed.
- These were:
  - **Samkhya**
    - Samkhya, literally 'count', seems to have originated first.
    - According to the early Samkhya philosophy, the presence of divine agency is not essential to the creation of the world. The world owes its creation and evolution more to Nature or prakriti than to God. This was a rational and scientific view.
    - Around the 4th century AD, in addition to prakriti, purusha or spirit was introduced as an element in the Samkhya system, and the creation of the world was attributed to both. According to the new view, Nature and the spiritual element together create the world. Thus, at the outset the Samkhya School of philosophy was materialistic, but later it tended to become spiritualistic.
    - A person can attain salvation through the acquisition of real knowledge, and his misery can be ended forever.
  - **Yoga**
    - A person can attain salvation through meditation and physical application.
    - Practice of control over pleasure, the senses, and bodily organs is central to this system.
    - In order to obtain salvation, physical exercises in various postures called asanas are prescribed, and a breathing exercise called pranayama is recommended.
  - **Nyaya**
    - Nyaya, or the school of analysis, was developed as a system of logic.
    - Salvation can be attained through the acquisition of knowledge.
    - The stress laid on the use of logic influenced Indian scholars who took to systematic thinking and reasoning.
  - **Vaisheshika**
    - The Vaisheshika School gives importance to the discussion of material elements or dravya. Earth, water, fire, air, and ether (sky), when combined, give rise to new objects.
    - The Vaisheshika School propounded the atom theory believing that all material objects are made up of atoms.
    - The Vaisheshika thus marked the beginning of physics in India but the scientific view was

diluted by a belief in god and spiritualism, and this school put its faith in both heaven and salvation.

- **Mimamsa**
  - Mimamsa literally means the art of reasoning and interpretation.
  - However, reasoning was used to provide justifications for various Vedic rituals, and the attainment of salvation was made dependent on their performance.
  - According to the Mimamsa School, the Vedas contain the eternal truth.
  - In order to attain salvation, the Mimamsa School strongly recommended the performance of Vedic sacrifices, which needed the services of priests and legitimized the social distance between the various varnas.
- **Vedanta**
  - Vedanta means the end of the Veda.
  - Vedanta philosophy is traced to the earlier Upanishads. According to it, Brahma is the reality and everything else is unreal (maya). The self (soul) or atma coincides with Brahma. Therefore, if a person acquires the knowledge of the self (atma), he acquires the knowledge of Brahma, and thus attains salvation.
  - Both Brahma and atma are eternal and indestructible.
  - The theory of karma came to be linked to Vedanta philosophy.

9. **Correct Option: (b)**

Explanation:

- **Statement 3 is incorrect:** The use of Pali language helped in the spread of Buddhism.

Supplementary Notes:

Special Features of Buddhism and Causes for its Spread

- Buddhism does not recognize the existence of god and soul.
- It appealed to the common people, and particularly won the support of the lower orders because it attacked the Varna system. People were accepted by the Buddhist order without any consideration of caste, and women too were admitted to the sangha and thus brought on a par with men. In comparison with Brahmanism, Buddhism was liberal and democratic.
- Buddhism particularly appealed to the people of the non-Vedic areas where it found virgin soil for conversion. The people of Magadha responded readily to Buddhism because they were looked down upon by the orthodox Brahmanas.
- The use of Pali, the language of people, contributed to the spread of Buddhism. It facilitated the spread of Buddhist doctrines amongst the common people.
- The personality of the Buddha and the method adopted by him to preach his religion helped the spread of Buddhism. He sought to fight evil by goodness and hatred by love and refused to be provoked by slander and abuse. He maintained his poise and calm under difficult circumstances and tackled his opponents with wit and presence of mind.

10. **Correct Option: (b)**

Explanation:

- **Statements 1 and 2 are incorrect:** Shankara considers Brahma to be without any attributes, but Ramanuja's Brahma possesses attributes.

Supplementary Notes:

- Vedanta means end of Veda. Brahmasutra of Badaryana compiled in 2nd cen. BC formed its basic text. Later 2 famous commentaries were written on it , one by Shankara in 9th century and other by Ramanuja in 12th century.
- Shankara considers Brahma to be without any attributes, but Ramanuja's Brahma possesses attributes.
- Shankara considers knowledge or jnana to be the chief means of salvation, but Ramanuja's road to salvation lies in practicing devotion/loving faith.

11. **Correct Option: (d)**

Explanation:

- All statements are correct

Supplementary Notes:

Geographical Setting

- Large-scale human settlements generally spread from west to east.
- Various reasons for this are:
  - The Himalayas are sufficiently high to shield India against invasions from the north. This was especially true in pre-industrial times when communications were very difficult. However, on the north-west, the Sulaiman mountain ranges, which are a southward continuation of the Himalayas, could be crossed through the Khyber, Bolan, and Gomal passes. The Sulaiman ranges are joined southward in Baluchistan by the Kirthar ranges which could be crossed through the Bolan Pass. Through these passes, two-way traffic between India and Central Asia has continued from prehistoric times onwards.
  - The foothills of the Himalayas lent themselves to easier clearance than the jungles on the alluvial soil of the plains. It was easy to cross rivers in these areas because of their narrower width, and hence the earliest routes skirted along the foothills

of the Himalayas from the west to the east. It was therefore natural that the earliest agricultural settlements were founded in the foothills and uplands, and trade routes followed the terai route.

- Proceeding from west to east, we find the annual rainfall gradually increasing from 25 cm to over 250 cm. The Indus vegetation based on 25 to 37 cm rainfall and possibly the western Gangetic vegetation based on 37 to 60 cm rainfall could be cleared with stone and copper implements and made fit for cultivation, but this was not possible in the case of the mid-Gangetic vegetation based on 60 to 125 cm rainfall, and certainly not in the case of the lower Gangetic and Brahmaputra vegetation based on 125 to 250 cm rainfall. The thickly forested areas, which also had hard soil, could be cleared only with the aid of iron implements which became available at a much later stage. Therefore, the natural resources of the less rainy western area were utilized first.

12. **Correct Option: (c)**

Explanation:

- **Statement 3 is incorrect:** No other country in the world could manufacture such steel swords as were made by Indian craftsmen. Indian swords were in great demand in entire region from Asia to Eastern Europe.

Supplementary Notes:
Craft & Industry

- Indians were great expert in art of making steel. This craft was first developed in India.
- India has been reputed for its iron and steel since ancient times. Literary accounts indicate that steel from southern India was rated as some of the finest in the world and was traded over ancient Europe, China, the Arab world and the Middle East.
- Indian steel was exported to many countries of the world since very early times and came to be called wootz in later times.
- Studies on wootz indicate that it was an ultra-high carbon steel with 1-2% carbon and was believed to have been used to fashion the Damascus blades with a watered steel pattern.
- Wootz steel also spurred developments in modern metallographic studies and also qualifies as an advanced material in modern terminology since such steels are shown to exhibit super-plastic properties.
- No other country in the world could manufacture such steel swords as were made by Indian craftsmen. Indian swords were in great demand in entire region from Asia to Eastern Europe.

13. **Correct Option: (c)**

Explanation:

- Both statements are correct

Supplementary Notes:
Sea Ports in Ancient India

- Broach and Sopara – were situated on the Western Coast while Arikamedu and Tamralipti were situated on Eastern Coast of India. Of all these ports Broach seems to have been the most important and flourishing.
- To it were brought not only the commodities produced in Satavahana kingdom but also the goods produced in the Shaka and the Kushana kingdom through the route known as Uttarpatha.

14. **Correct Option: (b)**

Explanation:

- **Statements 1 is incorrect:** There was no trade of metal in Rig Vedic Period
- **Statement 3 is incorrect:** Settlements were fortified.

Supplementary Notes:
Economy of Rig Vedic Period

- The Rig Vedic people possessed better knowledge of agriculture.
- Ploughshare is mentioned In the earliest part of the Rig Veda though some consider it an interpolation.
- Possibly, this ploughshare was made of wood. They were acquainted with sowing, harvesting and threshing and knew about the different seasons.
- There are so many references to the cow in the Rig Veda that the Rig Vedic Aryans seem to have been pastoral people.
- Most of their wars were fought for the sake of cows. The term for war in the Rig Veda is 'gavisthi' or search for cows.
- The cow seems to have been the most important form of wealth, and whenever we hear of gifts made to priests, it is stated in terms of cows and women slaves and never in terms of the measurement of land.
- The Rig Vedic people may have occasionally occupied pieces of land, but land did not form a well-established type of private property.
- The Rig Veda mentions such artisans as the carpenter, the chariot maker, the weaver, the leather worker, the pottel, etc. This indicates that they practised all these crafts.
- The term 'ayas', used for copper or bronze shows that metal-working was known but we have no clear evidence of the existence of trade.
- It is doubtful whether the Aryans were acquainted with sea or ocean, because the word 'samudra' mentioned in the Rig Veda mainly denotes a collection of water.
- At any rate the Aryans did not live in cities possibly they lived in some kind of fortified mud settlements which still await to be identified satisfactorily by the archaeologists.

CONCEPT REVISION

Here is the list of concepts that have been covered as part of the previous exercise. Revise and self-reflect on your concepts you covered.

- Different Schools of Philosophy ☐
- Jain Councils ☐
- Different Philosophers and their theories ☐
- Buddhism ☐
- Various Sea Ports ☐

2.5 MAURYAN EMPIRE

QUESTION

1. Consider the following statements regarding a dynasty of southern India

1. They ruled in the region of Maharashtra and Vidarbha after the Satavahana Dynasty.
2. They gave land grants on a large scale.
3. They are credited with taking Brahmin religion and it's ideas to the south.

The above given statements holds true for which of the given below?

(a) Pallavas (b) Vakatakas
(c) Chalukyas (d) Ikshvakus

SOLUTION

1. Correct Option: (b)

Supplementary Notes:

Formation of New States and Rural Expansion in the Peninsula

- In northern Maharashtra and Vidarbha (Berar), the Satavahanas were succeeded by the Vakatakas, a local power.
- The Vakatakas, who were brahmins themselves, are known from a large number of copper plate land grants issued to the Brahmanas.
- They followed the Brahmanical religion and performed numerous Vedic sacrifices.
- The important contribution of Vakataka culturally was that this kingdom became a channel for transmitting Brahmanical ideas and social institutions to southern India.

CONCEPT REVISION

Here is the list of concepts that have been covered as part of the previous exercise. Revise and self-reflect on your concepts you covered.

- Material culture ☐
- Taxation system ☐

2.7 GUPTA'S ERA

QUESTIONS

1. Which of the following were the causes of the disintegration of the Gupta Empire?

1. Rise of Hunas attacks
2. Decline of foreign trade
3. Concentration of power at the centre
4. Issue of land grants to Brahmana donees

Which of the above statements are correct?

(a) 1 and 2 only
(b) 1, 2 and 4 only
(c) 3 and 4 only
(d) 1, 2, 3 and 4

2. With reference to the economic history of ancient India, the term Vapi refers to:

(a) Water wheel used in the irrigation of land.
(b) Wasteland converted to cultivated land.
(c) Canal irrigation
(d) Tank irrigation

3. Consider the following statements with respect to religious developments during the Gupta Period:

1. The Gupta kings followed a policy of tolerance towards different religious sects.
2. Bhagavatism or Vaishnavism overshadowed Mahayana Buddhism during Gupta times.

Which of the above statements is/are correct?

(a) 1 only (b) 2 only
(c) Both 1 and 2 (d) Neither 1 nor 2

SOLUTIONS

1. **Correct Option: (b)**

Supplementary Notes:

Fall of Empire

- Some of the factors that contributed towards the disintegration of the Gupta Empire are as follows:
  - **Huna Invasions:** From the time of Kumaragupta-I the north-west borders had been threatened by the Hunas, a Central Asian tribe which was successfully moving in different directions and was establishing pockets of rule in northwestern, northern and western India. But their attacks were repulsed during that period. However, towards the end of the fifth century AD the Huna chief Tormana was able to establish his authority over large parts of western India and in central India. Mihirakula, his son, further extended the dominions. Thus, the Huna attacks caused a major blow to the Gupta authority, particularly in northern and western regions of the empire.
  - **Administrative Weaknesses:** The policy adopted by the Guptas in the conquered areas was to restore the authority of local chiefs or kings once they had accepted Gupta suzerainty. In fact, no efforts were made to impose a strict and effective control over these regions. Hence it was natural that whenever there was a crisis of succession or a weak monarchy within the Gupta Empire these local chiefs would re-establish their independent authority. This created a problem for almost I every Gupta King who had to reinforce his authority. Towards the end of the fifth century AD and beginning of sixth century AD taking advantage of the weak Gupta emperors, many regional powers asserted their authority, and in due course declared their independence.
  - **Decline of foreign trade:** Their income went down due to decline of foreign trade also due to migration of guilds of the silk weavers from Gujarat to Malwa, and their adoption of non-productive professions.
  - Besides these, there were many other reasons which contributed to the decline of Guptas. For example, it has been argued that the Guptas issued landgrants to the Brahamana donees and in this process surrendered the revenue and administrative rights in favour of the donees.
  - Further, it is believed that the samanta system, the samantas or minor rulers, who ruled as subordinates to the central authority, started to consolidate itself in the Gupta period. This is also believed to be the reason why Gupta administrative structure became so loose.
  - There is no doubt that divisions within the imperial family, concentration of power in the hands of local chiefs or governors, loose administrative structure of the empire etc. contributed towards the disintegration of the Gupta Empire.

2. **Correct Option: (c)**

Explanation:

Vapi

- The Gupta kings also took special care of irrigation purposes for the promotion of agricultural economy in the Gupta kingdom. We can see three types of irrigation during that time
  - Araghabhata- lift irrigation
  - Tadaga- tank irrigation
  - Vapi- canal irrigation

3. **Correct Option: (c)**

Explanation:

- Both statements are correct

Supplementary Notes:

Religious Developments during the Gupta Period

- Bhagavatism originated in post-Maurya times and centred around the worship of Vishnu or Bhagavata.
- Bhagavatism was marked by bhakti and ahimsa. Bhakti meant the offer of loving devotion.
- The new religion was sufficiently liberal to attract foreigners. It also appealed to artisans and merchants who became important under the Satavahanas and Kushans.
  - Krishna taught in the Bhagavadgita that even women, vaishyas, and shudras who were born of sin could seek refuge in him.
  - This religious text dealt with the Vaishnava teachings, as did the Vishnu Purana, and also to an extent the Vishnu Smriti.
- Bhagavatism or Vaishnavism over-shadowed Mahayana Buddhism by Gupta times.
  - It preached the doctrine of incarnation, or avatar. History was presented as a cycle of the ten incarnations of Vishnu.
  - A few Gupta kings were worshippers of Shiva, the god of destruction, but he came to the fore at a later stage, and does not seem to have been as important as Vishnu in the early phase of the Gupta rule.
  - Idol worship in the temples became a common feature of Hinduism from the Gupta period onwards.

- The Gupta kings followed a policy of tolerance towards different religious sects.
  - We find no example of the persecution of the followers of Buddhism and Jainism.
  - This was also due to the change in the character of Buddhism which had come to acquire many features of Brahmanism or Hinduism.

CONCEPT REVISION

Here is the list of concepts that have been covered as part of the previous exercise. Revise and self-reflect on your concepts you covered.

- Disintegration of Gupta Empire ☐
- Vapi ☐
- Religious developments ☐

2.8 POST-GUPTA ERA

QUESTIONS

1. Consider the following statements with respect to Sangam Age Economy:

1. Inland trading was conducted primarily through barter in busy market places by merchant associations and commercial lending institutions.
2. External trade was carried between South India and Hellenistic kingdom of Egypt and Arabia.

Which of the above statements is/are correct?

(a) 1 only (b) 2 only
(c) Both 1 and 2 (d) Neither 1 nor 2

2. Consider the following statements regarding the age of three empires

1. The Pala rulers had close cultural ties with Tibet.
2. Sanskrit poet Rajasekhar lived in the court of King Bhoj of the Pratihara Dynasty.
3. The kings of the Rashtrakuta Dynasty gave patronage to Shaiva, Vaishnavism and Jainism.

Which of the above statements is/are correct?

(a) 1 and 2 only (b) 1 and 3 only
(c) 2 and 3 only (d) 1, 2, and 3

3. Which of the following statements is/are correct?

1. During the tripartite struggle among the Palas, Pratiharas, and Rashtrakuta, the Palas could never occupy Kannauj, the then centre of power in the north India.
2. Despite Bihar and eastern Uttar Pradesh remained a bone of contention between the Palas and the Pratiharas, Bihar remained under the control of the Palas for most of the time.
3. Palas gave grants to large numbers of Brahmans from north India who flocked to Bengal.

Select the correct option using the codes given below:

(a) 1 and 2 only (b) 3 only
(c) 2 and 3 only (d) 1, 2 and 3

SOLUTIONS

1. Correct Option: (c)

Explanation:

- Both statements are correct

Supplementary Notes:

Sangam Era

- The economy of the Sangam era (200 BCE – 200 CE) describes the ancient economy of a region in southern India that mostly covers the present-day states of Tamil Nadu and Kerala.
- The main economic activities were agriculture, weaving, pearl fishery, manufacturing and construction. Paddy was the most important crop that was the staple cereal and served as a medium of exchange for inland trade. Pepper, millets, grams and sugarcane were other commonly grown crops.
- Madurai and Urayur were important centers for the textile industry; Korkai was the center of the pearl trade. Industrial activity flourished.
- Inland trading was conducted primarily through barter in busy market places by merchant associations and commercial lending institutions.
- Merchants formed associations that operated autonomously, without interference from the state.
- Both internal and foreign trade was well organized and briskly carried on in the Sangam Age. External trade was carried on between South India & Hellenistic kingdom of Egypt & Arabia.
- Agriculture was the main occupation and the chief crops were rice, cotton, ragi, sugarcane pepper, ginger, turmeric, cardamom, cinnamon, etc. Weaving, ship-building, metal working, carpentry, rope-making, ornament-making, making of ivory products, tanning, etc. were some of the handicrafts, which were widely practiced.

2. **Correct Option: (b)**

Explanation:

- **Statement 2 is incorrect:** Sanskrit poet Rajasekhar lived in the court of King Mahipal of the Pratihara Dynasty.

Supplementary Notes:

Northern India: Age of the Three Empires (800-1000 AD)

- The kings of the Rashtrakuta Dynasty were very tolerant hence they gave patronage to Shaiva, Vaishnavism and Jainism.
- The Pala rulers also had close cultural relations with Tibet. The noted Buddhist scholars, Santarakshita and Dipankara (called Atisa), were invited to Tibet, and they introduced a new form of Buddhism there.
- As result, many Tibetan Buddhists flocked to the universities of Nalanda and Vikramshila for study.
- Sanskrit poet Rajasekhar lived in the court of King Mahipal of the Pratihara Dynasty who was the grandson of King Bhoj.

3. **Correct Option: (c)**

Explanation:

- **Statement 1 is incorrect:** Trap in statement 1- Dharmapala once occupied Kanauj and held a grand durbar over there however, he could not hold the control.
- **Trap in statement 3:** Although the Palas were supporters of Buddhism, they also extended their patronage to Saivism and Vaishnavism. In fact, they gave grants to large numbers of Brahmans from north India who flocked to Bengal.

Supplementary Notes:

The Palas

- In eastern India, after the death of king Shashanka in c. 637 CE, a situation of political confusion prevailed in Bengal and adjoining areas. The region witnessed invasions by Yashovarmana of Kannauj, Lalitaditya of Kashmir, and even of a Chinese army. Bhaskaravarman, the ruler of Assam, conquered most of Bengal and the western territories of Bihar and Orissa came under the influence of Harsha. Subsequently, around 8th century CE, Gopala laid the foundation of Pala dynasty.
- He unified Bengal under his control, and even brought Magadha (Bihar) under his control. Gopala was succeeded by his son, Dharamapala. His reign was marked by a tripartite struggle between the Palas, the Pratiharas and the Rashtrakutas for the control of Kanauj and north India.
- The Pratihara ruler advanced upon Gaud (Bengal), but before a decision could be taken, the Pratihara ruler was defeated by the Rashtrakuta ruler, Dhruva, and was forced to seek refuge in the deserts of Rajasthan. Dhruva then returned to the Deccan. This left the field free for Dharmapala who occupied Kanauj and held a grand durbar which was attended by vassal rulers from Punjab, eastern Rajasthan, etc.
- Dharmapala could not, however, consolidate his power in north India. The Pratihara power revived under Nagabhatta II. Dharmapala fell back, but was defeated near Mongyr.
- Bihar and modern east Uttar Pradesh remained a bone of contention between the Palas and the Pratiharas. However, Bihar, in addition to Bengal, remained under the control of the Palas for most of the time.
- Failure in the north compelled the Pala rulers to turn their energies in other directions. Devapala, the son of Dharmapala, who succeeded to the throne in AD 810 and ruled for 40 years, extended his control over Pragjyotishpur (Assam) and parts of Orissa. Probably a part of modern Nepal was also brought under Pala suzerainty. Thus, for about a hundred years, from the middle of the eighth to the middle of the ninth century, the Pala rulers dominated eastern India. For some time, their control extended up to Varanasi.
- Their power is attested to by an Arab merchant, Sulaiman, who visited India in the middle of the ninth century, and wrote an account of it. He calls the Pala Kingdom Ruhma.
- Information about the Palas is also provided to us by Tibetan chronicles, although these were written in the seventeenth century. According to these, the Pala rulers were great patrons of Buddhist learning and religion. The Nalanda University which had been famous all over the eastern world was revived by Dharmapala, and 200 villages were set apart for meeting its expenses. He also founded the Vikramasila University which became second only to Nalanda in fame.
- The Palas built many viharas in which a large number of Buddhist monks lived. The Pala rulers also had close cultural relations with Tibet. The noted Buddhist scholars, Santarakshita and Dipankara (called Atisa), were invited to Tibet, and they introduced a new form of Buddhism there. As a result, many Tibetan Buddhists flocked to the universities of Nalanda and Vikramsila for study.
- Although the Palas were supporters of Buddhism, they also extended their patronage to Saivism and Vaishnavism. They gave grants to large numbers of Brahmans from north India who flocked to Bengal. Their settlements helped in the extension of cultivation in the area, and the transformation of many pastoralists and food-gatherers to settle down to cultivation.
- The Palas were astute diplomats and military conquerors. Their army was noted for its vast

war elephant cavalry. Their navy performed both mercantile and defensive roles in the Bay of Bengal. The empire enjoyed relations with the Srivijaya Empire, the Tibetan Empire and the Arab Abbasid Caliphate. Abbasid coinage found in Pala archaeological sites, as well as records of Arab historians, point to flourishing mercantile and intellectual contacts. Islam first appeared in Bengal during Pala rule, as a result of increased trade between Bengal and the Middle East.

CONCEPT REVISION

Here is the list of concepts that have been covered as part of the previous exercise. Revise and self-reflect on your concepts you covered.

- Sangam Age Economy ☐
- Three Empire Rule ☐

☐☐☐

3.

SOCIO-CULTURAL DEVELOPMENT OF ANCIENT INDIA

3.1 SOCIO-CULTURAL LIFE IN STONE AGE

QUESTIONS

1. Consider the following statements regarding the religious beliefs in Chalcolithic Cultures:

1. The worship of Mother Goddess and the bull was in vogue.
2. The bull cult seems to have been predominant in Malwa during the Ahar period.
3. A large number of naturalistic as well as stylised lingas have been found in most of the sites.

Which of the above statements is/are correct?

(a) 1 only (b) 1 and 2 only
(c) 1 and 3 only (d) 1, 2 and 3

2. The largest Copper Hoards has been recovered from which of the following sites of Chalcolithic cultures?

(a) Gungeria (b) Bithur
(c) Almora (d) Malwa

3. With reference to 'megalithic phase of South India' consider the following statements:

1. The Megalith graves were found to be located within the center of settlement like citadel of Indus Valley Civilization.
2. The Megalith people had advanced type of agricultural practices as shown by their agricultural tools.

Which of the above statement/s is/are correct?

(a) 1 only (b) 2 only
(c) Both 1 and 2 (d) Neither 1 nor 2

SOLUTIONS

1. Correct Option: (d)

Explanation:

- All statements are correct

Supplementary Notes:

- Religion was an aspect which interlinked all the Chalcolithic cultures. The worship of Mother Goddess and the bull was in vogue. The bull cult seems to have been predominant in Malwa during the Ahar period. A large number of these, both naturalistic as well as stylised lingas, have been found from most of the sites. The naturalistic ones may have served as votive offerings, but the small stylised ones may have been hung around the neck as the Lingayats do today.

2. Correct Option: (a)

Supplementary Notes:

- The largest hoard from Gungeria (Madhya Pradesh) comprises 424 pieces of copper objects and 102 thin sheets of silver. The main types of objects are various kinds of celts, harpoons, antennae swords, rings and anthropomorphs.

3. **Correct Option: (d)**

Explanation:

- **Statement 1 is incorrect:** The Megalith graves were found to be located outside from the settlement unlike citadel of Indus Valley Civilization.
- **Statement 2 is incorrect:** The Megalith people did not practice advanced type of agricultural practices as shown by the number and proportion of their agricultural tools.

Supplementary Notes:

Megalithic phase of South India

- Interestingly, all the phenomena of civilisational evolution do not emerge in a linear fashion in southern India, especially at the tip of the peninsula with the Kaveri delta as the nucleus zone, until about the 2nd century BCE.
- The Neolithic phase of south India, which was highlighted by the use of polished stone axe and blade tools, was succeeded by the Megalithic phase (around 1200 BCE–300 BCE).
- The upper portions of the peninsula were inhabited by people who were called the Megalith builders. Quite strangely, these people are identified not from their actual settlements, which are rare, but from their graves.
- These graves are called Megaliths, as they were encircled with mega/big pieces of stones and were, in most cases, located outside the settlement area.
- These Megalith burial sites have yielded the first iron objects from south India (which include arrowheads, daggers, swords, spearheads, tridents, battle axe, hoes, ploughshares, sickles, etc.). Besides these, lot of black and red ware pottery has been found buried in these Megaliths.
- These artifacts, along with food grains such as wheat and rice, found at various Megalithic sites, indicate that the Megalithic people followed agropastoral and hunting activities for their livelihood.
- They did not, in all likelihood, practice an advanced type of agriculture, since the number of agricultural tools found in the grave sites are lesser in number in comparison to tools meant for fighting and hunting.
- These Megaliths have been found in all upland areas of the peninsula, but their concentration is more in eastern Andhra and in Tamil Nadu.

CONCEPT REVISION

Here is the list of concepts that have been covered as part of the previous exercise. Revise and self-reflect on your concepts you covered.

- Religious beliefs of Chalcolithic Cultures ☐
- Largest Copper Hoards ☐
- Megalithic phase of South India ☐

3.2 INDUS VALLEY CIVILIZATION

QUESTION

1. **The most common motif found on the seals of Indus Valley Civilisation is**

(a) Elephant (b) Bull
(c) Unicorn (d) Rhinoceros

SOLUTION

1. **Correct Option: (c)**

Supplementary Notes:

- Unicorn is the most common motif found on the seals of Indus Valley civilization. It is a mythological animal and is also depicted in other cultures.
- Attempts have also been made to reconstruct religious beliefs and practices by examining seals, some of which seem to depict ritual scenes. Others, with plant motifs, are thought to indicate nature worship. Some animals – such as the one-horned animal, often called the "unicorn" – depicted on seals seem to be mythical, composite creatures. In some seals, a figure shown seated cross-legged in a "yogic" posture, sometimes surrounded by animals, has been regarded as a depiction of "proto-Shiva", that is, an early form of one of the major deities of Hinduism. Besides, conical stone objects have been classified as lingas.

CONCEPT REVISION

Here is the list of concepts that have been covered as part of the previous exercise. Revise and self-reflect on your concepts you covered.

- Harappan Town Planning ☐
- Seals and Sculpture of the Harappan Civilization ☐

- Traits linked to Aryan Culture ☐
- Decline of Harappan Culture ☐
- Evidence of worship ☐
- Major findings on different Harappan Sites ☐

3.3 FROM VARNA SYSTEM TO CASTE SYSTEM

QUESTIONS

1. Which one of the following stages of the life of man in Aryan Society in ascending order of age, is correct?

(a) Brahmacharya-Grihastha-Vanaprastha-Sanyasa
(b) Grihastha-Brahmacharya-Vanaprastha-Sanyasa
(c) Brahmacharya-Vanaprastha-Sanyasa-Grihastha
(d) Grihastha-Sanyasa-Vanaprastha-Brahmacharya

2. Which of the following sections of the Brahmanical society extended generous support to both Mahavira and Gautam Buddha in a view to improve their position in the society?

(a) Brahmanas (b) Kshatriyas
(c) Vaisyas (d) Sudras

3. The rigidity of Varna system was maintained by Brahmans by following which of these strategies ?

1. They asserted that Varna order were of divine origin.
2. They advised kings to ensure that the system is followed in his kingdom.
3. The system was reinforced by the stories told in religious text.

Which of the above statements is/are correct?

(a) 1 and 2 only (b) 2 and 3 only
(c) 1 and 3 only (d) 1, 2 and 3

4. Consider the following statements about the religious practices of Later Vedic culture:

1. Vishnu and Rudra, which were smaller deities in the Rig Veda, became extremely important.
2. People did not believe in idolatry.
3. People worshipped Gods in the forms of trees and animals.
4. Some of the important yajnas were – ashvamedha, vajapeya, rajasuya, etc.

Which of the above statements are correct?

(a) 1, 2 and 4 only (b) 2, 3 and 4 only
(c) 1 and 4 only (d) 1, 2, 3 and 4

5. Observe the following statements with reference to the society during Rig Vedic period:

1. Women enjoyed respectable position and they were allowed to take part in Sabhas and Samitis.
2. Child marriage was common.
3. The Varna system of social distinction became very rigid.

Which of the above statement(s) is/ are correct?

(a) 1 only (b) 2 only
(c) 1, 2 and 3 (d) None

6. Which of the following was not the women poet of Vedic civilization?

(a) Kavar Pentu (b) Lopamudra
(c) Apara (d) Gosha

7. Consider the following statements:

1. Although the later vedic society became more settled, it lost its social equality and freedom than the early vedic age.
2. Rig vedic people worshipped to gods for their spiritual upliftment and end of the miseries of existence.

Which of the above statements is/ are correct?

(a) 1 only (b) 2 only
(c) Both 1 and 2 (d) Neither 1 nor 2

8. Consider the following statements regarding common characteristics of eastern India society in 6th-7th century

1. Large scale writing were in practice
2. Absence of private property in land
3. Society based on Varna system

Which of the above statements is/are correct?

(a) 1 and 2 only (b) 1 and 3 only
(c) 2 and 3 only (d) 1, 2 and 3

9. Consider the following statements regarding foreign travellers:

1. According to Al-Biruni, the caste system was a unique feature of Indian society.
2. The main thrust of Ibn Battuta's travelogue was to show the prosperity of Indian cities.
3. According to Bernier, the majority of the urban population was from the middle class.

Which of the above statements is/are incorrect?

(a) 1 and 2 only (b) 1 and 3 only
(c) 2 and 3 only (d) 1, 2 and 3

10. Consider the following statements regarding the social structure of the early Vedic period:

1. The daughter could inherit the property only if she was the only child of her parents.

2. The society comprised of four Varnas based on birth.

Which of the above given statements is/are correct?

(a) 1 only (b) 2 only
(c) Both 1 and 2 (d) Neither 1 nor 2

11. With reference to the later Vedic period, consider the following statements:

1. Women were not permitted to attend Sabhas and Samitis.
2. The rituals and sacrifices became more elaborate in this period.
3. Marriage within the gotra was allowed.

Which of the above statements are correct?

(a) 1 and 2 only (b) 2 and 3 only
(c) 1 and 3 only (d) 1, 2 and 3

12. Consider the following statements regarding Varna system:

1. The word 'Varna' used to reflect the status of caste and person in society.
2. In the Rig Vedic period, people present at the lower level in the Varna system were employed as slaves, mainly in agricultural work.
3. Economic division was the mainstay of the Varna system in the Rig Vedic period.

Which of the above statements is/are incorrect?

(a) 1 only (b) 1 and 3 only
(c) 2 and 3 only (d) 1, 2 and 3

SOLUTIONS

1. Correct Option: (a)

Supplementary Notes:

- An Ashrama in Hinduism is one of four age-based life stages discussed in Indian texts of the ancient and medieval eras.
- The four ashramas in order are: Brahmacharya (student), Grihastha (householder), Vanaprastha (retired) and Sannyasa (renunciate).

2. Correct Option: (c)

Explanation:

- Option (c) is correct

Supplementary Notes:

- Vaisyas were ranked third in the Brahmanical society of Vedic period and they looked for some religion which would improve their position. They found religions propagated by Mahavira and Gautama Buddha most suitable for them and this is why they extended their generous support to them. The merchants, called the setthis, made handsome gifts to Gautama Buddha and his disciples. There were several reasons for it.
  - First, Jainism and Buddhism in the initial stage did not attach any importance to the existing Varna system.
  - Second, they preached the gospel of non-violence, which would put an end to wars between different kingdoms and consequently promote trade and commerce.
  - Third, the Brahmanical law-books, called the Dharmasutras, decried lending money on interest. A person who lived on interest was condemned by them. Therefore the Vaisyas, who lent money on account of growing trade and commerce, were not held in esteem and were eager to improve their social status.

3. Correct Option: (d)

Explanation:

- All the statements are correct

Supplementary Notes:

- The Brahmanas evolved two or three strategies for enforcing these norms. One, as we have just seen, was to assert that the Varna order was of divine origin. Second, they advised kings to ensure that these norms were followed within their kingdoms. And third, they attempted to persuade people that their status was determined by birth. However, this was not always easy. So prescriptions were often reinforced by stories told in the Mahabharata and other texts.

4. Correct Option: (d)

Explanation:

- **Statement 1 is correct:** The two outstanding Rig Vedic gods, Indra and Agni, lost their former importance. On the other hand, Prajapati, the creator, came to occupy the supreme position in the later Vedic pantheon. Some of the other minor gods of the Rig Vedic period also came to the forefront. Rudra, the god of animals, became important in later Vedic times, and Vishnu came to be conceived of as the preserver and protector of the people who now led a settled life rather than a semi-nomadic one
- **Statement 2 is correct:** Some objects began to be worshipped as symbols of divinity but did not believe in idolatry in later Vedic times.
- **Statement 4 is correct:** Sacrifices were accompanied by formulae that had to be carefully enunciated by the sacrificer. The sacrificer was known as the yajamana, the performer of yajna, and much of his success depended on the magical power of words uttered correctly during the sacrifices. Some rituals performed by the Vedic Aryans are common to the Indo-European peoples, but several of them seem to have been developed on the Indian soil. These formulae and sacrifices were invented, adopted, and elaborated by the priests called the Brahmanas

who claimed a monopoly of priestly knowledge and expertise. They invented numerous rituals, some of which were adopted from the non-Aryans. The reason for the invention and elaboration of the rituals is not clear, but mercenary motives cannot be ruled out. We hear that as many as 240,000 cows were given as dakshina or gift to the officiating priest in the rajasuya sacrifice.

5. **Correct Option: (a)**

Supplementary Notes:

- Political Structure during Rig Vedic Period:
  - Monarchical form of government with a king known as 'Rajan'.
  - Patriarchal families and 'Jana' was the largest social unit in Rig Vedic times.
  - Social grouping: kula (family) – grama – visu – jana.
  - Tribal assemblies were called Sabhas and Samitis. Examples of tribal kingdoms: Bharatas, Matsyas, Yadus and Purus.
  - Women enjoyed respectable position and they were allowed to take part in Sabhas and Samitis
- Social Structure during Rig Vedic Period:
  - Cattle especially cows became very important.
  - Monogamy was practiced but polygamy was observed among royalty and noble families.
  - There was no child marriage.
  - Social distinctions existed but were not rigid and hereditary.
- Religious Structure during Rig Vedic Period:
  - They worshipped natural forces like earth, fire, wind, rain, thunder, etc. by personifying them into deities.
  - Indra (thunder) was the most important deity. Other deities were Prithvi (earth), Agni (fire), Varuna (rain) and Vayu (wind).
  - Female deities were Ushas and Aditi.
  - There were no temples and no idol worship.

6. **Correct Option: (a)**

Supplementary Notes:

- Women of the Vedic period (circa 1500-1200 BCE), were epitomes of intellectual and spiritual attainments. The Vedas have volumes to say about these women, who both complemented and supplemented their male partners. When it comes to talking about significant female figures of the Vedic period. Women poets during Vedic civilization were Vishwawara, Apala, Gosha, and Lopamudra.

7. **Correct Option: (a)**

Explanation:

- **Statement 2 is incorrect:** Rig Vedic people worshipped mainly for the want of praja (children), pashu (cattle), food, wealth, heath, etc.

Supplementary Notes:

Features of Rig Vedic Society -

- The earliest text of the early Vedic period is the Rig Vedic Samhita.
- **Polity and Administration -**
  - The concept of polity developed in the Rig Vedic time, with reference to various units of habitation viz the janas, vis, gana, grama and kula.
  - Cattle and material wealth were the cause of battles, which invoked support of gods for battles. They strongly believed that prayers, sacrifices and rituals could offer support in their mundane life.
  - The polity of the Rig Vedic period was that of a tribal society.
  - The chief of the tribe was called 'rajan' and was the main political head. Rajan was a hereditary chief, perhaps elected by the assembly called 'samiti'.
  - The assemblies called sabha, samiti, vidhata and gana are mentioned in the Rig Veda.
    - Sabha was the assembly of elders or the elites;
    - Samiti was an assembly of people, and
    - Vidhata was the assembly of tribes.
  - The assemblies performed military and religious functions. Women attended the sabhas and vidhatas.
  - The king sought the support of the samiti and sabha for his activities.
- **Social Divisions:**
  - Vedic people distinguished themselves from the non-Aryan people. 'Varna' was the term used by Aryans to refer to colour and category.
  - 'Arya Varna' and 'Dasa Varna' are mentioned in the Rig Veda.
  - Dasas and Dasyus were conquered and treated as slaves. (They came to be considered sudras in the later period.)
  - Social class was classified into warriors, priests and common people.
  - Slavery was common and slaves were given as gifts to the priests, but there is no reference to wage labour.
  - Horse-drawn chariots and bronze objects were possessed by a few suggesting social distinction.
  - Vedic society was largely egalitarian initially, and social distinctions emerged later.
- **Tribe and Family**
  - Kinship was the basis of the social structure.
  - People were identified with specific clans, which formed the tribe or jana. (However the concept of Janapada did not exist.)

- Common people were referred to by the term 'vis'.
- The family (griha) was the main social unit within the tribe - headed by the grihapati and his wife was known as sapatni.
- The family structure at that point of time was perhaps a joint family.

- **Women**
  - Though women had a respectable position, it can possibly not be generalised.
  - Society was essentially patriarchal with a preference for male children and cattle.
  - Women attended assemblies and offered sacrifices.
  - Polyandry seems to have existed, and widow remarriage was also known.
  - People married at the age of 16–17, according to scholars, and there is little evidence of child marriage.
- **Economy - Agricultural**
  - There is archeological evidence for development of agriculture. Ploughshare is mentioned in the Rig Veda.
  - Field was known as kshetra, and krishi referred to ploughing. langla and sura referred to plough and sita meant the furrow created by ploughing.
  - Water for irrigation was probably drawn from wells by cattle driven water-lifts using pulleys.
  - People had the knowledge of different seasons, sowing, harvesting and threshing.
  - Barley (yavam) and wheat (godhuma) was cultivated.
- **Trade**
  - Trading activities were limited. Pan meant barter, which was the mode of exchange.
  - Dan and dakshina were the means of redistributing resources.
- **Transportation**
  - Horses, horse-drawn chariots and bullock carts were used.
  - References are also found regarding samudra (sea) and nau (boats).
- **Pastoralism**
  - Cattle rearing was an important economic activity, though agriculture was also practiced.
  - Cattle were considered wealth. The term gavishthi which means search for cows is mentioned in the Rig Veda with reference to war.
  - The donations to the priests were mainly cows.

Difference between early and later vedic societies:

- **Caste System** - Profession was the basis of the caste system in early vedic society but it became birth in the later vedic era, making it more rigid.
- **Shudra/Untouchables** Later vedic period introduced the concept of Shudras, whose main function was to serve the upper-caste.
- **Women** - The participation of women in different activities got reduced tremendously in the later vedic society, subjugating them to a more subordinate position and homely roles reducing their freedom.
- **Kingship** - Leadership became more stable in the later vedic period with the role of the kind transforming into more absolute and prominent.
- **Settlement** - The society shifted from pastoralist and semi-nomadic nature in early vedic to settled and agriculture centrist in the later vedic era.
- **Economy** - Early vedic society functioned mainly on barter system, which was added up with use of gold and silver coins in the later vedic period.

8. Correct Option: (b)

Explanation:

- **Statement 2 is incorrect:** Private property in land was present.

Supplementary Notes:

Civilization in Eastern India

- Although different parts of eastern India acquired prominence at different times, the formative phase: ranged from the fourth to seventh century.
- In this period writing, Sanskrit learning Vedic rituals, brahmanical Social classes, and state systems spread and developed in eastern Madhya Pradesh, in north;' Orissa, in West Bengal, In a.good part of Bangladesh and in Assam.
- For the first time in the fifth and sixth centuries we clearly notice large-scale writing, use of Sanskrit, formation of varna society, and progress of Buddhism and Brahmanism in the form of Saivism and Vaishnavlsm in this area.
- We find only the remnants of communal authority over land, but we can see the existence of private property in land, and the use of gold coins with which it could be purchased.
- All this presupposes an advanced food-producing economy.
- Apparently it was based on iron ploughshare agriculture, wet paddy cultivation, and knowledge of various crafts.

9. Correct Option: (d)

Explanation:

- **Statement 1 is incorrect:** According to Al-Biruni, the caste system was not a unique feature of Indian society.

- **Statement 2 is incorrect:** Ibn Battuta was not particularly concerned with explaining the prosperity of towns.
- **Statement 3 is incorrect:** According to Bernier, between the poorest of the poor and the richest of the rich, there was no social group or class worth the name.

Supplementary Notes:
Travellers and Their Understanding of Society

- Al-Biruni tried to explain the caste system by looking for parallels in other societies.
- He noted that in ancient Persia, four social categories were recognised: those of knights and princes; monks, fire-priests and lawyers; physicians, astronomers and other scientists; and finally, peasants and artisans.
- In other words, he attempted to suggest that social divisions were not unique to India.
- While Ibn Battuta was not particularly concerned with explaining the prosperity of towns, historians have used his account to suggest that towns derived a significant portion of their wealth through the appropriation of surplus from villages.
- Ibn Battuta found Indian agriculture very productive because of the fertility of the soil, which allowed farmers to cultivate two crops a year.
- He also noted that the subcontinent was well integrated with inter-Asian networks of trade and commerce, with Indian manufactures being in great demand in both West Asia and Southeast Asia, fetching huge profits for artisans and merchants.
- Indian textiles, particularly cotton cloth, fine muslins, silks, brocade and satin, were in great demand. Ibn Battuta informs us that certain varieties of fine muslin were so expensive that they could be worn only by the nobles and the very rich.
- Bernier described Indian society as consisting of undifferentiated masses of impoverished people, subjugated by a small minority of a very rich and powerful ruling class.
- Between the poorest of the poor and the richest of the rich, there was no social group or class worth the name. Bernier confidently asserted: "There is no middle state in India."

10. Correct Option: (a)

Explanation:

- **Statement 2 is incorrect:** The society comprised four varnas depending on one's profession and within a family; members could follow the professions of different varnas.

Supplementary Notes:
Society in the Rig Vedic Period

- In the Rig Vedic period the society comprised of four varnas depending on one's profession and within a family, members could follow the professions of different varnas.
- In the later Vedic period, varnas came to be birth-based rather than profession-based. The proliferation of professions gave rise to 'jatis'. But the jati system was not yet as rigid as it became during the period of the sutras.
- The unit of society was family, primarily monogamous and patriarchal. Child marriage was not in vogue. There are a few references to the freedom of choice in marriage. A widow could marry the younger brother of her deceased husband. The wife was the husband's partner in all religious and social ceremonies.
- The father's property was inherited by his son (patriarchy and patrilineal). The daughter could inherit it only if she was the only child of her parents. Right to property was known in moveable things like cattle, horse, gold and ornament and so also in an immoveable property like land and house.

11. Correct Option: (a)

Explanation:

- **Statement 3 is incorrect:** Marriage within the gotra was not permitted.

Supplementary Notes:
Later Vedic Period

- **Geographical Extent:** Extended to the whole of western UP, Ganga-Yamuna doab, and also penetrated to the Deccan, Vindhyas & South India.
- **Polity:** Royal power increased many folds. Rituals and sacrifices were performed to strengthen the king's position – Rajasuya (consecration ceremony), Vajpeya (chariot race), and Asvamedha (horse sacrifice).
- Women were not permitted to attend public assemblies like Sabhas and Samitis. Their position in society diminished.
- Institution of 'gotra' appears in later Vedic period. Marriage within the gotra was not permitted.
- The importance of prayers reduced and rituals and sacrifices became more elaborate.

12. Correct Option: (d)

Explanation:

- All statements are incorrect.

Supplementary Notes:
Varna System

- The Rig Veda shows some consciousness of the physical appearance of people in northwestern India in about 1500-1000 BC.
- Varna was the term used for colour, and it seems that the Aryans were fair and the indigenous inhabitants were dark in complexion.
- The factor which contributed most to the creation of social divisions was the conquest of the indigenous inhabitants by the Aryans.

- The dasas and the dasyus, who were conquered by the Aryans, were treated as slaves and sudras.
- The tribal chiefs and the priest acquired a larger share of the booty, and they naturally grew at the cost of the common people, which created social inequalities in the tribe.
- Gradually, the tribal society was divided into three groups; warriors, priests and the people, on the same pattern as in Iran.
- The fourth division called the sudras appeared towards the end of the Rig Vedic period, because it is mentioned for the first time in the tenth book of the Rig Veda, which is the latest addition.
- It is found that slaves were given as gifts to the priests. They were mainly women slaves employed for domestic purposes.
- It is clear that in Rig Vedic tribes, slaves were not used directly in agriculture or other producing activities.
- Tribal elements in society were stronger and social divisions based on collection of taxes or accumulation of landed property were absent.
- The society was still tribal and largely egalitarian.

CONCEPT REVISION

Here is the list of concepts that have been covered as part of the previous exercise. Revise and Self-reflect on your concepts you covered.

- Stages of life of a man in Aryan Society ☐
- Strategies followed to maintain Varna System ☐
- Condition of society during Rig Vedic Period ☐
- Women poet of Vedic Civilization ☐
- Characteristics of Eastern Indian Society in 6th-7th century ☐
- Varna System ☐
- Social structure of Early Vedic Period ☐

3.4 INDIAN SCHOOL OF PHILOSOPHY

QUESTIONS

1. With reference to Sant Kabir, consider the following statements:

1. He was a disciple of Ramanuja.
2. The hallmark of Kabir's works consists of his two line couplets (Doha).
3. He did not believe in any religious discrimination and readily accepted all the religions.

Which of the above statements are correct?

(a) 1 and 2 only (b) 1 and 3 only
(c) 2 and 3 only (d) 1, 2 and 3

2. Consider the following statements about Indian School of Philosophy:

1. It has rejected the idea of the existence of God.
2. It recognizes four material elements as the substance: earth, water, fire, and air.
3. It rejected the notion of an afterworld, karma, liberation (moksha).

Which of the following School of Philosophy best describes the above characteristic features?

(a) Sankhya
(b) Mimamsa
(c) Vaisheshika
(d) Charvaka

3. Which of these Schools of Philosophy view the earthly life as full of suffering and liberation is the supreme end of life?

1. Samkhya
2. Mimamsa
3. Vaisheshika
4. Nyaya

Select the correct answer using the code given below:

(a) 1 and 4 only (b) 1 and 3 only
(c) 2 and 3 only (d) 3 and 4 only

4. The Philosophy of Advaitvad in the cultural history of India is associated with which of the following?

(a) Shankaracharya (b) Nimbarka
(c) Basavanna (d) Madhavacharya

5. Consider the following statements:

1. Charvaka denies the operation of divine and supernatural agencies and makes man the centre of all activities.
2. Charvaka accepted the existence/reality of only those things that could be experienced by human senses and organs.
3. Charvaka's Philosophy is also known as Lokayata i.e., the Philosophy of the common people

Which of the above statement/s is/are correct?

(a) 1 only (b) 2 only
(c) 3 only (d) 1, 2 and 3

6. **Who founded the four mathas (i.e., monasetries) in the four corners of India?**
   (a) Shankaracharya
   (b) Ramanujacharya
   (c) Bhaskaracharya
   (d) Madhvacharya

7. **Consider the following:**
   1. The pioneer in preaching Nirguna Bhakti in medieval India was Ramananda.
   2. Surdas was the blind poet who worshipped Krishna.
   3. Adi Shankaracharya established four mathas in the four corners of India.

   Select the correct answer using the codes given below:
   (a) 1 and 2 only (b) 3 only
   (c) 1 and 3 only (d) 1, 2 and 3

8. **Match List I with List II:**

List I	List II
A. Bengal	1. Chaitanya
B. Sri Perumbudur	2. Ramananda
C. Amritsar	3. Ramanuja
D. Benaras	4. Ramdas

Select the correct answer using the code given below:

	A	B	C	D
(a)	2	4	3	1
(b)	2	3	4	1
(c)	1	4	3	2
(d)	1	3	4	2

9. **With reference to schools of Philosophy in India, consider the following statements about hetrodox traditons:**
   1. Ajivikas was founded by Makkali Gosala and they were follower of Niyati.
   2. The Charvaka school of Philosophy completely disregarded the otherworldly existence beyond this world that is inhabited by a person.
   3. Anekantavada is the fundamental doctrine of Buddhism that emphasises on the multiple routes of finding the truth.

   Which of the above statement/s is/are correct?
   (a) 1 and 2 only (b) 1 and 3 only
   (c) 2 and 3 only (d) 1, 2 and 3

10. **Which of the following statements is correct about the Shada Darshana?**
   1. The Samkhya, propounded by Rishi Jaimini, is the oldest of all among the Shada Darshana.
   2. The Vaisheshika school believes in the physicality of the universe which is created by five main elements: fire, air, water, earth and ether.
   3. As per the Nyaya Philosophy, one can verify the truth of a proposition by using logical tools like inference, hearing and analogy.

   Select the correct answer using the code given below:
   (a) 1 only (b) 2 only
   (c) 2 and 3 only (d) 1 and 3 only

11. **Consider the following statements:**
   1. He was the first Indian philosopher to provide a systematic theistic interpretation of the Philosophy of the Vedas.
   2. He provided an intellectual basis for the practice of bhakti.
   3. Shri-bhashya and Bhagavadgita-bhashya were written by him.

   Which of the following Indian philosophers has been described above?
   (a) Adi Shankaracharya
   (b) Madhavacharya
   (c) Ramanujacharya
   (d) Mandan Mishra

SOLUTIONS

1. **Correct Option: (c)**

Explanation:

- **Statement 1 is incorrect:** Swami Ramananda influence: Kabir Das' ideologies were greatly influenced by Vaishnava saint Swami Ramananda who accepted Kabir as his disciple.

Supplementary Notes:

Sant Kabir Das

- Sant Kabir Das was a very renowned saint, poet and social reformer of India who lived during the 15th century. His esteemed works and poems describe the greatness and oneness of the Supreme Being.
- He did not believe in any religious discrimination and readily accepted all the religions. Sant Kabir Das propagated that there is the presence of same Supreme Being in all religions.
- Sant Kabir Das was a highly acclaimed poet of his time. His writings significantly influenced the Bhakti movement. Some of his famous writings include 'Sakhi Granth', 'Anurag Sagar', 'Bijak' and 'Kabir Granthawali'.
- The hallmark of Kabir's works consists of his two line couplets (Doha), which reflect his deep philosophical thinking.
- A religious community known as 'Kabir Panth' was founded by him and the members of this forum are referred as 'Kabir Panthis', implying the followers of Kabir Das. He was admired by individuals of all faiths and his teachings are still alive and passed from generations.
- Swami Ramananda's influence: Kabir Das' ideologies were greatly influenced by Vaishnava saint Swami Ramananda who accepted Kabir as his disciple.

- The UP Tourism department has initiated to promote Maghar as a tourist destination where Hindus have built a temple in mem`ory of Kabir, while Muslims have constructed a mausoleum in his memory.

2. **Correct Option: (d)**

Supplementary Notes:

Charvaka School of Philosophy

- It is also called Lokayata, a quasi-philosophical Indian school of materialists who rejected the notion of an afterworld, karma, liberation (moksha), the authority of the sacred scriptures, the Vedas, and the immortality of the self.
- The Charvakas do not consider 'ether' as one of the five essential elements as it cannot be experienced through the perception. Hence, they say the universe consists of only four elements: fire, earth, water and air.
- Combinations of these elements produce all objects and phenomena of nature, both material and spiritual.
- The Charvakas decried religious superstition which kept the people ignorant and oppressed, and opposed their view of cognition as the result of sense perception to religious visions.

Samkhya

- This Philosophy holds that reality is constituted of two principles – one female and the other male – i.e. Prakriti and Purusha, respectively.
- Prakriti and Purusha are completely independent and absolute. According to this system, Purusha is mere consciousness; hence, it cannot be modified or changed. Prakriti, on the other hand, is constituted of three attributes, thought, movement and the change or transformation of these attributes brings about the change in all objects.
- It tries to establish some relationship between Purusha and Prakriti for explaining the creation of the universe. The propounder of this Philosophy was Kapila, who wrote the Samkhya sutra.

Mimamsa

- This Philosophy is basically the analysis of interpretation, application and the use of the text of the Samhita and Brahmana portions of the Veda.
- According to Mimamsa Philosophy, Vedas are eternal and possess all knowledge, and religion means the fulfilment of duties prescribed by the Vedas.
- This Philosophy encompasses the Nyaya-Vaisheshika systems and emphasizes the concept of valid knowledge. Its main text is known as the Sutras of Jaimini which have been written during the third century BC.

Vaisheshika

- This system is considered as the realistic and objective Philosophy of universe.
- The reality according to this Philosophy has many bases or categories which are substance, attribute, action, genus, distinct quality and inherence.
- Vaisheshika thinkers believe that all objects of the universe are composed of five elements–earth, water, air, fire and ether.
- They believe that God is the guiding principle.
- The living beings are rewarded or punished according to the law of karma, based on actions of merit and demerit.
- Creation and destruction of universe is a cyclic process and takes place in agreement with the wishes of God. Kanada wrote the basic text of Vaisheshika Philosophy.

3. **Correct Option: (d)**

Supplementary Notes:

Vaisheshika Philosophy

- It was founded by the sage Kanada.
- It propounded the atomic theory of its founder Kannada. At one time Vaisheshik was regarded as part of the Nyaya Philosophy since physics is part of science. But since physics is the most fundamental of all sciences, Vaisheshik was later separated from Nyaya and put forth as a separate Philosophy.
- It is a realistic and objective Philosophy of the universe.Vaisheshika school deals with metaphysics. It is an objective and realistic philosophy of the Universe. According to the Vaisheshika School of Philosophy, the universe is reducible to a finite number of atoms, Brahman being the fundamental force causing consciousness in these atoms.

Nyaya Philosophy

- Founder of this Philosophy is Gautam and the principles are mentioned in Nyaya Sutras.
- Nyaya Philosophy states that nothing is acceptable unless it is in accordance with reason and experience (scientific approach). Nyaya says that the world is real and the philosophy does not follow a monist view.
- It relies on several pramanas, i.e., means of obtaining true knowledge as its epistemology. According to it, the Pradhan Pramana or principal means of obtaining knowledge is Pratyaksha Pramana, i.e., the knowledge obtained through the 5 senses. There are also other pramanas like Anumana (inference, through which we can obtain true knowledge) and Shabda Pramana (a statement of an expert).
- **Statements 3 and 4 are correct:** Nyaya is a system of atomic pluralism and logical realism. It is allied to the Vaisheshika system which is regarded as 'Samanatantra or similar Philosophy'. Vaisheshika develops metaphysics and ontology. Nyaya develops logic and epistemology. Both agree in viewing the earthly life as full of suffering, as bondage of the soul

and liberation is absolute cessation of suffering, as the supreme end of life. Both agree that bondage is due to ignorance of reality and that liberation is due to right knowledge of reality.

Samkhya Philosophy

- Samkhya is the oldest philosphy. It was put forward by Kapila.
- Samkhya Philosophy provided the materialistic ontology for Nyaya and Vaisheshik, but there is very little original literature in Samkhya.
- It is generally believed that Samkhya Philosophy is dualistic and not monistic because it has two entities, purush (spirit) and prakriti (nature) in it. Samkhya emphasizes the attainment of knowledge of self by means of concentration and meditation.
- Samkhya holds that it is the self-knowledge that leads to liberation and not any exterior influence or agent.
- Samkhya forms the philosophical basis for yoga.
- In Samkhya, the necessity of God is not felt for epistemological clarity about the interrelationship between higher self, individual self, and the universe around us.

Mimamsa Philosophy

- It is based on sage Jaimini's Mimamsa Sutras.
- It lays emphasis on the performance of the 'yagya' for attaining various spiritual and worldly benefits. Hence, this philosophy relies on the Brahmana (and Samhita) part of the Vedas.
- This school of Philosophy believes in the complete authority of Vedas. It emphasizes the power of Yajnas and Mantras in sustaining the activities of the universe. It states that a human being can attain salvation only by acting in conformity with the principles of Vedas.

4. **Correct Option: (a)**

Supplementary Notes:

- **Advaitvad**
  - Advaita means non-duality. Its basic theme is that Brahman is the unchanging entity which alone is real while changing entities do not have absolute existence.
  - There is no difference between the Atman and the Brahman. The individual soul is not different from Brahman.
  - The world is an illusion (Maya) and only the self is real. A person who realises this attains Moksha (liberation of the soul).
  - The theory is also known as Monism.
- Shankaracharya propounded the theory of Advaitvad.
- Nimbarka propounded Dvaitvad (dualistic monism). According to him, the soul and the world are different from God but dependent on him.
- Basavanna is associated with Virashaivas. He believed that every human being is equal irrespective of gender or caste.
- Madhavacharya propounded the Dvait Philosophy, stating that the world is not an illusion and there is a difference between the Atman (one's own soul) and the Brahman (ultimate reality). He believed that liberation could be attained only through the grace of god.
- Ramanuja propounded the theory of Vishisht Advaita.

5. **Correct Option: (d)**

Explanation:

- All statements are correct.

Supplementary Notes:

Charvaka and the Materialistic View of Life

- Charvaka was the main expounder of the materialistic Philosophy which came to be known as the Lokayata, which means the ideas derived from the common people.
- It underlined the importance of intimate contact with the world (loka), and showed a lack of belief in the other world. Many teachings are attributed to Charvaka. He was opposed to the quest for spiritual salvation.
- He denied the existence of any divine or supernatural agency. He accepted the existence/reality of only those things that could be experienced by human senses and organs. This implied a clear lack of faith in the existence of Brahma and God.
- According to Charvaka, the Brahmanas manufactured rituals in order to acquire gifts (Dakshina). To discredit Charvaka, his opponents highlight only one of his teachings. According to it, a person should enjoy himself as long as he lives; he should borrow to eat well (i.e., take ghee).
- However, Charvaka's real contribution lies in his materialistic outlook. He denies the operation of divine and supernatural agencies and makes man the centre of all activities. The schools of Philosophy with emphasis on materialism developed in the period of an expanding economy and society between 500 BC and 300 AD.
- The struggle against the difficulties presented by nature in founding settlements and leading day-to-day life in the Gangetic plains and elsewhere led to the origin and growth of iron-based agricultural technology, the use of metal money, and the thriving of trade and handicrafts.
- The new environment gave rise to a scientific and materialistic outlook which was principally reflected in Charvaka's Philosophy and also figured in that of several traditional schools.

6. **Correct Option: (a)**

Supplementary Notes:

Mathas

- Matha is a Sanskrit word which also refers to a monastery in Buddhism and Jainism. The Matha tradition of Hinduism was involved in education, support studies, culture and also the place where many new texts were composed. Adi Shankara established four major mathas in different regions of India.
  - Govardhana Matha, Odisha – Rig Veda
  - Sharada Peetham, Karnataka – Yajur Veda
  - Dwaraka Pitha, Gujarat – Sama Veda
  - Jyotir Math, Uttarakhand – Atharva Veda

7. **Correct Option: (d)**

Explanation:

- All statements are correct.

Supplementary Notes:

Bhakti and Sufi Movements

- Nirguna Bhakti is the devotion towards a formless, all-encompassing God. The word 'Nirgun' means 'devoid of qualities,' referring to the lack of physical attributes in God. It is one of the two forms of devotion prevalent in Hinduism, the other one being Sagun Bhakti which sees God in a physical form. The pioneer in preaching Nirguna Bhakti in medieval India was Ramananda.
- Surdas (1483-1563): He was the disciple of Vallabhacharya of South India. He popularized the Krishna cult by singing songs glorifying Krishna's childhood. He was the author of the Sur Sagar, Sur Sarawali, etc.
- Adi Shankaracharya was a religious leader who propounded the Philosophy of Advaita. He established four Mathas, Jyotiramatha in Badrinath (Uttarakhand), Sharadapitha in Dwarika (Gujarat), Shringerimatha in Karnataka and Govardhanamatha in Puri (Odisha). He established them in four corners of the country with an objective to protect Indian culture, propagate Vedic Philosophy and strengthen the unity of India.

8. **Correct Option: (d)**

Supplementary Notes:

List I	List II
A. Bengal	1. Chaitanya
B. Sri Perumbudur	3. Ramanuja
C. Amritsar	4. Ramdas
D. Benaras	2. Ramananda

9. **Correct Option: (a)**

Explanation:

- **Statement 3 is incorrect:** Anekantavada is the fundamental doctrine of Jainism that emphasis on the multiple routes of finding the truth.

Supplementary Notes:

Ajivikas

- Buddhism and Jainism were not the only religions, which challenged Brahmanical dominance. According to the Buddhist sources, more than 62 sects and philosophies flourished in this period. One of these sects, known as the Ajivikas or 'Followers of the way of life,' were an ascetic order that started at the time of Buddha and Mahavira, and lasted until the 14th century.
- Ajivika was founded by Makkhali Gosala. Ajivikas were very popular in Magadha in the third century BC and Mauryan kings donated several caves (e.g., the Lomas Rishi Caves in the Barabar Hills in Bihar) in the honour of Ajivika monks.
- According to tradition, it is believed that for some six years, Mahavira's hardship was shared by Gosala, but ultimately the two quarreled and Gosala left Mahavira to found the sect of the Ajivikas (pre-determinism or 'niyati').
- His doctrines and those of his followers are known only from Buddhist and Jaina sources, which state that he was lowborn and died after a quarrel with Mahavira shortly before the Buddha died.
- The Ajivikas, who were rigid fatalists and determinists, supposedly, held that the affairs of the entire universe were ordered by a cosmic force called Niyati (meaning 'rule' or 'destiny' in Sanskrit) that determined all events, including an individual's fate, to the last detail and that barred personal efforts to change or accelerate improvement toward one's spiritual destiny.
- No human effort could have any effect against Niyati, and therefore, Karma is a fallacy. Nirvana was only reached after living through an immense number of lives, which proceeded automatically like the unwinding of a ball of thread, the last life being as an Ajivika monk.
- As a result of this static and melancholy view of the human condition, the Ajivikas practised austerities rather than pursue any purposeful goal.
- Some later Ajivikas worshipped Gosala as a divinity, and the tenet of Niyati developed into the doctrine that all change was illusory and that everything was eternally immobile.

Charvakas

- Its founder was Charvaka, the author of the Barhaspatya Sutras in the final centuries before the common era. It is characterised as a materialistic and atheistic school of thought.

- Lokayata refers to ideas derived from common people and it underlines the importance of intimate contact with the world (loka), while showing a lack of belief in the other world.
- It accepts direct perception as the surest method to prove the truth of anything. It thus recognises earth, water, fire, and air, but not ether, as it cannot be known by perception.
- Charvaka insists on joyful living and is opposed to the quest for spiritual salvation.
- He denies the existence of any divine or supernatural agency and accepts the existence reality of only those things which could be experienced by human senses and organs. Thus, there was a clear lack of faith in the existence of Brahman and God.
- According to Charvaka, the Brahmanas manufactured rituals for acquiring Dakshina (gifts).

Anekatvanda

- It is a Jaina doctrine an it literally means the doctrine of 'non-onesidedness' or 'manifoldness' or 'non-absolutism'.
- It is one of the basic principles of Jainism that encourages acceptance of relativism and pluralism.
- According to this doctrine, truth and reality are perceived differently from different points of view, and no single point of view is the complete truth. Jainas compare all attempts to proclaim absolute truth with Adhgajanyayah (the 'maxim of the blind men and elephant').

10. Correct Option: (c)

Explanation:

- **Statement 1 is incorrect:** The Samkhya, propounded by Kapila Muni, is the oldest of all among the Shada Darshana.

Supplementary Notes:

Orthodox Philosophy:

- This school believed that Vedas were the supreme revealed scriptures that hold the secrets to salvation. They did not question the authenticity of the Vedas. They had six sub-schools that were called the Shada Darshana. Following is the detailed discussion on the three of them-

Samkhya School

- This is the oldest school of Philosophy and was founded by Kapil Muni who is supposed to have written the Samkhya Sutra. The word 'Samkhya' or 'Sankhya' literally means 'count'.
- This school believed in dualism or dvaitavada, i.e., the soul and the matter are separate entities. This concept is the basis of all real knowledge. This knowledge can be acquired through three main concepts:
    - Pratyaksha – Perception
    - Anumana – Inference
    - Shabda – Hearing

Nyaya School

- As the name of the school suggests, they believed in the technique of logical thinking to achieve salvation.
- They considered life, death and salvation to be like mysteries that can be solved through logical and analytical thinking.
- Furthermore, they argue that acquiring 'real knowledge' can only accrue salvation.
- This school of thought was supposed to be founded by Gautama who is also identified as the author of the Nyaya Sutra.
- They argue that by using logical tools like inference, hearing and analogy, a human being could verify the truth of a proposition or statement.
- For example, when faced with a problem like:
    - There is fire in the jungle
    - Because there is emission of smoke
    - Everything that emits smoke has a component of fire in it.

Vaisheshika School

- The Vaisheshika school believes in the physicality of the Universe and is considered to be the realistic and objective Philosophy that governs the universe.
- The Upala Kanada who also wrote the basic text governing the Vaisheshika Philosophy is often considered the founder of this school.
- They argue that everything in the universe was created by the five main elements: fire, air, water, earth and ether (sky).
- These material elements are also called 'Dravya'. They also argue that reality has many categories, for example, action, attribute, genus, inherence, substance and distinct quality.

11. Correct Option: (c)

Supplementary Notes:

Ramanujacharya

- Ramanuja (1017–1137) was a Vedic spiritual leader, philosopher, and a mystic who is recognised as one of the most influential thinkers in Hinduism.
- He was the chief proponent of Vishishtadvaita. He was the first Indian philosopher to provide a systematic theistic interpretation of the Philosophy of the Vedas, and is famous for arguing for the epistemic and soteriological significance of bhakti, or devotion to a personal God.

- After a long pilgrimage, Ramanuja settled in Shrirangam, where he organized temple worship and founded centre to disseminate his doctrine of devotion to the god Vishnu and his consort Shri Lakshmi.
- He provided an intellectual basis for the practice of bhakti (devotional worship) in three major commentaries: the Vedartha-samgraha (on the Vedas, the earliest scriptures of Hinduism), the Shri-bhashya (on the Brahma-sutras), and the Bhagavadgita-bhashya (on the Bhagavadgita).

CONCEPT REVISION

Here is the list of concepts that have been covered as part of the previous exercise. Revise and Self-reflect on your concepts you covered.

- Samkhya ☐
- Mimamsa ☐
- Vaisheshika ☐
- Nyaya ☐
- Charvaka ☐
- Heterodox Traditions ☐

3.5 EMERGENCE OF BHAGWATISM, EXPANSION OF CASTEISM DURING GUPTA ERA

QUESTIONS

1. Consider the following statements regarding society in Gupta period:

1. As the Guptas were Vaishyas, the supremacy of the Brahamanas declined during this period.
2. The Greeks settled in the Indian subcontinent were expatriated back to their land.
3. All the tribals were given the status of Shudras.

Which of the above statements are incorrect?

(a) 1 and 2 only (b) 2 and 3 only
(c) 1 and 3 only (d) 1, 2 and 3

2. The castes proliferated into numerous sub-castes during Gupta Age because

1. Large number of foreigners had been assimilated into the Indian society.
2. Absorption of many tribal peoples into Brahmanical society.
3. Increased number of untouchables who were considered a Hindu caste.

Which of the above statements is/are correct?

(a) 1 and 2 only (b) 1 and 3 only
(c) 2 and 3 only (d) 1, 2 and 3

3. Consider the following about the status of women in Gupta period:

1. Women of higher Varna were free to earn livelihood but not the women of lower Varna
2. Women of higher Varna were free to live an independent life without male subordination

Which of the above statements is/are correct?

(a) 1 only (b) 2 only
(c) Both 1 and 2 (d) Neither 1 nor 2

4. The castes proliferated into numerous sub-castes in the Gupta period. What were the reasons behind it?

1. A large number of foreigners had been assimilated into Indian society, and each group of foreigners was considered a kind of caste.
2. There was the absorption of many tribal people into Brahmanical society through the process of land grants.
3. A large number of Chandalas was incorporated into the caste system.

Select the correct option using the codes given below:

(a) 1 and 2 only (b) 2 and 3 only
(c) 1 and 3 only (d) 1, 2 and 3

5. Consider the following statements regarding trade and economy during Gupta period:

1. The Romans learnt the art of growing silk from Indians which lowered the demand of Indian silk in Europe.
2. There was a rise of priestly landlord class at the cost of local tribal peasants in the Gupta period.
3. A substantial amount of virgin soil were brought to cultivation and better knowledge was applied in agriculture in the Gupta period.

Which of above statements is/are correct?

(a) 1 and 2 only
(b) 2 and 3 only
(c) 1 and 3 only
(d) 1, 2 and 3

SOLUTIONS

1. **Correct Option: (d)**

Explanation:

- **Statement 1 is incorrect:** The supremacy of the Brahmanas increased during this period.
- **Statement 2 is incorrect:** The Greeks settled in the Indian subcontinent were assimilated in the Indian society.
- **Statement 3 is incorrect:** The tribal head were given the status of Kshatriyas and other tribals were given the status of Shudras.

Supplementary Notes:

Society in Gupta period

- The structure of the society underwent change in the Gupta period. The Brahmana supremacy not only continued but rather increased in Gupta times.
- It is evident from the large number of land grants to the Brahmanas not only from the rulers (Brahmadeya) but from certain categories of other people too.
- In return of this favor and support, Brahmanas presented the Gupta kings as possessing attributes of Gods and tried to legitimize the position of the Guptas.
- The Guptas, who were originally Vaishyas, came to be looked upon as Kshatriyas by the Brahmanas.
- Since the Brahmadeya land was given along with administrative rights and tax exemptions, it resulted in creation of a new class of Brahmana landlords.
- The castes proliferated into numerous sub-castes in this period.
- A large number of foreigners had been assimilated into the Indian society and each foreigner was assigned a sub-caste. For instance, the various foreign ruling families of pre-Gupta period (of Greek/Scythian origins) were given semi-Kshatriya status.
- Similarly, the Hunas who invaded India during the early 5th century were also assimilated in Indian society as one of the 36 Rajput clans.
- With the extension of Brahmanical culture in distant and different areas, a large number of tribal communities were assimilated in the Brahmanical social structure of the Varna system.
- The foreigners and tribal heads were included as Kshatriyas, the ordinary tribals were given the status of Shudras.
- The social and economic status of Shudras improved during this period. They were now allowed to listen to the Ramayana, the Mahabharata, and the Puranas.
- They could also perform some domestic rituals that were earlier prohibited for them and could now even worship a new God called 'Krishna'.

2. **Correct Option: (a)**

Explanation:

- **Statement 3 is incorrect:** During this period, the untouchables increased in number, especially the Chandalas but it was not the reason for the castes proliferating into numerous sub-castes.

Supplementary Notes:

Social Activities in Gupta Era

- The castes proliferated into numerous sub-castes as a result of two factors: on the one hand a large number of foreigners had been assimilated into the Indian society and each group of foreigners was considered a kind of Hindu caste.
- Since the foreigners mainly came as conquerors they were given the status of the Kshatriya in society.
- The Hunas, who appeared in India towards the close of the fifth century, ultimately came to be recognized as one of the thirty-six clans of the Rajputs. Even now some Rajputs bear the title 'Huna'.
- The other reason for the increase in the number of castes was the absorption of many tribal peoples into Brahmanical society by way of land grants.
- To the ruling chiefs of the tribes was ascribed a respectable origin.
- But most of the rest of the tribal people were given a low origin, and every tribe now became a kind of caste in Hindu society.
- But during this period the untouchables increased in number, especially the Chandalas.
- The Chandalas appeared in society as early as the 5th century BC. By the 5th century AD their number had become so enormous and their disabilities so glaring that it attracted the attention of the Chinese pilgrim Fa-hien.

3. **Correct Option: (d)**

Explanation:

- Both the statement are wrong about status of women in Gupta period.

Supplementary Notes:

- They were allowed to listen to Ramayana, Mahabharata, Puranas and worship Krishna.
- Women of lower Varnas were free to earn livelihood but not the women of higher Varna.
- Higher order Varna followed polygamy because of their riches.
- Subordination of women of higher Varna as they were dependent on men for livelihood and had no property right.

4. **Correct Option: (a)**

Explanation:

- **Statement 3 is incorrect:** Chandalas were untouchables and out of the caste system, hence, statement 3 is eliminated.

Supplementary Notes:

Social Developments

- Large-scale land grants to the Brahmanas suggest that the Brahmana supremacy increased in Gupta times. The Guptas, who probably were originally Vaishyas, came to be looked upon as Kshatriyas by the Brahmanas. The Brahmanas presented the Gupta kings as possessing god-like attributes. All this helped to legitimize the position of the Gupta princes, who became great supporters of the Brahmanical order. The Brahmanas accumulated wealth on account of the numerous land grants made to them and therefore, claimed many privileges, which are listed in the Narada Smriti, the lawbook of Narada, a work of about the 5th century BC.
- The castes proliferated into numerous sub-castes as a result of these factors:
  - A large number of foreigners had been assimilated into Indian society, and each group of foreigners was considered a kind of caste. As the foreigners largely came as conquerors they were given the status of Kshatriya in society. The Hunas, who came to India towards the close of the 5th century, eventually came to be recognised as one of the thirty-six clans of the Rajputs. Even now, some Rajputs bear the title 'Huna'.
  - The other reason for the increase in the number of castes was the absorption of many tribal people into Brahmanical society through the process of land grants. The tribal chiefs were assigned a respectable origin, but most of their ordinary kinsmen were assigned a low origin, and every tribe became a kind of caste in its new incarnation. This process continues in some ways up to the present.
  - The position of Shudras improved during this period. They were now permitted to listen to recitations of the Ramayana, the Mahabharata, and the Puranas. The epics and the Puranas represented the Kshatriya tradition, whose myths and legends won loyalty to the social order. The Shudras could also worship a new God called 'Krishna' and were also permitted to perform certain domestic rites which naturally meant fees for the priests. This can all be linked to some improvement in the economic status of the Shudras. From the 7th century onwards, they were mainly represented as agriculturists; in the earlier period, they generally figured as servants, slaves, and agricultural labourers working for the three higher Varnas.
  - However, during this period, the number of untouchables increased, especially the Chandalas. The Chandalas entered the society as early as the 5th century BC. By the 5th century AD, their number had become so enormous and their disabilities so glaring that these attracted the attention of the Chinese pilgrim Fa-hien. He informed us that the Chandalas lived outside the village and dealt in meat and flesh. Whenever they entered the town, they struck a piece of wood to announce their arrival so that others might avoid them.

5. **Correct Option: (b)**

Explanation:

- **Statement 1 is incorrect:** Romans learnt the art of growing silk from Chinese.

Supplementary Notes:

Decline of Trade and Rise of Landed Class

- In contrast to earlier Gupta period, there occurred a decline of foreign trade in the Gupta period.
- Around 550 AD, the Romans learnt the art of growing silk from Chinese which affected India's trade with them. However, the demand of Indian silk was already low at that time in the Roman markets. In the mid 5th century, many guilds of the silk weavers from Gujarat migrated to Malwa and they adopted non-productive professions.
- In eastern and central MP, there was a rise in priestly landlord class at the cost of local peasants. These local tribal peasants were brought to the level of landless agriculture labourers. In central and western India also, the peasants were forced to become labourers. However, a substantial amount of virgin soil was brought to cultivation and better knowledge was applied in agriculture.

CONCEPT REVISION

Here is the list of concepts that have been covered as part of the previous exercise. Revise and self-reflect on your concepts you covered.

- Society in Gupta Period ☐
- Castes during Gupta Period ☐
- Status of women in Gupta period ☐
- Proliferation of sub-castes in Gupta Period ☐

MEDIEVAL HISTORY

Syllabus (MICRO TOPICS)

1. Political Structure of Medieval India

- Major Dynasties (750-1200) of Early Medieval India
  - The Pratiharas (8th to 10th Century)
  - The Palas (8th to 11th Century)
  - The Tripartite Conflict
  - The Senas (11th to 12th Century)
  - The Rajaputas
  - Pallavas
  - Chalukyas
  - Rashtrakutas
  - Indian Feudalism
  - Administration
  - Society and Culture
- Cholas and other South Indian Kingdoms
  - Chola Rulers and Political History
  - Chola Administration
  - Naval Expeditions of Cholas
  - Socio-Economic Life
  - The Cheras (9th to 12th Century)
  - The Yadavas (12th to 13th Century)
  - Contact with South-East Asia
- Early Muslim Invasions
  - The Arab Conquest of Sindh
  - Mahmud of Ghazni
  - Muhammad Ghori
- Delhi Sultanate
  - Slave Dynasty
  - Khalji Dynasty (1290-1320 AD)
  - Tughlaq Dynasty (1320-1414 AD)
  - Provincial Kingdoms and Resistance by Indian Chiefs
  - Sayyid Dynasty
  - Lodi Dynasty
  - Attacks by Mongols and other Turks
- Vijayanagara Empire
  - Sources
  - Political History
  - Administration
  - Development of the State
  - Five Main Provinces
- Foundation of Mughal Empire in India
  - The Timurids
  - The Timurid-Uzbek
  - Uzbek-Iran Conflict and Babur
  - Battle of Panipat
  - Babur's Advent into India
  - Babur and Rajputs
  - Babur and Afghan Chieftains
  - Humayun
  - Establishment of Second Afghan Empire in India (1540-1555)
- Expansion and Consolidation: 1556-1707
  - Territorial Expansion
  - Administrative Reorganisation
  - Territorial Expansion by Successors of Akbar
  - Policies towards Autonomous Chieftains
  - Relations with Central Asia and Persia
  - Relations with Uzbegs
  - Relations with Persia
    - Babur and Humayun
    - Akbar
    - Jahangir
    - Shah jahan
    - Aurangzeb and Northwest Frontier
- The Maratha and Other Indian States and Society in the 18th Century
  - The Marathas and their Policy of Expansion
  - Marathas and Mughal Relations
  - The Marathas and Nizam-ul-Mulk
  - Third Battle of Panipat
  - Shivaji (1627-1680)
  - Shivaji's Administration
  - Successors of Shivaji
  - The Peshwas (1713-1818)
  - Other Indian States (The Bhonsles, the Gaikwads, the Holkars, the Scindhias)
  - Marathas, English and Portuguese

2. Economic Conditions of Medieval India

- Economic Conditions in 750-1200 AD
  - Rise in Land Grants
  - Economy and the Decline of Trade
  - Decline of Towns

- Cholas and other South Indian Kingdoms
  - Trade and Commerce
  - Irrigation
  - Agriculture
  - Taxes
- Delhi Sultanate
  - Economic Measures
  - Urbanization
  - Trade, Industry and Merchants
  - Agrarian Measures
- Vijayanagara Empire
  - Foundation
  - Krishnadeva Raya
  - The Portuguese
  - Deccan Muslim States
  - Foreign Trade
  - Internal Trade and Urban Life
- Mughal Empire
  - Land-Revenue System
    - Dahsala System
    - Mansabdari
    - Jagirdari System
  - Nobility
  - Organisation of Trade and Commerce
  - Foreign Trade and European Traders
- The Maratha and Other Indian States and Society in the 18th Century
  - Economic Condition in 18th Century
  - Revenue System
  - Chauth and Sardeshmukhi

3. **Socio-Cultural Development of Medieval India**

- Socio-Cultural Developments in 750-1200AD
  - Evolution of Temple Architecture
  - Contact with South–East Asia
  - Influence of Buddhism Abroad
  - Development of Literary Works in Regional Languages
- Cholas and Other South Indian Kingdoms
  - Education and Literature
  - Temple Architecture
  - Growth in Sculptural Art
  - Growth of Literature
- Delhi Sultanate
  - Religion and Delhi Sultanate
  - Social Customs
  - Position of Women
  - Caste and Slavery
  - Architecture: New Structural Forms
  - Growth of Literature
  - Composite Culture
- Vijayanagar Empire
  - Role of Temples
  - Society and Culture
  - Literature and Arts
  - Vijayanagara Style of Architecture
- Mughal Empire
  - Architecture
  - Paintings
  - Development of Language and Literature
  - Religious Ideas and Beliefs
  - Din-i-Ilahi
  - Sufi Movement and Bhakti Movement
  - Vaishnavite Movement
  - Literature and Fine Arts
- The Maratha and Other Indian States and Society in the 18th Century
- Social and Cultural Life
- Impact of Bhakti Movement

4. POLITICAL STRUCTURE OF MEDIEVAL INDIA

4.1 CHOLAS AND OTHER SOUTH INDIAN KINGDOMS

QUESTIONS

1. **Consider the following statements with respect to Chola's social life:**
   1. Caste system was widely prevalent during the Chola period.
   2. The Devadasi system or dancing girls attached to temples emerged during this period.
   3. Both Shaivism and Vaishnavism continued to flourish during the Chola period.
   4. The practice of 'Sati' was prevalent among the royal families.

   Which of the above statements are correct?

   (a) 2 and 3 only (b) 1, 2 and 4 only
   (c) 2, 3 and 4 only (d) 1, 2, 3 and 4

2. **Pattini cult was established under which of the following dynasties?**

   (a) Cheras (b) Cholas
   (c) Pandyas (d) Chedis

3. **Which of the following features of the Chola administration is/are correct?**
   1. The arrangement of democratic local self-government was a distinct feature.
   2. Land revenue and trade tax were principal sources of income.
   3. The empire was divided into smaller provinces called mandalams and nadus which had administrative autonomy.
   4. The king was alone responsible for efficient administration of the Chola Empire.

   Select the correct answer using the code given below:

   (a) 2 only (b) 1 and 3 only
   (c) 1, 2 and 3 only (d) 2, 3 and 4 only

4. **Match List-I with List-II**

List-I (State)	List-II (Emblem)
A. Chera	1. Bow
B. Chola	2. Tiger
C. Pandya	3. Fish

   Select the correct answer using the code given below:

	A	B	C
(a)	1	2	3
(b)	3	2	1
(c)	3	1	2
(d)	2	1	3

5. **Consider the following statements:**
   1. The expedition of Rajendra Chola to Bengal followed in reverse the same route which the great conqueror Samudragupta had followed.

2. Both Rajaraja and Rajendra I converted the Bay of Bengal into 'Chola Lake' by constructing numerous temples with water tanks there.
3. The Chola rulers especially Rajaraja and his son adopted the practice of having inscriptions written on the walls of the temples, giving a historical narrative of their victories.

Which of the above statements are correct?

(a) 1 and 2 only (b) 2 and 3 only
(c) 1 and 3 only (d) 1, 2 and 3

6. Consider the following statements:

1. Pandya Kings of early south Indian kingdom had trade relationship with the Romans.
2. Puhar was the port city developed by Chola ruler Karikala.
3. The Chera Kingdom of South India never fought with the other two kingdoms of Chola and Pandya, and maintained peace through matrimonial alliance.

Which of the above statement/s is/are correct?

(a) 1 and 2 only (b) 1 and 3 only
(c) 2 and 3 only (d) 1, 2 and 3

7. Consider the following statements about Chalukyas and Pallavas conflict during the 6th-8th century:

1. They were trying to establish supremacy over the land lying between the Krishna and the Kaveri doab.
2. The Aihole inscription give us some idea about the struggle between Chalukyas and Pallavas
3. During the entire period of struggle, the Pallava kings never occupied the Chalukyas capital and always remained at bay.

Which of the above statement/s is/are incorrect?

(a) 1 only (b) 2 only
(c) 3 only (d) 1 and 3 only

8. Which of the following statements regarding the Chola Empire is/are correct?

1. The founder of the Chola Empire was a feudatory of the Rashtrakutas.
2. Their strong navy aided them to develop sea trade in the Indian Ocean and to conquer Sri Lanka and the Maldives.

Select the correct option using the codes given below:

(a) 1 only (b) 2 only
(c) Both 1 and 2 (d) Neither 1 nor 2

9. Regarding the local administration of the Chola Empire, consider the following pairs:

1.	Ur	The exclusive assembly of the Brahman residents
2.	Mahasabha	The general assembly of the local residents
3.	Agraharas	Rent free lands/villages

Which of the above pairs is/are correctly matched?

(a) 1 and 2 only (b) 2 and 3 only
(c) 3 only (d) 1, 2 and 3

10. He subjugated the Kadamba capital at Banavasi and compelled the Gangas of Mysore to acknowledge his suzerainty. He also conquered the entire area between the Krishna and the Godavari, which came to be known as the province of Vengi.

Which of the following rulers is described in above passage?

(a) Narshimhavarman
(b) Pushyamitra Shunga
(c) Vikramditya II
(d) Pulakeshin II

11. 'The southern end of the Indian peninsula situated south of the Krishna River was divided into three kingdoms: Chola, Pandya, and Chera'. In this context, consider the following statements.

1. The city of Puhar was founded by the Chola king Karikala.
2. Senguttuvan was a Chera king who invaded the north and crossed the Ganges.

Which of the above statements is/are correct?

(a) 1 only (b) 2 only
(c) Both 1 and 2 (d) None of the above

12. Consider the following statements regarding the Chola Government:

1. All the authority rested in King's hand with Council of Ministers to advise him.
2. The basic unit of administration was 'Nadu' which consisted of a number of villages.

Which of the above statements is/are correct?

(a) 1 only (b) 2 only
(c) Both 1 and 2 (d) Neither 1 nor 2

13. Consider the following statements regarding the village assemblies and their administration in Chola Empire:

1. Mahasabha was a gathering of the adult men in the Brahman villages called as Agraharams.
2. The affairs of the village were managed by an executive committee to which educated persons owning property were elected either by drawing lots or by rotation.

Which of the above statements is/are correct?

(a) 1 only (b) 2 only
(c) Both 1 and 2 (d) Neither 1 nor 2

14. Consider the following statements regarding Pala and Pratihara Empires:

1. The directly administered territories in the Pala and Pratihara empires were divided into Bhukti, Mandala and Rashtra.
2. The Uparika collected land revenue and maintained law and order.

Which of the above statements is/are correct?

(a) 1 only (b) 2 only
(c) Both 1 and 2 (d) Neither 1 nor 2

15. Which of the following statements is/are correct about Administration of the Cholas?

1. The Chola empire was divided into eight Mandalams.
2. The Mandalams were further divided into Kottams.

Select the correct answer using the code given below:

(a) 1 only (b) 2 only
(c) Both 1and 2 (d) Neither 1 nor 2

16. The famous 'Kadaram Campaign' was undertaken by which Indian Kingdom?

(a) Chalukyas (b) Pandyas
(c) Cholas (d) Hoysala

17. Hostilities between the powers to the north and to the south of the Tungabhadra river became a regular and recurrent feature during the early medieval times. This hostility pattern was seen between which of the following kingdoms?

1. Chalukya-Pallava
2. Pallava-Rashtrakutas
3. Rashtrakutas-Cholas

Select the correct answer using the code given below:

(a) 1 and 3 only (b) 1 and 2 only
(c) 2 and 3 only (d) 1, 2 and 3

18. Consider the following pairs:

Ruler		Kingdom
1. Dantidurga	-	Rashtrakutas
2. Mayurasharman	-	Kadamba
3. Harichandra	-	Gurjara-Pratihara

Which of the above given pairs are correctly matched?

(a) 1 and 2 only (b) 1 and 3 only
(c) 2 and 3 only (d) 1, 2 and 3

19. Consider the following statements regarding Chola kingdom:

1. They put greater stress on Dana (gift) than on Yajna (sacrifice).
2. During Cholas, 'ur' referred to the settlements of peasants.

Which of the above statements is/are correct?

(a) 1 only (b) 2 only
(c) Both 1 and 2 (d) Neither 1 nor 2

20. Consider the following statements regarding the rulers of Chera Dynasty:

1. King Karikalathe, the prominent king, introduced the Pattini cult in Tamil Nadu.
2. Senguttuvan was the first to send an embassy to China from South India.

Which of the above statements is/are correct?

(a) 1 only (b) 2 only
(c) Both 1 and 2 (d) Neither 1 nor 2

SOLUTIONS

1. Correct Option: (d)

Explanation:

- All statements are correct.

Supplementary Notes:

Chola's Social Life

- After the decline of the Sangam period, the Cholas became feudatories in Uraiyur.
- They became prominent in the 9th century and established an empire comprising the major portion of South India.
- Caste system was widely prevalent during the Chola period.
- Brahmins and Kshatriyas enjoyed special privileges.
- The inscriptions of the later period of the Chola rule mention two major divisions among the castes - Valangai and Idangai castes.
- However, there was cooperation among various castes and sub-castes in social and religious life.
- The position of women did not improve. The practice of 'Sati' was prevalent among the royal families.
- The Devadasi system, or dancing girls attached to temples, emerged during this period.
- Both Shaivism and Vaishnavism continued to flourish during the Chola period.
- A number of temples were built with the patronage of Chola kings and queens. The temples remained centres of economic activity during this period. The Mathas had great influence during this period.

2. Correct Option: (a)

Supplementary Notes:

Cheras Dynasty

- Cheras ruled over Malabar Coast. King Sengattuvan was the most popular king of Cheras. He was first to construct a temple for Kannagi and the first to introduce the Pattini cult. 'Rechar' was his title. Karur and Vanji were the two capital cities.

3. Correct Option: (c)

Explanation:

- **Statement 4 is incorrect:** The king was not solely responsible for efficient administration of the Chola Empire. There was a body of executive officers in the immediate and constant attendance on the king.

Supplementary Notes:

Chola Administration System

- The Chola administration system was very well organised and efficient.
- The administration of Chola Dynasty was essentially monarchical in character where the king was at

the helm of the administration and all executive, legislative and military powers rested with him.

- A council of ministers and other high officials were there to advice the king on the administration of Chola Empire.
- Even the princes of Chola Dynasty were to associate with the ruling king and were actively employed in war and peace. Since the Chola empire was a big one there were many administrative divisions for the efficient working of the government.
- The empire was divided into many divisions (Mandala).
- An important feature of the Chola administration was village autonomy. People of the village looked after the administration through their own elected representatives. This administrative system became famous during the Chola period.
- The arrangement of democratic local self-government was a distinct feature. One representative from each unit was elected for a period of one year. The members were elected through Kuduvalai (lucky draw system). Villagers assembled in the temple on the day of election. The names of candidates to be elected were written on palm leaves and put on a pot. Then a small boy was asked to pick leaves one after the other in the presence of everybody and thus the representatives were elected.
- Land revenue and trade tax were principal sources of income. An extensive resurvey was done around 1089 CE by the Chola king Kulottunga, recording the extents of lands and their assessment, boundaries of villages and the common rights inside the village, including the communal pastures.
- The king was not alone responsible for efficient administration of the Chola Empire. There was a body of executive officers in the immediate and constant attendance of the king.
- Revenue officials were responsible for the tax collection. The Chola government was very mindful of the need for the fair and accurate collection of tax to run the state machinery. The revenue records were not manuals of extortion, but carefully maintained records of land rights based on complete enquiries and accurate surveys, and were kept up-to-date by regular surveys.

4. **Correct Option: (a)**

Supplementary Notes:

Cheras

- The Cheras ruled over large parts of modern-day Kerala.
- Vanji was the capital of the Cheras.
- Musiri and Tondi were the important seaports in this period.
- The emblem of Cheras was the 'bow and arrow'.
- The first-century Pugalur inscriptions reference to 3 generations of Chera kings.
- Senguttuvan (2nd century CE) was the prominent ruler of the Chera Dynasty.
- The military achievements of Senguttuvan have been recorded in the epic Silapathikaram, which talks about his Himalayan expedition where he vanquished many rulers from northern India.
- Senguttuvan introduced the Pattini cult or the worship of Kannagi as the ideal wife.
- He was the first to send an ambassador to China from South India.

Cholas

- The Chola kingdom of the Sangam period stretched from the present-day Tiruchi district to Southern Andhra Pradesh.
- Initially, the capital of the Cholas was Uraiyur. Later, it was shifted to Puhar (also called Poompuhar).
- King Karikala was a prominent king of the Sangam Chola Dynasty.
- The insignia/emblem of the Cholas was 'tiger'.
- Pattinappalai written by Kadiyalur Uruttirangannanar depicts his life as well as military achievements.
- Various Sangam poems mention the Battle of Venni where he defeated an alliance of the Cheras, Pandyas and 11 smaller chieftains.
- Vahaipparandalai was another important battle fought by Karikala.
- Trade and commerce prospered during his rule.
- He also constructed irrigation tanks near river Kaveri to make water available for reclaimed land from the forest for farming.

Pandyas

- The Pandyas reigned over the Southern region of modern-day Tamil Nadu.
- Madurai was the capital of Pandyas.
- Their emblem was the 'Carp/Fish'.
- King Neduncheliyan was also called 'Aryappadai Kadantha Neduncheliyan'.
- According to mythology, the curse of the Kannagi, wife of Kovalan, burnt and destroyed Madurai.
- The socio-economic condition of the seaport of Korkai was mentioned in Maduraikkanji which was written by Mangudi Maruthanar.

5. **Correct Option: (c)**

Explanation:

- **Statement 2 is incorrect:** The Bay of Bengal was converted into 'Chola Lake' due to naval expeditions of the strong Chola navy.

Supplementary Notes:

Age of Rajaraja and Rajendra I

- The greatest Chola rulers were Rajaraja (985-1014 AD) and his son Rajendra I (1014-1044 AD).
- Rajaraja destroyed the Chera navy at Trivandrum, and attacked Quilon. He, then conquered Madurai and captured the Pandyan king. He also invaded Sri Lanka and annexed its northern part to his empire. These moves were partly motivated by his desire to bring the trade with the southeast Asian countries under his control. One of his naval exploits was the conquest of the Maldives. Rajaraja, annexed the north-western parts of the Ganga kingdom in Karnataka, and overran Vengi.
- Rajendra-I was appointed heir apparent in his father's lifetime, and had considerable experience in administration and warfare before his accession to the throne. He carried forward the annexationist policy of Rajaraja by completely overrunning the Pandyas and the Cheras, and including them in his empire. The conquest of Sri Lanka was also completed with the crown and royal insignia of the king and the queen of Sri Lanka being captured in a battle. Sri Lanka was not able to free itself from the Chola control for another 50 years.
- Rajaraja and Rajendra I marked their victories by erecting a number of Siva and Vishnu temples at various places. The most famous among those was the Brihadeshwara Temple at Tanjore which was completed in 1010 AD.
- The Chola rulers adopted the practice of having inscriptions written on the walls of these temples, giving a historical narrative of their victories. That is why we know a great deal more about the Cholas than their predecessors.
- One of the most remarkable exploits in the reign of Rajendra I was the march across Kalinga to Bengal, in which the Chola armies crossed the river Ganga, and defeated two local kings. This expedition, led by a Chola general, took place in 1022 AD and followed in reverse the same route, which the great conqueror Samudragupta had followed. To commemorate this occasion, Rajendra I assumed the title of Gangaikondachola (the Chola who conquered the Ganga). He built a new capital near the mouth of the Kaveri river and called it 'Gangaikondacholapuram' (the city of the Chola who conquered the Ganga).
- An even more remarkable exploit at the time of Rajendra I was the naval expeditions don't change against the revived Sri Vijaya empire. The Sri Vijaya empire, which had been revived in the 10th century, extended over the Malay Peninsula, Sumatra, Java and the neighbouring islands, and controlled the overseas trade route to China.
- The expeditions led to the conquest of Kadaram or Kedah and a number of other places in the Malay Peninsula and Sumatra. The Chola navy was the strongest in the area, and for some time the Bay of Bengal was converted into 'Chola Lake'.

6. **Correct Option: (a)**

Explanation:

- **Statement 3 is incorrect:** The history of the Cheras is a continuing battle with the Cholas and Pandyas. Later, the Chera kingdoms temporarily became friends and concluded a matrimonial alliance with Pandyas. But this was only temporary peace.

Supplementary Notes:

- The southern end of the Indian peninsula, situated to south of the Krishna river, was divided into three kingdoms: Chola, Pandya, and Chera or Kerala.
- The Pandyas are first mentioned by Megatheres, who says that their kingdom was celebrated for pearls. He also speaks of it being ruled by a woman, which suggests some matriarchal influence in Pandya society.
- Even Sangam Literature mentions Pandya rulers and describes the Pandya kingdom as wealthy and prosperous. The Pandya kings profited from trade with Roman Empire and even sent embassies to the Roman emperor Augustus.
- The Chola kingdom (which in early medieval times was also known as Cholamandalam/Coromandel) was situated to the north-east of the territory of the Pandyas and between the Pennar and the Velar rivers.
- Karikala was the greatest of all Chola kings, who founded its port city Puhar (modern Kaveripattanam which was a great centre of trade and commerce and had a large dock) and constructed 160 km of embankment along Kaveri river.
- The Cheras were situated to the west and north of the Pandyas. It was an important and prosperous kingdom owing to its trade with the Romans. It appears that the Romans had, in fact, set up two regiments at Muziris and Muchiri (near modern Kochi) to protect their interests and also built a temple of Augustus.
- The history of the Cheras is marked with continuous battle against the Cholas and the Pandyas.

7. **Correct Option: (d)**

Explanation:

- **Statement 1 is incorrect:** They were trying to establish supremacy over the land lying between the Krishna and the Tungabhadra doab.
- **Statement 3 is incorrect:** The Pallava king Narasimhavarman (630–68 AD) occupied the Chalukya capital at Vatapi in about 642 AD, when Pulakesin II was probably killed in a battle against

the Pallavas. Therefore, he assumed the title of Vatapikonda or the conqueror of Vatapi.

Supplementary Notes:

- The principal interest in the political history of peninsular India from the 6th to the 8th century centres around the long struggle for supremacy between the Pallavas of Kanchi and the Chalukyas of Badami.
- The Pandyas, who were in control of Madurai and Tirunelveli districts of Tamil Nadu, joined this conflict as a poor third. Although, both the Pallavas and the Chalukyas championed Brahmanism, performed Vedic sacrifices, and made grants to the Brahmanas, the two quarrelled with each other over plunder, prestige, and territorial resources.
- Both tried to establish supremacy over the land lying between the Krishna and the Tungabhadra. Time and again, the Pallava princes tried to cross the Tungabhadra, which formed the natural historic boundary between many a kingdom of the Deccan and the deep south.
- The struggle continued over a long period with varying fortunes. The first important event in this long conflict took place during the reign of Pulakeshin II (609–42 AD), the most famous Chalukya king.
- He is known to us from the eulogy written on him by the court poet Ravikirti in the Aihole inscription. This inscription is an example of the poetic excellence achieved in Sanskrit, and despite its exaggeration is a valuable source for the life of Pulakeshin.
- He subjugated the Kadamba capital at Banavasi and compelled the Gangas of Mysore to acknowledge his suzerainty. He also defeated Harsha's army on the Narmada and checked his advance towards the Deccan.
- In his conflict with the Pallavas, he almost reached the Pallava capital, but the Pallavas purchased peace by ceding their northern provinces to Pulakeshin II.
- Around 610 AD Pulakeshin II also conquered the entire area between the Krishna and the Godavari, which came to be known as the province of Vengi. Here, a branch, of the main dynasty was set up and is known as the eastern Chalukyas of Vengi. However, Pulakeshin's second invasion of Pallava territory ended in failure.
- The Pallava king Narasimhavarman (630–68 AD) occupied the Chalukya capital at Vatapi in about 642 AD, when Pulakesin II was probably killed in a battle against the Pallavas. Narasimhavarman assumed the title of 'Vatapikonda or the conqueror of Vatapi'. He is also said to have defeated the Cholas, the Cheras, the Pandyas, and the Kalabhras.

8. **Correct Option: (b)**

Explanation:

- **Statement 1 is incorrect:** The founder of the Chola empire was Vijayalaya, who was at first a feudatory of the Pallavas.

Supplementar y Notes:

The Rise of the Chola Empire

- The founder of the Chola empire was Vijayalaya, who was at first a feudatory of the Pallavas.
- He captured Tanjore in 850 AD. And by the end of the 9th century, the Cholas had defeated both the Pallavas of Kanchi (Tondaimandalam) and weakened the Pandyas, bringing the southern Tamil country under their control.
- But the Cholas were hard put to defend their position against the Rashtrakutas. Krishna III defeated the Chola king, and annexed the northern part of the Chola empire. This was a serious setback to the Cholas, but they rapidly recovered, particularly after the death of Krishna III in 965 AD and the downfall of the Rashtrakuta empire.
- They developed a strong navy, which further aided them to develop sea trade in the Indian Ocean and to conquer Sri Lanka and the Maldives Islands. They also defeated the kings of Malaya, Java and Sumatra.

9. **Correct Option: (c)**

Explanation:

- **Pair 1 is incorrect:** Ur was the general assembly of the local residents of non-Brahmadeya villages.
- **Pair 2 is incorrect:** Sabha or Mahasabha was the exclusive assembly of Brahmans.

Supplementary Notes:

Chola Government: Local Self-Government

- The Cholas were famous for their local self-government model, which can be considered as one of the earliest examples of the Panchayati Raj System. The village administration was very systematic and well developed. Regarding the assemblies of the villages, the Chola inscriptions mention:
  - Ur: The general assembly of the local residents of non-Brahmadeya villages (or Vellanvagai villages) to discuss matters without any formal rule or procedure. Nothing much is known about the composition of the Ur but generally, the members were less than ten. It dealt with various matters related to land maintenance such as land sale, gift, and tax exemptions.
  - Sabha or Mahasabha: Exclusive assembly of Brahmans/gatherings of the adult male members in the Agraharas, that is, rent-free Brahmadeya villages which enjoyed a large measure of autonomy. The membership was governed by

different criteria such as property ownership, family antecedents, learning and good conduct. The Mahasabha possessed the propriety rights over communal lands and controlled the private lands within its jurisdiction. It could raise loans for the village and levy taxes with the right to realise the revenue in cases of default by selling the lands in question by public auction.

- The affairs of the village were managed by an executive committee to which educated persons owning property were elected either by drawing lots or by rotation. These members had to retire every three years. There were other committees for helping in the assessment and collection of land revenue, for maintenance of law and order, justice, etc. One of the important committees was the tank committee which looked after the distribution of water to the fields. The Mahasabha could distribute new lands, and exercise ownership rights over them. It could also raise loans for the village and levy taxes. The self-government enjoyed by these Chela villages was a very fine system. To some extent, this system worked in the other villages as well. However, the growth of feudalism restricted their autonomy.

10. Correct Option: (d)

Supplementary Notes:

Pulakeshin II

- The first important event in long conflict between the Pallavas and the Chalukyas took place during the reign of Pulakeshin II (609–42 AD), the most famous Chalukya king.
- He subjugated the Kadamba capital at Banavasi and compelled the Gangas of Mysore to acknowledge his suzerainty. He also defeated Harsha's army on the Narmada and checked his advance towards the Deccan.
- In his conflict with the Pallavas, he almost reached the Pallava capital, but the Pallavas purchased peace by ceding their northern provinces to Pulakeshin II. Around 610 AD, Pulakeshin II also conquered the entire area between the Krishna and the Godavari, which came to be known as the province of Vengi.
- Here, a branch of the main dynasty was set up and is known as the 'eastern Chalukyas of Vengi'. However, Pulakeshin's second invasion of Pallava territory ended in failure. The Pallava king Narasimhavarman (630–668 AD) occupied the Chalukya capital at Vatapi in about 642 AD, when Pulakesin II was probably killed in a battle against the Pallavas. Narasimhavarman assumed the title of 'Vatapikonda or the conqueror of Vatapi'. He is also said to have defeated the Cholas, the Cheras, the Pandyas, and the Kalabhras.

11. Correct Option (c)

Explanation:

- Both statements are correct.

Supplementary Notes:

- **Chola**
  - The Chola kingdom, which came to be called Cholamandalam (Coromandel), in early medieval times, was situated to the north-east of the territory of the Pandyas, between the Pennar and the Velar rivers.
  - Their chief center of political power lay at Uraiyur, a place famous for cotton trade.
  - The famous king, Karikala, founded Puhar (coterminous with Kaveripattanam, the Chola capital) and constructed 160 km of embankment along the Kaveri River during the 2nd century AD.
  - They maintained an efficient navy.
- **Pandya**
  - The Pandya territory occupied the southernmost and the south-eastern portion of the Indian peninsula with Madurai in Tamil Nadu as its capital.
  - Sangam literature refers to the Pandya rulers. They were profited from trade with the Roman empire and sent ambassadors to the Roman emperor Augustus.
  - The Brahmanas enjoyed considerable influence, and the Pandya king performed Vedic sacrifices in the early centuries of the Christian era.
- **Chera**
  - The Chera or the Kerala country was situated to the west and north of the land of the Pandyas.
  - In the early centuries of the Christian era, the Chera state was as important as the states of the Cholas and Pandyas and owed its position to trade with the Romans.
  - The history of the Cheras is a continuous battle against the Cholas and the Pandyas.
  - According to the Chera poets, their greatest king was Senguttuvan, who is said to invade the north and crossed the Ganges, which seems an exaggeration.
  - After the 2nd century, Chera's power declined, and we know nothing of its history until the 8th century.

12. Correct Option: (c)

Explanation:

- Both statements are correct.

Supplementary Notes:

Chola Government

- The king was the most important person in the Chola administration. All authority rested in his hands, but he had a council of ministers to advise him. The kings often went on tours in order to oversee the administration.

- The Cholas maintained a large share of elephants, cavalry and infantry which were called the three limbs of the army. The infantry was generally armed with spears. Most of the kings had bodyguards who were sworn to defend the kings even at the cost of their lives.
- The Chola state included area of central control, and loosely administered areas under different types of local control.
- The state was interpersed with hill people and tribals. The basic unit of administration was the Nadu which consisted of a number of villages having close kinship ties and other close associations.
- The number of Nadus increased as fresh lands were brought under cultivation by means of irrigation works such as ponds, wells, etc., and by converting hill or tribal people into agriculturists.
- Grants to Brahmans and temples increased, both of which helped in expanding cultivation.

13. **Correct Option: (c)**

Explanation:

- Both statements are correct.

Supplementary Notes:

Village Assemblies During Chola

- There were two assemblies, called the Ur and the Sabha or Mahasabha.
- The Ur was a general assembly of the village.
- Mahasabha was a gathering of the adult men in the Brahman villages which were called Agraharams. These were villages with Brahman settlements in which most of the land was rent-free.
- These villages enjoyed a large measure of autonomy. The affairs of the village were managed by an executive committee to which educated persons owning property were elected either by drawing lots or by rotation.
- These members had to retire every three years. There were other committees for helping in the assessment and collection of land revenue, for maintenance of law and order, justice, etc.
- One of the important committees was the tank committee which looked after the distribution of water to the fields. The Mahasabha could distribute new lands, and exercise ownership rights over them.
- It could also raise loans for the village and levy taxes. The self-government enjoyed by these Chola villages was a very fine system. To some extent, this system worked in other villages as well.

14. **Correct Option: (b)**

Explanation:

- **Statement 1 is incorrect:** The directly administered territories in the Pala and Pratihara empires were divided into Bhukti and Mandala.

Supplementary Notes:

Pala and Pratiharas

- The directly administered territories in the Pala and Pratihara empires were divided into Bhukti (provinces), and Mandala or Visaya (districts).
- The governor of a province was called Uparika and the head of a district, Visayapati. The Uparika was expected to collect land revenue and maintain law and order with the help of the army. The Vvisayapati was also expected to do the same within his jurisdiction. During the period, there was an increase of smaller chieftains called Samantas or Bhogapatis, who dominated over a number of villages.
- The Visayapatis and these smaller chiefs tended to merge with each other, and later on, the word Samanta began to be used indiscriminately for both of them.
- In the Rashtrakuta kingdom, the directly administered areas were divided into Rashtra (provinces), Visaya and Bhukti. The head of Rashtra was called Rashtrapati, and he performed the same functions as the Uparika did in the Pala and Pratihara empires.
- The Visaya was like a modern district, and the Bhukti was a smaller unit to it. In the Pala and Pratihara empires, the unit below the Visaya was called Pattala.
- The precise role of these smaller units is not known. It seems that their main purpose was the realization of land revenue and some attention to law and order. Apparently, all the officials were paid by giving them grants of rent-free land.
- This tended to blur the distinction between local officials and the hereditary chiefs and smaller Vassals. Similarly, the Rashtrapati or governor sometimes enjoyed the status and title of a Vassal king.

15. **Correct Option: (a)**

Explanation:

- **Statement 2 is incorrect:** The Eastern Gangas ruled over Orissa.

Supplementary Notes:

Administration of the Cholas

- The Chola inscriptions generally refer to the king as Ko, Perumal, Perumal Adigal (the great one), Raja-Rajadhiraja and Ko-Konmai Kondan (king of kings).
- The king had all the authority rested in him and had a council of ministers to advise him.
- The kings were often compared with the gods either directly or with the use of double entendre.

- The kings often undertook tours in order to keep in better touch with the administration.
- The kings maintained large households and large palaces with banquet halls, spacious gardens and terraces.
- The large number of terms for offices and officials in the Chola inscriptions suggest an expansion of the administrative structure especially from the reign of Rajaraja I.
- The Cholas maintained a large army consisting of three limbs of elephants, cavalry and infantry (which was armed with spears).
- The large number of terms for offices and officials in the Chola inscriptions as compared to those of the Pallavas, Pandyas and Cheras suggest an expansion of the administrative structure especially from the reign of Rajaraja I (early 11th century).
- The empire known as Rajyam or Rastrayam was divided into eight mandalams (provinces) each governed by a governor/Viceroys who were generally princes of the royal blood or of noble families.
- Officials were generally paid by assigning them revenue-bearing lands.
- Some of the provinces were formed of principalities which had been annexed by the Cholas and some were the territories of the Vassal princes, who paid tribute and rendered service to the king in emergent situations.
- The provinces were further divided into Kottams or Valanadus which were again divided into Nadus (districts), each of which again consisted of a number of autonomous villages that played a key role in the Chola administration system.
- The administration was also greatly facilitated by the Shrenis or Pugas (guilds), which were like some autonomous corporate organisations having persons belonging to the same craft.
  - Mandalam/Province: Headed by Viceroy/Governor.
  - Kottam/Valandu
  - Nadus (district): also known as agricultural land.
  - Nattar: Assembly of the leading men of a Nadu or district.
  - Nagarattar/Nagaram: assembly of the Mercantile groups/Merchants.

16. Correct Option: (c)

Explanation:

- **Option (c) is correct:** Cholas undertook the famous Kadaram campaign in 1025-26 AD.

Supplementary Notes:

Kadaram Campign

- The Cholas were well known for their sustained naval policy from the days of Rajaraja to Kulottunga1, a rare feature in early Indian polity and politics. Rajaraja initiated the process by sending fleets to Ilam or Sri Lanka, the northern part of which came under the Chola rule. The Chola fleet became stronger during Rajenndra I's time when the entire island of Ilam was conquered.
- This campaign was followed by the most daring Chola raids, the Kadaram campaign in 1025-26 AD when no less than twelve areas in south-east Asia were conquered by the Chola fleet.

17. Correct Option: (d)

Explanation:

- All statements are correct.

Supplementary Notes:

The Hostility between Various Kingdoms

- During the early medieval times, hostilities between the powers to the north and to the south of the Tungabhadra river became a regular and recurrent feature that would develop into protracted battles without resulting in any long-term annexation of territories, a constant pattern of political struggle in south India.
- This pattern of struggle or rivalries among regional powers cut across dynastic changes and upheavals.
- This pattern was seen in the protracted struggle between Chalukya-Pallava, Pallava-Rashtrakuta, Rashtrakuta-Chola and Chola-Western Chalukya.

18. Correct Option: (d)

Explanation:

- All pairs are correctly matched.

Supplementary Notes:

Empires and Their Founders

- Gopala founded the Pala empire in 750 AD.
- The Rashtrakutas: 752-973 AD.
  - Dantidurg (752-756 AD) founded the kingdom. He fixed his capital at Malkhand.
- Mayurasharman founded the Kadambas of Vanavasi.
- The Dynasty of Gurjar Pratiharas was founded by Harichandra in 6th century AD.
- Guptas of Magadha was founded by Shri Gupta.

19. Correct Option: (c)

Explanation:

- Both statements are correct.

Supplementary Notes:

Chola Kingdom

- Cholas were mostly devotees of Shiva, though a few worshipped Vishnu and Buddhism. Jainism witnessed a decline. A peculiarity of the Chola religion was that greater stress was laid on Dana (gift) than on Yajna (sacrifice).

- Settlements of peasants, known as Ur, gradually became prosperous with the spread of irrigation agriculture. Groups of such villages formed larger units called Nadu.
- The village council and the Nadu had several administrative functions including dispensing justice and collecting taxes. Rich peasants of the upper caste exercised considerable control over the affairs of the Nadu under the supervision of the central Chola government.
- Chola kings gave some rich landowners titles like Muvendavelan (a Velan or peasant serving three kings), Araiyar (chief), etc. as markers of respect, and entrusted them with important offices of the state at the centre.

20. **Correct Option: (b)**

Explanation:

- **Statement 1 is incorrect:** Senguttuvan introduced the Pattini cult or the worship of Kannagi as the ideal wife in Tamil Nadu.

Supplementary Notes:

Cheras

- The Cheras controlled the central and northern parts of Kerala and the Kongu region of Tamil Nadu.
- Vanji was their capital and the ports of the west coast, Musiri and Tondi, were under their control.
- The emblem of Cheras was "bow and arrow".
- The Pugalur Inscription of the 1st century AD has reference to three generations of Chera rulers.
- The greatest ruler of Cheras was Senguttuvan, who belonged to the 2nd century AD.
- His military achievements have been chronicled in epic Silapathikaram, with details about his expedition to the Himalayas, where he defeated many north Indian rulers.
- Senguttuvan introduced the Pattini cult or the worship of Kannagi as the ideal wife in Tamil Nadu.
- He was the first to send an embassy to China from South India.

CONCEPT REVISION

Here is the list of concepts that have been covered as part of the previous exercise. Revise and Self-reflect on your concepts you covered.

- Chola's Social Life ☐
- Pattini Cult ☐
- Features of the Chola Administration ☐
- Conflict between Chalukyas and Pallavas ☐
- Pala and Pratihara Empires ☐
- Administration of the Chola ☐
- Rulers of Chera Dynasty ☐

4.2 EARLY MUSLIM INVASIONS

QUESTIONS

1. **Balban abandoned the policy of conquest and adopted the policy of consolidation. The reasons to do so was/were:**
   1. Threat of external invasion
   2. Internal revolts
   3. Indian Kings willing to throw off the Turkish rule
   4. His weak nature

   Select the correct answer using the code given below:

   (a) 1 and 4 only (b) 1 and 2 only
   (c) 1, 2 and 3 only (d) 1, 2, 3 and 4

2. **Consider the following statements regarding Mongols:**
   1. The Mongols ruled from the Jaxartes to the Caspian Sea and from Ghazni to Iran.
   2. The Mongols deliberately used terror as an instrument of war.
   3. The Mongols were able to bring almost the entire Punjab as well as Kashmir under their control.

   Which of the above statements is/are correct?

   (a) 1 and 2 only (b) 2 and 3 only
   (c) 1 and 3 only (d) 1, 2 and 3

3. **Consider the following statements:**
   1. Ilbari Turks were also called the Mameluk or Slave rulers
   2. After the death of Balban, Bengal and Bihar remained outside the control of Delhi.
   3. Balban could not consolidate the Turkish rule in eastern Rajasthan.

   Which of the above statements is/are correct?

(a) 1 and 2 only (b) 2 and 3 only
(c) 1 and 3 only (d) 1, 2 and 3

4. **Which of the following statements regarding trade and commerce in the early medieval India is/are incorrect?**
   1. Despite the fall of the Roman Empire, India's trade with the West was seriously affected.
   2. The chief Indian port for the trade with southeast Asia and China was Tamralipti.

   Select the correct option using the codes given below:

   (a) 1 only (b) 2 only
   (c) Both 1 and 2 (d) Neither 1 nor 2

5. **Consider the following statements about Mahmud Ghazni:**
   1. He is considered as the Hero of Islam.
   2. He made 17 raids to India.
   3. His most daring raids were Kanauj and Somnath temple in Gujarat.

   Select the correct option using the codes given below:

   (a) 1 and 2 only (b) 2 and 3 only
   (c) 1 and 3 only (d) 1, 2 and 3

6. **Consider the following statements regarding the Turkish Conquest of North India:**
   1. After the Ghaznavid conquest of Punjab, Sufis arrived in India.
   2. During this period, Chauhans captured Delhi from Tomars.

   Which of the above statements is/are correct?

   (a) 1 only (b) 2 only
   (c) Both 1 and 2 (d) Neither 1 nor 2

7. **Consider the following statements regarding the Battle of Tarain:**
   1. It was fought between Mahmud Ghazni and Prithviraja Chauhan.
   2. Prithviraja lost but was allowed to rule over Ajmer.

   Which of the above statements is/are incorrect?

   (a) 1 only (b) 2 only
   (c) Both 1 and 2 (d) Neither 1 nor 2

8. **Which of the following statements is/are correct regarding the era of Balban?**
   1. With Balban's accession to the throne, there began an era of strong, decentralized government.
   2. Balhan constantly sought to increase the prestige and power of the monarchy.
   3. Balban was the one who finally broke the power of the Chahalgani, i.e., the Turkish nobles.

   Select the correct answer using the codes given below:

   (a) 1 and 2 only (b) 2 and 3 only
   (c) 1 and 3 only (d) 1, 2 and 3

9. **Consider the following statements regarding Turkish king Balban:**
   1. The Persian festival of Nauroz was introduced by him.
   2. He is known to have included non-Turks to his administration.
   3. Balban followed the policy of 'Tolerance and Recognition' for building peace and control in the region.

   Which of the above statements is/are incorrect?

   (a) 1 and 2 only (b) 2 and 3 only
   (c) 3 only (d) 1, 2 and 3

10. **Which of the following statements is/are correct about the Muhammad Ghori and Mahmud of Ghazni?**
    1. Hindu Shahi kingdom of Jayapala was defeated in 1001 AD by Muhammad Ghori.
    2. Prithviraj Chauhan defeated Mahmud of Ghazni in Battle of Tarain in 1191 AD.

    Select the correct answer using the code given below:

    (a) 1 only (b) 2 only
    (c) Both 1and 2 (d) Neither 1 nor 2

SOLUTIONS

1. **Correct Option: (c)**

Supplementary Notes:

- **The Delhi Sultanate** – The Slave Dynasty: Ghiyas-ud-din Balban (1265-1287 AD), a Turkish slave noble, was the "ruler with an iron hand" who is considered the last ruler of the Slave Dynasty. Balban adopted a policy of consolidation rather than expansion. He was the first sultan who strove to make monarchy hereditary. Balban provided the Sultanate with an iron-willed ruler who aimed at consolidating the hinterlands. The fourth option is not correct in this question.

2. **Correct Option: (d)**

Explanation:

- All statements are correct.

Supplementary Notes:

The Mongols

- Although the Mongols were gradually able to bring almost the entire Punjab as well as Kashmir under their control, and to threaten Delhi, due to the firmness and vigour of the Turkish rulers, and their diplomacy, this threat was averted, and later, Punjab was recovered.
- However, the serious threat posed to the Sultanat of Delhi by the Mongols had a powerful effect on all the internal problems of the Sultanat.
- The Mongols attacked the Khwarizmi empire in 1218 AD. They ruthlessly sacked flourishing cities from the Jaxartes to the Caspian Sea and from Ghazni to Iran, and ravaged the countryside. Many Turkish soldiers went over to the side of the Mongols.

- The Mongols deliberately used terror as an instrument of war. Whenever a city refused to surrender or was conquered after putting up resistance, all the soldiers and a large number of their chiefs were slaughtered, and their women and children were sold into slavery. Even the civilians were not spared.

3. **Correct Option: (a)**

Explanation:

- **Statement 3 is incorrect:** Balban consolidated the Turkish rule in eastern Rajasthan, despite his other preoccupations.

Supplementary Notes:

- During the rule of the Ilbari Turks (sometimes called, the Mameluk or Slave rulers), the Sultans of Delhi had to face not only internal dissensions and foreign invasions, but internal rebellions as well.
- Delhi could not keep control over Bengal for long. After Balban's death, his son, Bughta Khan, who had been appointed the governor of Bengal, preferred to rule over that part rather than stake his life for the throne of Delhi.
- He, therefore, assumed independence and set up a dynasty which ruled over Bengal for the next 40 years. Thus, Bengal and Bihar remained outside the control of Delhi during the greater part of the 13th century.
- The bulk of the Punjab, too had passed under the control of the Mongols. The Turkish rule was not fully secure even in the Ganga doab. The Katehariya Rajputs who had their capital at Ahichchatra across the Ganga were a force to be reckoned with.

4. **Correct Option: (d)**

Explanation:

- Both statements are correct.

Supplementary Notes:

Trade and Commerce in 800-1200 AD

- The economic situation, especially trade and commerce in the country during this period is a matter of debate among historians. Some consider it to be a period of stagnation and decline, a setback both the foreign and long-distance trade within the country, decline of towns, and greater localism and regionalism. The virtual absence of gold coins till the 10th century is considered to be a proof of this.
- Suffice it to say that the fall of the Roman empire did not seriously affect India's trade with the West since two large empires, the Byzantine empire with its base in Constantinople, and the Sassanid empire based in Iran rose during the subsequent period. Both of them took keen interest in trade with India and the Indian Ocean region.
- After the rise of the Arab empire in the 7th century, the Arabs expanded the trade of the West to India, southeast Asia and China.
- Hence, gold and silver continued to come to India in return for its favourable trade. That is why India continued to be considered a country full of gold and silver, and hence, an attractive prize for foreigners to invade and trade with.
- The Indian merchants were organised in guilds, the most famous of them being the Manigraman and the Nandesi which had been active since early times. These guilds displayed a spirit of enterprise, engaging in retail and wholesale trade in many foreign countries.
- On account of its prosperity, China had become a main focus of trade in the Indian Ocean. The Chinese consumed enormous quantities of spices, which were imported from southeast Asia and India. Indian rulers, particularly the Pala and Sena rulers of Bengal, and the Pallava and Chola rulers of south India, tried to encourage this trade by sending a series of embassies to the Chinese emperors. The Chola ruler, Rajendra I, sent a naval expedition against Malaya and the neighbouring countries to overcome their interference in the trade with China. The chief Indian port for sailing to Java, Sumatra, etc., was Tamralipti (Tamluk) in Bengal.

5. **Correct Option: (d)**

Explanation:

- All statements are correct.

Supplementary Notes:

The Ghaznavids

- Mahmud ascended the throne (998-1030 AD) at Ghazni.
- He is considered a hero of Islam because he protected Ghazni empire from the Central Asian Turkish Tribal invaders who were not Muslims.
- In India, his memory is that of a plunderer and destroyer of temples.
- He made 17 raids to India.
- The initial raids were against the Hindushahi rulers who at the time held Peshawar and Punjab.
- His most daring raid was against Kanauj in 1018 AD and against the Somnath in Gujarat in 1025 AD.
- In Kanauj, he sacked and plundered both Mathura and Kanauj and returned via Bundelkhand.
- No attempt was made by the Mahmud to annex these areas.
- He marched from Multan across Rajputana in order to raid the rich temple at Somnath.

6. **Correct Option: (c)**

Explanation:

- Both statements are correct.

Supplementary Notes:

The Turkish Conquest of North India

- After the Ghaznavids conquest of Punjab, two types of relations emerged between the Muslims and the Hindus.
- One was the lure of plunder which resulted in raids to the Gangetic Valley and Rajputana by the successors of the Mahmud.
- At the 2nd level, the Muslim traders were allowed, even welcomed in the country, since they helped in strengthening the India's trade with the Central and West Asia.
- After this, the Muslim religious preachers called Sufis came to North India.
- Meanwhile, the Chauhans steadily grew in Northern India and they defeated many Turks and they also captured Delhi from the Tomars around the middle of the century.
- Thus, it brought them into conflict with the Ghaznavids rulers of the area.
- While Muizzudin Muhammad was running Multana and Uchch, a young lad ascended the throne at Ajmer. He was Prithviraja.
- He invaded the Bundelkhand area and defeated the Chandela rulers.

7. **Correct Option: (a)**

Explanation:

- **Statement 1 is incorrect:** It was fought between Muizzudin Muhammad and Prithviraja.

Supplementary Notes:

Battle of Tarain

- The conflict started with the rival claims on Tabarhinda.
- In the battle which was fought at Tarain in 1191 AD the Ghuri forces were completely routed and Muizzudin Muhammad's life was saved by the young Khalji horseman.
- Prithviraja now pushed on to Tabarhinda and conquered it.
- Little attempt was made by the Prithviraja to oust the Ghurids from Punjab.
- This gave time to the Muizzudin Muhammad to regroup his forces and make another bid for India.
- The IInd battle in Tarain in 1192 AD is regarded as the one of the turning points in Indian history.
- Muizzudin marched with 1,20,000 men and 10,000 mounted archers.
- As soon as Prithviraja realised the nature of the Ghurid threat, he appealed to all the Rajas of the northern India for help.
- In the battle a large number of Indian soldiers lost their lives.
- Prithviraja escaped but was captured near Saraswati. Turkish army captured the fortress of Hansi, Saraswati and Samana.
- They attacked and captured Ajmer.
- Prithivaraja was allowed to rule over Ajmer for some time.
- Soon he was executed and his son succeeded him.

8. **Correct Option: (b)**

Explanation:

- **Statement 1 is incorrect:** With Balban's accession to the throne, there began an era of strong, centralized government.

Supplementary Notes:

Era of Balban

- Balban's methods were often harsh and undesirable. But there is no doubt that with his accession to the throne, there began an era of strong, centralised government.
- Balban constantly sought to increase the prestige and power of the monarchy, because he was convinced that this was the only way to face the internal and external dangers facing him.
- It was an age in which authority and power was supposed to be the privilege of those born in noble houses or those who could boast of an ancient pedigree. Hence, Balban tried to strengthen his claim to the throne by declaring that he was the descendant of the legendary Iranian king Afrasiyab. In order to prove his claim to noble blood, Balban stood forth as the champion of the Turkish nobility.
- Balban was determined to finally break the power of the Chahalgani, i.e., the Turkish nobles, and to exalt the power and prestige of the monarchy.
- He did not hesitate even to poison his cousin, Sher Khan, to achieve this objective. At the same time, in order to win the confidence of the public, he administered justice with extreme impartiality.

9. **Correct Option: (b)**

Explanation:

- **Statement 2 is incorrect:** Balban is known to have been deeply racist and excluded non-Turks from administration.
- **Statement 3 is incorrect:** He followed the policy of "Blood and Iron" to gain control in the region.

Supplementary Notes:

Reign of Balban

- Balban ascended the throne of Delhi Sultanate in 1265 AD.

- He administered justice with extreme impartiality but was deeply racist and excluded non-Turks from administration. He stood forth as the champion of the Turkish nobility.
- Indian Muslims were not given important posts in the government. He appointed spies to monitor the activities of the nobles.
- Balban maintained a magnificent court and also introduced the Persian festival of Nauroz.
- During his reign, the law and order situation in the area around Delhi and in the doab had deteriorated.
- In the Ganga-Jamuna doab and Awadh, the roads were infested with robbers and dacoits, so much so, that the communication with the eastern areas had become difficult.
- He followed the policy of "Blood and Iron" to ouster the Rajput zamindars who had set up forts in the area by defying the government and the Mewatis, who had become so bold as to plunder people up to the outskirts of the city.
- These were ruthlessly hurled down and killed, the forests around Delhi cut down, and many military outposts (Thanas) were established there.

10. Correct Option: (a)

Explanation:

- **Statement 1 is incorrect:** Hindu Shahi kingdom of Jayapala (Punjab to Kabul) was defeated in 1001 AD by Mahmud of Ghazni.
- **Statement 2 is incorrect:** Prithviraj chauhan defeated Muhammad Ghori in Battle of Tarain, near Delhi in 1191.

Supplementary Notes:

Mahmud of Ghazni

- Mahmud of Ghazni is said to have made 17 raids to India, mainly aimed at rich temples and cities of north India
- North Indian frontier Hindu Shahi kingdom of Jayapala (Punjab to Kabul) was defeated in 1001 AD by Mahmud of Ghazni.
- His successor Anandpala also got defeated in Battle of Waihind (1008 AD).
- In the Battle of Waihind, Anandpala was supported by rulers of Kannauj & Rajasthan; as a result Mahmud got his rule established almost all over Punjab.
- **Mahmud of Gazni patronised poets:**
  - Firdausi who wrote Shahnamah.
  - Alberuni, the writer of Kitab-i-Hind.

Muhammad Ghori

- After the death of Mahmud, Ghori succeeded to the throne of Ghazni.
- In 1186, he attacked Punjab & captured it from "Khusro Malik", annexing it to his dominions.
- Realizing the urgency of situation, North Indian Hindu princes formed a confederacy under the command of Prithviraj Chauhan.
- Prithviraj Chauhan defeated Muhammad Ghori in Battle of Tarain, near Delhi in 1191 AD.
- In 1192, in IInd battle of Tarain, Prithviraj Chauhan was captured and killed, marking the establishment of Ist Muslim kingdom rule over Ajmer in India.
- Muhammad Ghori returned to Ghazni leaving his general Qutubuddin Aibak to make further conquests in India.
- Later, Aibak captured Delhi and Meerut and in 1193 AD, Ghori invaded Jayachandra, "Ruler of Kannauj" in battle of Chandwar or Ghardawala and annexed it, setting Turkish rule in north India.

CONCEPT REVISION

Here is the list of concepts that have been covered as part of the previous exercise. Revise and Self-reflect on your concepts you covered.

- Balban's policy of consolidation ☐
- Mongols ☐
- Trade & Commerce in Medieval India ☐
- Battle of Tarain ☐
- Turkish conquest of North India ☐

4.3 DELHI SULTANATE

QUESTIONS

1. Consider the following statements with respect to the Iltutmish reign:

1. He set up Iqtas under Iqtadars.
2. He introduced copper coinage called Jital.
3. He was the first Turkish ruler to introduce Arabic coinage.
4. He formed a band of administrative and military elite of forty members called Chihalgani.

Which of the above statements is/are correct?

(a) 2 only (b) 1 and 3 only
(c) 2, 3 and 4 only (d) 1, 2, 3 and 4

2. Consider the following description:

'He was one of the important rulers of his dynasty. He introduced 'Paibos' which is a form of salutation to the king by kissing his feet in the court. He believed in the Divine Right Theory of Kingship. He was also known to end the Chihalgani system and introduced a well-organized spy system'.

Which of the following rulers of Delhi Sultanate can be associated with the above description?

(a) Balram Shah (b) Qutubud - Din Aaibak
(c) Balban (d) Allaudin Khilji

3. Which of the following statements is/are correct about Mohammad-bin-Tughlaq?

1. He believed in political and administrative unity of India.
2. He opened up administration to all people on the basis of meritocracy.
3. He was the first to introduce token currency in the whole world.
4. He transferred his capital from Devagiri to Delhi.

Select the correct answer using the code given below:

(a) 1 and 2 only (b) 1, 2 and 4 only
(c) 3 and 4 only (d) 2, 3 and 4 only

4. Consider the following statements with reference to Sher Shah Suri's Administration:

1. Sher Shah's empire was divided into administrative units called Sarkars.
2. The State's share was one-third of the average produce and it was paid in cash or crop.
3. He borrowed ideas like the branding of horses from Alauddin Khilji's administration.

Which of the above statements is/are correct?

(a) 2 only (b) 1 and 2 only
(c) 2 and 3 only (d) 1, 2 and 3

5. Consider the following statements regarding Allauddin Khilji?

1. He was the first to introduce Nauroz festival in Sultanate court.
2. He started a system of branding horses called Dagh system.
3. He implemented the policy of direct land revenue collection from peasants.
4. He prohibited the use of wine.

Which of the above statements is/are correct?

(a) 1 and 2 only (b) 2 and 4 only
(c) 2, 3 and 4 only (d) 3 and 4 only

6. With reference to the history of India, consider the following pairs.

1. Diwan-i-Amir Kohi – Agricultural Department
2. Diwani-i-Wazarat – Revenue Department
3. Diwan-i-Riyasat – Army Department
4. Diwan-i-Arz – Market Control

Which of the above pairs is/are correctly matched?

(a) 1 and 2 only (b) 1 only
(c) 3 only (d) 2, 3 and 4 only

7. Consider the following statements:

1. Persian wheel is a mechanical water lifting device used in India since the Delhi Sultanate.
2. Adil Shahi rulers of Bijapur built various tanks and wells known as Bavdis.

Which of the above statements is/are correct?

(a) 1 only (b) 2 only
(c) Both 1 and 2 (d) Neither 1 or 2

8. Ibn Battuta, the famous Muslim explorer who came to India during regime of Mohammad bin Tughlaq, belonged to which country?

(a) Afghanistan (b) Morocco
(c) Iraq (d) Iran

9. Consider the following statements regarding Sher Shah Suri's administration:

1. Sher Shah's empire was divided into forty seven sarkars.
2. Chief Shiqdar (law and order) and Chief Munsif (judge) were the two officers in charge of the administration in each sarkar.
3. Each sarkar was divided into several Parganas.

Which of the above statements is/are correct?

(a) 1 only (b) 2 and 3 only
(c) 1 and 2 only (d) 1, 2 and 3

10. Who among the following rulers is known to have assumed the title of Caliph himself?

(a) Balban
(b) Alauddin Khalji
(c) Qutbuddin Mubarak Shah Khalji
(d) Mohammad bin Tughlaq

11. Consider the following statements regarding Tughlaqs:

1. Muhammad bin Tughlaq established the Tughlaq Dynasty.
2. Firuz Shah Tughlaq established four new towns – Firuzabad, Fatehabad, Jaunpur and Hissar.

Which of the above statements is/are correct?

(a) 1 only (b) 2 only
(c) Both 1 and 2 (d) Neither 1 nor 2

12. Consider the following statements about decline and disintergration of the Delhi Sultanate:

1. The rebellions in South India were the most serious and were organised by the local governors.
2. Firuz Tughlaq made no attempt to re-assert his authority over South India and the Deccan.
3. Firuz decreed that whenever a noble died, his son should be allowed to succeed to his position.

Which of the above statements is/are correct?

(a) 1 and 2 only (b) 2 and 3 only
(c) 1 and 3 only (d) 1, 2 and 3

13. Which of the following statements is/are correct regarding Firuz Tughlaq?

1. He tried to ban practices which the orthodox theologians considered un-Islamic.

2. He never prohibited the practice of Muslim women going out to worship at the graves of saints.
3. It was during the time of Firuz that jizyah became a separate tax.

Select the correct answer using the codes given below:

(a) 1 and 2 only (b) 2 and 3 only
(c) 1 and 3 only (d) 1, 2 and 3

14. "He was famously known as Lal Baksh. He assumed the title 'Sultan' and made his capital Lahore. He is also known to have built 'Arhai din ka Jhopara' in Ajmer. Quwwat-ul-Islam mosque was built by him in Delhi".

Which of the following rulers has been mentioned in the above quote?

(a) Qutub-ud-din Aibak
(b) Iltutmish
(c) Ghiyas-ud-din Balban
(d) Nasiruddin Mahmud

15. Consider the following statements regarding the Khilji Dynasty:

1. Ala-ud-din Khilji followed the divine right theory of kingship.
2. Nasiruddin Khusrau Shah was the only Hindu convert to sit on the throne of Delhi.

Which of the above statements is/are correct?

(a) 1 only (b) 2 only
(c) Both 1 and 2 (d) Neither 1 nor 2

16. With reference to the central administration of Delhi Sultanate, consider the following statements:

1. Naib headed the finance department, called Diwan-i-Wizarat.
2. The military department was headed by the Ariz-i-Mumalik who was responsible for recruiting the soldiers and administering the military department.
3. The Wazir practically enjoyed all the powers of the Sultan and exercised general control over all the departments.

Which of the above statements are incorrect?

(a) 1 and 2 only (b) 1 and 3 only
(c) 2 and 3 only (d) 1, 2 and 3

17. Consider the following statements regarding the rule of Iltutmish:

1. He shifted his capital from Lahore to Delhi.
2. The hereditary succession to Delhi Sultanate was initiated by Iltutmish.
3. He introduced coins of silver known as Jital and copper as Tanka.

Which of the above statements is/are correct?

(a) 1 and 2 only (b) 2 and 3 only
(c) 3 only (d) None of the above

18. Consider the following statements:

1. Qutbuddin Aibak played an important role in the expansion of the Turkish Sultanate in India.
2. The reign of Razya Sultan marked the beginning of a struggle for power between the monarchy and the Turkish chiefs, called 'the forty' or the chahalgani.

Which of the above statements is/are correct regarding Delhi Sultanate?

(a) 1 only (b) 2 only
(c) Both 1 and 2 (d) Neither 1 nor 2

19. Which of the following statements is/are correct regarding Delhi Sultanate?

1. Khaljis were non-Turks who had come to India in the time of the Ghurid invasion.
2. The Khaljis excluded the Turks from high offices, and the rise of the Khaljis to power ended the Turkish monopoly of high offices.
3. Jalaluddin Khalji was the first ruler of Delhi Sultanate who said, as the large majority of the people in India were Hindus, the state in India could not be a truly Islamic state.

Select the correct answer using the codes given below:

(a) 1 and 2 only (b) 2 and 3 only
(c) 1 and 3 only (d) 1, 2 and 3

20. Which of the following statements is/are correct regarding Muhammad bin Tughlaq?

1. He prepared to give high offices to people who belonged to noble families.
2. He transferred the capital from Delhi to Deogir.
3. He introduced the 'token currency'.

Select the correct answer using the codes given below:

(a) 1 and 2 only (b) 2 and 3 only
(c) 1 and 3 only (d) 1, 2 and 3

21. Which of the following statement is correct regarding the Lodi Dynasty?

(a) Sikander Lodhi laid the foundation of the Lodhi Dynasty in India in 1451.
(b) Ibrahim Lodhi wrote Persian verses under the name of 'Gulrakhi'.
(c) Bahlol Lodhi defeated Alauddin Alam Shah of the Sayyid Dynasty.
(d) Bahlol Lodhi introduced a new measurement yardstick, the Gazz-i-Sikandar, and a system of auditing of accounts.

22. Consider the following statements regarding the Sultan of Bijapur, Ibrahim Adil Shah II:

1. He composed a book called Kitab-i-Naurasin modes or ragas.
2. He built a new capital Nauraspur.

Which of the above statements is/are correct?

(a) 1 only (b) 2 only
(c) Both 1 and 2 (d) Neither 1 nor 2

23. 'Mohammad bin Tughlaq was known as an ill-fated idealist'. In this context consider the following events that occurred during his reign:

1. He is known to have transferred his capital from Delhi to Devagiri.
2. He issued copper coins at par with the value of the silver tanka coins.
3. Ibn Batuta acted as a Qazi in Delhi for eight years during his reign.
4. Fort of Adilabad was built under his rule.

Which of the above statements are correct?

(a) 1, 2 and 4 only (b) 1 and 3 only
(c) 2 and 3 only (d) 1, 2, 3 and 4

24. Consider the following statements with respect to the Lodhi Dynasty in India:

1. Bahlol Lodhi laid the foundation of the Lodhi Dynasty in India.
2. Sikandar Lodi wrote Persian verses under the name 'Gulrakhi'.

Which of the above statements is/are correct?

(a) 1 only (b) 2 only
(c) Both 1 and 2 (d) Neither 1 nor 2

25. Qutub-ud-din Aibak was the founder of the Slave Dynasty in India. In this contex, consider the following statements:

1. The first mosque in India was built by him.
2. He is known to have issued a large number of silver coins in India.
3. He started the construction of the Qutub Minar in Delhi.

Which of the above statements are correct?

(a) 1 and 2 only (b) 1 and 3 only
(c) 2 and 3 only (d) 1, 2 and 3

26. Arrange the following rulers of Slave Dynasty in the chronological order:

1. Bahram Shah
2. Nasiruddin Mahmud
3. Balban
4. Alauddin Masud Shah

Select the correct answer using the code given below:

(a) 1-2-3-4 (b) 3-1-4-2
(c) 1-4-2-3 (d) 3-2-4-1

27. Match the following:

List-I	List-II
A. Jalauddin Khalji	1. Deposed Malik Kafur
B. Alauddin Khalji	2. Settled New Musalmans near Delhi
C. Qutbuddin	3. Only Hindu convert Mubarak Shah to sit on the throne of Delhi
D. Nasiruddin	4. Renamed Chittor to Khusrau Khizrabad

Select the correct answer using the code given below:

	A	B	C	D
(a)	2	4	1	3
(b)	3	4	1	2
(c)	4	3	2	1
(d)	3	2	1	4

28. He was a King of Sultanate of Bijapur. He was very solicitous to the poor and had the title of 'Abla Baba' i.e. 'Friend of Poor'. He was deeply interested in music and composed a book called 'Kitab-i-Nauras' in which songs were set to various musical modes. He also built a new capital 'Nauraspur' in which a large number of musicians were invited to settle. He accorded patronage to all, including Hindu saints and temples and due to his broad approach; he came to be called 'Jagat Guru'.

Identify the personality described in the above passage?

(a) Adil Ali Shah
(b) Ibrahim Adil Shah II
(c) Muhammad Quli Qutub Shah
(d) Yusuf Adil Shah

29. With reference to Sher Shah Suri, the founder of Sur Empire, consider the following statements:

1. He made significant changes in the administrative divisions as compared to Delhi Sultanate by following a decentralized system of administration.
2. He introduced liberal policies like abolition of Jizyah.
3. He paid great attention to improvement of communications in his kingdom.

Which of the above statements is/are incorrect?

(a) 1 and 2 only (b) 2 only
(c) 2 and 3 only (d) None of the above

30. Arrange the following rulers of Saiyyad Dynasty in chronological order:

(a) Khizr Khan - Mubarak Shah - Muhammad Shah - Alauddin Alam Shah
(b) Mubarak Shah - Alauddin Alam Shah - Khizr Khan - Muhammad Shah
(c) Khizr Khan - Muhammad Shah - Alauddin Alam Shah - Mubarak Shah
(d) Alauddin Alam Shah - Khizr Khan - Mubarak Shah - Muhammad Shah

31. Jalaluddin Khalji laid the foundation of the Khalji Dynasty in India. In this context, consider the following statements:

1. He is known to have a benevolent attitude towards Hindus.
2. He maintained the policy of tolerance to win the goodwill of nobility.

Which of the above statements is/are correct?

(a) 1 only (b) 2 only
(c) Both 1 and 2 (d) Neither 1 nor 2

32. Match the following listed items given below:

List I	List II
A. Ghiyasuddin Tughlaq	1. Safarnama Rehla
B. Muhammad bin Tughluq	2. A Telugu Brahmin convert Wazir
C. Ibn Batuta	3. First sultan to start irrigation works
D. Khan-i-Jahan Maqbal	4 Diwan-i-amirkohi

Select the correct answer using the code given below:

	A	B	C	D
(a)	2	3	4	1
(b)	3	4	1	2
(c)	4	3	2	1
(d)	3	4	1	2

33. The death of Iltutmish created a political turmoil for accession to the throne. In this context, consider the following statements:

1. Razia Sultan seized the throne of Delhi Sultanate from Bahram Shah.
2. Malik Jamaluddin Yaqut is known to have imprisoned Razia at Qila Mubarak in Bathinda.

Which of the above statements is/are correct?

(a) 1 only (b) 2 only
(c) Both 1 and 2 (d) Neither 1 nor 2

34. Which of the following statements is incorrect regarding Alauddin Khalji?

(a) He is known to have refuted the suzerainty of the Caliph.
(b) Alauddin was the first ruler to fix land revenue in cash.
(c) The title of Tuti-i-Hind was given to him by Amir Khusrau.
(d) He followed the policy of ruthless governance to maintain his control over the state.

35. Match the following listed items with respect to central administration during the Delhi Sultanate period:

List I	List II
A. Diwan-i-Wizarat	1. Department of Correspondence
B. Diwan-i-Arz	2. Department of Religious Affairs
C. Diwan-i-Rasalat	3. Military Department
D. Diwan-i-Insha	4. Finance Department

Select the correct answer using the code given below:

	A	B	C	D
(a)	4	3	2	1
(b)	1	4	3	2
(c)	1	3	4	2
(d)	4	1	2	3

36. With reference to Iltutmish, which of the following statements is/are incorrect?

1. He shifted the capital from Lahore to Delhi.
2. He was the first to issue purely Arabic coinage of gold tanka.
3. He disposed of Aram Shah and became the Sultan with the name of Shamsuddin.
4. Turkan-i-Chahalgani was organized by him for administering the sultanate.

Select the correct answer using the code given below:

(a) 1 and 2 only (b) 2 only
(c) 3 and 4 only (d) None of the above

37. With respect to the provincial government during the sultanate period, arrange the following administrators in increasing order of their position and role in Sultanate bureaucracy:

(a) Muqti - Shiqdar - Amil - Muqaddam
(b) Muqaddam - Amil - Shiqdar - Muqti
(c) Shiqdar - Muqti - Amil - Muqaddam
(d) Amil - Muqti - Shiqdar – Muqaddam

38. With reference to the Sur Dynasty, consider the following statements:

1. The Battle of Chausa was fought between Akbar and Sher Shah Suri.
2. Sher Shah Suri appointed Diwan-i-Risalat for royal orders in the state.

Which of the above statement is/are correct?

(a) 1 only (b) 2 only
(c) Both 1 and 2 (d) Neither 1 nor 2

39. Consider the following statements regarding central administration during the Sultanate period:

1. Post of Wazir was the most powerful one as he exercised general control over all departments.
2. Chief Sadr was the head of both religious and judicial departments.
3. All the ministers remained in office during the pleasure of Sultan.

Which of the above statements is/are correct?

(a) 1 and 2 only (b) 2 and 3 only
(c) 3 only (d) 1, 2 and 3

40. Which of the following statements regarding Muhammad bin Tughlaq is/are correct?

1. He transferred his capital from Delhi to Daulatabad.
2. Ibn Batuta came to India during his reign.
3. He introduced a token currency system.

Select the correct answer using the code given below:

(a) 1 only (b) 1 and 3 only
(c) 3 only (d) 1, 2 and 3

41. Following are the departments under Sher Shah Suri. Match them correctly:

1. Diwan-i-wijarat (i) Finance Department
2. Diwan-i-arz (ii) Military Department
3. Diwan-i-insha (iii) Royal Secretariat
4. Diwan-i-Rasalat (iv) Department for religious and foreign affairs

Choose the correct option from the codes given below.

(a) 1-i, 2-ii, 3-iii, 4-iv
(b) 1-i, 2-iv, 3-iii, 4-ii
(c) 1-iii, 2-ii, 3-i, 4-iv
(d) 1-i, 2-iii, 3-ii, 4-iv

SOLUTIONS

1. **Correct Option: (d)**

Explanation:

- All statements are correct.

Iltutmish (1211-1236 AD)

- Iltutmish belonged to the Ilbari tribe and hence his dynasty was named as Ilbari Dynasty. His half-brothers sold him as a slave to Aibak, who made him his-son-in law by giving his daughter in marriage to him.
- In 1211 AD, Iltutmish defeated Aram Baksh and became Sultan. He shifted his capital from Lahore to Delhi. During the first ten years of his reign, he concentrated on securing his throne from his rivals.
- In the meantime, Temujin, popularly known as Chengiz Khan, the leader of the Mongols, started invading Central Asia. He defeated Jalaluddin Mangabarni, the ruler of Kwarizam. Mangabarni crossed the river Indus and sought asylum from Iltutmish.
- Iltutmish refused to give him shelter in order to save his empire from the onslaught of the Mongols. Fortunately for Iltutmish, Chengiz Khan returned home without entering into India. In fact, the Mongol policy of Iltutmish saved India from the wrath of Chengiz Khan. Iltutmish marched against Bengal and Bihar and reasserted his control over them.
- He nominated his daughter Raziya as his successor. Thus, the hereditary succession to Delhi Sultanate was initiated by Iltutmish. He patronized many scholars and a number of Sufi saints came to India during his reign.
- **Statement 1 is correct:** The Iqta system was a practice of tax farming under Iqtadars, which was introduced by Iltutmish in Delhi Sultanate. It was basically grant of revenue from a territory in lieu of salary. This grant was not hereditary and was subject to passing from officer to officer. Iqta system linked the farthest part of the Sultanate to the central government.
- Apart from completing the construction of Qutub Minar at Delhi, the tallest stone tower in India (238 ft.), he built a magnificent mosque at Ajmer.
- **Statement 2 is correct:** Iltutmish introduced the Arabic coinage into India. He introduced silver Tanka and copper Jital, the two coins of the Delhi Sultanate.
- **Statement 3 is correct:** Iltutmish was the first to introduce a "Pure Arabic Coin" in India. The Silver Tanka issued by Iltutmish weighed 175 grains. The silver tanka remained the basis of the modern rupee.
- **Statement 4 is correct:** Iltutmish had also created a new class of ruling elite of forty powerful military leaders, called the Forty or Chihalgani.

2. **Correct Option: (c)**

Supplementary Notes:

Delhi Sultanate (Balban):

- In 1266 AD Nasiruddin Mahmud died without issues and Balban ascended the throne.
- Balban's experience as the regent made him to understand the problems of Delhi Sultanate. He knew that the real threat to the monarchy was from the nobles called 'the Forty'. He was convinced that by enhancing the power and authority of the monarchy, he could handle the problems.
- According to Balban, the Sultan was God's shadow on earth and the recipient of divine grace. Balban introduced rigorous court discipline and new customs such as prostration and kissing the Sultan's feet to prove his superiority over the nobles.
- He also introduced the Persian festival of Nauroz to impress the nobles and people with his wealth and power. He stood forth as the champion of Turkish nobility.
- At the same time, he did not share power with other nobles. Indian Muslims were not given important post in the government.
- He appointed spies to monitor the activities of the nobles. Balban was determined to break the power of the Forty, the Turkish nobles. He spared only the most obedient nobles and eliminated all others by fair or foul means.
- Instead of expanding his kingdom, Balban paid more attention to the restoration of law and order. He established a separate military department, Diwan-i-Arz, and reorganized the army.
- The outskirts of Delhi were often plundered by the Mewatis. Balban took severe action against them and prevented such robberies. Robbers were mercilessly pursued and put to death. As a result, the roads became safe for travel.

3. **Correct Option: (a)**

Explanation:

- **Statement 3 is incorrect:** Kublai Khan of China was the first to mint token currency.

- **Statement 4 is incorrect:** He transferred his capital from Delhi to Devagiri.

Supplementary Notes:
Muhammad bin Tughlaq (1325-1351 AD)

- He was a very attractive character in the history of medieval India owing to his ambitious schemes and novel experiments.
- His enterprises and novel experiments ended in miserable failures because they were all far ahead of their time.
- He was very tolerant in religious matters. He maintained diplomatic relations with far off countries like Egypt, China and Iran.
- He also introduced many liberal and beneficial reforms. He believed in political and administrative unity of India. He opened up administration to all people on basis of meritocracy. But all his reforms failed.
- Muhammad bin Tughlaq was the only Delhi Sultan who had received a comprehensive literary, religious and philosophical education.
- He wanted to make Devagiri his second capital so that he might be able to control South India better. In 1327, he made extensive preparations for the transfer of royal household and the Ulemas and Sufis from Delhi to Devagiri, which was renamed as Daulatabad. When they resisted, the Sultan enforced his orders ruthlessly which caused great hardship to the population of Delhi. The distance between these two places was more than 1500 kilometres. Many people died during the rigorous journey in the summer. After two years, the Sultan abandoned Daulatabad and asked them to return to Delhi.
- In 1329-30 Muhammad bin Tughlaq introduced a token currency. There was a shortage of silver throughout the world in the 14th century. Kublai Khan issued paper money in China. In the same manner, Muhammad bin Tughlaq issued copper coins at par with the value of the silver tanka coins.
- Kublai Khan of China was the first to mint token currency.
- He transferred his capital from Delhi to Devagiri.
- But he was not able to prevent forging the new coins. The goldsmiths began to forge the token coins on a large scale. Soon the new coins were not accepted in the markets. Finally, Muhammad bin Tughlaq stopped the circulation of token currency and promised to exchange silver coins for the copper coins.

4. **Correct Option: (d)**

Explanation:

- All statements are correct.

Supplementary Notes:
Sher Shah Suri's Administration

- **Statement 1 is correct:** Although Sher Shah Suri ruled for five years, he organized a brilliant administrative system. Sher Shah's empire was divided into forty seven sarkars.
- Chief Shiqdar (law and order) and Chief Munsif (judge) were the two officers in charge of the administration in each sarkar. Each sarkar was divided into several parganas. Shiqdar (military officer), Amin (land revenue), Fotedar (treasurer) Karkuns (accountants) were in charge of the administration of each pargana. There were also many administrative units called Iqtas.
- The land revenue administration was well organized under Sher Shah. Land survey was carefully done. All cultivable lands were classified into three classes: good, middle and bad. The state's share was one-third of the average produce and it was paid in cash or crop. His revenue reforms increased the revenue of the state.
- Sher Shah introduced new silver coins called "Dam", and they were in circulation till 1835.
- Sher Shah had also improved the communications by laying four important highways. They were:
  1. Sonargaon to Sind
  2. Agra to Burhampur
  3. Jodhpur to Chittor and
  4. Lahore to Multan.

  Rest houses were built on the highways for the convenience of the travelers. Police was efficiently reorganized and crime was less during his regime.
- The military administration was also efficiently reorganized and Sher Shah borrowed many ideas like the branding of horses from Alauddin Khalji.

5. **Correct Option: (c)**

Explanation:

Statement 1 is incorrect: Balban was the first to introduce Nauroz festival in Sultanate court.

Supplementary Notes:
Reforms of Alauddin Khalji

- Alauddin Khalji maintained a large permanent standing army and paid them in cash from the royal treasury.
- **Statement 2 is correct:** He introduced the system of Dagh (branding of horses) and prepared Huliya (descriptive list of soldiers). In order to ensure maximum efficiency, a strict review of army from time to time was carried out.
- The introduction of paying salaries in cash to the soldiers led to price regulations popularly called as market reforms. Alauddin Khalji established four separate markets in Delhi, one for grain; another

for cloth, sugar, dried fruits, butter and oil; a third for horses, slaves and cattle; and a fourth for miscellaneous commodities. Each market was under the control of a high officer called Shahna-i- Mandi.

- The supply of grain was ensured by holding stocks in government store-houses. Regulations were issued to fix the price of all commodities. A separate department called Diwan-i-Riyasat was created under an officer called Naib-i-Riyasat.
- Every merchant was registered under the market department. There were secret agents called Munhiyans who sent reports to the Sultan regarding the functioning of these markets.
- The Sultan also sent slave boys to buy various commodities to check prices. Violation of regulations was severely punished.
- Balban was the first to introduce Nauroz festival in Sultanate court.
- Apart from market reforms, Alauddin Khalji took important steps in the land revenue administration. He was the first Sultan of Delhi who ordered for the measurement of land. Even the big landlords could not escape from paying land tax. Land revenue was collected in cash in order to enable the Sultan to pay the soldiers in cash. His land revenue reforms provided a basis for the future reforms of Sher Shah and Akbar.
- As part of his measures to prevent rebellions, Alauddin imposed prohibition, because he believed that the rampant use of alcoholic drinks enabled people to assemble, lose their senses and think of rebellion.

6. **Correct Option: (a)**

Explanation:

- **Statement 3 is not correctly matched:** Diwan-i-Riyasat. It referred to the department responsible for trade and commerce.
- **Statement 4 is not correctly matched:** Diwan-i-Arz referred to the army department.

Supplementary Notes:

- During the Sultanate period, different rulers started different administrative departments. Some of these were:
  - Diwan-i-Amir Kohi: It was the agricultural department started by Muhammad bin Tughluq.
  - Diwani-i-Wazarat: It referred to the revenue department.
  - Diwan-i-Riyasat: It referred to the department responsible for trade and commerce.
  - Diwan-i-Arz: It referred to the army department.
  - Diwan-i-Mustakhraj: Department of revenue to release arrears, established by Alauddin Khilji.
  - Diwan-i-Khairat: It was the charity department started by Feroz Tughluq.
  - Diwan-i-Risalat: It was related to the foreign affairs. and was also responsible for religious issues.
  - Diwan-i-Insha: It was associated with the government correspondence.

7. **Correct Option: (c)**

Explanation:

- Both statements are correct.

Supplementary Notes:

Water Management Structures from Medieval India

- The Persian Wheel is a mechanical water lifting device operated usually by draught animals like bullocks, buffaloes or camels.
- This device made its entry into India with the establishment of Delhi Sultanate. Baburnama gives a pictorial representation and a clear description of Persian wheel in use in the Punjab province.
- Other water management structures of Medieval India include Reservoirs, Johads, Baoris/Bers, Jhalaras, Step Wells and Water Temples.
- The Adil Shahi rulers made an elaborate arrangement of pure and wholesome water for the people of Bijapur and its suburbs.
- The water works, bearing ample testimony to the sophistication of the engineers of that period, are the most fascinating aspect of Bijapur.
- The principal tanks and wells in the town are Taj Bavadi, Chand Bavadi near the Shahapur gate, the Bari and Mubarak Khan's Bavadis in the southeast, the Masa and Nim Bavdis in Northeast quarter of city, Hal, Nagar and Jama Masjid Bavadis in southern part of the city.
- Most of Bijapur's tombs and mosques had also attached water structures which show the engineering achievement of Adil Shahis. These were actually the quarries used for building the structures and later converted into small bavadis.

8. **Correct Option: (b)**

Supplementary Notes:

Morocco

- Ibn Batutah was a Muslim Moroccan explorer. He is known for his extensive travels, accounts of which were published in the Rihla. Bathuta is considered one of the greatest travelers of all time. He came to India during the regime of Muhammad bin Tughlaq.

9. **Correct Option: (d)**

Explanation:

- All statements are correct.

Supplementary Notes:

Although his rule lasted for five years, he organized a brilliant administrative system. The central government consisted of several departments. The king was assisted by four important ministers:

- Diwan-i-Wizarat – also called as Wazir, in charge of Revenue and Finance.
- Diwan-i-Ariz – in charge of Army.
- Diwan-i-Rasalat – Foreign Minister.
- Diwan-i-Insha – Minister for Communications.
- Sher Shah's empire was divided into forty seven sarkars. Chief Shiqdar (law and order) and Chief Munsif (judge) were the two officers in charge of the administration in each sarkar. Each sarkar was divided into several parganas. Shiqdar (military officer), Amin (land revenue), Fotedar (treasurer) Karkuns (accountants) were in charge of the administration of each pargana. There were also many administrative units called Iqtas.

10. Correct option : (c)

Supplementary Notes:

- **The Delhi Sultanate – The Khilji Dynasty:** Qutb-ud-din Mubarak Shah Khilji was the third and last ruler of the Khilji Dynasty. He was the only ruler who assumed the title of Caliph himself.

11. Correct Option: (b)

Explanation:

- **Statement 1 is incorrect:** Ghiyasuddin Tughlaq established a new dynasty which ruled till 1412 AD.

Supplementary Notes:

The Tughlaqs

- The Tughlaqs provided three competent rulers: Ghiyasuddin, his son Muhammad bin Tughlaq (1324-51), and his nephew Firuz Shah Tughlaq (1351-88).
- The first two of these sultans ruled over an empire which comprised almost the entire country.
- The empire of Firuz was smaller but even then it was almost as large as that ruled over by Alauddin Khalji.
- After the death of Firuz, the Delhi Sultanat disintegrated and north India was divided into a series of small states.
- Although the Tughlaqs continued to rule till 1412, the invasion of Delhi by Timur in 1398 may be said to mark the end of the Tughlaq empire.

12. Correct Option: (d)

Explanation:

- All statements are correct.

Supplementary Notes:

- Firuz Tughlaq was faced with the problem of preventing the imminent break-up of the Delhi Sultanat. He adopted a policy of trying to appease the nobles, the army and the theologians, and of asserting his authority over only such areas which could be easily administrated from the centre.
- He, therefore, made no attempt to re-assert his authority over south India and the Deccan. He led two campaigns into Bengal, but was unsuccessful in both. Bengal, was thus, lost to the Sultanat.
- Even then, the Sultanat continued to be as large as it was during the early years of the reign of Alauddin Khalji. Firuz led a campaign against the ruler of Jajnagar (Orissa). He desecrated the temples there and gathered a rich plunder.
- Firuz was by no means a distinguished military leader. But his reign was a period of peace, and of quiet development. He decreed that whenever a noble died, his son should be allowed to succeed to his position, including his Iqta, and if he had no son, his son-in-law and in his absence, his slave.
- The rebellions in south India were the most serious. At first, these areas were organised by the local governors. The Sultan hurried to south India. Some time later, plague broke out in the army and two-thirds of the army perished in this plague.
- This was a blow from which Muhammad Tughlaq never recovered. Soon after the return of the Sultan from south India, there was another rebellion there; led by two brothers, Harihara and Bukka.

13. Correct Option: (c)

Explanation:

- **Statement 2 is incorrect:** He prohibited the practice of Muslim women going out to worship at the graves of saints.

Supplementary Notes:

Firuz Shah Tughlaq

- Firuz followed the policy of his predecessors in essentials. There is no reason to believe that he allowed the theologians to dictate the state policy.
- But he gave a number of important concessions to the theologians. He tried to ban practices which the orthodox theologians considered un-Islamic.
- Thus, he prohibited the practice of Muslim women going out to worship at the graves of saints. He persecuted a number of Muslim sects which were considered heretical by the theologians. It was during the time of Firuz that Jizyah became a separate tax.
- Earlier, it was a part of land revenue. Firuz refused to exempt the Brahmans from the payment of Jizyah since this was not provided for in the Sharia.
- Only women, children, disabled and the indigent who had no means of livelihood were exempt from it. Worse, he publicly burnt a Brahman for preaching to

the people, including Muslims, on the grounds that it was against the Sharia.

- On the same ground, he even ordered that the beautiful wall paintings at his palace be erased. However, he patronized music, and despite his orthodoxy, was fond of wine.

14. Correct Option: (a)

Explanation:

- Option (a) is correct.

Supplementary Notes:

Slave Dynasty

- Invasions by Mahmud of Ghazni and Mohd. Ghori into India ultimately resulted in the establishment of the Delhi Sultanate.
- Five different dynasties–the Slave, the Khalji, the Tughlaq, the Sayyids, and the Lodhis are collectively referred to as the Delhi Sultanate.
- Qutub-ud-din Aibak founded the Slave Dynasty (also called the Mameluk Dynasty) in India.
  - He assumed the title of 'Sultan' and made Lahore his capital.
  - He did not issue any coins and was formally recognized after three years.
  - He gave a lot of liberal donations and was famously known as 'Lakh Baksh' or giver of lakhs, for his Magnanimity.
  - The first mosque in India "Quwwat-ul-Islam" in Delhi was built by him. He is also known to have built 'Arhai din ka jhonpara' in Ajmer.
  - The construction of Qutub Minar was started by him (only the first storey) in the memory of the famous Sufi Saint, Khwaja Qutbuddin Bakthiyar Kaki. It was later completed by Iltutmish in around 1220 AD.

15. Correct Option: (c)

Explanation:

- Both statements are correct.

Supplementary Notes:

Khilji Dynasty

- Jalaluddin is known to have followed the policy of tolerance.
- He repelled the attack of the Mongols on Delhi Sultanate and allowed the converted Mongols to settle near Delhi who was called the 'New Musalmans'.
- Alauddin Khalji reversed Jalaluddin's policy of tolerance and pursued ruthless governance. Ala-ud-din followed the Divine Right Theory of Kingship.
- He made an expedition against Gujarat, Rajputana, and the Deccan states and is known to have renamed Chittor to Khizrabad after his son Khizr Khan.
- Malik Kafur was the favorite of Alauddin and he raised a minor son of Alauddin to the throne and imprisoned or blinded his other sons, without encountering any opposition from the nobles.
- Qutbuddin Mubarak Shah deposed of Malik Kafur to sit on the throne of Delhi after Alauddin.
- Soon after accession to the throne, Mubarak Shah was killed by Nasiruddin Khusrau.
- Nasiruddin Khusrau Shah was the only Hindu convert to sit on the throne of Delhi.
- In 1320, a group of officers led by Ghiyasuddin Tughlaq raised the banner of revolt which led to open rebellion and a battle was fought outside the capital in which Khusrau was defeated and killed.

16. Correct Option: (b)

Explanation:

- **Statement 1 is incorrect:** Wazir headed the finance department, called Diwan-i-Wizarat.
- **Statement 3 is incorrect:** The Naib practically enjoyed all the powers of the Sultan and exercised general control over all the departments.

Supplementary Notes:

Central Administration in the Sultanate Period

- The office of the Sultan was the most important in the Sultanate and he was the ultimate authority for the military, legal, and political matters.
- The Sultan was assisted by several ministers who headed different departments and aided in administration. These ministers were chosen by Sultan and they remained in office at his pleasure.
- The post of Naib was the most powerful one. The Naib practically enjoyed all the powers of the Sultan and exercised general control over all the departments.
- Next to him, was the Wazir, who headed the finance department, called Diwan-i-Wizarat.
- The military department was called Diwan-i-Arz. It was headed by the Ariz-i-Mumalik who was responsible for recruiting the soldiers and administering the military department.
- Diwan-i-Rasalat was the department of religious affairs, which dealt with pious foundations and gave stipends to deserving scholars and men of piety. Grants were made by this department also for the construction and maintenance of mosques, tombs, and madrasas. It was headed by chief Sadr who also functioned as Chief Qazi, as the head of the judicial department.
- The department of correspondence was called Diwan-i-Insha. All the correspondence between the ruler and the sovereigns of other states as well as with his subordinate officials was dealt with.

17. Correct Option: (a)

Explanation:

- **Statement 3 is incorrect:** Iltutmish introduced the Arabic coinage into India. He introduced silver Tanka and copper Jital, the two coins of the Delhi Sultanate.

Supplementary Notes:

Iltutmish (1211-1236)

- Iltutmish belonged to the Ilbari tribe and hence his dynasty was named as Ilbari Dynasty. His half-brothers sold him as a slave to Aibak, who made him his-son-in law by giving his daughter in marriage to him.
- In 1211, Iltutmish defeated Aram Baksh and became Sultan. He shifted his capital from Lahore to Delhi. During the first ten years of his reign, he concentrated on securing his throne from his rivals.
- In the meantime, Temujin popularly known as Chengiz Khan, the leader of the Mongols, started invading Central Asia. He defeated Jalaluddin Mangabarni, the ruler of Kwarizam. Mangabarni crossed the river Indus and sought asylum from Iltutmish.
- Iltutmish refused to give him shelter to save his empire from the onslaught of the Mongols. Fortunately for Iltutmish, Chengiz Khan returned home without entering into India. The Mongol policy of Iltutmish saved India from the wrath of Chengiz Khan. Iltutmish marched against Bengal and Bihar and reasserted his control over them.
- He nominated his daughter Raziya as his successor. Thus, the hereditary succession to Delhi Sultanate was initiated by Iltutmish. He patronized many scholars and several Sufi saints came to India during his reign.
- The Iqta system was a practice of tax farming under Iqtadars, which was introduced by Iltutmish in Delhi Sultanate. It was a grant of revenue from territory in place of salary. This grant was not hereditary and was subject to passing from officer to officer. Iqta system linked the farthest part of the Sultanate to the central government.
- Apart from completing the construction of Qutub Minar at Delhi, the tallest stone tower in India (238 ft.), he built a magnificent mosque at Ajmer.
- Iltutmish introduced the Arabic coinage into India. He introduced silver tanka and copper Jital, the two coins of the Delhi Sultanate.
- Iltutmish was the first to introduce a "Pure Arabic Coin" in India. The silver Tanka issued by Iltutmish weighed 175 grains. The silver Tanka remained the basis of the modern rupee.
- Iltutmish had also created a new class of ruling elite of forty powerful military leaders, called the Forty Chihalgani.

18. Correct Option: (c)

Explanation:

- Both statements are correct.

Supplementary Notes:

Struggle for the Establishment of a Strong Monarchy

- Muizzuddin (Muhammad of Ghur) was succeeded by Qutbuddin Aibak, a Turkish slave in 1206. He had played an important role in the expansion of the Turkish Sultanat in India after the Battle of Tarain. Another slave of Muizzuddin, Yalduz, succeeded at Ghazni. As the ruler of Ghazni, Yalduz claimed to rule over Delhi as well.
- This, however, was not accepted by Aibak who ruled from Lahore. But from this time, the Sultanate severed its links with Ghazni.
- This was fortunate, since it helped to prevent India being drawn into Central Asian politics. It also enabled the Delhi Sultanat to develop on its own without depending on countries outside India.
- In order to assert her claim Raziya had to contend against her brothers as well as against powerful Turkish nobles, and could rule only for three years. Though brief, her rule had a number of interesting features.
- It marked the beginning of a struggle for power between the monarchy and the Turkish chiefs, sometimes called 'the forty' or the Chahalgani. Iltutmish had shown great deference to these Turkish chiefs.

19. Correct Option: (c)

Explanation:

- **Statement 2 is incorrect:** The Khaljis who were of a mixed Turkish-Afghan origin, did not exclude the Turks from high offices, but the rise of the Khalji to power ended the Turkish monopoly of high offices.

Supplementary Notes:

- Jalaluddin Khalji ruled only for a brief period of six years. He tried to mitigate some of the harsh aspects of Balban's rule.
- He was the first ruler of the Delhi Sultanate to clearly put forward the view that the state should be based on the willing support of the governed, and that since the large majority of the people in India were Hindus, the state in India could not be a truly Islamic state.
- Many non-Turks such as the Khaljis, had come to India in the time of the Ghurid invasion.
- They never received sufficient recognition in Delhi and had to move to Bengal and Bihar for an opportunity for advancement.
- They also found employment as soldiers, many of them were being posted in the northwest to meet the Mongol challenge. In course of time, many Indian Muslims were admitted to the nobility.

20. **Correct Option: (b)**

Explanation:

- **Statement 1 is incorrect:** He gave high offices to people on the basis of merit, irrespective of whether they belonged to noble families or not.

Supplementary Notes:
Muhammad bin Tughlaq

- Muhammad bin Tughlaq was one of the most remarkable rulers of his age. He was deeply read in religion and philosophy, and had a critical and open mind.
- He conversed not only with the Muslim mystics, but also with the Hindu yogis and Jain saints such as Jinaprabha Suri. This was not liked by many orthodox theologians who accused him of being a 'rationalist', that is, one who was not prepared to accept religious beliefs as a matter of faith.
- He transferred the capital from Delhi to Deogir.
- Another step which Muhammad Tughlaq took during his time was the introduction of the 'token currency.
- Since money is merely a medium of exchange, all countries in the world today have token currencies – generally paper currency, so that they do not have to depend upon the supply of gold and silver.

21. **Correct Option: (c)**

Explanation:

- **Option (c) is correct:** Bahlol Lodhi laid the foundation of the Lodhi Dynasty in India in 1451 after defeating Alauddin Alam Shah of the Sayyid Dynasty.

Supplementary Notes:
Lodhi Dynasty

- Bahlol Lodhi laid the foundation of the Lodhi Dynasty in India in 1451 after defeating Alauddin Alam Shah of the Sayyid Dynasty. He considered himself one of the Afghan peers and not the king.
- He was succeeded by Sikander Lodhi whose real name was Nizam Khan.
- Sikander Lodhi was a good administrator. He laid many roads and provided many irrigational facilities for the benefit of the peasantry.
- Sikander Lodhi introduced a new measurement yardstick, the Gazz-i-Sikandar, and a system of auditing the accounts. However, he showed little tolerance towards the non-Muslims and re-imposed Jizya on them.
- Sikander Lodhi founded Agra in c.1504 CE and wrote Persian verses under the name 'Gulrakhi'.
- Ibrahim Lodhi was the eldest son of Sikander Lodhi. Babur marched against Delhi and defeated and killed Ibrahim Lodhi in the First Battle of Panipat (c.1526 CE).
- The Sultanate of Delhi, which had its birth on the battlefield of Tarain in c. 1192 CE, breathed its last in c.1526 CE, a few miles away on the battlefield of Panipat.

22. **Correct Option: (c)**

Explanation:

- Both statements are correct.

Supplementary Notes:
Ibrahim Adil Shah II

- The successor of Ali Adil Shah, Ibrahim Adil Shah II (1580-1627), ascended the throne of the Sultanate of Bijapur at the age of nine.
- He was very solicitous to the poor and had the title of 'Abla Baba' or 'Friend of the Poor'.
- He was deeply interested in music and composed a book called Kitab-i-Nauras in modes or ragas.
- He built a new capital, Nauraspur, in which a large number of musicians were invited to settle.
- In his songs, he freely invoked the goddess of music and learning, Saraswati. Due to his broad approach, he came to be called 'Jagat Guru'. He accorded patronage to all, including Hindu saints and temples. This included grants to Pandharpur, the centre of the worship of Vithoba, which became the centre of the Bhakti movement in Maharashtra.

23. **Correct Option: (d)**

Explanation:

- All statements are correct.

Supplementary Notes:
Mohammad bin Tughlaq

- Mohammad bin Tughlaq is considered an ill-fated idealist owing to his ambitious schemes and novel experiments.
- He transferred his capital from Delhi to Devagiri (Daulatabad), but the capital was shifted back to Delhi after two years because of the lack of water supply in Daulatabad.
- He modeled the idea of token currency on the basis of the Chinese ruler Kublai Khan who issued paper money in China.
- He issued copper coins at par with the value of the silver tanka coins. Later on, he repealed his verdict, and all coins were redeemed in silver/gold, making the treasury empty.
- During his reign, the famous traveler Ibn Batuta came to India in 1334 CE and acted as a Qazi at Delhi for eight years.
- He was the only Delhi Sultan who had received a comprehensive literary, religious, and philosophical education and is known to have built the fort of Adilabad and the city of Jahanpanah.

24. Correct Option: (c)

Explanation:

- Both statements are correct.

Supplementary Notes:

Lodhi Dynasty

- Bahlol Lodhi laid the foundation of the Lodhi Dynasty in India in 1451 after defeating Alauddin Alam Shah of the Sayyid Dynasty.
- He considered himself one of the Afghan peers and not the king.
- He was succeeded by Sikander Lodhi whose real name was Nizam Khan.
- Sikander Lodhi was a good administrator. He laid many roads and provided many irrigational facilities for the benefit of the peasantry.
- Sikander Lodhi introduced a new measurement yardstick, the Gazz-i-Sikandar, and a system of auditing the accounts. However, he showed little tolerance towards the non-Muslims and re-imposed Jizya on them.
- Sikander Lodhi founded Agra in c.1504 CE and wrote Persian verses under the name 'Gulrakhi'.
- Ibrahim Lodhi was the eldest son of Sikander Lodhi. Babur marched against Delhi and defeated and killed Ibrahim Lodhi in the First Battle of Panipat (c.1526 CE).
- The Sultanate of Delhi, which had its birth on the battlefield of Tarain in c. 1192 CE, breathed its last in c.1526 CE, a few miles away on the battlefield of Panipat.

25. Correct Option: (b)

Explanation:

Statement 2 is incorrect: Qutub-ud-din Aibak did not issue any coins during his rule.

Supplementary Notes:

Slave Dynasty

- Invasions by Mahmud of Ghazni and Mohd. Ghori into India ultimately resulted in the establishment of the Delhi Sultanate.
- Five different Dynasties–the Slave, the Khalji, the Tughlaq, the Sayyids, and the Lodhi's are collectively referred to as the Delhi Sultanate.
- Qutub-ud-din Aibak founded the Slave Dynasty (also called the Mameluk Dynasty) in India.
- He assumed the title of 'Sultan' and made Lahore his capital.
- He did not issue any coins and was formally recognized after three years.
- He gave a lot of liberal donations and was famously known as 'Lakh Baksh' or 'Giver of Lakhs' for his magnanimity.
- The first mosque in India "Quwwat-ul-Islam" in Delhi was built by him. He is also known to have built 'Arhai din ka jhonpara' in Ajmer.
- The construction of Qutub Minar was started by him (only the first storey) in the memory of the famous Sufi saint, Khwaja Qutbuddin Bakthiyar Kaki. It was later completed by Iltutmish in around 1220.

26. Correct Option: (c)

Explanation:

- **Option (c) is correct:** The correct chronological order is:
  - Bahram Shah
  - Alauddin Masud Shah
  - Nasiruddin Mahmud
  - Balban

Supplementary Notes:

Slave Dynasty Rulers

- The fall of Raziya paved way for Bahram Shah for the ascendancy with the support of noble elites, the Forty.
- However he was later murdered by his own army and the chiefs chose Alauddin Masud Shah, son of Ruknuddin Firuz Shah and nephew of Raziya Sultan to become the next ruler.
- He became infamous for his fondness for entertainment and wine.
- By the year 1246, the chiefs became upset with his increasing hunger for more power in the government and replaced him with Nasiruddin Mahmud, the grandson of Iltutmish.
- He had ascended to the throne with the aid of Ulugh Khan/Balban (member of the Chahalgani), who himself assumed the position of Naib (deputy or regent).
- Due to internal conflicts, as per historians such as Ibn Battuta and Isami, Balban poisoned his master Nasiruddin and ascended the throne in the year 1266.

27. Correct Option: (a)

Explanation:

List-I	List-II
A. Jalauddin Khalji	2. Settled New Musalmans near Delhi
B. Alauddin Khalji	4. Renamed Chittor as Khizrabad
C. Qutbuddin	1. Deposed Malik Mubarak Shah Kafur
D. Nasiruddin	3. Only Hindu convert Khusrau to sit on the throne of Delhi

Supplementary Notes:

Khalji Dynasty

- Jalaluddin is known to have followed the policy of tolerance.
- He repelled the attack of the Mongols on Delhi Sultanate and allowed the converted Mongols to settle near Delhi who were called the 'New Musalmans'.
- Alauddin Khalji reversed Jalaluddin's policy of tolerance and pursued ruthless governance.
- He made an expedition against Gujarat, Rajputana, and the Deccan states and is known to have renamed Chittor to Khizrabad after his son Khizr Khan.
- Malik Kafur was the favorite of Alauddin and he raised a minor son of Alauddin to the throne and imprisoned or blinded his other sons, without encountering any opposition from the nobles.
- Qutbuddin Mubarak Shah deposed Malik Kafur to sit on the throne of Delhi after Alauddin.
- Soon after accession to the throne, Mubarak Shah was killed by Nasiruddin Khusrau.
- Nasiruddin Khusrau Shah was the only Hindu convert to sit on the throne of Delhi.
- In 1320, a group of officers led by Ghiyasuddin Tughlaq raised the banner of revolt which led to open rebellion and a battle was fought outside the capital in which Khusrau was defeated and killed.

28. Correct Option: (b)

Supplementary Notes:

Ibrahim Adil Shah II

- The successor of Ali Adil Shah, Ibrahim Adil Shah II (1580-1627), ascended the throne of Sultanate of Bijapur at the age of nine.
- He was very solicitous to the poor, and had the title of 'Abla Baba' or 'Friend of the Poor'.
- He was deeply interested in music, and composed a book called Kitab-i-Nauras in which songs were set to various musical modes or ragas.
- He built a new capital, Nauraspur, in which a large number of musicians were invited to settle.
- In his songs, he freely invoked the goddess of music and learning, Saraswati. Due to his broad approach he came to be called 'Jagat Guru'. He accorded patronage to all, including Hindu saints and temples. This included grants to Pandharpur, the centre of the worship of Vithoba, which became the centre of the Bhakti movement in Maharashtra.

29. Correct Option: (a)

Explanation:

- **Statement 1 is incorrect:** Sher Shah did not make many changes in the administrative divisions prevailing since the Sultanate period. He apparently continued the central machinery of administration which had developed during the Sultanate period.
- **Statement 2 is incorrect:** Sher Shah did not initiate any new liberal policies. Jizyah continued to be collected from the Hindus.

Supplementary Notes:

Sher Shah and the Sur Empire (1540-1555)

- Sher Shah ascended the throne of Delhi at the age of 54. His original name was Farid and his father was a small Jagirdar at Jaunpur. The title of Sher Khan was given to him by his patron for killing a tiger or for services rendered.
- As a ruler, Sher Shah ruled the mightiest empire which had come into existence in north India since the time of Muhammad bin Tughlaq. His empire extended from Bengal to the Indus, excluding Kashmir. In the west, he conquered Malwa, and almost the entire Rajasthan.
- The Sur Empire may be considered in many ways as a continuation and culmination of the Delhi Sultanate, the advent of Babur and Humayun being in the nature of an interregnum.
- Amongst the foremost contributions of Sher Shah was his re-establishment of law and order across the length and breadth of his empire. He dealt sternly with robbers and dacoits and with zamindars who refused to pay land revenue or disobeyed the orders of the government.
- Sher Shah paid great attention to the improvement of communications in his kingdom. For e.g. he restored the old imperial road called the Grand Trunk Road, from the river Indus in the west to Sonargaon in Bengal. He also built a road from Agra to Jodhpur and Chittor, evidently linking up with the road to the Gujarat seaports. He built a third road from Lahore to Multan. For the convenience of travellers, Sher Shah built a sarai at a distance of every two Kos (about eight km) on these roads.
- Sher Shah also introduced other reforms to promote the growth of trade and commerce. In his entire empire, customs duty for goods was paid only at two places. His attempt to fix standard weights and measures and a uniform standard for coins all over the empire was also helpful for trade and commerce.
- Sher Shah did not make many changes in the administrative divisions prevailing since the Sultanate period. A number of villages comprised a Pargana. The Pargana was under the charge of the Shiqdar, who looked after law and order and general administration, and the Munsif or Amil who looked after the collection of land revenue. He apparently continued the central machinery of administration as he did not favor leaving too much authority in the hands of ministers.

- He paid special attention to the land revenue system. He insisted on measurement of the sown land. A crop rate (called ray) was drawn up, laying down the state's share of the different types of crops.
- Sher Shah did not initiate any new liberal policies. Jizyah continued to be collected from the Hindus.
- His nobility was drawn almost exclusively from the Afghans. Thus, the state under the Surs remained an Afghan institution based on race and tribe.

30. Correct Option: (a)

Explanation:

- **Option (a) is correct:** The correct chronology is: Khizr Khan - Mubarak Shah - Muhammad Shah - Alauddin Alam Shah.

Supplementary Notes:

Sayyid Dynasty

- Timur, the Mongol leader of Central Asia, head of Chagatai Turks, invaded India in c.1398 CE.
- Before his departure from India, Timur appointed Khizr Khan as the governor of Multan.
- Khizr Khan captured Delhi by defeating Daulat Khan of the Tughlaq Dynasty and founded the Sayyid Dynasty in c.1414 CE. However, he did not assume the title of the Sultan but was comfortable with Rayat-i-Ala.
- Khizr Khan was succeeded by his son, Mubarak Shah.
- Muhammad Shah was the third monarch of the Sayyid Dynasty which ruled the Delhi Sultanate. He succeeded his uncle, Mubarak Shah to the throne.
- Muhammad Shah died in 1445 and was succeeded by his son Alam Shah.
- He proved to be an incompetent Sultan and the weakest of the Sayyid princes.
- Alam Shah's Wazir, Hamid Khan, invited Bahlol Lodhi to take charge of the army and after realizing that it would be difficult to continue as Sultan, Alam Shah left for Badaun.

31. Correct Option: (c)

Explanation:

- Both statements are correct.

Supplementary Notes:

Jalaluddin Khalji

- Jalaluddin Khalji laid the foundation of the Khalji Dynasty in India in the year 1290.
- During Balban's reign, Jalaluddin had been the warden of the marches in north-west and had fought many successful battles against the Mongols.
- He was generous and also the first sultan of the Delhi Sultanate to have a benevolent attitude towards Hindus.
- He clearly put forward the view that the State should be based on the willing support of the governed.
- Jalaluddin followed the policy of tolerance to win the goodwill of the nobility by retaining the earlier nobility in his administration.
- For instance, Malik Chhajju, nephew of Balban, was allowed to remain the governor of Kara. When Chhajju revolted, it was suppressed, but he was pardoned.
- In the year 1292 CE, when Malik Chhajju revolted for the second time, he was replaced by his nephew and son-in-law, Alauddin Khalji.

32. Correct Option: (b)

Explanation:

- Option (b) is correct

List I	List II
A. Ghiyasuddin Tughlaq	3. First sultan to start irrigation work
B. Muhmmad bin Tughluq	4. Diwan-i-Amirkohi
C. Ibn Batuta	1. Safarnama Rehla
D. Khan-i-Jahan Maqbal	2. A Telugu Brahmin convert Wazir

Supplementary Notes:

Tughlaq Reign

- Ghiyasuddin Tughlaq was the first sultan to start irrigation works.
- Muhammad bin Tughluq set up a new department of Agriculture, "Diwan-i-Amirkohi". He launched a scheme by which Takkavi loans (loans for cultivation) were given to the farmers to buy seed and to extend cultivation.
- "Safarnama Rehla" was authored by Ibn Batuta which is one of the main sources of the information regarding the reign of Muhammad bin Tughluq in India.
- Firoz Shah Tughlaq had the unique distinction of being chosen as the Sultan by the nobles. So, his policy aimed to appease the nobles, the army, and theologians.
- He appointed Khan-i-Jahan Maqbal, a Telugu Brahmin convert as Wazir (prime minister). The Wazir helped the Sultan in his administration and maintained the prestige of the Sultanate during this period.

33. Correct Option: (d)

Explanation:

- **Statement 1 is incorrect:** Raziya, with the support of amirs of Delhi, seized the throne of the Delhi Sultanate from Firuz Shah, the eldest son of Iltutmish who was supported by the nobles.

- **Statement 2 is incorrect:** Altuniya (governor of Lahore) is known to have imprisoned Razia at Qila Mubarak in Bathinda.

Supplementary Notes:

Death of Iltutmish and his succession

- Iltutmish did not consider any of his sons worthy of the throne. So, he declared his daughter Razia as successor, deviating from normal practice.
- However, the eldest son of Iltutmish was put on the throne by nobles who wanted a puppet ruler.
- Raziya, with the support of amirs of Delhi, seized the throne of the Delhi Sultanate and Firuz Shah was put to death.
- She was the first and only female Muslim ruler of medieval India.
- Her attempts to create a counter nobility of non-Turks invited the wrath of the Turkish amirs.
- They were particularly incensed over her decision to appoint an Abyssinian slave, Malik Jamaluddin Yaqut, to important office of the Amir-i-Akhur (Superintendent of royal horses).
- The recruitment of a few other non-Turks to important posts further inflamed matters.
- Among others, Altuniya, the governor of Lahore was first to create trouble but was defeated.
- In the year 1240 CE, a serious rebellion broke out in Sirhind (Bhatinda) under Altuniya.
- Raziya, alongside Yaqut, marched against Altuniya, but on the way, Turkish followers of Altuniya murdered Yaqut and imprisoned Raziya at Qila Mubarak in Bathinda.
- In the meantime, the Turkish nobles put Bahram, another son of Iltutmish, on the throne.
- However, Raziya won over her captor, Altuniya, and after marrying him proceeded to Delhi. But she was defeated and killed on the way by Bahram Shah.

34. Correct Option: (c)

Explanation:

- **Option (c) is incorrect:** The title of 'Tuti-i-Hind' was given to Amir Khusrau by Alauddin Khalji.

Supplementary Notes:

Alauddin Khalji

- Alauddin Khalji was Jalaluddin's nephew and son-in-law.
- He treacherously murdered his father-in-law Jalaluddin Khalji near Kara and usurped the throne of Delhi.
- Jalaluddin's policy of tolerance was reversed by Alauddin Khalji, who awarded drastic punishments to all those who dared to oppose him. He decided to revive Balban's policies of ruthless governance.
- Alauddin adopted the title of Sikander-i-Azam and gave Amir Khusrau the title of Tuti-i-Hind (Parrot of India).
- He became the first ruler to fix land revenue in cash.
- His theory of kinship was secular, and he proclaimed "Kingship knows no Kinship". He is known for his inclusion of non-Turks in his service.
- He refuted the suzerainty of the Caliph and did not allow any power independent of the state to guide his policy.

35. Correct Option: (a)

Explanation:

- Option (a) is correct.

List I	List II
A. Diwan-i-Wizarat	4. Finance department
B. Diwan-i-Arz	3. Military department
C. Diwan-i-Rasalat	2. Department of religious affairs
D. Diwan-i-Insha	1. Department of correspondence

Supplementary Notes:

Central Administration in the Sultanate Period

- The office of the Sultan was the most important in the Sultanate and he was the ultimate authority for the military, legal, and political matters.
- The Sultan was assisted by a number of ministers who headed different departments and aided in administration. These ministers were chosen by Sultan and they remained in office at his pleasure.
- The post of Naib was the most powerful one. The Naib practically enjoyed all the powers of the Sultan and exercised general control over all the departments.
- Next to him, was the Wazir, who headed the finance department called Diwan-i-Wizarat.
- The military department was called Diwan-i-Arz. It was headed by the Ariz-i-Mumalik who was responsible for recruiting the soldiers and administering the military department.
- Diwan-i-Rasalat was the department of religious affairs, which dealt with pious foundations and gave stipends to deserving scholars and men of piety. Grants were made by this department also for the construction and maintenance of mosques, tombs, and madrasas. It was headed by chief Sadr who also functioned as chief Qazi, as the head of the judicial department.
- The department of correspondence was called Diwan-i-Insha. All the correspondence between the ruler and the sovereigns of other states as well as with his subordinate officials was dealt.

36. Correct Option: (b)

Explanation:

- **Statement 2 is incorrect:** Iltutmish was the first to issue purely Arabic coinage of silver tanka, which remains the basis of the modern rupee and copper Jital.

Supplementary Notes:

Iltutmish

- Iltutmish is known to be the real consolidator of Turkish rule in India.
- He belonged to the Ilbari tribe and hence, his Dynasty also known as the Ilbari Dynasty.
- He was the son-in-law of Qutbuddin Aibak and disposed of Aram Shah (son of Qutbuddin Aibak) and became the Sultan with the name of "Shamsuddin".
- After becoming Sultan, he shifted his capital from Lahore to Delhi.
- He divided his empire into Iqtas which included the assignment of land in lieu of salary. Every Iqtadars had to maintain law and order and collect revenue.
- "Turkan-i-Chahalgani" was organized by him as a new class of ruling elite of forty powerful military leaders, called the Forty.
- These were Turkish amirs (nobles) who advised and helped the Sultan in administering the Sultanate. The group was finally eliminated by Balban.
- He was the first to issue purely Arabic coinage of silver Tanka weighing 175 grains, which remains the basis of the modern rupee and copper Jital.

37. Correct Option: (b)

Explanation:

- **Option (b) is correct:** The correct order is Muqaddam – Amil – Shiqdar – Muqti.

Supplementary Notes:

Provincial Government in the Sultanate Period

- The provinces under the Delhi Sultanate were called Iqtas. They were headed by the Governor who was called "Muqtis or Walis". They were to maintain law and order and collect land revenue.
- The provinces were further divided into Shiqs (districts), which was under the control of the "Shiqdar".
- The next division subdivision was Pargana (sub-district), comprising a number of villages and was headed by the "Amil".
- The villages were grouped into units of 100 or 84 (traditionally called Chaurasi). The village remained the basic unit of the administration. The village headman was known as "Muqaddam or Chaudhri". The village accountant was called 'Patwari'

38. Correct Options: (b)

Explanation:

- **Statement 1 is incorrect:** The Battle of Chausa was a notable military engagement between the Mughal emperor, Humayun and the Afghan, Sher Shah Suri.

Supplementary Notes:

Battle of Chausa

- It was fought on 26 June 1539 at Chausa in modern-day Bihar.
- Humayun escaped from the battlefield to save his life. Sher Shah was victorious and crowned himself "Farīd al-Dīn Shēr Shah".

Sher Shah Suri

- The Tarikh-i-Sher Shahi (History of Sher Shah), by Abbas Khan Sarwani, provides detailed citations about Sher Shah's administration.
- Sher Shah also appointed four important ministers which are given:
  - ➤ Diwan-i-Wazarat : Financial Department
  - ➤ Diwan-i-Ariz : Military Department
  - ➤ Diwan-i-Risalat : Department for Religious Matters, Foreign Affairs
  - ➤ Diwan-i-Insha : Department for Royal Secretariat
- Rotation of officers across Empire was planned to keep a check on their performance. The rotation would occur every 2-3 years.
- Important places of the Kingdom under Sher Shah were connected by excellent roads for smoother military and trade movement.
- The longest of the roads, was called the Sadak-e-Azam or the "Badshahi Sadak" (which the British renamed as "Grand Trunk Road") and exists till date.
- Land was classified into three categories for calculating the revenue based on the yield and measurement of land – good, middle and bad.
- The famous Hindi work 'Padmavat' by Malik Muhammad Jayasi was written during his reign.

39. Correct Option: (b)

Explanation:

- **Statement 1 is incorrect:** Post of Naib was the most powerful one as he exercised general control over all departments.

Supplementary Notes:

Central Administration in the Sultanate Period

- The office of the Sultan was the most important in the Sultanate and he was the ultimate authority for the military legal, and political matters.
- The Sultan was assisted by a number of ministers who headed different departments and aided in administration. These ministers were chosen by Sultan and they remained in office at his pleasure.

- The post of Naib was the most powerful one. The Naib practically enjoyed all the powers of the Sultan and exercised general control over all the departments.
- Next to him, was the Wazir, who headed the finance department called Diwan-i-Wizarat.
- The military department was called Diwan-i-Arz. It was headed by the Ariz-i-Mumalik who was responsible for recruiting the soldiers and administering the military department.
- Diwan-i-Rasalat was the department of religious affairs, which dealt with pious foundations and gave stipends to deserving scholars and men of piety. Grants were made by this department also for the construction and maintenance of mosques, tombs, and madrasas. It was headed by Chief Sadr who also functioned as Chief Qazi, as the head of the judicial department.
- The department of correspondence was called Diwan-i-Insha. All the correspondence between the ruler and the sovereigns of other states as well as with his subordinate officials was dealt with by this department.

40. Correct Option: (d)

Explanation:

- All statements are correct.

Supplementary Notes:

Mohammad bin Tughlaq

- Mohammad bin Tughlaq is considered an ill-fated idealist owing to his ambitious schemes and novel experiments.
- Transferred his capital from Delhi to Devagiri (Daulatabad) but shifted back to Delhi after two years because of the lack of water supply in Daulatabad.
- He modeled the idea of token currency on the basis of the Chinese ruler Kublai Khan who issued paper money in China.
- Tughlaq, thus, issued copper coins at par with the value of the silver tanka coins. Later on, he repealed his verdict, and all coins were redeemed in silver/gold, making the treasury empty.
- During his reign, the famous traveler Ibn Batuta came to India in c.1334 CE and acted as a Qazi at Delhi for eight years.
- He was the only Delhi Sultan who had received a comprehensive literary, religious, and philosophical education and is known to have built the fort of Adilabad and the city of Jahanpanah.

41. Correct Option: (a)

Explanation:

- **Option (a) is correctly matched.**
    - Diwan-i-Wijarat (Finance Department);
    - Diwan-i-Arz (Military Department);
    - Diwan-i-Insha (Royal Secretariat); and
    - Diwan-i-Rasalat (Department for religious and foreign affairs).

Supplementary Notes:

Information regarding Sher Shah Suri

- The founder of the Suri Empire in the northern part of the Indian subcontinent, with its capital in Sasaram in modern-day Bihar.
- He introduced the currency of rupee.
- His reorganization of the empire laid the foundations for the later Mughal emperors, notably Akbar, son of Humayun.
- His empire occupied the whole of North India except Assam, Gujarat, Kashmir, and Nepal.
- He divided his whole empire into 47 divisions called 'Sarkars' and these were again subdivided into smaller administrative units called 'Parganas', which was in charge of various officers: Shiqdar – Military Officer, Amin – Land Revenue, Fotedar – Treasurer, Karkuns – Accountants.
- He established four main central departments:
    - Diwan-i-Wijarat (Finance Department);
    - Diwan-i-Arz (Military Department);
    - Diwan-i-Insha (Royal Secretariat); and
    - Diwan-i-Rasalat (Department for religious and foreign affairs).
- Iqtas were the various administrative units.
- He introduced a system of pure metal coins which came to characterise Mughal coinage (Silver coin) which was called 'Rupia'.
- He introduced copper coins which were called Dam, Half Dam and quarter Dam as per denomination.
- He introduced regular postal services.

CONCEPT REVISION

Here is the list of concepts that have been covered as part of the previous exercise. Revise and Self-reflect on your concepts you covered.

- Iltutmish Reign ☐
- Administration during the reign of Sher Shah Suri ☐
- Ibn Batutta ☐
- Decline of Delhi Sultanate ☐
- Khilji Dynasty ☐
- Central Administration of Delhi Sultanate ☐
- Lodhi Dynasty ☐
- Slave Dynasty ☐
- Saiyyad Dynasty ☐
- Sur Dynasty ☐

4.4 MUGHAL EMPIRE

QUESTIONS

1. Consider the following statements regarding contingents of Mughal administration:

1. Every noble had to bring his contingent for periodic inspection before persons appointed by the emperor.
2. For every ten cavalry men, the Mansabdar had to maintain twenty horses.

Which of the following statements is/are correct?

(a) 1 only (b) 2 only
(c) Both 1 and 2 (d) Neither 1 nor 2

2. Consider the following statements regarding Mughal Empire:

1. The authors of Mughal chronicles were invariably courtiers.
2. Due to cultural and intellectual contacts with Iran, Persian was made the leading language of the Mughal court.
3. The finished manuscript was seen in the court as a precious object of beauty, with little intellectual value.

Which of the above statements is/are correct?

(a) 1 and 2 only (b) 1 and 3 only
(c) 2 and 3 only (d) 1, 2 and 3

3. Consider the following description:

"He launched a prolonged campaign in the northwest frontier to recover Kandahar and other ancestral lands. He carved four Mughal provinces in the Deccan- Khandesh, Berar, Telangana and Daulatabad. His last years of reign were clouded by a bitter war of succession among his four sons".

Which of the following rulers best represents the above description?

(a) Jahangir (b) Dara Sikhoh
(c) Shah Jahan (d) Humayun

4. Which of the following pairs are correctly matched regarding Mughal Administration?

Designation Administration	Department/ Office
1. Muqqadam	1. Head of revenue in village
2. Amalguzar	2. Administrative head of district
3. Shiqdar	3. Administrative head of pargana
4. Kotwal	4. Trial of criminal cases

Select the correct answer using the code given below:

(a) 1, 2 and 4 only (b) 2 and 3 only
(c) 3 and 4 only (d) 1, 3 and 4 only

5. Which of the following reasons for the downfall of Mughal Empire is/are correct?

1. The religious and Deccan policies of the Aurangzeb.
2. The financial difficulties due to continuous wars.
3. The invasions of Nadir Shah and Ahmad Shah Abdali.

Select the correct answer using the code given below:

(a) 2 only (b) 3 only
(c) 1, 3 and 3 only (d) 1, 2 and 3

6. Which of the following pairs is/are correctly matched?

Battle		Rulers
1. Battle of Khanwa (1527)	-	Babur and Rana Sanga
2. Battle of Gogra (1529)	-	Jahangir and Afghans
3. Battle of Bilgram (1540)	-	Humayun and Sher Shah

Select the correct answer using the code given below:

(a) 2 only (b) 1 and 3 only
(c) 2 and 3 only (d) 1, 2 and 3

7. Consider the following statements with reference to Aurangzeb's reign:

1. He ended the Mughal practice of Jharokha Darshan.
2. He released an order to ban the music everywhere and arrest those who listen to the music.
3. He restarted the practice of engraving of Kalma on issued coins.

Which of the above statements is/are correct?

(a) 1 and 2 only (b) 3 only
(c) 2 and 3 only (d) 1, 2 and 3

8. Which of the following policies are associated with Akbar's administration?

1. Decree of Infallibility
2. Bandobast System
3. Dahsala System
4. Mansabdari

Select the correct answer using the code given below:

(a) 1 and 2 only (b) 2 and 3 only
(c) 2, 3 and 4 only (d) 1, 2, 3 and 4

9. The term 'Du-aspah Sih-aspah System' was used in the Medieval India with reference to:

(a) A new scaling device under which the salaries of mansabdars were put on a month scale.

(b) A unit of measurement of land under the Marathas dominions.
(c) Maintaining a large quota of soldiers by selected nobles without any change in their Jat rank.
(d) An espionage system in practice during the Mughal rule.

10. Consider the following statements regarding the Third Battle of Panipat:
1. It was fought between Marathas and Ahmad Shah Abdali.
2. Just after the battle, Marathas entered into treaty with Mughals for collecting Chauth all over India.
3. Division of the Mughal nobility in contending groups was one of the reason for the battle.

Which of the above statements is/are correct?
(a) 2 only (b) 3 only
(c) 1 and 3 only (d) 1, 2 and 3

11. Consider the following statements with respect to the Mughal administration:
1. The district in the Mughal administration was known as Sarkar.
2. Each Sarkar was further divided into various Suba, which were then divided into Pargana or Mahal.

Which of the above statements is/are correct?
(a) 1 only (b) 2 only
(c) Both 1 and 2 (d) Neither 1 nor 2

12. Consider the following:
Besides being a great conqueror and a diplomat, he was a successful administrator. He employed members of all castes and tribes to maintain balance among them. In matters of administration, he gave superior position to his civil officers as compared to military officers. He had a council of ministers named Asht Pradhan to advise him on the matters of the state.
Above description relates to which of the following rulers?
(a) Aurangzeb (b) Akbar
(c) Shivaji (d) Balban

13. Hira Vijay Suri, a Jain philosopher was awarded the title of "Jagatguru" by which emperor?
(a) Shah Jahan (b) Humayun
(c) Dara Shikoh (d) Akbar

14. Which of the following denotes the term "cushoons" during the medieval period?
(a) Chief Officer of Records Department
(b) Treasurer
(c) Rocket artillery brigades
(d) None of the above

15. Who among the following was named as "Zinda Pir" or " Living Saint" in Mughal India ?
(a) Humayun (b) Akbar
(c) Aurangzeb (d) Jahangir

16. Who among the following was the French explorer who visited court of Emperor Shah Jahan and left a detailed account of Takht-i-Taus (Peacock throne)?
(a) Jean-Baptiste Tavernier
(b) Geronimo Verroneo
(c) Pierre-Jean Grosley
(d) Jean-Paul Dubois

17. Consider the following statements regarding the military conquest of Babur, the founder of Mughal Empire in India:
1. On 21st April 1526, the first Battle of Panipat took place between Babur and Ibrahim Lodi,
2. Babur occupied Delhi and sent his son Humayun to seize Agra and Babur proclaimed himself as "Emperor of Hindustan".

Which of the above statements is/are correct?
(a) 1 only (b) 2 only
(c) Both 1 and 2 (d) Neither 1 nor 2

18. The battle of Chausa was fought between which of the following two rulers?
(a) Babur and Rana Sanga
(b) Humayun and Sher Khan
(c) Babur and Sher Khan
(d) Sher Khan and Rana Sanga

19. Who among the following was the Head of judicial department during the Mughal period?
(a) Qazi (b) Mir Bakhshi
(c) Mir Saman (d) Diwan

20. With reference to the prevalent system of administration during the reign of Akbar, which of the following statement is incorrect?
(a) Nasaq was a system of measurement and the assessment based upon that measurement.
(b) In the galla-bakhshi system, the produce was divided between the peasants and the state in fixed proportion.
(c) Zabti was a system of measurement and the assessment based upon that measurement.
(d) The zabti system is associated with Raja Todar Mal, and was sometimes called Todar Mal's bandobast.

21. Consider the following statements regarding Akbar's relation with Rajputs:
1. Akbar married the Rajput princess, the daughter of Raja Bharamal.
2. The Rajput policy of Akbar proved to be beneficial to the Mughal state as well as to the Rajputs.

Which of the above statements is/are correct?
(a) 1 only (b) 2 only
(c) Both 1 and 2 (d) Neither 1 nor 2

22. The famous battle between Babur and Rana Sanga is known as the battle of Khanwa is currently located in which of the following states of India?
(a) Uttar Pradesh (b) Madhya Pradesh
(c) Rajasthan (d) Haryana

23. Consider the following statements regarding the significance of Babur's advent into India:

1. Since the downfall of the Kushan Empire, Kabul and Qandahar became integral parts of an empire comprising north India.
2. Babur and his successors were able to give to India security from external invasions which strengthened India's foreign trade with China and the Mediterranean seaports.
3. Babur's advent led to rapid popularisation of gunpowder and artillery in India, thereby reducing the importance of forts.

Which of the above statements is/are correct?

(a) 1 only (b) 1 and 2 only
(c) 2 and 3 only (d) 1, 2 and 3

24. Amu Darya was a

(a) river of the Ancient period
(b) pond during Mughal time
(c) canal established by Aurangzeb
(d) None of the above

25. Consider the following statements regarding the failure of Mughals at Quandhar during the reign of Aurangzeb:

1. The failure of Mughals at Quandhar did not so much reflect the weakness of Mughal artillery, as has been asserted by some historians.
2. The failure of Mughals at Quandhar rather showed the inherent strength of Qandhar fort if held by a determined commander, and the ineffectiveness of medieval artillery against strong forts.
3. It was not so much the loss of Qandhar as the failure of the repeated Mughal efforts which affected the Mughal prestige.

Which of the above statements is/are correct?

(a) 1 only (b) 1 and 2 only
(c) 1 and 3 only (d) 1, 2 and 3

26. Mansabdars were

(a) Those who were holding ranks below 500 zats
(b) Those from above 500 and below 2500 zats
(c) Those holding ranks of 2500 and above zats
(d) Those holding ranks after the ruler

27. Match List I with List II:

List I	List II
A. Akbar	1. Moti Masjid at Agra
B. Jehangir	2. Buland Darwaza
C. Aurangzeb	3. Moti Masjid, Red Fort
D. Shah Jahan	4. Climax of Painting

Select the correct answer using the code given below:

	A	B	C	D
(a)	2	4	3	1
(b)	2	3	4	1
(c)	1	4	3	2
(d)	1	3	4	2

28. Match List I with List II:

List I	List II
A. Mir Bakshi	1. Head of Military
B. Mushriff	2. Master of ceremonies
C. Shiqdar	3. In-charge of law and order
D. Mir Tozak	4. Revenue Secretary

Select the correct answer using the code given below:

	A	B	C	D
(a)	2	4	3	1
(b)	2	3	4	1
(c)	1	4	3	2
(d)	1	3	4	2

29. With respect to the significance of Babur's advent into India, consider the following statements:

1. Babur not only tried hard to maintain Mughal influence on Badakhshan beyond the Hindukush Mountains, but even upto river Oxus.
2. The inclusion of Kabul and Qandahar in the empire created a favourable opportunity for the increase of India's share in the great trans-Asian trade.
3. The use of cannon and muskets in India was first used by Babur in the battle of Panipat.

Which of the above statement/s is/are correct?

(a) 1 and 2 only (b) 2 and 3 only
(c) 1 and 3 only (d) 1, 2 and 3

30. The Battle of Khanua was fought between which of the following rulers?

(a) Babur and Ibrahim Lodi
(b) Ibrahim Lodi and Rana Sangha
(c) Rana Sanga and Babur
(d) Babur and Rajputs

31. Which of the following pairs is/are correctly matched with respect to the travellers who came to India during the reign of Shah Jahan?

1. François Bernier: French physician
2. Jean-Baptiste Tavernier: French gem merchant
3. Niccolao Manucci: German adventurer

Select the correct option from the codes given below:

(a) 2 only (b) 3 only
(c) 1 only (d) 1 and 2 only

32. Consider the following statements regarding First Battle of Panipat:

1. It was fought between the forces of Babur and Bahlol Lodhi.
2. Tulghuma and the Araba Tactics were used in this battle by Babar.
3. It resulted in the end of Delhi Sultanate and beginning of Mughal rule in India.

Which of the above statements is/are correct?

(a) 1 and 2 only (b) 1 and 3 only
(c) 2 and 3 only (d) 1, 2 and 3

33. **With respect to the reign of Jahangir, consider the following statements:**
1. Like Akbar, Jahangir realised that conquest would not be lasting on the basis not of force but by securing the goodwill of the people.
2. Jahangir defeated his eldest son Khusrau at a battle near Lahore but he was shown sympathy and was released immediately.
3. In 1608, Jahangir posted Islam Khan to Bengal who handled the situation with great energy and foresight.

Which of the above statement/s is/are correct?
(a) 1 and 2 only (b) 2 and 3 only
(c) 1 and 3 only (d) 1, 2 and 3

34. **Shah Jahan had his own ambitions of which Jahangir was not unaware and later rebelled against him. Consider the following statements in this regard:**
1. The immediate cause of the rebellion was Jahangir's refusal to proceed to Qandhar which had been besieged by the Persians.
2. Shah Jahan had the full backing of the Deccan army and all the nobles posted there and also of his father-in law, Asaf Khan and a number of important nobles at the court.

Which among the above statement/s is/are incorrect?
(a) 1 only (b) 2 only
(c) Both 1 and 2 (d) Neither 1 nor 2

35. **Which of the following religious policy was not implemented by Aurangzeb?**
(a) He had pulled down several temples including the Chintamani temple of Ahmedabad which he replaced with a mosque.
(b) Aurangzeb abolished jizya (a type of tax) levied on Hindus.
(c) Hindus were not allowed to occupy high administrative or executive posts.
(d) Muslim traders were totally exempted from the payment of the toll tax.

36. **Which of the following are the reasons for the Decline of Mughal?**
1. Hindus and other groups were regarded as inferiors, excluded from the Mughal court, and heavily taxed.
2. The heavy taxes levied by Emperors impoverished the farming population.
3. The East India Company took political control of much of the Indian subcontinent.

Select the correct option from the codes give below:
(a) 1 and 2 only (b) 2 and 3 only
(c) 1 and 3 only (d) 1, 2 and 3

37. **Match the following:**

Officer	In-charge of Departments
A. Mir Bakhshi	1. Imperial Household
B. Mir Saman	2. Military Department
C. Chief Qazi	3. Revenue Department
D. Wazir	4. Judicial Department

Select the correct answer using the code given below:

	A	B	C	D
(a)	1	2	3	4
(b)	2	1	4	3
(c)	3	1	4	2
(d)	4	3	2	1

38. **With reference to the Battle of Panipat, consider the following statements:**
1. First Battle of Panipat laid the foundation of the Mughal Empire in India.
2. The Second Battle of Panipat was fought between the forces of Samrat Hem Chandra Vikramaditya, popularly called Hemu, and Akbar.

Which of the above statements are correct?
(a) 1 only (b) 2 only
(c) Both 1 and 2 (d) Neither 1 nor 2

39. **With reference to the Mughals advent in India, consider the following statements:**
1. The Battle of Khanwa marked the beginning of the Mughal Empire.
2. The Mughal emperor Humayun defeated Sher Shah Suri in the Battle of Chausa.

Which of the above given statements is/are correct?
(a) 1 only (b) 2 only
(c) Both 1 and 2 (d) Neither 1 nor 2

40. **Which of the following statements regarding the organization of the local government under the reign of Akbar are correct?**
1. Faujdar was in charge of law and order.
2. Jagirs were allotted to nobles and members of the royal family excluding the queens.
3. Income from khalisa villages went directly to the royal exchequer.

Select the correct answer using the code given below:
(a) 1 and 2 only (b) 1 and 3 only
(c) 2 and 3 only (d) 1, 2 and 3

41. **It was logical to expect a Mughal advance towards the Deccan after the consolidation of the empire in North India. Consider the following statements in this regard:**
1. At first, none of the Deccan states accepted Mughal suzerainty except Khandesh which was too near and exposed to the Mughals to resist.
2. The Mughal invasion to Ahmadnagar was led by prince Murad, who was the governor of Gujarat; and by Abdur Rahim Khan-i-Khanan.

Which of the above statement/s is/are correct?

(a) 1 only (b) 2 only
(c) Both 1 and 2 (d) Neither 1 nor 2

42. Which of the following is/are the significance of Babur's advent into India?

1. Security to India from external invasions
2. Introduction of arch and dome in region's architecture
3. Introduction and popularization of gunpowder and artillery in India
4. Establishment of tradition of garden building

Select the correct answer using the code given below:

(a) 1, 2 and 3 only (b) 2 and 4 only
(c) 1 and 4 only (d) 1, 2, 3 and 4

43. Consider the following statements regarding the organization of central and provincial governments under Akbar:

1. Akbar organized the central administration on the basis of division of powers between various departments.
2. Wazir was considered to be the head of nobility.
3. The provincial administration was organized on the model of central administration.

Which of the above statements is/are correct?

(a) 1 and 2 only (b) 1 and 3 only
(c) 2 only (d) 3 only

44. Consider the following statements:

1. The first Battle of Panipat was fought between Babur and Rana Sanga in 1526.
2. The Battle of Khanwa was fought between Babur and Ibrahim Lodi in 1527.
3. The Battle of Khanwa was more decisive than the Battle of Panipat as it secured Babur's position in the Delhi-Agra region.

Which of the above statements is/are correct?

(a) 1 and 2 only (b) 3 only
(c) 1, 2 and 3 (d) None of the above

45. Which among the following Mughal Emperor built a new city – 'Dinpanah' at Delhi?

(a) Babur (b) Humayun
(c) Akbar (d) Jahangir

46. Consider the following statements regarding organization of the local government during Akbar's reign:

1. Amalguzar was the officer-in-charge of law and order in a pargana.
2. Inam lands were those which were allotted to learned and religious men.

Which of the above statements is/are correct?

(a) 1 only (b) 2 only
(c) Both 1 and 2 (d) Neither 1 nor 2

47. The 'Dagh System' during Akbar's reign was employed to

(a) mark territorial boundaries of Mughal empire.
(b) mark the horses of sawars.
(c) mark the swords of each soldier.
(d) mark the divisions of land for revenue assessment.

48. Arrange the following battles fought by Mughals for establishing their empire in the correct chronological order?

1. Battle of Khanwa
2. Battle of Sirhind
3. Battle of Chausa
4. First Battle of Panipat

Select the correct answer using the code given below:

(a) 1-4-2-3 (b) 1-4-3-2
(c) 4-1-2-3 (d) 4-1-3-2

49. Consider the following statements:

1. Bairam Khan, an officer in the court of Humayun was given the title of Khan-i-Khanan.
2. The Afghan forces led by Hemu were defeated at Lahore by the Mughals.

Which of the above statements is/are correct?

(a) 1 only (b) 2 only
(c) Both 1 and 2 (d) Neither 1 nor 2

50. With reference to the Battle of Panipat, consider the following statements:

1. First Battle of Panipat marked the beginning of the Mughal Empire in India.
2. Akbar and Bairam Khan did not participate in the second battle of Panipat.
3. The result of third battle of Panipat did not impact Marathas' advances in the north.

Which of the above statements is/are correct?

(a) 1 and 2 only (b) 2 and 3 only
(c) 1 only (d) 1, 2 and 3

51. Consider the following statements regarding Akbar's Navratnas:

1. Ain-i-Akbari was written by Abul Fazl.
2. Babarnama was translated into Turkish by Abdul Rahim Khan-i-Khanan.
3. The work of translating Mahabharata into the Persian language was carried out by Faizi.

Which of the above statements are correct?

(a) 1 and 3 only (b) 2 and 3 only
(c) 1 and 2 only (d) 1, 2 and 3

52. Which of the following are the reasons for the decline of the Mughal Empire in India?

1. Weak successors
2. Power usurping nobility
3. Foreign invasions
4. Lack of strong finances

Select the correct option using the codes given below:

(a) 1 and 3 only (b) 2 and 4 only
(c) 1, 2 and 3 only (d) 1, 2, 3 and 4

53. Under which Mughal emperor's reign, artist Mir Sayyid Ali was present?

(a) Babur (b) Humayun
(c) Akbar (d) Shah Jahan

54. Consider the following pairs:

Author/Artists		Mughal Emperor
1. Abul Fazl	-	Akbar
2. Abdul Hamid Lahori	-	Humayun
3. Abdus Samad	-	Shah Jahan

Which of the above pairs is/are correctly matched?

(a) 1 only (b) 1 and 2 only
(c) 2 and 3 only (d) 1, 2 and 3

55. With reference to the Mughal dynasty, which of the following statements is/are correct:

1. They were Chaghtai Turks.
2. Turkish was their mother language.
3. The Mughal court chronicles were written in Persian language.

Select the correct answer using the code given below:

(a) 1 and 2 only (b) 2 and 3 only
(c) 1 and 3 only (d) 1, 2 and 3

56. Consider the following statements regarding the Mansabdari System:

1. It was a bureaucratic-cum-military system.
2. Mansabdars received their salaries as revenue assignments called jagirs.
3. Mansabdars used to reside in their own Jagirs for its effective administration.

Which of the statements given above is/are correct?

(a) 1 and 2 only (b) 2 and 3 only
(c) 3 only (d) 1, 2 and 3

57. Consider the following pairs regarding foreign traveller and Mughal ruler of that period:

Foreign Traveller		Mughal Ruler
1. Peter Mundy	–	Akbar
2. Jean Baptiste Tavernier	–	Jahangir
3. Giovanni Careri	–	Aurangzeb

Which of the above given pairs is/are correctly matched?

(a) 1 only (b) 1 and 2 only
(c) 2 and 3 only (d) 3 only

58. With reference to the chronicles of Mughal India, which of the following statement is correct?

(a) They present a continuous chronological record of events.
(b) They give a clear account of social life prevailing outside the court and empire.
(c) Mughal emperor commissioned the translations of Mahabharat and Ramayan into Turkish.
(d) None of the above

59. Following are some of the statements regarding Babur's invasion:

1. The first Battle of Panipat was fought between Babur and Sikander Lodi in 1526.
2. Babur used the canons and firearms as his war tactics.
3. After the war at Chanderi in 1528, he took on the title "Ghazi".

Which of the above statements are correct?

(a) 1 and 2 (b) 1, 2 and 3
(c) 2 only (d) 1 only

60. Which of the following battles re-established Humayun's reign in India?

(a) Battle of Chausa
(b) Battle of Sirhind
(c) Battle of Kanauj
(d) Battle of Khanua

61. Which of the following pairs is/are correctly matched?

Administrative positon		Department
1. Diwan-i-Wizarat	-	Defence or War Minister
2. Sadr-us-Suddar	-	Minister of Islamic Law
3. Diwan-I-lnsha	-	Correspondence Minister
4. Diwan-I-Arz	-	Foreign Affairs Minister.

Select the corrcct answer using the code given below:

(a) 1 and 2 (b) 2 and 3
(c) 3 and 4 (d) All the above

SOLUTIONS

1. Correct Option: (c)

Supplementary Notes:

Mughal administration

Mansabdari System:

- The Mansab is an Arabic word meaning rank or position or status. Thus, Mansabdari was a system in which the rank of a government official was determined. Every civil and military official was given a Mansab and was called a Mansabdar.
- There were two methods of making payments to the nobles; one was giving them Jagirs (land), wherefrom they got their salaries. The second was making cash payment to them.
- For every ten cavalry men, the Mansabdar had to maintain twenty horses. In the Mansabdari system, no Jagirs were granted for the purpose of paying salaries. A Mansabdar got his salary from the royal treasury.

2. **Correct Option: (a)**

Explanation:

- **Statement 3 is incorrect:** The finished manuscript was seen as a precious object, a work of intellectual wealth and beauty.

Supplementary Notes:

Mughal Courts and their Customs

- The authors of Mughal chronicles were invariably courtiers. The histories they wrote focused on events centred on the ruler, his family, the court and nobles, wars and administrative arrangements.
- Their titles, such as the Akbar Nama, Shahjahan Nama, Alamgir Nama, that is, the story of Akbar, Shah Jahan and Alamgir (a title of the Mughal ruler Aurangzeb), suggest that in the eyes of their authors the history of the empire and the court was synonymous with that of the emperor.
- Mughal court chronicles were written in Persian. Under the Sultans of Delhi, it flourished as a language of the court and of literary writings, alongside north Indian languages, especially Hindavi and its regional variants. As the Mughals were Chaghtai Turks by origin, Turkish was their mother tongue.
- It was Akbar who consciously set out to make Persian the leading language of the Mughal court. Cultural and intellectual contacts with Iran, as well as a regular stream of Iranian and Central Asian migrants seeking positions at the Mughal court, might have motivated the emperor to adopt the language.
- Persian was elevated to a language of empire, conferring power and prestige on those who had a command of it. It was spoken by the king, the royal household and the elite at court. Further, it became the language of administration at all levels so that accountants, clerks and other functionaries also learnt it.
- The finished manuscript was seen as a precious object, a work of intellectual wealth and beauty.
- It exemplified the power of its patron, the Mughal emperor, to bring such beauty into being.

3. **Correct Option: (c)**

Supplementary Notes:

Mughal Ruler - Shahjahan (1627-1658)

- Shah Jahan launched a prolonged campaign in the northwest frontier to recover Kandahar and other ancestral lands.
- The Mughal army lost more than five thousand lives during the successive invasions between 1639 and 1647. Then, Shah Jahan realized the futility of his ambition and stopped fighting.
- His Deccan policy was more successful. He defeated the forces of Ahmadnagar and annexed it. Both Bijapur and Golkonda signed a treaty with the emperor. Shah Jahan carved four Mughal provinces in the Deccan – Khandesh, Berar, Telungana and Daulatabad. They were put under the control of his son Aurangzeb.
- The last years of Shah Jahan's reign were clouded by a bitter war of succession among his four sons – Dara Shikoh (crown prince), Shuja (governor of Bengal), Aurangzeb (governor of Deccan) and Murad Baksh (governor of Malwa and Gujarat).
- Towards the end of 1657, Shah Jahan fell ill at Delhi for some time but later recovered. But the princes started fighting for the Mughal throne. Aurangzeb emerged victorious in this struggle. He entered the Agra fort after defeating Dara. He forced Shah Jahan to surrender. Shah Jahan was confined to the female apartments in the Agra fort and strictly put under vigil.
- But he was not ill-treated. Shah Jahan lived for eight long years lovingly nursed by his daughter Jahanara. He died in 1666 and buried beside his wife's grave in the Taj Mahal.

4. **Correct Option: (c)**

Supplementary Notes:

- **Statement 1 is incorrect:** Muqqadam was the village headman not head of revenue.
- **Statement 2 is incorrect:** During the reign of Akbar, the role of an official called Amalguzar was to make an assessment and collection of land revenue.

Muqaddam

- Muqqadam was the village headman, not head of revenue.
- He was the village headman, through whom the government dealt with the peasants. He was, by profession, a peasant of the village which he headed. He could sell and buy land for the village and settle the common treasury. His position was hereditary; however, it could also be bought and sold. He was not a government servant, but he could be dispossessed of his status by the revenue official.

Amalguzar

- During the reign of Akbar, the role of an official, called Amalguzar, was to make an assessment and collection of land revenue.
- Amalguzar or the revenue collector was the second most important official of a district. He was also required to punish robbers and other miscreants in order to protect the peasantry. The Bitikchi was an important assistant of Amalguzar. His duty was to prepare necessary papers and records regarding the nature of land and its produce, and it was on the basis of these records that the assessment was made by Amalguzar.

Shiqdar

- Shiqdar was responsible for maintaining law and order at the Pargana level and informing the state government about the same. He helped the Amil in revenue collection. He was also entitled to punish criminals.

Kotwal

- **Statement 4 is correct:** Kotwals was a title used in medieval India for the leader of a Kot or fort. Kotwals often controlled the fort of a major town or an area of smaller towns on behalf of another ruler. It was similar in function to a British India Zaildar. From Mughal times the title was given to the local ruler of a large town and the surrounding area. However, the title is also used for leaders in small villages as well. Kotwal has also been translated as chief police officer.

5. **Correct Option: (d)**

Explanation:

- All statements are correct.

Supplementary Notes:

Causes for the Downfall of the Mughals

- The Mughal Empire declined rapidly after the death of Aurangzeb. The Mughal court became the scene of factions among the nobles.
- The weakness of the empire was exposed when Nadir Shah imprisoned the Mughal Emperor and looted Delhi in 1739. The weak successors and demoralization of the Mughal army also paved the way for it.
- To some extent, the religious and Deccan policies of Aurangzeb contributed to its decline. The vastness of the empire became unwieldy.
- The financial difficulties due to continuous wars led to the decline. The neglect of the sea power by the Mughals was felt when the Europeans began to settle in India.
- The invasions of Nadir Shah and Ahmad Shah Abdali weakened the Mughal state.
- Thus, the decline and downfall of the Mughal Empire was due to the combination of political, social and economic factors.

6. **Correct Option: (b)**

Explanation:

- **Statement 2 is incorrect:** Battle of Gogra took place between Babur and Afghans in which Babur defeated the Afghans.

Supplementary Notes:

Battles in Medieval India

- Battle of Gogra took place between Babur and Afghans in which Babur defeated the Afghans.
- On 21st April 1526, the first Battle of Panipat took place between Babur and Ibrahim Lodi, in which the latter was killed. Babur occupied Delhi and sent his son, Humayun to seize Agra. Babur proclaimed himself as 'Emperor of Hindustan'.
- In 1527, the Battle of Khanwa took place between Babur and Rana Sangha of Mewar in which Babur won a decisive victory over him and assumed the title 'Ghazi'.
- In 1529, Babur defeated the Afghans in the Battle of Ghogra in Bihar.
- In 1539, the Battle of Chausa took place between Sher Khan and Humayun in which Sher Khan destroyed the Mughal army but Humayun escaped from there.
- Humayun reached Agra to negotiate with his brothers. But as they were not cooperative, Humayun was forced to fight with Sher Khan alone in the Battle of Bilgram in 1540. This battle was also known as the Battle of Kanauj.
- Humayun was thoroughly defeated by Sher Khan. After losing his kingdom, Humayun became an exile for the next fifteen years.

7. **Correct Option: (a)**

Explanation:

- **Statement 3 is incorrect:** Aurangzeb stopped engraving Kalma on coins, not restarted it.

Supplementary Notes:

Aurangzeb's Reign

- Aurangzeb stopped engraving Kalma on coins, not restarted it.
- Aurangzeb was a staunch and orthodox Muslim in his personal life. His ideal was to transform India into an Islamic state.
- He created a separate department to enforce moral codes under a high-powered officer called Muhtasib. Drinking was prohibited. Cultivation and use of bhang and other drugs were banned.
- Aurangzeb forbade music in the Mughal court. He released an order to ban the music everywhere and arrest those who listen to the music.
- He discontinued the practice of Jarokhadarshan, use of almanacs, the Mughal custom of weighing the emperor in gems and distributing the wealth to the poor on coronation anniversaries.
- He also discontinued the celebration of Dasarah and royal astronomers and astrologers were also dismissed from service.
- Initially, Aurangzeb banned the construction of new Hindu temples and repair of old temples. Then, he began a policy of destroying Hindu temples. In 1679, he reimposed jiziya and pilgrim tax. He was also intolerant of other Muslim sects. The celebration of Muharram was stopped.

8. **Correct Option: (d)**

Explanation:

- All statements are correct.

Supplementary Notes:

Akbar's Administrative Policies

- **Religious Policy:**
  - In the beginning of his life, Akbar was a pious Muslim. Soon after marrying Jodha Bai of Amber, he abolished the pilgrim tax and in 1562, he abolished jiziya. He allowed his Hindu wives to worship their own Gods. Later, he became a skeptical Muslim.
  - In 1575, he ordered for the construction of Ibadat Khana (House of worship) at his new capital, Fatepur Sikri. Akbar invited learned scholars from all religions like Hinduism, Jainism, Christianity and Zoroastrianism. He disliked the interference of the Muslim Ulemas in political matters. In 1579, he issued the "Infallibility Decree" by which he asserted his religious powers.
- **Land Revenue Administration:**
  - Akbar made some experiments in the land revenue administration with the help of Raja Todar Mal. The land revenue system of Akbar was called Zabti or Bandobast system.
  - It was further improved by Raja Todar Mal. It was known as Dahsala System which was completed in 1580. By this system, Todar Mal introduced a uniform system of land measurement. The revenue was fixed on the average yield of land assessed on the basis of past ten years. Payment of revenue was made generally in cash.
- **Mansabdari System:**
  - Akbar introduced the Mansabdari system in his administration. Under this system every officer was assigned a rank (mansab). The lowest rank was 10 and the highest was 5000 for the nobles. Princes of royal blood received even higher ranks.
  - The ranks were divided into two: Zat and Sawar. Zat means personal and it fixed the personal status of a person. Sawar rank indicated the number of cavalrymen a person was required to maintain. Every Sawar had to maintain at least two horses.
  - The Mansab rank was not hereditary. All appointments and promotions as well as dismissals were directly made by the emperor.

9. **Correct Option: (c)**

Supplementary Notes:

Du-aspah Sih-aspah System

- Jahangir and Shah Jahan introduced new systems into the original Mansabdari system of Akbar. While the system introduced by Jahangir was called du-aspah sih-aspah, the one brought out by Shah Jahan was the month-ratio or month-scale system.
- Du-aspah Sih-aspah system literally means trooper with two or three horses. Under this system, selected nobles could be allowed to maintain a large quota of soldiers, without making any change in their Jat rank.
- It implied that a Mansabdar or noble holding du-aspah sih-aspah rank had to maintain double the quota of troopers indicated by his Sawar rank. They were paid accordingly.

10. **Correct Option: (c)**

Explanation:

- **Statement 2 is incorrect:** The Peshwa entered into a treaty with the Mughul emperor in 1752 AD, and not after the third battle of Panipat. By it, the Mughul emperor gave the Marathas the right to collect chauth and sardeshmukhi from all over India and, in return, the Marathas were obliged to help the Emperor in times of need. Thus, the Marathas involved themselves directly with the politics at Delhi.

Supplementary Notes:

Third Battle of Panipat

- The most important event of the period of Balaji was the third battle of Panipat which was fought between the Marathas and Ahmad Shah Abdali, the ruler of Afghanistan in 1761 AD.
- The weakness of Mughul emperors, the division of the nobility in contending groups, the ambition of the Marathas to gain influence in the North were the primary causes of the third battle of Panipat.
- The Peshwa entered into a treaty with the Mughul emperor in 1752 AD, and not after the third battle of Panipat. By it, the Mughul emperor gave the Marathas the right to collect chauth and sardeshmukhi from all over India and, in return, the Marathas were obliged to help the Emperor in times of need. Thus, the Marathas involved themselves directly with the politics at Delhi.

11. **Correct Option: (a)**

Explanation:

- **Statement 2 is incorrect:** The Suba (province) was divided into Sarkars (districts).

Supplementary Notes:

- **Suba**
  - For the sake of administrative convenience, Akbar had divided the empire into various units. Provinces in the Mughal era were known as Suba.
  - In Akbar's reign, there were 12 provinces which were subsequently raised to 18 and finally to 20 in Aurangzeb's time.

- **Sarkar**
  - ➤ In Mughal period, the district was known as Sarkar.
  - ➤ Every Sarkar had a chief officer like Faujdar, Amalguzar, Qazi, Kotwal, Bitiqhi and Khajandar.
- **Pargana**
  - ➤ Every Sarkar was further divided into sub-districts which were known as Pargana.

12. Correct Option: (c)

Supplementary Notes:

Shivaji's Administration

- He had a council of ministers (Asht Pradhan) to advise him on the matters of the state but he was not bound by it. He could appoint or dismiss them. This appointment was subject to their efficiency. The Peshwa was the first among ministers. The word Peshwa stands for leader or senior one.
- Besides being a great conqueror and a diplomat, he was a successful administrator. He employed members of all castes and tribes to maintain balance among them. In matters of administration, he gave superior position to his civil officers as compared to military officers.

13. Correct Option: (d)

Supplementary Notes:

Acharya Hira Vijay Suri

- Acharya Hira Vijay Suri (1527 AD) was an important Jain Acharya. He belonged to Shvetambar sect of Jainism. He became the disciple of Vijayadana Suri in 1540 at the age of 13.
- He went to Devagiri – a center of Sanskrit learning in those days, for further education.
- He successively won the title of 'Pandit' in 1550,'Upadhyaya' in 1552 and of 'Acharya' (Suri) in 1553.
- Henceforth he was known as Hira Vijaya Suri in 1556, when his guru died, the Shvetambara community of Jainism selected him as their successer (bhattaraka).
- Akbar renounced hunting and restricted the practice of fishing with his influence. Therefore, he gave him the title of "Jagad-Guru" or world teacher in 1584.

14. Correct Option: (c)

Supplementary Notes:

Tipu Sultan

- Tipu Sultan organised his Rocket artillery brigades known as Cushoon's, Tipu Sultan expanded the number of servicemen in the various Cushoon's from 1500 to almost 5000.
- The Mysorean rockets utilised by Tipu Sultan, were later updated by the British and successively employed during the Napoleonic Wars.
- Tipu Sultan's father had expanded on Mysore's use of rocketry, making critical innovations in the rockets themselves and the military logistics of their use. He deployed as many as 1,200 specialised troops in his army to operate rocket launchers. These men were skilled in operating the weapons and were trained to launch their rockets at an angle calculated from the diameter of the cylinder and the distance to the target.
- The rockets had twin side sharpened blades mounted on them, and when fired en masse, spun and wreaked significant damage against a large army.
- Tipu greatly expanded the use of rockets after Hyder's death, deploying as many as 5,000 rocketeers at a time.
- The rockets deployed by Tipu during the Battle of Pollilur were much more advanced than those the British East India Company had previously seen, chiefly because of the use of iron tubes for holding the propellant; this enabled higher thrust and longer range for the missiles (up to 2 km range).

15. Correct Option: (c)

Supplementary Notes:

Aurangzeb

- Aurangzeb was called "Zinda Pir"or "Living Saint " in Mughal India.

16. Correct option (a)

Supplementary Notes:

Jean-Baptiste Tavernier

- Jean-Baptiste Tavernier, a French jeweller and traveller of the Mughal period has left a detailed account of Takht-i-Taus (Peacock throne). Peacock throne was a dazzling and spectacular display of Mughal architecture. Its construction was undertaken by the Emperor Shah Jahan and he personally spent a great deal of time and energy in the designing of the throne.

17. Correct Option: (c)

Explanation:

- Both statements are correct.

Supplementary Notes:

- On the eve of Babur's invasion of India, there were five prominent Muslim rulers – the Sultans of Delhi, Gujarat, Malwa, Bengal and the Deccan, and two prominent Hindu rulers – Rana Sanga of Mewar and the Vijayanagar Empire. Once again by the end of 1525, Babur started from Kabul to conquer India. He occupied Lahore easily by defeating its governor, Daulat Khan Lodi. Then, he proceeded against Delhi where Ibrahim Lodi was the Sultan. On 21st April 1526, the first Battle of Panipat took place between Babur and Ibrahim Lodi, who was killed in the battle. Babur's success was due to his cavalry and artillery.

Babur occupied Delhi and sent his son Humayun to seize Agra. Babur proclaimed himself as "Emperor of Hindustan".

- His subsequent victories over Rana Sanga and the Afghans secured his position as the ruler of India. Rana Sanga of Mewar was a great Rajput warrior. He marched against Babur, and in the Battle of Khanua (near Agra), held in 1527, Babur won a decisive victory over him. Babur assumed the title 'Ghazi'. In 1528, Babur captured Chanderi from another Rajput ruler Medini Rai. In the next year, Babur defeated the Afghans in the Battle of Gogra in Bihar.

18. Correct Option: (b)

Supplementary Notes:

- Humayun captured Gujarat from Bahadur Shah and appointed Askari as its governor. But soon, Bahadur Shah recovered Gujarat from Askari who fled from there. In the meantime Sher Khan became powerful in the east. Humayun marched against him, and in the Battle of Chausa, held in 1539, Sher Khan destroyed the Mughal army and Humayun escaped from there.
- Humayun reached Agra to negotiate with his brothers. But as they were not cooperative, Humayun was forced to fight with Sher Khan alone in the Battle of Bilgram in 1540. This battle was also known as Battle of Kanauj. Humayun was thoroughly defeated by Sher Khan. After losing his kingdom, Humayun became an exile for the next fifteen years.

19. Correct Option: (a)

Supplementary Notes:

- The fourth important department was the judicial department headed by the chief Qazi. This post was sometimes combined with that of the chief Sadr who was responsible for all charitable and religious endowments.

20. Correct Option: (a)

Supplementary Notes:

- A third system after zabti and galla-bakshi which was widely used in Akbar's time was nasaq. The historians are a bit uncertain about this system. It seems that it meant a rough calculation of the amount payable by the peasant on the basis of what he had been paying in the past. Hence, some modern historians think that it was merely a system of computing the peasant's dues, not a different system of assessment. Others think that it meant rough appraisement both on the basis of the inspection or the crops and past experience, and thereby fixing the amount to be paid by the village as a whole. It is also called 'kankut'.

21. Correct Option: (c)

Explanation:

- Both statements are correct.

Supplementary Notes:

- The Rajput policy of Akbar was notable. He married the Rajput princess, the daughter of Raja Bharamal. It was a turning point in the history of Mughals. Rajputs served the Mughals for four generations. Many of them rose to the positions of military generals. Raja Bhagawan Das and Raja Man Singh were given senior positions in the administration by Akbar.
- One by one, all Rajput states submitted to Akbar. But the Ranas of Mewar continued to defy despite several defeats. In the Battle of Haldighati, Rana Pratap Singh was severely defeated by the Mughal army led by Man Singh in 1576. Following the defeat of Mewar, most of the leading Rajput rulers had accepted Akbar's suzerainty. Akbar's Rajput policy was combined with a broad religious toleration. He abolished the pilgrim tax and later, the jiziya. The Rajput policy of Akbar proved to be beneficial to the Mughal state as well as to the Rajputs. The alliance secured to the Mughals the services of the bravest warriors. On the other hand, it ensured peace in Rajasthan and a number of Rajputs who joined the Mughal service rose to important positions.

22. Correct Option: (c)

Supplementary Notes:

- The Battle of Khanwa was fought on March 16, (1527), between Babur, founder of the Mughal empire in India on the one hand, and a combined Rajput army led by Rana Sanga, ruler of Mewar, on the other. It was the second of the series of three major battles, victories in which, gave Babur overlordship over north India in Bharatpur district in Rajasthan.
- The battle or Khanwa (1527) was fiercely contested. According to Babur, Sanga's forces exceeded 200,000 including 10,000 Arghan cavalrymen and an equal force fielded by Hasan Khan Mewati. As usual, these figures may be greatly exaggerated, though Babur's forces were undoubtedly inferior in number. Sunga made ferocious attacks on Babur's right and almost breached it. However, the Mughal artillery took a heavy toll of life, and slowly, Sanga's forces were pushed back. At this juncture, Babur ordered his soldiers in the centre, which had been sheltering behind their tripods, to launch an attack. The artillery also advanced behind the chained wagons. Sanga's forces were thus hemmed in and were defeated after a great slaughter. Rana Sanga escaped and wanted to renew the conflict with Babur. But he was poisoned by his own nobles who considered such a course to be dangerous and suicidal.

23. Correct Option: (d)

Explanation:

- All statements are correct.

Supplementary Notes:

- Babur's advent into India was significant from many points of view. For the first time since the downfall of the Kushan Empire, Kabul and Qandahar became integral parts of an empire comprising north India. Since these areas had always acted as staging places for an invasion of India, by dominating them, Babur and his successors were able to give to India security from external invasions for almost 200 years. Economically also, the control of Kabul and Qandahar strengthened India's foreign trade since these two towns were the starting points for caravans meant for China and the Mediterranean seaports. Thus, India could take a greater share in the great trans-Asian trade.
- In north India, Babur smashed the power of the Lodhis and of the Rajput confederacy led by Rana Sanga. Thereby, he destroyed the balance of power obtaining in the area. This was a long step towards the establishment of an all-India empire. However, a number of conditions had still to be fulfilled before this could be achieved. Babur showed what a skilled combination of artillery and cavalry could achieve. His victories led to rapid popularisation or gunpowder and artillery in India, thereby reducing the importance of forts.

24. Correct Option: (a)

Supplementary Notes:

- Amu Darya also called as the Amu River and historically known by its Latin name, Oxus, is a major river in Central Asian region. It is formed by the junction of the Vakhsh and Panj rivers, at Qaleh-ye Panjeh in Afghanistan, and flows from there north-westwards into what remains of the Aral Sea. In ancient times, the river was regarded as the boundary between Greater Iran and Turan.

25. Correct Option: (d)

Explanation:

- All statements are correct.

Supplementary Notes:

- The failure of Mughals at Quandhar did not so much reflect the weakness of Mughal artillery, as it has been asserted by some historians. It rather showed the inherent strength of Qandhar fort, if held by a determined commander, and the ineffectiveness of medieval artillery against strong forts (this was also the Mughal experience in the Deccan). It may, however, be argued that Shah Jahan's attachment to Qandhar was more sentimental than realistic. With the growing enfeeblement of both the Uzbeks and the Safavids, Qandhar no longer had the same strategic importance as it had earlier. It was not so much the loss of Qandhar as the failure of the repeated Mughal efforts which affected the Mughal prestige. But even this should not be unduly exaggerated, for the Mughal Empire remained, outwardly, at the height of its power and prestige during Aurangzeb's reign.

26. Correct Option: (a)

Supplementary Notes:

- There were sixty-six grades or mansabs from ten to ten thousand. But ranks above five thousand were reserved for princes. Persons holding ranks below 500 zat were called mansabdars, those from above 500 and below 2500 amirs, and those holding ranks of 2500 and above were called 'amir-i-umda' or 'amir-i-azam'. However, the word 'mansabdar' is sometimes used for all the three categories.

27. Correct Option: (a)

Supplementary Notes:

Mughal Art and Architecture

List I	List II
A. Akbar	2. Buland Darwaza
B. Jehangir	4. Climax of Painting
C. Aurangzeb	3. Moti Masjid, Red Fort
D. Shah Jahan	1. Moti Masjid at Agra

28. Correct Option: (c)

Explanation:

- Option (c) is correct:

List I	List II
A. Mir Bakshi	1. Head of Military
B. Mushriff	4. Revenue Secretary
C. Shiqdar	3. In-charge of law and order
D. Mir Tozak	2. Master of ceremonies

Supplementary Notes:

Mughal Administration

- The chief departments of the State were:
  - The Imperial Household under the Khan-i-Saman
  - The Exchequer under the Diwan
  - The Military Pay and Accounts Office under the Mir Bakshi
  - The Judiciary under the Chief Qazi
  - Religious Endowments and Charities under the Chief Sadr or Sadr-us-Sudur
  - The Censorship of Public Morals under the Muhtasib
  - The Diwan or Wazir was usually the highest officer in the State, being in sole charge of revenues and finance. The Bakhshi discharged a variety of functions. While he was the Paymaster-General of all the officers of the State, who "theoretically belonged to the military department", he was also responsible for the recruiting of the army, and for maintaining lists of mansabdars and other high officials; and when preparing for a battle,

he presented a complete muster-roll of the army before the Emperor.

- The Khan-i-Saman or the Lord High Steward had charge of the whole imperial household "in reference to both great and small things".
- The Muhtasibs or Censors of Public Morals looked after the enforcement of the Prophet's commands and the laws of morality.
- The other officers, somewhat inferior in status to those mentioned above, were the Mir Atish or Daroga-i-Topkhana (head of the artillery), the Daroga of Dak chowki (head of the correspondence departments), the Daroga of the Mint, the Mir Mal or the Lord Privy Seal, the Mustaufi or the Auditor-General, the Nazir-i-Buyutat or the Superintendment of the Imperial Workshop, the Mushriff or the Revenue Secretary, the Mir Bahri or the Lord of the Admiralty, the Mir Barr or the Superintendent of Forests, the Waqa-i-navis or news-reporters, the Mir Arz or the officer in charge of petitions presented to the Emperor, the Mir Manzil or the Quartermaster-General, and the Mir Tozak or the Master of Ceremonies.

29. **Correct Option: (a)**

Explanation:

- **Statements 3 is incorrect:** It was first used at Bajaur in 1519.

Supplementary Notes:

Significance of Babur's Advent into India

- The inclusion of Afghanistan in an empire-based on India was a development of capital importance. Although, Afghanistan was considered an integral part of India in antiquity, and was often called "Little India" even in medieval times, politically, it had not been a part of India after the downfall of the Kushan empire, followed by the defeat of the Hindu Shahis by Mahmud Ghazni.
- Since ancient times, Afghanistan had been the staging place for an onslaught on India. By keeping control of Afghanistan, and its two doors to India, Kabul and Qandahar, Babur and his successors safeguarded India from foreign invasion for 200 years.
- The control of Babur and his successors over Afghanistan made India a player in Central Asian politics. Powerful rulers of the area – Turan, Iran, Ottoman Turkey, and others kept close diplomatic contact with India, and also sought its support on occasions.
- On their part, Babur and the succeeding Mughal rulers kept a close watch on political developments in Central and West Asia by means of a constant exchange of envoys. Thus, with the arrival of Babur, a new phase began in India's foreign policy and strategic perception.
- Babur not only tried hard to maintain Mughal influence on Badakhshan beyond the Hindukush mountains, but even upto river Oxus. Following the defeat of the Uzbek ruler, Ubaidullah, by Shah Tehmasp at Jam in 1528, Babur even instructed Humayun to recover Samarqand with Iranian help, but had to give up when such help was not forthcoming.
- The inclusion of Kabul and Qandahar in the empire created a favourable opportunity for the increase of India's share in the great trans-Asian trade. By his victories over Ibrahim Lodi and Rana Sanga, Babur paved the way for the emergence of a new Indian empire, sweeping away the balance of power which had gradually emerged in the country during the 15th century.
- However, many steps were necessary for the emergence of such an empire. Humayun carried forward the task bequeathed to him by Babur, but a long step in this direction was taken by Sher Shah Suri, followed by Akbar.
- The introduction of cannon and muskets in India has generally been ascribed to Babur. Although gunpowder which is of Chinese origin was introduced into India from China, and was used for mining under the walls of the forts from the middle of the 13th century, its use for cannons and muskets was of European origin.
- Their use in Iran and Central Asia is generally dated back to the Ottomans at the battle of Chaldiran in 1514 against Shah Ismail. Babur quickly look it up by employing two Ottoman mastergunners in 1516, and mentions their first use at Bajaur in 1519. Its use in the battles of Panipat and Khanua, and other battles fought by Babur in India has been noted.

30. **Correct Option: (c)**

Supplementary Notes:

Battle of Khanwa, 1527

- Babur decided to take on Rana Sanga of Chittor, who as ruler of Mewar, had a strong influence over Rajasthan and Malwa.
- Babur selected Khanwa, near Agra, as a favourable site for this inevitable encounter.
- The ferocious march of Rana Sanga with a formidable force strengthened by Afghan Muslims, Mahmud Lodi, brother of Ibrahim Lodi, and Hasan Khan Mewati, ruler of Mewat, confronted the forces of Babur.
- With strategic positioning of forces and effective use of artillery, Babur defeated Rana Sanga's forces.
- This victory was followed by the capture of forts at Gwalior and Dholpur which further strengthened Babur's position.

31. **Correct Option: (d)**

Explanation:

- **Pair 3 is incorrectly matched:** Niccolao Manucci was an Italian writer.

Supplementary Notes:

Travellers in India

- Europeans like Bernier (French physician and traveller), Tavernier (French gem merchant and traveller), Mandelslo (German adventurer and traveller), Peter Mundy (English Trader) and Manucci (Italian writer and traveller) visited India during the reign of Shah Jahan and left behind detailed accounts of India.

32. **Correct Option: (c)**

Explanation:

- **Statement 1 is incorrect:** The First Battle of Panipat was fought between the forces of Babur and Ibrahim Lodhi.

Supplementary Notes:

Battle of Panipat

- The First Battle of Panipat was fought between the forces of Babur and Ibrahim Lodhi. The Battle was fought on April 21, 1526.
- The use of guns by troops of Babur helped them claim victory in the battle. The Lodi troops were lagging in terms of artillery skills and the sound emitted by canons frightened the war elephants of Lodi.
- Babur had outstanding tactics in his favour more than the weapons, which helped him emerge victorious in the battle. The placement of troops as planned by Babur helped them defeat such a large force of Lodi.
- Babur's new tactics introduced during this first battle of Panipat were the Tulghuma and the Araba. Tulghuma referred to the division of the army into the left, right and centre units, whereas the Araba referred to carts, that were used to launch cannon fire. This deadly combination was used by Babur dexterously to create havoc among Lodi's troops.
- The First Battle of Panipat resulted in the death of Ibrahim Lodi and also, the end of Lodi Dynasty and the Delhi Sultanate in India. Also, with the end of the Sultanate, the Mughal rule began in India.

33. **Correct Option: (c)**

Explanation:

- **Statement 2 is incorrect:** Jahangir defeated Khusrau at a battle near Lahore, and soon afterwards, the latter was captured and imprisoned.

Supplementary Notes:

Jahangir

- Jahangir, the eldest son of Akbar, succeeded to the throne without any difficulty, his younger brothers having died during the life-time of Akbar due to excessive drinking.
- However, shortly after Jahangir's succession, his eldest son, Khusrau, broke out into rebellion. Tussle between father and son for the throne was not unusual in those times.
- Jahangir himself had rebelled against his father, and kept the empire disturbed for some time. However, Khusrau's rebellion proved to be short-lived.
- Jahangir defeated him at a battle near Lahore, and soon afterwards, he was captured and imprisoned.
- Jahangir brought to an end the conflict with Mewar which had continued for four decades, and the struggle in the Deccan with Malik Ambar, who was not prepared to accept the settlement made by Akbar. There was conflict in the east, too.
- Although Akbar had broken the back of the power of the Afghans in this region. Afghan chiefs were still powerful in various parts of east Bengal.
- They had the support of many Hindu rajas of the region, such as the Raja of Jessore, Kamrup (western Assam), Cachar, etc.
- Towards the end of his reign, Akbar had recalled Raja Man Singh, the governor of Bengal, to the court, and during his absence, the Afghan chief, Usman Khan, and others found an opportunity to raise a rebellion.
- Jahangir sent back Man Singh for some time but the situation continued to worsen. In 1608, Jahangir posted to Bengal, Islam Khan, the grandson of Shaikh Salim Chishti, the famous sufi saint who was the patron saint of the Mughals.
- Though young in years, Islam Khan handled the situation with great energy and foresight. He won over many of the zamindars including the Raja of Jessore to his side, and fixed his headquarters at Dacca, which was strategically located, to deal with the rebels. To keep the area under full control, soon the provincial capital was transferred from Rajmahal to Dacca, which began to develop rapidly.
- Like Akbar, Jahangir realised that conquest would be lasting not on the basis of force but of securing the goodwill of the people. He, therefore, treated the defeated Afghan chiefs and their followers with consideration and sympathy.
- After some time, many of the princes and zamindars of Bengal detained at the court were released and allowed to return to Bengal. Even Musa Khan was released and his estates restored. Thus, after a long spell, peace and prosperity returned to Bengal.
- To cap the process, more Afghans now began to be inducted into the Mughal nobility. The leading Afghan noble under Jahangir was Khan-i-Jahan Lodi, who rendered distinguished service in the Deccan.

34. **Correct Option: (a)**

Explanation:

- **Statement 1 is incorrect:** The immediate cause of the rebellion was Shah Jahan's refusal to proceed to Qandhar which had been besieged by the Persians.

Supplementary Notes:

Shah Jahan's Rebellion

- The immediate cause of the rebellion was Shah Jahan's refusal to proceed to Qandhar, which had been besieged by the Persians.
- Shah Jahan was afraid that the campaign would be a long and difficult one and that intrigues would be hatched against him during his absence from the court.
- Hence, he put forward a number of demands such as full command of the army, which included the veterans of the Deccan, complete sway over the Punjab, control over a large number of important forts, etc.
- Jahangir was enraged by this attitude. Convinced that the prince was meditating rebellion, he wrote harsh letters, and took punitive steps which only made the situation worse, and resulted in an open breach.
- From Mandu, where he was stationed, Shah Jahan made a sudden dash on Agra in order to capture the treasures lodged there.
- Shah Jahan had the full backing of the Deccan army and all the nobles posted there. Gujarat and Malwa had declared for him, and he had the support of his father-in law, Asaf Khan, and a number of important nobles at the court.
- However, in the battle near Delhi, Shah Jahan was defeated by the forces led by Mahabat Khan. He was saved from complete defeat by the valiant stand of the Mewar contingent.
- Another army was sent to wrest Gujarat from Shah Jahan. Shah Jahan was hounded out of the Mughal territories and compelled to take shelter with his erstwhile enemies, the Deccani rulers.
- However, he crossed the Deccan into Orissa, took the governor by surprise, and soon Bengal and Bihar were under his control.
- Mahabat Khan was again pressed into service. He took energetic steps and compelled Shah Jahan to retreat in to the Deccan again.
- This time, he made an alliance with Malik Ambar, who was once again at war with the Mughals. However, soon Shah Jahan wrote abject letters of apology to Jahangir.
- Jahangir also felt that it was time to pardon and conciliate his ablest and most energetic son.

35. **Correct Option: (b)**

Explanation:

- **Statement (b) is incorrect:** Akbar had abolished jizya tax on the Hindus but Aurangzeb again levied this tax.

Supplementary Notes:

Aurangzeb's Religious Policies

- Even as a governor of Deccan he had pulled down several temples including the important 'Chintamani temple of Ahmedabad' which he replaced with a mosque. He followed this practice vigorously after becoming emperor of India.
- Akbar had abolished jizya tax on the Hindus but Aurangzeb again levied this tax. According to Elliot, the object of imposing the Jizya or poll tax "was to curb the infidels and to distinguish the land of the faithful from an infidel land."
- Aurangzeb's predecessors, especially Akbar had appointed a large number of Hindus in the various departments, but Aurangzeb followed the policy of removal of the Hindus from these jobs.
- The Hindus were not allowed to occupy high administrative or executive posts. But, as it resulted in the complete breakdown of the efficiency, the order was slightly modified, and the Hindus were allowed to work on certain limited posts in the revenue department.
- The Hindu traders were required to pay a toll tax of 5 per cent as against half of it paid by the Muslim traders. Later on Muslim traders were totally exempted from the payment of this tax.
- For destroying the culture of the Hindus, Aurangzeb destroyed their several educational institutions at Varanasi, Multan and Thatta. The Hindu children were not disallowed to study the fundamentals of their faith.
- For the Hindus, the only way to escape from the payment of various taxes like pilgrim tax, trade tax, Jizya, etc. was conversion to Islam. Getting jobs after conversion also became easier. The Hindu prisoners were freed on their conversion to Islam.
- Aurangzeb issued order that except Rajput, no Hindu could ride an elephant, a horse and a palanquin. The Hindus were not allowed to burn their dead on the banks of the river Sabarmati in Ahmedabad. Similar restrictions were placed at Delhi on the river Jamuna.

36. **Correct Option: (d)**

Explanation:

- All statements are correct.

Supplementary Notes:

Decline of Mughal

- In the later decades of the empire, Mughal emperors became more autocratic and intolerant. Hindus and other groups were regarded as inferiors, excluded from the Mughal court, and heavily taxed. Religious intolerance led to the destruction of Hindu and Sikh temples, and schools. These policies created widespread resentment and rebellion against the Mughals, fragmented their kingdom, and greatly weakened their rule.
- During Aurangzeb's reign (1658–1707), the economy of the Mughal Empire began to decline. The heavy taxes he levied impoverished the farming population. At the same time, there was a steady decay in the quality of Mughal government. Later, emperors showed little desire to govern or to invest their money in agriculture, technology or the military.
- In 1757, British forces defeated the nawab of Bengal and French forces at the Battle of Plassey. The East India Company thereafter took political control of much of the Indian subcontinent. During the Indian Mutiny of 1857–59, the British exiled the last Mughal emperor.

37. Correct Option: (b)

Officer	In-charge of Departments
A. Mir Bakhshi	2. Military Department
B. Mir Saman	1. Imperial Household
C. Chief Qazi	4. Judicial Department
D. Wazir	3. Revenue Department

Supplementary Notes:

Organization of Central and Provincial Governments During Reign of Akbar

- Akbar's system of the central government was based on the structure of government which had evolved under the Delhi Sultanate, but the functions of the various departments were carefully reorganized and meticulous rules and regulations were laid down for the conduct of affairs.
- Akbar reorganized the central machinery of administration based on the division of power between various departments and of checks and balances.
- The head of the Revenue Department was the Wazir. Under Akbar, generally, the Wazir did not hold a high Mansab. Many nobles held Mansabs which were higher than his. Thus, he was no longer the principal adviser to the ruler, but one who was an expert in revenue affairs. Thus, in practice, the concept of an all-powerful Wazir was given up. To emphasize this point, Akbar generally used the title of 'Diwan' or 'Diwan-i-Ala' in preference to the word Wazir.
- The head of the military department was called the Mir Bakhshi. It was the Mir Bakhshi and not the Diwan who was considered the head of the nobility. Recommendations for appointment to Mansabs or promotions etc. were made to the emperor through the Mir Bakhshi.
- The Mir Bakhshi was also the head of the intelligence and information agencies of the empire. Intelligence officers (barids) and news reporters (Waqia-Navis) were posted to all parts of the empire. Their reports were presented to the emperor at the court through the Mir Bakhshi.
- The third important officer was the Mir Saman. He was in charge of the imperial household, including the supply of all the provisions and articles for the use of the inmates of the haram or the female apartments.
- The fourth important department was the judicial department headed by the chief Qazi. This post was sometimes combined with that of the chief Sadr who was responsible for all charitable and religious endowments.

38. Correct Option: (c)

Explanation:

- Both statements are correct.

Supplementary Notes:

Battle of Panipat

- **First Battle of Panipat:** An overwhelmingly outnumbered Mughal force prevailed at Panipat. This was due to the resourcefulness of its commander, Babur, who demonstrated the use of field fortifications and his instinctive sense of value of firepower of gunpowder. The victory enabled him to lay the foundations for the Indian Mughal Empire.
- **Second Battle of Panipat:** The Second Battle of Panipat was fought between the forces of Samrat Hem Chandra Vikramaditya, popularly called Hemu, the Hindu king who was ruling North India from Delhi, and the army of Akbar, on November 5, 1556. It was a decisive victory for Akbar's generals Khan Zaman I and Bairam Khan. H.G.Keen writes; "Akbar and his guardian Bairam Khan did not participate in the battle and were stationed 5 Kos (8 miles) away from the war zone. Bairam Khan did not permit the 13 year old child king to be present in the battlefield in person, instead he was provided with a special guard of 5000 well trained and most faithful troops, and was stationed at a safe distance far behind the battle lines. He was instructed by Bairam Khan to flee towards Kabul for life in case the Mughal Army was routed in the battlefield."
- The result of the battle was the halting of Maratha advances in the north, and a destabilization of their territories, for roughly 10 years. This period of 10 years is marked by the rule of Peshwa Madhavrao, who is credited with the revival of Maratha

domination following the defeat at Panipat. In 1771, 10 years after Panipat, he sent a large Maratha army into North India in an expedition that was meant to (a) re-establish Maratha domination in North India, and, (b) punish refractory powers that had either sided with the Afghans, such as the Rohillas, or had shaken off Maratha domination after Panipat. The success of this campaign can be seen as the last saga of the long story of Panipat.

39. **Correct Option: (d)**

Explanation:

- **Statement 1 is incorrect:** The First Battle of Panipat marked the beginning of the Mughal Empire.
- **Statement 2 is incorrect:** In the Battle of Chausa, Humayun escaped from the battlefield to save his life. Sher Shah was victorious and crowned himself as the emperor.

Supplementary Notes:

Important Battles during Mughal Advent into India

- **First Battle of Panipat:** The First Battle of Panipat was fought between the invading forces of Babur and the Lodi Empire, which took place on 21 April 1526 in North India. It marked the beginning of the Mughal Empire. This was one of the earliest battles involving gun powder firearms and field artillery.
- **Battle of Khanwa:** The Battle of Khanwa was fought near the village of Khanwa, in Bharatpur District of Rajasthan, on March 16, 1527. It was fought between the invading forces of the first Mughal Emperor, Babur, and the Rajput forces led by Rana Sanga of Mewar, after the Battle of Panipat. The victory in the battle consolidated the new Mughal Dynasty in India.
- **Battle of Chausa:** The Battle of Chausa was a notable military engagement between the Mughal emperor, Humayun, and the Afghan, Sher Shah Suri. It was fought on 26 June, 1539 at Chausa, 10 miles southwest of Buxar in modern-day Bihar, India. Humayun escaped from the battlefield to save his life. Sher Shah was victorious and crowned himself the emperor.
- **Battle of Sirhind:** The Battle of Sirhind was fought between the Mughal Empire and the Suri Empire in 1555. After the death of Islam Shah Suri, the Suri Empire was in a civil war where various contenders to the throne fought each other for supremacy. Sikandar Shah Suri was occupied with his struggle against Ibrahim Shah Suri when Humayun mobilized an army from Kabul. On June 22, 1555, Humayun and Bairam Khan carried out a daring raid, defeated Sikandar Shah, and re-established their empire in India.

40. **Correct Option: (b)**

Explanation:

- **Statement 2 is incorrect:** Jagirs were allotted to nobles and members of the royal family including the queens.

Supplementary Notes:

Organization of Local Government Under the Reign of Akbar

- Akbar made hardly any changes in the organization of local government.
- The Pargana (tehsil) and the Sarkar (district) continued as before. The chief officers of the Sarkar were the Faujdar and the Amalguzar, the former being in charge of law and order, and the latter responsible for the assessment and collection of the land revenue.
- The territories of the empire were divided into Jagir, Khalisa, and Inam.
- Income from Khalisa villages went directly to the royal exchequer.
- The Inam lands were those which were allotted to learned and religious men.
- Jagirs were allotted to nobles and members of the royal family, including the queens.
- The Amalguzar was required to exercise general supervision over all types of holdings so that the imperial rules and regulations for the assessment and collection of land revenue were followed uniformly.

41. **Correct Option: (c)**

Explanation:

- Both statements are correct.

Supplementary Notes:

Mughal advance towards the Deccan

- In 1591, Akbar launched a diplomatic offensive. He sent embassies to all the Deccani states 'inviting' them to accept Mughal suzerainty.
- As might have been expected, none of the states accepted this demand, the only exception being Khandesh, which was too near and exposed to the Mughals to resist.
- Burhan Nizam Shah, the ruler of Ahmadnagar, was rude to the Mughal envoy; the others only made promises of friendship. It seemed that Akbar was on the verge of making a definite move in the Deccan.
- The necessary opportunity was provided to him when factional fighting broke out among the Nizam Shahi nobles following the death of Burhan in 1595.
- There were four candidates for the throne, backed by different parties. The strongest claim was that of Bahadur, son of the deceased ruler. Ibrahim Adil Shah II, the ruler of Bijapur, was inclined to support Bahadur's claim.

- Chand Bibi was the sister of Burhan, and the widow of the former ruler of Bijapur who was Ibrahim Adil Shah's uncle. She was a remarkable woman and had virtually ruled Bijapur for almost ten years when Ibrahim Adil Shah was a minor.
- She had gone to Ahmadnagar to condole the death of her brother Burhan, but she stayed on to take up with vigour the cause of her nephew, Bahadur, who was a minor.
- It was against this background that the leaders of the rival party, the Deccanis, invited the Mughals to intervene.
- The struggle which now began was really a struggle between Bijapur and the Mughals for the domination of Ahmadnagar state.
- The Mughal invasion was led by prince Murad, who was the governor of Gujarat; and by Abdur Rahim Khan-i-Khanan.
- The ruler of Khandesh was asked to cooperate. Due to factional fights among the Ahmadnagar nobles, the Mughals encountered little opposition till they reached the capital, Ahmadnagar.
- Chand Bibi shut herself up in the fort with the boy king, Bahadur. After a close siege of four months in which Chand Bibi played a valiant role, the two sides came to an agreement.
- They agreed to cede Berar to the Mughals in return for their recognition of the claim of Bahadur. Mughal suzerainty was also recognised. This was in 1596.

42. Correct Option: (c)

Explanation:

- **Statement 2 is incorrect:** Arches and Domes were introduced by Turks during the Delhi Sultanate.
- **Statement 3 is incorrect:** Gunpowder was already known in India before Babur's arrival. His victories led to rapid popularization of gunpowder and artillery in India.

Supplementary Notes:

Significance of Babur's Advent into India

- Babur's advent into India was significant from many points of view.
- For the first time since the downfall of the Kushana Empire, Kabul and Qandhar became integral parts of an empire comprising North India. Since these areas had always acted as staging places for an invasion of India by dominating them, Babur and his successors were able to give to India security from external invasions for almost 200 years.
- Economically, the control of Kabul and Qandhar strengthened India's foreign trade since these two towns were the starting points for caravans meant for China in the east, and the Mediterranean seaports in the west. Thus, India could take a greater share in the great trans-Asian trade.
- Babur introduced a new mode of warfare in India. Although gunpowder was known in India earlier, Babur showed what a skilled combination of artillery and cavalry could achieve. His victories led to rapid popularization of gunpowder and artillery in India.
- By his new military methods as well as by his personal conduct, Babur re-established the prestige of the Crown which had been eroded since the death of Firoz Shah Tughlaq. Although Sikandra Lodi and Ibrahim Lodi had tried to reestablish the prestige of the Crown, Afghan ideas of tribal independence and equality had resulted only in a partial success. Babur had the prestige of being a descendant of two of the most famous warriors of Asia, Changez and Timur. None of his nobles could, therefore, claim a status of equality with him.
- Babur was deeply learned in Persian and Arabic, and is regarded as one of the two most famous writers in the Turkish language which was his mother tongue. His famous memoirs, the Tuzuk-i-Baburi, is considered one of the classics of literature. His other works include a masnavi and the Turkish translation of a well-known Sufi work. He was a keen naturalist, and has described the flora and fauna of India in considerable detail. He laid out a number of formal gardens with running water, thereby establishing a tradition of building gardens.
- Babur introduced a new concept of the state which was to be based on the strength and prestige of the Crown, absence of religious and sectarian bigotry, and the careful fostering of culture and fine arts.

43. Correct Option: (b)

Explanation:

- **Statement 2 is incorrect:** It was the Mir Bakhshi and not the Diwan/Wazir, who was considered the head of the nobility.

Supplementary Notes:

Organisation of Central and Provincial Governments

- Akbar paid great attention to the organisation of the central and provincial governments. His system of central government was based on the structure of government which had evolved under the Delhi Sultanate, but the functions of the various departments were carefully reorganised and meticulous rules and regulations were laid down for the conduct of affairs.
- Akbar reorganised the central machinery of administration on the basis of the division of power between various departments and of checks and balances.
- The head of the revenue department was the Wazir. Under Akbar, generally the wazir did not hold a high

Mansab. Many nobles held Mansabs which were higher than his. Thus, he was no longer the principal adviser to the ruler, but one who was an expert in revenue affairs. Thus, in practice, the concept of an all-powerful Wazir had been given up. To emphasize this point, Akbar generally used the title of Diwan or Diwan-i-Ala in preference to the word Wazir.

- The head of the military department was called the Mir Bakhshi. It was the Mir Bakhshi and not the Diwan who was considered the head of the nobility. Recommendations for appointment to Mansabs or for promotions etc. were made to the emperor through the Mir Bakhshi.
- The Mir Bakhshi was also the head of the intelligence and information agencies of the empire. Intelligence officers (Barids) and news reporters (Waqia-Navis) were posted to all parts of the empire. Their reports were presented to the emperor at the court through the Mir Bakhshi.
- The third important officer was the Mir Saman. He was in charge of the imperial household, including the supply of all the provisions and articles for the use of the inmates of the haram or the female apartments.
- The fourth important department was the judicial department headed by the chief Qazi. This post was sometimes combined with that of the chief Sadr who was responsible for all charitable and religious endowments.
- Akbar divided the empire into twelve Subas in 1580. A governor (Subedar), a Diwan, a Bakhshi, a Sadr, a Qazi, and a Waqia-Navis were appointed to each of the provinces. Thus, an orderly government based on the principle of checks and balances was extended to the provinces.

44. Correct Option: (b)

Explanation:

- **Statement 1 is incorrect:** The first Battle of Panipat was fought between Babur and Ibrahim Lodi in 1526.
- **Statement 2 is incorrect:** The Battle of Khanwa was fought between Babur and Rana Sanga in 1527.

Supplementary Notes:

Battle of Panipat (20 April, 1526)

- The battle of Panipat is regarded as one of the decisive battles of Indian history. It was an inevitable conflict between Ibrahim Lodi and Babur. It broke the back of Lodi power, and brought under Babur's control the entire area upto Delhi and Agra. The treasures stored up by Ibrahim Lodi at Agra relieved Babur from his financial difficulties.
- Babur had to wage another two hard-fought battles, one against Rana Sanga of Mewar; and the other against the eastern Afghans, before he could consolidate his hold on this area.
- Viewed from this angle, the battle of Panipat was not as decisive in the political field as has been made out. Its real importance lies in the fact that it opened a new phase in the struggle for domination in north India.

Battle of Khanwa (1527)

- The establishment of an empire in the Indo Gangetic valley by Babur was a threat to Rana Sanga. Sanga set afoot preparations to expel Babur, at any rate, to confine him to the Punjab.
- Babur accused Rana Sanga of breach of agreement as he promised to join him against Ibrahim Lodi, but made no move while he (Babur) conquered Delhi and Agra.
- Having carefully selected a site, Babur entrenched himself at Khanwa about 40 km from Agra. The Battle of Khanwa was fiercely contested and resulted in defeat of Sanga's forces.
- The battle of Khanwa secured Babur's position in the Delhi-Agra region and thus was more decisive than the Battle at Panipat. Babur strengthened his position further by conquering the chain of forts – Gwalior, Dholpur, etc., and east of Agra. He also annexed large parts of Alwar from Hasan Khan Mewati.

45. Correct Option: (b)

Explanation:

- Option (b) is correct.

Supplementary Notes:

Humayun

- Humayun succeeded Babur in December 1530 at the young age of 23. He had to grapple with a number of problems left behind by Babur. The administration had not yet been consolidated, and the finances were precarious. The Afghans had not been subdued, and were nursing the hope of expelling the Mughals from India. Finally, there was the Timurid legacy of partitioning the empire among all the brothers.
- Humayun also had to deal with the rapid growth of power of the Afghans in the east and Bahadur Shah, the ruler of Gujarat in the west.
- In 1532, at a place called Dadrah, he defeated the Afghan forces which had conquered Bihar and overrun Jaunpur in eastern Uttar Pradesh. After this success, Humayun besieged Chunar which had recently come in the possession of an Afghan sardar, Sher Khan. Sher Khan, however, persuaded Humayun to allow him to retain possession of the fort and in return, he promised to be loyal to the Mughals, and sent one of his sons to Humayun as a hostage.
- After this, Humayun moved from Agra to Gwalior, and due to fear of Mughal intervention, Bahadur Shah patched up a treaty with the Rana, leaving the fort in his hands after extracting a large indemnity in cash and kind.

- During the next year and a half, Humayun spent his time in building a new city at Delhi, which he named 'Dinpanah'. The building of Dinpanah was meant to impress friends and foes alike. It could also serve as a second capital in case Agra was threatened by Bahadur Shah.

46. **Correct Option: (b)**

Explanation:

- **Statement 1 is incorrect:** Amalguzar was officer-in-charge for the assessment and collection of land revenue in Pargana.

Supplementary Notes:

Organization of Local Government Under Reign of Akbar

- Akbar made hardly any changes in the organization of local government.
- The Pargana (tehsil) and the Sarkar (district) continued as before. The chief officers of the Sarkar were the Faujdar and the Amalguzar, the former being in charge of law and order, and the latter responsible for the assessment and collection of the land revenue.
- The territories of the empire were divided into jagir, khalisa and inam.
- Income from khalisa villages went directly to the royal exchequer.
- The inam lands were those which were allotted to learned and religious men.
- Jagirs were allotted to nobles and members of the royal family including the queens.
- The amalguzar was required to exercise a general supervision over all types of holdings so that the imperial rules and regulations for the assessment and collection of land revenue were followed uniformly.

47. **Correct Option: (b)**

Supplementary Notes:

Dagh System

- During Akbar's reign great care was taken to ensure that, the Sawars recruited by the nobles were experienced and well-mounted. For this purpose, a descriptive roll (chehra) of the soldier was maintained, and his horse was branded with the imperial marks. This was called the 'dagh system'.
- Every noble had to bring his contingent for periodic inspection before persons appointed by the emperor for the purpose.
- The horses were carefully inspected and only good quality horses of Arabic and Iraqi breed were employed.
- Provision was made that the contingents of the nobles should be mixed ones drawn from all the group – Mughal, Pathan, Hindustani and Rajput. Thus, Akbar tried to weaken the forces of tribalism and parochialism. Only the Mughal and Rajput nobles were allowed to have contingents exclusively of Mughals or Rajputs.

48. **Correct Option: (d)**

Supplementary Notes:

Important Battles during Mughal Advent into India

- **First Battle of Panipat:** The First Battle of Panipat was fought between the invading forces of Babur and the Lodi Empire, which took place on 21 April 1526 in North India. It marked the beginning of the Mughal Empire. This was one of the earliest battles involving gun powder firearms and field artillery.
- **Battle of Khanwa:** The Battle of Khanwa was fought near the village of Khanwa, in Bharatpur District of Rajasthan, on March 16, 1527. It was fought between the invading forces of the first Mughal Emperor Babur and the Rajput forces led by Rana Sanga of Mewar, after the Battle of Panipat. The victory in the battle consolidated the new Mughal Dynasty in India.
- **Battle of Chausa:** The Battle of Chausa was a notable military engagement between the Mughal emperor, Humayun, and the Afghan, Sher Shah Suri. It was fought on 26 June 1539 at Chausa, 10 miles southwest of Buxar in modern-day Bihar, India. Humayun escaped from the battlefield to save his life. Sher Shah was victorious and crowned himself the emperor.
- **Battle of Sirhind:** The Battle of Sirhind was fought between the Mughal Empire and the Suri Empire in 1555. After the death of Islam Shah Suri, the Suri Empire was in a civil war where various contenders to the throne fought each other for supremacy. Sikandar Shah Suri was occupied with his struggle against Ibrahim Shah Suri when Humayun mobilized an army from Kabul. On June 22, 1555, Humayun and Bairam Khan carried out a daring raid, defeated Sikandar Shah and reestablished their empire in India.

49. **Correct Option: (a)**

Explanation:

- **Statement 2 is incorrect:** The Afghan forces led by Hemu were defeated at the 2nd Battle of Panipat in 1556 by the Mughals.

Supplementary Notes:

Akbar Ascendance to the Throne

- When Humayun fled to Iran, young Akbar was captured by his uncle, Kamran. He treated the child well on the whole. Akbar was re-united with his parents after the capture of Qandhar.
- When Humayun died, Akbar was at Kalanaur in Punjab, commanding operations against the Afghan rebels there. He was crowned at Kalanaur in 1556 at the young age of thirteen years and four months.

- Akbar succeeded to a difficult position. The Afghans were still strong beyond Agra, and were regrouping their forces under the leadership of Hemu for a final showdown. Kabul had been attacked and besieged. Sikandar Sur, the defeated Afghan ruler, was loitering in the Siwalik Hills.
- However, Bairam Khan, the tutor of Akbar and a loyal and favorite officer of Humayun, rose to the occasion. He became the wakil of the kingdom, with the title of Khan-i-Khanan, and rallied the Mughal forces.
- The battle between the Mughals and the Afghan forces led by Hemu, took place once again at Panipat (5 November, 1556) and the Afghans led by Hemu were defeated by Mughals. Thus, Akbar had virtually to reconquer his empire.

50. Correct Option: (a)

Explanation:

- **Statement 3 is incorrect:** The result of the battle was the halting of further Maratha advances in the north.

Supplementary Notes:

Battle of Panipat

- **First Battle of Panipat:** An overwhelmingly outnumbered Mughal force prevailed at Panipat. This was due to the resourcefulness of its commander, Babur, demonstrated his use of field fortifications and his instinctive sense of the value of the firepower of gunpowder. The victory enabled him to lay the foundations for the Indian Mughal Empire.
- **Second Battle of Panipat:** The Second Battle of Panipat was fought between the forces of Samrat Hem Chandra Vikramaditya, popularly called Hemu, the Hindu king who was ruling North India from Delhi, and the army of Akbar, on November 5, 1556. It was a decisive victory for Akbar's generals Khan Zaman I and Bairam Khan. H.G.Keen writes; "Akbar and his guardian Bairam Khan did not participate in the battle and were stationed 5 Kos (8 miles) away from the war zone. Bairam Khan did not permit the 13-year-old child king to be present in battlefield in person, instead he was provided with a special guard of 5000 well trained and most faithful troops and was stationed at a safe distance far behind the battlelines. He was instructed by Bairam Khan to flee towards Kabul for life in case the Mughal army was routed in the battlefield."
- The result of the battle was the halting of further Maratha advances in the north, and a destabilization of their territories, for roughly 10 years. This period of 10 years is marked by the rule of Peshwa Madhavrao, who is credited with the revival of Maratha domination following the defeat at Panipat. In 1771, 10 years after Panipat, he sent a large Maratha army into North India in an expedition that was meant to (a) re-establish Maratha domination in North India, and (b) punish refractory powers that had either sided with the Afghans, such as the Rohillas, or had shaken off Maratha domination after Panipat. The success of this campaign can be seen as the last saga of the long story of Panipat.

51. Correct Option: (d)

Explanation:

- All statements are correct.

Supplementary Notes:

Akbar's Navratnas

- Akbar was a great lover of artists and intellectuals.
- His passion for knowledge and interest in learning from great minds attracted him to men of genius to his court.
- Nine of these courtiers were known as Akbar's Navratnas (or nine jewels):
  - Abul Fazl
    - He wrote the famous 'Ain-i-Akbari' and 'Akbar Nama'. He also lead the Mughal imperial army in its wars in Deccan.
  - Faizi
    - He was a historian, Persian poet and Abul Fazl's brother.
    - He translated Lilavati into Persian (a work on mathematics), and under his supervision, the Mahabharata was translated into the Persian language.
  - Fakir Aziao Din
    - He was a Sufi mystic and one of the chief advisors of Akbar.
  - Tansen
    - He served as a court musician to King Ramachandra.
    - He accepted Islam at the hand of great Sufi mystic saint Muhammad Ghaus of Gwalior.
    - It is believed that he could bring rain and fire through singing the ragas Megh Malhar and Deepak respectively.
  - Raja Birbal/Mahesh Das
    - He was given the title of both Raja and Birbal.
    - He died fighting Yusuf Shahis on North-West frontier.
  - Raja Todar Mal
    - He was the finance minister and overlooked revenue system.
    - Introduced standard weights and measurements, revenue districts and officers.
    - He earlier worked under Sher Shah Suri.
    - In the year 1582 CE, Akbar, bestowed on him the title of 'Diwan-i-Ashraf'.

- Raja Man Singh
  - He was a Mansabdar and grandson of Akbar's father-in-law. He was Akbar's trusted general.
- Abdul Rahim Khan-i-Khanan
  - Great poet and son of Bairam Khan.
  - Although a Muslim by birth but was a devotee of Lord Krishna.
  - He translated Babarnama into Turki.
- Mirza Aziz Koka
  - He was also known as Khan-i-Azam or Kotaltash and was one of the leading nobles, and also the foster brother of Akbar. He also served as the Subedar of Gujarat.

52. Correct Option: (d)

Explanation:

- All statements are correct.

Supplementary Notes:

The decline of the Mughal Empire in India

- The combination of varied political, social, and economic factors led to the decline and the downfall of the Mughal Empire such as:
  - **Weak Successors:** None of Aurangzeb's successors could give any stability to the empire. They were absolutely inefficient and most of them were puppets in the hands of powerful nobles who ran the administration on their behalf. The wars of succession that plagued Delhi from c.1707 to 1719 CE too weakened the empire.
  - **Power usurping Nobility:** A major factor for the disintegration of the Mughal Empire was the infighting between the nobles. They had assumed a lot of powers and the course of politics and state activities were guided by their individual interests. The accession of weak rulers at the centre made them strong contenders for power.
  - **Ineffective Mughal Army, Neglect of Naval Power, and Foreign invasions:** The Mughal army gradually became inefficient and demotivated after losing many important battles. The neglect of naval power by the Mughals also cost them dearly. Further, the external invasions of Nadir Shah and Ahmad Shah Abdali not only took a heavy toll of the imperial treasury but also laid open the inefficiencies of the military and political administration.
  - **Lack of Strong finances:** Due to the emergence of many autonomous states, the revenue sources depleted, and due to continuous wars the treasury was further emptied.
  - **Orthodox rule of Aurangzeb:** The religious and Deccan policies of Aurangzeb contributed to the empire's decline. He was ambitious and wanted to increase the geographical limits of his empire with a hard-headed attitude towards the Marathas, Rajputs, and the Jats, which turned away these loyal warriors. His religious policy too, alienated the Hindus, which certainly had an adverse effect on the stability of the empire.

53. Correct Option: (b)

Explanation:

- **Option (b) is correct:** Mir Sayyid Ali and Abdus Samad were present in the court of Humayun.

Supplementary Notes:

Artists in the Mughal Court

- Mir Sayyid Ali and Abdus Samad were present in the court of Humayun.
- They migrated from Iran to Mughal court and accompanied Humayun to Delhi.

54. Correct Option: (a)

Explanation:

- Pairs 2 and 3 are incorrectly matched.

Author/Artists	Mughal Emperor
1. Abul Fazl	- Akbar
2. Abdul Hamid Lahori	- Shahjahan
3. Abdus Samad	- Humayun

Supplementary Notes:

Author/Artists in the Mughal Court

- Abdul Hamid Lahori, Abul Fazl and Abdus Samad were present in the courts of Shahjahan, Akbar and Humayun respectively.

55. Correct Option: (d)

Explanation:

- All statements are correct.

Supplementary Notes:

Mughal India

- The name 'Mughal' derives from Mongol. The term evokes the grandeur of an empire, it was not the name the rulers of the Dynasty chose for themselves.
- They referred to themselves as Timurids, as descendants of the Turkish ruler Timur on the paternal side.
- Babur, the first Mughal ruler, was related to Ghenghiz Khan from his mother's side. He spoke Turkish and referred derisively to the Mongols as barbaric hordes.
- As the Mughals were Chaghtai Turks by origin, Turkish was their mother tongue.
- Mughal court chronicles were written in Persian.
- Under the Sultans of Delhi, it flourished as a language of the court and of literary writings, alongside north Indian languages, especially Hindavi and its regional variants.

- It was Akbar who consciously set out to make Persian the leading language of the Mughal court.
- Cultural and intellectual contacts with Iran, as well as a regular stream of Iranian and Central Asian migrants seeking positions at the Mughal court, might have motivated the emperor to adopt the language.

56. **Correct Option: (a)**

Explanation:

- **Statement 3 is incorrect:** Mansabdars did not reside in or administer their own jagirs.

Supplementary Notes:

Mansabdari System

- Mansabdar refers to an individual who holds a Mansab, meaning a position or rank.
- It was a grading system used by the Mughals to fix: rank, salary and military responsibilities.
- Rank and salary were determined by a numerical value called 'zat'. The higher the zat, the more prestigious was the noble position in court and the larger his salary.
- The mansabdar's military responsibilities required him to maintain a specified number of sawar or cavalrymen. Mansabdars received their salaries as revenue assignments called jagirs.
- Mansabdars did not actually reside in or administer their jagirs. They only had rights to the revenue of their assignments which was collected for them by their servants while the mansabdars themselves served in some other part of the country.

57. **Correct Option: (d)**

Explanation:

- **Pair 1 and 2 are incorrectly matched:** Peter Mundy and Tavernier visited during the reign of Shahjahan.

Supplementary Notes:

Foreign Travellers During the Mughal Rule

- **Peter Mundy (1630–34 AD):** He was an Italian traveller to the Mughal empire in the reign of Shahjahan, who gives valuable information about the living standard of the common people in the Mughal Empire.
- **Jean Baptiste Tavernier (1638–1663 AD):** He was a French traveller, whose account covers the reign of Shahjahan and Aurangzeb.
- **Giovanni Careri:** He passed through India during the reign of Aurangzeb. He also provides a graphic account of the way silver travelled across the globe to reach India.

58. **Correct Option: (a)**

Explanation:

- **Option (a) is correct:** They present a continuous chronological record of events.

Supplementary Notes:

Chronicles of Mughal India

- The Mughal kings commissioned court historians to write accounts. These accounts recorded the events of the emperor's time.
- They present a continuous chronological record of events. They were a repository of factual information about the institutions of the Mughal state.
- The authors of Mughal chronicles were invariably courtiers. The accounts they wrote focused on events centered on the ruler, his family, the court and nobles, wars and administrative arrangements.
- Various chronicles such as the Akbar Nama, Shahjahan Nama, Alamgir Nama are the stories of Akbar, Shah Jahan, and Aurangzeb, respectively.
- Akbar Nama was written in Persian and Babur's memoirs were translated from Turkish into Persian as Babur Nama.
- Translations of Sanskrit texts such as the Mahabharata and the Ramayana into Persian were commissioned by the Mughal emperors. The Mahabharata was translated as the Razmnama (Book of Wars).

59. **Correct Option: (c)**

Explanation:

- **Statements 1 and 3 are incorrect:** The first Battle of Panipat was fought between Babur and Ibrahim Lodi, in 1526. After the war at Khanwa in 1527, Babus took on the title of "Ghazi".

Supplementary Notes:

Information regarding Babur's Invasion in India:

- Babur seized Kabul in 1504.
- In 1526, he defeated the Sultan of Delhi, Ibrahim Lodi, at Panipat and captured Delhi and Agra. The First Battle of Panipat marked the foundation of Mughal dominion in India.
- Babur conquered Delhi and sent his son Humayun to seize Agra.
- Babur announced himself as "Emperor of Hindustan".
- Cannons were an important addition in sixteenth-century warfare. Babur used them effectively in the first battle of Panipat.
- Gun powder technology was brought to India for warfare in the 14th century.
- Firearms were used for the first time in regions such as Gujarat, Malwa and Deccan and were used by Babur in early 16th century.
- In 1526, he defeated Ibrahim Lodi and his Afghan supporters at Panipat.
- In 1527, he defeated Rana Sanga, Rajput rulers and allies at Khanua.

- In 1528, he defeated the Rajputs at Chanderi and established control over Agra and Delhi before his death.
- He wrote his memoirs, Tuzuk-i-Baburi in Turki language.

60. Correct Option: (b)

Explanation:

- **Option (b) is correct:** In Iran Humayun received help from the Safavid Shah. He recaptured Delhi in Battle of Sirhind, in 1555.

Supplementary Notes:

Information regarding Humayun

- Humayun divided his inheritance according to the will of his father. His brothers were each given a province. The ambitions of his brother Mirza Kamran weakened Humayun's cause against Afghan competitors.
- Sher Khan defeated Humayun at Chausa (1539) and Kanauj (1540), forcing him to flee to Iran.
- In Iran, Humayun received help from the Safavid Shah. He recaptured Delhi in 1555 but died the next year after an accident in this building.
- Mir Sayyid Ali and Abdus Samad were the artists who accompanied Emperor Humayun to Delhi.
- Humayun Nama written by Gulbadan Begum. Gulbadan was the daughter of Babur, Humayun's sister and Akbar's aunt. Gulbadan could write fluently in Turkish and Persian.

61. Correct Option: (b)

Explanation:

- Pair 1 and 4 are incorrectly matched.

Supplementary Notes:

Administrative Department	Positon
A. Diwan-i-Wizarat	Prime Minister and Finance Minister
B. Sadr-us-Suddar	Minister of Islamic Law
C. Diwan-i-Insha	Correspondence Minister
D. Diwan-i-Arz	Defence or War Minister

CONCEPT REVISION

Here is the list of concepts that have been covered as part of the previous exercise. Revise and Self-reflect on your concepts you covered.

- Contingents of Mughal Administration ☐
- Different Administrative Offices ☐
- Reasons for downfall of Mughal Empire ☐
- Aurangzeb's Reign ☐
- Akbar's Administration ☐
- 'Du-aspah Sih-aspah system' ☐
- Third Battle of Panipat ☐
- Title of 'Jagatguru' ☐
- Term 'Cushoons' ☐
- 'Zinda Pir' ☐
- Battle of Chausa ☐
- Battle of Khanwa ☐
- Amu Darya ☐
- Significance of Babur's advent into India ☐
  Religious policy of Aurangzeb ☐
- 'Dagh System' ☐

4.5 VIJAYANAGARA EMPIRE

QUESTIONS

1. The 'Amara-Nayaka System' was a major political innovation of which of the following Medieval kingdoms?

(a) Pallavas (b) Pratiharas
(c) Chalukyas (d) Vijayanagara

2. Consider the following description:

"It was the only empire in Medieval India which employed women in state services. Women even went to battles and it was the only state that promoted widow remarriage".

Which of the following empires/kingdoms best represent the above description?

(a) Bahamani (b) Vijayanagara
(c) Rashtrakutas (d) Pallavas

3. Under Vijaynagara empire, a system of village organization comprising of 12 functionaries conducting every village affair refers to:

(a) Manyoms system (b) Auagar System
(c) Agaram style (d) Vidyaranya style

4. Which of the following battles was decisive in the decline of Vijayanagar Empire?
(a) Battle of Talikota
(b) Battle of Venni
(c) Battle of Chandawar
(d) Battle of Bilgram

5. The rulers of Vijayanagar promoted which of the following language?
(a) Hindi, Marathi and Sanskrit
(b) Malayalam, Tamil and Sanskrit
(c) Tamil, Telugu and Sanskrit
(d) Telugu, Urdu and Sanskrit

6. After victory over Vijaynagara, two of the following states Ahmadnagar, Bijapur and Golconda, claimed Sholapur. The states are:
(a) Ahmadnagar and Bijapur
(b) Golconda and Ahmadnagar
(c) Bijapur and Golconda
(d) None of the above

7. Sayana, an important commentator on Vedas was associated with which of the following empires?
(a) Chola Empire
(b) Vijayanagar Empire
(c) Hoyasala Empire
(d) Bahmani Empire

8. The Nayakas in the Vijayanagar Empire were ______:
(a) Central Ministers
(b) Military Chiefs controlling particular territories
(c) Cavalry soldiers
(d) Priests of large and powerful temples

9. Match the following pairs:

List I	List II
A. Harihara I and Bukka	1. Tuluva Dynasty
B. Krishan Deva Raya	2. Founded Vijaynagar Empire
C. Rana Khumbha	3. Sangeet Shiromani
D. Deva Raya II	4. Famous poet Srinatha

Select the correct answer using the code given below:
(a) A-2, B-1, C-3, D-4
(b) A-1, B-2, C-3, D-4
(c) A-4, B-3, C-2, D-1
(d) A-3, B-1, C-2, D-4

10. Consider the following statements:
1. The Telugu work Rayavachakamu gives interesting details about the Nayak system under Krishnadevaraya.
2. The Vijayanagara kings issued a large number of gold coins called Varaha.

Which of the above statement/s is/are correct regarding Vijayanagara Empire?
(a) 1 only (b) 2 only
(c) Both 1 and 2 (d) Neither 1 nor 2

11. Which of the following areas led to a conflict between Vijayanagar and the Bahmani Empire?
1. Raichur doab
2. Marathwada region
3. The deltaic region of Krishna-Godavari

Select the correct option using the codes given below:
(a) 1 and 2 only (b) 1 and 3 only
(c) 2 and 3 only (d) 1, 2 and 3

12. Consider the following statements regarding Vijayanagara empire:
1. Krishna Deva erected a well-developed naval structure.
2. Travelers like Barbosa, Nuniz give the details of the Vijayanagara Empire.
3. During the time of Krishna Dev Rai, independent creation of literature was started in Telugu language.

Which of the above statements is/are correct?
(a) 1 and 2 only (b) 1 and 3 only
(c) 2 and 3 only (d) 1, 2 and 3

13. Consider the following statements regarding the king of Vijayanagara Empire Krishna Deva Raya:
1. He restored the Bahmani Sultanate to Muhammad Shah, which was taken over by independent kingdoms of the Deccan Sultanate.
2. He acquired the title of Gajabetegara.
3. He was the author of Manucharitram.

Which of the above statements is/are correct?
(a) 1 and 2 only (b) 1 only
(c) 3 only (d) 1, 2 and 3

14. Arrange the following dynasties of Vijaynagar Empire in chronological order:
(a) Sangama - Tuluva - Saluva - Aravidu
(b) Sangama - Saluva - Tuluva - Aravidu
(c) Sangama - Aravidu - Tuluva - Saluva
(d) Saluva - Aravidu - Sangama - Tuluva

15. Consider the following statements with respect to social life during the Vijayanagar period:
1. Nayaks were army officers who were granted land in lieu of their services.
2. The practices of devadasi and sati were absent during this period.

Which of the above statements is/are correct?
(a) 1 only (b) 2 only
(c) Both 1 and 2 (d) Neither 1 nor 2

16. Who among the following is known to have acquired the title of Gajabetegara?
(a) Deva Raya II
(b) Harihara II
(c) Krishna Deva Raya
(d) None of the above

17. **Match the following literatures written during Vijayanagar period with their respective authors:**

List I	List II
A. Jambavati	1. Pingali Kalyanam Suranna
B. Manucharitam	2. Tenali Ramakrishna
C. Panduranga	3. Allasani Mahamatyam Peddanna
D. Garuda Puranam	4. Krishna Deva Raya

Select the correct answer using the code given below:

	A	B	C	D
(a)	1	2	3	4
(b)	2	4	1	3
(c)	3	1	2	4
(d)	4	3	2	1

18. **Consider the following statements with respect to Vijayanagar king Krishna Deva Raya:**
    1. He took the title of "Yavanarajya sthapanacharya" after defeating the Gajapati ruler Prataparudra.
    2. Amukthamalyadha is composed by him in Telugu.
    3. Eight eminent scholars of Telugu known as the 'Ashta diggajas' were present in his court.

    Which of the above statements are correct?

    (a) 1 and 2 only (b) 2 and 3 only
    (c) 1 and 3 only (d) 1, 2 and 3

19. **Consider the following statements:**
    1. The kingdom of Vijaynagara was divided into five parts namely Bijapur, Berar, Golkonda, Bidar and Ahmednagar.
    2. The battle of Talaikota was fought between conflict between the Vijaynagar kingdom and Bahmani Sultanate

    Which of the above statement is/are incorrect?

    (a) 1 only (b) 2 only
    (c) Both 1 and 2 (d) Neither 1 nor 2

20. **Vijaynagara Empire was defeated at the Battle of Talikota (1565) by the combined armies of:**

    (a) Bijapur, Bahamani, and Golconda
    (b) Bijapur, Bahamani, and Ahmadnagar
    (c) Bahamani, Ahmadnagar, and Golconda
    (d) Bijapur, Ahmadnagar, and Golconda

21. **Consider the following statements:**
    1. Harihara and Bukka were the founders of the Vijaynagara Empire.
    2. They were the contemporaries of Mohammad bin Tughlaq.

    Which of the above statements is/are correct?

    (a) 1 only (b) 2 only
    (c) Both 1 and 2 (d) Neither 1 nor 2

22. **Consider the following statements regarding the Amara-Nayaka system of the Vijaynagara Empire:**
    1. Amara-Nayaka system was a major political innovation of the Vijayanagara Empire that was influenced by the Iqta system of the Delhi Sultanate.
    2. Amara-Nayakas were military commanders who were given territories to govern without any financial responsibilities.

    Which of the above statements is/are correct?

    (a) 1 only (b) 2 only
    (c) Both 1 and 2 (d) Neither 1 nor 2

23. **Consider the following statements regarding Krishnadeva Raya:**
    1. He belonged to the Saluva Dynasty of the Vijayanagara Empire.
    2. He founded a sub-urban township called Nagalapuram.
    3. Abur Razzaq and Conti visited Vijayanagar empire during his tenure.

    Which of the above statements is/are correct?

    (a) 1 and 2 only (b) 2 only
    (c) 2 and 3 only (d) 1 and 3 only

24. **Consider the following characteristics of the Vijayanagara Empire:**
    1. The copper plate inscriptions were predominantly in Sanskrit language and Nagari script.
    2. The rulers of this kingdom issued gold coins called Varahas or Pagodas.
    3. A new style of architecture was developed under the rule called Provida style.

    Which of the above characteristics is/are correct?

    (a) 2 only (b) 1 and 2 only
    (c) 2 and 3 only (d) 1, 2 and 3

25. **Consider the following features of the Bahamani Kingdom:**
    1. The Sultans followed a Feudal type of administration.
    2. The kingdom was divided into many provinces called Tarafs.
    3. The Bahmani Sultans gave great attention to education.
    4. They discouraged Arabic and Persian learning.

    Which of the above statements is/are correct?

    (a) 1 and 2 only (b) 1, 2 and 3 only
    (c) 3 and 4 only (d) 2, 3 and 4 only

SOLUTIONS

1. **Correct Option: (d)**

Supplementary Notes:

Amara-Nayaka System

- The amara-nayaka system was a major political innovation of the Vijayanagara Empire.

- It is likely that many features of this sytem were derived from the iqta system of the Delhi Sultanate.
- There is an important role of this sytem in emergence of the Vijayanagara empire. This shows in the following points:
  - The amara-nayakas were military commanders who were given territories to govern by the Raya. They collected taxes and other dues from peasants.
  - The amar-nayak retained part of the revenue for personal use and for maintaining a stipulated contingent of horses and elephants.
  - These contingents provided the Vijayanagara kings with an effective fighting force with which they brought the entire southern peninsula under their control. Some of the revenue was also used for the maintenance of temples and irrigation works.
  - The amara-nayakas sent tribute to the king annually and personally appeared in the royal court with gifts to express their loyalty.
  - Kings occasionally asserted their control over them by transferring them from one place to another.

2. **Correct Option: (b)**

Supplementary Notes:

Position of Women in Vijayanagar Empire

- Women occupied a very honorable position in the Vijayanagar society. Some of them were very learned and were eminent litterateurs.
- Monogamy was the general practice, but kings and nobility followed polygamous practices.
- The widows could remarry.
- Women of the nobility and higher castes were carefully educated. Music and dancing formed an important part of their curriculum.
- Women were also wrestlers, astrologers, accountants, writers, musicians and even went to the battlefield.
- Another group of women were the courtesans who played a very important role in society. They fell under two classes: (a) those that were attached to the temples, and (b) those that lived independently. Their case was not homogeneous and it was open to women of any community to join their sisterhood. Courtesans were highly educated and cultured and no social stigma was attached to them.
- It was the only empire in Medieval India which employed women in state services.

3. **Correct Option: (b)**

Supplementary Notes:

Vijayanagara Administration

- The Auagar system was an important feature of the Vijayanagara village organization. It is the body of twelve functionaries, known as "Auagars". They conducted every village affair. They were granted tax free lands "manyoms", which they were to enjoy in perpetuity.
- The administration under the Vijayanagar Empire was well organised. The king enjoyed absolute authority in executive, judicial and legislative matters. He was the highest court of appeal.
- The succession to the throne was on the principle of hereditary. Sometimes usurpation to the throne took place as Saluva Narasimha came to power by ending the Sangama Dynasty. The king was assisted by a council of ministers in his day-to-day administration.
- The Empire was divided into different administrative units called Mandalams, Nadus, Sthalas and finally, into Gramas.
- The governor of Mandalam was called Mandaleswara or Nayak. Vijayanagar rulers gave full powers to the local authorities in the administration. Besides land revenue, tributes and gifts from vassals and feudal chiefs, customs collected at the ports, taxes on various profession were other sources of income to the government.
- Land revenue was fixed generally one-sixth of the produce. The expenditure of the government included personal expenses of king and the charities given by him, and military expenditure. In the matter of justice, harsh punishments such as mutilation and throwing to the elephants were followed.

4. **Correct Option: (a)**

Supplementary Notes:

Battle of Talikota (1565)

- Also known as the battle of Bannihatti, this battle is generally considered the signal for the end of Vijayanagar empire.
- It was fought after the death of Krishnadevaraya as his successors were weak and bitter amongst each other for acquiring the throne.
- As a result, the opposing powers joined hands against their common enemy – Vijayanagar.
- Aliya Ramaraya was the leader of the Vijayanagara troops. On the other hand was the coalition army of Shahi Sultans. – Adil Shahis of Bijapur, Nizam Shahis of Ahmadnagar, Kutub Shahis of Golconda and Barid Shahis of Bidar.
- Following formed the major and immediate reasons for the battle :
  - Shahi sultans and Vijayanagar had their mutual religious differences.
  - Region between Krishna and Tungabhadra river was fertile and sought after by both the powers.
  - Immediate Cause – Ali Adil Shah had demanded the return of Raichur from Aliya Ramaraya, who

instead refused its return and invited Shahi to the battlefield.

- The end result of the war was that Aliya Ramaraya was defeated blatantly and Vijayanagar lost its glory.

Battle of Venni (130 CE)

- This battle finds its mention in Sangam era's poems.
- It was fought by King Karikala (Sangam Chola ruler), who defeated an alliance of Cheras, Pandyas and 11 smaller chieftains.

Battle of Chandawar (1194)

- It was fought between Mohammad Ghori and Jaichand.
- Jaichand was defeated in this battle.

Battle of Bilgram (1540)

- Also known as the Battle of Kannauj, it was fought between Humayun and Sher Shah.
- By the end of this war, Sher Shah had captured Delhi and Agra; Humayun had to flee and seek refuge in Persia.

5. **Correct Option: (c)**

Supplementary Notes:

Vijayanagara Empire

- The Hazara Ramasami temple and Vittalaswamy temple was built during this period
- The bronze image of Krishnadeva Raya is a masterpiece.
- Sanskrit, Tamil, Telugu and Kannada literature were developed.
- Sayana wrote commentaries on Vedas.
- Krishnadevaraya wrote Amuktamalyada in Telugu and Usha Parinayam and Jambavathi Kalyanam in Sanskrit.

6. **Correct Option: (a)**

Supplementary Notes:

- Both Ahmadnagar and Bijapur claimed Sholapur which was a rich and fertile tract. Neither wars nor marriage alliances between the two could resolve the issue. Both the states had the ambition of conquering Bidar. Ahmadnagar also wanted to annex Berar in the north.

7. **Correct Option: (b)**

Supplementary Notes:

Vijayanagar Empire

- Sayana: was an important commentator on the Vedas. His commentary on the Rigveda was edited by Max Müller, 1849-1875. He flourished under the king Bukka I and his successor Harihara II in the Vijayanagar Empire of South India.

8. **Correct Option: (b)**

Supplementary Notes:

Nayakas in the Vijayanagara Empire

- Among those who exercised power in the empire were military chiefs who usually controlled forts and had armed supporters. These chiefs often moved from one area to another, and in many cases were accompanied by peasants looking for fertile land on which to settle. These chiefs were known as nayakas and they usually spoke Telugu or Kannada. Many nayakas submitted to the authority of the kings of Vijayanagara but they often rebelled and had to be subdued by military action.

9. **Correct Option: (a)**

List I	List II
A. Harihara I and Bukka	2. Founded Vijaynagar Empire
B. Krishan Deva	1. Tuluva Dynasty Raya
C. Rana Khumbha	3. Sangeet Shiromani
D. Deva Raya II	4. Famous poet Srinatha

10. **Correct Option: (c)**

Explanation:

- Both statements are correct.

Supplementary Notes:

Vijayanagara Empire

- Several Persian accounts written by the court historians of the Bahmani Sultanate, relating to Bahmani - Vijayanagar conflicts have survived.
- Though they contain some biased and exaggerated information they provide rare eye-witness accounts relating to the battles, the palace intrigues, the life and sufferings of the people on either side, etc. which are lacking in inscriptions.
- The Kannada and Telugu literature, like Manucharitram, Saluvabhyudayam, etc., patronized in the Vijayanagar court, give genealogical, political and social information.
- The Telugu work, Rayavachakamu gives interesting details about the Nayak system under Krishnadevaraya.
- The Vijayanagara kings issued a large number of gold coins called Varaha (also called 'Pon' in Tamil and 'Honnu' in Kannada).
- These gold coins have the images of various Hindu deities and animals like the bull, the elephant and the fabulous gandaberunda (a double eagle, sometimes holding an elephant in each beak and claw).
- The legend contains the king's name either in Nagari or in Kannada script.

11. **Correct Option: (d)**

Explanation:

- All statements are correct.

Supplementary Notes:

Vijayanagara Conflict with Bahamani

- There were constant conflicts between the Vijayanagar and the Bahamani kingdoms over the control of Raichur doab which was the land between rivers Krishna and Tungabhadra.
- This area was fertile and rich in mineral resources. The famous diamond mines of Golconda were located in the eastern part of the doab region.
- The geography of both the kingdoms was such that expansion was possible only across Tungabhadra in the Deccan.
- It appears that the battles between the two were not conclusive and the status quo was maintained.
- Sometimes, Bahamani had an advantage and sometimes, Vijayanagar had an advantage. For instance, in 1504, the Bahamani managed to reconquer the Raichur doab. However, with the ascent of Krishna Deva Raya, the Bahamanis lost Raichur, Mudkal, Nalgonda and other inland towns.
- An important result of these wars was that both the powers were so involved amongst themselves that they never realized the increasing power of the Portuguese on the coast of South India.
- Besides, continuous warfare exhausted the resources of both the states and weakened them.
- The other areas of conflict were the Marathwada region and the deltaic region of Krishna-Godavari.
- Both regions had fertile areas and important ports that controlled trade to the foreign countries.
- The fertile area in the Marathwada region was the Konkan belt that also had the port of Goa which was an important region for trade (export and import) especially import of horses from Iraq and Iran.
- Territorial and economic motives were the main causes of the war.

12. **Correct Option: (c)**

Explanation:

- **Statement 1 is incorrect:** The early Vijayanagara rulers, Krishna Deva seems to have paid scant attention to the development of a navy.

Supplementary Notes:

Climax of Vijayanagara Empire

- Unlike the Cholas and some of the early Vijayanagara rulers, Krishna Deva seems to have paid scant attention to the development of a navy.
- Krishna Deva was also a great builder. He built a new town near Vijayanagara and dug an enormous tank which was also used for irrigation purposes.
- He was a gifted scholar of Telugu and Sanskrit. Of his many works, only one in Telugu on polity and a drama in Sanskrit are available today.
- His reign marked a new era in Telugu literature when imitation of Sanskrit works gave place to independent works.
- He extended his patronage to Telugu, Kannada and Tamil poets alike.
- Foreign travellers like Barbosa, Paes and Nuniz speak of his efficient administration and the prosperity of the empire under his sway.

13. **Correct Option: (b)**

Explanation:

- **Statement 2 is incorrect:** Deva Raya II (1422-1446) was the greatest ruler of the Sangama Dynasty. He was called Immadi Deva Raya. In his inscriptions, he has the title of Gajabetekara (the elephant hunter).
- **Statement 3 is incorrect:** Allasani Peddanna is the author of Manucharitram and is also known as Andhra Kavitapitamaha.

Supplementary Notes:

Krishnadevaraya (1509–29)

- He was the greatest of the Vijayanagar rulers, also known as 'Abhinava Bhoja', 'Andhra Pitamah', 'Andhra Bhoja' (as he was a great patron of literature and art).
- He invaded the Raichur Doab and captured the city of Raichur in c.1520 CE.
- He restored the Bahmani Sultanate to Muhammad Shah, which was taken over by independent kingdoms of Deccan Sultanate and Krishna Deva himself took the title of 'Yavanarajya Sthapanacharya'.
- Ashtadiggajas was the collective title given to the eight Telugu poets in his court.
- The age of Ashtadiggajas is called Prabandha Age (AD 1540 to 1600). These poets were:
    - Allasani Peddanna
    - Nandi Thimmana
    - Madayyagari Mallana
    - Dhurjaty
    - Ayyalaraju Ramambhadrudu
    - Pingali Surana
    - Ramarajabhushanudu
    - Tenali Ramakrishna
- The most famous being Allasani Peddana who was honoured with the title 'Andhrakavitapitamaha'.
- Amuktamalyada is an epic poem in Telugu composed by Krishnadevaraya of the Vijayanagar Dynasty. Amuktamalyada translates to "A garland of pearls".

- Considered as a masterpiece, Amuktamalyada describes the story of the wedding of the Hindu Lord Vishnu and Andal – the Tamil Alvar poet and daughter of Periyalvar, at Srirangam.

14. Correct Option: (b)

Explanation:

- **Option (b) is correct:** The correct sequence is Sangama Dynasty – Saluva Dynasty – Tuluva Dynasty – Aravidu Dynasty.

Supplementary Notes:

Vijaynagar Empire

- The Vijayanagar kingdom constituted four dynasties — Sangama (c.1336–1485 CE), Saluva (c.1485–1503 CE), Tuluva (c.1503–1570 CE) and Aravidu (till the end of the 17th century).
- The foundation of Vijaynagar Empire in India was laid by Harihara and Bukka, the founders of Sangama Dynasty.
- These were originally feudatories of the Kakatiyas of Warangal and after their fall, they served as ministers in the Kampili state.
- These two brothers founded a new city of Vidyanagar or Vijayanagara (meaning 'city of victory') on the south bank of river Tungabhadra.
- The decline of the Hoysala kingdom enabled Harihara and Bukka to expand their newly founded kingdom. By c. 1346 CE, they brought the whole of the Hoysala kingdom under their control.
- Bukka succeeded his brother in c.1356 and ruled till 1377 CE. During his reign, the Sultanate of Madurai was eliminated in the year 1377 and the Vijaynagara kingdom comprised the whole of south India up to Rameshwaram, including the Tamil country as well as that of the Cheras (Kerala).

15. Correct Option: (a)

Explanation:

- **Statement 2 is incorrect:** The practices such as devadasi and sati were honoured during this period.

Supplementary Notes:

Social life during the Vijayanagar Period

- One of the important characteristics of the Vijayanagar administration was the 'Amara-nayaka' system. The top-grade officers of the army were known as Nayaks or Palaiyagars or Poligars.
- Nayakas officers were granted land (called amaram) in lieu of their services while soldiers were usually paid in cash.
- The nayaka was responsible for expanding agricultural activities in his amaram (area). The nayaka was also the commander of the forts.
- By the 17th century, several of these nayakas such as those of Tanjore and Madurai became independent and established separate states.
- The position of women was not much improved.
- Large number of women were employed in the royal palaces as dancers, domestic servants, and palanquin bearers.
- Sahagaman, i.e., Sati was honoured.
- The practice of devadasi (attachment of dancing girls to temples) was prevalent.
- Polygamy was prevalent among the royal families.

16. Correct Option: (a)

Explanation:

- **Option (a) is correct:** Deva Raya II is known to have acquired the title of Gajabetegara or "Hunter of elephants".

Supplementary Notes:

Deva Raya II

- Deva Raya II was the greatest of the Sangama Dynasty rulers who was an able administrator, an ambitious warrior, and a man of letters.
- He authored well-known works in the Kannada language (Sobagina Sone and Amaruka) and in the Sanskrit language (Mahanataka Sudhanidhi).
- He also wrote a commentary on the Brahmasutra.
- He acquired the title of Gajabetegara, which literally means "Hunter of Elephants", an honorific title that explained his addiction to hunting elephants or a metaphor referring to his victories against enemies who were as strong as elephants.

17. Correct Option: (d)

List I	List II
A. Jambavati Kalyanam	4. Krishnadevaraya
B. Manucharitam	3. Allasani Peddanna
C. Panduranga Mahamatyam	2. Tenali Ramakrishna
D. Garuda Puranam	1. Pingali Suranna

Supplementary Notes:

Literature during the Vijayanagar Period

- Krishna Deva Raya was great patron of literature and art.
- He himself authored:
  - Amukthamalyadha (epic poem in Telugu)
  - Jambavati Kalyanam (Sanskrit drama based on the Jambavati, one of the eight principal queen-consorts of Lord Krishna)
  - Ushaparinayam (Sanskrit drama)
- He adorned eight eminent scholars of Telugu known as the 'Ashta diggajas' in his court.

- Their contribution to literature includes:
  - Manucharitam and Harikathasaram by Allasani Peddanna (the greatest, who was also called Andhrakavita Pitamaga).
  - Panduranga Mahamatyam, authored by Tenali Ramakrishna.
  - Pingali Suranna, author of Garuda Puranam, Prabhavatee Pradyumnamu, Raghava Pandaveeyam and Kala-purnodayamu.

18. Correct Option: (d)

Explanation:

- All statements are correct.

Supplementary Notes:

Krishnadevaraya (1509–29)

- He was the greatest of the Vijayanagar rulers, and is also known as 'Abhinava Bhoja', 'Andhra Pitamah', 'Andhra Bhoja' (as he was great patron of literature and art).
- He invaded the Raichur Doab and captured the city of Raichur in c.1520 CE.
- He restored the Bahmani Sultanate to Muhammad Shah, which was taken over by independent kingdoms of Deccan Sultanate and Krishna Deva himself took the title of 'Yavanarajya sthapanacharya'.
- Ashtadiggajas was the collective title given to the eight Telugu poets in his court.
- The age of Ashtadiggajas is called Prabandha Age (AD 1540 to 1600).
- These poets were:
  - Allasani Peddanna
  - Nandi Thimmana
  - Madayyagari Mallana
  - Dhurjaty
  - Ayyalaraju Ramambhadrudu
  - Pingali Surana
  - Ramarajabhushanudu
  - Tenali Ramakrishna
- The most famous being Allasani Peddana honoured with the title 'Andhrakavitapitamaha'.
- Amuktamalyada is an epic poem in Telugu composed by Krishnadevaraya of the Vijayanagar Dynasty. Amuktamalyada translates to "A garland of pearls".
- Considered as a masterpiece, Amuktamalyada describes the story of wedding of the Hindu Lord Vishnu and Andal - the Tamil Alvar poet and daughter of Periyalvar, at Srirangam.

19. Correct Option: (a)

Explanation:

- **Statement 1 is incorrect:** The Bahmani Sultanate was divided into five parts namely, Bijapur, Berar, Golkonda, Bidar and Ahmednagar, not Vijaynagara empire.

Supplementary Notes:

The Bahamani Kingdom

- The bahamani minister Mahmud Gawain was the reason for the increase in the kingdoms' strength.
- Gawain suggested administrative reforms to improve control of sultan over nobles.
- The nobles disliked him and convinced the sultan to execute him.
- After Gawan's execution, the empire weakened. The provincial governors declared autonomy.
- Thus, five kingdoms were formed in 1526 viz. Ahmednagar, Golconda, Bidar, Bijapur and Berar.
- The confederacy of the four states of Bijapur, Ahmednagar, Golkunda and Bidar i.e., the allied forces fought against the ruler of Vijayanagara on January 23, 1565 at Bannihathi near Talikota.
- According to some historians this is called the Battle of Rakshi-Tangadi – the battle site marked by these two villages.

20. Correct Option: (d)

Explanation:

- **Option (d) is correct:** Vijayanagara forces were defeated at the Battle of Talikota (1565) by the combined armies of Bijapur, Ahmadnagar, and Golconda.

Supplementary Notes:

Battle of Talikota (1565)

- After the death of Krishnadeva Raya in 1529, his successors were troubled by rebellious nayakas or military chiefs. By 1542, the control at the centre had shifted to another ruling lineage, that of the Aravidu Dynasty of Vijayanagar empire, which remained in power till the end of the seventeenth century.
- During this period, the military ambitions of the rulers of Vijayanagara as well as those of the Deccan Sultanates resulted in shifting alignments. Eventually, this led to an alliance of the Sultanates against Vijayanagara.
- In 1565, Rama Raya, the chief minister of Vijayanagara, led the army into battle at Rakshasi-Tangadi (also known as Battle of Talikota), where his forces were routed by the combined armies of Bijapur, Ahmadnagar and Golconda.

21. Correct Option: (c)

Explanation:

- Both statements are correct.

Supplementary Notes:

Harihara and Bukka

- Harihara and Bukka founded the Vijayanagara Empire in 1336. They made Hampi as the capital city.

- Mohammad bin Tughlaq was the Sultan of Delhi from 1325-51. He was contemporary to Harihara and Bukka.
- Harihara and Bukka were nobles of the Kakatiya Kingdom of Warangal. They went to Kampili when Warangal was defeated by the Sultans of Delhi. When Muhammad Tughlaq invaded Kampili to give shelter to a Muslim rebel, he brought Harihara and Bukka to Delhi as his prisoners and converted them to Islam.
- Later, they returned to the Hindu fold at the initiative of the saint Vidyaranya.
- They also proclaimed their independence and founded a new city on the south bank of the Tungabhadra river. It was called Vijayanagar meaning 'city of victory'.

22. Correct Option: (a)

Explanation:

- **Statement 2 is incorrect:** Amara-Nayaka collected taxes and other dues from peasants, craftspersons, and traders in the area.

Supplementary Notes:

Amara-Nayaka system

- The Amara-Nayaka system was a major political innovation of the Vijayanagara Empire. It is likely that many features of this system were derived from the Iqta system of the Delhi Sultanate.
- The Amara-Nayakas were military commanders who were given territories to govern by the Raya. They collected taxes and other dues from peasants, craftspersons, and traders in the area.
- They retained part of the revenue for personal use and for maintaining a stipulated contingent of horses and elephants. These contingents provided the Vijayanagara kings with an effective fighting force with which they brought the entire southern peninsula under their control.
- Some of the revenue was also used for the maintenance of temples and irrigation works. The Amara-Nayak sent tribute to the king annually and personally, appeared in the royal court with gifts to express their loyalty.

23. Correct Option : (b)

Explanation:

- **Statement 1 is incorrect:** Krishnadeva Raya belonged to the Tuluva Dynasty of the Vijayanagara Empire.
- **Statement 3 is incorrect:** Abur Razzaq and Conti visited during the reign of Deva Raya II.

Supplementary Notes:

Krishnadeva Raya

- He was the greatest king of the Vijaynagar empire. He was a great warrior and military commander. He belonged to the Tuluva Dynasty.
- His rule was characterized by expansion and consolidation. Under his rule, the land between the Tungabhadra and Krishna rivers (the Raichur doab) was acquired (1512), the rulers of Orissa were subdued (1514), and severe defeats were inflicted on the Sultan of Bijapur (1520). Although the kingdom remained in a constant state of military preparedness, it flourished under conditions of unparalleled peace and prosperity.
- He is credited with building some fine temples and adding impressive gopurams to many important South Indian temples. He also founded a suburban township, after his mother, called Nagalapuram (near Vijayanagara).
- He is also known as 'Andhra Bhoja', for his patronage to art and literature. He was a scholar and also known as Abhinava Bhoja. He wrote the Telugu work 'Amuktamalyada' and a Sanskrit play 'Jambavati Kalyana'.
- Foreigners who visited the Vijaynagara empire during his tenure were Barbosa and Paes while others like Razzaq and Conti visited during the tenure of Deva Raya II.

24. Correct Option: (d)

Explanation:

- All statements are correct.

Supplementary Notes:

Vijayanagar Empire – Culture

- Vijayanagar kingdom was one of the important kingdoms in the medieval Indian history.
- The rulers were strict worshippers of the Hindu Gods and Goddess, but also tolerant towards the other religions.
- The emperors were great patrons of art and culture. The region influenced a development in the streams of music, literature and architecture.
- Gold coins issued in the form of Varaha–the boar – were called Pagodas or Varahas.
- The copper plate inscriptions were predominantly in Sanskrit language and Nagari script.
- Many temples built in the territories of the south represent the style of Vijaynagara kingdom – a unique style of 'Provida Style' emerged.

25. Correct Option: (b)

Explanation:

- **Statement 4 is incorrect:** The Bahamani Sultans were patrons of the Persian language, culture and literature, and some members of the dynasty became well-versed in the language and composed its literature in it.

Supplementary Notes:

Bahamani Kingdom

- The Bahmani Sultanate was a Muslim state of the Deccan in southern India and was one of the great medieval Indian kingdoms.
- Agriculture was the main economic activity of Bahmani kingdom for earning the main revenue of the state.
- The Bahmani kingdom flourished in architectural monuments.
- The Bahamani Sultans were patrons of the Persian language, culture and literature, and some members of the dynasty became well-versed in the language and composed its literature in that language. Thus, in the field of architecture, the Bahamanis paved way for the distinct style by inviting architects from Persia, Turkey, and Arabia and blended it with local styles. They encouraged Arabic and Persian learning.

CONCEPT REVISION

Here is the list of concepts that have been covered as part of the previous exercise. Revise and Self-reflect on your concepts you covered.

- 'Amara-Nayaka System' ☐
- System of Village Organization ☐
- Battle of Talikota ☐
- Languages ☐
- Sayana ☐
- Conflict between Vijayanagar and Bahmani Empire ☐
- Social life during Vijayanagar Period ☐
- Title of Gajabetegara ☐
- Features of Bahamani Kingdom ☐

4.6 MARATHAS AND OTHER INDIAN STATES AND SOCIETY

QUESTIONS

1. Which of the following statements regarding Shivaji's Administration is/are correct?

1. Chauth was an additional levy of ten percent on those lands which the Marathas claimed hereditary rights.
2. He was assisted by a council of ministers called Ashtapradhan.
3. Sardeshmukhi was one-fourth of the land revenue paid to the Marathas in order to avoid the Maratha raids.

Which of the above statements is/are correct?

(a) 1 and 2 only (b) 2 only
(c) 2 and 3 only (d) 1, 2 and 3

2. Which of the following kingdoms were involved during infamous Tripartite struggle for Kannauj?

1. The Pratiharas of Central India
2. The Paramaras of Malwa
3. The Rashtrakutas of Deccan
4. The Rathore of Kannauj
5. The Chandelas of Bundelkhand
6. The Palas of Bengal

Select the correct answer using the code given below:

(a) 2, 4 and 5 only (b) 1, 4 and 5 only
(c) 1, 3 and 6 only (d) 3, 5 and 6 only

3. Shivaji had formed a council of eight ministers that administered the Maratha empire. The council was named as:

(a) Nyaya Pradhan (b) Ashta Sena
(c) Ashta Siddhi (d) Ashta Pradhan

4. Consider the following statements regarding the policy of Ibrahim Adil Shah of Bijapur:

1. Ibrahim Adil Shah of Bijapur who ascended the throne in 1555, was the leading advocate of policy of winning over the Marathas to their side.
2. It is said that he entertained 30,000 Maratha auxiliaries (bargis) in his army, and showed great favour to the Marathas in the revenue system.
3. Ibrahim Adil Shah was supposed to have introduced Marathi in revenue accounts at all levels.

Which of the above statements is/are correct?

(a) 1 only (b) 1 and 2 only
(c) 1 and 3 only (d) 1, 2 and 3

5. Which of the following statements regarding Gurjara-Pratiharas are correct?

1. King Bhoja, the greatest Pratihara king, was a devotee of Vishnu and adopted the title of 'Adivaraha'.
2. According to the Arab travellers, the Pratihara rulers had the best cavalry in India.
3. The dissolution of the Pratihara empire was due to the frequent raids from the Arab armies of Sind.

Select the correct option using the codes given below:

(a) 1 and 2 only (b) 1 and 3 only
(c) 2 and 3 only (d) 1, 2, and 3

6. **Consider the following statements regarding the Marathas:**
1. The Marathas were a noble group who rose to prominence during the rule in that region of the sultans of Bijapur and Ahmadnagar.
2. Leaders in the religious and social fields of Maharashtra inspired the people to unite by preaching faith in one God and by condemning the caste system.
3. Marathas adopted the guerilla warfare which obstructed the deployment of large armies by the outside rulers.

Which of the following statement/s is/are correct?

(a) 1 only (b) 2 and 3 only
(c) 3 only (d) 1 and 2 only

7. **With reference to the Pala Empire, consider the following statements:**
1. The reign of Gopala was marked by the tripartite struggle for the control of Kanauj and north India.
2. Agama Shastra was composed by Gaudapada during the time of the Palas.

Which of the above statements is/are correct?

(a) 1 only (b) 2 only
(c) Both 1 and 2 (d) Neither 1 nor 2

8. **Consider the following statements regarding the Rajputs:**
1. With the breakup of Rashtrakutas a number of Rajput states came into existence in North India.
2. They were champions of Hinduism and patronized only Brahamanas.
3. They were responsible for the climax period of temple building in North India

Select the correct option using the codes given below:

(a) 1 and 2 only (b) 2 only
(c) 3 only (d) None of the above

9. **Consider the following statements regarding causes of the defeat of the Rajputs:**
1. The Rajputs were defeated in a short span of 15 years.
2. Growth of feudalism was the main reason for Rajputs' defeat.
3. Turks were strong because of Iqta and Khalisa system.

Select the correct option using the codes given below:

(a) 1 and 2 only (b) 2 and 3 only
(c) 1 and 3 only (d) 1, 2 and 3

10. **With reference to the nobility under the Mughals, consider the following statements:**
1. Nobility's aristocratic character did not provide avenues of promotion and distinction to lower sections of society.
2. The Marathas were ousted from nobility during the times of Aurangzeb.

Which of the above statements is/are correct?

(a) 1 only (b) 2 only
(c) Both 1 and 2 (d) Neither 1 nor 2

11. **Which of the following is/are not correct regarding Bajirao II?**
1. He fought the Third Battle of Panipat when Ahmad Shah Abdali invaded India.
2. He signed the Treaty of Bassein with the British in which Marathas lost the effective control of Maratha region.
3. He was defeated by the East India Company in the Third Anglo-Maratha War.

Select the correct answer using the code given below:

(a) 1 only (b) 2 only
(c) 1 and 2 only (d) 2 and 3 only

12. **Which among the following is/are the features of Maratha administration during Shivaji's rule?**
1. The king was assisted by a council of ministers called the Ashtapradhan.
2. These offices of ministers were hereditary.
3. Shivaji built a powerful navy.
4. Sardeshmukhi was an additional levy of ten percent paid to the Marathas in order to avoid the Maratha raids.

Select the correct answer using the code given below:

(a) 1 and 2 only (b) 1 and 3 only
(c) 3 and 4 only (d) 1, 2 and 4 only

13. **Consider the following statements regarding the Rajput clans:**
1. The Chandellas of Bundelkhand are popularly known as the Chauhans of Sambhar.
2. The Chahamanas of Shakambhari trace their descent to a mythical ancestor named Chandratreya, born of the moon.
3. Paramaras trace their lineage to the hero who seized Vashishtha's kamadhenu from Vishwamitra.

Which of the above statements is/are correct?

(a) 1 and 2 only (b) 3 only
(c) 1 and 3 only (d) 1, 2 and 3

14. **Consider the following statements regarding rise of Marathas with the decline of the Mughal Dynasty:**
1. Treaty of Purander was signed at an advantage to Shivaji.
2. Sambhaji supported the execution of Farukkh Siyar.
3. The title of Peshwa became prominent during the rule of Shahu.

Select the correct answer using the code given below:

(a) 1 and 2 only (b) 2 and 3 only
(c) 1 and 3 only (d) 3 only

15. Consider the following pairs:

Medieval Indian State		Present Region
1. Bahamani	-	Maharashtra
2. Jaunpur	-	Bihar
3. Vijaynagar	-	Orissa

Which of the above pair is/are incorrectly matched?

(a) 1 and 2 only (b) 2 only
(c) 2 and 3 only (d) None of the above

16. With reference to the nobility under the Mughals, consider the following statements:

1. Nobility because of its aristocratic character did not provide avenues of promotion to lower sections of society.
2. The Marathas were ousted from nobility during the times of Aurangzeb.
3. The nobility, though feudal in character, developed many characteristics of bureaucracy.

Which of the above statements is/are correct?

(a) 1 and 2 only (b) 2 only
(c) 3 only (d) 2 and 3 only

17. Regarding the Battle of Palkhed, which of these statments is/are correct?

1. It was fought between Peshwa Baji Rao II and Nizamul Mulk, Asaf Jah.
2. The Maratha had to face defeat and the treaty of Munji was signed.

Choose the correct option from the codes given below.

(a) 1 only (b) 2 only
(c) Both 1 and 2 (d) None of the above

18. Consider the following statements:

1. The Battle of Pratapgarh was fought between Afzal Khan and Shivaji.
2. The Battle of Plassey was fought during the reign of Alamgir II.
3. Nana Phadnavis defeated the British and signed the Treaty of Purandhar in c.1776 CE.

Which of the above statements is/are correct?

(a) 1 and 2 only (b) 3 only
(c) 1 and 3 only (d) 1, 2 and 3

19. Consider the following statements regarding the Sikh Gurus:

1. Guru Nanak Dev started the institution of Guru Ka Langar.
2. Guru Arjan Dev compiled the writings of Nanak Dev in Guru Granth Sahib in Gurmukhi Script.
3. Guru Ram Das founded the city of Amritsar.
4. Guru Gobind Singh Sahib created the Khalsa.

Which of the above statements are correct?

(a) 1 and 2 (b) 2 and 3
(c) 1, 3 and 4 (d) 2, 3 and 4

20. Consider the following description:

"The Maratha power reached its zenith under him. He initiated the system of confederacy among the Maratha chiefs in which each Maratha chief was assigned a territory which could be administered autonomously. As a result, many Maratha families became prominent and established their authority in different parts of India".

Which of the following rulers best represent the above description?

(a) Baji Rao II (b) Baji Rao I
(c) Balaji Viswanath (d) Sambhaji

SOLUTIONS

1. Correct option (b)

Explanation:

- **Statement 1 is incorrect:** Chauth was one fourth of the land revenue paid to the Marathas in order to avoid the Maratha raids.
- **Statement 3 is incorrect:** Sardeshmukhi was an additional levy of ten percent on those lands which the Marathas claimed hereditary rights.

Supplementary Notes:

Shivaji's Administration

- Chauth was one fourth of the land revenue paid to the Marathas in order to avoid the Maratha raids
- Sardeshmukhi was an additional levy of ten percent on those lands which the Marathas claimed hereditary rights.
- Shivaji was also a great administrator. He laid the foundations of a sound system of administration. The king was the pivot of the government.
- He was assisted by a council of ministers called Ashtapradhan. However, each minister was directly responsible to Shivaji.
  - Peshwa: Finance and general administration. Later he became the prime minister.
  - Sar-i-Naubat or Senapati: Military commander, an honorary post.
  - Amatya: Accountant General.
  - Waqenavis: Intelligence, posts and household affairs.
  - Sachiv: Correspondence.
  - Sumanta: Master of ceremonies.
  - Nyayadish: Justice.
  - Panditarao: Charities and religious administration.

- Most of the administrative reforms of Shivaji were based on the practices of the Deccan sultanates. For example, Peshwa was the Persian title.
- The revenue system of Shivaji was based on that of Malik Amber of Ahmadnagar.
- Lands were measured by using the measuring rod called 'kathi'. Lands were also classified into three categories – paddy fields, garden lands and hilly tracks. He reduced the powers of the existing Deshmuks and Kulkarnis. He appointed his own revenue officials called Karkuns.

2. **Correct Option: (c)**

Supplementary Notes:

Tripartite Struggle – Kannauj

- During the 8th century AD, a struggle for control over the Kannauj took place among three major empires of India namely the Palas, the Pratiharas and the Rastrakutas.
- The Palas ruled the eastern parts of India while the Pratiharas controlled the western India (Avanti-Jalaor region). The Rastrakutas ruled over the deccan region of India. The struggle for control over Kannauj among these three dynasties is known as the Tripartite struggle in Indian history.
- Their Tripartite struggle lasted nearly 200 years and weakened all of them and enabled the Turks to overthrow them.
- Both Dharmpala, the Pala king and Pratihara king, Vatsaraja clashed against each other for Kannauj. The latter emerged victorious but was defeated by Rashtrakuta King Dhruva I. However, the moment the Rashtrakuta King returned to his kingdom in south, Pala king Dharmapala took the advantage of the situation and captured Kannauj.

3. **Correct option (d)**

Supplementary Notes:

Ashta Pradhan

- Ashta Pradhan was a council of eight ministers that administered the Maratha empire. The council was formed in 1674 by founding Emperor Chhatrapati Shivaji. The term 'Ashta Pradhan' literally translates to 'the Prime Eight', from the Sanskrit 'ashta' (eight) and 'pradhan' (prime). The body discharged the functions of a modern council of ministers; this is regarded as one of the first successful instances of ministerial delegation in India. The council is credited with having implemented good governance practices in the Maratha heartland, as well as for the success of the military campaigns against the Mughal Empire.

4. **Correct Option: (d)**

Explanation:

- All statements are correct.

Supplementary Notes:

- Ibrahim Adil Shah of Bijapur who ascended the throne in 1555 was the leading advocate of this policy. It is said that he entertained 30,000 Maratha auxiliaries (bargis) in his army, and showed great favour to the Marathas in the revenue system. He is supposed to have introduced Marathi in revenue accounts at all levels. Apart from increasing his favours to old families, a few other families such as the Bhonsales who had the family name of Ghorpade, the Dafles (or Chavans), etc., also rose to prominence in Bijapur as a result of the policy of winning over the Marathas to their side.

5. **Correct Option: (a)**

Explanation:

- **Statement 3 is incorrect:** The dissolution was caused by the frequent attacks from the Rashtrakutas.
- **Trap:** The Gurjara-Pratiharas were instrumental in containing Arab armies from Sind.

Supplementary Notes:

The Pratiharas

- The Pratiharas who ruled over Kanauj for a long time are also called Gurjara-Pratiharas. Most scholars consider that they originated from the Gurjaras who were pastoralists and fighters, like the Jats.
- They established a series of principalities in central and eastern Rajasthan. They clashed with the Rashtrakutas for the control of Malwa and Gujarat, and later for Kanauj which implied control of the upper Ganga valley.
- The Pratiharas who first had their capital at Bhinmal gained prominence under Nagabhatta I who offered stout resistance to the Arab rulers of Sind who were trying to encroach on Rajasthan, Gujarat, Punjab, etc. The Arabs made a big thrust towards Gujarat but were decisively defeated by the Chalukyan ruler of Gujarat in 738. Although small Arab incursions continued, the Arabs ceased to be a threat thereafter.
- The efforts of the early Pratihara rulers to extend their control over the upper Ganga valley and Malwa were defeated by the Rashtrakuta rulers Dhruva and Gopal III. In 790 and again in 806-07, the Rashtrakutas defeated the Pratiharas, and then withdrew to the Deccan, leaving the field free for the Palas. Perhaps the main interest of the Rashtrakutas was the domination of Malwa and Gujarat.

Mihir Bhoja

- The real founder the Pratihara empire and the greatest ruler of the Dynasty was Bhoja. He rebuilt the empire, and by about 836, he had recovered Kanauj which remained the capital of the Pratihara empire for almost a century.

- Bhoja tried to extend his sway in the east but he was defeated and checkmated by the Pala ruler, Devapala. He then turned towards central India and the Deccan and Gujarat. This led to a revival of the struggle with the Rashtrakutas. In a sanguinary battle on the bank of the Narmada, Bhoja was able to retain his control over considerable parts of Malwa, and some parts of Gujarat. But he could progress no further in the Deccan. Hence, he turned his attention to the north again.
- According to an inscription, his territories extended to the western side of the river Sutlej.
- Bhoja was a devotee of Vishnu, and adopted the title of 'Adivaraha' which has been found inscribed in some of his coins. He is sometimes called Mihir Bhoja to distinguish him from Bhoja Paramara of Ujjain, who ruled a little later. Bhoja probably died in about 885. He was succeeded by his son Mahendrapala I. He had only 2000 elephants trained for war, but the best cavalry of any king in the country.
- He is also identified with the king Juzr in the travel accounts of the 9th century Arab merchant, Sulaiman, who describes his great military power and riches. He was appreciated by the Arab writer for keeping his empire safe from robbers. He was called King Baura by another Arab traveller, Al-Masudi.
- Arab travellers tell us that the Pratihara rulers had the best cavalry in India. Import of horses from Central Asia and Arabia was an important item of India's trade at that time. Following the death of Devapala and the weakening of the Pala empire, Bhoja also extended his empire in the east.
- The Pratiharas were patrons of learning and literature. The great Sanskrit poet and dramatist, Rajasekhara, lived at the court of Mahipala, a grandson of Bhoja. The Pratihara also embellished Kanauj with many fine buildings and temples. During the eighth and ninth centuries, many Indian scholars went with embassies to the court of the caliph at Baghdad. These scholars introduced Indian sciences, especially mathematics, algebra and medicine to the Arab world.
- The Pratiharas were well-known for their hostility to the Arab rulers of Sind. Despite this, it seems that the movement of scholars and goods between India and West Asia continued even during this period.
- Between 915 and 918, the Rashtrakuta king, Indra III, again attacked Kannauj, and devastated the city. This weakened the Pratihara empire, and Gujarat probably passed into the hands of the Rashtrakutas, for al-Masudi tells us that the Pratihara empire had no access to the sea. The loss of Gujarat, which was the hub of the overseas trade and the main outlet for north Indian goods to West Asian countries, was another blow to the Pratiharas. Another Rashtrakuta ruler, Krishna III, invaded north India in about 963 and defeated the Pratihara ruler. This was followed by the rapid dissolution of the Pratihara empire.

6. **Correct Option: (b)**

Explanation:

- **Statement 1 is incorrect:** The Marathas were a peasant warrior group that rose to prominence during the rule in that region of the sultans of Bijapur and Ahmadnagar.

Supplementary Notes:

Rise of the Marathas

- Initially deriving from the western Deccan, the Marathas were a peasant warrior group that rose to prominence during the rule in that region of the sultans of Bijapur and Ahmadnagar.
- Several prominent leaders in the religious and social fields of Maharashtra inspired the people to unite by preaching faith and Bhakti in one God and by condemning the caste system which had divided the society.
- Elphinstone has observed in this regard. "They (Marathas) are all active, laboriousy hardy and preserving. If they have none of the pride and dignity of the Rajput's, they have none of their indolence or want of worldly wisdom too.
- The broken ranges of the hills provided natural forts and the people were inspired to regard these forts as their mother-the seats of their protection.
- The location of Maharashtra and its physical features helped in the rise of Maratha power. The large part of Maratha land is a plateau where the Marathas had to struggle hard for their existence. This made the Marathas courageous and hard working.

7. **Correct Option: (b)**

Explanation:

- **Statement 1 is incorrect:** The reign of Dharmapala was marked by the tripartite struggle for the control of Kanauj and north India.

Supplementary Notes:

Pala Empire

- The Pala Empire was founded by Gopala, probably in AD 750 when he was elected king by the notable men of the area to end the anarchy prevailing there.
- Gopala was not born in a high, much less a royal family; his father probably was a soldier. He unified Bengal under his control and even brought Magadha (Bihar) under his control.
- Gopala was succeeded in AD 770 by his son, Dharmapala, who ruled till AD 810.
- His reign was marked by a tripartite struggle between the Palas, the Pratiharas and the Rashtrakutas for the control of Kanauj and north India.

- The Pratihara ruler advanced upon Gaud (Bengal), but before a decision could be taken, the Pratihara ruler was defeated by the Rashtrakuta ruler, Dhruva, and was forced to seek refuge in the deserts of Rajasthan. Dhruva then returned to the Deccan.
- This left the field free for Dharmapala who occupied Kanauj and held a grand darbar which was attended by vassal rulers from Punjab, eastern Rajasthan, etc.
- Sanskrit scholars were also patronized by the Pala kings. Gaudapada composed Agama Shastra during the time of the Palas.

8. Correct Option: (c)

Explanation:

- **Statement 1 is incorrect:** Rajputs states came into existence after breakup of Pratiharas in North India.
- **Statement 2 is incorrect:** They also patronized Jainism.

Supplementary Notes:

The Rajput states

- New section of rulers arose i.e Rajputs after the breakup of the Pratihara empire in North India.
- Most Imp: Gahadavalas of Kanauj, the Paramaras of Malwa and the Chauhans of Ajmer.
- Most of the Rajputs were the champions of the Hinduism, some also patronised Jainism.
- Gave rich donations and grants of land to the Brahamanas and the temples.
- The period after the 8th century and between the 10th and 12th century may be regarded as marking a climax period for the temple building in North India.
- The Nagara Style of temple building was most famous.
- Main centers of construction was Deccan and North India.

9. Correct Option: (d)

Explanation:

- All statements are correct.

Supplementary Notes:

Causes of the Defeat of the Rajputs

- They were defeated in short span of 15 years.
- Superiority of the Turks was more social and organisational.
- Growth of feudalism was the main reason for the weakened administrative position of India.
- Rulers had to depend more on various chiefs who rarely acted in coordination.
- On the other hand, the tribal structure of the Turks and the growth of Iqta and Khalisa system enabled the Turks to maintain large standing armies which could be kept for long time in the field.
- Perhaps, the Rajputs also lacked the mounted archers or heavy armed cavalary.
- In terms of personal bravery or fighting spirit, Rajputs were no way inferior than the Turks. Caste was certainly divisive but it did not prevent people from the lower castes from taking to soldiering.
- But they lacked in organisation and leadership.
- Rajputs also did not take any offensive action and try to push the Turks from the strategic lands they had occupied.
- Thus, they allowed Afghanistan and Punjab to remain under the hostile hands.

10. Correct Option: (d)

Explanation:

- **Statement 1 is incorrect:** Despite its aristocratic character, the nobility did provide an avenue of promotion and distinction to persons drawn from the lower section of society.
- **Statement 2 is incorrect:** Of the Hindu nobles, the Marathas formed more than half during Aurangzeb's reign.

Supplementary Notes:

Nobility under the Mughals

- Socially and economically, the Mughal nobility formed a privileged class. Theoretically, Mughal nobility were open to everyone. In practice, persons belonging to aristocratic families, whether they were Indians or foreigners, had a decided advantage.
- The bulk of the Mughal nobles were drawn from the homeland of the Mughals – Turan and from its neighboring areas, Tajikistan, Iran, etc., in the beginning.
- Babur tried to win the leading Afghan nobles to his side but the tussle between the Mughals and the Afghans continued in Bihar and Bengal even under Akbar. But from the times of Jahangir, more Afghans began to be recruited in the nobility.
- From the time of Akbar, Hindus also began to be inducted into the nobility on a regular basis. The largest section among them consisted of the Rajputs.
- The Rajputs who were recruited to the nobility were either hereditary rajas or belonged to aristocratic families related to or allied to the raja. Thus, their incorporation into the nobility strengthened its aristocratic character. Despite this, the nobility did provide an avenue of promotion and distinction to persons drawn from the lower section of society. This way, many kayasthas and khatris were employed at various levels in the central and provincial governments. A few of them were elevated to the position of a noble.
- Under Jahangir and Shah Jahan, the bulk of the nobles already consisted of those who had been born

in India. Simultaneously, the proportion of Afghans, Indian Muslims (Hindustanis), and Hindus in the nobility continued to rise. A new section among the Hindus which entered the nobility during the period were the Marathas. Jahangir was the first monarch who realized that the Marathas were 'the hub of affairs in the Deccan', and tried to win them over to his side. The policy was continued by Shah Jahan. Of the Hindu nobles, the Marathas formed more than half during Aurangzeb's reign.

- The Mughal nobility had a number of unusual features. Though often divided on ethnic lines, it formed a composite ruling class representing different regions and religions.
- It also tried to promote a composite culture by extending patronage to painters, musicians, poets, both Persian and Hindavi, and to scholars.
- Though essentially feudal in character, since land was its main source of income, it had developed many characteristics of a bureaucracy. It was also becoming more commercial and money-minded.

11. Correct Option: (a)

Explanation:

- **Statement 1 is incorrect:** The Third Battle of Panipat was fought during the regime of Balaji Baji Rao I/ Nana Sahib I.

Supplementary Notes:

The Office of the Peshwa

- The word 'Peshwa' probably originated in Persian, meaning 'foremost', and was introduced in Deccan by the Muslim rulers. Duties of a Peshwa were equal to that of a Prime Minister.

Balaji Vishwanath Bhatt (c.1713–1719 CE)

- He is known in history for making the post of the Peshwa hereditary.
- He got certain rights from the then Mughal Emperor, Farrukh Siyar, such as the recognition of Shahu as the Maratha king and the permission to collect chauth and sardeshmukhi from the six Mughal provinces of the Deccan, including the Carnatic and Mysore.

Baji Rao I (c.1720–1740 CE)

- He was the most famous of all nine Peshwas and also known as "Thorale", meaning 'Elder' Baji Rao.
- During his lifetime, he never lost a battle and formulated the policy of Northward expansion.
- He preached and popularised the idea of Hindu-padpadshahi (Hindu Empire) to secure the support of the Hindu chiefs against the common enemy, the Mughals.
- In c.1722 CE, he captured Salsette and Bassein from the Portuguese.
- He shifted the administrative capital from Satara to Pune in c.1728 CE.

Balaji Baji Rao I/Nana Sahib I (c.1740–1761 CE)

- Marathas fought the Third Battle of Panipat (c.1761 CE) when Ahmad Shah Abdali invaded India, in which the Marathas were defeated.

Sawai Madhav Rao (c.1774–1795 CE)

- He was merely 40 days old when crowned as Peshwa. The empire was managed by Nana Phadnavis.
- At the famous battle of Talegaon (c.1776 CE), Nana Phadnavis defeated the British and the famous treaty of Purandhar (c.1776 CE) and the treaty of Salbai (c.1782 CE) were signed. The treaty virtually restored the status quo except the fact that the English retained Salsette.

Baji Rao II (c.1796–1818 CE)

- Weakest and most incompetent Peshwa who signed the humiliating Treaty of Bassein with the British (c. 1802 CE), which gave the British effective control of not only the Maratha region but also of Deccan and western India.
- He was defeated by the East India Company in the Third Anglo– Maratha War in c.1818 CE after which the Peshwa's territory in central Maharashtra was annexed to the British East India Company's Bombay province and he was pensioned off.
- Nana Sahib (alias Dhondu Pant) was the adopted son of Baji Rao II and he participated in the famous Revolt of 1857.

12. Correct Option: (b)

Explanation:

- **Statement 2 is incorrect:** Under Shivaji, the offices of council of ministers were neither hereditary nor permanent.
- **Statement 4 is incorrect:** 'Sardeshmukhi' was paid on those lands on which the Marathas claimed hereditary rights whereas 'Chauth' was paid to the Marathas in order to avoid the Maratha raids.

Supplementary Notes:

Shivaji's Administration

- The administrative system of the Marathas was very much influenced by the administrative system of the Mughals and the Deccani states (adopted by Malik Amber of Ahmednagar and Mahmud Gawan of Bahmani Kingdom). The Maratha Kingdom was known as Swarajya or Mulk-e-Kadim.
- The king was the pivot of the government, who was assisted by a council of ministers called the Ashtapradhan.
- Under Shivaji, these offices were neither hereditary nor permanent and were also frequently transferred.
  - Peshwa – Finance and General Administration

- Sar-i-Naubat or Senapati – Military Commander
- Amatya/Majumdar – Accountant General
- Waqenavis – Intelligence and Police
- Surnavis or Chitnis or Sachiv – General Secretary, who also overlooked official correspondence
- Sumant/Dabir – Master of Ceremonies and Foreign Affairs
- Nyayadish – Justice
- Pandit Rao – Charities and Ecclesiastical Affairs

- The Marathas were famous for guerrilla warfare, along with the use of an innovative weapon, the Bagh naka.
- At the time of exigencies, peasants also functioned as part-time soldiers as they used to work for eight months in the field and performed war duty for four months.
- Shivaji also built a powerful navy.
- Chauth and Sardeshmukhi were two major sources of revenue:
  - Chauth: One fourth (1/4th of the land revenue) paid to the Marathas in order to avoid the Maratha raids.
  - Sardeshmukhi was an additional levy of ten percent, that is, 1/10 of standard land revenue on those lands on which the Marathas claimed hereditary rights.

13. **Correct Option: (b)**

Explanation:

- **Statement 1 is incorrect:** The Chahamanas of Shakambhari are popularly known as the Chauhans of Sambhar.
- **Statement 2 is incorrect:** The Chandellas of Bundelkhand trace their descent to a mythical ancestor named Chandratreya, born of the moon.

Supplementary Notes:

Rajput Clans

The Chahamanas/Chauhans

- The Chahamanas of Shakambhari, colloquially known as the Chauhans of Sambhar, ruled in parts of the present-day Rajasthan and its neighbouring areas between 7th and 11th centuries CE.
- They were the most prominent ruling family of the Chahamana clan.
- The Chahamanas originally had their capital at Shakambari, which is identical to modern Sambhar near Jaipur in the Sapadalaksa country (part of present-day Rajasthan).
- However, the later rulers moved the capital to Ajmer, and for this reason, they are also known as the Chahamanas (Chauhans) of Ajmer.
- They were originally feudatories of the Pratiharas and assumed independence during the reign of King Simharaja.

The Chandellas of Bundelkhand

- The Chandellas of Bundelkhand trace their descent to a mythical ancestor named Chandratreya, born of the moon.
- The Chandellas initially ruled as feudatories of the Gurjara-Pratiharas of Kannauj, and were involved in conflicts with the Pratiharas, the Palas, and the Kalachuris of Chedi (who bordered the Chandellas on the south).
- The Chandellas are well-known for their art and architecture, most notably for the fully developed Nagara-style temples at their original capital Khajuraho.
- The Lakshmana Temple (c. 930–950 CE), the Vishvanatha Temple (c. 999-1002 CE), and the Kandariya Mahadeva Temple (c. 1030 CE) were constructed during the reigns of Chandella rulers Yashovarman, Dhanga, and Vidyadhara, respectively.
- They also commissioned a number of water bodies, palaces and forts at other places, including their strongholds of Jayapura-Durga (modern Ajaigarh), Kalanjara (modern Kalinjar), and their later capital Mahotsava-Nagara (modern Mahoba).
- In the first quarter of the 9th century CE, the dynasty was founded by Nannuka, who was the ruler of a small kingdom and established his capital at Kharjjuravahaka (Khajuraho).

The Paramaras of Malwa

- The Paramaras of Malwa were originally based in the Mount Abu area of Rajasthan.
- According to tradition, the sage Vishwamitra stole Vashishtha's kama dhenu (wish-granting cow).
- In order to retrieve his cow, Vashishtha performed a sacrifice on Mount Abu and out of this sacrificial fire, emerged a hero who seized his cow and was named Paramara (slayer of enemies).
- He was thereafter crowned the king.
- The earliest known Paramara king, Upendra, was believed to be of the lineage of this hero.
- There are several branches of this dynasty, though the main branch ruled at Malwa, with its capital at Dhara (modern Dhar, MP).
- The c. 949 CE Harsola copper-plates issued by the Paramara king, Siyaka II, establish that the early Paramara rulers were feudatories of the Rashtrakutas of Manyakheta, and were probably established in the 10th century CE.
- The Paramara power rose and declined several times as a result of their struggles with the Chalukyas of Gujarat, the Chalukyas of Kalyani, the Kalachuris of Tripuri, and other neighbouring kingdoms.
- The later Paramaras moved their capital to Mandapa-Durga (now Mandu) after Dhara was sacked multiple times by their enemies.

- Malwa enjoyed a great level of political and cultural prestige under the Paramaras.
- The Paramaras were well-known for their patronage to poets and scholars and Bhoja was himself a renowned scholar. Most of the Paramara kings were Shaivites and commissioned several Shiva temples, although they also patronized Jain scholors.

14. Correct Option: (d)

Explanation:

- **Statement 1 is incorrect:** Treaty of Purander was signed in which Shivaji had to surrender 23 forts to the Mughals out of the 35 forts held by him. Hence, it was at Shivaji's disadvantage.
- **Statement 2 is incorrect:** Shahu supported the execution of Farukkh Siyar.

Supplementary Notes:

Shivaji and the Rise of Marathas

- In 1654, Shivaji captured forts in the Western Ghats and along the Konkan coast. Shivaji and his elder brother defeated invading armies of Adil Shah.
- Battle of Pratapgarh (c.1659) was fought between Afzal Khan (represented Adil Shah of Bijapur) and Shivaji, in which Shivaji killed Afzal Khan.
- Battle of Pavankhind (c.1660) was fought between Siddi Johar (represented Adil Shah of Bijapur) and Shivaji. A truce was made between Shivaji and Adil Shah acknowledging and formally recognising the independence of Shivaji's kingdom.
- In c.1663, Shivaji carried out a night attack on the camp of Shaista Khan (a governor of Shivaji), injuring Khan and killing his son.
- In c.1664, Shivaji sacked the rich port of Surat, an important Mughal trading city.
- Enraged Aurangzeb sent Raja Jai Singh of Amber and Diler Khan to destroy the Maratha power. They made elaborate preparations and succeeded in besieging the Purander fort.
- Shivaji opened negotiations with Jai Singh and the Treaty of Purander was signed in c.1665. According to this treaty, Shivaji had to surrender 23 forts to the Mughals out of the 35 forts held by him, and the remaining 12 forts were to be left to Shivaji on the condition of service and loyalty to the Mughal empire.
- He defeated Mughals in the Battle of Salher (c.1672) and crowned himself at Raigarh and assumed the title of 'Maharaja Chattrapati'.
- Shahu's period was marked by the ascendancy of a lineage of Chitpavan Brahmin ministers, who held the title of Peshwa (chief minister) and virtually came to control central authority.
- In c.1719, Shahu, under the advice of Peshwa Balaji Vishwanath, assisted the Saiyyad brothers in the execution of Farukkh Siyar and got his mother released. Soon after, he declared the independence of Maratha land.

15. Correct Option: (b)

Explanation:

- **Pair 2 is incorrectly matched:** Jaunpur – Uttar Pradesh

Supplementary Notes:

Bahamani Kingdom

- Bahamani and Vijayanagar, both these kingdoms were founded by officers of the Sultanate who had rebelled against the Sultan.
- Hasan led a rebellion against the Sultan and proclaimed the independence of the Bahmani kingdom.
- He took the title of Bahman Shah.
- The Bahmani kingdom included the whole of the northern Deccan up to the river Krishna.
- So, present region include Maharashtra, Telangana, Andhra Pradesh and part of Karnataka.

Jaunpur

- Jaunpur and Bengal, these two were the important regions of the Eastern India.
- Both of these were founded by governors of the Delhi Sultan who had later rebelled against the Sultanate.
- Jaunpur was ruled by the Sharqi kings. He had a great ambition i.e., to capture Delhi, which never happened.
- Later, Jaunpur became an important centre of Hindi literature and learning.
- Bengal was ruled by kings of different races; however, largely they were Turks and Afghans. All these kings were patrons of local culture and encouraged the use of the Bengali language.
- Jaunpur was located in present day Uttar Pradesh.

Vijaynagar

- Vijayanagara Kingdom was founded by two brothers Harihara and Bukka.
- In 1336, Harihara and Bukka conquered the territory of the Hoysala (i.e., modern Mysore State) and proclaimed themselves as an independent ruler of the Vijayanagara Kingdom.
- Harihara and Bukka made Hastinavati (modern Hampi) their capital.
- Krishnadeva Raya won the Gajapati kingdom in present day Orissa and extended the Vijayanagara empire to that region as well.
- Krishnadeva Raya defeated the Deccan Sultans in the battle of Diwani. He, then, invaded Raichur Doab (between Tungabhadra and Krishna river, known for its fertile soil) confronting Sultan of Bijapur, Ismail Adil Shah. He also captured Bidar.
- Vijayanagar Empire was spread in states of Andhra Pradesh, Karnatka, Tamil Nadu and parts of Kerala and Orrisa.

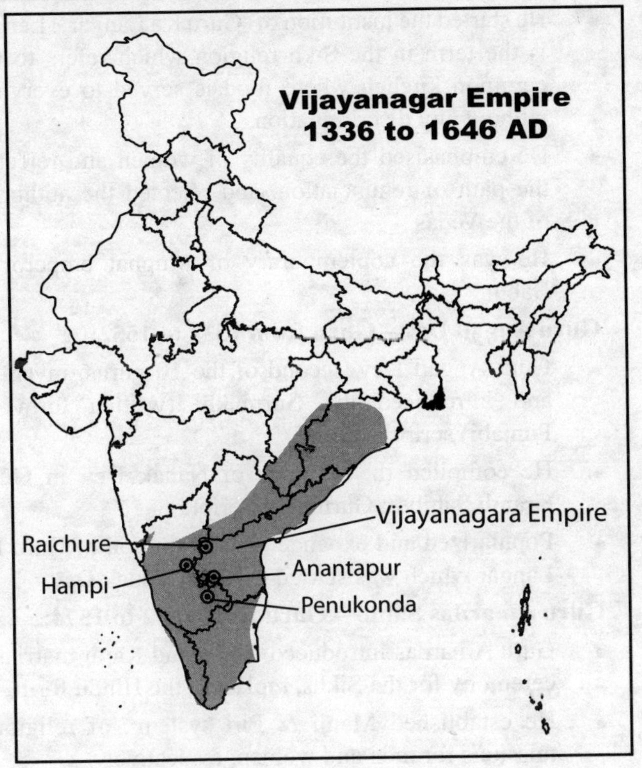

Map: 1.5.1

16. **Correct Option: (c)**

Explanation:

- **Statement 1 is incorrect:** Despite its aristocratic character, the nobility did provide an avenue of promotion and distinction to persons drawn from the lower section of society.
- **Statement 2 is incorrect:** Of the Hindu nobles, the Marathas formed more than half during Aurangzeb's reign.

Supplementary Notes:

Nobility under the Mughals

- Socially and economically, the Mughal nobility formed a privileged class. Theoretically, the doors of the Mughal nobility were open to everyone. In practice, persons belonging to aristocratic families, whether they were Indians or foreigners, had a decided advantage.
- To begin with, the bulk of the Mughal nobles were drawn from the homeland of the Mughals – Turan and from its neighboring areas, Tajikistan, Iran, etc.
- Babur tried to win the leading Afghan nobles to his side but the tussle between the Mughals and the Afghans continued in Bihar and Bengal even under Akbar. But from the time of Jahangir, more Afghans began to be recruited in the nobility.
- From the time of Akbar, Hindus also began to be inducted into the nobility on a regular basis. The largest section among them consisted of the Rajputs.
- The Rajputs who were recruited to the nobility were either hereditary Rajas or belonged to aristocratic families related to or allied to the Raja. Thus, their incorporation into the nobility strengthened its aristocratic character. Despite this, the nobility did provide an avenue of promotion and distinction to persons drawn from the lower sections of society. Thus, many Kayasthas and Khatris were employed at various levels in the central and provincial governments. A few of them were elevated to the position of a noble.
- Under Jahangir and Shah Jahan, the bulk of thc nobles already consisted of those who had been born in India. Simultaneously, the proportion of Afghans, Indian Muslims (Hindustanis), and Hindus in the nobility continued to rise. A new section among the Hindus which entered the nobility during the period were the Marathas. Jahangir was the first monarch who realized that the Marathas were 'the hub of affairs in the Deccan', and tried to win them over to his side. The policy was continued by Shah Jahan. Of the Hindu nobles, the Marathas formed more than half during Aurangzeb's reign.
- The Mughal nobility had a number of unusual features. Though often divided on ethnic lines, it formed a composite ruling class representing different regions and religions.
- It also tried to promote a composite culture by extending patronage to painters, musicians, poets, both Persian and Hindavi, and to scholars.
- Though essentially feudal in character, since land was its main source of income, it had developed many characteristics of a bureaucracy. It was also becoming more commercial and money-minded.

17. **Correct Option: (a)**

Explanation:

- **Statement 2 is incorrect:** In this battle, the Marathas defeated the Nizam.

Supplementary Notes:

Information regarding the Battle of Palkhed

- The Maratha-Nizam relations mark the most important phase in the history of Maharashtra during the 18th and 19th centuries because as the Subhedar of the Deccan, the founder of the ex-Hyderabad State, Nizam-ul-mulk Asaf Jah controlled more than 3/4th of the territory of the present Maharashtra.
- The Battle of Palkhed was fought on February 28, 1728 at the village of Palkhed, near Aurangabad between the Peshwa Baji Rao I and the Nizam-ul-mulk, Asaf Jah wherein, the Marathas defeated the Nizam.
- The battle plan was set by the withdrawal of Baji Rao's army from the southern reaches of the Maratha empire during May 1727. This was followed by

Shahu breaking off negotiations with the Nizam-ul-Mulk about restoration of the chauth.

- By the treaty of Munji Shivagaon, the Nizam was forced to make certain concessions.

18. Correct Option: (d)

Explanation:

- All statements are correct.

Supplementary Notes:

- The Battle of Pratapgarh (1659) was fought between Afzal Khan and Shivaji.
- Alamgir II grieved the death of Alivardi Khan, the famous Nawab of Bengal, who annually pledged 5 million dams to the imperial court. His successor Siraj-ud-Daula was recognised as the next Nawab of Bengal, but he faced internal rivals who refused to consider the Firman granted by Alamgir II to Siraj-ud-Daula. These internal conflicts would lead Siraj-ud-Daula to hastily annex Calcutta from the English East India Company, without the permission of the Mughal Emperor Alamgir II and Salabat Jung. Siraj-ud-Daula was quickly defeated by Clive who recaptured Calcutta and defeated Siraj-ud-Daula during the Battle of Plassey in the year 1757.
- After the annihilation of his entire army, Siraj-ud-Daula fled and was killed by the forces of the treacherous Mir Jafar. The deceased Siraj-ud-Daula's pretensions were criticised in the Mughal imperial court by Ghulam Husain Tabatabai, and Alamgir II refused to recognise Mir Jafar as the next Nawab of Bengal. In response to the imperial courts' decision, Mir Jafar, thus, consolidated an alliance with the manipulative Imad-ul-Mulk against the imperial family.
- On 1 March 1776, the Treaty of Purandar was signed between Nana Phadnavis, a Maratha minister and the Calcutta Council of the East India Company.

19. Correct Option: (c)

Explanation:

- **Statement 2 is incorrect:** He compiled the writings of Nanak Dev in Guru Granth Sahib in Gurmukhi Script.

Supplementary Notes:

Sikh Gurus

- The era of the ten gurus of Sikhism spans from the birth of Nanak Dev in 1469, through the life of Guru Gobind Singh. At the time of Guru Gobind Singh's death in 1708, he passed the title of Guru to the Sikh scripture, Guru Granth.

Guru Nanak Dev – Guru from 1469 to 1539:

- Guru Nanak Dev, first of the 10 gurus, founded the Sikh faith, introducing the concept of one God.
- He started the institution of 'Guru Ka Langar'. Langar is the term in the Sikh religion which refers to the common kitchen where food is served to everyone without any discrimination.
- He emphasised the equality of women and rejected the path of renunciation, and rejected the authority of the Vedas.
- He was the contemporary of Mughal emperor – Babur.

Guru Angad Dev – Guru from 1539 to 1552:

- Guru Angad Dev, second of the 10 gurus, invented and introduced the Gurmukhi (written form of Punjabi) script.
- He compiled the writings of Nanak Dev in Guru Granth Sahib in Gurmukhi Script.
- Popularized and expanded the institution of Guru ka Langar which was started by Guru Nanak Dev.

Guru Amardas Sahib – Guru from 1552 to 1574:

- Guru Amardas introduced the Anand Karaj marriage ceremony for the Sikhs, replacing the Hindu form.
- He established Manji & Piri system of religious missions for men and women, respectively.
- He strengthened the tradition of Guru Ka Langar.
- He also completely abolished amongst the Sikhs, the custom of Sati and purdah system.
- He was the contemporary of Mughal emperor – Akbar.

Guru Ram Das – Guru from 1574 to 1581:

- Guru Ram Das, fourth of the 10 gurus, founded the city of Amritsar.
- He started the construction of the famous Golden Temple at Amritsar, the holy city of the Sikhs.
- He requested the Muslim Sufi, Mian Mir to lay the cornerstone of the Harmandir Sahib.

Guru Arjan Dev – Guru from 1581 to 1606:

- He compiled the Adi Granth, the scriptures of the Sikhs.
- He completed construction of Sri Darbar Sahib also known as Golden Temple in Amritsar.
- He founded the town of Tarn Taran Sahib near Goindwal Sahib.
- He became the first great martyr in Sikh history when Emperor Jahangir ordered his execution. Thus, he was hailed as Shaheedan-de-Sartaj (The crown of martyrs).

Guru Har Gobind Sahib – Guru from 1606 to 1644:

- He was the son of Guru Arjan Dev and was known as a "soldier saint".
- He organised a small army and became the first Guru to take up arms to defend the faith.

- He waged wars against Mughal rulers Jahangir and Shah Jahan.

Guru Har Rai Sahib – Guru from 1644 to 1661:

- Though he was a man of peace, he never disbanded the armed sikh warriors who were earlier maintained by Guru Har Gobind.
- He gave shelter to Dara Shikoh, the eldest son of Mughal Ruler Shah Jahan, who was later persecuted by Aurangazeb.
- He cautiously avoided conflict with Emperor Aurangzeb and devoted his efforts to missionary work.

Guru Har Krishan Sahib – Guru from 1661 to 1664:

- Guru Har Krishan was the youngest of the Gurus. He was installed as Guru at the age of five.
- He was contemporary of Aurangzeb and summoned to Delhi by him under framed charges of anti-Islamic blasphemy.

Guru Tegh Bahadur Sahib – Guru from 1665 to 1675:

- He established the town of Anandpur.
- He opposed the forced conversion of the Hindu Kashmiri Pandits by Mughal ruler Aurangzeb and he was consequently persecuted for this.

Guru Gobind Singh Sahib – Guru from 1675 to 1708:

- He became Guru after the martyrdom of his father Guru Tegh Bahadur.
- He created the Khalsa in 1699, changing the Sikhs into a saint-soldier order for protecting themselves.
- Last Sikh Guru in human form and he passed the Guruship of the Sikhs to the Guru Granth Sahib.

20. Correct Option: (b)

Supplementary Notes:

Baji Rao I (1720-1740)

- Baji Rao was the eldest son of Balaji Viswanath. He succeeded his father as Peshwa at the young age of twenty. The Maratha power reached its zenith under him.
- He initiated the system of confederacy among the Maratha chiefs. Under this system, each Maratha chief was assigned a territory which could be administered autonomously. As a result, many Maratha families became prominent and established their authority in different parts of India.

CONCEPT REVISION

Here is the list of concepts that have been covered as part of the previous exercise. Revise and Self-reflect on your concepts you covered.

- Shivaji's Administration ☐
- Tripartite struggle for Kannauj ☐
- Policy of Ibrahim Adil Shah of Bijapur ☐
- Pala Empire ☐
- Rajputs ☐
- Gujaras & Pratiharas ☐
- Battle of Palkhed ☐
- Sikh Gurus ☐

☐☐☐

5. ECONOMIC CONDITIONS OF MEDIEVAL INDIA

5.1 ECONOMIC CONDITIONS AND REFORM IN SULTANATE PERIOD

QUESTIONS

1. **Consider the following statements regarding the administration under Sher Shah Suri:**
   1. The land revenue was one-third of the average produce and it was paid in cash or crop.
   2. He introduced new silver coins called "Dam".

   Which of the above statements is/are correct?

   (a) 1 only (b) 2 only
   (c) Both 1 and 2 (d) Neither 1 nor 2

2. **Which among the following was a new department of agriculture started by Muhammad-bin-Tughlaq?**

   (a) Diwan-i-Risalat (b) Diwan-i-Ashraf
   (c) Diwan-i-Kohi (d) Diwan-i-Mustkharaz

3. **Which of the following is/are the contributions of the Suri Dynasty?**
   1. The kingdom was divided into many administrative units called Sarkars.
   2. Sher Shah introduced mixed metal coins which were called Dams.
   3. The famous Hindi work Padmavat by Malik Muhammad Jayasi was written during his reign.
   4. The land revenue was one-third of the average produce and it was paid in cash or crop.

   Select the correct answer using the code given below:

   (a) 3 only (b) 3 and 4 only
   (c) 1, 3 and 4 only (d) 1, 2 and 4 only

4. **Consider the following statements regarding Sultanate Period:**
   1. To gain the throne in the Sultanate period, military power was the deciding factor and noble's opinion was a neglected element.
   2. Oil pressing and making of jaggery were the main village industries in Sultanate Period.

   Which of the above statements is/are incorrect?

   (a) 1 only (b) 2 only
   (c) Both 1 and 2 (d) Neither 1 nor 2

5. **Consider the following statements regarding peasants and rural gentry of Delhi sultanate.**
   1. Muqaddams and khuts misused their offices to force the ordinary peasants to pay their share of the land revenue also.
   2. Alauddin Khilji took stern action against muqaddams and khuts and curtailed many of their privileges.

Which of the above statements is/are correct?

(a) 1 only (b) 2 only

(c) Both 1 and 2 (d) Neither 1 nor 2

6. Consider the following statements regarding trade and industry under Delhi sultanate:

1. Currency system was strong and based on silver tanka and copper dirham.
2. Cambay in Gujarat was famous for raw silk and fine cotton cloth.
3. The production of textiles was also improved by the introduction of the spinning-wheel.

Which of the above statements is/are correct?

(a) 1 and 2 only (b) 1 and 3 only

(c) 2 and 3 only (d) 1, 2 and 3

7. Which of the following pairs are correctly matched?

1. Taquavi - Agricultural loans
2. Khams - 1/5 of the war booty
3. Kharaj - 1/10 of the produce of the land

Select the correct answer using the codes given below:

(a) 1 and 2 only (b) 2 and 3 only

(c) 1 and 3 only (d) All of the above

8. Consider the following statements:

1. Khuts and muqaddams were the revenue collectors during the reign of Alauddin Khilji.
2. Alauddin was the first monarch in the Sultanate who insisted that in the doab, land revenue would be assessed on the basis of measuring the land under cultivation.

Which of the above statements is/are correct?

(a) 1 only (b) 2 only

(c) Both 1 and 2 (d) Neither 1 nor 2

9. With reference to Delhi Sultanate's socio-economic system, consider the following statements:

1. Delhi Sultans classified lands as Iqta, Khalisa and Inam lands.
2. Unlike the Mughals, Delhi Sultans gave equal opportunities to Hindu nobles to occupy high positions in the government.
3. Jizya was collected as part of land tax and not as a separate tax during this period.

Which of the above statements is/are incorrect?

(a) 1 only (b) 2 only

(c) 1 and 3 only (d) 2 and 3 only

10. Consider the following statements with respect to the socio-economic system during the Sultanate period:

1. Khalisa was the land under the direct control of the Sultan.
2. Zimmis were the Turkish nobles who were positioned at high places in the Sultanate rule.

Which of the above statements is/are correct?

(a) 1 only (b) 2 only

(c) Both 1 and 2 (d) Neither 1 nor 2

11. Match the following listed taxes imposed by Firoz Shah Tughlaq:

Tax	Purpose
A. Sharb	1. Imposed on 10% of produce
B. Kharaj	2. 20% spoils of war
C. Zakat	3. Alms for Muslims
D. Khams	4. Irrigation tax

Select the correct answer using the codes given below:

	A	B	C	D
(a)	2	3	4	1
(b)	4	2	1	3
(c)	2	4	3	1
(d)	4	1	3	2

SOLUTIONS

1. Correct Option: (c)

Explanation:

- Both statements are correct.

Supplementary Notes:

Sher Shah Suri (1540-1545)

- Although his rule lasted for five years, he organised a brilliant administrative system. The central government consisted of several departments. The king was assisted by four important ministers:
    - Diwan-i-Wizarat – also called as Wazir, in charge of Revenue and Finance.
    - Diwan-i-Ariz – in charge of the Army.
    - Diwan-i-Rasalat – Foreign Minister.
    - Diwan-i-Insha – Minister for Communications.
- Sher Shah's Empire was divided into forty-seven sarkars.
- Chief Shiqdar (law and order) and Chief Munsif (judge) were the two officers in charge of the administration in each sarkar. Each sarkar was divided into several Parganas. Shiqdar (military officer), Amin (land revenue), Fotedar (treasurer) Karkuns (accountants) were in charge of the administration of each Pargana.
- There were also many administrative units called iqtas.
- The land revenue administration was well organised under Sher Shah. A land survey was carefully done. All cultivable lands were classified into three classes – good, middle, and bad. The state's share was one-

third of the average production and it was paid in cash or crop.

- His revenue reforms increased the revenue of the state. Sher Shah introduced new silver coins called "Dam" and they were in circulation till 1835.
- The military administration was also eifficiently reorganized and Sher Shah borrowed many ideas like the branding of horses from Alauddin Khalji.
- Sher Shah remained a pious Muslim and generally tolerant of other religions. He employed Hindus in important offices. He was also a patron of art and architecture. He built a new city on the banks of the river Yamuna near Delhi.
- Now the old fort called Purana Qila and its mosque is alone surviving. He also built a Mausoleum at Sasaram, which is considered as one of the masterpieces of Indian architecture.
- Sher Shah also patronized the learned men. Malik Muhammad Jayasi wrote the famous Hindi work Padmavat during his reign.

2. Correct Option: (c)

Supplementary Notes:

- The Delhi Sultanate – The Tughlaq Dynasty: Muhammad bin Tughlaq created a department of agriculture known as Diwan-i-Kohi . The main object of the department was to increase the land under cultivation.

3. Correct Option: (c)

Explanation:

- **Statement 2 is incorrect:** Sher Shah introduced new silver coins which were called Dams.

Supplementary Notes:

Sher Shah Suri (1540-1545)

- Although his rule lasted for five years, he organized a brilliant administrative system. The central government consisted of several departments. The king was assisted by four important ministers:
  - Diwan-i-Wizarat – also called as Wazir, in charge of Revenue and Finance
  - Diwan-i-Ariz – in charge of Army.
  - Diwan-i-Rasalat – Foreign Minister.
  - Diwan-i-Insha – Minister for Communications.
- Sher Shah's Empire was divided into forty seven sarkars.
- Chief Shiqdar (law and order) and Chief Munsif (judge) were the two officers in charge of the administration in each sarkar. Each sarkar was divided into several Parganas. Shiqdar (military officer), Amin (land revenue), Fotedar (treasurer) Karkuns (accountants) were in charge of the administration of each Pargana.
- There were also many administrative units called Iqtas.
- The land revenue administration was well organized under Sher Shah. Land survey was carefully done. All cultivable lands were classified into three classes – good, middle and bad. The state's share was one third of the average produce and it was paid in cash or crop.
- His revenue reforms increased the revenue of the state. Sher Shah introduced new silver coins called "Dam" and they were in circulation till 1835.
- The military administration was also efficiently reorganized and Sher Shah borrowed many ideas like the branding of horses from Alauddin Khalji.
- Sher Shah remained a pious Muslim and generally tolerant towards other religions. He employed Hindus in important offices. He was also a patron of art and architecture. He built a new city on the banks of the river Yamuna near Delhi. Now, the old fort called Purana Qila and its mosque is alone surviving. He also built a Mausoleum at Sasaram, which is considered as one of the masterpieces of Indian architecture.
- Sher Shah also patronized learned men. Malik Muhammad Jayasi wrote the famous Hindi work Padmavat during his reign.
- Sher Shah introduced new silver coins which were called Dams.

4. Correct Option: (a)

Explanation:

- **Statement 1 is incorrect:** Nobles opinion was also an important factor for gaining the throne.

Supplementary Notes:

- Though military strength was the main factor in succession to the throne. However, public opinion could not be ignored.
- Iltutmish no doubt was a great military leader, but he had the support of the Delhi nobles against Aibak's nomination of his son Aram Shah to the throne of Delhi.
- For fear of public opinion, the Khaljis could not dare to enter Delhi for a long time after deposing the successors of Balban, and built a new town called Siri.
- There were many village industries in the Sultanate Period such as oil-pressing, making of jaggery, weaving, and dyeing of clothes.

5. Correct Option: (c)

Explanation:

- Both statements are correct.

Supplementary Notes:

Peasants and Rural Gentry of Delhi Sultanate

- As before, peasants formed the overwhelming majority of the population.

- There were recurring famines and wars in different parts of the country, and these added to the hardships of the peasants.
- All the peasants did not live at the level of subsistence.
- Apart from the village artisans and share-croppers, there was a more prosperous section of people, who were owner cultivators of their lands.
- They were considered the original settlers of the village, and dominated the village panchayat.
- The village headmen (muqaddams) and smaller landlords (khuts) enjoyed a higher standard of life.
- In addition to their own holdings, they held lands for which they paid revenue at concessional rates.
- Sometimes, they misused their offices to force the ordinary peasants to pay their share of the land revenue also.
- These people were prosperous enough to ride on costly Arabi and Iraqi horses, wear fine clothes, and behave like members of the upper classes.
- Alauddin Khilji took stern action against them and curtailed many of their privileges. Even then they continued to enjoy a standard of life higher than that of the ordinary peasants.
- It seems that after the death of Alauddin, they were able to resume their own ways.

6. **Correct Option: (b)**

Explanation:

- **Statement 2 is incorrect:** Sonargaon in Bengal was famous for raw silk and fine cotton cloth (called muslin later on).

Supplementary Notes:

Trade, Industry and Merchants under Delhi Sultanate

- With the consolidation of the Delhi Sultanate and the improvement of communications, and the establishment of a sound currency system based on the silver tanka and the copper dirham, there was a definite growth of trade in the country.
- This was marked by the growth of towns and town life. Ibn Battuta calls Delhi the largest city in the eastern part of the Islamic world.
- He says that Daulatabad (Deogir) government, and economic and social life equalled Delhi in size – an index of the growth of trade between the north and the south.
- The other important cities of the times were Lahore and Multan in the northwest, Kara and Lakhnauti in the east, and Anhilwara (Patan) and Cambay (Khambayat) in the west.
- Bengal and the towns in Gujarat were famous for their fine quality fabrics.
- Cambay in Gujarat was famous for textiles and for gold and silver work.
- Sonargaon in Bengal was famous for raw silk and fine cotton cloth (called 'muslin' later on).
- There were many other handicrafts as well, such as leather work, metal work, carpet weaving, wood-work including furniture, stone-cutting, etc., for which India was famous.
- Some of the new crafts introduced by the Turks included the manufacturer of paper.
- The production of textiles was also improved by the introduction of the spinning-wheel.
- Cotton could be cleaned faster and better by wider use of the cotton carder's bow (dhunia).

7. **Correct Option: (d)**

Explanation:

- All pairs are correctly matched.

Supplementary Notes:

- Taquavi are (agricultural) loans that were granted by Mohammed-bin-Tughluq. But Firoz Tughluq cancelled all Taquavi (agricultural) loans.
- Khams – it is 1/5 of the warbooty, and Kharaj – is 1/10 of the produce of the land.

8. **Correct Option: (b)**

Explanation:

- **Statement 1 is incorrect:** Alauddin wanted that the landlords of the area, called khuts and muqaddams, should pay the same taxes as others.

Supplementary Notes:

- Apart from the control of the market, Alauddin took important steps in the field of land revenue administration.
- He was the first monarch in the Sultanate who insisted that in the doab, land revenue would be assessed on the basis of measuring the land under cultivation. This implied that the rich and the powerful in the villages who had more land could not pass on their burden to the poor. Alauddin wanted that the landlords of the area, called khuts and muqaddams, should pay the same taxes as others.
- Thus, they had to pay taxes on milch cattle and houses like the others, and forgo other illegal cesses which they were in the habit of realizing. In the picturesque language of Barani, 'the khatts and muqaddams could not afford to ride on rich caprisoned horses, or to chew betel leaves and they became so poor that their wives had to go and work in the houses of Muslims'.
- The policy of direct collection of land revenue by the state, based on measurement, could only succeed if the amils and other local officials were honest.

9. Correct Option: (d)

Explanation:

- **Statement 2 is incorrect:** The Hindu nobles were rarely given high positions in the government.
- **Statement 3 is incorrect:** In the beginning, jizya was collected as part of a land tax but Firoz Tughlaq separated it from the land revenue and collected jizya as a separate tax and levied it on Brahmans also.

Supplementary Notes:

Socio-Economic System during the Sultanate Period

- Delhi Sultans introduced reforms in the land revenue administration. The lands were classified into three categories:
  - **Iqta land:** Lands assigned to officials as iqtas instead of payment for their services.
  - **Khalisa land:** Land under the direct control of the Sultan and the revenues collected were spent for the maintenance of royal court and royal household.
  - **Inam land:** Land assigned or granted to religious leaders or religious institutions.
- Muslim society remained divided into several ethnic and racial groups. The Turks, Iranians, Afghans, and Indian Muslims developed as exclusive groups and there were no intermarriages between them.
- Hindu converts from lower castes were also not given equal respect. The Muslim nobles occupied high offices, and very rarely the Hindu nobles were given a high position in the government.
- The Hindus were considered 'zimmis' or protected people, for which they were forced to pay a tax called jizya. In the beginning, jizya was collected as part of a land tax.
- Firoz Tughlaq separated it from the land revenue and collected jizya as a separate tax and levied it on Brahmans also.

10. Correct Option: (a)

Explanation:

- **Statement 2 is incorrect:** The Hindus were considered zimmis or protected people, for which they were forced to pay a tax called jizya.

Supplementary Notes:

Socio-Economic System during the Sultanate Period

- Delhi Sultans introduced reforms in the land revenue administration. The lands were classified into three categories:
  - Iqta land: Lands assigned to officials as iqtas instead of payment for their services.
  - Khalisa land: Land under the direct control of the Sultan and the revenues collected were spent for the maintenance of royal court and royal household.
  - Inam land: Land assigned or granted to religious leaders or religious institutions.
- Muslim society remained divided into several ethnic and racial groups. The Turks, Iranians, Afghans, and Indian Muslims developed as exclusive groups and there were no intermarriages between them.
- Hindu converts from lower castes were also not given equal respect. The Muslim nobles occupied high offices and very rarely the Hindu nobles were given a high position in the government.
- The Hindus were considered zimmis or protected people, for which they were forced to pay a tax called jizya. In the beginning, jizya was collected as part of a land tax.
- Firoz Tughlaq separated it from the land revenue and collected jizya as a separate tax and levied it on Brahmans also.

11. Correct Option: (d)

Tax	Purpose
A. Sharb	4. Irrigation tax
B. Kharaj	1. Imposed on 10% of produce
C. Zakat	3. Alms for Muslims
D. Khams	2. 20% spoils of war

Supplementary Notes:

Economy under Firoz Shah Tughlaq

- Firoz Shah Tughlaq is known to have made the Iqtadari system hereditary which was introduced in India by Iltutmish. In this system, the officers were paid in land grants which were known as Iqtas which were given to them in specific territorial boundaries.
- He was the first Sultan to impose Sharb (irrigation tax). But at the same time, he built a number of canals and also set up a separate department of public works.
- He imposed other taxes like Kharaj on 10% of produce, Zakat as alms for Muslims and Khams which included 20% of the spoils of war for the royal treasury.

CONCEPT REVISION

Here is the list of concepts that have been covered as part of the previous exercise. Revise and Self-reflect on your concepts you covered.

- Economic Administration under Sher Shah Suri ☐
- Contribution of Sur Dynasty ☐
- Peasants and Rural gentry of Delhi Sultanate ☐
- Trade and Industry under Delhi Sultanate ☐
- Different taxes imposed ☐

5.2 ECONOMIC LIFE DURING MUGHAL PERIOD

QUESTIONS

1. **Kabuliyat and Patta as instruments of settlement were introduced during the reign of _______ ?**
   (a) Ghiyasuddin Mahmud Shah
   (b) Bahlul Khan Lodi
   (c) Sher Shah Suri
   (d) None

2. **The person who either controlled or collected revenue from a number of villages during the Mughal period was called:**
   (a) Sadi (b) Hazara
   (c) Toman (d) All of the above

3. **With reference to the salaries of Mansabdar, which of the following is not correct?**
   (a) The salaries of mansabdars were stated in rupees, they were generally not paid in cash, and but by assigning them a jagir.
   (b) The salaries of mansabdars were stated in rupees, they were generally paid in cash and not by assigning them a jagir.
   (c) Mansabdars preferred a jagir because cash payments were likely to be delayed and sometimes entailed a lot or harassment.
   (d) For purposes of assigning jagirs the revenue department had to maintain a register indicating the assessed income (Jama) or various areas.

4. **Which of the following statements is/are associated with the growth of trade during Mughals?**
   1. Gujarat was an entry point of foreign goods especially fine textiles and silk.
   2. The Seth and Bohra traders specialized in long distance trade, while local traders were called Baniks.
   3. The balance of trade was maintained by the export of gold and silver.

   Select the correct answer using the code given below:
   (a) 1 only (b) 3 only
   (c) 1 and 2 only (d) 1, 2 and 3

5. **'Polaj', 'Parauti' and 'Chachar' are the terms used in the context of:**
   (a) Revenue administration under Vijayanagara kingdom.
   (b) Military designations under Turkish rule.
   (c) Land revenue system under Mughal rule.
   (d) Irrigation schemes under Chola administration.

6. **With reference to Mansabdari System, consider the following statements:**
   1. It was a hereditary system showing a noble's civil and military capacity.
   2. The rank of 'Zat' indicated the number of cavalrymen of a person who was required to maintain.
   3. All appointments and promotions as well as dismissals were directly made by the emperor.

   Which of the above statements is/are incorrect?
   (a) 3 only (b) 1 and 2 only
   (c) 2 and 3 only (d) 1, 2 and 3

7. **Consider the following statements.**
   1. Jizya was the irrigation tax charged at the rate of 1/10th of the produce.
   2. Kharaj was the tax on mines, treasure trove and share in war booty.
   3. Ijarah referred to tax farming in Mughal India.

   Which of the above statements is/are incorrect?
   (a) 2 only (b) 1 and 2 only
   (c) 3 only (d) 1 and 3 only

8. **The portion of the actual produce fixed as state's share under the Zabti System of Mughals was:**
   (a) One-half (b) One-third
   (c) One-fourth (d) One-fifth

9. **The most important source of information about the agrarian conditions during Mughals is:**
   (a) Ain-i-Akbari
   (b) Akbarnama
   (c) Muntakhab-ul-Lubab
   (d) Tarikh-i-Ferishta

10. **Consider the following statements regarding the Zamindars of Mughal Period:**
    1. Personal ownership of land was very old in India .
    2. The tradition was that anyone who first brought land under cultivation was considered its owner.

    Which of the above statements is/are correct?
    (a) 1 only (b) 2 only
    (c) Both 1 and 2 (d) Neither 1 nor 2

11. **With reference to the Madad-i-Maash of Mughal period which of the following statements is correct?**
    (a) The land grants were received by king from the family of girl to whom the king had to marry.
    (b) The land grants received by a large class of religious divines and learned men in return for their services.
    (c) Such grants are called shasan in Maharashtra.
    (d) There was no provision for renewing of such grants by new ruler and they were not hereditary in practice.

12. **Consider the given 'statements' regarding the income and wages of peasants during the Mughal period:**

1. The village artisans were paid for their services by means of commodities which were fixed by custom.
2. The peasant who did not have his own ploughs and bullocks often tilled the land of the zamindars or the upper castes, and could eke out a bare existence.
3. The sixteenth century Hindi poet, Tulsidas has said that this type of cultivation was a source of misery.

Which of the above statement is/are correct?

(a) 1 only (b) 1 and 2 only
(c) 1 and 3 only (d) 1, 2 and 3

13. Which of the following statements is incorrect regarding the foreign trade and European traders under Mughals?

(a) With the help of Portuguese, the Dutch established themselves at Masulipatam, obtaining a farman from the ruler of Golconda in 1606.
(b) The Dutch joined the English in their new venture, exporting both calico and indigo from the Coromandel.
(c) The Britishers developed the export of saltpetre which supplemented the European sources for gun powder.
(d) Lahore and Multan were the major centres for India's overland trade.

14. Trade and commerce expanded in India during the seventeenth century due to a number of factors. Which of the following statements is/are correct regarding the same:

1. The Mughal rupee became a standard coin in India and abroad and thus helped India's trade.
2. The Mughals paid less attention to the development of roads and sarais.
3. Under the zabti system, the land revenue was assessed and required to be paid in kind.
4. Any trader could carry silver to the royal mint, and have coins in exchange on payment of a batta.

Which of the above statement/s is/are correct?

(a) 1 and 2 only (b) 2 and 3 only
(c) 1 and 4 only (d) 1, 2 and 4 only

15. Consider the following statements regarding socio-economic lifestyle of people under Mughal Empire:

1. The condition of peasants was miserable.
2. The merchants brought huge money from abroad.
3. There was decline of arts and crafts during Aurangzeb's reign.

Which of the following statements are correct?

(a) 1 and 2 only (b) 2 and 3 only
(c) 1 and 3 only (d) 1, 2 and 3

16. With reference to 'Mansabdari system', consider the following statements:

1. In this system, every officer was assigned a rank (mansab).
2. This system was hereditary.
3. All appointments and dismissals were directly made by the emperor.

Choose the correct answer using the codes given below:

(a) 1 and 2 only (b) 2 and 3 only
(c) 1 and 3 only (d) All of the above

17. Consider the following statements regarding the village life under Mughal rule:

1. Kamins were the landless peasants who often belonged to the untouchable class.
2. Khudkasht were the peasants who owned the land they tilled.
3. Muzarain were the tenants who paid land revenue at higher rates as compared to other classes of peasants.

Which of the above statements is/are incorrect?

(a) 1 only (b) 1 and 2 only
(c) 2 and 3 only (d) None of the above

18. Which of the following was/were the features of Inam grants made during the reign of Akbar?

1. Inam lands were granted to all persons irrespective of their religious faiths and beliefs.
2. Half of the inam lands consisted of cultivable wasteland.

Select the correct answer using the code given below:

(a) 1 only (b) 2 only
(c) Both 1 and 2 (d) Neither 1 nor 2

19. With reference to Dahsala or Zabti system of land revenue assessment, consider the following statements:

1. It was a system of ten year settlement but not a permanent one as the state retained the right of modification.
2. Peasants were given the choice of paying in cash or kind under this system.

Which of the above statements is/are correct?

(a) 1 only (b) 2 only
(c) Both 1 and 2 (d) Neither 1 nor 2

20. In fixing the land revenue during the reign of Akbar, continuity of cultivation was taken into account and land was divided into four categories. In this context, match the following:

List I		List II
A. Polaj	1.	Land uncultivated for 5 years or more
B. Parati	2.	Land which is temporarily uncultivated
C. Chachar	3.	Land always under cultivation
D. Banjar	4.	Land left fallow for 2-3 years

Select the correct answer using the code given below:

	A	B	C	D
(a)	2	1	4	3
(b)	3	2	4	1
(c)	4	2	3	1
(d)	2	4	3	1

21. Consider the following statements regarding the Mansabdari system:

1. Under this system, every officer was assigned a mansab which was divided into zat and sawar.
2. Princes of blood received higher mansabs.
3. Mansabdars were either assigned a jagir or paid in cash.
4. The system served the dual objective of organizing the nobility as well the army.

Which of the above statements are correct?

(a) 1 and 3 only (b) 2 and 4 only
(c) 2, 3 and 4 only (d) 1, 2, 3 and 4

22. A number of systems for land revenue assessments were followed during the reign of Akbar. In this context, consider the following statements:

1. Under the Dahsala system, both the average produce and prices prevailing over the last 10 years of crops were calculated.
2. Under the Nasaq system, the produce was divided between the peasants and state in fixed proportion.
3. Under the Batai system, the amount payable was calculated based on an assessment of what they have been paying in the past.

Which of the above statements is/are correct?

(a) 1 only (b) 1 and 2 only
(c) 2 and 3 only (d) 1, 2 and 3

23. With reference to Mansabdari system, which of the following pair is correctly matched?

1. Mansabdar – Person holding rank below 500 zat
2. Umda-i-Azam – Person holding rank from 500 to below 2500 zat
3. Amir – Person holding rank of 2500 zat and above

Select the correct answer using the codes given below:

(a) 1 only (b) 2 only
(c) 3 only (d) None of the above

24. Consider the following statements regarding Akbar's Mansabdari system:

1. The Mansab rank in the Akbar's administration was hereditary.
2. Zat rank indicated the number of cavalrymen a person was required to maintain.
3. Akbar's administration is known to have followed the chehra and dagh system.

Which of the above statements is/are correct?

(a) 1 and 2 only (b) 3 only
(c) 2 only (d) 1 and 3 only

25. Consider the following statements regarding the Zamindars in the Mughal India:

1. It had an exclusive representation from upper and intermediate castes.
2. Zamindars often received the support of the peasantry in their struggle against the states during the agrarian uprisings.

Which of the above statements is/are correct?

(a) 1 only (b) 2 only
(c) Both 1 and 2 (d) Neither 1 nor 2

26. Consider the following statements regarding the peasant community during the Mughal period:

1. Muzarian is an Indo-Persian term used to denote a peasant.
2. Peasants mobility was affected due to a rigid social system and excessive tax burden.

Which of the above statements is/are correct?

(a) 1 only (b) 2 only
(c) Both 1 and 2 (d) Neither 1 nor 2

27. Consider the following statements in context with Mughal rule in India:

1. During the Mughal rule, more people lived in urban than in rural areas.
2. Both peasants and landed elites were involved in agricultural production and hence claimed the right in the share of the produce.

Which of the above statements is/are correct?

(a) 1 only (b) 2 only
(c) Both 1 and 2 (d) Neither 1 nor 2

28. Consider the following statements:

1. This system was introduced by Todar Mal.
2. The revenue was fixed on the basis of prices of average of last 10 years.
3. The revenue could be given in cash and kind.
4. It was prevalent in most of the Mughal Empire.

Which of the following systems contains these characteristics?

(a) Zabti System
(b) Istamrari System
(c) Izara System
(d) Iqta System

29. Malikana or Nankar in the context of Medieval India refers to:

(a) Received assistance by zamindar on collecting revenue on behalf of the state.
(b) Land grants to people of religious assignments.
(c) A standardized method of collection based on rates of crops.
(d) A religious policy to curb the dominance of Ulema.

SOLUTIONS

1. **Correct option (c)**

Supplementary Notes:

Pathan Sultan Sher Shah Suri

- Pathan Sultan Sher Shah Suri (1540 – 1545) measured and classified land in terms of produce and introduced Kabuliyat and Patta as instruments of settlement. During Akbar's time, Todarmal made some reforms to this system and the whole Empire was divided into Suba, Sarkar, Pargana and Mahal.

2. **Correct Option: (d)**

Supplementary Notes:

- The terms Sadi, Hazara, and Toman quickly began to be used for persons who either controlled that number of villages or collected revenue of that account. The Mughal term Karori, i.e., a person who collected a kror of dam, was one such term.

3. **Correct Option: (b)**

Supplementary Notes:

- The salaries of Mansabdars were stated in rupees, they were generally not paid in cash, but by assigning them a Jagir. The working of the jagirdari system under Akbar has been already discussed. Mansabdars preferred a jagir because cash payments were likely to be delayed and sometimes entailed a lot or harassment. For purposes of assigning jagirs, the revenue department had to maintain a register indicating the assessed income (Jama) or various areas. The account, however, was not, indicated in rupees but in dams which was calculated at the rate of 40 dams per rupee. This document was called the jama-dami or assessed income based on dams.

4. **Correct Option: (c)**

Explanation:

Statement 3 is incorrect: The balance of trade was maintained by the import of gold and silver.

Supplementary Notes:

The Growth of Trade During Mughals

- The balance of trade was maintained by the import of gold and silver.
- The Indian trading classes were large in numbers and spread throughout the country. They were well organized and highly professional. Seth, Bohra traders specialized in long distance trade while local traders were called Banik.
- Another class of traders was known as Banjaras, who specialized in carrying bulk goods. The Banjaras used to move to long distances with their goods on the back of oxen. Bulk goods were also taken through rivers on boats.
- The trading community did not belong to one caste or religion. The Gujarati merchants included the Hindus, Jains and Muslims. In Rajasthan, Oswals, Maheshwaris and Agarwals came to be called the Marwaris.
- Multanis, Khatris and Afghanis conducted trade with central Asia. In south India, the Chettis on the Coramandal coast and the Muslim merchants of Malabar were the most important trading communities.
- Bengal exported sugar, rice as well as delicate muslin and silk. The Coramandal coast became a centre of textile production.
- Gujarat was an entry point of foreign goods. From there, fine textiles and silk were taken to north India. Indigo and food grains were exported from north India through Gujarat. It was also the distribution centre for luxury products of Kashmir, such as shawls and carpets.

5. **Correct Option: (c)**

Supplementary Notes:

Mughal Administration – Land Revenue System

- Under the Mughal Rule, the revenue was fixed on the average yield of land assessed on the basis of past ten years. The land was also divided into four categories:
- Polaj (cultivated every year).
- Parauti (once in two years).
- Chachar (once in three or four years).
- Banjar (once in five or more years).

6. **Correct Option: (b)**

Explanation:

- **Statement 1 is incorrect:** The Mansab rank was not hereditary.
- **Statement 2 is incorrect:** Sawar rank indicated the number of cavalrymen a person was required to maintain.

Supplementary Notes:

Mansabdari System

- The Mansab rank was not hereditary.
- Sawar rank indicated the number of cavalrymen a person was required to maintain.
- Akbar introduced the Mansabdari system in his administration. Under this system, every officer was assigned a rank (Mansab). The lowest rank was 10 and the highest was 5000 for the nobles. Princes of royal blood received even higher ranks.
- The ranks were divided into two – zat and sawar. Zat means personal and it fixed the personal status of a person. Sawar rank indicated the number of cavalrymen a person was required to maintain.

- Every Sawar had to maintain at least two horses.
- All appointments and promotions as well as dismissals were directly made by the Emperor.

7. **Correct Option: (b)**

Explanation:

- **Statement 1 is incorrect:** Jizya was the tax levied on non-Muslim subjects in return for the safety of their lives.
- **Statement 2 is incorrect:** Kharaj referred to the land tax realized from non-Muslims.

Supplementary Notes:

- **Jizya**
  - Jizya was a tax levied on non-Muslims in return for the protection of life and property and exemption from military services. Women, children, indigent and the Brahmanas were exempted from it.
  - It was started in India by Qutb-ud-din Aibak.
  - The Mughal ruler Akbar abolished this tax in the 16th century, only to be reintroduced by Aurangzeb in 1679.
- **Sharaf**
  - It was the irrigation tax charged at the rate of 1/10th of the produce. This was imposed by Firoz Tughlaq.
- **Kharaj**
  - It was the land tax realized from non-Muslims.
  - It was one of the most common agricultural taxes of the Delhi Sultanate.
- **Khums**
  - It was the tax on mines, treasure trove and share in war booty.
- **Ijarah**
  - The Ijara system meant revenue farming or tax farming in Mughal era.
  - Although the Mughals disapproved of this practice, and was sometimes farmed out in certain villages due to factors like peasants not having resources for undertaking cultivation, or owing to some calamity, cultivation could not be done.

8. **Correct Option: (b)**

Supplementary Notes:

Zabtl System

- Akbar's finance minister Todar Mal introduced a land revenue system whereby the aggregate of the rate of collection for 10 years from 1570 to 1580 was taken and one third of them was taken as the basis of assessment. This new system was called as Zabti System or Ain-i-Dahsala.

9. **Correct option (a)**

Supplementary Notes:

Ain-i-Akbari

- Ain-i-Akbari by Abul Fazal is the main source for today's historians to know about the structure of agrarian relations from the time of Akbar onwards.

10. **Correct Option: (c)**

Supplementary Notes:

- From the writings of Abul Fazi and other contemporary authors, it is clear that personal ownership of land was very old in India. The right of ownership in land depended mainly on succession. But new rights of ownership of land were being created all the time.
- The tradition was that anyone who first brought land under cultivation was considered its owner. There was plenty of cultivable waste-land (banjar) available in medieval times. It was not difficult for an enterprising group of people to settle a new village or to bring under cultivation the wetlands belonging to a village and become the owners of these lands.

11. **Correct Option: (b)**

Supplementary Notes:

- In addition to the Zamindars, there was a large class of religious divines and learned men who, in return for their services were granted tracts of land for its maintenance. Such grants were called 'milk of madad-i-maash' in Mughal terminology, and 'shasan' in Rajasthan.
- Although these grants were to be renewed by every ruler, they often became hereditary in practice. Many of the grantees held official positions such as that of the qazi, etc. Hence, they had both a rural and an urban base. Writers, historians, hakims, etc., were also often drawn from this section.

12. **Correct Option: (d)**

Explanation:

- All statements are correct.

Supplementary Notes:

- It has been estimated that the population in India at the beginning of the seventeenth century was about 125 million. Hence, there was an abundance of cultivable land available and it may be surmised that peasant proprietors were more numerous than the pahis and the village artisans.
- The village artisans were paid for their services by means of commodities which were fixed by custom. It is difficult to compute the average size of the holding of the peasant. The information available shows that there was a great deal of inequality in the villages. The peasant who did not have his own ploughs and bullocks often tilled the land of the zamindars or the upper castes, and could eke out a bare existence. Peasants of this type were called pahis.

- The sixteenth century Hindi poet, Tulsidas, has said that this type of cultivation was a source of misery. Whenever there was a famine – and famines were frequent – it was this class of peasants and the village artisans who suffered the most. The peasants who owned the land they tilled are called khudkasht. They paid land revenue at customary rates. Some of them had many ploughs and bullocks which they let out to their poorer brethren.

13. Correct Option: (a)

Explanation:

- **Statement (a) is incorrect:** Despite vehement Portuguese opposition, the Dutch established themselves at Masulipatam, obtaining a 'Farman' from the ruler of Golconda in 1606.

Supplementary Notes:

Foreign Trade and the European Traders

- During the seventeenth century, many other European traders, specially the Dutch, the English and later, the French came to India for purpose of trade.
- The Portuguese power had begun to decline during the second half of the sixteenth century. Despite vehement Portuguese opposition, the Dutch established themselves at Masulipatam, obtaining a Farman from the ruler of Golconda in 1606.
- They also established themselves in the Spice Islands (Java and Sumatra) so that by 1610, they predominated the spice trade.
- The cloth produced on the Coromandel coast was the most acceptable in Southeast Asia, and also cheapest to carry. Hence, the Dutch spread south from Masulipatam to the Coromandel Coast, obtaining Pulicat from the local ruler and making it a base of their operations.
- The Dutch joined the English in their new venture, exporting both calico and indigo from the Coromandel.
- The English also explored 'Lahri Bandar' at the mouth of the river Indus which could draw the produce of Multan and Lahore by transporting goods down the river Indus. But the trade there remained subsidiary to the Gujarat trade. More important were their efforts to develop the trade of Bengal and Orissa.
- The activities of the Portuguese and the Magh pirates in east Bengal made this development slow. However, by 1650, the English had set themselves up at Hoogly and at Balasore in Orissa, exporting from there raw silk and sugar in addition to textiles.
- Another item which was developed was the export of saltpetre which supplemented the European sources for gun powder. It was also used as a ballast for ships going to Europe. The best quality saltpetre was found in Bihar.
- Lahore and Multan were the major centres for India's overland trade. We are told that a large colony of traders, amounting to 10,000 lived in different parts of Iran.
- From Iran they spread to Bokhara and Samarqand and also to South Russia. Thus, there was a large colony of Indian traders at Baku and at Astrakhan at the mouth of the river Volga, who traded upto Moscow.
- There were colonies of Indian traders at 'Yarkand and Khotan' (modern Sinkiang) who helped in the trade from Punjab via Kashmir and Ladakh to China.

14. Correct Option: (c)

Explanation:

- **Statements 2 is incorrect:** The Mughals paid attention to roads and sarais. (Eliminating this option can fetch the answer).
- **Statements 3 is incorrect:** Under the zabti system, the land revenue was assessed and required to be paid in cash.

Supplementary Notes:

Organization of Trade and Commerce

- Trade and commerce expanded in India during the seventeenth century due to a number of factors. An important factor was the political integration of the country under Mughal rule and establishment of conditions of law and order over extensive areas.
- The Mughals paid attention to roads and sarais. Taxes were levied on goods at the point of their entry into the Empire.
- Road cesses or rahdari was declared illegal, though it continued to be collected by some of the local rajas.
- The Mughals minted silver rupees of high purity from mints scattered all over the Empire. Any trader could carry silver to the royal mint, and have coins in exchange on payment of a batta (discount).
- The Mughal rupee became a standard coin in India and abroad and thus helped India's trade. Some of the Mughal policies also helped in the commercialization of the economy, or the growth of a money economy.
- Salaries to the standing army as well as to many of the administrative personnel (but not to the nobles) were paid in cash.
- Under the zabti system, the land revenue was assessed and required to be paid in cash. Even when the peasant was given the option of choosing other methods of assessment, such as crop-sharing, the share of the state was, generally, sold in the villages with the help of grain dealers.
- It has been estimated that about 20 per cent of the rural produce was marketed, which was a high proportion.

15. **Correct Option: (d)**

Explanation:

- All statements are correct.

Supplementary Notes:

Socio-Economic Lifestyle of People under Mughal Empire:

- William Hawkins informs us that Jahangir possessed a huge amount of wealth and had a big treasure of jewels. The merchants also brought huge money from abroad.
- According to Sir Thomas Roe, the condition of peasants was miserable. He has also mentioned of huge treasure of gold and diamonds of Jahangir.
- Peter Mundy has observed that during Shah Jahan's reign, people in Deccan suffered great distress. He has further stated that the peasantry was in a miserable condition.
- Bernier states that the artisans and labourers were not treated well. There was decline of arts and crafts during Aurangzeb's reign.
- Ralph Fitch who came to India towards the end of the sixteenth century says that, at Banaras "people go naked save a little cloth bound about their middle."
- About the closing years of the 17th century during Aurangzeb's rule, economic condition of the country deteriorated. Sir J.N. Sarkar has observed, "there appeared a great economic impoverishment of India."

16. **Correct Option: (c)**

Explanation:

- **Statement 2 is incorrect:** The mansab rank was not hereditary.

Supplementary Notes:

Mansabdari system

- Akbar introduced the Mansabdari system in his administration.
- Under this system every officer was assigned a rank (mansab).
- The lowest rank was 10 and the highest was 5000 for the nobles.
- Princes of royal blood received even higher ranks.
- The ranks were divided into two – zat and sawar. Zat means personal and it fixed the personal status of a person.
- Sawar rank indicated the number of cavalrymen a person was required to maintain. Every sawar had to maintain at least two horses.
- All appointments and promotions as well as dismissals were directly made by the emperor. The mansab rank was not hereditary.

17. **Correct Option: (d)**

Explanation:

- All statements are correct.

Supplementary Notes:

Pattern of Village Life under Mughals

- It is difficult to compute the average size of the holding of the peasant. The information available to us shows that there was a great deal of inequality in the villages.
- The peasant who did not have his own ploughs and bullocks tilled the land of the zamindars or the upper castes, and could eke out a bare existence.
- The landless peasants and laborers often belonged to the class of people called 'untouchables' or kamin.
- Whenever there was a famine – and famines were frequent – it was this class of peasants and the village artisans who suffered the most.
- The peasants who owned the land they tilled were called 'khudkasht'. They paid land revenue at customary rates. Some of them had many ploughs and bullocks which they let out to their poorer brethren, the tenants or 'muzarain', who generally paid land revenue at a higher rate.
- These two groups were the largest section among the cultivators in the village. Thus, the village society was highly unequal.

18. **Correct Option: (c)**

Explanation:

- Both statements are correct.

Supplementary Notes:

Features of Inam Grants under Reign of Akbar

- Akbar separated the inam lands from the jagir and khalisa lands, and divided the Empire into six circles for purposes of grant of inam lands and their administration.
- Two features of the inam grants are noteworthy.
- First, Akbar made it a deliberate part of his policy to grant inam lands to all persons, irrespective of their religious faith and beliefs.
- Second, Akbar made it a rule that half of the inam land should consist of cultivable wasteland. Thus, the inam holders were encouraged to extend cultivation.

19. **Correct Option: (d)**

Explanation:

- **Statement 1 is incorrect:** Dahsala was neither a system of ten year settlement nor a permanent one as the state retained the right of modification.
- **Statement 2 is incorrect:** Under this system, the state's demand was stated in cash.

Supplementary Notes:

Dahsala or Zabti System

- In 1580, Akbar instituted a new system called 'Dahsala'. Under this system, the average produce of different crops as well as the average prices prevailing over the last ten (dah) years were calculated. One third of the average produce was the state share. The state demand was, however, stated in cash. This was done by converting the state share into money on the basis of a schedule of average prices over the past ten years.
- Later, a further improvement was made. Not only were local prices taken into account, parganas having the same type of productivity were grouped into separate assessment circles. Thus, the peasant was required to pay on the basis of local productivity as well as local prices.
- There were a number of advantages of this system. As soon as the area sown by the peasant had been measured by means of the bamboos linked with iron rings, the peasants as well as the state knew what the dues were. The peasant was given remission in the land revenue if crops failed on account of drought, floods, etc. The system of measurement and the assessment based upon it is called the zabti system. Akbar introduced this system in the area from Lahore to Allahabad and in Malwa and Gujarat. The dahsala system was a further development of the zabti system.
- The dahsala was not a ten-year settlement. Nor was it a permanent one with the state retaining the right to modify it. However, with some changes, Akbar's settlement remained the basis of the land revenue system of the Mughal Empire till the end or the seventeenth century.
- The zabti system is associated with Raja Todar Mal, and is sometimes called Todar Mal's bandobast. Todar Mal was a brilliant revenue officer who had first served under Sher Shah.
- The peasants were allowed to choose between Zabti and Batai under certain conditions. Thus, such a choice was given when the crops were ruined. Under Batai, the peasants were given the choice of paying in cash or in kind, though the state preferred cash. In case of crops such as cotton, indigo, oil seeds, sugarcane, etc., the state demand was invariably in cash. Hence, these were called 'cash crops'.

20. Correct Option: (b)

List I	List II
A. Polaj	3. Land always under cultivation
B. Parati	2. Land which is temporarily uncultivated
C. Chachar	4. Land left fallow for 2-3 years
D. Banjar	1. Land uncultivated for 5 years or more

Supplementary Notes:

Ascertainment of Produce per Bigha

- In fixing the land revenue, continuity of cultivation was taken into account.
- Land which remained under cultivation almost every year was called 'Polaj'.
- When it remained uncultivated it was called 'Parati' (fallow). Parati land paid at the full (polaj) rate when it was cultivated.
- Land which had been fallow for two to three years was called 'Chachar', and 'Banjar' if longer than that.
- These were assessed at concessional rates, the revenue demand gradually rising till the full or polaj rate was paid in the fifth or the eighth year. In this way, the state helped in bringing virgin and uncultivated wasteland under cultivation.
- Land was classified further into good, middling and bad. One-third of the average produce was the state demand, but it varied according to the productivity of the land, the method of assessment, etc.

21. Correct Option: (d)

Explanation:

- All statements are correct.

Supplementary Notes:

Mansabdari System and the Army

- Akbar would not have been able to expand his Empire and maintain his hold over it without a strong army. For this purpose, it was necessary for him to organize the nobility as well as his army. Akbar realized both these objectives by means of the mansabdari system.
- Under this system, every officer was assigned a rank (mansab). The lowest tank was 10, and the highest was 5000 for the nobles. Princes of the blood received higher mansabs.
- The ranks or mansabs were divided into two – zat and sawar. The word zat means personal status of a person and also the salary due to him. The sawar rank indicated the number of cavalry men (sawars) a person was required to maintain.
- A person who was required to maintain as many sawars as his zat rank was placed in the first category of zat rank; if he maintained half or more, then in the second category, and if he maintained less than half, then in the third category. Thus, there were three categories in every rank (mansab).
- The salary due to soldiers was added to the salary of the mansabdar, who was paid by assigning him a Jagir. Sometimes, the Mansabdars were paid in cash.
- The origins of the Mansabdari system can, perhaps, he traced back to Changez Khan who organized his army on a decimal basis, the lowest unit of command being ten, and the highest ten thousand (toman), whose commander was called 'Khan'.

- Persons were generally appointed at a low Mansab and gradually promoted, depending upon their merits and the favor of the emperor. A person could also be demoted as a mark of punishment.

22. **Correct Option: (a)**

Explanation:

- **Statement 2 is incorrect:** Under the Nasaq system, the amount payable was calculated based on an assessment of what they had been paying in the past.
- **Statement 3 is incorrect:** Under the Batai system, the produce was divided between the peasants and state in fixed proportion.

Supplementary Notes:

Land Revenue Administration under Akbar

- The most common and the oldest was called 'Batai' or 'Ghalla-bakhshi'. In this system, the produce was divided between the peasants and the state in fixed proportion. The crop was divided after it had been thrashed; or when it had been cut and tied in stacks, or while it was standing in the field.
- In 1580, Akbar instituted a new system called the dahsala. Under this system, the average produce of different crops as well as the average prices prevailing over the last ten (dah) years were calculated. One-third of the average produce was the state's share. The state demand was, however, stated in cash. This was done by converting the state share into money on the basis of a schedule of average prices over the past ten years.
- A third system which was widely used in Akbar's time was Nasaq. It was a rough calculation of the amount payable by the peasant on the basis of what he had been paying in the past.

23. **Correct Option: (a)**

Explanation:

- **Pair 2 and 3 are incorrectly matched:** Amirs were those who held ranks from 500 to below 2500, and those holding ranks of 2500 and above were called Amir-i-Umda or Umda-i-Azam.

Supplementary Notes:

Mansabdari System

- Under this system, every officer was assigned a rank (mansab). The ranks or mansabs were divided into two – zat and sawar.
- The word 'zat' means personal status of a person and also the salary due to him. The 'sawar' rank indicated the number of cavalry men (sawars) a person was required to maintain.
- A person who was required to maintain as many sawars as his zat rank was placed in the first category of zat rank; if he maintained half or more, then in the second category, and if he maintained less than half, then in the third category. Thus, there were three categories in every rank (mansab).
- Persons holding ranks below 500 zat were called 'Mansabdars', those from 500 to below 2500 were called 'Amirs', and those holding ranks of 2500 and above were called 'Amir-i-Umda' or 'Umda-i-Azam'.
- However, the word mansabdar is sometimes used for all the three categories.
- Apart from status, this classification had significance: an Amir or an Amir-i-Umda could have another amir or mansabdar serve under him, but a mansabdar could not do so. Thus, a person with a rank of 5000 could have under him a mansabdar up to a rank of 500 zat, and one with a rank of 4000 could have a mansabdar up to a rank of 400 zat, and so on.

24. **Correct Option: (b)**

Explanation:

- **Statement 1 is incorrect:** The Mansab rank was not hereditary.
- **Statement 2 is incorrect:** Sawar rank and not zat rank, indicated the number of cavalrymen a person was required to maintain.

Supplementary Notes:

Administration During Akbar's Reign

- Akbar is known to have introduced the Mansabdari system in his administration.
- Under this system, every officer (mansabdar) was assigned a rank (mansab).
- Princes of royal blood received even higher ranks, but the mansab rank was not hereditary.
- All appointments and promotions, as well as dismissals, were directly made by the emperor.
- The ranks were further divided into two – zat and sawar.
  - ➤ Zat means personal and apart from fixing the personal status of a person in the administrative hierarchy, it also decided salary due to him.
  - ➤ Sawar rank indicated the number of cavalrymen (sawars) a person was required to maintain.
- There were further three categories in every mansab (rank) based on the number of sawars each zat rank had to maintain.
- Mansabdar's position in the official hierarchy was decided by the zat rank.
- The 'chehra' (descriptive roll of every soldier) and 'dagh' system (branding of horses) was followed.
- Mughal Mansabdars formed the highest-paid service in the world.

25. **Correct Option: (b)**

Explanation:

- **Statement 1 is incorrect:** Lower castes and forest tribals also entered into the rank of zamindars.

Supplementary Notes:
The Zamindars

- Zamindars were people in the countryside that lived off agriculture but did not participate directly in the processes of agricultural production.
- They were landed proprietors who enjoyed certain social and economic privileges by virtue of their superior status in rural society. Caste was one factor that accounted for the elevated status of zamindars.
- They also derived their power from the fact that they could often collect revenue on behalf of the state, a service for which they were compensated financially. They had control over the military resources which added to their power.
- There was a slow process of zamindari consolidation which involved colonisation of new lands, by transfer of rights, by order of the state and by purchase. These were the processes which perhaps permitted people belonging to the relatively "lower" castes and forest tribal chiefs to enter into the rank of zamindars as zamindaris.
- Zamindars, although, were an exploitative class, their relationship with the peasantry had an element of reciprocity, paternalism and patronage.
- Zamindars often received the support of the peasantry in their struggle against the states during the agrarian uprisings.

26. Correct Option: (a)

Explanation:

- **Statement 2 is incorrect:** Peasants mobility was a feature of the Mughal agrarian society.

Supplementary Notes:
Peasant and their Land

- 'Raiyat' or 'Muzarian' was the term which Indo-Persian sources of the Mughal period frequently used to denote a peasant.
- There were two kinds of peasants: khud-kashta and pahi-kashta.
- 'Khud-kashta' were residents of the village in which they held their lands. The 'pahi-kashta', on the other hand, were non-resident cultivators who belonged to some other village but cultivated lands elsewhere on a contractual basis.
- Peasants became pahi-kashta either out of choice – for example when terms of revenue in a distant village were more favourable – or out of compulsion – for example, when forced by economic distress after a famine.
- Deep inequities on the basis of caste and other caste-like distinctions meant that the cultivators were a highly heterogeneous group.
- The relatively easy availability of uncultivated land and the competition over labour resources made peasants mobility very effective.

27. Correct Option: (b)

Explanation:

- **Statement 1 is incorrect:** During the Mughal rule, more people lived in rural areas than urban areas.

Supplementary Notes:
Society During Mughal period

- During the 16th and 17th centuries under the Mughal rule, about 85 per cent of the population of India lived in its villages.
- Mughal society was an agricultural society and village became the fundamental unit of it.
- Both peasants and landed elites were involved in agricultural production and claimed rights to a share of the produce.
- Rural India was not characterized by settled peasant production alone.
- Several kinds of areas such as large tracts of dry land hilly regions and forest areas which made up a substantial proportion of territory were not cultivable in the same way as the heartland of the Mughal Empire which was more fertile.

28. Correct Option: (a)

Explanation:

- **Option (a) is correct:** Zabti or Dahsala System has all the mentioned features.

Supplementary Notes:
Information regarding Dahasala or Zabti system

- Akbar introduced the Dahasala or Zabti system of land revenue collection in 1580-82 to alleviate the problems arising due to fixing prices every year and doing settlements of revenues of previous years.
- One-third of this average produce was fixed in Rupees per Bigha and fixed as share of the state (Mal). Rest two-third share was left to the cultivators (Kharaj).
- The settlement was based on the average prices and produces during the last ten years.
- The system prevailed from Allahabad to Lahore and in the provinces of Gujrat and Malwa.
- The agricultural land was classified into 4 different categories namely, Banjar: It is the land where no cultivation has been done for 5 or more years. Chachar: It is the land that has been left follow for 3-4 years. Parauti: It is the land left aside to become fertile again. Polaj: It is a fertile land where cultivation is done every year and not left fallow.
- The Parauti and Chachar lands were further divided into 3 sub-categories namely bad, middling and good. The average production of all these 3 categories were sum totalled as the normal production of one Bigha.
- The state demand in kind was given in 'Maunds' but for the conversion of the state demand from kind to cash, a separate schedule of cash revenue rates for

various crops was fixed, which was called Dastur-i-Amal.

- **Dahsala System** or **Zabti System** was introduced by Raja Todarmal, the able finance minister of Akbar.
- This remained a standard system of revenue assessment during the greater part of the Mughal Empire.

29. Correct Option: (a)

Supplementary Notes:

Administrative System – Malikana or Nankar

- Land grants to people of religious assignments are called Madad-i Maash. The standardized method of collection based on crops is called 'Zabti system'.
- Under the Zamindari system, a zamindar is responsible of collecting revenue on behalf of the state and the received assistance is called 'Malikana' or 'Nankar'. The religious policy by Akbar to curb the dominance of Ulema was the Mahzarnama.

CONCEPT REVISION

Here is the list of concepts that have been covered as part of the previous exercise. Revise and Self-reflect on your concepts you covered.

- Kabuliyat and Patta ☐
- Salaries of Mansabdar ☐
- Growth of trade during Mughals ☐
- 'Polaj', Parauti' and 'Chachar' ☐
- Zabti System ☐
- Madad-i-Maash ☐
- Village life under Mughal Rule ☐
- Features of Inam grants ☐
- Malikana ☐

5.3 ECONOMIC LIFE OF REGIONAL STATES IN INDIA

QUESTIONS

1. Who was the last Maratha chief to accept the subsidiary alliance of the British?

(a) Gaikwad (b) Scindia
(c) Holkar (d) Bhonsle

2. Consider the following statements:

1. Chauth was a tax collected by the Marathas from people living outside their kingdom.
2. Chauth and Sardesmukhi were novel inventions of the Maratha Empire under Shivaji.

Which of the above statements is/are correct?

(a) 1 only (b) 2 only
(c) Both 1 and 2 (d) Neither 1 nor 2

3. Which among the following was the single biggest item of import to the Vijayanagar Empire?

(a) Precious stones (b) Horses
(c) Luxury goods (d) Raw silk

4. The tax called 'Shisht' is associated with which of the following rulers?

(a) Shivaji
(b) Krishnadeva Raya
(c) Rajendra Chola
(d) Ballala-II

5. Which one of the following port served as international port for Kakatiya Dynasty, Kondaveedu Dynasty and Deva Raya-II of Vijayanagara Dynasty in the medieval times?

(a) Poompuhar (b) Motupalli
(c) Krishnapatnam (d) Machilipatnam

6. The most important reason for collection of "Chauth" and "Sardeshmukhi" by Marathas was:

(a) To increase the source of income
(b) To expand his territories
(c) To consolidate his political influence
(d) Because of the opposition of Muslim rulers

7. Consider the following statements regarding the economy of the Vijaynagara Empire:

1. Trade was contributing more to the revenue of the empire than agriculture.
2. The society was highly egalitarian.
3. Only gold coins were in circulation in the economy.

Which of the above statements is/are incorrect?

(a) 1 only (b) 1 and 2 only
(c) 2 and 3 only (d) 1, 2 and 3

8. Consider the following statements regarding Maratha ruler, Shivaji's, organisation of the army and the revenue system:

1. Regular soldiers were given salaries in cash.
2. The revenue system was patterned on the system of 'Malik Ambar'.
3. Shivaji abolished the Zamindari system.

Which of the above statements is/are correct?

(a) 1 only (b) 1 and 2 only
(c) 3 only (d) 1, 2 and 3

9. **With reference to the cultural contributions of the Deccan States, consider the following statements:**
1. Ali Adil Shah invited Christian missionaries to his court even before Akbar had done so.
2. Muhammad Quli Qutub Shah was a contemporary of Akbar who constructed Char Minar.
3. Gol Gumbaz, built by rulers of Bijapur, has the single largest dome ever constructed.

Which of the above statements is/are correct?

(a) 1 only (b) 1 and 2 only
(c) 2 and 3 only (d) 1, 2 and 3

10. **Consider the following statements regarding Pala Empire:**
1. This empire was founded by Dharmapala.
2. Dharmapala's reign was marked by a tripartite struggle between the Palas, the Pratiharas and the Rashtrakutas
3. This tripartite struggle was for the control of Kanauj and North India.

Which of the above statements is/are correct?

(a) 1 and 2 only (b) 3 only
(c) 2 and 3 only (d) 1, 2 and 3

SOLUTIONS

1. **Correct option (c)**

Supplementary Notes:

- The doctrine of subsidiary alliance was introduced by Marquess (or Lord) Wellesley, British Governor-General of India from 1798 to 1805 . Under this doctrine, Indian rulers under British protection surrendered control of their foreign affairs to the British. Hyderabad first signed it. The five Maratha chiefs entered into subsidiary alliance were as follows:
  - Peshava 1802
  - Scindia 1804
  - Gaekwa 1805
  - Bhonsle 1806
  - Holkar 1818
  - Chauth and Sardeshmukhi

2. **Correct Option: (a)**

Explanation:

- **Statement 2 is incorrect:** These taxes were not invented by Shivaji. The rulers of Deccan already knew about these. Koli Maharaja Som Shah of Ramnagar initiated it.

Supplementary Notes:

- Chauth and Sardesmukhi were the customary taxes under the reign of Shivaji. The outside area, whenever plundered by Marathas was to be levied the two taxes:
  - Chauth
    - It refers to one-quarter of the land revenue paid to the government, which was collected as a tax by the Marathas, from the people living outside the Maratha kingdom in return for which they were promised security against plunder and raid of their territories by the Marathas.
  - Sardesmukhi
    - Sardesmukhi was a tax equivalent to one-tenth of the land revenue levied by Marathas on those lands over which the Marathas claimed hereditary rights.
- These taxes were earlier being paid by Portuguese to the neighbouring kings of their territories as well to avoid conflicts with them. Hence, it was not introduced by Shivaji.

3. **Correct Option: (b)**

Supplementary Notes:

Horses

- Kings of Vijayanagar imported Arabian horses on a large scale in order to improve the breed of cavalry horses in their own districts. Thus, the single biggest item of import to the Vijayanagar Empire was horses.

4. **Correct Option: (b)**

Supplementary Notes:

Shisht

- The main source of revenue in the Vijayanagara Empire was the taxes on the land/farm. The land was well-surveyed. Normally, the land tax was one-third to one-sixth of the yield, depending upon the land category or crop quality.
- The tax called 'Shisht' (Rai-rekha) was the main source of state income.

5. **Correct Option: (b)**

Supplementary Notes:

Ports of Ancient History:

- Lothal Port: Harappan (Gujarat)
- Muziris Port: Kerala
- Poompuhar Port: Tamil Nadu
- Arikamedhu Port: Pondicherry (Tamil Nadu)
- Bharuch Port: Gujarat
- Calicut Port: Kerala
- Tuticorin Port: Tamil Nadu

Ports of Medieval History:

- Kakatiya Dynasty: Motupalli
- Chola Dynasty: Poompuhar, Arikamedhu, Nagapattinam
- Chera Dynasty: Muziris
- Pallava Dynasty: Mamallapuram
- Pandya Dynasty: Korkai, Madurai

- Vijayanagar Dynasty: Motupalli
- Kondaveedu Dynasty: Motupalli

6. **Correct Option: (a)**

Supplementary Notes:

- Shivaji collected the Chauth and Sardeshmukhi from the territory which was either under his enemies or under his own influence. The Chauth was one-fourth part of the income of a particular territory while the Sardeshmukhi was one-tenth. Shivaji collected these taxes simply by force of his arms. These constituted as the primary sources of income of Shivaji and helped in the extension of the power and territory of the Marathas.

7. **Correct Option: (d)**

- **Statement 1 is incorrect:** Agriculture was contributing more to the economy than industries and trade.
- **Statement 2 is incorrect:** The society was unequal and not egalitarian.
- **Statement 3 is incorrect:** Gold, copper and silver coins all were in circulation.

Supplementary Notes:

Vijaynagara Empire

- The economy of the Vijaynagara Empire was in very sound and healthy condition.
- The agriculture was in flourishing condition in Vijayanagar Empire. Agriculture was essentially the biggest contributor to the economy in ancient and medieval times.
- The agricultural wealth was supplemented by numerous industries, the most important of which were textiles, mining and metallurgy.
- The social condition of the Empire was not egalitarian as the houses of the ordinary people were made of thatch, but nonetheless, well-built and arranged according to occupations, in long streets with many open places.
- The Caste system was prevalent in the Empire. The Sati system was freely sanctioned by Brahmanas and was very common in the Vijayanagar Empire.
- Coins made up of copper, gold and silver were in use in the Vijayanagara Empire.

8. **Correct Option: (b)**

Explanation:

- **Statement 3 is incorrect:** Shivaji did not abolish the zamindari (deshmukhi) system, but awarded jagirs (mokasa) to his officials. However, Shivaji strictly supervised the 'mirasdars', that is, those with hereditary rights on land.

Supplementary Notes:

Shivaji's Organisation of the Army

- Shivaji preferred to give cash salaries to the regular soldiers, though sometimes the chiefs received revenue grants (saranjam).
- The plunder taken by each soldier during campaigns was strictly accounted for.
- The regular army (Paga) consisting of about 30,000 to 40,000 cavalry, as distinct from the loose auxiliaries (Silahdars), were supervised by Havaldars who received fixed salaries.
- The forts were carefully supervised, Mavali foot soldiers and gunners being appointed there.

Revenue System

- The revenue system seems to have been patterned on the system of Malik Ambar. A new revenue assessment was completed by Annaji Datto in 1679.
- It is not correct to think that Shivaji abolished the Zamindari (Deshmukhi) system, or that he did not award Jagirs (Mokasa) to his officials. However, Shivaji strictly supervised the mirasdars, that is, those with hereditary rights on land.
- Shivaji supplemented his income by levying a contribution on the neighbouring Mughal territories. This contribution which came to one-fourth of the land revenue, began to be called 'chauthai' (one-fourth) or 'chauth'.

9. **Correct Option: (d)**

Explanation:

- All statements are correct.

Supplementary Notes:

Cultural Contribution of Deccan States

- The Deccan states had a number of cultural contributions to their credit. Ali Adil Shah (d. 1580) loved to hold discussions with Hindu and Muslim saints and was called a Sufi. He invited Catholic missionaries to his court, even before Akbar had done so. He had an excellent library to which he appointed the well-known Sanskrit scholar, Waman Pandit.
- The successor of Ali Adil Shah, Ibrahim Adil Shah II (1580-1627) was deeply interested in music, and composed a book called Kitab-i-Nauras in which songs were set to various musical modes or ragas. He built a new capital, Nauraspur, in which a large number of musicians were invited to settle.
- Sultan Muhammad Quli Qutub Shah, a contemporary of Akbar, was very fond of literature and architecture. He wrote in Dakhani Urdu, Persian and Telugu and has left an extensive 'diwan' or collection. He was the first to introduce a secular note in poetry. Apart from the praise of God and the Prophet, he wrote about nature, love, and the social life of his day.

- In the field of architecture, Muhammad Quli Qutub Shah constructed many buildings, the most famous of which is the Char Minar. Completed in 1591-92, it stood at the centre of the new city of Hyderabad, founded by Muhammad Quli Qutub Shah. It had four lofty arches, facing the four directions. Its chief beauty was the four minarets which were four storied and 48 metre high. The double screen of arches had fine carvings.
- The rulers of Bijapur consistently maintained a high standard and an impeccable taste in architecture. The most famous Bijapur buildings of the period were the Ibrahim Rauza and the Gol Gumbaz.
- The former was a mausoleum for Ibrahim Adil Shah and shows the style at its best. The Gol Gumbaz, which was built in 1660 has the largest single dome ever constructed. All its proportions are harmonious, the large dome being balanced by tall, tapering minarets at the corner. It is said that a whisper at one side of the huge main room can be heard clearly at the other end.

10. Correct Option: (c)

Explanation:

- **Statement 1 is incorrect:** This empire was founded by Gopala.

Supplementary Notes:

Pala Empire

- The Pala Empire was founded by Gopala, probably in AD 750 when he was elected king by the notable men of the area to end the anarchy prevailing there.
- Gopala was not born in a high, much less a royal family, his father probably was a soldier. He unified Bengal under his control, and even brought Magadha (Bihar) under his control.
- Gopala was succeeded in AD 770 by his son, Dharamapala, who ruled till AD 810.
- His reign was marked by a tripartite struggle between the Palas, the Pratiharas and the Rashtrakutas for the control of Kanauj and north India.
- The Pratihara ruler advanced upon Gaud (Bengal), but before a decision could be taken, the Pratihara ruler was defeated by the Rashtrakuta ruler, Dhruva, and was forced to seek refuge in the deserts of Rajasthan. Dhruva then returned to the Deccan.
- This left the field free for Dharmapala who occupied Kanauj and held a grand Darbar which was attended by Vassal rulers from Punjab, eastern Rajasthan, etc.

CONCEPT REVISION

Here is the list of concepts that have been covered as part of the previous exercise. Revise and Self-reflect on your concepts you covered.

- Chauth & Sardesmukhi ☐
- 'Shisht' ☐
- International port of Kakatiya Dynasty ☐
- Shivaji's organisation of revenue system ☐
- Cultural contributions of Deccan States ☐

☐☐☐

6. SOCIO-CULTURAL DEVELOPMENT OF MEDIEVAL INDIA

6.1 CASTE SYSTEM AND FEUDALISM IN MEDIEVAL INDIA

QUESTIONS

1. **Which of the following group of society did not comprise the feudalism in medieval India?**
   (a) Local hereditary chiefs or military adventurers
   (b) Defeated rajas and their supporters
   (c) Government officers, paid in revenue-bearing villages
   (d) None of the above

2. **Consider the following features mentioned in historical accounts of foreign travelers who visited India in medieval times:**
   1. The bazaars were only places of economic transactions and not for socio-cultural activities.
   2. The lack of private property in land was the fundamental difference between Medieval India and Europe.
   3. Besides agricultural labor, women were not allowed to perform commercial activities.
   4. Large halls as Karkhanas or workshops were built for the artisans.

   Which of the above statements is/are correct?
   (a) 3 only (b) 1 and 3 only
   (c) 1, 2 and 4 only (d) 2, 3 and 4 only

3. **Consider the following features of the Bahamani Kingdom:**
   1. The Sultans followed a feudal type of administration.
   2. The kingdom was divided into many provinces called Tarafs.
   3. The Bahmani Sultans gave great attention to education.
   4. They discouraged Arabic and Persian learning.

   Which of the above statements is/are correct?
   (a) 1 and 2 only (b) 1, 2 and 3 only
   (c) 3 and 4 only (d) 2, 3 and 4 only

4. **Consider the following statements:**
   1. Firoz Shah Tughlaq strictly imposed the Jaziya on non-Muslims.
   2. Mohammad bin Tughlaq transferred his capital from Delhi to Devagiri permanently.
   3. Mohammad bin Tughlaq set up a new department of agriculture, Diwan-i-Amirkohi and launched a scheme of takkavi loans to the farmers to buy seed and to extend cultivation.

   Which of the above statement/s is/are correct?
   (a) 1 and 2 only (b) 2 and 3 only
   (c) 1 and 3 only (d) 1, 2 and 3

5. **Consider the following statements regarding society of 16th century:**
   1. The panchayat had to ensure that caste boundaries among the various communities inhabiting the village were upheld.
   2. In both civil and criminal matters, the State respected the decisions of jati panchayats.
   3. Remarriage was considered legitimate both among divorced and widowed women.

   Which of the above statements is/are correct?
   (a) 1 and 2 only (b) 1 and 3 only
   (c) 2 and 3 only (d) 1, 2 and 3

6. **The customs "Sijada" and "Paibos" were introduced by which of the following ruler?**
   (a) Bahram Shah
   (b) Nasiruddin Mahmud
   (c) Alauddin Masud Shah
   (d) None of the above

7. **Which of the following was/were the chief features of the Indian feudal economy and polity?**
   1. Slump in crafts, commerce, and urban decay resulted in stagnant rural economy.
   2. Excessive legal levies such as Vishti or forced labor on the peasantry community.
   3. Strong central and provincial political authority.

   Select the correct answer using the code given below:
   (a) 1 only (b) 1 and 2 only
   (c) 2 and 3 only (d) 1 and 3 only

SOLUTIONS

1. **Correct Option: (d)**

Supplementary Notes:

Nature of Society

- A number of important changes took place in Indian society during early medieval period.
- One of these was the growing power of a class of people who were variously called samanta, rana, rautta (rajput), etc., by the contemporary writers.
- Their origins were very different. Some were government officers who were increasingly paid not in cash but by assigning to them revenue-bearing villages. Others were defeated Rajas and their supporters who continued to enjoy the revenue of limited areas. Still others were local hereditary chiefs or military adventurers who had carved out a sphere of authority with the help of armed supporters. Still others were tribal or clan leaders. Thus, there was a hierarchy among them.
- The revenue assignments (called, 'bhoga' or 'fief') granted by a ruler to his officers and supporters were temporary in theory and were liable to be resumed whenever the ruler wanted. However, in practice this was rarely done, except in the case of outright rebellion or disloyalty. According to current notions, it was a sin to deprive even a defeated ruler of his lands. As a result, the kingdoms of this period included large areas dominated by defeated and subordinate rulers who were constantly on the lookout for reasserting their independence. Within the territories of these rulers, again, various officers looked upon their assignments as hereditary fiefs. In course of time, even various government offices began to be considered hereditary.
- The hereditary chiefs gradually assumed many of the functions of the government. They not only assessed and collected land revenue, but also assumed more and more administrative powers, such as the right of awarding punishments and exacting fines on their own, which earlier were generally considered royal privileges. They assumed the right to sublet their land to their followers without the prior permission of the ruler, thus increasing the number of people who drew sustenance from land without working on it themselves.
- Some historians call this type of a society 'feudal', although features of European feudalism, such as vassalage, serfdom, and manors did not exist in India. It is emphasised that the common feature between the two was that the society was dominated by a class of people who derived their income from the surplus produced by the peasant, but did not work on the land themselves. Also, that the position of the primary producer, the peasant, was a dependent one. A number of other historians prefer to call this society a 'medieval society'.

2. **Correct Option: (c)**

Explanation:

Statement 3 is incorrect: Not only women were allowed as agricultural and non-agricultural labourers, but they also performed in commercial activities.

Supplementary Notes:

Foreign Travellers' Account

- The bazaars were not the only places of economic transactions but also social and cultural activities.
- The lack of private property in land was the principal difference between medieval India and Europe.
- Not only women were allowed as agricultural and non-agricultural labourers, but they also performed commercial activities.
- Large halls as Karkhanas or workshops were built for the artisans.

3. **Correct Option: (b)**

Explanation:

Statement 4 is incorrect: They encouraged Arabic and Persian learning.

Supplementary Notes:

Bahamani Kingdom

- The Bahmani Sultanate was a Muslim state of the Deccan in southern India and was one of the great medieval Indian kingdoms.
- Agriculture was the main economic activity of Bahmani kingdom for earning the main revenue of the state.
- The Bahmani kingdom flourished in architectural monuments.
- The Bahamani Sultans were patrons of the Persian language, culture and literature, and some members of the dynasty became well-versed in that language and composed its literature in the language. Thus, in the field of architecture, the Bahamanis paved way for a distinct style by inviting architects from Persia, Turkey, and Arabia and blended it with local styles. They encouraged Arabic and Persian learning.
- **Administration:**
  - The Sultans followed a feudal type of administration.
  - Tarafs – The kingdom was divided into many provinces called Tarafs.
  - Tarafdar or Amir – Governor who controlled the Taraf.
- **Contribution to Education:**
  - The Bahmani Sultans gave great attention to education.
  - They encouraged Arabic and Persian learning.
  - Urdu also flourished during this period.

4. **Correct Option: (c)**

Explanation:

- **Statement 2 is incorrect:** Mohammad bin Tughlaq transferred his capital from Delhi to Devagiri but after two years, shifted back to Delhi due to lack of water supply.

Supplementary Notes:

Mohammad bin Tughlaq/Jauna Khan (c. 1325–51 CE):

- Transferred his capital from Delhi to Devagiri (Daulatabad) to have better administration, and forcibly moved the entire population to the new capital. But the capital was shifted back to Delhi after two years because of the lack of water supply in Daulatabad. The distance between these two places was more than 1500 kilometres and many people died during the rigorous journey in the summer.
- In order to overcome financial difficulties, Muhammad bin Tughlaq increased the land revenue (half the produce) on the farmers of Doab (land between Ganges and Yamuna rivers). It was an excessive and arbitrary step on the farmers. This measure proved to be ill-timed as the Doab was going through famine, followed by plague.
- Idea of token currency (using copper coins) model led on the basis of Chinese example (Kublai Khan issued paper money in China). Tughlaq, thus issued copper coins at par with the value of the silver tanka coins. Very few people exchanged gold/silver for copper and the tokens were easy to forge, which led to heavy losses. Later on, he repealed his verdict, and all coins were redeemed in silver/gold, making the treasury empty.
- Set up a new department of agriculture, Diwan-i-Amirkohi. He launched a scheme by which takkavi loans (loans for cultivation) were given to the farmers to buy seed and to extend cultivation.

Firoz Shah Tughlaq (c.1351–1388 CE):

- He had the unique distinction of being chosen as Sultan by the nobles. So, his policy aimed to appease the nobles, the army, and theologicians.
- He strictly followed the advice of the Ulemas in running the administration. As per the Islamic law, he levied the taxes. Jaziya was strictly imposed on non-Muslims.
- He not only revived the Iqtadari system but also made it hereditary. Soldiers were given land assignments (jagir system), and even their recruitment was made hereditary.
- He was the first Sultan to impose Sharb (irrigation tax). But at the same time, he built a number of canals and also set up a separate department of public works.

5. **Correct Option: (b)**

Explanation:

- **Statement 2 is incorrect:** In most cases, except in matters of criminal justice, the state respected the decisions of jati panchayats.

Supplementary Notes:

Society and Mughal Empire

- One important function of the panchayat was to ensure that caste boundaries among the various communities inhabiting the village were upheld. In eastern India, all marriages were held in the presence of the mandal.

- In other words, one of the duties of the village headman was to oversee the conduct of the members of the village community chiefly to prevent any offence against their caste.
- In addition to the village panchayat, each caste or jati in the village had its own jati panchayat.
- These panchayats wielded considerable power in rural society. In Rajasthan, jati panchayats arbitrated civil disputes between members of different castes.
- They mediated in contested claims on land, decided whether marriages were performed according to the norms laid down by a particular caste group, determined who had ritual precedence in village functions, and so on.
- In most cases, except in matters of criminal justice, the state respected the decisions of jati panchayats.
- The importance attached to women as a reproductive force also meant that the fear of losing control over them was great. According to established social norms, the household was headed by a male.
- Thus, women were kept under strict control by the male members of the family and the community. They could inflict draconian punishments if they suspected infidelity on the part of women.
- Marriages in many rural communities required the payment of bride-price rather than dowry to the bride's family.
- Remarriage was considered legitimate both among divorced and widowed women.

6. Correct Option: (d)

Explanation:

- **Option (d) is correct:** Customs such as "Sijada" and "Paibos" were introduced by Balban.

Supplementary Notes:

Balban Rule

- Balban was undoubtedly one of the main architects of the Delhi Sultanate, particularly, of its form of government and institutions.
- Balban's experience as the regent made him understand the problems of Delhi Sultanate. He knew that the real threat to monarchy was from the nobles called 'the Forty'.
- He was convinced that only by enhancing the power and authority of the monarchy, he could solve this problem.
- He got every member of the Iltutmish family killed and gave a deadly blow to Chahalgani.
- Balban introduced rigorous court discipline and new customs such as "Sijada" (prostration) and "Paibos" (kissing the Sultan's feet) to prove his superiority over the nobles.

7. Correct Option: (b)

Explanation:

- **Statement 3 is incorrect:** There was a weakening of central paramount power during the period of Indian feudalism.

Supplementary Notes:

Feudalism

- Feudalism was a kind of socio-political organisation which was based on land tenure given by the king to the Samantas who served their masters in various ways. In other words, feudalism was a part of the feudal society where the subordinate subjects showed loyalty to their lords and obtained from them a piece of land, thereby serving their master in various ways, seeking protection from them for their life and property.
- The parallelization of sovereignty could take place because of the dismemberment of the centralized political structure of the pre-feudal days.
- Chief features of the feudal economy were:
  - ➤ Conversion of royal and communal rights on land into the private holding of vassals.
  - ➤ Peasant bearing the burdens of numerous legal and extra-legal levies, including vishti or forced labor.
  - ➤ Slumps in crafts, commerce and urban decay resulting in the stagnant and enclosed village economy.

CONCEPT REVISION

Here is the list of concepts that have been covered as part of the previous exercise. Revise and Self-reflect on your concepts you covered.

- Accounts of Foreign Travellers ☐
- Bahamani Kingdom ☐
- Customs of 'Sijada' and 'Paibos' ☐
- Features of Indian feudal economy and polity ☐

6.2 EMERGENCE AND SPREAD OF ISLAM AND ITS IMPACT

QUESTIONS

1. **The concept of 'Zil-i-Illahi' or 'Shadow of God' introduced by Balban refers to:**
   (a) The rule of king on the basis of divine sanction and not answerable to anyone.
   (b) The idea of kingship, derived from Sassanid Persia.
   (c) The universal principle of harmony and peace.
   (d) The idea of a superior religion for masses.

2. **Which of the following best explains the term 'Kharaj'?**
   (a) Worship tax on Hindus
   (b) Education tax
   (c) Poll or a head tax
   (d) Individual Islamic land tax

3. **Consider the following statements regarding Jharokha system during Akbar's rule:**
   1. Akbar started his day with his appearance at the Jharoka of the palace.
   2. Large numbers of people assembled to present petitions to him, if necessary.

   Which of the above statements is/are correct?
   (a) 1 only (b) 2 only
   (c) Both 1 and 2 (d) Neither 1 nor 2

4. **With reference to the religious policy of Akbar, consider the following statements:**
   1. Akbar's attitude towards his Hindu subjects was guided by the policy of Sulh-i-Kul.
   2. The proceedings at Ibadat Khana were initially confined to Muslims only.
   3. Akbar propounded Tauhid-i-Ilahi which combined elements from other existing religions.

   Which of the above statements is/are correct?
   (a) 1 only (b) 1 and 2 only
   (c) 2 and 3 only (d) 1, 2 and 3

5. **Akbar introduced a number of social and educational reforms. Which of the following reforms were introduced by him in this regard?**
   1. Legalized widow remarriage
   2. Raised marriage age for both boys and girls
   3. Complete ban on practice of Sati
   4. Introduction of secular subjects

   Select the correct answer using the code given below:
   (a) 1 and 3 only (b) 1, 2 and 4 only
   (c) 2, 3 and 4 only (d) 1, 2, 3 and 4

6. **Consider the following statements regarding Aurangzeb's religious policy:**
   1. His invasions against Deccan Sultanate were partly a result of his non-tolerance towards other Muslim sects.
   2. He was a staunch Muslim but he allowed construction of new Hindu temples.

   Which of the above statements is/are correct?
   (a) 1 only (b) 2 only
   (c) Both 1 and 2 (d) Neither 1 nor 2

7. **Consider the following statements regarding Ibadat Khana:**
   1. Ibadat Khana or the Hall of Prayer was established at Agra.
   2. It was opened up for all the religions but later on was confined to Muslim scholars.

   Which of the above statements are correct?
   (a) 1 only (b) 2 only
   (c) Both 1 and 2 (d) None of the above

8. **Match the following:**

List I	List II
A. Sharia	1. Consensus of the community
B. Hadis	2. Traditions of the Prophet
C. Qiyas	3. Law governing Muslim community
D. Ijma	4. Reasoning by analogy

Select the correct answer using the code given below:

	A	B	C	D
(a)	2	3	1	4
(b)	3	2	4	1
(c)	4	1	2	3
(d)	3	4	1	2

SOLUTIONS

1. **Correct Option: (a)**

Supplementary Notes:

Zil-e-Ilahi

- Balban ascended the throne in 1266.
- He broke the power of Chalisa and resorted to the prestige of the crown. That was his greatest contribution towards the stability of the Sultanate.
- To keep himself well-informed, Balban appointed spies.
- He created a strong centralised army to deal with internal disturbances and to check Mongols who were posing a serious danger to Delhi Sultanate.

- He established the military department, Diwani-i-Arz.
- **Option (a) is correct:** The Persian court model influenced Balban's conception of Kingship. He took up the title of Zil-i-Ilahi (Shadow of God). He believed that he ruled on the basis of divine sanction and was not answerable to anyone.

2. **Correct Option: (d)**

Supplementary Notes:

Islamic Law – Kharaj

- Kharaj is a type of individual Islamic tax on agricultural land and its produce developed under Islamic law.
- It was first imposed only on non-Muslims but was later imposed on Muslims as well.

3. **Correct Option: (c)**

Explanation:

- Both statements are correct.

Supplementary Notes:

- In order to make himself accessible to the people as well as to the ministers, Akbar carefully divided his time. The day started with the emperor's appearance at the jharoka of the palace. Large numbers of people assembled daily to have a glimpse of the ruler, and to present petitions to him, if required.
- Akbar had initiated the practice of "Jharokha Darshan" and "Tuladan". The Mughal emperors wielded unlimited powers but they were not cruel or selfish. They believed that the prime duty of a king was to look after the welfare of his subjects. Akbar was generous and always used to listen personally to the complaints of the people. In the matter of administration, the king was assisted by several ministers. The ministers advised the emperor collectively as well as individually.

4. **Correct Option: (d)**

Explanation:

- All statements are correct.

Supplementary Notes:

State and Religion under Akbar

- Akbar followed a policy of broad religious toleration.
- In 1564, he abolished the Jizyah which was sometimes used by the Ulama to humiliate non-Muslims and was often considered a symbol of Muslim domination and superiority. He had earlier abolished the pilgrim tax, and the practice of forcible conversion of prisoners of war.
- The liberal principles of the empire were strengthened by bringing able Hindus into the nobility.
- Akbar's attitude towards his Hindu subjects is closely linked with his views of how a sovereign should behave towards his subjects. According to Abul Fazl, the office of a true ruler was a very responsible one which depended on divine illumination (Farr-i-Izadi). Hence, no one could stand between God and a true ruler. A true ruler was distinguished by a paternal love towards his subjects without distinction of sect or creed and it was his duty to maintain equilibrium in society by not allowing the dust of sectarian strife to rise. All this constituted what has been called the policy of Sulh-i-Kul or 'peace to all'.
- Akbar was deeply interested in religion and philosophy. In 1575, Akbar built a hall called 'Ibadat Khana' or 'the Hall of Prayer' at his new capital, Fatehpur Sikri. To this he called selected theologians, mystics and those of his courtiers and nobles who were known for their scholarship and intellectual attainments. The proceedings, at first, were confined to the Muslims and were later opened to people of all religions – Christians, Zoroastrians, Hindus, Jains, and even atheists.
- But Akbar was less successful in his effort to find a meeting ground between the votaries of different religions in the country. The debates in the Ibadat Khana had not led to a better understanding between different religions, but to greater bitterness, as the representatives of each religion denounced the others and tried to prove that their religion was superior to others. Hence, in 1582, Akbar discontinued the debates in the Ibadat Khana.
- Badayuni asserts that as a result, Akbar gradually turned away from Islam and set up a new religion which was compounded of many existing religions – Hinduism, Christianity, Zoroastrianism, etc. The word used by Abul Fazl and Badayuni for the so called new path was Tauhid-i-Ilahi which literally meant 'Divine Monotheism' which was later called as 'Din-i-Ilahi' or 'Divine Faith'.

5. **Correct Option: (b)**

Explanation:

- **Statement 3 is incorrect:** He stopped Sati, the burning of a widow, unless she herself, of her own free will, persistently desired it.

Supplementary Notes:

Social and Educational Reforms by Akbar

- Akbar introduced a number of social and educational reforms.
- He stopped Sati, the burning of a widow, unless she herself, of her own free will, persistently desired it. Widows of tender age who had not shared the bed with their husbands were not to be burnt at all.
- Widow remarriage was also legalised.
- Akbar was against anyone having more than one wife unless the first wife was barren.

- The age of marriage was raised to 14 for girls and 16 for boys.
- The sale of wines and spirits was restricted.
- Akbar also revised the educational syllabus, laying more emphasis on moral education and mathematics, and on secular subjects such as agriculture, geometry, astronomy, rules of government, logic, history, etc.
- He also gave patronage to artists, poets, painters and musicians, so much so that his court became famous for the galaxy of renowned people known as the 'Navaratnas'.
- However, not all these steps were, however, successful. As we know, the success of social legislation depends largely on the willing cooperation of the people. Akbar was living in an age of superstition and it seems that his social reforms had only limited success.

6. **Correct Option: (a)**

Explanation:

- **Statement 2 is incorrect:** He banned the construction of new Hindu temples and the repair of old temples and gradually started destroying Hindu temples.

Supplementary Notes:
Aurangzeb's Religious Policy

- Various rebellions took place during his reign due to his harsh religious policy. This included the rebellions of the Jat peasantry at Mathura, the Satnami peasantry in Punjab, and the Bundelas in Bundelkhand in c.1672 CE.
- He was a staunch and orthodox Muslim in his personal life and his ideal was to transform India into an Islamic state. Initially, he banned the construction of new Hindu temples and the repair of old temples, but later, he gradually started destroying Hindu temples. The celebrated temples of Keshava Rai at Mathura and Vishwanath temple at Banaras were reduced to ruins and mosques erected in their place.
- In c.1679 CE, he re-imposed jiziya and pilgrim tax.
- He was also not tolerant of other Muslim sects. The celebration of Muharram was stopped. In fact, his invasions against the Deccan Sultanate were partly due to his hatred of the Shia faith.

7. **Correct Option: (d)**

Explanation:

- **Both the Statements are incorrect:** A hall called 'Ibadat Khana' or the 'Hall of Prayer' was established at his new capital, Fatehpur Sikri. Akbar's quest for religious knowledge led to interfaith debates in the Ibadat Khana at Fatehpur Sikri between learned Muslims, Hindus, Jains, Parsis and Christians, and it continued till the end.

Supplementary Notes:
Information regarding Ibadat Khana

- In 1575, Akbar built a hall called 'Ibadat Khana' or 'the Hall of Prayer' at his new capital, Fatehpur Sikri.
- To this he called selected theologians, mystics and those of his courtiers and nobles who were known for their scholarship and intellectual attainments.
- Akbar discussed religious and spiritual topics with them.
- Akbar's quest for religious knowledge led to interfaith debates in the Ibadat Khana at Fatehpur Sikri between learned Muslims, Hindus, Jains, Parsis and Christians.
- This horrified the theologians, and all kinds of rumours began to circulate about Akbar's desire to forsake Islam.
- Instead of bringing credit, the Ibadat Khana brought growing discredit.
- In 1582, Akbar discontinued the debates in the Ibadat Khana. But he did not give up his quest for truth.

8. **Correct Option: (b)**

Explanation:

- Option (b) is correctly matched.

List I	List II
A. Sharia	3. Law governing Muslim community
B. Hadis	2. Traditions of the Prophet
C. Qiyas	4. Reasoning by analogy
D. Ijma	1. Consensus of the community

Supplementary Notes:
Islamic Traditions

- Ulama (plural of 'Alim') were scholars of Islamic studies. As preservers of this tradition, they performed various religious, juridical and teaching functions. They guided the Muslim rulers and ensured that they ruled according to Sharia.
- Sharia is the law governing the Muslim community. It is based on the Quran and the Hadis – the traditions of the Prophet including a record of his remembered words and deeds.
- With the expansion of Islamic rule outside Arabia, in areas where customs and traditions were different, Qiyas (reasoning by analogy) and Ijma (consensus of the community) were recognized as two other sources of legislation.
- Thus, the Sharia evolved from Quran, Hadis, Qiyas and Ijma.

CONCEPT REVISION

Here is the list of concepts that have been covered as part of the previous exercise. Revise and Self-reflect on your concepts you covered.

- Concept of 'Shadow of God' ☐
- Kharaj ☐
- Jharokha System ☐
- Religious policy of Akbar ☐
- Aurangzeb's religious policy ☐
- Ibadat Khana ☐

6.3 BHAKTI AND SUFI MOVEMENTS

QUESTIONS

1. Consider the following statements:

1. Alvars were devotees of Vishnu whereas Nayanars worshipped Shiva.
2. Nayanars and Alvars were patronized by Chola rulers.
3. Alvars and Nayanars promoted the distinctions of caste.

Which of the above statements is/are correct?

(a) 1 and 2 only
(b) 2 only
(c) 2 and 3 only
(d) 1, 2 and 3

2. Which of the following Bhakti saints was/were associated with Nirguna-Bhakti movement?

1. Adi Shankaracharya
2. Guru Nanak
3. Kabir
4. Tulsidas

Select the correct answer using the codes given below:

(a) 1 only (b) 1 and 2 only
(c) 1, 2 and 3 only (d) 1, 2, 3 and 4

3. In the context of Medieval Indian history, Barid-i-Mumalik or Munihiyan refers to:

(a) Artisans and Tradesmen
(b) Bodyguards of the Emperor
(c) The spy department or intelligence officers
(d) Officer-in-charge of state exchequer

4. Consider the following Bhakti Saints:

1. Tukaram
2. Jayadeva
3. Namdev

Who among the above belong to the state of Maharashtra?

(a) 1 and 2 only (b) 2 and 3 only
(c) 1 and 3 only (d) 1, 2 and 3

5. Consider the following Bhakti saints:

1. Kabir
2. Namdeva
3. Ramananda
4. Nanak

The correct chronological order of their appearance in Bhakti Movement is:

(a) 2 - 3 - 1 - 4 (b) 2 - 3 - 4 - 1
(c) 3 - 2 - 1 - 4 (d) 3 - 2 - 4 - 1

6. Match List-I with List-II :

List-I (Saint)	List-II (Region)
A. Chaitanya Mahaprabhu	1. Malabar
B. Guru Nanak	2. Maharashtra
C. Tukaram	3. Punjab
D. Shankaracharya	4. Bengal

Select the correct answer using the code given below:

	A	B	C	D
(a)	4	3	2	1
(b)	1	3	2	4
(c)	3	4	2	1
(d)	2	4	3	1

7. Match List-I with List-II:

List-I (Sufi Saints)	List-II (Silsilas)
A. Shaikh Nizamuddin	1. Qadiri Auliya
B. Bahauddin Zakariya	2. Suhrawardi
C. Mian Mir	3. Chisti
D. Ahmed Sirhindi	4. Naqshbandi

Select the correct answer using the code given below:

	A	B	C	D
(a)	3	2	1	4
(b)	3	4	2	1
(c)	2	1	3	4
(d)	1	2	3	4

8. Consider the following statements about Amir Khusrau:

1. He was a disciple (murid) of Nizamudddin Auliya.
2. He is regarded as 'Father of Qawwali'.

Which of the above statements is/are correct?

(a) 1 only (b) 2 only
(c) Both 1 and 2 (d) Neither 1 nor 2

9. Which of the following statements is incorrect regarding the development of religious ideas and beliefs during the Mughal Reign?

(a) To emphasise that the Guru combined both spiritual and worldly leadership in his person, Guru Arjun began to live in an aristocratic style.
(b) Dara Shikoh declared the Vedas to be 'heavenly books in point of time' and 'in conformity with the holy Quran'.
(c) The most renowned figure in the Muslim orthodox and revivalist movement of the time was Shaikh Ahmad Sirhindi.
(d) Tukaram asserted the privileges of the Brahmans stating that none other except the Brahmans had the right to read the scriptures or to preach.

10. Consider the following statements regarding development of Bhakti movement:

1. The Bhakti movement stressed the mystical union of the individual with God.
2. The development of popular Bhakti took place in South India between the 12th and the 14th century.
3. After becoming popular in South India, the Bhakti movement spread rapidly towards North India.

Which of the above statements is/are incorrect?

(a) 1 and 2 only (b) 1 and 3 only
(c) 2 and 3 only (d) 1, 2 and 3

11. Which actions of Sufi saints are influenced by Hindu and Buddhism?

1. Monastic organisation
2. Penance
3. Fasting and holding the breath

Select the correct option using the codes given below:

(a) 1 and 2 only (b) 1 and 3 only
(c) 2 and 3 only (d) 1, 2 and 3

12. Consider the following statements regarding Sufi movement:

1. It adhered to direct perception of mankind to God without any mediator.
2. It rejected outward religiosity.

Which of the above statements is/are correct?

(a) 1 only (b) 2 only
(c) Both 1 and 2 (d) Neither 1 nor 2

13. He was born in Tamil Nadu in the 11th century and was deeply influenced by the Alvars.

According to him, the best means of attaining salvation was through intense devotion to Vishnu . He propounded the doctrine of Vishishtadvaita or qualified oneness in that the soul even when united with the Supreme God remained distinct". The given paragraph is about which of the following Bhakti saints?

(a) Ramanuja (b) Shankara
(c) Basavanna (d) None of the above

14. Consider the following:

1. Surge in vernacular literature
2. Development of philosophies
3. Devotional transformation of society and inclusiveness

Which of the above is/are impact/s of Bhakti Movement?

(a) 2 and 3 only (b) 3 only
(c) 1 only (d) 1, 2 and 3

15. Consider the following statement regarding Sufi Silsilah in India:

1. Chishti Silsilah usually stayed away from State powers.
2. Quadariya Silsilah supported the concept of Wahadat-al-Wajud.
3. Naqshbandi Silsilah was established by Khwaja Bahauddin Naqshbandi in India.

Which of the above statements is/are correct?

(a) 1 only (b) 1 and 2 only
(c) 1, 2 and 3 (d) None of the above

16. Which of the following were the main features of the Bhakti Movement?

1. Intense love and devotion as the means of salvation.
2. Rejection of rituals and ceremonies.
3. Need for a true Guru to realize God.
4. Stressed on the idea of a personal connection with God.

Select the correct answer using the code given below:

(a) 1 and 2 only (b) 2, 3 and 4 only
(c) 1, 3 and 4 only (d) 1, 2, 3 and 4

17. Consider the following statements regarding philosophies of Sufism:

1. The concept of Wahadat-al-Wujud was coined by Ibn Arabi, while Wahadat-ul-Shujud was formulated by Ala-al-Dawlah Simnani.
2. The concept of Wahadat-al-Wujud means the 'Oneness of Existence', while the concept of Wahadat-ul-Shujud means the 'unity of appearance'.

Which of the above statements is/are incorrect?

(a) 1 only (b) 2 only
(c) Both 1 and 2 (d) Neither 1 nor 2

18. Consider the following statements regarding Sufism:

1. Sufism in Islam and Bhakti movement in Hindus brought both the communities closer to each other.
2. Beshara sufi order was bound by the Islamic laws whereas Bashara was not bound by the Islamic laws.
3. Sufism could not influence the masses as it restricted to the urban areas.

Which of the above statements is/are incorrect?

(a) 2 only (b) 3 only
(c) 2 and 3 only (d) 1, 2 and 3

19. Consider the following statements with respect to 'Great' and 'Little' Traditions:

1. Great Tradition emanated from dominant social categories like priests and rulers.
2. Little tradition refers to great tradition tailored according to regional and village conditions.

Which of the above statements is/are correct?

(a) 1 only (b) 2 only
(c) Both 1 and 2 (d) Neither 1 nor 2

20. Consider the following statements:

1. Sufism was initiated as a result of protest against the growing mysticism and asceticism of the Caliphate.
2. Sufi saints interpreted Quran based on their personal experiences.
3. The Sufis organized communities around a hospice called 'Dargah'.
4. Chisti order was named after its founder Khwaja Muinuddin Chisti.

Which of the above statements is/are incorrect?

(a) 2 only (b) 3 and 4 only
(c) 1 and 3 only (d) 1, 3 and 4 only

21. There is no evidence of anything resembling the compositions of Alvars and Nayanars in North India till the 14th century. In this context, consider the following statements:

1. Emergence of Rajput states
2. Establishment of Delhi Sultanate
3. Emergence of new urban centres

Which of the above statements can be the reason for absence of Bhakti Group in North India till 14th century?

(a) 1 only (b) 1 and 2 only
(c) 3 only (d) 1, 2 and 3

22. Historians often classify Bhakti and Sufi traditions into two broad categories. In this regard, consider the following statements:

1. Saguna is the concept of worshipping an abstract form of God.
2. Nirguna traditions focused on worship of specific deities in their anthropomorphic forms.

Which of the above statements is/are correct?

(a) 1 only (b) 2 only
(c) Both 1 and 2 (d) Neither 1 nor 2

23. Consider the following statements with respect to the Chisti Order:

1. It was the most influential of the groups of Sufis who migrated to India.
2. Both Amir Khusrau and Ziyauddin Barani were associated with Chisti order.
3. Sama or performance of mystical music was integral to the Chishtis.
4. Alauddin Khalji was the first sultan to visit the dargah of Khwaja Muinuddin.

Which of the above statements are correct?

(a) 1 and 3 only (b) 2 and 4 only
(c) 1, 2 and 3 only (d) 2, 3 and 4 only

24. With reference to Virashaiva tradition, consider the following statements:

1. It emerged in 12th century in Kerala, led by a saint named Basavanna.
2. The Virashaivas encouraged the remarriage of widows.
3. Their ideas were incorporated within Sanskrit tradition which led into culmination of Bhagvata Purana.
4. The Lingayats buried their dead as they believed in the theory of rebirth.

Which of the above statements is/are incorrect?

(a) 1 only (b) 2 and 4 only
(c) 1, 3 and 4 only (d) 1, 2, 3 and 4

25. The earliest Bhakti movements were led by Alvars and Nayanars. In this context, consider the following statements:

1. Alvars were the devotees of Shiva while Nayanars were the devotees of Vishnu.
2. Both Alvars and Nayanars initiated a movement of protest against the caste system.
3. Women devotees were present among Alvars while they were absent in Nayanars.
4. Opposition to Buddhism and Jainism is particularly marked in the compositions of Nayanars.

Which of the above statements are correct?

(a) 1 and 2 only (b) 1 and 4 only
(c) 2 and 4 only (d) 3 and 4 only

26. Consider the following statements about Virashaiva movement:

1. The movement was initiated by a Brahmana named Basavanna.
2. The Virashaivas were very critical towards Brahmanical ideas of caste, rituals and idol worship.
3. Even though they have advocated for equal rights of women, they were not supportive of remarriage of widows.

Which of the statements given above is/are correct?

(a) 1 and 2 only (b) 1 and 3 only
(c) 2 and 3 only (d) All the above

27. Consider the following statements about doctrine of Sufism:

1. It calls for spiritual self-development through service of mankind.

2. It discouraged materialism and believed in complete renunciation.
3. Sufi saints are organized into different orders called Silsilas.
4. It preaches faith and devotion to God unlike the Bhakti movement.

Which of the above statements are correct?

(a) 1 and 3 only (b) 1, 2 and 4 only
(c) 2, 3 and 4 only (d) 1, 2, 3 and 4

28. Which of the following statements is/are correct regarding the Alvars of the Bhakti movement?

1. They were the devotees of Lord Shiva and were called Shaivites.
2. They composed their poems and compositions in Tamil.
3. People from lower castes and women were prohibited to be part of the order.
4. They initiated a movement of protest against the caste system.

Select the correct answer using the code given below:

(a) 1 only (b) 2 and 4 only
(c) 1, 2 and 3 only (d) 2, 3 and 4 only

SOLUTIONS

1. **Correct Option: (a)**

Explanation:

Statement 3 is incorrect: The Alvars and Nayanars initiated a movement of protest against the caste system and the dominance of Brahmanas.

Supplementary Notes:

Alvars & Nayanars:

- Earliest Bhakti movements in South India were led by the Alvars (those who are "immersed" in devotion to Vishnu) and Nayanars (who were devotees of Shiva).
- They travelled from place to place singing hymns in Tamil in praise of their God.
- The Alvars and Nayanars initiated a movement of protest against the caste system and the dominance of Brahmanas.
- To some extent this is corroborated by the fact that bhaktas hailed from diverse social backgrounds ranging from Brahmanas to artisans and cultivators and even from castes considered "untouchable".
- The importance of the traditions of the Alvars and Nayanars was sometimes indicated by the claim that their compositions were as important as the Vedas.
- One of the major anthologies of compositions by the Alvars, the Nalayira Divyaprabandham, was frequently described as the Tamil Veda, thus claiming that the text was as significant as the four Vedas in Sanskrit that were cherished by the Brahmanas.
- In South India, one of the major themes in Tamil Bhakti hymns is opposition to Buddhism and Jainism, thus, patronized by Cholas.
- For example, the powerful Chola rulers (9th to 13th centuries) supported Brahmanical and Bhakti traditions by making land grants and constructing temples for Vishnu and Shiva.

2. **Correct Option: (c)**

Supplementary Notes:

Nirguna and Saguna

- The Bhakti movement of Hinduism saw two ways of imaging the nature of the divine (Brahman) – Nirguna and Saguna.
- Nirguna Brahman was the concept of the Ultimate Reality as formless, without attributes or quality. Saguna Brahman, in contrast, was envisioned and developed as with form, attributes and quality.
- The two had parallels in the ancient pantheistic unmanifest and theistic manifest traditions, respectively, and traceable to Arjuna-Krishna dialogue in the Bhagavad Gita.
- It is the same Brahman, but viewed from two perspectives, one from Nirguni knowledge-focus and other from Saguni love-focus, united as Krishna in the Gita.
- Nirguna bhakta's poetry were Jnana-shrayi, or had roots in knowledge. Saguna bhakta's poetry were Prema-shrayi, or with roots in love.
- Nirguna: Kabir, Nanak, Adi Shankaracharya, Dadu.

3. **Correct Option: (c)**

Supplementary Notes:

Barid-i-Mumalik

- Barid-i-Mumalik was the head of the information and intelligence department. Only a nobleman who enjoyed the fullest confidence of Sultan was appointed the chief Barid.
- The Barid-i-Mumalik had to keep information of all that was happening in the Sultanate.
- At local level there were Barids who used to send regular news concerning the matters of the State to the central office.
- Apart from Barids, another set of reporters also existed who were known as Munihiyan.

4. **Correct Option: (c)**

Explanation

- **Option (c) is correct:** Jayadeva is a Bhakti saint from Eastern Indian states of Bihar and Odisha.

Supplementary Notes:

Bhakti Movement – Maharashtra

- In Maharashtra, the Bhakti movement drew its inspiration from the Bhagavata Purana and the Siva Nathpanthis.
- Jnaneswar was a pioneer Bhakti saint of Maharashtra. His commentary on the Bhagavad Gita called Jnaneswari served as a foundation of the Bhakti ideology in Maharashtra. Arguing against caste distinctions he believed that the only way to attain God was through Bhakti.
- Vithoba was the God of this sect and its followers performed a pilgrimage to the temple twice a year. The Vithoba of Pandharpur became the mainstay of the movement in Maharashtra.
- Namdev (1270–1350) was another important Bhakti saint from Maharashtra. While he is remembered in the north Indian monotheistic tradition as a Nirguna saint, in Maharashtra he is considered to be part of the Varkari tradition (the Vaishnava devotional tradition).
- Some of the other important Bhakti saints of Maharashtra were the saints Choka, Sonara, Tukaram and Eknath.
- Tukaram's teachings are in the form of the Avangas (dohas), which constitute the Gatha, while Eknath's teachings that were in Marathi attempted to shift the emphasis of Marathi literature from spiritual to narrative compositions.

5. **Correct Option: (a)**

Supplementary Notes:

Bhakti Movement

- Despite being a proponent of the Warkari sect, Saint Namdev established religious unity across the country. Saint Namdeo was born in the year 1270 in the village of Narasi-Bamani, now located in the Hingoli District in Maharashtra. He was born to a tailor named Damasheti Relekar and his wife, Gonai.
- Ramananda, also called Ramanand or Ramadatta, (born c. 1400 – died c. 1470), North Indian Brahman (priest), held by his followers (Ramanandis) to be fifth in succession in the lineage of the philosopher-mystic Ramanuja.
- Kabir Das, a mystical poet and great saint of India, was born in the year 1440 and died in the year 1518.
- Sri Guru Nanak was born in 1469 in Talwandi, a village in the Sheikhupura district, 65 kms west of Lahore.

6. **Correct Option: (a)**

Saints

List-I (Saint)	List-II (Region)
A. Chaitanya	4. Bengal Mahaprabhu
B. Guru Nanak	3. Punjab
C. Tukaram	2. Maharashtra
D. Shankaracharya	1. Malabar

Supplementary Notes:

- The Bhakti Movement in Bengal was started by none other than Sri Chaitanya Mahaprabhu. In the beginning of Kali Yuga, the Bhakti Movement was prominent in South India due to the prevalence of the Sri Vaishnavas and Madhavas. Then in 1486, Sri Chaitanya Mahaprabhu appeared in Mayapur in Bengal.
- Guru Nanak, the founder of Sikhism was born on 15 April, 1469 at Rai Bhoi Ki Talvandi (modern-day Nankana Sahib, Punjab, Pakistan).
- Tukaram was another Bhakti saint of Maharashtra and was a contemporary of Sivaji. He is also referred to as Sant Tukaram, Bhakta Tukaram, Tukaram Maharaj, Tukobaand Tukobaraya. He was a 17th-century poet-saint of the Bhakti movement. Tukaram is best known for his Abhanga – devotional poetry and kirtans – community-oriented worship with spiritual songs. His poetry was devoted to Vitthala or Vithoba, an avatar of Hindu God Vishnu. His responsible for creating a background for Maratha nationalism.

7. **Correct Option: (a)**

Supplementary Notes:

Sufi Saints

- The word Silsila literally means a chain, signifying a continuous link between master and disciple, stretching as an unbroken spiritual genealogy to the Prophet Muhammad. It was through this channel that spiritual power and blessings were transmitted to devotees. Special rituals of initiation were developed in which initiates took an oath of allegiance, wore a patched garment, and shaved their hair.

List-I (Sufi Saints)	List-II (Silsilas)
A. Shaikh Nizamuddin	3. Chisti Auliya
B. Bahauddin Zakariya	2. Suhrawardi
C. Mian Mir	1. Qadiri
D. Ahmed Sirhindi	4. Naqshbandi

8. **Correct Option: (c)**

Explanation:

- Both statements are correct.

Supplementary Notes:

Amir Khusrau

- His real name was Abdul Hasan.
- He lived for 72 years, out of which 60 years he lived in the courts of as many as ten different rulers of the Delhi Sultanate.

- He was a poet as well as prolific musician. His primary language to write poems was Persian but he composed almost half a million verses in Persian, Turkish, Arabic, Braj Bhasha, Hindavi as well as the Khadi Boli. His Khaliq-e-Bari, which is known as oldest printed dictionary of the world deals with Hindi and Persian words. He is regarded as the "father of qawwali".
- He created a new literary style in Persian which came to be known as Sabaq-i-Hindi.
- He composed verses in Hindi as well and paved the way for the development of Urdu.
- He was a disciple of Nizamuddin Auliya, the famous Sufi saint of Chisti order.
- He introduced numerous Perso-Arabic ragas – aiman, sanam, ghura, etc.
- His five literary masterpieces – dedicated to Alauddin Khalji, Matula-Ui-Anwar, Shirin Khasrau, Laila Majnuri Ayina-i-Sikandri and Hasht Bihist.
- He is also credited with enriching Indian classical music by introducing Persian and Arabic elements in it, and was the originator of the khayal and tarana styles of music.
- Khayal later reached to its zenith during the times of Mohammad Shah Rangile and today is integral part of Hindustani classical music.

9. **Correct Option: (d)**

Explanation:

- **Statement (d) is incorrect:** Raghunandan asserted the privileges of the Brahmans stating that none other except the Brahmans had the right to read the scriptures or to preach.

Supplementary Notes:

Development of Religious Ideas and Beliefs

- The fifth guru, Arjun Das, completed the compilation of the Sikh scriptures called the 'Adi Granth' or 'Granth Sahib'.
- To emphasise that the guru combined both spiritual and worldly leadership in his person, Guru Arjun began to live in an aristocratic style.
- He erected lofty buildings at Amritsar, wore fine clothes, kept fine horses procured from Central Asia and maintained retainers in attendance.
- Despite some display of orthodoxy by Shah Jahan at the beginning of his reign and a few acts of intolerance, such as the demolition of 'new' temples, he was not narrow in his outlook which was further tempered towards the end of his reign by the influence of his liberal son, Dara.
- Dara, the eldest son of Shah Jahan, was by temperament a scholar and a Sufi who loved to discourse with religious divines.
- With the help of the Brahmans of Kasi, he got the Gita translated into Persian. But his most significant work was an anthology of the Vedas in the introduction to which Dara declared the Vedas to be 'heavenly books in point of time' and 'in conformity with the holy Quran'. Thus, he underlined the belief that there were no fundamental differences between Hinduism and Islam.
- The sentiments of the orthodox Hindus were echoed by Raghunandan of Navadwipa (Nadia) in Bengal.
- Considered to be the most influential writer on the Dharmashastras during the medieval period, Raghunandan asserted the privileges of the Brahmans stating that none others except the Brahmans had the right to read the scriptures or to preach.
- He ends by saying that, in the Kali Age there were only two Varnas – Brahmans and Shudras, the true Kshatriyas having disappeared long ago and the Vaishyas and others having lost their caste status due to the non-performance of appropriate duties.
- Ram Das of Maharashtra, who was later the spiritual guru of Sivaji, and who put forward a philosophy of activism, was equally vehement in assertion of the privileges of the Brahmans.
- Among the Muslims, too, while the trend of tauhid continued apace, and was supported by many leading Sufi saints, a small group of the orthodox Ulama denounced it, as also the liberal policies of Akbar. The most renowned figure in the Muslim orthodox and revivalist movement of the time was Shaikh Ahmad Sirhindi.
- A follower of the orthodox Naqshbandi school of Sufis which had been introduced in India during Akbar's reign, Shaikh Ahmad Sirhindi opposed the concept of pantheistic mysticism (tauhid) or unity of God and the created being, denouncing it as un-Islamic.

10. **Correct Option: (c)**

Explanation:

- **Statement 2 is incorrect:** The development of popular Bhakti took place in south India between the seventh and the twelfth century.
- **Statement 3 is incorrect:** Although there were many points of contact between south and north India, the transmission of the ideas of the Bhakti saints from south to north India was a slow and long drawn-out process

Supplementary Notes:

Cultural Development in India 1300-1500: Bhakti Movement

- The Bhakti movement which stressed the mystical union of the individual with God had been at work in India long before the arrival of the Turks.

- Although the seeds of Bhakti can be found in the Vedas, it was not emphasized during the early period. The idea of the adoration of a personal God, seems to have developed with the growing popularity of Buddhism.
- During the early centuries of the Christian era, under Mahayana Buddhism, the Buddha began to be worshipped in his 'gracious' (avalokita) form.
- The worship of Vishnu developed more or less at the same time. When many of the holy books, such as the Ramayana and the Mahabharata, were re-written during the Gupta times, Bhakti was accepted, along with jnana and karma, as one of the recognized roads to salvation.
- However, the development of popular Bhakti took place in south India between the 7th and the 12th century. As has been noticed earlier, the Saiva nayanars and the Vaishnavite alvars disregarded the austerities preached by the Jains and the Buddhists and preached personal devotion to God as a means of salvation.
- They disregarded the rigidities of the caste system and carried their message of love and personal devotion to God to various parts of south India by using the local languages.
- Although there were many points of contact between south and north India, the transmission of the ideas of the Bhakti saints from south to north India was a slow and long drawn-out process.
- Oddly enough, the very reasons which made the nayanars and alvars popular in the south limited their appeal outside the area, viz., the fact that they preached and composed in the local languages.
- Sanskrit was still the vehicle of thought in the country.
- The ideas of Bhakti were carried to the north by scholars as well as by saints.

11. Correct Option: (d)

Explanation:

- All statements are correct.

Supplementary Notes:

The Sufi Movement (Influence of Buddhist and Hindu Yogic Influence)

- Mystics, who are called Sufis, had risen in Islam at a very early stage. Most of them were persons of deep devotion who were disgusted by the vulgar display of wealth and degeneration of morals following the establishment of the Islamic empire.
- Hence, these saints wanted to have nothing to do with the State, a tradition which continued later on.
- Some of the early Sufis, such as the woman mystic Rabia (d. 8th century) and Mansur bin Hallaj (d. 10th century), laid great emphasis on love as the bond between God and the individual soul.
- The monastic organisation of the Sufis, and some of their practices such as penance, fasting and holding the breath are sometimes traced to the Buddhist and Hindu yogic influence.
- Buddhism was widely prevalent in Central Asia before the advent of Islam, and the legend of the Buddha as a saintly man had passed into the Islamic legend.
- Yogis continued to visit West Asia even after the advent of Islam and the yogic book, 'Amrit-Kund' had been translated into Persian from Sanskrit.
- Thus, Hindu and Buddhist practices and rituals seem to have been absorbed and assimilated by the Sufis even before they came to India.
- Whether, Buddhist philosophic ideas and Vedantist ideas had, in a significant manner, influenced Sufism is a matter of controversy. The origin of ideas is difficult to trace.
- The Sufi saints and many modern thinkers trace the Sufi ideas to the Quran. What is important to note here is that, irrespective of origin, there were many similarities in the ideas of the Sufis and the Hindu yogis and mystics about the nature of God, and His relationship with the soul, and the material world. This provided a basis for mutual toleration and understanding.

12. Correct Option: (c)

Explanation:

- Both statements are correct.

Supplementary Notes:

Sufi Movement

- The 10th century AD marks the important changes in the realm of ideas and beliefs in the Islamic religion – the rise of the Sufi mystic orders. It was mystical movement against orthodox practice in Islam with an aim to adhere the direct perception of mankind to God without any mediator.
- The core concept of Sufi Movement is Darikh-i-Duniya/Wahad-ul-Wahjud, meaning "Universal Brotherhood". It outwardly rejected the religion and emphasised love and devotion to God and compassion towards all fellow human beings.
- Mystics, who are called Sufis, were persons of deep devotion who were disgusted by the display of wealth and degeneration of morals following the establishment of the Islamic empire.
- The Sufis were organized in 12 orders or Silsilahs. A Silsilah was generally led by a prominent mystic who lived in a Khanqah or hospice along with his disciples.

- The Sufi saints made themselves popular by adopting musical recitations called "Sama", to create a mood of nearness to God. 'Qawwali' is the form of sufi devotional music popular in South Asia and Ghazal is a form of Qawwali.

13. Correct Option: (a)

Explanation:

- **Option (a) is correct:** The given paragraph is about Ramanuja.

Supplementary Notes:

Ramanuja

- He was born in Tamil Nadu in the 11th century, and was deeply influenced by the Alvars.
- According to him, the best means of attaining salvation was through intense devotion to Vishnu. He propounded the doctrine of Vishishtadvaita or qualified oneness in that the soul, even when united with the supreme God, remained distinct.
- He said that the ultimate reality is Brahman and that the soul and matter are his qualities. He expounded the grace of God as more important than knowledge.

14. Correct Option: (d)

Explanation:

- All statements are correct.

Supplementary Notes:

Bhakti Movement

- The Bhakti movement started in the 7th-8th century in Kerala and Tamil Nadu. Later, it spread to Karnataka, Maharashtra, and it reached north India in the 15th century. The Bhakti movement reached its peak in the 15th – and 17th century.

Major Impacts of Bhakti Movement

- **Surge in Vernacular Literature**
  - Bhakti Movement resulted in a surge in Hindu literature in regional/vernacular languages mainly in the form of devotional poems and music.
- **Development of Philosophies**
  - The Bhakti Movement led to development of different philosophies within the Vedanta school, ranging from dvaita to advaita.
- **Devotional Transformation of Society and Inclusiveness**
  - It led to devotional transformation of medieval Hindu society and pushed the early means to achieve salvation (Vedic rituals and ascetic lifestyles) to background and brought individualistic relationship with personally defined God on forefront.
  - Thus, salvation which was hitherto considered achievable only for Brahmins, Kshatriya and Vaishya castes, was not available to everyone. Thus, this movement provided inclusive path to spiritual salvation to women and members of Shudra and untouchable community.
  - In many ways, the impact was similar to that of Protestant Reformation of Christianity in Europe. It was able to evoke shared religiosity, direct emotional attachment to divine and pursuit of spiritual satisfaction without overhead of institutional super structures.
- **New Forms of Worship**
  - Bhakti Movement led to emergence of new forms of spiritual leadership and social cohesion such as community singing, chanting together of deity names, festivals, pilgrimages, and rituals, etc. many of which are in vogue even today.
  - It also led to new forms of voluntary social giving such as Seva (service), Dana (Charity) and Community Kitchens (Bhandra/Langar, etc.) Some of the temples and Gurudwaras adopted social functions such as helping poor, providing education by establishing charity schools, charity hospitals, relief in the aftermath of natural disasters etc.

15. Correct Option: (c)

Explanation:

- All statements are correct.

Supplementary Notes:

Chishti Silsilah

- The Chishti order was founded in India by Khwaja Muinuddin Chishti (AD 1143-1223). It began in Chist, a small town near heart in Afghanistan in AD 930. Khwaja Muinuddin Chishti established his khanqah in Ajmer to work for the poorest sections of the society.
- After his demise, every year an annual congregation (urs) is held at Ajmer. It is the most widespread among the Sufi orders. They usually stayed away from state powers. However, they were intrinsically linked and established khanqahs and dargahs in far-flung areas like Bengal and Multan.

Suhrawardi Silsilah

- This Silsilah was founded by Sheikh Shihabuddin Suhrawardi in Baghdad but it was established in India by Sheikh Bahauddin Zakariya (1182-1262) and was given the title of 'Sheikh-ul-Islam' by Iltutmish.
- They accepted royal patronage and amassed a lot of property. They believed that a Sufi should own the three attributes: property, knowledge, and hal (mystical enlightenment).

Qadariya Silsilah

- Its founder was Abdul Qadir Gilani (Pir Dastagir). Shah Namatullah introduced the Silsilah in India. It became popular in Punjab (esp. Sindh) The pirs of this order supported the concept of Wahadat-al-Wajud.

- Miyan Mir was one of the famous pirs of this silsilah and enrolled prince Dara Shikoh. His influence can be seen in the writing of Dara. Urdu poets Hasrat Mohani and Muhammad Iqbal belonged to this order.

Naqshbandi Silsilah

- The Naqshbandi order was established by Khwaja Bahauddin Naqshbandi in India. The most popular saint of the silsila was Sheikh Ahmed Sarhindi. He gave himself the title of 'Mujeddid Ali Saffani' or the reformer of the new millennium. It became popular during the reign of Akbar. It was radical in nature and had Aurangzeb as one of its followers.

16. Correct Option: (d)

Explanation:

- All statements are correct.

Supplementary Notes:

Main Features of the Bhakti Movement

- Intense love and devotion as the means of salvation.
- Unity of God (Universalism) and repeating the one true name again and again.
- Rejection of rituals and ceremonies.
- No caste discrimination and keeping an open mind on religious and gender issues. They allowed both men and women to seek salvation. They even took their meals together from the common kitchen.
- Using local and regional languages to spread their messages.
- They stressed on the idea of a personal God.
- Need of a true Guru (teacher) to realize God.
- They propagated equality and spirit of brotherhood like the Sufis.
- They despised priests who they thought were middlemen and instead focused on establishing a personal connection with God.

17. Correct Option: (d)

Explanation:

- Both statements are correct.

Supplementary Notes:

Philosophies of Sufism

- There are two different philosophies in Sufi mystical thought. One is the concept of Wahadat-al-Wujud or the 'Oneness of Existence' which was coined by Ibn Arabi.
- The philosophy emphasises that 'there is no true existence except the Ultimate Truth (God)' and that the only truth within the universe is God, and that all things exist within God only.
- The other is the concept of Wahadat-ul-Shujud or the 'unity of appearance'. This school was formulated by `Ala al-Dawlah Simnani', to attract many followers in India, including Ahmed Sirhindi who provided some of the most widely accepted formulations of this doctrine in the Indian sub-continent.
- He held that God and creation are not identical; rather, the latter is a shadow or reflection of the Divines' Name and Attributes when they are reflected in the mirrors of their opposite non-beings.

18. Correct Option: (c)

Explanation:

- **Statement 2 is incorrect:** Bashara sufi order obeyed the Islamic laws whereas Beshara was more liberal.
- **Statement 3 is incorrect:** Sufism took roots in both rural and urban areas.

Supplementary Notes:

Sufism

- Sufism or mysticism emerged in the 8th century. By the 12th century, the Sufis were organised in silsilahs (i.e., orders, which basically represented an unbreakable chain between the pir, the teacher, and the murids, the disciples). The four most popular silsilahs were the Chistis, Suhrawardis, Qadiriyahs, and Naqshbandis.
- There were two broad Sufi orders:
  - Bashara – Those who obeyed the Islamic laws.
  - Beshara – Those who were more liberal.
- Alongside the liberal and unorthodox Sufi movement, the Bhakti cult was gaining strength among the Hindus and these two parallel movements based on the doctrines of love and selfless devotion contributed a great deal in bringing both the communities of Hindus and Muslims closer together.
- Sufism took roots in both rural and urban areas and exercised a deep social, political, and cultural influence on the masses.

19. Correct Option: (c)

Explanation:

- Both statements are correct.

Supplementary Notes:

Great and Little Traditions

- The terms 'great' and 'little' traditions were coined by a sociologist named Robert Redfield in the 20th century to describe the cultural practices of the peasant societies.
- He founded that peasants observed rituals and customs that emanated from dominant social categories, including priests and rulers. He classified them as great traditions.
- The great traditions consist of the traditions contained in epics like Puranas and other classical Sanskritic works.

- At the same time, peasants followed local practices that did not necessarily correspond with those of great tradition. These he included them within the category of little tradition.
- The carriers of little tradition include story-tellers, poets, saints etc.

20. Correct Option: (d)

Explanation:

- **Statement 1 incorrect:** Sufism was initiated as a result of protest against the growing materialism of the Caliphate.
- **Statement 3 is incorrect:** The Sufis organized communities around a hospice called 'khanqah'.
- **Statement 4 is incorrect:** Chisti order was named after their place of origin – the town of Chist in Central Afghanistan.

Supplementary Notes:

Growth of Sufism

- In the early centuries of Islam, a group of religious minded people called Sufis turned to asceticism and mysticism in protest against the growing materialism of the Caliphate as a religious and political institution.
- They were critical of the dogmatic definitions and scholastic methods of interpreting the Quran and Sunna (traditions of the Prophet) adopted by theologians. Instead, they laid emphasis on seeking salvation through intense devotion and love for God by following His commands, and by following the example of the Prophet Muhammad whom they regarded as a perfect human being.
- The Sufis, thus, sought an interpretation of the Quran on the basis of their personal experience.
- By the 11th century Sufism evolved into a well-developed movement with a body of literature Quranic studies and Sufi practices.
- The Sufis began to organize communities around the hospice or khanqah (Persian) controlled by a teaching master known as 'Shaikh' (in Arabic), and 'Pir' or 'Murshid' (in Persian). He enrolled disciples (murids) and appointed a successor (khalifa). He established rules for spiritual conduct and interaction between inmates as well as between laypersons and the master.
- The word 'silsila' literally means a chain, signifying a continuous link between master and disciple, stretching as an unbroken spiritual genealogy to the Prophet Muhammad.
- When the Sufi teacher 'Shaikh' died, his tomb-shrine (Dargah, a Persian term meaning court) became the centre of devotion for his followers. This encouraged the practice of pilgrimage or ziyarat to his grave, particularly on his death anniversary or urs (or marriage, signifying the union of his soul with God).
- Most Sufi lineages were named after a founding figure. For instance, Qadri order was named after Shaikh Abdul Qadir Jilani. However, the Chisti order was named after their place of origin – the town of Chist in Central Afghanistan.

21. Correct Option: (d)

Explanation:

- All statements are correct.

Supplementary Notes:

Bhakti Movement in North India

- Historians have not found evidence of anything resembling the compositions of the Alvars and Nayanars till the 14th century in north India.
- Various factors account for this:
  - In north India, this was the period when several Rajput states emerged. In most of these states Brahmanas occupied positions of importance, performing a range of secular and ritual functions. There seems to have been little or no attempt to challenge their position directly.
  - At the same time other religious leaders like Naths, Siddhas and Jogis, who did not function within the orthodox Brahmanical framework, were gaining ground. Many of them came from artisanal groups, including weavers, who were becoming increasingly important with the development of organized craft production. Demand for such production grew with the emergence of new urban centres, and long-distance trade with Central Asia and West Asia.
  - Many of these new religious leaders questioned the authority of the Vedas, and expressed themselves in languages spoken by ordinary people.
  - A new element in the situation was the coming of the Turks which culminated in the establishment of the Delhi Sultanate (13th century). This undermined the power of many of the Rajput states and the Brahmanas who were associated with these kingdoms.

22. Correct Option: (d)

Explanation:

- **Statement 1 is incorrect:** Saguna traditions focused on worship of specific deities in their anthropomorphic forms.
- **Statement 2 is incorrect:** Nirguna is the concept of worshipping an abstract form of God.

Supplementary Notes:

Bhakti and Sufi Traditions

- Historians of religion often classify Bhakti traditions into two broad categories: Saguna (with attributes) and Nirguna (without attributes).

- Saguna included traditions that focused on the worship of specific deities such as Shiva, Vishnu and his avatars (incarnations) and forms of the goddess or Devi, all often conceptualized in anthropomorphic forms.
- Nirguna Bhakti, on the other hand, was worship of an abstract form of god.

23. Correct Option: (c)

Explanation:

- **Statement 4 is incorrect:** Muhammad bin Tughlaq (ruled, 1324-51) was the first Sultan to visit the dargah of Khwaja Muinuddin.

Supplementary Notes:

Chisti Order in the Subcontinent

- Among the many groups of Sufis who migrated to India in the late 12th century, the Chishtis were the most influential. This was because they adapted successfully to the local environment and adopted several features of Indian devotional traditions.
- Major teachers of Chisti Silsila were:

Sufi Teachers	Year of Death	Location of Dargah
Shaikh Muinuddin Sijzi	1235	Ajmer
Khwaja Qutubuddin Bakhtiyar Kaki	1235	Delhi
Shaikh Fariduddin Ganj-i-Shakar	1265	Ajodhan (Rajasthan)
Shaikh Nizamuddin Auliya	1325	Delhi
Shaikh Nasiruddin Chiragh-i-Delhi	1356	Delhi

- From morning till late night, people from all walks of life – soldiers, slaves, singers, merchants, poets, travelers, rich and poor, Hindu jogis (yogi) and qalandars – came seeking discipleship, amulets for healing, and the intercession of the Shaikh in various matters.
- Other visitors included poets such as Amir Hasan Sijzi and Amir Khusrau and the court historian Ziyauddin Barani, all of whom wrote about the Shaikh.
- Pilgrimage, called ziyarat, to tombs of Sufi saints is prevalent all over the Muslim world. This practice is an occasion for seeking the Sufi's spiritual grace (barakat).
- The most revered shrine is that of Khwaja Muinuddin, popularly known as "Gharib Nawaz" (comforter of the poor). It was evidently popular because of the austerity and piety of its Shaikh, the greatness of his spiritual successors, and the patronage of royal visitors. Muhammad bin Tughlaq (ruled, 1324-51) was the first Sultan to visit the shrine.
- Also, part of Ziyarat is the use of music and dance including mystical chants performed by specially trained musicians or qawwals to evoke divine ecstasy. The Sufis remember God either by reciting the Zikr (the Divine Names) or evoking His Presence through Sama (literally, "audition") or performance of mystical music.
- Sama was integral to the Chishtis, and exemplified interaction with indigenous devotional traditions.

24. Correct Option: (c)

Explanation:

- **Statement 1 is incorrect:** Virashaiva emerged in 12th century in Karnataka, led by a saint named Basavanna.
- **Statement 3 is incorrect:** The ideas of Tamil bhaktas (especially Vaishnavas) were incorporated within Sanskrit tradition which led into culmination of Bhagvata Purana.
- **Statement 4 is incorrect:** They ceremonially buried their dead but they questioned the theory of rebirth.

Supplementary Notes:

Virashaiva Tradition

- The 12th century witnessed the emergence of a new movement in Karnataka, led by a Brahmana named Basavanna (1106-68) who was a minister in the court of a Kalachuri ruler.
- His followers were known as Virashaivas (heroes of Shiva) or Lingayats (wearers of the linga). They worship Shiva in his manifestation as a linga, and men usually wear a small linga in a silver case on a loop strung over the left shoulder.
- Lingayats believe that on death the devotee will be united with Shiva and will not return to this world. Therefore, they do not practice funerary rites such as cremation, prescribed in the Dharmashastras. Instead, they ceremonially bury their dead.
- The Lingayats challenged the idea of caste and the "pollution" attributed to certain groups by Brahmanas, thus, winning them followers amongst those who were marginalized within the Brahmanical social order.
- They also questioned the theory of rebirth.
- The Lingayats also encouraged certain practices disapproved in the Dharmashastras, such as post-puberty marriage and the remarriage of widows.
- Most of the understanding of the Virashaiva tradition is derived from Vachanas (literally, sayings) composed in Kannada by women and men who joined the movement.
- This period also witnessed another major development. Many ideas of Tamil bhaktas (especially the Vaishnavas) were incorporated within

the Sanskrit tradition, culminating in the composition of the one of the best known Puranas, the Bhagavata Purana.

25. **Correct Option: (c)**

Explanation:

- **Statement 1 is incorrect:** Alvars were devotees of Vishnu while Nayanars were devotees of Shiva.
- **Statement 3 is incorrect:** Women devotees were present among both Alvars and Nayanars.

Supplementary Notes:

Alvars and Nayanars

- Some of the earliest Bhakti movements (c. 6th century) were led by the Alvars (literally, those who are "immersed" in devotion to Vishnu) and Nayanars (literally, leaders who were devotees of Shiva).
- They travelled from place to place singing hymns in Tamil in praise of their Gods.
- During their travels, the Alvars and Nayanars identified certain shrines as abodes of their chosen deities. Very often large temples were later built at these sacred places. These developed as centres of pilgrimage. Singing compositions of these poet-saints became part of temple rituals in these shrines, as did worship of the saints' images.
- Alvars and Nayanars initiated a movement of protest against the caste system and the dominance of Brahmanas or at least attempted to reform the system. This is corroborated by the fact that bhaktas hailed from diverse social backgrounds ranging from Brahmanas to artisans and cultivators and even from castes considered "untouchable".
- Alvars and Nayanars claimed that their compositions were as important as the Vedas. For instance, one of the major anthologies of compositions by the Alvars, the Nalayira Divyaprabandham, was frequently described as the Tamil Veda.
- Most striking feature of the Alvar and Nayanar traditions was the presence of women. For instance, the compositions of Andal, a woman Alvar, were widely sung and Karaikkal Ammaiyar, a woman Nayanar, adopted the path of extreme asceticism in order to attain her goal.
- One of the major themes in Tamil Bhakti hymns is the poets' opposition to Buddhism and Jainism. This is particularly marked in the compositions of the Nayanars. Historians explain this hostility as a result of competition between members of other religious traditions for royal patronage.

26. **Correct Option: (a)**

Explanation:

- **Statement 3 is incorrect:** The Lingayats also encouraged certain practices disapproved in the Dharmashastras, such as post-puberty marriage and the remarriage of widows.

Supplementary Notes:

- The 12th century witnessed the emergence of a new movement in Karnataka, led by a Brahmana named Basavanna (1106-68) who was a minister in the court of a Kalachuri ruler, called Virashaiva movement. His followers were known as Virashaivas (heroes of Shiva) or Lingayats (wearers of the linga).
- The Virashaiva movement challenged the idea of caste and the "pollution" attributed to certain groups by Brahmanas. They also questioned the theory of rebirth. These won them followers amongst those who were marginalised within the Brahmanical social order.
- The Virashaivas argued strongly for the equality of all human beings and against Brahmanical ideas about caste and the treatment of women. The Lingayats also encouraged certain practices disapproved in the Dharmashastras, such as post-puberty marriage and the remarriage of widows. Our understanding of the Virashaiva tradition is derived from Vachanas (literally, sayings) composed in Kannada by women and men who joined the movement.

27. **Correct Option: (a)**

Explanation:

- **Statement 2 is incorrect:** Sufism though discouraged materialism but did not believe in complete renunciation.

Supplementary Notes:

Sufism

- Sufism was a liberal reform movement within Islam. It had its origin in Persia and spread into India in the 11th century. The Sufis lay stress on inner purity.
- While the orthodox believe in blind observance of rituals, the Sufis consider love and devotion as the only means of attaining salvation.
- According to them, one must have the guidance of a Pir or Guru, without which spiritual development is impossible. Sufism also inculcated a spirit of tolerance among its followers.
- Other ideas emphasized by Sufism are meditation, good actions, repentance for sins, performance of prayers and pilgrimages, fasting, charity and suppression of passions by ascetic practices.
- Sufism, though discouraged materialism, did not believe in complete renunciation.
- These liberal and unorthodox features of Sufism had a profound influence on medieval Bhakti saints. In the later period, Akbar, the Mughal emperor, appreciated Sufi doctrines which shaped his religious outlook and religious policies.

- When the Sufi movement was becoming popular in India, about the same time the Bhakti cult was gaining strength among the Hindus. The two parallel movements based on the doctrines of love and selfless devotion contributed a great deal to bringing the two communities closer together. However, this trend did not last long.

28. Correct Option: (b)

Explanation:

- **Statement 1 is incorrect:** They were the devotees of Lord Vishnu and were called Vaishnavites.
- **Statement 3 is incorrect:** People from lower castes and women were not prohibited to be part of the order.

Supplementary Notes:

Bhakti Movement – Alvars

- Some of the earliest Bhakti Movements (c. 6th century) were led by the Alvars. Alvars were literally those who were immersed in devotion to Vishnu and Nayanars were the devotees of Shiva.
- They were the devotees of Lord Vishnu and were called Vaishnavites.
- They travelled from place to place singing hymns in Tamil in praise of their Gods.
- People from lower castes and women were not prohibited to be part of the order.
- They initiated a movement of protest against the caste system. Hence, the devotees hailed from diverse social backgrounds ranging from Brahmanas to artisans and cultivators and even from castes considered 'untouchable'.

CONCEPT REVISION

Here is the list of concepts that have been covered as part of the previous exercise. Revise and Self-reflect on your concepts you covered.

- Alvars and Nayanars ☐
- Nirguna-Bhakti Movement ☐
- Munihiyan ☐
- Amir Khusrau ☐
- Religious ideas during Mughal Reign ☐
- Development of Bhakti Movement ☐
- Sufi Movement ☐
- Sufi Silsilah ☐
- Virashaiva tradition ☐

☐☐☐

ART & CULTURE

Syllabus (MICRO TOPICS)

1. Visual Arts

- Architecture & Sculptures
  - Sculpture
    - Sculptures of Harappan Civilisation
    - Sculptures of Mauryan Age
    - Post-Mauryan Period
    - Jain Sculptures
    - Buddhist Sculpture
    - Gupta Sculpture
    - Medieval School of Sculpture
    - Modern Indian Sculpture
- Architecture in Ancient India
  - Harappan Period
  - Mauryan Architecture
  - Post-Mauryan Period Gupta Period
  - Temples of Khajuraho
  - Temples of Odisha
  - Temples of Gwalior
  - Temples of Gujarat
  - Temples of Rajasthan
  - Temples of Bengal
  - Temples of Assam
  - Temples of Himachal Pradesh
  - Temples of Jammu and Kashmir
  - Pallava Period
  - Chola Period
  - Pandya Temples
  - Vijayanagara Period
  - NayakaTemples
  - Temples of Kerala
  - Vesara Style
  - Hoysala Style
  - Rashtrakuta Period
- Indo-Islamic Architecture
  - Imperial Style Delhi Sultanat
  - Provincial Style
  - Mughal Style
  - Sikh Style of Architecture
  - Rajput Architecture
  - Salient features
- Modern Architecture
  - European Influence
  - Indo-Saracenic Architecture
  - Post-Independence Period
- Paintings, Pottery and Numismatic
  - Tradition of Mural Paintings in India
  - Tradition of Miniature Paintings in India
  - Paintings in the Deccan
  - Rajput School of Painting
  - Pahari School of Painting
  - Miniature Painting in South India
  - Regional Paintings
  - Modern Paintings
  - Contemporary Paintings
  - Ochre Coloured Pottery (OCP)
  - Black and Red Ware (BRW)
  - Painted Grey Ware (PGW)
  - Northern Black Polished Ware (NBPW)
  - Glazed and Unglazed Pottery

2. Performing Arts

- Music in India
- Main Pillars of Indian Music
- Forms of Indian Music
- Musical Instruments
- Institutions Related to Music
- Dances in India
  - Concept of Dance in India
  - Concept of Ashta Nayika
  - Eight Classical Dance Forms in India
  - Folk Dances
  - Modern Dances
- Indian Theatre and Puppetry
  - Classical Sanskrit Theatre
  - Regional Theatre
  - Modern Theatre
  - Renaissance of Indian Theatre
  - String Puppets
  - Shadow Puppets
  - Rod Puppets
  - Glove Puppets

- Modern Puppetry
- Tribal Puppetry

- Sports in India
    - Genesis of Martial Arts
    - Forms of Traditional Martial Arts

3. **Religion, Language and Literature**

- Religions in India
    - Pre-Vedic Religon
    - Hinduism
    - Buddhism
    - Jainism
    - Sikhism
    - Islam
    - Christianity
    - Zoroastrianism
    - Judaism
    - Philosophy in India
    - Bhakti Movement
    - Vaishnava Acharyas: Metaphysical Foundation
    - Other Saints of Bhakti Movement
    - Maharashtra Dharma
    - Sufism
- Languages and Literature in India
    - Sanskrit Literature
    - Pali Literature
    - Prakrit Literature
    - Tamil Literature
    - Telugu Literature
    - Malayalam Literature
    - Kannada Literature
    - Odia Literature
    - Assamese Literature
    - Bengali Literature
    - Gujarati Literature
    - Rajasthani Literature
    - Punjabi Literature
    - Marathi Literature
    - Hindi Literature
    - Persian Literature
    - Urdu Literature

4. **Miscellaneous**

- Indian Handicrafts
- Indian Universities
- Personalities Related to Culture
- Places of Cultural Interest
- Fairs and Festivals in India
- Cultural Institutions in India
- Awards and Honours Associated with Culture
- The Calendar
- The Eras
- Science and Technology in Ancient India
- UNESCO's List of Cultural Heritage in India
- Legal Provisions Related to the Protection and Promotion of Indian Culture and Heritage

7.

VISUAL ARTS

7.1 ARCHITECTURE & SCULPTURES

QUESTIONS

1. **With reference to Lion Capital at Sarnath, consider the following statements:**
   1. It was built by Ajatashatru in commemoration of Dhammachakra-pravartana of Buddha.
   2. The capital originally consisted of five component parts with the crowning element, Dharamchakra – a large wheel.

   Which of the above statement/s is/are correct?

   (a) 1 only (b) 2 only
   (c) Both 1 and 2 (d) Neither 1 nor 2

2. **Consider the following statements regarding Khajuraho Temples:**
   1. The Temples are famous for their Vesara-style architectural symbolism and erotic sculptures.
   2. These Temples were constructed by the Chandella rulers.
   3. These Temples got the status of UNESCO's World Heritage Sites in 1986.

   Which of the above statements are correct?

   (a) 1 and 2 only (b) 1 and 3 only
   (c) 2 and 3 only (d) 1, 2 and 3

3. **Consider the following statements related to the different types of sculptures:**
   1. Mathura School of Art used grey sandstone.
   2. Gandhara School of Art used spotted red sandstone.
   3. Amravati School of Art used white marble.

   Which of the above statement/s is/are correct?

   (a) 1 and 3 only (b) 2 and 3 only
   (c) 3 only (d) 1, 2 and 3

4. **Consider the following statements with reference to the seals found at Indus Valley Civilisation sites:**
   1. The standard Harappan seal was a square plaque indicating trade relations of the civilisation.
   2. Pashupati Seal was depicted with a human figure standing in the centre and animals around it.
   3. The seals show the dresses, ornaments, hair-styles of the people of that era.

   Which of the above statement/s is/are correct?

   (a) 1 Only (b) 2 and 3 Only
   (c) 1 and 3 Only (d) 1, 2 and 3

5. **Consider the following characteristic features with reference to a cave:**
   1. This rock-cut cave was carved out in Mauryan times.
   2. It belonged to Ajeevika sect.
   3. These are also known as Lomas Rishi caves.

Which of the following caves represents the above features?

(a) Ajanta caves (b) Barabar caves
(c) Elephanta caves (d) Bagh caves

6. Consider the following features of Dashavatara Temple located in Central India:

1. This Temple is in the panchayatana style of architecture.
2. Sculpture of Nara-Narayan shows the discussion between human soul and the eternal divine.
3. Gajendramoksha represents the Vishnu's discussion with the lord of elephants.

Which of the above features is/are correct?

(a) 1 and 2 only (b) 2 only
(c) 1 and 3 only (d) 1, 2 and 3

7. Which of the following statements related to the Temple architecture is/are correct?

1. Temples at Khajuraho in Central India is a UNESCO world heritage site.
2. Temples in West India were mainly constructed by Terracota and White Marbles.
3. In all the Temples in East India, the mount or vehicle of the Temple's main deity is placed axially before the sanctum.

Select the correct answer using the codes given below:

(a) 1 only (b) 2 only
(c) 1 and 3 only (d) 2 and 3 only

8. Consider the following statements regarding the Ashokan pillar at Sarnath:

1. It was built in the commemoration of the first sermon by the Buddha at Sarnath.
2. Sarnath column depicts four animals, namely, horse, cow, elephant and tiger.
3. The capital of the pillar is carved out of a single block of polished limestone.

Which of the above statement/s is/are correct?

(a) 1 only (b) 1 and 2 only
(c) 1 and 3 only (d) 1, 2 and 3

9. Which of the following is not the characteristic feature of the Gandhara School of Art?

(a) Lord Buddha is depicted in the form of `Swastika` mark.
(b) Buddha has been carved out in various Mudras.
(c) It was developed during the reign of Kushana emperor Kanishka.
(d) It gave more stress to the bodily features and external beauty.

10. Consider the following statements with reference to Nagara style of Temple Architecture:

1. They are enclosed within a compound wall or gateways.
2. The Garbhagriha is always located directly under the tallest tower.
3. The entire Temple is generally built on a stone platform with steps leading up to it.

Which of the above statement/s is/are correct?

(a) 2 and 3 only (b) 1 and 3 only
(c) 2 only (d) 1, 2 and 3

11. Statue of Equality is associated with:

(a) Sardar Vallabhai Patel
(b) Ramanujacharya
(c) Madhavacharya
(d) Nimbarka

12. Consider the following statements about Sardar Vallabhai Patel:

1. He was awarded Bharat Ratna soon after his death.
2. The first Rashtriya Ekta Diwas commemorates his 150th birth anniversary.
3. 'Run for Unity' campaign is associated with Rashtriya Ekta Diwas

Which of the above statement/s is/are correct?

(a) 1 only (b) 1 and 2 only
(c) 3 only (d) 1 and 3 only

13. With reference to the 'Rajput architecture', consider the following:

1. Forts were usually made by Rajputs on small hills to prevent the entry of any unwanted person.
2. The Rajputs had built the Rathas of Mahabalipuram, the Kailash Temple at Ellora and the engravements of Elephanta.

Which of the statements given above is/are incorrect?

(a) 1 only (b) 2 only
(c) Both 1 and 2 (d) Neither 1 nor 2

14. Which of the following is/are the features of Mauryan architechture?

1. Wood was the principal building material in the construction of the palaces.
2. The shaft of the pillars was made up of pieces of sandstone cemented together.
3. The Mauryan cave architecture had a poor finish owing to its initial stages of emergence of rock-cut architecture.

Select the correct answer using the codes given below:

(a) 1 only (b) 1 and 2 only
(c) 2 and 3 only (d) 1, 2 and 3

15. Which one of the following inscriptions of Ashoka refers to his name as "Devnampiyadasi" or "Priyadarshi"?

(a) Maski Rock Edict
(b) Sarnath Pillar Edict
(c) Rummindei Pillar Edict
(d) Nigalisagar Pillar Edict

16. Which of the following is/are the features of Jain sculptures?

1. Among the twenty-four Tirthankaras, only Mahavir and Parshvanatha are depicted in sculptures.

2. Digambara sculptures are naked without any beautification whereas Svetambara ones are clothed.

Select the correct answer using the codes given below.

(a) 1 only (b) 2 only
(c) Both 1 and 2 (d) Neither 1 nor 2

17. Consider the following statements:

1. They belong to Nagara style of Temple architecture
2. These are group of Temples of many faiths
3. They have extensive erotic sculptures
4. It is a UNESCO World Heritage Site

Which of the following Temples represents the above description?

(a) Khajuraho Temples
(b) Badami Aihole Temples
(c) Vijayanagar Temples
(d) Orissa Temples

18. Following are the description of a Temple style of ancient India

1. Exterior walls are lavishly decorated but interior walls are plain
2. No pillars are used
3. Temples are surrounded by walls/gateways

Which of the following Temples do the above statements describe?

(a) Sun Temple at Konark
(b) Modhera Sun Temple, Gujrat
(c) Kailashnath Temple at Kanchipuram
(d) Shore Temple at Mahabalipuram

19. 'Char Dhams' is a belief among Vaishnavite Hindus that visiting these sites helps achieve "Moksha". Which among the following Temple is associated with Char Dham:

(a) Dwarkadhish Temple, Dwarka
(b) Somnath Temple, Somnath
(c) Akshardham Temple, Gandhinagar
(d) Bhadreshwar Jain Temple, Kutch

20. Consider the following statements with respect to Buddhist Architecture:

1. Chaityas are the prayer halls.
2. Stupa is a place of worship which is constructed on relics.
3. Pipriwaha Stupa in Lumbini is the oldest among all stupas.
4. Bharhut stupa in Madhya Pradesh was built during Maurya Dynasty.

Which of the above statements are correct?

(a) 1 and 2 only (b) 1, 2 and 3 only
(c) 1, 3 and 4 only (d) 1, 2, 3 and 4

21. Which of the following statements are incorrect?

1. Mathura School of art is developed by Sunga Dynasty.
2. Amaravathi School of art is developed by Kushana Dynasty.
3. Gandhara School of art is developed by Sathavahana Dynasty.

Select the correct answer using the code given below:

(a) 1 and 2 only (b) 1 and 3 only
(c) 2 and 3 only (d) 1, 2 and 3

22. Which of the following Dynasty was the first to construct Hindu Temples in South India?

(a) Ikshvaku Dynasty
(b) Gupta Dynasty
(c) Maurya Dynasty
(d) Pandyas Dynasty

23. Which of the following statements regarding architecture during the Delhi Sultanate period is/are correct ?

1. Qutubuddin Aibak started work on the Qutub Minar and Iltutmish completed it.
2. The city Tughluqabad was founded by Muhammad Bin Tughlaq.
3. Alauddin Khalji built the Alai Darwaza with fine patterns and intricate decoration mark.

Select the correct answer using the codes given below:

(a) 2 only (b) 3 only
(c) 1 and 2 only (d) 1 and 3 only

24. Which of the following statement/s is/are correct?

1. Chanhudaro – It is the only Indus valley site without a citadel.
2. Kalibangan – There is no evidence of worship of mother Goddesses.
3. Surkotada – It gave definite evidence that Indus Valley people had knowledge of horse.
4. Rakhigarhi – It is the biggest Indus Valley site in India.

Select the correct answer using the code given below:

(a) 3 and 4 only (b) 1 only
(c) 1, 2 and 4 only (d) 1, 2, 3 and 4

25. Who built the magnificent rock-cut monolithic Kailasa Temple at Ellora?

(a) Danthidurga (b) Krishna I
(c) Amoghavarsha I (d) Krishna III

26. The cave Temples at Bhairavakonda and Sittanavasal belonged to

(a) Pallavas (b) Pushyabutis
(c) Pandyas (d) Cholas

27. Consider the following architectural buildings and their location:

Architectural Building	Locations
1. Nishat Bagh	1. Lahore
2. Panch Mahal	2. Fatehpur Sikri
3. Tomb of Ittimaddaulah	3. Sikandar
4. Tomb of Humayun	4. Delhi

Which of the above pairs are correctly matched?

(a) 1 and 2 only (b) 2 and 4 only
(c) 1, 3 and 4 only (d) 2, 3 and 4 only

28. Which of the following is correct about Sri Padmanabhaswamy Temple?

1. The Temple is built in the unique Chera style of architecture.
2. The main deity of the Temple is Lord Shiva.
3. It is located in Madurai, Tamil Nadu

Select the correct option using the codes given below:

(a) 1 only (b) 2 only
(c) 3 only (d) 1, 2 and 3

29. Consider the following statements about 'Group of Monuments at Pattadakal':

1. Pattadakal group of monuments are famous for their harmonious blend of architectural forms of northern and southern India.
2. The oldest Temple at Pattadakal is the simple but massive Sangamesvara built by Vijayaditya Satyasraya.
3. The Mallikarjuna and the Virupaksha Temples at Pattadakal, were built by two queens of Vikramaditya II, to commemorate the victory of the Chalukyas over the Pallavas.

Which of the above statement/s is/are correct?

(a) 1 and 2 only (b) 2 only
(c) 1, 2 and 3 (d) None of the above

30. Which of the following listed Temples are parts of 'Great Living Chola Temples'?

1. Brihadeeswarar Temple.
2. Airavateshwarar Temple.
3. Sri Ranganathaswamy Temple.

Select the correct option using the codes given below:

(a) 1, 2 and 3 (b) 2 and 3 only
(c) 1 only (d) 1 and 2 only

31. The site is locally known as 'Verul Leni' is located on the Aurangabad-Chalisgaon road at a distance of 30 km north-northwest of Aurangabad. It represents one of the largest rock-hewn monastic-Temple complexes in the entire world. It is also world famous for the largest single monolithic excavation in the world, the great Kailasa.

Which of the following UNESCO World Heritage sites is mentioned above?

(a) Kanheri Caves
(b) Ellora Caves
(c) Aurangabad Caves
(d) Bhaja Caves

32. Bijak, Sabad, Sakhi and Ramani are associated with which of the following?

(a) Meera Bai
(b) Saint Maluk Das
(c) Ramanujacharya
(d) Kabir

33. Some Buddhist rock-cut caves are called Chaityas while the others are called Viharas. What is the difference between the two?

(a) Vihara is a place of worship while Chaitya is the dwelling place of the monks.
(b) Chaitya is a place of worship while Vihara is the dwelling place of monks.
(c) Chaitya is a Stupa at the far end of the cave while Vihara is the hall axial to it.
(d) There is no material difference between the two.

34. With reference to the Thrissur pooram and Vadakkunnathan Temple, consider the following statements:

1. The Vadakkunnathan Temple has been declared as National Monument under Ancient Monuments and Archaeological Sites and Remains Act 1958.
2. The Thrissur pooram festival is brainchild of Raja Rama Varma, famously known as SakthanThampuran.

Which of the above statement/s is/are correct?

(a) 1 only (b) 2 only
(c) Both 1 and 2 (d) Neither 1 nor 2

35. "This site is different from other sites of Indus Valley Civilisation in terms of town planning that it has entry to the houses on the main street while in other sites have shown lateral entry."

Which of the following site has been described in the above quote?

(a) Lothal (b) Kalibangan
(c) Mohenjo-daro (d) Dholavira

36. Consider the following statements with reference to Nagara and Dravida styles of architecture.

1. Both these architectures are prominently from Southern India.
2. Nagara style has multiple shikhara, but the Dravida style has only one.
3. In the Nagara style, there is only one tower whereas the Dravida style has multiple towers.
4. Pedestals are higher than the ground in the Dravida style and at ground level in the Nagara style.

Which of the statements given above is/are incorrect?

(a) 1 and 4 only (b) 2 only
(c) 2 and 3 only (d) 1, 3 and 4

37. Consider the following statements:

1. Mathura School of Art was a purely indigenous development, patronised by the Kushan Dynasty.
2. Gandhara School of Art was patronised by the Sakas and depicted only images of Buddha.
3. Amravati School of Art depicted Buddha in symbols.

Which of the above statements are correct?

(a) 1 and 2 only (b) 2 and 3 only
(c) 1 and 3 only (d) 1, 2 and 3

38. Consider the following statements regarding Temples of Khajuraho:

1. Viewed from a distance, these Temples appear to be from a mountain range.
2. Chausath Yogini Temple was the first Temple built at Khajuraho and dedicated to Goddess Durga.
3. These Temples were made on a high platform called "Antarala".

Which of the above statement/s is/are correct?

(a) 1 and 2 only (b) 1 and 3 only
(c) 2 and 3 only (d) 1, 2 and 3

39. Consider the following statements about Katora Houz:

1. It is a cup-shaped water tank constructed inside the fortified walls of the Golconda Fort.
2. It was constructed in 1560 for the visit of King Ibrahim Quli Qutb Shah.

Which of the above statement/s is/are correct?

(a) 1 only (b) 2 only
(c) Both 1 and 2 (d) Neither 1 nor 2

40. Where has the world's largest monolithic statue of Buddha been installed?

(a) Bamiyan (b) Hyderabad
(c) Kandy (d) Lhasa

41. Which of the following materials was used in the Harappan seals?

1. Gold
2. Steatite
3. Silver
4. Wood

Select the correct answer using the code given below:

(a) 1 only (b) 2 only
(c) 2 and 3 only (d) 1, 2 and 3

42. The salient features of town planning in Harappan culture were:

1. System of town planning was on the lines of hexagonal view where streets and lanes together looked like honeycomb.
2. The large scale use of mud bricks and underground drainage system was remarkable.

Which of the above statement/s is/are correct?

(a) 1 only (b) 2 only
(c) Both 1 and 2 (d) Neither 1 nor 2

43. Gandhara School of Art came into existence among :

(a) Hinayana sect (b) Mahayana sect
(c) Vaishanava sect (d) Shaiva sect

44. Which one of the following does not appear on the abacus of the Sarnath Lion capital of Ashoka?

(a) Bull (b) Bear
(c) Elephant (d) Horse

45. With whose reign is the Gandhara School of Art associated?

(a) Kanishka
(b) Harsha
(c) Chandragupta Vikramaditya
(d) Ashoka

46. Consider the following statements regarding the town planning of the Harappan settlements:

1. The idea of settlement planning did not appear suddenly with the first large cities but was already well established in earlier period as has been revealed from the excavations at Kot Diji, Kalibangan, etc.
2. The basic layout at all these settlements was established along a grid that was defined by large streets running north south and east-west and fortification all around.

Which of the above statement/s is/are correct?

(a) 1 only (b) 2 only
(c) Both 1 and 2 (d) Neither 1 nor 2

47. Which among the following is a correct meaning of "Khanqah" ?

(a) Works of Poet Amir Khusro
(b) Court of Sikandar Lodi
(c) Birth place of Khwaja Muinud-din Chisti
(d) The place where Sufi Mystics lived

48. Consider the following statement about Ashokan edict:

1. Ashoka was the first ruler to speak directly to his people through the inscriptions
2. They are found only in India
3. The inscription were written in Brahmi script, Kharosthi script and Greek script

Which of the above statement/s is/are correct?

(a) 1 and 2 only (b) 2 and 3 only
(c) 1, 2 and 3 (d) 1 and 3 only

49. In which one among the following Ashokan edicts is the Kalinga war mentioned?

(a) Pillar edict VI (b) Rock edict XIII
(c) Rock edict XI (d) Pillar edict I

50. There are only two known examples of cave paintings of the Gupta period in Ancient India. One of these is the paintings of the Ajanta caves. Where is the other surviving example of Gupta paintings?

(a) Bagh Caves (b) Udaygiri Caves
(c) Ellora Caves (d) Bhimbetka Caves

51. The Allahabad Pillar inscription is associated with:

(a) Harshavardhan (b) Bimbisar
(c) Ashoka (d) Samudragupta

52. With reference to the art and archaeological history of India, which one among the following was made the earliest?

(a) Lingaraja Temple at Bhubaneswar
(b) Rock-cut Elephant at Dhauli
(c) Khajuraho Group of Monuments
(d) Qutub Minar

53. Consider the following statements:

1. Gandhara School of Art was developed due to Taxashila University.
2. Mahayana Buddhism developed due to Central Asian influence.
3. The Bodhisattvas are important component of Mahayana philosophy.

Which of the above statement/s is/are correct?

(a) 1 and 2 only (b) 1 only
(c) 2 and 3 only (d) 1, 2 and 3

54. With reference to the cultural history of India, the term Panchayatan refers to:

(a) Peitra dura style
(b) A religious sect
(c) A style of Temple construction
(d) An administrative functionary

55. Consider the following historical places:

1. Ajanta Caves
2. Lepakshi Temple
3. Bagh Caves

Which of the above places is / are also known for mural paintings?

(a) 1 only (b) 2 only
(c) 2 and 3 only (d) 1, 2 and 3

56. The National Emblem of India is adopted from which of the following pillars?

(a) Allahabad Pillar
(b) Sarnath Pillar
(c) Nandgarh Pillar
(d) None of the above

57. The Mughals built magnificent forts, palaces, gates, public buildings, mosques, baolis (water tank or well), etc. Consider the following statements regarding Mughal architecture:

1. The Gujarat style of architecture is used most widely in the palace built by Jahangir.
2. In the Panch Mahal, all the types of pillars used in various Temples were employed to support flat roofs.
3. Akbar was the first Mughal ruler who had the time and means to undertake construction on a large scale.

Which of the above statement/s is/are correct?

(a) 1 and 2 only (b) 2 and 3 only
(c) 1 and 3 only (d) 1, 2 and 3

58. Consider the following statements regarding Architecture of Vijaynagara Empire:

1. Kalyana Mandapam and Raya Gopurams are important features of it.
2. Vittala Swamy and the Hazara Ramaswamy Temples are the best examples of Vijayanagar empire architecture.
3. Bull was the most common animal to be depicted on the pillars.

Which of the above statement/s is/are correct?

(a) 1 and 2 only (b) 1 and 3 only
(c) 2 and 3 only (d) 1, 2 and 3

59. Consider the following statements regarding Mauryan architecture:

1. The pillars were usually made of chunar sandstone and consisted of four parts.
2. Mauryan architecture was inspired by Iranian architecture.
3. Sanchi Stupa is the oldest known stupa.

Which of the above statements are correct?

(a) 1 and 2 only (b) 1 and 3 only
(c) 2 and 3 only (d) 1, 2 and 3

60. Consider the following statements regarding Mathura School of Art

1. Sculptures were influenced by imageries of Hinduism only.
2. Usage of symbolism was the main characteristic of it.
3. In this school of art Buddha is shown in delighted mood with a face and head shaven.

Which of the above statements are correct?

(a) 1 and 2 only (b) 1 and 3 only
(c) 2 and 3 only (d) 1, 2 and 3

61. Which of the following statements is incorrect about the Gupta age Temples?

(a) It is marked the beginning of the Free Standing Temple Architecture.
(b) The basic, characteristic elements of the Indian Temple consisting of a square sanctum sanctorum and a pillared porch had emerged in the Gupta age.
(c) Nagara style and Dravida style began from the Gupta era.
(d) Dasavatar Temple at Deogarh which is entirely made up of Bricks belongs to Gupta age.

62. With reference to 'Dravida Style of Temple Architecture' consider the given figure:

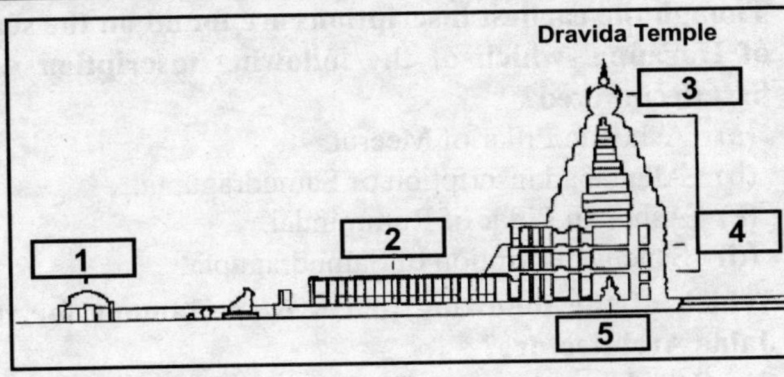

Which of the following is correctly matched?

(a) 1 – Amlak, 2 – Mandapa, 3 – Vimana, 4 – Shikhara, 5 – Garbhagriha
(b) 1 – Pitha, 2 – Mandapa, 3 – Shikhara, 4 – Vimana, 5 – Garbhagriha
(c) 1 – Gopuram, 2 – Vimana, 3 – Shikhara, 4 – Mandapa, 5 – Kalasha
(d) 1 – Gopuram, 2 – Mandapa, 3 – Shikhara, 4 – Vimana, 5 – Garbhagriha

63. Which of the following statements is correct about the Elephanta Caves?

1. It was originally a Jain site which was later dominated by Vaishnavism.
2. It was contemporary to Ajanta Caves.
3. It has been included in the UNESCO world heritage list of India.

Select the correct answer using the codes given below:

(a) 1 only (b) 2 only
(c) 3 only (d) 1, 2 and 3

64. Consider the following statements about Modern Architecture:

1. Iberian architectural style was introduced by French.
2. The Portuguese continued with their western tradition and did not introduced any variations using Indian architectural styles.
3. French brings about the concept of anonymous architecture which involves simple façade without much ornamentation.
4. Red sandstone and coarse limestone were primarily used in the Gothic Architecture.

Which of the above statement/s is/are incorrect?

(a) 1 only (b) 1 and 2 only
(c) 3 and 4 only (d) 1, 2 and 3 only

65. Consider the following statements regarding Hoyasaleshvara Temple:

1. It is a fine example of Vesara Style of Temple architecture.
2. The Temple is dedicated to Lord Vishnu.
3. It is located at Aihole in Karnataka.

Which of the above statement/s is/are incorrect?

(a) 1 only (b) 2 only
(c) 1 and 3 only (d) 2 and 3 only

66. With reference to the Temples outside India's present boundary, consider the following statements:

1. With spread of Indian culture in the South East Asian Region Temple were also erected that have the dominant elements of Dravidic style of Indian Temple architecture.
2. The Angkor group of Temples were built in the period of Sailendra kingdom Sumatra.
3. The Preah Vihar Temple is dedicated to manifestation of Lord Shiva and remained boundary dispute between Cambodia and Thailand, later awarded to Thailand by ICJ in 1962.

Which of the above statement/s is/are incorrect?

(a) 1 only (b) 1 and 2 only
(c) 2 and 3 only (d) 1, 2 and 3 only

67. What are the differences between Hindustani and Carnatic Schools of classical music?

1. While Hindustani Music is completely indigenous, Carnatic Music has foreign influence.
2. There is no freedom to improvise in Carnatic Music while there is a scope for variations in Hindustani Music.
3. Hindustani Music puts more emphasis on vocals than Carnatic Music.
4. While Hindustani Music has several sub-styles, there is no sub-style within Carnatic Music.

Select the correct answer using the codes given below:

(a) 1 and 3 only (b) 2 and 4 only
(c) 1, 2 and 3 only (d) 2, 3 and 4 only

68. Consider the following statements regarding the 'Indus Dancing Girl' statue:

1. It is the world's oldest bronze sculpture.
2. It depicts the girl standing in chowk posture.
3. It suggests that Indus artists knew metal blending and casting.

Which of the above statement/s is/are correct?

(a) 1 and 2 only (b) 1 and 3 only
(c) 3 only (d) 1, 2 and 3

69. Consider the following:

1. Use of minars
2. Use of human and animal figures
3. Use of foresightening techniques
4. Use of geometrical vegetal ornamentation

Which of the above is/are the features of Indo-Saracenic architecture?

(a) 1 only (b) 2 and 3 only
(c) 1, 3 and 4 only (d) 1, 2, 3 and 4

70. An important piece of Chola sculpture was the bronze sculpture of Nataraja. In this context consider the given statements:

1. Shiva in this sculpture is associated with the end of cosmic world.
2. Shiva is depicted as suppressing the ignorance of an individual.
3. The bhujangatrasita stance of Shiva which implies kicking away of illusion from devotee's mind.

Which of the above statement/s is/are correct?

(a) 1 only (b) 1 and 3 only
(c) 2 only (d) 1, 2 and 3

71. With reference to Pala School of Art, consider the following statements:

1. The Pala period witnessed the last great phase of Buddhist art in India.
2. Pala manuscripts mostly belong to Hinayana Buddhism.
3. The Pala paintings are characterised by sinuous line and subdued tones of colour.

Which of the above statements are correct?

(a) 1 and 2 only (b) 2 and 3 only
(c) 1 and 3 only (d) 1, 2 and 3

72. With reference to the history of Indian rock-cut architecture, consider the following statements:

1. The caves at Badami are the oldest surviving rock-cut caves in India.
2. The Barabar rock-cut caves were originally made for Ajivikas by the Emperor Chandragupta Maurya.
3. At Ellora, caves were made for different faiths.

Which of the above statement/s is/are correct?

(a) 1 only (b) 2 and 3 only
(c) 3 only (d) 1, 2 and 3

73. Consider the following pairs:

	Temple		Chief Deity
1.	Sree Padmana-Bhaswamy Temple	–	Lord Shiva
2.	Sabarimala Temple	–	Lord Ayyappan
3.	Vaikom Mahadeva Temple	–	Lord Vishnu

Which of the above pairs is/are correctly matched?

(a) 1 and 3 only (b) 2 only
(c) 1 and 2 only (d) 2 and 3 only

74. Which of the following statements regarding the Archaeological Survey of India is/are correct?

1. All archaeological activities in the country are regulated by it.
2. It also performs the epigraphical and numismatic studies.
3. William Jones was its first Director-General.

Select the correct option using the codes given below:

(a) 1 only (b) 1 and 2 only
(c) 2 and 3 only (d) 1, 2 and 3

75. Though the earliest inscriptions are found on the seals of Harappa, which of the following inscription was first deciphered?

(a) Ashokan Pillar of Meerut.
(b) Allahabad inscription of Samudragupta.
(c) Ashokan Pillar of Rummindai.
(d) Sanchi Inscription of Samudragupta.

76. Which of the following places is/are famous for the Jaina Architecture?

1. Pattadakal 2. Mount Abu
3. Girnar 4. Ajanta Caves
5. Pavapuri 6. Khajuraho

Select the correct answer using the code given bellow:

(a) 1, 2, 3, 5 and 6 only
(b) 2, 3, 4, 5 and 6 only
(c) 1, 3, 5 and 6 only
(d) All of the above

77. Consider the following statements:

1. The Temple is named after a nearby village, once a flourishing town and seaport.
2. This Temple, which has been mentioned in Skanda Purana, is situated on the banks of Pushpavati River.
3. Built during the reign of Chalukya King Bhima I, this Temple was attacked and damaged by Mahmud Ghazni.
4. Every year a dance festival is held during the third week of January in the backdrop of this Temple.

Identify the well-known Temple with the help of above given information:

(a) Khajuraho Temple
(b) Konark Sun Temple
(c) Modhera Sun Temple
(d) Chandrabhaga Temple, Jhalawar

78. Consider the following statements about Meenakshi Temple:

1. The current structure was built by Chera Rulers.
2. It is dedicated to Lord Shiva and Parvathi.

Which of the statements given above is/are correct?

(a) 1 only (b) 2 only
(c) Both 1 and 2 (d) Neither 1 nor 2

79. Taj Mahal is an architectural wonder built in Agra by Mughal Emperor Shah Jahan as a mausoleum of Mumtaz Mahal, his deceased wife. Which of the following is/are true regarding Taj Mahal's architecture?

1. Laid out in a Chahar Bagh style.
2. Use of Calligraphy to write Quranic verses.
3. Use of Pietra Dura and Tessellation.
4. Delicate carving of marble into Jalis.

Select the correct answer using the codes given below:

(a) 1 and 4 only (b) 2 and 3 only
(c) 3 and 4 only (d) All of the above

80. Which of the statement/s is/are correct regarding Archaeological Survey of India (ASI)?

1. It has been charged with preservation of the cultural heritage of our nation.
2. The provisions of the Ancient Monuments and Archaeological Sites and Remains Act, 1958 guide ASI.

Select the correct option using the codes given below:

(a) 1 only (b) 2 only
(c) Both 1 and 2 (d) Neither 1 nor 2

81. Which of the following is incorrect about the Chola Art and Architecture?

(a) The Dravidian style of the Temple architecture reached its zenith during the period of Chola Kingdom.
(b) The Temple erected during the period of the Chola generally did not have sculpture art on the walls.
(c) The Brihadeshwara Temple of Tanjore was completed during the time of Rajaraja Chola around 1009 AD.
(d) The presence of water tank inside the Temple enclosure was the unique feature of Temple build during the period of Cholas.

82. Which of the following statement/s is/are correct?

1. Although Buddhism ceased to receive royal patronage during the Gupta period, some viharas and stupas were constructed.
2. There was a change in the character of Buddhism which had come to acquire many features of Brahmanism in the Gupta period.

Select the correct option using the codes given below:

(a) 1 only (b) 2 only
(c) Both 1 and 2 (d) Neither 1 nor 2

83. Consider the following statements regarding impact of central Asian contact:

1. The building construction technique declined and did not reach the developed stage till the Mughal period.
2. The use of burnt brick was rare.
3. Red polished pottery came from central Asia.

Which of the above statement/s is/are incorrect?

(a) 1 only (b) 1 and 2 only
(c) 2 and 3 only (d) 1, 2 and 3

84. The figure of Chulakoka Devta is a notable specimen of which art?

(a) Mauryan Art (b) Sunga Art
(c) Kanvas Art (d) Mathura Art

85. Mauryan's contribution to art and architecture can be seen through.

1. Pillars 2. Rock Cut Caves
3. Sculptures 4. Pottery

Select the correct answer using the code given below:

(a) 1, 2 and 3 only (b) 1, 2 and 4 only
(c) 3 and 4 only (d) 1, 2, 3 and 4

86. Consider the following pairs:

Stage of Temple development		Features added
1. Second stage	-	Pradakshina path
2. Third stage	-	Shikharas
3. Fourth stage	-	Circular Temple

Which of the above pairs is/are correctly matched?

(a) 1 and 2 only (b) 2 only
(c) 1 and 3 only (d) 3 only

87. Which one of the following best describes the term Shalbhanjika seen in ancient India?

(a) A group of anonymous sculptures from the Nanda period.
(b) A type of Temple constructed in the Harappan period dedicated to Mother Goddess.
(c) It describes sculpture of a woman, with stylized feminine features, standing near a tree and grasping a branch.
(d) A mural painting of dying prince from the Ajanta caves.

88. Consider the following statements regarding the Indo-Islamic architecture:

1. Like Hindu architecture, the Indo-Islamic architecture too was congested and less spacious.
2. The mortar was used as a cementing agent in their constructions.
3. Indo-Islamic architecture avoided the use of human and animal figures.

Which of the above statements is/are correct?

(a) 1 and 3 only (b) 2 only
(c) 2 and 3 only (d) 1, 2 and 3

89. Consider the following statements regarding the Vijaynagara School of Architecture:

1. It was influenced by the Indo-Islamic style of Bijapur.
2. Secular buildings were also present inside the Temple complexes.

Which of the above statements is/are correct?

(a) 1 only (b) 2 only
(c) Both 1 and 2 (d) Neither 1 nor 2

90. Consider the following statements regarding the Ellora Caves:

1. It has monasteries associated with Buddhism, Jainism, and Brahmanism.
2. Double-storeyed caves are a unique achievement of Ellora caves as compared to single-storeyed caves of Ajanta.
3. Jaina caves at Ellora belong to the Swetambara sect.

Which of the above statements is/are correct?

(a) 1 only (b) 1 and 2 only
(c) 2 and 3 only (d) 3 only

91. Rekha-prasad, Phamsana and Valabhi terms are seen in ancient India Temple architecture refer to?

(a) Mandapas (b) Vahana
(c) Shikharas (d) Garbhagriha

92. Which of the following is/are the characteristics of Mathura Art?

1. Sculptures were made on white-spotted red stones.
2. It was purely indigenous in nature.
3. The new ideals of Hinayana Buddhism inspired the sculptors of this art.

Select the correct answer from the code given below:

(a) 1 only (b) 1 and 2 only
(c) 1 and 3 only (d) 2 and 3 only

93. Consider the following statements regarding the Orissa School of Architecture:

1. Shikhara is known as Jagmohana in this school.
2. Like Nagaras school, Temples are not surrounded by the Boundary wall.

Which of the above statement is/are incorrect?

(a) 1 only (b) 2 only
(c) Both 1 and 2 (d) Neither 1 nor 2

94. In Which of the following caves, the religious themes of Andhakasurvadha and Kalyanasundaram can be found?

(a) Sittanvasal Caves (b) Ajanta Caves
(c) Ellora Caves (d) Bagh Caves

95. Consider the following statements regarding the Pallava School of Architecture:

1. Under the Mahendra group, the mandaps divided into rathas.
2. Real structural Temple replaced rock-cut Temple under the Narasimha group.

Which of the above statements is/are correct?

(a) 1 only (b) 2 only
(c) Both 1 and 2 (d) Neither 1 nor 2

96. With reference to Indian Bronze Sculpture, consider the following statements:

1. The 'Dancing Girl' from Mohenjo-daro is the world's oldest bronze sculpture.
2. Bronze sculptures relating to both Hinduism and Buddhism are found in the Kashmir region.
3. Portrait sculptures made of bronze were made during the Pallava period.

Which of the above statements is/are correct?

(a) 1 only (b) 1 and 2 only
(c) 2 and 3 only (d) 1, 2 and 3

97. Consider the following statements regarding the Gandhara School of Art:

1. It represents a fusion of native and foreign elements.
2. The most notable of the Gandhara icons is that of the Buddha seated in the position of a yogi.
3. It is confined to incidents related to the life of Buddha.

Which of the above statements is/are correct?

(a) 1 and 2 only (b) 2 only
(c) 2 and 3 only (d) 1, 2 and 3

98. The architecture during the period of Delhi Sultanate can be categorized into imperial and provincial style. Consider the following statements in this regard:

1. The imperial style of architecture under the Khilji Dynasty is marked by the use of red sandstone.
2. Double domes in the imperial style were introduced by the Tughlaqs.
3. Jaunpur School of provincial architecture is characterized by extensive use of minars.

Which of the above statements is/are correct?

(a) 1 only (b) 1 and 2 only
(c) 2 and 3 only (d) 1, 2 and 3 only

99. What does the term Panchayatan signify in ancient India?

(a) The religious sect of Vaishnavism
(b) Temple style
(c) Port cities established during the Chola period
(d) Learning centres attached to an Temple

100. Consider the following statements:

1. Use of minars
2. Use of human and animal figures
3. Use of foresightening techniques
4. Use of geometrical vegetal ornamentation

Which of the above is/are the features of Indo-Saracenic architecture?

(a) 1 only (b) 2 and 3 only
(c) 1, 3 and 4 only (d) 1, 2, 3 and 4

101. Consider the following statements regarding the Satvahana Sculptures:

1. They reflect the influence of both the Gandhara and the Mathura School of Art.
2. They are iconic in nature with the absence of representation in human forms.
3. Eroticism is a predominant feature of these sculptures.

Which of the above statements are correct?

(a) 1 and 2 only (b) 2 and 3 only
(c) 1 and 3 only (d) 1, 2 and 3

102. Rekhapida, Pidhadeul, and Khakra are the features of which school of architecture?

(a) Pala and Sena Art (b) Hoysala Art
(c) Orissa Art (d) Nayaka Art

103. An example of Sunga Art of the second century BC. is the jovial figure of the dwarfish Yaksha carrying a bowl of abundance on his head. His round belly indicates that he is fully satisfied with his amulets warding off the evil spirit from his devotees.

Identify the cave where this figure was found?

(a) Karle Caves (b) Bagh Caves
(c) Pithalkhora Caves (d) Kondan Caves

104. Consider the following statements regarding the Vesara School of Architecture:

1. It combines the features of both Nagara school and Dravidian school.
2. Hoysala, Rashtrakutas, and Pallavas patronized this school.

Which of the above statements is/are correct?

(a) 1 only (b) 2 only
(c) Both 1 and 2 (d) Neither 1 nor 2

105. Which of the following statements are correct regarding the Lion Capital, Sarnath?

1. It was built in commemoration of the Dhammachakrapravartana by the Buddha
2. The whole capital has been adopted as the National Emblem of Independent India.
3. It is now kept in the archaeological museum at Sarnath.

Select the correct answer using the code given below:

(a) 1 and 2 only (b) 2 and 3 only
(c) 1 and 3 only (d) 1, 2 and 3

106. Consider the following statements regarding the Elephanta Caves:

1. It exclusively depicts Shaivite faith.
2. It is contemporary with Ajanta caves.

Which of the above statements is/are correct?

(a) 1 only (b) 2 only
(c) Both 1 and 2 (d) Neither 1 nor 2

107. Consider the following statements regarding the Sanchi Stupa:

1. The present stupa at Sanchi was originally constructed during Ashoka's reign.
2. Buddha never visited Sanchi during his lifetime.
3. Toranas at Sanchi were added during the Sunga period.
4. The Sanchi sculptures are, like Bharhut sculpture i.e. entirely naturalistic in the treatment of the human form.

Which of the above statements is/are correct?

(a) 1, 2 and 3 only (b) 2, 3 and 4 only
(c) 1, 2 and 4 only (d) 1, 2, 3 and 4

108. Sangharama in ancient India refers to:

(a) Market place for a priestly class in the Gupta period
(b) Monastery for Buddhist monastic community
(c) Religious sect originated during the post-Mauryan period
(d) A type of revenue collected on infertile land during Muryan period

109. Consider the following statements regarding the Ajanta Caves:

1. It has less number of Vihraras than Chaitya.
2. It is the only surviving example of a painting of the first century BCE.
3. It was patronised by Satvahanas, Vakatakas and Guptas.

Which of the above statements is/are correct?

(a) 1 only (b) 2 and 3 only
(c) 3 only (d) 1, 2 and 3

110. Consider the following statements:

1. Most of the constructions during Akbar's reign were made up of red sandstone.
2. Jahangir's reign saw a decline in Mughal architecture as he shifted his focus on paintings and other art forms.
3. The concept of hanging balcony belongs to the Sikh style of architecture.
4. Rajput architecture is characterized by the use of shallow cornices.

Which of the above statements are incorrect?

(a) 1 and 2 only (b) 1 and 3 only
(c) 2 and 4 only (d) 3 and 4 only

111. Consider the following statements regarding the difference between Ashokan Pillars and Achaemenian Pillars:

1. The shaft of the Ashokan pillars was monolithic while the shaft of Achaemenian pillars was made up of various types of sandstone.
2. The Ashokan pillars were generally attached to state buildings, while Achaemenian pillars were independently erected by royal diction.

Which of the above statements is/are correct?

(a) 1 only (b) 2 only
(c) Both 1 and 2 (d) Neither 1 nor 2

112. Consider the following statements regarding the styles of Temple architecture:

1. Unlike the Nagara Temples, the Dravidian Temples were surrounded by high boundary walls.
2. The entrance of a garbhagriha in a Nagara Temple had sculptures of Mithun's while that of Dravida Temple had river goddesses.
3. The presence of a water tank inside the Temple enclosure is a unique feature of the Dravidian style.

Which of the above statements are correct?

(a) 1 and 2 only (b) 2 and 3 only
(c) 1 and 3 only (d) 1, 2 and 3

113. Consider the following statements regarding the Bharhut Art:

1. The peculiar feature of this art is the absence of indigenous elements and is highly influenced by Greek Art.

2. The carvings represent minute details like decorative patterns on turbans or cloths which signify that knowledge of correct human anatomy existed.

Which of the above statements is/are incorrect?

(a) 1 only (b) 2 only
(c) Both 1 and 2 (d) Neither 1 nor 2

114. Consider the following statements regarding Markandeshwar group of Temples:

1. It is located on the bank of river Wainganga.
2. It belongs to Dravidian group of architecture.

Which of the above statements is/are correct?

(a) 1 only (b) 2 only
(c) Both 1 and 2 (d) Neither 1 nor 2

115. Consider the following statements regarding Ashokan Inscriptions:

1. Ashoka's name does not occur in any of his inscriptions and mentioned as 'devanampiya piyadasi'.
2. The title devanampiya or 'dear to gods' adopted by Ashoka was unique and was not adopted by his ancestors.

Which of the above statements is/are correct?

(a) 1 only (b) 2 only
(c) Both 1 and 2 (d) Neither 1 nor 2

116. With reference to the Art and Architecture during the Gupta Period, consider the following statements:

1. The gold coin issued by Samudragupta shows him playing the vina.
2. Gupta period was rich in terms of the architectural developments.
3. Ajanta paintings were built during the Gupta period.

Which of the above statements are correct?

(a) 1 and 2 only (b) 1 and 3 only
(c) 2 and 3 only (d) 1, 2 and 3

117. Consider the following statements with respect to Ashoka's edicts and inscriptions:

1. There is no reference to the teachings of the Buddha in the Greek and Aramaic versions of his inscriptions.
2. The inscriptions throw light on his external and domestic polices as well as the extent of his empire.

Which of the above statements is/are correct?

(a) 1 only (b) 2 only
(c) Both 1 and 2 (d) Neither 1 nor 2

118. With reference to sculptures of Indus Valley/Harappan Civilisation, consider the following statements:

1. All of the Harappan seals were square in shape and were made of steatite.
2. The terracotta sculptures are more in number as compared to bronze figures.
3. Northern Black Polished Ware was associated with the Indus Valley Civilisation.
4. Bones and baked clay were used to make ornaments by the Harappans.

Which of the above statements is/are incorrect?

(a) 1 only (b) 2 and 4 only
(c) 1, 2 and 3 only (d) 3 only

119. Which of the following are the features of Harappan town planning?

1. Streets arranged in a rectangular grid pattern
2. Higher citadel in east and lower town in west
3. Use of burnt bricks for construction
4. Doors and windows opening into main streets
5. Loosely covered drains alongside the main road

Select the correct answer using the code given below:

(a) 1 and 2 only (b) 1, 3 and 5 only
(c) 2, 3, and 4 only (d) 1, 2, 3, 4 and 5

120. Which of the following statements is incorrect with respect to the Delhi Sultanate art and architecture?

(a) Alai Darwaza at the entrance of Qutub Minar was built by Qutbuddin Mubarak Shah.
(b) Tomb of Ghyasuddin was built by Muhammad bin Tughlaq.
(c) Kotla fort at Delhi was the creation of Firoz Tughlaq.
(d) The palace complex called Tughlaqabad was built during the period of Ghyasuddin Tughlaq.

121. Which of the following case is correct regarding Magao Caves?

1. Mogao caves reveal pivotal India-China Buddhist link.
2. Mogao cave-Temples of Dunhuang are a World Heritage Site.

Which of the above statements is/are correct?

(a) 1 only (b) 2 only
(c) Both 1 and 2 (d) Neither 1 nor 2

122. Which of the following pairs are correctly matched?

1. Akbar - Buland Darwaza
2. Humayun - Jamali Mosque
3. Jahangir - Moti Masjid at Agra
4. Shah Jahan - Cimax of Painting.

Select the correct answer using the code given below:

(a) 1 and 3 only (b) 1 and 2 only
(c) 2 and 4 only (d) 3 and 4 only

123. Consider the following statements regarding Mauryan art and sculpture:

1. Ashoka's greatest innovation was the substitution of wood for stone.

2. The stone portrait of Ashoka was found at Kanaganahalli.
3. Lomasha Risi cave and Dhauli caves in the Barabara hills near Gaya present the rock-cut architecture of Mauryan times.

Which of the above statements is/are correct?
(a) 2 only (b) 1 and 2 only
(c) 1 and 3 only (d) 1, 2 and 3

124. Consider the following statements regarding rare life-size stucco Buddhist sculpture recently found in Telangana:
1. A life-size figurine represents a Bodhisattva
2. It is the biggest stucco sculpture found in India till date.

Which of the above statements is/are correct?
(a) 1 only (b) 2 only
(c) Both 1 and 2 (d) Neither 1 nor 2

125. Consider the following statements with reference to Harappan Phase:
1. Drainage systems were unique to the larger cities.
2. There are indications of complex decisions being taken and implemented in Harappan society.
3. Cholistan is one of the Mature Harappan sites.

Which of the above statements is/are correct?
(a) 1 only (b) 1 and 2 only
(c) 2 and 3 only (d) 1, 2 and 3

126. Consider the following statements regarding Vittala Temple:
1. It is known for its architecture of stone chariot and the musical pillars.
2. It is located in Masulipattnam.

Which of the above statements is/are correct?
(a) 1 only (b) 2 only
(c) Both 1 and 2 (d) Neither 1 nor 2

127. Consider the following statements regarding Ashokan Edicts:
1. Dhamma was the central theme of the edicts.
2. Edicts clearly defined the meaning of the term 'Dhamma' given by Ashoka.
3. It was first deciphered by James Princep.

Which of the above statements is/are correct?
(a) 1 and 2 only (b) 1 only
(c) 2 and 3 only (d) 1 and 3 only

128. Consider the following statements:
1. The mausoleum of Mohammed Adil Shah was built by architect Yaqut of Dabul.
2. The building has an amazing acoustical system.
3. It is built of **dark grey basalt** and decorated plaster work.

Which of the following monuments contain these characteristics?
(a) Gol Gumbad (b) Golconda Fort
(c) Char Minar (d) Ibrahim Rouza

129. Consider the following statements.
1. The main architectural features are classified in three orders, i.e., rekhapida, pidhadeul and khakra.
2. These Temples are a distinct substyle within the Nagara order.
3. These Temples usually have boundary walls.

Which of the following Temple architecture is being referred to here?
(a) Pala style (b) Kalinga style
(c) Garhwal style (d) None of the above

130. Who built the magnificent rock-cut monolithic Kailasa Temple at Ellora?
(a) Dantidurga (b) Krishna I
(c) Amoghavarsha I (d) Krishna III

SOLUTIONS

1. Correct Option: (b)

Supplementary Notes:

Lion Capital, Sarnath

- The Lion Capital discovered more than a hundred years ago at Sarnath, near Varanasi, is generally referred as Sarnath Lion Capital.
- **Statement 1 is incorrect:** It is one of the finest examples of sculpture from Mauryan period and was built by Ashoka in commemoration of 'Dhammachakrapravartana' or the first sermon of Buddha.
- **Statement 2 is correct:** Originally it consists of five components:
    - The pillar shaft.
    - The lotus bell or base.
    - A drum on the bell base with four animals proceeding clockwise (abacus).
    - Figure of four majestic addorsed (back to; back) lions
    - The crowning element, Dharamchakra/ Dharmachakra.

Figure: 7.1.1

2. **Correct Option: (c)**

Supplementary Notes:

Khajuraho Temples

- The Khajuraho group of monuments is a group of Hindu and Jain Temples in Madhya Pradesh (in Chhatarpur district).
- In Hindi language, "Khajura" means 'Date' and "Vahika" means 'Bearing'. In history, Khajuraho is also described with the name of Jejakbhukti.
- The Temple site is situated within Vindhya Mountain range in Central India.
- **Statement 2 is correct:** These temples were constructed by the Chandella rulers between AD 900 and 1130.
- **Statement 3 is correct:** These Temples got the status of UNESCO's World Heritage Sites in 1986.
- The Khajuraho Temples are made of sandstone, with a granite foundation that is almost hidden.
- **Statement 1 is incorrect:** The Temples are famous for their Nagara-style architectural symbolism and erotic sculptures.
- The Khajuraho group of Temples belongs to Vaishnavism School of Hinduism, Saivism School of Hinduism and Jainism.
- The Khajuraho Temples were reported for the first time by Abu Rihan al Biruni in AD 1022 and the Arab travellerIbn Battuta in AD 1335.

3. **Correct Option: (c)**

Supplementary Notes:

Gandhara School of Art:

- Gandhara Art was a combination of Hellenistic, West Asiatic and native elements.
- Greek and Roman techniques, modified according to Indian requirements, were employed in fashioning the Gandhara sculpture which truly represents Indian culture in a Western garb.
- Its area extended from Takshila in India to the Swat Valley in Pakistan and northwards to areas in Afghanistan.
- The Gandhara sculptors made images of Lord Buddha in the Greco-Roman style. The images of Buddha resembled Greek God Apollo. It gave more stress to the bodily features and external beauty.
- **Statement 2 is incorrect:** Early Gandhara School used bluish-grey sandstone while the later period saw the use of mud and stucco.
- In all the Buddha depicted in the Gandhara Art is shown making four types of hand gestures and this is a remarkable feature in this art. The gestures are as follows:

Abahayamudra	: Don't fear.
Dhyanamudra	: Meditation.
Dharmachakramudra	: A preaching mudra
Bhumisparshamudra	: Touching the earth

Amravati School of Art:

- The Amravati school of Art evolved during Satavahna period.
- **Statement 3 is correct:** The sculptures of Amaravati School were made using white marbles
- This school of art developed at Amravati, on the banks of the Krishna River in modern Andhra Pradesh.
- This school of art had great influence on art in Sri Lanka and South-East Asia as products from here were carried to those countries.
- Lord Buddha is depicted in the form of `Swastika` mark. This has been carved out on the cushioned seat over a throne that is situated under the Bodhi tree.

Mathura School of Art:

- Mathura School of Art is purely indigenous style. Mathura Art developed during post Maurya period (mainly during Shunga period) and reached its peak during the Gupta period (AD 325 to 600).
- **Statement 1 is incorrect:** The sculptures of Mathura School were made using spotted red sandstone.
- The traditional centre, Mathura, remained the main art production site whereas Sarnath and Kosambi also emerged as important centres of art production. Spotted red sandstone has been used in this school.
- Themes in the Mathura Art vary from Buddhist to Brahmanical to sometimes secular. More stress was given to the inner beauty and facial emotions rather than bodily gesture.
- Under the Mathura Art images of Vishnu and Shiva, Buddha, Yakshas, Yakshinis, Shaivite and Vaishnavite deities were found.

4. **Correct Option: (d)**

Supplementary Notes:

Seals of Indus Valley Civilisation:

- Archaeologists have discovered thousands of seals, usually made of steatite, and occasionally of agate, chert, copper, faience and terracotta, with beautiful figures of animals, such as unicorn bull, rhinoceros, tiger, elephant, bison, goat, and buffalo, etc.
- The purpose of producing seals was mainly commercial. It appears that the seals were also used as amulets, carried on the persons of their owners, perhaps as modern-day identity cards.
- **Statement 1 is correct:** The standard Harappan seal was a square plaque 2×2 square inches, usually

made from the soft riverstone, steatite. Every seal is engraved in a pictographic script which is yet to be deciphered. They all bear a great variety of motifs, most often of animals including those of the bull, with or without the hump, the elephant, tiger, goat and also monsters. Sometimes, trees or human figures were also depicted.

- **Statement 2 is correct:** The most remarkable seal is the Pashupati Seal, depicted with a figure in the centre and animals around. This seal depicts a human figure seated cross-legged. An elephant and a tiger are depicted to the right side of the seated figure, while on the left, a rhinoceros and a buffalo are seen. In addition to these animals, two antelopes are shown below the seat. Seals such as these date from between 2500 and 1500 BCE and were found in considerable numbers.
- **Statement 1 and Statement 3 are correct:** The seals show the culture and civilisation of the Indus Valley people. In particular, they indicate:
  - Dresses, ornaments, hair-styles of people.
  - Skill of artists and sculptors.
  - Trade contacts and commercial relations.
  - Religious beliefs.
  - Script.

5. **Correct Option: (b)**

Supplementary Notes:

Barabar Caves

- **Option (b) is correct:** The oldest examples of Mauryan rock-cut architecture in India are the Barabar caves, located in the Barabar Hills, in Jehanabad District of Bihar. There are four caves in Barabar dating back to reign of Ashoka (273-232 BC) and his grandson Dasaratha, initially for the Ajeevika sect. These are also known as Lomas Rishi Caves.
- **Four Caves at Barabar are as follows:**
  - **Lomas Rishi Cave:** This is the most popular Barabar cave. The decorative arch above the entrance (facade) of Lomas Rishi Cave was made in imitation of the wooden architecture of the time. This became a constant feature in the later Chaityas and is known as the Chaitya Arch. It also continued as a decorative motif in later Temples.
  - **Sudama Cave:** This cave known for the bow shaped arches and has Ashokan inscriptions.
  - **Karan Chaupar:** It has a single rectangular room with polished surfaces, contains inscription dating back to Maurya era.
  - **Visva Zopri:** There are two rectangular caves over there.

Ajanta Caves:

- These are another UNESCO World Heritage Site famous for ancient Buddhist paintings. Ajanta caves are located in the Aurangabad district of the state of Maharashtra, India. Comprising of 29 Buddhist cave monuments, excavated out of rocks, tracing back to the 2nd century BCE to around 480 or 650 CE, the site presents rock-cut sculptures and paintings of utmost brilliance.

Elephanta Caves:

- These are situated on the Elephanta Island near Mumbai city in the state of Maharashtra, India. This site comprises of five Hindu caves and two Buddhist caves that trace back to a period between 5th century and 8th century and excavated out of solid basalt rock. The Hindu caves of the site are dedicated to Lord Shiva and rock-cut sculptures of these caves represent the Shaiva Hindu sect.

Bagh caves:

- These are located on the bank of Baghani River in the Dhar district of Madhya Pradesh. These rock cut caves possess the most amazing paintings known to be made by ancient man. Out of the initial 9 caves, only 5 have been extant. The legend says that these caves were established by Buddhist monk Dataka. The caves were carved in late 4th century to 6th century AD.

6. **Correct Option: (a)**

Supplementary Notes:

Dashavatara Temple

- The Dashavatara Temple is an early 6th century Vishnu Hindu Temple located at Deogarh, Uttar Pradesh in the Betwa River valley in north-central India.
- It has a simple, one cell square plan and is one of the earliest Hindu stone Temples still surviving today. Built in the Gupta Period, the Dashavatara Temple at Deogarh shows the ornate Gupta style architecture.
- The Temple at Deogarh is dedicated to Vishnu, but includes in its small footprint images of Shiva, Parvati, Kartikeya, Brahma, Indra, River goddesses Ganga and Yamuna, as well as a panel showing the five Pandavas of the Hindu epic Mahabharata.
- The Temple was built out of stone and masonry brick. Legends associated with Vishnu are sculpted in the interior and exterior walls of the Temple. Also carved are secular scenes and amorous couples in various stages of courtship and intimacy.
- The Dashavatara Temple is locally known as Sagar marh, which literally means "the Temple on the tank", a name it gets from the square water pool cut into the rock in front.
- **Statement 1 is correct:** This Temple is in the panchayatana style of architecture where the main shrine is built on a rectangular plinth with four smaller subsidiary shrines at the four corners (making it a total number of five shrines, hence the name, panchayatana).

- **Statement 2 is correct:** Sculpture of Nara-Narayan – Shows the discussion between human soul and the eternal divine.
- **Statement 3 is incorrect:** Gajendra Moksha Carving on the northern wall represents Vishnu coming to the rescue of the Gajendra (elephant).

7. **Correct Option: (a)**

Supplementary Notes:

Khajuraho Group of Monuments

- It is a group of Hindu, Buddhist and Jain Temples in Madhya Pradesh about 175 km southeast of Jhansi.
- Statement 1 is correct: They are one of the UNESCO World Heritage Sites in India.
- Temples at Khajurao in Central India were devoted to Hindu gods. There are some Jain Temples as well as a Chausanth Yogini Temples also.
- The Temples are famous for their nagara-style architectural symbolism. Khajuraho's Temples are also known for their extensive erotic sculptures; the erotic expression is given equal importance in human experience as spiritual pursuit, and it is seen as part of a larger cosmic whole.
- Khajuraho's sculptures are highly stylised with typical features: they are in almost full relief, cut away from the surrounding stone, with sharp noses, prominent chins, long slanting eyes and eyebrows. The other notable example at Khajuraho is Kandariya Mahadeo Temple dedicated to Lord Shiva.

Temples in West India:

- **Statement 2 is incorrect:** The Temples in the western parts of India used stones such as sandstone, a grey to black basalt.
- The most exuberant and famed is the manipulatable soft white marble which is also seen in some of the tenth to twelveth century Jain Temples in Mount Abu and the fifteenth century Temple at Ranakpur.

Temples in East India:

- Terracota was used in East India. Eastern Indian Temples include those found in the North-East, Bengal and Odisha. Each of these three areas produced distinct types of Temples.
- The history of architecture in the North-East and Bengal is hard to study because a number of ancient buildings in those regions were renovated, and what survives now are later brick or concrete Temples at those sites.
- It appears that terracotta was the main medium of construction, and also for moulding plaques which depicted Buddhist and Hindu deities in Bengal until the seventh century.
- A large number of sculptures have been found in Assam and Bengal which shows the development of important regional schools in those regions.
- **Statement 3 is incorrect:** In most of the Temples architecture in East India, the mount or vehicle of the Temple's main deity is placed axially before the sanctum.

8. **Correct Option: (a)**

Supplementary Notes:

Ashokan pillar at Sarnath – Lion Capital of Sarnath:

- **Statement 1 is correct:** The Lion Capital at Sarnath, near Varanasi, is one of the finest examples of sculpture from the Mauryan period. It was built in commemoration of the historical event of the first sermon or the Dhammachakrapravartana by the Buddha at Sarnath, the capital was built by Ashoka.
- Statement 2 is incorrect: Sarnath column depicts four animals representing the four cardinal directions: a horse (west), an ox (east), an elephant (south), and a lion (north).
- Statement 3 is incorrect: The capital is carved out of a single block of polished sandstone.
- The Sarnath Column has three parts. First, a base of a lotus flower, the most ubiquitous symbol of Buddhism. Then, a drum on which four animals are carved representing the four cardinal directions: a horse (west), an ox (east), an elephant (south), and a lion (north).
- The motif of the chakra becomes significant as a representation of the Dhammachkra in the entire Buddhist art. Each animal figure, despite sticking to the surface, is voluminous, its posture creating movement in the circular abacus. Despite having limited space between each chakra, these animal figures display considerable command over the depiction of movement in a limited space.
- The abacus is supported by a bell-shaped base consisting of a lotus with dharmachakra, which perhaps symbolized the victory of righteousness over physical force. The superb modelling of the figures executed in a realistic manner with a certain stylisation, is invested with a great power and dignity, and reveals the aristocratic and international nature of Mauryan art.

Figure: 7.1.2

9. **Correct Option: (a)**

Supplementary Notes:

Gandhara School of Art:

- Gandhara Art was a combination of Hellenistic, West Asiatic and native elements.
- Greek and Roman techniques, modified according to Indian requirements, were employed in fashioning the Gandhara sculpture which truly represents Indian culture in a Western garb.
- **Option (c) is correct:** Its area extended from Takshila in India to the Swat Valley in Pakistan and northwards to areas in Afghanistan. It has been developed during the reign of Kushana Emperor Kanishka.
- **Option (d) is correct:** The Gandhara sculptors made images of Lord Buddha in the Greco-Roman style. The images of Buddha resembled Greek God Apollo. It gave more stress to the bodily features and external beauty.
- **Option (b) is correct:** In all the Buddha depicted in the Gandhara Art is shown making four types of hand gestures and this is a remarkable feature in this art. The gestures are as follows:

Abahayamudra	: Don't fear
Dhyanamudra	: Meditation
Dharmachakramudra	: A preaching mudra
Bhumisparshamudra	: Touching the earth

Amravati school of Art:

- The Amravati School of Art evolved during Satavahna period.
- This school of art developed at Amravati, on the banks of the Krishna River in modern Andhra Pradesh.
- This school of art had great influence on art in Sri Lanka and South-East Asia, as products from here were carried to those countries.
- **Option (a) is incorrect:** Lord Buddha is depicted in the form of `Swastika` mark. This has been carved out on the cushioned seat over a throne that is situated under the Bodhi tree.

Mathura School of Art:

- Mathura School of Art is purely indigenous style. Mathura Art developed during post Maurya peiod (mainly during Shunga period) and reached its peak during the Gupta period (AD 325 to 600).
- The traditional centre, Mathura, remained the main art production site whereas Sarnathand Kosambi also emerged as important centres of art production. Spotted red sandstone has been used in this school.
- Themes in the Mathura Art vary from Buddhist to Brahmanical to sometimes secular. More stress was given to the inner beauty and facial emotions rather than bodily gesture.
- Under the Mathura Art images of Vishnu and Shiva, Buddha, Yakshas, Yakshinis, Shaivite and Vaishnavite deities were found.

10. **Correct Option: (a)**

Explanation:

- **Statement 1 is incorrect:** It is the Dravida Temple is enclosed within a compound wall or gateway.

Supplementary Notes:

Nagara Style of Temple Architecture:

- This style of Temple architecture became popular in Northern India where Temple is structured on a large basement as seen in image .
- In Nagara Style an entire Temple is built on a stone platform with steps leading up to it.
- Unlike in South India (which is Dravidian Style) it does not usually have elaborate boundary walls or gateways.
- Anatomy of the Nagara Style
- **Sikhara:** While the earliest Temples had just one tower, or Shikhara, later Temples had several.
- **Statement 2 is correct:** Garbhagriha – The garbhagriha is always located directly under the tallest tower.
- There are many subdivisions of Nagara Temples depending on the shape of the shikhara.
  - **Latina Type** – Common name for the simple shikhara which is square at the base and whose walls curve or slope inward to a point on top is called the 'latina' or the rekha-prasada type of shikara.
  - **Phamsana Type** – Phamsana buildings tend to be broader and shorter than Latina ones. Their roofs are composed of several slabs that gently rise to a single point over the centre of the building, unlike the Latina ones which look like sharply rising tall towers.
  - **Valabhi Type** – These are rectangular buildings with a roof that rises into a vaulted chamber. The edge of this vaulted chamber is rounded, like the bamboo or wooden wagons that would have been drawn by bullocks in ancient times. They are usually called wagon vaulted buildings'.

11. **Correct Option: (b)**

Supplementary Notes:

Statue of Equality

- **Option (b) is correct:** The world's second tallest statue of a seated figure, at 216 feet of Bhakti saint Ramanujacharya is in Hyderabad, named as "Statue of Equality".
- Currently, the Great Buddha of Thailand is the tallest statue, at 302-feet.

- Once the Ramanujacharya statue is unveiled, it will become the second tallest, a distinction now held by the Guanyin figure on Mount Xiqiao in China's Guangdong region, at 203 feet.
- Rāmānuja's philosophical foundation was qualified monism and is called Vishishtadvaita in the Hindu tradition.
- His ideas are one of three subschools in Vedānta, the other two are known as Ādi Shankara's Advaita (absolute monism) and Madhvāchārya's Dvaita (dualism).
- Madhavacharya ranks with Sankaracharya and Ramanuja as one of the three principal philosophers of the Vedanta system. He propounded Dvaita or dualism. According to him, the final aim of man is the direct perception of Hari which leads to Moksha or eternal bliss.
- Nimbarka, was a younger contemporary of Ramanuja. He was worshipper of Krishna and Radha. He founded Dvaitadvaita or dualistic monism. He wrote Vedanta Parijata-saurabha, a commentary on Brahmasutras. He settled in Mathura.
- The Statue of Unity dedicated to the iron man of India Sardar Vallabhbhai Patel was unveiled by Prime Minister Shri Narendra Modi on 31st October 2018, the 143rd birth anniversary of Sardar Patel.
- The work of 182-meter tall statue was completed after round-the-clock work by 3,400 labourers and 250 engineers at Sadhu Bet Island on Narmada River in Gujarat.

12. **Correct Option: (c)**

Supplementary Notes:

- **Statement 2 is incorrect:** Rashtriya Ekta Diwas was observed nationwide for first time on 31st October 2014, to commemorate the 139th birth anniversary of Sardar Vallabhbhai Patel.
- **Statement 1 is incorrect:** Sardar Vallabhbhai Patel was posthumously awarded the Bharat Ratna, India's highest civilian honour, in 1991.
- **Statement 3 is correct:** 'Run for Unity' campaign: The Run for Unity campaign is a nationwide marathon that was organised on first Rashtriya Ekta Diwas. It was organized in all cities, towns and villages of India. This campaign was to pay tribute to the efforts made by Sardar Patel to unite India.
- Objective of commemoration of Rashtriya Ekta Diwas:
  - This day will create awareness among the people about Sardar Patel's contribution towards India's freedom struggle and ensuring national integration in India. He played a pivotal role in the merger of princely states with British ruled India to form a sovereign united country called India.

13. **Correct Option: (d)**

Supplementary Notes:

Rajput Architecture

- **Statement 1 is correct:** The Rajputs had built magnific fortresses at Chittorgarh, Amber (Jaipur), Jaisalmer, Jodhpur, Ranthambhor, Gwalior, and many other places. These forts were usually made on small hills and some barriers were also made to prevent the entry of any unwanted person. All the forts had magnificent walls and various towers.
- **Statement 2 is correct:** During 600 AD to 900 AD, the Rajputs had built the Rathas of Mahabalipuram, the Kailash Temple at Ellora and the engravements of Elephanta.
- During 900 AD to 1200 AD, they had developed the Pallava, Chola and Hoysala Temples. Also included are the Vishwanath and the Khandariya Temples, the Khajuraho Temples, the Surya Temple at Konark, the Lingaraj Temple at Bhubaneshwar, the Jagannath Temple in Puri and the Tejpala Temple at Mt. Abu. Amongst these, the Khajuraho Temples are considered the most beautiful, as those are made of pink buff-coloured and yellow fine grained sandstone.

14. **Correct Option: (a)**

Supplementary Notes:

Mauryan Architecture

- The Mauryan rulers commissioned a large number of architectural works for political as well as religious reasons. These works are referred to as Court Art.
- **Statement 1 is correct:** The Mauryan Empire was the first powerful empire to come to power in India. The capital at Pataliputra and the palaces at Kumrahar (three-storey wooden structure) were created to reflect the splendour of the Mauryan Empire. The palace of Chandragupta Maurya was inspired by the Achaemenid palaces at Persepolis in Iran. Wood was the principal building material. The palace walls were decorated with carvings and sculptures.
- **Statement 2 is incorrect:** Pillars were constructed as a symbol of the state or to commemorate battle victories. He also used pillars to propagate imperial sermons as well. On an average of 40 feet high, the pillars were usually made of chunar sandstone and comprised of four parts. A long shaft formed the base and was made up of a single piece of stone or monolith. On top of it lay the capital, which was either lotus shaped or bell shaped. The bell shaped capitals were influenced by the Iranian pillars, as was the highly polished and lustrous finish of the pillars. Above the capital, there was a circular or rectangular base known as the abacus on which an animal figure was placed.
- The shaft of Achaemenian pillars were made up of various pieces of sandstone cemented together and

were generally attached to the state buildings unlike the Mauryan pillars that were independently erected by royal diction.

- **Statement 3 is incorrect:** This period saw the emergence of rock-cut cave architectures. During the Mauryan period, these caves were generally used as viharas, i.e., living quarters, by the Jain and Buddhist monks. The caves during Mauryan period were marked by a highly polished finish of the interior walls and decorative gateways.

15. **Correct Option: (a)**

Supplementary Notes:

Ashokan Pillar Edicts

- **Option (a) is correct:** Ashoka refers to himself as "Devnampiyadasi" or "Priyadarshi" (both refer to the beloved of the Gods) in a rock edict located in Maski, Karnataka.
- **Option (b) is incorrect:** The most celebrated of the Ashokan pillars is the one erected at Sarnath, the site of Buddha's First Sermon where he shared the Four Noble Truths (the dharma or the law). Currently, the pillar remains where it was originally sunk into the ground, but the capital is now on display at the Sarnath Museum.
- **Option (c) is incorrect:** Rummindei Pillar inscription refers to Ashoka's visit to Lumbini & exemption of Lumbini from tax.
- **Option (d) is incorrect:** Nigalisagar Pillar inscription mentions that Ashoka increased the height of stupa of Buddha Konakamana to its double size.

16. **Correct Option: (b)**

Supplementary Notes:

Jain Sculptures

- **Statement 1 is incorrect:** The sculpture can depict any of the twenty-four tirthankaras with images depicting Parshvanatha, Rishabhanatha, or Mahāvīra being more popular. Jain sculptures are an example of Jain art. There is a long history of construction of Jain sculptures. Early examples include Lohanipur Torsos which has been regarded to be from the Maurya period, and images from the Kushan period from Mathura.
- **Statement 2 is correct:** There are a few differences in Digambara and Svetambara depiction of idols. Digambara images are naked without any beautification whereas Svetambara ones are clothed and decorated with temporary ornaments.
- Jainism spread in all over Tamil Nadu during Sangam Age. One of the Tamil literature, called Paripadal, probably belongs to 3rd century, mentions that there were propelling statues sculptured in stone for different deities in the Temple of God Murugan in Thirupparankundram. One among them was Jain statue. Others are Kaaman-Rathi (the deities of Love), Deity Indira (the king of so-called heavenly people according to Indian mythology), Agaligai (wife of Saint Gaudham), and Buddha.

17. **Correct Option: (a)**

- **Option (a) is correct:** The Khajuraho Group of Monuments are a group of Hindu and Jain Temples in Madhya Pradesh. The name 'Khajuraho' derived from Sanskrit word ('Kharjuravahaka') is the confluence of two words 'Kharjur' meaning date palm and 'Vahaka' meaning bearer. These are group of 25 Temples spread over an area of approximately 6 square km. There are 6 Temples dedicated to Lord Shiva, 8 Temples to Lord Vishnu, 1 each to Lord Ganesha and the Sun God, while 3 Temples are dedicated to Jain Tirthankaras.
- The largest of the Temples is the Kandariya Mahadeo Temple which is dedicated to the glory of Lord Shiva. Khajuraho is one of the four holy sites dedicated to the glory of Lord Shiva, the other three being Gaya, Kashi and Kedarnath which represent a tradition of tolerance and acceptance
- The Parasvanath, Adinath, Shantinath and Ghantai Temples are the ones dedicated to worshipping of the Jain Trithankaras.
- They are one of the UNESCO World Heritage Sites in India. The Temples are famous for their Nagara-style architecture and their erotic sculptures.

18. **Correct Option: (a)**

Unique features of Odisha School:

- Exterior walls are lavishly decorated through intricate cravings, but interior walls are plain.
- No use of pillars – Instead of pillars, iron gridders were used, to support roof.
- Shikhara is called Deul and is almost vertical till the top when it suddenly curves sharply inwards
- Option (a) is correct: Sun Temple at Konarak (c. AD. 1250). Built in the thirteenth century, it was conceived as a gigantic solar chariot with twelve pairs of exquisitely-ornamented wheels dragged by seven rearing horses. The Temple comprised a sanctum with a lofty (presumably over 68 m. high) sikhara, a jagamohana (30. m. square and 30. m. high) and a detached nata-mandira (hall of dance) in the same axis, besides numerous subsidiary shrines. The sanctum and the nata-mandira have lost their roof. The nata-mandira exhibits a more balanced architectural design than that of other Orissan Temples. The sanctum displays superb images of the Sun-god in the three projections which are treated as miniature shrines. The sanctum and the jagamohana together stand on a common platform studded with an intricate wealth of decorative ornaments and sculptures, often highly erotic.

19. Correct Option: (a)

Supplementary Notes:

- **Option (a) is correct:** The Char Dham ("four abodes") is a set of four pilgrimage sites in India. The Char Dham as defined by Adi Shankaracharya consists of four Vaishnavite pilgrimage sites
- Vaishnavite Hindus believe that visiting these sites helps achieve "Moksha" (salvation). It comprises Badrinath, Dwarka, Puri and Rameswaram. It is considered by Hindus that every Hindu must visit the char dhams during one's lifetime.
- All the given Temples are from Gujarat.
- About Dwadkadish Temple: Dedicated to Lord Dwarkadhish (a form of Lord Krishna), the Temple is 2500 years old. Located on confluence of Gomati River and Arabian Sea, the magnificent sandstone Temple has 5 floors, supported by 60 columns and has beautiful wonderful carvings.
- Dwarkadhish Temple is one of the Sapt Puris as per Hindu religion The Temple is also the 108th Divya Desam of Lord Vishnu. On the top of the Temple is a flag that has a sun and a moon on it, which is changed three times in a day. The present structure of the Temple was founded around 15th and 16th century.

20. Correct Option: (b)

Supplementary Notes:

Buddhist Architecture

- Buddhist religious architecture developed in the Indian subcontinent. Three types of structures are associated with the religious architecture of early Buddhism.
- **Statement 2 is correct:** Stupa: It is a place of worship which is constructed on relics. It is a representation of life being ephemeral, symbolized by half dome.
- **Statement 1 is correct:** Chaityas: They are prayer halls.
- **Viharas:** Viharas are the rest houses of Buddhist monks.
- **Statement 3 is correct:** Pipriwaha Stupa in Lumbini is the oldest among all stupas.
- Bharhut Stupa in Madhya Pradesh was built during Sunga Dynasty.
- **Statement 4 is incorrect:** Bharhut Stupa in Madhya Pradesh was built during Sunga Dynasty (not during Maurya Dynasty).

21. Correct Option: (c)

Supplementary Notes:

Schools of Art in Ancient India

- Three different school of art represent Buddhism
- **Statement 1 is correct:** Mathura School of Art: It was developed by Sunga Dynasty. It comprises of images of Buddha in sitting postures, in deep meditation.
- **Statement 2 is incorrect:** Gandhara School of Art: It was developed by Kushans. Here Buddha is shown with thick curly hair, drapes, Greek like, masculine physique modeled as Apollo.
- **Statement 3 is incorrect:** Amaravati School of Art: It was developed by Sathavahana Dynasty. It is the most decorative form. The art is depicted on white limestone slabs where the theme of Buddha's life is engraved in all kinds of posture.

22. Correct Option: (a)

Supplementary Notes:

Ikshvaku Dynasty

- **Option (a) is correct:** The Ikshvaku Dynasty was the first to construct Hindu Temples in South India.
- The Ikshvaku Dynasty, in Puranic literature, was a Dynasty founded by the legendary king Ikshvaku. Ikshvaku, literally means "bitter cucumber".
- The Dynasty is also known as Suryavamsa. Lord Rama belonged to the Ikshavaku Dynasty. Twenty-two out of the twenty-four Jain Tirthankaras belonged to this Dynasty.
- Rishabha is present in both Hindu as well as Jain mythology. Both refer to the same person.
- According to the Buddhist texts, Prince Siddhartha belonged to this Dynasty.
- The important personalities belonging to this royal house are Bharata, Harishchandra, Dilipa, Sagara, Raghu, Rama and Pasenadi. Although, both the Hindu Puranas and the Buddhist texts include Shuddodhana, Gautama Buddha and Rahula in their accounts of the Ikshvaku Dynasty, but according to the Buddhist texts, Mahasammata, an ancestor of Ikshvaku was the founder of this Dynasty, who was elected by the people as the first king of the present era.
- According to the Puranas, supreme preceptor of the Ikshvaku Dynasty was sage Vashishta.

23. Correct Option: (d)

Supplementary Notes:

Delhi Sultanate Architecture

- The art and architecture of the Delhi Sultanate period was distinct from the Indian style. The Turks introduced arches, domes, lofty towers or minarets and decorations using the Arabic script. They used the skill of the Indian stone cutters.
- They also added colour to their buildings by using marbles, red and yellow sand stones. In the beginning, they converted Temples and other structures demolished into mosques. For example, the Quwwat-ul-Islam mosque near Qutub Minar in Delhi was built by using the materials obtained from destroying

many Hindu and Jain Temples. But later, they began to construct new structures.

- **Statement 1 is correct:** The most magnificent building of the 13th century was the Qutub Minar which was founded by Aibek and completed by Iltutmish.
- This seventy one metre tower was dedicated to the Sufi saint Qutbuddin Bakthiyar Kaki. The balconies of this tower were projected from the main building and it was the proof of the architectural skills of that period.
- **Statement 2 is incorrect:** Tughlaq architecture is marked by the city Tughluqabad, founded by Ghiyasuddin Tughlaq, the Adilabad fort and the city of Jahanpana, built by Muhammad bin Tughluq, and the Ferozabad palace and fort built by Firoz Shah Tughlaq.
- **Statement 3 is correct:** Later, Alauddin Khalji added an entrance to the Qutub Minar called Alai Darwaza.
- The dome of this arch was built on scientific lines. The buildings of the Tughlaq period were constructed by combining arch and dome. They also used the cheaper and easily available grey colour stones. The palace complex called Tughlaqabad with its beautiful lake was built during the period of Ghyasuddin Tughlaq.

24. Correct Option: (d)

Supplementary Notes:

Important Sites of Indus Valley Civilisation

- As of 2008, over 1000 Indus Valley Civilisation sites have been discovered, of which 406 sites are in Pakistan and 616 sites in India, while some sites in Afghanistan are believed to be trading colonies.
- **Statement 1 is correct:** Chanhudaro: It was situated on right bank of river Indus, south of Mohenjo-daro. It was excavated by M G Majumdar. It was the only Indus valley site without citadel. Image of male dancer resembling Lord Shiva was found here.
- **Statement 2 is correct:** Kalibangan: It was situated on the banks of river Ghaghra in Rajasthan and was excavated by Dr A Ghosh. It was an important site for bangles and beads manufacturing. No evidence of worship of Mother Goddess could be traced here.
- **Statement 3 is correct:** Surkotada: Located on the banks of river Bhogavo in Gujarat, it was excavated by Jagapath Joshi. It is also a port city. It gave definite evidence that Indus Valley people had knowledge of horses as horse skeletons were found here.
- **Statement 4 is correct:** Biggest Indus Valley site in India is Rakhigarhi (Haryana).

25. Correct Option: (b)

Supplementary Notes:

- **Option (b) is correct:** Krishna I, a Rashtrakutas was also a great conqueror. He defeated the Gangas and the Eastern Chalukyas of Vengi. He built the magnificent rock-cut monolithic Kailasa Temple at Ellora.

26. Correct Option: (a)

Supplementary Notes:

Pallavas Dynasty

- The Pallavas introduced the art of excavating Temples from the rock. In fact, the Dravidian style of Temple architecture began with the Pallava rule. It was a gradual evolution starting from the cave Temples to monolithic rathas and culminated in structural Temples. The development of Temple architecture under the Pallavas can be seen in four stages. The cave Temples at Bhairavakonda and Sittanavasal also belonged to the Pallavan age.

27. Correct Option: (b)

Supplementary Notes:

Mughal Architecture

- **Statement 1 is incorrect:** Nishat Bagh is a terraced Mughal garden built on the eastern side of the Dal Lake, in the state of Jammu and Kashmir, India.
- **Statement 3 is incorrect:** Tomb of Itmaddaulah located at Agra.
- The Mughals were fond of laying gardens with running water. Some of the Mughal gardens such as the Nishat Bagh in Kashmir, the Shalimar Bagh at Lahore and the Pinjore garden in the Punjab have survived even today.
- **Statement 2 is correct:** At Fatehpur Sikri are Jodha Bai's palace and Panch Mahal with five storeys.
- Akbar's tomb at Sikandara near Agra was completed by Jahangir.
- Nur Jahan built the tomb of Ittimaddaulah at Agra.
- The Moti Masjid at Agra was built entirely in white marble.
- The Jama Masjid at Delhi was built in red sandstone.
- Tomb of Itmaddaulah at Agra.
- **Statement 4 is correct:** Humayun's tomb is the tomb of the Mughal Emperor Humayun in Delhi, India. The tomb was commissioned by Humayun's first wife in 1569-70. It was the first garden-tomb on the Indian subcontinent, and is located close to the Dina-panah Citadel, also known as Purana Qila (Old Fort), that Humayun founded in 1533. It was also the first structure to use red sandstone at such a scale. The tomb was declared a UNESCO World Heritage Site in 1993.

28. Correct Option: (a)

Explanation:

- **Statement 2 is incorrect:** The main deity of the Temple is Lord Vishnu.
- **Statement 3 is incorrect:** It is located in Thiruvananthapuram, Kerala.

Supplementary Notes:

Sree Padmanabhaswamy Temple

- Recently, the Supreme Court of India upheld the right of the Travancore royal family to manage the property of deity at Sree Padmanabhaswamy Temple in Thiruvananthapuram (Kerala).
- According to Historians, the Temple dates back to the 8th century but the present structure was built in the 18th century by the then Travancore Maharaja MarthandaVarma.
- The Temple was initially made of wood but later it was constructed with granite.
- The Temple is built in the unique Chera Style of architecture, and its main deity is Lord Vishnu who is found in the Anantha Shayana posture (reclined posture of eternal yoga) on Adishesha or king of all serpents.

29. Correct Option: (c)

Explanation:

- All statements is correct

Supplementary Notes:

Group of Monuments at Pattadakal

- Pattadakal group of monuments are famous for their harmonious blend of architectural forms of northern and southern India, situated in the southern State of Karnataka. Pattadakal, the capital of the Chalukya Dynasty of Medieval India, is 22 km away from Badami. This famous world heritage site consists of a group of ten major Temples, each displaying interesting architectural features.
- The Pattadakal monument built in the 7th and 8th centuries, was famous for royal coronation called 'Pattadakisuvolal'. Temples constructed here mark the blending of the Rekha Nagara Prasada and the Dravida Vimana styles of Temple building.
- The oldest Temple at Pattadakal is the simple but massive Sangamesvara built by Vijayaditya Satyaraya (AD. 697-733).
- The Mallikarjuna and the Virupaksha Temples at Pattadakal, were built by two queens of Vikaramaditya II, to commemorate the victory of the Chalukyas over the Pallavas.
- Virupaksha Temple, built by Queen Lokamahadevi, was originally called Lokeshwara. This Temple is built in the southern Dravida style and is the largest in the enclosure. It has a massive gateway and several inscriptions.
- Virupaksha Temple also served as a model for the Rashtrakuta ruler to carve out the great Kailasa at Ellora.
- Pattadakal also has a Jaina basadi of Rashtrakuta times with two beautiful elephants in front.
- The Group of Monuments at Pattadakal was listed as UNESCO World Heritage Site in 1987.

30. Correct Option: (d)

Explanation:

- **Statement 3 is incorrect:** The Sri Ranganathaswamy Temple is a Hindu Temple dedicated to Ranganatha, a form of the Supreme God, Maha Vishnu, located in Srirangam, Tiruchirapalli, Tamil Nadu, India, and is not part of Great Living Chola Temples.

Supplementary Notes:

Great Living Chola Temples

- The Great Living Chola Temples were built by kings of the Chola Empire, which stretched over all of South India and the neighbouring islands are part of UNESCOs World Heritage Sites. The site now includes the three great 11th and 12th century Chola Temples: the Brihadisvara Temple of Thanjavur, the Temple of Gangaikondacholapuram and the Airavatesvara Temple at Darasuram.
- The Temple of Gangaikondacholapuram, built by Rajendra I, was completed in 1035. Its 53-m vimana (sanctum tower) has recessed corners and a graceful upward curving movement, contrasting with the straight and severe tower at Thanjavur. It has six pairs of massive, monolithic dvarapalas statues guarding the entrances and bronzes of remarkable beauty inside.
- The Airavatesvara Temple complex at Darasuram was built by Rajaraja II around 1150 AD. It features a 24-m vimana and a stone image of Shiva. The Temples testify to the Cholas brilliant achievements in architecture, sculpture, painting, and bronze casting. One of the striking features of this Temple is Rajagambhira Thirumandapam - Royal Courtyard, with intricately carved pillars, long steps made of granite stones and elegant chariots drawn by horse – again hewn out of stone.
- The Brihadisvara Temple at Thanjavur is a Hindu Temple dedicated to Shiva. It is one of the largest South Indian Temples and an exemplary example of fully realized Tamil architecture. Built by Raja Raja Chola I between 1003 and 1010 AD. The original monuments of this 11th century Temple were built around a moat. It included gopura, the main Temple, its massive tower, inscriptions, frescoes and sculptures predominantly related to Shaivism, but also of Vaishnvaism and Shaktism traditions of Hinduism.
- The Sri Ranganathaswamy Temple is a Hindu Temple dedicated to Ranganatha, a form of the Supreme God, Maha Vishnu, located in Srirangam, Tiruchirapalli, Tamil Nadu, India, and is not part of Great Living Chola Temples. The Temple was first built by Dharma Varma Chola. Then, Later Kaveri river flood

destroyed the Temple vimanam and later the Early Chola King Killivalavan rebuilt the Temple complex present today.

31. Correct Option: (d)

Supplementary Notes:

Ellora Caves

- Ellora is a UNESCO World Heritage Site located 30 km Northwest in the Aurangabad district of Maharashtra, India.
- Ellora is one of the largest rock-cut monastery-Temple cave complexes in the world, featuring Hindu, Buddhist and Jain monuments, and artwork, dating from the 600–1000 CE period. Hindu and Buddhist caves in the Ellora monuments were built during the Rashtrakuta Dynasty, and the Jain caves were constructed by the Yadava Dynasty.
- There are nearly 100 caves in the hill range out of which 34 caves are famous and open to public and are visited by many tourists, out of which Caves 1 to 12 are Buddhist, Caves 13 to 29 are Brahmanical and Caves 30 to 34 are Jaina (Digambara Sect). They are all excavated from the basalt cliffs in the Charanandri Hills.
- The largest single monolithic rock excavation in the world, the Kailash Temple, a chariot shaped monument dedicated to Lord Shiva is in Cave 16. Temple's relief panels summarise the two major Hindu Epics.
- Funding for the construction of the monuments was provided by royal people, traders and the wealthy of the region.

Kanheri Caves

- The Kanheri Caves are a group of caves and rock-cut monuments cut into a massive basalt outcrop in the forests of the Sanjay Gandhi National Park, on the former island of Salsette in the western outskirts of Mumbai.

Aurangabad Caves

- The Aurangabad caves are twelve rock-cut Buddhist shrines located on a hill running roughly east to west.

Bhaja Caves

- Bhaja Caves is a group of 22 rock-cut caves dating back to the 2nd century BC located in the city of Pune, India.

32. Correct Option: (d)

Supplementary Notes:

- **Kabir (1398-1518 AD)**
  - Born near Varanasi, Kabir was one of the 12 disciples of Ramananda.
  - Bijak is a compilation of the sermons of Saint Kabir. It is the holy book of those who believe in the Kabirpanthi sect.
  - Sabad, Sakhi and Ramani refer to the compositions of Kabir but his dialogues with Dharmadasa are found in the book titled Amarmool.

33. Correct Option: (b)

Explanation:

- **Option (b) is correct:** Chaitya is a place of worship in the form of an assembly hall inside the cave whereas Viharas are the resident places for Buddhist monks and Ajivikas.

Supplementary Notes:

Chaityas and Viharas

- Viharas were for living, while Chaityas were meant for assemblies for discussions.
- Further, Chaityas were with Stupas, Viharas did not have Stupas.
- Both early Chaityas and Viharas were made by woods and later stone-cut Chaityas and Viharas were made.
- Chaitya was a rectangular prayer hall with a Stupa placed in the centre, the purpose was prayer. The Chaitya was divided into three parts, and had an apsidal ending, that is, a semicircular rear end, the central part of the hall (also called the nave) was separated from the two aisles by two rows of pillars. The Chaityas also had polished interior walls, semicircular roofs and horse-shoe shaped windows called the Chaitya windows.
- Viharas were the residences of the monks.

34. Correct Option: (c)

Explanation:

- Both statements are correct

Supplementary Notes:

Thrissur pooram and Vadakkunnathan Temple:

- Thrissur Pooram is an annual Hindu festival held in Kerala. It is celebrated on the day when the star sign "Pooram" occurs in the Malayalam month of "medam (April-May)".
- The festival was started by Raja Rama Varma, famously known as SakthanThampuran, the Maharaja of Cochin (1790–1805).
- The Pooram consists of ten Temples in and around Thrissur and is considered to be a ceremony where these deities come together to pay obeisance to Lord Shiva at the Vadakkunnathan Temple, located in the centre of the town.
- One of the hallmarks of the festival is the percussion ensemble consisting of traditional instruments like chenda, maddalam, edakka, thimila and kombu.

Vadakkunnathan Temple:

- It is a Hindu Temple dedicated to Lord Shiva at Thrissur, Kerala.

- It is a classic example of the architectural style of Kerala and has monumental towers on all four sides and also a kuttambalam.
- Mural paintings depicting various episodes from Mahabharata can be seen inside the Temple.
- The Temple has been accorded the status of a National Monument under the Ancient Monuments and Archaeological Sites and Remains Act 1958.

35. Correct Option: (a)

Supplementary Notes:

Lothal

- A different kind of town planning we found at Lothal; this city was divided into 6 sections and each section had a wide platform of earthen bricks. Lothal and Rangpur are two sites where historians found rice husk.
- The magnum opus of Lothal is an artificial dock. Lothal's dock—the world's earliest known, connected the city to an ancient course of the Sabarmati river on the trade route between Harappan cities in Sindh and the peninsula of Saurashtra when the surrounding Kutch desert of today was a part of the Arabian Sea. It was a vital and thriving trade centre in ancient times, with its trade of beads, gems and valuable ornaments reaching the far corners of West Asia and Africa.
- A bead making factory has also been found in Lothal. A seal from Iran has been found which indicates its link with overseas countries.
- Then, Lothal is different from other sites of Indus Valley Civilisation in terms of town planning in that it has entry to the houses on the main street while in other sites have shown lateral entry.

36. Correct Option: (d)

Explanation:

- Statement 1 is incorrect: Nagara is North Indian architecture, whereas Dravida is South Indian.
- Statement 3 is incorrect: Nagara style has multiple towers but Dravida style has only one.
- Statement 4 is incorrect: Pedestals are higher than the ground level in the Nagara style and at the ground level in the Dravida style.

Supplementary Notes:

- Although both the Nagara and Dravida architecture emerged from the Panchayatana style of architecture, there are various differences between the two.

Nagara Style

- The North Indian Temples are often classified as the Nagara Style of architecture. It is also found in the western, central and eastern parts of the Indian subcontinent.
- Distinctive features -
  - Multiple shikhara;
  - Multiple towers;
  - Curvilinear shape of the central tower;
  - Presence of mandap;
  - Sanctum is single or single storeyed and has Ganga and Yamuna rivers depicted in personified manner at its entrance;
  - Temple boundaries are not given much importance;
  - Pedestals higher than the ground;
  - Gopuram is not a prominent feature.
- Major substyles of Nagara architecture are Latina, Phamsana, Sekhari and Valabhi.

Dravidian Style

- This is a prominent style in the South Indian part of the Indian subcontinent.
- Distinctive features -
  - Only one shikhara;
  - Single tower;
  - Pyramid shape of the central tower;
  - Dwarpalas at the entrance of sanctum;
  - Mandaps not present;
  - Temple boundaries given equal or even higher importance;
  - Pedestals at the ground level;
  - Gopuram is one of the most prominent features.
- Its major sub-styles include Tamil, Karnataka and Andhra.

37. Correct Option: (c)

Explanation:

- Statement 2 is incorrect: Gandhara School of Art was patronised by the Kushans and depicted only images of Buddha.

Supplementary Notes:

Gandhara School of Art

- Gandhara School of Art is uniquely associated with the Greco-Roman style of art.
- This school depicted only images of Buddha.
- Location: Near present-day Peshawar
- Some characteristics of the Greco-Roman effect on Gandhara art include:
  - Halo around the head of Lord Buddha
  - Buddha's wavy hair
  - Ornaments
  - Drape and style of the garments
- The Gandhara School flourished during the Kushan Dynasty.
- Raw material used: Green phyllite and grey-blue mica.

Mathura School of Art

- The Mathura School of Art flourished under the Kushan Emperor Kanishka during the first century AD.
- Location of centres of production: Mathura, Sarnath and Kosambi
- Raw Material used : Spotted red sandstone.
- Hinduism, Buddhism and Jainism were the main religious motivations for the Mathura School of Art.

Amravati School of Art

- Amravati School of Art was patronised by the Ikshvakus and also by other groups, flourished for nearly six centuries starting from 200-100 BC.
- Buddhist art and a large religious complex of Buddhism grew around Amravati which represent the revival of uniquely different regional art styles.
- Symbolic representation of Buddha's life, the Buddha almost always being represented by a symbol, though in two or three places he is personified.
- Like the Sanchi Stupa, the Amaravati Stupa also has pradakshina patha enclosed within a vedika on which many narrative stories from the life of Buddha and bodhisattva dominate such episodes relating to the birth.
- Both religious and secular images were present in this style.
- Later, this style got transformed into Pallava and Chola architecture.

38. Correct Option: (a)

Explanation:

- **Statement 3 is incorrect:** Antarala is a vestibular entrance in the Temple.

Supplementary Notes:

Temples of Khajuraho

- The Chandela rulers developed a distinct style of Temple making of their own – known as Khajuraho School or Chandela School in the central part of India which belonged to Hindu as well as Jain religion. Example: Kandariya Mahadeva Temple, Lakshman Temple at Khajuraho, Chausath Yogini Temple.
- In these Temples, both the interior and exterior walls were lavishly decorated with carvings and sculptures that were generally erotic in their themes and drew inspiration from Vatsyayana's Kamasutra.
- These Temples were made of sandstone on a high platform and generally north and east facing.
- The Temples had three chambers – garbhagriha, mandapa and ardha-mandapa. Some Temples had a vestibular entrance to the garbhagriha known as antarala.
- The Panchayatan style of Temple making was followed in these Temples. Even the subsidiary shrines had rekha-prasad shikharas. This created an impression of a mountain range.

Chausath Yogini Temple

- It is dedicated to Goddess Durga and it is the first Temple built at Khajuraho. In this Temple, Goddess Durga is shown attended by 64 yoginis or female mystics.

39. Correct Option: (c)

Explanation:

- Both statements are correct

Supplementary Notes:

Katora Houz and Golconda fort

- Katora Houz, the 450-year old cup-shaped water tank is constructed inside the fortified walls of the Golconda Fort.
- Currently, it lies in a neglected state with water hyacinth fast spreading amid the trash that carpets the drain water.
- If the legend is to be believed the Katora Houz at Golconda was filled with rose water for the king Ibrahim Quli Qutb Shah who visited the place and enjoyed the ambience.
- Katora means 'bowl' in Urdu and the stone and mortar structure, constructed in 1560, was shaped like a bowl, hence the name.
- In its heyday it got water from dedicated underground pipes connected to the Talaab-e-Durg, now Durgam Cheruvu.
- The Qutb Shahi kings visited the place for recreational purpose.

40. Correct Option: (a)

Explanation:

- **Option (a) is correct**

Supplementary Notes:

- The Buddha of Bamiyan was a 6th-century monumental statue of Gautam Buddha carved into the side of a cliff in the Bamyan valley in the Hazarajat region of central Afghanistan. However it has now been destroyed.

41. Correct Option: (b)

Supplementary Notes:

- More than 2500 seals have been found. These are made of steatite. They mostly depict a single animal-unicorn bull, elephant, rhinoceros etc. but some also depict trees, semi-human and human figurines, in some cases participating in a ceremony.

42. Correct Option: (d)

Supplementary Notes:

- The Harappan Culture was distinguished by its system of town planning on the lines of the grid system – that is streets and lanes cutting across one another almost at right angles, thus dividing the city into several rectangular blocks. Harappa, Mohenjōdaro and Kalibangan each had its own citadel built on a high podium of mud brick. Below the citadel in each city lay a lower town containing brick houses, which were inhabited by the common people. The large-scale use of burnt bricks in almost all kinds of constructions and the absence of stone buildings are the important characteristics of the Harappan culture. Another remarkable feature was the underground drainage system connecting all houses to the street drains which were covered by stone slabs or bricks.

43. Correct Option: (b)

Supplementary Notes:

- The Gandhara School of Art developed in first century AD along with Mathura School during reign of Kushana emperor Kanishka. Both Shakas and Kushanas were patrons of Gandhara School, which is known for the first sculptural representations of the Buddha in human form. The art of the Gandhara school was primarily Mahayana and shows Greco-Roman influence.

44. Correct Option: (b)

Supplementary Notes:

- The Sarnath Pillar consists of a canopy representing an inverted bell-shaped lotus flower, a short cylindrical abacus with four 24-spoked, 4 animals (Elephant, bull, horse, lion)

Figure 7.1.3

45. Correct Option: (a)

Explanation

- The Gandhara School of Art had also developed in first century AD along with Mathura School during reign of Kushana emperor Kanishka. Both Shakas and Kushanas were patrons of Gandhara School, which is known for the first sculptural representations of the Buddha in human form. The art of the Gandhara School was primarily Mahayana and shows Greco-Roman influence.
- Gandhara School was based on Greco-Roman norms encapsulating foreign techniques and an alien spirit. It is also known as Graeco-Buddhist School of art. The foreign influence is evident from the sculptures of Buddha in which they bear resemblance to the Greek sculptures. Grey sandstone (Blue-grey Mica schist to be precise) is used in Gandhara School of Art.
- The Bamyan Buddha of Afghanistan were the example of the Gandhara School.
- Gandhara Style has naturalism in body form, drapery, and pictorial scale.
- The male figures are shown with musculature, drapery with sharp flowing folds,wavy curled hair and sharp features.
- The extended ears are merely due to the downward thrust of the heavy ear-rings worn by a prince or magnate.
- There is a standardisation of composition, pose of figures and other incidents from the life of Buddha.
- Bodhisattva icons that portrayed Buddhahood and form one of the most important elements of Mahayana Buddhism was prevalent in this era. These male figures are shown standing or seated and wear a dhoti like lower garment, the torso is bare except for the shawl like length of cloth over the shoulder.
- One of the distinguishing features is the depiction of paradise such as Sukhavati which was part of the Paradise cult within Buddhism prevalent in North West India during the Kushana period.
- There were also female statures, corresponding to city goddesses.

46. Correct Option: (c)

Supplementary Notes:

- The overall layout of the Indus Saraswati cities is distinguished by the orientation of streets and buildings, according to the cardinal directions – east-west, and north-south. The idea of settlement planning did not appear suddenly with the first large cities but was already well established in earlier period as has been revealed from the excavations at Kot Diji, Kalibangan, Harappa, Rahman Dheri, Nausharo etc. The basic layout at all these settlements was established along a grid that was defined by large streets running north south and east-west and fortification all around.

47. Correct Option: (d)

Supplementary Notes:

- Khanqah , zawiyahs, or tekke is a building designed specifically for gatherings of a Sufi brotherhood, or tariqa, and is a place for spiritual retreat and character reformation.

48. Correct Option: (d)

Supplementary Notes:

- **Statement 1 is correct:** Ashoka was the first king in the Indian history who has left his records engraved on stones.
- **Statement 2 is incorrect:** The Ashokan inscriptions are found at 47 places in different regions of India, Nepal, Pakistan, and Afghanistan.
- **Statement 3 is correct:** Ashokas inscriptions were written in four different scripts, namely: Greek languages and scripts used in Afghanistan area; Aramaic languages and scripts used in West Asia; Prakrit language and Kharosthi script used in Pakistan area; and Prakrit language and Brahmi script used in rest of the inscriptions.

49. Correct Option: (b)

Supplementary Notes:

Ashoka

- **Option (b) is correct:** The vivid description of Kalinga War is given in 13th Rock Edict. After the war of Kalinga Ashoka realized the gravity of war and the event had a profound impact on his mind. He vowed to never wage such war and also directed his sons and grandsons. The 13th Rock Edict mentions Ashoka's remorse after the war and his changed attitude from Digvajay to Dhammavijay. Ashoka adopted Buddhism in 9th year of his reign after winning Kalinga. He was inspired by Nigrodha, a boy monk. Later, he came in contact with Moggaliputta Tissa. Later his brother Tissa, queen Karuvaki also adopted Buddhism.

50. Correct Option: (a)

Supplementary Notes:

Gupta Empire: Art and Culture

- **Option (a) is correct:** The Gupta period was famous for vast progress in area of art, science and literature and due to this progress it has been called "a golden age". The Gupta period covers an important place in the history of Indian art and architecture. The following are the highlights of the art and culture of Gupta Empire.
- Most remarkable was the Bhitari monolithic pillar of Skandagupta.
- Nagara and Dravidian Styles of Art came during this period.
- There was absence of growth of Gandhara Style.
- But Mathura's one pleasant standing Buddha statue shows a little Greek Style.
- The Temple at Deogarh near Jhansi, the sculptures in the Temple at Garhwas which is near Allahabad were great source of showing effects of the Gupta Art.
- The unearthed statue of Buddha at Sarnath is a symbol of Gupta Art.
- Most of the paintings are seen at Bagh Caves near Gwalior which shows the greatness and preciseness of Gupta Art.
- The paintings of Ajanta mostly demonstrate the life of the Buddha.
- Kalidasawas was a great poet and playwriter during Chandragupta II. His masterpiece was the Shakuntala. His other plays are Malavikagnimitra, Vikramorvasiya and Kumarasambhava. His two lyrics are Ritusamhara and Meghaduta.
- During the Gupta period metallurgy also made a wonderful growth. The craftsmen were expert in their art of casting metal statues and pillars.
- The most antique item in Sultanganj is the huge copper statue of Buddha. This is now kept at Birmingham museum, was of seven and a half feet height and a ton weight. The Delhi Iron Pillar of the Gupta period is rust free even today.
- Chandragupta II and his successors also issued gold, silver and copper coins.
- Samudragupta was a great poet. Samudragupta patronized Harisena. Harisena was one of the scholars.
- Dandin was the author of Kavyadarsa and Dasakumaracharita.
- Vasavadatta was written by Subhandhu.
- Visakadatta was other renowned author of this period. He was the author of two dramas: Mudrarakshasa and Devichandraguptam.
- Sudraka was a renowned poet. He wrote his book 'Mrichchakatika'.
- Bharavi's Kritarjuniya is the story of discriminations between Arjuna and Siva.
- The Buddhist author Amarasimha created Amarakosa.

51. Correct Option: (d)

Supplementary Notes:

Allahabad Pillar Inscription

- **Option (d) is correct:** Samudragupta's court poet and minister Harisena composed the Allahabad pillar Inscription or Prayag Prasasti. The Pillar was an Ashokan Pillar erected by Ashoka sixth century before him. This Inscription is a eulogy of Samudragupta and mentions about the conquests of Samudragupta and boundaries of the Gupta Empire. As per this inscription, Samudragupta defeated 9 kings in North, 12 Kings in South, and reduced all the Atavika states to vassalage.

52. Correct Option: (b)

Supplementary Notes:

- Varaha image at Udayagiri is 5th century AD creation: Udayagiri is best known for a series of rock-cut sanctuaries and images excavated into hillside in the early years of the fifth century CE. The site is notable for its ancient monumental relief sculpture of Hindu god Vishnu, in his incarnation as the boar-headed Varaha, rescuing the earth symbolically represented by Bhudevi clinging to the boar's tusk as described in Hindu mythology. The site has important inscriptions of the Gupta Dynasty belonging to the reigns of Chandragupta II (c. 375-415) and Kumaragupta I (c. 415-55).

- Rock-cut Monuments at Mahabalipuram are 7th century AD creation: Architecture under Pallava Dynasty is significant because it demonstrates the later development of the Dravidian Style of architecture. The architecture of the Pallavas is classified into two periods. The earliest architecture of the Pallavas are the rock cut Temples which dates back to 610-690AD under the reign of the Mamalla rulers and the architecture of the structural Temples dates back to 690-900AD and these flourished under the Rajasimha Empire. The Temples were mostly dedicated to Lord Shiva.
- The rock cut Temples of Mahabalipuram are the most magnificent features of Pallava architecture. It was built under the patronage of king Narasimhavarman I of the Mamalla period and thus it is also referred to as Mamallapuram. The first phase of the Pallava architecture is influenced by the Buddhist monasteries and chaitya halls.
- Lingaraja Temple at Bhubaneswar was created in 11th AD.The Lingaraja Temple, datable to about 1000 AD, is perhaps the most marvellous Temple ever erected the grandest and the loftiest (above 36.50 m. high) marking the culmination of the architectural activities at Bhubaneswar. This Temple consists of the sanctum sanctorum, a closed hall, a dancing hall and a hall of offerings, the last two being later additions.
- Rock-cut Elephant at Dhauli was created during Ashoka's reign (272-231 BC). This is the oldest among the four. Dhauli is located in the ancient territory of Kalinga, now the state of Odisha, which the emperor Ashoka Maurya (reigned 272-231 BC) conquered with appalling loss of life in about 260 BC. Rock-cut Elephant at Dhauli is one of oldest monument which sculpted elephant facing east. The prime Buddhist attractions of Dhauli are the rock edicts of the Indian emperor Ashoka. These rock edicts are on the northern face of the southern range and primarily carry instructions for local administrators to rule with gentleness and justice.

53. Correct Option: (c)

Supplementary Notes:

- **Statement 2 is correct:** Mahayana Buddhism and Hinayana Buddhism both originated in Buddhism but they differ in practice. Hinayana Buddhism practices on enlightening of each person, his or her self, while Mahayana seeks to enlighten all living beings. Despite of having existed in the primitive Buddhism, Mahayana Buddhism was not an independent branch. Its doctrines were improved by Nagarjuna, Asanga, and Vasubandhu. Mahayana, as a result has risen in influence in large areas of China, Northeast Asia, and Vietnam. It was the aggressive development of Mahayana Buddhism, together with the demand of international trading that made the Silk Road as an effective missionary tool. The network of routes linked Buddhist centers from India to Central Asia, crossed Himalaya ranges, and Taklimakan desert to the Chinese continent. There were many Buddhist centers formed along the Silk Road such as, Bamiyan (Afghanistan), Khotan, Kucha, Turfan, Dunhuang, Pengcheng, Luojang, Longmen (China), etc. during Buddhism's religious development and they mark the golden era of Mahayana Buddhist art. However, at present there are only four centers left in Bamiyan, Dunhuang, Yungang, and Longmen – from Mahayana Buddhism's expansion period.
- **Statement 3 is correct:** Mahayana or "great vehicle" believes in the heavenliness of Buddha and Idol worship of Buddhas and Bodhisattvas embodying Buddha Nature. Zen, Pure Land, Tiantai, and Nichiren, Shingon and Tibetan Buddhism are traditions of Mahayana. Mahayana believed in universal liberation from suffering for all beings (hence the "Great Vehicle"). Ultimate aim of Mahayana is "spiritual upliftment". It allows salvation to be alternatively obtained through the grace of the Amitābha Buddha by having faith and devoting oneself to mindfulness of the Buddha. It believes in mantras. Language of Mahayana was predominantly Sanskrit.

54. Correct Option: (c)

Supplementary Notes:

Panchayatana

- **Option (c) is correct:** Panchayatana is an architectural style where the main shrine is built on a rectangular plinth with four smaller subsidiary shrines at the four corners thus making it a total of five shrines–i.e., Pancha.
- Examples of Panchayatana Temples:
  - Kandariya Mahadeva Temple in Khajuraho
  - Brahmeswara Temple in Bhubaneswar
  - Jagdish Temple in Udaipur
  - Lakshmana Temple in Khajuraho
  - Lingaraja Temple in Bhubaneswar
  - Arasavalli Temple near Srikakulam District of Andhra Pradesh near Visakhapatnam. Main shrine dedicated to Aditya. Subsidiary shrines dedicated to Ganesh, Shiva, Parvati and Vishnu.

- ➤ Dashavatara Temple in Deogarh, Uttar Pradesh. It should be the oldest panchayatana Temple in India.
- ➤ Nabaratna Temple in Pantchupi
- ➤ Shiva Panchayatana Temple in Tumbadi, Tumkur district. Subsidiary shrines dedicated to Lakshmi Narasimha, Vinayaka, Parvati and Surya
- ➤ Gondeshvara Temple, in Sinnar, Maharashtra

55. Correct Option: (d)

Supplementary Notes:

Mural Painting

- Indian Mural Paintings are paintings made on walls of caves and palaces. These pieces of art are symbolic of the life, culture and traditions of the people of the contemporaneous periods.
- **Statement 1, 2 and 3 are correct:** The art on the caves of Ajanta, Ellora and Elephanta and also on the Bagh Caves and Sittanvasal are vivid reminders of great art that flourished centuries ago.

56. Correct Option: (b)

Supplementary Notes:

National Emblem of India

- **Option (b) is correct:**
- The National Emblem is the graphic representation of the Lion Capital that originally graced the top of the Ashok Stambh or Ashoka Pillar at Sarnath, along with the National Motto written below it.
- The Lion Capital crowning the Ashok Pillar is carved out of a single block of yellow sandstone and features four Asiatic Lions sitting back to back, but the two dimensional representation of National Emblem depicts only 3, the fourth lion is hidden from view.
- The four lions stand on a short cylindrical base that has four Ashok Chakras corresponding to each lion bust and reliefs of four more animals in between them – the lion, the bull, the elephant and the galloping horse.
- In the 2D form of the National Emblem, only one Ashok Chakra is visible in the front with the galloping horse on the left and the bull on the right of it.The Ashok Chakra is actually a form of the Buddhist Dharma Chakra.
- Representative of: The Republic of India
- Based on: The Lion Capital of the Ashoka Pillar in Sarnath, Uttar Pradesh
- Motto: Satyameva Jayate/Truth Alone Triumphs
- Adopted by: Madhav Sawhney
- Adopted on: January 26, 1950

57. Correct Option: (b)

Explanation:

- **Statements 1 is incorrect:** The Gujarat style of architecture is used most widely in the palace built by Akbar.

Supplementary Notes:

Mughal Architecture

- Akbar was the first Mughal ruler who had the time and means to undertake construction on a large scale.
- He built a series of forts, the most famous of which is the fort at Agra. Built in red sandstone, this massive fort had many magnificent gates.
- For their forts, the Mughals drew on the developed Indian tradition of fort-building, such as the ones at Gwalior, Jodhpur, etc.
- The climax of fort-building was reached at Delhi where Shah Jahan built his famous Red Fort.
- In 1572, Akbar commenced a palace-cum-fort complex at Fatehpur Sikri, 36 kilometres from Agra, which he completed in eight years.
- Built atop a hill, along with a large artificial lake, it included many buildings in the style of Gujarat and Bengal. These included deep caves, balconies, and fanciful kiosks.
- In the Panch Mahal built for taking the air, all the types of pillars used in various Temples were employed to support flat roofs.
- The Gujarat style of architecture is used most widely in the palace built probably for his Rajput wife or wives. Buildings of a similar type were also built in the fort at Agra, though only a few of them have survived.
- Akbar took a close personal interest in the work of construction both at Agra and Fatehpur Sikri.
- Persian or Central Asian influence can be seen in the glazed blue tiles used for decoration in the walls or for tiling the roofs.
- But the most magnificent building was the mosque and the gateway to it called the Buland Darwaza (the lofty gate) built to commemorate Akbar's victory in Gujarat. The gate is in the style of what is called a half-dome portal.
- Towards the end of Jahangir's reign began the practice of putting up buildings entirely of marble and decorating the walls with floral designs made of semi-precious stones.
- This method of decoration, called pietra dura, became even more popular under Shah Jahan who used it on a large scale in the Taj Mahal.

58. Correct Option: (a)

Explanation:

- **Statement 3 is incorrect:** The horse was the most common animal to be depicted on the pillars.

Supplementary Notes:

Architecture of Vijayanagar empire

- The Temple building activity of the Vijayanagar rulers produced a new style, called the Vijayanagar style. Though often characterized as Dravida Style, it had its own distinct features.

- The distinct features of the architecture were the pillars and the complicated manner in which they were sculptured.
- The horse was the most common animal to be depicted on the pillars.
- The Temples had a Mandapam or open pavilion with a raised platform, generally meant for seating the deity on special occasions.
- It also had a Kalyana Mandapam with elaborately carved pillars.
- The most magnificent of the Temples in this style are in Hampi (Vijayanagar). Vittala Swamy and the Hazara Ramaswamy Temples are the best examples.
- The Raya Gopurams, towers in commemoration of the visit of emperors in different corners of the empire, are also important examples of architecture of the period.

59. Correct Option: (a)

Explanation:

- Statement 3 is incorrect: Piprahwa Stupa is the oldest known stupa.

Supplementary Notes:

Mauryan Architecture

- During the time of Ashoka, the inscription of pillars as a symbol of the state or to commemorate battle victories – assumed a great significance.
- He also used pillars to propagate imperial sermons as well.
- On an average of 40 feet high, the pillars were usually made of chunar sandstone and consisted of four parts.
- A long Shaft formed the base and was made up of a single piece of stone or monolith.
- On top of it lay the capital, which was either lotus shaped or bell shaped.
- The bell shaped capitals were influenced by the Iranian pillars, as was the highly polished and lustrous finish of the pillars.
- Above the capital, there was a circular or rectangular base known on the abacus on which an animal figure was placed.
- Stupas were burial mounds prevalent in India from the Vedic period.
- It is a conventional representation of a funeral cumulus in which relics and ashes of the dead were kept.
- During the period of Ashoka, the art of stupas reached its climax. Almost 84,000 stupas were erected during his period.
- Although a Vedic tradition, stupas were popularised by the Buddhists. After the death of Buddha, 9 stupas were erected. 8 of them had the relics of Buddha at their medhi while the ninth had the pot in which the relics were originally kept.
- The core of the stupa was made of unburnt brick while the outer surface was made by using burnt bricks, which were then covered with a thick layer of plaster.
- The medhi and the toran were decorated by wooden sculptures. Devotees walk around the pradakshina patha or open ambulatory passageway as a token of worship.
- Sanchi Stupa in Madhya Pradesh is the most famous of the Ashokan stupas. Piprahwa Stupa in Uttar Pradesh is the oldest one.

60. Correct Option: (c)

Explanation:

- **Statement 1 is incorrect:** Sculptures were influenced by imageries of Hinduism, Buddhism and Jainism.

Supplementary Notes:

Mathura School of Art

- The Mathura School flourished on the banks of the river Yamuna in the period between 1st and 3rd centuries BC.
- The sculptures of the Mathura School were influenced by the stories and imageries of all three religions of the time – Buddhism, Hinduism and Jainism.
- The images were modelled on the earlier Yaksha images found during the Mauryan period.
- The Mathura School showed a striking use of symbolism in the images.
- The Hindu Gods were represented using their avayudhas. For example, Shiva is shown through linga and mukhalinga. Similarly, the halo around the head of Buddha is larger than in Gandhara School and decorated with geometrical patterns.
- Buddha is shown to be surrounded by two Bodhisattavas – Padmapani holding a lotus and Vajrapani holding a thunderbolt.
- It was developed indigenously and not influenced by external cultures.
- The sculptures of Mathura School were made using spotted red sandstone.
- It has Influence of all three religions of the time, i.e. Hinduism, Jainism and Buddhism.
- It was patronised by Kushana rulers. Developed in and around Mathura, Sonkh and Kankalitila. Kankalitila was famous for Jain sculptures.
- Buddha is in a delighted mood with a face and head shaven.
- Buddha is sitting in Padmasana with different mudras and his face reflects grace.

61. **Correct Option: (d)**

Explanation:

- **Statement (d) is incorrect:** Dasavatar Temple at Deogarh is earliest example of stone Temple.

Supplementary Notes:

Gupta early Temples

- During Gupta Era, the rock cut architecture reached its zenith and this era marked the beginning of the Free Standing Temple Architecture.
- Most of the Temples built in the Gupta era were carved with representations of Gods (mainly avatara of Vishnu and Lingams) and Goddesses.
- The most important Temple of Gupta era is Dasavatar Temple of Deogarh, Uttar Pradesh.
- Dasavatara Temple is located in Deogarh Village in Lalitpur town in Uttar Pradesh.
- The Temple was discovered by Captain Charles Strahan and was named so by Alexander Cunningham.
- It depicts the 10 avatara of Vishnu. It is a large and elaborate edifice with typical Temple art of Guptas (without Shikhara) and cubical Garbhagriha.
- This Temple has also been linked to the "Sarvatobhadra Temple" mentioned in the Vishnudharmottara Purana by several scholars.
- In the Gupta period, the basic, characteristic elements of the Indian Temple consisting of a square sanctum sanctorum and a pillared porch had emerged.
- The Shikhara was not much prominent in the early Gupta Temples but was prominent in later Gupta era.
- There was a single entrance or mandapa or Porch.
- Gupta style Temple was modeled on the architectural norms of the Mathura school.
- Some Other Notes about Gupta Temples Sanchi Temple at Tigawa has a flat roof.
- Dasavatar Temple at Deogarh , Bhitargaon Temple and Mahadev Temple at Nachna Kuthar have a square tower of Shikhara.
- Maniyar Math at Rajgriha is a circular Temple of Gupta era.
- Main style of Temple architecture in i.e. Nagara style and Dravida style actually began from the Gupta era.
- The earliest stone Temple with Shikhara is Dasavatar Temple at Deogarh.
- The Bhitargaon Temple at Kanpur is entirely made up of Bricks.
- Some other Gupta era Temples
  - Vishnu Temple of Tigawa Jabalpur
  - Shiva Temple of Bhumara
  - Mukund Darra Temple of Kota
  - Lakshaman Temple of Raipur
  - Shiva Temple of Koh
  - Bhitari Temple at Ghazipur

62. **Correct Option: (d)**

Explanation:

- **Option (d) is correct:** The correctly matched figure is as follows:
  - Gopuram
  - Mandapa
  - Shikhara
  - Vimana
  - Garbhagriha

Supplementary Notes:

Dravidian Temple Architecture

- Unlike the Nagara Temple, the Dravida Temple is enclosed within a compound wall.
- The front wall has an entrance gateway in its centre, which is known as a gopuram.
- After the gopuram and before the garbhagriha there lies a portico or colonnaded hall that incorporates space for a large number of worshippers and is known as a mandapa. This is well developed in the Dravidian Style Temples.
- The shape of the main Temple tower known as vimana in Tamil Nadu is like a stepped pyramid that rises up geometrically rather than the curving shikhara of North India.
- In the South Indian Temple, the word 'shikhara' is used only for the crowning element at the top of the Temple which is usually shaped like a small stupika or an octagonal cupola— this is equivalent to the amlak and kalasha of North Indian Temples.
- Whereas at the entrance to the North Indian Temple's garbhagriha, it would be usual to find images such as mithunas and the river goddesses, Ganga and Yamuna, in the south you will generally find sculptures of fierce dvarapalas or the door-keepers guarding the Temple.
- It is common to find a large water reservoir, or a Temple tank, enclosed within the complex.
- Subsidiary shrines are either incorporated within the main Temple tower, or located as distinct, separate small shrines beside the main Temple.
- The North Indian idea of multiple shikharas rising together as a cluster was not popular in South India. At some of the most sacred Temples in South India, the main Temple in which the garbhagriha is situated has, in fact, one of the smallest towers. This is because it is usually the oldest part of the Temple.
- With the passage of time, the population and size of the town associated with that Temple would have increased, and it would have become necessary to make a new boundary wall around the Temple.

- This would have been taller than the last one, and its gopurams would have been even loftier. So, for instance, the Srirangam Temple in Tiruchirapally has as many as seven 'concentric' rectangular enclosure walls, each with gopurams.
- The outermost is the newest, while the tower right in the centre housing the garbhagriha is the oldest.
- Temples became rich administrative centres, controlling vast areas of land.
- Just as there are many subdivisions of the main types of Nagara Temples, there are subdivisions also of Dravida Temples. These are basically of five different shapes: square, usually called kuta, and also caturasra; rectangular or shala or ayatasra; elliptical, called gaja-prishta or elephantbacked, or also called vrittayata, deriving from wagonvaulted shapes of apsidal chaityas with a horse-shoe shaped entrance facade usually called a nasi; circular or vritta; and octagonal or ashtasra.
- Generally speaking, the plan of the Temple and the shape of the vimana were conditioned by the iconographic nature of the consecrated deity. So it was appropriate to build specific types of Temples for specific types of icons. It must, however, be remembered that this is a simplistic differentiation of the subdivisions. Several different shapes may be combined in specific periods and places to create their own unique style.

63. Correct Option: (c)

Explanation:

- **Statement 1 is incorrect:** It was originally a Buddhist site which was later dominated by Shaivite faith.
- **Statement 2 is incorrect:** It was contemporary to Ellora Cave (and not the Ajanta Cave).

Supplementary Notes:

Elephanta Caves

- The Elephanta Caves located near Mumbai are dominated by the Shaivite faith. This cave system also contains Buddhist site which is relatively older than Shaivite caves.
- It is contemporary with Ellora, and its sculptures show slenderness in the body, with stark light and dark effects.
- It was included in the UNESCO World Heritage List in the year of 1987.

64. Correct Option: (a)

Explanation:

- **Statement 1 is incorrect:** Iberian architectural style was introduced by the Portuguese (This question can also be answered using the knowledge of geography as Portugal is located on the Iberian Peninsula).

Supplementary Notes:

Modern Architecture

- The arrival of Europeans also brought with them a wealth of architectural style that dominated the Modern Indian architecture since their arrival.
- The Portuguese brought with them the Iberian Style of structure. They also introduced the concept of 'Patio Houses" and 'Baroque Style" developed in the 16th century in Europe.
- The Portuguese continued with their western tradition and did not introduced any variations using Indian architectural styles. E.g., Se Cathedral in Goa, Diu Fort etc.
- Bricks was main material used by the Portuguese and roof was made up of woods.
- The French brought with them the urban city planning with them. They also introduced the concept of anonymous architecture which involves simple façade without much ornamentation.
- The Indo-Gothic style also known as Victorian Style was unique blend of Indian, Persian, and Gothic style of architecture. Red sandstone and coarse limestone were primarily used in the Gothic Architecture.

65. Correct Option: (d)

Explanation:

- **Statement 2 is incorrect:** The Hoyasaleshvara Temple is dedicated to Lord Hoyasalas and Shiva as Nataraja.
- **Statement 3 is incorrect:** It is located at Halebid in Karnataka.

Supplementary Notes:

Hoysaleshvara Temple

- The Hoysaleshvara Temple (Lord of the Hoysalas) at Halebid in Karnataka was built in dark schist stone by the Hoysala king in 1150.
- Hoysala Temples are sometimes called hybrid or vesara as their unique style seems neither completely dravida nor nagara, but somewhere in between.
- They are easily distinguishable from other medieval Temples by their highly original star-like ground-plans and a profusion of decorative carvings.
- Dedicated to Shiva as Nataraja, the Halebid Temple is a double building with a large hall for the mandapa to facilitate music and dance. A Nandi pavilion precedes each building.

66. Correct Option: (c)

Explanation:

- **The statement 1 is correct:** So, using elimination method the correct answer is option (c).
- **Statement 2 is incorrect:** The Angkor group of Temples were built in the period of Khmer Empire of Cambodia.

- **Statement 3 is incorrect:** The Preah Vihar Temple is dedicated to manifestation of Lord Shiva and remained boundary dispute between Cambodia and Thailand. Later awarded to Cambodia by ICJ in 1962.

Supplementary Notes:

Temples outside India

- With the spread of Indian culture in the South East Asian Region, temples were also erected that had the dominant elements of Dravida style of Indian Temple architecture with some distinct local flavor as well.
- The Indians began to colonize the East Asia in the Gupta period. It was further encouraged by the Pallavas.
- Cambodia was colonized by Indians in the first century AD. This influenced the native people called the Khemeres. Thus, the ruling Dynasty was known as Khmers/Khamboja.
- The most famous Temple was the Temple of Lord Vishnu built by Suryavarman II, most famous Khmer ruler, in the capital city of Angkor. It was popularly called as Angkorwat Temple. It is the largest Hindu Temple in the world.
- The Preah Vihar Temple is dedicated to manifestation of Lord Shiva and remained boundary dispute between Cambodia and Thailand, later awarded to Cambodia by ICJ in 1962. It is also included in the UNESCO's World Heritage List.

67. Correct Option: (b)

Explanation:

- **Statement 1 is incorrect:** Carnatic music is completely indigenous while Hindustani music has Arabic and Persian influence.
- **Statement 3 is incorrect:** Carnatic music puts more emphasis on vocals.

Supplementary Notes:

Classical Music

- The two distinct schools of Indian Classical Music are:
  - Hindustani Music: practiced in northern parts of India.
  - Carnatic Music: practiced in southern parts of India.

Points of Difference	Hindustani Music	Carnatic Music
Influence	Arab, Persian, and Afghan	Indigenous
Freedom	Scope for artists to improvise, hence there is scope for variations	No freedom to improvise
Sub-styles	There are several sub-styles, which led to the emergence of 'Gharanas'	Only one particular style of singing
Need for Instruments	Equally important as vocals	More emphasis on vocal music
Ragas	6 major ragas	72 ragas
Time	Adheres to time	Doesn't adhere to any time
Instruments	Tabla, Sarangi, Sitar and Santoor	Veena, Mrindangum, and Mandolin
Association to Parts of India	North India	Usually South India

68. Correct Option: (b)

Explanation:

- **Statement 2 is incorrect:** The girl in the statue stands in a 'tribhanga', dancing posture with the right hand on her hip.

Supplementary Notes:

Dancing Girl

- The Dancing Girl is the world's oldest bronze sculpture.
- Found in Mohenjo-daro, this four-inch figure depicts a naked girl wearing only ornaments, which include bangles in the left arm, and amulet and bracelet on the right arm.
- She stands in a 'tribhanga' dancing posture with the right hand on her hip.
- The statue, recovered in excavation from 'HR area' of Mohenjo-daro, is suggestive of two major breakthrough, one, that the Indus artists knew metal blending and casting and perhaps other technical aspects of metallurgy, and two, that as a well-developed society, Indus people had innovated dance and other performing arts as modes of entertainment.

69. Correct Option: (c)

Explanation:

- **Statement 2 is incorrect:** This architecture avoided the use of human and animal figures as Muslims are forbidden to replicate living forms on any surface.

Supplementary Notes:

Indo-Islamic Architecture

- By 12th century AD, the throne of Delhi had been occupied by an Islamic ruler and in the subsequent years, Indian architecture underwent a massive change. Thus we see a confluence of Persian Style with the Indian Style. Hence, it is known as the Indo-Islamic architecture of Indo-Saracenic architecture.

- The salient features of this architecture include:
  - The use of arch and domes gained prominence. It was known as the 'Arcuade' style of architecture and replaced the traditional Trabeat style of architecture.
  - The Islamic rulers introduced the use of minars around the mosques and the mausoleums.
  - Mortar was used as a cementing agent in their constructions.
  - The Indo-Islamic architecture avoided the use of human and animal figures.
  - While the Hindu architecture had become too congested, the Indo – Islamic architecture introduced spaciousness, massiveness and breadth to it.
  - While the previous structures used sculptures as means of decoration, the Indo-Islamic architecture used calligraphy as means of decoration.
  - Arabesque method was also used for decoration which was characterized by use of geometrical vegetal ornamentation and by a continuous stem which split regularly, producing a series of counterpoised, leafy, secondary stems creating decorative patterns.
  - The architecture of this period heavily used the principles of geometry – from decorative pattern to imbibing a sense of symmetry.
  - The buildings had intricate jaali works, which signifies the importance of light in Islamic religion.
  - An important feature of the architecture during this period was the use of water in the premises of the constructions in the form of courtyard pools, fountains and small drains for religious, cooling and decorative purposes.
  - The Islamic rulers introduced the Charbagh style of gardening.
  - The architectures of these times also used the pietra dura technique for the inlay of precious stones and gems into the stone walls.
  - Another unique feature was the use of foresightening technique in the buildings, such that the inscriptions appear to be closer than it really is.

70. Correct Option: (d)

Explanation:

- All statements are correct

Supplementary Notes:
Nataraja Sculpture

- The bronze casting technique and the making of bronze images of traditional icons reached a high stage of development in South India during the medieval period. Chola bronzes are the most sought after collectors' items by art lovers all over the world. An important piece of Chola sculpture was the sculpture of Nataraja in the 'Tandava' dance posture. Shiva is thus associated with the end of the cosmic world.
- Features of the Nataraja sculpture are:
  - In this Chola period bronze sculpture Shiva has been shown balancing himself on his right leg and suppressing the 'apasmara', the demon of ignorance or forgetfulness, with the foot of the same leg.
  - At the same time, he raises his left leg in bhujangatrasita stance, which represents 'tirobhava' that is kicking away the veil of maya or illusion from the devotee's mind.
  - His four arms are outstretched and the main right hand is posed in 'abhaya hasta' or the gesture reassuring the devotee to not be afraid.
  - The upper right holds the 'damaru' his favorite musical instrument to keep on the beat tala. All creation springs from the great sound of 'damaru'.
  - The upper left hand carries a flame which represents destruction while the main left hand is held in dola hasta and connects with the 'abhaya hasta' of the right hand.
  - His hair locks fly on both the sides touching the circular 'jvala mala' or the garland of flames which surrounds the entire dancing figuration.

71. Correct Option: (c)

Explanation:

- **Statement 2 is incorrect:** The surviving examples of the Pala illustrated manuscripts mostly belong to the Vajrayana School of Buddhism.

Supplementary Notes:
Pala School of Art

- The earliest examples of miniature painting in India exist in the form of illustrations to the religious texts on Buddhism executed under the Palas of eastern India and the Jain texts executed in western India during the 11th–12th centuries AD.
- The Pala period (750 AD to the middle of the 12th century) witnessed the last great phase of Buddhism and Buddhist art in India.
- The surviving examples of the Pala illustrated manuscripts mostly belong to the Vajrayana School of Buddhism.
- The Pala painting is characterized by sinuous lines and subdued tones of color. It is a naturalistic style which resembles the ideal forms of contemporary bronze and stone sculpture and reflects some feeling of the classical art of Ajanta.

- The Pala Art came to a sudden end after the destruction of the Buddhist monasteries at the hands of Muslim invaders in the first half of the 13th century. Some of the monks and artists escaped and fled to Nepal, which helped in reinforcing the existing art traditions there.

72. Correct Option: (c)

Explanation:

- **Statement 1 is incorrect:** Badami Caves are not the oldest caves in India, but caves at Bhimbetka is the oldest surviving example.
- **Statement 2 is incorrect:** The Barabar Caves built during 3rd century BCE belonged to the period of Ashoka and his son Dasaratha.

Supplementary Notes:

Rock-cut Architecture

- During the Mauryan period, these caves were generally used as viharas, i.e. living quarters, by the Jain and Buddhist monks. While the early caves were used by the Ajivika sect, later, they became popular as Buddhist monasteries. The caves during the Mauryan period were marked by a highly polished finish of the interior walls and decorative gateways. Barabar and Nagarjuni Caves in Bihar were formed during the time of Dasharath, grandson of Ashoka.
- Ellora Caves are located nearly 100 kms away from Ajanta caves in the Sahyadri ranges of Maharashtra. It is a group of 34 caves – 17 Brahmanical, 12 Buddhist and 5 Jain. These set of caves were developed during the period between 5th and 11th centuries AD (newer as compared to Ajanta Caves) by various guilds from Vidarbha, Karnataka and Tamil Nadu. Hence, the caves reflect a natural diversity in terms of theme and architectural styles.
- The Badami cave Temples are a complex of Hindu and Jain cave Temples located in Badami, a town in the Bagalkot district in northern part of Karnataka, India. The caves are considered an example of Indian rock-cut architecture, especially Badami Chalukya architecture, which dates from the 6th century. The Badami cave Temples represent some of the earliest known examples of Hindu Temples in the Deccan region.

73. Correct Option: (b)

Explanation:

- Pair 2 is correctly matched

Supplementary Notes:

Temples in Kerala

- Sree Padmanabhaswamy Temple in Thiruvananthapuram dates back to the 8th century but the present structure was built in the 18th century by the then Travancore Maharaja Marthanda Varma. The Temple is built in the unique Chera style of architecture, and its main deity is Lord Vishnu who is found in the Anantha Shayana posture (reclined posture of eternal yoga) on Adishesha or king of all serpents. It is known to be one of the 108 holy Temples associated with Vaishnavism in India.
- Sabarimala is a Hindu pilgrimage center located at the Periyar Tiger Reserve in the Western Ghat, Kerala. The Sabarimala shrine is an ancient Hindu Temple of Lord Ayyappan, who is also known as Sasta or Dharmasasta. The Temple is a prominent pilgrimage site among the Hindu devotees in the state of Kerala. It witnesses the second largest seasonal pilgrimage after the Islamic holy site of Mecca in Saudi Arabia.
- Vaikom Mahadeva Temple is an ancient Temple in Kerala dedicated to Lord Shiva. The Temple is popular for its annual Vaikathashtami festival. The Shiva Linga here is believed to be from the Treta Yuga (the second of the four yugas, or ages of humankind) and is considered as one of the oldest Temples in Kerala.

74. Correct Option: (b)

Explanation:

- **Statement 3 is incorrect:** Alexander Cunningham became its first Director-General.

Supplementary Notes:

Archaeological Survey of India (ASI)

- The Archaeological Survey of India (ASI) under the Ministry of Culture is the premier organisation for archaeological researches and protection of the cultural heritage of the nation. Maintenance of ancient monuments and archaeological sites and remains of national importance is the prime concern of the ASI. Besides, it regulates all archaeological activities in the country as per the provisions of the Ancient Monuments and Archaeological Sites and Remains Act, 1958. It also regulates Antiquities and Art Treasure Act, 1972.
- For the maintenance of ancient monuments and archaeological sites and remains of national importance, the entire country is divided into 29 circles.
- It was founded in 1861 by Alexander Cunningham who also became its first Director-General.
- Its major activities inter-alia are as under:
  - Conducting archaeological explorations and excavations;
  - Maintenance, conservation and preservation of protected monuments and archaeological sites and remains of national importance;
  - Chemical preservation of monuments and antiquarian remains;
  - Architectural survey of monuments;

- ➤ Epigraphical and numismatic studies;
- ➤ Setting up and re-organisation of Site Museums;
- ➤ Training in Archaeology;
- ➤ Bringing out archaeological publications;
- ➤ Archaeological expeditions outside India;
- ➤ Horticulture operation in and around ancient monuments and sites;
- ➤ Implementation and regulation of – The Ancient Monuments and Archaeological Sites and Remains Act, 1958, the Antiquities and Art Treasures Act, 1972, etc.

75. Correct Option: (a)

Supplementary Notes:

- The earliest inscriptions are found on the seals of Harappa belonging to about 2500 BC. They have not been deciphered so far.
- The oldest inscriptions deciphered so far were issued by Ashoka in the third century BC. An Ashokan pillar inscription was found by Firoz Shah Tughlaq in Meerut.
- He brought it to Delhi and asked the pandits of his empire to decipher it, but they failed to do so. The same difficulty was faced by the British when in the last quarter of the eighteenth century they discovered Ashokan inscriptions.
- These epigraphs were first deciphered in 1837 by James Prinsep, a civil servant in the employment of the East India Company in Bengal.

76. Correct Option: (a)

Explanation:

- **Statement 4 is incorrect:** Ajanta Caves are related to Buddhism not Jainism, however Ellora Caves are related to both as well as Hinduism.

Supplementary Notes:

- Monuments at Pattadakal include Jain Temple – Jaina Narayana built in 9th century. This three-storeyed Temple with the two lower storeys being functional, is the last in the Temple series at Pattadakal.
- Mount Abu is famous for Dilwara Jain Temple consisting of five major Temples devoted to five Jain Tirthankaras.
  - ➤ Shri Adinath Temple or Vimal Vasahi Temple – Oldest of all. Dedicated to Shri Adinathji, 1st Tirthankar, it was built by Vimal Shah, Minister of Solanki ruler of Gujarat in 1031 AD.
  - ➤ Shri Neminathji Temple or Luna Vasahi Temple - built in 1230 AD by two brothers known as Tejpal and Vastupal. Dedicated to Shri Neminathji.
  - ➤ Shri Parshavanath Temple or Khartar Vasahi Temple – Dedicated to Shri Parshavanathji
  - ➤ Shri Rishabnathji Temple or Peethalhar Temple – built by Bhima Shah, a minister from rulers of Gujarat. Called Peethalhar as most of the statues are built using 'Pittal' (Brass Metal). Dedicated to Shri Rishabhnathji.
  - ➤ Shri Mahaveer Swami Temple – Dedicated to Shri Mahaveer Swamiirnar:
- The Jain Temples at Girnar attract time, since the caves here house rock paintings, created by man from as early as about 15,000 years ago in vivid and panoramic detail. The rock paintings have numerous layers belonging to various epochs of time, ranging from the Upper Palaeolithic, Mesolithic Age to the protohistoric, early historic and medieval periods. The most ancient scenes here believed to be commonly belonging to the devotees of both Shwetambar and Digambar sects of Jainism. The two important Jain Temples here are the Mallinath and Neminath. Rectangular Neminath Temple, completed between 1128 CE and 1159 CE. Neminath (the 22th Tirthankar) is carved in black marble with jewelled eyes. The courtyard is filled with sculptures. While the Mallinath Temple dedicated to the 19th Tirthankar was built in 1231 CE by Vastupal and Tejpal. Mallinath is shown in blue colour.
- Pawapuri Nalanda (Bihar) – Lord Mahavira breathed his last at this place, and was cremated here. A marble Temple, the "Jalmandir", built in the middle of a tank, and another Jain Temple Samosharan are major pilgrimage spots.
- Khajuraho Group of Monuments are a group of Hindu and Jain Temples.

77. Correct Option: (c)

Supplementary Notes:

- Modhera is a village in Gujarat situated on the banks of Pushpavati river. It was once a flourishing town and seaport. Modhera Sun Temple is situated here, which finds a mention in Skanda Purana. It is a Monument of National Importance maintained by Archaeological Survey of India. Having resemblance to Konark Sun Temple, it was so designed that the first rays of the sun fell on the image of Surya, the Sun God, at equinoxes.
- Temple was constructed in 1026-27 AD during the reign of Chalukya King Bhima I (1022-1063 AD) and was later attacked and damaged by Mahmud of Ghazni. An annual festival of Indian classical dances is organized by the Tourism Corporation of Gujarat in month of January, in the backdrop of this Temple.
- Some of the famous Sun Temples of India are listed in the following table:

S.No.	Sun Temple	Location
1.	Konark Sun Temple	Konark, Puri (Odisha)
2.	Sun Temple	Modhera, Mehsana (Gujarat)
3.	Martand Sun Temple	Martand, Anantnag (J&K)
4.	Dakshinaarka Temple	Gaya, Bihar
5.	Surya Pahar Temple	Golapara, Assam
6.	Suryanarayana Swamy Temple	Arasavalli, Srikakulam, Andhra Pradesh
7.	Suryanaar Temple	Kumbhakonam, T.N.
8.	Balaji Sun Temple or Brahmanya Dev Temple	Unao, Datia (M.P.)

78. Correct Option: (b)

Explanation:

- **Statement 1 is incorrect:** The initiative to rebuild the structure was taken by first Nayak king of Madurai, Viswanatha Nayak (1559–1600) under the supervision of Ariyanatha Mudaliar, the prime minister of the Nayak Dynasty and the founder of the Poligar System. The original design by Vishwanatha Nayak in 1560 was substantially expanded to the current structure during the reign of Thirumalai Nayak (1623–55).

Supplementary Notes:

Meenakshi Temple

- The Temple is dedicated to Goddess Meenakshi or Parvathi and Lord Shiva.
- Meenakshi Sundareswarar Temple in Madurai has been adjudged the best 'Swachh Iconic Place' (clean place) in India. Ten spots were identified by the Central government as part of the 'Swachh Iconic Places' initiative earlier this year.

79. Correct Option: (d)

Explanation:

- All statements are correct

Supplementary Notes:

The Taj Mahal

- The Taj Mahal is considered to be the greatest architectural achievement in the whole range of Indo-Islamic architecture.
- It was built by Mughal Emperor Shah Jahan in the memory of his wife Mumtaz Mahal with construction started in 1632 AD and completed in 1648 AD.
- Chahar Bagh or Chah Bagh is a Persian style layout of gardens brought to India by Mughals and subsequently updated according to Indian conditions. In Indian scenario it meant a square walled garden divided into four by intersecting water channels. Generally main buildings were built in the middle of garden.
- Taj Mahal is built on one of the extremes of this on river front.
- Calligraphy (decorative handwriting) was an ornamental decoration done on surface of building, usually using Quranic verses. In Taj Mahal, the art of calligraphy is used with the inlay of jasper in white marble. This technique of embellishment is beautifully used to enhance beauty of structure.

Figure: 7.1.4

- Pietra Dura (cut-and-fit technique) is inlaying technique of semiprecious stones of various colours, including lapis lazuli in highly formalized and intertwining geometric and floral designs.

Figure: 7.1.5

- While Tesselation (Mosaic Design) is an arrangement of shapes, especially of polygons, closely fitted together in a repeated pattern without gaps or overlapping.

- Both these techniques are used in Taj Mahal construction.
- Jali work is also a part of the building.

Figure: 7.1.6

80. Correct Option: (c)

Explanation:

- Both statements are correct

Supplementary Notes:

The Archaeological Survey of India

- The Archaeological Survey of India (ASI) is directly under the aegis of the Ministry of Culture and it is the foremost institution for archaeological researches conducted across India.
- It has been charged with preservation of the cultural heritage of our nation.
- Its focus is on the preservation of physical and tangible heritage that is accumulated in the ancient monuments and archaeological sites.
- The provisions of the Ancient Monuments and Archaeological Sites and Remains Act, 1958, guide ASI.
- Another major legislation that directs the working of the ASI, is the Antiquities and Art Treasure Act, 1972.
- This Act directs ASI to prevent the illegal export of Indian antiquities from our nation.
- Although the ASI is charged with the control over all heritage sites across the nation, for the smooth functioning, the entire country has been divided into 24 Circles, which concentrate on preservation of monuments under their jurisdiction.
- ASI employs many trained archaeologists, architects, conservators, epigraphists, etc.
- They have other institutions under their aegis like the Museums, Excavation branches, Epigraphy branches, Building Survey Projects, Horticulture branch, Temple Survey Projects, etc.
- One of the more specialised and one in the kind project by the ASI is their Underwater Archaeology Wing.
- The ASI also has several diplomas and degrees for studying archaeology from the Institute of Archaeology in New Delhi.

81. Correct Option: (b)

Explanation:

- **Statement 2 is incorrect:** The Cholas also made rich contribution to art of sculpture. The walls of Chola Temple such as the Tanjore and Gangaikondacholapuram contain numerous icons of large size with fine execution.

Supplementary Notes:

Chola Art and Architecture

- The Dravidian style of the Temple architecture reached its zenith during the period of Chola Kingdom.
- The Brihadeshwara Temple of Tanjore is a fine example of Temple architecture of this period. It was completed during the time of Rajaraja Chola around 1000 AD.
- Feature of Dravida Style Temple Built during the Chola Kingdom:
  - Unlike the Nagara Temples, they were surrounded by high boundary wall.
  - The front wall had a high entrance gateway known as gopuram.
  - The Temple was laid down in the panchayatan style.
  - The spire is in the form of a stepped pyramid that rises up linearly. This is called as vimana.
  - The assembly hall was connected with the garbhagriha by a vestibule tunnel known as antrala.
  - The presence of water tank inside the Temple enclosure was the unique feature of Temple built during the period of Cholas.

82. Correct Option: (c)

Explanation:

- Both statements are correct

Supplementary Notes:

Buddhism and Brahmanism during Gupta Period

- Buddhism ceased to receive royal patronage during the Gupta period. Fa-hien gives the impression that this religion was flourishing, but in reality it was not as important during the Gupta period as it had been in the days of Ashoka and Kanishka. However, some stupas and viharas were constructed, and Nalanda was established by Kumaragupta and became the center of Buddhist education.

- The Gupta kings followed a policy of tolerance towards different religious sects. We find no example of the persecution of the followers of Buddhism and Jainism. This was also due to the change in the character of Buddhism which had come to acquire many features of Brahmanism or Hinduism.

83. **Correct Option: (b)**

Explanation:

- **Statement 1 is incorrect:** Building construction techniques got advanced.
- **Statement 2 is incorrect:** The use of burnt brick was common.

Supplementary Notes:

Impact of Central Asian Contact: Structures and Pottery

- The Shaka-Kushan phase registered a distinct advance in building activities.
- Excavations have revealed several layers of structures, sometimes more than half a dozen at various sites in north India.
- In them we find the use of burnt bricks for flooring and that of tiles for both flooring and roofing. But the use of surkhi and tiles may not have been adopted from outside.
- The period is also marked by the construction of brickwalls. Its typical pottery is red ware, both plain and polished, with medium to fine fabric.
- Red pottery techniques were widely known in Central Asia, and they are found even in regions like Farghana which were on the peripheries of the Kushan cultural zone.
- The distinctive pots are sprinklers and spouted channels.

84. **Correct Option: (b)**

Explanation:

- **Option (b) is correct:** The figure of Chulakoka Devta is a notable specimen of Sunga Art among the several deities of fertility and other scenes sculptured on the railing pillars of Bharhut, representing its indigenous character and folk quality.

Supplementary Notes:

Sunga Art

- After the decline of the Mauryan Empire, the Sungas succeeded to power in circa 185 BC. They ruled the central and eastern parts of Northern India. Their native style, distinguished by its simplicity and folk appeal is best represented in monolithic free-standing sculptures of Yakshas and Yakshis.
- The figure of Chulakoka Devta is a notable specimen of Sunga Art among the several deities of fertility and other scenes sculptured on the railing pillars of Bharhut, representing its indigenous character and folk quality.
- She stands gracefully on an elephant with her arms and one leg entwined around a flowering tree, as she is a tree goddess. The profuse jewelry and the mode of wearing the undergarment and the head-dress demonstrate the feminine fashion of the period.

85. **Correct Option: (d)**

Explanation:

- All statements are correct

Supplementary Notes:

Art and Architecture of Mauryan Period

- The Mauryan contribution to art and architecture was significant. Ashoka is known to have built 84,000 stupas to commemorate various events of Buddha's life.
- Ashokan edicts were inscribed on stone pillars that were made of single columns of polished sandstone and had capitals on their top. The best preserved of all Ashokan edicts stands at Lauriya Nandangarh (Bihar). This thirty-two feet tall column has an almost fifty ton seated lion capital placed on its top, an engineering feat worth admiring.
- The bull capital from Rampura is also another fine example of Mauryan sculpture. The most famous capital is the one at Sarnath, which shows four lions and the Dharmachakra.
- Besides pillars, few Mauryan figures have also come to light. The most well-known of these is the Yakshi from Didarganj. The beauty of these figures lies in the exactness of their workmanship and in the fact that they appear to be made from one single stone.
- A noteworthy aspect of Mauryan architecture is the rock cut caves. The Lomash Rishi (with its impressive entrance) and the Sudama Caves are examples of such architecture. These caves cut from solid rock were provided by Ashoka for non-Buddhist monks. These caves marked the beginning of the rock-cut architecture which was patronised by later rulers too. His rock edicts were inscribed in the local language and the local script.
- Pottery of the Mauryan period is generally referred to as Northern Black Polished Ware (NBPW). They were characterised by the black paint and highly lustrous finish and were generally used as luxury items. They have often been referred to as the highest level of pottery.

86. **Correct Option: (a)**

Explanation:

- Pair 3 is incorrectly matched:

Stage of Temple development	Features added
A. Second stage	Pradakshina path
B. Third stage	Shikharas
C. Fourth stage	Rectangular Temple

Supplementary Notes:

Progression of Temple Development

There are generally five stages of Temple development in India.

First Stage:

- The Temples had a flat roof.
- The Temples were square in shape.
- The portico was developed on shallow pillars.
- The entire structure was built on low platforms.

- Second stage:
  - Temples were higher or raised.
  - Most important addition was a cover ambulatory passageway around the sanctum sanctorum or garbhagriha. The passageway was used as a pradakshina path.
- Third stage:
  - This stage saw the emergence of shikharas in place of a flat roof. However, they were still quite low and almost square, i.e. curvilinear.
  - Panchayatan Style of Temple making was introduced.
- Fourth stage:
  - Main shrine became more rectangular.
- Fifth stage:
  - Introduction of circular Temples with shallow rectangular projections.

87. Correct Option: (c)

Explanation:

- Option (c) is correct

Supplementary Notes:

Shalbhanjika

- A salabhanjika is the sculpture of a woman, displaying stylized feminine features, standing near a tree and grasping a branch.
- The Salbhanjika is portrayed in the eastern Torana of Sanchi stupa. It is one of the loveliest female figures in the whole of Indian art.
- She is holding the branch of a mango tree, with her left hand, while the right hand is adroitly adjusted within the holds of a big branch of the tree, which itself merges into her draperies and jewelry. Posed securely within the framework of the lush fruit-bearing tree, she also gives the effect of almost flying off from the tree into outer space.
- She is one of the loveliest fantasies of carvers whose imaginations floated women as flying spirits soaring towards the heavens.

88. Correct Option: (c)

Explanation:

- **Statement 1 is incorrect:** Indo-Islamic architecture introduced spaciousness, massiveness, and breadth to Indian architecture.

Supplementary Notes:

Indo-Islamic Architecture

- It had a confluence of Indian and Persian Styles.
- Some of the features of Indo-Islamic architecture are:
  - The use of arch and domes gained prominence during this period.
  - The Islamic rulers introduced the use of minars around the mosques and the mausoleums.
  - The mortar was used as a cementing agent in its construction.
  - Indo-Islamic architecture avoided the use of human and animal figures.
  - While the Hindu architecture had become too congested, the Indo-Islamic architecture introduced spaciousness, massiveness, and breadth to it.
  - While the previous structures used sculptures as a means of decoration, the Indo-Islamic architecture used calligraphy as a means of decoration.
  - An important feature of the architecture during this period was the use of water in the premises of the constructions in the form of courtyard pools fountains and small drains.
  - The Islamic rulers introduced the Charbagh Style of gardening, in which a square block was divided into four adjacent identical gardens.
  - The architectures of these times also used the pietra dura technique for the inlay of precious stones and gems into the stone walls.

89. Correct Option: (c)

Explanation:

- Both statements are correct

Supplementary Notes:

Vijaynagara Architecture

- The rulers of the Vijayanagara Empire (1335-1565 AD) were great patrons of art and architecture with capital at Hampi (Karnataka).
- They combined the features of Chola, Hoysalas, Pandyas, Chalukyas architectural styles. Under them, the architectural style started to be influenced by the Indo-Islamic style of Bijapur, which in turn was reflected in the Temples built during this period.
- The features of the Temples were:
  - The walls of the Temples were highly decorated with carvings and geometrical patterns.
  - Gopurams, which were previously present on the front side, were now built on all the sides.

- ➤ Monolithic rock pillars.
- ➤ Temple pillars have a mythical creature Yali (Horse) engraved in them.
- ➤ The enclosing walls was larger.
- ➤ More than one mandap were built in each Temple. The central mandap came to be known as Kalyan mandap.
- ➤ The concept of secular buildings inside the Temple premises was also introduced during this period.
- ➤ Temple complex is enclosed by boundaries.
- Vittalsami Temple, Lotus Mahal, Virupaksha Temple in Hampi, Raghunatha Temple in Hampi, etc. reflect the Vijaynagar architecture.

90. Correct Option: (a)

Explanation:

- Statement 2 is incorrect: Triple storey caves are a unique achievement at Ellora.
- Statement 3 is incorrect: Jaina Caves at Ellora belong to the Digambara sect.

Supplementary Notes:

Ellora Caves

- It is one of the largest rock-cut monastery-Temple cave complexes in the world, featuring Buddhist, Hindu, and Jain monuments.
- The entire group of more than 34 caves was excavated during the period from the 5th - 6th centuries to 12th - 13th centuries AD.
- The Buddhist caves (nos. 1-12) were excavated between the 5th and the 8th centuries AD.
- The Brahmanical group of caves (nos. 13-29) was excavated between the 7th and 10th centuries AD. The famous Kailasa Temple in this group is attributed to the Rashtrakuta king, Krishna I (circa. AD. 757 - 783). The Jain Caves (nos. 30-34) were excavated between 10th and 13th centuries AD.
- Jaina caves belong to the Digambara sect.
- Ajanta also has double-storeyed caves but at Ellora, the triple storey is a unique achievement.

91. Correct Option : (c)

Explanation:

- **Option (c) is correct**

Supplementary Notes:

Style of Temple architecture

- The basic form of the Hindu Temple comprises Sanctum Sanctorum, Mandapa, Shikhara, and vahana.
- The Shikharas were generally of three types:
  - ➤ Latina or Rekha-prasad: They were square at the base and the walls curve inward to a point on the top.
  - ➤ Phamsana: They had a broader base and were shorter in height than the Latina ones. They slope upwards on a straight line.
  - ➤ Valabhi: They had a rectangular base with the roof rising into vaulted chambers. They were also called wagon-vaulted roofs.

92. Correct Option: (b)

Explanation:

- **Statement 3 is incorrect:** The new ideals of Mahayana Buddhism inspired the sculptors of Mathura art.

Supplementary Notes:

Mathura Art

- Mathura art refers to a particular school of Indian art starting in the 2nd century BCE, which centered on the city of Mathura, in central northern India, during a period in which Buddhism, Jainism together with Hinduism flourished in India.
- The Mathura school was contemporaneous with a second important school of Kushana art, that of Gandhara in the northwest. About the 1st century CE, each area appears to have evolved separately its own representations of the Buddha. The Mathura images are related to the earlier yaksha (male nature deity) figures.
- Important characteristics of the Mathura School of Art:
  - ➤ Buddhist to Brahmanical to the sometimes secular theme.
  - ➤ More stress is given to the inner beauty and facial emotions rather than bodily gesture.
  - ➤ Sculptures were made on white-spotted red stones.
  - ➤ These were not influenced by Greco-Roman techniques to that extent.
  - ➤ Several Brahmanical deities were first crystallized by this school.
  - ➤ They were depicted as more human and less spiritual. It was wholly influenced by Indian sculptures.
  - ➤ In Mathura art tradition, Buddha image has longer earlobes, thicker lips, wider eyes and prominent noses.
- The new ideals of Mahayana Buddhism inspired the sculptors. According to Indian authorities, the creation of the Buddha image was the greatest contribution of the artists of this school. The tradition of this school extended to not only the images of Buddha but to the images of the Hindu pantheon of gods.
- Unlike the Gandhara School, this school was purely indigenous in its origins and reached its zenith.

93. Correct Option: (c)

Explanation:

- **Statement 1 is incorrect:** The shikharas in the Odisha school were known as Rekhadeuls.
- **Statement 2 is incorrect:** Temples of this school were surrounded by a boundary wall as in the Dravidian Style of Temple architecture.

Supplementary Notes:

Orissa School of Architecture

- It is a sub-school of Nagara architecture.
- **Some of its features are:**
  - The exterior walls were lavishly decorated with intricate carvings, but interior walls were plain.
  - There was no use of pillars on the porch. Iron girders were used instead to support the roof.
  - The mandap was known as Jagmohan in this region.
  - Temples were surrounded by a boundary wall as in the Dravidian Style of Temple architecture.
  - Their architectural features are classified into three orders, i.e., rekhapida, pidhadeul, and khakra.
  - The shikharas in the Odisha School was known as rekhadeuls. They were almost vertical roofs which suddenly curved inwards sharply.
- Example: Sun Temple at Konark (also known as Black Pagoda as the first rays of the Sun entered the garbhagriha through the sea-facing pagoda.

94. Correct Option : (c)

Supplementary Notes:

Ellora Caves

- It is one of the largest rock-cut monastery-Temple cave complexes in the world, featuring Buddhist, Hindu, and Jain monuments.
- The Brahmanical group of caves (nos. 13 - 29) was excavated between the 7th and 10th centuries AD.
- Many of the Brahmanical caves at Ellora are dedicated to Shaivism, but the images of both Shiva and Vishnu and their various forms according to Puranic narrative are depicted. Among the Shaivite themes, Ravana shaking Mount Kailash, Andhakasurvadha, Kalyanasundaram are profusely depicted whereas, among the Vaishnavite themes, the different avatars of Vishnu are depicted.

95. Correct Option: (d)

Explanation:

- **Statement 1 is incorrect:** Under Narasimhavarman, the mandapas were now divided into separate rathas.
- **Statement 2 is incorrect:** Under Rajsimhavarman, the development of real structural Temples was started in the place of rock-cut Temples.

Supplementary Notes:

Pallava School of Architecture

- Temple architecture in South India began under the Pallava rulers.
- The Temples developed during the Pallava Dynasty reflected the stylistic taste of the individual rulers and can be classified into four stages chronologically.
- **Mahendra group:**
  - This was the first stage of Pallava Temple architecture. The Temples built under Mahendravarman were basically rock-cut Temples.
- **Narasimha group:**
  - This represented the second stage of the development of Temple architecture in South India. The rock-cut Temples were decorated with intricate sculptures. Under Narasimhavarman, the mandapas were now divided into separate rathas.
- **Rajsimha group:**
  - Rajsimhavarman led the third stage of Temple development. Under him, the development of real structural Temples was started in place of rock-cut Temples. Example: Shore Temple at Mahabalipuram, Kailashnath Temple at Kanchipuram, etc.
- **Nandivarman group:**
  - This was the fourth stage of Temple development during the Pallava Dynasty. The Temples built under him were smaller in size. The features were almost similar to the Dravidian style of Temple architecture.

96. Correct Option: (b)

Explanation:

- **Statement 3 is incorrect:** Portrait sculptures made of bronze were made during the Vijayanagar period in Andhra Pradesh.

Supplementary Notes:

Indian Bronze Sculpture

- The Harappan civilisation saw a wide-scale practice of bronze casting. The bronze statues were made using "lost wax technique" or "Cire Perdue".
- The Dancing Girl is the world's oldest bronze sculpture datable to 2500 BCE. Found in Mohenjo-daro, this four-inch figure depicts a naked girl wearing only ornaments, which include bangles in the left arm, and amulet and bracelet on the right arm. She stands in a 'tribhanga' dancing posture with the right hand on her hip.
- A famous hoard of Jain bronzes was found at Akota, on the outskirts of Baroda, dated between 5th -7th CE. These bronzes were often subsequently inlaid with silver and copper to bring out the eyes, crowns

and details of the textiles on which the figures were seated.

- Many standing Buddha images with right hand in abhaya mudra were cast in North India, particularly Uttar Pradesh and Bihar, during the Gupta and Post-Gupta periods.
- Vakataka bronze images of the Buddha from Maharashtra are contemporary with the Gupta period bronzes. They show the influence of the Amaravati style of Andhra Pradesh in the 3rd CE. The additional importance of the Gupta and Vakataka bronzes is that they were portable and monks carried them from place to place for the purpose of individual worship or to be installed in Buddhist viharas.
- Himachal Pradesh and Kashmir regions also produced bronze images of Buddhist deities as well as Hindu gods and goddesses have a very distinct style in comparison with bronzes from other parts of India.
- A noteworthy development is the growth of different types of iconography of Vishnu images. Four-headed Vishnu, also known as Chaturanana or Vaikuntha Vishnu, was worshipped in these regions. While the central face represents Vasudeva, the other two faces are that of Narasimha and Varaha.
- The Narasimha avatar and Mahishasuramardini Durga images of Himachal Pradesh are among the very dynamic bronzes from that region.
- Among the Pallava Period bronzes of the eighth century is the icon of Shiva seated in ardhaparyanka asana (one leg kept dangling). The right hand is in the achamana mudra gesture, suggesting that he is about to drink poison.
- Some of the most beautiful and exquisite statues were produced during the Chola period in Tamil Nadu from the 10th – 12th CE.
- During the sixteenth century, known as the Vijayanagar period in Andhra Pradesh, the sculptors experimented with portrait sculpture in order to preserve knowledge of the royal patron for posterity. For e.g. at Tirupati, life-size standing portrait statues were cast in bronze, depicting Krishnadevaraya with his two queens, Tirumalamba and Chinnadevi.

97. Correct Option: (a)

Explanation:

- **Statement 3 is incorrect:** A majority of sculptures portray Buddha's life and incidents related to his life, but the Gandhara sculptors did not confine themselves to this only.

Supplementary Notes:

Gandhara School of Art

- Gandhara art represents the art that developed and spread in the northwestern part of India from the 1st Century BC to the 4th Century AD.
- Gandhara School was based on Greco-Roman norms encapsulating foreign techniques and an alien spirit. It is also known as the Graeco-Buddhist School of Art.
- Gandhara art presents some of the earliest images of the Buddha. The Gandhara Art flourished during the Kushana rule in India. It was during his reign that Gandhara School of Art flourished.
- It represents a fusion of native and foreign elements. The great strength of the classical elements in the art of the Gandhara province is best seen in portrait heads and the representations of classical deities which found their way into the Buddhist Art of north-western India.
- The distinguishing Gandhara sculpture is the standing or seated Buddha.
- Most of the Gandhara reliefs portray episodes from the life of the Buddha or scenes from Buddhist legends, yet the Gandhara sculptors did not confine themselves to this only. The bodhisattvas or Buddhist saints portrayed in the art are shown with a bare upper body, skirt, scarves, jewels and long hair. This contrast between the Buddha as the sacred being who has achieved enlightenment, and the bodhisattva who is on the road to this goal, is found in the Buddhist Art of entire Asia.

98. Correct Option: (a)

Explanation:

- **Statement 2 is incorrect:** Double domes in the imperial style were introduced by the Lodhi Dynasty.
- **Statement 3 is incorrect:** Jaunpur School of provincial architecture is characterized by the absence of minars.

Supplementary Notes:

Architecture during Delhi Sultanate

- During the period of Delhi Sultanate (1206-1526 AD), architecture can be categorized into two broad categories:
  - Imperial Style Architecture
    - The Imperial Style of architecture flourished from 1191 to 1557 AD under the various dynasties that ruled during this period. Each ruler imparted certain flavors of his own, but the broad stylisation remained the same.
    - The Slave Dynasty remained in power from 1206 to 1290 AD. During this period, most of the constructions were remodeling of the existing Hindu structures. They also started the erection of a number of monuments, Qutub Minar being a prime example.
    - The constructions during the period of Khilji Dynasty (1290-1320 AD) are marked by the use of red sandstone. Also, the prominence

of Arcuade style began from this period. Mortar began to be used prominently in all the constructions as a cementing agent.

- During the period of Tughlaq Dynasty the focus was more on strength of the building rather than on decoration. A new style of construction known as "batter" was introduced which was characterized by sloping walls to give more strength to the building. Some construction works were undertaken using grey sandstone.
- Only tombs were commissioned under the Lodhi Dynasty. One important feature of architecture during this period was the introduction of double domes which consisted of a hollow dome inside the top dome.

➤ **Provincial School of Architecture**

- During this period, the Indo-Islamic style started to influence the local architectural styles as well. Bengal, Jaunpur and Mandu became important seats of architectural development.
- The Bengal School of Architecture was characterized in its use of bricks and black marble. The mosques built during this period continued the use of sloping 'Bangla roofs', which was previously used for Temples.
- Mandu is a typical representation of the medieval provincial style of art and architecture. It was a complex mix of official and residential-cum-pleasure palace, pavilions, mosques, artificial reservoirs, embattlements, etc. In spite of the size or monumentality, the structures were very close to nature, designed in the style of arched pavilions, light and airy, so that these buildings did not retain heat. Local stone and marble were used to great advantage. Mandu is a fine example of architectural adaptation to the environment.
- Jaunpur architecture avoided the use of minars. A unique feature of the buildings here is the use of bold and forceful characters painted on huge screens in the centre and side bays of the prayer hall.

99. Correct Option: (b)

Supplementary Notes:

Panchayatan Style

- Panchayatana Style of Temple architecture is the one where the main shrine is surrounded by four subsidiary shrines.
- The main Temple was square with an elongated mandap in front of it, giving it a rectangular shape. The subsidiary shrines were placed opposite to each other on either side of the mandap giving the ground plan a crucified shape.
- Example: Dashavatar Temple at Deogarh (UP), Durga Temple at Aihole (Karnataka), etc.

100. Correct Option: (c)

Explanation:

- **Statement 2 is incorrect:** This architecture avoided the use of human and animal figures as Muslims are forbidden to replicate living forms on any surface.

Supplementary Notes:

Indo-Islamic Architecture

- By 12th century AD, the throne of Delhi had been occupied by an Islamic ruler and in the subsequent years, Indian architecture underwent massive change.
- New elements, such as calligraphy, ornamentation using inlay work, etc., were introduced to reflect the tastes and preferences of the new rulers and certain flavors of local architecture were also retained.
- Thus we see a confluence of Persian Style with the Indian Style. Hence, it is known as the Indo-Islamic architecture of Indo-Saracenic architecture.
- The salient features of this architecture include:
  - ➤ The use of arch and domes gained prominence. It was known as the 'Arcuade' Style of architecture and replaced the traditional Trabeat Style of architecture.
  - ➤ The Islamic rulers introduced the use of minars around the mosques and the mausoleums.
  - ➤ The mortar was used as a cementing agent in their constructions.
  - ➤ Indo-Islamic architecture avoided the use of human and animal figures.
  - ➤ While the Hindu architecture had become too congested, the Indo-Islamic architecture introduced spaciousness, massiveness, and breadth to it.
  - ➤ While the previous structures used sculptures as a means of decoration, the Indo-Islamic architecture used calligraphy as a means of decoration.
  - ➤ Arabesque method was also used for decoration which was characterized by the use of geometrical vegetal ornamentation and by a continuous stem which split regularly, producing a series of counterpoised, leafy, secondary stems creating decorative patterns.
  - ➤ The architecture of this period heavily used the principles of geometry – from decorative patterns to imbibing a sense of symmetry.
  - ➤ The buildings had intricate jaali works, which signifies the importance of light in the Islamic religion.
  - ➤ An important feature of the architecture during this period was the use of water in the premises of the constructions in the form of courtyard pools, fountains and small drains for religious, cooling and decorative purposes.

- The Islamic rulers introduced the Charbagh style of gardening.
- The architectures of these times also used the pietra dura technique for the inlay of precious stones and gems into the stone walls.
- Another unique feature was the use of fore-sightening technique in the buildings, such that the inscriptions appear to be closer than it really is.

101. Correct Option: (b)

Explanation:

- Statement 2 is incorrect: Satavahana sculptures are not iconic.

Supplementary Notes:

Satvahana Sculptures

- The Satavahana Empire was the successor of the Mauryan Empire in Deccan. In the first century BC the Satavahana Dynasty rose in eminence in Deccan for the following three centuries.
- The Satavahana sculptures at Amaravati reflect the influence of both the Gandhara and the Mathura School of Art. Eroticism is also a predominant feature of these Satavahana sculptures. Spontaneous energy, grace, and dynamism ooze out of the carved stone figures.
- The theme of nature and related things are most charmingly depicted through the art of carving with emphasis on vigor, activity, and grace. The erotic sculptures are less in numbers but can be marked with their presence.
- One of the main features of Satavahana sculptures is that these are not iconic. Satavahana sculpture denies any representation in human form. Throughout the sculptures, the main theme is of showing various episodes revolving around the Buddha and his life.

102. Correct Option: (c)

Explanation:

- Option (c) is correct

Supplementary Notes:

Orissa School of Architecture

- It is a sub-school of Nagara architecture.
- Some of its features are:
  - The exterior walls were lavishly decorated with intricate carvings, but interior walls were plain.
  - There was no use of pillars on the porch. Iron girders were used instead to support the roof.
  - The mandap was known as Jagmohan in this region.
  - Temples were surrounded by a boundary wall as in the Dravidian style of Temple architecture.
  - Their architectural features are classified into three orders, i.e., rekhapida, pidhadeul, and khakra.
  - Example: Sun Temple at Konark (also known as Black Pagoda as the first rays of the Sun entered the garbhagriha through the sea-facing pagoda).

103. Correct Option: (c)

Explanation:

- **Option (c) is correct:** A good example of Sunga art of the second century BC is the jovial figures, the dwarfish Yaksha from the Pithalkhora caves in Central India, carrying a bowl of abundance on his head.

Supplementary Notes:

Sunga Art

- The Shunga school viewed the human body as the centre of life. It attempted to reproduce on sculptured stone not only the actual features but the feelings of living men and women portrayed against the beauty and harmony of their lives.
- A good example of Sunga art of the second century BC is the jovial figures, the dwarfish Yaksha from the Pithalkhora caves in Central India, carrying a bowl of abundance on his head. The care-free broad smile on his face and his round belly indicate that he is fully satisfied in all respects. The two amulets strung on his necklace ward off evil spirits from his devotees.
- The back of his right-hand bears an inscription giving the name of the sculptor as Krishnadasa who was a goldsmith by profession. Generally, Indian art is an anonymous art, as the sculptor or the artist never sought to glorify himself.

104. Correct Option: (a)

Explanation:

- **Statement 2 is incorrect:** Three prominent dynasties who made Vesara style Temples are Chalukyas, Hoysalas and Rashtrakutas.

Supplementary Notes:

Vesara School of Architecture

- It is also known as the Karnataka School of Architecture and was conceptualized under the later Chalukya rulers in the mid-seventh century AD.
- It combined features of both Nagara School and Dravidian School and resulted in a hybridized style. Some of its features are:
  - Emphasis on vimana and mandapa
  - Open ambulatory passageway
  - The pillars, doorways and the ceilings were decorated with intricate carvings.
- Three prominent dynasties who made Vesara style Temples are:
  - Chalukyas of Badami and Kalyani.
  - Rashtrakutas (750-983 AD). For Example, Kailashnath Temple in Ellora, etc.

- Hoysala Dynasty (1050-1300 AD). For example, Temples at Halebid, Belur etc.

- Influence of Nagara Style is in Curvilinear Shikhara and square base of Vesara Temples.
- Influence of Dravida Style is seen in intricate carvings and sculptures, design of Vimana and Step or terraced Shikara of Vesara Temples.

105. Correct Option: (c)

Explanation:

- **Statement 2 is incorrect:** The capital without the crowning wheel and the lotus base has been adopted as the National Emblem of Independent India.

Supplementary Notes:

The Lion Capital, Sarnath

- The Lion Capital was discovered more than a hundred years ago at Sarnath, near Varanasi, which is generally referred to as Sarnath Lion Capital. This is one of the finest examples of sculpture from the Mauryan period.
- Built in commemoration of the historical event of the first sermon or the Dhammachakrapravartana by the Buddha at Sarnath, the capital was built by Ashoka.
- The capital originally consisted of five component parts: (i) the shaft (which is broken in many parts now), (ii) a lotus bell base, (iii) a drum on the bell base with four animals proceeding clockwise, (iv) the figures of four majestic addorsed lions, and (v) the crowning element, Dharamchakra, a large wheel, was also a part of this pillar.
- However, this wheel is lying in a broken condition and is displayed in the site museum at Sarnath.
- The capital without the crowning wheel and the lotus base has been adopted as the National Emblem of Independent India.
- Now kept in the archaeological museum at Sarnath, the capital has four lions firmly seated back to back on a circular abacus. The lion figures of the capital are very impressive and massive.
- Being a pillar image, it was conceived to be viewed from all the side, thus there are no boundations of fixed viewpoints. A lion capital has also been found at Sanchi but is in a dilapidated condition. The motif of lion-capital-pillar continued even in the subsequent period.

106. Correct Option: (d)

Explanation:

- **Statement 1 is incorrect:** Elephanta has two groups of caves – Buddhist and Shaivite.
- **Statement 2 is incorrect:** Elephanta caves are contemporary with Ellora Caves.

Supplementary Notes:

Elephanta Caves

- The Elephanta Caves (natively known as Gharapurichi Leni, basically Gharapuri) are a network of sculpted caves located on Elephanta Island or Gharapuri (literally the city of caves) in Mumbai.
- It consists of two groups of caves—the first is a large group of five Hindu caves, the second, a smaller group of two Buddhist caves.
- The Hindu caves contain rock cut stone sculptures, representing the Shaiva Hindu sect, dedicated to Lord Shiva.
- It is contemporary with Ellora, and its sculptures show slenderness in the body, with stark light and dark effects.
- There are legends that suggest that the great warrior Prince of Chalukya Dynasty – Pulkesin ll built the Lord Shiva shrine, to celebrate his victory.
- There are sculptured compartments in this cave with remarkable images of Ardhanarisvara, Kalyana-Sundara Shiva, Ravana lifting Kailasa, Andhakari-Murti (slaying of Andhaka demon) and Nataraja Shiva.

107. Correct Option: (c)

Explanation:

- **Statement 3 is incorrect:** Toranas (gateways) at Sanchi was built by the Satvahana Dynasty.

Supplementary Notes:

Sanchi Stupa

- The Sanchi Stupa is one of India's primary Buddhist sites and contains some of the oldest stone structures in the country.
- The principal monument of Sanchi, "The Great Stupa" or Stupa 1 was constructed under the commission of Mauryan Emperor, Ashoka the Great in around 3rd Century BCE. Around the same time, Ashoka Pillar was also erected which was made up of finely polished sandstone.
- Buddha never visited Sanchi.
- The four signature torans – embellished with scenes from the Jataka Tales, Ashoka's visit to the Bodhi tree, the war for Buddha's relics, etc – were later additions, constructed by the Satavahanas between the 1st century BCE and 1st century CE.
- Sanchi sculptures are magnificently decorative, and provide the most wonderful picture of Indian life and thought. The low relief of Barhut evolved in Sanchi. The composition is more thoughtful and there are no empty spaces. There is no vanishing point or reduction

to create depth. Important elements are at the bottom of the relief while the top one is supposed to be further away from the viewer. The Sanchi sculptures are, like those of Bharhut, entirely naturalistic in the treatment of the human form.

108. Correct Option: (b)

Explanation:

- **Option (b) is correct:** Sangharama is monastery for the Buddhist monastic community.

Supplementary Notes:

Sangharama

- Sangharama is a Sanskrit word meaning "Temple" or "monastery", the place, including its garden or grove, where dwells the Sangha, the Buddhist monastic community.

109. Correct Option: (b)

Explanation:

- **Statement 1 is incorrect:** Ajanta has twenty-nine caves. Out of those 29, only four are Chaitya and rest are vihara.

Supplementary Notes:

Ajanta Caves

- Ajanta is the most famous cave site in India. It is located in the Aurangabad District of Maharashtra State. Ajanta has twenty-nine caves.
- It has four chaitya caves datable to the earlier phase, i.e., the second and the first century BCE (Cave Nos. 10 and 9) and the later phase, i.e., the fifth century CE (Cave Nos. 19 and 26).
- Chaityas are the place of worship whereas Viharas are used by wandering monks to rest during the rainy season.
- Large chaitya viharas are decorated with sculptures and paintings. Ajanta is the only surviving example of a painting of the first century BCE and the fifth century CE.
- The paintings cover the walls, pillars, and ceilings to illustrate scenes from the life of Buddha and his previous lives, comprising the jatakas and avadanas.
- It was patronised by Satavahanas, Vakatakas and Guptas.

110. Correct Option: (d)

Explanation:

- **Statement 3 is incorrect:** The concept of a hanging balcony belongs to the Rajput style of architecture.
- **Statement 4 is incorrect:** Sikh style architecture is characterized by the use of shallow cornices.

Supplementary Notes:

Mughal Architecture

- The Mughals were great patrons of art and architecture. Under them, architecture regained its place of importance, as new buildings were built with great vision and artistic inspiration.
- Akbar took a keen interest in the development of art and architecture during his reign. The principal feature of the constructions during Akbar's reign was the use of red sandstone. He also introduced the use of the 'Tudor arch' (four-centered arches).
- Agra Fort was one of the first constructions that started during the reign of Akbar. However, most of the structures present inside the fort were done during the reign of Shah Jahan. The gardens inside the fort are built using the Charbagh style.
- One of the highlights of Indo-Islamic architecture was the creation of a new capital city by Akbar at Fatehpur Sikri. Important buildings inside the city include Buland Darwaza, Salim Chisti's Tomb, Panch Mahal, Ibadat Khana, etc.
- During the reign of Jahangir, architecture took a back seat as he focused more on paintings and other forms of art. However, he oversaw the construction of some noteworthy monuments including Akbar's tomb in Sikandra. He also built his own tomb at Lahore. Further, he developed a number of gardens during his reign, e.g. the Shalimar Bagh in Kashmir.

Sikh Style Architecture

- Sikh style of architecture developed in the region of modern day Punjab. It was heavily influenced by the Mughal style of architecture. Some of the features of the Sikh school are:
  - The use of multiple Chhatris or kiosks on the top of the construction.
  - Use of shallow cornices.
  - The buildings had fluted domes, which were generally covered by brass and copper guilds for decoration and support.
  - The arches were decorated by the use of numerous foliations.

Rajput Style of Architecture

- The Rajput constructions of the period were also influenced by the Mughal style, but were unique in the size and scope of their constructions. They generally undertook the building of imposing palaces and forts. Some of the unique features of Rajput architecture are as follows:
  - They introduced the concept of hanging balcony, which were constructed in all shapes and sizes.
  - The cornices were built in the shape of an arch such that the shadow took the shape of a bow.

111. Correct Option: (a)

Explanation:

- **Statement 2 is incorrect:** The Ashokan pillars were independently erected by royal diction while Achaemenian pillars were generally attached to state Buildings.

Supplementary Notes:

Difference between Ashokan Pillars and Achaemenian Pillars

Basis	Ashokan Pillars	Achaemenian Pillars
Composition	The shaft of the Ashokan pillars was monolithic, i.e. they were inscribed from a single piece of stone, mainly chunar sandstones.	The shaft of Achaemenian pillars was made up of various pieces of sandstone cemented together.
Location	The Ashokan pillars were independently erected by royal diction.	The Achaemenian pillars were generally attached to state Buildings.

112. Correct Option: (c)

Explanation:

- **Statement 2 is incorrect:** The entrance of a garbhagriha in a Nagara Temple had sculptures of river goddesses (Ganga and Yamuna) while that of Dravida Temple had sculptures of Dwaarpal, Mithun and Yakshas.

Supplementary Notes:

Temple Architecture

- Nagara style of architecture was a distinct style of Temple architecture developed in the northern parts of India by the 5th century AD.
- Some of the features of the Nagara style are:
  - The Temples generally followed the Panchayatan style of Temple making, which consisted of subsidiary shrines laid out in a crucified ground plan with respect to the principal shrine.
  - Presence of assembly halls or mandaps in front of the principal shrine.
  - Outside the garbhagriha, images of the river goddesses, Ganga and Yamuna, were placed.
  - There were no water tanks or reservoirs present in the Temple premises.
  - The Temples were generally built on upraised platforms.
- Dravida style of architecture was a distinct style of Temple architecture developed in southern parts of India.
- Ome of the features of Dravida style are:
  - the Dravidian Temples were surrounded by high boundary walls.
  - The front wall had a high entrance gateway known as the gopuram.
  - The entrance of the garbhagriha had sculptures of Dwaarpal, Mithun and yakshas.
  - In the Dravidian style, the spire is in the form of a stepped pyramid that rises up linearly rather than curved. It is known as vimana.
  - The presence of a water tank inside the Temple enclosure was a unique feature of the Dravidian style.

113. Correct Option: (c)

Explanation:

- **Statement 1 is incorrect:** The art of Bharhut primarily represents the central Indian indigenous elements.
- **Statement 2 is incorrect:** The life-size carvings of yakshas and devatas show the sculptor's zeal for representing minute details, such as marks painted on the body or decorative patterns on turban or cloth, though knowledge of correct human anatomy is absent.

Supplementary Notes:

Bharhut Sculpture

- Bharhut art, post-Mauryan art, is vital and sophisticated. All the figures in the panels are dignified, refined and lively, radiating delight. Men and women are graceful, animals are vigorous and the vegetation is joyous. The figures are all characterized by certain rigidity and are completely archaic in character. The exquisite precision of caring, the delight in surface decoration and the essentially shallow character of the relief make it appear likely that the sculpture is a translation into stone of woodcarver's or ivory carver's technique.
- The sculptured railing at Bharhut – although clearly derived from its wooden prototypes –provides a firm starting point for observing salient stylistic and iconographic characteristics of Indian art. The railings contain numerous birth stories of the Buddha's previous lives or Jataka tales. The Bharhut Stupa represents the aniconic phase of Buddhist art.
- The art of Bharhut primarily represents the central Indian indigenous elements. The round human faces, wearing elaborate headdresses, the flat bodily forms, and the absence of proper perspective are the main features of this art.
- The compositions usually lack symmetry. There is a tendency towards overcrowding. The Bharhut art, primarily meant for the masses, is more inclined toward the folk elements than the refined aesthetic sense. The linear treatment of human figures with a rough depiction of the costumes is, however, compensated by the graphic details of interesting scenes and decorative patterns.

- The life-size carvings of yakshas and devatas show the sculptor's zeal for representing minute details, such as marks painted on the body or decorative patterns on turban or cloth, though knowledge of correct human anatomy is absent.

114. Correct Option: (a)

Explanation:

- **Statement 2 is incorrect:** It belongs to Nagara group of Temples of North India.

Supplementary Notes:

Mini Khajuraho

- The Archaeological Survey of India is restoring the Markandeshwar group of Temples in the Gadchiroli district of Maharashtra.
- This group of Temples were built between the 9th and 12th centuries and may have had up to 24 different Temples.
- It gets its name from the main Temple dedicated to Lord Shiva called Markandeshwar or Markandadeo Temple, which lies in Markanda village on the banks of the Wainganga river.
- They are famously known as the 'mini Khajuraho' or 'Khajuraho of Vidarbha'. They belong to the Saiva, Vaishnava and Sakti faith.
- The Temples belong to the Nagara group of the Temple of North India with ardhamandapa, mandapa, antarala, and garbhagriha forming the component of entire setup.
- It is believed that a lightning strike about 200 years ago led to the partial collapse of the shikhara. Then a Gond ruler about 120 years ago tried to restore the Temple.

115. Correct Option: (d)

Explanation:

- **Statement 1 is incorrect:** Ashoka's name does not occur only in those inscription found in north or north-west India.
- **Statement 2 is incorrect:** The title 'Devanampiya' or 'dear to gods' adopted by Ashoka was not unique but also adopted by his ancestors.

Supplementary Notes:

Ashokan Inscriptions

- The history of Ashoka is reconstructed on the basis of his inscriptions which is thirty nine in number. These inscription are classified into Major Rock Edicts, Minor Rock Edicts, Separate Rock Edicts, Major Pillar Edicts, and Minor Pillar Edicts.
- The name Ashoka occurs in copies of Minor Rock Edict I found at three places in Karnataka and at one in MP. Thus, altogether, the name Ashoka occurs four times.
- It is significant that Ashoka's name does not occur in any of his inscriptions from north or north-west India.
- The inscriptions which do not carry his name mention only 'devanampiya piyadasi', dear to the gods, and leave out the name Ashoka. The title devanampiya or 'dear to gods' adopted by Ashoka was not unique but also adopted by his ancestors. However, 'piyadasi' or 'good looking' seems to have been his unique title.
- Ashokan inscriptions have been found in India, Nepal, Pakistan, and Afghanistan. Altogether, they appear at forty-seven places, and the total number of versions is 182, including two edicts which are considered spurious.
- It is significant that Ashokan inscriptions which were generally located on ancient highways, have been found at six places in Afghanistan. Composed in Prakrit, they were written in Brahmi script in the greater part of the subcontinent. However, in the north-western part of the subcontinent they appeared in Aramaic language and Kharoshthi script, and in Afghanistan they were written in both Aramaic and Greek scripts and languages.
- He was the first Indian king to speak directly to the people through his inscriptions which carry royal orders. The inscriptions throw light on Ashoka's career, his external and domestic policies, and the extent of his empire.

116. Correct Option: (b)

Explanation:

- **Statement 2 is incorrect:** Gupta period was poor in terms of architecture.

Supplementary Notes:

Gupta Architecture

- The Gupta period was poor in terms of architecture.
  - All that we find are a few Temples made of brick in UP and a stone Temple.
  - The brick Temples of Bhitargaon in Kanpur, Bhitari in Ghazipur, and Deogarh in Jhansi may be mentioned.
  - The Buddhist University at Nalanda was set up in the fifth century, and its earliest structure, made of brick, relates to this period.

Gupta Art

- The Gupta period is called the Golden Age of ancient India.
- Guptas possessed a large quantity of gold and they issued the largest number of gold coins which were called "dinaras" in their inscriptions.
- After the conquest of Gujarat, the Guptas issued a large number of silver coins mainly for local exchange, in which silver occupied an important position under the Western Kshatrapas.

- In contrast to those of the Kushans, the Gupta copper coins are very few in number. This would suggest that the use of money did not touch the common people as much as it did under the Kushans.

- Both Samudragupta and Chandragupta II were patrons of art and literature.
    - Samudragupta is represented on his coins playing the lute (vina), and Chandragupta II is credited with maintaining in his court nine luminaries.
- Buddhism gave great impetus to art in Maurya and post-Maurya times.
    - During the Gupta period a life-size copper image of the Buddha of more than 6 feet was made. It was discovered at Sultanganj near Bhagalpur, and is now displayed in Birmingham.
    - During the Gupta period beautiful images of the Buddha were fashioned at Sarnath and Mathura, but the finest specimens of Buddhist art in Gupta times are the Ajanta paintings.
    - They depict various events in the life of Gautama Buddha and the previous Buddhas whose birth stories are related in the Jatakas.
- As the Guptas supported Brahmanism, images of Vishnu, Shiva, and some other Hindu gods were fashioned for the first time during their period.
    - At many places, the entire pantheon is portrayed with the chief god at the centre surrounded by his retainers and subordinates.
    - The leading god is represented as large in size, with his retainers and subordinate gods drawn on a smaller scale.
    - This reflects clear social hierarchy and discrimination.

117. Correct Option: (c)

Explanation:

- Both statements are correct

Supplementary Notes:

Ashoka's Edicts

- There are a total of 33 inscriptions primarily classified into Major Rock Edicts, Minor Rock Edicts, Separate Rock Edicts, Major Pillar Edicts, and Minor Pillar Edicts.
- The edicts of the earlier half of his reign were inscribed on conveniently located rock surfaces and were widely distributed throughout the empire, especially in the areas of public settlements where people could easily read these edicts. Hence these are referred to as the Minor and Major Rock Edicts.
- Pillar edicts were mostly inscribed in the latter parts of his reign and were on well-polished sandstone monolithic pillars.
- These sandstones were quarried from the sites of Chunar, near Varanasi.
- Each pillar was surmounted with a finely sculpted animal capital and was largely confined to the Ganges plain.
- In his inscriptions, Brahmi, Kharosthi, Prakrit, Aramaic, and Greek languages have been used.
- These inscriptions were deciphered by James Prinsep in 1837 CE.
- There is no reference to the teachings of the Buddha in the Greek and Aramaic versions.
- Ashoka's inscriptions do not contain certain key ideas associated with the Buddha's teaching, such as the Eight-Fold Path, the Four Noble Truths, and the goal of Nibbana.
- However, there is definite Buddhist core ideology in his dhamma-focussed inscriptions.
- He was the first Indian king to speak directly to the people through his inscriptions which carry royal orders. The inscriptions throw light on Ashoka's career, his external and domestic polices, and the extent of his empire.

118. Correct Option: (c)

Explanation:

- **Statement 1 is incorrect:** While most of the Harappan seals were square triangular, rectangular and circular seals have also been found. Also besides steatite, chert, copper and terracotta seals have also been found.
- **Statement 2 is incorrect:** Compared to the bronze figures, the terracotta sculptures are less in number.
- **Statement 3 is incorrect:** Plain Pottery and Red-and-black pottery is associated with Indus Valley Civilisation.

Supplementary Notes:

Sculptures of Harappan Civilisation

- The Harappan sculptors were extremely adept at handling three dimensional volumes. The most commonly found were seals, bronze figures and potteries.
- **Seals:**
    - Archaeologists have found numerous seals of different shapes and sizes all across the excavation sites.
    - While most seals are square, it was found that triangular, rectangular and circular seals were also used. Steatite, a soft stone found in the river beds, was although the most common material used to make seals, yet agate, chert, copper, faience and terracotta seals have also been found.
    - Some instances of copper, gold and ivory seals have also been found.
    - Most seals have inscriptions in a pictographic script that is yet to be deciphered.

- Seals were primarily used for commercial purposes and helped in communication.
- Some seals with a hole on them have been found on dead bodies. This indicates they might have been used as amulets.
- Mathematical images have also been found on some seals, which might have been used for educational purposes as well.

- **Bronze Figures:**
  - The Harappan Civilisation saw a wide scale practice of bronze casting. The bronze statues were made using "lost wax technique" or "Cire Perdue". Bronze dancing girl of Mohenjo-daro, bronze bull of Kalibangan, etc. are examples of bronze figures.
- **Terracotta:**
  - Terracotta refers to the use of fire baked clay for making sculptures.
  - Compared to the bronze figures, the terracotta sculptures are less in number and crude in shape and form.
- **Pottery:**
  - The potteries found at the excavation sites can be broadly classified into two kinds – plain pottery and painted pottery. The painted pottery is also known as Red-and-Black pottery.
  - Most of the potteries that have been found are very fine wheel-made wares, with a very few being handmade.
- **Ornaments:**
  - The Harappans used a large variety of materials, from precious metals and gemstones to bones and even baked clay, to make ornaments.
  - Both men and women wore ornaments like necklaces, fillets, armlets and finger rings. Girdles, earrings and anklets were worn only by women.
  - The people of the time were conscious of fashion as well, as can be inferred from the different styles of hair and beard.

119. Correct Option: (b)

Explanation:

- **Statement 2 is incorrect:** Higher citadel in west and lower town in east.
- **Statement 4 is incorrect:** Doorways and windows rarely opened out into the main street, but faced side lanes to protect from the view of the passers-by.

Supplementary Notes:

Harappan Town Planning

- The Harappan culture was distinguished by its system of town planning. The overall layout of the Indus-Saraswati cities is distinguished by the orientation of streets and buildings, according to the cardinal directions – east-west, and north-south, thus forming a grid system, with roads cutting across one another virtually at right angles. Even the width of these streets was in a set ratio.
- Both Harappa and Mohenjōdaro had a higher western citadel or acropolis, and this was possibly occupied by members of the ruling class. Below the citadel in each city lay a lower town in the east with brick houses that were inhabited by the common people.
- The use of burnt bricks in the Harappan cities is remarkable because in the contemporary buildings of Egypt dried bricks were primarily used. We find the use of baked bricks in contemporary Mesopotamia, but they were used to a much larger extent in the Harappan cities. The doors windows were made of wood and mats.
- Doorways and windows rarely opened out into the main street, but faced side lanes. The view into the house was blocked by a wall or a room around the front door. This was done to protect the activities in the central courtyard from the view of passers-by.
- Many houses were at least two storied and some scholars think that some of the houses may have been three storied.
- Almost every house had a bathroom, and in some cases there is evidence of bathrooms on the first floor.
- The most striking feature of Harappan civilisation is the advanced drainage system. Small drains ran from each house and were connected to larger drains running alongside the main roads. The drains were loosely covered to allow regular cleaning and maintenance. The importance placed on health and hygiene – both public and private is quite impressive.

120. Correct Option: (a)

Explanation:

- **Option (a) is incorrect:** Alai Darwaza was built by Alauddin Khalji in 1311 and is made of red sandstone.

Supplementary Notes:

Sultanate Art and Architecture

- The art and architecture of the Delhi Sultanate period were distinct from the Indian style. The Turks introduced arches, domes, lofty towers, or minarets and decorations using the Arabic script.
- The most magnificent building of the 13th century was Qutub Minar, which was started by Aibak and completed by Iltutmish.
- Later, Alauddin Khalji added an entrance to the Qutub Minar called Alai Darwaza. The dome of this arch was built on scientific lines.
- The buildings of the Tughlaq period were constructed by combining arch and dome. The palace complex called Tughlaqabad with its beautiful lake was built during the period of Ghyasuddin Tughlaq.
- Muhammad bin Tughlaq built the tomb of Ghyasuddin on a high platform.

- The Kotla fort at Delhi was the creation of Firoz Tughlaq.

121. Correct Option: (c)

Explanation:

- Both statements are correct

Supplementary Notes:

Mogao Caves

- Dunhuang in China was a major point of intersection along the ancient Silk Road.
- Silk Road had played a foundational role in bringing about the Indian-China confluence of the past.
- Dunhuang houses the famous Mogao Caves.
- These caves are replete with Buddhist art and are located in the desert.
- The early caves show greater Indian and Western influence, while during the Tang Dynasty (618-906 C.E.), the influence of the Chinese painting styles of the imperial court is apparent.
- The art also reflects the changes in religious beliefs and rituals at the pilgrim site.
- In the early caves, jataka tales (previous lives of the Historical Buddha) were commonly depicted. During the Tang Dynasty, Buddhism became very popular.
- In terms of art, it was the Graeco-Buddhist Gandhara School, known for depicting Buddha in human form, that finally reached China, heavily influencing the emergence of what became known as Serendian art, embodying a powerful Chinese artistic tradition as well.
- The Mogao Caves are the best known of the Chinese Buddhist grottoes and, along with Longmen Grottoes and Yungang Grottoes, are one of the three famous ancient Buddhist sculptural sites of China.
- Mogao Caves reveal pivotal India-China Buddhist link.
- Mogao cave-Temples of Dunhuang are a World Heritage Site.

122. Correct Option: (b)

Explanation:

- Pair 3 and 4 are incorrectly matched:

A. Akbar	-	Buland Darwaza
B. Humayun	-	Jamali Mosque
C. Jahangir	-	Cimax of Painting
D. Shah Jahan	-	Moti Masjid at Agra

123. Correct Option: (a)

Explanation:

- **Statement 1 is incorrect:** Ashoka's greatest innovation was the substitution of stone for wood.
- **Statement 3 is incorrect:** Lomasha Risi Cave is located in the Barabara hills near Gaya whereas Dhauli Caves are near Bhubaneswar, Odisha.

Supplementary Notes:

Mauryan Art and Sculpture

- In the Mauryan period, important beginnings were made in rock-cut and stupa architecture.
- Ashoka's greatest innovation was the substitution of stone for wood and brick. Ashokan pillars at Rampurva, Lauriya Nandangarh, and Sarnath present excellent examples of stone sculptures that developed in this period. All these pillars are circular and monolithic, and are made of sandstone found at Chunar, near Mirzapur in UP.
- The Maurya period also saw the beginning of rock-cut architecture. The rock-cut architecture of Lomasha Risi Cave in the Barabara hills near Gaya, and the majestic Dhauli Caves (near Bhubaneswar, Odisha which contains the rock sculpture of the front part of an elephant) is magnificent.
- The famous Vajrasana (throne of meditation) at the Mahabodhi Temple at Bodh Gaya probably belonged to this period.
- Among several stone and terracotta sculptures of this period, the polished stone sculpture of a female known as the Didarganj Yakshini (demi-gods and spirits; Yakshinis are generally regarded as fertility deities, and the female counterpart of Yakshas, who were the deities connected with water, trees, forest, wilderness, and fertility) is the most famous one.
- Another important polished Chunar sandstone sculpture is of the torso of a nude male figure found at Lohanipur in Patna.
- The stone portrait of Ashoka found at Kanaganahalli (near Sannati, Karnataka) is also spectacular.
- Universities of Taxila, Ujjain, and Varanasi were the famous centres of learning.
- In the field of literature, Bhadrabahu's Kalpasutra is attributed to the Mauryan period. Lomasha Risi and Sudama Caves of Gaya are other great examples of wooden architectural heritage.

124. Correct Option: (c)

Explanation:

- Both statements are correct

Supplementary Notes:

Rare life-size stucco Buddhist sculpture in Telangana

- Indian archaeologists recently unearthed a rare life-sized stucco sculpture from a Buddhist site at Phanigiri in Suryapet, Telangana.
- Till date it is the biggest stucco sculpture found in India. It is about 1.73 metres in height and 35 cm in width.
- As per archaeologists, the life-size figurine represents a Bhodhisattva in Jathaka Chakra.
- It was created nearly 1,700 years ago by craftsmen at Phanigiri at peak of Ikshavaku Dynasty.

125. Correct Option: (c)

Explanation:

- **Statement 1 is incorrect:** Drainage systems were not unique to the larger cities, but were found in smaller settlements as well.

Supplementary Notes:

Harappan Phase

- **Drainage:**
  - About the drains, Mackay noted: "It is certainly the most complete ancient system as yet discovered." Every house was connected to the street drains. The main channels were made of bricks set in mortar and were covered with loose bricks that could be removed for cleaning. In some cases, limestone was used for the covers. House drains first emptied into a sump or cesspit into which solid matter settled while waste water flowed out into the street drains. Very long drainage channels were provided at intervals with sumps for cleaning. It is wonder of archaeology that "little heaps of material, mostly sand, have frequently been found lying alongside drainage channels, which shows ... that the debris was not always carted away when the drain was cleared".
  - Drainage systems were not unique to the larger cities, but were found in smaller settlements as well.
- **Decision Making:**
  - There are indications of complex decisions being taken and implemented in Harappan society. Take for instance, the extraordinary uniformity of Harappan artefacts as evident in pottery, seals, weights and bricks. Notably, bricks, though obviously not produced in any single centre, were of a uniform ratio throughout the region, from Jammu to Gujarat. We have also seen that settlements were strategically set up in specific locations for various reasons. Besides, labour was mobilised for making bricks and for the construction of massive wall sand platforms.
- **Cholistan:**
  - There is evidence that by c. 1800 BCE most of the Mature Harappan sites in regions such as Cholistan had been abandoned. Simultaneously, there was an expansion of population into new settlements in Gujarat, Haryana and western Uttar Pradesh

126. Correct Option: (a)

Explanation:

- **Statement 2 is incorrect:** Vittala Temple is located in Hampi.

Supplementary Notes:

Vittala Temple, Hampi

- The Vittala Temple or Vitthala Temple in Hampi is an ancient monument that is well-known for its exceptional architecture and unmatched craftsmanship.
- It is considered to be one of the largest and the most famous structure in Hampi.
- The Temple is located in the north eastern part of Hampi, near the banks of the Tungabhadra River.
- The iconic Temple has amazing stone structures such as the incomparable stone chariot and the fascinating musical pillars.
- This predominant monument of Hampi is a major attraction of the ruined town and is a must-see for visitors and tourists.

127. Correct Option: (d)

Explanation:

- **Statement 2 is incorrect:** Ashoka spoke of several features of Dhamma in his edicts. He did not clearly define what Dhamma was.

Supplementary Notes:

Ashokan Edicts

- The great Emperor Ashoka, the third monarch of the Maurya Dynasty converted to Buddhism after witnessing the horrific effects of war in Kalinga. He became a champion and patron of Buddhism and strove to spread Dhamma throughout his empire and beyond.
- He erected pillars and edicts all over the subcontinent and even in modern-day Afghanistan, Nepal, Bangladesh, and Pakistan to spread the Buddha's word. James Prinsep, a British antiquary and colonial administrator was the first person to decipher Ashoka's edicts. These inscriptions are the first tangible evidence of Buddhism.
- More than religious discourses, they talk about the moral duties of the people, how to conduct life, Ashoka's desire to be a good and benevolent ruler, and about Ashoka's work towards this end.
- Ashoka used Dhamma as an ideology for ensuring coalescence in the empire. Dhamma became the central theme of the edicts issued by Ashoka.
- He categorically called himself an 'upasaka' or a lay Buddhist devotee. The minor rock edict at Maski more specifically labels him as a lay worshipper of the Buddha. The edicts leave little room for doubt about Ashoka's personal leaning to Buddhism.
- Ashoka used edicts to explain various features of the Dhamma such as respect towards elders, generosity towards Brahmanas and those who renounced worldly life, treating slaves and servants kindly, and respect for religions and traditions other than one's own.

- Ashoka only spoke of Dhamma's various features rather than defining it.

128. Correct Option: (a)

Explanation:

- **Option (a) is correct:** All these are the features of Gol Gumbad.

Supplementary Notes:

Information regarding Culture Contribution of Deccan States

- The Deccan Sultanates contributed greatly in the fields of art, music, literature and architecture.
- One such cultural contribution includes the development of the Dakhani language which was originated under the rulers of the Bahmani Kingdom. The language was drawn from Arabic, Persian, Marathi, Kannada and Telugu and later developed into an independent literary and spoken language known as Dakhani Urdu.
- Flourishment of the Deccani miniature paintings in the courts of Ahmadnagar, Bijapur and Golconda along with the construction of the architectural splendours like Char Minar and Gol Gumbaz is another major cultural contribution of the Deccan Sultanates.
- Gol Gumbad is situated in Bijapur, district of Karnataka.
- It is the mausoleum of Muhammed Adil Shah, the 7th sultan of the Adil Shahi Dynasty of Bijapur (1498-1686).
- The tomb is a complex building such as a gateway, a Naqqar Khana, a mosque and a sarai located within a large walled garden.
- Gumbad is a square building topped with a circular drum over which rests a majestic dome, giving the building its nomenclature.
- It is built of dark grey basalt and decorated plaster work. The dome of Gol Gumbad is the largest in the world.
- The building has an amazing acoustical system. Along with the drum of the dome, there is a whispering gallery where sounds get magnified and echoed many times over.
- While its structural peculiarities of dome, arches, geometric proportions and load bearing techniques suggest Timurid and Persian styles, it is made of local material and is decorated with surface embellishments popular in Deccan.

129. Correct Option: (b)

Supplementary Notes:

- The main architectural features of Odisha Temples are classified in three orders, i.e., rekhapida, pidhadeul and khakra. Most of the main Temple sites are located in ancient Kalinga—modern Puri District, including Bhubaneswar or ancient Tribhuvanesvara, Puri and Konark.
- The Temples of Odisha constitute a distinct substyle within the nagara order. In general, here the shikhara, called deul in Odisha, is vertical almost until the top when it suddenly curves sharply inwards. Deuls are preceded, as usual, by mandapas called jagamohana in Odisha.
- Odisha Temples usually have boundary walls.

130. Correct Option: (b)

Explanation:

- Option (b) is correct: Krishna I was also a great Rashtrakutas conqueror. He defeated the Gangas and the Eastern Chalukyas of Vengi. He built the magnificent rock-cut monolithic Kailasa Temple at Ellora.

CONCEPT REVISION

Here is the list of concepts that have been covered as part of the previous exercise. Revise and self-reflect on your concepts you covered.

- Disintegration of Gupta Empire ☐
- Lion Capital at Sarnath ☐
- Khajuraho Temples ☐
- Mathura School of Art ☐
- Gandhara School of Art ☐
- Amravati School of Art ☐
- Seals found at Indus Valley Civilisation ☐
- Rock-cut caves ☐
- Dashvatara Temple ☐
- Temple Architecture ☐
- Rajput Architecture ☐
- Monolithic Kailasa Temple ☐
- Cave Temple ☐
- 'Great living Chola Temples' ☐
- 'Group of Monuments at Pattadakal ☐
- World's largest monolithic statue of Buddha ☐
- Katora houz ☐
- 'Khanqah' ☐
- Allahabad Pillar Inscription ☐
- Architecture of Vijaynagar Empire ☐
- Modern Architecture ☐
- Bronze statue of Nataraja ☐
- Chulakoka Devta ☐
- Bharhut Art ☐
- Satavahana Sculptures ☐
- Harappan town planning ☐

7.2 PAINTINGS, POTTERY AND NUMISMATIC

QUESTIONS

1. With reference to the caves in India, which of the following statement/s is/are correct?

1. The Lakhudiyar cave paintings in Jammu and Kashmir belong to Palaeolithic age.
2. Bhimbetka caves are located in the Vindhya Hills in Madhya Pradesh.
3. Ellora Caves are located in Chamadari Hills.

Select the correct answer using the codes given below:

(a) 1 only (b) 2 and 3 only
(c) 1 and 3 only (d) 1, 2 and 3

2. Which of the following is/are the characteristic features of the pre-historic art?

1. Animal figures were represented in their paintings.
2. Paintings mainly depicted socio-economic life of people of that era.

Select the correct answer using the code given below:

(a) 1 only (b) 2 only
(c) Both 1 and 2 (d) Neither 1 nor 2

3. Which of the following statements regarding Mughal School of painting is/are correct?

1. During the reign of Akbar, paintings were based on the Mahabharata, Ramayana and Persian epics.
2. During the reign of Shah Jahan, paintings were based on nature such as birds, flowers, animals, etc.
3. During the reign of Jahangir, themes were based on musical parties, ascetics gathered around a fire, etc.

Select the correct answer using the code given below:

(a) 1 only (b) 2 and 3 only
(c) 1 and 3 only (d) 1, 2 and 3

4. Which of the following pairs is/are correctly matched?

Paintings		Patronized by
1. Ahmednagar Paintings	-	Hussain Nizam Shah I.
2. Bijapur Paintings	-	Ali Adil Shah I.
3. Golconda Paintings	-	Qutb Shahi rulers.

Select the correct answer using the code given below:

(a) 1 only (b) 1 and 3 only
(c) 2 only (d) 1, 2 and 3

5. Which of these pairs is/are correctly matched?

Historic Age		Pottery type
1. Chalcolithic	-	Black and Red ware pottery
2. Harappan	-	Polished ware with rough surface
3. Vedic	-	Painted Gray ware
4. Later Vedic		North Black Polished ware

Select the correct answer using the code given below:

(a) 1 only (b) 1, 2 and 3 only
(c) 2 and 4 only (d) 1, 2, 3 and 4

6. Which of the following Pre-Historic Period Paintings show mutual exchange of requirements of the cave dwellers (hilly region) with settled agricultural communities of the plains?

(a) Palaeolithic (b) Mesolithic
(c) Chalcolithic (d) Neolithic

7. Consider the following statements related to the coinage of ancient era:

1. The Gupta Empire produced large numbers of gold coins depicting the Gupta kings performing rituals.
2. Kushan coins contained inscriptions of Siva, Buddha and Kartikeya.
3. The Turkish Sultans of Delhi introduced Islamic Calligraphy on coins for the first time in India.

Which of the above statement/s is/are correct?

(a) 2 only (b) 1 and 2 only
(c) 2 and 3 only (d) 1, 2 and 3

8. Consider the following statement regarding Deccan School of Painting:

1. It was inspired by Mughal School of Painting.
2. They are mainly embellished with precious and semi-precious stones.

Which of the following statement/s is/ are incorrect?

(a) 1 only (b) 2 only
(c) Both 1 and 2 (d) Neither 1 nor 2

9. Consider the following statements regarding Thanjavur Paintings:

1. It has the influence of Deccani, Vijayanagar, Maratha and even European styles of painting.
2. It has been recognized as a Geographical indication by the Government of India.
3. It is well known for its famous gold coating which prolongs the life of the artefact.

Which of the above statement/s is/are correct?

(a) 2 only (b) 2 and 3 only
(c) 1 and 3 only (d) 1, 2 and 3

10. Consider the following with reference to the 'Mural Paintings in India':

1. The earliest surviving paintings in the Indian subcontinent are from Harappan period.
2. Murals paintings depict mainly religious themes of Buddhist, Jain and Hindu religions.

Which of the statements given above is/are correct?

(a) 1 only (b) 2 only
(c) Both 1 and 2 (d) Neither 1 nor 2

11. With reference to 'Pahari School of Painting', consider the following:

1. Pahari painting is an Indian painting done mostly in fresco forms.
2. Mughal painting grew out of the Pahari painting.
3. Bundi school of painting is an example of Pahari painting.

Which of the statements given above is/are incorrect?

(a) 1 only (b) 1 and 3 only
(c) 2 and 3 only (d) 1, 2 and 3

12. Consider the following statements with reference to the unique Pietra Dura style of Art:

1. It includes floral designs made of semi-precious stones on the White Marble walls.
2. The Pietra Dura style was used on a large scale in the Moti Masjid.

Which of the above statement/s is/are correct?

(a) 1 only (b) 2 only
(c) Both 1 and 2 (d) Neither 1 nor 2

13. Consider the following pairs:

Folk Paintings:		**State**
A. Patachitra Painting	:	Odisha
B. Patua Art	:	Maharashtra
C. Paitkar Painting	:	Bengal

Which of the pairs given above is/are correctly matched?

(a) 1 only (b) 2 only
(c) 2 and 3 only (d) 1, 2 and 3

14. Consider the following statements regarding cave paintings in India:

1. Ajanta Caves is the only surviving example of painting of the first century BC.
2. Sittannavasal is a rock-cut Jain Temple of the Pandyan era.
3. The world's oldest known cave paintings are found at Bhimbhetka.

Which of the above statements are correct?

(a) 1 and 2 only (b) 2 and 3 only
(c) 1 and 3 only (d) 1, 2 and 3

15. The painting of Bodhisattva Padmapani is one of the most famous and oft-illustrated paintings at:

(a) Ajanta (b) Badami
(c) Bagh (d) Ellora

16. Consider the following statements about Ashokan Edicts:

1. They are mostly written in Pali in Brahmi script.
2. They mention that medical care provision is an important function of the state.
3. They provide crucial information about the Mauryan Empire.

Which of the above statements is/ are correct?

(a) 3 only (b) 2 and 3 only
(c) 1 and 2 only (d) 1, 2 and 3

17. The silver coins of the Gupta period were known as

(a) Dinar (b) Rupyaka
(c) Satamana (d) Karsharpana

18. The decimal numeral system, including the concept of zero was invented in India during the period of which one of the following dynasties?

(a) Saka (b) Gupta
(c) Pala (d) Chola

19. With reference to the Indian history of art and culture, match the following pairs:

List I		**List II**
1. A grand image	-	Mount Abu of Buddha's Mahaparinirvana
2. Huge image of	-	Udayagiri Varaha Avatar (boar incarnation) of Vishnu - sculpted on rock
3. "Arjuna's	-	Mamallapuram & Penance" "Descent of Ganga"

Which of the pairs given above is/are correctly matched?

(a) 1 and 2 only (b) 3 only
(c) 2 and 3 only (d) 1, 2 and 3

20. Which of the following folk painting styles started from paintings of mud walls of huts?

(a) Madhubani (b) Phad
(c) Kolam (d) Warli

21. Which of the following region is not matched correctly with painting?

(a) Kalighat – West Bengal
(b) Phad – Rajasthan
(c) Kalamkari – Bihar
(d) Madhubani – Bihar

22. Consider the following statements regarding Indo Greek coins:

1. Coins were mainly made of silver, copper, nickel and lead.
2. Coins of Greek Kings in India were bilingual.
3. Only the king had the right to issue coins and the same currency was accepted in his kingdom.

Which of the above statement/s is/are correct?

(a) 1 and 2 only (b) 1 and 3 only
(c) 2 and 3 only (d) 1, 2 and 3

23. **If you find a coin from a Gupta period, you can see inscribed in it:**
1. Hunting king
2. Pictures of Hindu goddesses
3. King performing ashvamedha

Select the correct option using the codes given below:
(a) 1 and 2 only (b) 1 and 3 only
(c) 2 and 3 only (d) 1, 2 and 3

24. **Consider the following statement:**
1. Alauddin Khalji is best remembered for the experiment of market control through the introduction of token currency in the form of bronze and copper coins.
2. The silver tanka and copper jital was introduced by Iltutmish.

Which of the above statement/s is/are incorrect?
(a) 1 only (b) 2 only
(c) Both 1 and 2 (d) Neither 1 nor 2

25. **Consider the following statement pertaining to Mughal Coins:**
1. Akbar issued the "Ilahi coins" to propagate his new religious idea of Din-e-Illahı.
2. Zodiac sign on the coins was minted during the time of Shahjahan.
3. Sher Shah Suri introduced the "Rupya" which was made up of silver and weighed around 11 gms.

Which of the above statement/s is/are incorrect?
(a) 1 only (b) 2 only
(c) 3 only (d) 2 and 3 only

26. **With reference to miniature paintings in South India, consider the following statements:**
1. South Indian miniatures differ from North Indian ones due to their heavy use of gold.
2. Most of the Tanjore paintings depicted smiling Krishna in various poses.

Which of the above statement is/are correct?
(a) 1 only (b) 2 only
(c) Both 1 and 2 (d) Neither 1 nor 2

27. **Consider the following statements regarding 'Painted Grey Ware':**
1. It is associated with Harrapan Valley civilisation.
2. It has a glossy surface with a thin core and ware was usually unpainted.
3. It succeeded the Northern Black Polished Ware culture.

Which of the above statement/s is/are incorrect?
(a) 1 only (b) 1 and 3 only
(c) 2 and 3 only (d) 1, 2 and 3

28. **Consider the following statements regarding Sittanavasal cave paintings:**
1. They depict Buddhist and Jataka tales.
2. The paintings in these caves belong to Chola period.
3. The central element of the paintings in Sittanavasal is a pond with lotuses.

Which of the above statement/s is/are incorrect?
(a) 1 only (b) 1 and 2 only
(c) 2 and 3 only (d) 1, 2 and 3

29. **Consider the following statements regarding the paintings of Mughal era:**
1. Paintings in this period glorified the ruler rather than depicting God.
2. The Mughal paintings reached its zenith in the period of Akbar.
3. Jahangir established a formal artistic studio called Tasvir Khana where the artists developed their own styles.

Which of the above statement/s is/are correct?
(a) 1 only (b) 1 and 2 only
(c) 1 and 3 only (d) 2 and 3 only

30. **With reference to the folk paintings in India, consider the following statements:**
1. Kalighat paintings have a close resemblance to the mural paintings of Bhimbetka.
2. Warli paintings are first of its kind in the country to express subaltern sentiments.
3. Pattachitra paintings are inspired from Jagannath and Vaishnava cult.

Which of the above statement is/are correct?
(a) 1 and 2 only (b) 2 only
(c) 1 and 3 only (d) 3 only

31. **Which of the following pairs is/are correctly matched?**

Paintings	Patronized by
1. Ahmednagar Paintings	1. Hussain Nizam Shah I.
2. Bijapur Paintings	2. Ali Adil Shah I.
3. Golconda Paintings	3. Qutb Shahi rulers.

Select the correct answer using the code given below:
(a) 1 only (b) 1 and 3 only
(c) 2 only (d) 1, 2 and 3

32. **Consider the following statements about Bhimbetka cave painting:**
1. The rock paintings have numerous layers belonging to various epochs of time, ranging from the Upper Palaeolithic to medieval periods.
2. Both animals and humans were depicted in these painting.

Which of the above statements is/are true?
(a) 1 only (b) 2 only
(c) Both 1 and 2 (d) Neither 1 nor 2

33. **Even though the medieval period was dominated by the Mughal style of paintings, numerous imperial schools developed their own styles. In this context, consider the following statements:**

1. The famous Bani-Thani painting belongs to the Bundi School.
2. Kangra art, like the art of Ajanta is essentially an art of line.

Which of the above statements is/are correct?

(a) 1 only (b) 2 only
(c) Both 1 and 2 (d) Neither 1 nor 2

34. With reference to miniature paintings in south India, consider the following statements:

1. South Indian miniatures differ from north Indian ones due to their heavy use of gold.
2. South Indian miniatures concentrated on painting the rulers who patronized them.

Which of the above statements is/are correct?

(a) 1 only (b) 2 only
(c) Both 1 and 2 (d) Neither 1 nor 2

35. Consider the following statements regarding Red and Black Pottery:

1. It used black colour to paint the background and red paint was used to draw designs.
2. Trees, birds, animal figures and geometrical patterns were the recurring themes on them.

Which of the above statements is/are correct?

(a) 1 only (b) 2 only
(c) Both 1 and 2 (d) Neither 1 nor 2

36. With reference to the Seals of Indus Valley Civilisation, consider the following statements:

1. Steatite was the most common material used to make seals.
2. Pictographic script inscribed on the seals is not yet deciphered.
3. The common animal motifs found on seals were a unicorn, humped bull, rhinoceros, tiger, cow, etc.

Which of the above statements are correct?

(a) 1 and 2 only (b) 1 and 3 only
(c) 2 and 3 only (d) 1, 2 and 3

37. An important piece of Chola sculpture was the bronze sculpture of Nataraja. In this context consider the following statements:

1. Shiva in this sculpture is associated with the end of the cosmic world.
2. Shiva is depicted as suppressing the ignorance of an individual.
3. The bhujangatrasita stance of Shiva implies kicking away illusion from the devotee's mind.

Which of the above statements is/are correct?

(a) 1 only (b) 1 and 3 only
(c) 2 only (d) 1, 2 and 3

38. Mural paintings were executed on walls of caves or Temple walls. In light of this, consider the following statements:

1. Each woman is characterized by a different hairstyle in the Ajanta cave paintings.
2. The paintings in Ellora caves are related to Buddhism, Jainism, and Hinduism.
3. Sittanavasal Caves in Tamil Nadu are known for the paintings in the Jain Temples.

Which of the above statements is/are correct?

(a) 1 only (b) 1 and 3 only
(c) 2 only (d) 1, 2 and 3

39. Consider the following statements regarding pre-historic paintings:

1. The pre-historic paintings were generally executed on rocks.
2. The most common scene depicted in these paintings is of group hunting.
3. Animals are only drawn in bold outline while human bodies are filled in completely.
4. Bhimbetka in Madhya Pradesh is an important site for these paintings.

Which of the above statements is/are correct?

(a) 1 and 3 only (b) 1, 2 and 4 only
(c) 2 and 4 only (d) 1, 2, 3 and 4

40. Consider the following statements with reference to the role of Central Asia in Indian history:

1. Indo-Greeks were first to use gold coins.
2. Patanjali in his Mahabhasya refers to the Kushanas as Anirvasita Shudras'.
3. An inscription at Takht-i- Bahi, recovered near Peshawar is related to Parthians.
4. Shaka Kshatrapas were involved in continuous conflict with the Satavahanas.

Which of the above statements is/are correct?

(a) 1, 3 and 4 only (b) 1, 2 and 3 only
(c) 2, 3 and 4 only (d) 1, 2, 3 and 4

41. As per Indian Cultural history "Kulhadar Group" is associated with?

(a) A group of musicians in North West India
(b) A group of miniature paintings
(c) Classical vocalists of South India
(d) Monuments built using pietra dura tradition in Central India

SOLUTIONS

1. Correct Option: (b)

Supplementary Notes:

The different caves are explained below

Lakhudiyar cave paintings:

- **Statement 1 is incorrect:** The rock shelters on banks of the River Suyal at Lakhudiyar, about twenty kilometres on the Almora-Barrachina road (Uttarkhand), bear these prehistoric paintings. 'Lakhudiyar' literally means one lakh caves. The paintings here can be divided into three categories: man, animal and geometric patterns in white, black and red ochre. Humans are represented in stick-like forms.

Bhimbetka caves:

- **Statement 2 is correct:** Among the earliest cave shelters, the largest and most spectacular rock-shelter is located in the Vindhya hills at Bhimbetka in Madhya Pradesh. These hill ranges are full of Palaeolithic and Mesolithic remains. Bhimbetka is located forty five kilometres south of Bhopal, in an area of ten square kilometres, having about eight hundred rock shelters, five hundred of which bear paintings.

Ellora Caves:

- **Statement 3 is correct:** Another important cave site located in Aurangabad District is Ellora. It is located a hundred kilometres from Ajanta and has thirty-two Buddhist, Brahmanical and Jain caves. It is a unique art-historical site in the country as it has monastries associated with the three religions dating from the fifth century CE onwards to the eleventh century CE. The famous Ellora caves are located in the lap of the Chamadari hills.

2. **Correct Option: (c)**

Supplementary Notes:

Some of the characteristics of these early paintings are:

- **Statement 1 is correct:** The paintings of the Upper Palaeolithic phase are linear representations, in green and dark red, of huge animal figures, such as bisons, elephants, tigers, rhinos and boars besides stick-like human figures. A few are wash paintings but mostly they are filled with geometric patterns. The green paintings are of dancers and the red ones of hunters.
- Wavy lines, rectangular filled geometric designs and a group of dots also can be seen.
- Superimposition of paintings – earliest is black, then red and later white.
- The paintings mainly consist of man's struggle for survival. Hunting scenes pre-dominate.
- Paintings have 3 motifs – MAN, ANIMAL and GEOMETRIC PATTERN.
- The largest number of paintings belong to Period II that covers the Mesolithic paintings. During this period the themes multiply but the paintings are smaller in size. Hunting scenes predominate.
- **Statement 2 is correct:** The hunting scenes depict people hunting in groups, armed with barbed spears, pointed sticks, arrows and bows. In some paintings these primitive men are shown with traps and snares probably to catch animals.
- Some of the animal paintings, especially in the hunting scenes, show a fear of animals, but many others show a feeling of tenderness and love for them. There are also a few engravings representing mainly animals.
- Though animals were painted in a naturalistic style, humans were depicted only in a stylistic manner. Women are painted both as nude and clothed. The young and the old equally find place in these paintings. Children are painted running, jumping and playing. Community dances provide a common theme.

3. **Correct Option: (a)**

Supplementary Notes:

Mughal School of Painting

- Mughal School of Painting: Considered to be a landmark in the history of painting in India the Mughal School of Painting originated in the reign of Akbar in 1560 AD.
- **Akbar:**
    - Akbar was keenly interested in the art of painting and architecture. While a boy he had taken lessons in drawing. In the beginning of his rule an atelier of painting was established under the supervision of two Persian masters, Mir Sayyed Ali and Abdul Samad Khan, who were originally employed by his father Humayun.
    - **Statement 1 is correct:** A large number of Indian artists from all over India were recruited to work under the Persian masters. The paintings were based on the Mahabharata, Ramayana and Persian epics.
    - Some of the famous painters in Akbar's court includes Dasvanth, Miskina, Nanha, Knha, Basawan, Manohar, Doulat, Mansur, Kesu, Bhim Gujarati, Dharam Das, Madhu, Surdas, Lal, Shankar Goverdhan and Inayat.
- **Jahangir:**
    - Under his reign painting acquired greater charm, refinement and dignity. He had great fascination for nature and took delight in the portraiture of birds, animals and flowers.
    - Miniature form of painting executed during the period of Jahangir. The miniature is marked by the spirit of action and dramatic movement created in the fighting scene.
    - **Statement 2 is incorrect:** Besides a number of durbar scenes, portraits, bird, animal and flower studies were also executed during his period. The famous painters of Jahangir are Aqa Riza, Abul Hasan, Mansur, Bishan Das, Manohar, Goverdhan, Balchand, Daulat, Mukhlis, Bhim and Inayat.

- **Shah Jahan:**
  - The Mughal painting maintained its fine quality. But the style, however, became over-ripe during the later period of his rule. Portraiture was given considerable attention by his painters.
  - Statement 3 is incorrect: Apart from portrait, other paintings showing groups of ascetics and mystics and a number of illustrated manuscripts were also executed during his period. During the reign of Shahjahan themes were based on musical parties, ascetics gathered around a fire, etc.
  - The well-known artists of his period are Bichiter, Chaitaraman, Anup Chattar, and Mohammed Nadir of Samarquand, Inayat and Makr.

A miniature in the collection of the National Museum depicts a gathering of Sufis (Muslim divines) who are seen seated in an open space and engaged in discussion. It displays supple naturalism of the Mughal style of the Shah Jahan period. The drawing is refined and the colours have subdued tones. The background is green and the sky is in golden colour. The borders show floral designs in golden colour. The miniature is assigned to circa 1650 AD.

4. **Correct Option: (d)**

Supplementary Notes:

The Deccani Schools (1560-1800 AD)

- **Ahmednagar:**
  - **Statement 1 is correct:** The patronage was given by the Hussain Nizam Shah I of Ahmednagar (1553-1565).
  - The colours used in the painting being rich and brilliant are different from those used in the northern paintings.
  - The Persian influence can be seen in the high horizon, gold sky and the landscape.
  - Some other fine examples of the Ahmednagar painting are the "Hindola Raga" of about 1590 AD and portraits of Burhan Nizam Shah II of Ahmednagar (1591-96 AD) and of Malik Amber of about 1605 AD existing in the National Museum, New Delhi and other museums.
- **Bijapur:**
  - **Statement 2 is correct:** In Bijapur, painting was patronised by Ali Adil Shah I (1558-80 AD) and his successor Ibrahim II (1580-1627 AD).
  - The rich colour scheme, the palm trees, animals and men and women all belong to the Deccani tradition.
  - The profuse use of gold colour, some flowering plants and arabesques on the top of the throne are derived from the Persian tradition.
  - It is believed that a number of the Ragamala paintings were commissioned in various museums and private collections. A few contemporary portraits of Ibrahim II are also available in several museums.
- **Golconda:**
  - **Statement 3 is correct:** The paintings were patronized by the Muhammad Quli Quta Shah (1580-1611).
  - The paintings show dancing girls entertaining the company.
  - One of the miniatures illustrated shows the king in his court watching a dance performance. He wears the white Muslim coat with embroidered vertical band, a typical costume associated with the Golconda court. Gold colour has been lavishly used in painting the architecture, costume, jewellery and vessels, etc.
  - Other outstanding examples of the Golconda painting are "Lady with the Myna bird".

5. **Correct Option: (d)**

Supplementary Notes:

Different Types of Potteries

- **Neolithic Age:** The first reference of pottery is found in this age. Naturally it is hand-made pottery but during the later period foot-wheel is also used.
- **Pair 1 is correct:** Chalcolithic Age: The first metal age. People of this age used different kinds of pottery. Black and red ware seems to have been widely used. Cultures like Ahar-Banas showed the presence of Black and Red ware pottery with white linear designs.
- **Pair 2 is correct:** Harappan Civilisation: Polished Ware Pottery with rough surface. Both polished and unpolished type of pottery existed. Pottery generally has a red surface and is wheel thrown although handmade ones too exist.
- **Pair 3 is correct:** Early Vedic Era: The early Vedic age saw the emergence of Painted Grey Ware (PGW) Culture. The Rig Vedic sites have PGW but iron objects and cereals are absent.
- **Pair 4 is correct:** Later Vedic Era – NBPW: The later Vedic people were acquainted with 4 types of pottery – Black-and-red ware, black-slipped ware, painted grey ware and red ware. Towards the very end of Later Vedic Age around 6th century BC, we see the emergence of 2nd phase of urbanisation (1st being Indus Valley Civilisation). This era marked the beginning of the Northern Black Polished Ware (NBPW).

6. **Correct Option:(c)**

Supplementary Notes:

Chalcolithic Paintings

- **Option (c) is correct:** The paintings of this period reveal the association, contact, and mutual exchange of requirements of the cave dwellers of this area with settled agricultural communities of the Malwa plains. Many a time Chalcolithic ceramics and rock paintings bear common motifs, e.g., cross-hatched squares, lattices. Pottery and metal tools are also shown. But the vividness and vitality of the earlier periods disappear from these paintings.

Palaeolithic Paintings:

- Linear representation in green and red colour of animal figures.

Mesolithic Paintings:

- Besides showing fear of animals, they also show a feeling of tenderness and love for them. Some of the animal paintings, especially in the hunting scenes, show a fear of animals, but many others show a feeling of tenderness and love for them. There are also a few engravings representing mainly animals. Though animals were painted in a naturalistic style, humans were depicted only in a stylistic manner.

Neolithic Paintings:

- Designs of swastika, cruciform and running animals on terracotta figurines.

7. **Correct Option: (d)**

Supplementary Notes:

Coinage in Different Eras:

- **Statement 1 is correct:** The Gupta Empire produced large numbers of gold coins depicting the Gupta kings performing various rituals. This tradition of engraved coins continued till the arrival of the Turkish Sultanate in North India.
- **Statement 2 is correct:** Earliest Kushan coinage is generally attributed to Vima Kadphises. The Kushan coins generally depicted iconographic forms drawn from Greek, Mesopotamian, Zorastrian and Indian mythology.
- Siva, Buddha and Kartikeya were the major Indian deities portrayed. Kushan gold coins influenced subsequent issues, notably those of the Guptas.
- **Statement 3 is correct:** Turkish Sultans of Delhi (by 12th century AD) replaced the royal designs of Indian kings with Islamic calligraphy. The currency – made in gold, silver and copper – was now referred to as tanka, with the lower valued coins being called jittals.

Information Related to Coins:

- The study of coins is known as numismatics. It not only includes visual elements such as script and images on the coins but also metallurgical analysis Ancient coins were mostly minted in metals such as copper, silver, gold and lead.
- The earliest coins found in India contained certain symbols and were called punch-marked coins. They were made of silver and copper (c. sixth century BC onwards).
- The first coins to bear the names and images of rulers were issued by the Indo-Greeks, who established control over the north-western part of the subcontinent (c. second century BC).
- The first gold coins were issued by the Kushanas in first century AD.

8. **Correct Option: (c)**

Supplementary Notes:

Deccan School of Painting:

- **Statement 1 and 2 are incorrect:** Deccan School developed in 16th and 17th centuries. Early centers of their growth were Ahmednagar, Bijapur and Golconda. Initially it developed independent of Mughal influence. Later, in 17th and 18th century the painting came under their influence.
- The Deccani painting initially absorbed influences of the northern tradition of the pre-Mughal painting of Malwa, and of the southern tradition of the Vijayanagar School of Painting.
- The colors of the Deccani schools paintings are rich and brilliant and are different from those of the northern painting.
- Distinctive features of the Deccani paintings of the 18th and 19th centuries are observed in the treatment of the ethnic types, costumes, jewellery, flora, fauna, landscape and colours.

Ahmednagar School of Painting:

- This school was patronized by Hussain Nizam Shah I of Ahmednagar.
- The significant illustrated manuscript is 'Tarif-i-Hussain Shahi'.
- These paintings exhibited Persian influence like the landscape, gold sky, and high horizon.

Bijapur School of Painting:

- The Bijapur School of Painting was patronized by Ali Adil Shah I and his successor Ibrahim II.
- Notable work is Najum-al-ulum (Stars of Sciences).
- The painting exhibits rich color scheme, animals, the palm trees, men, and women belongs to the Deccan tradition.

Golconda School of Painting:

- The patrons of the Golconda school of Paintings were the Qutb Shahi rulers.
- The first notable work was done during the times of Muhammad Quli Qutab Shah.
- There is a deep impact on Iranian art on the Golconda miniature paintings.
- Two more notable paintings in Golconda paintings are the 'Lady with the Myna bird' and the 'Lady smoking Hooka'.

Hyderabad School of Painting:

- Hyderabad school of Painting belongs to the 3rd quarter of the 18th.
- It was developed in 1724 after the foundation of Asaf Jahi Dynasty by Chin Qilij Khan and Nizam-ul-Mulk.
- "Princes in the company of maids" is a famous painting belonging to the Hyderabad School of Painting.

9. **Correct Option: (d)**

Supplementary Notes:

Thanjavur Paintings

- It is a classical South Indian painting style, which was inaugurated from the town of Thanjavur and spread across the adjoining and geographically contiguous old Tamil country.
- **Statement 1 is correct:** It has the influence of Deccani, Vijayanagar, Maratha and even European or Company styles of painting.
- Thanjavur paintings are characterised by rich, flat and vivid colors, simple iconic composition, glittering gold foils overlaid on delicate but extensive gesso work and inlay of glass beads and pieces or very rarely precious and semi-precious gems.
- **Statement 3 is correct:** The gold foil used liberally in Thanjavur paintings serves two objectives: the glitter makes the painting more attractive, and it also prolongs the life of the artefact.
- Essentially serving as devotional icons, the subjects of most paintings are Hindu gods, goddesses, and saints. Episodes from Hindu Puranas, Sthala-puranas and other religious texts were visualised, sketched or traced and painted with the main figure or figures placed in the central section of the picture. It is surrounded by several subsidiary figures, themes and subjects. There are also many instances when Jain, Sikh, Muslim, other religious and even secular subjects were depicted in Tanjore paintings.
- **Statement 2 is correct:** It has been recognized as a Geographical indication by the Government of India in 2007-08.
- A team of researchers have found a solution that uses Raman spectroscopy to tell whether the foil used in the paintings is made of gold or some other cheaper material. The researchers tested ten 'gold foils' and found only three to be genuine. In the case of paintings, only one or two out of ten turned out to be genuine gold foil.
- **Raman spectroscopy:** It is a spectroscopic technique which is used to analyze vibrational, rotational, and other low-frequency modes in a system. Raman spectroscopy is commonly used in the branch of chemistry to provide a fingerprint by which molecules can be identified.

10. **Correct Option: (b)**

Supplementary Notes:

Mural Paintings

- **Statement 1 is incorrect:** The earliest surviving mural paintings in the Indian subcontinent are those of Ajanta. The paintings here were made in two phases. The oldest date to around the 2nd century BC. The marvellous latter phase was around the 5th century AD, under the patronage of the Vakatakas who ruled the Deccan.
- The history of Indian murals starts in ancient and early medieval times, from the 2nd century BC to 8th-10th century AD. There are more than 20 known locations around India containing murals from this period, mainly natural caves and rock-cut chambers. The highest achievements of this time are the caves of Ajanta, Bagh, Sittanavasal, Armamalai Cave (Tamil Nadu), Ravan Chhaya rock shelter, Kailasanatha Temple in Ellora Caves.
- **Statement 2 is correct:** Murals from this period depict mainly religious themes of Buddhist, Jain and Hindu religions. There are though also locations where paintings were made to adorn mundane premises, like the ancient theatre room in Jogimara Cave and possible royal hunting lodge circa 7th-century AD – Ravan Chhaya rock shelter.

11. **Correct Option: (d)**

Supplementary Notes:

Pahari School of Painting

- **Statement 1 is incorrect:** Pahari painting is an umbrella term used for a form of Indian painting, done mostly in miniature forms, originating from Himalayan hill kingdoms of North India, during 17th-19th century, notably Basohli, Mankot, Nurpur, Chamba, Kangra, Guler, Mandi, and Garhwal.
- The Pahari School developed and flourished during 17th-19th centuries stretching from Jammu to Almora and Garhwal, in the sub-Himalayan India, through Himachal Pradesh. Each created stark variations within the genre, ranging from bold intense Basohli Painting, originating from Basohli in Jammu and Kashmir, to the delicate and lyrical Kangra paintings, which became synonymous to the style before other schools of paintings developed.
- The Kangra style reached its pinnacle with paintings of Radha and Krishna, inspired by Jayadev's Gita Govinda.
- **Statement 2 is incorrect:** Pahari painting grew out of the Mughal painting, though this was patronized mostly by the Rajput kings who ruled many parts of the region, and gave birth to a new idiom in Indian painting.

- **Statement 3 is incorrect:** Bundi painting is an important school of the Rajasthani Style of Indian miniature painting that lasted from the 17th to the end of the 19th century.

12. Correct Option: (a)

Supplementary Notes:

Pietra Dura Style of Art

- **Statement 2 is Incorrect:** The Pietra Dura method was used on a large scale in the Taj Mahal, not Moti Masjid. Though Moti Masjid was also made of white marble.
- Pietra dura is an Italian phrase that means "hard stone," and usually refers to the technique of creating intricate inlaid pictures from shaped colored stones.
- **Statement 1 is correct:** This architectural style wholly of white marble with floral designs made of semi-precious stones on the walls.
- This method became more popular during the reign of Shah Jahan.

13. Correct Option: (a)

Explanation:

- **Statement 2 is incorrect:** Patua Art – Bengal
- **Statement 3 is incorrect:** Paitkar Painting – Jharkhand

Supplementary Notes:

Folk Paintings: State

- Patachitra or Pattachitra is a traditional form of cloth-based scroll painting, based in the eastern Indian state of Odisha. These paintings are based on Hindu mythology and specially inspired by Jagannath and Vaishnava sect The painters do not use pencil or charcoal for the preliminary drawings. On the surface of the painting fine, lacquer is applied to have a glossy finish. Patachitra on palm leaf is known as Tala Pattachitra. Raghurajpur in Odisha is known for this art form.
- Patua Art is an ancient art form of Bengal. The painting tradition of Patuas was started as a village tradition as painters of scrolls. The Bengal Patua artworks are detailed graphic accounts of stories waiting to be told. They can be categorised into social, general, mythological, religious, political, environmental and historical groups. Some Patuas belongs to Hindus, while others belong to Muslims and Buddhists.
- The Paitkar paintings are also popularly known as the scroll paintings of Jharkhand and have long been used in storytelling performances and in socio-religious customs. The old form of painting has cultural association with Ma Mansa goddess. The paintings that belong to this form have a common subject of what happens to human life after death. The art is present in Amadubi village (Village of Paitkar) since ancient times.

14. Correct Option: (a)

Explanation:

- **Statement 3 is incorrect:** Recently, world's oldest known cave painting (painted at least 45,500 years ago) was found in the limestone cave of Leang Tedongnge, Indonesia.

Supplementary Notes:

Cave paintings

- Recently, World's oldest known cave painting (painted at least 45,500 years ago) was found in the limestone cave of Leang Tedongnge, Indonesia.
- Ajanta Caves is the only surviving example of painting of the first century BCE. The subject matter of these paintings is almost exclusively Buddhist except for decorative patterns on the ceilings and the pillars. The first Buddhist cave monuments at Ajanta date from the 2nd and 1st centuries BCE. During the Gupta period (5th-6th centuries AD), many more richly decorated caves were added to the original group.
- Sittannavasal is a rock-cut Jain Temple of the Pandyan era (9th century) near Pudukkottai. These cave paintings are dedicated to the Jain themes and symbolism.
- Saspol caves are amazing rock-cut Temples from the 13th-15th century AD situated at Leh. The dominant color here is bright blue, but the paintings themselves represent an exciting fusion of Tibetan and Indian Buddhist art.
- Jogimara caves were made around the 1st century BC at Chhattisgar. Contrary to other ancient Indian cave paintings these drawings are not related to religion. Paintings show dancing couple, fish and elephant figures, seen also an unclear painting of chariot.

15. Correct Option: (a)

Supplementary Notes:

Ajanta cave paintings

- The Ajanta caves were inscribed by the Buddhist monks, under the patronage of the Vakataka kings – Harishena being a prominent one. The figures in these caves were done using fresco painting and demonstrate considerable naturalism. The colours were obtained from local vegetation and minerals. The outlines of the paintings were done in red colour and then the inside was painted. One of thes triking features is the absence of blue colour in the paintings. The paintings in the Ajanta caves predominantly narrate the Jataka tales. These are Buddhist legends describing the previous births of the Buddha.
- The famous paintings of Padmapani and Vajrapani Bodhisattvas under Buddhism are found in Ajanta Caves.

16. **Correct Option: (b)**

Explanation:

- **Statement 1 is incorrect:** The edicts are mostly written in Prakrit and Magadhi in Brahmi script.

Supplementary Notes:

Ashokan Edicts

- Ashokan edicts are an important source of information about the Mauryan empire along with the extent of the vast empire over which Ashoka ruled.
- There are 33 edicts comprising 14 Major Rock Edicts, 2 known as Kalinga Edicts, 7 Pillar Edicts, some Minor Rock Edicts and a few Minor Pillar Inscriptions.
  - Major Rock Edicts – From Kandahar in Afghanistan, Shahbazgarhi and Mansehra in northwest Pakistan to Uttarakhand district in the north, Gujarat and Maharashtra in the west, Odisha in the east and as far south as Karnataka and Kurnool district in Andhra Pradesh.
  - Minor Pillar Inscriptions – Found as far north as Nepal (near Lumbini).
- The edicts were written mostly in the Brahmi script and in Magadhi and Prakrit.
  - The Kandahar inscriptions are in Greek and Aramaic, while the two inscriptions in north-west Pakistan are in Kharosthi script.
- The Ashokan edicts stress his belief in peace, righteousness, justice and his concern for the welfare of his people.

Dharmic State through Ashokan Edicts

- Ashoka's rule gives us an alternative model of a righteous king and a just state.
- Major mentions of his edicts are mentioned below –
  - Major Rock Edict 3 – Instructions to his officials to go on tours every five years to instruct people in dhamma.
  - Kalinga Rock Edict 1 – Officials should recognise their own responsibilities and strive to be impartial and see to it that men were not imprisoned or tortured without good reason.
  - Major Rock Edict 6 – The king should be advised and informed promptly wherever he might be.
  - Major Rock Edicts 7 and 12 – All religions should coexist and the ascetics of all religions were honoured.
  - Major Rock Edict 2 – Providing medical care should be one of the functions of the state, the emperor ordered hospitals to be set up to treat human beings and animals.
  - Preventing unnecessary slaughter of animals and showing respect for all living beings.
  - All the people were his children and he wished for his people what he wished for his own children, that they should obtain welfare and happiness in this world and the next.

17. **Correct Option: (b)**

Supplementary Notes:

- The silver coins issued by the Guptas were called Rupaka. The silver coins based on Sakas of Ujjaini weighing 32-36 grains were called Rupaka. A silver coin which weighed about 180 grains are called Satamana.

18. **Correct Option: (b)**

Supplementary Notes:

- Aryabhata was an outstanding scholar of the Gupta age. His most original contribution was that the eclipses were not the work of Shani (Saturn), as believed by some astrologers, but caused by the shadow of the earth falling on the moon, therefore, asserting the movement of earth on its own axis around the sun, as was known in Vedic times. Aryabhata was the first to utilize sign functions, numbers and the use of zero in astronomy. He discovered an accurate formula to measure the decrease or increase in the duration of two consecutive days.

19. **Correct Option: (c)**

Supplementary Notes:

- **Pair 1 is incorrect:** In Cave 26, Ajanta of 5th century AD, there is a grand image of Buddha's Mahaparinirvana with numerous celestial musicians above and the sorrowful figures of his followers below.
- **Pair 3 is correct:** Mamallapuram hosts India's largest and most dramatic relief-sculpture. It represents the celebrated myth of the descent of the river Ganga from heaven to earth. The Great Penance, is carved on a giant granite rock wall 27 meters wide and 9 meters tall, and was believed to be initiated during the reign of the Pallava King Mahendra Varman, 7th century CE.
- **Pair 2 is correct:** The most famous carving at Udayagiri (near Vidisha, Madhya Pradesh) is a five-foot (or so) tall statue of Vishnu's Boar Avatar (showing rescuing the Earth, who is hanging on his tusk), with the worshipful masses standing in homage by the sides. This image was in the personal Temple of King Chandra Gupta II (ruled 376-415 CE).

20. **Correct Option: (a)**

Supplementary Notes:

Madhubani Painting

- **Option (a) is correct:**
- The Madhubani Painting was traditionally done on freshly plastered mud walls and floors of huts, but

now they are also done on cloth, handmade paper and canvas.

- Madhubani paintings are made from the paste of powdered rice.
- Madhubani painting has remained confined to a compact geographical area and the skills have been passed on through centuries, the content and the style have largely remained the same.
- And that is the reason for Madhubani painting being accorded the coveted GI (Geographical Indication) status.
- Madhubani paintings also use two-dimensional imagery, and the colors used are derived from plants. Ochre and lampblack are also used for reddish brown and black respectively.

21. Correct Option: (c)

Supplementary Notes:

Kalamkari Paitings

- Option (c) is incorrectly matched:
- Kalamkari is a type of hand-painted or block-printed cotton textile, produced in Indian states of Andhra Pradesh and Telangana. Only natural dyes are used in Kalamkari and it involves twenty three steps.
- There are two distinctive styles of kalamkari art in India – Srikalahasti style and the Machilipatnam style.

22. Correct Option: (a)

- **Statement 3 is incorrect:** Various tribes and dynasties also issued coins.This question can be done by elimination. If we eliminate Statement 3, option a will be the answer.

Supplementary Notes:

Indo-Greek coins

- The reign of Indo-Greeks was from 180 BC to around 10 AD. The Indo-Greeks introduced the fashion of showing the bustor head of the ruler on the coins.
- The legends on their Indian coins were mentioned in two languages – in Greek on one of the sides and in Kharosthi on the other side of the coin.
- The Greek gods and goddesses commonly shown on the Indo-Greek coins were Zeus, Hercules, Apollo and Pallas Athene.
- The initial series used images of Greek deities but later coins had images of Indian deities as well.
- These coins are significant because they carried detailed information about the issuing monarch, the year of issue and sometimes an image of the reigning king.
- Coins were mainly made of silver, copper, nickel and lead. The coins of the Greek kings in India were bilingual, i.e., written in Greek on the front side and in Pali language (in Kharosthi script) on the back.
- Later, Indo-Greek Kushan kings introduced the Greek custom of engraving portrait heads on the coins.
- Kushan coins were adorned with a helmeted bust of the king on one side, and the king's favourite deity on the reverse.
- The coins issued by Kanishka employed only Greek characters.
- The extensive coinage of the Kushan Empire also influenced a large number of tribes, dynasties and kingdoms, which began issuing their own coins.

23. Correct Option: (d)

Explanation:

- **Option (d) is correct:** Gupta coins had all three pictures inscribed in it.

Supplementary Notes:

Coins in Gupta Age

- The Gupta Age (319 AD–550 AD) marked a period of great Hindu revival.
- The Gupta coins were mainly made of gold, although they issued silver and copper coins too.
- Silver coins were issued only after Chandragupta II overthrew the Western Satraps. There were many types and varieties of Gupta gold coins.
- On one side of these coins, we find the king standing and making oblations before an altar, playing the veena, performing ashvamedha, riding a horse or an elephant, slaying a lion or a tiger or a rhinocerous with a sword or bow, or sitting on a couch.
- On the other side is the Goddess Lakshmi seated on a throne or a lotus seal, or the figure of the queen herself.
- The inscriptions on the coins were all in Sanskrit (Brahmi script) for the first time in the history of coins.
- Gupta rulers issued coins depicting the emperors not only in martial activities like hunting lions/tigers, posing with weapons, etc., but also in leisurely activities like playing a Veena, with reverse side of the coin having images of Goddess Lakshmi, Durga, Ganga, Garuda and Kartikeya.
- The end of Gupta rule in the sixth century due to a Hun invasion ushered in a period of uncertainty when again a number of local kingdoms rose in different regions issuing region-specific coins which were poor in both metallic content and artistic design.
- Thus, during a long period stretching till the thirteenth century, a mix of designs borrowed not only from the Kushana–Gupta pattern but also from foreign designs, were employed by these dynasties in Western, Eastern, Northern and Central India.
- South India developed a different coin paradigm moving towards a gold standard which was inspired from the Roman gold coins, which arrived in the region during the first three centuries of the first millennium.

24. Correct Option: (a)

Explanation:

- **Statement 1 is incorrect:** Alauddin Khalji is best remembered for the experiment of market control through the fixation of cost of various commodities BUT the introduction of token currency in the form bronze and copper coins was done by Muhammad bin Tughlaq.

Supplementary Notes:

Turkish and Delhi Sultanate Coins

- Muhammad bin Tuqhlaq was best remembered for the failed experiment of introduction of Token Currency. There was a shortage of silver in the world in the 14th century. Qublai Khan of China had already successfully experimented with a token currency. Ghazan Khan, a Mongol ruler, also experimented with token currency.
- Muhammad bin Tughlaq also introduced a bronze coin which was to have same value as the silver tanka.
- It was failed due to newness of the system and he could not prevent people from forging new coins.
- The silver tanka and Copper jital were introduced by Iltutmish.

25. Correct Option: (b)

Explanation:

- **Statement 2 is incorrect:** Zodiac sign on the coins was minted during the time of Jahangir.

Supplementary Notes:

Mughals Coinage

- The standard gold coins of the Mughal were the Mohur of about 170 to 175 grains.
- Abul Fazal in Ain-e-Akabari indicated that a Mohur was equivalent to 9 rupees.
- The Silver rupee which was an adoption from Sher Shah's currency was the most famous of all Mughal coins.
- Akbar issued the "Ilahi coins" to propagate his new religious Idea of Din-e-Illahi.
- Jahangir showed the legend in a couplet in the coins. In some of his coins, he added the name of his beloved wife Noorjahan.
- The most famous of his coin had the images of zodiac signs, e.g. Cancer.

26. Correct Option: (c)

Explanation:

- Both statements are correct

Supplementary Notes:

Miniatures in South India

- The trend of making miniature paintings was already prevalent in the South Indian states and it developed in the early medieval period.
- These were different from the North Indian schools owing to the heavy use of gold in these paintings. Furthermore, they concentrated on painting divine creatures much more than painting the rulers who patronized them.
- Some of the major schools are:
  - Tanjore Paintings
    - The Thanjavur or Tanjore School is famous for the special style of decorative paintings. The Maratha rulers patronized them during the 18th century.
    - They are mostly created on glass and board instead of cloth and vellum preferred in north India and are unique because of the use of brilliant colour patterns and the liberal use of gold leaf. They used many types of gemstones and cut glasses for embellishments to create larger than life images.
    - Most of the paintings depicted smiling Krishna in various poses and various major events in his life.
  - Mysore Paintings
    - The major theme of the Mysore paintings is the depiction of Hindu gods and goddesses.
    - The unique part of these paintings is that they had two or more figures in each painting and one figure predominates all the others in size and colour.
    - Furthermore, even the technique of making these paintings is very different from the North Indian styles. They use the 'gesso paste', which is a mixture of zinc oxide and Arabic gum. This gives a particular base to the painting that develops sheen on the background.
    - They counter it with the use of muted colours that are not so bright so as to counteract the background.

27. Correct Option: (d)

Explanation:

- **Statement 1 is incorrect:** Painted Grey Ware (1200-600 BC) and Northern Back Polished Ware (700-200 BC) were the main archaeological culture of Iron Age Pottery that succeeded late Harappan Culture in the Indian subcontinent.
- **Statement 2 is incorrect:** Northern Black Polished Ware was a luxury style of burnished pottery used by elites and the NBP Wares were of well levigated (smooth paste) clay, has a glossy surface with a thin core and ware was usually unpainted.
- **Statement 3 is incorrect:** Northern Black Polished Ware (NBPW) succeeded Painted Grey Ware (PGW) culture and many of the PGW settlements grew into

large towns and cities of Northern Black Polished Ware period.

Supplementary Notes:
Painted Grey Ware (PGW)

- Painted Grey Ware (1200-600 BC) and Northern Black Polished Ware (700-200 BC) were the main archaeological culture of Iron Age Pottery that succeeded the Harappan Culture in the Indian subcontinent.
- PGW culture lasted roughly 600 years (1200 BC to 600 BC) in the Ghaggar-Hakra Valley and Western Gangetic Plain.
- There have been more than 1100 PGW sites discovered and most of them were small farming villages, several dozen sites emerged as relatively bigger settlements and had characteristics of Towns. The period of PGW culture corresponds to the middle or late Vedic period i.e. Kuru-Panchala Kingdom.
- Painted Grey Ware is the successor of the Black and Red Ware (BRW) in the Western Gangetic Plain and it is contemporary with the continuation of the BRW Culture in Central India and Eastern Gangetic Plain.
- The PGW culture majorly being associated with village and town settlements, ivory-working, domesticated horses, the advent of iron metallurgy was characterized by a style of fine, grey pottery painted with geometric patterns in black.

28. **Correct Option: (b)**

Explanation:

- **Statement 1 is incorrect:** These famous rock-cut caves are known for the paintings in the Jain Temples. These murals have close resemblance to Bagh and Ajanta paintings.
- **Statement 2 is incorrect:** Some scholars believe that these caves belong to the Pallava period, when king Mahendravarman I excavated the Temple, while the others attribute them when Pandya ruler renovated the shrine in the 7th century.

Supplementary Notes:
Sittanavasal Cave Paintings

- Located 16 km northwest of Pudukkottai town in Tamil Nadu, these famous rock-cut caves are known for the paintings in the Jain Temples. These murals have close resemblance to Bagh and Ajanta paintings.
- The paintings are not only on the walls but also on the ceiling and pillars. The paintings are with the theme of Jain Samavasarana (Preaching Hall).
- The medium used for painting is vegetable and mineral dyes and is done by putting colors on the surface of thin wet lime plaster. The common colors include yellow, green, orange, blue, black, and white.
- The central element of the paintings in Sittanavasal is a pond with lotuses. Flowers in this pond are collected by monks. Also, are shown ducks, swans, fishes, and animals. This scene shows Samavasarana - an important scene in Jain religion.
- Samavasarana is a special, beautiful audience hall where Tirthankaras delivered sermons after they reached realisation (kevala-gnana). Bulls, elephants, apsaras and gods gathered in this audience hall to witness this grand scene.

29. **Correct Option: (a)**

Explanation:

- **Statement 2 is incorrect:** The Mughal paintings reached its zenith in the period of Jahangir.
- **Statement 3 is incorrect:** Akbar established a formal artistic studio called Tasvir Khana where the artists developed their own styles.

Supplementary Notes:
Mughal Era Paintings

- The paintings made in the Mughal period had a distinctive style as they were drawing from Persian antecedents. There was a change in colour palette, themes and forms.
- The focus shifted from depicting the god to glorifying the ruler and showing his life. They focused on hunting scenes, historical events and other court related paintings.
- The Mughal paintings brought together Persian naturalistic style with the opulence of a great Dynasty and created some beautifully illustrated folios.
- Akbar was responsible for establishment of an entire department devoted to the paintings and scribing of his documents. He established a formal artistic studio called Tasvir Khana where the artists were hired on salary and they developed their own styles.
- The Mughal paintings reached its zenith in the period of Jahangir. He was a naturalist by nature and preferred the paintings of flora and fauna, i.e. birds, animals, trees and flowers. He emphasised on bringing naturalism to portrait painting. One of the unique trends that developed in this period was of decorated margins around the paintings that were sometimes as elaborate as the paintings themselves.

30. **Correct Option: (d)**

Explanation:

- **Statement 1 is incorrect:** Warli paintings have a close resemblance to the mural paintings of Bhimbetka.
- **Statement 2 is incorrect:** Kalighat paintings are first of its kind in the country to express subaltern sentiments.

Supplementary Notes:

Folk Paintings in India

- Kalighat paintings were done by the rural migrants who settled around the Kalighat Temple in the then British capital (Calcutta). Water colours were used on mill paper using brushes made of calf and squirrel hair. The painted figures has a plaque-like effect on neutral background given the shaded contours and articulated movements. Originally, the paintings depicted religious note, especially Hindu Gods and Goddesses. Over time, these paintings were used to express social sentiments. Kalighat paintings are considered first of its kind in the country to express subaltern sentiments and address customers directly.
- Warli painting comes from the people occupying mainly the Gujarat-Maharashtra border. These paintings have close resemblance to the mural paintings of Bhimbetka in Madhya Pradesh that date back to the pre-historic period. These ritualistic paintings have a central motif of a chaukat or chauk, which is surrounded by scenes portraying fishing, hunting, farming, dances, animals, trees and festivals. Among the Goddesses, Palaghata (goddess of fertility) is drawn and among the male gods, those spirits that have taken human form are represented.
- A traditional painting of Odisha, the name Pattachitra comes from a Sanskrit word 'patta', which means canvas/cloth and 'chitra' means picture. The paintings show a mix of classical and folk elements, with a bias towards the latter. The base of the painting is treated cloth while the colours used comes from natural sources including burnt coconut shells, Hingula, Ramaraja and lamp black. No pencil or charcoal is used, rather brush is used to draw the outlines in red or yellow after which the colours are filled. The background is decorated with foliage and flowers and the paintings have a intricately worked frame. Once the final lines are drawn, the painting is given a coating of lacquer to give it a glossy finish. The themes of these paintings are inspired from Jagannath and Vaishnava cult, sometimes from Shakti and Shaiva cults.

31. Correct Option: (d)

Explanation:

- All pairs are correctly matched

Supplementary Notes:

- The Deccani Schools (1560-1800 AD) Ahmednagar: The patronage was given by the Hussain Nizam Shah I of Ahmednagar (1553-1565).
- The colours used in the painting being rich and brilliant are different from those used in the northern paintings.
- The Persian influence can be seen in the high horizon, gold sky and the landscape.
- Some other fine examples of the Ahmednagar painting are the "Hindola Raga" of about 1590 AD and portraits of Burhan Nizam Shah II of Ahmednagar (1591-96 AD) and of Malik Amber of about 1605 AD. existing in the National Museum, New Delhi and other museums.
- **Bijapur:** In Bijapur, painting was patronised by Ali Adil Shah I (1558-80 AD) and his successor Ibrahim II (1580-1627 AD). The rich colour scheme, the palm trees, animals and men and women all belong, to the Deccani tradition.
- The profuse use of gold colour, some flowering plants and arabesques on the top of the throne are derived from the Persian tradition. It is believed that a number of the Ragamala paintings were commissioned in various museums and private collections. A few contemporary portraits of Ibrahim II are also available in several museums.
- **Golconda:** The paintings were patronized by the Muhammad Quli Quta Shah (1580-1611). The paintings show dancing girls entertaining the company. One of the miniatures illustrated shows the king in his court watching a dance performance. He wears the white Muslim coat with embroidered vertical band, a typical costume associated with the Golconda court. Gold colour has been lavishly used in painting the architecture, costume, jewellery and vessels etc.
- Other outstanding examples of the Golconda painting are "Lady with the Myna bird".

32. Correct Option: (c)

Explanation:

- Both statements are correct

Supplementary Notes:

Bhimbetka

- Bhimbetka is a natural art gallery and an archaeological treasure. For miles together, the footsteps of the prehistoric man can be easily discerned upon the sands of time, since the caves here house rock paintings, created by man from as early as about 15,000 years ago in vivid and panoramic detail.
- The rock paintings have numerous layers belonging to various epochs of time, ranging from the Upper Palaeolithic, Mesolithic Age to the protohistoric, early historic and medieval periods. The most ancient scenes here believed to be commonly belonging to the Mesolithic Age. These magnificent paintings can be seen even on the ceiling of the rock shelters located at daunting heights.
- The themes of paintings found here are of great variety, ranging from mundane events of daily life in those times to sacred and royal images. These include hunting, dancing, music, horse and elephant

riders, animal fighting, honey collection, decoration of bodies, and other household scenes. They include both animal and human being.

33. **Correct Option: (b)**

Explanation:

- **Statement 1 is incorrect:** The famous Bani Thani painting belongs to the Kishangarh School.

Supplementary Notes:

Regional Schools of Art

- Even though the medieval period was dominated by the Mughal style of painting, the sub-imperial schools developed a space for them by developing their own styles. They remembered their Indian roots and a penchant for colorful paintings as opposed to the more naturalistic Mughal style.
- The different schools and styles that developed in this period were:
  - **Kishangarh School of Painting**
    - Paintings at Kishangarh are associated with the most romantic legends – Sawant Singh and his beloved Bani Thani, and of the intertwining of lives and myths, romance and bhakti.
    - It is sometimes argued that the women in 'Bani Thani' is said to resemble the character of Radha. She has a distinctive profile and has large and lustrous eyes, thin lips and a pointed chin. Her odhni or headgear defines her side profile. This became the unique painting associated with the Kishangarh School.
  - **Kangra School of Painting**
    - After the decline of the Mughal Empire, many artists trained in the Mughals style migrated to the Kangra region as they got patronage by Raja Govardhan Singh in 1774. It led to the birth of Guler-Kangra School of paintings.
    - This school reached its zenith under the patronage of Raja Sansar Chand.
    - Its chief features are delicacy of line, brilliance of color and minuteness of decorative details, like the art of Ajanta, Kangra art is essentially an art of the line.
    - The Kangra painters made use of pure colors like yellow, red and blue.
    - The central theme of Kangra painting is live and its sentiments are expressed in a lyrical style full of rhythm, grace and beauty.
    - The recurring theme of Kangra painting whether it portrays one of the six seasons or modes of music, Radha and Krishana or Siva and Parvati is the love of man for woman and of woman for man.

34. **Correct Option: (a)**

Explanation:

- **Statement 2 is incorrect:** South Indian miniatures concentrated on painting divine creatures rather than the rulers who patronized them.

Supplementary Notes:

Miniatures in South India

- The trend of making miniature paintings was already prevalent in the South Indian states and it developed in the early medieval period.
- These were different from the north Indian schools owing to the heavy use of gold in these paintings. Furthermore, they concentrated on painting divine creatures much more than painting the rulers who patronized them.
- Some of the major schools are:
  - **Tanjore Paintings**
    - The Thanjavur or Tanjore School is famous for the special style of decorative paintings. The Maratha rulers patronized them during the 18th century.
    - They are mostly created on glass and board instead of cloth and vellum preferred in north India and are unique because of the use of brilliant colour patterns and the liberal use of gold leaf. They used many types of gemstones and cut glasses for embellishments to create larger than life images.
    - Most of the paintings depicted smiling Krishna in various poses and various major events in his life.
  - Mysore Paintings
    - The major theme of the Mysore paintings is the depiction of Hindu gods and goddesses.
    - The unique part of these paintings is that they had two or more figures in each painting and one figure predominates all the others in size and colour.
    - Furthermore, even the technique of making these paintings is very different from the north Indian styles. They use the 'gesso paste', which is a mixture of zinc oxide and Arabic gum. This gives a particular base to the painting that develops sheen on the background.
    - They counter it with the use of muted colours that are not so bright so as to counteract the background.

35. **Correct Option: (b)**

Explanation:

- **Statement 1 is incorrect:** It used red colour to paint the background and glossy black paint was used to draw designs.

Supplementary Notes:

Pottery

- The potteries found at the excavation sites can be broadly classified into two kinds – plain pottery and painted pottery.
- The painted pottery is also known as Red and Black pottery as it used red colour to paint the background and glossy black paint was used to draw designs and figures on the red background. Trees, birds, animal figures and geometrical patterns were the recurring themes of the paintings.
- Most of the potteries that have been found are very fine wheel-made wares, with a very few being handmade. Some examples of polychrome pottery have also been found, though very rare.
- The potteries were used for three main purposes: Plain pottery was used for household purposes, mainly storage of grains and water. Miniature vessels, generally less than half an inch in size, were used for decorative purposes.
- They are so marvellously crafted that even now they evoke awe. Some of the potteries were perforated – with a large hole in the bottom and small holes across the sides. They might have been used for straining liquor.

36. Correct Option: (a)

Explanation:

- **Statement 3 is incorrect:** No evidence of cow has been found on any seal.

Supplementary Notes:

Seals

- Archaeologists have found numerous seals of different shapes and sizes all across the excavation sites of Indus Valley Civilisation.
- While most seals are square, it was found that triangular, rectangular and circular seals were also used.
- Steatite, a soft stone found in the river beds, was although the most common material used to make seals, yet agate, chert, copper, faience and terracotta seals have also been found. Some instances of copper, gold and ivory seals have also been found.
- Most seals have inscriptions in a pictographic script that is yet to be deciphered. The script was written mostly from right to left, but, bi-directional writing style i.e., right to left on one line and left to right on another line has also been found.
- Animal impressions were also there, generally five, which were carved intaglio on the surfaces. The common animal motifs were unicorn, humped bull, rhinoceros, tiger, elephant, buffalo, bison, goat, markour, ibex, crocodile, etc. However, no evidence of cow has been found on any seal.
- Seals were primarily used for commercial purposes and helped in communication. Discovery of various seals in Mesopotamia and various sites such as Lothal points to the fact that seals were extensively used for trade.
- Some seals with a hole on them have been found on dead bodies. This indicates that they might have been used as amulets, carried on the persons of their owners, probably used as some form of identification.
- Mathematical images have also been found on some seals, which might have been used for educational purposes as well. Seals with symbol similar to 'Swastika' design have also been found.

37. Correct Option: (d)

Explanation:

- All statements are correct

Supplementary Notes:

Nataraja Sculpture

- The bronze casting technique and the making of bronze images of traditional icons reached a high stage of development in South India during the medieval period. Chola bronzes are the most sought after collectors' items by art lovers all over the world. An important piece of Chola sculpture was the sculpture of Nataraja in the Tandava dance posture. Shiva is thus associated with the end of the cosmic world.
- Features of the Nataraja sculpture are:
  - In the Chola period, bronze sculpture Shiva has been shown balancing himself on his right leg and suppressing the 'apasmara', the demon of ignorance or forgetfulness, with the foot of the same leg.
  - At the same time, he raises his left leg in bhujangatrasita stance, which represents 'tirobhava' that is kicking away the veil of 'Maya' or illusion from the devotee's mind.
  - His four arms are outstretched and the main right hand is posed in 'Abhaya hasta' or the gesture reassuring the devotee to not be afraid.
  - The upper right holds the 'damaru' his favorite musical instrument to keep on the beat tala. All creation springs from the great sound of damaru.
  - The upper left hand carries a flame which represents destruction while the main left hand is held in 'dola hasta' and connects with the 'abhaya hasta' of the right hand.
  - His hair locks fly on both the sides touching the circular 'jvala mala' or the garland of flames which surrounds the entire dancing figuration.

38. Correct Option: (d)

Explanation:

- All statements are correct

Supplementary Notes:
Mural Paintings in India

- The works on the walls or a solid structure are referred to as Murals.
- Most of the mural paintings are either in natural caves or in rock-cut chambers.
- The paintings follow a theme, the most common being Hindu, Buddhist and Jain.
- The Mural paintings are unique because of their sheer size. They cannot be contained on paper and need to be executed on the walls of large structures, usually caves and Temple walls.
- **Ajanta Cave Paintings**
  - One of the oldest surviving murals of the Indian subcontinent, Ajanta caves were carved in 4th century AD out of volcanic rocks. It consists of a set of 29 caves, carved in a horse-shoe shape.
  - The walls of the caves have both murals and fresco paintings (painted on wet plaster).
  - The paintings portray human values and social fabric along with styles, costumes, and ornaments of that period.
  - The emotions are expressed through hand gestures.
  - The unique feature of the paintings is that each female figure has a unique hairstyle. Even animals and birds are shown with emotions.
  - The common themes of these paintings range from Jataka stories to life of Buddha to elaborate decorative patterns of flora and fauna. Graceful poses of humans and animals adorn the walls of the caves.
  - The medium of painting was vegetable and mineral dyes. The outline of the figures is red ochre, with contours of brown, black or deep red.
- **Ellora Cave Paintings**
  - The mural paintings in the Ellora caves are found in five caves, mostly limited to Kailasa Temple.
  - The earlier paintings show Vishnu with his consort Lakshmi borne through the clouds by Garuda, the celestial bird. The later paintings, made in Guajarati style, depict procession of Shaiva holy men.
  - The paintings are related to all three religions (Buddhism, Jainism and Hinduism).
- **Sittanavasal Cave Paintings**
  - Located in Tamil Nadu, these famous rock-cut caves are known for the paintings in the Jain Temples. These murals have close resemblance to Bagh and Ajanta paintings.
  - The paintings are not only on the walls but also on the ceiling and pillars.
  - The medium used for painting is vegetable and mineral dyes, and is done by putting colors on surface of thin wet lime plaster.
  - The central element of the paintings in Sittanavasal is a pond with lotuses. Flowers in this pond are collected by monks; there are shown ducks, swans, fishes and animals. This scene shows Samavasarana an important scene in Jain religion.

39. Correct Option: (b)

Explanation:

- **Statement 3 is incorrect:** The animals are drawn in bold outline, and the bodies are sometimes filled in completely or partially with crosshatching. Human figures in simple outline forms as well as with hatched body are depicted.

Supplementary Notes:
Prehistoric Rock Art

- The people of the Palaeolithic and Mesolithic Ages practiced painting. The pre-historic paintings were generally executed on rocks and these rock engravings were called Petroglyphs.
- Almost all the rock-shelters in India occupied by the Upper Palaeolithic and Mesolithic people, and many others as well contain rock-paintings depicting a variety of subjects, chiefly animals, or scenes including both people and animals.
- Some of the important rock-painting sites are Murhana Pahar in Uttar Pradesh, Bhimbetka, Adamgarh, and Lakha Juar in Madhya Pradesh and Kupagallu in Karnataka. Bhimbetka in MP is a striking site having over 500 painted rock shelters distributed in an area of 10 sq. km. and the rock paintings extend from the Upper Palaeolithic to the Mesolithic Age and in some series even up to recent times.
- Animals are the most frequently depicted subject either alone or in large and small groups and are shown in various poses. The animals are drawn in bold outline, and the bodies are sometimes filled in completely or partially with crosshatching.
- Depiction of human figures in rock paintings is quite common. These are in simple outline forms as well as with hatched body. The humans are shown in various activities, such as dancing, running, hunting, playing games and engaging in battle.
- One of the most common scenes depicted in these paintings is of group hunting and several paintings depict grazing activity and riding scenes.
- The colours used in making these drawings are deep red, green, white and, yellow.

40. Correct Option: (a)

Explanation:

- **Statement 2 is incorrect:** Patanjali in his Mahabhasya refers to the Shakas as 'Anirvasita (pure) Shudras'.

Supplementary Notes:

Contact with Central Asia:

- **Indo-Greeks:** In the beginning of the 2nd century BCE, the Indo-Greeks were the first to invade India. They occupied a large part of north-western India, much larger than that conquered by Alexander, and it is believed that they pushed forward to as far as Ayodhya and Pataliputra. They were the first to issue gold coins and much of their lineage is determined on the basis of excavated coins which include coins of sliver, copper, and nickel as well.
- **Shaka:** 'Shaka' is the Indian term used for the people called the Scythians, who originally belonged to Central Asia. Patanjali in his Mahabhasya refers to the Shakas as 'Anirvasita (pure) Shudras'
- **Parthians:** Originally, the Parthians lived in Iran and invaded India at the beginning of the Christian era. Gondophernes/Guduvhara (mentioned in an inscription dated 45 CE found at Takht-i-Bahi, recovered from Mardan near Peshawar) was the most famous and important Parthian king, and it was during his reign that St. Thomas came to India to propagate Christianity.
- **Shaka Kshatrapas:** It is believed that the Shaka Kshatrapas were involved in continuous conflict with the Satavahanas for the suzerainty over Deccan, and control over the western seaport areas frequently changed hands. For instance, the Nashik and Pune areas seem to have been conquered by either Nahapana or his predecessors from the Satavahanas.

41. Correct Option: (b)

Explanation:

- The finest examples of painting belonging to the first half of the 16th century are, however, represented by a group of miniatures generally designated as the "Kulhadar Group". This group includes illustrations of the 'Chaurapanchasika' – "Fifty Verses of the Thief" by Bilhan, the Gita Govinda, the Bhagavata Purana and Ragamala. The style of these miniatures is marked by the use of brilliant contrasting colours, vigorous and angular drawing, transparent drapery and the appearance of conical caps 'Kulha' on which turbans are worn by the male figures.

42. Correct Option: (b)

Explanation:

- **Statement 1 is incorrect:** In the year 1665, the Treaty of Purandar was signed between Jai Singh and Shivaji.

Supplementary Notes:

Information regarding the Treaty of Purandar

- In the year 1665, the Treaty of Purandar was signed between Jai Singh and Shivaji.
- The treaty had following sections – (i) Shivaji Maharaj would pay Badshah, a tax of 23 lakh hons (coins) annually. (ii) 23 of his 40 forts are to be handed over to Mughals. He had to give up his forts at Purandar, Rudramal, Konda, Lohagad, Isagad, Tung, Tikona, Rohid, Nardurga, Mahuli, Bhandardurga, Palaskhol, Rupgad, Bakhtgad, Morabkhan, Manikgad, Saroopgad, Sakargad, Marakgad, Ankola, Songad, and Maangad. (iii) He has to pay a visit to honour the Badshah on the occasion of his 53rd birthday. (iv) Maharaj will aid the Mughals (with 2000 cavalry and 7000 infantry) during the campaigns against Adil Shah. (v) Sambhaji Raje has to command a force of 5000 under Mughals.
- Amongst several demands, the treaty had required the Maratha ruler to give up Fort Kandhana to the Mughals.
- After it was taken over by the Mughals, the fort was guarded by Rajput, Pathan and Arab troop guards and was said to be impenetrable.
- This deeply disturbed and enraged Shivaji's mother Rajmata Jijabai. Upon knowing this, Shivaji entrusted Taanaji, the only man he could think of capable of reconquering the fort Kondhana at any cost.

CONCEPT REVISION

Here is the list of concepts that have been covered as part of the previous exercise. Revise and Self-reflect on your concepts you covered.

- Features of prehistoric art ☐
- Mughal School of Painting ☐
- Evolution of pottery ☐
- Coinage of Ancient Age ☐
- Deccan School of Painting ☐
- Thanjavur Painting ☐
- Mural Paintings ☐
- Pahari School of Painting ☐
- Pietra Dura style of ART ☐
- Folk Paintings ☐
- Decimal numeral system ☐
- Indo Greek coins ☐
- Sittanavasal Cave paintings ☐
- Bhimbetka Cave paintings ☐
- Chola Sculpture ☐
- "Kulhadar Group" ☐

☐☐☐

8. PERFORMING ARTS

8.1 MUSIC IN INDIA

QUESTIONS

1. **Consider the following statements regarding Kamaicha:**
   1. It is a bowed lute played by the manganiars of West Rajasthan.
   2. It links the sub-continent to Western Asia and Africa.

   Which of the above statement/s is/are correct?

   (a) 1 only (b) 2 only
   (c) Both 1 and 2 (d) Neither 1 nor 2

2. **Consider the following Statements regarding Pahari School of Indian Paintings:**
   1. It flourished in the Pahari region which comprised the present State of Himachal Pradesh, parts of Punjab, Jammu and Kashmir and Uttar Pradesh.
   2. Kishangarh School of Paintings was part of this school.

   Which of the above statement/s is/are correct?

   (a) 1 only (b) 2 only
   (c) Both 1 and 2 (d) Neither 1 nor 2

3. **Consider the following statements regarding Carnatic music:**
   1. Carnatic Music gives more importance to literary aspects of singing as compared to Hindustani music.
   2. Purandara Dasa is considered Pitahmaha of the Carnatic music.

   Which of the above statement/s is/are incorrect?

   (a) 1 only (b) 2 only
   (c) Both 1 & 2 (d) Neither 1 nor 2

4. **With reference to eminent classical singer Girija Devi, consider the following statements:**
   1. She is the founder of Benaras Gharana.
   2. She is a recipient of all categories of Padma awards.

   Which of the above statement/s is/are correct?

   (a) 1 only (b) 2 only
   (c) Both 1 and 2 (d) Neither 1 nor 2

5. **With reference to the history of 'Music in India', consider the following statements:**
   1. The main instruments of Hindustani music are sitar, veena and sarod.
   2. The main instruments used in Carnatic music are mridhangam, veena and violin.
   3. The main emphasis in Carnatic music is on vocal while in Hindustani music the focus is both on vocal and instruments.

   Which of the statements given above is/are correct?

   (a) 3 only (b) 1 and 3 only
   (c) 2 and 3 only (d) 1, 2 and 3

6. **In Medieval India, the terms 'Narnal', 'Gajal' and 'Shutrnal' were often associated with:**
   (a) Several types of Mughal light artillery.
   (b) Various ranks in the administration of Rajputs.
   (c) Poetic renditions of Sufi Saints.
   (d) Various types of Maratha War strategies.

7. **With reference to Carnatic Music, consider the following statements:**
   1. It has developed in the south Indian states of Tamil Nadu, Kerala, Andhra Pradesh and Karnataka.
   2. Thyagaraja is considered to be the father of Carnatic music.
   3. Shamashastri is one of the "trinity" of Carnatic music.

   Which of the above statement is/are correct?
   (a) 1 and 2 only (b) 3 only
   (c) 1 and 3 only (d) 1, 2 and 3

8. **Consider the following statements regarding Chaitanya Mahaprabhu:**
   1. He popularised musical gathering or kirtan as a special form of mystic experience.
   2. He rejected the scriptures or idol-worship.

   Which of the above statement is/are incorrect?
   (a) 1 only (b) 2 only
   (c) Both 1 and 2 (d) Neither 1 nor 2

9. **Consider the following statements regarding Dhrupad and Khyal:**
   1. Taan is the main feature of Dhrupad and Alap of khyal.
   2. Sultan Mohammad Sharqi gave patronage to Khyal and Emperor Akbar to Dhrupad.

   Which of the above statement/s is/are incorrect?
   (a) 1 only (b) 2 only
   (c) Both 1 and 2 (d) Neither 1 nor 2

10. **Consider the following statements regarding Ajanta and Ellora Caves:**
    1. A sculpture on the wall of Kailash Temple depicting Ravana shaking Mount Kailasha is part of Ellora caves.
    2. Blue colour is absent from Ajanta Cave paintings.

    Which of the above statement/s is/are correct?
    (a) 1 only (b) 2 only
    (c) Both 1 and 2 (d) Neither 1 nor 2

11. **Which of the following pairs is/are not correctly matched?**

Regional Music	Region
1. Pankhida	Karnataka
2. Lotia	Telengana
3. Chhakri	Haryana

    Select the correct answer using the code given below:
    (a) 1 only (b) 2 only
    (c) 1 and 3 only (d) 1, 2 and 3

12. **Which of the following is/are not a form of music?**
    1. Pada 2. Javali
    3. Pallavi 4. Kamaicha

    Select the correct answer using the codes given below:
    (a) 1 and 4 only (b) 2 and 3 only
    (c) 4 only (d) All of the above

13. **The term 'Sushira Vadya' refers to:**
    (a) Membrane-based musical instruments.
    (b) Solid musical instruments that do not require any tuning.
    (c) String-based musical instruments.
    (d) Wind-based musical instruments.

14. **Swara, Raga, and Tala are the three main pillars of Indian classical music. In this regard, consider the following statements:**
    1. Swara is the smallest gradation of pitch representing the quality of frequency.
    2. Raga forms the basis of melody.
    3. Tala forms the basis of rhythm.

    Which of the above statements is/are correct?
    (a) 1 only (b) 1 and 2 only
    (c) 2 and 3 only (d) 1, 2 and 3

15. **With reference to the different style of singing in Hindustani music, consider the following statements:**
    1. Dhrupad includes the use of Sanskrit syllables and is of Temple origin.
    2. The origin of the Khayal style of singing is attributed to Amir Khusrau.
    3. Thumri is semi-classical Indian music revolving around the love for Shiva.

    Which of the above statements is/are correct?
    (a) 1 only (b) 1 and 2 only
    (c) 2 and 3 only (d) 1, 2 and 3

16. **What are the differences between Hindustani and Carnatic Schools of Classical Music?**
    1. While Hindustani music is completely indigenous, Carnatic music has foreign influence.
    2. There is no freedom to improvise in Carnatic music while there is a scope for variations in Hindustani music.
    3. Hindustani music puts more emphasis on vocals than Carnatic music.
    4. While Hindustani music has several sub-styles, there is no sub-style within Carnatic music.

    Select the correct answer using the code given below:
    (a) 1 and 3 only (b) 2 and 4 only
    (c) 1, 2 and 3 only (d) 2, 3 and 4 only

17. **M. S. Subbalakshmi was famous vocalist for which form of Classical Music?**
    (a) Hindustani
    (b) Carnatic
    (c) Quwwali
    (d) Both Carnatic and Hindustani

18. **With reference to the different styles of singing in Hindustani music, consider the following statements:**
1. Dhrupad includes the use of Sanskrit syllables and is of Temple origin.
2. Thumri is semi-classical Indian music revolving around the love for Shiva.

Which of the above statements is/are correct?

(a) 1 only (b) 2 only
(c) Both 1 and 2 (d) Neither 1 nor 2

SOLUTIONS

1. **Correct Option: (c)**

Supplementary Notes:

Kamaicha

- **Statement 1 is correct:** The Kamaicha is a bowed lute played by the manganiars of West Rajasthan. The whole instrument is one piece of wood, the spherical bowl extending into a neck and fingerboard; the resonator is covered with leather and the upper portion with wood. There are four main strings and a number of subsidiary ones passing over a thin bridge.
- **Statement 2 is correct:** The Kamaicha links the sub-continent to Western Asia and Africa and is considered by some scholars to be the oldest instrument, with the exception of the Ravana Hasta or Ravana Hasta Veena.
- The varieties of upright bowed instruments are generally seen in the northern areas of the country. In these there are again two varieties, the fretted and the non-fretted.

2. **Correct Option: (a)**

Explanation:

Supplementary Notes:

- **Statement 1 is correct:** The Pahari region comprises the present State of Himachal Pradesh, some adjoining areas of the Punjab, the area of Jammu in the Jammu and Kashmir State.
- Pahari paintings of India can be divided into two distinct categories, on the basis of their geographical range, namely:
  - Basohli and Kulu Style (Influenced by Chaurpanchasika Style)
  - Guler and Kangra Style (Based on cooler colors and refinement)
- **Statement 2 is incorrect:** Kishangarh Style of painting is part of the Rajput schools of painting itis essentially a synthesis of Mughal and local style. The theme of this style comprised of the representation of the affection between Krishna and Radha.

3. **Correct Option: (a)**

Supplementary Notes:

Carnatic music

- It is a system of music associated with the southern part of Indian sub-continent, while the Hindustani music is associated with North India and is deeply influenced by Persian and Islamic music system.
- **Statement 2 is correct:** In Hindustani music, the language used is quite formal and words are not articulated clearly. The reason for this was that concerts usually occurred in Muslim courts where reference to Hindu gods was underplayed in order to keep it a secret. In Carnatic songs the saints are revered and the words are very clear and well-articulated. The meaning and pronunciation of the words is very important in conveying the mood of the performer. Thus Carnatic Music gives more importance to literary aspects of singing.
- **Statement 3 is correct:** The advent of Purandaradasa, in the year 1484, marked a very important landmark in the development of Carnatic music. He effected such a thorough systematisation and refinement in the art, that, up to the present day, it has remained the same. He has been justly termed as "Carnatic Sangeeta Pitamaha". He was not merely a composer but a Lakshanakara of the highest caliber. He introduced the Malavagowla scale as the basic scale for music instruction. He also framed graded exercises, forming part of the series of lessons to beginners of music. This system prevails even today in the teaching of music. The Svaravalis, Janta varisas, the Suladi Sapta tala alankaras and gitams, composed by Purandaradasa, form the basis for mastery in the art. Among the compositional types, he has to his credit numerous lakshya gitams and lakshna gitams, tana varnams, tillanas, suladis, ugabhogas, vritta namas and kirtanas. His kirtanas are popularly referred to as Dasara Padas or Devarnamas.

4. **Correct Option: (b)**

Supplementary Notes:

Girija Devi

- The word gharana comes from the Hindi word 'ghar' which is derived from Sanskrit for Griha, which means 'house'. The music Gharanas are also called styles. These schools or Gharanas have their basis in the traditional mode of musical training and education. Every Gharana has its own distinct features. The main area of difference between Gharanas is the manner in which the notes are sung.
- **Gwalior Gharana:** This is the oldest among all the Khayal Gayaki (vocal) styles. The distinctive feature of this style of singing has been noted as its lucidity and simplicity. Exponents – Bal Krishna Balchal Karanjikar, Vishnu Digambar Paluskar, Pandit Omkarnath Thakur, Veena Sahasrabuddhe and Malini Rajurkar
- **Benaras Gharana:** Statement 1 is incorrect: The Benaras Gharana evolved as a result of the great lilting style of khayal singing known by Thumri singers of Benaras and Gaya.

- Founder – Pt Gopal Mishra
- Exponents – Rajan Mishra, Sajan Mishra, Girija Devi.

- **Agra Gharana:** The Agra Gharana places great importance on developing forcefulness and deepness in the voice so that the notes are powerful and resonant.
  - Exponents – The important singers of this Gharana are Faiyyaz Khan, Latafat Hussein Khan and Dinkar Kakini.
- **Kirana Gharana:** It derives its name from the birthplace of Abdul Kharim Khan of Kirana near Kurukshetra
  - Exponents – Hirabhai Barodekar, Begum Akhtar, Pandit Bhimsen Joshi, Gangubai Hangal and Prabha Atre.
- **Jaipur - Atrauli Gharana:** The most distinctive feature of the Jaipur Gharana can be best described as its complex and melodic form which arises out of the involutedly and undulating phrases that comprise the piece.
  - Exponents – Alladiya Khan, Mallikarjun Mansur, Kesarbhai Kerkar, Kishori Amonkar, Shruti Sadolikar, Padma Talwalkar and Ashwini Bhide Deshpande.
- **Rampur Sahaswan Gharana:** In the Rampur Sahaswan Gharana there is a stress on the clarity of swara in this style and the development, and elaboration of the raga is done through a stepwise progression.
  - Exponents – Ghulam Mustafa Khan, Ustad Nissar Hussain Khan, Ustad Rashid Khan, Sulochana and Brihaspati.
- **Patiala Gharana:** Patiala Gharana is regarded as an offshoot of the Delhi Gharana. The Patiala Gharana is characterized by the use of greater rhythm play and by Layakari with the abundant use of Bols.
  - Founders – Ustad Fateh Ali Khan and Ustad Ali Baksh
  - Exponents – Bade Ghulam Ali Khan, Ajoy Chakravarti, Raza Ali Khan, Beghum Akhtar, Nirmala Devi, Naina Devi, Parveen Sultana and others.
- **Delhi Gharana:** The Delhi Ghaana was represented by Tanras Khan and Shabbu Khan. The highlights of Delhi Gharana are pleasing vistaar and exquisite compositions.
  - Founders – Ustad Mamman Khan
  - Exponents – Some of the notable exponents of Delhi Gharana are Chand Khan, Nasir Ahmed Khan, Usman Khan, Iqbal Ahmed Khan and Krishna Bisht.
- **Bhendi Bazaar Gharana:** The most distinctive feature of the Bhendi Bazaar Gharana is the presentation of Khayal, which is open voice, using Akar. There is a stress on breath-control and singing of long passages in one breath is highly regarded in this Gharana
  - Exponents – The important singers of this Gharana are Ustad Aman Ali Khan, Shashikala Koratkar and Anjanibai Malpekar.
- **Mewati Gharana:** The Mewati Gharana gives importance to developing the mood of the raga through the notes forming it and its style is Bhava Pradhan. It also gives equal importance to the meaning of the text.
  - Exponents – The exponents of the Mewati Gharana are Pandit Jasraj, Moti Ram, Mani Ram, Sanjeev Abhyankar and others.
- **Statement 2 is correct:** She is a recipient of all the Padma awards:

Award Name	Award Category	Year	Field
Padma Shri	Civilian Award	1972	Arts
Padma Bhushan	Civilian Award	1989	Arts
Padma Vibhushan	Civilian Award	2016	Arts

5. **Correct Option: (c)**

Explanation:

- **Statement 1 is incorrect:** Hindustani classical music is the traditional music of northern regions of the Indian subcontinent. It may also be called North Indian classical music or sastriya sangit. Besides vocal music, which is considered to be of primary importance, its main instruments are the sitar and sarod (not veena). Classical music can be divided into melody and rhythm; there is no concept of harmony.
- **Statement 2 is correct:** Carnatic music is usually performed by a small ensemble of musicians, consisting of a principal performer (usually a vocalist), a melodic accompaniment (usually a violin), a rhythm accompaniment (usually a mridangam), and a tambura, which acts as a drone throughout the performance. Other typical instruments used in performances may include the ghatam, kanjira, morsing, venu flute, veena, and chitraveena. The greatest concentration of Carnatic musicians is to be found in the city of Chennai. Various Carnatic music festivals are held throughout India and abroad, including the Madras Music Season, which has been considered to be one of the world's largest cultural events.

- **Statement 3 is correct:**

Areas of differences	Carnatic	Hindustani
Ragas	72 Ragas	6 Major Ragas
Instruments	Veena, Mridangam and Mandolin	Tabla, Sarangi, Sitar and Santoor
Influence	Indigenous	Afghan Persian and Arab
Sub-styles	Only one particular prescribed style of singing	Several sub-styles
Freedom	Freedom to improvise	Scope to do variations and improvise
Vocal and instruments	Both have equal importance	More importance to vocal music

6. **Correct Option: (a)**

Supplementary Notes:

'Narnal', 'Gajal' and 'Shutrnal'

- **Option (a) is correct:** There were several types of Mughal light artillery. If carried on the back of a man, they were called narnal; if carried on backs of elephants- gajal, if on backs of camels- shutrnal.

7. **Correct Option: (c)**

Explanation:

- **Stsatement 2 is incorrect:** Purandardas is considered to be the father of Carnatic music.

Supplementary Notes:

Carnatic Music

- Carnatic music or Carnatic sangeet is the South Indian classical music. Carnatic music has a rich history and tradition and is one of the gems of world music.
- Carnatic Sangeet has developed in the South Indian states of Tamil Nadu, Kerala, Andhra Pradesh and Karnataka. These states are known for their strong presentation of Dravidian culture.
- Purandardas (1480-1564) is considered to be the father of Carnatic music. To him goes the credit of codification of the method of Carnatic music. He is also credited with creation of several thousand songs.
- Another great name associated with Carnatic music is that of Venkat Mukhi Swami. He is regarded as the grand theorist of Carnatic music. He also developed "Melankara", the system for classifying south Indian ragas.
- It was in the 18th century that Carnatic music acquired its present form. This was the period that saw the "trinity" of Carnatic music; Thyagaraja, Shamashastri and Muthuswami Dikshitar compile their famous compositions.
- Numerous other musicians and composers have also enriched the tradition of Carnatic music.
- Some other notable Carnatic music exponents are Papanasam Shivan, Gopala Krishna Bharati, Swati Tirunal, Mysore Vasudevachar, Narayan Tirtha, Uttukadu Venkatasubbair, Arunagiri Nathar and Annamacharya.
- In Carnatic music there is a very highly developed theoretical system. It is based upon a complex system of Ragam (Raga) and Thalam (Tala).
- Raga is basically the scale and the seven notes of this scale are Sa Re Ga Ma Pa Dha and Ni. Though unlike a simple scale there are definite melodic restrictions and compulsions.
- The Ragams are classified into various modes. These modes are referred to as mela, which are 72 in number. The Tala (thalam) is the rhythmic foundation of the Carnatic music.

8. **Correct Option: (b)**

Explanation:

- **Statement 2 is incorrect:** He did not reject the scriptures or idol-worship, though he cannot be classified as a traditionalist.

Supplementary Notes:

Cultural development in India 1300-1500: Vaishnavite movement

- Apart from the non-sectarian movement led by Kabir and Nanak, the Bhakti movement in North India developed around the worship of Rama and Krishna, two of the incarnations of the god Vishnu.
- They used the love between Radha and Krishna in an allegorical manner to depict the relationship of love, in its various aspects, between the individual soul and the supreme soul.
- Like the early Sufis, Chaitanya popularised musical gathering or kirtan as a special form of mystic experience in which the outside world disappeared by dwelling on God's name.
- According to Chaitanya, worship consisted of love and devotion and song and dance which produced a state of ecstasy in which the presence of God could be realised. Such a worship could be carried out by all, irrespective of caste or creed.
- The writings of Narsinha Mehta in Gujarat, of Meera in Rajasthan, of Surdas in western Uttar Pradesh and of Chaitanya in Bengal and Orissa reached extraordinary heights of lyrical fervour and of love which transcended all boundaries, including those of caste and creed.
- These saints were prepared to welcome into their fold everyone, irrespective of caste or creed. This is

seen most clearly in the life of Chaitanya. Born and schooled in Nadia which was the centre of Vedantic rationalism, Chaitanya's tenor of life was changed when he visited Gaya at the age of twenty-two and was initiated into the Krishna cult by a recluse. He became a god-intoxicated devotee who incessantly uttered the name of Krishna. Chaitanya is said to have travelled all over India, including Vrindavan, where he revived the Krishna cult. But most of his time was spent at Gaya.

- He did not reject the scriptures or idol-worship, though he cannot be classified as a traditionalist.

9. **Correct Option: (a)**

Explanation:

- **Statement 1 is incorrect:** Alap is the main features of dhrupad and taan of khyal.

Supplementary Notes:

Dhrupad and Khyal

- It is one of the oldest and grandest forms of Hindustani classical music and finds mention even in Natyashastra (200 BC–200 AD).
- It is said that dhrupad owes its roots to older forms like Prabhanda and Dhruvapada.
- The name is derived from 'dhruva' and 'pada,' which means that it denotes both verse form of the poetry and the style in which it is sung.
- Although Dhrupad consolidated its position as a classical form of music in the 13 th century, it reached its zenith in the court of emperor Akbar.
- He employed and patronised musical masters like Baba Gopal Das, Swami Haridas and Tansen, who was considered to be one of the Navaratna or nine gems of the Mughal court.
- It is also speculated that Baiju Bawra sang at the court of Akbar.
- We find evidence of singers who mastered Dhrupad in the court of Raja Man Singh Tomar situated in Gwalior.
- It became the major form of singing in the medieval period but fell in a state of decline in the 18 th century.
- Dhrupad is essentially a poetic form that is incorporated into an extended presentation style that is marked by precise and overt elaboration of a raga.
- Dhruva literally means 'unmoving'. It implies the return of the Swara (tonal), Kala (time) and Shabda (textual) trajectories to a fixed point.
- Dhrupad starts with Alap which is sung without words. The tempo rises gradually, and it is the major part of the performance.
- The alap evokes a mood in the audience that coincides with the mood of the raga that is chosen.
- It is pure music without the distraction of words.
- Then after some time Dhrupad begins and Pakhawaj is played.
- Dhrupad includes use of Sanskrit syllables and is of Temple origin.
- Dhrupad compositions usually have 4 to 5 stanzas and are performed by a duo.
- Generally two male vocalists perform Dhrupad style of performances.
- Tanpura and Pankhawaj usually accompany them.
- Dhrupad singing can be further divided into four forms on the basis of vanis or banis that they perform:

Khyal

- The word 'Khyal' is derived from Persian and means "idea or imagination".
- The origin of this style was attributed to Amir Khusrau.
- This form is popular amongst the artists as this provides greater scope for improvisation.
- Khyal is based on the repertoire of short songs ranging from two to eight lines.
- Generally, a Khyal composition is also referred to as a 'Bandish'.
- Sultan Mohammad Sharqi gave the biggest patronage to Khyal in the 15 th century.
- One of the most unique features of Khyal is the use of taan in the composition
- Because of this, Alap is given much less room in the Khyal music as compared to Dhrupad.
- A typical Khyal performance uses two songs:
  - Bada Khyal: sung in the slow tempo
  - Chhota Khyal: sung in the fast tempo
- In most cases, every singer renders the same bandish differently, while keeping the text and raga as constant.
- Usually, the theme for these Khyal bandish is romantic in nature.
- They sing about love, even if they are related to the divine creatures.
- It may be praising God or a particular king. Exceptional Khyal compositions are composed in the praise of Lord Krishna.

10. **Correct Option: (c)**

Explanation:

- Both statements are correct

Supplementary Notes:

Ajanta Caves

- Ajanta is a series of rock-cut caves in the Sahyadri ranges on Waghora river near Aurangabad in Maharashtra.

- There are a total of 29 caves of which 25 were used as Viharas or residential caves while 4 were used as Chaitya or prayer halls. The caves were developed in the period between 200 BC to 650 AD.
- The Ajanta caves were inscribed by the Buddhist monks, under the patronage of the Vakataka kings – Harishena being a prominent one.
- The figures in these caves were done using fresco painting and demonstrate considerable naturalism.
- The colours were obtained from local vegetation and minerals.
- The outlines of the paintings were done in red colour and then the inside was painted.
- One of the striking features is the absence of blue colour in the paintings.
- Cave No. 16 is one of the most elegant specimens of cave architecture.
- The paintings are generally themed around Buddhism – the life of Buddha and Jataka stories.
- Of the 29 caves, 5 were developed during the Hinayana phase while the remaining 24 were developed during the Mahayana phase of Buddhism.
- Reference of the Ajanta Caves can be found in the travel accounts of Chinese Buddhist travellers Fa hien and Hieun Tsang.
- Some prominent sculptures of Ajanta Caves are:
    - Mahaparinirvana of Buddha in Cave No. 26.
    - Naga king and his consort in Cave No. 19

Ellora Caves:

- Ellora caves are another important site of cave architecture.
- It is located nearly 100 kms away from Ajanta caves in the Sahyadri ranges of Maharashtra.
- It is a group of 34 caves – 17 Brahmanical, 12 Buddhist and 5 Jain.
- These set of caves were developed during the period between 5th and 11th centuries AD (newer as compared to Ajanta Caves) by various guilds from Vidarbha, Karnataka and Tamil Nadu.
- Hence, the caves reflect a natural diversity in terms of theme and architectural styles.
- Caves 1–12: Buddhist Caves; 13–29: Hindu Caves 30–34: Jain (Digambara sect).
- Some of the prominent caves in Ellora are:
- Cave No. 10 is a Buddhist Chaitya cave known as Vishwakarma Cave or carpenter's cave. Buddha is seated in Vyakhyana Mudra here and Bodhi tree is carved at his back.
    - Cave No. 14 is themed "Raavan ki khai".
    - Cave No. 15 is Dashavatar Temple.
    - Cave No. 16 is Kailash Temple dedicated to Lord Shiva. It was developed under the patronage of Rashtrakuta king Krishna I and was carved out of a monolith, and even has a courtyard.
    - In cave no 16, there is also a sculpture on the wall of Kailash Temple depicting Ravana shaking Mount Kailasha. It is considered one of the masterpieces of Indian sculpture.
    - Dhumar Lena in Cave 29
    - Rameshwar Temple in Cave 21
    - Two famous Jain caves are Indra Sabha (Cave 32) and Jagannath Sabha (Cave 33).

11. Correct Option: (d)

Explanation:

- All pairs are incorrectly matched

Regional Music	Region
A. Pankhida	Rajasthan
B. Lotia	Rajasthan
C. Chhakri	Kashmir

Supplementary Notes:

Regional Music

- **Pankhida, Rajasthan:** Sung by the peasants of Rajasthan while doing work in the fields, the peasants sing and speak while playing algoza and manjira. The literal meaning of the word 'Pankhida' is lover.
- **Lotia, Rajasthan:** 'Lotia' is sung in the chaitra month during the festival - 'Lotia'. Women bring lotas (a vessel to fill water) and kalash (a vessel considered to be auspicious to fill water during worship) filled with water from ponds and wells. They decorate them with flowers and come home.
- **Chhakri, Kashmir:** Chhakri is a group song which is the most popular form of Kashmir's folk music. It is sung to the accompaniment of the noot (earthen pot) rababs, sarangi and tumbaknari (an earthen pot with high neck).

12. Correct Option: (c)

Explanation:

- **Option (c) is correct:** The Kamaicha is a bowed lute played by the manganiars of West Rajasthan.

Supplementary Notes:

- **PADA:** Padas are scholarly compositions in Telegu and Tamil. Though they are composed mainly as dance forms, they are also sung in concerts, on account of their musical excellence and aesthetic appeal. A padam also has the sections, 24 angeet, anupallavi and charana. The music is slow-moving and dignified. There is a natural flow of music and, sustained balance between the words and the music is maintained throughout.
- **JAVALI:** A javali is a composition belonging to the sphere of light classical music. Sung both in concert programmes and dance concerts, the javalis are

popular because of the attractive melodies in which they are composed. In contrast to the padas which portray divine love, javalis are songs which are sensuous in concept and spirit. They are generally set in madhyama kala.

- **PALLAVI:** This is the most important branch of creative music. It is in this branch of manodharma 24 angeeta, that the musician has ample opportunities of displaying his or her creative talents, imaginative skill, and musical intelligence. The term Pallavi is coined from the initial syllables of the three words: Padam, meaning words; Layam, meaning time and Vinyasam, meaning variations. The words chosen for a Pallavi may be either in Sanskrit, Telugu or Tamil and may be on any theme, though the devotional is always preferred.
- **KAMAICHA:** The Kamaicha is a bowed lute played by the manganiars of West Rajasthan. The whole instrument is one piece of wood, the spherical bowl extending into a neck and fingerboard; the resonator is covered with leather and the upper portion with wood. There are four main strings and a number of subsidiary ones passing over a thin bridge. The kamaicha links the sub-continent to Western Asia and Africa and is considered by some scholars to be the oldest instrument, with the exception of the Ravana Hatta or Ravana Hasta Veena.

13. Correct Option: (d)

Supplementary Notes:

Musical Instruments

- There are four major traditional categories of musical instruments depending upon the type of instruments that are included in it. They are:
  - **Awanad/Avanaddha Vadya**
    - These are the membranophone instruments as they contain an outer membrane, which is beaten to take out particular musical sounds.
    - These are also known as percussion instruments as one has to strike them to generate musical sound.
    - They generally have one or two faces covered with hiding or skin.
    - Generally, the musical instruments included in this category are Tabla, Drum, Dhol, Congo, Mrindangum, etc.
  - **Sushira Vadya**
    - These are the aerophones, i.e. this category includes all the wind instruments.
    - The most common instruments include Bansuri (flute), Shehnai, Pungi, Ninkirns, etc.
    - Shehnai is a double reeded wind instrument with a widening tube towards the end. It is one of the oldest wind instruments in India.
  - **Ghana Vadya**
    - It is the genre of the solid instruments that do not require any tuning.
    - They are also called the Idiophone instruments.
    - The most popular examples of Ghana Vadya are Manjira, Jaltarang, Kanchtarang, Jhanj, Khartal, etc.
    - The function of these instruments is to keep rhythm and time with the song that is being sung.
  - **Tata Vadya**
    - These are the Chordophones or the string instruments that function best when their sound is modified by hand.
    - Examples include Sitar, Veena, and Violin etc.

14. Correct Option: (c)

Explanation:

- **Statement 1 is incorrect:** A Shruti is the smallest gradation of pitch representing the quality of frequency. Swara is used to define the 'note' or 'scale degree' in a composition.

Supplementary Notes:

Anatomy of Indian Music

- Before one delves into the different types and kinds of Indian music it is necessary to understand the anatomy of Indian classical music.
- There are three main pillars of Indian classical music: Raga, tala, and Swara.
- **Swara:**
  - In the ancient period, the term "Swara" was associated with the recitation of the Vedas. Over time, the term is used to define the 'note' or 'scale degree' in a composition.
  - In the Natyasastra, Bharata has divided the swaras into a twenty-two notes scale.
  - Currently, the notational system of the Hindustani music is defined by these abbreviated swaras – Sa, re, ga, ma, pa, dha, ni. The Seven Swaras together are called Saptak or Sargam.
  - The Swara differs from Shruti. A Shruti is the smallest gradation of pitch representing the quality of frequency. There are 22 Shrutis or microtones out of which only 12 are audible. These 12 are seven Suddha Swaras and five Vikrita Swaras.
- **Raga:**
  - The word 'raga' comes from the Sanskrit word 'Ranj', which literally means to delight or to make happy and satisfy a person.
  - The ragas form the basis of the melody.

- The basic element necessary for the working of a raga is the note on which they are based.
- The reason behind the creation of ragas was to evoke emotional responses in the performer and the audience. These emotions, which are evoked through the singing and playing of instruments, are called Rasas.

- **Tala:**
  - The rhythmic groupings of beats are called 'Tala'.
  - These rhythmical cycles range from three to 108 beats.
  - Tala thus becomes the basis of the rhythm.
  - The tempo of the 'tala', which keeps the uniformity of the time span, is called the 'laya'.

15. Correct Option: (b)

Explanation:

- **Statement 3 is incorrect:** Thumri is semi-classical Indian music inspired by the Bhakti movement and revolves around the girl's love for Krishna.

Supplementary Notes:

Hindustani Music

- The Hindustani branch of music focuses more on the musical structure and the possibilities of improvisation in it. The Hindustani branch adopted a scale of 'Shudha Swara Saptaka' or the 'Octave of Natural notes'.
- There are ten main styles of singing in Hindustani music like the 'Dhrupad', 'Dhamar', 'Hori', 'Khayal', 'Tappa', 'Chaturanga', 'Ragasagar', 'Tarana', 'Sargam' and 'Thumri'.
- **Dhrupad:**
  - It is one of the oldest and grandest forms of Hindustani classical music and finds its mention even in Natyashastra (200 BC–200 AD).
  - Although Dhrupad consolidated its position as a classical form of music in the 13th century, it reached its zenith in the court of Akbar. He employed and patronized musical masters like Baba Gopal Das, Swami Haridas, and Tansen, who was considered to be one of the Navaratna or nine gems of the Mughal court. It is also speculated that Baiju Bawra sang at the court of Akbar.
  - Dhrupad is essentially a poetic form that is incorporated into an extended presentation style that is marked by the precise and overt elaboration of a raga.
  - Dhrupad includes the use of Sanskrit syllables and is of Temple origin.
  - Generally, two male vocalists perform Dhrupad style of performances.
- **Khayal:**
  - The origin of this style was attributed to Amir Khusrau.
  - This form is popular amongst the artists as this provides greater scope for improvisation.
  - One of the unique features of Khayal is the use of 'taan' in the composition. Because of this, Alap is given much less room in the Khayal music as compared to Dhrupad.
- **Thumri:**
  - It is based on mixed ragas and is commonly considered to be semi-classical Indian music.
  - The compositions are either romantic or devotional in nature. This was inspired by the Bhakti movement so much that the text usually revolves around the girl's love for Krishna.
  - The language of the composition is usually Hindi or Awadhi dialect or the Braj Bhasha dialect.
  - The compositions are usually sung in a female voice.

16. Correct Option: (b)

Explanation:

- **Statement 1 is incorrect:** Carnatic music is completely indigenous while Hindustani music has Arabic and Persian influence.
- **Statement 3 is incorrect:** Carnatic music puts more emphasis on vocals.

Supplementary Notes:

Classical Music

- The two distinct schools of Indian Classical Music are:
  - Hindustani Music: practiced in northern parts of India
  - Carnatic Music: practiced in southern parts of India

Points of Difference	Hindustani Music	Carnatic Music
Influence	Arab, Persian and Afghan	Indigenous
Freedom	Scope for artists to improvise, hence there is scope for variations	No freedom to improvise
Sub-styles	There are several sub-styles which led to emergence of 'Gharanas'	Only one particular style of singing
Need for Instruments	Equally important as vocals	More emphasis on vocal music

Ragas	6 major ragas	72 ragas
Time	Adheres to time	Doesn't adhere to any time
Instruments	Tabla, Sarangi, Sitar and Santoor	Veena, Mrindangum and Mandolin
Association to Parts of India	North India	Usually South India

17. Correct Option: (d)

Supplementary Notes:

- Madurai Shanmukhavadivu Subbulakshmi (also known as M.S.; September 16, 1916 – December 11, 2004) was an Indian Carnatic singer from Madurai, Tamil Nadu. She was the first musician ever to be awarded the Bharat Ratna, India's highest civilian honour.
- M.S. Subbulakshmi began her Carnatic classical music training under her mother Shanmugavadivu; and later in Hindustani classical training under Pandit Narayan Rao Vyas.

18. Correct Option: (a)

Explanation:

- **Statement 2 is incorrect:** Thumri is semi-classical Indian music revolving around the love for Lord Krishna.

Supplementary Notes:

Hindustani Music

- The Hindustani branch of music focuses more on the musical structure and the possibilities of improvisation in it. The Hindustani branch adopted a scale of 'Shudha Swara Saptaka' or the 'Octave of Natural Notes'.

Dhrupad:

- It is one of the oldest and grandest forms of Hindustani classical music and finds its mention even in Natyashastra (200 BC–200 AD).
- Although Dhrupad consolidated its position as a classical form of music in the 13th century, it reached its zenith in the court of Akbar. He employed and patronized musical masters like Baba Gopal Das, Swami Haridas, and Tansen, who was considered to be one of the Navaratna or nine gems of the Mughal court. It is also speculated that Baiju Bawra sang at the court of Akbar.
- Dhrupad is essentially a poetic form that is incorporated into an extended presentation style that is marked by the precise and overt elaboration of a raga.
- Dhrupad includes the use of Sanskrit syllables and is of Temple origin.
- Generally, two male vocalists perform Dhrupad style of performances.

Thumri:

- It is based on mixed ragas and is commonly considered to be semi-classical Indian music.
- The compositions are either romantic or devotional in nature. This was inspired by the Bhakti movement so much that the text usually revolves around the girl's love for Krishna.
  - The language of the composition is usually Hindi or Awadhi dialect or the Braj Bhasha dialect.
  - The compositions are usually sung in a female voice.

CONCEPT REVISION

Here is the list of concepts that have been covered as part of the previous exercise. Revise and self-reflect on your concepts you covered.

- Kamaicha ☐
- Carnatic Music ☐
- Classical Singers ☐
- Terms –'Narnal','Gajal' and 'Shutrnal' ☐
- Chaitanya Mahaprabhu ☐
- Dhrupad and Khyal ☐
- Regional Music ☐
- 'Sushira Vadya' ☐
- Swara,Raga and Tala ☐
- Different singing styles in Hindustani Music ☐

8.2 DANCES IN INDIA

QUESTIONS

1. With reference to Odissi dance form consider the following statements:

1. Tribangha posture is an important feature of this dance style.
2. It was patronized mainly by the Jain King Kharvela.

Which of the above statement/s is/are correct?

(a) 1 only (b) 2 only
(c) Both 1 and 2 (d) Neither 1 nor 2

2. Which of the following pairs are correctly matched?

Folk Dance		State
1. Rouff	-	Maharashtra
2. Raut Nacha	-	Chhattisgarh
3. Ghumura	-	Rajasthan
4. Puli Kali	-	Kerala

Select the correct answer using the code given below:

(a) 1 and 3 only (b) 2 and 4 only
(c) 1 and 2 only (d) 3 and 4 only

3. Which of the following pairs related to the musical instruments is/are correctly matched?

Instruments		Features
1. Tata Vadya	-	Sound is produced by the vibration of a string.
2. Reed instruments	-	Sound is produced by blowing air into an hollow column.
3. Avanaddha vadya	-	Sound is produced by striking animal skin.

Select the correct answer using the code given below:

(a) 1 and 2 only (b) 2 and 3 only
(c) 1 and 3 only (d) 1, 2 and 3

4. With reference to the 'folk dances in India', consider the following statements:

1. Kalbelia is a folk dance performed by the women of the Kalbelia community of Bihar.
2. Alkap is a rural dance-drama performance of Gujarat and Rajasthan.
3. Thangta is the exclusive dance form of Nagaland

Which of the statements given above are incorrect?

(a) 1 and 2 only (b) 1 and 3 only
(c) 2 and 3 only (d) 1, 2 and 3

5. With reference to Odissi Dance, consider the following statements:

1. One of the positions is the tribhanga imitating a square which is a very masculine stance with the weight of the body equally balanced.
2. The other position is chowk which is a very feminine stance where the body is deflected at the neck, torso and the knees.
3. The dance form is known as mobile sculpture.

Which of the above statement/s is/are correct?

(a) 1 and 2 only (b) 3 only
(c) 2 and 3 only (d) 1, 2 and 3

6. Consider the following statements regarding History of Indian classical dance:

1. Tandava is symbolic to the feminine features of dance as an art form.
2. Lasya is symbolic to the male aspects of dance.

Which of the above statement/s is/are incorrect?

(a) 1 only (b) 2 only
(c) Both 1 and 2 (d) Neither 1 nor 2

7. Consider the following:

1. One of the principal mudras of this dance is 'Kataka Mukha Hasta' in which the three fingers are joined to symbolise 'Om'.
2. Varnam is a combination of dance and emotions, and synchronised with tala and raag, to express the story is the most important part of this dance.
3. Rukmini Devi Arundale was famous artist of this classical dance

Which of the following classical dance is mentioned in the above statements?

(a) Kuchipudi (b) Bharatnatyam
(c) Kathakali (d) Kathak

8. Consider the following description:

This Mudra indicates fearlessness. The right hand is raised to shoulder height with arm bent. The palm of the right hand faces outwards and the fingers are upright and joined".

Identify the Mudra related to Buddha described in the above passage:

(a) Dhyan Mudra (b) Abhaya Mudra
(c) Anjali Mudra (d) Karana Mudra

9. Consider the following statements regarding Natya Shastra:

1. The first formal mention of dance is found in Bharata Muni's Natya Shastra.
2. As, per Natya Shastra, there are two basic aspects of Indian classical dance, Nritya, and Natya.

Which of the above statements is/are incorrect?

(a) 1 only (b) 2 only
(c) Both 1 and 2 (d) Neither 1 nor 2

10. **Which of the following folk dance is/are inscribed in Representative List of Intangible Cultural Heritage of Humanity?**
1. Chhau 2. Kalbelia
3. Garba
Select the correct answer using the code given below:
(a) 1 and 2 only (b) 2 only
(c) 1 and 3 only (d) 1, 2 and 3

11. **Match the following:**

Classical Dance	State
A. Kathakali	1. Andhra Pradesh
B. Kathak	2. Assam
C. Sattriya	3. Uttar Pradesh
D. Kuchipudi	4. Kerala

Select the correct answer using the code given below:

	A	B	C	D
(a)	3	4	1	2
(b)	3	4	2	1
(c)	4	3	2	1
(d)	4	3	1	2

12. **As per Abhinaya Darpan, the famous treatise on dance, an act has been broken into three basic elements. In this context, consider the following pairs:**
1. Nritya – Basic dance steps
2. Natya – Dramatic representations
3. Nritta – Emotions evoked through dance
Which of the above pair is/are correctly matched?
(a) 1 and 3 only (b) 2 an 3 only
(c) 2 only (d) 1, 2 and 3

13. **Consider the following statements regarding the Odissi dance:**
1. The caves of Udayagiri-Khandagiri provide some of the earliest examples of this dance form.
2. Jatiswaram, Shabdam, Varnam, etc are some of the elements of this dance.
3. This dance is accompanied by Hindustani classical music.
Select the correct answer using the code given below:
(a) 1 and 2 only (b) 2 and 3 only
(c) 1 and 3 only (d) 1, 2 and 3

14. **Consider the following statements:**
1. Bhavai involves women balancing nine brass pitchers or earthen pots on their head as they dance,feet on the perimeter of a brass plate or on the top of a glass.
2. In Chari, women are attired in traditional outfit and dance while balancing brass chari on their heads, along with a lighted lamp in it.
3. Chang dance form is the fast-paced rhythmic beats of the chang instrument, upon which a group of men dance.
Which of the given statements is/are correct?
(a) 1 and 2 only (b) 2 only
(c) 1 and 3 only (d) All of the above

15. **Koodiyattam is a form of:**
(a) Sacred Theatre (b) Organic Painting
(c) Traditional Dance (d) Martial Art

16. **Consider the following statements regarding Sattriya dance:**
1. Khol and Flute are the main instruments played in this dance.
2. It combines the elements of Lasya and Tandava.
Which of the above statements is/are correct?
(a) 1 only (b) 2 only
(c) Both 1 and 2 (d) Neither 1 nor 2

SOLUTIONS

1. **Correct Option: (c)**
Supplementary Notes:
Odissi
- Odissi derives its name from 'Odra Nirtya' mentioned in NatyaShastra. Khandariya-Udayagiri caves provide some of the early examples of Odissi dance.
- Statement 2 is correct: It was patronized mainly by the Jain King Kharvela and primarily performed by Maharis.
- Kabichanda Kallicharan Patnaik revived this dance form after the independence. Later efforts of Charles Fabri and Indrani Rehman bought International acclaim to this dance form.
- Mudras and postures for expressing emotions are similar to that of Bharatanatyam.
- Statement 1 is correct: The three bent form of dance called Tribangha posture is an important feature of Odissi.
- Odissi dance performs Natya combined with an element of dancing and acting.
- It is a unique representation of gracefulness, beauty, and sensuality.
- Geometrical shapes and patterns are created with dancers body. Hence it is called 'Mobile Sculpture'.
- Elements of Odissi includes:
  - Mangalcharan: It is the beginning of the dance.
  - Batunirtya: It comprises of dancing.
  - Pallavi: It includes the facial expression and representation of the song.
  - Tarijham: Pure dance before the conclusion.
    - Odissi dance music is Hindustani.
    - Water is symbolized in this dance form.
    - Guru Pankaj Charan Das, Guru Kelu Charan Mohapatra etc. are the main proponents of this dance form.

2. **Correct Option: (b)**

Supplementary Notes:

Different Dance Forms and Their States

- **Rouff:**
  - **Pair 1 is incorrect:** Rouff is the most well liked customary folk dance of Kashmir. This good looking ballet shape elegances at all the celebratory events and particularly at Ramzan and Id days.
  - It is executed by the group of girls that face each other when dancing. It is considered both as an artistic and visual treat. This welcoming dance form is basically carried out by Kashmiri women in order to welcome the spring season.
  - This dance is enthused by an insect bee. The dance form thus depicts the lovemaking of the bees that can clearly be seen when it is portrayed.
- **Raut Nacha:**
  - It is a dance performed by yadava/yaduvanshis, a caste which considers themselves to be descendants of Krishna. For them it is as a symbol of worship to Krishna.
  - They perform the dance at the time of 'dev udhni ekadashi'. It is believed that it is time of awakening of Gods after brief rest according to Hindu panchaang (calendar).
  - **Pair 2 is correct:** The dance is a close resemblance of Krishna's dance or raas leela. It is a folk dance of the Indian state Chhattisgarh.
- **Ghumura:**
  - **Pair 3 is incorrect:** It is a folk dance of the Indian state, Orissa. As per ancient mythological texts, Ghumura was a war dance of the Gods and Demons.
  - The Ghumura Janma Bidhan was written by the poet Kandarpa Panda in the year 1954, describing the Ghumara dance. Ghumura, which is a form of a drum, is said to be a combination of Lord Shiva's Damru and Goddess Saraswati's Veena that was created to kill the demon Mahishasura by Goddess Durga.
  - During the epic battle of Mahabharata, Ghumura was used as a war musical instrument by the Gods and the Goddesses. It is also said that Ghumura was used to produce the war music for the Lanka King Ravana, as noted in another Hindu mythological epic, Ramayana.
- **Puli Kali:**
  - **Pair 4 is correct:** It is a recreational folk art from the state of Kerala. It is performed by trained artists to entertain people on the occasion of Onam, an annual harvest festival, celebrated mainly in Kerala.
  - On the fourth day of Onam celebrations (Nalaam Onam), performers painted like tigers and hunters in bright yellow, red, and black dance to the beats of instruments like Udukku and Thakil. Literal meaning of Pulikkali is the 'play of the tigers' hence the performance revolve around the theme of tiger hunting.

3. **Correct Option: (d)**

Supplementary Notes:

Tata Vadya:

- **Pair 1 is Correct:** It is a category of instruments in which sound is produced by the vibration of a string or chord.
- These vibrations are caused by plucking or by bowing on the string which has been pulled taut.
- This is further classified based on the mode of playing – by friction with a bow like the Violin, Sarangi, Dilruba, Esraj etc.
- Ravanastram is one of the earliest known bowed instrument by plucking the string like the veena, rudra veena, gotuvadyam, sitar, sarod, guitar, mandolin, harp, (tambura, ektar-drone instruments) etc. by striking with a hammer or a pair of sticks like gettuvadyam, swaramandala.

Reed Instruments:

- Pair 2 is correct: Reed instruments like the Shehnai, Nadaswaram, etc. have one or two reeds inserted in the hollow beak or tube of the instrument, which vibrate when air is blown into them.
- In this type of instrument the reeds are bound together with a gap between them before inserting into the body of the instrument.
- The body of the tube is conical in shape narrow at the blowing end and opening out gradually with a metallic bell at the farther end to enhance the volume of the sound.
- A set of spare reeds, an ivory or silver needle for adjusting and cleaning the reeds are also hung from the mouth piece of the instrument.

AvanaddhaVadya:

- Pair 3 is correct: In the Avanaddha Vadya category of instruments, sound is produced by striking the animal skin which has been stretched across an earthern or metal pot or a wooden barrel or frame.
- The earliest references to such instruments have been found in the Vedas where there is mention of Bhumi Dundhubhi; this was a hollow pit dug in the ground and covered with the hide of a buffalo or ox which was stretched across the pit.
- The tail of the animal was used for striking the animal hide and thus sound was produced.
- Drums have been divided into different categories on the basis of their shapes and structure as also

the position and placement for playing. The main categories are – oordhwaka, ankya, alingya and the waisted or the damaru family of drums.

4. **Correct Option: (d)**

Supplementary Notes:

- **Statement 1 is incorrect:** Kalbelia or Kabeliya is one of the most sensuous dance forms of Rajasthan, performed by a tribe of the same name. They are famous for their dance which is an integral part of their culture. Both men and women in the tribe participate in this activity to celebrate joyfully occasionally.
- **Statement 2 is incorrect:** Alkap is a form of Bengali folk performance popular in the districts of Murshidabad, Malda and Birbhum in West Bengal and Chapai Nawabganj, Randajshahi in Bangladesh.
- **Statement 3 is incorrect:** Huyen langlon is an Indian martial art from Manipur. In the Meitei language, huyen means war while langlon or langlong can mean net, knowledge or art. Huyen langlon consists of two main components: thang-ta (armed combat) and sarit sarak (unarmed fighting). The primary weapons of huyen langlon are the thang (sword) and ta (spear).

5. **Correct Option: (b)**

Explanation:

- **Statement 1 is incorrect:** The chowk is a position imitating a square – a very masculine stance with the weight of the body equally balanced.
- **Statement 2 is incorrect:** The tribhanga is a very feminine stance where the body is deflected at the neck, torso, and knees.

Supplementary Notes:

Odissi Dance

- Odissi is known as the oldest dance form of India based on archaeological evidence. The reason is the bass reliefs of 1st century BC in the Udaygiri caves.
- The Natya Shastra speaks of the dance from this region and refers to it as Odra-Magadhi. Characterized by various Bhangas (Stance), which involves stamping of the foot and striking various postures as seen in Indian sculptures. The common Bhangas are Bhanga, Abanga, Atibhanga, and Tribhanga.
- The techniques of movement are built around the two basic postures of the Chowk and the Tribhanga. The chowkis a position imitating a square – a very masculine stance with the weight of the body equally balanced. The tribhanga is a very feminine stance where the body is deflected at the neck, torso, and knees.
- There are three traditions of the Odissi Dance viz. Mahari, Gotipua and Nartaki Schools.
- The dance form is also known as mobile sculpture, as the dancers create intricate geometrical patterns with their bodies.

6. **Correct Option: (c)**

Explanation:

- **Statement 2 is incorrect:** Lasya – It denotes grace, bhava, rasa and abhinaya. It is symbolic to the feminine features of dance as an art form.
- **Statement 3 is incorrect:** Tandava – This is symbolic to the male aspects of dance and has more emphasis on rhythm and movement.

Supplementary Notes:

History of Indian Classical Dance

- According to Bharata's Natya Shastra, when Lord Brahma was requested by the Gods to create a pastime, he combined certain aspects of the four Vedas and created a fifth Veda known as Natya Veda.
- Natya is an amalgamation of dance, drama and music and included Pathya (words) from Rig Veda, Abhinaya (gestures) from Yajur Veda, Geet (music) from Sam Veda and Rasa (emotions) from Atharva Veda.
- This highlights the divine importance attached to dance in the Indian cultural tradition. From Shiva's tandava dance, which signifies the cycle of creation, preservation and destruction, to the feminine response of Parvati, Indian mythology is replete with examples of dance forms and expressions.
- Similarly, the engravings of community dancing at Bhimbetka and the sculpture of Bronze dancing girl of the Harappan civilisation highlights the importance of dance as means of social entertainment.
- The first formal mention of dance is found in Bharata Muni's famous work Natya Shastra which gives a most comprehensive and vivid treatise on the various facets of Indian classical dance.
- The work was compiled in between 200 BCE and 2nd century AD and describes in detail the techniques, postures, emotions, ornaments, stage and even the audience.
- Bharata Muni describes dance as the 'complete art' encompassing within its scope all other forms of art – music, sculpture, poetry and drama.
- As per Natya Shastra, there are two basic aspects of Indian classical dance:
  - Lasya: It denotes grace, bhava, rasa and abhinaya. It is symbolic to the feminine features of dance as an art form.
  - Tandava: This is symbolic to the male aspects of dance and has more emphasis on rhythm and movement.
- As per Abhinaya Darpan, Nandikeshwara's famous treatise on dance, an act has been broken into three basic elements:

- Nritta: It refers to the basic dance steps, performed rhythmically but devoid of any expression or mood.
- **Natya:** It means dramatic representations and refers to the story that is elaborated through the dance recital.
- **Nritya:** Nritya refers to the sentiment and the emotions evoked through dance. It includes the mime and the different methods of expression including mudras in the dance. Nandikeshwara further elaborates the Nayaka-Nayika Bhav, in which the eternal deity is seen as the hero or Nayaka and the devotee who performs the dance is the heroine of the act, the Nayika.

7. **Correct Option: (b)**

Explanation:

- **Option (b) is the correct:** All these features are of Bharatnatyam.

Supplementary Notes:

Features of Bharatnatyam

- Oldest among all classical dance forms, Bharatnatyam derives its name from Bharata Muni and 'natyam' which means dance in Tamil.
- However, other scholars have ascribed the name 'Bharata' to 'Bhava', 'Raga' and 'Taal'.
- The origins of this dance form can be traced back to 'Sadir' – the solo dance performance of the Temple dancers or 'devadasis' in Tamil Nadu, hence it was also referred to as 'Dashiattam'.
- With the decline of the Devadasi system, the art too became nearly extinct. However, the efforts of E. Krishna Iyer, a prominent freedom fighter, revived this dance form.
- Previously, this dance form was performed by solo female dancers; it has since become increasingly popular among male and group artists as well. Rukmini Devi Arundale, another famous proponent of Bharatnatyam, is remembered for giving global recognition to the dance.
- Some of the important features of Bharatnatyam are:
  - In the early nineteenth century, four dance teachers of Thanjavur defined the elements of a Bharatnatyam recital.
  - They are:
    - Alarippu: It is an invocatory piece of performance which includes basic dance postures and is accompanied with rhythmic syllables. It is meant to seek the blessings of God.
    - Jatiswaram: It is the Nritta component and is devoid of expressions. It includes the different poses and movements.
    - **Shabdam:** It is the dramatic element with expressed words, which includes the abhinaya in the song. It is generally in praise of the glory of God.
    - **Varnam:** It is the Nritya component. It is a combination of dance and emotions, and is the most important part of the whole performance. It is synchronised with tala and raag, to express the story.
    - **Padam:** It refers to a mastery over the abhinaya (expression) of the spiritual message, by the artist. Music becomes light, dance becomes emotional.
    - **Jawali:** These are short love-lyrics performed at a faster tempo.
    - **Thillana:** It is the concluding stage of the performance, and comprises pure dance (Nritta) with exuberant movement and intricate rhythmic variations.
  - The four Thanjavur teachers, known as the 'Tanjore quartet', are Chiniah, Ponniah, Vadivelu and Shivanandam. Under them, Bharatnatyam also came to be known as Tanjore natyam.
  - Bharatnatyam is often referred to as the 'fire dance', as it is the manifestation of fire in the human body. Most of the movements in Bharatnatyam resemble that of a dancing flame.
  - In this dance form, equal emphasis is given on both the Tandava and Lasya aspects of dance, with major emphasis on 'mudras'.
  - One of the principal mudras is 'Kataka Mukha Hasta' in which the three fingers are joined to symbolise 'Om'.
  - In a Bharatnatyam recital, the knees are mostly bent and the weight is equally distributed across both the feet.
  - It is also characterised by the 'Ekcharya lasyam' style in which one dancer plays many different roles. Famous proponents: Yamini Krishnamurthy, Lakshmi Viswanathan, Padma Subramaniam, Mrinalini Sarabhai, Mallika Sarabhai, etc.

8. **Correct Option: (b)**

Supplementary Notes:

Mudras of Buddha

- **Abhaya Mudra:** It indicates fearlessness. The right hand is raised to shoulder height with arm bent. The palm of the right hand faces outwards and the fingers are upright and joined. The left hand hangs downwards by the side of the body. This gesture was shown by Buddha immediately after attaining enlightenment.
- **Dhyana Mudra:** Indicates meditation and is also called 'Samadhi' or 'Yoga' Mudra. It depicts Buddha

with both the hands in the lap, with the back of the right hand resting on the palm of the left hand with fingers extended. In many statues, the thumbs of both hands are shown touching at the tips, thus forming a mystic triangle. It signifies attainment of spiritual perfection. This Mudra was used by Buddha during the final meditation under the bodhi tree.

- Anjali Mudra: Greetings, devotion, and adoration. Both hands close to the chest, palms and fingers joined against each other vertically. It is common gesture used in India to greet people (Namaste). It signifies adoration of the superior and considered a sign of regards with deep respect.
- Karana Mudra: It indicates warding off evil. Hand is stretched out, either horizontally or vertically, with the palm forward. The thumb presses the folded two middle fingers but the index and little fingers are raised straight upwards. It signifies expelling demons and negative energy. The energy created by this Mudra helps remove obstacles such as sickness or negative thoughts

9. **Correct Option: (b)**

Explanation:

- **Statement 2 is incorrect:** As per Natya Shastra, there are two basic aspects of Indian classical dance, Lasya, and Tandava.

Supplementary Notes:

Natya Shastra

- Natya is an amalgamation of dance, drama, and music and include Pathya (words) from Rig Veda, Abhinaya (gestures) fromYajur Veda, Geet (music) from Sam Veda and rasa (emotions) from Atharva Veda.
- This highlights the divine importance attached to dance in the Indian cultural tradition. From Shiva's tandava dance, which signifies the cycle of creation, preservation, and destruction, to the feminine response of Parvati, Indian mythology is replete with examples of dance forms and expressions.
- Similarly, the engravings of community dancing at Bhimbetka and the sculpture of the Bronze dancing girl of the Harappan civilisation highlights the importance of dance as a means of social entertainment.
- The first formal mention of dance is found in Bharata Muni's famous work Natya Shastra which gives most comprehensive and vivid treatise on the various facets of Indian classical dance. The work was compiled between 200 BCE and 2nd century AD and describes in detail the techniques, postures, emotions, ornaments, stage and even the audience.
- Bharata Muni describes dance as the 'complete art' encompassing within its scope all other forms of art – music, sculpture, poetry and drama.
- As per Natya Shastra, there are two basic aspects of Indian classical dance.
    - Lasya – It denotes grace, bhava, rasa and abhinaya. It is symbolic to the feminine features of dance as an art form.
    - Tandava – This is symbolic to the male aspects of dance and has more emphasis on rhythm and movement.

10. **Correct Option: (a)**

Explanation:

- **Statement 3 is incorrect:** Garba is not inscribed in Representative List of Intangible Cultural Heritage of Humanity.

Supplementary Notes:

Chhau

- The word 'Chhau' originates from 'Chhaya' meaning shadow. It is a form of mask dance that uses vigorous martial movements to narrate mythological stories. Some narrations also use natural themes such as Sarpa nritya (serpent dance) or Mayur Nritya (peacock dance).
- There are three main styles of Chhau dance – Saraikella Chhau in Jharkhand, Mayurbhanj Chhau in Odisha and Purulia Chhau in West Bengal. Of these, Mayurbhanj Chhau artists don't wear masks.
- In 2010, UNESCO inscribed Chhau in the Representative List of Intangible Cultural Heritage of Humanity.

Kalbelia

- It is a sensuous folk dance performed by the women of the Kalbelia community of Rajasthan. The costumes and dance moves are similar to that of the serpents. 'Been' (wind instrument played by snake charmers) is the popular musical instrument of this dance form.
- The UNESCO has inscribed Kalbelia folk songs and dances in the Representative List of the Intangible Cultural Heritage of Humanity in 2010.

11. **Correct Option: (c)**

Classical Dance	State
A. Kathakali	4. Kerala
B. Kathak	3. Uttar Pradesh
C. Sattriya	2. Assam
D. Kuchipudi	1. Andhra Pradesh

Supplementary Notes:

Kathakali

- In the Temples of Kerala, two forms of dance-drama, Ramanattam and Krishnattam, evolved under the patronage of feudal lords, narrating episodes from Ramayana and Mahabharata.

Kathak

- Tracing its origins from the Ras Leela of Brajbhoomi, Kathak is the traditional dance form of Uttar Pradesh.

Sattriya

- Sattriya dance in modern-form was introduced by the Vaishnava saint Shankaradeva in the 15th century AD in Assam.

Kuchipudi

- Originally performed by group of actors going from village-to-village, known as Kusselavas, Kuchipudi derives its name from the Andhra village of Kusselavapuri or Kuchelapuram. In 17th century, Siddhendra Yogi formalized and systematized the tradition.

12. Correct Option: (c)

Explanation:

- **Pair 1 is incorrectly matched:** Nritya – Emotions evoked through dance
- **Pair 3 is incorrectly matched:** Nritta – Basic dance steps

Supplementary Notes:

Abhinaya Darpan

- As per Abhinaya Darpan, Nandikeshwara's famous treatise on dance, an act has been broken into three basic elements:
  - **Nritta:** It refers to the basic dance steps, performed rhythmically but devoid of any expression or mood.
  - **Natya:** It means dramatic representations and refers to the story that is elaborated through the dance recital.
  - **Nritya:** Nritya refers to the sentiment and the emotions evoked through dance. It includes the mime and the different methods of expression including mudras in the dance.
- Nandikeshwara further elaborates the Nayaka-Nayika Bhav, in which the eternal deity is seen as the hero or Nayaka and the devotee who performs the dance is the heroine of the act, the Nayika. There are nine rasas or emotions that are expressed through the dance.

13. Correct Option: (c)

Explanation:

- **Statement 2 is incorrect:** These are the elements of Bharatnatyam Classical Dance.

Supplementary Notes:

Odissi

- The caves of Udayagiri-Khandagiri provide some of the earliest examples of Odissi dance. The dance form derives its name from the 'Odra nritya' mentioned in Natya Shastra.
- It was primarily practised by the 'maharis' and patronised by the Jain king Kheravela.
- With the advent of Vaishnavism in the region, the Mahari system became defunct. Instead, young boys were recruited and dressed as females to continue the art form. They came to be known as 'Gotipuas'.
- Another variant of this art, 'Nartala' continued to be practised at the royal courts.
- The elements of Odissi dance form include:
  - Mangalacharan or the beginning where a flower is offered to mother earth.
  - Batu Nritya comprising of the dance. It has the Tribhanga and the Chowk postures.
  - Pallavi which includes the facial expressions and the representation of the song.
  - Tharijham consisting of pure dance before the conclusion.
  - The concluding item is of two types. Moksha includes joyous movements signifying liberation. Trikhanda majura is another way of concluding, in which the performer takes leave from the gods, the audience and the stage.
- Odissi dance is accompanied by Hindustani classical music and instruments generally used are Manjira (Cymbals), Pakhawaj (Drums), Sitar, Flute, etc.
- The dance form symbolises the element of water.
- The lyrics of Gita Govinda, written by Jayadeva, is used along with compositions of some local poets.
- The woman dancer wears an elaborate hair-style, silver jewellery, long necklace, etc.

14. Correct Option: (d)

Explanation:

- All statements are correct

Supplementary Notes:

Bhavai

- Bhavai is Rajasthan's ritualistic dance, which is usually performed by women belonging to Kalbelia, Jat, Meena, Bhil or Kumhar tribal communities of the state.
- The dance involves women balancing eight to nine brass pitchers or earthen pots on their head as they dance and twirl with their feet on the perimeter of a brass plate or on the top of a glass.
- The dance is accompanied by male performers singing and playing instruments, such as harmonium, sarangi and dholak.
- Because of its high level of difficulty and complexity, it takes years for the performer to master the dance form.

Chari

- Chari is another ritualistic dance that primarily belongs to the Saini community of Ajmer and Gujjar's of Kishangarh.
- Enacted by women, it is usually performed on special occasions, such as the birth of a male child, marriage or festival.
- It symbolises joy as well as representing the ritual of collecting water in chari, which means pot. The women are attired in traditional outfit and dance while balancing brass chari on their heads, along with a lighted lamp in it. The dance is accompanied by sounds of dholak, harmonium and nagada (percussion instrument).

Chang

- The centrepiece of Rajasthan's Holi festival, Chang is a lively folk dance that originated from the Shekhawati region (Bikaner, Churu, Jhunjhunu and Sikar).
- Also called as Dhamal, the highlighted characteristic of this dance form is the fast-paced rhythmic beats of the chang instrument (a type of tambourine), upon which a group of men dance, sing and carouse.
- Another notable feature is that some men dress up like women – donning traditional attire and performing ghoomar.

15. **Correct Option: (a)**

Supplementary Notes:

Koodiyattam

- Koodiyattam or Kutiyattam is a form of sacred theater traditionally performed in Hindu Temples in the state of Kerala, India.
- Performed in the Sanskrit language or an early form of Prakrit, it is believed to be at least two thousand years old, making it the oldest living theater tradition in the world.
- Koodiyattam blends ritual, sacred traditional precepts, and rehearsed elements with creative improvisation.
- Complicated gesture language, chanting, and exaggerated expressions of the face and eyes are complemented by elaborate headdresses and makeup.

16. **Correct Option: (c)**

Explanation:

- Both statements are correct

Supplementary Notes:

Sattriya Dance

- In the 15th century AD, Vaishnava saint of Assam, Shankaradeva introduced the Sattriya form of dance.
- Sattriya derives its name from the Vaishnava Monastries known as Sattras.
- It focuses more on the devotional aspect of dance, and narrates the mythological stories of Vishnu.
- The dance form is performed in a group by male monks known as Bhokots as part of their daily rituals.
- Khol and flute are the main instruments played in Sattriya dance.
- Rhythmic syllables and dance postures along with footwork has been given greater emphasis in Sattriya dance.
- It combines the elements of Lasya and Tandava.
- There is a strict guideline laid down for the hand gestures and footwork in Sattriya dance.
- Gayan-Bhayanar Nach and Kharmanar Nach are two streams evolved in modern times.

CONCEPT REVISION

Here is the list of concepts that have been covered as part of the previous exercise. Revise and self-reflect on your concepts you covered.

- Odissi Dance form ☐
- Folk Dances in India ☐
- Various Instruments and their features ☐
- History of Indian Classical Dance ☐
- Natya Shastra ☐
- Intangible Cultural Heritage of Humanity ☐
- Classical Dances ☐
- Abhinaya Darpan ☐

8.3 INDIAN THEATRE AND PUPPETRY

QUESTIONS

1. **Which of the following statements regarding traditional theatre is incorrect?**
   (a) Swang is a music based theatre popular in Haryana.
   (b) Bhand Pather is a theatre popular in Kashmir.
   (c) Jatra is a musical play theatre in Bengal.
   (d) Dashavatra is folk theatre of Odisha.

2. **Which of the following statements regarding Puppetry is incorrect?**
   (a) String puppets allows greater flexibility and are hence more articulative in nature.
   (b) Shadow puppets are pressed against the screen, with a strong source of light and hence showcase flat figures.
   (c) Rod puppets are manipulated and controlled by rods from above.
   (d) Glove puppets are manipulated and controlled by hand directly.

3. **Consider the following statements with respect to the "plays" produced during Gupta period:**
   1. All these plays were of comedies and there were no tragedy plays.
   2. Characters of the higher and lower classes do not speak same language.
   3. Women and Shudras featuring in these plays use prakrit while the higher classes use Sanskrit.

   Which of the above statements are correct?
   (a) 1 and 2 only (b) 1 and 3 only
   (c) 2 and 3 only (d) 1, 2 and 3

4. **It is the most theatrical shadow puppetry and is a popular form of entertainment in the Odisha. The puppet is made of deerskin and depicts bold and dramatic postures. They do not have any joints attached to them. Use of non human puppets such as trees and animals is common.**
   Which of the following puppetry is mentioned above?
   (a) Ravanchhaya
   (b) Chamadyacha Bahulya
   (c) Tolpava Kuthu
   (d) Tolu Bommalatta

5. **Consider the following statements regarding Bhaona theatre form:**
   1. Bhaona owes its origin to the unique genre of plays, evolved by Vaishnava saint Sankardeva.
   2. In Bhaona cultural glimpses of Mathura and Brindavan can be seen.
   3. It is a kind of dance-drama with songs and dialogues in Brajavali.

   Which of the statements given above is/are correct?
   (a) 1 only (b) 2 and 3 only
   (c) 1 and 3 only (d) 1, 2 and 3

6. **Which of the following statement/s is/are correct regarding Traditional Theatre forms of India?**
   1. Dashavatar is a folk theatre form practised in the Konkan region of Maharashtra and Goa, in which ten incarnations of Lord Vishnu are depicted.
   2. Nacha is a popular folk theatre of West Bengal, where Comedy is an essential aspect.
   3. Mudiyettu is a ritual theatre form of Kerala where mythological tale of Mohini and Bhasmasur is the main subject.

   Select the correct answer using the codes given below:
   (a) 1 only (b) 2 and 3 only
   (c) 3 only (d) All of the above

7. **Ravanachhaya is a type of**
   (a) Scroll type from Western Rajasthan
   (b) A popular folk dance form of Jharkhand
   (c) Shadow Puppet Theatre form of Odisha
   (d) Textile from Maharashtra

8. **Consider the following statements about -**
   1. Vikramorvasiya is a Sanskrit drama written by Kalidasa which contains the love affairs of Vikram and Urvashi.
   2. Nagananda, a Sanskrit play written by Harshvardhana, is the story of how prince Jimutavahana gives up his own body to stop a sacrifice of serpents to the divine Garuda.

   Which of the above statement/s is/are correct?
   (a) 1 only (b) 2 only
   (c) Both 1 and 2 (d) Neither 1 nor 2

9. **It is the most theatrical of shadow puppetry and is a popular form of entertainment in the Odisha region. The puppets are made of deer skin and depict bold dramatic postures. They do not have any joints attached to them, making it a more complex art. There is the use of non-human puppets, such as trees and animals as well".**
   The above passage describes which of the following forms of Indian puppetry?
   (a) Tholu Bommalata (b) Pavakoothu
   (c) Ravanchhaya (d) Gombeyatta

10. **Consider the following pairs:**
    1. Kundhei – String Puppet
    2. Pavakoothu – Shadow Puppet
    3. Yampuri – Glove Puppet
    4. Gombeyatta – Rod Puppet

Which of the above pairs is/are correctly matched?

(a) 1 only (b) 1 and 4 only
(c) 2 and 3 only (d) 3 only

11. Consider the following statements regarding Classical Sanskrit Theatre:

1. Classical Sanskrit plays always had a happy ending.
2. The protagonists of these plays were males who would always achieve the object of his desire.
3. The rigid orthodoxy of these plays was a reason for the decline of this theatre.

Which of the above statements is/are correct?

(a) 1 only (b) 1 and 3 only
(c) 3 only (d) 1, 2 and 3

SOLUTIONS

1. Correct Option: (d)

Supplementary Notes:

Traditional Theatre

- **Swang:**
  - **Option (a) is correct:** Swang is a music based theatre popular in Haryana. Originally, the theatre form **Swang**, was mainly music-based.
  - The softness of emotions, accomplishment of rasa along with the development of character can be seen in this theatre form.
  - The two important styles of Swang are from Rohtak and Haathras. In the style belonging to Rohtak, the language used is Haryanvi (Bangru) and in Haathras, it is Brajbhasha.
  - Religious stories and folk tales are enacted by a group of ten or twelve persons in an open area or an open-air theatre surrounded by the audience. Swang as an art of imitation means Rang-Bharna, Nakal-Karna. Swang can be considered as the most ancient folk theatre form of India that further lead to the origin of Nautanki, Saang, and Tamasha originated from the Swang traditions.
- **Bhand Pather:**
  - **Option (b) is correct:** It is the traditional theatre form of Kashmir which is a unique combination of dance, music and acting.
  - Satire, wit and parody are preferred for inducing laughter. In this theatre form, music is provided with surnai, nagaara and dhol. Since the actors of Bhand Pather are mainly from the farming community, the impact of their way of living, ideals and sensitivity is discernible.
- **Jatra:**
  - **Option (c) is correct:** Fairs in honour of gods, or religious rituals and ceremonies have within their framework musical plays known as Jatra. This form was born and nurtured in Bengal.
  - Krishna Jatra became popular due to Chaitanya's influence. Later, however, worldly love stories too, found a place in Jatra. The earlier form of Jatra has been musical. Dialogues were added at later stage. The actors themselves describe the change of scene, the place of action, etc.
- **Dashavatar:**
  - **Option (d) is incorrect:** It is the most developed theatre form of the Konkan and Goa regions.
  - The performers personify the ten incarnations of Lord Vishnu – the god of preservation and creativity. The ten incarnations are Matsya (fish), Kurma (tortoise), Varaha (boar), Narsimha (lion-man), Vaman (dwarf), Parashuram, Rama, Krishna (or Balram), Buddha and Kalki. Apart from stylized make-up, the Dashavatar performers wear masks of wood and papier mache.

2. Correct Option: (c)

Supplementary Notes:

Puppetry

- **String Puppets:**
  - **Option (a) is correct:** India has a rich and ancient tradition of string puppets or marionettes. Marionettes having jointed limbs controlled by strings allow far greater flexibility and are, therefore, the most articulate of the puppets.
  - Rajasthan, Orissa, Karnataka and Tamil Nadu are some of the regions where this form of puppetry has flourished.
- **Shadow Puppets:**
  - **Option (b) is correct:** Shadow puppets are flat figures. They are cut out of leather, which has been treated to make it translucent. Shadow puppets are pressed against the screen with a strong source of light behind it.
  - The manipulation between the light and the screen make silhouettes or colourful shadows, as the case may be, for the viewers who sit in front of the screen. This tradition of shadow puppets survives in Orissa, Kerala, Andhra Pradesh, Karnataka, Maharashtra and Tamil Nadu.
- **Rod Puppets:**
  - **Option (c) is incorrect:** Rod puppets are an extension of glove-puppets, but often much larger and supported and manipulated by rods from below. This form of puppetry now is found mostly in West Bengal and Orissa.
- **Glove Puppets:**
  - Glove puppets, are also known as sleeve, hand or palm puppets. The head is made of either papier

mache, cloth or wood, with two hands emerging from just below the neck. The rest of the figure consists of a long – flowing skirt.

- **Option (d) is correct:** These puppets are like limp dolls, but in the hands of an able puppeteer, are capable of producing a wide range of movements. The manipulation technique is simple. The movements are controlled by the human hand the first finger inserted in the head and the middle finger and the thumb are the two arms of the puppet. With the help of these three fingers, the glove puppet comes alive.
- The tradition of glove puppets in India is popular in Uttar Pradesh, Orissa, West Bengal and Kerala.

3. **Correct Option: (d)**

Supplementary Notes:

Gupta Period

- **All the statements are correct:** Literature reached its climax in the Gupta period. Two things can be noticed about the plays produced in India in Gupta period. First these are comedies. We do not come across any tragedies. Secondly, Characters of the higher and lower classes do not speak same language. Women and Shudras featuring in these plays use Prakrit, while the higher classes use Sanskrit.

4. **Correct Option: (a)**

Supplementary Notes:

Ravanchhaya

- It is the most theatrical shadow puppetry and is a popular form of entertainment in the Odisha region.
- The narratives are mainly based on the epics of Ramayana and Mahabharata, Puranas, local myths and tales. They communicate significant messages to the rural community besides entertainment.
- The puppets are crafted from either goat or deer skin. They do not have any joints attached to them. Use of non human puppets such as trees and animals is common. They are manipulated from behind the screen, where lighting is provided to cast shadows.
- Puppet performances are a part of festivals, celebrations of special occasions and rituals, and sometimes staged to ward off evil spirits and to invoke the rain gods in times of drought in rural areas.
- There are six shadow puppet theatre traditions across different regions in India, which are locally known as: Chamadyacha Bahulya in Maharashtra, Tolu Bommalatta in Andhra Pradesh, Togalu Gombeyatta in Karnataka, Tolu Bommalattam in Tamil Nadu, Tolpava Kuthu in Kerala and Ravanchhaya in Orissa.
- All the above are part of the National List for Intangible Cultural Heritage drafted by the Ministry of Culture.

5. **Correct Option: (d)**

Explanation:

- **All statements are correct**

Supplementary Notes:

Bhaona

- Bhaona is a presentation of the Ankia Naat of Assam. It has got its roots embedded in the Vaishnav monasteries or Satras.
- Bhaona owes its origin to the unique genre of plays, evolved by 15th Century Vaishnav saint Sankardeva and his disciple Madhavdeva, and is a kind of dance-drama with songs and dialogues in Brajavali.
- In Bhaona cultural glimpses of Assam, Bengal Orissa, Mathura and Brindavan can be seen. The Sutradhaar, or narrator begins the story, first in Sanskrit and then in either Brajboli or Assamese.

6. **Correct Option: (a)**

Explanation:

- **Statement 2 is incorrect:** Nacha is a noted folk theatre form in Chhattisgarh, performed in all areas except Sarguja and Baster regions.
- **Statement 3 is incorrect:** Mudiyettu is a ritual theatre form of Kerala based on the mythological tale of the battle between Goddess Kali and Darika, an evil king.

Supplementary Notes:

- Dashavatar is a folk theatre form practised by agriculturists in the Sindhudurg district of southern Maharashtra and Northern Goa.
- The term Dashavatar refers to the ten incarnations of Lord Vishnu, the Hindu God of preservation. The ten incarnations are 'matsya' (fish), 'kurma' (tortoise), 'varaha' (boar), 'narasimha' (lion-man), 'vaman' (dwarf), Parashuram, Ram, Krishna, Buddha and Kalki. Some of the features of this folk theatre are-
  - It is performed during the annual festival of the village deity in the Temple premises after midnight, without any technical props.
  - Each character enters the stage from behind a curtain held by two persons.
  - The Dashavatar performance comprises two sessions, the Poorva-Ranga(the initial session) and the Uttara-Ranga (the latter session).
  - The Poorva-Ranga is the preliminary presentation that precedes the performance proper. The Poorva-Ranga is the story about the killing of the demon Shankhasur. This act also includes the characters of Lord Ganesha, Riddhi, Siddhi, a Brahmin, Sharada (the goddess of learning), Brahmadev and Lord Vishnu.
  - The Uttara-Ranga, known as Akhyaan is considered to be the main performance based on

Hindu mythological tales, highlighting one of the ten incarnations of Lord Vishnu.

- The performance uses bright make-up and costumes.
- It is accompanied by three musical instruments: a Paddle Harmonium, Tabla and Zanj (cymbals)

- Nacha is a noted folk theatre form in Chhattisgarh, performed in all areas except Sarguja and Baster regions. Nacha performances are usually held during the night where comedy is an essential part. Sometimes themes on social issues are also incorporated to create awareness.
- There are four different forms of Nacha of which Baithe Saaj Nacha is the most popular form,while for other three (Khare Saaj Nacha, Gandawa Nacha and Dewar Nacha) performing troupes are very few. In Dewar Nacha, the female roles are performed by women artists while in other three forms, these roles are enacted by male artists dressed in female costumes and makeup.
- Mudiyettu is a ritual theatre form of Kerala based on the mythological tale of the battle between Goddess Kali and Darika, an evil king. It is also a part of Intangible Cultural Heritage of Humanity (Representative List). Being a community ritual, entire village participates in it.

7. **Correct Option: (c)**

Supplementary Notes:

- Ravanachhaya is a shadow puppet theatre form of Odisha. There are six shadow puppet theatre traditions across different regions in India. Having distinct regional identities, languages and dialects in which they are performed, they share common aesthetics and themes. The puppets are crafted from either goat or deer skin.
- The narratives are mainly based on the epics of Ramayana and Mahabharata, Puranas, local myths and tales. The performance begins with an invocation on a ritually set up stage in a village square or a Temple courtyard. Stock characters provide comic relief. They are manipulated from behind the screen, where lighting is provided to cast shadows. Puppet performances are a part of festivals, celebrations of special occasions and rituals, and sometimes staged to ward off evil spirits and to invoke the rain gods in times of drought in rural areas.

8. **Correct Option: (c)**

Explanation:

- Both statements are correct

Supplementary Notes:

Kalidasa wrote following Sanskrit Plays:

- **Malavikagnimitram:** The love story of Malavika a maiden of Queen and Agnimitra the son of Pushyamitra Shunga.
- **Vikramorvasiya:** Love story of Vikram and Urvasi.
- **Abhigyana Shakuntala:** the recognition of Shakuntala.

Harshavardhana: He is also attribute to have written the following Sanskrit plays.

- **Ratnavali:** This is about the love story of princess Ratnavali, daughter of the king of Ceylon and king Udayana. We find here, the mention of celebration of Holi for the first time.
- **Nagananda:** The story of how prince Jimutavahana gives up his own body to stop a sacrifice of serpents to the divine Garuda. One unique character in this drama is invocation to Lord Buddha in the Nandi verse.
- **Priyadarsika:** The union of Udayana and Priyadarshika, daughter of King Dridhavarman.

9. **Correct Option: (c)**

Supplementary Notes:

Indian Puppetry

- **Ravanchhaya:** It is the most theatrical of shadow puppetry and is a popular form of entertainment in the Odisha region. The puppets are made of deer skin and depict bold dramatic postures. They do not have any joints attached to them, making it a more complex art. There is the use of non-human puppets, such as trees and animals as well. The Ravanchhaya artists are thus extremely trained in their art – creating a lyrical and sensitive theatrical narration.
- **Pavakoothu:** It is the traditional glove puppet show of Kerala. It originated in the period around 18th century AD. The puppets are decorated with colorful headgears, feathers and face paints, which is evidence of a heavy influence of Kathakali dance form. The plays are themed around narrations of Ramayana and Mahabharata.
- **Tholu Bommalata:** It is the shadow theatre of Andhra Pradesh. The show is accompanied by a classical background in the music and themed around mythological and devotional tales of the epics and Puranas. The puppets are larger in size and colored on both sides.
- **Gombeyatta:** It is the traditional puppet show of Karnataka. They are styled and designed on the various characters of the Yakshagana theatres. A unique feature of this puppetry is that more than one puppeteer is used to manipulate the puppets.

10. **Correct Option: (a)**

Explanation:

- **Pair 2, 3 and 4 are incorrectly matched:** Pavakoothu is related to glove puppet, Yampuri is related to rod puppet and Gombeyatta is related to string puppet.

Supplementary Notes:
Indian Puppetry

- Puppetry in India can be broadly classified into four categories:
  - **String Puppets**
    - The puppets are generally 8-9 inch miniature figures chiseled out of wood.
    - Oil colour is used to paint the wood with skin colour and add other facial features such as eyes, lips, nose, etc.
    - Small wooden pipes are created with the body to form the limbs. The body is then covered with colorful miniature dress and stitched.
    - Miniature jewelries and other accessories are attached to give a realistic feel.
    - Strings are attached to small holes in the hands, head and back of the body which are then controlled by the puppeteer.
    - Examples include Kathputli, Kundhei, Gombeyatta, and Bommalattam.
  - **Shadow Puppets**
    - Shadow puppets are flat figures cut out of leather.
    - The figures are painted identically on both sides of the leather.
    - The puppets are placed on a white screen with light falling from behind, creating a shadow on the screen.
    - The figures are manipulated so that the silhouettes created on the blank screen create telling imagery.
    - Examples include Tholu Bommalata, Ravanchhaya and Togalu Gombeyatta.
  - **Glove Puppets**
    - Glove puppets are also known as sleeve, hand or palm puppets.
    - They are small figures with head and arms wearing a long, flowing skirt as costume.
    - The puppets are generally made of cloth or wood, but some variations of paper puppet has also been seen.
    - The puppeteer wears the puppet as glove, manipulating the head with his index finger.
    - The two hands are manipulated using the thumb and the middle finger – giving life and expression to the originally limp puppet.
    - Example includes Pavakoothu.
  - **Rod Puppets**
    - Rod puppets are larger variations of glove puppet and are controlled by rods by the puppeteer from behind a screen.
    - It is mainly popular in the region of Eastern India.
    - Examples include Yampuri and Putul Nachh.

11. Correct Option: (d)

Explanation:

- All statements are correct

Supplementary Notes:
Classical Sanskrit Theatre

- Theatre in India began as a narrative art form, which encompassed a concoction of music, dance, and acting. Recitation, dance, and music were integral parts of the theatre.
- In the classical Sanskrit tradition, plays were categorized into ten types – namely Anka, Bhana, Dima, Ithamgra, Nataka, Prahasana, Prakarna, Svakarna, Vithi, and Vyayog. Natyashastra describes only two of these – Nataka and Prakarna.
- Classical Sanskrit plays were bound by some rigid conventions:
  - They were generally four to seven-act plays.
  - They always had happy endings.
  - The portrayal of the tragedy was almost rare.
  - The protagonist was a male who would always achieve the object of his desire at the end.
  - The plays had well-defined opening, progression, development, pause, and conclusion.
- The reasons for decline of Sanskrit theatre include:
  - As Sanskrit dramatists began to diverge towards poetry, the lyrical writings started gaining popularity over the dramatic works.
  - The rigid orthodoxy of the Sanskrit theatre restricted the creative space of new playwrights who turned to other forms.
  - As Sanskrit became more and more embellished, it lost popularity among the masses. It was increasingly confined to the religious sphere and among the Brahmins, while other languages such as Pali and Prakrit took its place.
  - With the advent of Muslim rulers, Sanskrit theatre took a definite backseat, as dance and music gained patronage.

CONCEPT REVISION

Here is the list of concepts that have been covered as part of the previous exercise. Revise and self-reflect on your concepts you covered.

- Plays during Gupta Period ☐
- Ravanchhaya ☐
- Bhaona theatre form ☐
- Traditional theatre forms of India ☐
- Different forms of puppetry ☐
- Classical Sanskrit Theatre ☐

8.4 SPORTS IN INDIA

QUESTIONS

1. **Consider the following statements regarding Tholu Bommalata:**
   1. It is the traditional puppetry art form of Karnataka.
   2. It is an example of shadow puppet style of puppetry.

   Which of the above statement/s is/are correct?

   (a) 1 only (b) 2 only
   (c) Both 1 and 2 (d) Neither 1 nor 2

2. **Consider the following statements regarding 'Hornbill Festival':**
   1. It is celebrated in the first week of November.
   2. The festival coincides with the statehood day of Nagaland
   3. The Great Hornbill is the state bird of Nagaland.

   Which of the above statement/s is/are correct?

   (a) 1 only (b) 2 only
   (c) 1 and 3 only (d) 1, 2 and 3

3. **In which of the following state Teesta Rangit Tourism Festival is celebrated:**

   (a) Sikkim (b) West Bengal
   (c) Odisha (d) Assam

4. **Consider the following statements on Kumbh Mela:**
   1. It is the largest peaceful congregation of pilgrims on Earth.
   2. It is organised at Haridwar only.
   3. The Chinese traveller Hiuen Tsang described this ritual.

   Which of the above statement/s is/are correct?

   (a) 1 only (b) 1 and 3 only
   (c) 2 and 3 only (d) 1, 2 and 3

5. **With reference to 'The First World Orange Festival', which of the following statement(s) is/are correct?**
   1. The maiden event was hosted by West Bengal Government in Darjeeling.
   2. Its main objective is to create awareness and linkages which will eventually help in the growth of farmers and their value chain.

   Select the correct answer using the code given below.

   (a) 1 only (b) 2 only
   (c) Both 1 and 2 (d) Neither 1 nor 2

6. **With reference to 'Bharat Parv', which of the following statement(s) is/are correct?**
   1. The Ministry of Culture has been designated as the nodal Ministry for organizing the event.
   2. Its prime objective is to generate a patriotic mood and promote the rich cultural diversity of the country.

   Select the correct answer using the code given below.

   (a) 1 only (b) 2 only
   (c) Both 1 and 2 (d) Neither 1 nor 2

7. **Consider the following statements regarding Chapchar Kut festival:**
   1. It is a festival celebrated in the state of Mizoram.
   2. It is a harvest festival named after a bamboo that has been dried and cut.

   Which of the above statement/s is/are correct?

   (a) 1 only (b) 2 only
   (c) Both 1 and 2 (d) Neither 1 nor 2

8. **Kheer Bhawani is a**

   (a) Geographical tag holding local sweet delicacy of Madhya Pradesh.
   (b) Prestigious Saree variant of Kerala weaved from banana leaves.
   (c) Annual festival of Jammu and Kashmir dedicated to the Goddess Kheer Bhawani.
   (d) Famous painting of Mughal style.

9. **Consider the following statements regarding Yoga:**
   1. Yoga consists of a series of poses, other techniques designed to help individuals build self-realisation.
   2. Yoga is inscribed in the representative list of the Intangible Cultural Heritage of Humanity.
   3. Yoga day is celebrated on June 21st because it is the shortest day in the Northern Hemisphere.

   Which of the above statement/s is/are correct?

   (a) 1 only (b) 1 and 2 only
   (c) 2 and 3 only (d) 1, 2 and 3

10. **'Losar Festival' is celebrated in which state?**

    (a) Jammu & Kashmir
    (b) Uttar Pradesh
    (c) Sikkim
    (d) Arunachal Pradesh

11. **Consider the following statements about Animal Sports in India:**
    1. Kambala is an annual Buffalo Race held traditionally in coastal Karnataka.
    2. Bulbul Fight is organized during Bhogali Bihu, the harvest festival of West Bengal.
    3. Jallikattu is held during the Pongal festival in Tamil Nadu.

    Which of the above statements are correct?

    (a) 1 and 2 only (b) 2 and 3 only
    (c) 1 and 3 only (d) 1, 2 and 3

12. Bathukamma is the state festival of which state?

(a) Tamil Nadu (b) Nagaland
(c) Rajasthan (d) Telangana

13. With reference to 'Sangai Festival', consider the following statements:

1. It is an annual festival celebrated in the state of Nagaland.
2. The festival is named after the endangered brow-antlered deer Sangai.

Which of the statement(s) given above is/are correct?

(a) 1 only (b) 2 only
(c) Both 1 and 2 (d) Neither 1 nor 2

14. Consider the following pairs:

Festival	**State**
A. Ambubachi festival	**1. Maharashtra**
B. Gudi Padwa	**2. Assam**

Which of the pairs given above is/are correctly matched?

(a) 1 only (b) 2 only
(c) Both 1 and 2 (d) Neither 1 nor 2

15. With reference to the 'Sankalp Parv-Sankalp se Siddhi', consider the following statements:

1. It is organized by the Ministry of Water Resources, River Development & Ganga Rejuvenation.
2. Its objective is to ensure effective abatement of pollution and rejuvenation of the river Ganga.

Which of the statements given above is/are incorrect?

(a) 1 only (b) 2 only
(c) Both 1 and 2 (d) Neither 1 nor 2

16. Consider the following statements regarding Sunburn Festival:

1. It is India's biggest Electronic Dance Music Festival.
2. The venue for 2018 was Goa.

Which of the above statement/s is/are correct?

(a) 1 only (b) 2 only
(c) Both 1 and 2 (d) Neither 1 nor 2

17. Consider the following statements regarding Ganga Sagar Mela:

1. It is organized during Makar Sankranti festival.
2. It is celebrated in the State of Bihar.
3. Pilgrims visit Kapilmuni Temple during this occasion.

Which of the above statements are correct?

(a) 1 and 2 only (b) 2 and 3 only
(c) 1 and 3 only (d) 1, 2 and 3

18. Consider the following statements regarding Nabakalebar Rath Yatra:

1. It is the festival that marks the demise and rebirth of Lord Jagannath of Puri.
2. It is celebrated once in every four years.

Which of the above statement/s is/are correct?

(a) 1 only (b) 2 only
(c) Both 1 and 2 (d) Neither 1 nor 2

19. Wangala Festival is the harvest festival of which of the following States?

(a) Telangana
(b) Andhra Pradesh
(c) Meghalaya
(d) Arunachal Pradesh

20. With reference to "Swachh Paryatan", consider the following statements:

1. It's aim is to keep monuments clean and protected.
2. It's a mobile application.

Which of the above statement/s is/are correct?

(a) 1 only (b) 2 only
(c) Both 1 and 2 (d) Neither 1 nor 2

21. 'Tholu bommalata' is a traditional art of:

(a) Mizoram
(b) Odisha
(c) Andhra Pradesh
(d) Gujarat

22. 'Nazhu festival' the major festivals of the Pochury tribe celebrated in the month of February belongs to which state?

(a) Manipur
(b) Mizoram
(c) Arunachal Pradesh
(d) Nagaland

23. In which of the following states the Cheery Blossom Mao Festival was celebrated?

(a) Arunachal Pradesh
(b) Meghalaya
(c) Manipur
(d) Mizoram

24. Consider the following pairs:

Festival	**State**
1. Bathukamma	Telangana
2. Hornbill festival	Mizoram
3. Pandharpur Wari	Kerala
4. Lui-Ngai-Ni	Manipur

Which of the above pairs are correctly matched?

(a) 1 and 3 only (b) 2 and 4 only
(c) 2 and 3 only (d) 1 and 4 only

25. With reference to recently organized Thumbimahotsavam in India, consider the following statements:

1. It was a state Dragonfly festival organized in Tamil Nadu.
2. It was organized by WWF India along with the Bombay Natural History Society.
3. 'Pantalu' was the official mascot of the festival.

Which of the given statements are correct?

(a) 1 and 2 only (b) 2 and 3 only
(c) 1 and 3 only (d) 1, 2 and 3

26. Which of the following pairs are correctly matched?

Harvest Festivals		States
1. Wangala	:	Meghalaya
2. Hareli	:	Assam
3. Kut	:	Manipur
4. Onam	:	Tamil Nadu

Select the correct option using the codes given below:

(a) 1 and 2 only (b) 3 and 4 only
(c) 1 and 3 only (d) 1, 2, 3 and 4

27. Consider the following statements about Therukoothu.

1. It is the most popular form of martial art of Andhra Pradesh.
2. It is mostly performed to please rain God to achieve a rich harvest.

Which of the statements given above is/are correct?

(a) 1 only (b) 2 only
(c) Both 1 and 2 (d) Neither 1 nor 2

28. India has one of the oldest and largest film industries in the world. Directorate of Film Festivals is entrusted with some of the functions related to this industry. Which of the following are its responsibilities?

1. Organizing the International Film Festival of India (IFFI).
2. Participation in International Film Festivals abroad
3. Awarding the National Awards for films
4. Shortlisting of awardees for Dadasaheb Phalke Award

Select the correct answer using the code given below:

(a) 1, 3 and 4 only (b) 3 and 4 only
(c) 1 and 2 only (d) 1, 2, 3 and 4

29. Consider the following statements:

1. Kambala a traditional buffalo race organized during monsoon months in coastal Karnataka.
2. Tuluva landlords are the main sponsors of Kambala race.

Which of the above statement/s is/are correct?

(a) 1 only (b) 2 only
(c) Both 1 and 2 (d) Neither 1 nor 2

30. Match the following:

Martial Art	State
A. Kalaripayattu	1. Punjab
B. Gatka	2. Mizoram
C. Pari-Khanda	3. Bihar
D. Inbuan Wrestling	4. Kerala

Select the correct answer using the code given below:

	A	B	C	D
(a)	2	3	4	1
(b)	1	4	3	2
(c)	3	4	2	1
(d)	4	1	3	2

31. Consider the following statements regarding the Pushkaram Festival:

1. It is an annual festival celebrated at shrines along the banks of South Indian rivers only.
2. Mahapushkaram occurs once in 500 years.

Which of the above statements is/are correct?

(a) 1 only (b) 2 only
(c) Both 1 and 2 (d) Neither 1 nor 2

32. Nabakalebar festival is associated with which of the following Temples in India?

(a) Meenakshi Temple, Madurai
(b) Brihadisvara Temple, Tanjore
(c) Somnath Temple, Gujarat
(d) Jagannath Temple, Puri

33. Consider the following pairs:

Festival		State
1. Ambubachi Mela	–	Jammu & Kashmir
2. Kharchi Festival	–	Tripura
3. Chamliyal Mela	–	Assam

Which of the above pairs is/are correctly matched?

(a) 1 and 2 only (b) 2 only
(c) 3 only (d) 1, 2 and 3

34. Consider the following statements regarding UNESCO's List of Intangible Cultural Heritage in India:

1. Kumbh Mela is the latest addition to the Representative List of the Intangible Cultural Heritage of Humanity in India.
2. Sangeet Natak Academy is the nodal body involved in the preparation of nomination dossiers for representative list of UNESCO.

Which of the above statements is/are correct?

(a) 1 only (b) 2 only
(c) Both 1 and 2 (d) Neither 1 nor 2

35. Match the following:

Festival	State
A. Hornbill Festival	1. Manipur
B. Chapchar Kut Festival	2. Meghalaya
C. Wangala Festival	3. Mizoram
D. Sangai Festival	4. Nagaland

Select the correct answer using the code given below:

	A	B	C	D
(a)	4	3	2	1
(b)	4	3	1	2
(c)	3	1	4	2
(d)	3	4	2	1

36. Consider the following statements regarding the Kheer Bhawani Festival:

1. It is celebrated by the Gaddis and Bakarwal tribes of Kashmir valley.
2. It is mentioned in Kalhana's Rajtarangini.

Which of the above statements is/are correct?

(a) 1 only (b) 2 only
(c) Both 1 and 2 (d) Neither 1 nor 2

37. It is a colorful and vibrant festival celebrated by women with flowers that grow exclusively in each region. Different, unique seasonal flowers are arranged in concentric layers in the shape of a Temple gopuram thus forming a beautiful flower stack. The festival celebrates the inherent relationship between earth, water, and human beings".

Which among the following festival is described in the above passage?

(a) Mahapushkaram (b) Bathukamma
(c) Losar (d) Bonalu

38. Which of the following statements is incorrect about Khelchawa Festival?

(a) Tiwa tribals celebrate Khelchawa festival in Assam.
(b) This festival is celebrated every five years.
(c) The festival is held at the close of the harvest season.
(d) Goats are sacrificed during the festival as a mark of respect for their local deity Lampha Raja.

39. Which of the following Martial Arts and their region is/are correctly matched?

1. Kalaripayattu was originated in state of Andhra Pradesh.
2. Silambam staff fencing is art of Tamil Nadu.
3. Thang-ta martial art belongs to West Bengal.

Select the correct answer using the code given below:

(a) 1 and 2 only (b) 2 only
(c) 1 and 3 only (d) 2 and 3 only

SOLUTIONS

1. Correct Option: (b)

Supplementary Notes:

Tholu Bommalata:

- **Statement 1 is incorrect and Statement 2 is correct:** Tholu Bommalata is the shadow puppet theatre tradition of the state of Andhra Pradesh.
- Tholu Bommalata literally means "the dance of leather puppets".
- The puppets are large in size and have jointed waist, shoulders, elbows and knees.
- They are coloured on both sides. Hence, these puppets throw coloured shadows on the screen. The music is dominantly influenced by the classical music of the region.
- The puppeteers make up some of the various entertainers who perform all night and usually reenact various stories from Hindu epics such as the Ramayana and Mahabharata and Puranas.
- Its performers are the part of a group of wandering entertainers and peddlers who pass through villages during the course of a year and offer to sing ballads, tell fortunes, sell amulets, perform acrobatics, charm snakes, weave fishnets, tattoo local people and mend pots.
- Years ago, the art was active in the four districts of Rayalaseema, especially in the border villages of Karnataka and Andhra Pradesh.
- However currently, there are only 6-8 troops left in all those areas that are still taking up the leather puppetry as the prime livelihood.

2. Correct Option: (b)

Supplementary Notes:

Hornbill Festival

- **Statement 2 is correct:** The Hornbill Festival began in the Naga Heritage village of Kisama. The festival coincides with the Statehood Day of Nagaland which is observed on December 1.
- It is tourism promotional extravaganza to revive, protect and preserve the richness and uniqueness of the Naga heritage. It is also called as the 'Festival of Festivals'.
- **Statement 1 is incorrect:** Hornbill Festival is celebrated in Nagaland every year in the first week of December. It is one of the biggest indigenous festivals of the country.
- The festival is a tribute to Hornbill, the most admired and revered bird for the Nagas for its qualities of alertness and grandeur.
- The majestic bird is closely identified with the social and cultural life of the Nagas as reflected in tribal folklore, dances and songs.
- It is organized by the State Tourism and Art & Culture Departments. It is also supported by the Union Government.
- The Hornbill Festival provides a colourful mixture of dances, performances, crafts, parades, games, sports, food fairs and religious ceremonies.
- It was established on 1st December 1963 and was inaugurated by the then President Dr. S Radhakrishnan.
- Former President Ram Nath Kovind inaugurated 18th edition (01-12-2017 to 10-12-2017) of the Hornbill Festival at the Naga Heritage Village in Kisama, Nagaland. The festival coincided with 54th statehood day of Nagaland.
- **Statement 3 is incorrect:** Statebird of Nagaland is Blyth's tragopan is a Schedule–I bird, according to Wildlife (Protection) Act, 1972 and classified as Vulnerable (VU) by the IUCN.

3. **Correct Option: (b)**

Supplementary Notes:

Teesta Rangit Tourism festival:

- **Option (b) is correct:** The Teesta Rangit Tourism festival was held in separate phases in different places of Darjeeling and Kalimpong districts of West Bengal.
- This festival is organized by Gorkhaland Territorial Administration (GTA) and Darjeeling state tourism department and information and cultural affairs department.
- About Gorkhaland Territorial Administration (GTA):
  - Purpose – administrative body for the Darjeeling and Kalimpong hills
  - Headquarters – Darjeeling
  - Chairman – Binoy Tamang

4. **Correct Option: (b)**

Supplementary Notes:

Kumbh Mela

- **Statement 1 is correct:** Kumbh Mela (the festival of the sacred Pitcher) is the largest peaceful congregation of pilgrims on earth, during which participants bathe or take a dip in a sacred river.
- Devotees believe that by bathing in the Ganges one is freed from sins liberating her/him from the cycle of birth and death. Millions of people reach the place without any invitation. The congregation includes ascetics, saints, sadhus, aspirants-kalpavasis and visitors.
- **Statement 2 is incorrect:** The festival is held at Allahabad, Haridwar, Ujjain and Nasik by rotation and is attended by millions of people irrespective of caste, creed or gender. The normal Kumbh Mela is held every 3 years, the Ardh (half) Kumbh Mela is held every six years at Haridwar and Allahabad (Prayag) while the Purna (complete) Kumbh mela takes place every twelve years, at four places Prayag (Allahabad), Haridwar, Ujjain, and Nashik, based on planetary movements. The Maha Kumbh Mela is celebrated at Prayag after 144 years (after 12 'Purna Kumbh Melas').
- **Statement 3 is correct:** The Chinese traveler Xuanzang (Hiuen Tsang) describes a ritual organized by Emperor Shiladitya (identified with Harsha) at the confluence of two rivers, in the kingdom of Po-lo-ye-kia (identified with Prayaga). He also mentions that many hundreds took a bath at the confluence, to wash away their sins.
- As it is held in four different cities in India, it involves different social and cultural activities, making this a culturally diverse festival. Knowledge and skills related to the tradition are transmitted through ancient religious manuscripts, oral traditions, historical travelogues and texts produced by eminent historians.
- However, the teacher-student relationship of the sadhus in the ashrams and akhadas remains the most important method of imparting and safeguarding knowledge and skills relating to Kumbh Mela.

5. **Correct Option: (b)**

Supplementary Notes:

World Orange Festival

- **Statement 1 is incorrect:** The First World Orange Festival was held in December 2017 at Nagpur, Maharashtra involving multiple activities, including trips to orange orchards, orange installations by art students, recipe contests, music festivals, cultural parades and lots more.
- The festival is conceptualised and organised by Taplight and supported by the Maharashtra Government and Maharashtra Tourism Development Corporation (MTDC).
- **Statement 2 is correct:** The main objective of World Orange Festival is to create awareness and linkages which will eventually help in the growth of farmers and their value chain, encourage and empower the hard work done by farmers to produce oranges of the best quality and to buoy the identity of the 'Orange City' to the world and up the brand value of Nagpur oranges on a global level and thereby bringing more income to the farmers.
- From a business angle it focuses on exhibitions, seminars and the participation of orange farmers from 10 other states in the country. International orange cultivators and technology experts from Israel, Turkey and South Africa will also attend the fest.

6. **Correct Option: (b)**

Supplementary Notes:

Bharat Parv

- **Statement 1 is incorrect:** The 'Bharat Parv' event was organized by the Government of India at the Red Fort, Delhi from 26th to 31st January, 2018 as part of the Republic Day 2018 celebrations. The Ministry of Tourism has been designated as the nodal Ministry for the event.
- **Statement 2 is correct:** The prime objective of organizing the event is to generate a patriotic mood, promote the rich cultural diversity of the country and to ensure wider participation of the general public.
- The highlights of the event include:
  - Display of Republic Day Parade Tableaux, Performances by the Armed Forces Bands (Static as well as dynamic), a Multi-Cuisine Food Court,

Craft Mela, Cultural Performances from different regions of the country and Photo Exhibition by the Directorate of Advertising and Visual Publicity (DAVP).

- The Cultural Performances include choreographed Fork/ Tribal Dances and Music arranged through the North Zonal Cultural Centre as well as performances by cultural troupes from the different States/UTs of the country. The Food Court will have stalls set up by the States/UTs, National Association of Street Vendors of India (NASVI) showcasing street food from different regions as well as by the Institutes of Hotel Managements and ITDC.
- The Craft Mela with 50 stalls will showcase the diverse handicrafts of the country, arranged by the State Governments and Ministry of Textiles through the office of the Development Commissioner of Handicrafts. There will be Theme State Pavilions where each State would showcase their strengths along with tourism products. DAVP is also setting up an exhibition on the theme "Naya Bharat Hum Karke Rahenge". A live 'Cookery Demonstration Area' is being set up in the food court to promote cuisines of different states of India.

7. **Correct Option: (c)**

Supplementary Notes:

Chapchar Kut Festival:

- **Statement 1 is correct:** It is celebrated across Mizoram to mark the beginning of the spring.
- It is one of the oldest festivals of Mizoram and is a unique blend of ancient and modern festivity.
- Chapchar Kut is estimated to have started in 1450-1700 AD in Suaipui village in Myanmar, where Mizo population was huge. It was celebrated to thank the God for saving the people from harm during the clearing of forest. During the festival people would dance, eat meat and drink Zu (rice beer) throughout the day.
- **Statement 2 is correct:** Chapchar Kut festival is a harvest festival named after a bamboo that has been drying and cut. In local language, "Kut" means festival and there are two more festivals connected with the different agricultural cycle, Mim Kut and Pawl Kut. During the month of February, farmers cut bamboo forests to create space for jhum or seasonal farming.
- Chapchar refers to the process of drying the bamboos so that they can be burnt later. For subsequent farming, they have to wait. So, they celebrate this free time by dancing and feasting.

8. **Correct Option: (c)**

Supplementary Notes:

Kheer Bhawani Festival

- **Option (c) is correct:** "Zesht Ashtami" or Kheer Bhawani festival is an annual Mata Kheer Bhawani celebration of mainly the Pandit community in Srinagar, Jammu & Kashmir.
- The devotees of the Goddess fast and gather the Kheer Bhawani shrine at Tulmula village constructed over a sacred spring on the eighth day of the full moon in the month of May/June.
- The name 'Kheer Bhawani' is derived from the fact that thousands of devotees offer milk and "Kheer" or pudding to the sacred spring, as they believe the pudding turns black to warn of impending disaster. According to belief, the Goddess changes the colour of the spring's waters, which are ascribed to different manifestations of the Goddess.
- The Kheer Bhawani Temple is dedicated to the Goddess. Rajnya Devi, popularly known as Kheer Bhawani Goddess Ragnya Devi is symbolised as a sacred spring at Tulmula village.
- Going back in history the goddess Raganya can be traced back to the ancient text of "Rajatarangini" by Kalhana who mentions of a certain location containing many natural springs in a marshy land. Interestingly, this is the many spring location of Ganderbal, where till date the Temple of the goddess stands. In the book, the location is referred to as Mata Ragini Kund. The associated mythology explains the same narrative with a little bit more of a story element of the goddess choosing to preside at this same spot many centuries ago having disillusioned by Ravana's way of life, hence moving her base from Lanka to Kashmir.
- In the last half century the pilgrimage has become the most important for Kashmiri Brahmans who come here from all over the State and even from outside. Kheer Bhawani is considered to be the presiding deity of most of the Kashmiri Brahmans.

9. **Correct Option: (b)**

Supplementary Notes:

Yoga

- Yoga is based on unifying the mind with the body and soul to allow for greater mental, spiritual and physical wellbeing, the values of yoga form a major part of the community's ethos.
- Statement 1 is correct: Yoga consists of a series of poses, meditation, controlled breathing, word chanting and other techniques designed to help individuals build self-realisation, ease any suffering they may be experiencing and allow for a state of liberation.
- Yoga literally means the union of the two principal entities. The origin of yoga is found in the Yogasutra of

Patanjali believed to have been written in the second century BC. By purifying and controlling changes in the mental mechanism, yoga systematically brings about the release of purusha from prakriti.

- Yogic techniques control the body, mind and sense organs. Thus this philosophy is also considered a means of achieving freedom or mukti.
- This freedom could be attained by practising self-control (yama), observation of rules (niyama), fixed postures (asana), breath control (pranayama), choosing an object (pratyahara) and fixing the mind (dharna), concentrating on the chosen object (dhyana) and complete dissolution of self, merging the mind and the object (Samadhi). Yoga admits the existence of God as a teacher and guide.
- **Statement 2 is correct:** Yoga is inscribed in 2016 on the Representative List of the Intangible Cultural Heritage of Humanity.
- **Statement 3 is incorrect:** The Northern solstice is the moment when the sun reaches its highest position with reference to the North Pole. This makes 21st June the longest day in the Northern Hemisphere.

10. Correct Option: (a)

Supplementary Notes:

Losar Festival

- The traditional festival of Losar was celebrated in Ladakh region of Jammu and Kashmir to mark the beginning of New Year in this Himalayan region.
- The 10-day-long festival began with illumination of religious and residential places and by visiting monasteries for prayer.
- The Losar festival marks the beginning of New Year in Ladakh and Tibet region and falls in December. Losar is Tibetan word for 'new year'.
- It is considered to be the most important festival of the region. It is an important social and religious celebration in Ladakh. Ladakhi Buddhists make religious offering before their deities in the domestic shrines or in the Gompas.
- A medley of cultural events, ancient rituals and also traditional performances are performed during this festival.
- There is blaring music events accompanied with dancing and celebration, dinner with relatives. Houses are decorated with good luck signs.
- Prayer flags are hoisted in important religious places to welcome the new year.

11. Correct Option: (c)

Supplementary Notes:

- **Statement 2 is incorrect:** Bhogali Bihu is a festival of Assam not West Bengal. Bulbul fight is organized during this harvest festival

Bulbul Fight

- Unlike large mammals fights, Bulbul fight is associated with members of smaller species, the Bulbuls. It is organized on the day of Makar Sankranti which coincides with Assam's harvest festival Bhogali Bihu.
- People of surrounding villages catch bulbul chicks and rear them for a few weeks before they are taken to the Temple premises on Makar Sankranti, the owners of the winners get various prizes.
- There is no betting on the fights. Some birds do sustain injuries during the fight. Those that lose are let off after trimmings the crest so that they do not enter a contest again.

Kambala

- **Statement 1 is correct:** Kambala is an annual Buffalo Race held (during Navaratri)as a part of tradition under the auspices of local landlords and households in coastal Karnataka.
- The 'track' used for Kambala is a paddy field filled with slush and mud. The contest takes place between two pairs of buffaloes, each pair raced in wet rice fields.
- Traditionally, it is sponsored by local Tuluva landlords and households in the coastal districts of Dakshina Kannada and Udupi and along Kasargod district of Kerala, a region collectively known as Tulu Nadu.

Jallikattu

- **Statement 3 is correct:** This festival which is intrinsic to the culture and tradition of Tamil Nadu is practiced as a part of Pongal celebrations which occurs annually in January.
- In this a bull is released into a crowd of people and multiple human participants attempt to grab the large hump on the bull's back with both arms and hang on to it while the bull attempts to escape.
- Participants hold the hump for as long as possible, attempting to bring the bull to a stop. In some cases, participants must ride long enough to remove flags on the bull's horns.

In News:

- There is increasing conflict between law, tradition and duties of citizens. The law at public debate is Prevention of Cruelty to Animals Act, 1960. All the festivals in the question had been banned by respective High Court while Jallikatu was reprimanded by Supreme Court as well. A recent revised amendment with notification from State Governments were passed to accommodate massive protests and address sentiments of the locals.

12. **Correct Option: (d)**

Supplementary Notes:

Bathukamma

- **Option (d) is correct:** Bathukamma is a nine-day floral festival of Telangana traditionally celebrated by women across the state during Durga Navratri. A beautiful flower stack is arranged in a unique style in shape of a Temple, which usually consists of seasonal flowers, having medicinal values.
- It is the state festival of Telangana and represents the cultural spirit of Telangana.
- In Telugu, 'Bathukamma' means 'Mother Goddess come Alive' symbolizing the patron Goddess of womanhood. The festival is also regarded as the Spring Festival of Goddess Gauri. It is dedicated to Goddess Parvati as it is believed that Goddess Sati returned as Goddess Parvati. The festival is celebrated with joy and happiness as there are dance performances, music, dramas etc.
- Every year this festival is celebrated as per Telugu version of Hindu calendar in the Bhadrapada Amavasya, also known as Mahalaya Amavasya, usually in September–October of Gregorian calendar.

13. **Correct Option: (b)**

Explanation:

Manipur Sangai Festival

- **Statement 1 is incorrect:** Every year the State of Manipur celebrates the "Manipur Sangai Festival" from 21st to 30th November.
- **Statement 2 is correct:** The 'Festival' is named after the State animal, Sangai, the endangeredbrow-antlered deer found only in Manipur.
- The festival is labelled as the grandest festival of the State today and helps promote Manipur as a world class tourism destination. Every edition of the festival showcases the tourism potential of the state in the field of Arts & Culture, Handloom, Handicrafts, Indigenous Sports, Cuisine, Music and Adventure sports of the state etc.
- The State's classical dance form, 'Ras Leela' is quite famous all over the world for its distinctiveness from any other dance forms in India. The Ras Leela will form an important part of the dance performances at the Manipur Sangai Festival 2018 besides the various other folk dance performances like the Kabui Naga dance, Bamboo dance, Maibi dance, Lai Haraoba dance, Khamba Thoibi dance, etc. which will be showcased.
- Unlike the previous editions of the festival, the 2018 edition of the Manipur Sangai Festival will be organized at different locations in Imphal and Bishnupur District keeping in view, the increasing number of visitors to the state during the festival.

14. **Correct Option: (d)**

Supplementary Notes:

Ambubachi Festival

- **Pair 1 is incorrect:** The annual Ambubachi ('issuing forth of water') Mela is the biggest religious congregation in the northeast of India at Kamakhya Temple, Assam.
- It is the celebration of the menstruation of Mother Earth. The common notion is that Ambubachi Mela is the celebration of the annual menstruation of Goddess Kamakhya.
- All Temples in the surrounding areas remain closed for the first 3 days – the menstruation period of the Goddess. The cleansing happens on the 4th day, the Temple is opened, and devotees receive blessings and prasad.
- The prasad known as Rakta Bastra is a red cloth which is believed to be soaked in the menses of the Goddess.
- Goddess Kamakhya is Goddess Kameshwari (source as well as the fulfilment of all the desires of mankind).

Losar Festival

- **Pair 2 is correct:** The traditional festival of Losar is celebrated in Ladakh region of Jammu and Kashmir, Tibet and by Monpa tribe of Arunanchal Pradesh majorly to mark the beginning of New Year in this Himalayan region. The 10-day-long festival began with illumination of religious and residential places and by visiting monasteries for prayer and religious offering before their deities.
- Losar is Tibetan word for 'new year'. It is an important social and religious celebration in Ladakh. The rites and the rituals that are followed during the Losar is an interesting amalgamation of the Buddhist and the pre Buddhist Bon religious practices.
- A medley of cultural events, ancient rituals, traditional performances, music accompanied with dancing and celebration and dinner with relatives are performed during this festival. There is blaring music events and houses are decorated with good luck signs. Prayer flags are hoisted in important religious places to welcome the New Year.
- Chang, a local barley beer is a popular drink for the Losar celebrations and grain from the harvest is kept for its brewing, as a part of preparations for the Losar celebrations. People wear new clothes and adorn themselves in new jewellery to enhance the festive mood in the air. The slaughtering of the goats and the sheep which were kept reserved for the festivities are done with a ritual to mark the beginning of the Losar celebrations.
- The variation of the festival in Nepal is called Lhochhar and is observed about eight weeks earlier than the Tibetan Losar.

Gudi Padwa

- **Pair 3 is incorrect:** Gudi Padwa is a New Year celebration in Maharashtra, celebrated in the first month of Chaitra.
- The festival marks the beginning of Vasant Ritu and New Year according to the Hindu calendar. Gudi Padwa also marks the completion of harvesting of Rabi crops.
- It is said to mark the day when Brahma created the world after the great flood. Lord Brahmais worshipped on this day and the Gudi, Brahma's flag (also called Brahmadhvaj), is hoisted in every house as a symbolic representation of Rama's victory over Ravana.
- This day is celebrated with different names and for different reasons. In Andhra Pradesh and Telangana, it's called Ugadi in Karnataka, it's called Yugadi. It's celebrated as Cheti Chand by the Sindhi community, Navreh in Kashmir and Sajibu Nongma Panba Cheiraoba in Manipur.

15. Correct Option: (c)

Supplementary Notes:

Sankalp Parva-Sankalp se Siddhi

- **Statement 1 is incorrect:** 'Sankalp Parva-Sankalp se siddhi' (Attainment through Resolve) is a major cultural event organized by the Ministry of Culture.
- **Statement 2 is incorrect:** The aim of the celebration is to appeal to the youth and other stakeholders to come forward and join hands for working for a new India by 2022 as the nation would be observing 75th anniversary of the Quit India Movement in August 2022, and will complete 75 years as an independent nation.
- The New India Movement 2017-2022 envisions an India free from Poverty, Corruption, Terrorism, Communalism, Casteism and Un-cleanliness.

16. Correct Option: (a)

Supplementary Notes:

Sunburn Festival

- **Statement 1 is correct:** Sunburn Festival, India's biggest Electronic Dance Music Festival, attracts more than 3,50,000 people and hundreds of artists every year.
- After years of being held on Vagator Beach in Goa, it has shifted its venue to the hills of Pune and rebranded itself to Sunburn Hills.
- **Statement 2 is incorrect:** The venue for Sunburn Festival in 2018 is the Oxford Golf Resort in Pune, located on the Mumbai-Bangalore highway.
- Sunburn festival was started in the year 2007 as the brainchild of Nikhil Chinapa and Percept Entertainment.
- The festival showcases handpicked artists, along with some of the most renowned DJ's from across the world. Some of the genres of music which make the event an exciting and lively one are Trance, House, Techno, Drum & Bass, Psy-trance and others.
- Another big draw of the festival is the huge line-up of international celebrities who attend it.

17. Correct Option: (c)

Supplementary Notes:

Ganga Sagar Mela:

- **Statement 1 is correct and Statement 2 is incorrect:** Ganga Sagar Mela, also known as Ganga Sagar Yatra or Ganga Snan, is the annual gathering of Hindu pilgrims to take holy dip in River Ganga before she merges in the Bay of Bengal Sea during Makar Sankranti at Sagar Island or Sagardwip in West Bengal, India.
- The Gangasagar fair begins a couple of day early and ends on the day after Sankranti. Hindu pilgrims from India and around the world arrive at Sagar Island to take a holy dip in sacred waters of Ganga River before she merges in the Bay of Bengal.
- Thousands of Hindus take holy dip at the auspicious time on Makar Sankranti day morning and offer prayers to Lord Surya (sun god). The holy dip is believed to wash the sins away and lead to the attainment of Moksha.
- **Statement 3 is correct:** After performing Ganga Snan, pilgrims visit the Kapilmuni Temple situated nearby. This is an ancient Temple and is one of its kinds in India.
- Devotees start to arrive in the first week of January and the venue attracts maximum pilgrims on the Makar Sankranti day.

18. Correct Option: (a)

Supplementary Notes:

Nabakalebar Rath Yatra

- **Statement 1 is correct:** Nabakalebara festival is an ancient ritual that is observed in the Shree Jagannath Temple at Puri, Odisha at predefined time according to Hindu Calender.
- Naba means new and Kalebara is body. In this festival, the idols of Lord Jagannath, Balabhadra and Subhadra are replaced by new idols as it is believed that Lord Shree Jagannath adornes new body during Nabakalebara.
- **Statement 2 is incorrect:** It usually comes in every twelve to nineteen years based on the auspicious two months of Ashadha in a year called as Purusottam month as per the Hindu calendar.
- President Ram Nath Kovind has released ₹ 1,000 and ₹ 10 commemorative coins on the occasion of Nabakalebar festival at a function held in Puri, Odisha.

19. **Correct Option: (c)**

Supplementary Notes:

Wangala Festival

- **Option (c) is correct:** Wangala Festival of Meghalaya is the most popular festival among the Garos of Meghalaya, India. Wangala festival is a harvest festival held in honour of Saljong, the Sun God of fertility. The celebration of the Wangala Festival marks the end of a period of toil, which brings good output of the fields. It also signifies the onset of winter.
- Also known as a 100-drums festival, Wangala Festival is the occasion when the tribals offer sacrifices to please their main deity Saljong – the Sun God.
- It is generally celebrated for two days and sometimes continues for even a week. The ceremony performed on first day is known as "Ragula" which is held inside the house of the chief. On the second day known as "Kakkat", people, young and old dressed in their colourful costumes with feathered headgears dance to the tune of music played on long oval-shaped drums.
- This is the occasion to relax and for days the hills and valleys echo with the extraordinary beat of drums. The popular dance forms are performed during the festival. It has certain subtle variations, the main motif being a queue of two parallel lines – one of men and other of women clad in their festive fineries. Young and old join the festivities with equal enthusiasm. While the men beat the drums, the line moves forward in rhythmic accord. The 'orchestra' of men includes drums, gong and flutes, punctuated by the sonorous music of an primitive flute made of buffalo horn. There is a notable sense of tempo in the performers, both young and old, and the energetic dance leaves a lasting impression upon the beholder.
- Basically, the Wangala festival is a way to preserve and promote the cultural identity of Garos in Meghalaya. This is one way to exhibit the culture and tradition of the region.

20. **Correct Option: (c)**

Supplementary Notes:

Swachh Paryatan App:

- **Statement 1 and 2 are correct:** Union Government has launched 'Swachh Parayatan' mobile application to keep tourist places clean.
- The project is being implemented by the Union Ministry of Tourism through Delhi eGovernance Society (DeGS) and National Informatics Centre (NIC).
- Initially the application facility will be available for 25 Adarsh Smarak Monuments protected by Archaeological Survey of India (ASI).
- The mobile app will be monitored by the project monitoring unit of Swachh Bharat Mission in the Union Ministry of Tourism.
- This mobile app will enable citizens, tourists to take photograph of garbage seen at the monument and upload it on the app along with their remarks.
- On uploading images and remarks in the app, it will send an SMS to the ASI Nodal officer concerned with the monument, to take further action to clean the garbage.
- Thereafter, the Nodal Officer will send confirmation about the redressal of the complaint through an SMS.
- Initially, this application will be available only on Android Phones and later it will be made available on Apple and Microsoft platforms.

21. **Correct Option: (c)**

Supplementary Notes:

Tholu bommalata

- Tholu bommalata literally means the (dance of leather dolls). It is a shadow theatre tradition of Andhra Pradesh, Telangana and parts of Karnataka.
- Among the many traditions, Tholu bommalata puppets are definitely the most peculiar for their large sizes. The heights of these puppets range from 120 to 180 centimetres; and at times almost two meters as well. Dimensions can vary according to regional traditions. In different areas of Andhra Pradesh and Telangana, there are differences in aspects and techniques of puppetry.
- Dolls are fashioned of translucent, coloured leather. These are projected on a small screen, like colour photographic transparencies. Animals, birds, gods, and demons dominate the screen. The puppeteer manipulates them from behind with two sticks. Strong lamps are arranged so that the size, position, and angle of the puppets change with the distance of the light.

22. **Correct Option: (d)**

Supplementary Notes:

Nazhu Festival

- The Nazu festival is one of the major festivals of the Pochury tribe of Nagaland and is celebrated in the month of February. This festival usually lasts for 10 days and is held before the sowing of seeds.
- It is celebrated in Phek, which is a district in Nagaland, and the festival is organized by the department of tourism.
- This festival is a time when people celebrate by singing and dancing on the beats of tribal music.
- The festival is defined by various functions and stages of preparation. The most symbolic and unique element common to all is heralding of Nazhu, with the

erection of a bamboo totem Awuthrüu, that resembles a giant wind chime hung from a tall bamboo.

- The major dance performed at the time of this festival is Khupielilie dance. This dance has beautiful hand gestures and many tourists come to the state to view this festival and its beautiful dance. The whole outlook of this festival is less of rituals and more of pure entertainment and competition.
- The Nazu festival is listed in the National List for Intangible Cultural Heritage drafted by the Ministry of Culture under Social practices, rituals and festive events category.

23. Correct Option: (c)

Supplementary Notes:

- In Manipur, the Cherry Blossom Mao Festival was held at Senapati district marking the beginning of pink season in the district.
- The Mao area of Senapati district in Manipur is known for Cherry Blossom, a plant which is popularly known as Sakura in Japan.
- The Manipur government started organizing the festival every year from 2017 onward.
- The festival is held every year in Shillong, the capital of Meghalaya, to celebrate the unique autumn flowering of the Himalayan cherry blossoms and mark the beginning of India's version of autumn.
- However this year, the authority decided to scale down the festival due to COVID-19 pandemic and cancelled the 5th edition of the festival.

24. Correct Option: (d)

Explanation:

- **Pair 2 is incorrectly matched:** Hornbill Festival - Nagaland
- **Pair 3 is incorrectly matched:** Pandharpur Wari - Maharashtra

Supplementary Notes:

Important Cultural Festivals of Different States

State	List of Indian Festivals
Andhra Pradesh	Dasara, Ugadi, Deccan Festival, Brahmotsavam
Arunachal Pradesh	Reh, Boori Boot, Myoko, Dree, Pongtu, Losar, Murung, Solang, Mopin, Monpa festival
Assam	Ambubachi, Bhogali Bihu, Baishagu, Dehing Patkai, Porag Festival
Bihar	Chhath Puja, Bihula
Chhattisgarh	Maghi Purnima, Bastar Dussehra
Goa	Sunburn festival, Ladain, Mando
Gujarat	Navratri, Janmashtami, Kutch Utsav, Uttarayana, Ashadhi Bij
Himachal Pradesh	Rakhadumni, Gochi Festival
Haryana	Baisakhi, Surajkund International Crafts Mela
Jammu and Kashmir	Har Navami, Chhari, Bahu Mela, Dosmoche, Mela Kheerbhawani, Chamliyal Mela
Jharkhand	Karam Utsav, Holi, Rohini, Tusu
Karnataka	Mysore Dasara, Ugadi
Kerala	Onam, Vishu
Madhya Pradesh	Lok-rang Utsav, Tejaji, Khajuraho festival
Meghalaya	Nongkrem festival, Khasis festival, Wangla, Sajibu Cheiraoba
Maharashtra	Ganesh Utsav, Gudi Padva, Pandharpur Wari
Manipur	Yaoshang, Porag, Chavang Kut, Lui-Ngai-Ni
Mizoram	Chapchar kut, Zo Kutpui
Nagaland	Hornbill festival, Moatsu Festival
Odisha	Rath Yatra, Raja Parba, Nukahai
Punjab	Lohri, Baisakhi
Rajasthan	Gangaur, Teej, Bundi
Sikkim	Losar, Saga Dawa
Tamil Nadu	Pongal, Thaipusam, Natyanjali Festival
Telangana	Bonalu, Bathukamma, Nagoba Jatara
Tripura	Kharchi Puja
West Bengal	Durga Puja
Uttaranchal	Ganga Dussehra
Uttar Pradesh	Ram Navmi, Ganga Mahotsav, Navaratri, Khichdi

25. **Correct Option: (b)**

Explanation:

- **Statement 1 is incorrect:** It was organized in Kerala and not Tamil Nadu.

Supplementary Notes:

Thumbimahotsavam

- Recently Thumbimahotsavam 2020, the first-ever state Dragonfly festival was organized in Kerala.
- It was organized by the WWF India, Bombay Natural History Society along with National Biodiversity Board, United Nations Environment Programme and IUCN – Centre for Environment Conservation.
- The official mascot of the festival was 'Pantalu'.
- Dragonfly Festival was first started in 2018 for educating and informing people public about the integral role that dragonflies play in our ecosystem.
- World Wide Fund for Nature (WWF) is an international non-governmental organisation founded in 1961 and headquartered in Gland, Switzerland.
- It organizes 'Earth Hour' annually to encourage people to turn off electric equipment for an hour as symbolism to protect our planet earth.
- Living Planet Report is published by WWF based on a Living Planet Index and ecological footprint analysis.

26. **Correct Option: (c)**

Harvest Festivals		States
A. Wangala	:	Meghalaya
B. Hareli	:	Chhattisgarh
C. Kut	:	Manipur
D. Onam	:	Kerala

Supplementary Notes:

Major Harvest Festivals

- Hareli is celebrated largely in districts of Chattisgarh during the monsoon (Sawan) months of the year i.e. from July to August. During this festival, the members of the tribes pray to cows, motherland, farming equipment and crops and celebrate the upcoming season with lots of social and cultural events and gatherings.
- Kut festival is a major post harvest festival celebrated in the month of November by Kuki-Chin tribes. The annual festival is a leading festival of Manipur.
- Wangala (also known as The Hundred Drums Festival, Wanma, Wanma Rongchua) is a harvest festival celebrated by the Garo tribe, who live in Meghalaya, Nagaland and Assam.
- Onam festival is the grand carnival of Kerala, celebrated during the month of Chingam (August–September). The ancient festival has a significance of homecoming of the legendary Emperor Mahabali and harvest of rice and rain flowers in Kerala.

27. **Correct Option: (b)**

Explanation:

- **Statement 1 is incorrect:** Therukoothu, the most popular form of folk drama of Tamil Nadu, literally means "street play". It is not a martial art form.

Supplementary Notes:

Therukoothu

- Therukoothu, the most popular form of folk drama of Tamil Nadu, literally means "street play".
- It is mostly performed at the time of annual Temple festivals of Mariamman (Rain goddess) to achieve rich harvest.
- At the core of the extensive repertoire of Therukoothu there is a cycle of eight plays based on the life of Draupadi. Kattiakaran, the Sutradhara of the Therukoothu performance, gives the gist of the play to the audience and Komali entertains the audience with his buffoonery.

28. **Correct Option: (d)**

Explanation:

- **All statements are correct**

Supplementary Notes:

- Directorate of Film Festivals was set up by the Government of India in 1973. It functions under Ministry of Information and Broadcasting.
- Responsibilities of Directorate of Film Festivals (DFF) are:
  - The International Film Festival of India
  - The National Film Awards
  - The Dadasaheb Phalke Award
  - Participation in International Film Festivals abroad
  - Cultural Exchange Programme and organizing screening of Indian films through the missions abroad
  - Selection of Indian Panorama.
  - Special film expositions on behalf of the Govt. in India
  - Print collection and documentation

29. **Correct Option: (b)**

Explanation:

- **Statement 1 is incorrect:** It is organized between November to March.

Supplementary Notes:

Kambala

- Kambala is a traditional buffalo race in paddy fields filled with slush and mud which generally takes place in coastal Karnataka (Udupi and Dakshina Kannada) from November to March.

- Traditionally, it is sponsored by local Tuluva landlords and households in the coastal districts. Tuluva people are an ethnic group native to Southern India. They are native speakers of the Tulu language.

30. Correct Option: (d)

Martial Art	State
A. Kalaripayattu	4. Kerala
B. Gatka	1. Punjab
C. Pari-Khanda	3. Bihar
D. Inbuan Wrestling	2. Mizoram

Supplementary Notes:

Martial Arts in India

- **Kalaripayattu:** One of the oldest martial arts in India, Kalaripayattu, although practiced in most parts of southern India, originated in the state of Kerala in the 4th century AD. Kalari, a Malayalam word, refers to a specific type of school/gymnasium/training hall where martial arts are practiced or taught (in this case it's Kalaripayattu). Its most important key is footwork; it also includes kicks, strikes and weapon-based practice. Even women practice this art. Even though Kalaripayattu is used as a means of unarmed self-defense and a way to achieve physical fitness today, it is still rooted in the traditional rituals and ceremonies.
- **Pari-Khanda:** Pari-Khanda, created by Rajputs, is a form of martial art from Bihar. It involves fighting using sword and shield. Still practiced in many parts of Bihar, its steps and techniques are widely used in Chhau dance. In fact this martial art forms the basis of Chhau dance in which all its elements are absorbed. The name of this martial art consists of two words, 'Pari' that means shield while 'khanda' refers to sword, thus the use of both sword and shield in this art.
- **Gatka:** Gatka is a weapon based martial art form, performed by the Sikhs of Punjab. The name 'Gatka' refers to the one whose freedom belongs to grace. Gatka features the skillful use of weapons, including stick, Kirpan, Talwar and Kataar. The attack and defense in this art form is determined by the various positions of hands and feet and the nature of weapon used. It is displayed on a number of celebrations in the state including fairs.
- **Inbuan Wrestling:** A native martial art form of Mizoram, Inbuan Wrestling is believed to have its genesis in 1750 AD in Dungtlang village. It has very strict rules that prohibit stepping out of the circle, kicking and knee bending. The way to win this is by lifting the opponent off their feet, while stringently adhering to the rules. It also involves catching of the belt (worn around their waist) by the wrestlers. This art form was regarded as a sport only after the people of Mizoram migrated from Burma to Lushai hills.

31. Correct Option: (d)

Explanation:

- **Statement 1 is incorrect:** It is an annual festival dedicated to the worshiping of rivers. It is celebrated at shrines along the banks of 12 major sacred rivers in India.
- **Statement 2 is incorrect:** Mahapushkaram occurs once in 144 years.

Supplementary Notes:

Pushkaram

- Pushkaram is an Indian festival dedicated to the worshiping of rivers.
- It is also known as Pushkaralu (in Telugu), Pushkara (in Kannada) or Pushkar.
- It is celebrated at shrines along the banks of 12 major sacred rivers in India, like Ganga, Yamuna, Indus, Godavari, Krishna etc, in the form of ancestor worship, spiritual discourses, devotional music, and cultural programs.
- The celebration happens annually, once in 12 years along each river.
- Each river is associated with a zodiac sign, and the river for each year's festival is based on which sign Jupiter is in at the time.
- This year the festival will be held at the banks of Brahmaputra river in Assam.
- The 'Pushakaram' is similar to the 'Kumbh Mela' performed alongside rivers elsewhere in the country and taking a holy dip is the main ritual of the festival.
- Mahapushkaram takes place once in 144 years. The last time it took place was in 2015 during Godavari mahapushakaram.

32. Correct Option: (d)

Explanation:

- **Option (d) is correct:** The Nabakalebara is an ancient ritual associated with the Jagannath Temple.

Supplementary Notes:

Nabakalebar festival

- The Nabakalebara is an ancient ritual associated with the Jagannath Temple at Puri, Odisha, when the Idols of Lord Jagannath, Balabhadra, Subhadra and Sudarshan are replaced by a new set of idol's.
- A year with an extra Ashadhamasa/month as per Hindu Calendar is considered auspicious for conducting the ceremony. This usually occurs every twelve to nineteen years.
- The Deities are made from a special type of Neem wood known as DaruBramha.
- The most recent ceremony was in 2015, following the 1996 ceremony.

33. **Correct Option: (b)**

Explanation:

- **Pair 1 is incorrectly matched:** Ambubachi Mela – Assam
- **Pair 3 is incorrectly matched:** Chamliyal Mela – Jammu and Kashmir

Supplementary Notes:

Kharchi Festival

- It is one of the most popular festivals in Tripura and is celebrated at Puran Agartala in Temple premises of 14 gods. The word 'Kharchi' is derived from the word 'Khya' which means earth thus Kharchi Puja is basically done to worship earth. It's a week-long royal Puja which falls in month of July on 8th day of new moon and attracts thousands of people.

Ambubachi Mela

- The Ambubachi Mela is celebrated in the capital city of Guwahati, in the northeastern state of Assam in India. The Ambubachi Mela is the most important festival of the Kamakhya Temple of Guwahati. The Ambubachi is a ritual of asceses observed with "Tantrik means". It is believed that the presiding goddess of the Temple, Devi Kamakhya, the Mother Shakti, goes through her annual cycle of menstruation during this time stretch.

Chamliyal Mela

- It is celebrated at Chamliyal border shrine along the International Border (IB). The fair takes place at the shrine of Baba Dalip Singh Manhas, a saint popularly known as Baba Chamliyal, in Samba district in Jammu and Kashmir.

34. **Correct Option: (c)**

Explanation:

- **Both statements are correct**

Supplementary Notes:

Intangible Cultural Heritage

- UNESCO's 2003 Convention for the Safeguarding of the Intangible Cultural Heritage proposes five broad domains in which intangible cultural heritage are manifested:
  - Oral traditions and expressions, including language as a vehicle of the intangible cultural heritage
  - Performing arts
  - Social practices, rituals, and festive events
  - Knowledge and practices concerning nature and the universe
  - Traditional craftsmanship

Intangible Cultural Heritage in India

- A total of 13 Intangible Cultural Heritage (ICH) elements from India have been inscribed to date on UNESCO's Representative List of the Intangible Cultural Heritage of Humanity with Kumbh Mela being the latest addition in 2017.
- For inclusion of an element in the UNESCO's Representative List of Intangible Cultural Heritage, the state parties are required to submit nomination dossier on the relevant element for evaluation and examination of the UNESCO Committee.
- The Ministry of Culture has appointed the Sangeet Natak Akademi, an autonomous organisation under the Ministry of Culture, as a nodal officer for matters relating to the intangible cultural heritage including for preparation of the nomination dossiers for the Representative List of UNESCO.

35. **Correct Option: (a)**

Festival	State
A. Hornbill Festival	4. Nagaland
B. Chapchar Kut Festival	3. Mizoram
C. Wangala Festival	2. Meghalaya
D. Sangai Festival	1. Manipur

Supplementary Notes:

Important Festivals in North-East India

- **Hornbill Festival:** To encourage inter-tribal interaction and to promote the cultural heritage of Nagaland, the Government of Nagaland organizes the Hornbill Festival every year in the first week of December. It is also called 'Festival of Festivals'. The festival is named after the Indian hornbill, the large and colorful forest bird which is displayed in the folklore of most of the state's tribes. Visitors can enjoy the colorful performances, crafts, sports, local food fairs, games, and ceremonies, besides traditional arts which include paintings, wood carvings, and sculptures throughout the festival.
- **Chapchar Kut Festival:** It is a spring festival, which is the most important festival and the only one regularly observed during the first week of March in Mizoram. On this day people of all ages, young and old, men and women dressed in their colorful costumes and distinctive head gears and jewelry, assemble and perform various folk dances, singing traditional songs accompanied by beating of drums, gongs, and cymbals. Some dances are strictly martial danced by strong virile warriors with their weapons and trophies. One dance perennially popular is the Cheraw or the "bamboo dance" so-called as long bamboo staves are used for this dance.
- **Wangala Festival:** The Wangala is the most significant festival of the Garo clans of Meghalaya which is performed after the harvesting is over, generally in the month of October to November. It is a "Thanksgiving" ceremony to Misi Saljong, also

known as Pattigipa Ra'rongipa (The Great Giver) for having blessed the human beings with a rich harvest of the season.

- **Sangai Festival:** Every year the State of Manipur celebrates the "Manipur Sangai Festival" from 21st -30th November. The festival is named after the State animal, Sangai, the brow-antlered deer found only in Manipur. It started in the year 2010 and has grown over the years into a big platform for Manipur to showcase its rich tradition and culture to the world. The festival is labeled as the grandest festival of the State today and helps promote Manipur as a world-class tourism destination.

36. Correct Option: (b)

Explanation:

- **Statement 1 is incorrect:** It is celebrated by the Kashmiri Pandits at the famous Ragnya Devi Temple.

Supplementary Notes:

Kheer Bhawani Festival

- It is an annual festival celebrated by the Kashmiri Pandits at the famous Ragnya Devi Temple in Jammu and Kashmir's Ganderbal district on the occasion of Shukla Paksha Ashtami.
- The Temple often referred to as the most important Temple for the Kashmiri Hindus in the state is constructed over a sacred spring, which is believed to have water changing colors.
- The festival witnessed a rare reunion of two separated communities of the valley – Muslims and Pandits. The festival is fast emerging as a source of healing relationships between Pandits and Muslims of Kashmir.
- Local Muslim shopkeepers sell earthenware lamps, marigold flowers and other puja paraphernalia at the Temple.
- Kheer Bhawani is mentioned in Kalhana's Rajtarangini. He writes that the sacred spring of Tulmulla is situated on marshy ground. The name of the spring is Mata Ragini Kund. The site is also mentioned in Ain-i-Akbari by Abul Fazl.

37. Correct Option: (b)

Supplementary Notes:

Bathukamma Festival

- Bathukamma is a colorful and vibrant festival of Telangana and celebrated by women, with flowers that grow exclusively in each region. This festival is a symbol of Telangana's cultural identity.
- Bathukamma that means 'Mother Goddess come Alive' is celebrated towards the end of monsoon and heralds the abundance that nature has to offer. The festival begins on the day of Mahalaya Amavasya and is celebrated with much fanfare for nine days. The final day of Bathukamma, known as Pedha or Saddula Bathukamma falls two days before Dussehra.
- Bathukamma is a beautiful flower stack, arranged with different unique seasonal flowers most of them with medicinal values, in seven concentric layers in the shape of Temple gopuram.
- Bathukamma celebrates the inherent relationship between earth, water, and human beings.

38. Correct Option: (d)

Explanation:

- **Option (d) is correct:** Pigs are sacrificed during the festival as a mark of respect for their local deity known as Lampha Raja.

Supplementary Notes:

Khelchawa Festival

- Tiwa tribals celebrate Khelchawa festival in Assam.
- This festival is celebrated every five years.
- The festival is held at the close of the harvest season in the month of April.
- After the harvesting season is over Tiwa community celebrates the festival for a good harvest.
- The festival also celebrates the efforts of young boys becoming an adult.
- Pigs are also sacrificed during the festival as a mark of respect for their local deities collectively known as Lampha Raja.
- Tiwa tribesmen are recognized as a Scheduled Tribe within the State of Assam.
- They are also found in the states of Meghalaya, Manipur and Arunachal Pradesh. They speak Tibeto Burman language.
- Further, they are divided into two sub-groups namely Hill Tiwas and Plain Tiwas.
- Tiwa tribesmen take part in dance during the Khelchawa festival in Karbi Anglong district of Assam.

39. Correct Option: (b)

Explanation:

- **Statements 1 and 3 are incorrect**

Supplementary Notes:

Martial Arts

- Kalaripayattu is one of the most ancient martial art originated in Kerala state in 4th century AD.
- Silambam a kind of staff fencing is modern and scientific martial art of Tamil Nadu.
- Thang-ta and Saritsarat–is armed martial art created by Meiti people of Manipur.

CONCEPT REVISION

Here is the list of concepts that have been covered as part of the previous exercise. Revise and self-reflect on your concepts you covered.

- Tholu Bommalata ☐
- Hornbill Festival ☐
- Teesta Rangit Tourism Festival ☐
- Kumbh Mela ☐
- 'First world Orange festival' ☐
- 'Bharat Parv' ☐
- Chapchar Kut festival ☐
- Kheer Bhawani ☐
- Yoga ☐
- 'Losar Festival' ☐
- Animal sports in India ☐
- Bathukamma ☐
- 'Sangai Festival' ☐
- 'Sankalp Parv-Sankalp se Siddhi' ☐
- Sunburn Festival ☐
- Ganga Sagar Mela ☐
- Nabakalebar Rath Yatra ☐
- Wangala Festival ☐
- 'Swachh Paryatan' ☐
- 'Tholu bommalata' ☐
- 'Nazhu festival' ☐
- Cherry Blossom Mao Festival ☐
- Thumbimahotsavam ☐
- Harvesting festivals ☐
- Therukoothu ☐
- Different forms of Martial Art ☐
- Pushkaram Festival ☐
- Khelchawa festival ☐
- Martial Arts and their region ☐

☐☐☐

9. RELIGION, LANGUAGE & LITERATURE

9.1 RELIGIONS IN INDIA

QUESTIONS

1. **Which of the following is/are not the salient features of the Vajrayana Buddhism?**
   1. Its predominant in China, Nepal, Bhutan and Mongolia.
   2. It combines Mahayana ideals with a body of esoteric knowledge and tantric practice.

   Select the correct answer using the codes given below:

   (a) 1 only (b) 2 only
   (c) Both 1 and 2 (d) Neither 1 nor 2

2. **Which of the following are the Jewels of Jainism which constitutes the path to liberation?**
   1. Right Faith
   2. Right Knowledge
   3. Right Conduct
   4. Right Livelihood
   5. Right Mindfulness

   Select the correct answer using the codes given below:

   (a) 1, 3 and 5 only (b) 1, 2 and 3 only
   (c) 1, 2 and 4 only (d) 2, 3 and 4 only

3. **Which of the following Buddhist Mudras and their meanings is/are correctly matched?**

Mudra	Meaning
1. Dharmacakra Mudra	- Gesture of Teaching.
2. Varada Mudra	- Gesture of Compassion
3. Vitaka Mudra	- Gesture of Warding off Evil

   Select the correct answer using the code given below:

   (a) 1 only (b) 2 and 3 only
   (c) 1 and 2 only (d) 1, 2 and 3

4. **Consider the following statements about International Buddhist Conclave:**
   1. It is organized every two years.
   2. Since inception the conclave is organized in India only
   3. The theme of 2018 edition is—'Buddha Path – The Living Heritage'

   Which of the above statements are correct?

   (a) 1 and 3 only (b) 2 and 3 only
   (c) 1 and 2 only (d) 1, 2 and 3

5. **Consider the following statements related to Vaishanvism:**
   1. Vaishanvism became powerful movement in South India especially under the Alvars.
   2. The first Vaishnava philosopher was Ramanuja Acharya, who introduces visistaadvaitha siddhantha.

3. Key texts in Vaishnavism include the Upanishads, the Pancaratra (Agama) texts and the Bhagavata Purana.

Which of the above statement/s is/are correct?

(a) 1 only (b) 2 only
(c) 2 and 3 only (d) 1, 2 and 3

6. Consider the following statements regarding the Sikh Gurus:

1. Guru Nanak Dev started the institution of Guru Ka Langar.
2. Guru Arjan Dev compiled the writings of Nanak Dev in Guru Granth Sahib in Gurmukhi Script.
3. Guru Ram Das founded the city of Amritsar.
4. Guru Gobind Singh Sahib created the Khalsa.

Which of the above statements are correct?

(a) 1 and 2 only (b) 2 and 3 only
(c) 1, 3 and 4 only (d) 2, 3 and 4 only

7. Who was the first Sanskrit scholar in Buddhism ?

(a) Ashwaghosha
(b) Acharya Nagarjuna
(c) Amarasimha
(d) Buddhaghosha

8. With reference to Bhagavatism, consider the following statements :

1. Bhagavatism centered on the worship of Vishnu and originated in post-Maurya times.
2. Bhagavatism was marked by Bhakti and Ahimsa.
3. Bhagavatism overshadowed Mahayana Buddhism by Gupta times.

Which of the above statement/s is/are correct?

(a) 3 only (b) 1 and 3 only
(c) 2 and 3 only (d) 1, 2 and 3

9. Which of the following is/are the causes for decline of Buddhism in India?

1. The concept of incarnation made Buddhism lose its identity.
2. Advent of Islam with the emergence of the slave Dynasty led to decline of Buddhism.
3. Lack of security made Buddhism move to Nepal.

Select the correct answer using the code give below:

(a) 2 only (b) 2 and 3 only
(c) 1 and 3 only (d) 1, 2 and 3

10. Consider the following statements:

1. Ananda recited Vinaypitaka and Upali recited Suttapitaka.
2. During 2nd Buddhist Council, Buddhism got divided into two sects: Mahasangiks and Sthiravadins.
3. Moggaliputra Tissa composed Abhidamma Pitaka that dealt with Buddhist philosophy.
4. During 4th Buddhist Council, Buddhism got divided into Mahayana and Hinayana.

Which of the above statements are correct?

(a) 1, 3 and 4 only (b) 1, 2 and 4 only
(c) 2, 3 and 4 only (d) 1, 2, 3 and 4

11. Consider the following statements related to Gupta's contribution in Art and Architecture:

1. Gupta introduced the Nagara style of architecture.
2. Gupta continued the Ajanta cave painting tradition at Bagh caves.

Which of the above statement/s is/are correct?

(a) 1 only (b) 2 only
(c) Both 1 and 2 (d) Neither 1 nor 2

12. Consider the following statements regarding Sthanakvas:

1. It is a sub-sect of Digambara sect in Jainism.
2. They practice their religious duties in temples.
3. They do not believe in idol worship at all.

Which of the above statement/s is/are correct?

(a) 1 only (b) 1 and 2 only
(c) 2 and 3 only (d) 3 only

13. Consider the following statements regarding Tenets of Buddhism:

1. There exists a supreme god or deity in Buddhism.
2. 'Dukkha' and its extinction are central to the Buddha's doctrine.

Which of the above statement/s is/are correct?

(a) 1 only (b) 2 only
(c) Both 1 and 2 (d) Neither 1 nor 2

14. "Sallekhana" is a religious practice followed in Jainism. Which one of the following options correctly describe it?

(a) It is related to Anekantavada.
(b) Jaina's sixteen noble fold path to liberation.
(c) Jaina religious ritual of fasting to death.
(d) None of the above

15. Consider the following statements about Sant Ravidas.

1. Sant Ravidas was disciple of Ramananda and contemporary of Kabir.
2. He is considered the founder of the 21st-century Ravidassia religion.
3. His hymns are included in the Guru Granth Sahib.

Which of the above statement/s is/are correct?

(a) 1 only (b) 1 and 2 only
(c) 2 and 3 only (d) 1, 2 and 3

16. Which among the following is not among the three protective deities around Buddha that are depicted in Ajanta caves?

(a) Avalokiteśvara (b) Manjusri
(c) Samantabhadra (d) Vajrapani

17. Which of the following statement/s is/are correct?

1. Jainism condemns the varna system.
2. Buddhism does not recognize the existence of god and soul.

Select the correct answer using the code given below:

(a) 1 only (b) 2 only
(c) Both 1 and 2 (d) Neither 1 nor 2

18. Which of the following are common features between Jainism and Buddhism?

1. Practice of extreme penance and austerity
2. Non-violence
3. Belief in varna system
4. Belief in right action

Select the correct answer using the code below:

(a) 2 and 4 only (b) 1, 3 and 4 only
(c) 1 and 2 only (d) 4 only

19. Consider the following statements regarding Zen Buddhism

1. It's related to the Hinyana branch of Buddhism.
2. The essence of Zen Buddhism is that all human beings are Buddha.
3. The most common way of teaching in Zen Buddhism for enlightenment is communication directly from master to pupil.

Which of the above statement/s is/are correct?

(a) 1 and 2 only (b) 1 and 3 only
(c) 2 and 3 only (d) 1, 2 and 3

20. In the religious and cultural history of India, "ekantika-dharma" is related to:

(a) Buddhism (b) Jainism
(c) Lokayata (d) Bhagavata

21. Consider the following statements regarding Buddhism in Gupta Period:

1. Buddhism no longer received royal patronage in the Gupta period.
2. Fa-hien gives the impression that Buddhism was in a declining state.
3. Earliest structure of Nalanda University belongs to Gupta period.

Which of the above statement/s is/are correct?

(a) 1 and 2 only (b) 1 and 3 only
(c) 2 and 3 only (d) 1, 2 and 3

22. The principle that distinguishes Jainism from Buddhism is the

(a) practice of the eight-fold path
(b) rejection of the infallibility of the Vedas
(c) attribution of a soul to all beings and things
(d) belief in rebirth

23. Which one of the following is not included in the eight-fold path of Buddhism?

(a) Right speech
(b) Right contemplation
(c) Right desire
(d) Right conduct

24. Consider the following places:

1. Lumbini 2. Bodh Gaya
3. Sarnath 4. Kushinagar

In the context of the life of Buddha, the correct chronological sequence of these places is:

(a) 1 - 2 - 3 - 4 (b) 1 - 2 - 4 - 3
(c) 2 - 1 - 3 - 4 (d) 2 - 1 - 4 - 3

25. Who among the following Bahmani rulers built the famous Gol Gumbaj at Bijapur?

(a) Muhammd Adil Shah
(b) Mahmud Gawan
(c) Yusuf Adil Shah
(d) Ismail Adil Shah

26. Consider the following statements about Jain Philosophy:

1. Principal of Ahimsa is derived from the Jain Philosophy
2. Jain did not believed in the cycle of birth and death based on Karma

Which of the above statement/s is/are correct?

(a) 1 only (b) 2 only
(c) Both 1 and 2 (d) Neither 1 nor 2

27. Consider the following statement about Buddha's teaching:

1. The Buddha regarded the social world as the creation of humans rather than of divine origin
2. Buddha emphasized on individual agency to attain Nibbana

Which of the above statement/s is/are correct?

(a) 1 only (b) 2 only
(c) Both 1 and 2 (d) Neither 1 nor 2

28. Match the following pairs:

List 1	List 2
A. Eight fold path	i. Tantras
B. Vajrayana	ii. Jainism
C. Digambara	iii. Buddhism
D. Buddha's first sermon	iv. Sarnath

Select the correct answer using the code given below:

(a) A-ii, B-i, C-iii, D-iv
(b) A-i, B-ii, C-iii, D-iv
(c) A-iv, B-iii, C-ii, D-i
(d) A-iii, B-i, C-ii, D-iv

29. Consider the following statements about Buddhism:

1. The women were not admitted in the Buddhist Sanghas.
2. The Middle Path was laid down by the Buddha.
3. The Buddha was born at Lumbini.
4. According to the Buddha, desire is the root cause of all evils.

Which of the given statement/s is/are correct?

(a) 1 and 2 only (b) 2 and 3 only
(c) 2, 3, and 4 only (d) 3 and 4 only

30. Consider the following statements:

1. Mahavira was a contemporary of Buddha.
2. The first Buddhist council was held during the reign of King Ashoka.
3. Buddhism accepted the superiority of Brahmanas.

Which of the above statement/s is/are correct?

(a) 1 and 2 only (b) 2 only
(c) 2 and 3 only (d) 1 only

31. Consider the following statements:

1. Mahavira did not believe in the existence of God.
2. Buddhism believes in the ideas of eternal self or soul (Atman) and eternity.

Which of the above statement/s is/are correct?

(a) 1 only (b) 2 only
(c) Both 1 and 2 (d) Neither 1 nor 2

32. Consider the following statements

1. Both Buddhism and Jainism were formed by Kshatriyas.
2. Mahayana Buddhism believes in idol worship while Hinayana does not.

Which of the above statement/s is/are correct?

(a) 1 only (b) 2 only
(c) Both 1 and 2 (d) Neither 1 nor 2

33. Consider the following statements regarding Pre-Vedic Religion:

1. The earliest traces of some form of religion in the Indian sub-continent were discovered at the excavated sites of the Harappan Civilisation.
2. Vedism is the oldest stratum of religious activity in India for which there exist written materials.

Which of the following statement/s is/are correct?

(a) 1 only (b) 2 only
(c) Both 1 and 2 (d) Neither 1 nor 2

34. Consider the following statements regarding Pre-Vedic Religion:

1. People believed in the sanctity of the creative force and venerated the male and female aspects of divinity.
2. The nature of the religious beliefs and practices of the Aryans is known from the Atharva Veda.

Which of the following statement/s is/are correct?

(a) 1 only (b) 2 only
(c) Both 1 and 2 (d) Neither 1 nor 2

35. Consider the following statements regarding Hindu sect:

1. Vallabhacharya sect, founded by Vallabha, opposed fasts and self-mortification.
2. Aghori Panth cult was founded by Bhrama Giri and they worship Shiva.
3. Dashnami Sampraday cult, founded by Shankracharya, are the worshipers of Lord Vishnu.

Which of the above statement/s is/are correct?

(a) 1 and 2 only (b) 2 and 3 only
(c) 1 and 3 only (d) 1, 2 and 3

36. Regarding Buddhist sects, consider the following statements:

1. The followers of Hinayana believe in the original traditions of Buddha.
2. According to Mahayana, Bodhisattva was potential Buddha and everybody could achieve salvation.
3. Vajrayana sect believed that salvation can be achieved by acquiring magical powers.

Which of the above statement/s is/are correct?

(a) 1 and 2 only (b) 2 and 3 only
(c) 1 and 3 only (d) 1, 2 and 3

37. Consider the following statements regarding Buddhism:

1. Buddhism was an organized religion where education was given state patronage
2. Buddhism is/was the state religion of Tibet, China and Japan.

Which of the above statement/s is/are correct?

(a) 1 only (b) 2 only
(c) Both 1 and 2 (d) Neither 1 nor 2

38. Consider the following statements regarding Jainism:

1. The Jain texts were written in Pali and were finally compiled in the sixth century AD in Valabhi, Gujarat.
2. The Digambara believed that the monks should not wear cloth and that the women cannot attain salvation.
3. Upangas, Chhedab and Malasutras are some of the important works in Jain literature.

Which of the above statement/s is/are correct?

(a) 1 and 2 only (b) 2 and 3 only
(c) 1 only (d) 1, 2 and 3

39. Which of the following Sikh sects are correctly matched with their founders:

1. Nirankari Sect : Dyal Das
2. Radha Soami Sect : Shiv Dayal
3. Namdhari Sect : Arjun Singh

Choose the correct option from the codes given below:

(a) 1 and 2 only (b) 3 only
(c) 1 and 3 only (d) 2 only

40. Which of the following statements is incorrect regarding Islam/Muslim sect?

(a) The migration of Prophet Mohammad to Madina from Mecca in AD 622 marked the beginning of the Hijira Era.

(b) Pilgrimage to Madina is one of the five fundamental principles of Islam.
(c) Within the Islamic tradition the rise of Wahabis represented an active oppositionist sect whereas the Bahais were more of a passive and withdrawing kind.
(d) Both the Bhakti and the Sufi movements believed that all humans are equal, God is supreme and devotion to God is the only way to achieve salvation.

41. Christians also have a number of denominations and sects. Consider the following statements regarding the same:

1. A section of the community felt that the Church and society are in a state of crisis and demanded reforms came to be known as Protestant.
2. The Eastern Orthodox Churches recognize the authority of Bible alone.

Which of the above statement/s is/are correct?

(a) 1 only (b) 2 only
(c) Both 1 and 2 (d) Neither 1 nor 2

42. Consider the following statements:

1. The Zoroastrianism is a polytheistic religion developed in Persia around 7th century BC
2. They believe in the supreme authority of the God called as Angra Mainyu.
3. Dakhma is place where dead bodies are left to be eaten by Dakhma Nashini.

Which of the above statement/s is/are incorrect?

(a) 1 only (b) 2 only
(c) 3 only (d) 1 and 2 only

43. Consider the following statement:

1. Bnei Menashe Jews live in Cochin and have genealogies to the Menashe or the Menasseh Tribe, which was one of the 10 lost tribes of the Jews.
2. Bene Ephraim is a small group of Telugu-speaking Jews who converted to Judaism in the 1980s.
3. As per the Judaism, the Sefer Torah was given to Prophet Jacob/Israel on the Mt Sinai.

Which of the above statement/s is/are incorrect?

(a) 1 only (b) 2 only
(c) 1 and 3 only (d) 1, 2 and 3

44. Which of the following statement/s is/are correct regarding the Chisti Order?

1. The saints of Chisti Order lived in poverty and lead a hermit life.
2. It was established in India by Khwaja Qutbuddin Bakhtiyar Kaki.

Select the correct answer using the code given below:

(a) 1 only (b) 2 only
(c) Both 1 and 2 (d) Neither 1 nor 2

45. Consider the following statements about Sufi orders:

1. Ba-shara are those who followed the Islamic Law.
2. Be-shara are those who were not bound by the Islamic Law.

Which of the above statement/s is/are incorrect?

(a) 1 only (b) 2 only
(c) Both 1 and 2 (d) Neither 1 nor 2

46. According to Buddhism, which of the following characteristics are the 'marks of existence'?

1. Dukkha 2. Anitya
3. Anatma

Select the correct option using the codes given below:

(a) 1 and 2 only (b) 2 and 3 only
(c) 1 and 3 only (d) 1, 2 and 3

47. Which of the following is/are the basic theory of Vishishtadvaita?

1. It states the each soul has different characteristics.
2. By this philosophy Brahman is characterized by multiple forms.
3. The liberation can be obtained only by true knowledge of Brahman.

Select the correct option using the codes given below:

(a) 1 only (b) 2 only
(c) 1 and 3 only (d) 1, 2 and 3

48. Which of the following is/are not part of the three Jewels or triratna of Jainism?

(a) Right action (conduct)
(b) Right knowledge
(c) Right faith.
(d) Right character

49. Consider the following statements about Jainism.

1. It did not recognise the existence of gods except the jina (Mahavira).
2. Jainism did not condemn the Varna system.

Which of the above statement/s is/are correct?

(a) 1 only (b) 2 only
(c) Both 1 and 2 (d) Neither 1 nor 2

50. Which of the following statement is incorrect about Buddhism?

(a) Buddha did not involve in the discussions regarding soul (atman) and brahma.
(b) Buddha preached middle path in life by avoiding excess of both luxury and austerity.
(c) Buddhism recognized the existence of gods and soul (atman).
(d) Buddhism rejected the Varna system.

51. Consider the following statements regarding Jainism:

1. It stressed on equality and rejected the caste system.
2. Doctrine of Anekant is related to Jainism.

Which of the above statement/s is/are incorrect?

(a) 1 only (b) 2 only
(c) Both 1 and 2 (d) Neither 1 nor 2

52. Which of the following statement/s is/are incorrect?

1. Bhadrabahu was an exponent of Digambara sect whereas, Sthulabhadra was of Shvwetambara sect.
2. Svetambaras have made a departure from Mahavira's teachings while Digambaras strictly follow his teachings.

Select the correct option using the codes given below:

(a) 1 only (b) 2 only
(c) Both 1 and 2 (d) Neither 1 nor 2

53. Which of the following statements is incorrect?

(a) The development of Hinayana Buddhism led to the composition of numerous texts in what is now known as Buddhist Hybrid Sanskrit.
(b) Tantric Buddhism is sometimes described as offering a shortcut to enlightenment.
(c) The Sthaviravadins followed strict monastic life and rigid disciplinary laws.
(d) The concept of Bodhisattva is the result of Mahayana Buddhism.

54. Consider the following statements:

1. Ashoka appointed dhamma mahamatras to propagate Buddhism in foreign countries.
2. There was a clear demarcation between Asoka's own commitment as a Buddhist and his policy of Dhamma.
3. Ashoka's dhammalipis covered not only religion and morality but also embraced social and administrative matters.

Which of the above statements are correct?

(a) 1, 2, and 3 (b) 1 and 3 only
(c) 1 and 2 only (d) 2 and 3 only

55. Which of the following statements is incorrect about the Mahayana branch of Buddhism?

(a) Prosperity in trade was the main reason for its rise.
(b) Kanishka was the patron of the Mahayana branch.
(c) Buddha's statue began to be worshiped in place of the Buddhist emblems.
(d) With the increase in donations, more people started attracting towards Buddhist monasteries.

56. Which of the following features in the Gandhara Art style were influenced by the Greek Roman Style?

1. Halo around the head of Buddha
2. Forehead lines
3. Buddha's wavy hair

Select the correct option using the codes given below:

(a) 1 only (b) 1 and 2 only
(c) 2 and 3 only (d) 1, 2 and 3

57. Consider the following statements regarding Mahavira:

1. Mahavira is considered 23rd and the last Tirthankara.
2. Mahavira was the first person in the Indian subcontinent to be idolized.

Which of the above statement/s is/are incorrect?

(a) 1 only (b) 2 only
(c) Both 1 and 2 (d) Neither 1 nor 2

58. Which of the following statements regarding the life of Buddha is/are correct?

1. As the cities which Buddha visited did not assume any urban character then his existence is not supported by any archaeological evidence.
2. He was called Buddha just after the event of 'Dharmachakra Pravartana' took place.
3. He attained 'Mahaparinirvan' in the capital the Malla Mahajanpada.

Select the correct option using the codes given below:

(a) 2 only (b) 2 and 3 only
(c) 1 and 3 only (d) 1, 2 and 3

59. Consider the following statements:

1. Buddha rejected the authority of the Vedas as well as the law of 'karma'.
2. 'Nirvana', according to Buddha, means the shedding of all desires, and ending of all the sufferings.
3. He did not believe in the existence of soul.

Which of the above statement/s is/are correct?

(a) 1 only (b) 1 and 2 only
(c) 2 and 3 only (d) 1, 2 and 3

60. Consider the following statements regarding the spread of Buddhism:

1. A new form of Buddhism, known as Mahayana Buddhism developed during the rule of Kanishka.
2. Theravada Buddhism was more popular in Sri Lanka, Myanmar, Thailand, and other parts of Southeast Asia including Indonesia.

Which of the above statement/s is/are correct?

(a) 1 only (b) 2 only
(c) Both 1 and 2 (d) Neither 1 nor 2

61. With reference to the religious practices in India, the "Sammitiyas" sect belongs to which religion?

(a) Buddhism
(b) Jainism
(c) Hinduism
(d) None of the above

62. The twelfth century witnessed the emergence of a new movement in Karnataka, led by a Brahmana named Basavanna. In this context, consider the following statements:

1. His followers were known as Virashaivas or Lingayats.
2. They supported the caste system and various social practices of Hindus.
3. The Virshaivas is a Shaivite sect in Hinduism.

Which of the given statements are correct?

(a) 1 and 2 only (b) 1 and 3 only
(c) 2 and 3 only (d) 1, 2 and 3

63. Which of the following statements is/are correct regarding Principles of Jainism?

1. Like Buddhism, it condemns the Varna system.
2. It principally aims at the attainment of freedom from worldly bonds.
3. Satya, Ahimsa and Asteya are considered as Triratna of Jainism.

Select the correct answer using the code given below:

(a) 1 and 2 only (b) 2 only
(c) 1 and 3 only (d) None of the above

64. One of the major causes of the spread of Jainism in South India is said to have been the great famine that took place in Magadha 200 years after Mahavira's death. In this context, consider the following statement:

1. Many Jainas migrated to the south under the leadership of Sthalabahu.
2. The southern Jainas began to be called digambaras and the Magadhans shvetambaras.

Which of the above statement is/are incorrect?

(a) 1 only (b) 2 only
(c) Both 1 and 2 (d) Neither 1 nor 2

65. Paticca-Samuppada is the fundamental principle among which of the following?

(a) Jainism (b) Shaivism
(c) Ajivika (d) Buddhism

66. As per Buddhist Philosophy, the universe is:

1. Transient 2. Sorrowful
3. Soulless

Select the correct answer using the code given below:

(a) 1 and 2 only (b) 2 and 3 only
(c) 1 and 3 only (d) 1, 2 and 3

67. Consider the following statements regarding Zoroastrianism:

1. It is a monotheistic religion which believes in one eternal god.
2. Their sacred text is called Zend Avesta and fire along with water are seen as symbol of purity.

Which of the above statements is/are correct?

(a) 1 only (b) 2 only
(c) Both 1 and 2 (d) Neither 1 nor 2

68. Consider the following description:

"He was instrumental in establishing Vajrayana Buddhism in Tibet around the 8th century CE. He was a missionary monk who went from Nalanda to convert Tibetans to Buddhism in the 8th century. He is also known as the 'Second Buddha' ".

Identify the monk described in the above passage:

(a) Padmasambhava
(b) Shantarakshita
(c) Sakya Sri Bhadra
(d) Danaseela

69. Which of the following deities find their mention in Rig Veda?

1. Indra 2. Agni
3. Usha 4. Rudra
5. Vak

Select the correct answer using the code given below:

(a) 1 and 2 only (b) 3, 4 and 5 only
(c) 1, 2 and 3 only (d) 1, 2, 3, 4 and 5

70. Consider the following statements regarding Brahmanas and Aranyakas:

1. Both Aranyakas and Brahamanas are attached to the Vedas.
2. Brahmanas describe the rituals and sacrifices involved in the Vedas from various perspectives.

Which of the above statements is/are correct?

(a) 1 only (b) 2 only
(c) Both 1 and 2 (d) Neither 1 nor 2

71. Consider the following statements regarding the Vajrayana Buddhism:

1. It evolved as a movement within Hinayana Buddhism.
2. This school considers Buddha as an ordinary person.
3. It was influenced by primitive local cults and practices.

Which of the above statements is/are correct?

(a) 1 only (b) 1 and 2 only
(c) 2 and 3 only (d) 3 only

72. With reference to the International Buddhist Conclave, consider the following statements:

1. The conclave is organized biennially by the Ministry of Tourism to boost tourism to Buddhist sites in India.
2. The theme for the latest edition of the conclave was "Buddha Path – The Living Heritage".

Which of the above statements is/are correct?

(a) 1 only (b) 2 only
(c) Both 1 and 2 (d) Neither 1 nor 2

73. Consider the following pairs:

Symbols	**Events in Buddha's life**
1. Stupa	Parinirvana
2. Bodhi Tree	Nirvana
3. Horse	Mahabhinishkramana

Which of the above pairs are correctly matched?

(a) 1 and 2 only (b) 2 and 3 only
(c) 1 and 3 only (d) 1, 2 and 3

74. Consider the following statements regarding the state of Nirvana in Buddhism:

1. It has no definite location.
2. It is transient.
3. It is part of the universe.

Which of the above statements are incorrect?

(a) 1 and 2 only (b) 2 and 3 only
(c) 1 and 3 only (d) 1, 2 and 3

75. Consider the following statements regarding the second Buddhist Council:

1. It was held at Patliputra.
2. The monastic order was divided into Mahayan and Hinayana section in this council.

Which of the above statements is/are correct?

(a) 1 only (b) 2 only
(c) Both 1 and 2 (d) Neither 1 nor 2

76. Consider the following statements regarding Sallekhana:

1. It is a religious practice of voluntarily fasting to death by gradually reducing the intake of food and liquids.
2. It can be performed by both Jain ascetics and householders.

Which of the above statements is/are correct?

(a) 1 only (b) 2 only
(c) Both 1 and 2 (d) Neither 1 nor 2

77. Which of the following statements is incorrect about Mangu Matt?

(a) It is a place of historical significance for the Jain community.
(b) It is in proximity to Sri Jagannath Temple.
(c) It was built by Mangu Das, an ardent disciple of Guru Nanak.
(d) Guru Nanak came to this place in Puri in 1550 and offered 'Arati' to Lord Jagannath.

78. Consider the following statements regarding 'Doctrines of Jainism':

1. Principle of Syadavada is also known as the doctrine of non-one-sidedness.
2. Principle of Anekantavada emphasises on the relativity of all knowledge.
3. Principle of Pancha Mahavrata deals with the 5 great vows of a Jaina.

Which of the above statements is/are correct?

(a) 3 only (b) 1 and 3 only
(c) 2 only (d) 1, 2 and 3

79. Consider the following statements regarding Buddhism and Brahmanism in India:

1. Both Brahmanism and Buddhism emphasised the virtues of carrying out familial obligations.
2. While the Buddhism monks did not consider the Varna system, Brahmanas conferred Varna system based on the birth of the individual.

Which of the above statements is/are correct?

(a) 1 only (b) 2 only
(c) Both 1 and 2 (d) Neither 1 nor 2

80. With reference to Ajivikas sect, consider the following statements:

1. It was an ascetic order that was founded by Makkhali Gosala.
2. They were against Brahmanical dominance.
3. They followed the principle of niyati or pre-determinism stating the fallacy of karma.

Which of the above statements are correct?

(a) 1 and 2 only (b) 2 and 3 only
(c) 1 and 3 only (d) 1, 2 and 3

81. Consider the following statements regarding the Lingayats and Siddhas:

1. The Lingayats were worshippers of Shiva.
2. The Siddha saints were mostly Vaishnavites.

Which of the above statements is/are correct?

(a) 1 only (b) 2 only
(c) Both 1and 2 (d) Neither 1 nor 2

82. In Ancient India, terms prithivisthana, antarikshasthana and dyusthana refer to?

(a) Temple courtyard
(b) Educational courses
(c) Vedic gods
(d) Market places

83. With reference to the history of philosophical thoughts in India, consider the following statements regarding Vedanta school:

1. The theory of karma was closely linked to the Vedanta philosophy.
2. It lays emphasis on Brahmagyan, hence relies on the Upanishad part of the Vedas.

Which of the statements given above is /are correct?

(a) 1 only (b) 2 only
(c) Both 1 and 2 (d) Neither 1 nor 2

84. "He emerged as one of the leading proponents of Vaishnavism in Assam. His teachings, often known as the Bhagavati Dharma, focused on absolute surrender to the supreme deity. He emphasized the need for naam kirtan; recitation of name of Lord in satsanga or congregations of pious devotees his major composition includes the Kirtana-ghosha". Identify the personality discussed in the above passage:

(a) Manikkavachakar (b) Shankaradeva
(c) Jnanadeva (d) Ramananda

85. Which of the following were the causes for the rise of Jainism and Buddhism?

1. Introduction of new agricultural economy in north-eastern India.
2. The complex and expensive rituals and sacrifices advocated in the Later Vedic period were not acceptable to the common people.

Select the correct answer using the code given below:

(a) 1 only (b) 2 only
(c) Both 1 and 2 (d) Neither 1 nor 2

86. With reference to the Buddhist Councils, consider the following statements:

1. The first Buddhist Council was presided by Mogaliputta Tissa.
2. Second Buddhist Councils was conducted under the patronage of King Ashoka of Maurya Dynasty.

Which of the above statements is/are correct?

(a) 1 only (b) 2 only
(c) Both 1 and 2 (d) Neither 1 nor 2

SOLUTIONS

1. Correct Option: (d)

Supplementary Notes:

Vajrayana Buddhism:

- **Statement 1 is correct:** The Vajrayana tradition of Buddhism spread to China, Mongolia, Bhutan and Tibet.
- Vajrayana Buddhists recognise a large body of Buddhist Tantras, some of which are also included in Chinese and Japanese collections of Buddhist literature, and versions of a few even in the Pali Canon.
- **Statement 2 is correct:** It includes practices that make use of mantras, dharanis, mudras, mandalas and the visualisation of deities and Buddhas. It also combines Mahayana ideals with a body of esoteric knowledge and tantric practice.
- According to Vajrayāna scriptures, the term Vajrayāna refers to one of three vehicles or routes to enlightenment.

Buddhism split into two schools:

- The Mahayana or the Great Wheel and the Hinayana or the Small Wheel. The former believed in image worship, rituals and Bodhisattvas, (incarnations of Buddha) while the latter continued the practices of the earlier Buddhism.
- **Hinayana Buddhism:** It does not believe in idol worship and tries to attain individual salvation through self-discipline and meditation. They consider Buddha to be mortal and his teachings were ethical values that defined the way humans should live.
- **Mahayana Buddhism:** They believed in an Eternal Buddha who will live forever and is like a god who is unending. They followed the Boddhisattva concept of salvation of all conscious individuals. The Mahayana followers believe in idol or image worship of Buddha.

2. Correct Option: (b)

Supplementary Notes:

Jewels of Jainism

Jainism emphasizes on Ratnatraya (triple gems of Jainism) which constitutes the path to liberation. These are as follows:

- **Option 1 is correct:** Right faith (Samyak Darshana)
- **Option 2 is correct:** Right knowledge (Samyak Gyana)
- **Option 3 is correct:** Right conduct (Samyak Charitra)

3. Correct Option: (c)

Supplementary Notes:

Buddhist Mudras

- **Statement 1 is correct:** The Gesture of Teaching (Dharmacakra Mudra) with both hands in front of the breast tips of the index finger and the thumps touching.
- **Statement 2 is correct:** The Gift bestowing Gesture of Compassion (Varada Mudra) with the right hand pendant with the palm turned outwards.
- **Statement 3 is incorrect:** Vitaka Mudra - Gesture of Debate
- The Gesture of Meditation (Samadhi Mudra) with both hands resting on the lap, palms upwards.
- The Gesture of Fearlessness (Abhaya Mudra) with the right hand slightly elevated, the palm turned outwards, also called the Gesture of Renunciation.
- The Gesture of Debate explaining the Buddha's teachings (Vitaka Mudra) with the hands raised and the tips of the forefingers and the thumbs touch each other.
- The Gesture Warding off Evil (Tarjani Mudra) with forefinger and little finger outstretched.

4. Correct Option: (d)

- **Statement 1 is correct:** The International Buddhist Conclave (held every two years) is to showcase and project the Buddhist Heritage in India and boost tourism to the Buddhist sites in the country and cultivate friendly ties with countries and communities interested in Buddhism.
- India has a rich ancient Buddhist Heritage with several important sites associated with the life of Lord Buddha.
- Buddha Path refers to the extraordinary teachings of the Buddha which is called the Middle Path whose practice brings purity of mind and leads to Peace, Happiness and Harmony within and also in the Society as well.
- International Buddhist Conclave is organised biennially by the Ministry of Tourism, Government of India.

- **Statement 2 is correct:** The earlier International Buddhist Conclaves (IBC) were organized in New Delhi and Bodhgaya (February 2004), Nalanda and Bodhgaya (February 2010), Varanasi and Bodhgaya (September 2012), Bodhgaya and Varanasi (September 2014) and in Sarnath/Varanasi and Bodhgaya (October 2016).
- Note that in every IBC, Bodhgaya is chosen as one of the places.
- **Statement 3 is correct:** The theme of the 6th edition (in 2018) is "Buddha Path – The Living Heritage".

5. **Correct Option: (d)**

Supplementary Notes:

Vaishanvism

- **Statement 1 is correct:** Vaishnavism became a powerful movement in South India especially in Tamillakam under the Alvars.
- They composed devotional literature in Tamil on Vaishnavism called Prabandha.
- **Statement 2 is correct:** Acharya's were the Vaishnav philosophers. The first Vaishnava philosopher was Ramanuja Acharya. He introduced visista advaitha siddhantha. Other renowned Acharya's were Madhava and Vallabhacharya.
- **Statement 3 is correct:** Key texts in Vaishnavism include the Vedas, the Upanishads, the Bhagavad Gita, the Pancaratra (Agama) texts and the Bhagavata Purana.

6. **Correct Option: (c)**

Supplementary Notes:

Sikh Gurus

- The era of the ten gurus of Sikhism spans from the birth of Nanak Dev in 1469, through the life of Guru Gobind Singh. At the time of Guru Gobind Singh's death in 1708, he passed the title of Guru to the Sikh scripture, Guru Granth.

Guru Nanak Dev – Guru from 1469 to 1539:

- Guru Nanak Dev, first of the 10 gurus, founded the Sikh faith, introducing the concept of one God.
- He started the institution of Guru Ka Langar. Langar is the term in the Sikh religion refers to the common kitchen where food is served to everyone without any discrimination.
- He emphasized the equality of women and rejected the path of renunciation, and he rejected the authority of the Vedas.
- He was the contemporary of Mughal emperor Babur.

Guru Angad Dev – Guru from 1539 to 1552:

- Guru Angad Dev, second of the 10 gurus, invented and introduced the Gurmukhi (written form of Punjabi) script.
- **Statement 2 is incorrect:** He compiled the writings of Nanak Dev in Guru Granth Sahib in Gurmukhi Script.
- Popularized and expanded the institution of Guru ka Langar which was started by Guru Nanak Dev.

Guru Amardas Sahib – Guru from 1552 to 1574:

- Guru Amardas introduced the Anand Karaj marriage ceremony for the Sikhs, replacing the Hindu form.
- He established Manji & Piri system of religious missions for men and women respectively.
- He strengthened the tradition of Guru Ka Langar.
- He also completely abolished amongst the Sikhs, the custom of Sati and purdah system.
- He was the contemporary of Mughal emperor - Akbar.

Guru Ram Das – Guru from 1574 to 1581:

- Guru Ram Das, fourth of the 10 gurus, founded the city of Amritsar.
- He started the construction of the famous Golden Temple at Amritsar, the holy city of the Sikhs.
- He requested the Muslim Sufi, Mian Mir to lay the cornerstone of the Harmandir Sahib.

Guru Arjan Dev – Guru from 1581 to 1606:

- He compiled the Adi Granth, the scriptures of the Sikhs.
- He completed construction of Sri Darbar Sahib also known as Golden Temple in Amritsar.
- He founded the town of Tarn Taran Sahib near Goindwal Sahib.
  - He became the first great martyr in Sikh history when Emperor Jahangir ordered his execution. Thus, he was hailed as Shaheedan-de-Sartaj (The crown of martyrs).

Guru Har Gobind Sahib – Guru from 1606 to 1644:

- He was the son of Guru Arjan Dev and was known as a "soldier saint".
- He organised a small army and became the first Guru to take up arms to defend the faith.
- He waged wars against Mughal rulers Jahangir and Shah Jahan.

Guru Har Rai Sahib – Guru from 1644 to 1661:

- Though he was a man of peace, he never disbanded the armed sikh warriors who were earlier maintained by Guru Har Gobind.
- He gave shelter to Dara Shikoh, the eldest son of Mughal Ruler Shah Jahan, who was later persecuted by Aurangazeb.
- He cautiously avoided conflict with Emperor Aurangzeb and devoted his efforts to missionary work.

Guru Har Krishan Sahib – Guru from 1661 to 1664:

- Guru Har Krishan was the youngest of the Gurus. He was installed as Guru at the age of five.
- He was contemporary of Aurangazeb and summoned to Delhi by him under framed charges of anti-Islamic blasphemy.

Guru Tegh Bahadur Sahib – Guru from 1665 to 1675:

- He established the town of Anandpur.
- He opposed the forced conversion of the Hindu Kashmiri Pandits by Mughal ruler Aurangazeb and he was consequently persecuted for this.

Guru Gobind Singh Sahib – Guru from 1675 to 1708:

- He became Guru after the martyrdom of his father Guru Tegh Bahadur.
- He created the Khalsa in 1699, changing the Sikhs into a saint-soldier order for protecting themselves.
- Last Sikh Guru in human form and he passed the Guruship of the Sikhs to the Guru Granth Sahib.

7. **Correct Option: (a)**

Supplementary Notes:

Ashwaghosha

- **Option (a) is correct:** Ashwaghosha was a Buddhist philosopher, dramatist, poet and orator from India. He was born in Saketa in northern India. He is believed to have been the first Sanskrit dramatist, and is considered the greatest Indian poet prior to Kalidasa. He was the most famous in a group of Buddhist court writers, whose epics rivalled the contemporary Ramayana. Whereas much of Buddhist literature prior to the time of Ashwaghosa had been composed in Buddhist Hybrid Sanskrit, Ashwaghosha wrote in Classical Sanskrit. First Sanskrit scholar in Buddhism was Ashwaghosha. He wrote Buddha Charita, which is the first kavya in Sanskrit literature. He was also a singer, a dramatist and a short story teller.

8. **Correct Option: (d)**

Supplementary Notes:

Bhagavatism

- **Statement 1 is correct:** Bhagavatism centered on the worship of Vishnu and originated in post-Maurya times.
- Vishnu was the minor God in Vedic times. He represented the sun and also fertility cult.
- **Statement 2 is correct:** Bhagavatism was marked by Bhakti and Ahimsa.
- Bhakti meant the offer of loving devotion. It was a kind of loyalty offered by a tribal to his chief or by a subject his king.
- Ahimsa or non-killing of animals suited the agricultural society.
- **Statement 3 is correct:** Bhagavatism or Vaishnavism overshadowed Mahayana Buddhism by Gupta times. It preached the doctrine of incarnations, or Avatar.

9. **Correct Option: (d)**

Supplementary Notes:

Buddhism

- **Causes of decline for Buddhism in India:** The decline of Buddhism in India, the land of its birth, occurred for a variety of reasons such as sectarian conflicts within Buddhism, a loss in public and royal support for Buddhism, socio-political developments, gains by competing Indian religions such as Hinduism and Jainism, and the invasions of India from central Asia.
- **Statement 1 is correct:** The concept of incarnation made Buddhism lose its identity.
- **Statement 2 is correct:** Advent of Islam with the emergence of the Slave Dynasty led to decline of Buddhism. Bhaktiar Khilji destroyed Buddhist stupas and Nalanda.
- **Statement 3 is correct:** Lack of security made Buddhism move to Nepal.
- Unpopularity – without prosperity and wealth.

10. **Correct Option: (c)**

Supplementary Notes:

Buddhism

- **Statement 1 is incorrect:** Ananda recited Suttapitaka – Code of conduct of, morals, and principles for Buddhist monks. Upali recited Vinaypitaka – code of conduct for sanghas.
- **Statement 2 is correct:** 2nd Buddhist council was held in 383 at Vaishali, which was presided over by Sabbakami and patronized by Kalasoka, the greatest king of Sishunaga Dynasty. Here Buddhism got divided into two sects: Mahasanghikas - who favoured changes and Sthiravadins or Theravadins – who advocated no changes and were followers of holders.
- **Statement 3 is correct:** Moggaliputra Tissa composed Abhidhammapitaka that dealt with Buddhist philosophy.
- **Statement 4 is correct:** 4th Buddhist council was held in first century AD at Kundlavana in Srinagar. It was presided over by Vasumitra and Ashwaghosha and patronized by Kanishka. During this council Buddhism got divided into Mahayana and Hinayana.

11. **Correct Option: (c)**

Supplementary Notes:

Gupta's Administration

- Gupta's age considered as the golden age, as it was a period in which remarkable progress was made in art, architecture, literature, astronomy and medicine.
- In architecture, the Gupta's were the first to start the construction of temples in North India.
- **Statement 1 is correct:** Gupta's introduced the Nagara style of architecture.
- The Gupta's temples were found at Gaya, Varanasi, Paharpur, Mathura and Debgarh.
- In the field of sculpture, the Royal Boar was the best specimen of Gupta sculpture found on Gupta temples.

- **Statement 2 is correct:** Gupta's continued the Ajanta cave painting tradition at Bagh Caves. The main cave structure of this age belongs to Ajanta, Ellora, Bagh and Andhra Country.

12. **Correct Option: (d)**

Explanation:

- **Statement 1 is incorrect:** Sthanakvas is a sub-sect of Svetambara sect.
- **Statement 2 is incorrect:** They practice their religious duties in prayer-halls, not in temples.

Supplementary Notes:

Sthanakvas

- The Svetambara sect has also been split into three main sub-sects:
  - Murtipujaka,
  - Sthanakvasi, and
  - Terapanthi
- The Sthanakvasi arose from the Svetambaras through the Lonka sect of Jainism. Some of the members of the Lonka sect disapproved of the ways of life of their ascetics, declaring that they lived less strictly than Mahavira would have wished.
- Hence, a Lonka sect layman, Viraji of Surat, received initiation as a Yati, i.e., an ascetic, and won great admiration on account of the strictness of his life. Many people of the Lonka sect joined this reformer.
- They took the name of Sthanakvasi, meaning those who do not have their religious activities in temples but carry on their religious duties in places known as Sthanakas – prayer-halls.
- The Sthanakvasi do not believe in idol-worship at all. As such they do not have temples but only sthanakas, that is, prayer halls, where they carry on their religious fasts, festivals, practices, prayers, discourses, etc.
- Further, the ascetics of Sthanakvasi cover their mouths with strips of cloth for all the time and they do not use the cloth of yellow or any other color (of course, except white).
- Moreover, the Sthanakvasi admit the authenticity of only 31 of the scriptures of Svetambaras.
- Furthermore, the Sthanakvasi do not have faith in the places of pilgrimage and do not participate in the religious festivals of Murtipujaka Svetambaras.
- The Svetambara Sthanakvasi are spread in different business centers in India but they are found mainly in Gujarat, Punjab, Harayana and Rajasthan.

13. **Correct Option: (b)**

Explanation:

- **Statement 1 is incorrect:** There is no supreme god or deity in Buddhism.

Supplementary Notes:

Tenets of Buddhism

- Buddha asked his followers to avoid the two extremes of indulgence in worldly pleasure and the practice of strict abstinence and asceticism.
- He ascribed instead the 'Madhyam Marg' or the middle path which was to be followed.
- According to him everyone was responsible for their own happiness in life, stressing upon the individualistic component of Buddhism.
- The main teachings of Buddhism are encapsulated in the basic concept of four noble truths or ariya-sachchani and eightfold path or astangika marg.
- Dukkha and its extinction are central to the Buddha's doctrine. Suffering is not limited to the actual pain but also to the potential to experience these things.
- The essence of Buddhism is the attainment of enlightenment. It points to a way of life that avoids self-indulgence and self-denial. There is no supreme god or deity in Buddhism.
- The ultimate goal of Buddha's teaching was the attainment of nibbana which was not a place but an experience, and could be attained in this life.

14. **Correct Option: (c)**

Explanation:

- **Statement (c) is correct**

Supplementary Notes:

Sallekhana:

- Recently in the Uttara Kannada district 2 Nisadis (memorial stone) have been found belonging to 12th century at Hiregutti village in Kumta of Uttara Kannada district which were black in colour showing connection of Karnataka with Jaina Religion .
- In addition to these two Nisadis, other inscriptions belonging to Buddhism and Shaivism were also found there. Both the Nisadis have images of ascetics in meditation and women who performed Sallekhana.
- It is the Jaina practice of embracing the death voluntarily when both householders and ascetics foresee that the end of the life is very near either due to the old age, incurable disease, severe famine, attack from the enemy or wild animal, etc.
- At such time one overcomes all the passions and abondons all the worldly attachments by observing austerities such as gradually abstaining from the food and the water and simultaneously meditating on the true nature of the Self until the soul parts the body.
- An approximate assessment of the remaining span of the life is necessary in order to adjust to the nature of the fasting.
- He should endure all the hardships, but if he falls ill or for any other reason can not maintain the peace of

mind, then he should give up Sallekhana and resume taking foods and other activities.

15. Correct Option: (d)

Explanation:

- All statements are correct

Supplementary Notes:

Guru Ravidas

- He was a mystic poet during the time of Bhakti Movement.
- He belonged to an untouchable caste and suffered a lot of atrocities as a result.
- His famous disciples was the saint, Mirabai.
- Guru Ravidas Jayanti is celebrated on Magh Purnima, which is the full moon day in the Hindu calendar month of Magha.
- He was disciple of the bhakti saint-poet Ramananda.
- He was contemporary of the bhakti saint-poet Kabir.
- His hymns are included in the Guru Granth Sahib.
- He was also contemporary of Guru Nanak.
- Based on his teachings he started a religion called the Ravidassia religion, or Ravidassia Dharam.
- He taught about the omnipresence of God and said that a human soul is a particle of God and hence Ravidas rejected the idea that people considered lower caste cannot meet God.
- He said in his teachings that the only way to meet God was to free the mind from the duality.

16. Correct Option: (c)

Supplementary Notes:

Bodhisattva

- Bodhisattva is the one who has generated Bodhicitta (a spontaneous wish and a compassionate mind) to attain Buddhahood for the benefit of all sentient beings. It believes in Universal liberation and is a concept under Mahayana Buddhism.
- Buddha in his previous births was Bodhisattva as contemplated in Jataka tales and the stories depict the various attempts of the bodhisattva to embrace qualities like self-sacrifice and morality.
- On the path to become a Buddha, a bodhisattva proceeds through ten grounds or bhumis namely great joy, stainless, luminous, radiant, very difficult to train, obviously transcendent, gone afar, immovable, god discriminating wisdom and Cloud of Dharma. By passing these 10 bhumis, he becomes an enlightened one.
- Important 8 Bodhisattvas are as follows:
  - **Avalokiteśvara:** One of the three protective deities around Buddha. He is described as holding Lotus flower and is also known as Padmapani. The painting can be found at Ajanta Caves. He is the most acknowledged among all the Bodhisattvas.
  - **Manjusri:** One of three protective deities around Buddha is also depicted in Ajanta Caves. He is associated with the Wisdom of Buddha and is a male Bodhisattva with a wielding sword in his hand.
  - **Vajrapani:** One of three protective deities around Buddha and is also depicted in Ajanta Caves. Vajrapani is contemplated to manifest all the powers of Buddha as well as the power of all five tathagatas.
  - **Samantabhadra:** Associated with practice and meditation. Together with the Buddha and Manjusri, he forms the Shakyamuni trinity in Buddhism.
  - **Ksitigarbha:** He is depicted as a Buddhist monk and took vow not to achieve Buddhahood till the hell is completely emptied.
  - **Maitreya:** A future Buddha who will appear on Earth in the future, achieve complete enlightenment and teach the pure dharma. Laughing Buddha is said to be an incarnation of Maitreya.
  - **Akasagarbha:** Associated with element of space.

17. Correct Option: (b)

Explanation:

- **Statement 1 is incorrect:** Jainism did not condemn the Varna system, as Buddhism did. According to Mahavira, a person is born in a high or a lower Varna in consequence of the sins or the virtues acquired by him in the previous birth.

Supplementary Notes:

Jainism

- Rejected the authority of Vedas & objected to Vedic rituals & sacrifices.
- The doctrine of ascetism & renunciation was carried to great lengths by the practice of starvation, nudity and other forms of self-tortures (Penance for all sins committed).
- Mahavira did not condemn the Varna system as Buddhism did. As according to Mahavira, a person born in higher or lower varna is the consequences of the sins of past life and through penance and meritorious life they can attain liberation.
- Jainism mainly aimed at the freedom of individuals from worldly bonds.

Buddhism

- Buddha did not believe in God or the soul.
- Stressed on karma and ahimsa.
- He was against the varna system. Buddha taught in Pali.

18. Correct Option: (a)

Explanation:

- Option (a) is correct

Supplementary Notes:

Doctrines of Jainism

- Jainism taught five doctrines -
  - Non-violence;
  - Not to speak a lie;
  - Not to steal;
  - Not to acquire property; and
  - Observance of continence (brahmacharya)
- Jainism attached the utmost importance to ahimsa or non-injury to living beings.
- Jainism recognised the existence of gods but placed them lower than jina. However, it did not condemn the varna system as Buddhism did.
- According to Mahavira, a person is born in high or low varna as per the sins or virtues of his previous birth. Through meritorious work, members of lower castes can also attain liberation.
- Triratna of Jainism – According to Jainism, freedom can be obtained from the worldly bonds without any rituals but by following:
  - Right Knowledge
  - Right Faith
  - Right Actions

Doctrines of Buddhism

- Buddha did not believe in fruitless controversies as regarding the soul (atman) and Brahman. He rather addressed himself to the worldly problems.
- Gautama Buddha recommended the eight-fold path (ashtangika marga) for the elimination of human misery. It consisted of right observation, right determination, right speech, right action, right livelihood, right exercise, right memory and right meditation.
- Main code of social conduct by Buddha are -
  - Do not covet the property of others;
  - Do not commit violence;
  - Do not use intoxicants;
  - Do not speak a lie; and
  - Do not indulge in corrupt practices.

19. Correct Option: (c)

Explanation:

- **Statement 1 is incorrect:** Zen Buddhism is related to the Mahayana branch.

Supplementary Notes:

Zen Buddhism

- Zen is the way the Chinese word Ch'an is pronounced in Japan. 'Ch'an' is the Chinese pronunciation of the Sanskrit word Dhyana, which means (more or less) meditation.
- Zen Buddhism is a mixture of Indian Mahayana Buddhism and Taoism. It began in China, spread to Korea and Japan, and became very popular in the West from the mid-20th century.
- The essence of Zen is attempting to understand the meaning of life directly, without being misled by logical thought or language.
- The essence of Zen Buddhism is that all human beings are Buddha, and that all they have to do is to discover that truth for themselves.
- Zen Buddhists pay less attention to scripture as a means of learning than they do to various methods of practising Zen. The most common way of teaching is for enlightenment to be communicated directly from master to pupil.

20. Correct Option: (d)

Explanation:

- **Option (d) is correct:** The Bhagavata School was referred to as ekantika-dharma ("religion with one object"—i.e., monotheism).

Supplementary Notes:

The Origin and Development of the Bhagavata Sect

- Bhagavata (Sanskrit: "One Devoted to Bhagavat [God]") Member of the earliest Hindu sect of which there is any record, representing the beginnings of theistic devotional worship (bhakti) in Hinduism and of modern Vaishnavism (worship of the god Vishnu).
- The Bhagavata system was a highly devotional faith centred upon a personal god, variously called Vishnu, Vasudeva, Krishna, Hari, or Narayana.
- The school was referred to as ekantika-dharma ("religion with one object"—i.e., monotheism).
- The Bhagavatas believed in simple rites of worship and condemned Vedic sacrifices and austerities.
- The Bhagavata sect originated among the Yadava people of the Mathura area of northern India in the 2nd and 1st centuries BCE. From there it spread as the tribes migrated to western India and the northern Deccan and then into South India.
- The sect continued to be prominent within Vaishnavism until at least the 11th century CE, when bhakti was revitalized by the great theologian Ramanuja.
- The Bhagavadgita (1st–2nd century CE) is the earliest and finest exposition of the Bhagavata system. By the time of the Bhagavadgita, Vasudeva (Krishna), the hero of the Yadava clan, was identified with the Vedic god Vishnu.
- Later, the deified sage Narayana, whose followers were originally called Pancharatras, was assimilated,

and, still later, the pastoral and amorous Krishna was added to the multiplicity of traditions.

- The sect contributed greatly to the spread of image worship among upper-class Hindus.
- Few early Vaishnava images are still extant, but those that have survived are mainly from the Mathura area; perhaps the earliest is the image of Balarama, the half brother of Krishna, attributed to the 2nd–1st century BCE.

21. Correct Option: (b)

Explanation:

- **Statement 2 is incorrect:** Fa-hien gives the impression that Buddhism was in a very flourishing state.

Supplementary Notes:

Cultural development in 6th-7th century (Buddhism)

- Buddhism no longer received royal patronage in the Gupta period.
- Fa-hien gives the impression that Buddhism was in a very flourishing state.
- But in reality Buddhism was not so important in the Gupta period as it was in the days of Ashoka and Kanishka. Especially it suffered in Magadha.
- The Buddhist university at Nalanda was set up in the fifth century, and its earliest structure, made of brick, belongs to Gupta period.

22. Correct Option: (c)

Supplementary Notes:

- The two religions also have differing views about the soul. The soul, according to Jainism is more universal. It is present in all things may it be the living and non-living things. All elements in the universe wind, earth, fire and water also have their own respective souls. Buddhism believes otherwise because the soul is said to reside in living things only like animals and plants and that inanimate objects don't have any.

23. Correct Option: (c)

Supplementary Notes:

- The Noble Eightfold Path
- Right understanding (Samma ditthi)
- Right thought (Samma sankappa)
- Right speech (Samma vaca)
- Right action (Samma kammanta)
- Right livelihood (Samma ajiva)
- Right effort (Samma vayama)
- Right mindfulness (Samma sati)
- Right concentration (Samma samadhi)

24. Correct Option: (a)

Supplementary Notes:

- Siddhartha Gautama, the Lord Buddha, was born in 623 BC in the famous gardens of Lumbini, which soon became a place of pilgrimage. Among the pilgrims was the Indian emperor Ashoka, who erected one of his commemorative pillars there.
- Bodh Gaya is a religious site and place of pilgrimage associated with the Mahabodhi Temple Complex in Gaya district in the Indian state of Bihar. It is famous as it is the place where Gautama Buddha is said to have obtained Enlightenment (Pali: bodhi) under what became known as the Bodhi Tree.
- Sarnath was the place where first sermon of Lord Buddha was given. One of the holiest places of Budhaism. It is the place where Lord Buddha gave his first sermon.
- According to Buddhist tradition, Buddha died at Kuśinārа (present-day Kushinagar), which became a pilgrimage centre. It was at abandoned jungles of Kuśinārа of the Malla kingdom. The Buddha believed that Kushinara was a land once ruled by a righteous wheel-turning king and hence appropriate place for him to die.

25. Correct Option: (a)

Supplementary Notes:

Gol Gumbaz

- It is situated in the Bijapur district of Karnataka.
- It is the mausoleum of Muhammed Adil Shah, the 7th sultan of the Adil Shahi Dynasty of Bijapur (1498-1686).
- Built by the ruler himself, it is a striking edifice in spite of being unfinished.
- The tomb is a complex building such as a gateway, a Naqqar Khana, a mosque and a sarai located within a large walled garden.
- Gumbad is a square building topped with a circular drum over which rests a majestic dome, giving the building its nomenclature.
- It is built of dark grey basalt and decorated plaster work.
- The dome of Gol Gumbad is the largest in the world.
- The building has an amazing acoustical system. Along with the drum of the dome, there is a whispering gallery where sounds get magnified and echoed many times over.
- Gol Gumbad is a fine convergence of many styles located in medieval India.
- While its structural peculiarities of dome, arches, geometric proportions and load bearing techniques suggest Timurid and Persian styles, it is made of local material and is decorated with surface embellishments popular in Deccan.

26. Correct Option: (a)

Supplementary Notes:

- **Statement 1 is correct:** The principle of ahimsa, emphasised within Jainism, has left its mark on Indian thinking as a whole.

- **Statement 2 is incorrect:** According to Jaina teachings, the cycle of birth and rebirth is shaped through karma. Asceticism and penance are required to free oneself from the cycle of karma. This can be achieved only by renouncing the world; therefore, monastic existence is a necessary condition of salvation.

27. **Correct Option: (c)**

Supplementary Notes:

- **Statement 1 is correct:** According to Buddhist philosophy, the world is transient (anicca) and constantly changing; it is also soulless (anatta) as there is nothing permanent or eternal in it. Within this transient world, sorrow (dukkha) is intrinsic to human existence. The Buddha regarded the social world as the creation of humans rather than of divine origin. Therefore, he advised kings and gahapatis to be humane and ethical. Individual effort was expected to transform social relations.
- **Statement 2 is correct:** The Buddha emphasised individual agency and righteous action as the means to escape from the cycle of rebirth and attain self-realisation and nibbana, literally the extinguishing of the ego and desire – and thus end the cycle of suffering for those who renounced the world.

28. **Correct Option: (d)**

Supplementary Notes:

Buddhism and Jainism

- Option (d) is correct:

List I	**List II**
A. Eight Fold Path	iii. Buddhism
B. Vajrayana	i. Tantras
C. Digambara	ii. Jainism
D. Buddha's first sermon	iv. Sarnath

29. **Correct Option: (c)**

Supplementary Notes:

Buddhism

- **Statement 1 is incorrect:** The rules made for the Buddhist sangha were written down in a book called the Vinaya Pitaka. Men and women who joined the sangha led simple lives. Those who joined the sangha included brahmins, kshatriyas, merchants, labourers, barbers, courtesans, children and slaves.
- **Statement 2 is correct:** According to Buddha the best course to be pursued by an individual is the Middle Path (Madhyama Pratipat or Tatha Grah Marg). Buddha laid stress on truth, charity, purity and control over passions and advocated for cardinal virtues i.e. Maitri (Love), Karuna (Passion), Mudita (joy at other's success) and Upeksha (Equanimity) towards all living being in order to lead a better life in the next birth. Besides, one should avoid pursuing bad instincts such as ill-will, anger, deceit, jealousy, arrogance etc. One should not steal, speak lie or get drunk or have illicit relations. Thus, Buddha preached moral and ethical conduct for the common man.
- **Statement 3 is correct:** Gautama Buddha was born in 563 BC in Lumbini (now in Nepal) in the Sakya Kshatriya clan of Kapilvastu. He was the son of Suddhodana, who seems to have been the elected ruler of Kapilvastu, and headed the republican clan of the Shakyas. His mother, Maya was a princess from the Koshalan Dynasty. Maya died in child-birth and the little Siddhartha was brought up by his aunt and stepmother Prajapati Gautami.
- **Statement 4 is correct:** Lord Buddha emphasized Four Noble Truths to mankind. He said that the world is full of suffering. All sufferings have a cause: desire, ignorance and attachment are the causes of suffering. The suffering could be removed by destroying its cause. In order to end suffering, one must know the right path. This path is the Eight Fold Path.

30. **Correct Option: (d)**

Supplementary Notes:

Buddhism and Jainism

- **Statement 1 is correct:** Gautama Buddha or Siddhartha was a contemporary of Vardhamana Mahavira, the 24th Tirthankara of Jainism.
- **Statement 2 is incorrect:** First Buddhist Council was held soon after the Mahaparinirvana of the Buddha, around 483 BC under the patronage of King Ajatshatru with the monk Mahakasyapa presiding, at Rajgriha, in the Sattapani Cave. The idea was to preserve and codify Buddha's teachings (Sutta) and rules for disciples (Vinaya). Ananda, one of the great disciples of Buddha recited Suttas and Upali, another disciple recited Vinaya.
- **Statement 3 is incorrect:** Buddha's liberal and democratic approach quickly attracted the people of all sections. His attack on the caste system and the supremacy of the Brahmanas was welcomed by the lower orders. Irrespective of caste, creed and sex, people were welcomed in the new order. Buddha rejected the authority of the Vedas and condemned animal sacrifices. He detested the complex and meaningless rituals. He strongly believed that sacrifices and rituals could neither help a person to wash away his sins nor benefit any sinner by performing various ritualistic practices.

31. **Correct Option: (a)**

Supplementary Notes:

Buddhism and Jainism

- **Statement 1 is correct:** Mahavira didn't believe in the existence of God. Jains believe that every soul is divine and has the potential to achieve God-consciousness. Any soul which has conquered its own inner enemies and achieved the state of Supreme Being is called jina (Conqueror or Victor). Jainism is the path to achieve this state.

- Buddha neither accepted nor rejected the existence of God. He was a practical reformer who took note of the realities of the day. He said that everything is transient in this Universe. There is no immortal soul. The Universe is soulless. The transmigration is no transmigration of soul. In transmigration nothing passes over from one life to another – only a new life arises as part of events which include the old or rather it is the reaction of one's own actions. He believed that one's ignorance makes a person believe in existence of God or soul and this ignorance creates desire in man, then leads to action and that action leads to impulse to be born again to satisfy desire. This leads to chain of birth and rebirth which is the primary cause of misery of a man. The chain of ignorance, desire, attachment etc. can be snapped by knowledge or Gyan.
- **Statement 2 is incorrect:** Buddhism did not believe in the ideas of eternal self or soul (Atman) and eternity. Soul is treated as an ever changing entity.

32. Correct Option: (c)

Supplementary Notes:

Buddhism and Jainism

- **Statement 1 is correct:** Buddha belonged to a small gana known as the Sakya gana, and was a kshatriya. Vardhamana Mahavira was a contemporary of Buddha. He was a kshatriya prince of the Lichchhavis, a group that was part of the Vajji sangha.
- **Statement 2 is correct:** Hînayâna is the orthodox, conservative schools of Buddhism. Did not believe in idol worship and tried to attain individual salvation through self-discipline and meditation. Mahayana Buddhism, also known as the Great Vehicle, is the form of Buddhism prominent in North Asia, including China, Mongolia, Tibet, Korea, and Japan. This sect believes in the heavenliness of Buddha and believes in idol worship.

33. Correct Option: (c)

Explanation:

- Both statements are correct

Supplementary Notes:

Pre-Vedic Religion

- Vedic religion, also called Vedism, takes its name from the collections of sacred texts known as the Vedas.
- Vedism is the oldest stratum of religious activity in India for which there exist written materials. It was one of the major traditions that shaped Hinduism.
- The earliest traces of some form of religion in the Indian sub-continent were discovered at the excavated sites of the Harappan Civilisation (also known as the Indus-Valley Civilisation) that is dated to have flourished between C. 3000-1700BC.
- The term 'Veda' means "knowledge" in that they are thought to contain the fundamental knowledge relating to the underlying cause of, function of, and personal response to existence.

34. Correct Option: (a)

Explanation:

- **Statement 2 is incorrect:** The nature of the religious beliefs and practices of the Aryans is known from the Rig Veda.

Supplementary Notes:

Pre-Vedic Religion

- From the archaeological findings in the pre and proto-historic sites it seems that these people believed in the sanctity of the creative force and venerated the male and female aspects of divinity.
- They were worshippers of the forces of nature like the sun and the moon. This belief is also partly substantiated by the early literature of the Aryans.
- The nature of the religious beliefs and practices of the Aryans is also known from the Rig Veda, They believed in many gods like Indra, Varuna, Agni, Surya and Rudra.
- Sacrifices, and ritual offering of food and drink to fire in honour of the Gods, constituted the main religious practices. The Sama Veda and the Yajur Veda elaborated the different aspects of the sacrificial acts and this ritualism was further elaborated in the Brahmanas.
- The Atharva Veda contained a great deal of animistic beliefs.

35. Correct Option: (a)

Explanation:

- **Statement 3 is incorrect:** Dashnami Sampraday are the followers of Lord Shiva. So, eliminating this option we can find the answer.

Supplementary Notes:

Hindu Sects

- Sects of Vallabhacharya and Chaitanya
  - These two sects were most popular in Western India (Vallabhacharya) and Eastern India (Chaitanya).
  - Vallabhacharya sect was founded by Vallabha a Telugu Brahmin. He taught his disciples not to turn their backs to worldly pleasures. He opposed fasts and self-mortification. Their gurus also lead a comfortable life.
  - The followers of Chaitanya were to lead a simple and humble life. They believed in singing devotional songs and dancing as a way of worship.

Shaiva Sects

- **Dashnami Sampradaya:** In the eighth century Shankracharya gave a new turn to Shaivism. He established a very important cult called Dashnami Sampradaya. Dashnamis are also known as Vedic Saivas.
  - Before the establishment of Dashnami order, Tantrik Shaivas such as Kanphatas, Aghoris, Kalamukhis and Kapaliks dominated the Shaiva cult.
  - Shankaracharya organized the Dashnami order which includes the following ten categories of Sanyasis: 1) Giri 2) Puri 3) Bharti 4) Vana 5) Parvathi 6) Aranya 7) Sagara 8) Tirtha 9) Ashram 10) Saraswati.
  - Shankaracharya established four seg monastic centres, namely, Jyotir Peeth, Shringeri Peeth, Govardhan Peeth and Dwarka or Sharda Peeth in North, South, East and West, respectively.
  - For the smooth functioning of the Mathas, area, direction, sampradaya, Dashnami order, deities to be worshipped, pilgrimage, Veda, Mahasakya (great saying), Gotra and jurisdiction of each monastic centre was fixed.
  - Dashnami sanyasis are divided into two broad sections, namely, Dandadharis (staff holders) and pammhansas (holding no staff).
  - Out of the ten subsects of Dashnami order, Sanyasis of only three that is, Tirtha, Ashram and Saraswati are allowed to hold staff and the rest called Paramhansas are not allowed to do so.
- **Kanphata or Nath Panthi:** This sect forms the part of Tantrik Shaivism. Kanphatas pierce their ears and insert ear-rings in them.
  - Gorakh Nath is regarded to be the reorganiser of this cult. This cult is believed to have been founded by Sati Nath.
  - The chief scripture of this cult is "Hath Yoga Pradipika". Kanphatas regard Shiva as the supreme reality. Salvation lies in the union with Shiva. In Nath Sampradaya, Nath yoga and Tantra are recommended as the most appropriate means of salvation.
- **Aghori Panth:** The sect is also known as Aghor Panth or Augar Panth and the followers are call Aghoris or Aughars. This cult was founded by Bhrama Giri, a disciple of Gorakhnath.
  - The name of the cult is derived from the word 'Aghor' meaning non-terrifying. The epithet Aghor is usually used for Shiva. Thus, it is clear that Aghor Panthi means an ascetic who worships Shiva.
  - Aghoris are found all over India and move about all the year round. The Aghori smears himself with the ashes of the funeral pyre.
  - He wears the frontal mark denoting the unity of the Hindu triad. He also wears a Rudraksha rosary and a necklace of stone. Some wear rosary of human teeth too.
- **Vir Shaiva or Lingayat Sampraday:** Lingayats are mostly found in southern India. The name of this cult has been derived from the word linga (Phallus symbol).
  - A true lingayat wears on his body a small silver box containing a stone linga which is a symbol of his faith and the loss of which means spiritual death.
  - It is worn by both male and female members of the sect. Of the Hindu sects, Lingayats or Vir Shaivas acknowledge Shiva whose symbol, the linga they wear on their person.
  - They are against caste system. All wearers of the lingas are proclaimed equal in the eyes of the God. They prohibit child marriage and stand for widow remarriage. They bury their dead.
- **Kapalika Panth:** Though almost dying now this sect was widely prevalent in ancient India. Kapaliks are expert Tantriks. They wear some rosaries and live naked near Ghats.
  - They take their food from the human skull. They eat meat and drink wine without hesitation.
  - The deity of Kapaliks is Kal Bhairav. Though the number of Kapaliks is very small, they are spread all over India.

36. Correct Option: (d)

Explanation:

- All statements are correct

Supplementary Notes:

Buddhist Sects

- Buddha taught that the cause of all human suffering is desire. It is important to control and overcome desire.
  - This could be achieved by following the Eightfold Path, which means Right Conduct, Right Speech, Right Action, Right Means of Livelihood, Right Effort, Right Mindfulness, Right Meditation, Right Resolution and Right View. Buddha also preached in the language of the common people, i.e., Pali and Prakrit and laid stress on a life of virtues and morals.
- After the Gautama Buddha several Buddhist councils were held to debate the questions of faith and religious order.
- These gave rise to two main schools of thought. Later on a third one also emerged. These are Hinayana, Mahayana and the Vajrayana.

- The followers of Hinayana believe in the original traditions of Buddha. They recognized only a fured body of canonical literature.
- Their main literature was limited to tripitaka (three baskets). There are Vinay Pitaka, Sutta Pitaka and Abhidhamma Pitaka.
- The Mahayana claimed their own doctrines and practices as belonging to Bodhisatva (enlightened being). They called themselves Mahayana.
- Bodhisattva according to them was potential Buddha and everybody could achieve it. They believed that accumulated merit of bodhisattva could be transferred to help those who wanted to achieve salvation.
- The Hinayana do not accept deity worship while the Mahayana introduced the idea of deity worship.
- The Tantrayana or Vajrayana sect incorporates mystic and magical dimension. They believed that salvation can be achieved by acquiring magical powers called Vajra (thunderbolt)

37. Correct Option: (c)

Explanation:

- Both statements are correct

Supplementary Notes:

Buddhism

- Buddhism was an organized religion. There were Sanghas for the Buddhist monks. Viharas were made for the monks to live in. Education was given state patronage along with the Sangha as a result of which great universities like Nalanda came up over a period of time. Buddhism spread into many countries of the world.
- Acharya Kamalasheel of Nalanda University was invited by the king of Tibet. After his death, the Tibetans embalmed his body and kept it in a monastery in Lhasa.
  - Another distinguished scholar was Jnanabhadra. He went to Tibet with his two sons to preach Dharma. A monastery was founded in Tibet on the model of Odantapuri University in Bihar.
  - The head of the Vikramashila University was Acharya Ateesha, also known as Dipankara Shreejnana. He went to Tibet in the eleventh century and gave a strong foundation to Buddhism in Tibet.
  - Thonmi Sambhota, a Tibetan minister was a student at Nalanda when the Chinese pilgrim Huien-tsang visited India. Thonmi Sambhota studied there and after going back, he preached Buddhism in Tibet.
  - A large number of Tibetans embraced Buddhism. Even the king became a Buddhist. He declared Buddhism as the State religion. Among the noteworthy teachers, Kumarajiva was active in the fifth century.
- In the fourth century AD Wei Dynasty came to power in China. Its first Emperor declared Buddhism as the state religion.
  - This gave an impetus to the spread of Buddhism in China. Thousands of Sanskrit books were translated into Chinese.
  - Braving the hazards of a long and perilous journey they came to visit the land of the Buddha.
  - They stayed in India and collected Buddhist relics and manuscripts related to Buddhism and learnt about it staying at the various educational centres.
- The story of Indian culture in Japan is believed to go back to more than fifteen hundred years. But the earliest historical evidence of Indian culture going to Japan is from AD 552.
  - At that time, the Korean Emperor sent a Buddhist statue, sutras, instruments for worship, artists, sculptors, painters and architects as gifts for the Japanese Emperor. Soon, Buddhism was given the status of State Religion.
  - Thousands of Japanese became monks and nuns. Sanskrit was accepted as the sacred language in Japan.
  - Monks were given special training to write the Sanskrit syllables and mantras. The script in which all these are written is known as 'Shittan'. Shittan is believed to be Siddham, the script that gives 'siddhi' (accomplishment).

38. Correct Option: (b)

Explanation:

- **Statement 1 is incorrect:** The Jain texts were written in Prakrit. So, this statement can be eliminated easily and answer can be found.

Supplementary Notes:

Jainism

- The founder of Jainism is believed to be Rishabhadeva, the first of the twenty four tirthankaras and as the last tirthankara, Mahavira developed and gave final shape to the Jain doctrines. The Jains lay great emphasis on severe penance and asceticism.
- Lord Mahavira asked them to take five vows – not to tell lies; not to injure life; not to own property; not to steal; and to maintain chastity (celibacy). He also asked the Jains to follow the three-fold path of Right belief, Right Conduct and Right Knowledge.
- After Mahavira there emerged differences among his followers over many religious questions. As a result two main sects – the Digarnbara (sky clad) and Swetambara (white clad) emerged.

- The Digambara believed that the monks should not wear cloth, while Swetambara believed in wearing white cloth. The Digambara also believed that the women cannot attain salvation.
- A number of subsects also emerged in due course. Many of these rejected the practice of image worship of the Jina or Mahavira.
- The Jain texts were written in Prakrit and were finally compiled in the sixth century AD in Valabhi in Gujarat.
- The important works are known as Angas, Upangas, Prakirnas, Chhedab Sutras and Malasutras.
- Among the important Jain scholars, reference may be made to Haribhadra Suri (eighth century AD) and Hemchandra Suri (twelfth century AD).
- Jainism helped in the growth of a rich literature comprising poetry, philosophy and grammar.
- These works contain many passages which help us to reconstruct the political history of eastern Uttar Pradesh and Bihar. The Jain texts refer repeatedly to trade and traders.

39. Correct Option: (a)

Explanation:

- **Pair (3) is incorrectly matched:** Namdhari sect was founded by Balak Singh.

Supplementary Notes:

Sikhism

- The rise of sects in Sikhism was more in the form of religious reform and movements. Many of these sects had both Sikhs and Hindus as members. The Nirankaris, Radha Soamis of Beas and the Namdharis are some prominent sects.
- The Nirankari sect was started by Dyal Das, a merchant of Peshawar. He opposed idol worship and disapproved of going on pilgrimages and performing Brahminical rituals. He saw the God as formless - nirankar. To begin with his followers came from Khatri, Arora and Bania castes. In due course they acquired the system of Gurus and developed their own, places of worship. They recognized many gurus other than ten Sikh Gurus.
- Radha Soami sect was founded by Shiv Dayal a Hindu banker of Agra. He included doctrines of both Hinduism and Sikhism. The main difference with Sikhism is that they believe in a living guru. The sect was divided into a number of sub sects like Radha Soamis of Dayal Bagh (Agra) and of Beas (Punjab). They also have separate religious places. Their discourse continues to draw heavily from the Adi Granth of Sikhs.
- Namdhari sect was founded by Balak Singh of village Hazro in North West Frontier region. They developed different forms of worship, and dress code. The followers of the sect chanted hymns and worked themselves into a state of frenzy and emitted loud shrieks (Kuks) and therefore came to be known as Kukas.

40. Correct Option: (b)

Explanation:

- **Statement (b) is the correct answer:** Pilgrimage to Mecca is one of the five fundamental principles of Islam.

Supplementary Notes:

Islam

- The Muslims first came to India in the eighth century AD mainly as traders. They were fascinated by the socio-cultural scenario in this country and decided to make India their home.
- The traders who came to India from Central and West Asia and carried back with them traces of Indian science and culture.
- As a result, they became cultural ambassadors of India by disseminating this knowledge to the Islamic world and from there to Europe.
- The immigrant Muslims also entered into matrimonial alliances with the local people and learned to live together in harmony. There was mutual exchange of ideas and customs.
- The Hindus and Muslims influenced each other equally in dress, speech, manners, customs and intellectual pursuits. The Muslims also brought with them their religion, Islam which had a deep impact on Indian society and culture.
- Prophet Mohammad preached Islam in the seventh century AD in Arabia. He was born in AD 571 in the Quraysh tribe of Arabia. He migrated to Madina from Mecca in AD 622, and this marked the beginning of the Hijira Era.
- According to the Muslim belief, Quran is the message of Allah revealed to Mohammad through his archangel Gabriel.
- The five fundamental principles of Islam are:
  - Tauhid (belief in Allah)
  - Namaz (prayers, five times a day)
  - Roza (fasting in the month of Ramzan)
  - Zakat (giving of alms)
  - Haj (pilgrimage to Mecca)
- Prophet Mohammad's sayings are preserved in what is called the Hadith or Hadees. After his death the Caliphate was established. There were four pious Caliphs.
- Islam talked of equality, brotherhood, and the existence of one God. Its arrival particularly made a

profound impact on the traditional pattern of Indian society.

- The rise of both the Bhakti and the Sufi movements contributed immensely in this regard. Both the Bhakti and the Sufi movements believed that all humans are equal, God is supreme and devotion to God is the only way to achieve salvation.
- The Muslims are divided into a large number of sects and subsects. In India the Sunnis, the Shias, the Bohras, the Ahmediyas are a few bigger sects. Within these sects there are sub-sects.
- The Wahabis are considered subsect of Sunnis. Ismaili Bohras of the Bohra sect. Many of these started as cults around some individuals, but in due course they developed into sects.
- Within the Islamic tradition, the rise of Wahabis represented an active oppositionist sect whereas the Bahais were more of a passive and withdrawing kind.

41. Correct Option: (a)

Explanation:

- **Statement 2 is incorrect:** The Protestant Churches recognize the authority of Bible alone.

Supplementary Notes:

Christianity

- Christians also have a number of denominations and sects. However, a major divisions came in the 16th century during the reformation movement in Europe.
- A section of the community felt that the Church and society are in a state of crisis. They demanded reforms in such a situation and came to be called as Protestants. They organized themselves under a separate Church.
- The Protestant Churches recognize the authority of Bible alone, whereas the Roman Catholic and Eastern Orthodox Churches also recognize their church tradition as authoritative besides the Bible.
- In India, most of the Christian sect and subsects exist under the two major denominations, the Catholics and the Protestants.
- According to tradition, Christianity was brought to India by Saint Thomas in the first century AD.
- According to legends, the Parthian king Gondophernes (C. 19–45 A.C.) sent a messenger to Syria to look for a skilful architect who would build for him a new city. The messenger returned with St. Thomas, who converted him and many members of his court to Christianity. The truth of the legend is doubtful.
- It was most probably the frequent trade and movement between India and the West which was responsible for bringing this disciple of Lord Christ to India.
- The merchants, traders and even craftsmen frequently travelled along popular land and sea routes. St. Thomas preached Christianity in many parts of India. He was killed at Mylapore (near Madras). The tomb of St. Thomas is still to be found at the same place.
- A large community of Christians known as Syrian Christians continue to reside in Kerala even today.

42. Correct Option: (d)

Explanation:

- **Statement 1 is incorrect:** The Zoroastrianism is a monotheistic religion developed in Persia around 7th century BC
- **Statement 2 is incorrect:** They believe in one eternal god whose name is Ahura Mazda who is the epitome of just behaviour and goodness. There is a spirit of malice and bad behaviour called Angra Mainyu.

Supplementary Notes:

Zoroastrianism

- This religion has its origin in Persia by the Prophet Zarathustra around 6–7 BCE.
- They are a monotheistic religion who believe in one eternal god whose name is Ahura Mazda who is the epitome of just behaviour and goodness. There is a spirit of malice and bad behaviour called Angra Mainyu. These two keep fighting with each other and this is an eternal struggle and one day good will win over evil and that will be the last day.
- They are commonly known as Parsis and are presently amongst the smallest (and rapidly shrinking) communities in India. They live mostly in Mumbai, Goa and Ahmedabad.
- Their fire temples called Atash Bahram are rare and only eight known temples exist in the entire country.
- They worship fire but also consider air, water and earth to be sacred elements. They believe that dead matter is a corrupting element to everything and hence, they place the dead bodies in the open to be eaten by the vultures. These open spaces are called 'Dakhma' and the vultures that eat them are called 'Dakhma Nashini'. The only space known in India where they are left are the 'Towers of Silence' in Mumbai. Now-a-days, people have even started cremating or burying their dead.

43. Correct Option: (c)

Explanation:

- **Statement 1 is incorrect:** Bnei Menashe Jews live in the Manipur and have genealogies to the Menashe or the Menasseh Tribe, which was one of the 10 lost tribes of the Jews.
- **Statement 3 is incorrect:** As per the Judaism, the Sefer Torah was given to Prophet Moses on the Mt. Sinai.

Supplementary Notes:

Judaism

- It is one of the oldest religions. The followers of Judaism are called Jews. It is also a monotheistic religion that believes in one God. Their religion predates Christianity and Islam. In fact, these two religions have borrowed a lot from Judaic philosophies.
- The Jews believe in Yahweh or the one true God who was instituted by Abraham.
- Their religious book is called the Torah, which is also the first five books of the Old Testament or Bible. Apart from these another set of compilations of legal and ethical writings and a brief history of Jewish history is called the Talmud.
- They have separate prayer halls and synagogues (place for worship). They follow religious services called the Eliyahu-hanavi or the thanksgiving to Elijah the Prophet. Abraham was the ancestor of all Jews and propounded that those who followed the injunctions of God would be blessed. His son Isaac and grandson Jacob (who was also called Israel) were also blessed by God.
- God sent Moses to the Earth and gave him the Ten Commandments or the Sefer Torah at the Mt. Sinai, which clarified how Israelis (it is a term used for Jews who were the children of Jacob or Israel) should live.
- Jacob had 12 children who became the ancestors of the 12 tribes referred to as Bene Israel or the 'Children of Israel'. The Sefer Torah has 613 percepts, which explain how to live a pious Jewish life, and this also forms the first five sections of the Old Testament. During the prayers, all male Jews have to wear a tsisith or the thread of prayer shawls. The Jews also believe in the day of judgment when the Messiah would come to take the pious to the heaven and the evil would be relegated to hell.

India and Jewish Community

- The first Jewish settlers came to the western coast of India and although they are numerically small, there are five major Jewish communities in India - the Malayalam speaking Cochinis and the Marathi-speaking Bene Israel. The third group is of the Baghdadi Jews who came from West Asia as traders and settled mainly around Mumbai, Pune and Kolkata.
- The fourth group is the Bnei Menashe or the Manipuri Jews. They have created genealogies to the Menashe or the Menasseh Tribe, which was one of the 10 lost tribes of the Jews. They live on the border of India and Myanmar in Manipur and Mizoram and they claim that they were enslaved and sold to the Assyrians and managed to escape to China from where they came and settled on the border of India. They call themselves the 'Children of Menasseh' or those who believe in Jesus Christ. These Bnei Menashe comprise Mizo, Kuki and Chin tribes there.
- The last amongst them is of the Bene Ephraim which is a small group of Telugu-speaking Jews who converted to Judaism in the 1980's.

44. Correct Option: (a)

Explanation:

- **Statement 2 is incorrect:** It was established in India by Khwaja Muinuddin Chisti.

Supplementary Notes:

Chisti Order

- The Saints of Chisti Order lived in poverty and lead a hermit life. They did not accept State service. This order is primarily followed in Afghanistan and Indian Subcontinent. The Chisti order in India was established in India by Khwaja Muinuddin Chisti in 1192, shortly after the death of Prithvi Raj Chauhan. He died in 1236 and his tomb in Ajmer was constructed by Ghiasuddin Khalji of Malwa. Mohammed bin Tuqlaq visited the tomb and later it came under State Management during Mughal Ruler Akbar's reign.
- One of the other notable Sufi saints was Khwaja Qutbuddin Bakhtiyar Kaki who organized work in Delhi and the contemporary Delhi Sultanate Ruler was Illtutmish who was deeply devoted to Chisti Order.
- Another famous Sufi saint was Nizamuddin Auliya and he adopted yogic breathing exercises, so much so that the yogis called him sidh or 'perfect.' Auliya's famous disciple was Amir Khusrow who is called as "father of Qawwali" and "Parrot of India" and introduced the Ghazal Style to India.
- After the death of Nasruddin Chiragh-i-Delhi in the 14th century, the chistis order declined.

45. Correct Option: (d)

Explanation:

- Both statements are correct

Supplementary Notes:

Sufi Movement

- The 10th century AD marks the important changes in the realm of ideas and beliefs in the Islamic religion – the rise of the Sufi mystic orders.
- The core concept of Sufi Movement is Darikh-i-Duniya/Wahad-ul-wahjud, meaning "Universal Brotherhood". It outwardly rejected the religion and emphasized love and devotion to God and compassion towards all fellow human beings.
- Mystics, who are called Sufis, were persons of deep devotion who were disgusted by the display of wealth and degeneration of morals following the establishment of the Islamic empire.
- The Sufis were organized in 12 orders or Silsilahs. A Silsilah was generally led by a prominent mystic

who lived in a Khanqah or hospice along with his disciples.

- The Sufi orders are broadly divided into two: Ba-shara – Those who followed the Islamic Law and Be-shara – Those who were not bound by the Islamic Law.
- The Sufi saints made themselves popular by adopting musical recitations called "Sama", to create a mood of nearness to God. Qawwali is the form of sufi devotional music popular in South Asia and ghazal is a form of Qawwali.

46. Correct Option: (d)

Explanation:

- All statements are correct

Supplementary Notes:

The Three Marks of Existence

- Buddhists believe that there are three characteristics that are common across everything in life. These are known as the Three Marks of Existence. The Three Marks of Existence are important as they can help Buddhists to achieve nibbana (salvation) and end suffering.
- They are called dukkha (suffering), anitya (Impermanence) and anatma (no soul).
- Dukkha: Life does not necessarily provide people with what they want and things are always changing. Therefore, people usually do not achieve complete satisfaction as everything has limitations, which causes them to be dissatisfied.
- Anitya: There is no fixed sense of self because everything is constantly changing. Another way of expressing this is the idea that people have no soul.
- Anatma: Things in life are always changing. Nothing stays the same as everything is subject to change.

47. Correct Option: (b)

Explanation:

- **Statement 1 is incorrect:** By this, all souls are alike in their quality.
- **Statement 3 is incorrect:** It advocates Bhakti to attain the salvation.

Supplementary Notes:

Vishishtadvaita

- This philosophy was pioneered by Ramanujacharya during the 11th century. Vishishtadvaita literally means the Unique Advaita, that is, Advaita with some amendments.
- While it accepts Brahman as the unified whole, it states He is characterized by multiple forms. According to Ramanujacharya, souls are intrinsically the same and all souls are alike in their quality.
- It doesn't see the world as simply illusion, which would make it separate from Brahman. The material world is a part of Brahman's nature.
- Vishishtadvaita advocates Bhakti to attain God.

48. Correct Option: (d)

Supplementary Notes:

Jainism

- Jainism was mainly aims at the attainment of freedom from worldly bonds.
- No ritual is required for acquiring such liberation. It can be obtained through right knowledge, right faith and right action.
- These three are considered to be the three jewels or triratna of Jainism.

Right faith – Samyak darshan

- This doesn't mean believing what you're told, but means seeing (hearing, feeling, etc.) things properly, and avoiding preconceptions and superstitions that get in the way of seeing clearly.

Right knowledge – Samyak jnana

- This means having an accurate and sufficient knowledge of the real universe – this requires a true knowledge of the five (or six) substances and nine truths of the universe – and having that knowledge with the right mental attitude.

Right conduct – Samyak charitra

- This means living your life according to Jain ethical rules, to avoid doing harm to living things and freeing yourself from attachment and other impure attitudes and thoughts.

49. Correct Option: (b)

Explanation:

- **Statement 1 is incorrect:** Jainism recognised the existence of the gods but placed them lower than jina.

Supplementary Notes:

Jainism

- Jainism recognised the existence of the gods but placed them lower than jina.
- Jainism did not condemn the varna system, as buddhism did. According to Mahavira, a person is born in a high or in a lower varna in consequence of sins or the virtues acquired by him in previous birth. In his opinion, through pure and meritorious life members of the lower castes can attain liberation.

50. Correct Option: (c)

Explanation:

- **Statement (c) is incorrect:** Buddhism does not recognise the existence of god and soul. This can be taken as a kind of revolution in the history of Indian religions.

Supplementary Notes:
Buddhism

- Buddha was a practical reformer who took note of the realities of the day. He did not involve himself in fruitless controversies regarding the soul (atman) and the Brahma.
- Buddha recommended eight-fold path for the elimination of human misery. If a person follows this path, he would not be depend on the machinations of the priests and will be able to reach his destination. Buddha taught that a person should avoid the excess of both luxury and austerity. He prescribed the middle path.
- Buddhism does not recognise the existence of god and soul. This can be taken as a kind of revolution in the history of Indian religions.
- Buddhism also attracted the support of the lower orders as it attacked the varna system. People were taken into the Buddhist order without any consideration of caste.

51. Correct Option: (a)

Explanation:

- **Statement 1 is incorrect:** Jainism did not reject the caste system.

Supplementary Notes:
Teachings of Mahavira

- Mahavira rejected Vedic principles. He did not believe in God's existence.
- According to him, the universe is a product of the natural phenomenon of cause and effect.
- He believed in Karma and transmigration of the soul. The body dies but the soul does not.
- One will be punished or rewarded as per one's karma.
- Advocated a life of austerity and non-violence.
- Stressed on equality but did not reject the caste system, unlike Buddhism. But he also said that man may be 'good' or 'bad' as per his actions and not birth.
- Asceticism was taken to a great length. Starvation, nudity, and self-mortification were expounded.
- Two elements of the world: Jiva (conscious) and Atma (unconscious):
  - Right conduct (observance of five vows)
  - Ahimsa (non-violence)
  - Satya (truth)
  - Asteya (no stealing)
  - Parigraha (no acquiring of property)
  - Brahmacharya (abstinence). It was given by Mahavira himself.
  - A Jina is said to possess 'Avadhijnana' (Superhuman cognition or psychic power).
  - Jaina doctrine insists that: Reality is Anekanta (Manifold).
  - Sat (Being) has three aspects – Substance (Dravya), Quality (Guna), and Mode (Paryaya).
  - Jaina Doctrine of Anekantavada mentions the manifold nature of reality.

52. Correct Option: (d)

Explanation:

- Both statements are correct

Supplementary Notes:
Sects of Jainism

- The followers of Bhadrabahu, after their return from Sravanabelgola to Magadha refused to acknowledge the canon holding that all the 14 purvas were lost. Moreover, a wide gulf had developed between those who emigrated and those who stayed in Magadha. In order to sort out these differences and to compile the principal teachings of Jainism, a council was convened in Pataliputra, but the Jains who had returned from the south boycotted it and refused to accept its decisions. From now onwards, the southerners began to be called Digambaras and the Magadhans Svetambaras. The latter had become accustomed to wearing white garments and made a departure from Mahavira's teachings, while the former still continued going naked and strictly followed his teachings.
- Digambaras follow all the five constraints (Ahimsa, Satya, Asteya, Aparigraha and Brahmacharya) as per the teachings of Mahavira, unlike Svetambaras, who follow the preachings of Prasvanatha, i.e., they believe in only four restraints (except Brahmacharya) to be followed to attain Kevalya.
- Bhadrabahu was an exponent of Digambara sect whereas, Sthulabhadra was of Shwetambara.
- During the later years further, splits took place among both the sections, the most important of them being one that renounced idol worship altogether and devoted itself to the worship of the scriptures. They were called the Terapanthis among the Svetambaras and the Samaiyas among the Digambaras.

53. Correct Option: (a)

Explanation:

- **Statement (a) is incorrect:** The development of Mahayan Buddhism led to the composition of numerous text what is known as Buddhist-Hybrid Sanskrit.

Supplementary Notes:
Buddhist sects

- In the second Council held at Vaisali, the Buddhist order was split into two schools namely: Sthaviravadins, and Mahasangikas.
  - The Sthaviravadins followed strict monastic life and rigid disciplinary laws as originally prescribed.

- ➤ The group which followed modified disciplinary rules was called the Mahasangikas.
- Later Buddhist schools included Theravada (Hinayana), Mahayana, Vajrayana, etc.

Hinayana

- It means the lesser vehicle.
- The school includes the followers of the original preaching of the Buddha. It is more of an orthodox school.
- They did not believe in idol or image worship of Buddha.
- They believe in individual salvation and try to attain individual salvation through self-discipline and meditation. Ultimate aim of Hinayana is thus nirvana.
- The Hinayana scholars used Pali language to interact with the masses.

Mahayana

- It means the greater vehicle.
- It developed after the Fourth Buddhist Council, during Kanishka reign.
- The Mahayana followers believe in idol or image worship of Buddha.
- The concept of Bodhisattva is the result of Mahayana Buddhism.
- The Mahayana scholars predominantly used Sanskrit as a language.
- The development of Mahayana Buddhism led to the composition of numerous avadanas (life history and teachings). Most of these texts were composed in what is now known as Buddhist Hybrid Sanskrit with the sole objective of communicating the teachings of Mahayana Buddhism to the people. Examples of important books of this genre were Mahavastu and Divyavadana.

Vajrayana

- An offshoot of Mahayana Buddhism, the origins of Tantric Buddhism can be traced to ancient Hindu and Vedic practices as well, including esoteric ritual texts designed to achieve physical, mental, and spiritual breakthroughs.
- Tantric Buddhism is sometimes described as offering a shortcut to enlightenment. Because some practices subverted mainstream Buddhism and Hinduism, engaging in acts otherwise considered taboo, its practitioners were secretive.
- According to the Vajrayani tantrikas, supreme knowledge, which amounted to supreme bliss, could be realized through the sexual union of the male and female. Spiritualism was thus inverted to justify eroticism in art and literature.

54. Correct Option: (d)

Explanation:

- **Statement 1 is incorrect:** Ashoka appointed dhammamahamatras to propagate dharma among various social groups, including women in his empire. Statement 1 can be eliminated.

Supplementary Notes:

Ashoka's Internal Policy and Buddhism

- Ashoka was converted to Buddhism as a result of the Kalinga war.
- According to tradition, he became a monk, made huge gifts to the Buddhists, and undertook pilgrimages to the Buddhist shrines.
- His visits to Buddhist shrines are also suggested by the dhamma yatras mentioned in his inscriptions.
- According to tradition, Ashoka held the third Buddhist Council (sangiti) and missionaries were sent not only to South India but also to Sri Lanka, Myanmar (Burma), and other countries to convert the people there. Brahmi inscriptions of the second and first centuries BC have been found in Sri Lanka.
- Ashoka set a very high ideal for himself, and this was the ideal of paternal kingship. He repeatedly asked his officials to tell his subjects that the king looked upon them as his children. As agents of the king, the officials were also asked to take care of the people.
- Ashoka appointed dhammamahamatras to propagate dharma among various social groups, including women, and appointed rajukas for the administration of justice in his empire.
- Ashoka disapproved of rituals, especially those observed by women. He forbade killing certain birds and animals, prohibited the slaughter of animals in the royal kitchen, and forbade the slaughter of animals in sacrifices.
- Ashoka's dharma was not however a narrow dharma and cannot be regarded as a sectarian faith. His Kandahar Greek inscription preaches amity between the sects.
- Ashoka's inscriptions are called dhammalipi, which cover not only religion and morality but also embrace social and administrative matters. They can be compared to the Dharmashastras or law-books written in Sanskrit under Brahmanical influence.
- Though the dhammalipis were written in Prakrit under Buddhist influence, they try to regulate the social order like the Dharmashastras.
- The Ashokan edicts can be also compared to the shasanas or royal edicts issued in Sanskrit by the brahmanized kings. The broad objective was to preserve the social order. He ordained that people should obey their parents, pay respect to the

brahmanas and Buddhist monks, and show mercy to slaves and servants. Above all, the dhammalipi asks the people to show firm devotion (dridha bhakti) or loyalty to king.

- These instructions are found in both the Buddhist and Brahmanical faiths.
- Ashoka taught people to live and let live. He emphasized compassion towards animals and proper behaviour towards relatives. His teachings were meant to strengthen the institution of family and the existing social classes. He held that if the people behaved well, they would go to heaven, but never said that they would attain nirvana, which was the goal of Buddhist teachings.
- Ashoka's teachings were thus intended to maintain the existing social order on the basis of tolerance. He does not seem to have preached any sectarian faith.
- Therefore, one must make a distinction between Asoka's policy of Dhamma which stressed on social responsibility and Asoka's own commitment as a Buddhist; the policy of Dhamma was an earnest attempt at solving some of the problems that a complex society faced.

55. Correct Option: (d)

Explanation:

- **Statement (d) is incorrect:** People started leaving Buddhist monasteries due to lack of discipline.

Supplementary Notes:

Origin of Mahayana Buddhism

- Indian religions underwent changes in post-Mauryan times partly due to a big leap in trade and artisanal activity and partly due to the large influx of people from Central Asia.
- Buddhism was especially affected. The monks and nuns could not afford to lose the cash donations from the growing body of traders and artisans concentrated in towns.
- The Buddhists welcomed foreigners who were non-vegetarians. All this meant laxity in the day-to-day living of the nuns and monks who led a sparse life.
- They now accepted gold and silver, took to non-vegetarian food and wore elaborate robes. Discipline became so slack that some renunciates even deserted the religious order or the Sangha and resumed the householder's life.
- This new form of Buddhism came to be called the Mahayana or the Great Wheel.
- In the old puritan Buddhism, certain things associated with the Buddha were worshipped as his symbols but now Budha was idolized.
- Images worship in Buddhism seems to have led to this practice in brahmanism on a large scale. With the rise of the Mahayana the old puritan school of Buddhism came to be known as the Hinayana or the Lesser Wheel.
- For the Mahayana, Kanishka became its great patron. He convened a council in Kashmir. The members of the council composed 3,00,000 words, which thoroughly explained the three pitakas or collections of Buddhist literature.
- Kanishka set up many other stupas to perpetuate the memory of the Buddha.

56. Correct Option: (d)

Explanation:

- All statements are correct

Supplementary Notes:

The Greco-Roman effect on Gandhara Art can be traced through:

- Halo around the head of Lord Buddha
- Buddha's wavy hair
- The forehead lines
- Ornaments
- Drape and style of the garments

Gandhara and Mathura Schools of Art

- This style of art was closely associated with Mahayana Buddhism and hence the main theme of this art was Lord Buddha and Bodhisattvas.
- Thus, it can be conjectured that in idea and conception this style was Indian and in execution it was foreign.
- One example of the Gandhara style of art is the Bamiyan Buddha statues.
- It mostly flourished in the areas of Afghanistan and present North-Western India.
- The prominent locations were Taxila, Peshawar, Begram, and Bamiyan.
- The period around which the Gandhara School of Art flourished could be said to be from the 1st century BCE to 4th century CE.
- There was extensive use of black stone and stucco. Stucco was a kind of plaster that was used for many structures including the freestanding ones under this style of art.
- The free-standing structures included many chaityas, Viharas, and stupas.
- The striking feature of the Gandhara School of Art shows a very realistic and natural depiction of features in perfection.
- Although it was dominated by the themes of Lord Buddha, however, there were images on other subjects also such as the images of the Greek God Apollo and certain kings as well.
- Thus, Gandhara School of Art can be said as an influence and culmination of both the Indian as well as foreign traditions due to its strategic location.

- The influence of the Gandhara Art also spread to Mathura.
- Mathura produced beautiful images of the Buddha, but it is also famous for the headless erect status of Kanishka whose name is inscribed on its lower part.
- It also produced several stone images of Vardhamana Mahavira.
- The Mathura School of Art flourished in the early centuries of the Christian era and its products made of red sandstone are found even outside Mathura.
- Beautiful Buddhist caves were constructed out of rocks in Maharashtra.
- In Andhra Pradesh, Nagarjunakonda and Amaravati became great centres of Buddhis art, and the stories connected with the Buddha came to be portrayed in numerous panels.
- The earliest panels dealing with Buddhism are found at Gaya, Sanchi and Bharhut and belong to the second century BC.

57. Correct Option: (c)

Explanation:

- **Statement 1 is incorrect:** Mahavira was 24th tirthankara.
- **Statement 2 is incorrect:** Buddha was first person to be idolized.

Supplementary Notes:

Birth and Life of Mahavira (540-468 BC)

- Jainism is a very ancient religion. As per some traditions, it is as old as the Vedic religion.
- The Jain tradition has a succession of great teachers or Tirthankaras.
- There were 24 Tirthankaras, the last of whom was Vardhaman Mahavira.
- The first Tirthankara is believed to be Rishabhanath or Rishabhadev.
- The 23rd Tirthankara was Parshvanatha who was born in Varanasi. He may have lived in the 8th or 7th century BC.
- All the Tirthankaras were Kshatriyas by birth.
- Founder of Jainism – Vardhamana Mahavira (539-467 BC) considered the last Tirthankara.
- He was born at Kundagrama near Vaishali. His parents were Kshatriyas. Father – Siddhartha (Head of Jnatrika Clan); Mother – Trishala (Sister of Lichchhavi chief Chetaka). Chetaka's daughter married Haryanka King Bimbisara.
- He was married to Yasoda and had a daughter Anojja or Priyadarsana.
- At the age of 30, Vardhaman renounced his home and became a wandering ascetic.
- He also observed self-mortification.
- After 13 years of penance, he attained the highest spiritual knowledge called Kevala or jina.
- He attained this at Jimbhikagrama village under a Sal tree at the age of 42. This is called Kaivalya. Thereafter, he was called Mahavira, Jina, Jitendriya (one who conquered his senses), Nigrantha (free from all bonds), and Kevalin.
- He preached his teachings for 30 years and died at Pava (near Rajagriha), aged 72.

58. Correct Option: (c)

Explanation:

- **Statement 2 is incorrect:** He was called Buddha just after he attained the supreme knowledge (Enlightenment or Nirvana).

Supplementary Notes:

Birth and Life of Buddha

- According to the tradition he was born in 567 BC in a Shakya Kshatriya family in Lumbini in Nepal near Kapilavastu, which is identified with Piprahwa in Basti district and is close to the foothills of Nepal. Gautama's father seems to have been the elected ruler of Kapilavastu, and headed the Shakya republican clan. His mother was a princess from the Koshalan Dynasty. Thus, like Mahavira, Gautama too belonged to a noble family. Born in a republic, he also inherited some egalitarian beliefs.
- In order to find a solution to the misery of mankind, he left home at the age of 29. This event is called renunciation (mahabhinishkramana). He spent six years as a wandering ascetic.
- He practised rigid austerities and resorted to different kinds of self-torture to find the truth. Ultimately abandoning this, he went to Uruvela (near, modem Bodh Gaya on the banks of Niranjiina river) and sat under a pipal tree (Bodhi tree). Here he attained the supreme knowledge (Enlightenment or Nirvana) on the 49th day of his continuous meditation. Since then, he was called the Buddha (the enlightened one).
- From here he proceeded to the Deer Park at Sarnath near Varinasi and gave his first sermon which is known as 'Dharmachakra Pravartana' (setting in motion the wheel of Dharma).
- Asvajit, Upali, Mogallana. Sari-putra and Ananda were the first five disciples of Buddha. Soon he started visiting various places to propagate his sermon. He visited Sarnath, Mathura, Rajgir, Gaya and Pataliputra. Kings like Bimbisara, Ajatasatru (Magadha), Prasenajita (Kosala) and Udayana (Kausambi) accepted his doctrines and became his disciples. He also visited Kapilavastu and converted his foster mother and his son Rahul to his faith.
- At the age of 80 (486 BC), he died (mahaparinirvana) at Kusinagara in Deoria District in Uttar Pradesh, the capital of the Malla.

- However, as in the case of Vardhamana Mahavira, the existence of Gautama Buddha in the sixth century BC is not supported by archaeological evidence. The cities Kaushambi, Shravasti, Varanasi, Vaishali, and Rajgriha, which the Buddha visited, did not assume any urban character until the fifth century BC

59. Correct Option: (c)

Explanation:

- **Statement 1 is incorrect:** Buddha laid great emphasis on the law of 'karma'.

Supplementary Notes:

Teachings of Buddha

- The basic teachings of Buddha are contained in Four Noble Truths, and Eight-Fold Path.
- The following are the Four Noble Truths:
  - The world is full of sufferings.
  - All sufferings have a cause: desire, ignorance and attachment are the causes of sufferings.
  - The suffering could be removed by destroying its cause.
  - In order to end sufferings, one must know the right path. This path is the Eight-Fold Path (Ashtangika Marga).
- The Eight-Fold Path consists of the following principles:
  - **Finding the right view:** It is to understand that the world is filled with sorrow generated by desire. The ending of desire will lead to the liberation of the soul.
  - **Right aim:** It seeks to avoid the enjoyment of the senses and luxury. It aims to love humanity and increase the happiness of others.
  - **Right speech:** It seeks to emphasise the speaking of truth always.
  - **Right action:** It is understood to be unselfish action.
  - **Right livelihood:** It instructs that a man should live by honest means.
  - **Right effort:** It is the proper way of controlling one's senses so as to prevent bad thoughts. It is through correct mental exercises that one can destroy desire and attachment.
  - **Right mindfulness:** It is the understanding of the idea that the body is impermanent and meditation is the means for the removal of worldly evils.
  - **Right concentration:** The observation of it will lead to peace. Meditation will unravel the real truth.
- Buddha rejected the authority of the Vedas and condemned animal sacrifices.
- Buddhism laid great emphasis on the law of 'karma'. According to this law, the present is determined by the past actions. The condition of a man in this life and the next depends upon his own actions. Every individual is the maker of his own destiny. Thus, the doctrine of karma is the essential part of the teachings of Buddha.
- Buddha preached 'nirvana', the ultimate goal in the life of a man. It means the shedding of all desires, and ending of sufferings, which finally leads to freedom from rebirth. By the process of elimination of desires, one can attain 'nirvana'. Therefore, Buddha preached that annihilation of desire is the real problem. Prayers and sacrifices will not end the desire. So, unlike the emphasis on rituals and ceremonies in Vedic religion, he laid emphasis on the moral life of an individual.
- He did not involve himself in fruitless controversies regarding the soul (atman) and Brahma which raged in his time, but addressed himself to worldly problems. He was more concerned about the individual and his actions.
- He taught that a person should avoid an excess of both luxury and austerity, and prescribed the middle path.

60. Correct Option: (c)

Explanation:

- Both statements are correct

Supplementary Notes:

The Spread of Buddhism

- The most famous Kushana ruler was Kanishka, who ruled around 1900 years ago. He organised a Buddhist council, where scholars met and discussed important matters. Ashvaghosha, a poet who composed a biography of the Buddha, the Buddhacharita, lived in his court. Ashvaghosha and other Buddhist scholars now began writing in Sanskrit.
- A new form of Buddhism, known as Mahayana Buddhism, now developed. This had two distinct features. Earlier, the Buddha's presence was shown in sculpture by using certain signs. For instance, his attainment of enlightenment was shown by sculptures of the peepal tree.
- The second change was a belief in Bodhisattvas. These were supposed to be persons who had attained enlightenment.
- Once they attained enlightenment, they could live in complete isolation and meditate in peace. However, instead of doing that, they remained in the world to teach and help other people.
- The worship of Bodhisattvas became very popular, and spread throughout Central Asia, China, and later to Korea and Japan.
- Buddhism also spread to western and southern India, where dozens of caves were hollowed out of hills for monks to live in.

- Buddhism also spread south eastwards, to Sri Lanka, Myanmar, Thailand, and other parts of Southeast Asia including Indonesia. The older form of Buddhism, known as Theravada Buddhism was more popular in these areas.

61. Correct Option: (a)

Supplementary Notes:

Sammitiyas

- It was one of the sects of lesser vehicle of Buddhism.
- They rejected the doctrine of soullessness and to postulate a sort of soul in the person, which passes from life to life.

62. Correct Option: (b)

Explanation:

- **Statement 2 is incorrect:** They rejected the caste system and various social practices of Hindus.

Supplementary Notes:

Virshaiva Movement/ Lingayats

- The Virshaivas is a Shaivite sect in Hinduism that emerged in the 12th century AD in Karnataka during the reign of Kalachuri Dynasty.
- They opposed the elaborate rituals prescribed by Hindu priests.
- They also rejected the caste system and various social practices of Hindus.
- It was initiated by Basavanna and was assisted by Allamaprabhu and Akkamaha Devi.
- They wanted a more egalitarian society and greater individual freedom.
- The followers are called Virshaiva (heroes of Shiva) or the Lingayats (wearers of Shivalinga).

63. Correct Option: (b)

Explanation:

- **Statement 1 is incorrect:** It did not condemn the varna system as Buddhism did.
- **Statement 3 is incorrect:** Right knowledge, right faith, and right action are considered to be the three jewels or Triratna of Jainism.

Supplementary Notes:

Doctrines of Jainism

- Jainism taught five doctrines: (i) do not commit violence, (ii) do not tell a lie, (iii) do not steal, (iv) do not hoard, and (v) observe continence (brahmacharya).
- Jainism recognized the existence of the gods but placed them lower than the Jina, and did not condemn the varna system as Buddhism did. According to Mahavira, a person is born in a high or in lower varna as a consequence of his sins committed or virtues acquired by him in his previous birth.
- Mahavira looks for human values even in a chandala. In his opinion, by leading a pure and meritorious life, members of the lower castes can achieve liberation.
- Jainism principally aims at the attainment of freedom from worldly bonds. No ritual is necessary for such liberation. It can be obtained through the right knowledge, right faith, and right action. These three are considered to be the three jewels or Triratna of Jainism.
- Jainism prohibited the practice of war and even agriculture for its followers because both involve the killing of living beings. Eventually, the Jainas principally confined themselves to trade and mercantile activities.

64. Correct Option: (a)

Explanation:

- **Statement 1 is incorrect:** Jainas migrated to the South under the leadership of Bhadrabahu.

Supplementary Notes:

Spread of Jainism

- According to a late tradition, the spread of Jainism in Karnataka is attributed to Chandragupta Maurya (322–298 BC). The emperor became a Jaina, gave up his throne, and spent the last years of his life in Karnataka as a Jaina ascetic, but this tradition is not corroborated by any other source.
- The second cause of the spread of Jainism in South India is said to have been the great famine that took place in Magadha 200 years after Mahavira's death. The famine lasted for twelve years, and in order to protect themselves, many Jainas migrated to the south under the leadership of Bhadrabahu, though the rest of them stayed back in Magadha under the leadership of Sthalabahu. The emigrant Jainas spread Jainism in South India.
- At the end of the famine, they returned to Magadha, where they developed differences with the local Jainas. Those who returned from the South claimed that even during the famine, they had strictly observed the religious rules.
- They alleged too that the Jaina ascetics living in Magadha had violated those rules and had become lax. In order to sort out these differences and to compile the principal teachings of Jainism, a council was convened in Pataliputra, modern Patna, but the Jainas who had returned from the South boycotted it and refused to accept its decisions.
- From now onwards, the southern began to be called digambaras and the Magadhans, shvetambaras.

65. Correct Option: (d)

Supplementary Notes:

Buddhism

- Paticca-samuppada (Pali: "dependent origination") Sanskrit pratitya-samutpada, the chain, or law, of dependent origination, or the chain of causation—a fundamental concept of Buddhism describing the causes of suffering (dukkha) and the course of events that lead a being through rebirth, old age, and death.

66. **Correct Option: (d)**

Explanation:

- All statements are correct

Supplementary Notes:

Buddhism

- According to Buddha, human misery is ultimately due to the delusion of selfhood.
- The ignorance primarily concerns the fundamental nature of the universe, which has three salient characteristics:
  - Full of sorrow (dukkha)
  - Transient (anicca)
  - Soulless (anatta)
- Buddhists would not claim that there is no happiness in the world, but that in some form or other sorrow is inevitable in every aspect of life.
- There is no abiding entity anywhere in this transient universe. Every being or object, however stable and homogenous it may appear, is, in reality, transient and composite.
- The universe is soulless. In transmigration, nothing passes over from one life to another—only a new life arises as part of the chain of events which includes the old.

67. **Correct Option: (c)**

Explanation:

- Both statements are correct

Supplementary Notes:

Zoroastrianism

- This religion has its origin in Persia by the Prophet Zarathustra around 6-7 BCE. It is a monotheistic religion which believes in one eternal god whose name is Ahura Mazda who is the epitome of just behaviour and goodness. Fire along with water are seen as symbol of purity in Zoroastrian religion
- There is a spirit of malice and bad behaviour called Angra Mainyu. These two keep fighting with each other and this is an eternal struggle and one day, good will win over evil and that will be the last day.
- The first contact of the Zoroastrians with India was in 936 AD when they fled from Iran because of the Islamic invasions. They are commonly known as Parsis and are presently amongst the smallest (and rapidly shrinking) communities in India. They live mostly in Mumbai, Goa, and Ahmedabad.
- Their fire temples called Atash Bahram are rare and only eight known temples exist in the entire country.
- Their sacred text called Zend Avesta is written in old Avestan and consists of 17 sacred songs (gathas) and the Athuna Vairyo (sacred chant), which was supposedly written by Zarathustra himself. The translations of these texts and compiled glossaries are called Zend.

68. **Correct Option: (a)**

Explanation:

- **Option (a) is correct:** Guru Padmasam-bhava is described in the above passage.

Supplementary Notes:

Guru Padmasambhava

- Guru Padmasambhava is an important figure in Buddhism who was instrumental in establishing Vajrayana Buddhism in Tibet around the 8th century CE.
- He was a missionary monk who went from Nalanda to convert Tibetans to Buddhism in the 8th century.
- The Vajrayana tradition continues to survive and flourish because of his efforts. This is one reason why he is also known as the 'Second Buddha'.
- His yogic style and royal robes remind to embrace all the delights of life as long as we live in human form. At the same time, his monastic robes remind to not get too caught up in sensual and carnal pleasures, otherwise, one can end up being hedonistic or materialistic, seeking satisfaction only from the outside world and believing with almost religious certainty that all fun comes from outside.
- Recently, the Orissa government built a massive 9-feet-high stone statue of Padmasambhava in the Gajapati district.

69. **Correct Option: (d)**

Explanation:

- All statements are correct

Supplementary Notes:

Rig Veda

- The Rig Veda is the oldest existing Veda amongst the other four. It consists of 1028 individual Sanskrit hymns.
- It is said to be one of the first extensive compositions in any Indo-European language that has survived for our perusal. Historians argue that it was compiled around 1200-900 BC
- The focus of this Veda is on worldly prosperity and natural beauty. The text is organised in 10 books, known as Mandalas, of varying age and length.
- Furthermore, each mandala comprises of several Suktas or hymns, which are usually for sacrificial purposes. Most of the hymns concentrate on the themes of life, death, creation, sacrifice and seeking godly pleasure or soma.

- The entire Rig Vedic hymns are dedicated to several deities, in particular to their chief deity, Indra. The other prominent Gods mentioned in the Rig Veda are Agni (God of fire), Varuna (God of water), Rudra (God of wind/storm), Aditya (a form of Sun God), Vayu (God of air) and the Ashwini twins.
- There are several hymns dedicated to female Goddesses too; like Usha (Goddess of Dawn), Prithvi (Goddess of the earth) and Vak (the Goddess of speech).

70. Correct Option: (a)

Explanation:

- **Statement 2 is incorrect:** Aranyakas describe the rituals and sacrifices involved in the Vedas from various perspectives.

Supplementary Notes:

Brahmanas

- The Brahmanas are part of the Hindu Sruti (revealed knowledge) literature. Each Veda has a Brahmana attached to it, which is essentially a collection of texts with commentaries on the particular Veda.
- They are usually a mixture of legends, facts, philosophy and detailed explanations of Vedic rituals. They also consist of instructions as to how to properly conduct rituals and enunciate the science of sacrifice. They also explain the symbolic significance of the sacred words used in the rituals.
- Although historians disagree on the dating of the Brahmanas, it is usually pegged to be composed and compiled between 900-700 BC As mentioned above, each Veda has its accompanying Brahmana.

Aranyakas

- The Aranyakas are also texts attached to the Vedas and they describe the rituals and sacrifices involved in the Vedas from various perspectives.
- They are said to be compilations of ritualistic information on the birth and death cycles as well as the complexity of the soul.
- It is argued that holy and learned men, called Munis, who preferred to dwell within the limits of the forests, taught them.

71. Correct Option : (d)

Explanation:

- **Statement 1 is incorrect:** Vajrayana Buddhism evolved as a movement within Mahayana Buddhism.
- **Statement 2 is incorrect:** In Vajrayana, the Buddha is not considered as a person, rather he is a mirror to our own mind.

Supplementary Notes:

Vajrayana Buddhism

- It arose as a major movement within Mahayana Buddhism around the 7th century.
- The Vajrayana, literally the "Diamond Vehicle" or the "Thunderbolt Vehicle," understands itself to be an esoteric form of Mahayana Buddhism with an accelerated path to enlightenment.
- A major technique associated with Vajrayana Buddhism is the use of prayer and meditation focused on a single, personal deity. This school of Buddhism also places greater emphasis on rituals, formulated behaviors, repetitive speech, and so forth, as compared to other sub-groups of Mahayana.
- Buddha's teaching in Vajrayana is about the mind itself. These direct teachings that Buddha gave are for those who have a special kind of confidence. They understand that they can only perceive perfection outside because they have the same innate perfection inside. In Vajrayana, the Buddha is not considered a person; rather he is a mirror to our own mind. The teachings point out the mind's perfect qualities directly. They are often known as Buddhist Tantra.
- The main deity is Tara.
- This school believes in Tantra's, Mantras and Yantras superiority due to being a faster vehicle to liberation containing many skillful methods of tantric ritual.
- It was also influenced by the primitive local cults and practices, which was finally established in Tibet in the 11th century, as a result of missions sent from the great Vajrayana monastery of Vikramshila, in Bihar.
- The Vajrayana also includes the Theravada and Mahayana teachings.
- Pala rulers of Bengal were great patrons of Vajrayana Buddhism.

72. Correct Option: (c)

Explanation:

- Both statements are correct

Supplementary Notes:

International Buddhist Conclave

- The Ministry of Tourism, Government of India, has been organizing the International Buddhist Conclave biennially since 2004.
- The 6th International Buddhist conclave was recently inaugurated in New Delhi by the President.
- The aim of the Conclave was to showcase and project the Buddhist Heritage in India and boost tourism to the Buddhist sites in the country and cultivate friendly ties with countries and communities interested in Buddhism.
- The Conclave was organized by the Ministry of Tourism in collaboration with the State Governments of Maharashtra, Bihar and Uttar Pradesh.
- The theme for the 6th International Buddhist Conclave was "Buddha Path – The Living Heritage".

- Buddha Path or the Eight-Fold Path refers to the extraordinary teachings of the Buddha which is also called the Middle Path and when practiced it brings the purity of mind and leads to Peace, Happiness, and Harmony within and also in the society as well.
- Buddha Path also refers to the Eight Great Places of Buddhist Heritage.
- The earlier International Buddhist Conclaves were organized in New Delhi and Bodh Gaya (February 2004), Nalanda and Bodh Gaya (February 2010), Varanasi and Bodh Gaya (2012 and 2014) and in Sarnath/Varanasi and Bodh Gaya (October 2016).

73. Correct Option: (d)

Explanation:

- All pairs are correctly matched

Supplementary Notes:

Important Symbols in Buddhism

Symbols	Events in Buddha's life
A. Stupa	Parinirvana
B. Bodhi Tree	Nirvana
C. Horse	Mahabhinishkramana
D. Wheel	Dhammachakraparivartan
E. Lotus & Bull	Birth

74. Correct Option: (b)

Explanation:

- **Statement 2 is incorrect:** It is the only stable entity in Buddhism.
- **Statement 3 is incorrect:** It's not a part of the universe.

Supplementary Notes:

Nirvana in Buddhism

- Buddha described Nirvana as the highest state of profound well-being a human is capable of attaining. The mind awakens from delusion, is liberated from bondage, is cleansed of all its defilements, becomes entirely at peace, experiences the complete cessation of suffering, and is no longer reborn.
- It is the only stable entity in the old school of Buddhism such as Sthaviravada.
- It is difficult to understand for one who has not experienced it.
- Nirvana is the only state of rest in this transient universe. This may seem like a paradox but it is not as Nirvana was outside the universe and only underlay it.
- Nirvana has no definite location, but it may be realised anywhere and at any time, while still in flesh. The man who once achieves Nirvana never again loses it, and when he dies he passes to this state forever, in his parinirvana, his Final blowing out.

75. Correct Option: (d)

Explanation:

- **Statement 1 is incorrect:** It was held at Vaisali.
- **Statement 2 is incorrect:** The monastic order broke into two sections: Sthaviravadins and Mahasanghikas at the second council.

Supplementary Notes:

Second Buddhist Council

- The Second Buddhist Council was held after the 100 years of Lord Buddha's death. It is believed to be held in 386 CE and was held at Vaishali.
- The schism rose within the order ostensibly over monastic discipline. The order broke into two sections, the orthodox Sthaviravadins (Believers in the teaching of the elders) and Mahasanghikas (Members of the great community).
- Sthaviravadins felt they were in keeping with the original spirit of the Buddha's teachings whereas Mahasanghika interpreted Buddha's teachings more liberally, but in a way that they felt was more true to his intentions.

76. Correct Option: (c)

Explanation:

- Both statements are correct

Supplementary Notes:

Sallekhana

- Sallekhana is embracing death voluntarily when both householders and ascetics foresee that the end of the life is very near either due to the old age, incurable disease, severe famine, attack from the enemy or wild animal, etc.
- At such time one overcomes all the passions and abandons all the worldly attachments by observing austerities such as gradually abstaining from the food and the water and simultaneously meditating on the true nature of the self until the soul parts the body.
- An approximate assessment of the remaining span of life is necessary in order to adjust to the nature of the fasting. He should endure all the hardships, but if he falls ill or for any other reason cannot maintain the peace of mind, then he should give up Sallekhana and resume taking foods and other activities.
- Sallekhana is also known by the other names like Samnyas-Marana, Samadhi-Marana, etc.
- In 2015, the Rajasthan High Court banned the practice, considering it a suicide. Later that year, the Supreme Court of India stayed the decision of the Rajasthan High Court and lifted the ban on Sallekhana.

77. Correct Option: (a)

Explanation:

- **Option (a) is incorrect:** Mangu Mutt is a place of historical significance for the Sikh community.

Supplementary Notes:

Mangu Mutt is a place of historical significance for the Sikh community

- It was within 75 metres of 'Meghanad Prachir' of Sri Jagannath Temple and needed to be demolished for creation of a heritage corridor.
- The Mutt is located in front of Simhadwar of the 12th-century shrine at the entrance of Dolamandap Sahi.
- The two-storied building, constructed with mortar and limestone powder over 100 years back, was declared unsafe by the administration a decade ago.
- Mangu Mutt, though not connected directly with Sri Jagannath Temple, connects Srikhetra with the founder of Sikh religion Guru Nanak.
- Guru Nanak came to Puri in 1550 and offered 'Arati' to Lord Jagannath on the sand dune where the Mutt now stands.
- In 1552, Guru Nanak's son Sri Chand too offered prayers to the Lord at the same place.
- The Mutt was built in the 17th century by a famous saint of Udasin sect of Sikh faith and an ardent disciple of Guru Nanak, Mangu Das.
- Interestingly, a marble statue of Sri Chand, the only one in India, is worshipped in the Mutt.
- The verses used by Guru Nanak while praying and conducting Arati of Lord Jagannath are recited in the Mutt.
- The verses were later included in the holy book of the Sikhs, the Guru Granth Sahib.
- The Arati verses are recited in all gurudwaras.

78. Correct Option: (a)

Explanation:

- **Statement 1 is incorrect:** Principle of Anekantavada is also known as the doctrine of non-one-sidedness.
- **Statement 2 is incorrect:** Principle of Syadavada emphasises on the relativity of all knowledge.

Supplementary Notes:

Doctrines of Jainism

- The core of Jaina doctrine is expressed in the following principles:
  - Principle of Anekantavada or the doctrine of manifold nature of reality.
    - It is literally the doctrine of 'non-one-sidedness'. According to this doctrine, truth and reality are perceived differently from different points of view, and no single point of view is a complete truth.
  - Principle of Syadavada or the theory of conditioned predication.
    - It emphasises on the relativity of all knowledge. According to this doctrine, all judgments are conditional, holding good only in certain conditions, circumstances, or senses.
  - Principle of Nayavada or the theory of partial standpoints.
    - It signifies the system of describing reality from different points of view.
  - Principle of Triratna
    - A Jaina must follow the three jewels of Jaina ethics, popularly called Triratna. These are Right faith, Right knowledge and Right conduct.
  - Principle of Pancha Mahavrata or the five great vows.
    - In order to help attain Triratna one must observe Pancha Mahavrata or the five great vows. These are Non-violence (Ahimsa), Truth (Satya), Non-stealing (Asteya), Chastity (Brahmacharya) and Non-possession (Aparigraha)
  - Principle of Ahimsa or the doctrine of non-violence.

79. Correct Option: (a)

Explanation:

- **Statement 2 is incorrect:** Buddhist monks also considered the Varna system but it was based on the action/ work of an individual and not on the birth.

Supplementary Notes:

Buddhism and Brahmanism

- The Buddhist monks considered varna based on action, unlike the Brahmanas, who conferred on it a divine sanction, dividing people based on birth.
- Though Buddhism was certainly more inclusive than the Brahmanical tradition, yet it supported social order based on classes and did not aim at abolishing social differences.
- For instance, Buddhist tradition rules placed conditions for entry into the sangha such as the ban on the entry of debtors, slaves, and soldiers without permission from their respective masters.
- Similarly, both Brahmanism and Buddhism emphasised on the virtues of carrying out familial obligations, protecting private property and respecting political authority.
- Both Buddhism and Brahmanism also did not participate directly in production and lived on alms given by society.

80. Correct Option: (d)

Explanation:

- All statements are correct

Supplementary Notes:

Ajivikas

- Ajivikas or 'followers of the way of life,' were an ascetic order that started at the time of Buddha and Mahavira, and lasted until the 14th century.
- They challenged Brahmanical dominance.
- Ajivika was founded by Makkhali Gosala.
- Ajivikas were very popular in Magadha in the third century BCE and Mauryan kings donated several caves in the honour of Ajivika monks.
- The Ajivikas, who were rigid fatalists and determinists, supposedly held that the affairs of the entire universe were ordered by a cosmic force called niyati (pre-determinism or destiny in Sanskrit).
- According to them, niyati determined all events, including an individual's fate, to the last detail and that barred personal efforts to change or accelerate improvement toward one's spiritual destiny.
- No human effort could have any effect against niyati, and therefore karma is a fallacy.
- As per them, Nirvana was only reached after living through an immense number of lives, which proceeded automatically like the unwinding of a ball of thread, the last life being as an Ajivika monk.
- As a result of this static and melancholy view of the human condition, the Ajivikas practised austerities rather than pursue any purposeful goal.
- Some later Ajivikas worshipped Gosala as a divinity.

81. Correct Option: (a)

Explanation:

- **Statement 2 is incorrect:** The Siddha saints were mostly Shaiva.

Supplementary Notes:

Lingayat

- Lingayat or Vir Shaiva was a popular movement which arose during the 12th century.
- Its founder was Basava and his nephew Channabasava, who lived at the court of the Kalachuri kings of Karnataka.
- The Lingayats were worshippers of Shiva and established their faith after bitter disputes with the Jainas.
- They strongly opposed the caste system and child marriage, and rejected feasts, fasts, pilgrimage and sacrifices.
- They supported widow remarriage.

Siddhas

- It is also pertinent to mention the Siddhas (or Sittars) of Tamil Nadu, who held contrasting views with the Bhakti tradition, although some of their ideologies are considered to have originated during the first Sangam Age.
- Their attitude against idol worship and their stress on yoga and right conduct distinguished them from the Bhakti cults.
- They believed in the oneness of the transcendental being (monotheism) in the world as well as in charity towards men.
- The Siddha saints were mostly Shaiva, who professed and practised an unorthodox type of sadhana (spiritual practices) to attain liberation.
- A siddha obtains yogic powers called siddhi by constant practice of certain yogic disciplines and tapasya.
- Along with that, they also used rasayanas, which were substances that were said to transform the body to make it potentially deathless, and a particular type of pranayama (breathing practice).

82. Correct Option: (c)

Supplementary Notes:

Vedic Gods

- Aryans personified natural forces like coming of the rains, the appearance of the sun and the moon, and the existence of the rivers, mountains, and looked upon them as living beings to whom they attributed human or animal attributes.
- We have a large number of such divinities in the Rig Veda, which is replete with hymns composed in their honor by the poets of sundry families.
- The Vedic gods can be classified into three categories, namely terrestrial (prithivisthana), aerial or intermediate (antarikshasthana), and celestial (Ayutthaya).
- Prithivi, Agni, Soma, Brihaspati, and rivers belong to the first category; Indra, Apam-napat, Rudra, Vayu-Vata, Prujanya, and Apah (water) to the second and Dyaus, Varuna, Mitra, Surya, Savitri, Pushan, Vishnu, the Adityas, Ushas and the Asvins to the third.
- Indra and Varuna (the supreme cosmic and moral ruler) stan; out, in that order, pre-eminent above the rest. Agni and Soma were also popular deities. Agni was revered as the messenger between the earth and heaven. Further, Agni is the only God who is regarded as present among all the categories of Gods.
- The dominant mode of worshipping the gods was through the recitation of prayers and the performance of sacrifices. Prayers played an important part in Rig Vedic times, both collective and individual. Originally every tribe or clan was the votary of a special god. It seems that prayers were offered to the gods in the chorus by the members of an entire tribe.

83. Correct Option: (c)

Explanation:

- Both statements are correct

Supplementary Notes:
Vedanta Philosophy

- The theory of karma is closely linked to Vedanta philosophy, which signifies that in his present birth a person has to bear the consequences of his actions performed in his previous birth.
- The core message of Vedanta is that every action must be governed by the discriminating faculty that is the intellect. The mind can make mistakes, but the intellect lets us know if the action is in our interest or not.
- According to Vedanta, the world is Maya (illusion) and there is only one reality, Brahman. Therefore, it lays emphasis on brahmagyan, and relies on the Upanishads.
- While Purva Mimansa discusses the fire sacrifices of the Vedic rituals in the Samhitas and the Brahmanas, Vedanta throws light on the esoteric teachings of the Aranyakas (the forest scriptures) and the Upanishads.

84. Correct Option: (b)

Supplementary Notes:
Shankaradeva

- In the late 15th century, Shankaradeva emerged as one of the leading proponents of Vaishnavism in Assam.
- His teachings, often known as the Bhagavati dharma because they were based on the Bhagvata Gita and Bhagvata Purana, focused on absolute surrender to the supreme deity (i.e. Vishnu).
- He emphasized the need for naam kirtan, recitation of name of Lord in satsanga or congregations of pious devotees.
- He also encouraged the establishment of satra or monasteries for the transmission of spiritual knowledge, and naam ghar or prayer halls.
- His major compositions include the Kirtana-ghosha.

85. Correct Option: (c)

Explanation:

- Both statements are correct

Supplementary Notes:
Causes for the rise of Jainism and Buddhism

- Caste system became rigid and it created inequality in the society. The varna-divided society seems to have generated tensions. The Kshatriyas, who acted as rulers, however, reacted strongly against the ritualistic domination of the Brahmanas, and seem to have led a kind of protest movement against the importance attached to birth in the Varna system.
- The complex and elaborative rituals and sacrifices advocated in the Later Vedic period were not acceptable to the common people Also it became expensive.
- Blind faith and superstitions created confusion in the minds of people.
- Introduction of new agricultural economy in north-eastern India.
- The use of iron tools made possible clearance, agriculture and large settlements. The agricultural economy based on the iron ploughshare required the use of bullocks, and it could not flourish without animal husbandry.
- But the Vedic practice of killing cattle indiscriminately in sacrifices stood in the way of the progress of new agriculture. The cattle wealth slowly decimated because the cows and bullocks were killed in numerous Vedic sacrifices. The tribal people living on the southern and eastern fringes of Magadha also killed cattle for food. But if the new agrarian economy had to be stable this killing had to be stopped.

86. Correct Option: (b)

Explanation:

- **Statement 1 is incorrect:** The monk who presided over the first council was Mahakassapa.

Supplementary Notes:
Buddhists Councils (Table 3.1.1)

TABLE: 3.1.1 - Buddhists Councils

Council	Period	Place	Patronaged By	Presided By	Important Events
First	483 BC	Sattapani cave at Rajgriha	King Ajatshatru	Mahakasyapa, a monk	It was held to preserve Buddha's teachings/Sutta and rules for disciples. Compilations were made of the Buddha's rules of Vinaya (monastic discipline), and the sutras (instructive aphorisms).
Second	383 BC	Vaishali	King Kalasoka	Sabakami	It was held to settle the disagreements of different subdivisions (Sthaviravada, Mahasanghika, and Sarvastivada).

Third	250 BC	Pataliputra	King Ashoka	Moggaliputta Tissa	The teachings of Buddha were classified into 3 baskets as Abhidhamma Pitaka was established in this council, and they were known as "Tripitaka".
Fourth	72 AD	Kashmir	King Kanishka	Vasumitra and Asvaghosha	In this council, 2 sects of Buddhism came into existence: Hinayana and Mahayana.

CONCEPT REVISION

Here is the list of concepts that have been covered as part of the previous exercise. Revise and self-reflect on your concepts you covered.

- Features of Vajrayana Buddhism ☐
- Jewels of Jainism ☐
- Buddhist Mudras and their meaning ☐
- International Buddhist Conclave ☐
- Vaishnavism ☐
- First Sanskrit Scholar in Buddhism ☐
- Bhagavatism ☐
- Decline of Buddhism in India ☐
- Sthanakvas ☐
- Tenets of Buddhism ☐
- 'Sallekhana' ☐
- Sant Ravidas ☐
- Common features between Jainism and Buddhism ☐
- Zen Buddhism ☐
- 'Ekantika-dharma' ☐
- Distinguishing feature between Jainism and Buddhism ☐
- Eight-fold path of Buddhism ☐
- Buddha's teachings ☐
- Jain philosophy ☐
- Hindu sect ☐
- Pre-Vedic Religion ☐
- Sikh sects ☐
- Islam sect ☐
- Zoroastrian ☐
- Chisti order ☐
- Sufi orders ☐
- Basic theory of Vishishtadvaita ☐
- Paticca-Samuppada ☐
- Brahmanas and Aranyakas ☐
- Vajrayana Buddhism ☐
- International Buddhist Conclave ☐
- Symbols depicting events in Buddha's life ☐
- 'Mangu Matt' ☐
- Lingayats and Siddhas ☐
- Ajivikas sect ☐

9.2 LANGUAGES AND LITERATURE IN INDIA

QUESTIONS

1. Which of the following statements about Harappan Civilisation are correct?

1. Harappan Script is written from Right to Left.
2. Stone buildings are not seen in Harappan Civilisation.
3. The figure of the bearded man or the "priest king" was found at Mohenjo Daro.
4. Most of the seals were made of Lapis Lazuli Stone.

Select the correct answer using the code given below:

(a) 1, 2 and 4 only (b) 2, 3 and 4 only
(c) 1 and 4 only (d) 1, 2 and 3 only

2. Which of the following statement/s is/are correct about Puranas?

1. It focuses on the divine Hindu trinity Gods: Brahma, Vishnu and Mahesh.
2. The Puranas narrate the incidents of various influential kings.
3. The Puranas discuss about the geography of the world thus helping in understanding of the physical features.

Select the correct answer using the code given below:

(a) 1 and 2 only
(b) 2 only
(c) 2 and 3 only
(d) 1, 2 and 3

3. Which of the following statements regarding Harappan culture is/are incorrect?

1. Egyptian culture used burnt bricks for architecture whereas Harappan culture used baked bricks.
2. Harappan script is not alphabetical but mainly pictographic.
3. Harappans did not use metal money; instead trade was through barter system.

Select the correct answer using the code given below:

(a) 1 only (b) 2 and 3 only
(c) 1 and 3 only (d) None

4. Arrange the following literary works in chronological order starting from the earliest:

1. Rig Veda
2. Natyashashtra
3. Vedangas
4. Atharva Veda

Select the correct answer using the code given below:

(a) 1-2-3-4 (b) 1-4-3-2
(c) 1-2-4-3 (d) 1-4-2-3

5. Consider the following statements regarding Buddhist literature:

1. Sutta Pitaka is a compilation of sayings of Buddha.
2. Vinay Pitaka is a compilation of rules of Sangha.
3. Abhidhamma Pitaka is a compilation of philosophies of Dhamma.

Which of the above statements are incorrect?

(a) 1 and 3 only (b) 2 and 3 only
(c) 1, 2 and 3 (d) None

6. Which of the following pairs is/are incorrectly matched?

Bhakti Movement		Literary Language
1. Namdev	-	Marathi
2. Tulsidas	-	Avadhi
3. Kabir	-	Bhojpuri
4. Narsi Mehta	-	Bangla

Select the correct answer using the code given below:

(a) 2 and 3 only (b) 1 and 4 only
(c) 2 and 4 only (d) 4 only

7. Which of the following scientists and their works is correctly matched?

(a) Aryabhatta calculated the value of 'Pi'.
(b) Kanad gave the atomic theory.
(c) Charak gave the concepts of plastic surgery and cataract operation.
(d) Bhaskaracharya introduced negative numbers and operations on zero into mathematics.

8. Which of the following statements related to the ancient scientific developments is/are incorrect?

1. Dhanvantari was the Raj Vaidya (royal doctor) in the court of Kanishka.
2. Varahamihira was the Indian astronomer during the Yashodharman Vikramaditya reign.
3. Unani Tibb system of medicine flourished in India during the medieval period.

Select the correct answer using the code given below:

(a) 1 only (b) 1 and 2 only
(c) 1 and 3 only (d) 2 and 3 only

9. Consider the following statements regarding Ancient Indian Literature:

1. Lord Buddha used Sanskrit language in his sermons.
2. Jain literature was primarily written in Prakrit having moral instructions.
3. Panchatantra was mainly written in Hindi Language.

Which of the above statement/s is/are correct?

(a) 1 only (b) 2 and 3 only
(c) 2 only (d) 1, 2 and 3

10. In the context of contribution of Christian Missionaries (since beginning of 16th century) in the development of Indian literature, consider the following statements:

1. They established lithographic printing press for printing literature in local languages.
2. They published dictionaries and grammar in several local languages.
3. They established Schools and Colleges in which they also taught the local languages, apart from English.

Select the correct answer using the code given below:

(a) 1 and 2 only (b) 1 and 3 only
(c) 1 only (d) 1, 2 and 3

11. Consider the following statements about 'National Mission on Manuscripts'.

1. It deals with documentation, conservation, preservation and digitisation of manuscripts of India.
2. It is a part of Project Mausam.
3. It is organized under the aegis of Ministry of Culture.

Which of the above statements are correct?

(a) 1 only (b) 2 only
(c) 1 and 3 only (d) 2 and 3 only

12. With reference to the 'Pali literature', consider the following statements:

1. Pali literature is concerned mainly with Mahayana Buddhism.
2. The Sanskrit language is much older than Pali.
3. Pali is an Indo Aryan language.

Which of the statements given above is/are correct?

(a) 1 only (b) 1 and 3 only
(c) 2 and 3 only (d) 1, 2 and 3

13. Which one of the following Upanishad talks about the childhood of Lord Krishna for the first time?

(a) Chandogya Upanishad
(b) Katha Upanishad
(c) Kena Upanishad
(d) Jabala Upanishad

14. Who was the author of 'Gathasaptasati or Sattasai in Prakrit?

(a) Simuka (b) Satakarni 1
(c) Hala (d) Kharawela

15. Consider the following statements with respect to the Vedic literature:

1. No Brahmins ever recites Atharva Veda.
2. Rig Veda's main theme is the prayers addressed to different Gods.
3. The priest who recites Samaveda is called Hotri.
4. The Gayatri mantra is part of Samaveda.

Which of the above statements are correct?

(a) 2 and 4 only (b) 1 and 2 only
(c) 2 and 4 only (d) 1, 2, 3 and 4

16. Which of the following statements with respect to Yajur Veda is/are correct?

1. It is the Veda of sacrificial formulas consisting of prose mantras.
2. The Yajur Veda hymns were called Sukta.
3. It also glorifies the curative powers of herbs and waters.

Select the correct answer using the code given below:

(a) 1 and 2 only (b) 1 and 3 only
(c) 1 only (d) 1, 2 and 3

17. Which of the following pairs of the famous literary works and their authors are correctly matched?

Literary Work		Author
1. Rajatarangini	-	Jayadeva
2. Gita Govindam	-	Kalhana
3. Kathaa Sarita Sagara	-	Somadeva
4. Siddhanta Shiromani	-	Bhaskaracharya
5. Prithiviraj Raso	-	Chand Bardai

Select the correct answer using the code given below

(a) 3, 4 and 5 only (b) 2, 3 and 5 only
(c) 1, 2, 4 and 5 only (d) 1, 3 and 5 only

18. Though the earliest inscriptions are found on the seals of Harappa, which of the following inscription was first deciphered?

(a) Ashokan Pillar of Delhi
(b) Allahabad inscription of Samudragupta
(c) Ashokan Pillar of Rummindei
(d) Sanchi inscription of Samudragupta

19. Which of the following text was first to talk about the development of fine arts and Buddhism in Deep South India?

(a) Silappadigaram
(b) Manimekalai
(c) Saivagachintamani
(d) Tolkappiyam

20. Which of the following statement/s is/are correct regarding the Santhali language?

1. It has been added to the 8th Schedule of the constitution by 92nd Amendment to the Indian constitution.
2. It is the first tribal language that has its own Wikipedia edition in its own script.

Select the correct answer using the code given below:

(a) 1 only (b) 2 only
(c) Both 1 and 2 (d) Neither 1 nor 2

21. Consider the following statements regarding the coins used during Mauryan Period as per Arthasastras:

1. Punch-marked coins, were started only during the Maurya period.
2. The silver coins were called panas and the copper coins were called mashakas.

Which of the above statement/s is/are correct?

(a) 1 only (b) 2 only
(c) Both 1 and 2 (d) None of the above

22. Consider the following statements about Scheduled Languages:

1. Sindhi was included as an official language by amending thc 8th schedule in 1967.
2. Hindi written in Devanagari script is to be the official language of the Union.

Which of the above statement/s is/are correct?

(a) 1 only (b) 2 only
(c) Both 1 and 2 (d) Neither 1 nor 2

23. Consider following statements with reference to Sangam period:

1. Tolkappiyam is considered as the earliest of Tamil literary work.
2. During the Sangam period, hereditary monarchy was the form of government.

Which of the above statement/s is/are correct?

(a) 1 only (b) 2 only
(c) Both 1 and 2 (d) Neither 1 nor 2

24. With reference to Vedic literature, consider the following statements:

1. Brahmanas are prose texts containing details about Vedic rituals and philosophies.
2. Aranyakas are texts that embody philosophical meditations of hermits and ascetics.

Which of the above statement/s is/are correct?

(a) 1 only (b) 2 only
(c) Both 1 and 2 (d) Neither 1 nor 2

25. Patanjali is well-known for the compilation of:
(a) Yoga Sutra (b) Panchatantra
(c) Brahma Sutra (d) Ayurveda

26. Which among the following is the sacred book of the Buddhists?
(a) Upanishad (b) Vedas
(c) Tripitaka (d) Agams

27. Which among the following is called 'The Bible of Tamil Land'?
(a) Kural (b) Tolkappiyam
(c) Silappadikaram (d) Manimekalai

28. Which of the following statements are correct with regard to the writings of Harrapan people?
1. The Harappans used ideograms i.e., a graphic symbol or character to convey the idea directly
2. Some inscriptions are thought to have followed boustrophedonic style.
3. The inscriptions are thought to have been mostly written from left to right

Select the correct answer using the code given below:
(a) 1 and 2 only (b) 2 and 3 only
(c) 1 and 3 only (d) 1, 2 and 3

29. Consider the following statements regarding the four Vedas:
1. Rig Veda is a collection of hymns
2. Sam Veda is a collection of songs mostly taken from Rig Veda
3. Atharva Veda is a collection of sacrificial formulae

Which of the above statement/s is/are correct?
(a) 1 only (b) 1 and 2 only
(c) 2 and 3 only (d) 1, 2 and 3

30. Chaitra 1 of the national calendar based on the Saka Era corresponds to which one of the following dates of the Gregorain calendar?
(a) 22nd March (or 21st March)
(b) 15th May (or 16th May)
(c) 31st March (or 30th March)
(d) 21st April (or 20th March)

31. Consider the following statement regarding the Brahamana text of Vedic Civilisation:
1. The Brahamanas are the collection of ancient Vedic texts with commentaries on the hymns of the four Vedas.
2. The Brahamanas contain details about the meaning of Vedic hymns, their applications, stories of their origins, etc.
3. Chandogya Brahmana, one of the oldest Brahmana includes eight suktas (hymns) for the ceremony of marriage and rituals at the birth of a child.

Which of the above statement/s is/are correct?
(a) 1 only (b) 1 and 2 only
(c) 2 and 3 only (d) 1, 2 and 3

32. The text 'Tolakappiyam' is related to:
(a) Administration (b) Law
(c) Grammar (d) None of these

33. Consider the following literary works:
1. Kumar Sambhavam
2. Mudrarakshasa
3. Raghuvamsa
4. Ritusamhara

Which of the above were the works of Kalidasa?
(a) 1, 2 and 3 only (b) 2, 3 and 4 only
(c) 1, 3 and 4 only (d) 1, 2 and 4 only

34. 'Mrichhakatika' was written by:
(a) Vikramaditya (b) Sudraka
(c) Kalhana (d) Banabhatta

35. Who among the following wrote the Sanskrit Grammar?
(a) Kalidasa (b) Charka
(c) Panini (d) Arayabhatt

36. The ninth mandala of the Rig Veda Samhita is devoted wholly to :
(a) Varuna (b) Soma
(c) Urvashi (d) Indra

37. Consider the following statements about the Northern Black Polished Ware (NBPW) phase :
1. Rice was the staple diet of the NBPW phase.
2. Peasants knew about paddy transplantation.
3. The NBPW phase marked the beginning of the second urbanisation.
4. Burnt bricks and ring wells were used in the NBPW phase.

Which of the above statements are correct?
(a) 2 and 3 only (b) 3 and 4 only
(c) 1, 2 and 3 only (d) 1, 2 , 3 and 4

38. Match the following pairs:

List I	List II
A. Vatsayana	i. Engineer
B. Agesilaus	ii. Medical Science
C. Vasumitra	iii. Kamasutra
D. Charaka	iv. Philosopher

Select the correct answer using the code given below:
(a) A-i, B-iii, C-iv, D-ii
(b) A-iii, B-i, C-iv, D-ii
(c) A-ii, B-iv, C-i, D-iii
(d) A-iv, B-iii, C-i, D-ii

39. Many Jain scholars contributed to the growth of Kannada and Sanskrit literature. Match the following literature with their Jain Scholars:

Literature	Scholars
A. Dharmanathapurana	1. Vedanatha Desika
B. Dharma Parikshe	2. Madhava

C. Parasara Smriti Vyakhya	3. Uritta Vilasa
D. Yadavabhyudayam	4. Madhavacharya

Choose the correct option from the codes given below:

(a) A-1, B-2, C-3, D-4
(b) A-2, B-4, C-3, D-1
(c) A-2, B-3, C-4, D-1
(d) A-1, B-3, C-4, D-2

40. Which of the following pairs are correctly matched?

1. Upanishad	Deals with knowledge and Spirituality
2. Aranyaka	Ritualistic and Sacrificial Action
3. Atharva Veda	Atharvangirasa
4. Mahakavya	Bhagwad and Vishnu Purana
5. Yajur Veda	Vajasaneyi and Taittiriya Samhita

Select the correct answer using the code given below:

(a) 1, 2, and 3 only (b) 1, 4 and 5 only
(c) 2, 3, 4 and 5 only (d) 1, 2, 3 and 5 only

41. With reference to the "Buddhist literature", consider the following statements:

1. The Sutta Pitakas are the texts that are supposed to contain what the Buddha himself said.
2. The Vinaya Pitakas contains rules for monks and nuns of the monastic order (Sangha).
3. Dipavamsa and the Mahavamsa, are the canonical text written in Pali, both contain historical cum mythical account of the Buddha's life, Buddhist councils, Ashoka, and arrival of Buddhism to Sri Lanka.
4. Milindapanho is a collection of Dialogue between the King Meander and Buddhist monk Nagasena

Which of the above statement/s is/are correct?

(a) 1 and 2 only (b) 1 and 3 only
(c) 2, 3 and 4 only (d) 1, 2 and 4 only

42. Which of the following statements about "Jaina literature" is incorrect?

1. Complication of the entire canonical literature of Jainism is traditionally believed to have taken place at a council held in Vallabhi in Gujarat
2. The Jaina Agamas were written in Ardha-magadhi Pali language.

Select the correct option using the code given below:

(a) 1 only (b) 2 only
(c) Both 1 and 2 (d) Neither 1 nor 2

43. Which of the following is statement about "Zoroastrian literature" is incorrect?

(a) The most important text of Zoroastrianism is Avesta dealing with religious belief, practice and instruction.
(b) The Avesta is written in the Avestan language which is currently spoken in the region of Northern Iran at the foothill of Albruz Moountains.
(c) Yasna, Gathas, Visperad, Yashts, Siroza, Nyayeshes are the parts of the Avesta.
(d) Denkard is regarded as the Encyclopedia of the Zoroastrianism. However, it does not have a divine status.

44. Consider the following statements:

1. Adi Granth was compiled by Bhai Gurdas under the aegis of the last guru, Guru Arjan Dev.
2. Guru Granth Sahib contains the teachings of the Sikh Gurus only.
3. Adi Granth is regarded as the Eleventh and final spiritual authority of the Sikhs.
4. Janamsakhis contain the mythological stories of the first guru Guru Nanak.

Which of the above statement/s is/are incorrect?

(a) 1 and 4 only (b) 1, 2 and 3 only
(c) 2, 3 and 4 only (d) 1, 2 and 4 only

45. Consider the following:

1. To them the path to salvation lay in meditation on the formless Ultimate Reality and the realisation of oneness with it.
2. They advocated intense training of the body and mind.
3. They became particularly popular among high castes.

Which of the above statement/s is/are correct regarding Nathpanthis, Siddhas and Yogis?

(a) 2 and 3 only (b) 3 only
(c) 1 and 2 only (d) 1, 2 and 3

46. Consider the following statements about Kabir:

1. His teachings were based on a complete, indeed vehement, rejection of the major religious traditions
2. He openly ridiculed all forms of external worship of only Brahmanical Hinduism.
3. He believed in a formless Supreme God.

Which of the above statement/s is/are correct?

(a) 2 and 3 only (b) 1 and 3 only
(c) 1 only (d) 1 and 2 only

47. Consider the following statements regarding Tamil Literature

1. Agam and Puram are two major schools of Sangam Literature.
2. Tamil saint Thiruvallurar had contributed the 'Kural' to the Sangam literature.

Which of the above statement/s is/are correct?

(a) 1 only (b) 2 only
(c) Both 1 and 2 (d) Neither 1 nor 2

48. Which of the following books is not written by any ruler?

1. Tarikh-e-Firuz Shahi.
2. Tuzuk-i-Babari
3. Humayunnama
4. Akbarnama
5. Padshahnama

Select the correct option using the codes given below:

(a) 1, 2 and 4 only (b) 1, 2 and 3 only
(c) 2, 3, 4 and 5 only (d) 1, 3, 4 and 5 only

49. Consider the following pairs regarding Modern literature:

1. Bharatendu Harishchandra – Andher Nagari
2. Bankim Chandra Chatterjee – Anand Math
3. Waris Shah – Heer-Ranjha

Which of the above pairs is/are correctly matched?

(a) 1 and 2 only (b) 1 and 3 only
(c) 2 and 3 only (d) 1, 2 and 3

50. Consider the following statements regarding development of science and technology in ancient India:

1. Atharva Veda mentioned cure for diseases like diarrhoea, sores, cough, leprosy, fever and seizure.
2. Takshila and Varanasi emerged as the centres for medicinal learning.
3. Indian philosophers conceived the idea of splitting an atom.

Which of the above statement/s is/are correct?

(a) 1 and 2 only (b) 1 and 3 only
(c) 2 and 3 only (d) 1, 2 and 3

51. Consider the following statements regarding Ancient India:

1. Yukti Kalpa Taru book deals with the various techniques used in ship building during ancient times.
2. The present form of Judo and karate originated from Kalaripayat, an ancient martial arts form.

Which of the above statement/s is/are correct?

(a) 1 only (b) 2 only
(c) Both 1 and 2 (d) Neither 1 nor 2

52. Consider the following statements:

1. Mahabhasya of Sudraka is a defence of grammarian Panini.
2. Mricchakatika is a drama by Patanjali that contains characters from all stratas of society.

Which of the above statement/s is/are correct?

(a) 1 only (b) 2 only
(c) Both 1 and 2 (d) Neither 1 nor 2

53. Consider the following statements regarding Nalanda University:

1. Nalanda was an acclaimed Mahavihara in the ancient kingdom of Magadha.
2. It flourished under the patronage of Gupta rulers.
3. It lost its importance under the Pala Dynasty.

Which of the above statement/s is/are correct?

(a) 2 only (b) 1 and 2 only
(c) 3 only (d) 1 and 3 only

54. Consider the following statements:

1. Santhali has become the first Indian tribal language to get a Wikipedia edition in its own script.
2. All the classical languages of India are included in the eighth schedule of the constitution.

Which of the above statement is/are correct?

(a) 1 only (b) 2 only
(c) Both 1 and 2 (d) Neither 1 nor 2

55. Consider the following statements:

1. Sulvasutra written by Baudhayana is one of the earliest texts on mathematics.
2. Apastamba, a 2nd century BC text deals with practical arithmetic.
3. Brahmgupta in his book Brahmasputa Siddhantika mentioned zero for the first time as a number.
4. Goladhyaya is one of the section of Siddhanta Shiromani written by Bhaskaracharya.

Which of the above statement/s is/are incorrect?

(a) 1 only (b) 2 only
(c) 3 and 4 only (d) None of the above

56. Consider the following statements:

1. Uttarayana and Dakshinayana are two halves of lunar Hindu calendar.
2. Vikram Samvat is a solar calendar based on ancient Hindu calendar.

Which of the above statement/s is/are correct?

(a) 1 only (b) 2 only
(c) Both 1 and 2 (d) Neither 1 nor 2

57. Which one of the following scientists and their works is correctly matched?

(a) Aryabhatta calculated the value of 'Pi'.
(b) Kanada gave the atomic theory.
(c) Charak gave the concepts of plastic surgery and cataract operation.
(d) Bhaskaracharya introduced negative numbers and operations on zero into mathematics.

58. Consider the following statements regarding Indian notational system during ancient India:

1. Indian notational system was adopted by Greeks from Indians who spread it to the western world.
2. Indian numerals are called Arabic in English, but Arabs themselves called their numerals hindsa.
3. Indian numerals are found on the inscriptions of Indus Valley Civilisation.

Which of the above statement/s is/are correct?

(a) 1 only (b) 2 only
(c) 1 and 3 only (d) 2 and 3 only

59. Which of the following statements is incorrect regarding ancient India?

(a) Avadana literature was related to Mahayana Buddhism.

(b) Saundarananda was written in Pali by Ashvaghosha.

(c) The oldest example of kavya style belongs to the 2nd century AD was found in Junagarh.

(d) Vatsyayana's Kamasutra shows the tableau of urban life.

60. Consider the following information regarding a literary work:

1. The play narrates the ascent of the king Chandragupta Maurya to power in Northern India with the aid of Chanakya.
2. It is a great piece of work written by Vishakhadatta.

Which piece of literary work is being referred to here?

(a) Rajatarangini (b) Mudrarakshasha
(c) Arthashashtra (d) Meghdoot

61. Which of the following pairs are correctly matched?

1. Brihatasamhita: Varahmihira
2. Romaka Sidhanta: Aryabhatta
3. Brahmasphuta-siddhant: Brahmagupta

Select the correct option using the codes given below:

(a) 1 and 2 only (b) 2 and 3 only
(c) 1 and 3 only (d) 1, 2 and 3

62. Which of the following statement/s is/are incorrect?

1. Arthashastra was finally compiled during Chandragupta's reign.
2. Palibothra was a term used for wooden wall in the Mauryan Age.

Select the correct option using the codes given below:

(a) 1 only (b) 2 only
(c) Both 1 and 2 (d) Neither 1 nor 2

63. Match the following:

List-I	List-II
A. Vikramorvasiya	1. Bhavabhuti
B. Uttara Ramacharitam	2. Bhasa
C. Devi Chandraguptam	3. Kalidasa
D. Swapnavasavadatta	4. Vishakhdutta

Select the correct answer using the code given below:

	A	B	C	D
(a)	1	3	2	4
(b)	3	1	4	2
(c)	1	4	3	2
(d)	4	2	3	1

64. Languages in India can be classified into major subgroups. Consider the following statements in this regard:

1. The majority of languages spoken in India belong to the Indo-Aryan group.
2. Sikkimese and the Assamese belong to the Sino-Tibetan group of languages.
3. Austric group of languages are older than Indo-Aryan languages.

Which of the above statements is/are correct?

(a) 1 and 3 only (b) 1 only
(c) 2 and 3 only (d) 1, 2 and 3

65. Consider the following statements regarding the Hindi Language:

1. It has its direct origin in the Prakrit language.
2. It got its biggest boost from the Bhakti movement.
3. Prithviraj Raso was the first Hindi book.

Which of the above statements is/are incorrect?

(a) 1 only (b) 1 and 2 only
(c) 2 and 3 only (d) None of the above

66. Consider the following statements regarding the development of Sanskrit language:

1. Ashvagosha's Buddhacharita was written in Sanskrit.
2. Panini's Asthadhyayi is the oldest book related to Sanskrit grammar.

Which of the above statements is/are correct?

(a) 1 only (b) 2 only
(c) Both 1 and 2 (d) Neither 1 nor 2

67. Consider the following pairs:

1. Nagarjuna– Chemistry
2. Bhasakaracharya – Mathematics
3. Narayan Pandit – Medicine

Which of the above pairs is/are correctly matched?

(a) 1 and 2 only (b) 2 and 3 only
(c) 1 only (d) 1, 2 and 3

68. Consider the following statements regarding Sangam Literature:

1. It is called as Sangam literature as assemblies were organised where poets, bards, and writers would flock from various parts of South India.
2. These assemblies were organised by the Kingdom of Pandya.

Which of the above statements is/are correct?

(a) 1 only (b) 2 only
(c) Both 1 and 2 (d) Neither 1 nor 2

69. With reference to the Buddhist Literature 'Tripitakas', consider the following statements:

1. The Sutta Pitaka covers the rules and regulations, which should be followed by the Buddhist monks.
2. The Abhidhamma Pitaka concentrates on the philosophy and metaphysics.

Which of the above statements is/are correct?

(a) 1 only (b) 2 only
(c) Both 1 and 2 (d) Neither 1 nor 2

70. Consider the given statements with reference to Vinaya Pitaka:

1. It is the collection of the Buddha's sermons on matters of doctrine and ethics.
2. It was recited by Upali, a Buddha disciple.
3. It was compiled at the first Buddhist Council at Rajgriha.

Which of the above statements is/are correct?

(a) 1 and 2 only (b) 2 only
(c) 1 and 3 only (d) 2 and 3 only

71. Match the following:

Vedas	Characteristic
A. Rigveda	1. Collection of sacrificial formulae
B. Samveda	2. Collection of hymns
C. Yajurveda	3. Collection of spells and charms
D. Atharvaveda	4. Collection of songs

Select the correct answer using the code given below:

	A	B	C	D
(a)	1	3	4	2
(b)	4	1	2	3
(c)	2	4	1	3
(d)	3	2	4	1

72. Match the following:

Terminology	Feature
A. Vishti	1. Book on astronomy
B. Kumaramatyas	2. Part of provincial and local administration system
C. Vishayas	3. Important officers in the Gupta empire
D. Romaka Sidhanta	4. Forced labour

Select the correct answer using the code given below:

	A	B	C	D
(a)	4	2	3	1
(b)	2	4	1	3
(c)	4	3	2	1
(d)	3	4	1	2

73. The Gupta period is remarkable for the production of literary works. In this context, consider the following statements:

1. Bhasa was the author of a drama called Dradiracharudatta.
2. Amarakosha was compiled by Amarasimha.

Which of the above statements is/are correct?

(a) 1 only (b) 2 only
(c) Both 1 and 2 (d) Neither 1 nor 2

74. Which of the following statements regarding Harappan Civilisation is/are correct?

1. Harappans were both phallus and animal worshipers.
2. Harappan script is largely pictographic which has not been deciphered yet.

Select the correct answer using the code given below:

(a) 1 only (b) 2 only
(c) Both 1 and 2 (d) Neither 1 nor 2

75. Match the following:

Books	Writers
A. Malavikagnimitram	1. Bilhana
B. Mudrarakshasha	2. Banabhatta
C. Vikramankadevacharita	3. Kalidasa
D. Harshacharita	4. Vishakha datta

Select the correct answer using the code given below:

	A	B	C	D
(a)	2	3	4	1
(b)	1	4	3	2
(c)	3	4	1	2
(d)	4	1	3	2

76. Match the following literatures related to the Delhi Sultanate period with their Authors:

List I	List II
A. Kitab-ul-Hind	1. Alberuni
B. Khazain-ul-Futuh	2. Amir Khusrau
C. Tarikh-i-Firoz Shahi	3. Barani
D. Tabaqat-i-Nasari	4. Minhaj-us-Siraj

Select the correct answer using the code given below:

	A	B	C	D
(a)	1	2	3	4
(b)	3	4	1	2
(c)	1	3	2	4
(d)	4	2	3	1

77. Arthashastra is considered as one of the most reliable literary source of ancient India. In this context, consider the following statements:

1. It is a treatise on statecraft and economic policy written by Vishnugupta.
2. It consists of 7 books dealing with both internal administration and interstate relations during the Mauryan age.
3. It is written in Prakrit language.
4. The manuscript of Arthashastra was first discovered and studied by R. Shama Shastri.

Which of the above statements are correct?

(a) 1 and 3 only (b) 2 and 3 only
(c) 1 and 4 only (d) 2 and 4 only

78. Which of the following correctly describes the findings of Megasthenes's Indica?

1. There were no slaves in India during the Gupta period.

2. The Pandyas were first mentioned by Megasthenes.
3. The king was at the head of the government and assisted by a council of ministers.
4. The administration of the armed forces was carried on by a board of thirty officers divided into six committees.

Select the correct answer using the code given below:

(a) 1 only (b) 3 and 4 only
(c) 2, 3 and 4 only (d) 1, 2, 3 and 4

79. Which of the following pairs are correctly matched?

Famous Book	Author
1. Shah Jahan Nama	- Inayat Khan
2. Ain-i-Akbari	- Jahangir
3. Humayunnama	- Gulbadan Begam
4. Tuzuk-i-Jahangiri	- Abul Fazl

Select the correct answer using the code given below:

(a) 1 and 3 only (b) 1 and 2 only
(c) 2 and 4 only (d) 3 and 4 only

80. Consider the following statements regarding the Vedic literature:

1. Sama Veda contains magic spells to ward off the evil spirits.
2. Yajur Veda is related to sacrifices made for god.
3. Rig Veda is included in UNESCO list of World Human Heritage literature.

Which of the above statements is/are correct?

(a) 1 and 2 only (b) 2 and 3 only
(c) 1 and 3 only (d) 1, 2 and 3

81. Which of the following statements is/are correct about the works of Bhaskara II?

1. Siddhanta Shiromani and Ganitasarasangraha are the main works of Bhaskara II.
2. While Lilavati discusses concept of zero, Bijaganita deals with arithmetic.

Select the correct answer using the code given below:

(a) 1 only (b) 2 only
(c) Both 1and 2 (d) Neither 1 nor 2

82. Consider the following statements regarding the Later Vedic age/texts:

1. Term Janapada was used for the first time during this age.
2. Increase in the proliferation of sedentary agricultural settlements.
3. Aitareya Brahmana has described the eastward journey of Videgha Mathava from the banks of Sarasvati to the Sadanira river.

Which of the above statements is/are correct?

(a) 1 and 2 only (b) 2 only
(c) 3 only (d) 1,2 and 3

83. With reference to 'Badshah Nama', consider the following statements:

1. It was written by Abdul Hamid Lahori.
2. It gives detailed account of reign of Mughal emperor Jahangir.

Which of the above statements is/are correct?

(a) 1 only (b) 2 only
(c) Both 1 and 2 (d) Neither 1 nor 2

84. What is Nastaliq?

(a) It is a calligraphic style with long horizontal strokes.
(b) It was a form of record-keeping in Mughal court.
(c) It was a form of tax paid by the Hindus during Mughal period.
(d) It was a style of dome-making during Mughal period.

85. Consider the following statements:

1. Harappan script is regarded as pictographic.
2. The Harappan script was boustrophedon, written from left to right and right to left in alternate lines.

Which of the above statements is/are correct?

(a) 1 only (b) 2 only
(c) Both 1 and 2 (d) Neither 1 nor 2

86. Which among the following anthologies contains 'Four Thousand Sacred Compositions'?

(a) Tevaram
(b) Nalayira Divyaprabandham
(c) Tirumurai
(d) Shunya Sampadane

87. The term 'Pallichchhandam' mentioned in chola inscriptions refers to:

(a) Land gifted to Brahmanas
(b) Land gifted to temples
(c) Land of non-Brahamana peasant proprietors
(d) Land donated to Jain institutions

88. It a descriptive linguistic treatise which covered the whole of Sanskrit language's grammar (including for the Vedic part) and also word formation rules in "sutra" format.

Which among the following literary work has been discussed in above passage?

(a) Nyaya Sutra (b) Amarakosha
(c) Astadhyayi (d) Rajatarangini

89. Consider the following statements regarding the Ain-i-Akbari of Abul Fazl:

1. The book deals with secular matters such as fiscal and revenue administration of the empire but remained silent on religious traditions of the people.
2. It is an extraordinary document because it hardly shows any mathematical errors in revenue collections.

Which of the above statements is/are incorrect?

(a) 1 only (b) 2 only
(c) Both 1 and 2 (d) Neither 1 nor 2

90. The term 'Karnataka Samrajyamu' is used to describe which kingdom of Medieval India?

(a) Hoysala (b) Chalukya
(c) Yadava (d) Vijaynagara

91. With reference to Alamgir Nama, consider the following statements:

1. It gives the account of Auragzeb's reign.
2. It was compiled by Muhammad Kazim.

Which of the above statements is/are incorrect?

(a) 1 only (b) 2 only
(c) Both 1 and 2 (d) Neither 1 nor 2

92. Which of the following statements regarding Consider the following pairs:

1. Abhijnana Shakuntalam - Vishakhadatta
2. Mudrarakshasha - Kalhana
3. Rajatarangini - Bilhana

Which of the above pairs is/are correctly matched?

(a) 1 only (b) 2 and 3 only
(c) 3 only (d) None of the above

93. With reference to Sangam literature, consider the following pairs:

1. Silappathikaram – Sittalai Sattanar
2. Manimegalai – Elango Adigal
3. Tolkappiyam – Tolkappiyar

Which of the above pairs is/are correctly matched?

(a) 3 only (b) 1 and 2 only
(c) 2 only (d) 1, 2 and 3

94. Match the following:

Upanishads	Features
A. Aitareya Upanishad	1. Contains Satyameva Jayate
B. Chandogya Upanishad	2. The story of Nachiketa and Yama
C. Katha Upanishad	3. Deals with rhythm and chanting of Mantras
D. Mundaka Upanishad	4. Talks about the creation of Atman (Soul) and Consciousness

Select the correct answer using the code given below:

	A	B	C	D
(a)	4	3	2	1
(b)	3	4	1	2
(c)	2	1	4	3
(d)	1	2	3	4

95. Consider the following statements regarding the development of the Sanskrit language:

1. Ashvagosha's Buddhacharita was written in Sanskrit.
2. Panini's Asthadhyayi is the oldest book related to Sanskrit grammar.

Which of the above statements is/are correct?

(a) 1 only (b) 2 only
(c) Both 1 and 2 (d) Neither 1 nor 2

SOLUTIONS

1. Correct Option: (d)

Explanation:

- **Statement 1 is correct:** Two scientists working at The Institute of Mathematical Sciences, Chennai, (IMSc) have studied the Indus script and calculated that it must flow from right to left.
- **Statement 2 is correct:** Large scale use of Burnt Bricks and absence of Stone Buildings.
- **Statement 3 is correct:** Seated male sculpture, or "Priest King" from Mohenjo-daro. Fillet or ribbon headband with circular inlay ornament on the forehead and similar but smaller ornament on the right upper arm. The two ends of the fillet fall along the back and though the hair is carefully combed towards the back of the head, no bun is present. The flat back of the head may have held a separately carved bun as is traditional on the other seated figures, or it could have held a more elaborate horn and plumed headdress.
- **Statement 4 is Incorrect:** Most of the seals were made of Steatite Stone.

2. Correct Option: (d)

Supplementary Notes:

Puranas

- The word Purana means 'that which renews the old' and is almost always mentioned along with Itihasa.
- Statement 1 is correct: It contains the stories of the kings, heroes, sages, and demigods, but it focuses on the divine Hindu trimurti or trinity/three Gods: Brahma, Vishnu and Mahesh.
- **Statement 2 is correct:** The Puranas also narrate the incidents of various influential kings, their supremacy as well as the rivalry between princely clans.
- These are ancient Indian mythological texts, which consist of the narrative stories about the creation of the universe and illustrate its history till the supposed destruction of the universe.
- There are 18 major Puranas (Mahapuranas) and each gives prominence to a particular deity and expound on the philosophical and religious concepts related to them. Some of the more prominent and well-known Puranas are Bhagvata, Brahma, Vayu, Agni, Garuda, Padma, Vishnu and Matsya.
- **Statement 3 is correct:** These contain anecdotes about the social, cultural and religious life of post-Vedic India and provide the historians with critical information about the geography, history and the dynastic genealogies.

3. **Correct Option: (a)**

Supplementary Notes:

Harappan culture:

- **Statement 2 is correct:** Harappan script is not alphabetical but mainly pictographic. This script has not been deciphered yet, so not much information is available about the social life, customs etc.
- **Statement 1 is incorrect:** The main features of town planning in Harappan culture were usage of burnt bricks, well planned straight roads and a system of drainage. The Egyptian used dries bricks.
- The practice of burying the dead.
- Houses with kitchens and wells, tanks or water reservoirs.
- Presence of wheel-made pottery.
- A fortified citadel at most of the cities. The number of the citadels varies.
- **Statement 3 is correct:** Harappan did not use metal money; instead trade was through barter system. Use of standard weights and measurement throughout the civilisation.

4. **Correct Option: (b)**

Supplementary Notes:

Indian Literature

- **Option (b) is correct:** Rig Veda – Atharvaveda – Vedangas – Natyashashtra
- **Rigveda:** It is an ancient Indian collection of Vedic Sanskrit hymns. It is one of the four canonical sacred texts of Hinduism known as the Vedas. The text is a collection of 1,028 hymns and 10,600 verses, organized into ten books (Mandalas). The Rigveda was composed in the northwestern region of the Indian subcontinent, most likely between c. 1500 and 1200 BCE.
- **Atharva Veda:** It is the 'knowledge storehouse of atharvas' as, the procedures for everyday life". The text is the fourth Veda, but has been a late addition to the Vedic scriptures of Hinduism. The Atharvaveda was likely compiled as about 1200 BCE - 1000 BCE.
- **Vedanga:** Six technical subjects related to the Vedas are traditionally known as Vedanga "limbs of the Veda". The Vedangas likely developed towards the end of the Vedic period, around or after the middle of the 1st millennium BCE.
- **Natyasastra:** Some post-Vedic texts, including the Mahabharata, the Natyasastra and certain Puranas, refer to themselves as the "fifth Veda". Its first complete compilation is dated to between 200 BCE and 200 CE.

5. **Correct Option: (d)**

Supplementary Notes:

Buddhist Literature

- **Tripitaka:** Tripitaka or Three Baskets is a traditional term used for various Buddhist scriptures. It is known as Pali Canon in English. The three pitakas are Sutta Pitaka, Vinaya Pitaka and Abhidhamma Pitaka
- **Statement 1 is correct:** Suttapitaka (Pali: "Basket of Discourse") is extensive body of texts constituting the basic doctrinal section of the Buddhist canon. It consists of more than 10,000 Suttas (discourses) delivered by the Buddha and his close disciples during and shortly after the Buddha's forty-five year teaching career, as well as many additional verses by other members of the Sangha.This also deals with the first Buddhist council which was held shortly after Buddha's death, dated by the majority of recent scholars around 400 BC
- **Statement 2 is correct:** The Vinaya Pitaka, is the textual framework upon which the monastic community (Sangha) is built. It includes not only the rules governing the life of every Theravada bhikkhu (monk) and bhikkhuni (nun) but also a host of procedures and conventions of etiquette that support harmonious relations, both among the monastics themselves, and between the monastics and their lay supporters, upon whom they depend for all their material needs. It is thus also called as Book of Discipline.
- **Statement 3 is correct:** Abhidhamma pitaka: Abhidhamma pitaka deals with the philosophy and doctrine of Buddhism appearing in the suttas. However, it does not contain the systematic philosophical treatises but a detailed reworking. They represent a development in a rationalistic direction of summaries or numerical lists. The topics dealt with in Abhidhamma books include ethics, psychology, and epistemology.

6. **Correct Option: (d)**

Supplementary Notes:

Narsi Mehta:

- **Pair 4 is Incorrect:** Narsi Mehta: Gujarati
- He hailed from Gujarat where the Bhakti movement had travelled to and then farther off to Kutch and Sind through Rajasthan and Punjab. He was a Vaishnava devotee and sang the praises of Lord Krishna. He is especially revered in Gujarati literature, where he is acclaimed as its Adi Kavi. His bhajan Vaishnav Jan was Mahatma Gandhi's favourite and has become synonymous to him.

Namdev:

- He was a poet-saint from Maharashtra, who is significant to the Varkari sect of Hinduism. He used the Marathi language to convey their beliefs rather than using the traditional Sanskrit language that was essentially used by the Brahmin priests. Namdev was influenced by Vaishnavism, and became widely known in India for his devotional songs set to music (bhajan-kirtans).

Tulsidas:

- He was a realized soul and saint, poet, often called reformer and philosopher from Ramanandi Sampradaya, in the lineage of Jagadguru Ramanandacharya renowned for his devotion to the Lord Shri Rama. Tulsidas wrote several popular works in Sanskrit and Awadhi; he is best known as the author of the epic Ramcharitmanas, a retelling of the Sanskrit Ramayana based on Rama's life in the vernacular Awadhi dialect of Hindi.

Kabir:

- He was a 15th-century Indian mystic poet and saint, whose writings influenced Hinduism's Bhakti movement and his verses are found in Sikhism's scripture Guru Granth Sahib. His early life was in a Muslim family, but he was strongly influenced by his teacher, the Hindu bhakti leader Ramananda. Kabir's poems were in vernacular Hindi, borrowing from various dialects including Avadhi, Braj, Bhojpuri.

7. **Correct Option: (b)**

Supplementary Notes:

- **Option (a) is Incorrect:** Baudhayan calculated the value of 'pi'.
- **Option (c) is Incorrect:** Susruta gave the concepts of plastic surgery and cataracts operation.
- **Option (d) is Incorrect:** Brahmagupta introduced negative numbers and operations on zero into mathematics.

Baudhayan:

- He was the first one ever to arrive at several concepts in Mathematics, which were later rediscovered by the western world. The value of pi was first calculated by him.
- As you know, pi is useful in calculating the area and circumference of a circle. What is known as Pythagoras theorem today is already found in Baudhayan's Sulva Sutra, which was written several years before the age of Pythagoras.

Aryabhatta:

- Aryabhatta was a fifth century mathematician, astronomer, astrologer and physicist. He was a pioneer in the field of mathematics.
- At the age of 23, he wrote Aryabhattiya, which is a summary of mathematics of his time. There are four sections in this scholarly work. In the first section he describes the method of denoting big decimal numbers by alphabets. In the second section, we find difficult questions from topics of modern day Mathematics such as number theory, geometry, trigonometry and Beejganita (algebra). The remaining two sections are on astronomy.
- Aryabhatta showed that zero was not a numeral only but also a symbol and a concept. Discovery of zero enabled Aryabhatta to find out the exact distance between the earth and the moon. The discovery of zero also opened up a new dimension of negative numerals.

Kanad:

- Kanad was a sixth century scientist of Vaisheshika School, one of the six systems of Indian philosophy.
- **Option (b) is correct:** His atomic theory can be a match to any modern atomic theory.
- According to Kanad, material universe is made up of kanas, (anu/atom) which cannot be seen through any human organ. These cannot be further subdivided. Thus, they are indivisible and indestructible.

Charak:

- Charak is considered the father of ancient Indian science of medicine.
- He was the Raj Vaidya (royal doctor) in the court of Kanishka.
- His Charak Samhita is a remarkable book on medicine. It has the description of a large number of diseases and gives methods of identifying their causes as well as the method of their treatment.
- He was the first to talk about digestion, metabolism and immunity as important for health and so medical science.
- In Charak Samhita, more stress has been laid on removing the cause of disease rather than simply treating the illness. Charak also knew the fundamentals of genetics. Don't you find it fascinating that thousands of years back, medical science was at such an advanced stage in India.

Bhaskaracharya:

- Bhaskaracharya was the leading light of 12th century. He was born at Bijapur, Karnataka. He is famous for his book Siddanta Shiromani.
- It is divided into four sections: Lilavati (Arithmetic), Beejaganit (Algebra), Goladhyaya (Sphere) and Grahaganit (mathematics of planets).
- Bhaskara introduced Chakrawat Method or the Cyclic Method to solve algebraic equations. This method was rediscovered six centuries later by European mathematicians, who called it inverse cycle. In the nineteenth century, an Englishman, James Taylor, translated Lilavati and made this great work known to the world.

8. **Correct Option: (a)**

Supplementary Notes:

Dhanvantari

- **Statement 1 is incorrect:** Dhanvantari was the noted physician in the court of Chandragupta Vikramaditya.

Varahamihira

- He was an Indian astronomer, mathematician, and astrologer who lived in Ujjain.
- **Statement 2 is correct:** He is considered to be one of the "Nine Jewels" (Navaratnas) of the court of legendary ruler Yashodharman Vikramaditya of Malwa.
- He made great contributions in the fields of hydrology, geology and ecology. He was one of the first scientists to claim that termites and plants could be the indicators of the presence of underground water.
- He gave a list of six animals and thirty plants, which could indicate the presence of water. Another theory, which has attracted the world of science is the earthquake cloud theory given by Varahmihira in his Brihat Samhita. He has tried to relate earthquakes to the influence of planets, undersea activities, underground water, unusual cloud formation and abnormal behaviour of animals.
- Another field where Varahamihira's contribution is worth mentioning is Jyotish or Astrology. Astrology was given a very high place in ancient India and it has continued even today.

The Unani Tibb System of Medicine

- It flourished in India during the medieval period. Ali-bin-Rabban summarized the whole system of Greek medicine as well as the Indian medical knowledge in the book, Firdausu-Hikmat.
- **Statement 3 is correct:** The Unani medicine system came to India along with the Muslims by about the eleventh century and soon found patronage for its growth.
- Hakim Diya Muhammad compiled a book, Majiny-e-Diyae, incorporating the Arabic, Persian and Ayurvedic medical knowledge.

9. **Correct Option:(c)**

Supplementary Notes:

Literature in Pali and Prakrit:

- Pali and Prakrit were the spoken languages of Indians after the Vedic period. Prakrit in the widest sense of the term was indicative of any language that in any manner deviated from the standard one i.e. Sanskrit. Pali is a combination of various dialects.These were adopted by Buddhist and Jain sects in ancient India as their sacred languages.

Pali:

- **Statement 1 is correct:** Lord Buddha (500 BC) used Pali to give his sermons. This was also the common mans' language to reach the masses. All the Buddhist canonical literature is in Pali which includes Tripitaka (threefold basket) the first basket, Vinaya Pitaka, the second basket, Sutta Pitaka and the third basket, the Abhidhamma Pitaka.
- The Jataka Kathas are non-canonical Buddhist literature in which stories relating to the former births of the Buddha (Bodhi-sattva or the would-be Buddha) are narrated. These stories propagate Buddhist religious doctrines and are available in both Sanskrit and Pali.

Prakrit:

- **Statement 2 is correct:** Like the Buddhist stories, the Jain tales, in general, are didactic in character. They are written in some forms of Prakrit.
- Prakrit is well known for Gathasaptashati (700 verses) by Hala (300 AD), the best example of erotic literature. It is a compilation of 700 verses along with his own contribution of 44 poems. The characteristic of Prakrit poetry is its subtlety; the inner meaning (Hiyaali) is its soul.

Panchatantra:

- **Statement 3 is incorrect:** It is an ancient Indian work of political philosophy, in the form of a collection of interrelated animal fables in Sanskrit verse and prose, arranged within a frame story.
- The surviving work is dated to about 300 BCE, but the fables are likely much more ancient.
- It is likely a Hindu text and based on older oral traditions with "animal fables that are as old as we are able to imagine".

10. **Correct Option: (d)**

Supplementary Notes:

Role of Christian Missionaries

- **Statement 2 is correct:** The contribution of the Christian Missionaries in the development of Indian literature was no less significant. They published dictionaries and grammar in several local languages. These books helped these missionaries as much as they helped the writers in the local languages.
- **Statement 1 is correct:** Lithographic printing press: were introduced in India in the beginning of the nineteenth century. Missionaries established them to propagate the practice of their religion and convent Indians into Christian fold. They had established these presses for printing literature in local languages for the benefit of the new, and would-be converts.
- **Statement 3 is correct:** The establishment of Schools and Colleges by the Missionaries: Besides English, the missionaries also taught the local languages. Perhaps

their aim was to spread Christianity but they also produced a newly educated class, who had a desire to read their literature. Thus, the role of missionaries cannot be ignored while writing the history of Indian languages and literature.

11. **Correct Option: (c)**

Supplementary Notes:

National Mission on Manuscripts

- **Statement 1 is correct:** The National Mission for Manuscripts (NMM) was established in the year 2003 by the Ministry of Culture to document, preserve and digitize the vast manuscript wealth of India.
- These documented repository will be made available to researcher and scholars (not to everyone) through a Trusted Digital Repository. The ultimate object of the Mission is to establish a Digital Manuscripts Repository in which researchers and scholars can view and consult the manuscripts to understand our past in its totality.
- **Statement 2 is incorrect:** Project Mausam is a project which aims to explore the Indian Ocean 'world'–by collecting archaeological and historical research and document the diversity of cultural, commercial and religious interactions in the Indian Ocean.
- **Statement 3 is correct:** It also aims to promote research on themes related to the study of Maritime Routes. This is also an initiative of Ministry of Culture to be implemented by the Archaeological Survey of India. It is largely to enhance India's soft power as a counter to China's One Belt One Road initiative.

12. **Correct Option: (c)**

Supplementary Notes:

- **Statement 1 is incorrect:** Pali literature is concerned mainly with Theravada Buddhism, of which Pali is the traditional language. The earliest and most important Pali literature constitutes the Pali Canon, the scriptures of Theravada school.
- **Statement 2 is correct:** Sanskrit is a language of ancient India with a documented history of about 3,500 years.
- **Statement 3 is correct:** Pali is a Middle Indo-Aryan language native to the Indian subcontinent. It is widely studied because it is the language of the Pali Canon or Tipiṭaka, and is the sacred language of some religious texts of Hinduism and all texts of Theravada Buddhism. The earliest archaeological evidence of the existence of canonical Pali comes from Pyu city-states inscriptions found in Burma dated to the mid 5th to mid 6th century CE.

13. **Correct Option: (a)**

Supplementary Notes:

Upanishads

- The Upanishads, part of the Vedas, are ancient Sanskrit texts that contain some of the central philosophical concepts and ideas of Hinduism, some of which are shared with religious traditions like Buddhism and Jainism.
- Upanishads numbering 108 are also known as Vedanta. They are part of every Veda.
- Katha Upanishad deals with the concept of death in terms of dialogues between Nachiketa , his father and the Lord of Death, Yama.
- **Option (a) is correct:** Chandogya Upanishad, talks about the childhood of lord Krishna for the first time.
- Kena Upanishad talks about Uma or Parvati.
- Jabala Upanishad – Varnasharma dharmas were mentioned in this.

14. **Correct Option: (c)**

Supplementary Notes:

Satavahana Dynasty

- **Option (c) is correct:** Hala, 17th ruler Satavahana Dynasty, was the author of 'Gathasaptasati' or, Sattasai in Prakrit. The text contains the love lures. Gathasaptasati is an ancient collection of Indian poems in Prakrit language. The poems are about love and love's joy. They are written as frank monologues usually by a married woman, or an unmarried girl. They often express her unrequited feelings and longings to her friend, mother or another relative, lover, husband or to herself. Many poems are notable for describing unmarried girls daring for secret rendezvous to meet boys in ancient India, or about marital problems with husbands who remains emotionally a stranger to his wife and bosses over her, while trying to have affairs with other women.

15. **Correct Option: (b)**

Supplementary Notes:

Vedas

- Religious literature - 4 Vedas, 108 Brahamanas, Aranyakas, 108 Upanishads, 6 Vedangas.
- **Statement 2 is correct:** Rigveda: It is first text in the world literature and first text in Indo-European language. Its main theme is the prayer addressed to different Gods.
- **Statements 4 is incorrect:** Rigveda is the most important Veda as Gayatri mantra is a part of it (not Samaveda).
- **Statement 3 is incorrect:** Sama Veda: It is full of ragas or tunes. it is first text to deal with Indian music – Sangeethashastra. The priest who recites Samaveda is known as Udgata.
- **Yajur Veda:** It deals with rituals and ceremonies. This text is composed in prose.
- The priest who recites Yajurveda is known as Adhvaryu.

- **Statement 1 is correct:** Atharva Veda: It was composed entirely by Non-Aryans. Its themes include witchcraft, sorcery and invoking evil spirits. No Brahmins ever recites Atharva Veda.

16. **Correct Option: (c)**

Supplementary Notes:

Vedas

- **Statement 1 is correct:** Yajur Veda – It is the Veda of sacrificial formulas consisting of prose mantras.
- Yajur Veda refers to acts of worship such as oblations made into Agni (fire); each mantra that is recited is also accompanied by an action within the sacrifice. There are two major renditions of this Veda known as the Krishna (black) and Shukla (white).
- **Statement 2 is incorrect:** The Rigveda includes more than a thousand hymns, called sukta or well-said.
- The hymns are in the praise of various gods and goddesses. The three gods are especially important are Agni, the god of fire; Indra, a warrior god; and Soma, a plant from which a special drink was prepared.
- The people who composed the hymns described themselves as Aryas and called their opponents Dasa or Dasyus. The Rig Veda was being composed in the north-west of the subcontinent.
- Atharva Veda glorifies the curative powers of herbs and water.
- **Statement 3 is incorrect:** Atharva Veda glorifics the curative powers of herbs and water.

17. **Correct option :(a)**

Supplementary Notes:

Literary Works and Authors

- **Statement 1 is incorrect:** Kalhana's wrote Rajatarangini.
- Jayadeva's Gita Govindam were popular literary works during Rajaput period.
- **Statement 3 is correct:** Somadeva wrote Kathasaritasagar.
- **Statement 4 is correct:** Bhaskaracharya wrote Siddhanta Shiromani, a book on astronomy.

Rajatarangini-Kalhana.

- **Statement 2 is incorrect:** Gita Govindam-Jayadeva.
- **Statement 5 is correct:** Chand Bardai, the court poet of Prithviraj Chauhan, wrote Prithviraj Raso in which he refers to the military exploits of Prithviraj Chauhan.

18. **Correct Option: (a)**

Supplementary Notes:

Ashokan Pillar

- **Option (a) is correct:** The earliest inscriptions are found on the seals of Harappa belonging to about 2500 BC. They have not been deciphered so far. The oldest inscriptions deciphered so far were issued by Ashoka in the third century BC. An Ashokan pillar inscription was found by Firoz Shah Tughlaq in Meerut. He brought it to Delhi and asked the pandits of his empire to decipher it, but they failed to do so. The same difficulty was faced by the British when in the last quarter of the eighteenth century they discovered Ashokan inscriptions. These epigraphs were first deciphered in 1837 by James Prinsep, a civil servant in the employment of the East India Company in Bengal.

19. **Correct Option: (b)**

Supplementary Notes:

Sangam Literature

- Manimekalai by the poet Chithalai Chathanar, is one of The Five Great Epics of Tamil Literature according to later Tamil literary tradition. Manimekalai is a poem in 30 cantos. Its story is a sequel to another of the Five Great Epics, Silappatikaram, and tells the story of the daughter of Kovalan and Madhavi, who became a Buddhist nun and text was first to talk about the development of fine arts and Buddhism in Deep South India. The aim of the author, Seethalai Saathanar was to compare Buddhism favorably with the other prevailing religions in South India in order to propagate Buddhism. He criticizes Hinduism, and exposes the weaknesses of the other contemporary Indian religions, while praising the Buddha's Teaching, the Dharma, as the most perfect religion.

20. **Correct Option: (c)**

Explanation:

- Both statements are correct

Supplementary Notes:

Santhali Language

- By 92nd Constitutional Amendment Act, 2003, Bodo, Maithili, Dogri and Santhali were added to the 8th Schedule of the Indian Constitution.
- It is an Austroasiatic-Munda language spoken mostly by tribals in Odisha.
- 'Santhali' reverberated in Rajya Sabha for the first time in 67 years since its inception when BJD MP Sarojini Hembram spoke in the language of the tribal community Santhals.
- It is the first tribal language that has its own Wikipedia edition in its own script.
- It is written in Ol Chiki script and spoken by 6.4 million people, according to the 2001 census, in India alone and its speakers live mostly in Jharkhand, West Bengal, Odisha and Assam.
- It is also spoken in Bangladesh and Nepal.

Smart Solution:

- Language added by the 92nd amendment to the Indian Constitution are BDMS (Bodo, Dogri, Maithili and Santhali).

21. Correct Option: (d)

Explanation:

- Statement (d) is correct

Supplementary Notes:

Punch Marked Coins:

- It is evident that the first coins were minted in India just before 5th century BC
- The punch marked coins started being used during the times of Mahajanpadas. It is in 500–600 BC, silver became abundantly available, of which most of it came from Afghanistan and Persia as a result of international trade.
- Silver coins were available in three types, namely Tuthatat of Tutha mountain, Gandika from Burma, and Kambu from Afghanistan's Kamboja.
- So a large amount of silver and copper coins as well coins were used during the Mauryan Period. Certain symbols such as the crescent-on-arches, tree-in-railing, and peacock-on-arches have been associated with the Maurya kings.
- As per the Arthashastra, silver coins (with some amount of alloying) called panas and copper coins called mashakas were used during that time.

22. Correct Option: (c)

Explanation:

- Both statements are correct

Supplementary Notes:

Scheduled Languages in India

- There are 22 languages in the Eighth Schedule of Constitution.
- Article 346 says that Hindi in Devanagari script is the official language. However, English is also allowed to be used as official language.
- Hindi written in Devanagari script is to be the official language of the Union.
- But, the form of numerals to be used for the official purposes of the Union has to be the international form of Indian numerals and not the Devanagari form of numerals.
- As per Articles 344(1) and 351 of the Indian Constitution, the eighth schedule includes the recognition of the 22 languages.
- Of these languages, 14 were initially included in the Constitution.
- Subsequently, Sindhi was added in 1967 by 21st constitutional amendment act.
- Konkani, Manipuri and Nepali were added in 1992 by 71st Constitutional Amendment Act; and Bodo, Dogri, Maithili and Santali were added in 2003 by 92nd Constitutional Amendment Act.

23. Correct Option: (c)

Explanation:

- Both statements are correct

Supplementary Notes:

Sangam Polity and Administration

- During the Sangam period hereditary monarchy was the form of government.
- Each of the dynasties of Sangam Age had a royal emblem – tiger for the Cholas, carp/Fish for the Pandyas, and bow for the Cheras.
- The king was assisted by a wide body of officials who were categorised into five councils.
- They were ministers (amaichar), priests (anthanar), envoys (thuthar), military commanders (senapathi), and spies (orrar).
- The military administration was efficiently organized and a regular army was associated with each ruler.
- The chief source of state's income was land revenue while a custom duty was also imposed on foreign trade.
- Major source of fulfilling the royal treasury was the booty captured in wars.
- The roads and highways were maintained and guarded to prevent robbery and smuggling.

Sangam Literature

- The Sangam literature includes Tolkappiyam, Ettutogai, Pattuppattu, Pathinenkilkanakku, and two epics named – Silappathikaram and Manimegalai .
- Tolkappiyam was authored by Tolkappiyar and is considered the earliest of Tamil literary work. Though it is a work on Tamil grammar but it also provides insights on the political and socio-economic conditions of the time.
- Ettutogai (Eight Anthologies) consist of eight works – Aingurunooru, Narrinai, Aganaooru, Purananooru, Kuruntogai, Kalittogai, Paripadal and Padirruppatu.
- The Pattuppattu (Ten Idylls) consists of ten works – Thirumurugarruppadai, Porunararruppadai, Sirupanarruppadai, Perumpanarruppadai, Mullaippattu, Nedunalvadai, Maduraikkanji, Kurinjip-patttu, Pattinappalai and Malai-padukadam.
- Pathinenkilkanakku contains eighteen works about ethics and morals. The most important among these works is Tirukkural authored by Thiruvalluvar, the great Tamil poet and philosopher.

24. Correct Option: (c)

Explanation:

- Both statements are correct

Supplementary Notes:

Vedic Literature

- The Vedic literature had grown in the course of many centuries and was handed down from generation to generation by word of mouth.

- It consists of three successive classes of literary creations. These three classes are:
  - **The Vedas:** A collection of hymns, prayers, charms, litanies and sacrificial formulae.
  - **The Brahmanas:** These are prose texts which contain details about the meaning of Vedic hymns, their applications, stories of their origins, etc. In a way these contain details about rituals and philosophies.
  - **Aranyakas and Upanishads:** These are partly included in the Brahmanas or attached there to, and partly exist as separate works. They embody philosophical meditations of the hermits and ascetics on soul, god, world etc.
- The Brahmanas, the Aranyakas and the Upanishads are attached to one or the other of the four Vedas.

25. Correct Option: (a)

Explanation:

Supplementary Notes:

- The Yoga Sūtras of Patañjali are a collection of 196 Indian sutras (aphorisms) on the theory and practice of yoga. The Yoga Sutras were compiled prior to 400 CE by Sage Patanjali who synthesized and organized knowledge about yoga from older traditions.

26. Correct Option: (c)

Explanation:

Supplementary Notes:

- Three months after Buddha's passing to Maha Parinibbana, his Chief Disciple led 500/1000 Arahat - fully enlightened ones and certified the teaching of Buddha – Dhamma. Among the 84,000 of Dhamma body, 2,000 were came from his disciples.
- Buddha's half brother (same father and their mothers were siblings) retold the teaching and the Arahats approved them. They either heard, presented at that time of the teaching or those individuals were living proof of practicing those Dhamma and became enlightened.
- Those certified teaching were not written down immediately. At that time, the script wasn't invented or fully developed yet.
- The duties of the monk includes memorizing them and teaching back to fellow monks.
- When they were finally written down, there were fewer people with good memory because of famine, disaster, decease, etc. and couldn't afford to lose teaching, and this three baskets full of text writing on palm leaves came out.
- They are called Tipitaka or three baskets or also known as Pali Canon because of having been written in Pali language.

27. Correct Option: (a)

Explanation

- The Tirukkural or shortly the Kural, is a classic Tamil text consisting of 1,330 couplets or Kurals, dealing with the everyday virtues of an individual.
- It is one of the two oldest works now extant in Tamil literature in their entirety, the other being the Tolkappiyam.
- Considered one of the greatest works ever written on ethics and morality, chiefly secular ethics, it is known for its universality and non-denominational nature.
- It was authored by Valluvar, also known in full as Thiruvalluvar. The text has been dated variously from 300 BCE to 5th century CE. The traditional accounts describe it as the last work of the third Sangam, but linguistic analysis suggests a later date of 450 to 500 CE.
- Traditionally praised as "the Universal Veda" and "the Universal Code of Conduct," the Kural emphasizes on the vital principles of non-violence, moral vegetarianism or veganism, human brotherhood, absence of desires, path of righteousness and truth, and so forth, besides covering a wide range of subjects such as moral codes of rulers, friendship, agriculture, knowledge and wisdom, sobriety, love, and domestic life.
- The work is commonly quoted in vegetarian conferences, both in India and abroad.
- The Kural is one of the most important works in the Tamil language and is often called "the masterpiece of Tamil Literature.
- This is reflected in some of the other names by which the text is given by, such as the Work of Three Books, Modern Veda, Divine Work, Faultless Word, and Tamil Veda.

28. Correct Option: (a)

Supplementary Notes:

- The inscriptions are thought to have been mostly written from right to left, but sometimes follow boustrophedonic style.
- A written pictographic language also existed as is evidenced by the Indus scripts written on clay seals. We see rectangular Harappan seals in the Indus region, round Harappan seals in Bahrain and one combination Harappan script/Akkadian illustration cylinder seal in Mesopotamia, which is further evidence of intercultural contact.
- The scripts appeared as early as c. 3300-2800 BC in the Ravi Phase at Harappa. We can assume with some degree of confdence that these were used in trade to mark ownership. However, the Indus seals are not extensive, there is no Rosetta stone-like object and it is different from any other known languages.

- Recent studies suggest that the Harappan script consists of about 400 signs and that it was written from right to left. However, the script has not been deciphered as yet. We do not know the language they spoke, though scholars believe that they spoke "Brahui", a dialect used by Baluchi people in Pakistan today. However further research alone can unveil the mystery and enable us to know more about the Harappan script.

29. Correct Option: (b)

Supplementary Notes:

- The Vedas: A collection of hymns, prayers, charms, litanies and sacrificial formulae. There are four Vedas, namely:
- Rig Veda – a collection of hymns
- Sam Veda – a collection of songs mostly taken from Rig Veda
- Yajur Veda – a collection of sacrificial formulae
- Atharva Veda - a collection of spells and charms
- The Vedas formed the earliest segment of Vedic literature and amongst the Vedas, Rig Veda is the oldest.

30. Correct Option: (a)

Explanation

- The national calendar of India is based on the Saka Calendar which has been adopted as the official civil calendar besides the Gregorian calendar.
- The Saka era is believed to have been founded by King Shalivahana of the Shatavahana Dynasty. The fact that the Saka era marks the commemoration of King Shalivahana's major military victories has been based on popular legends but hardly has any historical fact. The historical consensus is that it began at the 78th year of the Common Era. Earliest evidence of association between Shalivahana and the Saka era was substantiated by the 1222 CE Kannada work Udbhatakavya by Somaraja. Works like the Muhurta-Martanda suggests that the beginning of Saka Era is calculated from the birth of Shalivahana, while the Kalpa Pradipa written in 1300 CE suggests that it marks the victory of Shalivahana over Vikramaditya.

Structure

- The Saka Calender is based on luni-solar reckoning of time. The calendar consists of 365 days and 12 months like the normal Gregorian calendar. Chaitra is the first month of the year beginning on March 22 which is the day after the Spring Equinox. During leap years, the starting day of Chaitra corresponds with March 21.
- The names of the months in Saka Calendar are:
  - Chhaitra (March 21–April 20)
  - Vaishakha (April 21–May 21)
  - Jyeshtha (May 22–June 21)
  - Ashadha (June 22–July 22)
  - Shravana (July 23–August 22)
  - Bhaadra (August 22–September 22)
  - Ashwin (September 23–October 22)
  - Kartika (October 23–November 21)
  - Agrahayana (November 22–December 21)
  - Pausha (December 22–January 20)
  - Magha (January 21–February 19) and
  - Phalguna (February 20–March 20/21)
- The month of Chaitra has generally 30 days but there are 31 days during leap years. The months of Vaishakha, Jyeshtha, Ashadha, Shravana, Bhaadra, have 31 days while the rest have 30 days. This is done by taking into account the ellipticity of earth's orbit around the sun. To convert years in AD to Saka years, 78 must be subtracted for a date till December 31 and 79 for dates later to that.

31. Correct Option: (d)

Supplementary Notes:

- The Brahmanas are primarily a digest incorporating myths, legends, and the exposition of rituals in the Vedas and in some cases philosophy. Each Vedic shakha (school) has its own Brahmana, many of which have been lost.
- A total of 19 Brahmanas are extant at least in their entirety: two associated with the Rigveda, six with the Yajurveda, ten with the Samaveda and one with the Atharvaveda. Additionally, there are a handful of fragmentarily preserved texts. They vary greatly in length; the edition of the Shatapatha Brahmana fills five volumes of the Sacred Books of the East.

32. Correct Option: (c)

Explanation

- Tolkappiyam is the earliest available work in Tamil. It deals with the Tamil language. Having three sections, the first two deal with language (linguistics) and the third about the subject matters referred to in Tamil literature, the behavior of the Tamils. Each section has been divided into nine chapters.
- The author of the work is Tolkappiyar (Tholkaappiyar). He lived in the fifth century BC according to reliable sources based on Ainthiram, a school of Sanskrit grammar before Panini. In course of time, possibly before the fourth century AD, some layers have been inserted in between the work which can be identified in intensive study.

33. Correct Option: (c)

Supplementary Notes:

- The Gupta period marked the brilliant phase of Indian literature whether in poetry, drama, grammar or prose.

- The wonderful corpus of literature is the visible product of the system of education and learning.
- The Puranas, eighteen in number, preserved the traditions, legends, moral codes, religious and philosophical principles and itihas. The smritis are metrical texts containing the rules and regulations and laws for the guidance and governance of society. They are based on dharmasutras and grihyasutras of Vedic literature. But additions and alterations have been done to make them suitable to the changing conditions of society. They are written in verse. The phase of writing of commentaries on the smritis-begins after the Gupta period.
- The compilation of the two great epics, Ramayana arid Mahabharata was completed by the fourth century AD.
- The philosophical works of the period are many and varied in character such as philosophic works of Mahayana and other schools of Buddhist thoughts and those of various Saiva and Vaishnav school.
- In the field of kavya or poetical works, the name of Kalidasa stands foremost. Kalidasa graced the court of Chandragupta II. He is credited with having written the best works in poetry, dramma as well as in prose. His kavyas such as Meghaduta, Raghuvamsa and Kumarasambhava, and dramas such as Abhijnashakuntalam are considered to be among the best literary works in the world Malavikagnimitram, Abhijnanashakuntalam and Vikramorvasiyam the three other famous plays of Kalidas.
- In the field of drama, Bhasa, Sudraka, Kalidas and Bhavabhuti are the most noteworthy. Sudraka is the author of Mrichchakatika – 'Little clay cart'. His play deals with the love of a brahman with the beautiful daughter of a courtesan and is considered one of the best plays of ancient India. Vishakhadatta's two plays: Mudrarakshasa and Devichandraguptam, which are the two best known historical plays. Bhavabhuti's works are Uttararama-charita, Malati-Madhava etc.
- In prose, earliest notable works are Dasakumaracharita by Dandin and Vasavadatta of Subandhu. One of the most famous works is Panchatantra, written by Vishnu Sharma, which was translated into Persian and Arabic in the eighth century AD and has been translated in almost all European languages since then.

34. Correct Option: (b)

Explanation

- Mricchakatika, or Mrichchhakatika (The Little Clay Cart) is a ten-act Sanskrit drama attributed to Śūdraka, an ancient playwright generally thought to have lived sometime between the 3rd century BC and the 5th century AD and identified by the prologue as a Kshatriya king as well as a devotee of Siva who lived for 100 years.
- The play is set in the ancient city of Ujjayini during the reign of the King Pālaka, near the end of the Pradyota Dynasty that made up the first quarter of the fifth century BC
- The central story is that of noble but impoverished young Brahmin, Sanskrit: Cārudatta, who falls in love with a wealthy courtesan or nagarvadhu, Sanskrit: Vasantasenā. Despite their mutual affection, however, the couple's lives and love are threatened when a vulgar courtier, Samsthānaka, also known as Shakara, begins to aggressively pursue Vasantasenā.
- Rife with romance, comedy, intrigue and a political subplot detailing the overthrow of the city's despotic ruler by a shepherd, the play is notable among extant Sanskrit drama for its focus on a fictional scenario rather than on a classical tale or legend

35. Correct Option: (c)

Supplementary Notes:

- Paṇini wrote a descriptive linguistic treatise called "Aṣṭadhyayi" which covered the whole of Sanskrit language's grammar (including for the Vedic part) and also word formation rules in "sutra" format.

36. Correct Option: (b)

Supplementary Notes:

- **Option b is correct:** The ninth Mandala of the Rigveda, also called the Soma Mandala, has 114 hymns, and is entirely devoted to Sóma Pávamāna, "Purifying Soma", the sacred potion of the Vedic religion. Similar to Mandala 8, it cannot be dated within the relative chronology of the Rigveda as a whole; dealing with the Soma cult, a practice reaching back into Proto-Indo-Iranian times (late 3rd millennium BC), some of its hymns may contain the very oldest parts of the Rigveda, while other hymns may be rather recent relative to the other books.

37. Correct Option: (d)

Supplementary Notes:

- **Statement 3 and 4 are correct:** Archaeologically, the fifth century BC marks the beginning of the Northern Black Polished Ware (NBPW) phase in the Gangetic plains, and this was a very glossy, shining type of pottery.
- The Harappan towns had disappeared in 1900 BC Following that, for about 1500 years, no towns were established in India. However, from about 1200 BC we notice settlements in the doab and the neighbouring areas. We find two types of settlements in the lower doab in 1000–600 BC, based on size and location. In the same area and on the same basis, four types of settlements are located some parts. This settlement hierarchy is regarded as the most important indicator of urbanisation The NBPW phase marked the beginning of the second urbanisation in India.

- **Statement 1 and 2 are correct:** Rice was the staple cereal produced in eastern UP and Bihar during this period. Various types of paddy and paddy fields are described in the Pali texts. Although rice was used in India in the second and third millennia BC, like iron, it became far more effective in the NBPW phase. The use of the term shali for transplantation is found in the Pali, Prakrit, and Sanskrit texts of the period, and it appears that large-scale paddy transplantation began in the age of the Buddha

38. Correct Option: (b)

Supplementary Notes:

List I	List II
A. Vatsayana	iii. Kamasutra
B. Agesilaus	i. Engineer
C. Vasumitra	iv. Philosopher
D. Charaka	ii. Medical Science

39. Correct Option: (c)

Supplementary Notes:

Literature	Scholars
A. Dharmanathapurana	2. Madhava
B. Dharma Parikshe	3. Uritta Vilasa
C. Parasara Smriti	4. Madhavacharya Vyakhya
D. Yadavabhyudayam	1. Vedanatha Desika

Supplementary Notes:

Jain Scholars

- Apart from Telugu, Vijayanagara rulers extended their patronage to Kannada and Sanskrit writers as well. Many Jain scholars contributed to the growth of Kannada literature.
- Madhava wrote Dharmanathapurana on the fifteenth tirthankara.
- Another Jain scholar, Uritta Vilasa, wrote Dharma Parikshe.
- The Sanskrit works by the period include Yadavabhyudayam by Vedanatha Desika and Parasara Smriti Vyakhya by Madhavacharya.

40. Correct Option: (d)

Explanation:

- **Pair 4 is incorrect:** The Mahabharata and The Ramayana are the two great epics which are also called as Mahakavya.

Supplementary Notes:

The Vedas:

- The word 'Veda' signifies knowledge and the texts are actually about providing humans about knowledge to conduct their entire life on earth and beyond.
- It is written in highly stylised poetic style and the language is full of symbols and myths.
- The Vedas were initially handed down orally by generations of Brahmin families but it is estimated by historians that they were compiled around 1500 BC-1000 BC
- There are four major Vedas: Rig Veda, Yajur Veda, Sama Veda and Atharva Veda. The Brahmanas, the Upanishads and the Aranyakas accompany each Veda.

Rig Veda

- The Rig Veda is the oldest existing Veda amongst the other four.
- It consists of 1028 individual Sanskrit hymns. It is said to be one of the first extensive composition in any Indo-European language that has survived for our perusal.
- Historians argue that it was compiled around 1200-900 BC
- The focus of this Veda is on worldly prosperity and natural beauty. The text is organised in 10 books, known as Mandalas, of varying age and length. Furthermore, each mandala comprises of several Suktas or hymns, which are usually for sacrificial purposes.

Atharva Veda

- This Veda is also known as Brahma Veda and has been attributed to two rishis called Atharvah and Angira, respectively. Because of its association with the two rishis, in the olden times it was also called Atharvangirasa. While it is mostly concerned with peace and prosperity of the human society and covers all aspects of a man's daily life, it specifically focuses on treatment of several ailments

Yajur Veda

- The name 'Yajus' signifies 'sacrifice' and this Veda concentrates on rites and mantras of different types of sacrifices that were prevalent in the Vedic times. There are two major recensions (samhita) of the Yajur Veda: Shukla (white/pure) and Krishna (black/dark). These samhita's are also called: Vajasaneyi Samhita and Taittiriya Samhita. The Yajur Veda is predominantly a ritual Veda as it acts like a guide book for the rishis/priests who conduct sacrificial rituals.

Sama Veda

- Sama Veda has been named after 'Saman' (melody) and it concentrates on melody or songs. While the entire text has 1875 hymns, historians argue that 75 are original and the rest have been taken from the Sakala branch of the Rig Veda.

Arayankas

- The Arayankas are also texts attached to the Vedas and they describe the rituals and sacrifices involved in the Vedas from various perspectives. They are said to be compilations of ritualistic information on the birth and death cycles as well as the complexity of the soul.

Upanishads

- Interestingly, the term 'Upanishad' or u (at), pa (foot), ni (down) and s(h)ad (to sit), i.e. to sit down near (the teacher), describes the text completely.
- These are treatises written in Sanskrit and give an account of the Vedas in predominantly monastic and mystical terms. As they are generally the last part of the Vedas, they are also known as Vedanta or 'end (anta) of the Veda'.
- The Upanishads are said to have the 'truth' about human life and show the way towards human salvation or moksha. They continue to talk about the abstract and philosophical problems faced by mankind, especially about the origin of this universe, supposed origin of the mankind, life and death cycle and the material and spiritual quests of man.

The Mahabharata and The Ramayana

- These two great epics are also called Mahakavya as they have become a part of the collective memory of those who follow the Hindu religion.

Ramayana

- The most famous and revered recension of the Ramayana is by the sage Valmiki who is also called as Adikavi or the first amongst the poets. By the same logic Ramayana is called Adikavya or the first amongst the poetry. The Ramayana consists of 24,000 verses and is divided into seven books, called Khandas. It is considered as an epic as it presents the details of the war between Lord Rama and demon king Ravana over the kidnapping of Rama's wife, Sita.

Mahabharata

- The Mahabharata has several versions, but the most popular one is penned by Ved Vyas. It was written in Sanskrit and initially had 8,800 verses. This version was called 'Jaya' or the story of 'victory'. The story is based on the conflict between the Kauravas and the Pandavas over the right to claim the throne of Hastinapur. The sutradhar of the story is Lord Krishna.
- The Mahabharata also consists of an important didactical text of Hindus, i.e., the Bhagwata Gita. This text is like a concise guide to Hindu religions' philosophical dilemmas and even acts like a guide to mankind on how to live a righteous life. Most of the text is a dialogue between Lord Krishna and the Pandava prince Arjuna about the duties of a man, warrior and prince.

41. Correct Option: (d)

Explanation:

- **Statement 3 is incorrect:** Dipavamsa and the Mahavamsa, are the non-canonical texts written in Pali, both contain historical cum mythical account of the Buddha's life, Buddhist councils, Ashoka, and arrival of Buddhism to Sri Lanka.

Supplementary Notes:

Buddhist Canonical and Non-canonical Literatures

- Buddhist literature is generally divided into canonical and noncanonical texts.
- Canonical texts are those texts that are directly linked to Gautama Buddha in one way or another. However, differences exist among various Buddhist schools as to which texts are canonical.
- They can simply be understood as books which lay down the basic tenets and principles of Buddhism, such as, the Tipitakas (Three Pitakas, also known as the Pali canon).
- Non-canonical texts or semi canonical texts are texts that are not the sayings of the Buddha, but commentaries and observations on canonical texts, treatise on the Dharma/Dhammapada historical information, quotes, definitions, grammars, and other writings in Pali, Tibetan, Chinese, and other East Asian languages.

The Tripitakas

- The Tipitaka (in Pali) and Tripitaka (in Sanskrit) meaning 'The Three Baskets/Collections' is one of the earliest compilations of Buddhist teachings written (originally) on long, narrow leaves.
- All branches of Buddhism have the Tripitaka as part of their core scriptures, which comprises three books — the Sutta (conventional teaching), the Vinaya (disciplinary code), and the Abhidhamma (moral psychology).
  - The Sutta Pitaka (Sutra/Basket of Discourses): This contains the Buddha's discourses on various doctrinal issues in dialogue form. These doctrines deal with morality and righteous dharma. These texts are also known as 'Buddhavacana' or 'the word of the Buddha', as it refers to texts that are supposed to contain what the Buddha himself said. With the exception of few sutras, the authority of this text is accepted by all Buddhist schools.
  - The Vinaya Pitaka (Discipline Basket): This contains rules for monks and nuns of the monastic order (Sangha).
  - The Abhidhamma Pitaka (Basket of Higher Teachings): This contains a thorough study and systemisation of the teachings of the Sutta Pitaka through summaries, questions and answers, lists, etc. It concentrates on the philosophy and metaphysics. It also contains discussions on various topics like ethics, theory of knowledge and psychology.

- **Some important non-canonical texts are:**
    - **Milindapanho:** written in Pali, it consists of a dialogue on various philosophical issues between the Indo-Greek king Milinda/Menander and the monk Nagasena.
    - **Dipavamsa and the Mahavamsa:** written in Pali, both contain historical cum mythical account of the Buddha's life, Buddhist councils, Ashoka, and arrival of Buddhism to Sri Lanka
    - **Nettipakarana:** The Book of Guidance, which gives a connected account of the Buddha's teachings
    - **Visuddhimagga:** The Path to Purity, written by Buddhaghosa, deals with development from purity of discipline to nibanna/enlightenment
    - Nidanakatha: first connected life story of Buddha
    - **Mahavastu:** written in mixed Sanskrit–Prakrit, it lays down the sacred biography, i.e., hagiography of the Buddha.

42. Correct Option: (b)

Explanation:

- **Statement 2 is incorrect:** The Jaina Agamas were written in Ardha-magadhi. It is a dialect of the Prakrit not Pali.

Supplementary Notes:

Jain Literature

- They can be broadly divided into two major categories; Canonical or religious texts called Jain Agamas or Agama and non-canonical literary works.
- Jain Agamas
    - They are the sacred texts and are said to be the teachings of the Jain tirthankars. They are said to be originally compiled by the Gandharas who were immediate disciples of Mahavira. These texts are important for Svetambaras.
    - The present Angas are said to re-compiled in a council of monks of Svetambaras sect held in Vallabhi (Gujarat) during mid-5th century AD.
    - The Digamabara sect believes that original teachings were lost long ago and they do not accept the authority of Agamas compiled in Valabhi.
    - Agamas comprised of 46 texts. They are 12 Angas, 12 Upangas, 10 Prakirnakas, 4 Mulasutras, 6 Chedasutras, 2 Chulika Sutras.
    - They were written in Ardha-Magadhi Prakrit language.
    - The Angas teach reverence for all forms of life, strict codes of vegetarianism, asceticism, compassion and non-violence.

43. Correct Option: (b)

Explanation:

- **Statement 2 is incorrect:** The Avesta is written in the Avestan language which is now extinct. The Northern Iran at the foothill of Albruz Moountains has multilingual culture.

Supplementary Notes:

Zoroastrian literature:

- During the reign of Sassanid Empire in Iran, the religion went through reforms and lots of texts were written and re-interpreted.
- The most important text is called Avesta, which is a collection of various texts written and compiled over a period of time dealing with religious beliefs, practices and instruction.
- It was written in the Avestan language which is now extinct. It is similar to Sanskrit. It was compiled in its final form during the Sasanian rule of Iran, probably in 4th century CE.
- In the Avesta, Yasna is a collection of texts and has 72 chapters and is of great importance. Among them, the five chapters "Gathas are containing 17 hymns are the most revered ones, and are supposed to be written by Zoroaster himself. Yasna is the most important ceremony of the faith. Other parts of the Avesta are Visperad, Yashts, Siroza, Nyayeshes, etc.
- Some other important texts other than Avesta are:
    - **Denkard:** It is a collection of books and contains various aspects of the faith. It is regarded as the Encyclopaedia of the Zoroastrianism. It does not have a divine status. It was written in 10th century.
    - **Bundahishn:** It literally means "Primal Creations". It gives details about the theory of creation in the religion. It contains astronomical ideas and theories. The battles of 'Ahura Mazda' and 'Angra Mainyu' are also mentioned. Most of the chapters were written in the 8th and 9th centuries.

44. Correct Option: (b)

Explanation:

- **Statement 4 is correct.** So, through elimination method one can arrive at the right answer which is option (b).
- **Statement 1 is incorrect:** Adi Granth was compiled by Bhai Gurdas under the aegis of the fifth guru, Guru Arjan Dev in 1604.
- **Statement 2 is incorrect:** Guru Granth Sahib contains the teachings of the Sikh Gurus and the teachings of Bhakti saints, called 'Bhagats', like Ramananda, Namadev, etc.
- **Statement 3 is incorrect:** Guru Granth Sahib is regarded as the Eleventh and final spiritual authority of the Sikhs.

Supplementary Notes:

Sikh literature:

- Sikhism is relatively a new religion established in 15th century, and is based on the teachings of Guru Nanak. The beliefs and philosophies of Sikhism are written in the sacred scripture, Guru Granth Sahib.
- Gurbani is the composition and hymns of Sikh Gurus and the Guru Granth Sahib.
- The important literary works related to Sikhism are:
  - **Adi Granth:** It was compiled by Bhai Gurdas under the aegis of the fifth guru, Guru Arjan Dev in 1604. It is written in Gurumukhi script. It is a predecessor to Guru Granth Sahib. The book contains the teachings of the Sikh Gurus and fifteen Bhagats of Bhakti and Sufi traditions.
  - **Guru Granth Sahib:** Adi Granth was further expanded in 1678 under the tenth guru Guru Gobind Singh. It is of great regard to the Sikhs. It is regarded as the Eleventh and final spiritual authority of the Sikhs. It is written in Gurumukhi script and is in a language called 'Sant Bhasa'. Sant Bhasa contains words from various languages like Punjabi, Apabhramsa, Hindi, Braj Bhasa, Sanskrit, Khadiboli and Persian. The book also contains the teachings of thirteen Bhakti saints, called 'Bhagats', like Ramananda, Namadev, Ravidas, Parmanand, Sain, Surdas etc. and two Muslim Bhagats-Kabir and Baba Farid.
  - **Dasam Granth:** It is believed that the hymns written by Guru Gobind Singh (Tenth Guru) are compiled in this book, however many do not agree with this. These contain fables and Puranic stories. Some hymns of the book are supposed to be offered in the daily prayers called "Nit-Nem".
  - **Janamsakhis:** These books contain the mythological and exaggerated stories of the first guru, Guru Nanak. The most popular book is "Bhai Bala Janamsakhi". Others are Miharban Janam Sakhi and Adi Janam Sakhi.

45. Correct Option: (c)

Explanation:

- **Statement 3 is incorrect:** They became particularly popular among low castes.

Supplementary Notes:

Nathpanthis, Siddhacharas and Yogis

- A number of religious groups that emerged during this period criticised the rituals and other aspects of conventional religion and the social order, using simple, logical arguments. Among them were the Nathpanthis, Siddhacharas and Yogis.
- They advocated renunciation of the world. To them, the path to salvation lay in meditation on the formless Ultimate Reality and the realisation of oneness with it. To achieve this they advocated intense training of the mind and body through practices like yogasanas, breathing exercises and meditation.
- These groups became particularly popular among "low" castes. Their criticism of conventional religion created the ground for devotional religion to become a popular force in northern India.

46. Correct Option: (b)

Explanation:

- **Statement 2 is incorrect:** His teachings openly ridiculed all forms of external worship of both Brahmanical Hinduism and Islam, the pre-eminence of the priestly classes and the caste system.

Supplementary Notes:

Kabir

- Kabir, who probably lived in the fifteenth-sixteenth centuries, was one of the most influential saints. He was brought up in a family of Muslim julahas or weavers settled in or near the city of Benares (Varanasi).
- We get to know of his ideas from a vast collection of verses called 'sakhis' and 'padas' said to have been composed by him and sung by wandering bhajan singers. Some of these were later collected and preserved in the Guru Granth Sahib, Panch Vani and Bijak.
- Kabir's teachings were based on a complete, indeed vehement, rejection of the major religious traditions. His teachings openly ridiculed all forms of external worship of both Brahmanical Hinduism and Islam, the pre-eminence of the priestly classes and the caste system.
- The language of his poetry was a form of spoken Hindi widely understood by ordinary people. He also sometimes used cryptic language, which is difficult to follow.
- Kabir believed in a formless Supreme God and preached that the only path to salvation was through bhakti or devotion. Kabir drew his followers from among both Hindus and Muslims.

47. Correct Option: (c)

Explanation:

- Both statements are correct

Supplementary Notes:

Tamil (Sangam) Literature

- 'Sangam' means fraternity and this literature was very popular amongst the masses.
- This literature is a collection of works that contains approximately 2381 poems that have been attributed to 473 poets and there is a corpus of literature written by 102 poets that remains anonymous.

- The poets included men and women from different classes of society.
- The literary tradtion was so popular that the period between 300 BC and 300 AD, during which most of these were composed and compiled, is often called Sangam period.
- There are two major schools of Sangam literature:
  - aham/agam which is the 'inner field' and concentrates on the abstract discussion of human aspects like love, sexual relations, etc.
  - The second school is the 'puram' or the 'outer field' which discusses the human experiences like social life, ethics, valour, customs, etc.
- This literature bears the name 'Sangam' because the kingdom of Pandya organised assemblies where poets, bards and writers would flock from various parts of South India.
- These assemblies were called 'Sangamas' and the literature produced in the duration of these assemblies was called Sangam literature.
- There were three Sangams organized over a period of 600-700 years. However, the conclusive historical account of the first two Sangams are not available.
- The first and second Sangams are considered legends and myths by many scholars.
- It is also interesting to see that in the extant Sangam literature, around 30,000 lines of poetry, has been arranged in eight anthologies called Ettuttokoi.
- These were further divided into two groups; the older and the more historically relevant group is called the Patinenkil Kanakku (eighteen lower collections) and the second is Pattupattu (the ten songs).
- The very famous and revered Tamil saint Thiruvallurar had contributed the 'Kural' to the Sangam literature.
- It has been now translated in several languages and is divided into three parts which discuss the epics, polity-governance and love.
- Another famous female saint who contributed to Sangam literature is Avvaiyar. Apart from the Sangam literature, there are many well-known texts written in Tamil.

48. Correct Option: (d)

Explanation:

- **Option (d) is correct:** This question can be done by elimination technique. Tuzuk-I-Babari was written by Babar in Turkish language hence option d is the only choice left.

Supplementary Notes:

Medieval Literature

- Several different trends emerged in the medieval period, which affected the languages, and dialects that emerged.
- This period also sees the development of Hindi from the ancient apabhramsa language.
- During Mughal rule Persian became the mode of communication of the court.
- One of the finest Persian poets is Amir Khusrau Dehlavi (Amir Khusrau of Delhi). Apart from his Diwan (collection of poetry in Persian), he also wrote Nuh Sipihr and the Masnavi Duwal Rani Khizr Khan, that is a tragic love poem.
- In the Delhi Sultanate, multiple texts were written in Persian.
- Most of them were concerned with creating histories for the rulers.
- Zia-ud din Barani is amongst the top historians of that period and he wrote Tarikh-e-Firuz Shahi.
- Another famous historian was Minhajus Siraj.
- There are several travel accounts written by famous travellers like Ibn Batuta (Moroccan traveller) that explain the socio-political scenario of the period.
- The production and dissemination of literature in Persian shot up in the Mughal period.
- Mughal emperor Babar wrote Tuzuk-I-Babari in Turkish, which is his autobiography and gives us important information about the Mughal conquest of India.
- One of the greatest sources about the period of Jahangir was Tuzuk-I-Jahangiri.
- Another important work is Humayun-nama which gives an account of his life and struggles to get the throne, written by half-sister of Humayun, Gulbadan Begum.
- The greatest emperor of this period was Akbar and Ain-e Akbari and Akbarnama written by his court historian Abul Fazl, are the best examples of literature of this period.
- Two major examples are the Mahabharata which when translated into Persian was called Razmnama.
- One of highly illustrated works from this period is called Hamzanama, which depicts the story of the mythical Persian hero, Amir Hamza.
- Malik Muhammad Jayasi also composed his Padmavat in this period.
- Other major writers of this period include Badauni, who wrote on ethics of political rule and Faizi who was considered a master of Persian poetry.
- In Aurangzeb's period, several satirists like Mir Jafar Zatalli wrote their Kulliyat (collection of verses).
- Texts like Tabqat-i-Alamgiri give us a good idea about the period of eighteenth century.
- Padshahnama was written by Abdul Hamid Lahori. It is about Shah Jahan.

49. Correct Option: (d)

Explanation:

- All pairs are correctly matched

Supplementary Notes:

Modern literature

- **Hindi**
  - With the coming of the British, the focus of literature changed. This change occurred phenomenally in Hindi prose writing where there was a zest to go back to the classics and be inspired by Sanskrit.
  - This zest was combined with the nationalistic fervour. Bharatendu Harishchandra wrote his most famous drama Andher Nagari (City of Darkness) in 1850s and this became a major play, which has been reproduced several times. Another very famous nationalist work is Bharat Durdasha.
  - The movement to make Hindi the national language, which would link all regions, was spearheaded by Swami Dayanand. Although he wrote quite a lot in Gujarati, his most famous work in Hindi is Satyartha Prakash.
  - Prem Chand wrote many anthologies in Hindi and Urdu and his famous works include Godan, Bade Bhhaiya, etc.
- **Bengali and Assamese Literature**
  - The zenith of nationalist Bengali literature was achieved by the writing of Bankim Chandra Chatterjee. His work Anand Math was hugely popular, so much so that Vande Mataram, our national song, is an excerpt taken from this novel.
  - The first Indian to win a Nobel Prize was also a writer in Bengali, Rabindranath Tagore. He got this award for his Bengali masterpiece Geetanjali in 1913.
  - Sharat Chandra Chatterjee, Qazi Nazrul Islam and R. C Dutta made important contributions to Bengali literature.
  - Shankardev composed devotional poetry in Assamese. In context of the modern Assamese literature, two major scholars namely Padmanaba Gohain Barua and Lakshmi Nath Bezbarua, have made their mark.
- **Punjabi**
  - It was composed in two major scripts: Persian and Gurmukhi.
  - One of the greatest texts of the world is the religious book of the Sikhs: the Adi Granth and a majority of it is in Gurmukhi. It also comprises of Dohas of Kabir, Dadu and Nanak in Hindi or Braj, but it is a very composite text. Guru Gobind Singh, who contributed to the Adi Granth, had also written Savaiyyas (poetry) in Punjabi.
  - The local literature took heavily to love stories and epics like Sohni-Mahiwal, Sassi-Punnu and the very famous Heer-Ranjha, which was composed by Waris Shah.
  - Modern Punjabi literature was also affected by nationalistic writing and Bhagat Singh's legendary 'Rang de Basanti Chola' is a classic example of this trend.

50. Correct Option: (d)

Explanation:

- All statements are correct

Supplementary Notes:

Science and technology through ages

- **Medicine**
  - During the Vedic times, Ashwini Kumars were the practisioners of medicine and were given the divine status.
  - Dhanvantari was the God of medicine. Atharva Veda was the first book where we find mention about the diseases, their cure and medicines.
  - Atharva Veda mentioned cure for many of the diseases which include diarrhoea, sores, cough, leprosy, fever and seizure. However, the era of practical and more rational cure to diseases emerged around 600 BC
  - Takshila and Varanasi emerged as the centres for medicinal learning.
  - Charak Samhita (deals with Ayurveda) by Charak Sushruta Samhita (deals with Surgery) by Sushruta. Before them, Atreya and Agnivesa had already dealt with principles of Ayurveda way back in 800 BCE.
- **Physicsand Chemistry**
  - From the Vedic times, the materials on the Earth have been classified into panchbhootas.
  - These panch mahabhootas were identified with human senses of perception.
    - Earth (prithvi) with smell
    - Fire (agni) with vision
    - Air (maya) with feeling
    - Water (apa) with taste
    - Ether (akasha) with sound
  - It has been perceived that the material world comprises of these five elements.
  - Philosophers were of the view that except ether, all other four were physically palpable and therefore, they comprised miniscule particles of matter.
  - The last miniscule matter which could not be further subdivided was called Parmanu.
  - There are five different types of parmanu for five different elements.

- Hence it can be inferred that Indian philosophers conceived the idea of splitting an atom.
- Indian philosophers Kanada and Pakudha Katyayana in 6th century BC, first coined the idea of atoms and the material world being constituted of atoms.
- Kanada explained that the material world is made up of kana which cannot be seen through the human organs.
- They cannot be further subdivided and are indestructible as even said by modern atomic theory.

51. Correct Option: (c)

Explanation:

- Both statements are correct

Supplementary Notes:

Science and Technology through ages

- **Ship Building and Navigation**
  - There have been many references of maritime activities by Indians during ancient times.
  - Sanskrit and Pali literature had a mention of ship building and navigation activities.
  - In the theological folklore of Hinduism, the Satyanarayan Puja talks of a sea merchant who was caught in a storm and prayed to the lord that if he is saved then he will offer puja to Lord Satyanarayana.
  - Yukti Kalpa Taru is a treatise in Sanskrit which deals with the various techniques used in ship building during ancient times.
  - The book contains minute details about the types of ships, their sizes and the types of material used to build those ships.
  - Indian builders possessed good knowledge about the materials used for ship building during ancient times.
- Famous Sports of India during ancient times:
  - **Kalaripayat:** It was a martial art from Kerala which was transmitted to China in 5 th century BC by a sage called Bodhidharma. The present form of Judo and karate did originate from Kalaripayat.
  - **Chess:** The game was known as "Chaturanga" meaning four bodies.
  - It was played with counters and Aksha (dice). It was also called Astapada meaning game of eight steps. Chaturanga finds its mention in the famous epic Mahabharata where this game was played between Kauravas and the Pandavas.

52. Correct Option: (d)

Explanation:

- **Statement 1 is incorrect:** Mahabhasya of Patanjali is a monumental work in the tradition of Paninian grammar.
- **Statement 2 is incorrect:** The Mricchakatika (the clay-cart) by Sudraka (248 AD) presents a remarkable social drama with touches of grim reality.

Supplementary Notes:

Mahabhasya and Mrichhakatika

- The Mricchakatika (the clay-cart) by Sudraka (248 AD) presents a remarkable social drama with touches of grim reality. The characters are drawn from all stratas of society, which include thieves and gamblers, rogues and idlers, courtesans and their associates, police constables, mendicants, and politicians. In Act III an interesting account of a burglary is given in which stealing is treated as a regular art. The interlinking of a political revolution with the private affairs of the two lovers adds new charm to the play.
- Mahabhasya of Patanjali is a monumental work in the tradition of Paninian grammar. Patanjali explains a large number of sutras of Panini and Katyayana's varttika thereupon.

53. Correct Option: (b)

Explanation:

- **Statement 3 is incorrect:** Nalanda continued to flourish as a centre of learning under the Pala Dynasty (8th–12th centuries), and it became a centre of religious sculpture in stone and bronze. Nalanda was probably sacked during Muslim raids in Bihar (c. 1200) and never recovered

Supplementary Notes:

Nalanda University

- Nalanda was an acclaimed Mahavihara, a large Buddhist monastery in the ancient kingdom of Magadha (modern-day Bihar) in India. The site is located about 95 kilometres southeast of Patna near the town of Bihar Sharif, and was a centre of learning from the fifth century CE to1200 CE. It is a UNESCO World Heritage Site.
- The highly formalized methods of Vedic learning helped inspire the establishment of large teaching institutions such as Taxila, Nalanda, and Vikramashila which are often characterised as India's early universities.
- Nalanda flourished under the patronage of the Gupta Empire in the 5th and 6th centuries and later under Harsha, the emperor of Kannauj.
- The liberal cultural traditions inherited from the Gupta age resulted in a period of growth and prosperity until the ninth century. The subsequent centuries were a time of gradual decline, a period during which the tantric developments of Buddhism became most pronounced in eastern India under the Pala Empire.

54. Correct Option: (c)

Explanation:

- Both statements are correct

Supplementary Notes:

Languages & Literature in India

- Santhali is written in Ol Chiki script and spoken by 6.4 million people, according to the 2001 census, in India alone and its speakers live mostly in Jharkhand, West Bengal, Odisha and Assam. It is also spoken in Bangladesh and Nepal. In 2018 it got its own Wikipedia edition and become the first tribal language to achieve this feat.
- Currently there are six languages that enjoy the 'Classical' status in India: Tamil (2004), Sanskrit (2005), Kannada (2008), Telugu (2008), Malayalam (2013), and Odia (2014). All these languages are also included in the 8 schedule of constitution.

55. Correct Option: (b)

Explanation:

- **Statement 2 is incorrect:** Apastamba deals with practical geometry.

Supplementary Notes:

Science and Technology in Ancient India

- Apastamba in the second century BC introduced the concepts of practical geometry involving acute angles, obtuse angles and right angles . This knowledge of angles helps in construction of fire altars in those times.
- Sulvasutra written by Baudhayana is one of the earliest texts on mathematics.
- Brahmgupta in his book Brahmasputa Siddhantika mentioned zero for the first time as a number.
- Goladhyaya is one of the section of Siddhanta Shiromani written by Bhaskaracharya.

56. Correct Option: (d)

Explanation:

- **Statement 1 is incorrect:** They are two halves of the solar year.
- **Statement 2 is incorrect:** Vikram Samvat is a lunar calendar.

Supplementary Notes:

The Calendar & the Eras

- Uttarayana and dakshiyana are two halves of the solar year. Uttarayana is God's Day which falls between Paush (January) to Ashadh (June) while Dakshiyana is God's Night falls (between July to December).
- Vikram Samvat is a lunar calendar based on ancient Hindu calendar.

57. Correct Option: (b)

Supplementary Notes:

Scientists and Their Works

- **Baudhayan:**
  - He was the first one ever to arrive at several concepts in Mathematics, which were later rediscovered by the western world. The value of pi was first calculated by him.
  - As you know, pi is useful in calculating the area and circumference of a circle. What is known as Pythagoras Theorem today is already found in Baudhayan's Sulva Sutra, which was written several years before the age of Pythagoras.
- **Aryabhatta:**
  - Aryabhatta was a fifth century mathematician, astronomer, astrologer and physicist. He was a pioneer in the field of mathematics.
  - At the age of 23, he wrote Aryabhattiya, which is a summary of mathematics of his time. There are four sections in this scholarly work. In the first section he describes the method of denoting big decimal numbers by alphabets. In the second section, we find dificult questions from topics of modern day Mathematics such as number theory, geometry, trigonometry and Beejganita (algebra). The remaining two sections are on astronomy. Aryabhatta showed that zero was not a numeral only but also a symbol and a concept. Discovery of zero enabled Aryabhatta to find out the exact distance between the earth and the moon. The discovery of zero also opened up a new dimension of negative numerals.
- **Kanad:**
  - Kanada was a sixth century scientist of Vaisheshika School, one of the six systems of Indian philosophy.
  - His atomic theory can be a match to any modern atomic theory.
  - According to Kanada, material universe is made up of kanas, (anu/atom) which cannot be seen through any human organ. These cannot be further subdivided. Thus, they are indivisible and indestructible.
- **Charak:**
  - Charak is considered the father of ancient Indian science of medicine.
  - He was the Raj Vaidya (royal doctor) in the court of Kanishka.
  - His Charak Samhita is a remarkable book on medicine. It has the description of a large number of diseases and gives methods of identifying their causes as well as the method of their treatment.

- He was the first to talk about digestion, metabolism and immunity as important for health and so medical science.
- In Charak Samhita, more stress has been laid on removing the cause of disease rather than simply treating the illness. Charak also knew the fundamentals of Genetics. Don't you find it fascinating that thousands of years back, medical science was at such an advanced stage in India.

- **Bhaskaracharya:**
  - Bhaskaracharya was the leading light of 12th Century. He was born at Bijapur, Karnataka. He is famous for his book Siddanta Shiromani.
  - It is divided into four sections: Lilavati (Arithmetic), Beejaganit (Algebra), Goladhyaya (Sphere) and Grahaganit (mathematics of planets).
  - Bhaskara introduced Chakrawat.
  - Method or the Cyclic Method is a means to solve algebraic equations. This method was rediscovered six centuries later by European mathematicians, who called it inverse cycle. In the nineteenth century, an English man, James Taylor, translated Lilavati and made this great work known to the world.

58. Correct option : (b)

Explanation:

- **Statement 1 is incorrect:** Indian notational system was adopted by Arabs from Indians who spread it to the western world including Greeks.
- **Statement 3 is incorrect:** Before these numerals appeared in the West, they had been used in India for centuries. Indian numerals are found in the inscriptions of Ashoka, which were written in the 3rd century BC. However at the time of Indus Valley Civilisation pictographic script was in use which has not yet been deciphered.

Supplementary Notes:

Indian Notational System

- In the field of mathematics the ancient Indians made 3 contributions : Notation system, Decimal system, Use of zero.
- Indian notational system was adopted by Arabs from Indians who spread it to the western world including Greeks. So Greeks learnt it from the Arabs.
- Indian numerals are called Arabic in English, but Arabs themselves called their numerals 'hindsa'.
- Before these numerals appeared in the West they had been used in India for centuries. Indian numerals are found in the inscriptions of Ashoka, which were written in the 3rd century BC. However at the time of Indus Valley Civilisation pictographic script was in use which had not yet been deciphered.

59. Correct Option: (b)

Explanation:

- **Statement (b) is incorrect:** Saundarananda was written in Sanskrit not Pali.

Supplementary Notes:

Literature and Learning

- The earliest specimen of Kavya Style is found in the Junagadh inscription of Rudradaman in Kathiawar in about AD 150.
- Ashvaghosha enjoyed the patronage of the Kushans. He wrote the Buddhacharita.
- He also composed the Saundarananda, which is a fine example of Sanskrit Kavya.
- The progress of Mahayana Buddhism led to the composition of numerous avadana.
- One objective was to preach the teachings of Mahayana Buddhism to the people.
- Some of the important books of this genre were the Mahavastu and the Divyavadan.
- The Greeks contributed to the development of the Indian theatre by introducing the use of the curtain. Since the curtain was borrowed from the Greeks it came to be known as yavanika.
- Yavanika was derived from the term Yavana, which was a Sanskritized form of Ionian, a branch of the Greeks known to the ancient Indians.
- The best example of secular literature appears in the Kamasutra of Vatsayayan.
- Attributed to the third century AD, it is the earliest work on erotics dealing with sex and love-making.
- It gives us a picture of the life of a city-bred person or nagarat who lived in a period of driving urbanism.

60. Correct Option: (b)

Supplementary Notes:

- The Mudrarakshasa, a historical play in Sanskrit by Vishakhadatta (4th century CE) narrates the ascent of the king Chandragupta Maurya to power in Northern India with the aid of Chanakya, his Guru and chief minister.
- Rajatarangini (Sanskrit: "River of Kings") is a historical chronicle of early India, written by Kalhana.
- Sanskrit work by the Kashmiri Brahman Kalhana composed in 1148. It is justifiably considered to be the best and most authentic work of its kind. It covers the entire span of history in the Kashmir region from the earliest times to the date of its composition.
- The Arthashastra was written by Kautilya (also known as Chanakya) an Indian statesman and philosopher, chief advisor and Prime Minister of the Indian Emperor Chandragupta, the first ruler of the Mauryan

Empire. The Arthashastra summarizes the political thoughts of Kautilya. The book contains detailed information about specific topics that are relevant for rulers who wish to run an effective government. Diplomacy and war (including military tactics) are the two points treated in most detail but the work also includes recommendations on law, prisons, taxation, irrigation, agriculture, mining, fortifications, coinage, manufacturing, trade, administrations, diplomacy, and spies.

- Meghaduta (literally meaning "cloud messenger") is a lyric poem written by Kalidasa, considered to be one of the greatest Sanskrit poets in India. A short poem of only 111 stanzas, it is one of Kalidasa`s most illustrious works. Meghaduta is separated into two parts – Purvamegha (Previous cloud) and Uttaramegha (Consequent cloud).

61. **Correct Option: (c)**

Supplementary Notes:

Science and Technology

- In mathematics, the period saw, in the fifth century, a work called Aryabhatiya written by Aryabhatta who belonged to Pataliputra. It appears that this mathematician was well versed in various kinds of calculations. Aryabhatta displays an awareness of both the zero system and the decimal system. A Gupta inscription of AD 448 from Allahabad district suggests that the decimal system was known in India at the beginning of the fifth century. Aryabhatta was followed by Varahamihira (born 505 AD), who recorded the works of Aryabhatta and older astronomical findings in his classic work Brihatasamhita.
- In the field of astronomy, another book called Romaka Sidhanta was compiled by Varahamihira, its title indicating that it was influenced by Greek and Roman ideas. Brahmagupta, (born 598 AD) was an excellent scientist, and wrote Brahmasphuta-siddhant.
- The Gupta craftsmen distinguished themselves by their work in iron and bronze. Bronze images of the Buddha began to be produced on a considerable scale because of the knowledge the smiths had of advanced metal technology.
- With regard to iron objects, the best example is the iron pillar found at Mehrauli in Delhi. Manufactured in the fourth century AD, the pillar has not gathered any rust over the subsequent fifteen centuries which is a great tribute to the technological skill of the craftsmen, although the arid conditions in Delhi may also have contributed to its preservation. It was impossible to produce such a pillar in any iron foundry in the West until about a century ago. It is a pity that the later Indian craftsmen could not develop this knowledge further.

62. **Correct Option: (c)**

Explanation:

- **Statement 1 is incorrect:** Arthashastra was compiled after the Mauryan rule.
- **Statement 2 is incorrect:** Pataliputra (Patna) was called as Palibothra by Megasthenes.

Supplementary Notes:

Imperial Organisation of Mauryan Empire

- The Mauryas organized a very elaborate system of administration. We know about this from the account of Megasthenes (Indika) and the Arthashastra of Kautilya.
- Megasthenes was a Greek ambassador sent by Seleucus to the court of Chandragupta Maurya. He lived in the Maurya capital of Pataliputra and wrote an account not only of the administration of the city of Pataliputra but also of the Maurya Empire as a whole.
- Megasthenes's account does not survive in full, but quotations from it occur in the works of several subsequent Greek writers. These fragments have been collected and published in the form of a book entitled Indika, which throws valuable light on the administration, society, and economy of Maurya times.
- Megasthenes's account can be supplemented by the Arthashastra of Kautilya. Although the Arthashastra was finally compiled a few centuries after Maurya rule, some of its books contain material that provides authentic information about the Maurya administration and economy. These two sources enable us to draw a picture of the administrative system of Chandragupta Maurya.
- The empire was divided into a number of provinces, and each of these was placed under a prince who was a scion of the royal Dynasty. The provinces were divided into still smaller units, and arrangements were made for both rural and urban administration.
- Megasthenes states that numerous cities existed in India, but he considered Pataliputra to be the most important. He calls it Palibothra. This Greek term means a city with gates. According to him, Pataliputra was bounded by a deep ditch and a wooden wall crowned with 570 towers, and had 64 gates.
- According to Kautilya, the central government maintained about two dozen departments of state, which controlled social and economic activities at least in the areas that were in proximity to the capital. The most striking feature of Chandragupta's administration was its maintenance of a huge army.

63. **Correct Option: (b)**

List-I	List-II
A. Vikramorvasiya	3. Kalidasa
B. Uttara Ramacharitam	1. Bhavabhuti
C. Devi Chandraguptam	4. Vishakhdutta
D. Swapnavasavadatta	2. Bhasa

Supplementary Notes:

Works of Kalidasa

- Malavikagnimitra (The love story of Malavika a maiden of Queen and Agnimitra, the son of Pushyamitra Shunga)
- Vikramorvasiya (Love story of Vikram and Urvasi)
- Abhigyana Shakuntala (the recognition of Shakuntala)

Sudraka

- Mricchakatika (The Little Clay Cart) – Love affair of young brahmin Charudatta with a wealthy courtesan.

Vishakhdutta

- Mudra Rakshasa (is a political drama and narrates ascent of king Chandragupta Maurya to power in India)
- Devi Chandraguptam

Bhavabhuti

- Uttara Ramacharitam (the later life of Rama). It was written in 700 AD.

Bhasa

- Swapnavasavadatta (Vasavadatta in the dream), Pancharatra, Urubhanga (story of Duryodhana during and after his fight with Bhima.

64. **Correct Option: (a)**

Explanation:

- **Statement 2 is incorrect:** The Assamese belongs to Indo-Aryan group of languages.

Supplementary Notes:

Classification of Indian Languages

- Languages in India are classified into the following major sub-groups:
- **Indo-Aryan Group of Languages**
  - It is a branch of the larger Indo-European family which came to India with the advent of the Aryans. It is the largest language group of India and around 74% of the Indians speak those languages which belong to this group.
  - Sanskrit, Prakrit, Hindi, Assamese, Bengali, Punjabi, etc. belong to this group
- **Dravidian Group of Languages**
  - This group comprises mainly of the languages spoken in the southern part of India. Around 25% of the Indian population is covered under this group.
  - Among these 21 languages of the Dravidian Group, the four major languages of the Dravidian group are:
    - Telugu (numerically the largest of all Dravidian languages)
    - Tamil (the oldest and purest form of language)
    - Kannada
    - Malayalam (smallest and the youngest of the Dravidian group)
- **Sino-Tibetan Group of Languages**
  - Languages under this group belong to Mongoloid family and stretch to all over the Himalayas, North Bihar, and North Bengal, Assam and up to the North-Eastern frontiers of the nation.
  - These languages are considered to be older than the Indo-Aryan languages and are referred to in the oldest Sanskrit literature as Kiratas.
  - Sikkimese, Bhutia, Ladhaki, Kinnauri, Ahom, etc. are the languages in this group.
- **Austric Group of Languages**
  - Languages under this group belong to the Austro-Asiatic sub-family which are represented by the languages of Munda or Kol group and spoken in Central, Eastern, and North-Eastern India.
  - The existence of these languages have been much before the advent of the Aryans and was referred to in ancient Sanskrit literature as Nisadas.
  - Santhali is the most important language in this group. With the exceptions of Khasi and Santhali, all Austro-Asiatic languages on Indian Territory are endangered.

65. **Correct Option: (a)**

Explanation:

- **Statement 1 is incorrect:** It is evolved from Apabhramsa Language which was evolved from Prakrit.

Supplementary Notes:

Hindi and its Dialects

- Hindi as we know it today, evolved between the 7th and 14th centuries from Apabhramsa, which was evolved from Prakrit.
- The language got its biggest boost with the Bhakti movement, which shunned the use of Sanskrit as it was the language of the Brahmins and common people did not use it.
- Hence, they started writing in the language of the people and from the twelfth century onwards we see a sharp rise in regional languages like Bengali, Hindi, Marathi, Gujarati, etc.
- For a long time, Hindi literature was in the shadow of its Sanskrit antecedents, but Prithviraj Raso was

the first Hindi book and it documents the life and challenges faced by Prithviraj Chauhan.

- The bulk of the work is poetry by Bhakti writers like Kabir who is famous for his dohas (couplets) that are used by the common people of India even today.
- Tulsidas produced couplets in Braj and was peppered by Persian. He became immortal by writing Ramcharitmanas, one of the most revered Hindu texts.
- Lord Krishna's life also became the subject of various medieval poets like Surdas who wrote Sur Sagar about Krishna's infancy and adolescent affairs with the gopis. Rahim, Bhushan, and Raskhan also wrote about the devotion to Lord Krishna. Mirabai is also famous as the woman who renounced the world for Lord Krishna and wrote Bhakti poetry for him. Bihari's Satsai is also famous in this regard.

66. Correct Option: (c)

Explanation:

- Both statements are correct

Supplementary Notes:

Indo-Aryan Group of Languages

- **Old Indo-Aryan Group**
  - Sanskrit evolved out of old Indo-Aryan group languages. This group had its development around 1500 BC
  - The development of Sanskrit grammar began with Panini in 400 BC with his book Asthadhyayi being the oldest book in Sanskrit grammar.
  - Some of the Buddhist literature belonging to Mahayana and the Hinayana school are even written in the Sanskrit language. The book Mahavastu of the Hinayana school is a treasure of stories. Lalitavistara, the most sacred Mahayana text, and Ashvagosha's Buddhacharita were also written in Sanskrit.
  - The chaste form of Sanskrit developed between 300 BC to 200 BC It was a refined version of Vedic Sanskrit. The first evidence of the use of Sanskrit can be found in the inscriptions of Rudradamana at Junagarh in the present Southern Gujarat region.
  - In the field of Sanskrit literature, the Gupta period is known as the period of unique creation. This is because of the fact that there has been a variety of literary works developed during this reign. Another important aspect of it is related to ornate style in literary works. Many of the places developed during Gupta period is also written in Sanskrit.

67. Correct Option: (a)

Explanation:

- **Pair 3 is incorrectly matched:** Narayan Pandit – Mathematics

Supplementary Notes:

Narayan Pandit

- In the Medieval period, Narayan Pandit produced works of mathematics which include Ganitakaumudi and Bijaganitavatamsa.

Nagarjuna

- One of the famous alchemists of ancient times was Nagarjuna. He was an expert in transforming the base metals into gold. Born in Gujarat in 931 AD, Nagarjuna was blessed with this power of changing base metals into gold and extraction of "Elixir of life" as per the beliefs of the people.

Bhaskaracharya

- Bhaskaracharya was one of the leading mathematicians in the 12th century AD. He wrote the book Siddhanta Shiromani.

68. Correct Option: (c)

Explanation:

- Both statements are correct

Supplementary Notes:

Sangam Literature

- 'Sangam' means fraternity and this literature was very popular amongst the masses. This literature is a collection of works that contains approximately 2381 poems that have been attributed to 473 poets and there is a corpus of literature written by 102 poets that remains anonymous.
- The poets included men and women from different classes of society. The literary tradition was so popular that the period between 300 BC and 300 AD, during which most of these were composed and compiled, is often called the Sangam period.
- There are two major schools of Sangam literature:
  - aham/agam which is the 'inner field' and concentrates on the abstract discussion of human aspects like love, sexual relations, etc.
  - The second school is the 'Puram' or the 'outer field' which discusses human experiences like social life, ethics, valour, customs, etc.
- This literature bears the name 'Sangam' because the kingdom of Pandya organised assemblies where poets, bards, and writers would flock from various parts of South India.
- These assemblies were called 'Sangamas' and the literature produced in the duration of these assemblies was called Sangam literature.

- There were three Sangams organized over a period of 600-700 years. However, the conclusive historical account of the first two Sangams is not available.
- The first and second Sangams are considered legends and myths by many scholars.

69. Correct Option: (b)

Explanation:

- **Statement 1 is incorrect:** The Sutta Pitaka contains dialogues and speeches of the Buddha that deal with morality and righteous dharma.

Supplementary Notes:

Buddhist Literature

- Buddhist literature can be divided into Canonical and Noncanonical works. The Canonical literature consists of 'Triptikas' or baskets (of knowledge). The three Tripitakas are:
  - Vinaya Pitaka, which covers the rules and regulations, which should be followed by the Buddhist monks.
  - The Sutta Pitaka contains dialogues and speeches of the Buddha that deal with morality and righteous dharma.
- The Abhidhamma Pitaka concentrates on the philosophy and metaphysics. It also contains discussions on various topics like ethics, the theory of knowledge and psychology.

70. Correct Option: (d)

Explanation:

- **Statement 1 is incorrect:** Sutta Pitaka is the great collection of the Buddha's sermons on matters of doctrine and ethics.

Supplementary Notes:

Buddhist Council

- The first Buddhist Council was held soon after the mahaparinirvana of the Buddha, around 400 BC under the patronage of King Ajatshatru with the monk Mahakasyapa presiding, at Rajgriha.
- The idea was to preserve Buddha's teachings and rules for disciples.
- Vinaya Pitaka is the collection of rules of the monastic order.
- Upali, one of the chief disciples of Buddha recited Vinayaka Pitaka.
- Sutta Pitaka is the great collection of the Buddha's sermons on matters of doctrines and ethics.
- Sutta Pitaka was recited by Ananda, a great disciple of Buddha.

71. Correct Option: (c)

Explanation:

- Option (c) is correct

Vedas	Characteristic
A. Rigveda	2. Collection of hymns
B. Samveda	4. Collection of songs
C. Yajurveda	1. Collection of sacrificial formulae
D. Atharvaveda	3. Collection of spells and charms

Supplementary Notes:

The Vedas

- Vedas are a collection of hymns, prayers, charms, litanies and sacrificial formulae.
- The Vedas formed the earliest segment of Vedic literature and amongst the Vedas, Rigveda is the oldest.
- There are four Vedas, namely:
  - Rigveda - a collection of hymns
  - Samveda - a collection of songs mostly taken from Rig Veda
  - Yajurveda - a collection of sacrificial formulae
  - Atharvaveda - a collection of spells and charms

72. Correct Option: (c)

Terminology	Feature
A. Vishti	4. Forced labour
B. Kumaramatyas	3. Important officers in the Gupta empire
C. Vishayas	2. Part of provincial and local administration system
D. Romaka Sidhanta	1. Book on Astronomy

Supplementary Notes:

Life During the Gupta Period

- There was a general increase in the number of land taxes and various other burdens during the Gupta rule. For example, whenever the royal army passed through the countryside, the local people had to feed it. The peasants had also to supply animals, food grains, furniture, etc., for the maintenance of royal officers on duty in rural areas.
- In central and western India, the villagers were also subjected to forced labor called "Vishti" by the royal army and officials.
- Gupta bureaucracy.
  - The most important officers in the Gupta empire were the "Kumaramatyas".
  - They were appointed by the king in the home provinces and possibly paid in cash.
  - As the Guptas were possibly vaishyas, recruitment was not confined to the upper varnas only, but several offices were combined in the hands of the same person, and posts became hereditary.
  - This naturally weakened royal control.

- The empire was divided into divisions called bhuktis, and each bhukti was placed under the charge of an uparika.
- The bhuktis were divided into districts (vishayas), which were placed under the charge of a vishayapati.

- The period also witnessed the developments in the field of mathematics and astronomy. For e.g. Aryabhatiya was written by Aryabhata.
- "Romaka Sidhanta", a book which on astronomy was compiled in the same period its title indicating that it was influenced by Greek and Roman ideas.

73. Correct Option: (c)

Explanation:

- Both statements are correct

Supplementary Notes:

Gupta Period

- The Gupta period is remarkable for the production of secular literature, which consisted of a fair degree of ornate court poetry.
- Bhasa was an important poet in the early phase of the Gupta period and wrote thirteen plays. He wrote in Sanskrit, but his dramas also contain a substantial amount of Prakrit. He was the author of a drama called "Dradiracharudatta", which was later refashioned as Mrichchhakatika or the Little Clay Cart by Shudraka.
- The Gupta period also saw the development of Sanskrit grammar based on the work of Panini and Patanjali. This period is particularly memorable for the compilation of Amarakosha by Amarasimha, who was a luminary in the court of Chandragupta II. This lexicon is learnt by heart by students learning Sanskrit in the traditional way.
- Gupta period became particularly famous due to the work of Kalidasa who lived in the second half of the fourth and the first half of the fifth century. He was the greatest poet of classical Sanskrit literature and wrote Abhijnanashakuntalam which is very highly regarded in world literature.

74. Correct Option: (c)

Explanation:

- Both statements are correct

Supplementary Notes:

Harappan Civilisation

- Religious Practices
  - In Harappa numerous terracotta figurines of women have been found. In one figurine, a plant is shown growing out of the embryo of a woman. The image probably represents the goddess of earth, and was intimately connected with the origin and growth of plants. The Harappans, therefore, looked upon the earth as a fertility goddess.
  - There is also an evidence of worship of male deity. A male deity, "the prototype of the historic Siva," is portrayed on a seal with three faces, seated on a low throne in the typical posture of a Yogi, with two animals on each side - elephant and tiger on right and rhinoceros and buffalo on left, and two deer standing under the throne. The depiction shows Siva as Pashupati.
  - There are the evidnces of the prevalence of the phallus worship, which in later times became so intimately connected with Shiva. Numerous symbols of the phallus and female sex organs made of stone have been found in Harappa, and were possibly meant for worship.
  - The people of the Indus region also worshipped trees. The depiction of a deity is represented on a seal amidst branches of the pipal.
  - Animals like one horned unicorn, humped bull etc. were also worshipped in Harappan times.
- **Script**
  - The Harappan script is not alphabetical but largely pictographic and has not been deciphered yet.
  - Some scholars opine that Harappan inscriptions present 3 logosyllablic writing system, where a sequence of two or more signs would represent a complete word, a syllable or a sound and sometimes even a sentence of several words and grammatical indicators.
  - The script was written from right to left. When the inscription was of more than one line it could be first line from right to left and second from left to right.

75. Correct Option: (c)

Books	**Writers**
A. Malavikagnimitram	3. Kalidasa
B. Mudrarakshasha	4. Vishakhadatta
C. Vikramankadevacharita	1. Bilhana
D. Harshacharita	2. Banabhatta

Supplementary Notes:

Literary Sources

- The works of Kalidasa comprise kavyas and dramas, the most famous of which is Abhijnanashakuntalam. Besides being great creative compositions, they provide us with glimpses of the social and cultural life of the Guptas.
- Kalidasa's Malavikagnimitram is based on some events of the reign of Pusyamitra Sunga, a Dynasty which followed the Mauryas.
- Mudrarakshasha, a play written by Vishakhadatta, also gives a glimpse of society and culture.

- Banabhatta's Harshacharita throws light on many historical facts about which we could not have known otherwise.
- Bilhana's Vikramankadevacharita describes the victories of the later Chalukya king Vikramaditya.
- Rajatarangini by Kalhana is the best illustration of history writing appreciated by modern historians. His critical method of historical research and impartial treatment of the historical facts have earned him a great respect among the modern historians.

76. Correct Option: (a)

Explanation:

- Option (a) is correct

List I	List II
A. Kitab-ul-Hind	1. Alberuni
B. Khazain-ul-Futuh	2. Amir Khusrau
C. Tarikh-i-Firoz Shahi	3. Barani
D. Tabaqat-i-Nasari	4. Minhaj-us-Siraj

Supplementary Notes:

Literature in the Sultanate Period

- The Delhi Sultans patronised learning and literature. Many of them had great love for Arabic and Persian literature Barani's Tarikh-i-Firoz Shahi contains the history of Tughlaq Dynasty.
- Minhaj-us-Siraj wrote Tabaqat-i-Nasari, a general history of Muslim dynasties up to c.1260 CE.
- Amir Khusrau (c.1252–1325 CE) was the most famous Persian writer of this period.
- Amir Khusrau's Khazain-ul-Futuh speaks about Alauddin's conquests. His famous work, the Tughlaq Nama, deals with the rise of Ghiyasuddin Tughlaq.
- Alberuni's Kitab-ul-Hind is the most famous work wherein he comments on Indian sciences, Hindu religious beliefs, customs, and social organisation.

77. Correct Option: (c)

Explanation:

- **Statement 2 is incorrect:** It consists of 15 books (also called Adhikaranas) dealing with both internal administration and interstate relations during the Mauryan age.
- **Statement 3 is incorrect:** It is written in Sanskrit language.

Supplementary Notes:

Kautilya's Arthashastra

- The Arthashastra summarises the political thoughts of Chandragupta Maurya's chief minister Kautilya, also known as Chanakya or Vishnugupta, who is often compared to the Italian Renaissance writer Niccolo Machiavelli (the author of The Prince). It is written in Sanskrit language.
- The title Arthashastra, a Sanskrit word, literally means 'the science of material wellbeing', though it is also accepted as 'the science of statecraft'.
- It consists of 15 books (Adhikaranas), out of which the first five deal with tantra (internal administration), and next eight with avapa (interstate relations). The final two books deal with other miscellaneous topics.
- The manuscript of Kautilya's Arthashastra was first discovered and studied by R. Shama Shastri.
- The Arthashastra of Kautilya considers sovereignty, ministers, populated territory, forts, treasury, force, and friends to be the organs of the state.
- According to Kautilya, the republics or samghas are considered as the obstacles to the growth of the empire.
- Although the Arthashastra was finally compiled a few centuries after Maurya rule, some of its books contain material that provides authentic information about the Mauryan administration and economy.
- The book contains detailed information about specific topics that are relevant for rulers who wish to run an effective government. Diplomacy and war (including military tactics) are the two points treated in most detail but the work also includes recommendations on law, prisons, taxation, irrigation, agriculture, mining, fortifications, coinage, manufacturing, trade, administration, and spies.
- The ideas expressed by Kautilya in the Arthashastra are completely practical and unsentimental.
- Kautilya openly writes about controversial topics such as assassinations. He also writes about the moral duty of the king and stresses on paternal despotism as he summarizes the duty of a ruler.

78. Correct Option: (c)

Explanation:

- **Statement 1 is incorrect:** As per Indica, there were no slaves in India during the Mauryan period.

Supplementary Notes:

Megasthenes's Indica

- Indica is an account left by a Greek ambassador, Megasthenes, sent by Seleucus Nikator to the court of Chandragupta Maurya.
- He lived in the Mauryan capital of Pataliputra and wrote an account not only of the administration of the city of Pataliputra but also of the Maurya Empire as a whole.
- According to Megasthenes, the king was at the head of the government and assisted by a council of ministers whose members were noted for wisdom. There is nothing to show that their advice was binding on him.
- The administration of the armed forces, according to Megasthenes, was carried on by a board of thirty

officers divided into six committees, each committee consisting of five members. It seems that each of the six wings of the armed forces, the army, the cavalry, the elephants, the chariots, the navy, and the transport, was assigned to the care of a separate committee.

- Megasthenes states that he did not notice any slaves in India, but there is little doubt that there had been domestic slaves from Vedic times onwards. It seems that during the Maurya period slaves were engaged in agricultural work on a large scale.
- Megasthenes speaks of the wooden structure at the Maurya capital Pataliputra. Excavations show that logs of wood were also used as an important line of defence against flood and invasion.
- The Pandyas are first mentioned by Megasthenes, who says that their kingdom was celebrated for pearls. He also speaks of it being ruled by a woman, which suggests some matriarchal influence in Pandya society.
- The major faults of Megasthenes' work were mistakes in details, the uncritical acceptance of Indian folklore, and a tendency to idealise Indian culture by the standards of Greek philosophy.
- However, Megasthenes did identify two of the most important aspects of the Indian caste system: endogamy and hereditary occupation.

79. Correct Option: (a)

Explanation:

- Pairs 2 and 4 are incorrectly matched:

	Famous Book	Author
1.	Shah Jahan Nama	- Inayat Khan
2.	Ain-i-Akbari	- Abul Fazl
3.	Humayunnama	- Gulbadan Begam
4.	Tuzuk-i-Jahangiri	- Jahangir

80. Correct Option: (b)

Explanation:

- **Statement 1 is incorrect:** Sama Veda is collection of verses taken from the Rig Veda.

Supplementary Notes:

Vedic Literature

- The Rig Veda is a collection of 1,028 hymns, divided into 10 Mandals (books). They are the earliest compositions and hence, they depict the life of the Early Vedic people in India.
- The Rig Veda has been included by the UNESCO in the list of literature signifying World Human Heritage.
- The Sama Veda is the collection of verses mostly taken from the Rig Veda, but arranged in a poetic form to facilitate singing. It is a collection of 1,810 melodies, and also contains the famous Dhrupada raga, later sung by Tansen.
- The Yajur Veda deals with the procedure for the performance of sacrifices.
- The Atharva Veda is a collection of magic spells and charms to ward off the evil spirits and diseases.
- The Brahmanas describe the rules for the performance of sacrificial ceremonies. Each Veda has several Brahmanas attached to it. The most important Brahmana is the Satpatha Brahmana, which is attached to the Yajur Veda and is the most exhaustive.
- Aranyakas are called the 'forest books' as they were written mainly by hermits living in the jungles for their pupils. They deal with mysticism and philosophy and oppose sacrifice.

81. Correct Option: (d)

Explanation:

- **Statement 1 is incorrect:** Ganitasara-sangraha is the work of Mahaviracharya
- **Statement 2 is incorrect:** While Lilavati deals with arithmetic, Bijaganita discusses concept of zero

Supplementary Notes:

Bhaskara II

- Some advances were made in the field of mathematics as the 9th century Ganitasarasangraha of Mahaviracharya and the Lilavati of Bhaskar II was written during this period (c.1150 CE), which remained a standard text for a long time.
- Bhaskara II (c.1114–1185 CE), the greatest mathematician of medieval India and astronomer, was born in Bijapur in modern Karnataka.
- His main work, the Siddhanta Shiromani, (Sanskrit for "Crown of Treatises") is divided into four parts:
  - **Lilavati:** Deals with arithmetic and covers calculations, progressions, measurement, permutations, and other topics.
  - **Bijaganita:** Deals with algebra, and under this section, Bhaskara discusses concepts such as zero, infinity, positive and negative numbers, and indeterminate equations including (the now called) Pell's equation.
  - **Grahagaita:** Deals with the mathematics of the planets, and while treating the motion of planets, he considers their instantaneous speeds and also arrives at an approximation. Bhaskara accurately defined many astronomical quantities, including, for example, the length of the sidereal year, the time that is required for the Earth to orbit the Sun, as 365.2588 days.
  - **Goladhyaya:** Deals with mathematics of the spheres.

82. Correct Option: (a)

Explanation:

- **Statement 3 is incorrect:** Satapatha Brahmana has described the journey of Videgha Mathava from the banks of Sarasvati to the Sadanira river.

Supplementary Notes:

Later Vedic Age

- The Later Vedic Period also known as Post-Rigvedic age, commenced with the emergence of agriculture as the principal economic activity.
- The age witnessed the composition of three later Veda Samhitas namely, the Samveda Samhita, the Yajurveda Samhita, the Atharvaveda Samhita as well as Brahmanas and the Upanishads of all the four Vedas and later on the two great epics—the Ramayana and the Mahabharata.
- The center of Vedic civilisation now shifted from Saraswati to Ganga.
- The expansion of people towards the east is indicated in a legend of Satapatha Brahmana – how Videgh Madhav migrated from Saraswati region, the land of Vedic Culture, crossed Sadanira (modern Gandak river), the eastern boundary of Kosala and came to the land of Videha (modern Tirhut).
- The eastward spread of the Vedic culture has a direct relationship with the proliferation of sedentary agricultural settlements in the Ganga valley.
- During Rigvedic times agglomeration of the Kulas or the families led to the formation of the 'Jana' or 'Vis' that was marked not by the a fixed residence or territory, but by the kinship organisation whereas later Vedic texts acquaint us for the first time with the term Janapada literally where the jana or people first set its feet, meaning a settlement or more precisely a rural settlement.

83. Correct Option: (a)

Explanation:

- **Statement 2 is incorrect:** It gives detailed account of the reign of Mughal emperor Shahjahan.

Supplementary Notes:

Badshah Nama

- Abdul Hamid Lahori is known as the author of the Badshah Nama. Emperor Shahjahan, hearing of his talents, commissioned him to write a history of his reign modelled on the Akbar Nama.
- The Badshah Nama is the official history in three volumes (daftars) of ten lunar years each.
- Lahori wrote the first and second daftars comprising the first two decades of the emperor's rule (1627-47); these volumes were later revised by Sadullah Khan, Shah Jahan's wazir. Infirmities of old age prevented Lahori from proceeding with the third decade which was then chronicled by the historian Waris.

84. Correct Option: (a)

Explanation:

- **Option (a) is correct:** Nastaliq is a calligraphic style with long horizontal strokes.

Supplementary Notes:

Nastaliq

- Calligraphy is an art of handwriting. It is considered as a skill of great importance. It was practised using different styles. Akbar's favourite was the nastaliq, a fluid style with long horizontal strokes.
- It is written using a piece of trimmed reed with a tip of five to 10 mm called qalam, dipped in carbon ink (siyahi). The nib of the qalam is usually split in the middle to facilitate the absorption of ink.

85. Correct Option: (c)

Explanation:

- All statements are correct

Supplementary Notes:

Harappan Script

- The Harappan script has 400 to 500 signs and it is generally agreed that it is not an alphabetic form of writing but pictographic.
- Some scholars opine that Harappan inscriptions present 3 logosyllabic writing system, where a sequence of two or more signs would represent either a complete word, a syllable or a sound and sometimes even a sentence of several words and grammatical indicators.
- The script was written from right to left. When the inscription was of more than one line it could be first line from right to left and second from left to right.
- There are nearly 400 specimens of Harappan signs on seals and other materials such as copper tablets, axes, and pottery.
- Most of the inscriptions on seals are small, a group of few letters.
- The language of Harappans is at present still unknown and will remain so until the Harappan script is read/understood.
- While some scholars connect it to Dravidian languages and others to Indo-Aryan and Sanskrit yet there is no consensus till now

86. Correct Option: (b)

Supplementary Notes:

Compositions of Alvar Saints

- Both Alvars and Nayanars claimed that their compositions were as important as the Vedas. For instance, one of the major anthologies of compositions by the Alvars, the Nalayira Divyaprabandham, was frequently described as the Tamil Veda.

- By 10th century, the compositions of 12 Alvars were compiled in an anthology known as the Nalayira Divyaprabandham (or 'Four Thousand Sacred Compositions').
- The poems of Appar, Sambandar and Sundarar form the 'Tevaram', a collection that was compiled and classified in the 10th century on the basis of the music of the songs.

87. Correct Option: (d)

Explanation:

- **Option (d) is correct:** 'Pallichchhandam' refers to the land donated to Jaina institutions.

Supplementary Notes:

Types of land

- Chola inscriptions mention several categories of land.
  - **Vellanvagai:** Land of non-Brahmana peasant proprietors
  - **Brahmadeya:** Land gifted to Brahmanas
  - **Shalabhoga:** Land for the maintenance of a school
  - **Devadana, Tirunamattukkani:** Land gifted to temples
  - **Pallichchhandam:** Land donated to Jaina institutions

88. Correct Option: (c)

Explanation:

- Option (c) is correct

Supplementary Notes:

Astadhyayi

- Panini wrote a descriptive linguistic treatise called "Astadhyayi" which covered the whole of Sanskrit language's grammar (including for the Vedic part) and also word formation rules in "sutra" format.

89. Correct Option: (c)

Explanation:

- Statement 1 is incorrect: The book also covers the cultural and religious traditions of the empire.
- Statement 2 is incorrect: Numerous errors in totalling of fiscal numbers have been detected.

Supplementary Notes:

Ain-i-Akbari

- It was the culmination of a large historical, administrative project of classification undertaken by Abul Fazl at the order of Emperor Akbar. It was completed in 1598.
- The book gives detailed accounts of the organisation of the court, administration and army, the source of revenue and the physical layout of the province of Akbar's empire and the literary, cultural and religious traditions of the people
- It is made up of five books (daftars), of which the first three books describe the administration. The first book, called manzil-abadi, concerns the imperial household and its maintenance.
- The second book, sipah-abadi, covers the military and civil administration and the establishment of servants. This book includes notices and short biographical sketches of imperial officials (mansabdars), learned men, poets and artists.
- The third book, mulk-abadi, is the one which deals with the fiscal side of the empire and provides rich quantitative information on revenue rates, followed by the "Account of the Twelve Provinces". This section has detailed statistical information, which includes the geographic, topographic and economic profile of all subas and their administrative and fiscal divisions (sarkars, parganas and mahals), total measured area, and assessed revenue (jama).
- The fourth and fifth books (daftars) deal with the religious, literary and cultural traditions of the people of India and also contain a collection of Akbar's "auspicious sayings.
- The book was much more than a reproduction of official papers.
- Oral testimonies were also incorporated in the book after being cross-checked and verified.
- Historians who have carefully studied the Ain-i-Akbari point out that it is not without its problems. Numerous errors in totalling have been detected. These are ascribed to simple arithmetic slips.
- By providing fascinating glimpses into the structure and organisation of the Mughal Empire and by giving quantitative information about its products and people, Abul Fazl achieved a major breakthrough in the tradition of medieval chroniclers who wrote mostly about remarkable political events – wars, conquests, political machinations, and Dynasty turmoil.
- This literary work completely departed from above tradition, as it recorded information about the empire and the people of India, and thus constitutes a benchmark for studying India at the turn of the seventeenth century.

90. Correct Option: (d)

Explanation:

- **Option (d) is correct:** Vijaynagara empire has been described as the 'Karnataka Samrajyamu'.

Supplementary Notes:

Vijaynagara Empire

- Harihara and Bukka founded the Vijayanagara Empire in 1336.
- They made Hampi as the capital city.
- Four dynasties – Sangama, Saluva, Tuluva and Aravidu – ruled Vijayanagar from AD 1336 to 1672.

- Vijaynagara Empire has been described as the 'Karnataka Samrajyamu' by the contemporaries.

91. Correct Option: (d)

Explanation:

- Both statements are correct

Supplementary Notes:

Alamgir Nama

- Alamgir Nama is the story of Alamgir (a title of the Mughal ruler Aurangzeb).
- It is a as history of the first ten years of Aurangzeb's reign compiled by Muhammmad Kazim.

92. Correct Option: (d)

Explanation:

- **Pair 1 is incorrectly matched:** Abhijnana Shakuntalam – Kalidasa
- **Pair 2 is incorrectly matched:** Mudrarakshasha – Vishakhadatta
- **Pair 3 is incorrectly matched:** Rajatarangini – Kalhana

Supplementary Notes:

Literary Sources

- The works of Kalidasa comprise kavyas and dramas, the most famous of which is Abhijnanashakuntalam. Besides being great creative compositions, they provide us with glimpses of the social and cultural life of the Guptas.
- Kalidasa's Malavikagnimitram is based on some events of the reign of Pusyamitra Sunga, a Dynasty which followed the Mauryas.
- Mudrarakshasha, a play written by Vishakhadatta, also gives a glimpse of society and culture.
- Banabhatta's Harshacharita throws light on many historical facts about which we could not have known otherwise.
- Bilhana's Vikramankadevacharita describes the victories of the later Chalukya king Vikramaditya.
- Rajatarangini by Kalhana is the best illustration of history writing appreciated by modern historians. His critical method of historical research and impartial treatment of the historical facts have earned him a great respect among the modern historians.

93. Correct Option: (a)

Explanation:

- **Pair 1 is incorrectly matched:** Silappathikaram – Elango Adigal.
- **Pair 2 is incorrectly matched:** Manimegalai – Sittalai Sattanar.

Supplementary Notes:

Sangam Literature

- Tolkappiyam was authored by Tolkappiyar and is considered the earliest of Tamil literary work. Though it is a work on Tamil grammar it also provides insights on the political and socio-economic conditions of the time.
- Ettutogai (Eight Anthologies) consist of eight works – Aingurunooru, Narrinai, Aganaooru, Purananooru, Kuruntogai, Kalittogai, Paripadal and Padirruppatu.
- Pattuppattu (Ten Idylls) consists of ten works – Thirumurugarruppadai, Porunararruppadai, Sirupanarruppadai, Perumpanarruppadai, Mullaippattu, Nedunal-vadai, Maduraikkanji, Kurinjip-pattu, Pattinappalai and Malaipadukadam.
- Pathinenkilkanakku contains eighteen works about ethics and morals.
- Of the two epics, Silappathikaram is written by Elango Adigal and Manimegalai by Sittalai Sattanar.

94. Correct Option: (a)

Upanishads	**Features**
A. Aitareya Upanishad	4. Talks about the creation of Atman (Soul) and Consciousness
B. Chandogya Upanishad	3. Deals with rhythm and chanting of Mantras
C. Katha Upanishad	2. The story of Nachiketa and Yama
D. Mundaka Upanishad	1. Contains Satyameva Jayate

Supplementary Notes:

Upanishads

- **Aitareya Upanishad** – Talks about the creation of Atman (Soul) and Consciousness
- **Chandogya Upanishad** – Deals with rhythm and chanting of Mantras
- **Katha Upanishad** – The story of Nachiketa and Yama
- **Mundaka Upanishad** – Contains Satyameva Jayate
- **Brihadaranyaka Upanishad** – Talks about the transmigration of Atman; passages on metaphysics and ethics.

95. Correct Option: (c)

Explanation:

- Both statements are correct

Supplementary Notes:

Indo-Aryan Group of Languages

Old Indo-Aryan Group

- Sanskrit evolved out of old Indo-Aryan group languages. This group had its development around 1500 BC
- The development of Sanskrit grammar began with Panini in 400 BC with his book Asthadhyayi being the oldest book in Sanskrit grammar.

- Some of the Buddhist literature belonging to Mahayana and the Hinayana school are even written in the Sanskrit language. The book Mahavastu of the Hinayana School is a treasure of stories. Lalitavistara, the most sacred Mahayana text, and Ashvagosha's Buddhacharita were also written in Sanskrit.
- The chaste form of Sanskrit developed between 300 BC to 200 BC It was a refined version of Vedic Sanskrit. The first evidence of the use of Sanskrit can be found in the inscriptions of Rudradamana at Junagarh in the present Southern Gujarat region.
- In the field of Sanskrit literature, the Gupta period is known as the period of unique creation. This is because of the fact that there has been a variety of literary works developed during this reign. Another important aspect of it is related to the ornate style in literary works. Many of the places developed during the Gupta period is also written in Sanskrit.

CONCEPT REVISION

Here is the list of concepts that have been covered as part of the previous exercise. Revise and self-reflect on your concepts you covered.

- Harappan Scripts ☐
- Puranas ☐
- Buddhist literature ☐
- 'National Mission on Manuscript' ☐
- Ancient Indian Literature ☐
- 'Pali Literature' ☐
- Vedic Literature ☐
- Santhali Language ☐
- Scheduled Languages ☐
- The bible of Tamil Land ☐
- Jain Literature ☐
- Zoroastrian Literature ☐
- Modern Literature ☐
- Tamil Literature ☐
- Indian notational system ☐
- Development of Sanskrit language ☐
- 'Tripitakas' ☐
- Sangam Literature ☐
- Upanishads and their features ☐

9.3 MISCELLANEOUS

QUESTIONS

1. Which of the following statements regarding different cultural awards is/are correct?

1. Jnanpith Award is bestowed only to Indian writers writing in Indian languages mentioned in the Eighth Schedule of Indian Constitution.
2. Tagore Award is given for outstanding achievement in fostering harmony and universalism and values of cultural harmony.
3. Saraswati Award is given to outstanding literary work in Hindi, authored and published by an Indian citizen.

Select the correct answer using the codes given below:

(a) 1 and 2 only (b) 2 and 3 only
(c) 2 only (d) 1, 2 and 3

2. Which of the following statements regarding Central Board of Film Certification (CBFC) is/are correct?

1. It is a statutory body under the Ministry of Information and Broadcasting.
2. It regulates the public exhibition of cinema in all Indian languages.

Select the correct answer using the code given below:

(a) 1 only (b) 2 only
(c) Both 1 and 2 (d) Neither 1 nor 2

3. Consider the following statements related to the National Culture Fund (NCF):

1. NCF mobilizes resources from government, non-government agencies, private institutions and individuals for the restoration of cultural heritage.
2. Donations to the National Culture Fund are eligible for 100% tax benefit under Income Tax Act subject to limits.

Which of the above statement/s is/are correct?

(a) 1 only (b) 2 only
(c) Both 1 and 2 (d) Neither 1 nor 2

4. Consider the following statements regarding Fairs and Festivals in India:

1. Pongal is the harvest festival of Kerala.
2. Makar Sankranti is a harvest festival which marks the beginning of Sun's journey from Northern Hemisphere to Southern Hemisphere.
3. Gangasagar Mela is the most important fair celebrated in West Bengal.
4. Good Friday marks the birthday of Jesus Christ.

Which of the above statement/s is/are correct?

(a) 1 and 3 only (b) 3 only
(c) 3 and 4 only (d) 1, 3 and 4 only

5. Which of the following statement/s is/are correct related to schemes launched by the Government of India?

1. Swacch Bharat – Swachch Smarak initiative is to preserve and protect national parks and biosphere reserves.
2. Swachch Bharat – Swachch Pakwan initiative is to promote hygienic street food vendors and improve hospitatility services.
3. Swachh Bharat – Swachh Paryatan is an initiative by Ministry of Tourism to assess the requirement of Tourist guides at all popular tourist sites.

Select the correct answer using the code given below:

(a) 1 only (b) 2 only
(c) 2 and 3 only (d) 1, 2 and 3

6. With reference to the UNESCO World Heritage Sites of India, which of the following statement/s is/are correct?

1. The Walled City of Ahmedabad is a World Heritage City.
2. Jantar Mantar, Delhi is one of the World Heritage Sites.
3. Kanchenzunga National Park is the only Mixed Heritage Site in India.

Select the correct answer using the code given below:

(a) 1 only (b) 1 and 2 only
(c) 1 and 3 only (d) 1, 2 and 3

7. Consider the following statements regarding Deen Dayal Hastakal Sankul:

1. It is a trade facilitation centre for handicrafts at Varanasi.
2. The Sankul will facilitate the promotion of handicrafts and handlooms in international market only.

Which of the above statement/s is/are correct?

(a) 1 only (b) 2 only
(c) Both 1 and 2 (d) Neither 1 nor 2

8. Consider the following statements regarding Incredible India 2.0 Campaign:

1. It marks a shift to market specific promotional plans and product specific creative with greater focus on digital presence and social media.
2. It is functional under the Ministry of Electronics and Information Technology.

Which of the above statement/s is/are correct?

(a) 1 only (b) 2 only
(c) Both 1 and 2 (d) Neither 1 nor 2

9. Match the following pairs:

	GI Tag		State
1.	Shahi Litchi	-	Bihar
2.	Boku Chaul	-	Assam
3.	Alphonso Mango	-	Maharastra
4.	Wooden Mask	-	Madhya Pradesh

Which of the pairs given above is/are incorrectly matched?

(a) 1 only (b) 2 and 3 only
(c) 3 and 4 only (d) 4 only

10. Consider the following statements about 'National Virtual Library of India'

1. It is an initiative by Ministry of Human Resource Development.
2. It involves network of IITs, C-DAC, IGNOU for its execution.
3. It is being implemented as a part of National Mission on Libraries.

Which of the following statement/s is/are correct?

(a) 1 and 3 only (b) 1 and 2 only
(c) 3 only (d) 2 and 3 only

11. Consider the following statements about the list, 'Global Geopark Network cities'.

1. They are recognized by UNESCO.
2. There are no Global Geopark sites from India in the list.
3. They are recognised for being 'landscapes of international geological significance'.

Which of the following statement/s is/are correct?

(a) 1 and 2 only (b) 2 only
(c) 1 and 3 only (d) 1, 2 and 3

12. Consider the following statements about UNESCO Creative Cities Network.

1. This is an initiative started under Paris Climate Agreement.
2. Indian cities – Kanpur, Bangalore and Chandigarh are part of this network.
3. Its objectives are in synergy with Sustainable Development Goals 2030.

Which of the above statement/s is/are correct?

(a) 1 only (b) 2 and 3 only
(c) 3 only (d) 1 and 2 only

13. Consider the following statements about Muziris Heritage Project:

1. It is the largest Heritage Conservation Project in India.
2. Muziris, the port city finds its name mentioned in Sangam literature.

Which among the following statement/s is/are correct?

(a) 1 only (b) 2 only
(c) Both 1 and 2 (d) Neither 1 nor 2

14. Consider the following statements about Gandhi Heritage Mission:

1. It is an initiative of Government of Gujarat.
2. It is based on the recommendation of a panel, headed by Gopalkrishna Gandhi.
3. It will build a Portal (E-Library) on Gandhiji's life and achievements.

Which of the above statements are correct?

(a) 1 and 2 only (b) 2 and 3 only
(c) 1 and 3 only (d) 1, 2 and 3

15. Which among the following is/are not a mission under Ministry of Culture?

1. National Mission on Monuments and Antiquities
2. National Mission on Manuscripts
3. National Mission on Libraries
4. Gandhi Heritage Sites Mission

Select the correct answer using the code given below:

(a) 2 and 3 only (b) 3 and 4 only
(c) 1 and 2 only (d) None

16. Which of the following statement/s is/are correct about recently launched Sanskriti App?

1. It is an initiative of Ministry of Culture
2. It helps to view cultural events of India through mobile app.

Select the correct answer using the code given below:

(a) 1 only (b) 2 only
(c) Both 1 and 2 (d) Neither 1 nor 2

17. With reference to National Mission for Cultural Mapping of India, consider following statements

1. It is an initiative of Ministry of Human Resource Development.
2. It aims to develop an objective Cultural map of India.
3. It is to be inaugurated in 2019 to commemorate 150th Birth Anniversary of M.K. Gandhi.
4. "Design for Desire and Dream" is the theme associated with this mission.

Which of the above statement/s is/are correct?

(a) 3 and 4 only (b) 2 and 4 only
(c) 1 and 3 only (d) 2 only

18. Which among the following statements about International Council on Monuments and Sites (ICOMOS) is/are correct?

1. It is an organisation under United Nations.
2. There are no Indian board members in ICOMOS.
3. Kerala Heritage Rescue initiative is launched by ICOMOS.

Select the correct answer using the code given below:

(a) 1 and 2 only (b) 2 only
(c) 2 and 3 only (d) 3 only

19. Which among the following events is/are held permanently in India?

1. World Sanskrit Conference
2. World Hindi Conference
3. International Buddhist Conclave
4. World Kannada Conference

Select the correct answer using the codes given below:

(a) 1 and 2 only (b) 3 only
(c) 3 and 4 only (d) 2 only

20. Consider the following statements about Lalit Kala Academy:

1. Lalit Kala Akademi functions as the apex body and promote the cultural heritage of India in music, dance and drama.
2. The Lalit Kala Akademi promote and propagate understanding of Indian art only within territories of the country.
3. National School of Drama is a theatre training institute set up by Lalit Kala Akademi.

Which of the statements given above is/are incorrect?

(a) 3 only (b) 1 and 2 only
(c) 1 and 3 only (d) 1, 2 and 3

21. Consider the following statements regarding the National List of Intangible Cultural Heritage:

1. The list is based on UNESCO's 2003 Convention for the safeguarding of the Intangible Cultural Heritage.
2. Kumbh Mela has been categorised under social practices, rituals and festive events.

Which of the above statement/s is/are correct?

(a) 1 only (b) 2 only
(c) Both 1 and 2 (d) Neither 1 nor 2

22. The Mughals made distinctive contribution in the field of painting. Consider the following statements regarding the same:

1. The Rajasthan style of painting combined the themes and earlier traditions of Jain school of painting with Mughal forms and styles.
2. Daswant and Basawan were two of the famous painters of Humayun's court.
3. Aurangzeb's lack of interest in painting led to the development of painting in the states of Rajasthan and the Punjab hills.

Which of the above statement/s is/are correct?

(a) 1 and 3 only (b) 2 only
(c) 1 only (d) 2 and 3 only

23. With respect to language, literature and music under Mughals, consider the following statements:

1. The translation of the Mahabharata was carried out under the supervision of Faizi.
2. A Mughal noble, Abdur Rahim Khan-i-Khanan, produced a fine blend of Bhakti poetry with Persian ideas of life and human relations.

3. Aurangzeb banished singing from his court, but not playing of musical instruments.

Which of the above statement/s is/are correct?

(a) 3 only (b) 2 only
(c) 1 only (d) 1, 2 and 3

24. Consider the following statements regarding Arabic and Persian literature during Delhi sultanate:

1. The Arabic language was widely spread and became the language of the people.
2. Persian, was introduced with the arrival of the Turks in India during the 14th century.

Which of the above statement/s is/are incorrect?

(a) 1 only (b) 2 only
(c) Both 1 and 2 (d) Neither 1 nor 2

25. Which of following have written their literary works mainly in Sanskrit?

1. Ramanuja 2. Hemachandra Suri
3. Nammalvar

Select the correct option using the codes given below:

(a) 1 and 2 only (b) 1 and 3 only
(c) 2 and 3 only (d) 1, 2 and 3

26. Consider the following statements regarding Regional languages:

1. The use of the common language by the Bhakti saints was an important factor in the rise of these languages.
2. Hindi, Bengali and Marathi languages, trace their origin back to the eighth century.
3. Marathi was one of the administrative languages in the Bahmani kingdom.

Which of the above statement/s is/are correct?

(a) 1 and 2 only (b) 1 and 3 only
(c) 2 and 3 only (d) 1, 2, and 3

27. Which of the following statements regarding the Buddhist literature is/are incorrect?

1. Both Kailashnatha temple at Kanchipuram and the Brihadeswara temple at Tanjore are fine examples of the Dravida Architecture and were constructed by Rajaraja.
2. Kamban, whom wrote Tamila Ramayana, is believed to have lived at the court of a Chola king

Select the correct option using the codes given below:

(a) 1 only (b) 2 only
(c) Both 1 and 2 (d) Neither 1 nor 2

28. Which of the following set is part of UNESCO list of intangible cultural heritage of humanity?

(a) Kalamkari, Oggukatha, Traditions associated with funerals of Idu Mishimi Tribe
(b) Kumbh mela, Songs of Shaman, Sowa-Rigpa
(c) Kutiyattam, Mudiyettu, Chhau dance
(d) Sattriya Dance and Theatre, The Festival of Salhesh, Sankheda Nu Lakh Kam

29. Consider the following statements:

1. Ancient Monuments Preservation Act was passed during the reign of Lord Curzon.
2. National Monument authority was set up under the provisions of Ancient Monuments Preservation Act.
3. Under the existing rules areas up to 200 meters in the vicinity of ancient and historical monuments are prohibited area while area up to 400 meters is considered regulated area.

Which of the above statement/s is/are correct?

(a) 1 only (b) 1 and 2 only
(c) 2 and 3 only (d) 1, 2 and 3

30. Consider the following statements regarding The Indian Council for Cultural Relations (ICCR):

1. It was established to conduct programmes that promote Indian culture on an international platform.
2. It was established in 1950 by first president Dr Rajendra Prasad.

Which of the above statement/s is/are incorrect?

(a) 1 only (b) 2 only
(c) Both 1 and 2 (d) Neither 1 nor 2

31. Consider the following statements regarding Sahitya Academy:

1. It was established in 1954.
2. It undertakes literary activities in 22 Indian languages which are mentioned in the constitution.
3. It gives Bhasha Samman Award for significant contribution to the languages recognised by the Academi.

Which of the above statement/s is/are incorrect?

(a) 1 and 2 only (b) 1 and 3 only
(c) 2 and 3 only (d) 1, 2 and 3

32. Which of the following cultural sites of India are included in UNESCO'S List of Tangible World Heritage Sites?

1. Ajanta Caves 2. Sun Temple
3. Fatehpur Sikri

Select the correct option using the codes given below:

(a) 1 and 2 only (b) 1 and 3 only
(c) 2 and 3 only (d) 1, 2 and 3

33. Which of the following is included recently in UNESCO'S List of Intangible Cultural Heritage?

(a) Sankirtan (b) Koodiyattam
(c) Yoga (d) Kumbh Mela

34. Consider the following statements:

1. The national cultural fund was created through an act of parliament.

2. The Council of National Cultural Fund is chaired by the prime minister of India.
3. Donations to the National Culture Fund will be eligible for tax benefits under the Income Tax Act.

Which of the above statement is/are correct?

(a) 1 only (b) 1 and 2 only
(c) 3 only (d) 1, 2 and 3

35. With reference to PRASAD scheme, consider the following statements:

1. It is a central sector scheme aiming at integrated development of selected pilgrimage destinations in a sustainable manner.
2. The scheme was launched by the Ministry of Tourism.

Which of the above statement/s is/are correct?

(a) 1 only (b) 2 only
(c) Both 1 and 2 (d) Neither 1 nor 2

36. With reference to the Rashtriya Sanskriti Mahotsav, 2019, consider the following statements:

1. 10th Rashtriya Sanskriti Mahotsav was held in Tehri, Uttarakhand.
2. It is organised by the Ministry of Culture under the Ek Bharat Shrestha Bharat initiative to enhance mutual understanding and bonding among diverse culture.

Which of the above statements is/are correct?

(a) 1 only (b) 2 only
(c) Both 1 and 2 (d) Neither 1 nor 2

37. Which of the following statements regarding the HRIDAY scheme is/are correct?

1. It aims at preserving and revitalizing the soul and the unique character of the heritage cities in India.
2. It supports core heritage linked civic infrastructure projects for revitalisation of urban infrastructure.
3. It is a scheme of the Ministry of Culture.

Select the correct answer using the code given below:

(a) 1 and 2 only (b) 2 only
(c) 1 and 3 only (d) 3 only

38. With reference to various cultural institutions in India, consider the following statements:

1. The Archeological Survey of India is the premier institution for the preservation of tangible as well as intangible cultural heritage in India.
2. The Indira Gandhi National Centre for Arts is an autonomous organisation concentrating on visual and performing arts.
3. The Centre for Cultural Resources and Training is responsible for linking education with culture.

Which of the above statements is/are correct?

(a) 1 only (b) 1 and 2 only
(c) 2 and 3 only (d) 1, 2 and 3

39. Consider the following statements regarding the diseases and origin of Medicine in Ancient India:

1. Yajur Veda is the first book that deal with medicine diseases and its cure.
2. Dhanvantari is considered as the God of medicine.
3. Takshila and Varanasi emerged as the centres for medicinal learning.

Which of the above statements is/are incorrect?

(a) 1 and 2 only (b) 1 only
(c) 2 and 3 only (d) None of the above.

40. Consider the following statements regarding Paryatan Parv:

1. It is a nationwide festival spreading the principle of 'Tourism for All'.
2. Dekho Apna Desh, Tourism for All and Tourism & Governance are the three components of Paryatan Parv.

Which of the above statements is/are correct?

(a) 1 only (b) 2 only
(c) Both 1 and 2 (d) Neither 1 nor 2

41. Bharat Parv is a five-day event hosted on the eve of:

(a) Independence Day
(b) Republic Day
(c) Gandhi Jayanti
(d) National Unity Day

42. Consider the following statements:

1. Swadesh Darshan Scheme aims at providing improved visitor amenities at select monuments.
2. Adarsh Smarak Scheme aims at the integrated development of theme-based circuits.
3. Both Swadesh Darshan and Adarsh Smarak schemes were launched by the Ministry of Tourism.

Which of the above statements is/are incorrect?

(a) 1 and 2 only (b) 2 and 3 only
(c) 3 only (d) 1, 2 and 3

43. Recently, which of the following products were given the GI tag by the Geographical Indications Registry?

1. Dindigul Lock 2. Kandangi Saree
3. Tirur betel leaf

Select the correct answer using the codes given below:

(a) 1 and 2 only (b) 2 and 3 only
(c) 1 and 3 only (d) 1, 2 and 3

44. With reference to the Saka Calendar, consider the following statements:

1. It has the same number of months like Vikram era.
2. It begins on 22nd March every year.

Which of the above statements is/are correct?

(a) 1 only (b) 2 only
(c) Both 1 and 2 (d) Neither 1 nor 2

45. The term 'Ghumot' was seen in the news recently. In this context, consider the following statements:

1. It is an indigenous traditional percussion instrument made from an earthen vessel.
2. It is widely played during Ganesh Chaturthi Aarties.
3. It will be notified as a heritage instrument of Maharashtra.

Which of the above statements is/are correct?

(a) 1 only (b) 1 and 2 only
(c) 2 and 3 only (d) 1, 2 and 3

46. Consider the following statements:

1. Sangeet Natak Academy is the apex body for preserving and promoting performing arts in India.
2. Sahitya Academy is India's premier literary institution that promotes literature in the Schedule VIII languages only.

Which of the above statements is/are correct?

(a) 1 only (b) 2 only
(c) Both 1 and 2 (d) Neither 1 nor 2

47. Consider the following statements regarding various missions run by the Ministry of Culture:

1. National Mission on Manuscripts aims to establish a digital National Manuscripts Library at Indira Gandhi National Centre for Arts (IGNCA).
2. National Mission on Monuments and Antiquities aims to create a National Register on Built Heritage and Sites.
3. Archeological Survey of India is the nodal agency to implement the National Mission on Libraries.

Which of the above statements is/are correct?

(a) 1 and 2 only (b) 1 and 3 only
(c) 2 only (d) 1, 2 and 3

48. Consider the following statements about Minaret of Jam:

1. It is located in Ghur province in western Afghanistan.
2. It is a UNESCO World Heritage Site

Which of the above statements is/are Correct?

(a) 1 only (b) 2 only
(c) Both 1 and 2 (d) Neither 1 nor 2

49. Which of the following statements is/are correct about Pravasi Teerth Darshan Yojana?

1. People selected under this scheme would be taken to religious places of all major Hindu religious places in India.
2. People of Indian-origin aged 25 to 45 can apply and avail the benefits under the scheme.

Select the correct answer using the code given below:

(a) 1 only (b) 2 only
(c) Both 1 and 2 (d) Neither 1 nor 2

SOLUTIONS

1. Correct Option: (c)

Supplementary Notes:

Literary Awards

- **Jnanpith Award:**
  - It is India's highest literary honor. Its name has been taken from Sanskrit words Jnana and Pitha which means knowledge-seat.
  - **Statement 1 is incorrect:** It is bestowed upon any Indian citizen who writes in any 22 official languages of India mentioned in VIII Schedule of Constitution of India and English. The award was instituted in 1961 and is given by Bharatiya Jnanpith.
- **Saraswati Samman:**
  - **Statement 3 is Incorrect:** It is an annual award bestowed upon Indian citizen for his outstanding literary work written in any 22 Indian language mentioned in Schedule VIII of Constitution and published during last 10 years.
  - It is named after an Indian goddess of learning and is considered to be among the highest literary awards in India.
  - It was instituted in 1991 by the K. K. Birla Foundation. It consists of Rs. 15 lakh, a citation and a plaque.
  - Candidates are selected from literary works published in the previous ten years by a panel that included scholars and former award winners.
- **The Tagore Award:**
  - **Statement 2 is correct:** It is an award given in commemoration of the 150th birth anniversary of the Nobel laureate Rabindranath Tagore (1861-1941) for cultural harmony.
  - Established in 2011 by the Government of India, it is given for outstanding achievement in fostering harmony and universalism and values of cultural harmony especially in conflict or extreme situations through innovative systems/strategies and which have an enduring and transformational impact.
  - This award carries an amount of Rupees One Crore, a Citation in a Scroll, a Plaque as well as an exquisite traditional handicraft/handloom item.
- **Vyas Samman**
  - The Vyas Samman award was instituted by the K.K. Birla Foundation in 1991. It is awarded annually to outstanding literary work in Hindi authored and published in past 10 years by an Indian citizen.

2. **Correct Option: (c)**

Supplementary Notes:

Central Board of Film Certification (CBFC):

- **Statement 1 is correct:** Central Board of Film Certification (CBFC) is a statutory body under Ministry of Information and Broadcasting.
- **Statement 2 is correct:** It regulates the public exhibition of films in all Indian languages under the provisions of the Cinematograph Act 1952.
- **Vision:** To ensure the good and healthy entertainment in accordance with the provisions of the Cinematograph Act 1952 and the Cinematograph (Certification) Rules 1983.
- Films can be publicly exhibited in India only after they have been certified by the Central Board of Film Certification.
- The Board consists of non-official members and a Chairman (all of whom are appointed by Central Government) and functions with headquarters at Mumbai. It has nine Regional offices, one each at Mumbai, Kolkata, Chennai, Bangalore, Thiruvananthapuram, Hyderabad, New Delhi, Cuttack and Guwahati.
- The Regional Offices are assisted in the examination of films by Advisory Panels.
- The members of the panels are nominated by Central Government by drawing people from different walks of life for a period of 2 years.

3. **Correct Option: (c)**

Supplementary Notes:

National Culture Fund (NCF):

- It is under the Ministry of Culture, and aims at inviting the participation of the Corporate Sector, Non-Government agencies, State Governments, Private/Public Sector and individuals in the task of promoting, protecting and preserving India's cultural heritage both tangible and intangible.
- The broad guiding principles of the NCF are:
  - NCF sanctions grants to Government and Non-Government Organisations largely out of interest accrued on the Corpus Fund and out of the contributions of the donors.
  - Financial assistance under the NCF is given to Government or Non-Government Organisations to foster India's contemporary culture as well as cultural heritage and to bring both within the reach of the largest possible number of its citizens.
  - Assistance is, however, not provided to those organisations that are already in receipt of financial assistance from attached/subordinate offices or autonomous organisations under the Ministry of Culture or under any scheme of the Ministry.
  - **Statement 1 is correct:** NCF mobilize resources from government, non-government agencies, private institutions and individuals for the restoration of cultural heritage.
  - NCF strives to keep in readiness a number of projects requiring funding and shall, from time to time, renew, upgrade and add to them. The donors are free to choose any projects or suggest new ones for funding and support.
  - **Statement 2 is correct:** The donations / contributions to NCF are eligible for 100% tax deduction under the Income Tax Act, 1961 subject to the limits and conditions prescribed in the said Section and relevant Rules.

4. **Correct Option: (b)**

Supplementary Notes:

Fairs & Festivals:

- India being an agriculture country, where 70% of population of India live in villages and depend on agriculture. Therefore most of the big event of fair and festivals are related to cultivation.
- **Statement 1 is incorrect:** Pongal: It is a harvest festival dedicated to the Sun God. Pongal is one of the most important festivals celebrated by Tamil people in the Indian state of Tamil Nadu, the Indian Union Territory of Puducherry, and the country of Sri Lanka, as well as Tamils worldwide. The day marks the start of the sun's six-month-long journey northwards (the Uttaraayanam).
- **Statement 2 is incorrect:** Makar Sankranti: It is a harvest festival when farmers bring home their harvest. It marks the beginning of Sun's journey from Southern to Northern Hemisphere. It is a festival day in the Hindu calendar, in reference to deity Surya (sun). It is observed each year in January. It marks the first day of sun's transit into the Makara (Capricorn), marking the end of the month with the winter solstice and the start of longer days.
- **Statement 3 is correct:** Gangasagar Mela: The Sagar Island, also known as Gangasagar or Sagardwip, is a place of Hindu pilgrimage in West Bengal. Every year on the day of Makar Sankranti, hundreds of thousands of Hindus gather to take a holy dip at the confluence of river Ganges and Bay of Bengal and offer prayers in the Kapil Muni Temple.
- **Statement 4 is incorrect:** Good Friday: It is a Christian holiday observing the crucifixion of Jesus and his death at Calvary. It is observed during Holy Week as part of the Paschal Triduum on the Friday preceding Easter Sunday, and may coincide with the Jewish observance of Passover. It is also known as Holy Friday, Great Friday, and Black Friday.

5. **Correct Option: (b)**

Supplementary Notes:

Schemes Related to Culture

Swachh Bharat-Swachh Smarak

- **Statement 1 is incorrect:** This is an initiative to see a cleaner India for protecting and preserving the sanctity of monuments of national heritage.
- To aid this, Ministry of Tourism launched a special e-poster with Prime Minister's message requesting the tourists and the people of the nation to wholeheartedly engage themselves in the cleanliness of their surroundings and help create a Swachh Bharat, Swachh Smarak.

Swachh Bharat- Swachh Pakwan (Hunar Zaika)

- The street food vendors constitute a significant percentage of the hospitality service providers, are part of the Indian milieu through the ages and have a pan India presence.
- **Statement 2 is correct:** This program is aimed at upgrading the skills and hygiene standards of Street Food Vendors, so that they become a distinctive aspect of the Indian tourism.
- The Ministry of Tourism is partnering with the National Association of Street Vendors of India (NASVI) for the specific purpose of orientation, skill testing and certification of the vendors.

Swachh Bharat-Swachh Paryatan

- **Statement 3 is incorrect:** Ministry of Tourism has requested all States/UTs to assess the requirement of toilet facilities at all popular tourist sites, provide a list of existing non-functional toilets already constructed, identify an agency for construction and maintenance and follow the standardized model on the lines of Build and Operate pattern for construction of wayside amenities.
- The Ministry has also launched a mobile application to keep tourist places clean.This mobile app will enable citizens, tourists to take photograph of garbage seen at the monument and upload it on the app along with his or her remarks.
- On uploading images and remarks in the app, it will send an SMS to the Archeological Survey of India Nodal Officer concerned with the monument to take further action to clean the garbage.Thereafter, the Nodal Officer will send confirmation about the redressal of the complaint through an SMS.

6. **Correct Option: (c)**

Supplementary Notes:

- Statement 2 is incorrect: Jantar Mantar, Jaipur is one of the World Heritage sites.

UNESCO World Heritage List:

- **Jantar Mantar, Jaipur**
  - The Jantar Mantar (name derived from "Yantra Mantra" (instruments and formulae) in Jaipur is a collection of Astronomical instruments, built by Maharaja Sawai Jai Singh II at his then new capital, Jaipur, between 1727 and 1734.
  - It is modeled after the one that he had built at the Mughal capital of Delhi (which is the earliest).
  - The astronomical observations can be seen with naked eyes, which makes it extraordinary.
  - In all there are five such facilities at different locations, including the ones at Delhi and Jaipur. It is Jaipur and not Delhi that is declared as World Heritage Site by UNESCO. The Jaipur observatory is the largest and best preserved of these and has a set of some 20 main fixed instruments built in masonry.
  - In News: in 2016 Jantar Mantar was declared as World Heritage Site.
- **Walled City of Ahmedabad:**
  - Statement 1 is correct: This city founded by Sultan Ahmad Shah in the 15th century is located on bank of Sabarmati River. It is called Walled City because neighborhoods have clusters of centuries-old residences.
  - It presents a rich architectural heritage from the sultanate period, notably the Bhadra citadel, the walls and gates of the Fort city and numerous mosques and tombs as well as important Hindu and Jain temples of later periods.
  - The urban fabric is made up of densely-packed traditional houses (pols) in gated traditional streets (puras) with characteristic features such as bird feeders, public wells and religious institutions. The city continued to flourish as the capital of the State of Gujarat for six centuries, up to the present.
  - In 2017 ,UNESCO declared this city as World Heritage City, the first Indian city to make it to the list. (Hence)
  - Note:Mahatma Gandhi began his struggle for freedom for India from the British Raj in Ahmedabad.
  - In News: Ahmedabad has been organising a daily Heritage Walk from the early 19th century Swaminarayan temple in Kalupur to the famous 15th century Jama Masjid. Popularly known as 'Mandir to Masjid' the route encompasses 20 main spots besides numerous areas and aspects of the old city
- **Kanchenzunga National Park:**
  - The KNP exhibits one of the widest altitudinal ranges of any protected area worldwide.
  - **Statement 3 is correct:** Kanchenzunga National Park (lies partly in Nepal and partly in Sikkim) is

the only "Mixed Heritage Site" in India included in UNESCO's World Heritage List.

- Mixed Heritage criteria means it manifests outstanding universal values of both Natural and Cultural significance.
- There are numerous glaciers inside the National Park with the Zemu glacier being the most significant one. The area is home to most endemic and rare species of flora and fauna including the Snow Leopard and Himalayan Tahr.
- World's third highest peak and India's highest is located Mt. Kanchenzunga is located within KNP.
- The KNP lies within the Himalaya global biodiversity hotspot and displays an unsurpassed range of sub-tropical to alpine ecosystems due to high altitudal variations.
- **The cultural significance:** KNP is home to a sacred site of one of the world's leading religious traditions, Buddhism. The multi-layered sacred landscape of Khangchenzunga and the cultural and religious relevance of the hidden land is specific to Sikkim and is a unique example of co-existence and exchange between different religious traditions and people. It is because of these heterogeneous mix that this was declared under Mixed Heritage Site.
- The indigenous religious and cultural practices of the Lepcha with regard to the ecology and the specific properties of local plants, which stand as an outstanding example of traditional knowledge and environmental preservation.

7. **Correct Option: (a)**

Supplementary Notes:

Deen Dayal Hastakal Sankul:

- **Statement 1 is correct:** Deendayal Hastkala Sankul is a trade facilitation centre for handicrafts at Varanasi.
- **Statement 2 is incorrect:** The Sankul will facilitate the weavers/ artisans/exporters in promotion of handlooms/handicrafts in both domestic and international markets.
- The Crafts Museum in the Sankul will preserve the traditional handloom/handicrafts products of Varanasi and showcase the handloom & handicraft products.
- The Sankul consists of the automated BMS (Building Management Systems), power backup, and system to protect fire, central air conditioner, ventilation systems, lifts and escalators to help the people to move in the center. The center is centrally monitored by CCTV system for security and safety.

8. **Correct Option: (a)**

Supplementary Notes:

Incredible India 2.0

- **Statement 1 is correct and Statement 2 is incorrect:** Ministry of Tourism launched "Incredible India 2.0 Campaign" which marks a shift from the present generic promotions being undertaken across the world, to market specific promotional plans and product specific creatives, with greater focus on digital presence and social media.
- The Incredible India 2.0 Campaign is being released in the prime existing markets as well as important potential markets. Niche tourism products like Heritage Tourism, Adventure Tourism, Cruise Tourism, Rural Tourism, Wellness & Medical Tourism, MICE, Golf, etc. are being promoted through the Incredible India 2.0 Campaign.

9. **Correct Option: (d)**

Supplementary Notes:

Wooden Mask of Kushmandi

- West Bengal is famous for its unique art form and the mask is one of these art forms. Mainly there are two types of mask - Wooden Mask and Mask made of paper and pulp.
- The wooden masks are found in the northern part of Bengal. Kushmundi of Dakshin Dinajpur is home to 250 crafts persons who are involved in making wooden masks locally called as "Mukha," inexorably linked to the Gombhira dance.
- Bold and demonic look is the characteristic feature of the masks.
- The ecstatic wooden mask of Kushmandi in Dakshin Dinajpur district is associated with the Rajbangshi community of the area.
- The wood is generally sourced from the Gamar trees as it is a soft wood.

Boka chaul

- Its a native rice of the State of Assam which is well-known for its unique property of preparation by just soaking it in water at room temperature. It is a variety of rice grown in many parts of lower Assam, including Nalbari, Barpeta, Goalpara, Kamrup, Darrang, Dhubri, Chirang, Bongaiagoan, Kokrajhar and Baksa.
- It is grown mostly for personal consumption by farmers and is sold in farming areas for ₹ 60-80 per kg as opposed to ₹ 100-150 per kg across towns and cities.
- Traditionally in Assamese culture, at the eleventh hour of arrival of guests or during the need of savouring homemade light dishes at any undecided moments or at the time of guerrilla warfare in want of hurriedly consumable dishes Boka Chaul has always been the first preference that can be easily prepared without requiring any fuel.

Alphonso Mango

- Better known as 'Hapus' in Maharashtra, these mangoes are demanded in domestic and international markets for their taste and pleasant fragrance /vibrant colour.

Shahi Litchi

- Its cultivated mainly in North Bihar (Muzaffarpur, Samastipur, Vaishali, East Champaran and Begusarai) Shahi litchi has juicy aril with very good sugar acid blend and aroma.
- According to agriculture scientists, due to high calcium content in the soil, litchi is better in these areas. A total of 3 lakh metric tonnes of different varieties of litchi were produced in Bihar in 2017-18, out of which 60 per cent were Shahi litchis.

10. **Correct Option: (d)**

Supplementary Notes:

- **Statement 2 and statement 3 are correct:** National Virtual Library of India is a project set up by the Ministry of Culture, Government of India under the National Mission on Libraries.
- The execution of the project is carried out by multiple institutions including:
- IITB (Indian Institute of Technology Bombay), Mumbai
- CDAC (Centre for Development of Advanced Computing), Pune
- Indira Gandhi National Open University), New Delhi.
- It is a project in the larger vision of putting information of the entire Indian cultural heritage in the digital Web world.
- The main goal of this project is to create, collect, encode, and collate various digital artifacts related to Indian culture, in the form of a portal, and to allow relevant information access through web-based search.
- Note:Centre for Development of Advanced Computing (C-DAC) is the premier R&D organisation of the Ministry of Electronics and Information Technology (MeitY) for carrying out R&D in IT, Electronics and associated areas

11. **Correct Option: (d)**

Supplementary Notes:

UNESCO Global Geoparks:

- **Statement 1 and 3 are correct:** Global Geoparks are single, unified geographical areas where sites and landscapes of international geological significance which are managed with a holistic concept of protection, education and sustainable development.
- At present, there are 140 UNESCO Global Geoparks in 38 countries.
- **Statement 2 is correct:** Lonar Lake in Maharashtra and St Mary's Island and Malpe beach in the coastal Karnataka were recently refered by Geological Survey of India-GSI's as candidates for UNESCO Global Geopark Network Status.

Lonar Lake

- Located at Lonar in Buldhana district of Maharashtra, this is the only known meteorite crater in basaltic rock. It is relatively young at just 50,000 years old and was created during Pleistocene Epoch. This lake lies in a basalt impact structure and is both saline and alkaline in nature.

St. Mary's Island

- St. Mary's Islands is also known as Coconut Island and Thonsepar. These are a set of four small islands in the Arabian Sea off the coast of Malpe in Udupi of Karnataka. It is estimated to be an 88 million year old formation that goes back to a time when Greater India broke away from Madagascar.

12. **Correct Option: (c)**

- **Statement 1 is incorrect:** The UNESCO Creative Cities Network (UCCN) was created in 2004 to promote cooperation with and among cities that have identified creativity as a strategic factor for sustainable urban development.
- The Network covers seven creative fields: Crafts and Folk Arts, Media Arts, Film, Design, Gastronomy, Literature and Music.
- **Statement 2 is incorrect:** Chennai (added for its 6000 year old Musical Tradition) the third Indian city on the list of UNESCO Creative Cities list. Varanasi (added as City of Music), Jaipur (City of Crafts and Folk Art).
- **Statement 3 is correct:** Urban areas are today's principal breeding grounds for the development of new strategies, policies and initiatives aimed at making culture and creativity a driving force for sustainable development and urban regeneration through the stimulation of growth and innovation and the promotion of social cohesion, citizen well-being and inter-cultural dialogue.
- Towards this the Creative Cities Network of UNESCO, works as a platform for reflection on the role of creativity in sustainable development but also as a breeding ground of action and innovation, which can help in the implementation of the 2030 Agenda for Sustainable Development.

13. **Correct Option: (c)**

Supplementary Notes:

Muziris Heritage Project

- Muziris was an ancient sea port on the Malabar Coast in Kerala which served as one of the world's greatest trading center in East. The port was used for trade of goods ranging from spices to precious stones with Greeks, Romans and rest of the World during 3rd century BC to 4th century AD.
- **Statement 2 is correct:** The port also has its name mentioned in the Sangam literature and is also designated as the first place from where Christianity

entered India. Besides all these, the Muziris region was well known for its warmth and hospitality towards people of all cultures and religions. With the passage of time, the port lost its glory and identity.

- **Statement 1 is correct:** Muziris Heritage Project is India's largest Heritage conservation project. This is to bring back the past glory and to revive its lost legacy.

14. **Correct Option: (b)**

Supplementary Notes:

- **Staement 1 is incorrect:** Gandhi Heritage Mission is an initiative of Government of India which seeks to restore, preserve the legacy of all places associated with Gandhi's life and also digitise it. This is done by declaring such sites as 'Gandhi Heritage Sites'.
- **Statement 2 is correct:** It was launched in 2008 on the recommendation of a government constituted panel headed by Gandhi's grandson Gopalkrishna Gandhi.
- **Staement 3 is correct:** Among its major recommendations were the establishment of Gandhi Heritage Sites Mission, and the development of a website, containing a catalogue of Gandhi's heritage,to be run and maintained by the Sabarmati Ashram in Ahmedabad.
- Under the Mission 39 sites have been identified. These include Rajkot and Porbandar in Gujarat, Tilak Ghat in Chennai, Mani Bhavan in Mumbai, Beliaghat in Kolkata, Yervada Jail in Pune and the place in Madurai where Gandhi adopted loin-cloth as his only clothing. It includes some foreign locations in South Africa, United Kingdom, Mauritius, Myanmar, Sri Lanka, Pakistan and Bangladesh.

15. **Correct Option: (d)**

Supplementary Notes:

Important Missions Working under Ministry of Culture:

- National Mission on Monuments and Antiquities
- National Mission on Manuscripts
- National Mission on Libraries
- Gandhi Heritage Sites Mission.

National Mission on Monuments and Antiquities:

- Documentation and Creation of suitable database on India's heritage and sites for information and dissemination to planners, researchers etc. and for better management of such cultural resources.
- To promote awareness and sensitize people concerning the benefits of preserving the historical and cultural aspects of built heritage, sites and antiquities.
- Help in developing synergy between institutions like Archaeological Survey of India, State Departments, concerned Institutions and NGOs to generate close interaction.

National Mission on Manuscripts (NMM)-inception in 2003

- India has the largest repository of manuscripts in the world. Hence, conservation becomes more important.
- NMM's mandate is to identify, document, conserve and make accessible the manuscript heritage of India. It is a national effort for logical, radical and urgent response to a very contemporary challenge – of reclaiming the inheritance contained in manuscripts, often in a poor state of preservation.
- National Mission for Manuscripts is first national initiative which is comprehensive in the world and caters to the need of conserving manuscripts and disseminating knowledge contained therein.
- Its motto 'Conserving the Past for the Future'.

National Mission on Libraries:

- National Mission on Libraries seeks to transform India into a knowledge based society.
- Public libraries have a major role to play in realizing this goal. Towards this end Public Library System & Services are revamped to provide digital content-based services to the citizens at large.
- Raja Rammohan Roy Library Foundation has been declared as the nodal agency for the National Mission on Libraries for administrative, logistic, planning and budgeting purposes.

Gandhi Heritage Sites Mission

- Gandhi Heritage Mission is an initiative of Government of India under Ministry of Culture which seeks to restore, preserve the legacy of all places associated with Gandhi's life and also digitise it. This is done by declaring such sites as 'Gandhi Heritage Sites'.
- It was launched in 2008 on the recommendation of a government constituted panel headed by Gandhi's grandson Gopalkrishna Gandhi.
- Among its major recommendations were the establishment of Gandhi Heritage Sites Mission, and the development of a website, containing a catalogue of Gandhi's heritage,to be run and maintained by the Sabarmati Ashram in Ahmedabad.
- Under the Mission 39 sites have been identified. These include Rajkot and Porbandar in Gujarat,Tilak Ghat in Chennai, Mani Bhavan in Mumbai, Beliaghat in Kolkata,Yervada jail in Pune and the place in Madurai where Gandhi adopted loin-cloth as his only clothing. It includes some foreign locations in South Africa, United Kingdom, Mauritius, Myanmar, Sri Lanka, Pakistan and Bangladesh.

16. **Correct Option: (c)**

Supplementary Notes:

- **Statement 1 and 2 are correct:** Sanskriti is a Mobile App (launched by Ministry of Culture) to view cultural events of India to everyone having smartphones (free of cost).

- The main categories of events that can be viewed are Music, Theatre, Dance, Exhibitions, Film Shows, Literature, Lectures and Programs for children.
- The apps (downloadable from Google play store) gives the list of events and automatically detects current location of the mobile and the city is selected accordingly. User can also select city of his choice and see the listings.

17. Correct Option: (b)

Supplementary Notes:

- **Statement 1 and 3 are incorrect:** There is a need to have a consolidated database of information about cultural assets and resources i.e. cultural inventory at one place for essential planning, sustainable economic development and for preserving the scattered and extinct art forms. Towards this end, Ministry of Culture , Government of India has launched the following program during (150th Birth Centenary of Pandit Deen Dayal Upadhyay).

National Mission on Cultural Mapping of India

- The mission aims at converting the vast and widespread cultural canvas of India into an objective cultural map, designing a mechanism to fulfill the aspirations of the whole artist community of the nation and preserving the rich cultural heritage of this country in the form of a cultural repository of artists and art forms.
- Encompasses data mapping, demography building formalising the processes and bringing all the cultural activities under one web based umbrella for better results.
- The Mission seeks to open a direct channel of communication of artists with the Government and peer to peer communication among artists for talent honing and handholding of each other.

Objectives:

- **Statement 2 and 4 are correct:**
  - Establish the cultural mapping (i.e. database of cultural assets and resources) via running nationwide cultural awareness programme called Hamari Sanskriti Hamari Pahchan Abhiyan for the development of all art forms and artists.This Abhiyan will take care of their aspirations & needs by providing a robust mechanism under "Design for Desire and Dream" project.
  - The Mission will run the Abhiyan also by arranging "Sanskritik Pratibha Khoj Samaroh Din" at various levels of this project.
  - Establish a National Cultural Working Place (NCWP) portal for obtaining information, knowledge sharing, participation, performance and awards in the field of all art forms.
  - To provide support in effective utilisation of financial & intellectual resources, minimising wastage of time in talent scouting and providing an opportunity for developing cultural inventory including artistes and art forms.
  - Ranking/Certification of attainments of any kind at any level acquired through formal or non-formal means in conventional or non-conventional art forms.
  - Systematically building a comprehensive database of the capabilities of every individual artist over a period of time and developing a need based schemes/ provisions of Scholarship/Grants/ Awards etc.
  - All time availability of desired database on cultural assets and resources at village, district, State and national levels for self-paced learning.
  - Identify places where platforms like Kala Grams, Craft Melas, etc. may be developed for sharing of ideas, techniques, and resource pooling for planned development and promotion of cultural tourism.
  - Development of GIS (Geographical Information System) based resource inventory Standardisation & Quality Assurance of e-Content to make them world class.
  - Spreading Digital Literacy for teacher empowerment and encouraging teachers/gurus to be available on the internet for guidance/ mentoring of the artists along with online evaluation processes for artists. 16. Development of interfaces for other cognitive faculties which would also help physically challenged artists. These efforts may cut across all the content generation activities.

18. Correct Option: (d)

Supplementary Notes:

- **Statement 1 is incorrect:** ICOMOS (International Council on Monuments and Sites) is an international association that works for the conservation and protection of cultural heritage around the world and offers advice to UNESCO on world heritage sites
- When the Indian state of Kerala and neighbouring districts of Karnataka were hit by the most devastating floods in nearly a century, conservation architects banded together to begin the arduous process of documenting and rescuing affected cultural heritage:buildings, movable objects, crafts, landscapes, libraries and cultural traditions and rituals.
- **Statement 3 is correct:** With the help of ICOMOS India, the Kerala Heritage Rescue Initiative was initiated using a crowdmap to collect data on damaged cultural heritage of all types.

- The information collected through this survey was used to help in visualizing the location, extent and degree of damage and subsequently prioritizing emergency interventions to damaged heritage through evacuation, salvage and stabilisation.
- **Statement 2 is incorrect:** Dr Rohit Jigyasu, conservation and risk management professional and president of ICOMOS India was elected as the Vice-President of ICOMOS. He is the first Indian to get elected to the bureau of ICOMOS. Toshiyoko Kono from Japan has been elected as the President.

19. **Correct Option: (c)**

Supplementary Notes:

World Hindi Conference

- **Statement 2 is incorrect:** World Hindi Conference (Vishva Hindi Sammelan) is a world conference on Hindi language. The conference consists of several Hindi scholars, writers and laureates from different parts of the world to contribute the language.The objective of the Conference is to deliberate on how Hindi could be a medium of serving mankind in the prevailing environment and having imbibed the spirit of 'Seva propounded by Mahatma Gandhi, how Hindi could get recognized in the UN and move forward as a world language serving the cause of humanity. Further, how could it give to the world the motto of 'Vasudhaiva Kutumbakam' which is at the root of the Indian culture, thereby infusing the feeling of 'one world one family'.

World Sanskrit Conference

- **Statement 1 is incorrect:** Several Sanskrit scholars from major Indian universities perceived that the International Congress of Orientalises "did not allow sufficient scope for full discussion of Sanskrit and allied subjects". These scholars approached the Government of India, which arranged to convene the first World Sanskrit Conference at New Delhi in March 1972. Since then it has been held in North America, Europe, Asia and Australia.

International Buddhist Conclave

- **Statement 3 is correct:** The International Buddhist Conclave (held biennaly) is to showcase and project the Buddhist Heritage in India and boost tourism to the Buddhist sites in the country and cultivate friendly ties with countries and communities interested in Buddhism.
- India has a rich ancient Buddhist Heritage with several important sites associated with the life of Lord Buddha.
- Buddha Path refers to the extraordinary teachings of the Buddha which is called the Middle Path whose practice brings purity of mind and leads to Peace, Happiness and Harmony within and also in the Society as well.
- International Buddhist Conclave is organised biennially by Ministry of Tourism, Government of India.
- The earlier International Buddhist Conclaves were organized in New Delhi and Bodh Gaya (February 2004), Nalanda and Bodh Gaya (February 2010), Varanasi and Bodh Gaya (September 2012), Bodh Gaya and Varanasi (September 2014) and in Sarnath/ Varanasi and Bodh Gaya (October 2016).
- Note that in every IBC – Bodh Gaya is chosen as one of the places.
- The theme of the 6th edition (in 2018) is "Buddha Path – The Living Heritage".

World Kannada Conference

- **Statement 4 is correct:** World Kannada Conference is always held within Karnataka.

20. **Correct Option: (d)**

Supplementary Notes:

Lalit Kala Academy

- **Statement 1 is incorrect:** Sangeet Natak Akademi functions as the apex body of the performing arts in the country to preserve and promote the vast cultural heritage of India expressed in music, dance and drama. It also works with governments and art academies in states and territories of the country.
- **Statement 2 is incorrect:** The Lalit Kala Akademi or National Academy of Art is India's national academy of fine arts. It is an autonomous organisation, established in New Delhi in 1954 by Government of India to promote and propagate understanding of Indian art, in and outside the country.
- Lalit Kala Akademi provides scholarships and a fellow program, and sponsors and organises exhibitions in India and overseas. It publishes a bilingual journal. It is funded by the Union Ministry of Culture. Its headquarters are at Ravindra Bhawan, Ferozshah Road, New Delhi.
- In April 2015, Government of India took over management control of Lalit Kala Akademi citing complaints regarding alleged administrative and financial irregularities in its functioning.
- **Statement 3 is incorrect:** National School of Drama (or NSD) is a theatre training institute situated at New Delhi, India. It is an autonomous organisation under Ministry of Culture, Government of India. It was set up in 1959 by the Sangeet Natak Akademi, and became an independent school in 1975.

21. **Correct Option: (c)**

Supplementary Notes:

National List of Intangible Cultural Heritage (ICH)

- It is an attempt to recognize the diversity of Indian culture embedded in its intangible heritage.

- It aims to raise awareness about the various intangible cultural heritage elements from different states of India at national and international level and ensure their protection.
- Based on UNESCO's 2003 Convention for the Safeguarding of the Intangible Cultural Heritage, this list has been classified into five broad domains in which intangible cultural heritage is manifested.
- **Categories**
  - Oral traditions and expressions, including language as a vehicle of the intangible cultural heritage
  - Performing arts
  - Social practices, rituals and festive events
  - Knowledge and practices concerning nature and the universe
  - Traditional craftsmanship
- **Kumbh Mela**
  - It is a mass congregation of generally Hindu pilgrims in which people gather to take a bath/dip in a sacred river.
  - The geographical location for the Kumbh Mela spans across four cities within India.
  - In Madhya Pradesh it is held in Ujjain with the site of observation being the banks of sacred river Shipra.
  - It is categorised under social practices, rituals and festive events.

22. Correct Option: (a)

Explanation:

- **Statements 2 is incorrect:** Daswant and Basawan were two of the famous painters of Akbar's court.

Supplementary Notes:

Mughal Painting

- The Mughals made distinctive contribution in the field of painting. They introduced new themes depicting the court, battle scenes and the chase, and added new colours and new forms.
- Apart from the Jains, some of the provincial kingdoms, such as Malwa and Gujarat extended their patronage to painting during the fifteenth century. But a vigorous revival began only under Akbar.
- While at the court of the shah of Iran, Humayun had taken into his service two master painters who accompanied him to India. Under their leadership, during the reign of Akbar, a painting workshop was set up in one of the imperial establishments (karkhanas).
- A large number of painters, many of them from the lower castes, were drawn from different parts of the country. From the beginning, both Hindus and Muslims joined in the work. Thus, Daswant and Basawan were two of the famous painters of Akbar's court.
- The school developed rapidly, and soon became a celebrated centre of production. Apart from illustrating Persian books of fables, the painters were soon assigned the task of illustrating the Persian text of the Mahabharata, the historical work Akbar Nama, and others.
- Indian themes and Indian scenes and landscapes, thus, came in vogue and helped to free the school from Persian influence.
- Mughal painting reached a climax under Jahangir who had a very discriminating eye. It was a fashion in the Mughal school for the faces, bodies and feet of the people in a single picture to be painted by different artists.
- Jahangir claims that he could distinguish the work of each artist in a picture. Apart from painting hunting, battle and court scenes, under Jahangir special progress was made in portrait painting and paintings of animals. Mansur was the great name in this field. Portrait painting also became fashionable.
- While the tradition continued under Shah Jahan, Aurangzeb's lack of interest in painting led to a dispersal of the artists to different places of the country. This helped in the development of painting in the states of Rajasthan and the Punjab hills.
- The Mughal tradition of painting was, however, revived during the eighteenth century under the patronage of the successors of Aurangzeb.
- The Rajasthan style of painting combined the themes and earlier traditions of western India or Jain school of painting with Mughal forms and styles. Thus, in addition to hunting and court scenes, it had paintings on mythological themes, such as the dalliance of Krishna with Radha, the barahmasa (seasons) or the ragor (melodies). The Pahari school continued these traditions.

23. Correct Option: (d)

Explanation:

- All statements are correct

Supplementary Notes:

Language, Literature and Music under Mughals

- Persian prose and poetry reached a climax under Akbar's reign. Abul Fazl who was a great scholar and a stylist, as well as the leading historian of the age, set a style of prose-writing which was emulated for many generations.
- The leading poet of the age was his brother, Faizi, who also helped in Akbar's translation department. The translation of the Mahabharata was carried out under his supervision.

- Utbi and Naziri were the two other leading Persian poets. Though born in Persia, they were among the many poets and scholars who migrated from Iran to India during the period and made the Mughal court one of the cultural centres of the Islamic world. Hindus also contributed to the growth of Persian literature.
- From the time of Akbar, Hindi poets began to be attached to the Mughal court. A leading Mughal noble, Abdur Rahim Khan-i-Khanan, produced a fine blend of Bhakti poetry with Persian ideas of life and human relations. Thus, the Persian and the Hindi literary traditions began to influence each other.
- But the most influential Hindi poet was Tulsidas who venerated Rama as a god and hero, and he used a dialect of Hindi spoken in the eastern parts of Uttar Pradesh.
- Pleading for a modified caste system based not on birth but on individual qualities, Tulsidas was essentially a humanistic poet who upheld family ideals and complete devotion to Rama as a way of salvation open to all, irrespective of caste
- Akbar patronised Tansen of Gwalior who is credited with composing many new melodies (ragas). Jahangir and Shah Jahan as well as many Mughal nobles followed this example.
- There are many stories about the burial of music by the orthodox Aurangzeb. Recent research shows that Aurangzeb banished singing from his court, but not playing of musical instruments. In fact, Aurangzeb himself was an accomplished veena player.
- Music in all forms continued to be patronised by Aurangzeb's queens in the haram and by the princes and nobles. That is why the largest number of books on classical Indian music in Persian were written during Aurangzeb's reign.

24. Correct Option: (c)

Explanation:

- **Statement 1 is incorrect:** In India, the use of Arabic remained largely confined to a narrow circle of Islamic scholars and philosophers.
- **Statement 2 is incorrect:** With the arrival of the Turks in India during the tenth century, a new language, Persian, was introduced in the country.

Supplementary Notes:

Cultural development in India 1300-1500: Arabic and Persian literature

- Although the greatest amount of literature and scientific works produced by the Muslims was in Arabic which was the language of the Prophet.
- However, the Turks who came to India were deeply influenced by the Persian language which had become the literary and administrative language of Central Asia from the tenth century onwards.
- In India, the use of Arabic remained largely confined to a narrow circle of Islamic scholars and philosophers, most of the original literature on the subject being written in Arabic.
- In course of time, digests of the Islamic law were prepared in Persian with the help of Indian scholars.
- The most well-known of these were prepared in the reign of Firuz Tughlaq. But Arabic digests continued to be prepared, the most famous of these being the Fatawa-i-Alamgiri, or the Digest of Laws prepared by a group of jurists in the reign of Aurangzeb.
- With the arrival of the Turks in India during the tenth century, a new language, Persian, was introduced in the country.
- There was a resurgence of the Persian language in Iran and Central Asia from the tenth century onwards and some of the greatest poets of the Persian language, such as Firdausi and Sadi, lived and composed their works between the tenth and fourteenth centuries.
- From the beginning, the Turks adopted Persian as the language of literature and administration in the country. Thus, Lahore emerged as the first centre for the cultivation of the Persian language.
- However, the most notable Persian writer of the period was Amir Khusrau. Born in 1252 at Patiali (near Badayun in western Uttar Pradesh), Amir Khusrau took pride in being an Indian.
- Khusrau wrote a large number of poetical works, including historical romances. He experimented with all the poetical forms and created a new style of Persian which came to be called the sabaq-i-hindi or the style of India.

25. Correct Option: (a)

Explanation:

- **Option (3) is incorrect:** Nammalvar is one of the 12 alvar saints of Tamil Nadu. He contributed to Divya Pabhandam which represent (in Tamil language) the 4 Sanskrit Vedas.

Supplementary Notes:

Cultural development in India 1300-1500: Sanskrit literature

- Sanskrit continued to be a vehicle for higher thought and a medium for literature during the period under review. Following the great Sankara, works in the field of philosophy by Ramanuja, Madhava, Vallabha, etc., continued to be written in Sanskrit.
- The speed with which their ideas were widely disseminated and discussed in different parts of the country showed the important role which Sanskrit continued to play during the period.

- There was a network of specialised schools and academies in different parts of the country, including areas under Muslim domination.
- In fact, many of them took advantage of the introduction of paper to reproduce and disseminate older texts.
- Thus, some of the oldest available texts of the Ramayana and the Mahabharata written on paper belong to the period between the eleventh and twelfth century.
- Besides philosophy, works in the field of kavya (poetical narrative), drama, fiction, medicine, astronomy, music, etc., continued to be written in Sanskrit.
- A large number of commentaries and digests on the Hindu law (Dharmashastras) were prepared between the twelfth and the sixteenth century.
- The great Mitakshara of Vijnaneshwar, which forms one of the two principal Hindu schools of law, cannot be placed earlier than the twelfth century.
- Another famous commentator was Chandeshwar of Bihar who lived in the fourteenth century.
- The Jains, too, contributed to the growth of Sanskrit.
- Hemachandra Suri was the most eminent of these.
- Nammalvar is one of the 12 alvar saints of Tamil Nadu. He contributed to Divya Pabhandam which represent (in Tamil language) the 4 Sanskrit Vedas.

26. Correct Option: (d)

Explanation:

- All statements are correct

Supplementary Notes:

Cultural development in India 1300-1500: Regional languages

- During this period, literary works of high quality were produced in many of the regional languages as well.
- Many of these languages, such as Hindi, Bengali and Marathi, trace their origin back to the eighth century or so.
- Some others, such as Tamil, were much older. The rise to maturity of many of these languages and their use as means for literary works may be considered a striking feature of the medieval period.
- There were many reasons for this. Perhaps, with the loss of prestige by the Brahmans, Sanskrit also lost some of its prestige.
- The use of the common language by the Bhakti saints was, undoubtedly, an important factor in the rise of these languages.
- Later, when the Delhi Sultanate broke up, local languages, in addition to Persian, continued to be used for administrative purposes in many of the regional kingdoms.
- Thus, literature in Telugu developed in South India under the patronage of the Vijayanagara rulers.
- Marathi was one of the administrative languages in the Bahmani kingdom, and later, at the court of Bijapur.
- In course of time, when these languages had reached a certain stage of development, some of the Muslim kings gave them patronage for literary purposes also.

27. Correct Option: (a)

Explanation:

- **Statement 1 is incorrect:** Kailashnatha Temple was built by Rajasimha or Narasimhavarman II, a ruler of the Pallava Dynasty at Kanchipuram.

Supplementary Notes:

Cholas: Cultural Life

- The Chola rule saw the further growth and climax of the Bhakti Movement which we have discussed separately. The movement was closely linked to temples.
- The extent and resources of the Chola empire enabled the rulers to build great capitals, such as Tanjore, Gangaikonda Cholapuram, Kanchi, etc.
- The temple architecture in the south reached its climax under the Cholas. The Dravida Style of Temple architecture came into vogue which laid emphasis on the building of storey upon storey above the chief deity room (garbhagriha). The temple had a pillared hall called 'mandapa' with elaborately carved pillars and flat roof which was mostly used as an audience hall and a place for other activities such as ceremonial dances by devadasis. The temple, apart from serving as place of worship, also functioned as the hub of social and cultural life. The temple had lofty and elaborate gates called gopurams. A fine example of Dravida style architecture is the 8th century temple of Kailashnatha(built by a Rajasimha or Narasimhavarman II, a ruler of the Pallava Dynasty) at Kanchipuram. Similarly, the Brihadeswara temple (by Rajaraja) at Tanjore is another fine specimen of Dravida style.
- The art of sculpture attained a high standard in south India during this period. One example of this was the giant statue of Gomateshwara at Sravana Belgola. Another aspect was image-making which reached in zenith in the dancing figure of the Siva, called Nataraja. The Nataraja figures of this period, particularly those in bronze, are considered masterpieces.
- The rulers of the various dynasties also patronized arts and letters during this period. While Sanskrit was regarded as the language of high culture and a number of kings as well as scholars and court poets wrote in it, a remarkable feature of the period was the growth of literarure in the local languages of India. A number of popular saints called Nayanmars and Alvars who

were devotees of Siva and Vishnu respectively, flourished in the Tamil kingdoms between the sixth and the ninth centuries.

- The age of Kamban who is placed in the second half of the eleventh and the early part of the twelfth century is regarded as a golden age in Tamil literature. Kamban's Ramayana is considered a classic in Tamil literature. Kamban is believed to have lived at the court of a Chola king.

28. Correct Option: (c)

Supplementary Notes:

Intangible cultural list of humanity

- 13 traditions until now are included in UNESCO list of intangible cultural list of humanity:
  - Tradition of Vedic chanting
  - Ramlila, the traditional performance of the Ramayana
  - Kutiyattam, Sanskrit theatre
  - Ramman, religious festival and ritual theatre of the Garhwal Himalayas.
  - Mudiyettu, ritual theatre and dance drama of Kerala
  - Kalbelia folk songs and dances of Rajasthan
  - Chhau dance
  - Buddhist chanting of Ladakh: the recitation of sacred Buddhist texts in the trans-Himalayan Ladakh region, Jammu and Kashmir.
  - Sankirtana, ritual singing, drumming and dancing of Manipur
  - Traditional brass and copper craft of utensil making among the Thatheras of Jandiala Guru, Punjab
  - Yoga
  - Nawrouz
  - Kumbh Mela

29. Correct Option: (a)

Explanation:

- **Statement 2 is incorrect:** It has been set up under the Ancient Monuments and Archaeological Sites and Remains AMASR (Amendment and Validation) Act, 2010.
- **Statement 3 is incorrect:** The rules made under AMASR act stipulate that area in the vicinity of the monument, within 100 meters is prohibited area. The area within 200 meters of the monument is regulated category.

Supplementary Notes:

Protection and Promotion of Indian Culture and Heritage

- One of the most remarkable acts passed during the times of Lord Curzon was the Ancient Monuments Preservation Act of 1904. This act made any injury to the protected monuments an offence punishable under the law.
- National Monuments Authority (NMA) under the Ministry of Culture, Govt. of India has been set-up as per provisions of The Ancient Monuments and Archaeological Sites and Remains AMASR (Amendment and Validation) Act, 2010.
- The rules made under AMASR act stipulate that area in the vicinity of the monument, within 100 meters is prohibited area. The area within 200 meters of the monument is regulated category.

30. Correct Option: (b)

Explanation:

- **Statement 2 is incorrect:** It was established by Maulana Abul Kalam Azad.

Supplementary Notes:

Indian Council for Cultural Relations

- The Indian Council for Cultural Relations (ICCR) is under the aegis of the Ministry of Culture and was established to conduct programmes that promote Indian culture on an international platform.
- Maulana Abul Kalam Azad, who firmly believed in promoting cultural exchanges with other countries and cultures, established it in 1950.
- ICCR focuses on the formulation and implementation of the programmes and policies that are deeply rooted in the external cultural relations between India and other nations. With globalisation, the platforms of cultural exchanges among nations have taken various forms.
- ICCR funds various programmes relating to visual and performing arts that are international in their appeal.
- They provide grants in support of programmes like the Jazz Festival in New Delhi, the North-East Music Festival in Guwahati, etc. The programmes are an integral way of establishing and developing relations with similar national and international organisations that focus in the field of culture.
- The major focus of ICCR is to promote international friendship, promote cultural exchange between nations, generate healthy competition and exchange, and in turn blend the new and old features of the Indian culture.

31. Correct Option: (c)

Explanation:

- **Statement 2 is incorrect:** It also recognises languages which are not mentioned in the constitution like Rajasthani.
- **Statement 3 is incorrect:** Bhasha Samman is given for significant contribution in the languages not

recognised by the Academi and to those who have contributed to Ancient and Medieval literature.

Supplementary Notes:

Sahitya Academy

- The Government of India established the "National Academy of Letters" or the Sahitya Academi in 1954.
- The primary function of this organisation was to work as a national organisation to promote literary culture in India, to foster and co-ordinate literature in all the Indian languages and to overall promote the national unity of the country.
- It is an autonomous organisation, which undertakes literary activities in over 24 Indian languages. Apart from the 22 languages that are mentioned in the Constitution of India, the Sahitya Academi gives recognition to two more languages: English and Rajasthani.
- They have several awards and fellowships that honor the great contribution made to linguistic development by writers. Some of these awards are:
- Bhasha Samman: For significant contribution to the languages not recognised by the Academi and to those who have contributed to Ancient and Medieval literature.
- Dr. Anand Coomaraswamy Fellowship: Those who have worked on the field of art, especially in Ancient India.
- Premchand Fellowship: Those who have contributed to the literature in Hindi.
- For the last few years their collective focus has shifted to the preservation of the oral and tribal literature.
- Our ancient society and traditional knowledge was transferred as oral knowledge and that needs to be preserved for the coming generations.
- It has also tried to reach to a wider audience through the organisation of literary gatherings like: Samvad, Meet the Author, Kathasandi, Mulakat, Asmita, etc.

32. Correct Option: (d)

Explanation:

- **Option (d) is correct:** All of these are included in UNESCO'S List of Tangible World Heritage Sites in India.

Supplementary Notes:

UNESCO'S List of Tangible World Heritage Sites in India

- **Cultural Sites**
  - ➤ Ajanta Caves (Maharashtra)
  - ➤ Ellora Caves (Maharashtra)
  - ➤ Taj Mahal (Uttar Pradesh)
  - ➤ Agra Fort (Uttar Pradesh)
  - ➤ Sun Temple, Konark (Odisha)
  - ➤ Group of Monuments at Mahabalipuram (Pancha Ratha, Shore Temple, Arjuna's Penance or Descent of the Ganges, Caves Temples, etc) (Tamil Nadu)
- **Churches and Convents of Goa**
  - ➤ Khajuraho group of Monuments (Madhya Pradesh) (Group of Hindu and Jain temples which include Kandariya Mahadeva temple, Vishvanatha temple, Lakshmana temple, Chausath Yogini temple, etc. of Hindu origin and Parshvanatha, Adinath and Shantinatha temples, etc. of Jain origin).
- **Fatehpur Sikri (Uttar Pradesh)**
  - ➤ Group of Monuments at Hampi, Karnataka (Krishna temple complex, Narasimha, Ganesa, Hemakuta group of temples, Achyutaraya temple complex, Vitthala temple complex, Pattabhirama temple complex, Lotus Mahal complex, etc.).
- **Elephanta Caves (Maharashtra)**
  - ➤ Group of Monuments at Pattadakal (Karnataka) (Nine Hindu temples and one jain temple which includes Virupaksha temple, Papanatha temple, etc.).
  - ➤ Great Chola Temples [Brihadeshwara Temple, Thanjavur (Tamil Nadu), Airavateshvara Temple, Darasuram (Tamil Nadu)].
  - ➤ Buddhist Monuments at Sanchi, Madhya Pradesh (Great Stupa, Ashokan Pillar, Shunga Pillar, Siri Satakarni inscriptions of Satavahana period, various other Stupas, etc.).
  - ➤ Humayun's Tomb (Delhi).
  - ➤ Qutub Minar and it Monuments (Delhi).
  - ➤ Darjeeling Himalayan Railway (West Bengal) (Under Mountain Railways of India) 2002.
  - ➤ Mahabodhi Temple Complex, Bodh Gaya (Bihar) 2003.
  - ➤ Rock shelters of Bhimbetka (Madhya Pradesh) 2004.
  - ➤ Chhatrapati Shivaji Terminus or Victoria Terminus, Mumbai (Maharashtra).
  - ➤ Champaner-Pavagadh Archaeological Park (Gujarat).
  - ➤ Nilgiri Mountain Railways (under Mountain Railways of India).
  - ➤ Red Fort Complex (Delhi).
  - ➤ Kalka-Shimla Railway (Himachal Pradesh) (under Mountain Railways of India).
  - ➤ Jantar Mantar, Jaipur (Rajasthan).
- **Six Hill Forts of Rajasthan**
  - ➤ Chittorgarh
  - ➤ Ranthambhore
  - ➤ Jaisalmer
  - ➤ Kumbhalgarh

- Amber
- Gagron
- Rani ki Vav (The Queen's Stepwell), (Gujarat)
- The Achitectural work of Le Corbusier (Capital Complex, Chandigarh)
- Archeological site of Nalanda Mahavihara (Nalanda University), (Bihar)
- Historic city of Ahmedabad.

- **Natural Sites**
  - Manas Wildlife Sanctuary (Assam), 1985
  - Kaziranga National Park (Assam), 1985
  - Keoladeo National Park, Bharatpur (Rajasthan), 1985 4 Sundarban National Park (West Bengal), 1987
  - Nanda Devi National Park (1988) and Valley of Flowers (Uttarakhand), 2005
  - Western Ghats, 2012 (Sub-clusters include Agasthyamalai, Periyar, Anamalai, Nilgiri, Talakaveri, Kudremukh and Sahyadri)
  - Great Himalayan National Park (Himachal Pradesh), 2014
  - Khangchendzonga National Park (Sikkim) (2016) (Note: Khangchendzonga National Park is under the mixed category)

33. **Correct Option: (d)**

Explanation:

- Option (d) is correct

Supplementary Notes:

UNESCO's List of Intangible Cultural Heritage:

- The list is made up of those intangible heritage elements that help demonstrate diversity of cultural heritage and raise awareness about its importance. The list was established in 2008 when Convention for Safeguarding of the Intangible Cultural Heritage came into effect. UNESCO maintains three lists under its "Intangible Cultural Heritage" banner: the list of intangible cultural heritage in need of urgent safeguarding, the list of the intangible cultural heritage of humanity and the register of good safeguarding practices.
- Some of the criteria for inclusion in the representative list are if the inscription of the element will ensure visibility and awareness of it and if the element has been nominated after having "the widest possible participation" of the community, group or individuals concerned and with their free, prior and informed consent.

From India the Intangible Cultural Heritages added into this list include:

- Tradition of Vedic chanting
- Ramlila, the traditional performance of the Ramayana
- Kutiyattam, Sanskrit theatre
- Ramman, religious festival and ritual theatre of the Garhwal Himalayas.
- Mudiyettu, ritual theatre and dance drama of Kerala
- Kalbelia folk songs and dances of Rajasthan
- Chhau dance
- Buddhist chanting of Ladakh: recitation of sacred Buddhist texts in the trans-Himalayan Ladakh region, Jammu and Kashmir.
- Sankirtana, ritual singing, drumming and dancing of Manipur
- Traditional brass and copper craft of utensil making among the Thatheras of Jandiala Guru, Punjab
- Yoga
- Nawrouz
- Kumbh Mela

34. **Correct Option: (c)**

Explanation:

- **Statement 1 is incorrect:** It was set up in India as a Trust under the Charitable Endowment Act, 1890.
- **Statement 2 is incorrect:** Its council is chaired by the Minister of culture.

Supplementary Notes:

National Culture Fund (NCF)

- The National Culture Fund (NCF) was established as a funding mechanism distinct from the existing sources and patterns of funding for the arts and culture in India. It will enable institutions and individuals to support arts and culture directly as partners with its government.
- NCF was set up by the Government of India as a Trust under the Charitable Endowment Act, 1890 through a Gazette Notification.
- Its council is chaired by the Minister of Culture.
- The donation to NCF will be eligible for tax benefit under section 10 (23C) (iv) and 80 G (2) of the Income Tax Act.

35. **Correct Option: (c)**

Explanation:

- Both statements are correct

Supplementary Notes:

PRASAD Scheme

- Pilgrimage Rejuvenation and Spiritual Augmentation Drive (PRASAD) is a central sector scheme that focuses on identifying and developing the pilgrim sites across the country to enrich the religious tourism experience.
- It was launched by the Ministry of Tourism.

- The scheme shall be 100% centrally funded for the project components undertaken for public funding. Efforts will be made to achieve convergence with other schemes of Central and State governments and also to leverage the voluntary funding available for Corporate Social Responsibility (CSR).
- It aims at integrated development of pilgrimage destinations in a planned, prioritized and sustainable manner to provide complete religious tourism experience.
- 12 cities namely Amaravati (Andhra Pradesh), Gaya (Bihar), Dwarka (Gujarat), Amritsar (Punjab), Ajmer (Rajasthan), Kanchipuram (Tamil Nadu), Velankanni (Tamil Nadu), Puri (Odisha), Varanasi (Uttar Pradesh), Mathura (Uttar Pradesh), Kedarnath (Uttarakhand) and Kamakhya (Assam) have been identified for development under the scheme.
- The scheme has the following objectives:
  - Harness pilgrimage tourism for its direct and multiplier effect upon employment generation and economic development.
  - Enhance tourist attractiveness in a sustainable manner by developing world-class infrastructure in religious destinations.
  - Promote local art, culture, handicraft, cuisine, etc. to generate livelihood in identified places.

36. Correct Option: (b)

Explanation:

- **Statement 1 is incorrect:** 10th Rashtriya Sanskriti Mahotsav was held in Jabalpur, MP.

Supplementary Notes:

Rashtriya Sanskriti Mahotsav, 2019

- 10th Rashtriya Sanskriti Mahotsav is being held in Jabalpur, MP. It is organised by the Ministry of Culture under the Ek Bharat Shrestha Bharat initiative.
- Rashtriya Sanskriti Mahotsav was conceived in the year 2015. It is organised with an intent to showcase the rich cultural heritage of the country in all its rich and varied dimensions, viz, Handicrafts, Cuisine, Painting, Sculpture and Performing Arts-Folk, Tribal, Classical and Contemporary – all in one place.
- The Ek Bharat Shreshtha Bharat programme was launched by the Prime Minister on October 31, 2016, to promote engagement amongst the people of different States and UTs so as to enhance mutual understanding and bonding between people of diverse cultures, thereby securing stronger unity and integrity of India.

37. Correct Option: (a)

Explanation:

- **Statement 3 is incorrect:** HRIDAY is a scheme of Ministry of Housing and Urban Affairs.

Supplementary Notes:

HRIDAY Scheme

- The Ministry of Housing and Urban Affairs, Government of India, launched the National Heritage City Development and Augmentation Yojana (HRIDAY) scheme in 2015, with a focus on holistic development of heritage cities focusing not just on maintenance of monuments but on advancement of the entire ecosystem including its citizens, tourists, and local businesses.
- The scheme aims to preserve and revitalize the soul of the heritage city to reflect the city's unique character by encouraging aesthetically appealing, accessible, informative & secured environments.
- The scheme is being implemented in 12 identified Cities namely, Ajmer, Amaravati, Amritsar, Badami, Dwarka, Gaya, Kanchipuram, Mathura, Puri, Varanasi, Velankanni and Warangal in mission mode.
- HRIDAY is a central sector scheme, where 100% of funding will be provided by the Government of India.
- The scheme supports the development of core heritage civic infrastructure projects which shall include revitalisation of urban infrastructure for areas around heritage assets identified/ approved by the Ministry of Culture, Government of India and State Governments.
- It also seeks beautification in an inclusive and integrated manner with a focus on cleanliness, livelihoods, skills, safety, security, accessibility and faster service delivery of heritage cities.

38. Correct Option: (c)

Explanation:

- **Statement 1 is incorrect:** The Archeological Survey of India is the premier institution for the preservation of only physical and tangible cultural heritage.

Supplementary Notes:

Archeological Survey of India

- The Archaeological Survey of India (ASI) is directly under the aegis of the Ministry of Culture and it is the foremost institution for archaeological researches conducted across India.
- It has been charged with the preservation of the cultural heritage of our nation. Its focus is on the preservation of physical and tangible heritage that is accumulated in the ancient monuments and archaeological sites.
- The provisions of the Ancient Monuments and Archaeological Sites and Remains Act, 1958, guide ASI.

Indira Gandhi National Centre for Arts

- The Indira Gandhi National Centre for the Arts, established in memory of Smt. Indira Gandhi is visualized as a centre encompassing the study and experience of all the arts – each form with its own integrity, yet within a dimension of mutual interdependence, interrelated with nature, social structure and cosmology.

- It is an autonomous institution that concentrates on research, conservation, display and dissemination of arts.
- Although they concentrate on visual and performing art, yet they also promote critical and creative literature.

Centre for Cultural Resources and Training

- The Centre for Cultural Resources and Training (CCRT) is one of the premier institutions working in the field of linking education with culture.
- Established in 1979, pioneered by Smt. Kamaladevi Chattopadhyay and Dr. Kapila Vatsyayan, it functions as an autonomous organisation under the aegis of Ministry of Culture, Government of India.
- CCRT has been contributing to the strengthening of the foundation of the nation by making education culture-based and meaningful.
- CCRT's main thrust is to make a variety of training programmes for in-service teachers, teacher educators, educational administrators and students throughout the country. It also organizes special training programmes for physically and mentally challenged children.

39. Correct Option: (b)

Explanation:

- **Statement 1 is incorrect:** Atharva Veda was the first book where we find a mention about medicine.

Supplementary Notes:

Medicine

- During the Vedic times, Ashwini Kumars were the practitioners of medicine and were given divine status. Dhanvantari was the God of medicine.
- Atharva Veda was the first book where we find a mention of the diseases, its cure, and medicines. According to it, the diseases were caused by the demons and spirits entering into the human body and can be cured by magical charms and spells. Atharva Veda mentioned cure for many of the diseases which include diarrhea, sores, cough, leprosy, fever, and seizure.
- However, the era of practical and more rational cure to diseases emerged around 600 BC Takshila and Varanasi emerged as the centres for medicinal learning.

40. Correct Option: (c)

Explanation:

- Both statements are correct

Supplementary Notes:

Paryatan Parv

- The Ministry of Tourism, Government of India, in collaboration with other Central Ministries, State Governments and stakeholders organizes "Paryatan Parv" across the country.
- The event was organized with the objective of drawing focus on the benefits of tourism, showcasing the cultural diversity of the country and reinforcing the principle of "Tourism for All".
- Paryatan Parv 2019 is dedicated to the 150th Birth Anniversary of Mahatma Gandhi.
- The three components of Paryatan Parv are:
  - **Dekho Apna Desh:** To encourage Indians to visit their own country. In the run-up to the parv, several activities have been organized across the country like photography contest covering tourism attractions and experiences, promotion on social media, tourism related quiz, essay, debate and painting competitions for students. General public engagement for the event will be promoted through the MyGov platform.
  - **Tourism for All:** Tourism Events at sites across all States in the country are being organized. The activities at these sites will include illumination in and around the sites, cultural programmes of dance, music, theatre, story telling, sensitisation programmes for stakeholders around the sites, tourism exhibitions, showcasing culture, cuisine and handicrafts/handlooms, guided heritage walks, etc.
  - **Tourism & Governance:** Interactive Sessions & Workshops with Stakeholders on varied themes have been organized across the country as a part of the Paryatan Parv activities.

41. Correct Option: (b)

Supplementary Notes:

Bharat Parv

- Bharat Parv is a five-day event hosted as part of the Republic Day celebrations. Bharat Parv organized at Red Fort, Delhi aims to generate a patriotic fervor and promote the rich cultural diversity of the country.
- Bharat Parv showcases the spirit of Ek Bharat Shreshtha Bharat. The important attractions of Bharat Parv are:
  - Replica of the Statue of Unity.
  - Gandhi Gram in which 10 painting artists will create paintings on the theme of the Ideology of Mahatma Gandhi.
  - Display of Republic Day parade tableaux
  - Performances by the Armed Forces bands.
  - Theme based State Pavilions where each state showcases its strength along with its tourism products.
- Bharat Parv has been organized by the Ministry of Tourism in collaboration with other Central Ministries and State Governments.

42. Correct Option: (d)

Explanation:

- **Statement 1 is incorrect:** Swadesh Darshan Scheme aims at the integrated development of theme-based circuits.
- **Statement 2 is incorrect:** Adarsh Smarak Scheme aims at providing improved visitor amenities at select monuments.
- **Statement 3 is incorrect:** Swadesh Darshan is a scheme of Ministry of Tourism, while Adarsh Smarak is a scheme of Ministry of Culture.

Supplementary Notes:

Swadesh Darshan Scheme

- Ministry of Tourism in 2015 launched the Swadesh Darshan Scheme for developing critical tourism infrastructure in the country in a sustainable and inclusive manner to make India into a world-class tourist destination.
- The focus under the scheme is to develop public facilities like last-mile connectivity, tourist reception centers wayside amenities, solid waste management, illumination, landscaping, parking, etc. where private sector is not willing to invest.
- This scheme is envisioned to synergize with other Government of India schemes like Swachh Bharat Abhiyan, Skill India, Make in India, etc. with the idea of positioning the tourism sector as a major engine for job creation, driving force for economic growth, building synergy with various sectors to enable tourism to realize its potential.
- Under the Swadesh Darshan scheme, 15 thematic circuits have been identified for development namely: North-East India Circuit, Buddhist Circuit, Himalayan Circuit, Coastal Circuit, Krishna Circuit, Desert Circuit, Tribal Circuit, Eco Circuit, Wildlife Circuit, Rural Circuit, Spiritual Circuit, Ramayana Circuit, Sufi Circuit, Tirthankar Circuit and Heritage Circuit.

Adarsh Smarak Yojana

- It is a scheme of Ministry of Culture launched in 2014 for providing improved visitor amenities, especially for the physically challenged.
- The Archaeological Survey of India has identified 25 monuments for the Adarsh Smarak Scheme for upgradation of tourist-related amenities.
- The salient features of the scheme are as under:
  - To make monument visitor friendly
  - To upgrade/provide washrooms, drinking water, signage and cafeteria, and Wi-Fi facility
  - To provide Interpretation and audio video centres
  - To streamline wastewater and garbage disposal and rainwater harvesting system
  - To make the monument accessible to differently-abled
  - To implement Swachh Bharat Abhiyan

43. Correct Option: (d)

Explanation:

- All statements are correct

Supplementary Notes:

GI Tag

- The products — the Dindigul lock and the Kandangi saree — were given the GI tag by the Geographical Indications Registry in Chennai.
- The Dindigul locks are known for their superior quality and durability. The locks are made of iron and brass and are entirely handmade. It is unique as each lock is designed with different lever pattern. The Dindigul city is also called as 'Lock City'.
- Kandangi sarees are hand-woven cotton sarees manufactured in Karaikudi taluk in the Sivaganga district of Tamil Nadu. They are made up of high-quality cotton from Coimbatore. Kandangi cotton sarees are made by weavers of Devanga Chettiars for women of the Chettiar community also referred to as Nakarathars or Nattukottai Chettiars. The main characteristic of these sarees is its bright colours that hold strong.
- Kerala's Tirur betel leaf has also been awarded a Geographical Indication (GI) tag. Tirur betel vine from Kerala, which is mainly cultivated in Tirur, Tanur, Tirurangadi, Kuttippuram, Malappuram and Vengara block panchayaths of Malappuram district, is valued both for its mild stimulant action and medicinal properties.

44. Correct Option: (a)

Explanation:

- **Statement 2 is incorrect:** It begins on 22nd March every year except in Gregorian leap years when it starts on 21st March.

Supplementary Notes:

Saka Samvat

- This calendar form was initiated by King Shalivahan in 78 AD. It was also known as the Saka era as it is to this tribe that Shalivahan belonged. Historians do have confusion about whether Shalivahan was Saka himself or conquered Sakas.
- The Saka Calendar is both solar and lunar with lunar months and solar years and has the same number of months as the Vikram era has.
- However, the months commence in different periods here. Its year zero begins near the vernal equinox of the year 78.
- Saka Calendar begins on 22nd March every year except in Gregorian leap years when it starts on 21st March.

- Saka calendar has a year with a fixed number of days in each month. However, the names of months in both calendars are the same.
- Saka calendar starts with Chaitra followed by Vaisakha, Jyeshtha, Ashadha, Shravana, Bhadrapada, Ashwina, Kartika, Margshisha, Pausha, Magha, and Phalguna. The number of days in a Saka year is 365.

45. **Correct Option: (b)**

Explanation:

- **Statement 3 is incorrect:** It will be notified as a heritage instrument of Goa.

Supplementary Notes:

Ghumot to be Goa's Heritage Instrument

- Ghumot, Goa's indigenous traditional percussion instrument made from an earthen vessel, will be notified as a heritage instrument of Goa.
- The instrument was banned due to the use of the skin of the endangered monitor lizard for the drum membrane.
- In recent years, ghumot makers have started using goatskin instead.
- The ban is applicable to the use of any animal listed in the Wildlife (Protection) Act, 1972, and that the goat is not one of them.
- Ghumot is widely played during Ganesh Chaturthi Aarties.
- A smaller form of ghumot is generally used as the main accompaniment to the 'Burrakatha' a folk, storytelling tradition of Andhra Pradesh.

46. **Correct Option: (a)**

Explanation:

- **Statement 2 is incorrect:** Sahitya Academy is India's premier literary institution that promotes literature in English and Rajasthani besides the Schedule VIII languages.

Supplementary Notes:

Sahitya Academy

- Sahitya Academy, India's National Academy of Letters, was established in 1954 by the Government of India.
- It was registered as a society on 7 January 1956, under the Societies Registration Act, 1860.
- As India's premier literary institution, the academy preserves and promotes literature contained in 24 Indian languages recognized by it through awards, fellowships, grants, publications, literary programmes, etc.
- Besides the 22 languages enumerated in the Constitution of India, the Sahitya Akademi has recognized English and Rajasthani as languages in which its programme may be implemented.
- The academy also undertakes literary exchange programmes with various countries across the globe to promote Indian literature beyond the shores of India.

Sangeet Natak Academy

- The Sangeet Natak Akademi - India's national academy for music, dance, and drama - is the first National Academy of the Arts set-up by the Government of India in 1952.
- The Academy's charter of functions was expanded along the original lines in 1961 when the Sangeet Natak Akademi was reconstituted by the Government as a society and registered under the Societies Registration Act of 1860.
- Since its inception the Akademi has been functioning as the apex body of the performing arts in the country, preserving and promoting the vast intangible heritage of India's diverse culture expressed in the forms of music, dance and drama.
- It also looks after several institutions, which focus primarily on either dance or music or drama. For example, they administer the National School of Drama that was set up in 1959 for focused work on dramatics in India.

47. **Correct Option: (a)**

Explanation:

- **Statement 3 is incorrect:** Raja Rammohan Roy Library Foundation is the nodal agency to implement the National Mission on Libraries.

Supplementary Notes:

National Mission on Manuscripts (NMM)

- The National Mission for Manuscripts (NMM) was launched by the Ministry of Culture in the year 2003 with the objectives to survey, document, and conserve/preserve, digitize and publish the Indian Manuscripts.
- The final objective of the Mission is to establish a digital National Manuscripts Library at Indira Gandhi National Centre for the Arts (IGNCA) at which scholars and researchers can view the digital copies of the Indian Manuscripts.
- National Mission for Manuscripts is first such national-level comprehensive initiative in the world which caters to the need of conserving manuscripts and disseminating knowledge contained therein.

National Mission on Monuments and Antiquities (NMMA)

- It was launched in 2007 by the Ministry of Culture and Archaeological Survey of India (ASI) is the nodal agency for NMMA to implement the various activities all over the country.
- The mission expects to create a Nationall Register on Built Heritage & Sites and a National Register on Antiquities.

National Mission on Libraries

- Public libraries have a major role to play in realizing this goal. In order to revamp the Public Library System & Services, and to provide digital content-based services to the citizens at large, the Ministry of Culture has launched the scheme of National Mission on Libraries (NML).
- Raja Rammohan Roy Library Foundation has been declared as the nodal agency for the National Mission on Libraries for administrative, logistics, planning and budgeting purposes.
- The Scheme has the following four components:
  - ➤ Creation of National Virtual Library (NVLI)
  - ➤ Setting up of NML Model Libraries
  - ➤ Quantitative & Qualitative Survey
  - ➤ Capacity Building for library professionals

48. Correct Option: (c)

Explanation:

- Both statements are correct

Supplementary Notes:

Minaret and Archaeological Remains of Jam

- The Minaret of Jam is a UNESCO World Heritage Site
- The 65m-tall Minaret of Jam is a graceful, soaring structure, dating back to the 12th century.
- Covered in elaborate brickwork with a blue tile inscription at the top, it is noteworthy for the quality of its architecture and decoration, which represent the culmination of an architectural and artistic tradition in this region.
- Its impact is heightened by its dramatic setting, a deep river valley between towering mountains in the heart of the Ghur province in western Afghanistan.

49. Correct Option: (d)

Explanation:

- **Statement 1 is incorrect:** People selected under this scheme would be taken to religious places of all major religions in India.
- **Statement 2 is incorrect:** People of Indian-origin aged 45 to 65 can apply and avail the benefits under the scheme.

Supplementary Notes:

Pravasi Teerth Darshan Yojana

- In order to strengthen connections with the Indian diaspora this scheme is launched.
- A group of Indian diaspora will be taken on a government-sponsored tour of religious places in India twice a year.
- People of Indian-origin aged 45 to 65 can apply and avail the benefits under the scheme.
- Those selected would be taken to religious places of all major religions in India.
- The first batch of 40 people participated in the Pravasi Bharatiya Divas 2019 held in Varanasi.
- The government will bear all the expenses including the airfare from their country of residence.
- The Scheme accords first preference to people from Girmitiya countries such as Mauritius, Fiji, Suriname, Guyana, Trinidad and Tobago, and Jamaica.
- Girmitiya's are the descendants of indentured Indian labourers brought to Fiji, Mauritius, South Africa, East Africa, the Malay Peninsula, Caribbean and South America (Trinidad and Tobago, Guyana and Suriname) to work on sugarcane plantations for the prosperity of the European settlers.
- The term Girmitiya was coined by the father of the nation, Mahatma Gandhi who referred to himself as first Girmitiya. The countries where these indentured Indian labourers settled are known as Girmitiya countries.

CONCEPT REVISION

Here is the list of concepts that have been covered as part of the previous exercise. Revise and Self-reflect on your concepts you covered.

- Cultural awards ☐
- Central Board of Film Certification ☐
- Fairs & Festivals ☐
- World Heritage Sites of India ☐
- Deen Dayal Hastakal Sankul ☐
- Incredible India 2.0 Campaign ☐
- GI Tag ☐
- 'National Virtual Library of India' ☐
- 'Global Geopark Network Cities' ☐
- UNESCO Creative Cities Network ☐
- Muziris Heritage Project ☐
- Gandhi Heritage Mission ☐
- Sanskriti App ☐
- National Mission for Cultural Mapping of India ☐
- International Council on Monuments and Sites ☐
- Lalit Kala Academy ☐
- Indian Council for Cultural Relations ☐
- PRASAD Scheme ☐
- HRIDAY Scheme ☐
- Paryatan Parv ☐
- Saka Calender ☐

☐☐☐